Main Cities of Europe 2007

Commitments

"This volume was created at the turn of the century and will last at least as long".

This foreword to the very first edition of the MICHELIN Guide, written in 1900, has become famous over the years and the Guide has lived up to the prediction. It is read across the world and the key to its popularity is the consistency of its commitment to its readers, which is based on the following promises.

THE MICHELIN GUIDE'S COMMITMENTS :

Anonymous inspections: our inspectors make regular and anonymous visits to hotels and restaurants to gauge the quality of products and services offered to an ordinary customer. They settle their own bill and may then introduce themselves and ask for more information about the establishment. Our readers' comments are also a valuable source of information, which we can then follow up with another visit of our own.

Independence: Our choice of establishments is a completely independent one, made for the benefit of our readers alone. The decisions to be taken are discussed around the table by the inspectors and the editor. The most important awards are decided at a European level. Inclusion in the Guide is completely free of charge.

Selection and choice: The Guide offers a selection of the best hotels and restaurants in every category of comfort and price. This is only possible because all the inspectors rigorously apply the same methods.

Annual updates: All the practical information, the classifications and awards are revised and updated every single year to give the most reliable information possible.

Consistency: The criteria for the classifications are the same in every country covered by the Michelin Guide.

... and our aim: to do everything possible to make travel,holidays and eating out a pleasure, as part of Michelin's ongoing commitment to improving travel and mobility.

Dear Reader

Welcome to the 26th edition of the 'Main Cities of Europe' guide.

This guide is aimed primarily at the international business traveller who regularly journeys throughout Europe but it is equally ideal for those wishing to discover the delights of some of Europe's most romantic and culturally stimulating cities for a weekend break or special occasion.

Entry in the Michelin Guide is completely free of charge and it continues to be compiled by our professionaly trained teams of full-time inspectors from across Europe who make their assessments anonymously in order to ensure complete impartiality and independence. Their mission is to check the quality and consistency of the amenities and services provided by the hotels and restaurants throughout the year and our listings are updated annually in order to ensure the most up-to-date information.

Most of the establishments featured have been hand-picked from our other national guides and therefore our European selection is, effectively, a best-of-the-best listing.

In addition to the user-friendly layout the guide contains key thematic words which succinctly convey the style of the establishment; practical and cultural information on each country and each city; suggestions on what to see, where to shop and where to spend the evening.

Thank you for your support and please continue to send us your comments. We hope you will enjoy travelling with the 'Main Cities of Europe' guide 2007.

Consult the Michelin Guide at
www.ViaMichelin.com
and write to us at:
themichelinguide-europe@uk.michelin.com

Contents

Contents

COUNTRIES

Classification & Awards

CATEGORIES OF COMFORT

The Michelin Guide selection lists the best hotels and restaurants in each category of comfort and price. The establishments we choose are classified according to their levels of comfort and, within each category, are listed in order of preference.

	Luxury in the traditional style
	Top class comfort
	Very comfortable
	Comfortable
	Quite comfortable
	Traditional pubs serving good food
	Tapas bars
	Other recommended accommodation
without rest.	This hotel has no restaurant
with rm	This restaurant also offers accommodation

THE AWARDS

To help you make the best choice, some exceptional establishments have been given an award in this year's Guide. They are marked or and **Rest**.

THE BEST CUISINE

Michelin stars are awarded to establishments serving cuisine, of whatever style, which is of the highest quality. The cuisine is judged on the quality of ingredients, the skill in their preparation, the combination of flavours, the levels of creativity, the value for money and the consistency of culinary standards.

Exceptional cuisine, worth a special journey
One always eats extremely well here, sometimes superbly.

Excellent cooking, worth a detour

A very good restaurant in its category

RISING STARS

These establishments, listed in red, are the best in their present category. They have the potential to rise further, and already have an element of superior quality; as soon as they produce this quality consistently, and in all aspects of their cuisine, they will be hot tips for a higher award. We've highlighted these promising restaurants so you can try them for yourselves; we think they offer a foretaste of the gastronomy of the future.

GOOD FOOD AT MODERATE PRICES

Bib Gourmand
Establishments offering good quality cuisine at reasonable prices (the actual price limit varies from country to country according to the relative costs).

PLEASANT HOTELS AND RESTAURANTS

Symbols shown in red indicate particularly pleasant or restful establishments: the character of the building, its décor, the setting, the welcome and services offered may all contribute to this special appeal.

to **Pleasant hotels**

to **Pleasant restaurants**

OTHER SPECIAL FEATURES

As well as the categories and awards given to the establishment, Michelin inspectors also make special note of other criteria which can be important when choosing an establishment.

LOCATION

If you are looking for a particularly restful establishment, or one with a special view, look out for the following symbols:

Quiet hotel

Very quiet hotel

Interesting view

Exceptional view

WINE LIST

If you are looking for an establishment with a particularly interesting wine list, look out for the following symbol:

Particularly interesting wine list
This symbol might cover the list presented by a sommelier in a luxury restaurant or that of a simple restaurant where the owner has a passion for wine. The two lists will offer something exceptional but very different, so beware of comparing them by each other's standards.

Facilities & Services

30 rm	Number of rooms
A/C	Air conditioning (in all or part of the establishment)
	Establishment with areas reserved for non-smokers.
	Establishment at least partly accessible to those of restricted mobility
	Meals served in garden or on terrace
SAT	Satellite TV
	Wireless Internet access
Spa	Wellness centre: an extensive facility for relaxation and well-being
	Sauna – Exercise room
	Swimming pool: outdoor or indoor
	Garden
	Tennis court
150	Equipped conference room: maximum capacity
4/40	Private dining rooms (minimun and maximum capacity)
P P	Valet parking – Garage – Car park, enclosed parking
	No dogs allowed (in all or part of the establishment)
May-October	Dates when open, as indicated by the hotelier
M	Nearest metro station

Prices

These prices are given in the currency of the country in question. Valid for 2007 the rates shown should only vary if the cost of living changes to any great extent.

SERVICE AND TAXES

Except in Greece, Hungary, Poland and Spain, prices shown are inclusive, that is to say service and V.A.T. included. In the U.K. and Ireland, s = service included. In Italy, when not included, a percentage for service is shown after the meal prices, eg. (16 %).

MEALS

Meals 40/56	Set meal prices
Carte	"à la carte" meal prices

HOTEL

86 rm 🕴 650/750	Lowest and highest price for a comfortable single
🕴🕴 750/890	and a best double room
☕ 60/120	Prices include breakfast (where not included in rate)

BREAKFAST

☕ 20	Price of breakfast

CREDIT CARDS

	Credit cards accepted by the establishment:
AE ⓓ MC VISA	American Express – Diners Club – MasterCard – Visa

How to use this guide

PRACTICAL & TOURIST INFORMATION

Pages with practical information on every country and city: public transport, tourist information offices, main sites and attractions (museums, monuments, theatres, etc), with a directory of shop addresses and examples of local specialities to take home.

RESTAURANTS

XXXXX à X

The most pleasant : in red.

STARS

✿✿✿ Worth a special journey.

✿✿ Worth a detour.

✿ A very good restaurant.

Establishment named in red : "Rising Star".

RESTAURANTS & HOTELS

The country is indicated by the coloured strip down the side of the page: dark for restaurants, light for hotels.

HOTELS

🏨🏨🏨🏨🏨 à 🏨

The most pleasant : in red.

BIB GOURMAND ☺

Good food at moderate prices.

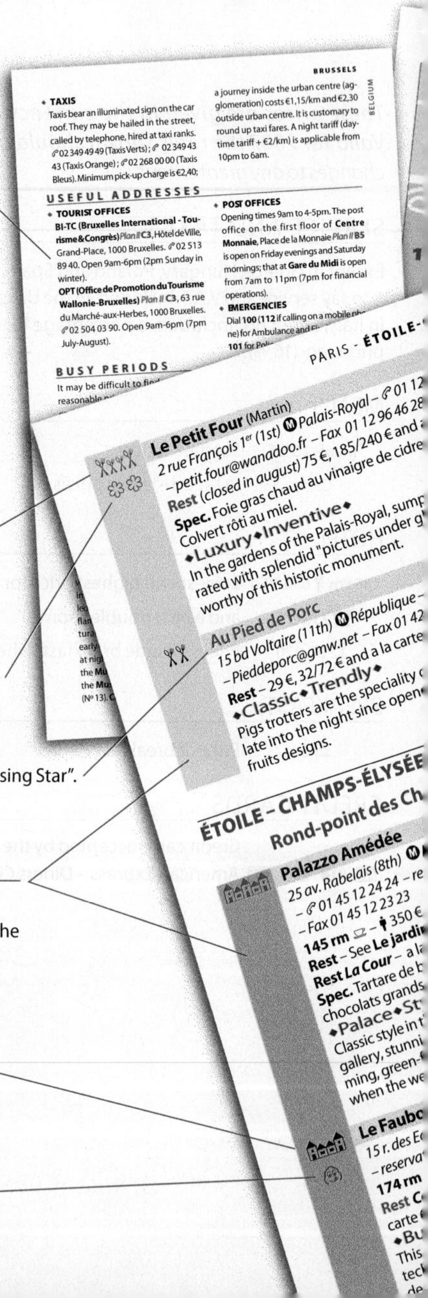

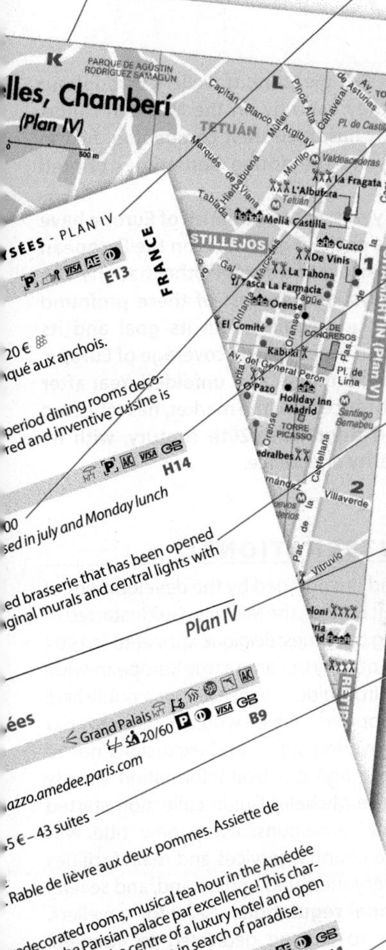

LOCATING THE ESTABLISHMENT

Location on the town plan, with principal sights.

LOCATION

The city, the district, the map.

ADDRESS

All the information you need to make a reservation and find the establishment.

FACILITIES & SERVICES

See also p.12.

DESCRIPTION OF THE ESTABLISHMENT

Atmosphere, style and character.

CLASSIFICATION BY DISTRICT

With the corresponding plan number.

PRICES

See also p.13.

KEY WORDS

If you're looking for a specific type of establishment, look out for these words. They aim to encapsulate the key 'theme' of the hotel or restaurant – the type of cooking, style of establishment, décor or atmosphere – in no more than three words, guiding you quickly to the type of hotel or restaurant that you are looking for.

The Michelin Guide and Europe

Whether it be for business or pleasure, travellers throughout Europe know that they can rely on the Michelin Guide. For over a century, it has been their companion, first in France and then beyond the dotted borderlines printed on the Michelin maps.
Over the last hundred years, the boundaries of Europe have been extended and the circle of gold stars on the European flag has had to adjust in order to welcome other nations. The Michelin Guide has always kept abreast of these profound changes on the ground, in keeping with its goal and its motto: *serving the traveller*. Indeed, in its coverage of Europe, it has witnessed the history of the continent as it unfolded. Year after year, the guide's publication, or absence from the market, has reflected the great upheavals experienced during the 20th century, with its vicissitudes, crises, eras of prosperity and peace.

THE MICHELIN GUIDE: MULTILINGUAL AND INTERNATIONAL

Inspired by its success in France and encouraged by the development of the automobile industry throughout Europe, the Michelin Guide started to spread the concept to neighbouring countries: *Belgique* appeared in 1904 – the second volume in what would quickly become a true European-wide collection. The following year, a third guide – *Benelux* – was published. The collection began to adopt an approach which would include **tourist information**, with new sections covering sights and excursions not to be missed, in addition to the advice and practical information already in the guides. At the same time, the Michelin Guide collection started to espouse Michelin's international ambitions: every new title was published in the language(s) of the country, services and main facilities were indicated by **symbols** that everyone could understand, and several pages were devoted to **international regulations** useful for travellers. Consequently readers could refer to a page dedicated to «General European Traffic Rules», for example, with specific information regarding

which side of the road to drive on in every European country. It is interesting to note that, at the time, the Michelin Guide included Turkey as part of Europe, with information about traffic in that country.

MICHELIN TRAVELS ABROAD

The Michelin Guide began to expand throughout Europe and use other languages. In 1908 *The Michelin Guide to France* was published, an **adaptation in English** of the original French guide, and two years later two new titles were published: *Deutschland und Schweiz* and *España y Portugal*. The following year (1911) three more guides were published, expanding the collection still further: *British Isles, Alpes et Rhin*, and the exotic *Les pays du Soleil*, covering not only the Côte d'Azur, Corsica and Italy, but also North Africa and Egypt! And that same year, all of these guides were translated into English.

This unprecedented expansion marked the start of the company's desire to spread throughout Europe and North Africa. Proof of the successful formula of the Michelin Guides was summed up in an advertising poster of the era showing Bibendum – the Michelin Man – proudly demonstrating that the total number of copies of the Michelin guide collection, if piled up, would be equivalent to 60 times the height of St Paul's Cathedral in London!

Success was then interrupted in 1939, with the start of the **Second World War**. From 1940 to 1944, the absence of the guide revealed the torment which Europe was going through. When the guide finally reappeared, it was *«for official use only»*, printed in Washington to accompany the officers of the Allied forces during the Normandy Landings.

FROM A EUROPEAN COLLECTION…

The 1950s brought new growth, with Michelin maps now covering all of Western Europe. But it was in the 1960s that the Michelin Guide collection really started to take on a **European dimension**, taking a step by step approach to expansion. In 1964, after a half century's absence, *Deutschland* reappeared (without the GDR and East Berlin), followed ten years later by *Great Britain & Ireland*. Meanwhile, the shorter *Paris* and *London* guides appeared on the shelves, based on information taken from the national guides, and revealing an interest in large **European capital cities**. In order to remain the indispensable companion for travellers throughout Europe, the guides would from then on follow the model of *France*: enhanced with more information, including a **rigorous selection of fine restaurants**.

...TO A GUIDE FOR EUROPE

Means of transport were becoming more and more diversified and journey times were shortening considerably, encouraging faster travel and trips made more often and over longer distances than ever before. Michelin needed to bring tourists and business travellers alike a guide which covered the relevant areas, and at the same time cross the borders of the new Europe to the north and to the east.

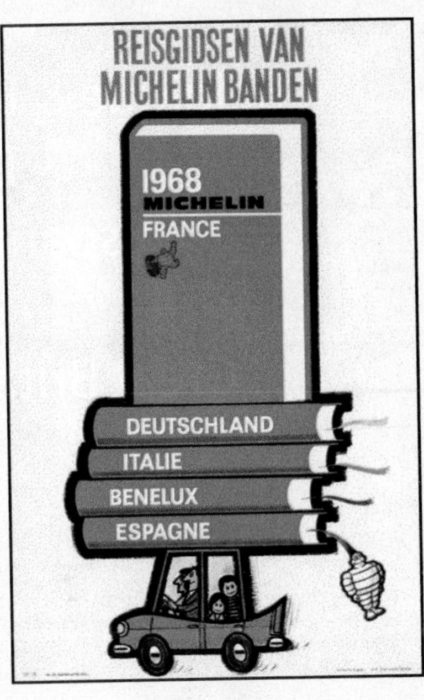

1982 saw the chance to do this. The first guide devoted to Europe was born of a **partnership** with *Times-Life Magazine* and appeared under the title *20 Cities/Villes EUROPE.* The guide was written in English and twenty thousands copies were published. The selection of establishments adopted for the guide took the best hotel and restaurant addresses in each category from the «country» guides, following the criteria guaranteeing **a constant level of quality**, above and beyond specific national considerations.

The huge success of this first edition led the company to repeat the experience. The following year, Copenhagen and Vienna were included in the guide: until then, no guide existed which covered these cities, and the more global title *Main Cities of Europe* was adopted in 1984 with more than 50 towns and cities – some of them capitals, but also the other large influential cities in **15 countries**.

Who does not recognise the famous red cover of the Michelin Guide today? Since the beginning of the 20th century, the Guide has established itself throughout Europe thanks to quality service and up-to-date selection. From Oslo to Athens, Lisbon to Budapest, the 12 titles in the collection (not including the latest, *New York City*) suggest nearly 30 700 hotels and 18 200 restaurants, including nearly 1 400 starred restaurants, and 1 200 town plans. With new introductions and practical information on every country and every town and city selected, the 2006 vintage of *Main Cities of EUROPE* offers you the very best. Happy reading and bon voyage with Michelin!

AUSTRIA
ÖSTERREICH

PROFILE

◆ **Area:**
83 853 km²
(32 376 sq mi).

◆ **Population:**
8 150 000 inhabitants (est. 2005), density = 97 per km².

◆ **Capital:**
Vienna (conurbation 1 892 000 inhabitants).

◆ **Currency:**
Euro (€); rate of exchange: € 1 = US$ 1.25 (Nov 2006).

◆ **Government:**
Parliamentary republic and federal state (since 1955). Member of European Union since 1995.

◆ **Language:**
German.

◆ **Specific public holidays:**
Epiphany (6 January); Corpus Christi (late May/June); National Day (26 October); Immaculate Conception (8 December); St. Stephen's Day (26 December).

◆ **Local Time:**
GMT + 1 hour in winter and GMT + 2 hours in summer.

◆ **Climate:**
Temperate continental with cold winters – high snow levels – and warm summers (Vienna: January: 0°C, July: 20°C).

Vienna

◆ **International dialling Code:**
00 43 followed by area code without initial 0 and then the local number.

◆ **Emergency:**
Police: ✆ **133**;
Medical Assistance: ✆ **144**;
Fire Brigade: ✆ **122.**

◆ **Electricity:**
220 volts AC, 50Hz; 2-pin round-shaped continental plugs.

FORMALITIES

Travellers from the European Union (EU), Switzerland, Iceland and the main countries of North and South America need a national identity card or passport (America: passport required) to visit Austria for less than three months (tourism or business purpose). For visitors from other countries a visa may be required, in addition to a passport, especially for those wishing to stay for longer than three months. We advise you to check with your embassy before travelling.

A valid driving licence is essential. An international driving licence is required for drivers from 80 countries, mainly in South America, Africa, Asia, Middle East and Pacific Islands. Third party insurance is the minimum cover required by Austrian legislation but it is advisable to take out fully comprehensive cover (Green Card).

MAJOR NEWSPAPERS

For Austria and Vienna the daily newspapers with the widest distribution are *Neue Kronenzeitung, Die Presse, Der Standard, Die Wiener Zeitung* and *Kurier.*

USEFUL PHRASES

ENGLISH	**GERMAN**
Yes	**Ja**
No	**Nein**
Good morning	**Guten Morgen**
Goodbye	**Auf Wiedersehen**
Thank you	**Danke**
Please	**Bitte**
Excuse me	**Verzeihung**
I don't understand	**Ich verstehe nicht**

HOTELS

→ CATEGORIES

Accommodation ranges from luxurious 5-star international hotels and well-appointed first class hotels to smaller, family-run guesthouses (pensions), which are frequently part of a residential building, and bed and breakfast establishments.

→ PRICE RANGE

The price is per room. Between April and October and in December it is advisable to book in advance.

→ TAX

Included in the room price.

→ CHECK OUT TIME

Usually between 11am and noon.

→ RESERVATIONS

By telephone or by Internet. A credit card number may be required.

→ TIP FOR LUGGAGE HANDLING

At the discretion of the customer (about €1 per bag).

→ BREAKFAST

It is often not included in the price of the room and is generally served between 7am and 10am. Most hotels offer a self-service buffet but usually it is possible to have continental breakfast served in the room.

Reception	**Empfang**
Single room	**Einzelzimmer**
Double room	**Doppelzimmer**
Bed	**Bett**
Bathroom	**Bad**
Shower	**Dusche**

RESTAURANTS

In addition to formal restaurants, you will also find a range of establishments for eating and drinking in a pleasant, relaxed atmosphere. **Keller**, similar to German beer cellars, are lively and informal and serve cold meals or a daily special with white wine or beer. **Gasthäuser** or **Weinhäuser**, known as **Beisel** in Vienna, offer regional cuisine at reasonable prices. **Weinstuben** are charming taverns where you can enjoy local wine and light meals. In wine-growing villages around Vienna (Grinzing, Nussdorf, Sievering, Gumpoldskirchen), the **Heurigen** offer cold snacks or complete meals and sometimes feature traditional **Schrammelmusik**. The **Buschenschenken** are similar establishments in Styria.

Breakfast	**Frühstück**	7am – 10am
Lunch	**Mittagessen**	11.30pm – 2pm
Dinner	**Abendessen**	6.30pm – 10-11pm, sometimes later

→ RESERVATIONS

Reservations are usually made by phone, fax or Internet. For famous restaurants (including Michelin starred restaurants), it is advisable to book several days, even weeks, in advance. A credit card number or a phone number may be required as guarantee.

→ THE BILL

The bill (check) includes a service charge (10-15%) and VAT in hotels and restaurants. If you are pleased with the service, it is customary to add a tip (5-10%).

Drink or aperitif	**Getränk oder Aperitif**
Meal	**Mahlzeit**
Appetizer, first course, starter	**Vorspeise**
Main dish	**Hauptgericht**
Main daily special	**Tagesgericht**
Dessert	**Nachtisch**
Water	**Wasser**
Wine (red, white, rosé)	**Wein (rot, weiss, rosé)**
Beer	**Bier**
Bread	**Brot**
Meat (rare, medium, well-done)	**Fleisch(blutig, mittel, gut durchgebraten)**
Fish	**Fisch**
Salt/pepper	**Salz/Pfeffer**
Cheese	**Käse**
Vegetables	**Gemüse**
Hot/cold	**heiss/kalt**
The bill (check) please	**Die Rechnung, bitte**

LOCAL CUISINE

The blend of the culinary traditions from countries of the former Austro-Hungarian Empire gives a special distinction to Austrian cooking. Fresh products and regional specialities from lowland and mountain areas are also notable features. Meals are substantial: soup (sometimes with Frittaten – pancake strips, or Leberknödel – liver dumplings) is followed by a main dish, almost always consisting of meat, fried in breadcrumbs or boiled, accompanied by salad and stewed fruit. Dumplings (Knödel) may be served instead of vegetables. The liberal use of spices in many dishes reveals Middle Eastern influences. The most famous dish, Wiener Schnitzel – breaded fillet of veal – is served with sautéed potatoes or potato salad. There are several types of goulash: Rindsgulasch, a paprika-flavoured stew of Hungarian origin; Erdäpfelgulasch, a potato stew served with frankfurters. Tafelspitz is a classic dish of boiled beef with horseradish sauce.

In **Carinthia**, game is accompanied by fresh cranberries picked in the mountains, wild mushrooms from the forests and full-bodied red wine. Among its special dishes are Saure Suppe – soup made with several meats and herbs, sweet and soured cream, flavoured with fennel, aniseed and saffron; Kasnudel – ravioli with curds and mint, meat, spinach, potatoes, mushroom or prunes; and Schlikkrappen – pastry pockets with a filling of offal and fresh herbs. The lake district of Salzkammergut in **Upper Austria** is famous for its freshwater fish – trout, carp, pike-perch and other varieties found nowhere else. **Salzburg** makes the most of its rural and sophisticated traditions: exquisite cheeses, home-cured pork, cured brook trout. **Styria** is well known for its 'black gold' – oil made from pumpkin seeds. Styrian lamb dishes and duck or chicken fried in egg and breadcrumbs are particularly tasty. The food of the **Tyrol** shows the influence of neighbouring Swabia, Carinthia and Friuli. Liver and bacon dumplings (Tirolerleberknödel or Speckknödel) are typical. In **Vorarlberg**, follow the Bregenzerwald Cheese Route (there are 30 varieties) which takes in hill farms and alpine dairy farms producing Bergkäse. Käsespätzle are gnocchi with grated cheese and topped with fried onion rings.

Austria is famous for the great variety of cakes, sweets and desserts **(Mehlspeisen)** accompanied by lashings of whipped cream. Sachertorte is a rich chocolate cake with a thin layer of apricot jam and covered with chocolate icing; Linzertorte is made with almonds and apricot or raspberry jam filling; Kaiserschmarren are morsels of raisin pancakes served with plum preserve. Other favourites are Strudel, turnover filled with apples or cream cheese and currants; plum or apricot fritters; apricot dumplings; Palatschinken, thin pancake filled with apricot jam or chocolate sauce; and a sweet soufflé (Salzburger Nockerl).

DRINK

Vineyards cultivated in Lower Austria, Weinviertel, Burgenland and Styria produce excellent wines. White wines include **Grüner Veltliner, Sauvignon blanc, Riesling, Welschriesling**. The district of **Wachau** in the Danube Valley produces wines with a delicate bouquet – Spitz, Dürnstein, Weissenkirchen, Krems, Langenlois. New wine called Heuriger is drunk in typical establishments known as Heurigen in Vienna and Buschenschenken in Styria. Red wines, especially the **Pinot Noir**, the **Zweigelt,** the **St. Laurent** and the **Blaufränkischer,** are of high quality. The best-known red wines come from **Burgenland**.

Beer is also drunk with meals. Austrians enjoy a variety of fruit and herbal spirits – **Slivovitz** (plums), **Kirsch** (cherries), **Himbeergeist** (raspberries).

VIENNA
WIEN

Population: 1 573 000 (conurbation 1 892 000) – Altitude: 156m

P. Bénet/MICHELIN

Vienna, an imperial city for over six centuries, epitomises elegance and sophistication. The profusion of splendid Baroque palaces and churches, interesting buildings in a variety of styles, ornate fountains and decorative sculpture creates an overwhelming aura of opulence. The elegant shops, fashionable coffee-houses and restaurants, pedestrian areas and grand avenues entice visitors to browse and while away the time pleasantly.

The Emperors and aristocratic families were discerning patrons of the arts and attracted the luminaries of the time – composers, musicians, artists and architects – to the city. Over the centuries Vienna has retained its considerable prestige as a leading artistic centre as evidenced by its magnificent art collections, excellent museums, and prestigious opera house and concert halls.

Vienna, which was an outpost of the Roman Empire and later withstood countless Turkish onslaughts, remained the easternmost centre of European culture until the collapse of the communist ideology. The city has found an international role as the permanent seat of OPEC, the organisation of petroleum-exporting countries, and as the third permanent centre of the United Nations after New York and Geneva.

WHICH DISTRICT TO CHOOSE

In the historic part of the city graced by the elegant patrician mansions around **the Hofburg** *Plan II* **D2** and the area near **Stephansdom** *Plan II* **E2** you will find luxurious establishments and stylish hotels. There are excellent hotels near the main station in **Landstrasse** *Plan I* **B3**; hotels of a good standard and comfortable pensions with all amenities near the Rathaus *Plan I* **A3**, in the University district, the Museums Quartier, Mariahilferstrasse *Plan II* **C3**, Währingerstrasse *Plan II* **C1** and near the Prater in Lassalle Strasse *Plan I* **B2**. For sophisticated cuisine look no further than the historic centre, in the streets around **Graben**,

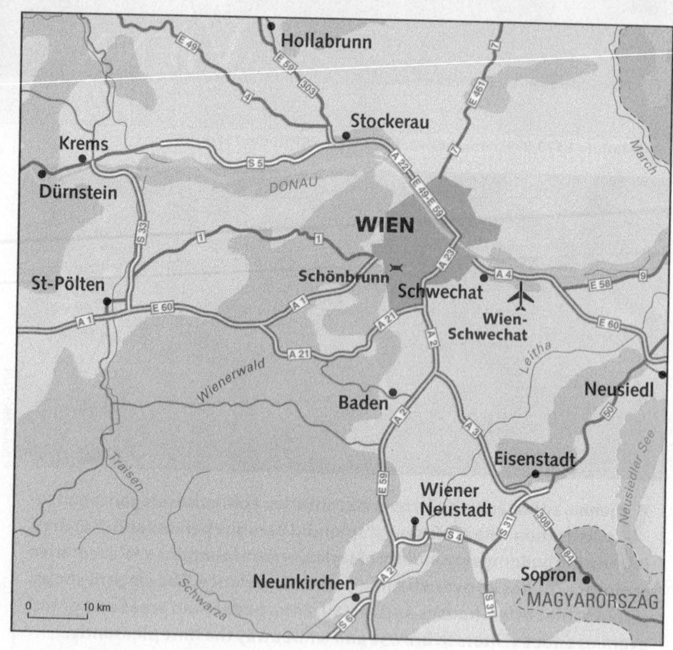

Kohlmarkt *Plan II* **D2**, **Kärntner Strasse.** Fashionable establishments are numerous in the **Fleischmarkt** and **Freyung** *Plan II* **E2-D2** districts. There are plenty of simple, traditional eateries in the **Spittelberg**, in the University district, in **Stubenring** *Plan II* **E2**, **Praterstr.** *Plan II* **F1**, at **Copa Cagrana** in Donau City.

PRACTICAL INFORMATION

ARRIVAL – DEPARTURE

Wien-Schwechat Airport – 19 km (12 mi) from the city centre. ✆ 01 70 07 22 233 (24hr). www.viennaairport.com

From the airport to the city centre – By **express train** to Wien Mitte: every 30min, time: 16min. €8 single, €15 return trip (reduction with Vienna Card). Check-in including boarding card possible (up to 24hr prior to departure) – except for travel to the USA – and separate CAT platform at Wien Mitte. ✆ 01 25 250, www.cityairporttrain.com

There are also regular train services to/from Wien Mitte, Praterstern/Wien Nord and Handelskai which all link up with the metro. By taxi: about €30; ask about special airport rates. By express bus: to/from Schwedenplatz/Rotenturmstr.–Postgasse, every 30 min, time: 20min; to/from Südbahnhof, every 30min, time: 20min; to/from Westbahnhof, every 30min, time:

35min; to/from Vienna International Centre (Donau City), every 90min, time: 25min; fare €6 single, €11 return trip (reduction with Vienna Card). ✆ 05 17 17, www.postbus.at (bus); www.oebb.at (express train).

Railway Stations – Westbahnhof *Plan I* **A3**: trains for Hungary, western Austria and most of Western and Northern Europe. **Südbahnhof** *Plan I* **B3**: trains to Berlin, Italy and Eastern Europe. www.oebb.at

TRANSPORT

→ BUS, METRO AND TRAM

The **Vienna Card** (Wien-Karte), which allows unlimited travel on the whole of the city's public transport network for 72hr and gives a discount to sights, cafés and restaurants, shops and heurigers, can be purchased from the Tourist Office, at your hotel or from ticket offices of the Vienna Transport Authority. €18.50. There are Rover tickets €5 (24hr), €12 (72hr), €1.50 single. ✆ 01 79 09 100, www.wienerlinien.at

→ TAXIS

Allow €7-10 for a short journey. It is customary to give a tip. Radio Taxis ✆ 31 300, 40 100, 60 160. The base fare is €2.50 during the day, Sunday and public holidays (€2.60 at night; radio taxi surcharge €2).

USEFUL ADDRESSES

→ TOURIST INFORMATION

Albertinaplatz 1 *Plan II* **D3**. ✆ 01 24 555, www.vienna.info.at; open 9am-7pm daily. Also at Rathaus, Westbahnhof, Südbahnhof, Airport, Nordeinfahrt/Florisdorfer Brücke (Donauinsel exit).

→ POST OFFICES

Opening times Mon-Fri 8am-noon and 2pm-6pm. Some open longer hours: the main post office in Fleischmarkt 19 *Plan II* **E2** (24hr), those at Franz-Joseph-Bahnhof, Althahnstr.10 7am-10pm (9-2am Sat-Sun), Südbahnhof, Wiedner Gürtel 1a Mon-Sat 7am-10pm, and Westbahnhof, Europaplatz 1/Mariahilferstr. 132 daily 7am-10pm (9am-8pm Sat-Sun).

→ BANKS/CURRENCY EXCHANGE

Banks open Mon-Fri, 8am-12.30pm and 1.30pm-3pm (5.30pm Thur). There are cash dispensers, which require a PIN, all over the city. Credit cards are widely accepted. Bureaux de change often charge high commissions.

→ EMERGENCY

Police ✆ **133;** Fire Brigade ✆ **122;** Ambulance Service ✆ **144.**

EXPLORING VIENNA

It is possible to visit the main sights and museums in three to four days.

Museums and other sights are usually open from 9-10am to 5-6pm. Some close on Mondays or Tuesdays and at lunchtime.

VISITING

Hofburg *Plan II* **D2** – The sumptuous residence of the Habsburgs: imperial apartments, porcelain and silver collections. Do not miss the **Winter Riding School** (Spanische Reitschule) and the **Treasury** (Schatzkammer).

Stephansdom *Plan II* **E2** – The magnificent Gothic cathedral is the symbol of Vienna. Views from the towers.

Schloss Schönbrunn – The imperial summer palace with ornate rococo decoration and fine gardens. View form the Gloriette.

Karlskirche – A splendid domed Baroque church with harmonious interior and decoration.

Kunsthistorisches Museum *Plan II* **C3** – The outstanding collections of fine arts of the Habsburg dynasty presented in a splendid building.

Secessiongebäude *Plan II* **D3** – An avant-garde building topped by a gilded dome (Beethoven frieze by Klimt).

Belvedere *Plan I* **B3** – Two magnificent Baroque palaces, built for Prince Eugene of Savoy, house excellent museums: **Baroque art** (Lower Belvedere), **Medieval art** (Orangery), **19C-20C Austrian and international art** (Upper Belvedere). French-style gardens with ornate fountain.

Tour of the Ring – Take circular tram Lines 1, 2 from Schottenring/Dr.K.-Lueger Ring: Votivkirche, University, Rathaus, Parliament, Burgtheater, Volksgarden, Heldenplatz, Neue Burg colonnade, Maria Theresien Platz, Burggarten, Opera House, Stadtpark, Museum of Applied Arts, Post Office Savings Bank.

Jugendstil buildings – Examples of modern European architecture. **Secession building** *(see above)*. **Wagner Pavillons** (Karlsplatz *Plan II* **E3**). Linke Wienzeile apartments (Majolikahaus, Medallionhaus) *Plan II* **D3**, Postsparkasse *Plan II* **E2**, Looshaus, 3 Michaelerplatz *Plan II* **D2**. Kirche an Steinhof and Wagner Villas (Penzing).

Boat trips on the Danube from Schwedenplatz *Plan II* **E1**.

Views from Donauturm (Danube Tower), the Ferris Wheel in the Prater, heights of Kahlenberg, and Leopoldsberg.

GOURMET TREATS

If you feel peckish during the day, stop at a typical Würstel-Stand (sausage stand): *Albertina*, 1 Albertinaplatz, *Hoher Markt*, 1 Hoher Markt/Marc-Aurelstr., *Zur Oper*, Kärtner Str. 42. Try *Trzesniewski*, Dorotheergasse 1, a traditional snack bar where the waitresses wear lace bonnets.

Be sure to visit a traditional Viennese coffee house to sample the speciality coffees and cakes or have a drink and a meal. Some are genuine institutions: *Demel*, Kohlmarkt 14, *Central*, Herrengasse 14, *Sacher*, Philarmonikerstr. 4, *Landtmann*, Dr.-Karl-Leuger-Ring 4, *Dommayer*, Dommayergasse 2, *Diglas*, Wollzeile 10, *Café Museum*, Friedrichstr. 6, *Kleines Café*, Franziskanerplatz 3.

Head for the pubs and bars around **Ruprechstkirche** and **Rudolfplatz** *Plan II* **E1** should you wish to go out **for a drink or for the evening.** The in-crowd frequents *Blaustern*, Döblinger Gürtel 2, *Casablanca*, Rabensteig 8, *Loos-Bar*, Kärtner Str.10. Other popular venues are *Cantino*, Seilerstätte 30, *Fischerbräu*, Billrothstr. 17, *Krah Krah*, Rabensteig 8. *Spittelberg* is another lively area. You can also visit the Heuriger district – **Grinzing** *Plan I* **A1**, **Heiligenstadt** *Plan I* **A1**, **Neustift, Nussdorf** or **Sievering** – or the 'city Heuriger' such as *Esterházykeller*, Haarhof 1, and *Zwölf Apostelkeller*, Sonnenfelgasse 3.

SHOPPING

Shops and malls usually open Mon-Fri, 9am-6.30pm, Sat 9am-5pm; many are open until 9pm on Thur and 7.30pm on Fri.

Plan II **D2** – For luxury and designer shops visit **Kärntner Strasse**, **Graben**, **Kohlmarkt, Neuer Markt** and **Tuchlau-**

ben. Viennese fashion designers are located in **Seilergasse** (no 7 *Helmut Lang*), **Singerstrasse** (no 7 *Michel Meyer*, no 4 *Schellakann*), **Jasomirgottstrasse** (no 5 *Doris Ainedeter*), **Spiegelgasse** (no 19 *Wiener Blut* – knitwear). The major department stores are: *Steffl*, 1 Kärntner Strasse, *Braum am Graben*, 8 Kärntner Ring, *Ringstrassen Galerien*, 5-7 Kärntner Ring, *Peek und Cloppenburg*, Mariahilferstr. 26-30. The lively **Mariahilferstrasse** *Plan II* **C3** and the side streets are famous for trendy fashions and accessories. Visit *Meinl am Graben*, Graben 19, for fine foods and wines.

MARKETS – **Naschmarkt,** Linke Wienzeile *Plan II* **D3** (Mon-Sat, 6.30am-6pm; flea market Sat 6am-6pm). **Karmelitermarkt**, Krummbaumgasse / Leopoldgasse/Haidgasse *Plan II* **D1** – the Orient in Vienna (Mon-Fri 6am-6.30pm, Sat 6am-2pm). **Am Hof** (Mar-Christmas, Fri-Sat 10am-8pm). **Craft market** at Spittelberggasse *Plan II* **C3**, Sat Apr-Nov, also **Christmas market**, late Nov-Christmas.

WHAT TO BUY – Porcelain, glass, Loden coats, Dirndl, leather goods, jewellery, confectionery and cakes (Sachertorte, Demel Torte, Imperialtorte).

ENTERTAINMENT

Vienna lives up to its cultural reputation with a number of prestigious venues:

Staatsoper *Plan II* **D3**: opera.

Burgtheater *Plan II* **C2**: concerts and shows.

Volksoper *Plan II* **C1**: opera and operettas sung in German, musical comedies.

Volkstheater *Plan II* **C2**: contemporary plays.

Theater an der Wien *Plan II* **D3**: Viennese operettas, ballets.

Wiener Konzerthaus *Plan II* **E3**: international orchestras and soloists.

NIGHTLIFE

Explore the **Bermuda triangle** (around Judengasse *Plan II* **D2**) for bars and nightclubs; listen to live music at *Arena*, Baumgasse 80, *Passage*, Burgring 1, venues under the arches – metro stops Thaliastrasse to Nussdorfer Strasse; dance the night away at *Flex*, 1 Donaukanal/ Augartbrücke, *Volksgarten Clubdisco*, Burgring 1. Try your luck at *Casino Wien*, Kärntner Strasse 41.

AUSTRIA

HISTORICAL CENTRE

Plan II

Imperial

rest rm 120

Kärntner Ring 16 ✉ 1015 – Ⓜ Karlsplatz – ✆ (01) 50 11 03 56 – hotel.imperial@luxurycollection.com – Fax (01) 50 11 04 10 – www.starwoodhotels.com/imperial

E3

138 rm – †640/730 € ††640/730 €, ☕ 35 € – 30 suites

Rest *Imperial* – *(closed July - mid August) (dinner only) (booking advisable)* Carte 43/85 €

Rest *Café Imperial* – Carte 31/54 €

♦ Palace ♦ Grand Luxury ♦ Historic ♦

The "Württemberg-Palais" from 1873 is the gem of Viennese architecture: ornate, luxurious, and decorated with antiques of the highest quality. A stylish and classic restaurant. Viennese coffee-house atmosphere in the Café.

Palais Coburg

rm 150

Coburgbastei 4 ✉ 1010 – Ⓜ Stubentor – ✆ (01) 51 81 80 – hotel.residenz@palais-coburg.com – Fax (01) 51 81 81 00 – www.palais-coburg.com

E2

35 suites ☕ – †490/2140 € ††490/2140 €

Rest *Restaurant Coburg* – see below

Rest *Gartenpavillon* – ✆ *(01) 51 81 88 70* – Carte 22/43 €

♦ Grand Luxury ♦ Historic ♦ Modern ♦

This impressive, carefully restored palace from 1840 offers sumptuously furnished and technologically equipped accommodation that meets the highest standards. Pleasantly bright: a garden pavilion in the form of a conservatory, with rattan chairs.

Grand Hotel

rm 250

Kärntner Ring 9 ✉ 1010 – Ⓜ Karlsplatz – ✆ (01) 51 58 00 – sales@grandhotelwien.com – Fax (01) 5 15 13 12 – www.grandhotelwien.com

E3

205 rm – †335/435 € ††385/485 €, ☕ 29 € – 11 suites

Rest *Le Ciel* – ✆ *(01) 5 15 80 91 00 (closed Sunday)* Menu 40/75 € – Carte 46/66 €

Rest *Unkai* – ✆ *(01) 5 15 80 91 10 (closed Monday lunch)* Menu 27/95 € – Carte 32/57 €

Rest *Grand Café* – ✆ *(01) 5 15 80 91 20* – Menu 24 € – Carte 27/42 €

♦ Grand Luxury ♦ Classic ♦

The glittering world of the Belle Epoque is revived here and the refined rooms of this luxurious hotel are tastefully elegant. The gentile Le Ciel restaurant overlooks the rooftops of Vienna. Beautiful terrace. Sushi and sashimi at "Unkai".

Sacher

rm 50

Philharmonikerstr. 4 ✉ 1010 – Ⓜ Karlsplatz – ✆ (01) 51 45 60 – wien@sacher.com – Fax (01) 51 45 68 10 – www.sacher.com

D3

152 rm – †313/550 € ††376/613 €, ☕ 29 € – 7 suites

Rest *Anna Sacher* – *(closed Monday)* Menu 57/82 € – Carte 54/77 €

Rest *Rote Bar* – Carte 33/64 €

♦ Grand Luxury ♦ Traditional ♦ Classic ♦

This hotel in the heart of Vienna, built in 1876, combines tradition and luxury. Exquisite antiques and paintings add to the refined ambiance. Modern fitness room. Anna Sacher: classic and elegant. Red velvet is all around you: the red bar with traditional cuisine.

Bristol

rest rm 80

Kärntner Ring 1 ✉ 1015 – Ⓜ Karlsplatz – ✆ (01) 51 51 60 – hotel.bristol@luxurycollection.com – Fax (01) 51 51 65 50 – www.luxurycollection.com/bristol

D3

140 rm – †410/530 € ††410/530 €, ☕ 30 € – 10 suites

Rest *Korso* – see below – **Rest *Sirk*** – Carte 28/56 €

♦ Grand Luxury ♦ Traditional ♦ Classic ♦

This hotel offers superb service and a stylish ambiance from the lounge to the guest rooms. The luxurious Prince of Wales suite is well worth seeing. The Sirk restaurant offers a beautiful view of the State Opera House.

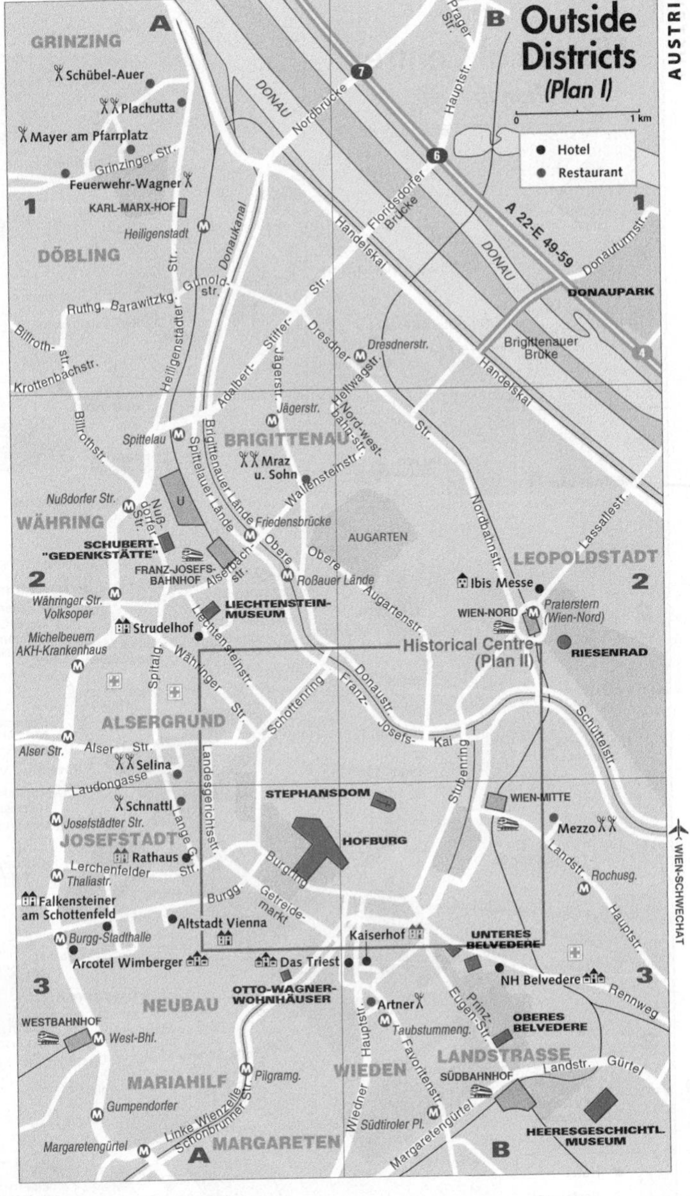
Outside Districts
(Plan I)
0
1 km
Hotel
Restaurant
GRINZING
Schübel-Auer
Plachutta
Mayer am Pfarrplatz
Grinzinger Str.
Feuerwehr-Wagner
KARL-MARX-HOF
Heiligenstadt
DÖBLING
Donaukanal
DONAU
Nordbrücke
Prager Str.
Hauptstr.
Floridsdorfer Brücke
Handelskai
A 22-E 49-59
Donauturmstr.
DONAUPARK
Brigittenauer Brücke
Gunoldstr.
Ruthg.
Barawitzkg.
Billrothstr.
Krottenbachstr.
Heiligenstädter Str.
Adalbert-Stifter-Str.
Jägerstr.
Dresdner Str.
Dresdnerstr.
Hellwagstr.
Nord-west-bahn-str.
Spittelau
BRIGITTENAU
Mraz u. Sohn
Wallensteinstr.
Spittelauer Lände
Brigittenauer Lände
Nußdorfer Str.
Nußdorfer Str.
WÄHRING
Friedensbrücke
AUGARTEN
Nordbahnstr.
Lassallestr.
LEOPOLDSTADT
SCHUBERT-"GEDENKSTÄTTE"
FRANZ-JOSEFS-BAHNHOF
Alserbachstr.
Obere
Roßauer Lände
Obere Augartenstr.
Ibis Messe
Währinger Str. Volksoper
LIECHTENSTEIN-MUSEUM
WIEN-NORD
Praterstern (Wien-Nord)
Strudelhof
Liechtensteinstr.
Michelbeuern AKH-Krankenhaus
Historical Centre (Plan II)
RIESENRAD
Spitalg.
Währinger Str.
Schottenring
Franz-Josefs-Kai
Donaustr.
ALSERGRUND
Schüttelstr.
Alser Str.
Selina
Laudongasse
Landesgerichtsstr.
Stubenring
STEPHANSDOM
WIEN-MITTE
Schnattl
Lange G.
Josefstädter Str.
JOSEFSTADT
HOFBURG
Mezzo
Landstr.
Rochusg.
WIEN-SCHWECHAT
Rathaus
Lerchenfelder Str.
Thaliastr.
Burgring
Falkensteiner am Schottenfeld
Burgg.
Getreidemarkt
Hauptstr.
Altstadt Vienna
Burgg-Stadthalle
Kaiserhof
UNTERES BELVEDERE
Arcotel Wimberger
Das Triest
NH Belvedere
Rennweg
OTTO-WAGNER-WOHNHÄUSER
NEUBAU
Artner
Prinz-Eugen-Str.
WESTBAHNHOF
West-Bhf.
Taubstummeng.
OBERES BELVEDERE
LANDSTRASSE
Favoritenstr.
Wiedner Hauptstr.
WIEDEN
Landstr. Gürtel
SÜDBAHNHOF
MARIAHILF
Pilgramg.
Gumpendorfer
Linke Wienzeile
Schönbrunner Str.
Südtiroler Pl.
Margaretengürtel
HEERESGESCHICHTL. MUSEUM
Margaretengürtel
MARGARETEN

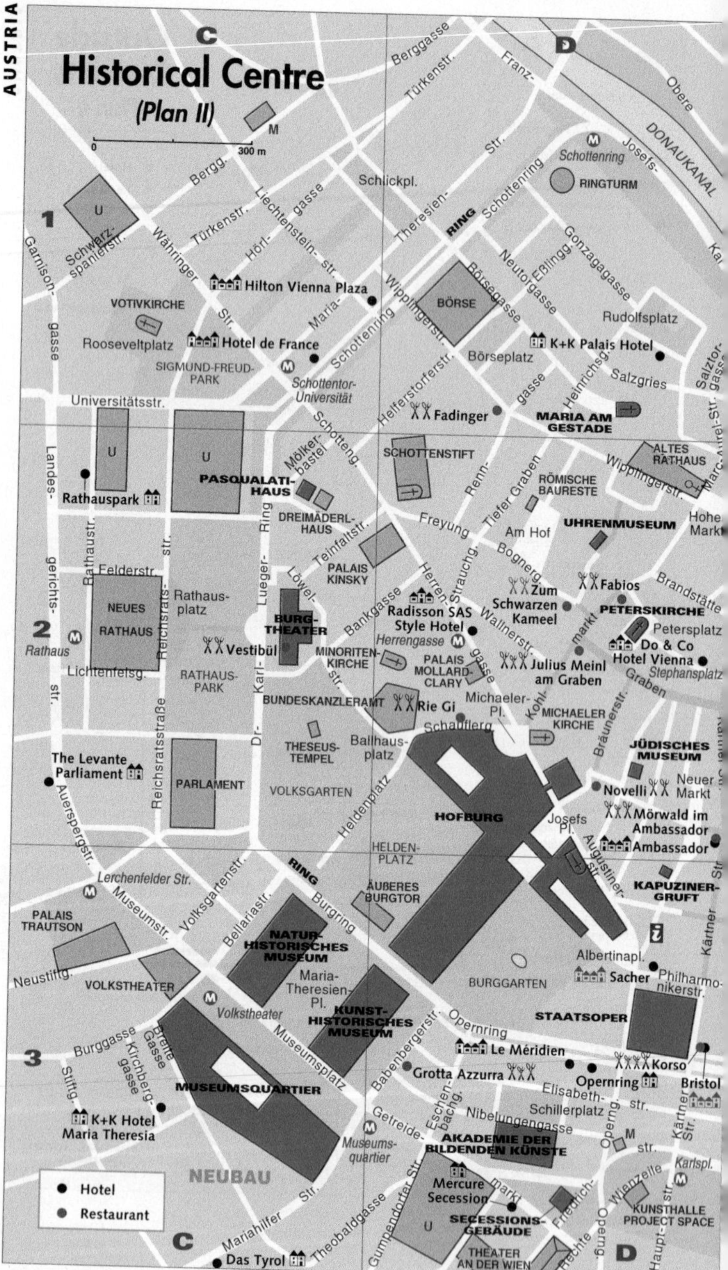

Historical Centre

(Plan II)

0 300 m

C
D
1
2
3

Schlickpl.
Berggasse
Türkenstr.
Franz-Josefs-
Obere DONAUKANAL
Schottenring
RINGTURM
Theresien-Str.
RING
Schwarz-spanierstr.
Bergg.
Garnison-gasse
Währinger Str.
Liechtenstein-str.
Hörl-gasse
Hilton Vienna Plaza
Maria-
Wipplingerstr.
BÖRSE
Börsegasse
Neutorgasse
Eßlingg.
Gonzagagasse
Rudolfsplatz
VOTIVKIRCHE
Rooseveltplatz
Hotel de France
SIGMUND-FREUD-PARK
Schottentor-Universität
Helferstorferstr.
Börseplatz
K+K Palais Hotel
Salzgries
Heinrichsg.
Salztor-gasse
Universitätsstr.
Fadinger
MARIA AM GESTADE
Marc-Aurel-Str.
U
Landes-gerichts-str.
Mölker-bastei
Schotteng.
SCHOTTENSTIFT
Renn-gasse
ALTES RATHAUS
PASQUALATI-HAUS
RÖMISCHE BAURESTE
Tiefer Graben
Rathauspark
DREIMÄDERL-HAUS
Freyung
Am Hof
UHRENMUSEUM
Hohe Markt
Rathausstr.
Teinfaltstr.
PALAIS KINSKY
Bognerg.
Felderstr.
Reichsrats-str.
Rathaus-platz
Dr.-Karl-Lueger-Ring
Löwel-
Herren-
Strauchg.
Zum Schwarzen Kameel
Fabios
Brandstätte
PETERSKIRCHE
NEUES RATHAUS
Rathaus
Vestibül
BURG-THEATER
Bankgasse
Radisson SAS Style Hotel
Herrengasse
Wallnerstr.
markt
Petersplatz
Do & Co Hotel Vienna
Stephansplatz
Graben
Lichtenfelsg.
RATHAUS-PARK
MINORITEN-KIRCHE
PALAIS MOLLARD-CLARY
Julius Meinl am Graben
BUNDESKANZLERAMT
Rie Gi
Michaeler-Pl.
Kohl-
MICHAELER KIRCHE
Schauflerg.
Bräunerstr.
THESEUS-TEMPEL
Ballhaus-platz
JÜDISCHES MUSEUM
The Levante Parliament
Reichsratsstraße
PARLAMENT
VOLKSGARTEN
Heldenplatz
HOFBURG
Novelli
Neuer Markt
Mörwald im Ambassador
Josefs Pl.
Ambassador
Augustiner-str.
Auerspergstr.
HELDEN-PLATZ
Lerchenfelder Str.
Volksgartenstr.
RING
ÄUßERES BURGTOR
KAPUZINER-GRUFT
Museumstr.
Burgring
PALAIS TRAUTSON
Bellariastr.
NATUR-HISTORISCHES MUSEUM
Kärtner Str.
Albertinapl.
Neustiftg.
VOLKSTHEATER
Maria-Theresien-Pl.
Sacher
Philharmo-nikerstr.
BURGGARTEN
Volkstheater
KUNST-HISTORISCHES MUSEUM
STAATSOPER
Burggasse
Breite Gasse
Kirchberg-gasse
Museumsplatz
Opernring
Babenbergerstr.
Le Méridien
Stiftg.
MUSEUMSQUARTIER
Grotta Azzurra
Korso
Opernring
Bristol
Elisabeth-str.
Eschen-bachg.
Schillerplatz
K+K Hotel Maria Theresia
Getreide-markt
Nibelungengasse
Operng.
M
Museums-quartier
AKADEMIE DER BILDENDEN KÜNSTE
Karlspl.
NEUBAU
Gumpendorfer Str.
Mercure Secession
Friedrich-str.
Wienzeile
KUNSTHALLE PROJECT SPACE
Mariahilfer Str.
Theobaldgasse
SECESSIONS-GEBÄUDE
Rechte
Operng.
Haupt-str.
THEATER AN DER WIEN
Das Tyrol

● Hotel
● Restaurant

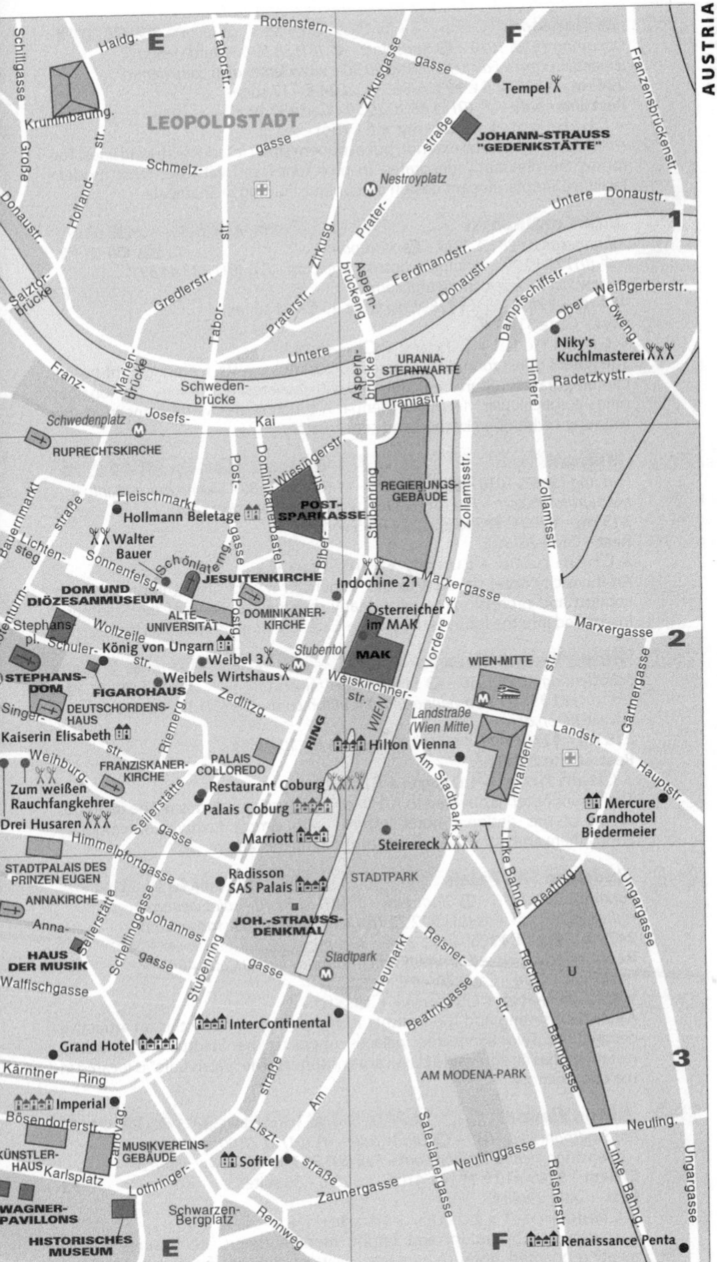
LEOPOLDSTADT
JOHANN-STRAUSS "GEDENKSTÄTTE"
Tempel
Nestroyplatz
URANIA-STERNWARTE
Niky's Kuchlmasterei
Schwedenplatz
RUPRECHTSKIRCHE
POST-SPARKASSE
REGIERUNGS-GEBÄUDE
Hollmann Beletage
Walter Bauer
JESUITENKIRCHE
Indochine 21
DOM UND DIÖZESANMUSEUM
ALTE UNIVERSITÄT
DOMINIKANER-KIRCHE
Österreicher im MAK
MAK
König von Ungarn
Weibel 3
Weibels Wirtshaus
Stubentor
WIEN-MITTE
STEPHANS-DOM
FIGAROHAUS
DEUTSCHORDENS-HAUS
Landstraße (Wien Mitte)
Kaiserin Elisabeth
Hilton Vienna
FRANZISKANER-KIRCHE
PALAIS COLLOREDO
Zum weißen Rauchfangkehrer
Restaurant Coburg
Palais Coburg
Mercure Grandhotel Biedermeier
Drei Husaren
Marriott
Steirereck
STADTPALAIS DES PRINZEN EUGEN
Radisson SAS Palais
STADTPARK
ANNAKIRCHE
JOH.-STRAUSS-DENKMAL
HAUS DER MUSIK
Stadtpark
InterContinental
Grand Hotel
AM MODENA-PARK
Imperial
KÜNSTLER-HAUS
MUSIKVEREINS-GEBÄUDE
Sofitel
WAGNER-PAVILLONS
HISTORISCHES MUSEUM
Renaissance Penta
RING
WIEN
E
F
1
2
3

Le Méridien

180 VISA AE

Opernring 13 ✉ 1010 – Ⓜ Karlsplatz – ✆ (01) 58 89 00 – info.vienna@lemeridien.com – Fax (01) 5 88 90 90 90 – www.lemeridien.com/vienna

294 rm – 325/365 € 325/365 €, 24 € – 17 suites **D3**

Rest *Shambala* – ✆ *(01) 5 88 90 70 50* – Carte 33/46 €

♦ Chain hotel ♦ Luxury ♦ Stylish ♦

A classical grand-hotel exterior, but a modern smart interior with bold lines. The rooms are pleasantly decorated in pale tones and with the most modern facilities. Simple, elegant design and unique lighting in Shambala.

InterContinental

rm 470 VISA AE

Johannesgasse 28 ✉ 1037 – Ⓜ Stadtpark – ✆ (01) 71 12 20 – vienna@ichotelsgroup.com – Fax (01) 7 13 44 89 – www.vienna.intercontinental.com

453 rm – 289/365 € 289/365 €, 25 € – 61 suites **E3**

Rest – Carte 31/47 €

♦ Chain hotel ♦ Luxury ♦ Classic ♦

The hotel's guest rooms are tailored to business guests, featuring light-toned, contemporary furniture and equipped with the latest technology. The top floor offers a spectacular view over Vienna. A touch of the Mediterranean at this restaurant with open kitchen and conservatory.

Marriott

rm 300 VISA AE

Parkring 12a ✉ 1010 – Ⓜ Stadtpark – ✆ (01) 51 51 80 – vienna.marriott.info@marriotthotels.com – Fax (01) 67 36 – www.viennamarriott.com **E2**

313 rm – 290 € 290 €, 24 € – 5 suites

Rest – Carte 26/56 €

♦ Chain hotel ♦ Luxury ♦ Functional ♦

An inner-city hotel devoted to the "American way of life", it impresses with comfort and professional service. Many rooms have views of the Stadtpark. Integrated into the lobby is the Garten-Café, offering international dishes.

Hilton Vienna Plaza

rm 60 VISA AE

Schottenring 11 ✉ 1010 – Ⓜ Schottentor-Universität – ✆ (01) 31 39 00 – info.vienna-plaza@hilton.com – Fax (01) 31 39 02 20 09 – www.hilton.at

218 rm – 170/390 € 170/390 €, 25 € – 10 suites **C1**

Rest – Carte 27/40 €

♦ Chain hotel ♦ Luxury ♦ Functional ♦

The "Grandhotel" is devoted to Art Deco and classic modernism. The generous rooms of this designer hotel impress with simple luxury. Contemporary atmosphere and attractive table settings in the restaurant.

Radisson SAS Palais

rm 190

Parkring 16 ✉ 1010 – Ⓜ Stadtpark – ✆ (01) 51 51 70 – sales.vienna@radissonsas.com – Fax (01) 5 12 22 16 – www.vienna.radissonsas.com

247 rm – 260 € 260 €, 23 € – 39 suites **E3**

Rest *Le siècle* – *(closed Saturday lunch - Sunday lunch)* Carte 46/87 €

Rest *Palais Café* – Carte 26/46 €

♦ Chain hotel ♦ Luxury ♦ Classic ♦

An historic setting and the stylishly furnished rooms make this an attractive destination. Two connected palaces opposite the Stadtpark. "Le siècle" restaurant has an agreeable classical atmosphere. The "Palais Café" is located in the conservatory.

Hilton Vienna

rm 475 VISA AE

Am Stadtpark 3 ✉ 1030 – Ⓜ Landstraße – ✆ (01) 71 70 00 – reservation.vienna@hilton.com – Fax (01) 7 13 06 91 – www.hilton.de

579 rm – 145/410 € 145/410 €, 25 € – 36 suites **F2**

Rest – Carte 29/48 €

♦ Chain hotel ♦ Luxury ♦ Modern ♦

A spacious lobby atrium and bright, modern rooms are features of this meeting-oriented hotel. A fantastic view of the city from the top floor. Contemporary and welcoming atmosphere.

Hotel de France

Schottenring 3 ✉ 1010 – Ⓜ Schottentor-Universität – ✆ (01) 31 36 80 – defrance@austria-hotels.at – Fax (01) 3 19 59 69 – www.hoteldefrance.at **C1**

195 rm – 160/280 € 195/315 €

Rest – *(closed Saturday - Sunday)* Carte 20/40 €

◆ Luxury ◆ Classic ◆

A classic city hotel. Guests enjoy well-presented rooms, some decorated with Viennese period furniture, some with modern furnishings. Spacious maisonettes on the top floor. In this modern bistro, guests enjoy simple meals.

Ambassador

Kärntner Str. 22 ✉ 1010 – Ⓜ Stephansdom – ✆ (01) 96 16 10 – office@ambassador.at – Fax (01) 5 13 29 99 – www.ambassador.at **D2**

86 rm – 233/426 € 295/534 €, 20 €

Rest *Mörwald im Ambassador* – see below

◆ Business ◆ Classic ◆

A successful symbiosis of beautiful period furniture, some antique, with hi-tech. Themed rooms are named after famous characters.

Renaissance Penta

Ungargasse 60 ✉ 1030 – ✆ (01) 71 17 50 – renaissance.penta.vienna@renaissancehotels.com – Fax (01) 7 11 75 81 43 – www.renaissancehotels.com/viese **F3**

339 rm – 145/280 € 145/280 €, 21 €

Rest – Carte 23/35 €

◆ Chain hotel ◆ Functional ◆

Even non-riders are welcome in the neo-classicist, historically listed building of the former imperial military riding school. Bright, functional rooms with burl wood furniture. The elegant Borromäus restaurant.

Do & Co Hotel Vienna

Stephansplatz 12, (6th floor) ✉ 1010 – Ⓜ Stephansplatz – ✆ (01) 2 41 88 – hotel@doco.com – Fax (01) 24 18 84 44 – www.doco.com **D2**

43 rm – 310/350 € 310/350 €

Rest – Carte 35/49 €

◆ Business ◆ Design ◆

At the Stephansdom is this modern designer hotel in a glass building. Natural light combines charmingly with the tasteful décor. This 7th floor restaurant offers Euro-Asian cuisine prepared in an open kitchen. Terrace with views of the Dom.

Radisson SAS Style Hotel

Herrengasse 12 ✉ 1010 – Ⓜ Herrengasse – ✆ (01) 22 78 00 – info.style@radissonsas.com – Fax (01) 2 27 80 77 – www.style.vienna.radissonsas.com **D2**

78 rm – 208/285 € 208/285 €, 22 €

Rest *Sapori* – ✆ *(01) 2 27 80 78 (closed August, Sunday and Bank Holidays, June - August also Saturday lunch)* Menu 35 € (lunch)/60 € – Carte 40/51 €

◆ Business ◆ Stylish ◆

Fine modern interiors are evident from the rotunda-like hall, through to the elegant rooms of this former bank building. A former basement vault is home to the Sapori. Italian cuisine.

Das Triest

Wiedner Hauptstr. 12 ✉ 1040 – Ⓜ Karlsplatz – ✆ (01) 58 91 80 – office@dastriest.at – Fax (01) 5 89 18 18 – www.dastriest.at *Plan I* **B3**

72 rm – 205 € 260 € – 4 suites

Rest – *(closed 2 - 7 January, 29 July - 15 August and Saturday lunch, Sunday)* Menu 40 € – Carte 28/42 €

◆ Business ◆ Design ◆

The rooms, designed by Terence Conran, feature blue armchairs and desks with modem connection. Functional, yet homely, without clutter. A modern ambience of mirrors welcomes you to the Italian cuisine in the restaurant.

NH Belvedere without rest

Rennweg 12a ✉ 1030 – ☎ (01) 2 06 11 – nhbelvedere@nh-hotels.com – Fax (01) 2 06 11 15 – www.nh-hotels.com Plan I **B3**

114 rm – 🚹104/195 € 🚹🚹104/195 €, ☕ 15 €

◆ Chain hotel ◆ Modern ◆

A modern hotel in the classicist building of the former State Printing Office. Impressive rooms, some with views of the Botanic Gardens, bistro with snacks.

Arcotel Wimberger

Neubaugürtel 34 ✉ 1070 – Ⓜ Burgg Stadthalle – ☎ (01) 52 16 50 – wimberger@arcotel.at – Fax (01) 52 16 58 11 – www.arcotel.at/wimberger Plan I **A3**

225 rm – 🚹259 € 🚹🚹259/274 €, ☕ 15 € – 7 suites

Rest – Carte 21/41 €

◆ Business ◆ Functional ◆

After it was destroyed by fire, the old "Hotel Wimberger Opfer" was reborn as a modern hotel for business travellers, with rooms furnished in attractive natural wood. The restaurant "Maskerade" is decorated with items from a former ballroom.

The Levante Parliament

Auerspergstr. 9 ✉ 1080 – Ⓜ Lerchenfelder Str. – ☎ (01) 22 82 80 – parliament@thelevante.com – Fax (01) 2 28 28 28 – www.thelevante.com **C2**

70 rm ☕ – 🚹160/210 € 🚹🚹195/273 € – **Rest** – *(closed Sunday)* Carte 20/40 €

◆ Townhouse ◆ Design ◆

Hidden behind the stone façade is this hotel with linear-modern design throughout. Glass art objects add interesting touches. Rooms with the most modern facilities. The minimalist hotel serves international cuisine.

Kaiserhof without rest

Frankenberggasse 10 ✉ 1040 – Ⓜ Karlsplatz – ☎ (01) 5 05 17 01 – wien@hotel-kaiserhof.at – Fax (01) 5 05 88 75 88 – www.hotel-kaiserhof.at Plan I **B3**

74 rm ☕ – 🚹130/185 € 🚹🚹165/260 € – 3 suites

◆ Traditional ◆ Art Deco ◆

Located in a small side street is this attractive house from 1896 which appeals with tastefully decorated rooms with high ceilings. Attractive bar area serving snacks.

Hollmann Beletage without rest

Köllnerhofgasse 6 ✉ 1010 – Ⓜ Schwedenplatz – ☎ (01) 9 61 19 60 – hotel@hollmann-beletage.at – Fax (01) 9 61 19 60 33 – www.hollmann-beletage.at **E2**

16 rm ☕ – 🚹130/170 € 🚹🚹130/170 €

◆ Townhouse ◆ Design ◆

A classic townhouse is home to this small designer hotel with private atmosphere. Clean linear design and interesting detail dominate the modern ambience.

K+K Hotel Maria Theresia without rest

Kirchberggasse 6 ✉ 1070 – Ⓜ Volkstheater – ☎ (01) 5 21 23 – kk.maria.theresia@kuk.at – Fax (01) 5 21 23 70 – www.kkhotels.com **C3**

123 rm ☕ – 🚹180 € 🚹🚹240 €

◆ Business ◆ Modern ◆

Located in the artists' quarter of Spittelberg, this hotel also has especially nice rooms with views of Vienna. The bar in the spacious lobby offers a small menu.

Kaiserin Elisabeth without rest

Weihburggasse 3 ✉ 1010 – Ⓜ Stephansplatz – ☎ (01) 51 52 60 – info@kaiserinelisabeth.at – Fax (01) 51 52 67 – www.kaiserinelisabeth.at **E2**

63 rm ☕ – 🚹122/165 € 🚹🚹208/230 €

◆ Traditional ◆ Classic ◆

Both Mozart and Wagner were guests at this hotel near the Stephansdom, in operation since 1809. Elegant, dark timber furniture in a style from the turn of the last century.

Mercure Grandhotel Biedermeier without rest

Landstraßer Hauptstr. 28, (at Sünnhof) 60 VISA AE
✉ 1030 – Ⓜ Landstraße – ✆ (01) 71 67 10 – h5357@accor.com
– Fax (01) 71 67 15 03 – www.mercure.com **F2**
202 rm – 151/231 € 178/340 €, 15 € – 12 suites
♦ Chain hotel ♦ Classic ♦
This hotel is located in a town house with a delightful arcade. All of the rooms are tastefully decorated with Biedermeier-style cherry-wood furniture.

König von Ungarn rm 15 VISA AE

Schulerstr. 10 ✉ 1010 – Ⓜ Stephansplatz – ✆ (01) 51 58 40 – hotel@kvu.at
– Fax (01) 51 58 48 – www.kvu.at **E2**
33 rm – 142/162 € 203 €
Rest – *(dinner only)* Carte 24/36 €
♦ Traditional ♦ Classic ♦
Located behind the Stephansdom is this classically decorated 16C building, with lots of style and warm colours. Don't miss the attractive courtyard! Follow Mozart's footsteps: This establishment is located in the house where Mozart once lived.

Das Tyrol without rest VISA AE

Mariahilfer Str. 15 ✉ 1060 – Ⓜ Museumsquartier – ✆ (01) 5 87 54 15
– reception@das-tyrol.at – Fax (01) 58 75 41 59 – www.das-tyrol.at **C3**
30 rm – 109/209 € 149/259 €
♦ Family ♦ Modern ♦
This lovingly restored corner building is home to tastefully decorated rooms with modern furnishings. Paintings by Viennese artists adorn the walls.

Altstadt Vienna without rest VISA AE

Kirchengasse 41 ✉ 1070 – Ⓜ Volkstheater – ✆ (01) 5 26 33 99 – hotel@
altstadt.at – Fax (01) 5 23 49 01 – www.altstadt.at *Plan I* **A3**
42 rm – 109/169 € 129/189 € – 7 suites
♦ Traditional ♦ Stylish ♦
Each room in this patrician house has its own character. Well-appointed rooms with high ceilings, parquet, and select objets d'art.

Sofitel rm 60 VISA AE

Am Heumarkt 35 ✉ 1030 – Ⓜ Stadtpark – ✆ (01) 71 61 60 – h1276@accor.com
– Fax (01) 71 61 68 44 – www.sofitel.com **E3**
211 rm – 130/290 € 150/290 €, 18 €
Rest – Carte 24/41 €
♦ Chain hotel ♦ Functional ♦
Elements of art nouveau and Gustav Klimt reproductions lend the rooms an agreeable ambience. Timeless natural wood and modern technical facilities. Lovely: the Pullmann Bar. International and Viennese dishes are served in the restaurant.

Rathauspark without rest 30 VISA AE

Rathausstr. 17 ✉ 1010 – Ⓜ Rathaus – ✆ (01) 40 41 20 – rathauspark@
austria-trend.at – Fax (01) 40 41 27 61 – www.austria-trend.at/rhw **C2**
117 rm – 138/175 € 199/248 €
♦ Business ♦ Classic ♦
An attractive stuccoed entrance welcomes guests to this smart hotel from 1880. The mostly high-ceilinged rooms are decorated with modern elegance. An original lift.

Falkensteiner Am Schottenfeld without rest

Schottenfeldgasse 74 ✉ 1070 100 VISA AE
– Ⓜ Burgg Stadthalle – ✆ (01) 5 26 51 81 – schottenfeld@falkensteiner.com
– Fax (01) 52 65 18 11 60 – www.falkensteiner.com *Plan I* **A3**
95 rm – 133/144 € 169/185 €
♦ Business ♦ Modern ♦
Modern interiors from the large lobby through to the pleasantly decorated rooms, with light furnishings and good facilities. The hotel is integrated into a row of houses.

AUSTRIA

K+K Palais Hotel without rest
Rudolfsplatz 11 ✉ 1010 – Ⓜ Schwedenplatz – ✆ (01) 5 33 13 53 – kk.palais.hotel@kuk.at – Fax (01) 5 33 13 53 70 – www.kkhotels.com
D1
66 rm – 🛉180 € 🛉🛉240 €
◆ Traditional ◆ Functional ◆
Functional, yet homely rooms and warm breakfast room at this historic city villa. The Stephansdom and the underground are close by.

Rathaus without rest
20 VISA AE
Lange Gasse 13 ✉ 1080 – Ⓜ Rathaus – ✆ (01) 4 00 11 22 – office@hotel-rathaus-wien.at – Fax (01) 4 00 11 22 88 – www.hotel-rathaus-wien.at
closed 22 - 27 December
Plan I **A3**
33 rm – 🛉118/138 € 🛉🛉148/198 €, ☕ 13 €
◆ Family ◆ Design ◆
The 1890 building has been combined with modern design. Wine is the theme here and each room is named after an Austrian wine-grower. Wine lounge.

Strudlhof without rest
150 P VISA AE
Pasteurgasse 1 ✉ 1090 – Ⓜ Währinger Str.-Volksoper – ✆ (01) 3 19 25 22 – hotel@strudlhof.at – Fax (01) 31 92 52 28 00 – www.strudlhof.at
Plan I **A2**
84 rm ☕ – 🛉135/169 € 🛉🛉179/199 €
◆ Business ◆ Functional ◆
This hotel offers comfortable, well-equipped rooms. A stylish setting for your business function.

Opernring without rest
VISA AE
Opernring 11 ✉ 1010 – Ⓜ Karlsplatz – ✆ (01) 5 87 55 18 – hotel@opernring.at – Fax (01) 5 87 55 18 29 – www.opernring.at
D3
35 rm ☕ – 🛉140/200 € 🛉🛉155/280 €
◆ Business ◆ Classic ◆
Opposite the State Opera House is this hotel with its pretty art nouveau façade. Spacious rooms combine homeliness with the functionality of modern hotels.

Mercure Secession without rest
30 VISA AE
Getreidemarkt 5 ✉ 1060 – Ⓜ Museumsquartier – ✆ (01) 58 83 80 – h3532@accor.com – Fax (01) 58 83 82 12 – www.mercure.com
D3
70 rm ☕ – 🛉141 € 🛉🛉176 €
◆ Chain hotel ◆ Functional ◆
Thanks to its central location, this residence is a great base for discovering the city. The rooms are homely and comfortable. Apartments also available.

Ibis Messe
rm 100 VISA AE
Lassallestr. 7a ✉ 1020 – Ⓜ Praterstern – ✆ (01) 21 77 00 – h2736@accor.com – Fax (01) 21 77 05 55 – www.ibishotels.com
Plan I **B2**
166 rm – 🛉66 € 🛉🛉81 €, ☕ 9 €
Rest – Carte 16/25 €
◆ Chain hotel ◆ Functional ◆
Contemporary, functional rooms with light-coloured furnishings, close to the Prater park. Guests enjoy spacious desks and excellent modern technology.

Steirereck (Reitbauer)
40 VISA AE
Am Heumarkt 2 (at Stadtpark) ✉ 1030 – Ⓜ Stadtpark – ✆ (01) 7 13 31 68 – wien@steirereck.at – Fax (01) 71 33 16 82 – www.steirereck.at
closed Saturday - Sunday, Bank Holidays
F2
Rest – *(booking advisable)* Menu 45 € (lunch)/95 € – Carte 53/79 €
Spec. Gebratene Gänseleber mit Cox-Orange Apfel. Reh mit Wald- und Wiesenaromaten. Lamm mit Pastinaken und gerollter Nudel.
◆ Contemporary ◆ Design ◆
This unusual restaurant in the Stadtpark, on the Wien River, offers large set menus each evening in an exclusive setting.

XXXX ✿ **Restaurant Coburg** – Hotel Palais Coburg
Coburgbastei 4 ✉ 1010 – Ⓜ Stubentor – ✆ (01) 51 81 88 00 – restaurant@palais-coburg.com – Fax (01) 51 81 88 18 – www.palais-coburg.com
closed Sunday - Monday, Bank Holidays E2
Rest – *(dinner only)* Menu 68/106 € – Carte 55/69 €
Spec. Wolfsbarschfilet mit marinierten Linsen und Kräutersalat. Wachtelbrust mit Kohlrabi und jungen Erbsen. Lammrücken mit Olivenkruste und grünen Bohnenkernen.
♦ French ♦ Formal ♦
This elegant restaurant with lovely vaulted ceiling and sumptuous table settings is the scene for the culinary joy of Christian Petz's classical cuisine. Professional service.

XXXX ✿ **Korso** – Hotel Bristol
Kärntner Ring 1 ✉ 1015 – Ⓜ Karlsplatz – ✆ (01) 51 51 65 46 – Fax (01) 51 51 65 75 – www.luxurycollection.com/bristol
closed August and Saturday lunch D3
Rest – Menu 47 € (lunch)/115 € – Carte 51/89 €
Spec. Filet vom Bachsaibling mit "eingebrannten" Kartoffeln. Riesling-Kalbsbeuscherl mit Semmelflan. Zitronennudeln mit Kaviar.
♦ Austrian ♦ Formal ♦
The visual focus in this classic restaurant is the illuminated onyx wall. Equally classical is the menu with regional elements.

XXX **Mörwald im Ambassador**
Kärntner Str. 22 (1st floor) ✉ 1010 – Ⓜ Stephansplatz – ✆ (01) 96 16 11 61 – ambassador@moerwald.at – Fax (01) 96 16 11 60 – www.moerwald.at
closed Sunday and Bank Holidays D2
Rest – *(booking advisable)* Carte 50/78 €
♦ Contemporary ♦ Friendly ♦
Guests enter this elegant restaurant through a bar in the hotel atrium. The large glass window front is opened in summer. International cuisine.

XXX **Drei Husaren**
Weihburggasse 4 ✉ 1010 – Ⓜ Stephansplatz – ✆ (01) 51 21 09 20 – office@drei.husaren.at – Fax (01) 5 12 10 92 18 – www.drei-husaren.at E2
Rest – Menu 33 € (lunch)/79 € – Carte 40/64 €
♦ International ♦ Formal ♦
In a side street near the Stephansdom is this long-standing Viennese gourmet restaurant. International cuisine and Viennese classics.

XXX **Niky's Kuchlmasterei** with rm
Obere Weissgerberstr. 6 ✉ 1030 – ✆ (01) 7 12 90 00 30
– office@kuchlmastererei.at – Fax (01) 7 12 90 00 16 – www.kuchlmasterei.at
closed Sunday and Bank Holidays except December F1
6 suites – †240 € ††240 €, ☕ 13 €
Rest – Menu 29 € (lunch)/51 € – Carte 35/58 €
♦ International ♦ Cosy ♦
The interior of this special restaurant is captivating with its rich décor and numerous original artworks. An attractive terrace and enormous wine cellar. Individually decorated, exclusive suites.

XXX **Julius Meinl am Graben**
Graben 19, (1st floor) ✉ 1010 – Ⓜ Stephansplatz – ✆ (01) 5 32 33 34 60 00 – restaurant@meinlamgraben.com – Fax (01) 5 32 33 34 12 90 – www.meinlamgraben.at
closed Sunday and Bank Holidays D2
Rest – *(booking essential)* Menu 34 € (lunch)/85 € (dinner) – Carte 45/67 €
♦ International ♦ Friendly ♦
Classic cuisine in an exclusive delicatessen, rich in tradition. The window seats provide a lovely view of the Graben and Pestsäule.

XXX

Grotta Azzurra

VISA MC AE

Babenbergerstr. 5 ✉ 1010 – Ⓜ Museumsquartier – ✆ (01) 5 86 10 44 – office@grotta-azzurra.at – Fax (01) 5 86 10 44 15 – www.grotta-azzura.at

D3

Rest – Carte 27/41 €

♦ Italian ♦ Friendly ♦

Austria's oldest Italian restaurant has been in existence since the beginning of the Fifties. Artistic Murano glass and mosaics create a special atmosphere.

XX

Mraz & Sohn

P VISA MC

Wallensteinstr. 59 ✉ 1200 – Ⓜ Friedensbrücke – ✆ (01) 3 30 45 94 – Fax (01) 3 50 15 36 – www.mraz-sohn.at

closed 3 weeks August, 24 December - 6 January and Saturday - Sunday, Bank Holidays

Plan I **A2**

Rest – *(booking advisable)* Menu 38/87 € – Carte 41/52 €

Spec. Gänseleber mit Essiglinsen in Karamelcreme. Ochsenfilet und Ochsenschlepp geschmort auf Majoran-Pilzragout. Alles Schokolade.

♦ Contemporary ♦ Fashionable ♦

Both the characterful décor and the creative cuisine at this family-run establishment are modern. Friendly service. Interesting wine cellar.

XX

Selina

VISA MC AE

Laudongasse 13 ✉ 1080 – Ⓜ Rathaus – ✆ (01) 4 05 64 04 – Fax (01) 4 08 04 59 – www.selina.at

Plan I **A2**

Rest – Menu 44/81 € – Carte 25/55 €

♦ Seasonal cuisine ♦ Friendly ♦

In a modern and elegant atmosphere punctuated with artwork and classical elements, refined cuisine as well as Mediterranean and eastern specialities are served.

XX

Novelli

VISA MC AE

Bräunerstr. 11 ✉ 1010 – Ⓜ Herrengasse – ✆ (01) 5 13 42 00 – novelli@haslauer.at – Fax (01) 5 13 99 74 – www.novelli.at

closed Sunday

D2

Rest – *(booking advisable)* Menu 25 € (lunch)/49 € – Carte 33/53 €

♦ Mediterranean ♦ Trendy ♦

Experience the Italian way of life in a refined atmosphere: a Mediterranean ambiance accompanies classic Mediterranean cuisine with an emphasis on Italian flavours.

XX

Vestibül

VISA MC AE

Dr. Karl-Lueger-Ring 2, (at Burgtheater) ✉ 1010 – Ⓜ Herrengasse – ✆ (01) 5 32 49 99 – restaurant@vestibuel.at – Fax (01) 5 32 49 99 10 – www.vestibuel.at

closed Saturday lunch, Sunday and Bank Holidays, July - August also Saturday dinner

C2

Rest – Menu 39 € – Carte 27/47 €

♦ International ♦ Friendly ♦

In a side wing of the Burgtheater is this stylish restaurant decorated with marble and stucco. Spoil yourself with good regional and Mediterranean cuisine.

XX

Walter Bauer

AC VISA MC AE

Sonnenfelsgasse 17 ✉ 1010 – Ⓜ Stubentor – ✆ (01) 5 12 98 71 – restaurant.walter.bauer@aon.at – Fax (01) 5 12 98 71

closed Holy week, 23 July - 17 August and Saturday - Monday lunch, Bank Holidays

E2

Rest – *(booking advisable)* Menu 50/90 € – Carte 44/55 €

Spec. Jakobsmuscheln mit Schalotten und Limone. Gefüllter Ochsenschwanz. Mousse von Ziegenfrischkäse mit karamellisierten Oliven und Marillen.

♦ International ♦ Cosy ♦

This restaurant with pretty cross-vaulting is found in a 14C old town building. Intimate atmosphere and professional service. Creative cuisine with regional influences.

Zum weißen Rauchfangkehrer

Weihburggasse 4 ✉ 1010 – Ⓜ Stephansplatz – ✆ (01) 5 12 34 71
– rauchfangkehrer@utanet.at – Fax (01) 5 12 34 71 28
– www.weisser-rauchfangkehrer.at
closed early July - early September and Sunday - Monday
Rest – *(dinner only) (booking advisable)* Carte 43/65 € **E2**

◆ Austrian ◆ Cosy ◆

Four charming dining rooms in this long-standing guesthouse, each in its own style. Enjoy authentic Viennese cuisine. Very friendly service.

Fabios

Tuchlauben 6 ✉ 1010 Wien – Ⓜ Stephansplatz – ✆ (01) 5 32 22 22
– fabios@fabios.at – Fax (01) 5 32 22 25
– www.fabios.at
closed Sunday except Bank Holidays **D2**
Rest – *(booking advisable)* Carte 40/62 €

◆ Mediterranean ◆ Trendy ◆

Warm wood tones and bold lines set the scene in this modern restaurant at the end of the pedestrian zone. Mediterranean cuisine.

Indochine 21

Stubenring 18 ✉ 1010 – Ⓜ Stubentor – ✆ (01) 5 13 76 60
– restaurant@indochine.at – Fax (01) 5 13 76 60 16
– www.indochine.at **E2**
Rest – Menu 40/75 € – Carte 40/71 €

◆ Asian influences ◆ Fashionable ◆

A trendy city location, where a piece of colonial Indo-China is recreated. High-class fusion cooking, Asiatic with French accents.

Zum Schwarzen Kameel

Bognergasse 5 ✉ 1010 – Ⓜ Herrengasse – ✆ (01) 5 33 81 25
– info@kameel.at – Fax (01) 5 33 81 25 23 – www.kameel.at
closed Sunday and Bank Holidays **D2**
Rest – *(booking essential)* Menu 27 € (lunch)/62 €
– Carte 32/58 €

◆ International ◆ Friendly ◆

Located in a house dating back to 1618, this charming restaurant offers beautiful Art Nouveau style and a one-of-a-kind Viennese coffee-house atmosphere. Gourmet shop.

RieGi

Schauflergasse 6 ✉ 1010 – Ⓜ Herrengasse – ✆ (01) 5 32 91 26
– world@barbaro.at – Fax (01) 5 32 91 26 20
– www.riegi.at
closed 24 July - 15 August and Sunday - Monday, Bank Holidays **D2**
Rest – Menu 38/68 € – Carte 44/56 €
Spec. Spargelsavarin mit Morcheln und gebratenen Langostinos. Gedämpftes Doradenfilet mit gefüllten Calamari und Saubohnen. Topfenpalatschinken mit Erdbeer-Rhabarber.

◆ International ◆ Friendly ◆

The restaurant near the Hofburg is decorated with modern art and an ornate illuminated ceiling. International cuisine with Mediterranean touches.

Fadinger

Wipplingerstr. 29 ✉ 1010 – Ⓜ Schottentor-Universität
– ✆ (01) 5 33 43 41 – restaurant@fadinger.at – Fax (01) 5 32 44 51
– www.fadinger.at
closed Saturday, Sunday and Bank Holidays **D1**
Rest – *(booking advisable)* Menu 19 € (lunch)/55 € (dinner)
– Carte 25/49 €

◆ Viennese cuisine ◆ Friendly ◆

Attractive location in the centre, close to the Börse: colourful watercolours suit the lively, vibrant atmosphere. The menu is international and regional.

Mezzo

Esteplatz 6 ✉ 1030 – Ⓜ Rochusgasse – ☎ (01) 7 15 51 48 – mezzo@mezzo.cc – Fax (01) 7 15 51 48 – www.mezzo.cc – closed 6 - 20 August, 23 December - 6 January and Saturday lunch - Sunday, Bank Holidays Plan I **B3**

Rest – Menu 27/54 € – Carte 26/44 €

♦ International ♦ Fashionable ♦

Modern-minimalist décor in warm tones. This restaurant in a townhouse on the edge of the centre offers an international menu with Mediterranean and regional influences.

Österreicher im MAK

Stubenring 5, (at Museum MAK) ✉ 1010 Wien – Ⓜ Stubentor – ☎ (01) 7 14 01 21 – office@oesterreicherimmak.at – Fax (01) 7 10 10 21 – www.oesterreicherimmak.at **F2**

Rest – Carte 23/36 €

♦ Austrian ♦ Trendy ♦

Historical architecture and clean modern design combine in the Museum für Angewandte Kunst. Chef Helmut Österreicher prepares regional specialities.

Schnattl

Lange Gasse 40 ✉ 1080 – Ⓜ Rathaus – ☎ (01) 4 05 34 00 – Fax (01) 4 05 34 00 closed 2 weeks after Easter, 2 weeks end August and Saturday - Sunday, Bank Holidays Plan I **A3**

Rest – Carte 33/48 €

♦ Austrian ♦ Cosy ♦

This small, well-presented restaurant with a simple but pleasant ambience is located on the edge of the inner city. The courtyard deck is particularly nice.

Weibels Wirtshaus

Kumpfgasse 2 ✉ 1010 – Ⓜ Stubentor – ☎ (01) 5 12 39 86 – Fax (01) 5 12 39 86 – www.weibel.at **E2**

Rest – *(booking advisable)* Carte 25/39 €

♦ Regional ♦ Cosy ♦

Small alcoves typify the very cosy atmosphere in this tavern located in Vienna town centre. Viennese cuisine is featured on the menu.

Weibel 3

Riemergasse 1 ✉ 1010 – Ⓜ Stubentor – ☎ (01) 5 13 31 10 – Fax (01) 5 13 31 10 – www.weibel.at – closed Sunday - Monday **E2**

Rest – *(dinner only) (booking advisable)* Menu 55 € – Carte 38/50 €

♦ Spanish ♦ Rustic ♦

The small restaurant offers a cosy, tavern-like atmosphere, a menu featuring mainly Spanish cuisine and a comprehensive wine list.

Artner

Floragasse 6 ✉ 1040 – Ⓜ Taubstummengasse – ☎ (01) 5 03 50 33 – restaurant@artner.co.at – Fax (01) 5 03 50 34 – www.artner.co.at closed Saturday lunch, Sunday and Bank Holidays lunch Plan I **B3**

Rest – Menu 30/47 € – Carte 25/42 €

♦ International ♦ Minimalist ♦

Dark wooden floors and smart lines characterise the simple, modern décor in this restaurant. International cuisine, with some regional dishes. Good-value lunch menu.

Tempel

Praterstr. 56 ✉ 1020 – Ⓜ Nestroyplatz – ☎ (01) 2 14 01 79 – restaurant.tempel@utanet.at – Fax (01) 2 14 01 79 closed 23 December - 7 January and Saturday lunch, Sunday - Monday

Rest – Menu 14 € (lunch)/37 € – Carte 26/32 € **F1**

♦ Regional ♦ Friendly ♦

This small, quite simple bistro-style restaurant is somewhat hidden in a courtyard. International cuisine. Changing daily set lunch menus.

OUTER DISTRICTS

Plan I

Landhaus Fuhrgassl-Huber without rest

Rathstr. 24, (by Krottenbachstr. A1) ✉ 1190
– ✆ (01) 4 40 30 33 – landhaus@fuhrgassl-huber.at – Fax (01) 4 40 27 14
– www.fuhrgassl-huber.at
closed 1 week February
38 rm – 🛉85/88 € 🛉🛉125/135 €

◆ Family ◆ Cosy ◆

This family-run hotel in a lovely location offers homely country-house style rooms. Very good breakfast buffet: in summer also in the courtyard.

Eckel

35

Sieveringer Str. 46, (by Billrothstr. A1) ✉ 1190
– ✆ (01) 3 20 32 18 – restaurant.eckel@aon.at – Fax (01) 3 20 66 60
– www.restauranteckel.at
closed 2 weeks August, 24 December - mid January and Sunday - Monday
Rest – Carte 24/40 €

◆ Austrian ◆ Rustic ◆

This country house is a combination of bright and welcoming décor and more traditional dark wood-panelling. Regular guests enjoy the regional and classical cuisine, and the pretty terrace.

Plachutta with rm

Heiligenstädter Str. 179 ✉ 1190 – ✆ (01) 3 70 41 25 – nussdorf@plachutta.at
– Fax (01) 3 70 41 25 20 – www.plachutta.at
closed end July - mid August **A1**
4 rm – 🛉55 € 🛉🛉85 €, 8 €
Rest – Carte 24/44 €

◆ Viennese cuisine ◆ Friendly ◆

This friendly establishment is devoted to the joys of beef: hearty soups are served in copper pots, with "Schulterscherzel", "Hüferschwänzel", and other fine cuts.

Schübel-Auer

Kahlenberger Str. 22, (Döbling) ✉ 1190 – ✆ (01) 3 70 22 22
– daniela.somloi@schuebel-auer.at – Fax (01) 3 70 22 22
– www.schuebel-auer.at
closed 23 December - 1 February and Sunday - Monday **A1**
Rest – *(open from 4pm)* Carte 12 €

◆ Buffet ◆ Cosy ◆

Built in 1642 as a wine-grower's house with mill, this traditional building was carefully renovated in 1972 and then lovingly furnished. Courtyard terrace.

Feuerwehr-Wagner

Grinzingerstr. 53, (Heiligenstadt) ✉ 1190 – ✆ (01) 3 20 24 42
– heuriger@feuerwehrwagner.at – Fax (01) 3 20 91 41
– www.feuerwehrwagner.at **A1**
Rest – *(open from 4pm)* Carte 12 €

◆ Buffet ◆ Cosy ◆

This typical "Heurige" (traditional Austrian wine tavern) is greatly appreciated by regulars. Cosy, rustic décor with dark wood and simple tables. Particularly nice: the terraced garden.

Mayer am Pfarrplatz

Pfarrplatz 2, (Heiligenstadt) ✉ 1190 – ✆ (01) 3 70 12 87 – mayer@pfarrplatz.at
– Fax (01) 3 70 47 14 – www.mayer.pfarrplatz.at
closed 21 December - 18 January **A1**
Rest – *(dinner only)* Menu 15 €

◆ Buffet ◆ Cosy ◆

A textbook "Heurige" (traditional Austrian wine tavern): rustic furnishings, traditional Viennese folk music, and an attractive courtyard terrace. Of note: Beethoven lived here in 1817!

AUSTRIA

AT THE AIRPORT

NH Vienna Airport

Hotelstr. 1 ✉ 1300 Wien – ✆ (01) 70 15 10
– nhviennaairport@nh-hotels.com
– Fax (01) 7 01 51 95 71 – www.nh-hotels.com
500 rm – †160/360 € ††160/360 €, ☕ 18 €
Rest – Carte 26/40 €
♦ Chain hotel ♦ Functional ♦
The clean, elegant design of the spacious foyer and the tasteful, modern, well-equipped rooms, some in classic style, are attractive features. The open plan of the restaurant "nhube" is smartly presented. With buffet.

BELGIUM

BELGIQUE - BELGIË

PROFILE

◆ **Area:**
30 513 km²
(11 781 sq mi)

◆ **Population:**
10 710 000 inhabitants (est. 2005), nearly 55% Flemish, 33% Walloons and about 10% foreigners. Density = 351 per km².

◆ **Capital:**
Brussels (conurbation 4 477 000 inhabitants).

◆ **Currency:**
Euro (€); rate of exchange: € 1 = US$ 1.31 (Nov 2006).

◆ **Government:**
Constitutional parliamentary monarchy (since 1830) and a federal state (since 1994). Member of European Union since 1957 (one of the 6 founding countries).

◆ **Languages:**
French (Wallonia), Flemish (Flanders), German (Eastern cantons); most Belgians also speak English.

◆ **Specific public holidays:**
National Day (21 July), Armistice Day 1918 (11 November).

◆ **Local Time:**
GMT + 1 hour in winter and GMT + 2 hours in summer.

◆ **Climate:**
Temperate maritime with cool winters and mild summers (Brussels: January: 2°C, July: 18°C); more continental towards the Ardennes. Rainfall evenly distributed throughout the year.

◆ **International dialling Code:**
00 32 followed by local number without the initial **0.** Electronic directories: www.skynet.be, www.belgacom.be

◆ **Emergency:**
Police: ✆ **101**; Medical Assistance and Fire Brigade: ✆ **100**; Police or Medical Assistance from cellular phones : ✆ **112**.

◆ **Electricity:**
220 volts AC, 50Hz; 2-pin round-shaped continental plugs.

FORMALITIES

Travellers from the European Union (EU), Switzerland, Iceland and the main countries of North and South America need a national identity card or passport (America: passport required) to visit Belgium for less than three months (tourism or business purpose). For visitors from other countries a visa may be required, in addition to a passport, especially for those wishing to stay for longer than three months. We advise you to check with your embassy before travelling.

A valid driving licence is essential. International driving licence is required for drivers from 80 countries, mainly in South America, Africa, Asia, Middle East and Pacific Islands. Third party insurance is the minimum cover required by Belgian legislation but it is advisable to take out fully comprehensive cover (Green Card).

MAJOR NEWSPAPERS

The main French-language dailies are *Le Soir, La Libre Belgique, La Dernière Heure - Les Sports, La Capitale, La Meuse* and *La Nouvelle Gazette*. The main Dutch-language dailies: *Het Laatste Nieuws, De Morgen, De Standaard, Het Nieuwsblad, Het Volk and De Gentenaar.* Daily German-language paper: *Grenz-Echo.*

USEFUL PHRASES

ENGLISH	FRENCH	DUTCH
Yes	**Oui**	**Ja**
No	**Non**	**Nee**
Good morning	**Bonjour**	**Goedemorgen**
Goodbye	**Au revoir**	**Tot ziens**
Thank you	**Merci**	**Dank u, bedankt**
Please	**S'il vous plaît**	**Alstublieft**
Excuse me	**Excusez-moi**	**Neemt U mij niet kwalijk**
I don't understand	**Je ne comprends pas**	**Ik begrijp het niet**

HOTELS

→ CATEGORIES

Accommodation ranges from luxurious 5-star international hotels, to smaller, family-run guesthouses and bed and breakfast establishments. The Benelux star rating is conferred on the application of the owner.

→ PRICE RANGE

The price is per room. There is little difference between the price of a single and a double room.

Between April and October it is advisable to book in advance. From November to March prices may be slightly lower, some hotels offer special cheap rates and some may be closed. In Brussels hotel chains offer lower weekend rates in the low season.

→ TAX

Included in the room price.

→ CHECK OUT TIME

Usually between 11am and noon.

→ RESERVATIONS

By telephone or by Internet. A credit card number may be required.

→ TIP FOR LUGGAGE HANDLING

At the discretion of the customer (about €1 per bag).

→ BREAKFAST

It is often not included in the price of the room and is generally served between 7am and 10am. Most hotels offer a self-service buffet but usually it is possible to have continental breakfast served in the room.

Reception	**Reception**	**Receptie**
Single room	**Chambre simple**	**Eenpersoonskamer**
Double room	**Chambre double**	**Kamer met tweepersoonsbed**
Bed	**Lit**	**Bed**
Bathroom	**Salle de bains**	**Badkamer**
Shower	**Douche**	**Douche**

RESTAURANTS

Besides the traditional **restaurants** there are **brasseries, bistros, 'estaminets'** (typical popular cafés serving beer mainly), **taverns, cafés** and **'friteries'** which serve simpler fare.

Breakfast	**Petit-déjeuner**	**Het ontbijt**	7am – 10am
Lunch	**Déjeuner**	**Middagmaal**	12.30pm – 2-3pm
Dinner	**Dîner**	**Avondeten**	6.30pm – 10-11pm sometimes later

NB: in French-speaking regions in Belgium and Luxembourg it is common practice to use the term 'déjeuner' for breakfast, 'dîner' for the midday meal and 'souper' for the evening meal.

Belgian restaurants offer fixed price menus (starter, main course and dessert) or à la carte. Menus are usually printed in French, Dutch and sometimes in English. A fixed price menu is usually less expensive than a meal with the same number of courses selected from the à la carte menu.

It is not uncommon for restaurants to offer a combined food and wine selection in addition to their usual menus ; wine is served by the glass and usually as much as you can drink. There is a shorter or simpler menu on offer at lunchtime than in the evening and sometimes two different menus: one for lunch and another for dinner.

→ RESERVATIONS

Reservations are usually made by phone, fax or Internet. For famous restaurants (including Michelin starred restaurants), it is advisable to book several days – or weeks in some instances – in advance. A credit card number or a phone number may be required as guarantee.

→ THE BILL

The bill (check) includes service charge and VAT. Tipping is optional but, if you are particularly pleased with the service, it is customary to round up the total to an appropriate figure – 10% in larger restaurants and the value of the small change elsewhere.

Drink or aperitif	**Apéritif**	**Aperitief**
Appetizer	**Mise en bouche**	**Hapje**
Meal	**Repas**	**Maaltijd**
First course, starter	**Entrée**	**Voorgerecht**
Main dish	**Plat principal**	**Hoofdgerecht**
Main dish of the day	**Plat du jour**	**Dagschotel**
Dessert	**Dessert**	**Nagerecht**
Water	**Eau**	**Water**
Wine (red, white, rosé)	**Vin (rouge, blanc, rosé)**	**Wijn (rode, witte, rosé)**
Beer	**Bière**	**Bier**
Bread	**Pain**	**Brood**

Meat (rare, medium, well done)	**Viande (bleu, saignant, à point)**	**Vlees (rood, saignant, gaar)**
Fish	**Poisson**	**Vis**
Salt/pepper	**Sel/poivre**	**Zout/peper**
Cheese	**Fromages**	**Kaas**
Vegetables	**Légumes**	**Groenten**
Hot/cold	**Chaud/froid**	**Heet/koud**
The bill (check) please	**L'addition SVP**	**De rekening alstublieft**

LOCAL CUISINE

Belgium's culinary traditions are among the finest in Europe and while in many respects Belgian cuisine is similar to that of France, its regional specialities lend it a special distinction. Typical dishes include **waterzooi** (chicken or fish stew), **Flanders hochepot** (casserole of pork, beef or mutton), **oie à la mode de Visé** (goose with a garlic sauce), **anguilles au vert** (eel sautéed in butter with chopped herbs), **boulets liégeois** (meatballs in a sauce with sirop de Liège), **carbonades flamandes** (beef braised in beer), **lapin aux pruneaux** (rabbit stewed with prunes) or **à la Gueuze** (with particular beer). **Potée** (stew with potatoes and vegetables served with pork chops, knuckle of ham or sausages) and **stoemp**, a Brussels variant, are very popular home-cooked dishes. Ardennes ham, shrimp rissoles, hop shoots in a mousseline sauce, chicory or Brussels **witloof** (endive) with ham, au gratin or braised, Flanders asparagus served with parsley and chopped hardboiled eggs are also delicious. **Zeeland mussels** and **schrimps** served with a plate of chips fried to perfection are particularly tasty. In the shooting season venison from the Ardennes is served with a medley of wild mushrooms as accompaniment.

The country produces an amazing variety of **cheese** (Herve, Maredsous, Chimay, Orval, Brussels). Delicious cheesy snacks include **doubles** (pancakes filled with cheese), **potkès** or boulettes de Huy (salty cheese from Huy). There are also plenty of delicious tarts to savour, among them **Lierse vlaaikens** (from Lier), **tarte au maton** (fromage frais, buttermilk and almonds), **flamiche** (with local cheese), **djote** (with whitebeet, cheese, eggs, lardons) and **tarte au stofé** (fromage frais, eggs, almonds and potato). Pralines (chocolates), **waffles** from Brussels and Liège, marzipan and sirop de Liège spread are great treats.

DRINK

Beer is the national drink though most restaurant meals are accompanied by wine. There is an extensive variety of local beers known as **'spéciales'**, as a general term, as distinct from ordinary lagers or 'Pils'.

Among the special beers, you should sample the abbey beers (**bières d'abbaye** – Maredsous, Affligem, Floreffe, Corsendonk, Val Dieu, St-Feuillien, Grimbergen, Leffe, etc.) and in particular an authentic Trappist beer (**bière trappiste**, appellation contrôlée reserved for the production of 6 abbeys – the most famous are Orval, N.-D. de Scourmont at Chimay, N.-D. de Saint-Rémy at Rochefort and Westmalle).

The famous speciality of the Brussels region, **lambics, gueuzes** and **krieks** (cherry-flavoured) are the same type of refreshing, slightly sour beer, which is naturally fermented without the addition of yeast (cork stoppers are used for the best bottles).

Fruit and plain **gin** (genever) are widely available as well as a variety of spirits and liqueurs (Elixir d'Anvers, Mandarine Napoléon, etc.)

BRUSSELS

BRUXELLES/BRUSSEL

Population (est. 2005): 133 000 (conurbation 4 477 000) – Altitude: about 100m

SGM/COLORISE

Brussels is a cosmopolitan city famous for its warm and friendly atmosphere. The Belgian capital is a place of contrasts reflecting its rich and turbulent history and multicultural influences as well as its pivotal role as the seat of NATO, WEU, the European Union institutions and several multinational companies. Brussels comprises 19 local districts or communes with vibrant local communities and their own distinctive charm. The majority of the population speaks French and some 15% are Dutch (Flemish) speakers.

From the historic city centre, wide avenues and boulevards lead to the surrounding areas which have been extensively redeveloped. Major building projects symbolize the dynamism of the city which is known as the capital of Art Nouveau. The delightful parks and gardens are tranquil havens from the bustling pace of life.

The people enjoy the good life and the reputation of Belgian artists and designers grows apace. An endearing aspect of the national character is revealed in the originality and quirky humour of the comic strips.

WHICH DISTRICT TO CHOOSE

The various districts of Brussels are well-endowed with places to stay, restaurants, sights and attractions.

A great concentration of **hotels, restaurants** and **brasseries** is located in the Grand'Place area, known as the "Îlôt sacré" *Plan IV* **M2**. This quartier is particularly charming and the small streets all around recall the quarter's history. Rue des Bouchers and Petite rue des Bouchers *Plan IV* **M1** are lined with many popular restaurants. Beware, however, many tourists traps also exist in this area, and we suggest you stick to those restaurants listed in the following pages.

For a gourmet meal with fresh seafood direct from the North Sea, choose one of the many restaurants in the quartier Ste-Catherine *Plan IV* **M1** where fish shops are located. Shrimp rissoles, croquettes de crevettes grises (starter), and succulent soles Meunière (main dish) are some of the tasty offerings.

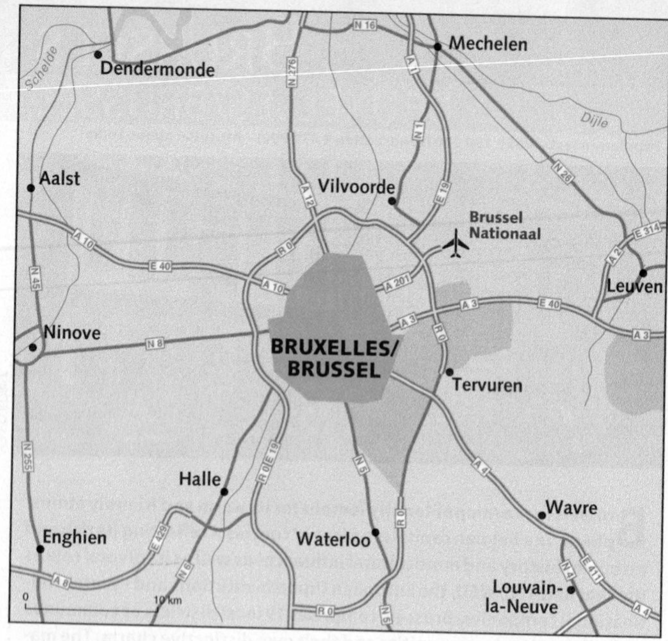

Quartier Louise *Plan III* **K3**, a busy commercial district with luxury shops, has many comfortable hotels and restaurants. Those who prefer simple cooking and a convivial atmosphere will be well served in quartier des Marolles *Plan IV* **M3**, a working-class district and in the adjacent quartier des Sablons where antique shops are to be found. Restaurants near Halles St-Géry *Plan IV* **L1**, the latest fashionable area, welcome a young and trendy crowd.

PRACTICAL INFORMATION

ARRIVAL – DEPARTURE

Brussels-National Airport in Zaventem – About 14 km (8 mi) from the city centre. ✆ 02 753 77 53; 0900 70 000 (7am-10pm); info@brusselsairport.be; www.brusselsairport.be

From the airport to the city centre – By **taxi**: €30 + charge for luggage. By **train**: Airport City Express to Bruxelles-Nord, Bruxelles-Centrale and Bruxelles-Midi every 20min. Time: 25min. ✆ 02 528 28 28. Fares €2.80. By **bus** B12. Fare €3.00. ✆ 02 515 20 20.

Main Stations – Bruxelles-Midi *Plan II* **E3** is the main interchange for international services. ✆ 02 528 28 28 (8am-8pm; Sat-Sun 9am-5.30pm); www.sncb.be; www.b-rail.be

TRANSPORT

→ METRO, BUS AND TRAM

Tickets are available from metro stations, STIB/MIVB offices, selected newsagents and tourist information centres. All tram and bus stops are request stops. A single short distance ticket costs €1.50; 5-10 journey cards and one-day travelcards are availa-

For **pralines** (chocolates), **massepain** (marzipan sold mostly in winter), **speculoos** (sweet, spicy biscuits) and other delicacies visit *Wittamer*, pl. du Grand-Sablon 6; *Dandoy*, rue au Beurre 31; *Planète Chocolat*, rue du Lombard 24; *Mary*, rue Royale 73; *Godiva*, Grand'Place 22; *Marcolini*, pl. du Grand-Sablon 39; *Neuhaus*, galerie de la Reine 25.

SHOPPING

Stores are usually open from 10am to 6-7pm. On Friday some department stores close at 8-9pm. In many districts, some shops also open on Sunday and/or in the evening.

Galeries Saint Hubert *Plan IV* **M2**: 3 shopping arcades under one roof: luxury stores and boutiques, bookshops. **Boulevard Anspach, place de Broukère, boulevard A. Max** *Plan IV* **M1. Rue Neuve** *Plan IV* **M2**: boutiques, department stores. **Rue Dansaert** *Plan IV* **L1**: trendy fashion boutiques. **Avenue Louise, avenue de la Toison d'Or. Boulevard de Waterloo** *Plan II* **F3**: luxury shops, couture houses. **Porte de Namur, rue de Namur** *Plan IV* **N3**: upmarket off-the-peg boutiques. **Rue du Midi** *Plan IV* **M2**: stamps, coins, musical instruments and other items. **Place du Grand Sablon and surroundings** *Plan IV* **M3**: antique shops and art galleries.

MARKETS – *See above "Different facets of the city".*

WHAT TO BUY – Brussels lace, fine glassware, earthenware, pewter, silver, diamonds, Tintin memorabilia, almond bread (marzipan), speculoos, Belgian pralines and chocolates, beers.

ENTERTAINMENT

The Bulletin, a weekly publication *(Thursdays)* in English, is a good source of information. *MAD*, the weekly supplement to *Le Soir*, and the monthly magazines *Kiosque* and *Tram 81* publish complete entertainment listings for Brussels.

CONCERT HALLS – **Théâtre Royal de la Monnaie** *Plan IV* **M1. Palais des Beaux-Arts** *Plan IV* **N2. Conservatoire royal de musique** *Plan IV* **M3**.

OTHER VENUES – **Ancienne Belgique** *Plan IV* **M1. Cirque Royal** *Plan IV* **N1. Forest National** *Plan I* **A3. Halles de Schaerbeek** *Plan I* **C2. Le Botanique** *Plan II* **F1**.

NIGHTLIFE

Brussels by Night available from the tourist offices lists clubs and discotheques near the **Grand'Place** *Plan IV* **M2, Marolles** *Plan IV* **M3, Sablons** and **Midi-Lemonnier** districts, near the **Atomium** *Plan I* **B1** and in the **Upper Town** and university districts.

Quartier de la Bourse, the focal point for the local youth, in particular around **Halles-St-Géry** and in **Rue Dansaert** *Plan IV* **L1**, is very lively late into the night.

Environs of Brussels (Plan I)

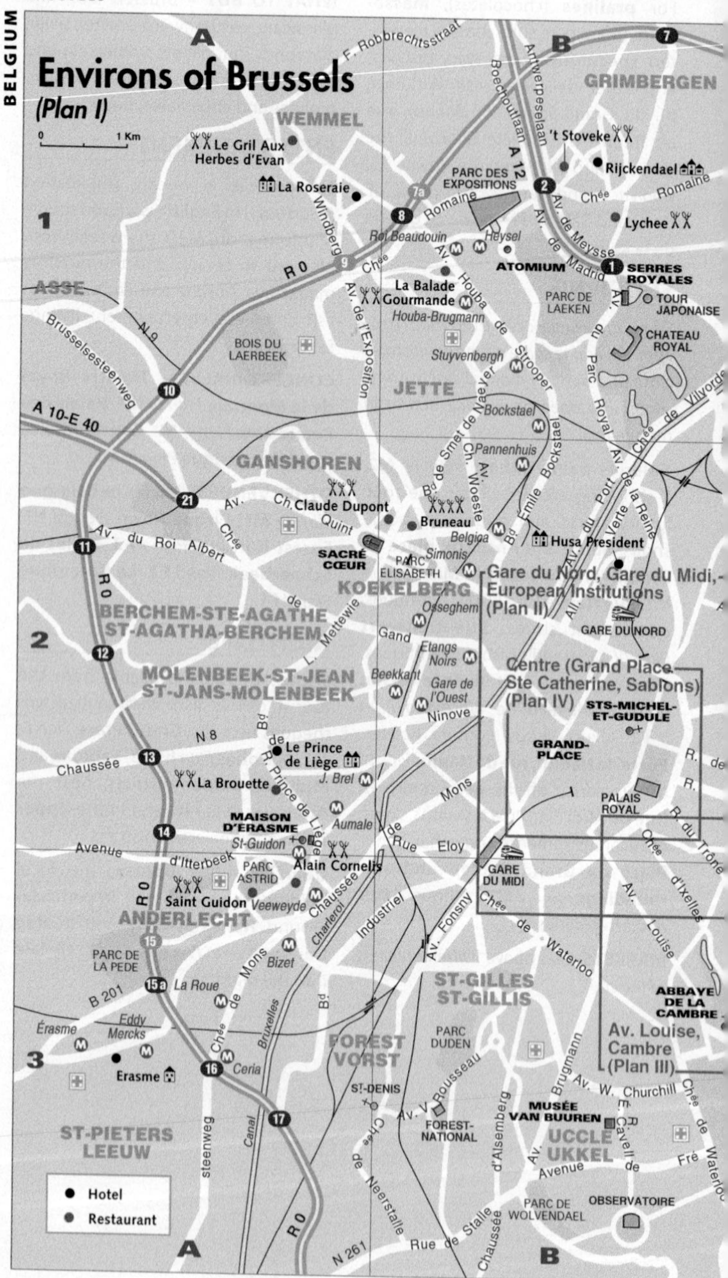

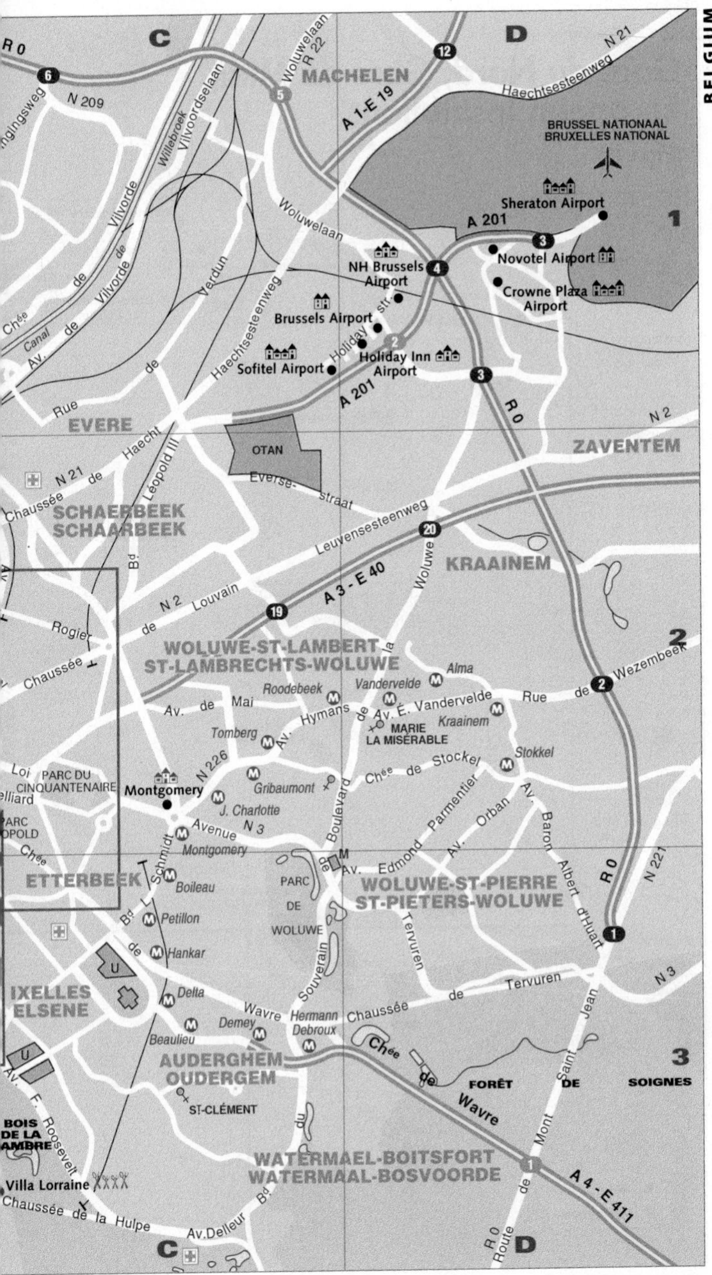
MACHELEN
BRUSSEL NATIONAAL
BRUXELLES NATIONAL
Sheraton Airport
Novotel Airport
Crowne Plaza Airport
NH Brussels Airport
Brussels Airport
Holiday Inn Airport
Sofitel Airport
EVERE
OTAN
ZAVENTEM
SCHAERBEEK
SCHAARBEEK
KRAAINEM
WOLUWE-ST-LAMBERT
ST-LAMBRECHTS-WOLUWE
MARIE LA MISÉRABLE
PARC DU CINQUANTENAIRE
Montgomery
ETTERBEEK
PARC DE WOLUWE
WOLUWE-ST-PIERRE
ST-PIETERS-WOLUWE
IXELLES
ELSENE
AUDERGHEM
OUDERGEM
ST-CLÉMENT
FORÊT DE SOIGNES
WATERMAEL-BOITSFORT
WATERMAAL-BOSVOORDE
Villa Lorraine
A 1-E 19
A 201
A 3 - E 40
A 4 - E 411
R 0
N 2
N 3
Leuvensesteenweg
Haechtsesteenweg
Woluwelaan
Chaussée de Louvain
Chaussée de Wavre
Chaussée de Tervuren
Chaussée de la Hulpe

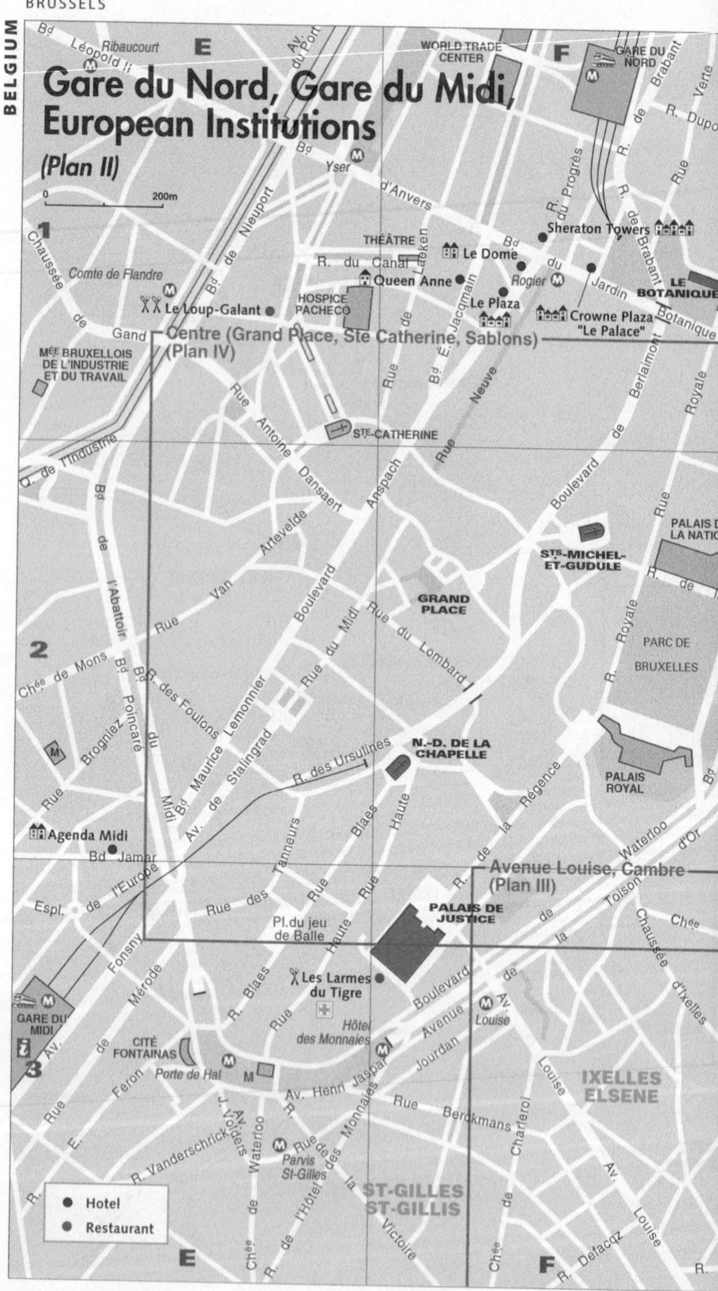
Gare du Nord, Gare du Midi, European Institutions
(Plan II)
0
200m
E
F
1
2
3
Bd Léopold II
Ribaucourt
Av. du Port
WORLD TRADE CENTER
GARE DU NORD
Bd Yser
d'Anvers
Bd de Nieuport
Chaussée de Gand
Comte de Flandre
Le Loup-Galant
THÉÂTRE
R. du Canal
Queen Anne
Le Dome
HOSPICE PACHECO
Le Plaza
Bd du Jardin Botanique
Rogier
Sheraton Towers
Crowne Plaza "Le Palace"
LE BOTANIQUE
R. de Brabant
R. Dupont
Rue Verte
R. du Progrès
Rue de Laeken
Bd É. Jacqmain
Centre (Grand Place, Ste Catherine, Sablons) (Plan IV)
Mée BRUXELLOIS DE L'INDUSTRIE ET DU TRAVAIL
Q. de l'Industrie
Rue Antoine Dansaert
STE-CATHERINE
Rue Neuve
Boulevard de Berlaimont
Rue Royale
Boulevard Anspach
STS-MICHEL-ET-GUDULE
PALAIS DE LA NATION
R. de la Loi
Bd de l'Abattoir
Rue Van Artevelde
GRAND PLACE
Boulevard
Rue du Midi
Rue du Lombard
R. Royale
PARC DE BRUXELLES
Chée de Mons
Bd Poincaré
Bd du Midi
R. des Foulons
Bd Maurice Lemonnier
Av. de Stalingrad
Rue Brogniez
R. des Ursulines
N.-D. DE LA CHAPELLE
PALAIS ROYAL
Rue Haute
Rue Blaes
Rue des Tanneurs
R. de la Régence
Agenda Midi
Bd Jamar
Bd de Waterloo
Avenue Louise, Cambre (Plan III)
Espl. de l'Europe
Rue des
PALAIS DE JUSTICE
Pl.du jeu de Balle
Toison d'Or
Av. de la Toison d'Or
Chée
Av. Fonsny
Rue Mérode
R. Blaes
Les Larmes du Tigre
Hôtel des Monnaies
Chaussée d'Ixelles
Boulevard de Waterloo
Avenue Louise
GARE DU MIDI
CITÉ FONTAINAS
Porte de Hal
Jourdan
Av. Louise
Rue E. Feron
Av. Henri Jaspar
Rue Berckmans
IXELLES ELSENE
Av. J. Volders
R. Vanderschrick
Parvis St-Gilles
Rue de la Victoire
R. de l'Hôtel des Monnaies
Chée de Waterloo
Chée de Charleroi
ST-GILLES ST-GILLIS
R. Defacqz
Hotel
Restaurant
M

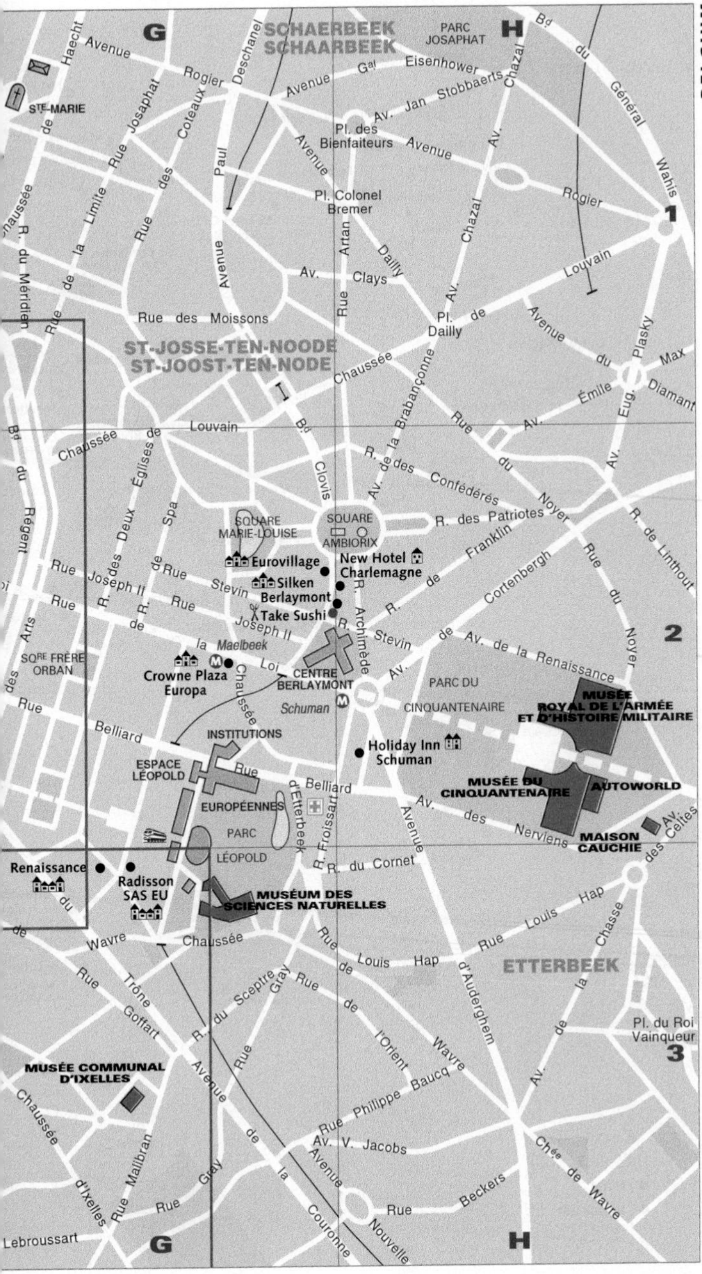
G
H
1
2
3
SCHAERBEEK
SCHAARBEEK
PARC JOSAPHAT
STE-MARIE
ST-JOSSE-TEN-NOODE
ST-JOOST-TEN-NODE
ETTERBEEK
Pl. des Bienfaiteurs
Pl. Colonel Bremer
Pl. Dailly
SQUARE MARIE-LOUISE
SQUARE AMBIORIX
Eurovillage
New Hotel Charlemagne
Silken Berlaymont
Take Sushi
Crowne Plaza Europa
Maelbeek
CENTRE BERLAYMONT
Schuman
SQRE FRÈRE ORBAN
INSTITUTIONS EUROPÉENNES
ESPACE LÉOPOLD
PARC LÉOPOLD
Holiday Inn Schuman
PARC DU CINQUANTENAIRE
MUSÉE ROYAL DE L'ARMÉE ET D'HISTOIRE MILITAIRE
MUSÉE DU CINQUANTENAIRE
AUTOWORLD
MAISON CAUCHIE
Renaissance
Radisson SAS EU
MUSÉUM DES SCIENCES NATURELLES
MUSÉE COMMUNAL D'IXELLES
Pl. du Roi Vainqueur
Avenue Rogier
Avenue Gal Eisenhower
Av. Jan Stobbaerts
Bd du Général Wahis
Avenue Paul Deschanel
Rue Josaphat
Rue des Coteaux
Rue de la Limite
Chaussée de Haecht
R. du Méridien
Avenue Clays
Rue Artan
Dailly
Av. Chazal
Chaussée de Louvain
Rue des Moissons
Av. de la Brabançonne
Avenue du Diamant
Av. Émile Max
Av. Eug. Plasky
Rue du Noyer
Bd Clovis
R. des Confédérés
R. des Patriotes
R. de Franklin
Av. de Cortenbergh
R. de Linthout
Chaussée de Louvain
Rue des Deux Églises
R. de Spa
Bd du Régent
Rue Joseph II
Rue Stevin
R. Archimède
R. Stevin
Av. de la Renaissance
Rue de la Loi
Chaussée d'Etterbeek
Rue des Arts
Rue Belliard
R. Froissart
Avenue d'Auderghem
Av. des Nerviens
Av. des Celtes
R. du Cornet
Rue Louis Hap
Chaussée de Wavre
Rue du Trône
Rue Goffart
R. du Sceptre
Rue Gray
Rue de l'Orient
Rue Philippe Baucq
Av. V. Jacobs
Avenue de la Couronne
Avenue Nouvelle
Rue Beckers
Chée de Wavre
Av. de la Chasse
Chaussée d'Ixelles
Rue Malibran
Lebroussart

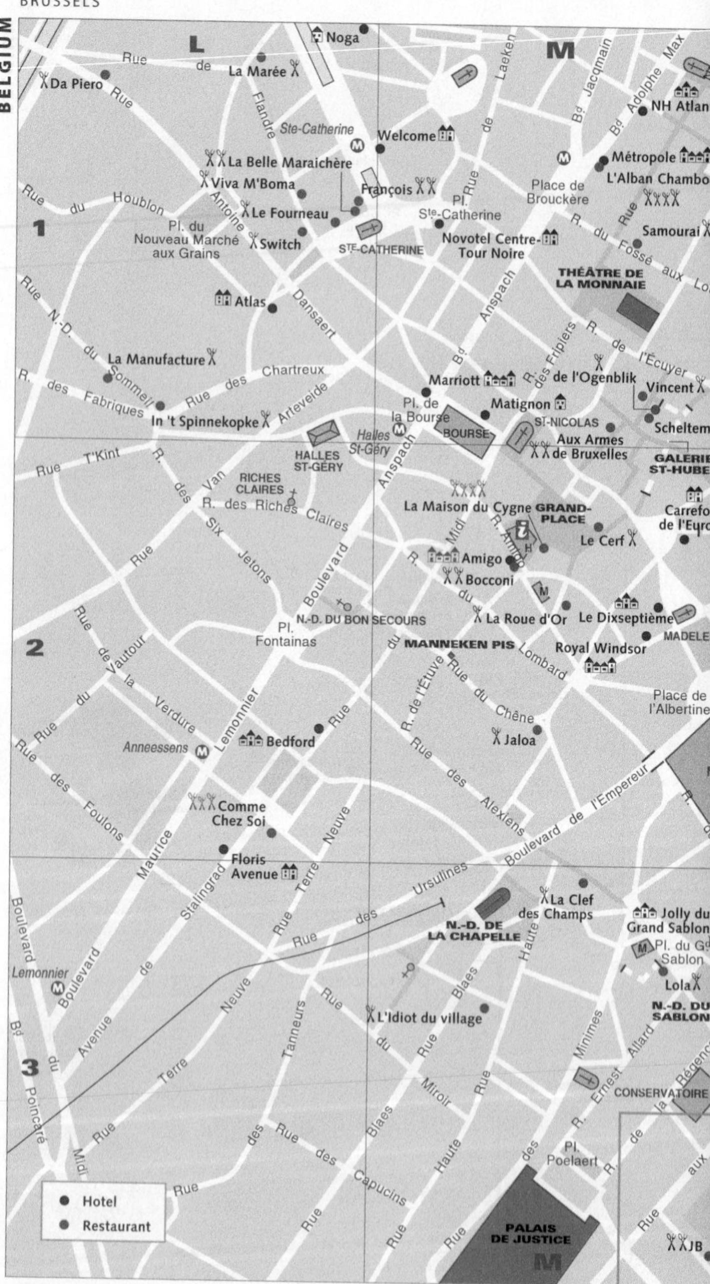
L
M
1
2
3
Noga
La Marée
Da Piero
Ste-Catherine
Welcome
La Belle Maraichère
Viva M'Boma
François
Le Fourneau
Switch
Pl. du Nouveau Marché aux Grains
Pl. Ste-Catherine
STE-CATHERINE
Novotel Centre-Tour Noire
Place de Brouckère
Métropole
L'Alban Chambo
Samourai
NH Atlan
THÉATRE DE LA MONNAIE
Atlas
La Manufacture
Marriott
de l'Ogenblik
Vincent
Matignon
Pl. de la Bourse
BOURSE
ST-NICOLAS
Scheltem
Aux Armes de Bruxelles
GALERIE ST-HUBE
In 't Spinnekopke
Halles St-Géry
HALLES ST-GÉRY
RICHES CLAIRES
La Maison du Cygne
GRAND-PLACE
Carrefo de l'Euro
Le Cerf
Amigo
Bocconi
La Roue d'Or
Le Dixseptième
N.-D. DU BON SECOURS
Pl. Fontainas
MANNEKEN PIS
Royal Windsor
MADELE
Place de l'Albertine
Jaloa
Bedford
Anneessens
Comme Chez Soi
Floris Avenue
La Clef des Champs
Jolly du Grand Sablon
N.-D. DE LA CHAPELLE
Pl. du Gd Sablon
Lemonnier
Lola
N.-D. DU SABLON
L'Idiot du village
CONSERVATOIRE
Pl. Poelaert
PALAIS DE JUSTICE
JB
Hotel
Restaurant

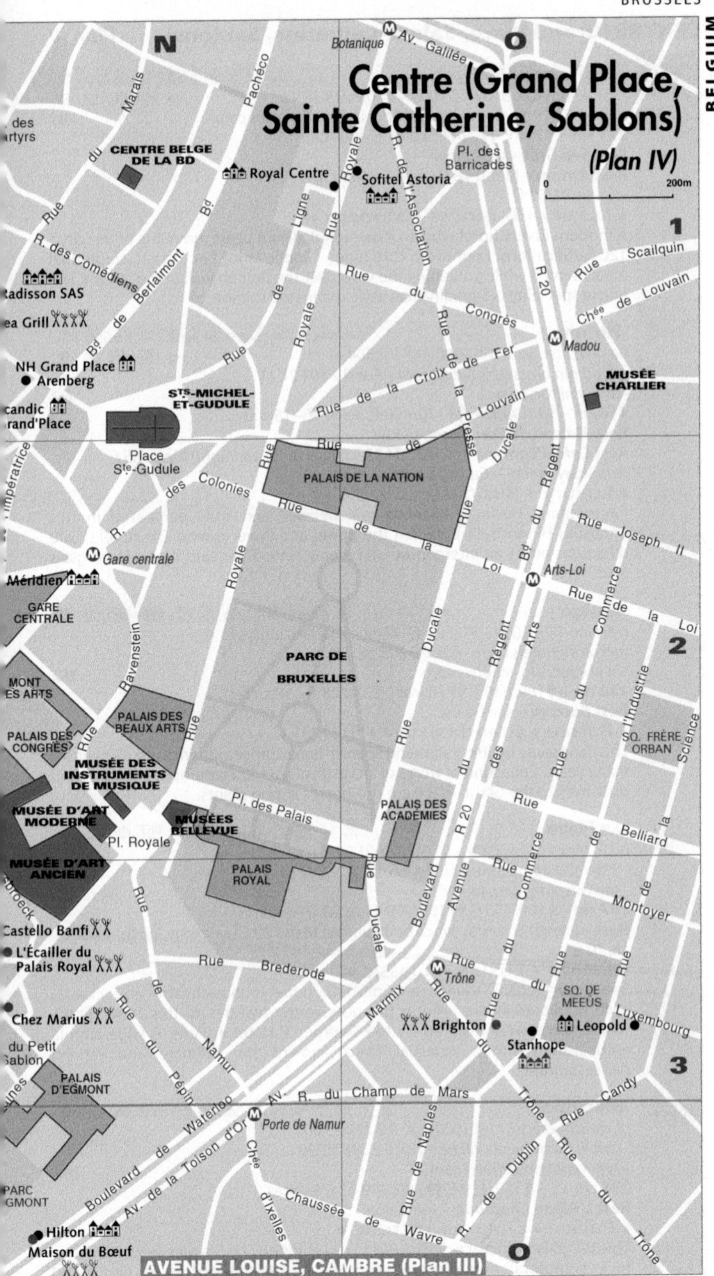

AVENUE LOUISE, CAMBRE (Plan III)

BELGIUM

CENTRE (Grand Place, Sainte-Catherine, Sablons) *Plan IV*

Radisson SAS Royal
420
r. Fossé-aux-Loups 47 ✉ 1000 – ✆ 0 2 219 28 28
– Fax 0 2 219 62 62 – www.royal.brussels.radissonsas.com **N1**
271 rm – †214 € ††214 €, ☕ 25 € – 10 suites
Rest *Sea Grill* – see below
Rest *Atrium* – Menu 18 € (weekday lunch)
– Carte 34/57 €
♦ Luxury ♦ Business ♦ Modern ♦
A modern luxury hotel whose glass-roofed atrium bears remnants of the city's 12C fortifications. Four room categories. "Comic strip" bar. Classic, traditional meals served while you enjoy the view over the Roman wall in the atrium. The house speciality is Scandinavian-style marinated salmon.

Hilton
< town, rest 650
bd de Waterloo 38 ✉ 1000 – ✆ 0 2 504 11 11
– fbadmin.brussels@hilton.com – Fax 0 2 504 21 11
– www.hilton.com **N3**
416 rm – †170/490 € ††170/490 €, ☕ 32 € – 15 suites
Rest *Maison du Bœuf* – see below
Rest *Café d'Egmont* – *✆ 0 2 504 13 33 (open until midnight)* Menu 35 € (weekday lunch) – Carte 38/58 €
♦ Luxury ♦ Business ♦ Classic ♦
International business clientele will be well and truly pampered in this imposing Hilton built between the upper and lower towns. The hotel's Café d'Egmont offers an intercontinental menu, served beneath its Art Deco glass roof.

Amigo
160
r. Amigo 1 ✉ 1000 – ✆ 0 2 547 47 47 – enquires.amigo@roccofortehotels.com – Fax 0 2 513 52 77
– www.roccofortehotels.com **M2**
156 rm – †189/640 € ††189/670 €, ☕ 28 € – 18 suites
Rest *Bocconi* – see below
♦ Palace ♦ Grand Luxury ♦ Stylish ♦
This handsome building showing Spanish Renaissance influence was a prison for many years. Collection of works of art on display, chic, contemporary rooms and proximity to the Grand-Place are this hotel's strong points.

Le Plaza
600
bd A. Max 118 ✉ 1000 – ✆ 0 2 278 01 00
– esterel@leplaza-brussels.be – Fax 0 2 278 01 01
– www.leplaza-brussels.be *Plan II* **F1**
187 rm – †109/450 € ††109/479 €, ☕ 29 € – 6 suites
Rest – *(closed Saturday lunch and Sunday)* Menu 29 € (weekday lunch) – Carte 48/70 €
♦ Palace ♦ Luxury ♦ Classic ♦
Spacious, elegant rooms, a superb Baroque lounge-theatre and classic-style public areas are among the noteworthy features of this 1930s hotel, whose plans were inspired by the Georges V Hotel in Paris. A wide cupola embellished with a celestial fresco crowns the intimate and refined bar-restaurant.

Métropole
500
pl. de Brouckère 31 ✉ 1000 – ✆ 0 2 217 23 00
– info@metropolehotel.be – Fax 0 2 218 02 20
– www.metropolehotel.com **M1**
284 rm ☕ – †359/419 € ††389/449 € – 14 suites
Rest *L'Alban Chambon* – see below
♦ Palace ♦ Luxury ♦ Historic ♦
This 19C palace on place de Brouckère was eulogised by Jacques Brel. Impressive foyer, sumptuous period lounges and delicate Art Nouveau frescoes discovered in 2004.

Sofitel Astoria

r. Royale 103 ✉ *1000* – ✆ *0 2 227 05 05* – *H1154@accor.com* – *Fax 0 2 217 11 50* – *www.sofitel.com* **O1**

106 rm – 🛉119/250 € 🛉🛉139/395 €, ☕ 25 € – 12 suites – **Rest *Le Palais Royal*** – *(closed 15 July-16 August, 20 December-10 January, Friday dinner, Saturday and Sunday)* Menu 44 € (weekday lunch), 45/72 € bi – Carte 51/78 €

♦ Palace ♦ Luxury ♦ Historic ♦

Emperor Hiro Hito, Churchill and Dali have all stayed at this elegant Belle Époque palace. Sumptuous lounges, bedrooms adorned with period furniture, and a bar with an "Orient Express" atmosphere. Meals for the modern palate and classic, refined decor at Le Palais Royal restaurant.

Royal Windsor

r. Duquesnoy 5 ✉ *1000* – ✆ *0 2 505 55 55* – *resa.royalwindsor@warwickhotels.com* – *Fax 0 2 505 55 00* – *www.royalwindsorbrussels.com* **M2**

249 rm – 🛉135/450 € 🛉🛉135/450 €, ☕ 25 € – 17 suites

Rest – Menu 14 € (weekday lunch) – Carte 24/40 €

♦ Luxury ♦ Business ♦ Stylish ♦

Luxury, comfort and refinement characterise this grand hotel in the historic centre, which tends to attract Belgium's fashion victims (you have been warned). Impeccable service. Contemporary bar-restaurant striving for a colonial ambience. Modern cuisine.

Marriott

r. A. Orts 7 (opposite the Stock Exchange) ✉ *1000* – ✆ *0 2 516 90 90* – *Fax 0 2 516 90 00* – **214 rm** – 🛉119/459 € 🛉🛉119/459 €, ☕ 25 € – 4 suites – **Rest** – ✆ 0 2 516 90 90 *(closed Saturday lunch and Sunday)* Menu 19 € bi (weekday lunch) – Carte approx. 45 € **M1**

♦ Chain hotel ♦ Business ♦ Functional ♦

Luxurious hotel situated in front of the Stock Exchange. Its imposing turn-of-the-century façade, interior public areas and rooms were given a facelift in 2002. Modern brasserie where the usual international fare is served with a contemporary touch. Kitchens and rotisserie opening onto the dining area.

Le Méridien

Carrefour de l'Europe 3 ✉ *1000* – ✆ *0 2 548 42 11* – *info.brussels@lemeridien.com* – *Fax 0 2 548 40 80* – *www.lemeridien.com/brussels* **N2**

216 rm – 🛉165/465 € 🛉🛉165/465 €, ☕ 25 € – 8 suites

Rest *L'Épicerie* – *(closed mid July-mid August, late December, Saturday lunch and Sunday dinner)* Menu 52 € (weekday lunch) – Carte 53/72 €

♦ Chain hotel ♦ Business ♦ Stylish ♦

The hotel's majestic neo-Classical façade stands opposite the Gare Centrale. Gleaming interior decor, with elegant bedrooms boasting the very latest in facilities. The restaurant menu is distinctly modern, and offers a cuisine inspired by the New World and its spices.

Le Dixseptième without rest

r. Madeleine 25 ✉ *1000* – ✆ *0 2 517 17 17* – *info@ledixseptieme.be* – *Fax 0 2 502 64 24* – *www.ledixseptieme.be* **M2**

18 rm ☕ – 🛉150/300 € 🛉🛉170/400 € – 6 suites

♦ Family ♦ Luxury ♦ Stylish ♦

As its name indicates, this old town house dates from the 17C, when the Spanish Ambassador occupied its rooms. Elegant lounges and large bedrooms furnished with antiques from different periods.

NH Atlanta

bd A. Max 7 ✉ *1000* – ✆ *0 2 217 01 20* – *nhatlanta@nh-hotels.com* – *Fax 0 2 217 37 58* – *www.nh-hotels.com* **M1**

234 rm – 🛉84/325 € 🛉🛉84/325 €, ☕ 21 € – 7 suites – **Rest** – *(closed Saturday lunch and Sunday lunch)* Menu 12 € (weekday lunch) – Carte approx. 35 €

♦ Chain hotel ♦ Business ♦ Modern ♦

This neo-Classical 1930s building just a stone's throw from the nostalgic passage du Nord and place de Brouckère has huge rooms and a panoramic breakfast room on the 6th floor. The modern brasserie serves a range of French and Italian cuisine.

BELGIUM

Bedford rest rest 450 VISA

r. Midi 135 ✉ 1000 – ✆ 0 2 507 00 00 – info@hotelbedford.be – Fax 0 2 507 00 10 – www.hotelbedford.be **L2**

318 rm – 260/340 € 300/380 € – 8 suites

Rest – Menu 36/56 € bi – Carte 37/51 €

♦ Traditional ♦ Business ♦ Classic ♦

Just a short walk from the Manneken Pis and 500m/550yd from the Grand-Place, this hotel houses major seminar facilities and well-appointed rooms. Franco-Belgian cuisine served in a large dining area with British-inspired decor.

Jolly du Grand Sablon 150 VISA

r. Bodenbroek 2 ✉ 1000 – ✆ 0 2 518 11 00 – jollyhotelsablon@jollyhotels.be – Fax 0 2 512 67 66 – www.jollyhotels.com **M3**

187 rm – 269/329 € 294/354 € – 6 suites

Rest – *(closed 20 July-20 August and Sunday)* Carte 26/45 €

♦ Chain hotel ♦ Business ♦ Stylish ♦

This Italian-owned hotel is located just a stone's throw from the city's prestigious royal museums. Spacious lobby area, well-appointed rooms, plus meeting rooms with all the facilities. The restaurant offers Italian cuisine, buffets and Sunday brunch accompanied by music.

Royal Centre without rest VISA

r. Royale 160 ✉ 1000 – ✆ 0 2 219 00 65 – hotel@royalcentre.be – Fax 0 2 218 09 10 – www.royalcentre.be **N1**

73 rm – 99/220 € 119/240 €

♦ Chain hotel ♦ Business ♦ Classic ♦

This hotel near to the EU institutions has a marble entrance hall and reception area, comfortable living room and contemporary-style rooms of varying sizes housed on eight floors.

Carrefour de l'Europe without rest 200 VISA

r. Marché-aux-Herbes 110 ✉ 1000 – ✆ 0 2 504 94 00 – info@carrefoureurope.net – Fax 0 2 504 95 00 **M2**

59 rm – 99/270 € 99/290 € – 5 suites

♦ Traditional ♦ Business ♦ Functional ♦

This modern hotel just off the Grand-Place is in keeping with the harmony of the city's architecture. Bedrooms slightly on the drab side, but of a good standard nonetheless.

NH Grand Place Arenberg 80 VISA

r. Assaut 15 ✉ 1000 – ✆ 0 2 501 16 16 – nhgrandplace@nh-hotels.com – Fax 0 2 501 18 18 – www.nh-hotels.com **N1**

155 rm – 75/220 € 75/260 €, 19 €

Rest – *(closed Saturday and Sunday)* Menu 20 € (weekday lunch)/30 € – Carte 21/32 €

♦ Chain hotel ♦ Business ♦ Modern ♦

This hotel is well-placed for exploring the heart of the city around the Grand-Place. The modern bedrooms are functional yet welcoming, and typical of the NH chain. Contemporary-style restaurant serving international cuisine with modern overtones.

Scandic Grand'Place rm 70 VISA

r. Arenberg 18 ✉ 1000 – ✆ 0 2 548 18 11 – grand.place@scandic-hotels.com – Fax 0 2 548 18 20 – www.scandic-hotels.com **N1**

100 rm – 75/259 € 75/289 €

Rest – *(closed Saturday lunch and Sunday lunch)* Carte 20/33 €

♦ Chain hotel ♦ Business ♦ Functional ♦

This new hotel close to the Grand-Place and accessible via the luxurious Galeries St-Hubert has public areas decorated with wood and an atrium giving onto rooms with a Scandinavian feel. A soberly-designed, yet welcoming and light modern brasserie.

Floris Avenue without rest

av. de Stalingrad 25 ✉ 1000 – ✆ 0 2 548 98 38
– floris.avenue@grouptorus.com
– Fax 0 2 513 48 22 – www.grouptorus.com L2

47 rm – 56/205 € 61/215 €

♦ Luxury ♦ Cosy ♦

The interior of this traditional mansion has been modernised to include a trendy lobby lit with large bay windows; a light, modern bar and breakfast room; and spacious, contemporary guestrooms.

Novotel Centre-Tour Noire

r. Vierge Noire 32 ✉ 1000 – ✆ 0 2 505 50 50 225
– H2122@accor.com – Fax 0 2 505 50 00 – www.accorhotels.com/be

217 rm – 115/210 € 115/210 €, 15 € M1

Rest – Menu 30 € bi – Carte 23/37 €

♦ Chain hotel ♦ Business ♦ Functional ♦

This chain hotel is built around the remains of the city's first defensive walls, including a tower restored in the spirit of Eugène Viollet-le-Duc. The rooms are being overhauled in stages. Contemporary-style brasserie serving good basic cuisine.

Welcome without rest

quai au Bois à Brûler 23 ✉ 1000 – ✆ 0 2 219 95 46
– info@hotelwelcome.com – Fax 0 2 217 18 87
– www.hotelwelcome.com M1

16 rm – 85/140 € 95/180 €

♦ Traditional ♦ Family ♦ Stylish ♦

A hotel with charming rooms, each of which has a decor inspired by an exotic land, such as Egypt, Kenya, Congo, China, Bali, Tibet, Japan and India.

Atlas without rest

30

r. Vieux Marché-aux- Grains 30 ✉ 1000 – ✆ 0 2 502 60 06 – info@atlas.be
– Fax 0 2 502 69 35 – www.atlas.be L1

88 rm – 70/175 € 75/250 €

♦ Traditional ♦ Business ♦ Classic ♦

This 18C hotel (modernised inside) stands on a small square in a festive neighbourhood full of Belgian fashion boutiques. Most of the rooms look onto an inner courtyard.

Agenda Midi without rest

bd Jamar 11 ✉ 1060 – ✆ 0 2 520 00 10 – midi@hotel-agenda.com
– Fax 0 2 520 00 20 – www.hotel-agenda.com *Plan II* E2

35 rm – 75/99 € 75/114 €

♦ Traditional ♦ Business ♦ Classic ♦

This hotel building is just a short distance from the Gare du Midi TGV railway station. Reliable accommodation at bargain prices. Breakfast buffet served in an inviting room decorated in warm tones.

Noga without rest

r. Béguinage 38 ✉ 1000 – ✆ 0 2 218 67 63 – info@nogahotel.com
– Fax 0 2 218 16 03 L1

19 rm – 70/90 € 85/105 €

♦ Traditional ♦ Family ♦ Functional ♦

A friendly hotel in a fine townhouse in a quiet area of the city. A pleasant lounge, bar with a nautical decor, attractive rooms and a stairway decorated with portraits of Belgian royalty.

Queen Anne without rest

bd E. Jacqmain 110 ✉ 1000 – ✆ 0 2 217 16 00 – info@queen-anne.be
– Fax 0 2 217 18 38 – www.queen-anne.be *Plan II* F1

60 rm – 75/170 € 80/205 €

♦ Traditional ♦ Family ♦ Minimalist ♦

This glass-fronted hotel is located on a main road. Ask for one of the small, recently refurbished rooms: sober, fresh and discreet designer features.

BELGIUM

Matignon without rest
r. Bourse 10 ✉ 1000 – ✆ 0 2 511 08 88 – hotelmatignon@skynet.be – Fax 0 2 513 69 27 – www.hotelmatignon.be **M1**
37 rm – †85/105 € ††85/105 €
◆ Traditional ◆ Family ◆ Classic ◆
This hotel next to the Stock Exchange has well-maintained rooms, including a dozen junior suites. Mainly popular with tourists.

XXXX ✿✿ **Sea Grill** – Hotel Radisson SAS Royal
r. Fossé-aux-Loups 47 ✉ 1000 – ✆ 0 2 217 92 25 – marc.meremans@radissonsas.com – Fax 0 2 227 31 27 – www.seagrill.be
closed 31 March-9 April, 21 July-15 August, 27 October-4 November, 17-25 February, Saturday and Sunday **N1**
Rest – Menu 49 € (weekday lunch), 77/215 € bi – Carte 63/137 €
Spec. Manchons de crabe royal, huile d'olive. Turbot rôti à l'arête, béarnaise d'huîtres. Homard breton à la presse.
◆ Seafood ◆ Cosy ◆
A warm, Scandinavian-influenced ambience, ambitious fish-dominated menu, excellent wine cellar, plus a lounge offering a good choice of cigars. Impeccable, friendly service.

XXXX **La Maison du Cygne** ⇔4/100
r. Charles Buls 2 ✉ 1000 – ✆ 0 2 511 82 44 – info@lamaisonducygne.be – Fax 0 2 514 31 48 – www.lamaisonducygne.be
closed 21 July-16 August, late December, Saturday lunch and Sunday **M2**
Rest – Menu 40 € (weekday lunch)/85 € – Carte 66/141 €
◆ French traditional ◆ Formal ◆
This 17C house on the Grand-Place was originally the headquarters of the Butchers' Guild. Roasting spit on view, traditional cuisine concocted with modern flourishes and excellent wine list.

XXXX **Maison du Bœuf** – Hotel Hilton ⇔20
1st floor, bd de Waterloo 38 ✉ 1000 – ✆ 0 2 504 11 11 – fpadmin.brussels@hilton.com – Fax 0 2 504 21 11 – www.hilton.com **N3**
Rest – Menu 55 € (weekday lunch), 58/68 € – Carte 78/118 €
◆ French traditional ◆ Formal ◆
The traditional cuisine served in the Hilton's gastronomic restaurant is in keeping with its opulent decor. Excellent wine list and views of the Parc d'Egmont.

XXXX ✿✿ **Bruneau** ⇔4/40 (dinner)
av. Broustin 75 ✉ 1083 – ✆ 0 2 421 70 70 – restaurant_bruneau@skynet.be – Fax 0 2 425 97 26 – www.bruneau.be
closed 1-10 February, August, Tuesday, Wednesday and Thursday holidays *Plan I* **B2**
Rest – Menu 45 € (weekday lunch), 95/150 € bi – Carte 66/202 €
Spec. Javanais de foie d'oie et anguille fumée aux pommes. Ravioles de céleri à la truffe et essences aromatiques. Ris de veau en habit de dentelle et truffes.
◆ Contemporary ◆ Cosy ◆
This renowned restaurant has achieved a perfect balance of innovation and tradition while at the same time maintaining its commitment to local products. Prestigious wine-list. Summer terrace.

XXXX **L'Alban Chambon** – Hotel Métropole ⇔50/70
pl. de Brouckère 31 ✉ 1000 – ✆ 0 2 217 23 00 – info@metropolehotel.be – Fax 0 2 218 02 20 – www.metropolehotel.com
closed 16 July-15 August, Saturday, Sunday and Bank Holidays **M1**
Rest – Menu 39 € (weekday lunch)/85 € – Carte 64/102 €
◆ French traditional ◆ Retro ◆
This restaurant is named after the architect who designed it. Light, classic cuisine served in a former ballroom embellished with period furniture.

LOUIS ROEDERER
CHAMPAGNE

XXX ✿✿
Comme Chez Soi
AC ⇔4/34 VISA MC AE D

pl. Rouppe 23 ✉ 1000 – ✆ 0 2 512 29 21 – info@commechezsoi.be – Fax 0 2 511 80 52 – www.commechezsoi.be
closed 10 April, 1-30 July, 30 October, 23 December-7 January, 20 February, Sunday, Monday and Wednesday lunch **L2**
Rest – *(booking essential)* Menu 67/168 € – Carte 72/277 €
Spec. Asperges et langoustines "a la plancha", sauce à la bière blanche. Fondant de joue de veau et croustillant de foie de canard à la truffe d'été. Ananas caramélisé, coulis de fruits et glace à la crème de calisson.
♦ French traditional ♦ Retro ♦
Founded in 1926, this famous Brussels restaurant has a Belle Epoque atmosphere and Art Nouveau decor influenced by the Belgian architect Victor Horta. Elaborate, classical dishes.

XXX ✿✿
Claude Dupont
⇔6/24 VISA MC AE D

av. Vital Riethuisen 46 ✉ 1083 – ✆ 0 2 426 00 00 – claudedupont@belgacom.net – Fax 0 2 426 65 40
closed July, Monday and Tuesday *Plan I* **A2**
Rest – Menu 45 € (weekday lunch), 70/110 € – Carte 59/115 €
Spec. Poissons de la Mer du Nord en bouillabaisse, rouille et croûtons (April-September). Écrevisses sautées, mirepoix bordelaise au vin (May-June). Méli-mélo de homard aux pommes et curry.
♦ French traditional ♦ Friendly ♦
A master-class in culinary invention. The accolades and awards on display in the entrance hall are thoroughly deserved. Classic dining area.

XXX ✿
L'Écailler du Palais Royal (Hahn)
AC VISA MC AE D

r. Bodenbroek 18 ✉ 1000 – ✆ 0 2 512 87 51 – lecaillerdupalaisroyal@skynet.be – Fax 0 2 511 99 50 – www.lecaillerdupalaisroyal.be
closed August, Christmas-New Year, Sunday and Bank Holidays **N3**
Rest – Carte 65/130 €
Spec. Rémoulade de crabe royal aux courgettes. Sole Colbert à la mousseline de crevettes. Glace vanille au miel.
♦ Seafood ♦ Cosy ♦
Cosy, smart oyster bar frequented by diplomats, politicians and business people. Comfortable benches, chairs and a bar counter on the ground floor; round tables upstairs.

XX
Aux Armes de Bruxelles
AC ⇔10/150 VISA MC AE D

r. Bouchers 13 ✉ 1000 – ✆ 0 2 511 55 98 – arbrux@beon.be – Fax 0 2 514 81 14 – www.armesdebruxelles.be
closed 18 June-16 July and Monday **M1**
Rest – *(open until 11 p.m.)* Menu 23 € bi (weekday lunch), 31/46 € – Carte 28/60 €
♦ Traditional ♦ Brasserie ♦
A veritable Brussels institution at the heart of the historic centre, this family-run restaurant established in 1921 focuses on the resolutely Belgian. Rooms in contrasting styles.

XX
Bocconi – Hotel Amigo
⇔10/160 VISA MC AE D

r. Amigo 1 ✉ 1000 – ✆ 0 2 547 47 15 – restaurantbocconi@roccofortehotels.com – Fax 0 2 547 47 67 – www.ristorantebocconi.com **M2**
Rest – *(open until 11 p.m.)* Menu 27 € (weekday lunch)/50 € – Carte 42/54 €
♦ Italian ♦ Design ♦
This fine Italian restaurant is in a luxury hotel near the Grand-Place. Inside, the design is that of a modern brasserie. The cuisine features appetising Italian classics.

XX
François
AC ⇔15/35 VISA MC AE D

quai aux Briques 2 ✉ 1000 – ✆ 0 2 511 60 89 – Fax 0 2 512 06 67 – www.restaurantfrancois.be
closed 1-15 April, 15-31 August, Sunday and Monday **L1**
Rest – Menu 25 € (weekday lunch), 35/39 € – Carte 40/92 €
♦ Seafood ♦ Friendly ♦
Seafood restaurant and fishmonger run by the same family since the 1930s. The maritime interior is enlivened with nostalgic photos.

La Belle Maraîchère
12/50 VISA AE

pl. Ste-Catherine 11 ✉ 1000 – ✆ 0 2 512 97 59 – Fax 0 2 513 76 91 – www.labellemaraichere.com – closed 2 weeks carnival, mid July-early August, Wednesday and Thursday – **Rest** – Menu 33/52 € – Carte 34/87 € **M1**

♦ Seafood ♦ Family ♦

This convivial restaurant with a slightly dated charm is without a doubt one of the most reliably good-value eats in the neighbourhood. Tasty classic cuisine with a penchant for fish and seafood.

Castello Banfi
30/50 VISA AE

r. Bodenbroek 12 ✉ 1000 – ✆ 0 2 512 87 94 – iktarea@hotmail.com – Fax 0 2 512 87 94 – www.castellobanfi.be
closed Easter week, last 3 weeks August, Sunday and Monday **N3**
Rest – Menu 29 € (weekday lunch)/55 € – Carte 53/84 €

♦ Italian ♦ Fashionable ♦

The menu at this gastronomic restaurant, hidden behind a 1729 façade, encompasses culinary and viticultural specialities from both France and Italy. The name refers to a large Tuscan wine estate.

JB
12/35 VISA AE

r. Grand Cerf 24 ✉ 1000 – ✆ 0 2 512 04 84 – restaurantjb@tele2.be – Fax 0 2 511 79 30 – www.restaurantjb.be
closed Saturday lunch and Sunday **M3**
Rest – Menu 32 € bi/43 € bi – Carte 46/60 €

♦ Traditional ♦ Family ♦

This friendly, family-run restaurant has nothing to do with the famous Scottish whisky! Appetising classic menu including good set menus.

Chez Marius
6/35 VISA AE

pl. du Petit Sablon 1 ✉ 1000 – ✆ 0 2 511 12 08 – info@chezmarius.be – Fax 0 2 512 27 89 – www.chezmarius.be
closed 20 July-20 August, Saturday and Sunday **N3**
Rest – Menu 25 € (weekday lunch), 43/50 € – Carte 46/84 €

♦ Traditional ♦ Friendly ♦

This restaurant opposite the Petit Sablon opened in 1965. Provençal cuisine is served in three classically arranged and very spruce rooms. Small terrace in front.

Le Loup-Galant
8/24 VISA AE

quai aux Barques 4 ✉ 1000 – ✆ 0 2 219 99 98 – loupgalant@swing.be – Fax 0 2 219 99 98 – closed 1 week Easter, 1-15 August, 24-31 December, Sunday and Monday *Plan II* **E1**
Rest – Menu 15 € (weekday lunch), 30/53 € bi – Carte 38/49 €

♦ Traditional ♦ Rustic ♦

You can spot this old house at one end of the Vismet thanks to its yellow walls and the gold statue of St Michel on the façade of the next house. Classic meals served in a rustic decor of chimney piece and exposed beams.

La Manufacture
30/120 VISA AE

r. Notre-Dame du Sommeil 12 ✉ 1000 – ✆ 0 2 502 25 25 – info@manufacture.be – Fax 0 2 502 27 15 – www.manufacture.be
closed Saturday lunch and Sunday **L1**
Rest – *(open until 11 p.m.)* Menu 14 € (weekday lunch), 32/70 € bi – Carte 30/50 €

♦ Contemporary ♦ Brasserie ♦

Metal, wood, leather and granite have all been used to decorate this trendy brasserie occupying the workshop of a renowned leather manufacturer. Contemporary cuisine.

De l'Ogenblik
16/25 VISA AE

Galerie des Princes 1 ✉ 1000 – ✆ 0 2 511 61 51 – ogenblik@scarlet.be – Fax 0 2 513 41 58 – www.ogenblik.be – closed Sunday and Bank Holidays lunch
Rest – *(open until midnight)* Menu 51/71 € bi – Carte 45/66 € **M1**

♦ Traditional ♦ Bistro ♦

This restaurant housed in an old café is known for its classic cuisine and bistro-style. Popular with the local business community. The same chef has worked here since 1975.

Samourai

r. Fossé-aux-Loups 28 ✉ 1000 – ☎ 0 2 217 56 39 – Fax 0 2 771 97 61
– www.restaurant-samourai.be
closed 14 July-16 August, Tuesday and Sunday lunch **M1**

Rest – Menu 22 € (weekday lunch), 46/70 € – Carte 43/89 €

♦ Japanese ♦ Exotic ♦

A Japanese restaurant established more than 30 years ago near the Théâtre de la Monnaie. Authentic, varied menu. Rooms with Japanese decor on several floors.

La Roue d'Or

r. Chapeliers 26 ✉ 1000 – ☎ 0 2 514 25 54 – roue.dor@hotmail.com
– Fax 0 2 512 30 81
closed mid July-mid August **M2**

Rest – *(open until midnight)* Menu 12 € (weekday lunch) – Carte 37/50 €

♦ Traditional ♦ Brasserie ♦

A typical old café with a convivial atmosphere where the culinary emphasis is on staple Belgian brasserie fare. Surrealist wall paintings in the genre of Magritte and a superb clock in the dining area.

Scheltema

⇔30/80

r. Dominicains 7 ✉ 1000 – ☎ 0 2 512 20 84 – scheltema@skynet.be
– Fax 0 2 512 44 82 – www.scheltema.be – *closed Christmas and Sunday*

Rest – *(open until 11.30 p.m.)* Menu 19 € (weekday lunch), 34/43 € – Carte 36/84 € **M1**

♦ Traditional ♦ Brasserie ♦

Situated in the Ilot Sacré district, this attractive old brasserie specialises in traditional and contemporary seafood dishes. Lively atmosphere and retro-style wood furnishings.

Jaloa

⇔8/30

pl. de la Vieille Halle aux Blés 31 ✉ 1000 – ☎ 0 2 512 18 31 – contact@jaloa.com
– www.jaloa.com
closed 21 July-6 August, Wednesday, Saturday lunch and Sunday **M2**

Rest – *(open until 11 p.m.)* Menu 16 € (weekday lunch), 33/85 € bi – Carte 45/79 €

♦ Contemporary ♦ Wine bar ♦

A long, narrow dining room in an old house near the Brel Museum with minimalist modern decor and a view of the kitchen. Contemporary cuisine and background music.

Da Piero

⇔35/45

r. Antoine Dansaert 181 ✉ 1000 – ☎ 0 2 219 23 48 – *closed August and Sunday*

Rest – *(open until 11 p.m.)* Menu 16 € (weekday lunch), 26/40 € bi – Carte 29/67 € **L1**

♦ Italian ♦ Rustic ♦

A pleasant family-run "ristorante" serving antipasti, a classic Italian à la carte menu, and reasonably-priced lunch and fixed menus.

La Marée

⇔6/20

r. Flandre 99 ✉ 1000 – ☎ 0 2 511 00 40 – Fax 0 2 511 86 19 – www.lamaree-sa.com
closed 15 June-15 July, Christmas, New Year, Monday and Tuesday **L1**

Rest – Carte 25/60 €

♦ Seafood ♦ Family ♦

The friendly atmosphere and unpretentious cuisine and decor of this restaurant account for its popularity. Open kitchen, where the chef prepares freshly delivered fish and seafood.

Switch

r. Flandre 6 ✉ 1000 – ☎ 0 2 503 14 80 – Fax 0 2 502 58 78
closed first 3 weeks August, Christmas, New Year, Sunday and Monday

Rest – Menu 28/38 € – Carte approx. 35 € **L1**

♦ Contemporary ♦ Bistro ♦

In this modern, original bistro diners are able to choose how they would like the basic ingredients of their meal cooked, as well as the individual flavouring and side dishes.

BELGIUM

Le Fourneau

pl. Ste-Catherine 8 ✉ 1000 – ✆ 0 2 513 10 02 – Fax 0 2 513 10 07
closed Christmas, New Year, Tuesday and Sunday lunch **L1**
Rest – Carte approx. 30 €
♦ Contemporary ♦ Trendy ♦
Good Mediterranean cuisine served around a circular bar with an open kitchen. Choices include a range of tapas as a first course and main dishes priced by weight. No reservations.

In 't Spinnekopke

pl. du Jardin aux Fleurs 1 ✉ 1000 – ✆ 0 2 511 86 95 – info@spinnekopke.be – Fax 0 2 513 24 97 – www.spinnekopke.be
closed Saturday lunch and Sunday **L1**
Rest – *(open until midnight)* Menu 14 € bi (weekday lunch), 42 € bi/55 € bi – Carte 29/53 €
♦ Regional ♦ Bistro ♦
This charming, typical tavern is esteemed for its good bistro-style atmosphere and regional cuisine which does justice to the Belgian tradition.

Le Cerf

Grand'Place 20 ✉ 1000 – ✆ 0 2 511 47 91 – Fax 0 2 546 09 59
closed 15 July-15 August, Saturday and Sunday **M2**
Rest – *(open until 11.30 p.m.)* Menu 23 € bi (weekday lunch), 46 € bi/54 € bi – Carte 35/54 €
♦ Traditional ♦ Cosy ♦
The decor of this grand old residence (1710) is a mix of wood, stained glass, fireplace and warm fabrics, giving an overall intimate and hushed feel. Two tables overlooking the Grand-Place.

Vincent

r. Dominicains 8 ✉ 1000 – ✆ 0 2 511 26 07 – info@restaurantvincent.com – Fax 0 2 502 36 93 – www.restaurantvincent.com
closed first 2 weeks August and 2-12 January **M1**
Rest – *(open until 11.30 p.m.)* Menu 13 € (weekday lunch), 27/37 € – Carte 23/69 €
♦ Tavern/bistro ♦ Retro ♦
Savour the typical Brussels atmosphere of this nostalgic rotisserie adorned with painted ceramic-tile frescoes. Local dishes to the fore, with meat and mussels specialities.

Viva M'Boma

r. Flandre 17 ✉ 1000 – ✆ 0 2 512 15 93 – closed 1-16 August, 1-8 January, Sunday, Monday dinner, Tuesday dinner and Wednesday **L1**
Rest – Carte approx. 31 €
♦ Regional ♦ Bistro ♦
This modern "canteen" serves typical Belgian dishes, which are also sold in its adjoining delicatessen (tripe is a speciality). Tables are close together and the walls are decorated with tiles. Small hidden terrace.

Lola

pl. du Grand Sablon 33 ✉ 1000 – ✆ 0 2 514 24 60 – restaurant.lola@skynet.be – Fax 0 2 514 26 53 – www.restolola.be – closed first week August, Christmas and New Year – **Rest** – *(open until 11.30 p.m.)* Carte 35/55 € **M3**
♦ Contemporary ♦ Trendy ♦
This convivial brasserie with its contemporary decor devotes its energies to the latest culinary trends. Choose between sitting on benches, chairs or at the bar.

La Clef des Champs

r. Rollebeek 23 ✉ 1000 – ✆ 0 2 512 11 93 – info@clefsdeschamps.be – Fax 0 2 502 42 32 – www.clefdeschamps.be
closed Sunday dinner and Monday **M3**
Rest – Menu 16 € (weekday lunch), 32/53 € bi – Carte 41/49 €
♦ Regional ♦ Friendly ♦
Pleasant, family-run restaurant, completely renovated in 2006. Decor includes large mirrors, crystal chandeliers, white wall panelling, and stylish chairs with openwork backs.

L'Idiot du village

r. Notre Seigneur 19 ✉ 1000 – ✆ 0 2 502 55 82
closed 20 July-20 August, 23 December-3 January, Saturday and Sunday
Rest – *(open until 11 p.m.)* Menu 15 € (weekday lunch) – Carte 38/58 € **M3**
♦ Traditional ♦ Bistro ♦
Service with a smile, eclectic, pleasingly kitsch decor, a warm ambience, bistro-style cuisine with an original, modern touch, astute wine-list and friendly service.

Les Larmes du Tigre 10/16

r. Wynants 21 ✉ 1000 – ✆ 0 2 512 18 77 – Fax 0 2 502 10 03 – www.leslarmesdutigre.be
closed Tuesday and Saturday lunch *Plan II* **E3**
Rest – Menu 11 € (weekday lunch)/35 € – Carte 26/37 €
♦ Thai ♦ Exotic ♦
Thai cuisine has been served in this mansion close to the Palais de Justice for 20 years. Parasols adorn the ceiling. Sunday buffet (lunch and dinner).

QUARTIER LOUISE-CAMBRE *Plan III*

Conrad 650

av. Louise 71 ✉ 1050 – ✆ 0 2 542 42 42 – brusselsinfo@conradhotels.com – Fax 0 2 542 42 00 – www.conradhotels.com **J1**
254 rm – †229/599 € ††254/624 €, ☕ 33 € – 15 suites
Rest *Loui* – *(closed July-August, Saturday lunch, Sunday lunch and Monday lunch)* Carte 48/66 €
Rest *Café Wiltcher's* – Menu 35 € (weekday lunch) – Carte 43/70 €
♦ Grand Luxury ♦ Business ♦ Classic ♦
An upmarket hotel brilliantly arranged inside a 1900s mansion. Excellent bedrooms with classic furnishings; full range of seminar and leisure facilities. The trendy restaurant Loui has a contemporary menu showing a variety of culinary influences, and a "lounge" ambience. The café serves popular lunch buffets.

Bristol Stephanie rest 400

av. Louise 91 ✉ 1050 – ✆ 0 2 543 33 11 – hotel_bristol@bristol.be – Fax 0 2 538 03 07 – www.bristol.be **J1**
139 rm – †130/410 € ††157/435 €, ☕ 27 € – 3 suites
Rest – *(closed 14 July-2 September, 15 December-6 January, Saturday and Sunday) (buffets)* Menu 42 € bi (weekday lunch) – Carte 43/62 €
♦ Luxury ♦ Business ♦ Classic ♦
The very pleasant guestrooms of this luxury property occupy two interlinked buildings. Three superb suites adorned with typical Norwegian furniture. Contemporary dining in a Scandinavian-inspired ambience. Buffet options also available.

Le Châtelain 180

r. Châtelain 17 ✉ 1000 – ✆ 0 2 646 00 55 – info@le-chatelain.net – Fax 0 2 646 00 88 – www.le-chatelain.net **J2**
107 rm – †350/450 € ††375/475 €, ☕ 25 € – 2 suites
Rest – *(closed Saturday and Sunday lunch)* Carte 35/48 €
♦ Luxury ♦ Business ♦ Functional ♦
A new hotel with large, modern rooms featuring the very latest equipment and facilities. Superb reception area, well-equipped fitness room and a small garden. The restaurant offers a range of continental dishes, as well as Asian specialities.

Warwick Barsey rest 50

av. Louise 381 ✉ 1050 – ✆ 0 2 641 51 11 – res.warwickbarsey@warwickhotels.com – Fax 0 2 641 51 55 – www.warwickbrussels.com **K3**
94 rm – †114/310 € ††114/310 €, ☕ 22 € – 5 suites
Rest – *(closed 17 July-20 August, Saturday lunch and Sunday)* Menu 16 € (weekday lunch)/35 € – Carte 37/62 €
♦ Luxury ♦ Business ♦ Stylish ♦
A characterful hotel near the Bois de la Cambre skilfully refurbished in a style inspired by the Second Empire. Elegant public areas and plush, well-appointed rooms. Personalised service. Neo-classical decor in the Jacques Garcia-designed restaurant-lounge.

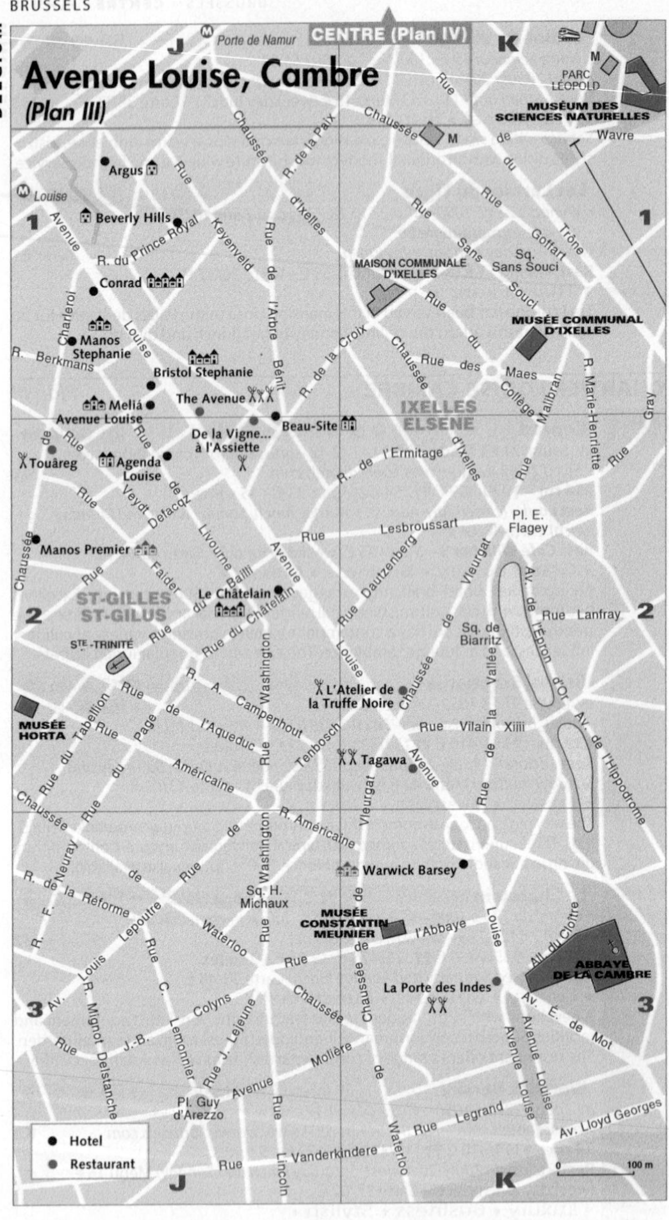
Avenue Louise, Cambre
(Plan III)
CENTRE (Plan IV)
Porte de Namur
Louise
Argus
Beverly Hills
Conrad
Manos Stephanie
Bristol Stephanie
Meliá Avenue Louise
The Avenue
De la Vigne... à l'Assiette
Beau-Site
Touâreg
Agenda Louise
Manos Premier
Le Châtelain
ST-GILLES ST-GILUS
STE-TRINITÉ
MUSÉE HORTA
L'Atelier de la Truffe Noire
Tagawa
Warwick Barsey
Sq. H. Michaux
MUSÉE CONSTANTIN MEUNIER
La Porte des Indes
ABBAYE DE LA CAMBRE
IXELLES ELSENE
MAISON COMMUNALE D'IXELLES
MUSÉE COMMUNAL D'IXELLES
PARC LÉOPOLD
MUSÉUM DES SCIENCES NATURELLES
Sq. Sans Souci
Pl. E. Flagey
Sq. de Biarritz
Pl. Guy d'Arezzo
Hotel
Restaurant
100 m

BELGIUM

Manos Premier

chaussée de Charleroi 102 ✉ 1060 (dinner) VISA AE
– ☎ 0 2 537 96 82 – manos@manoshotel.com – Fax 0 2 539 36 55
– www.manoshotel.com **J2**
45 rm ☕ – †295 € ††320 € – 5 suites
Rest *Kolya* – *(closed 24 December-7 January, Saturday lunch and Sunday) (open until 11 p.m.)* Menu 15 € (weekday lunch), 35/45 € – Carte 35/55 €
♦ Luxury ♦ Business ♦ Stylish ♦
A graceful late-19C town house adorned with sumptuous Louis XV and Louis XVI furniture. Ask for a room overlooking the garden. Authentic Turkish baths. Veranda restaurant, chic yet cosy lounge-bar, and an appealing patio.

Manos Stéphanie without rest

chaussée de Charleroi 28 ✉ 1060 – ☎ 0 2 539 02 50 – manos@manoshotel.com
– Fax 0 2 537 57 29 – www.manoshotel.com **J1**
50 rm ☕ – †245 € ††270 € – 5 suites
♦ Traditional ♦ Business ♦ Functional ♦
A hotel offering inviting rooms in a classic style with modern touches and white-leaded wood furnishings. Breakfast room crowned with a cupola.

Meliá Avenue Louise without rest

r. Blanche 4 ✉ 1000 – ☎ 0 2 535 95 00 25 VISA AE
– karin.jongman@solmelia.com – Fax 0 2 535 96 00 – www.solmelia.com
80 rm – †100/260 € ††100/260 €, ☕ 22 € **J1**
♦ Chain hotel ♦ Business ♦ Functional ♦
This hotel is recommended for its cosy atmosphere and the elegantly British feel of its rooms, as well as its public areas, which include a snug, wood-panelled lounge.

Agenda Louise without rest

r. Florence 6 ✉ 1000 – ☎ 0 2 539 00 31 – louise@hotel-agenda.com
– Fax 0 2 539 00 63 – www.hotel-agenda.com **J2**
37 rm ☕ – †118 € ††130 €
♦ Traditional ♦ Business ♦ Functional ♦
This recently renovated hotel offers guests reasonably-sized rooms, many of which have standard mahogany-coloured furnishings and are decorated with warm-toned, colour-coordinated fabrics.

Beau-Site without rest

r. Longue Haie 76 ✉ 1050 – ☎ 0 2 640 88 89 – info@beausitebrussels.com
– Fax 0 2 640 16 11 – www.beausitebrussels.com **J1-2**
38 rm ☕ – †65/159 € ††75/169 €
♦ Traditional ♦ Business ♦ Functional ♦
100m/110yd from the city's most elegant avenue. This family-run hotel occupies a small corner building and is simple, functional and welcoming. Fairly spacious rooms.

Beverly Hills without rest

r. Prince Royal 71 ✉ 1050 – ☎ 0 2 513 22 22 40 VISA AE
– Fax 0 2 513 87 77 – www.hotelbeverlyhills.be **J1**
34 rm ☕ – †89/119 € ††99/139 €
♦ Traditional ♦ Business ♦ Functional ♦
This hotel is situated in a quiet road close to avenue de la Toison d'Or and avenue Louise. The rooms are functional and well kept. Fitness room and sauna.

Argus without rest

r. Capitaine Crespel 6 ✉ 1050 – ☎ 0 2 514 07 70 – Fax 0 2 514 12 22
– www.hotel-argus.be **J1**
42 rm ☕ – †60/165 € ††60/195 €
♦ Traditional ♦ Business ♦ Functional ♦
Located in the upper town, this hotel has simple, standard rooms with soundproofing. The breakfast room is decorated with Art Deco-style stained glass. Good value for money.

BELGIUM

XXXX

Villa Lorraine

av. du Vivier d'Oie 75 ✉ 1000 – ✆ 0 2 374 31 63 – info@villalorraine.be – Fax 0 2 372 01 95 – www.villalorraine.be
closed 9-30 July and Sunday Plan I **C3**
Rest – Menu 55 € (weekday lunch), 85/150 € bi – Carte 74/155 €
♦ French traditional ♦ Formal ♦
A fine restaurant established in 1953 on the edge of the Bois de la Cambre woods. Classic setting and a prestigious wine cellar. Gorgeous terrace in the shade of a chestnut tree.

XXX

The Avenue

4/60 VISA MC AE

av. Louise 156 ✉ 1050 – ✆ 0 2 642 22 22 – info@andre-dhaese.be – Fax 0 2 642 22 25 – www.andre-dhaese.be
closed 29 July-20 August, 22-31 December, Saturday and Sunday **J1**
Rest – Menu 45/150 € bi – Carte 71/92 €
♦ Contemporary ♦ Formal ♦
This restaurant occupying a luxurious, elegant mansion serves inventive cuisine in a contemporary setting, with an open kitchen. Excellent choice of quality wines, terrace and classical-style rooms on the first floor.

XX

Tagawa

10/14 P VISA MC AE

av. Louise 279 ✉ 1050 – ✆ 0 2 640 50 95 – o.tagawa@tiscali.be – Fax 0 2 648 41 36 – www.restaurant-tagawa.be
closed Saturday lunch and Sunday **K2**
Rest – Menu 20 € (weekday lunch), 38/80 € – Carte 19/68 €
♦ Japanese ♦ Minimalist ♦
This simply furnished Japanese restaurant is worth tracking down inside one of the city's shopping galleries. Western and Oriental (tatami mats) seating, plus a sushi bar. Private parking.

XX

La Porte des Indes

8/100 VISA MC AE

av. Louise 455 ✉ 1050 – ✆ 0 2 647 86 51 – brussels@laportedesindes.com – Fax 0 2 375 44 68 – www.laportedesindes.com – closed Sunday lunch
Rest – Menu 17 € (weekday lunch), 38/48 € – Carte 32/59 € **K3**
♦ Indian ♦ Exotic ♦
If your taste-buds fancy a change, head for La Porte des Indes, with its exotic, deliciously flavoured cuisine. The restaurant interior is decorated with Indian antiques.

X

L'Atelier de la Truffe Noire

VISA MC AE

av. Louise 300 ✉ 1050 – ✆ 0 2 640 54 55 – luigi.ciciriello@truffenoire.com – Fax 0 2 648 11 44 – www.atelier.truffenoire.com – closed 1 week Easter, first 2 weeks August, first week January, Sunday and Monday dinner **K2**
Rest – *(open until 11 p.m.)* Carte 42/108 €
♦ Brasserie ♦ Fashionable ♦
A modern bistro whose originality and success lie in its fast service and truffle-based gourmet menu. Varied à la carte dishes showing Italian influence. Small terrace.

X

De la Vigne... à l'Assiette

VISA MC AE

r. Longue Haie 51 ✉ 1000 – ✆ 0 2 647 68 03 – Fax 0 2 647 68 03
closed 21 July-20 August, Saturday lunch, Sunday and Monday **J2**
Rest – Menu 14 € (weekday lunch), 21/35 € – Carte 35/49 €
♦ Contemporary ♦ Bistro ♦
Copious portions and innovative cuisine at this "gastro-bistro", which has a good selection of reasonably priced wines from around the world and knowledgeable staff.

X

Touâreg

P VISA MC AE

chaussée de Charleroi 80 ✉ 1060 – ✆ 0 2 534 54 00 – info@letouareg.be – Fax 0 2 534 54 74 – closed Saturday lunch and Sunday **J2**
Rest – Menu 13 € (weekday lunch), 25/49 € – Carte 30/39 €
♦ Moroccan ♦ Minimalist ♦
North African specialities served in three simple, modern dining rooms where indigo blue - the colour of the Tuareg - dominates. Guests may also dine on the large, enclosed terrace.

EUROPEAN INSTITUTIONS *Plan II*

Stanhope
square de Meëus 4 ✉ 1000 – ✆ 0 2 506 90 12 – Fax 0 2 512 17 08 – www.stanhope.be – closed 21-27 December Plan IV **O3**
99 rm – 155/375 € 195/375 €, ☕ 25 € – 9 suites – **Rest Brighton** – see below
◆ Grand Luxury ◆ Traditional ◆ Stylish ◆
Relive the splendour of the Victorian era in this town house with a distinctly British feel. Choose from a variety of room categories: the suites and split-level rooms are superb.

Renaissance
r. Parnasse 19 ✉ 1050 – ✆ 0 2 505 29 29 – renaissance.brussels@renaissancehotels.com – Fax 0 2 505 25 55 – www.renaissancebrussels.com
256 rm – 85/489 € 85/489 €, ☕ 25 € – 6 suites **G3**
Rest – *(closed Saturday lunch, Sunday lunch and Bank Holidays lunch)*
Menu 19 € (weekday lunch) – Carte 29/47 €
◆ Chain hotel ◆ Business ◆ Modern ◆
This hotel enjoys a good location on the edge of the European institutions district. Modern, well-appointed rooms, excellent business, conference and leisure facilities, plus a full range of hotel services. Good service. The brasserie offers a traditional choice, including a lunch menu served over three sittings.

Radisson SAS EU
r. Idalie 35 ✉ 1050 – ✆ 0 2 626 81 11 – info.brusseleu@radissonsas.com – Fax 0 2 626 81 12 – www.brussels.eu.radissonsas.com **G3**
145 rm – 79/193 € 79/193 €, ☕ 25 € – 4 suites
Rest – *(closed Saturday lunch and Sunday lunch) (open until 11 p.m.)* Menu 17 € (weekday lunch) – Carte 26/52 €
◆ Chain hotel ◆ Business ◆ Stylish ◆
This new, ultra-modern hotel has three types of guestrooms - Fresh, Chic and Fashion. Mainly business and EU clientele. Classical, contemporary cuisine is served either at table or at the bar in the trendy restaurant.

Montgomery
av. de Tervuren 134 ✉ 1150 – ✆ 0 2 741 85 11 – reservations@eurostarsmontgomery.com – Fax 0 2 741 85 00 – www.eurostarshotels.com
61 rm – 360 € 360 €, ☕ 20 € – 2 suites Plan I **C2**
Rest – Menu 25 € (weekday lunch) – Carte 25/46 €
◆ Luxury ◆ Business ◆ Stylish ◆
An elegant, discreet hotel with theme-based rooms (Asian, nautical or romantic decor), lovely penthouses, lounge-library, fitness room and sauna. Attentive service. The cuisine in the snug restaurant will find favour with aficionados of modern cuisine.

Crowne Plaza Europa
r. Loi 107 ✉ 1040 – ✆ 0 2 230 13 33 – brussels@ichotelsgroup.com – Fax 0 2 230 03 26 **G2**
238 rm – 260/380 € 260/380 €, ☕ 25 € – 2 suites
Rest ***The Gallery*** – *(closed Saturday lunch and Sunday lunch) (buffets)*
Menu 19 € (weekday lunch) – Carte 26/56 €
◆ Chain hotel ◆ Business ◆ Functional ◆
A twelve-storey hotel, located a few steps from the main European institutions. Comfortable rooms, modern lobby, business centre and full conference facilities. The Gallery offers a choice of classic and contemporary cuisine as well as buffets.

Silken Berlaymont
bd Charlemagne 11 ✉ 1000 – ✆ 0 2 231 09 09 – hotel.berlaymont@hoteles-silken.com – Fax 0 2 230 33 71 – www.hotelsilkenberlaymont.com
212 rm – 110/325 € 110/325 €, ☕ 25 € – 2 suites **G2**
Rest ***L'Objectif*** – Menu 20 € (weekday lunch), 29/43 € – Carte 35/47 €
◆ Chain hotel ◆ Business ◆ Functional ◆
This newly built chain hotel comprises two modern, inter-connected buildings with fresh, well-kept contemporary rooms. The interior decor follows a theme of contemporary photography. The menu is varied and the appetisers original.

Eurovillage
130 VISA
bd Charlemagne 80 ✉ 1000 – ✆ 0 2 230 85 55 – reservation@eurovillage.be – Fax 0 2 230 56 35 – www.eurovillage.be **G2**
96 rm – †318 € ††386 € – 4 suites
Rest – *(closed Friday dinner, Saturday and Sunday lunch)* Menu 21 € (weekday lunch) – Carte 29/45 €
♦ Traditional ♦ Functional ♦
A modern hotel building alongside a verdant park offering three room categories and good seminar and business facilities. Spacious lounge areas. Classic, traditional cuisine served in the modern setting of the restaurant.

Leopold
rest 80 VISA
r. Luxembourg 35 ✉ 1050 – ✆ 0 2 511 18 28 – reservations@hotel-leopold.be – Fax 0 2 514 19 39 – www.hotel-leopold.be *Plan IV* **O3**
111 rm – †140/240 € ††160/390 €
Rest *Salon Les Anges* – *(closed Saturday lunch and Sunday) (lunch only in July-August)* Menu 35 € (weekday lunch) – Carte 49/64 €
♦ Traditional ♦ Business ♦ Classic ♦
This continually expanding and improving hotel boasts well-appointed bedrooms, smart public areas, a winter garden where breakfast is served. A classic menu is on offer in the hushed Salon Les Anges restaurant; a variety of dishes served in the relaxed brasserie.

Holiday Inn Schuman
VISA
r. Breydel 20 ✉ 1040 – ✆ 0 2 280 40 00 – hotel@holiday-inn-brussels-schuman.com – Fax 0 2 282 10 70 – www.holiday-inn.com/brusselsschuman **H2**
57 rm – †295/495 € ††315/515 €, ☕ 20 € – 2 suites
Rest – Menu 37/65 € bi – Carte 31/41 €
♦ Chain hotel ♦ Business ♦ Functional ♦
Hotel named after a renowned pro-European politician, who would surely have appreciated this hotel offering rooms with a high level of comfort, perfect for those on European business. Traditional meals served in a simple room with parquet floors and bare wooden tables.

New Hotel Charlemagne
40 VISA
bd Charlemagne 25 ✉ 1000 – ✆ 0 2 230 21 35 – brusselscharlemagne@new-hotel.be – Fax 0 2 230 25 10 – www.new-hotel.be **H2**
68 rm – †99/425 € ††99/425 €, ☕ 21 €
Rest – *(residents only)*
♦ Traditional ♦ Business ♦ Functional ♦
This practical small hotel between Square Ambiorix and the Centre Berlaymont is popular with EU staff. Reception, lounge-bar and breakfast room on the same floor.

Brighton – Hotel Stanhope
VISA
r. Commerce 9 ✉ 1000 – ✆ 0 2 506 90 35 – brighton@stanhope.be – Fax 0 2 512 17 08 – www.stanhope.be
closed 9-17 April, 14 December-9 January, Saturday and Sunday *Plan IV* **O3**
Rest – Menu 39 € (weekday lunch), 45/66 € bi – Carte 53/105 €
♦ French traditional ♦ Formal ♦
An elegant hotel whose dining room with a refined English-style decor is inspired by Brighton's Royal Pavilion. Pleasant patio with a terrace open in fine weather.

Take Sushi
VISA
bd Charlemagne 21 ✉ 1000 – ✆ 0 2 230 56 27 – Fax 0 2 231 10 44
closed 23-31 December, Saturday and Sunday lunch **G2**
Rest – Menu 14 € (weekday lunch), 22/65 € bi – Carte 26/46 €
♦ Japanese ♦ Exotic ♦
This corner of Japan has existed at the heart of the city's European institutions district for more than 20 years. Japanese decor, background music and small garden. Sushi bar and fixed menus.

GARE DU NORD — *Plan II*

Sheraton Towers

600 VISA

pl. Rogier 3 ✉ 1210 – ✆ 0 2 224 31 11 – reservations.brussels@sheraton.com – Fax 0 2 224 34 56 – www.sheraton.com **F1**

486 rm – 109/375 € 109/375 €, 25 € – 22 suites

Rest – *(closed Saturday lunch and Sunday lunch) (buffets)* Menu 31 € (weekday lunch), 30/55 € bi – Carte 42/61 €

♦ Grand Luxury ♦ Business ♦ Modern ♦

With its full range of facilities, the imposing Sheraton has won over a business clientele, international travellers and conference-goers. Spacious standard rooms, plus club rooms and numerous suites. Attractive contemporary bar. Classic, traditional meals in the dining area facing the place Rogier. Lunch buffet.

Crowne Plaza "Le Palace"

600 VISA

r. Gineste 3 ✉ 1210 – ✆ 0 2 203 62 00 – info@cpbxl.be – Fax 0 2 203 55 55 **F1**

356 rm – 350 € 350 €, 26 € – 1 suite

Rest – Menu 18 € (weekday lunch)/35 € – Carte approx. 40 €

♦ Chain hotel ♦ Business ♦ Functional ♦

A Belle Époque-style palace embellished with period furniture in which several rooms have preserved the spirit of the 1900s. Attractive, opulent-looking public areas and contemporary, Art Nouveau-inspired rooms. Restaurant with a modern take on 1900s-style decor; international cuisine.

Husa President

rm 380 VISA

bd du Roi Albert II 44 ✉ 1000 – ✆ 0 2 203 20 20 – info.president@husa.es – Fax 0 2 203 24 40 – www.husa.es Plan I **B2**

281 rm – 75/300 € 75/300 €, 20 € – 16 suites

Rest – *(closed Saturday in July-August and Sunday)* Menu 21 € (weekday lunch) – Carte 37/59 €

♦ Traditional ♦ Business ♦ Functional ♦

An imposing hotel at one end of Brussels' "Manhattan", close to the Gare du Nord (North Station) and the World Trade Center. The public areas are spacious and the rooms very comfortable. The relaxed restaurant classic menu includes several fixed options and good daily suggestions.

Le Dome (annex Le Dome II)

rm 80 VISA

bd du Jardin Botanique 12 ✉ 1000 – ✆ 0 2 218 06 80 – dome@skypro.be – Fax 0 2 218 41 12 – www.hotel-le-dome.be **F1**

125 rm – 82/218 € 96/350 €

Rest – Menu 16 € (weekday lunch) – Carte 24/52 €

♦ Traditional ♦ Business ♦ Retro ♦

The dome crowning the 1900s-style façade overlooks the lively place Rogier. Art Nouveau-inspired decor in the hotel's public areas and rooms. A modern brasserie with mezzanine serving traditional Belgian fare, including salads and snacks.

GARE DU MIDI — *Plan I*

Le Prince de Liège

rm 25 VISA

chaussée de Ninove 664 ✉ 1070 – ✆ 0 2 522 16 00 – reception.princedeliege@coditel.net – Fax 0 2 520 81 85 – www.proximedia.com/web/prince-de-liege.html **A2**

32 rm – 75/100 € 98/115 €

Rest – *(closed Saturday lunch and Sunday dinner)* Menu 16 € (weekday lunch) – Carte 29/48 €

♦ Family ♦ Inn ♦ Functional ♦

The rooms at this family-run hotel located alongside a major road junction are functional, double-glazed and offer good value for money. The third-floor rooms are more recent. Bar-restaurant serving simple, classic à la carte choices, with menus and seasonal suggestions highlighted on boards.

Erasme

70 P VISA AE

rte de Lennik 790 ✉ 1070 – ✆ 0 2 523 62 82 – info@hotelerasme.be – Fax 0 2 523 62 83 – www.hotelerasme.be **A3**

74 rm – 62/198 € 62/249 €

Rest – *(closed 1-15 August and 24 December-3 January)* Menu 16 € (weekday lunch) – Carte 19/40 €

♦ Chain hotel ♦ Business ♦ Functional ♦

A chain hotel on the outskirts of the city, 1km/0.6mi beyond the ring road, with a choice between standard (small) and executive rooms (bigger). Fitness facilities and seminar rooms. Tavern-style restaurant with a varied international menu.

Saint Guidon

10/600 P VISA

av. Théo Verbeeck 2, 1st floor, in the R.S.C. Anderlecht football stadium ✉ 1070 – ✆ 0 2 520 55 36 – saint-guidon@skynet.be – Fax 0 2 523 38 27

closed 15 June-15 July, Christmas-New Year, Saturday, Sunday and at home matches **A3**

Rest – *(lunch only)* Menu 32 € (weekday lunch)/57 € bi – Carte 56/98 €

♦ Contemporary ♦ Formal ♦

This restaurant, situated on the second floor of Anderlecht's football stadium draws in supporters of the famous football club. The plush dining area is next to the stands but overlooks the car park.

Alain Cornelis

VISA AE

av. Paul Janson 82 ✉ 1070 – ✆ 0 2 523 20 83 – alaincornelis@skynet.be – Fax 0 2 523 20 83 – www.alaincornelis.be

closed 1 week Easter, 27 July-16 August, late December, Wednesday dinner, Saturday lunch and Sunday **A3**

Rest – Menu 30/65 € bi – Carte 30/43 €

♦ Traditional ♦ Friendly ♦

A classically bourgeois restaurant with a traditional wine-list. The terrace to the rear is embellished with a small garden. Fixed menus, à la carte and dishes of the month.

La Brouette

6/12 VISA AE

bd Prince de Liège 61 ✉ 1070 – ✆ 0 2 522 51 69 – info@labrouette.be – Fax 0 2 522 51 69 – www.labrouette.be

closed 16 July-15 August, Saturday lunch, Sunday dinner and Monday **A2**

Rest – Menu 25 € (weekday lunch), 42/69 € bi – Carte 35/52 €

♦ Contemporary ♦ Design ♦

This restaurant's grey and burgundy interior has given it a more modern feel. The flower arrangements on the tables are exhibited on the walls in photos. The owner is also the sommelier.

ATOMIUM QUARTER

Plan I

Rijckendael

rm 60 P VISA AE

J. Van Elewijckstraat 35 ✉ 1853 Strombeek-Bever – ✆ 0 2 267 41 24 – restaurant.rijckendael@vhv-hotels.be – Fax 0 2 267 94 01 – www.rijckendael.be **B1**

49 rm – 99/165 € 99/200 €, 16 €

Rest – *(closed last 3 weeks July-first week August)* Menu 23 € (weekday lunch), 36/65 € bi – Carte 37/61 €

♦ Traditional ♦ Business ♦ Functional ♦

This hotel of modern design is located in a residential area a short walk from the Atomium and Heysel stadium. Well-appointed rooms. Private car park. Restaurant with a rustic feel housed in a small former farmhouse (1857). Classic, traditional meals.

La Roseraie

Limburg Stirumlaan 213 ✉ 1780 Wemmel – ✆ 0 2 456 99 10 – hotel@laroseraie.be – Fax 0 2 460 83 20 – www.laroseraie.be **A1**

8 rm – 107/207 € 130/254 € – **Rest** – *(closed Saturday lunch, Sunday dinner and Monday)* Menu 22 € (weekday lunch)/29 € – Carte 41/53 €

♦ Family ♦ Inn ♦ Personalised ♦

A warm welcome awaits you at this 1930s villa transformed into a family-run hotel offering impeccably maintained rooms decorated along different themes: African, Japanese, Roman etc. Traditionally furnished dining room with a piano which is home to lobsters!

't Stoveke

4/10

Jetsestraat 52 ✉ 1853 Strombeek-Bever – ✆ 0 2 267 67 25 – info@tstoveke.be – www.tstoveke.be

closed mid August-mid September, late December-early January, Tuesday and Wednesday **B1**

Rest – Menu 25 € (weekday lunch), 40/86 € bi

♦ Traditional ♦ Family ♦

Modern-style restaurant occupying an early-20C building in a residential district near the Parc des Expositions. Traditional, classic cuisine with a simple, modern touch.

Le Gril aux Herbes d'Evan

10/15

Brusselsesteenweg 21 ✉ 1780 Wemmel – ✆ 0 2 460 52 39 – Fax 0 2 461 19 12

closed 24 December-1 January, Monday in July-August, Saturday lunch and Sunday **A1**

Rest – Menu 35 € (weekday lunch), 50/90 € bi – Carte 58/87 €

♦ Traditional ♦ Fashionable ♦

This small villa perched on a hilltop has a terrace and a large garden. Classic cuisine and a wine-list that does justice to the reputation of French vineyards.

Lychee

r. De Wand 118 ✉ 1020 – ✆ 0 2 268 19 14 – Fax 0 2 268 19 14

closed Monday except Bank Holidays **B1**

Rest – *(open until 11 p.m.)* Menu 15 € (weekday lunch), 19/30 € – Carte 17/35 €

♦ Chinese ♦ Exotic ♦

This Chinese restaurant between the Chinese Pavilion and the Roman road has been serving its Cantonese dishes for more than 25 years. A wide choice of fixed menus and a very reasonably-priced lunch.

La Balade Gourmande

8

av. Houba de Strooper 230 ✉ 1020 – ✆ 0 2 478 94 34 – Fax 0 2 479 89 52

closed 1 week carnival, 2 weeks September, Wednesday dinner, Saturday lunch and Sunday **B1**

Rest – Menu 17 € (weekday lunch)/32 €

♦ Contemporary ♦ Friendly ♦

The fixed-menu options at this local restaurant cover a cross-section of traditional dishes prepared with a modern eye. Decor dominated by red fabrics.

AIRPORT & OTAN *Plan I*

Sheraton Airport

600

at airport (North-East by A 201)

✉ 1930 Zaventem – ✆ 0 2 710 80 00 – reservations.brussels@sheraton.com – Fax 0 2 710 80 80 – www.sheraton.com/brusselsairport **D1**

292 rm – 109/395 € 109/395 €, 25 € – 2 suites

Rest *Concorde* – *(closed Saturday)* Menu 55 € bi (weekday lunch)/40 € – Carte 44/63 €

♦ Chain hotel ♦ Business ♦ Modern ♦

The closest luxury hotel to the airport, offering comfort and numerous services, this is a popular choice with business customers from around the world. Contemporary international à la carte menu at the Concorde, which shares a vast atrium with a bar serving buffets.

BELGIUM

Crowne Plaza Airport

Da Vincilaan 4 ✉ 1831 Diegem – ✆ 0 2 416 33 33 – cpbrusselsairport@ichotelsgroup.com – Fax 0 2 416 33 44 – www.crowneplaza.com/cpbrusselsarpt 400 **D1**

311 rm – 195/355 € 195/355 €, 21 € – 4 suites

Rest – *(closed Friday dinner, Saturday and Sunday lunch)* Menu 21 € (weekday lunch) – Carte 34/82 €

♦ Chain hotel ♦ Business ♦ Modern ♦

Part of the Crowne Plaza chain, this hotel is located in a business park close to the airport. Central atrium, comfortable, well-equipped rooms as well as good conference facilities and neat gardens. The restaurant offers a choice of contemporary dishes including a buffet lunch option.

Sofitel Airport

Bessenveldstraat 15 ✉ 1831 Diegem – ✆ 0 2 713 66 66 – H0548@accor.com – Fax 0 2 721 43 45 – www.sofitel.com 300 **C1**

125 rm – 375 € 375/450 €, 21 €

Rest ***La Pléiade*** – *(closed Friday dinner, Saturday and Sunday lunch)* Menu 25 € (weekday lunch) – Carte 42/53 €

♦ Chain hotel ♦ Business ♦ Functional ♦

A top-of-the-range chain hotel alongside a motorway 4km/2.5mi from Zaventem airport with quiet, inviting rooms, seven meeting rooms and some leisure facilities. Friendly bar and a restaurant decked out like a luxury brasserie.

NH Brussels Airport

De Kleetlaan 14 ✉ 1831 Diegem – ✆ 0 2 203 92 52 – nhbrusselsairport@nh-hotels.com – Fax 0 2 203 92 53 – www.nh-hotels.com 80 **D1**

234 rm – 90/300 € 90/300 €, 19 €

Rest – *(closed 20 July-10 August, Friday dinner, Saturday and Sunday) (buffets)* Menu 15 € (weekday lunch)/30 € – Carte 33/58 €

♦ Chain hotel ♦ Business ♦ Functional ♦

A distinctly modern-looking business hotel in the business district close to the airport. Rooms well soundproofed against the nearby railway. Contemporary-style lounge bar and restaurant serving cuisine from around the world as well as fixed buffet menus.

Holiday Inn Airport

Holidaystraat 7 ✉ 1831 Diegem – ✆ 0 2 720 58 65 – hibrusselsairport@ichotelsgroup.com – Fax 0 2 720 41 45 – www.benelux.ichotelsgroup.com 490 **D1**

310 rm – 75/230 € 75/270 €, 21 € – **Rest** – Carte 33/42 €

♦ Chain hotel ♦ Business ♦ Functional ♦

A 1970s hotel close to the airport. The rooms are due an overhaul. Comprehensive range of facilities for business or for pleasure. International cuisine is served at the restaurant on the first floor, and simple meals and snacks at the bar downstairs.

Novotel Airport

Da Vincilaan 25 ✉ 1831 Diegem – ✆ 0 2 725 30 50 – H0467@accor.com – Fax 0 2 721 39 58 – www.accorhotels.com/be rest 100 **D1**

209 rm – 180/186 € 180/186 €, 15 €

Rest – Carte 28/40 €

♦ Chain hotel ♦ Business ♦ Functional ♦

Ideal for those with an early flight to catch. No surprises in the identical bedrooms, which conform to the Novotel's usual criteria. Seminar rooms and outdoor pool.

Brussels Airport

Berkenlaan 4 ✉ 1831 Diegem – ✆ 0 2 721 77 77 – info@goldentulipairport.be – Fax 0 2 721 55 96 – www.goldentulipairport.be rm rest 100 **D1**

100 rm – 89/193 € 89/233 €, 16 €

Rest – *(closed Saturday and Sunday)* Carte 28/46 €

♦ Chain hotel ♦ Business ♦ Functional ♦

The delightful rooms are well-maintained and spotlessly clean. Modern decor in the restaurant, where the emphasis is on conventional dishes. A haven of peace and quiet for stopover or transit passengers.

ANTWERP

ANVERS - ANTWERPEN

Population (est. 2004): 455 300 – Altitude: sea level

J. Malburet / MICHELIN

Antwerp is Belgium's largest port, its main trading city and a major industrial centre but it remains in many ways a typical old Flemish town with narrow streets, spacious squares, imposing guildhalls and fine old buildings.

The vibrant city is a shoppers' paradise; its fashion designers have made their mark on the international scene. It is also renowned as the world diamond centre which has attracted a large Jewish population over the centuries. The members of the orthodox community in traditional dress are a common sight in the city. People of various origins (India, Lebanon, Armenia, Asia and Africa) working in the diamond trade create a mosaic of cultures.

Its name is said to be derived from the word *handwerpen* meaning 'to throw a hand' from the legend of a giant slain by a Roman soldier who cut off the former's hand and threw it into the river. From the 13C Antwerp flourished as a trading and cultural centre which attracted famous painters, sculptors, architects as well as the intellectual élite. Decline set in owing to political and religious struggles whilst under Austrian and French occupation and it was only in the 20C that Antwerp experienced steady economic growth and regained its prestige.

WHICH DISTRICT TO CHOOSE

For elegant **accommodation** you may choose to stay around Grote Markt *Plan II* **D1** and the area near the cathedral in the old town where charming 16C houses have been beautifully converted. You will also find comfortable hotels in De Keyserlei *Plan II* **F2** near Central Station and in the Diamond district. Het Zuid (South Quarter) with its lovely Art Nouveau buildings offers pleasant hotels in a vibrant district. There are also business hotels in the port area to the north of the city.

For **cafés**, **brasseries** and **restaurants** visit the areas around Grote Markt, Meir *Plan II* **E2**, Central Station *Plan II* **F2**, the Quartier Latin *Plan II* **E2** and Het Zuid *Plan II* **C3** which is the trendy district of Antwerp.

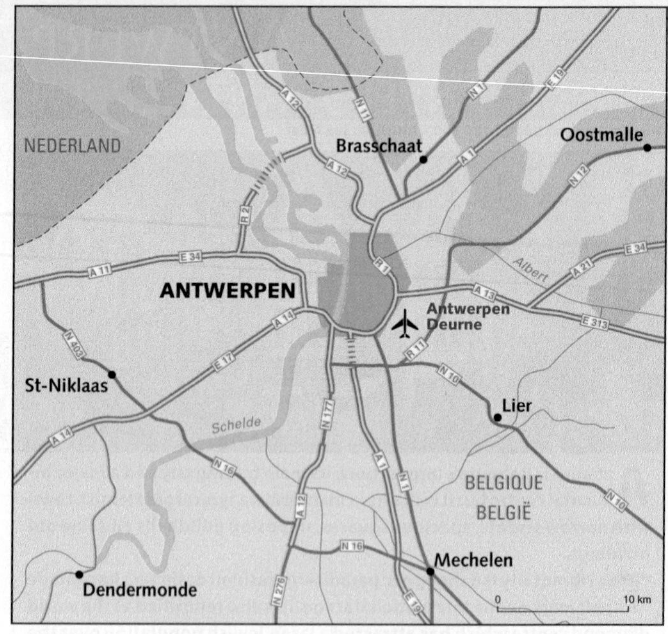

PRACTICAL INFORMATION

ARRIVAL

Via Zaventem airport (Brussels) – Take the SN Brussels Airlines shuttle to Central Station (Keyserlei 45). Approx. 45min; departure from Zaventem each precise hour from 7am to 11pm; from Antwerpen each precise hour from 5.30am to 10pm. Single ticket €8, return ticket €15; tickets sold in shuttle bus. ✆ 070 35 11 11; www.flysn.com

Via the airport of Antwerpen-Deurne – Take bus No 16 to Pelikaanstraat, next to Central Station.

Railway Stations – Both international and inter-city trains stop in **Antwerpen-Centraal** *Plan II* **F2** and **Antwerpen-Berchem** stations; www.sncb.be

TRANSPORT

→ BUS AND TRAM

The **Dagpas Stadt** (city day pass), which gives unlimited travel on the whole of the city's public transport network, is obtainable on board buses and trams and from De Lijn kiosks. Information: De Lijn, ✆ 03 218 14 11; www.delijn.be

→ TAXIS

Allow €7-10 for a short journey. It is customary to round up taxi fares. *Antwerp Taxi* ✆ 03 238 38 38; *Antwerpse Taxicentrale* ✆ 03 216 16 16.

USEFUL ADDRESSES

→ TOURIST OFFICES

Tourism Antwerp, Grote Markt 13 *Plan II* **D1**; ✆ 03 232 01 03; www.visi

tantwerpen.be; open 9am to 5.45pm (4.45pm Sundays and public holidays); closed 1 Jan and 25 Dec. **Centraal Station** (hall 2) *Plan II* **F2**. **Tourism Federation of the Province of Antwerp**, Koningin Elisabethlei 16 *Plan III* **G1** ✆ 03 240 63 73; www.tpa.be

→ POST OFFICES

Main Post Office: corner of Schoenmarkt and Nationalestraat *Plan II* **D2**, open Monday to Friday, 9am to noon and 2 to 5pm.

→ BANKS / CURRENCY EXCHANGE

Banks open Monday to Friday, 9am-4pm. There are cash dispensers all over the city.

→ EMERGENCY

Police ✆ **101**. Fire Brigade and Medical Emergency Service ✆ **100** (✆ **112** when calling from a mobile phone).

EXPLORING ANTWERP

It is possible to visit the main sights and museums in two days.

Museums and other sights are usually open from 9-10am to 5pm. Some close on Mondays.

VISITING

Boat trips on the Schelde (Escaut) starting from Steenplein *Plan II* **C1**.

Grote Markt *Plan II* **D1** – A charming square lined with the splendid 16C Town Hall and 16C-17C guildhalls.

Kathedraal *Plan II* **D2** – The largest cathedral in Belgium (14C-16C), crowned by a soaring tower, contains several works by Rubens.

Museum Plantin-Moretus *Plan II* **C2** – The house and printing works built by the famous 16C printer Christophe Plantin, complete with antique furnishings, engravings, manuscripts and early editions.

Rubenshuis *Plan II* **E2** – The home and studio of Antwerp's greatest painter.

Koninklijk Museum voor Schone Kunsten *Plan II* **C3** – The collections of the Royal Museum of Fine Art: European painting from the 14C to the present day, including Flemish Primitives, Rubens, the Belgian School, Expressionists and Surrealists.

Modemuseum (MOMU) *Plan II* **D2** – An innovative display on the evolution of fashion will delight admirers of fashion and design.

Nationaal Scheepvaartmuseum (Het Steen) *Plan II* **C1** – A fascinating exhibition traces maritime and river life with a collection of boats on display in the maritime park. It is housed in a fortress which is the oldest building in Antwerp.

Museum van Hedendaags Kunst Antwerpen (MuKHA) *Plan II* **D2** – A collection of contemporary art by Belgian and international artists housed in a converted grain silo and warehouse.

Provinciaal Diamantmuseum *Plan II* **F2** – An illuminating presentation on the use and transformation of diamonds and the history of diamonds in Antwerp. Diamond workshop and dazzling collection of precious jewels.

Brouwershuis (Brewers' Hall) *Plan I* **A1** – The 16C seat of the brewers' guild: horse treadmill, water-raising system, reservoirs, workshop and Council chamber with walls clad with 17C gilded leather.

Wijk Zurenborg *Plan III* **H1** – An impressive array of town houses built in revival, eclectic and Art Nouveau styles in several streets around Cogels-Osylei.

GOURMET TREATS

Most restaurants serve classic **French cuisine** but Antwerp is a cosmopolitan city where you will find a whole range of European and exotic dishes and the latest food trends. Typical **Flemish specialities** include stewed eel in chervil sauce, mussels in various sauces, dishes with rabbit or beef stew and chicory. To enjoy **frites with mayonnaise**, visit *Fritkot Max*, Groenplaats 12, a traditional 'frituur' (chip shop) which serves golden chips in a paper cone as in the old days. For all you need to know about 'frying' do not miss the tiny museum (photos, lithographs, cartoons, etc. – first floor) which celebrates this Belgian tradition. **Worstenbrood** (sausage rolls), **appelbollen** (apple balls), **roggeverdommeke** (rye/raisin bread), **wafels** and **smoutebollen** (fried dough balls) are delicious snacks.

Beer drinkers will enjoy **'bolleke'**, a special amber-coloured brew, produced by the De Koninck brewery. It is a time-honoured custom to sample a 'bolleke' or a 'keuninkske' at Café *De Pelgrim*, Boomgaardstraat 8.

SHOPPING

Diamonds are forever! Visit *Diamondland Plan II* **F2** and the numerous jewellers in the **diamond district** for that special gift. Look for the logo of the Antwerp Diamond and Jewellery Association (ADJA). More affordable specialities are Antwerpse handjes, small chocolates with filling and also available in biscuit form, Antwerps gebak (a biscuit or cake with almonds, apricot jam and sugar icing) and Semini biscuit (a sweet biscuit with sesame seed and a marzipan image of the Antwerp fertility symbol Semini). Antwerp Elixir is a sweet liqueur made with herbs.

Luxury and designer shops – The pedestrian avenue **Meir** *Plan II* **E2**, **De Keyserlei** *Plan II* **E2**, **Frankrijklei** *Plan II* **E2**, **Huidevetterstraat** *Plan II* **D2** and adjoining streets (Wiegstraat, Groendalstraat, Korte Gasthuisstraat). You will find the shops of the fashion designers *Chris Mesdagh, Ann De Meulemeester, Dirk Bikkembergs* in **Lombardenvest** *Plan II* **D2** and **Steenhouwersvest** *Plan II* **D2**. *Dries van Noten* has a shop in Modepaleis, **Nationalestraat** *Plan II* **D2**.

Antiques – Kloosterstraat *Plan II* **C2**, Steenhouwersvest *Plan II* **D2**, Hoogstraat *Plan II* **C1**, Hopland *Plan II* **E2**, Leopoldstraat *Plan II* **D2**, Mechelsesteenweg *Plan II* **E3**.

MARKETS – **Vogelenmarkt** (Bird Market, on Sunday morning) and **Exotic Market** (on Saturdays) on Theaterplein *Plan II* **E2**. **Vrijdagmarkt** (antiques and rare objects) *Plan II* **D2** on Wednesday and Friday mornings.

ENTERTAINMENT

Antwerp has a rich concert and theatre tradition.

Bourla Theatre *Plan II* **D2** – Classical concerts and theatre.

Koningin Elisabethzaal *Plan II* **F2** – Concerts and shows.

Arenberg Cultural Centre (Antwerpsesteenweg 59) – Cabaret and chanson productions.

De Muze *Plan II* **D2** – Live jazz in a converted warehouse.

NIGHTLIFE

Plan II **C1-D1** – Consult the publication *Weekup* (in French and Flemish) available in bars and other public places.

Bars with terraces, cafés with live music, pubs, clubs, discotheques, karaoke bars abound around **Groenplaats**, **Grote Markt** and along **Jordaenskaai** and **Ernest Van Dijckkaai** on the **banks of the Scheldt**, along **Koningin Astridplein** *Plan II* **F2**, in the neighbourhood of the **Centraal Station** (Franklin Rooseveltplaats, De Coninckplein, Statiestraat, Offerandestaat) and in bustling **Het Zuid** *Plan II* **C3** which boasts literary cafés.

The Grand Horta Café, Hopland 2 is a stylish designer café and *Den Engel*, Grote Markt 3, is a city institution.

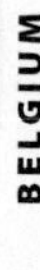

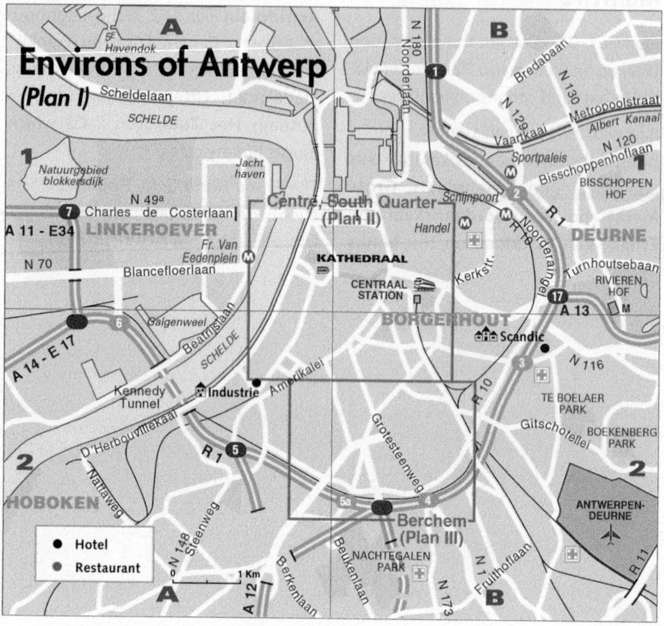

Environs of Antwerp
(Plan I)

● Hotel
● Restaurant

CENTRE (Old Town and Main Station) *Plan II*

Hilton
1000 VISA

Groenplaats – ✆ 0 3 204 12 12 – fb-antwerp@hilton.com
– Fax 0 3 204 12 13
– www.hilton.com **D2**
199 rm – 159/349 € 159/349 €, 25 € – 12 suites
Rest *Terrace-Café* – Menu 27 € (weekday lunch)/45 € – Carte 48/63 €
♦ Chain hotel ♦ Luxury ♦ Stylish ♦
This luxury hotel occupies a fine early-20C building which started life as a department store. Large, well-appointed rooms, plus pleasant public areas. Views of the cathedral and lively Groenplaats from the Terrace Café with its comprehensive menu.

Astrid Park Plaza
500 VISA

Koningin Astridplein 7 ✉ 2018 – ✆ 0 3 203 12 34
– appres@pphe.com – Fax 0 3 203 12 51
– www.parkplaza.com **F2**
225 rm – 119/165 € 119/265 €, 20 € – 3 suites
Rest – Menu 31/59 € – Carte 25/46 €
♦ Chain hotel ♦ Business ♦ Design ♦
This four-star hotel, its original architectural design the work of Michael Graves, is on a busy square near the central railway station. Impeccable, spacious and well-appointed rooms and modern public areas. Bright restaurant serving contemporary recipes.

Radisson SAS Park Lane
rest 600

Van Eycklei 34 – 2018 – 0 3 285 85 85 – guest.antwerp@radissonsas.com – Fax 0 3 285 85 86 – www.antwerp.radissonsas.com **E3**

160 rm – 130 € 130/185 €, 24 € – 14 suites

Rest – Carte 36/54 €

♦ Chain hotel ♦ Traditional ♦ Stylish ♦

This luxury hotel is well-located on a main road away from the centre, opposite a public park. Full range of tailored facilities and services for its mainly business clientele. Small dining room serving classic international cuisine.

De Witte Lelie without rest

Keizerstraat 16 – 0 3 226 19 66 – hotel@dewittelelie.be – Fax 0 3 234 00 19 – www.dewittelelie.be

closed Christmas and New Year **D1**

7 rm – 195/275 € 265/345 € – 3 suites

♦ Family ♦ Luxury ♦ Personalised ♦

Quiet and full of charm, this small "grand hotel" is spread across several 17C houses. Cosy, elegantly decorated rooms, in addition to an inviting patio.

't Sandt
100

Het Zand 17 – 0 3 232 93 90 – reservations@hotel-sandt.be – Fax 0 3 232 56 13 – www.hotel-sandt.be **C2**

27 rm – 140/270 € 155/285 € – 2 suites

♦ Family ♦ Luxury ♦ Stylish ♦

The fine Rococo façade of this impressive 19C residence contrasts starkly with the sober, contemporary decor of its interior. Delightful, Italianate winter garden and roomy, elegant guest accommodation.

Theater
50

Arenbergstraat 30 – 0 3 203 54 10 – info@theater-hotel.be – Fax 0 3 233 88 58 – www.vhv-hotels.be **E2**

122 rm – 110/220 € 130/240 €, 20 € – 5 suites

Rest – *(closed 21 July-14 August, 22 December-1 January, Saturday, Sunday and Bank Holidays)* Menu 17 € (weekday lunch) – Carte 33/45 €

♦ Business ♦ Classic ♦

A modern, comfortable hotel with an ideal location at the heart of the old city, just a short distance from the Bourla theatre and Rubens' house. Spacious bedrooms decorated in warm tones. Characterful restaurant featuring a small menu from around the world.

Rubens without rest

Oude Beurs 29 – 0 3 222 48 48 – hotel.rubens@glo.be – www.hotelrubensantwerp.be **D1**

35 rm – 145/175 € 145/255 € – 1 suite

♦ Traditional ♦ Business ♦ Classic ♦

A quiet and friendly renovated hotel near the Grand-Place and cathedral. Some rooms overlook the inner courtyard, which is flower-decked in summer.

Hyllit without rest
150

De Keyserlei 28 (access by Appelmansstraat) 2018 – 0 3 202 68 00 – info@hyllithotel.be – Fax 0 3 202 68 90 – www.hyllithotel.be **E2**

123 rm – 100/205 € 125/230 €, 17 € – 4 suites

♦ Business ♦ Modern ♦

Intimate public areas, spacious bedrooms and junior suites, and a good view of Antwerp's rooftops from the bright breakfast room and two large terraces.

De Keyser without rest
120

De Keyserlei 66 2018 – 0 3 206 74 60 – info@dekeyserhotel.be – Fax 0 3 232 39 70 – www.vhv-hotels.be **F2**

120 rm – 110/180 € 130/200 €, 20 € – 3 suites

♦ Chain hotel ♦ Business ♦ Classic ♦

Easily accessible and advantageously located close to the railway station and a metro line. Cosy, modern bedrooms.

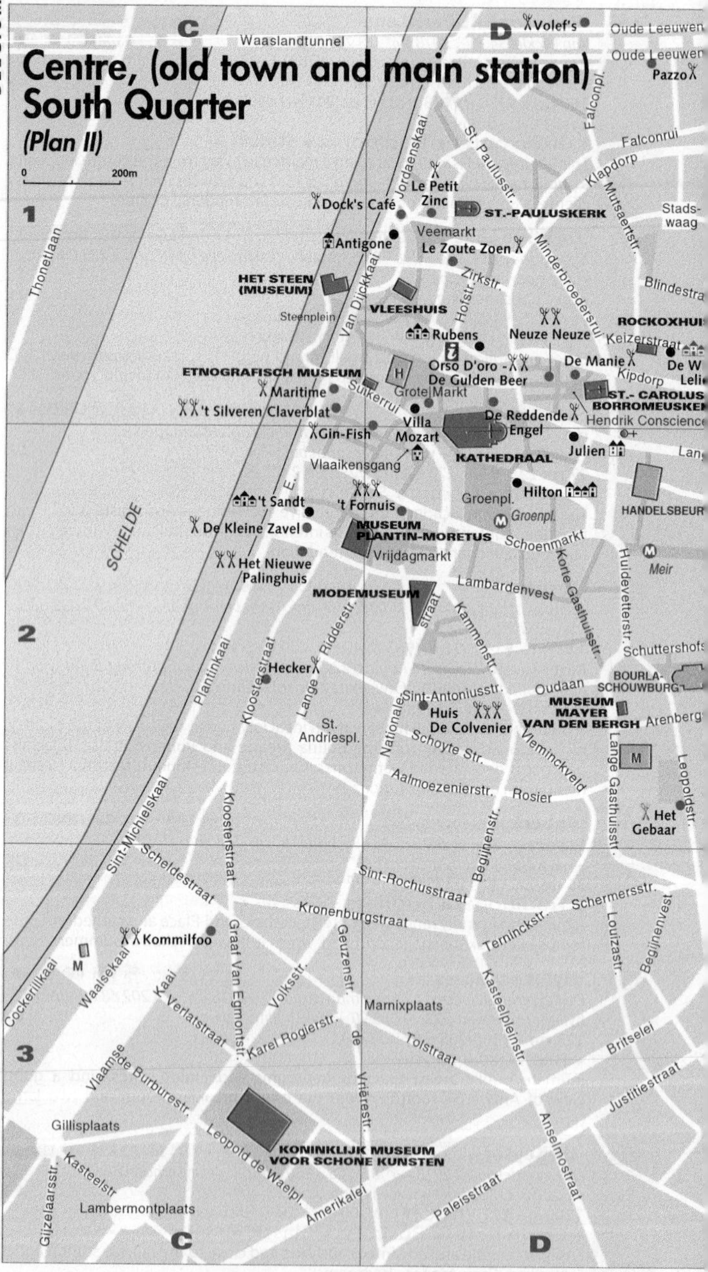

Centre, (old town and main station) South Quarter

(Plan II)

0 200m

C
D
1
2
3

Waaslandtunnel
Volef's
Oude Leeuwenrui
Oude Leeuwenrui
Pazzo
Falconpl.
Falconrui
Klapdorp
Mutsaertstr.
Stadswaag
St. Paulusstr.
Jordaenskaai
Le Petit Zinc
Dock's Café
ST.-PAULUSKERK
Veemarkt
Antigone
Le Zoute Zoen
Minderbroedersrui
Zirkstr.
Blindestraat
Thonetlaan
HET STEEN (MUSEUM)
Van Dijckkaai
VLEESHUIS
Hofstr.
Steenplein
Rubens
Neuze Neuze
ROCKOXHUIS
Keizerstraat
Orso D'oro
De Gulden Beer
De Manie
De W
Lelie
Kipdorp
ETNOGRAFISCH MUSEUM
H
Maritime
Suikerrui
Grote Markt
ST.- CAROLUS BORROMEUSKERK
't Silveren Claverblat
Villa
Mozart
De Reddende Engel
Hendrik Conscienceplein
Gin-Fish
KATHEDRAAL
Julien
Lange
Vlaaikensgang
E.
't Sandt
't Fornuis
Groenpl.
Groenpl.
Hilton
HANDELSBEURS
SCHELDE
De Kleine Zavel
MUSEUM PLANTIN-MORETUS
Schoenmarkt
Het Nieuwe Palinghuis
Vrijdagmarkt
Meir
Huidevettersstr.
Lambardenvest
MODEMUSEUM
straat
Korte Gasthuisstr.
Kammenstr.
Lange Riddersstr.
Plantinkaai
Kloosterstraat
Hecker
Schuttershofstr.
BOURLA-SCHOUWBURG
Oudaan
Sint-Antoniusstr.
MUSEUM MAYER VAN DEN BERGH
Arenbergstr.
Huis De Colvenier
St. Andriespl.
Nationalestr.
Schoyte Str.
Vleminckveld
Lange Gasthuisstr.
M
Leopoldstr.
Aalmoezenierstr.
Rosier
Het Gebaar
Sint-Michielskaai
Kloosterstraat
Begijnenstr.
Scheldestraat
Sint-Rochusstraat
Schermersstr.
Kronenburgstraat
Terninckstr.
Louizastr.
Begijnenvest
Kommilfoo
Graaf Van Egmontstr.
Geuzenstr.
M
Waalsekaai
Kaai
Volksstr.
Kasteelpleinstr.
Cockerillkaai
Verlatstraat
Marnixplaats
Karel Rogierstr.
de
Tolstraat
Britselei
Vlaamse
de Burburestr.
Vrièrestr.
Justitiestraat
Gillisplaats
Leopold de Waelpl.
KONINKLIJK MUSEUM VOOR SCHONE KUNSTEN
Anselmostraat
Kasteelstr.
Gijzelaarsstr.
Lambermontplaats
Amerikalei
Paleisstraat
C
D

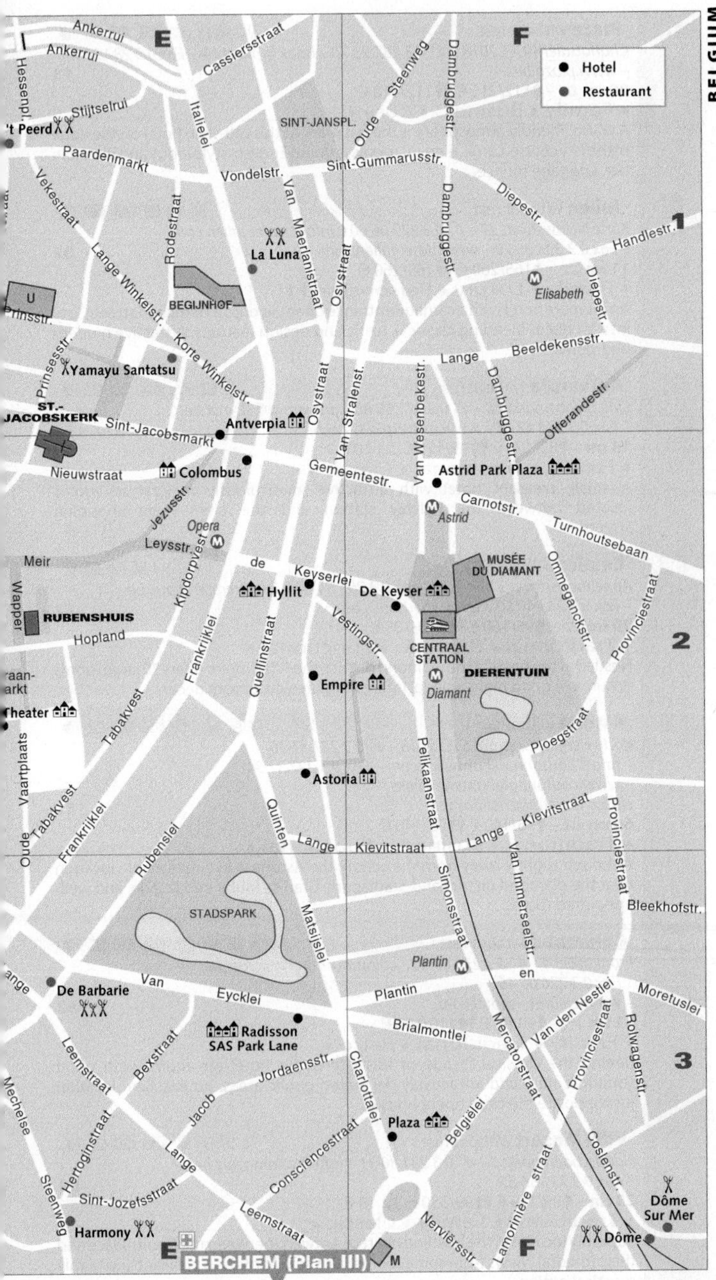

E
F
Hotel
Restaurant
Ankerrui
Cassiersstraat
Steenweg
Oude
Dambruggestr.
Hessenpl.
Stijtselrui
't Peerd
SINT-JANSPL.
Italielei
Paardenmarkt
Vondelstr.
Sint-Gummarusstr.
Diepestr.
Vekestraat
Van Maerlanistraat
Rodestraat
La Luna
Osystraat
Handlestr.
Lange Winkelstr.
BEGIJNHOF
Elisabeth
Prinsstr.
Korte Winkelstr.
Lange Beeldekensstr.
Prinsesstr.
Yamayu Santatsu
Van Stralenst.
Van Wesenbekestr.
Offerandestr.
ST.-JACOBSKERK
Sint-Jacobsmarkt
Antverpia
Nieuwstraat
Colombus
Gemeentestr.
Astrid Park Plaza
Carnotstr.
Astrid
Jezusstr.
Opera
Turnhoutsebaan
Leysstr.
Meir
de Keyserlei
MUSÉE DU DIAMANT
Ommeganckstr.
Kipdorpvest
Hyllit
De Keyser
Provinciestraat
Wapper
RUBENSHUIS
Vestingstr.
Quellinstraat
Hopland
CENTRAAL STATION
DIERENTUIN
Frankrijklei
Empire
Diamant
Theater
Tabakvest
Ploegstraat
Pelikaanstraat
Astoria
Vaartplaats
Oude
Quinten
Lange Kievitstraat
Van Immerseelstr.
Frankrijklei
Rubenslei
Simonsstraat
Bleekhofstr.
STADSPARK
Matsijslei
Plantin
Plantin en Moretuslei
De Barbarie
Van Eycklei
Radisson SAS Park Lane
Brialmontlei
Van den Nestlei
Rolwagenstr.
Leemstraat
Bexstraat
Jordaensstr.
Charlottalei
Mercatorstraat
Mechelse Steenweg
Jacob
Hertoginstraat
Plaza
Belgiëlei
Lange Leemstraat
Conscienceestraat
Coslenstr.
Sint-Jozefsstraat
Lamorinière straat
Dôme Sur Mer
Harmony
Nerviërsstr.
Dôme
BERCHEM (Plan III)
M
1
2
3

Plaza without rest

Charlottalei 49 ✉ 2018 – ✆ 0 3 287 28 70 – book@plaza.be – Fax 0 3 287 28 71 – www.plaza.be **F3**

80 rm ☕ – 🚹112/215 € 🚹🚹112/310 €

◆ Family ◆ Business ◆ Cosy ◆

A warm, friendly atmosphere is the hallmark of this old-style hotel on the edge of the city centre. Large, elegant rooms, a grand English-style lobby and Victorian bar. Luggage service.

Julien without rest

Korte Nieuwstraat 24 – ✆ 0 3 229 06 00 – info@hotel-julien.com – Fax 0 3 233 35 70 – www.hotel-julien.com **D2**

11 rm ☕ – 🚹165/260 € 🚹🚹165/260 €

◆ Family ◆ Luxury ◆ Personalised ◆

An intimate hotel with a carriage entrance opening onto a tramlined street. Cosy interior decor blending classical, rustic and design features. Attractive modern bedrooms.

Antverpia without rest

Sint-Jacobsmarkt 85 – ✆ 0 3 231 80 80 – antverpia@skynet.be – Fax 0 3 232 43 43 – www.antverpia-hotel.be **E1**

18 rm – 🚹87/124 € 🚹🚹99/175 €, ☕ 10 €

◆ Family ◆ Traditional ◆ Classic ◆

A small, pleasant hotel with attractive, meticulously maintained rooms located between the railway station and the city's main shopping streets.

Empire without rest

Appelmansstraat 31 ✉ 2018 – ✆ 0 3 203 54 00 – info@empirehotel.be – Fax 0 3 233 40 60 – www.vhv-hotels.be **E2**

70 rm ☕ – 🚹95/160 € 🚹🚹110/185 €

◆ Traditional ◆ Business ◆ Functional ◆

Nestled at the heart of the diamond district, the Alfa Empire offers 70 large rooms ensuring a good night's sleep. Interesting breakfast room decor.

Astoria without rest

Korte Herentalsestraat 5 ✉ 2018 – ✆ 0 3 227 31 30 – info@carltonhotel-antwerp.com – Fax 0 3 227 31 34 – www.carltonhotel-antwerp.com

closed Christmas holidays **E2**

66 rm ☕ – 🚹95/140 € 🚹🚹95/140 €

◆ Traditional ◆ Business ◆ Functional ◆

Although slightly away from the action, the Astoria is in a reasonable location near the diamond district and Stadtspark. Granite lobby and façade, and well-appointed rooms.

Colombus without rest

Frankrijklei 4 – ✆ 0 3 233 03 90 – colombushotel@skynet.be – Fax 0 3 226 09 46 – www.columbushotel.com **E2**

32 rm ☕ – 🚹90/97 € 🚹🚹110/117 €

◆ Family ◆ Traditional ◆ Retro ◆

Behind the classical façade of this city-centre hotel are rooms with good soundproofing and attractively decorated public areas. An excellent location just opposite the city's opera house.

Villa Mozart without rest

Handschoenmarkt 3 – ✆ 0 3 231 30 31 – info@villamozart.be – Fax 0 3 231 56 85 **D1**

25 rm – 🚹89/139 € 🚹🚹99/350 €, ☕ 13 €

◆ Traditional ◆ Family ◆ Classic ◆

Superbly located in the bustling heart of Antwerp between the Grand-Place and the cathedral (views from some rooms), this small hotel is a pleasant and highly practical option.

Antigone without rest

Jordaenskaai 11 – 0 3 231 66 77 – info@antigonehotel.be – Fax 0 3 231 37 74 – www.antigonehotel.be **D1**

21 rm – 75/95 € 85/110 €

◆ Traditional ◆ Family ◆ Classic ◆

A simple, but perfectly comfortable and adequate hotel housed in a bourgeois-style building near the Schelde River and Steen Museum. Individually decorated rooms.

't Fornuis (Segers)

10

Reyndersstraat 24 – 0 3 233 62 70 – fornuis@skynet.be – Fax 0 3 233 99 03 closed August, Christmas-New Year, Saturday and Sunday **D2**

Rest – *(booking essential)* Menu 88 € – Carte 65/95 €

Spec. Carpaccio de veau, sauce au thon. Ragoût de sole, foie gras, pâtes et champignons. Blanquette d'agneau au citron vert.

◆ Traditional ◆ Rustic ◆

This restaurant, occupying a fine 17C residence, offers an ambitious menu that is highly personalised and presented in theatrical fashion by the feisty chef! Rustic decor.

Huis De Colvenier

4/100

Sint-Antoniusstraat 8 – 0 3 226 65 73 – info@colvenier.be – Fax 0 3 227 13 14 – www.colvenier.be

closed carnival week, August, Saturday lunch, Sunday and Monday **D2**

Rest – Menu 65 € bi (weekday lunch), 75 € bi/100 € bi – Carte 65/90 €

◆ Traditional ◆ Retro ◆

This restaurant is housed in an elegant townhouse dating from 1879. It offers spruce dining areas embellished with attractive wall paintings, a charming winter garden and fine wines. Attentive service.

De Barbarie

6/50

Van Breestraat 4 2018 – 0 3 232 81 98 – barbarie@resto.be – Fax 0 3 231 26 78 – www.barbarie.be – closed first week Easter, first 2 weeks September, late December, Saturday lunch, Sunday and Monday **E3**

Rest – Menu 40/110 € bi – Carte 62/121 €

◆ Traditional ◆ Fashionable ◆

The creative menu here includes several duck specialities, accompanied by an attractive wine list. Fine collection of silver tableware. Outdoor restaurant.

Neuze Neuze

8/16

Wijngaardstraat 19 – 0 3 232 27 97 – neuzeneuze@pandora.be – Fax 0 3 225 27 38 – www.neuzeneuze.be – closed first 2 weeks August, first week January, Wednesday lunch, Saturday lunch and Sunday **D1**

Rest – Menu 25 € (weekday lunch), 50/78 € bi – Carte 40/77 €

◆ Traditional ◆ Rustic ◆

An intimate setting where the clientele ranges from business people to couples on dates. Separate banqueting rooms. Copious cuisine and refined service.

La Luna

Italiëlei 177 – 0 3 232 23 44 – info@laluna.be – Fax 0 3 232 24 41 – www.laluna.be – closed 1 week Easter, 29 July-20 August, Christmas-New Year, Sunday and Monday **E1**

Rest – *(dinner only)* Carte 42/53 €

◆ Contemporary ◆ Trendy ◆

Refined setting with a lunar design by Jean De Meulder (1996), delicious cuisine featuring French, Italian and Japanese influences, and a good selection of wines.

De Gulden Beer

5/35

Grote Markt 14 – 0 3 226 08 41 – Fax 0 3 232 52 09 closed Wednesday **D1**

Rest – Menu 25 € (weekday lunch), 40/90 € bi – Carte 37/64 €

◆ Italian ◆ Friendly ◆

This old house with its crow-step gables stands on the Grand-Place. Inviting Italian menu and pleasant views from the terrace and the bay windows on the first floor.

BELGIUM

XX

Harmony

6/12 VISA

Mechelsesteenweg 169 ✉ 2018 – ✆ 0 3 239 70 05 – info@diningroomharmony.com – Fax 0 2 343 48 61 – www.diningroomharmony.com
closed 22 July-9 August, Christmas, New Year, Wednesday and Saturday lunch **E3**
Rest – Menu 23 € (weekday lunch), 30/75 € bi – Carte 42/61 €
♦ Contemporary ♦ Fashionable ♦
The contemporary cuisine on offer here is in harmony with the decor of modern filtered lighting, fluted pilasters, lattice-work chairs and plain table setting.

XX

Het Nieuwe Palinghuis

VISA

Sint-Jansvliet 14 – ✆ 0 3 231 74 45 – hetnieuwepalinghuis@skynet.be – Fax 0 3 231 50 53 – www.hetnieuwepalinghuis.be
closed June, 1-18 January, Monday and Tuesday **C2**
Rest – Menu 36 € (weekday lunch), 36/95 € bi – Carte 40/149 €
♦ Seafood ♦ Family ♦
Eel takes pride of place in this fish and seafood restaurant, whose walls are adorned with nostalgic images of old Antwerp. Good choice of affordable wines.

XX

't Silveren Claverblat

VISA

Grote Pieter Potstraat 16 – ✆ 0 3 231 33 88 – Fax 0 3 231 31 46
closed July, Tuesday, Wednesday and Saturday lunch **C1**
Rest – Menu 42/72 € bi – Carte approx. 65 €
♦ Traditional ♦ Rustic ♦
A well-established and renowned restaurant in a typical 16C building in the old quarter. A limited number of tables and concise menu of classic à la carte choices.

XX

Dôme (Burlat)

VISA

Grote Hondstraat 2 ✉ 2018 – ✆ 0 3 239 90 03 – info@domeweb.be – Fax 0 3 239 93 90 – www.domeweb.be – closed 2 weeks August, 25 December-3 January, Saturday lunch, Sunday and Monday **F3**
Rest – Menu 30 € (weekday lunch)/59 € – Carte 54/89 €
Spec. Minestrone d'écrevisses au basilic (June-September). Sole pochée au beurre salé, crème de laitue. Tarte au chocolat.
♦ Contemporary ♦ Retro ♦
Ambitious contemporary cuisine is served in this restaurant with an impressive neo-Baroque dome and circular dining area, which was once a chic café (19C). Excellent sommelier.

XX

't Peerd

4/10 VISA

Paardenmarkt 53 – ✆ 0 3 231 98 25 – resto-t-peerd@yahoo.com – Fax 0 3 231 59 40 – www.tpeerd.be – closed 2 weeks Easter, Tuesday and Wednesday – **Rest** – Menu 39 € – Carte 44/77 € **E1**
♦ Traditional ♦ Friendly ♦
This characterful small restaurant is embellished in equestrian decor, providing a hint of the house specialities. Studied wine list, attentive service and local ambience.

X

De Manie

10/26 VISA

H. Conscienceplein 3 – ✆ 0 3 232 64 38 – demanie@euphonynet.be – Fax 0 3 232 64 38 – closed 15 August-2 September, Wednesday, Sunday lunch in school holidays and Sunday dinner **D1**
Rest – Menu 27 € (weekday lunch), 41/76 € bi – Carte 48/63 €
♦ Traditional ♦ Cosy ♦
On a pleasant square by the St-Charles-Borromée church, the De Manie's old façade is fronted by a summer terrace. Modern-rustic interior with mezzanine. Contemporary cuisine.

Dock's Café

Jordaenskaai 7 – ✆ 0 3 226 63 30 – info@docks.be – Fax 0 3 226 65 72 – www.docks.be – closed Saturday lunch **D1**

Rest – *(open until 11 p.m.)* Menu 15 € (weekday lunch), 24/30 € – Carte 31/72 €

♦ Brasserie ♦ Trendy ♦

A sense of travel pervades this seafood bar-cum-brasserie with its futurist, maritime decor. Dining room with mezzanine and neo-Baroque staircase. Reservation recommended.

De Kleine Zavel – Hotel 't Sandt

Stoofstraat 2 – ✆ 0 3 231 96 91 – Fax 0 3 231 79 01
closed 24-25 December, 1 January and Saturday lunch **C2**

Rest – Menu 20 € (weekday lunch), 35/75 € bi – Carte 38/62 €

♦ Brasserie ♦ Bistro ♦

Contemporary cuisine served in a typical bistro ambience, with plain tables, a bar, wooden decor and bare floorboards. Friendly atmosphere and attractive lunch menu.

De Reddende Engel

Torfbrug 3 – ✆ 0 3 233 66 30 – de.reddende.engel@telenet.be – Fax 0 3 233 73 79 – www.de-reddende-engel.be
closed mid August-mid September, Tuesday, Wednesday and Saturday lunch

Rest – Menu 26/40 € bi – Carte 29/51 € **D1**

♦ Regional ♦ Rustic ♦

A 17C house close to the cathedral is the setting for this friendly, rustic restaurant serving classic French cuisine with southern influence. Bouillabaisse a speciality.

Le Petit Zinc (Grootaert)

Veemarkt 9 – ✆ 0 3 213 19 08 – philippe.grootaert@pandora.be – Fax 0 3 213 19 08 – www.pzinc.be
closed 1 week Easter, 16-31 August, Saturday and Sunday **D1**

Rest – Menu 20 € (weekday lunch)/64 € – Carte 62/105 €

Spec. Salade d'artichaut aux truffes (May-October). Velouté de petits pois, escargots et cuisses de grenouilles. Confit d'épaule d'agneau, jardinière de légumes.

♦ Traditional ♦ Bistro ♦

A convivial local bistro with closely packed small tables, slate menus featuring tasty, traditional dishes, and attentive service.

Le Zoute Zoen

Zirkstraat 17 – ✆ 0 3 226 92 20 – lezoutezoen@telenet.be – Fax 0 3 231 01 30
closed Monday and Saturday lunch **D1**

Rest – Menu 18 € (weekday lunch), 27/65 € bi – Carte 30/45 €

♦ Traditional ♦ Bistro ♦

The menu in this cosy, intimate "gastro-bistro" offers unique value for money in Antwerp. A range of copious contemporary dishes served by efficient, friendly staff.

Gin-Fish (Garnich)

Haarstraat 9 – ✆ 0 3 231 32 07 – Fax 0 3 231 08 13
closed 10 June-1 July, 1-15 January, Sunday and Monday **D1-2**

Rest – *(dinner only) (booking essential)* Menu 60/75 € bi

Spec. Préparations avec la marée du jour. Glace tournée minute.

♦ Seafood ♦ Friendly ♦

Good seafood dishes prepared before you, behind the counter where guests dine. As the chef is working in full view, he errs on the side of caution by offering only one fixed menu. Lovely staff.

Het Gebaar

Leopoldstraat 24 – ✆ 0 3 232 37 10 – hetgebaar@pandora.be – Fax 0 3 293 72 32 – closed Sunday, Monday and Bank Holidays **D2**

Rest – *(lunch only)* Carte approx. 33 €

♦ Innovative ♦ Cosy ♦

This friendly restaurant occupies an old, cottage-style house near the Botanical Gardens. Inventive, "molecular" cuisine and elegant desserts.

BELGIUM

Maritime

Suikerrui 4 – ☎ 0 3 233 07 58 – restaurant.maritime@pandora.be – Fax 0 3 233 07 58 – www.maritime.be
closed Wednesday and Thursday
Rest – Carte 35/58 €

C1

♦ Seafood ♦ Friendly ♦
As its name would suggest, fish and seafood reign supreme here with some of the city's best mussels and eel in season. A good choice of Burgundies and attentive service.

Hecker

Kloosterstraat 13 – ☎ 0 3 234 38 34 – info@hecker.be – Fax 0 2 343 48 61 – www.hecker.be
closed 22 July-9 August, 23 December-6 January, Monday lunch and Wednesday
Rest – Menu 17 € (weekday lunch)/48 € – Carte 37/52 €

C2

♦ Contemporary ♦ Bistro ♦
This modern bistro sharing its walls with an antiques shop offers a small menu which is both original and enticing. A good choice of wines from around the world.

Pazzo

12/50

Oude Leeuwenrui 12 – ☎ 0 3 232 86 82 – pazzo@skynet.be – Fax 0 3 232 79 34 – www.pazzo.be
closed 15 July-15 August, late December-early January, Saturday and Sunday
Rest – *(open until 11 p.m.)* Menu 20 € (weekday lunch) – Carte 32/52 €

D1

♦ Contemporary ♦ Wine bar ♦
A lively dockside restaurant occupying a former warehouse converted into a modern brasserie, where the emphasis is on contemporary dishes and wines chosen to complement the cuisine.

Dôme Sur Mer

Arendstraat 1 ✉ 2018 – ☎ 0 3 281 74 33 – info@domeweb.be – Fax 0 3 239 93 90 – www.domeweb.be
closed 2 weeks September, 24 December-5 January, Saturday lunch, Sunday and Monday
Rest – *(open until midnight)* Carte 30/67 €

F3

♦ Seafood ♦ Brasserie ♦
This grand residence has been transformed into an "über-trendy" seafood brasserie with designer decor of bright white set off by the blue of a row of aquariums containing goldfish.

Yamayu Santatsu

10/15

Ossenmarkt 19 – ☎ 0 3 234 09 49 – Fax 0 3 234 09 49
closed first 2 weeks August, Sunday lunch and Monday
Rest – Menu 14 € (weekday lunch), 47/53 € – Carte 25/57 €

E1

♦ Japanese ♦ Minimalist ♦
This compact and constantly reliable Japanese restaurant and sushi bar is well known to aficionados of Asian cuisine. Quality products and an extensive menu choice.

Volef's

Oude Leeuwenrui 23 – ☎ 0 3 213 33 33 – info@volefs.be – Fax 0 3 213 34 43 – www.volefs.be
closed 30 July-17 August, Saturday lunch, Sunday and Monday dinner
Rest – Menu 23 € (weekday lunch), 28/33 € – Carte 24/46 €

D1

♦ Contemporary ♦ Fashionable ♦
International, "fusion"-style cuisine served in the contemporary ambience of an old mansion which has been completely modernised. Charming courtyard terrace.

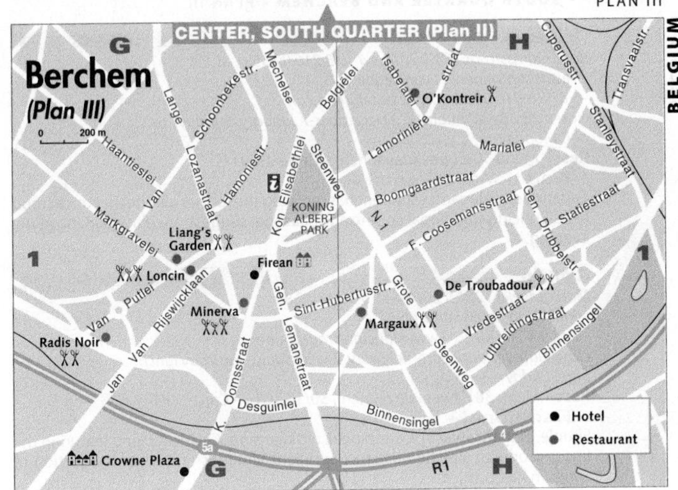

SOUTH QUARTER AND BERCHEM *Plan III*

Crowne Plaza

G. Legrellelaan 10 ✉ 2020 – ✆ 0 3 259 75 00 – cpantwerp@ichotelgroup.com – Fax 0 3 216 02 96 – www.crowneplaza.be G1

256 rm – 114/225 € 114/225 €, 21 € – 6 suites

Rest *Plaza One for two* – Menu 32/47 € bi – Carte 37/50 €

♦ Chain hotel ♦ Business ♦ Modern ♦

This international hotel close to a motorway exit offers pleasantly decorated, well-appointed rooms with a contemporary feel. Good conference facilities and 24-hour service. Full à la carte menu available in the restaurant and snacks are served in the lively lounge bar.

Firean

Karel Oomsstraat 6 ✉ 2018 – ✆ 0 3 237 02 60 – info@hotelfirean.com – Fax 0 3 238 11 68 – www.hotelfirean.com

closed 28 July-20 August and 22 December-7 January G1

12 rm – 139/149 € 167/228 €

Rest *Minerva* – see below

♦ Luxury ♦ Family ♦ Art Deco ♦

A charming, quiet hotel with a patio occupying an Art Deco-style residence close to the Koning Albert Park. Rooms decorated with stylish antique furniture. Attentive service.

Industrie without rest

Emiel Banningstraat 52 – ✆ 0 3 238 66 00 – sleep@hotelindustrie.be – Fax 0 3 238 86 88 – www.hotelindustrie.be *Plan I* **A2**

13 rm – 60/75 € 80/87 €

♦ Family ♦ Business ♦ Classic ♦

A charming small hotel occupying two mansions close to two of the city's finest museums. Compact but well-appointed rooms with a touch of individuality.

BELGIUM

XXX **Minerva** – Hotel Firean

Karel Oomsstraat 36 ✉ 2018 – ✆ 0 3 216 00 55
– restaurantminerva@skynet.be
– Fax 0 3 216 00 55 – www.hotelfirean.com
closed 28 July-20 August, 22 December-7 January, Sunday and Monday G1

Rest – Menu 50 € (weekday lunch) – Carte 49/91 €

♦ Traditional ♦ Formal ♦

This modern, elegant restaurant has replaced the former garage that once stood here. Enticing traditional cuisine and seasonal suggestions. Easy parking in the evening.

XXX **Loncin**

Markgravelei 127 ✉ 2018 – ✆ 0 3 248 29 89
– info@loncinrestaurant.be
– Fax 0 3 248 38 66 – www.loncinrestaurant.be
closed late January-early February, 2 weeks July, Saturday lunch and Sunday G1

Rest – Menu 38 € (weekday lunch), 50/102 € bi – Carte 50/147 €

♦ Traditional ♦ Family ♦

Simple, elegant style in a traditional, old mansion. Classical menu featuring the finest products, prestigious crus, excellent vintages and a good selection of wines in half bottles.

XX **Liang's Garden**

Markgravelei 141 ✉ 2018 – ✆ 0 3 237 22 22 – Fax 0 3 248 38 34
closed 3 weeks July and Sunday G1

Rest – Menu 24 € (weekday lunch)/40 € – Carte 30/73 €

♦ Chinese ♦ Exotic ♦

This attractive mansion houses one of Antwerp's oldest Chinese restaurants. A bourgeois setting with a few Asian touches. Menu featuring Peking duck specialities.

XX **Kommilfoo**

Vlaamse Kaai 17 – ✆ 0 3 237 30 00 – kommilfoo@resto.be
– Fax 0 3 237 30 00
closed 15 June-15 July, Saturday lunch, Sunday and Monday *Plan II* C3

Rest – Menu 30 € (weekday lunch), 48/50 € – Carte 47/75 €

♦ Traditional ♦ Rustic ♦

Located opposite a large, free car park a stone's throw from three museums, this former warehouse has been transformed into a restaurant that is sober yet modern in design, with a menu that is equally contemporary.

XX **Radis Noir**

Desguinlei 186 ✉ 2018 – ✆ 0 3 238 37 70 – radisnoir@skynet.be
– Fax 0 3 238 39 07 – www.radisnoir.be
closed 28 January-7 February, 22 July-15 August, Wednesday dinner, Saturday lunch, Sunday and Bank Holidays G1

Rest – Menu 30 € (weekday lunch), 48/56 € – Carte 51/66 €

♦ Traditional ♦ Fashionable ♦

This bourgeois house on a busy street near the new Palais de Justice has been transformed into a restaurant with designer-influenced decor. Concise yet regularly updated menu.

XX **De Troubadour**

Driekoningenstraat 72 ✉ 2600 Berchem – ✆ 0 3 239 39 16
– info@detroubadour.be – Fax 0 3 230 82 71
– www.detroubadour.be
closed 3 first weeks August, Sunday and Monday H1

Rest – Menu 25 € (weekday lunch)/33 € – Carte 33/68 €

♦ Contemporary ♦ Friendly ♦

Intelligently composed menus are a strongpoint of this pleasantly modern restaurant where the charismatic owner ensures a warm and friendly atmosphere.

XX

Margaux 8/20

Terlinckstraat 2 ✉ 2600 Berchem – ✆ 0 3 230 55 99 – restaurant.margaux@skynet.be – Fax 0 3 230 40 71 – www.restaurant-margaux.be
closed Easter, last week September, Christmas holidays, Sunday and Monday

H1

Rest – Menu 31 € (weekday lunch), 35/55 € – Carte 35/57 €

♦ Contemporary ♦ Brasserie ♦

This old house situated in a residential district has been completely refurbished inside, with the addition of a new courtyard terrace enclosed by low hedging and furnished in teak. Steak tartare is the house speciality.

X

O'Kontreir 12/25 VISA AE

Isabellalei 145 ✉ 2018 – ✆ 0 3 281 39 76 – info@okontreir.com – Fax 0 3 237 92 06 – www.okontreir.com
closed Saturday lunch, Sunday lunch, Monday and Tuesday **H1**

Rest – Menu 25 € (weekday lunch)/45 € – Carte 38/55 €

♦ Contemporary ♦ Trendy ♦

The O'Kontreir serves creative, contemporary and well-presented dishes in a distinctly modern setting in the city's Jewish quarter. Japanese tableware and background music.

AT THE AIRPORT

Plan I

Scandic 230 P VISA AE

Luitenant Lippenslaan 66 ✉ 2140 Borgerhout – ✆ 0 3 235 91 91 – info-antwerp@scandic-hotels.com – Fax 0 3 235 08 96 – www.scandic-hotels.com/antwerp **B2**

200 rm – †80/180 € ††80/180 € – 4 suites

Rest – Menu 30 € (weekday lunch) – Carte 30/48 €

♦ Chain hotel ♦ Business ♦ Functional ♦

A renovated chain hotel with a good location along the ring road, close to Borgerhout railway station, the Sterchshof Museum (Zilvercentrum) and a golf course. Business centre. Modern brasserie with an equally contemporary menu and attractive teak terrace.

Ter Elst 500 P VISA AE

Terelststraat 310 (by N 173) ✉ 2650 Edegem – ✆ 0 3 450 90 00 – info@terelst.be – Fax 0 3 450 90 90 – www.terelst.be
closed Christmas and New Year

54 rm – †105/120 € ††120/135 €

Rest *Couvert Classique* – *(closed also 2 July-10 August and Sunday)* Menu 35 € (weekday lunch) – Carte 36/46 €

♦ Family ♦ Business ♦ Functional ♦

Opened in 1995, this hotel and conference centre also offers sports facilities in a nearby complex. The hotel has a modern auditorium and large, functional guestrooms. Rustic ambience in the restaurant, which serves traditional cuisine and has a good selection of wines.

CZECH REPUBLIC

ČESKÁ REPUBLIKA

PROFILE

- **Area:** 78 864 km² (30 449 sq mi).
- **Population:** 10 241 000 inhabitants (est. 2005), density = 130 per km².
- **Capital:** Prague (population 1 141 000 inhabitants).
- **Currency:** Czech crown (Kč); rate of exchange: CZK 100 = € 3.58 = US$ 4.73 (Nov 2006).
- **Government:** Parliamentary republic (since 1993). Member of European Union since 2004.
- **Language:** Czech; also German and English.
- **Specific public holidays:** Liberation Day (8 May); St. Cyril and St. Methodius Day (4 July); Martyrdom of Jean Hus (5 July); Czech Statehood Day (28 September); Independence Day (28 October); Freedom and Democracy Day (17 November); Boxing Day (26 December).
- **Local Time:** GMT + 1 hour in winter and GMT + 2 hours in summer.
- **Climate:** Temperate continental with cold winters and warm summers (Prague: January: 0°C, July: 20°C).

Prague

- **International Dialling Code:** **00 420** followed by area code (Prague: 2, Brno: 5, etc.) and then the local number.
- **Emergency:** Police: ✆ **158**; Ambulance: ✆ **155**; Fire Brigade: ✆ **150**.
- **Electricity:** 220 volts AC, 50Hz; 2-pin round-shaped continental plugs.

FORMALITIES

Travellers from the European Union (EU), Switzerland, Iceland and the main countries of North and South America need a national identity card or passport (America: passport required) to visit Czech Republic for less than three months (tourism or business purpose). For visitors from other countries a visa may be required, in addition to a passport, especially for those wishing to stay for longer than three months. We advise you to check with your embassy before travelling.

Driving licences of most countries are recognized in the Czech Republic. If in doubt it is advisable to obtain an international driving licence. Third party insurance is the minimum cover required by Czech legislation but it is advisable to take out fully comprehensive cover (Green Card). To use motorways and similar roads in the Czech Republic you must buy a sticker (vignette) at a border crossing and display it on the car windscreen.

MAJOR NEWSPAPERS

The most important daily newspapers of the Czech Republic are *Mladá fronta Dnes, Právo, Hospodářské noviny, and Lidové noviny.* Popular press: *Blesk. Prague*

Post is a paper printed in English and *Prager Zeitung* a weekly newspaper printed in German.

USEFUL PHRASES

ENGLISH	CZECH
Yes	**Ano**
No	**Ne**
Good morning	**Dobré ráno**
Goodbye	**Na shledanou**
Thank you	**Děkuji**
Please	**Prosím**
Excuse me	**S dovolením**
I don't understand	**Nerozumím**

HOTELS

→ CATEGORIES

The range of accommodation in the Czech Republic has improved considerably over the past decade. Large towns and resorts and in particular Prague now offer luxury class and comfortable modern hotels as well as traditional hotels which have been renovated to a good standard. Pensions are usually family-run. Private accommodation (residence) is also available.

→ PRICE RANGE

The price is per room. There are few single rooms and a supplement is charged for single occupancy of a double room. Prices are 20% cheaper off season and rates in de luxe hotels can be negotiated down by 10-20%. In Prague it is advisable to book in advance in the high season.

→ TAX

Taxes (19%) and service charges included in the room price.

→ CHECK OUT TIME

Usually between 10am and noon.

→ RESERVATIONS

By telephone or fax or by Internet. Make sure you obtain a written confirmation by letter, fax or email.

→ TIP FOR LUGGAGE HANDLING

At the discretion of the customer.

→ BREAKFAST

It is often not included in the price of the room and is generally served between 6am and 10.30am. Most hotels offer a self-service continental buffet but hot dishes are charged extra. It is usually possible to have continental breakfast served in the room.

Reception	**recepce**
Single room	**jednolůžkový pokoj**
Double room	**Dvoulůžkový pokoj**
Bed	**Postel**
Bathroom	**Koupelna**
Shower	**sprcha**

RESTAURANTS

Besides the conventional restaurants **(restaurace)**, look out for **vinárny** (wine restaurants) which have an intimate, often traditional, old time atmosphere and where the emphasis is on the wine list. **Pivnice**, **hospody** or **hostinec** are pubs and taverns serving draught beer and traditional meat platters, with a friendly ambience and informal service. **Kavárny** (cafés) serve snacks, sweet pastries and some hot dishes. In less expensive restaurants and in pubs it is normal to share a table if the place is busy (but ask first). Often there are long communal tables for 10-12 people. It is increasingly common for restaurants to offer a set menu **(standardní menu)** as well as à la carte meals at lunchtime and in the evening.

Breakfast	**Snídaně**	6am – 10.30am
Lunch	**oběd**	noon – 2-3pm
Dinner	**večeře**	7pm – 9-11pm, sometimes later

➜ RESERVATIONS

It is not generally necessary to make a reservation unless the place is very popular. However it is advisable to phone in advance for smart restaurants.

➜ THE BILL

The bill (check) does not include a service charge in restaurants. However be wary of hidden charges – cover charge and items like bread, condiments and the little tit-bits at the start of the meal which you may have thought were complimentary. Tipping is not mandatory but it is customary to round up the bill to a reasonable amount or add a 10% tip if you are pleased with the service. Credit cards are accepted in an increasing number of restaurants but it is better to make sure before you order a meal.

Drink or aperitif	**Aperitiv**
Meal	**jídlo**
Appetizer, starter	**předkrm**
Main dish	**hlavní chod**
Main dish of the day	**nabídka dne**
Dessert	**moučník**
Water	**voda**
Mineral water (still, sparkling)	**Minerálka (neperlivá/perlivá)**
Wine (red, white, rosé)	**víno (červené, bílé, rosé)**
Beer	**pivo**
Bread	**chleba**
Meat (rare, medium, well-done)	**maso (krvavý, středně udělaný, dobře udělaný)**
Fish	**ryby**
Salt/pepper	**sůl/pepř**
Cheese	**sýr**
Vegetables	**zelenina**
Hot/cold	**teplý/studený**
The bill (check) please	**učet prosím**

LOCAL CUISINE

Although the robust Czech cooking is the antithesis of healthy eating with its emphasis on meat dishes, dumplings and cream, with few overcooked vegetables, some effort is being made towards a healthier lifestyle. Some traditional dishes are likely to find favour with most diners. A meal often starts with soup **(polévka)** as a light broth or thick with potatoes, vegetables and meat. Some of the favourites are: **bramborová polévka s houbami** (potatoes, mushrooms, bacon, cabbage, spices), **česneková polévka or česnečka** (garlic), **kuřecí polévka s nudlemi** (chicken noodle), **hovězí polévka s játrovými knedličky** (beef with liver dumplings), **zelná polévka or zelňačka** (sauerkraut). Tasty starters may be smoked pork **(uzené)**, eggs (vejce), **Prážká Šunka** (thin slices of ham garnished with cucumber and horseradish), ham and cheese in a sandwich, ham stuffed with cream or cheese and horseradish.

Popular meats are chicken (kuře), pork (vepřové), beef (hovězí), duck (kachna), goose (husa) which are either roasted (na rostu), fried (smažený) or breaded and served with a garnish (**obloha** – pickled cabbage, carrots, beets and lettuce) and side dishes – boiled/roasted potatoes **(vařené/opékané brambory)**, mashed potatoes **(bramborová kaše)**, potato salad **(bramborový salát)**, rice **(rýže)**, dumplings **(houskové knedlíky)** or potato dumplings **(bramborové knedlíky)**. Although fish is not very common, trout (pstruh), cod (treska) and mackerel (makrela) are well worth trying. Carp (kapr) is a traditional Christmas dish.

Classic main dishes include **hovězí pečeně** (roast beef stuffed with diced ham, peas, onion, spices), **svíčková pečeně na smetaně** (beef in a cream sauce), **Šunka po stavočesku** (boiled beef Bohemian style), **guláš** (goulash with dumplings), **smažený/vepřový řísek** (veal/pork Wiener schnitzel), **vepřová s knedlíkem a se zelím** (loin of pork with dumplings and sauerkraut).

For dessert you can sample **palačinky**, pancakes filled with fruit and cream or ice cream **(zmrzlina)**; **jablečný závin** (apple strudel); **jablka v županu** (baked apple in flaky pastry with cinnamon and raisins) and **Švestokové/borůvkové knedlíky** (plum/blueberry dumplings).

DRINK

The Czech Republic is the land of beer **(pívo)** and several types of beer are usually on offer. The most common are draught light beer **(světlé)** and dark blends **(tmave)** which are sweeter. The best known are **Pizenský Prazdroj** (Pilsner Urquell) and **Budějovický Budvar** (Budweiser) but Gambrinus, Krusovice, Radegast, Velkopopovicky kozel or Staropramen are equally good.

The main wine-growing area is Moravia but wine is also produced around Mělník, north of Prague, in Bohemia. Moravian wines are perfectly acceptable. Riesling, Müller-Thurgau or Veltliner grapes are used for white wines (*polusuché* – medium dry, *suché* – dry). **Rulandské** is a good dry white made from the Pinot grape. Red wines tend to be light-bodied **(Frankovka, Vavřinecké)**. **Burčák** is a young, sweet white wine drunk in Prague in the autumn.

Czech spirits are very popular. **Becherovka** is a bitter-sweet herbal liqueur, which is served as an aperitif or with tonic water. **Borovička** and **Slivovice** (plum brandy) are firm favourites.

PRAGUE

PRAHA

Population (est. 2005): 1 141 000 – Altitude: 250m

P. Bénet / MICHELIN

Prague, the capital of the Czech Republic, has been aptly described as 'Stověžatá Praha', hundred-spired Prague, and the skyline is punctuated by countless towers and turrets, spires and belfries, cupolas and pinnacles, often of extraordinary exuberance in design. The city has transformed itself into a European metropolis and has recaptured its vibrancy. It boasts an array of romantic monuments evocative of its long history and set in beautiful natural surroundings.

The site on the banks of the River Vltava was settled by a prehistoric people, followed by Slav tribes. In the 9C, a princely seat was built on the rocky promontory which became known as Hradčany. After the first timber bridge spanned the river in the 10C, the city developed apace. Malá Strana grew in the 13C and in mid-14C Emperor Charles IV gave Prague its present character as the city spread to the Nové Město (New Town). Splendid palaces were built in a variety of styles in 16-18C. In the 19C the population expanded rapidly as industrial activity grew and by the turn of the 20C Prague was a prosperous city full of gaiety. The war years and communism brought many vicissitudes which came to an end with the Velvet Revolution of 1989. After the birth of the Czech Republic in 1993, Prague regained its proud status as capital.

WHICH DISTRICT TO CHOOSE

For a central location choose Staré Město *Plan II* **G2** where there is a good selection of luxury and medium-priced hotels. In the delightful surroundings of Malá Strana *Plan II* **F2** romantic old houses have been converted into elegant establishments and if you prefer a quiet area there are some smart hotels in Hradčany *Plan II* **E1**. Expensive new hotels in the Jewish Quarter enjoy a view of the Vltava. Modern hotels are located near Wenceslas Square. If you choose to stay in the business hotels on the outskirts make sure you are near a metro station for convenience.

Staré Město is the area for lively **cafés and restaurants** but prices are fairly high. There are excellent restaurants in Malá Strana which take full advanta-

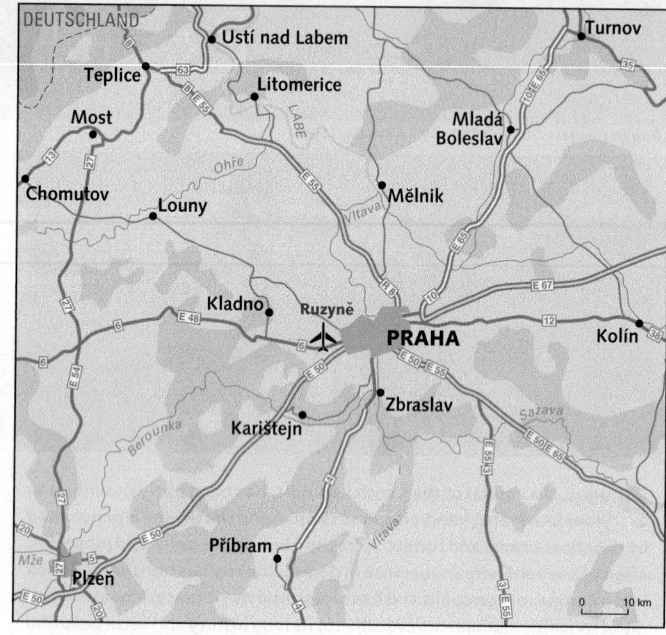

ge of the riverside location and views and with prices to match. Explore the backstreets north of Celetná *Plan II* **G2**, south of Karlova and south of Národní for moderately-priced eateries. Vinohrady *Plan II* **H2** is a residential area with cosy neighbourhood restaurants.

Prague's café culture is a great experience when going out **for a drink or for the evening**: *Obecní dům*, Náměstí Republicky 5 *Plan II* **H1**; *Café Europa*, Václavské náměsti 25 *Plan II* **H2**; *Slavia*, Smetanovo nábřeží 2 *Plan II* **G2**; *Café Milena*, Staroměstské náměsti 22.

PRACTICAL INFORMATION

ARRIVAL – DEPARTURE

Ruzyně (Prague Airport) – 20 km (12.5 mi) west of the city. ✆ 220 113 314.

From the airport to the city centre – By **taxi**: taxis display the 'Airport Cars' sign. Fare about Kč650. FIX registered taxis: ✆ 02 2056 1788. By **shuttle bus**: operated by *Cedaz* Bus to Terminal Náměstí Republiky every 30min. Fare Kč90; or directly to your hotel (1-4 passengers). Information desk for both taxis and shuttle bus in Arrivals Hall. ✆ 220 114 296. Or by **bus** nos. 119 and 254 to Dejvická metro station. **Night bus** services operated by *DP Praha*, ✆ 220 115 404.

Main Stations – International trains stop at **Hlavní nádraží** *Plan II* **H2** but some stop at the suburban stations at **Holešovice** *Plan I* **C1** and **Smíchov** *Plan I* **B3**, both with metro stations.

TRANSPORT

→ BUSES, TRAMS AND METRO

Public transport is convenient and inexpensive. Tourist passes are available for 1, 3, 7 and 15 days: Kč80 to Kč320. Passes are sold at ticket offices at some metro stations and from the Tourist Offices.

→ TAXIS

Although regulations specify rates, it is not uncommon to be overcharged. Make sure you establish the fare before getting into the car. It is advisable to order a taxi by phone from a reputable taxi firm. *AAA Radiotaxi* ✆ 140 14; *Citytaxi* ✆ 257 257 257; *Credit Taxi* ✆ 235 300 300; *Dimotaxi* ✆ 800 513 306; *Halotaxi* ✆ 244 114 411.

USEFUL ADDRESSES

→ TOURIST OFFICES

PIS Pražská Informační služba, entrance of Old Town Hall, Staroměstskě Náměstí *Plan II* **G2**. ✆ 1244. There are other offices at Lucerna Passage Vodickova 36, main railway station (Hlavní Nádrazí) and seasonally on the ground floor of the Mala Straná end of Charles Bridge. www.pis.cz

→ POST OFFICES

Open Mon-Fri 8am-5pm. Main Post Office, Jindřišská 14 *Plan II* **H2**, Mon-Fri 7am-8pm. There is a 24-hr post office at Masaryk Station (Masarykovo nádraží) *Plan II* **H1**.

→ BANKS/CURRENCY EXCHANGE

Banks are usually open Mon-Fri, 8am-5pm. There are exchange offices in convenient locations in Prague but their charges are fairly high; some in the old city are open 24hr a day. It is strongly advised against changing money other than at banks, exchange offices or authorised offices such as large hotels, tourist offices etc. Credit cards are becoming more widely accepted.

→ PHARMACY

Several open 24hr. The most central is at Belgická 37. ✆ 2251 9731.

→ EMERGENCY

Police ✆ **158** (National Police); ✆ **156** (City Police); Fire Brigade ✆ **150**; Ambulance ✆ **155**.

EXPLORING PRAGUE

It is possible to visit the main sights and museums in three days.

Museums and other sights are usually open from 9-10am to 5-6pm. Most close on Mondays and some may also close on public holidays, for long lunch hours and early in the afternoon.

VISITING

Boat trip on the River Vltava starting from Čech Bridge (Čechův most) *Plan II* **G1** and from the quayside at Rašínovo nábřeží *Plan II* **G3**.

Hradčany *Plan II* **E1** – The castle district with a vast square, palaces, churches and small streets. St Vitus Cathedral **(Katedrála sv. Víta)** – 14C-20C. Treasures of Bohemian art: silver reliquary, the Gothic St Wenceslas' Chapel, Crown Jewels. Royal Palace **(Královský Palác)** – 11C-16C. Residence of the Kings of Bohemia: Vladislav Chamber and equestrian staircase. The Church of St George **(Bazilika sv.Jiří)**: Baroque west front and fine Romanesque sanctuary. The convent **(Jiřský**

klášter) houses the National Gallery of Ancient Czech Art. Picturesque Gold Alley **(Zlatá Ulička)**. Belvedere **(Letohrádek Královnyanny)** – views. **Schwarzenberg Palace** – frescoes, soaring gables, Museum of Army History. National Gallery **(Národní Galérie)** – collection of European art. **Loreta** church. Strahov Monastery **(Strahovský Klášter)** – Literature Museum: Philosophy Room and Theology Room.

Malá Strana *Plan II* **F2** – Picturesque lower town with medieval network of narrow streets and squares. 14C Charles Bridge **(Karlův Most)**. St Nicholas' Church **(Sv. Mikuláš)** with ornate interior. The charming **Nerudova** lined with Renaissance, Baroque and Rococo mansions. The splendid 17C Wallenstein Palace **(Valdštejnský Palác)**. Vrtba Palace and Baroque gardens **(Vrtbovský Palác-Vrtbovská Zahrada)**.

Staré Město *Plan II* **G2** – A maze of streets and squares with the Town Hall **(Staroměstská radnice)** dominating Staroměstskě Náměstí (astronomical clock, Jan Hus monument, market). Panoramic views from the tower of the former town hall. Around Náměstí Jana Palacha stand the **Rudolfinium** concert hall and a museum of decorative arts **(Uměleckoprůmyslové muzeum – UPM)**. The imposing **Klementinum** houses the University of Prague. On the attractive Celetná Ulice stand the Cubist Black Madonna House **(Dům U černé Matky boži)** and the 14C Powder Tower **(Česká Lidova Řemesla)**. The Gothic St Agnes Convent **(Anežský klášter)** – collection of medieval art.

Nové Město *Plan II* **G2** – Gold Cross on the tree-lined Wenceslas Square **(Václavské Náměstí)**. Jan Palach Memorial. Model of Prague in the City Museum **(Muzeum hlavního města Prahy)**.

Josefov *Plan II* **G1** – The oldest Jewish ghetto in Europe. Solemn, inspiring synagogues **(Staronová and Pinkasova Synagóga)**, Old Jewish Cemetery **(Starý židovský hřbitov)**. Pařížská Boulevard lined with Art Nouveau buildings.

Environs – Imperial Karlštejn Castle **(Hrad Karlštejn** – *30km/19mi SW***)**. Early-14C Konopiště Castle **(Zámek Konopiště** – *40km/25mi SW***)**.

SHOPPING

Shops are generally open Mon-Fri, 8-9am to 6-7pm, Sat 8-9am to 6-8pm and Sun 10am-6pm, possibly with a break at lunchtime.

Nearly all the shops of interest to visitors, including major department stores, are concentrated in the city centre, particularly in the pedestrian streets like **Celetná** *Plan II* **G2**, **Na příkopě**, **Melantrichova**, **Krapova** and **Nerudova** *Plan II* **F2**.

Craft shops – Bohemian garnets: *Granát*, Dlouhá 30. Glass and porcelain: *Skio Bohemia*, Na příkopě 17; *Dana Bohemia*, Staroměstskě náměstí 16; *Bohemia Crystal*, Celetná 5 and Parížská 12; *Celetná Crystal*, Celetná 15; *Moser*, Na příkopě 12 and shops along **Karlova** and side streets. Wooden toys and marionettes: *Pohádka*, Celetná 32; *Fantasia Kubénova*, Rytířská 19; *Česká lidová řemesa*, Melantrichova 17.

Boutiques, perfumeries, fashion shops – Visit the shopping arcades (pasáž): *Darex obchodní dům*, Václavské náměstí 11; *Lucerna pasáž*, Štěpánská 61, Vodičkova 36; *Černá růže*, Na příkopě 12.

Antiques – There are antique shops all over the city. For quality goods, visit the auction house *Dorotheum*, Ovocný trh 2.

For antiquarian books, maps and prints: *Antikvariát Galerie Můstek*, 28 října 13; *Antikvariát Karel Křenek*, Celetná 31.

Gourmet shops – For Czech specialities and wines: *Dům lahůdek*, Malé náměstí 3.

MARKETS – Open-air market in **Havelská** (Mon-Fri 7.30am-6pm, Sat-Sun 8.30pm-6pm) and by Národní třída metro station (daily 7.30am-7pm).

WHAT TO BUY – Embroidery, Bohemian garnets, Bohemian glass, ceramics, craft goods, food and wine.

ENTERTAINMENT

Venues for musical events include the great concert halls, gardens, churches and many other places. Consult *Cultural Events* published by the Prague Tourist Office and the weekly *The Prague Post* for listings of events.

Státní Opera Praha *Plan II* **H2**: State Opera – opera and ballet.

Národní divadio *Plan II* **G2**: National Theatre – drama, opera and ballet.

Stavovské divadio *Plan II* **G2**: Drama, opera and ballet.

Hudební divadio v Karlině *Plan 1* **C1**: Operettas, musicals.

Rudolfinum *Plan II* **G1** and **Obecní dům** *Plan II* **H1**: Classical music.

Klub Lávka *Plan II* **G2**: Music by Mozart in period costume.

Divadio v Celetné *Plan II* **G2**: Black Theatre performances.

National Marionette Theatre *Plan II* **G2**: Puppet shows for adults and children.

NIGHTLIFE

There are great pubs and bars with live music and entertainment in Staré Město, along the riverside and on both sides of Charles Bridge such as *Pivnice U Sv. Tomáše*, Letenská 12; *U Flekŭ*, Křemencová 9/11; *U Medvickŭ*, Na Perštýně 7; *U kalicha*, Na bojišti 12; *U zlatého tygra*, Husova 17. Jazz fans will enjoy *Agharta Jazz Centre*, Zelená 16; *Batalion Music Club*, 28 října 3; *Lávka Club*, Novotného lávka 1; *Lucerna Music Bar*, Vodickova 3-6; *Metropolitan Jazz Club*, Jungmannova 14. You should be aware that Prague has become very popular with stag and hen parties which can become quite boisterous as the night wears on.

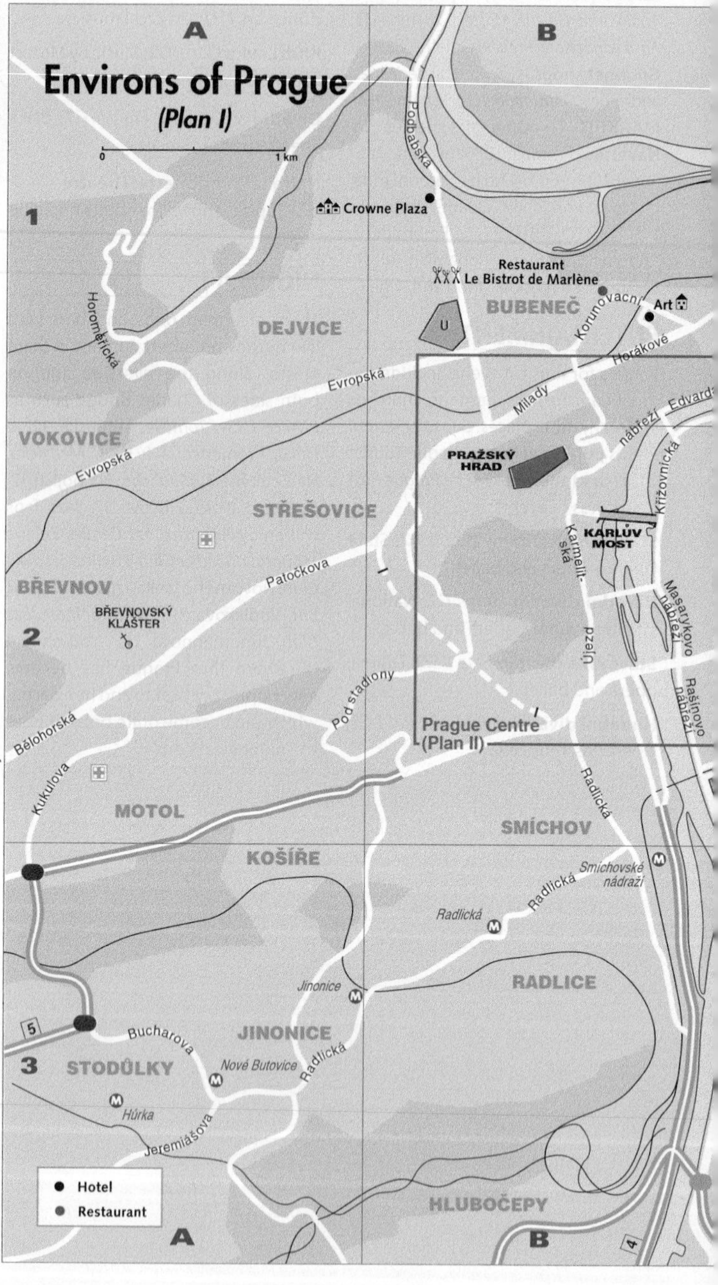
Environs of Prague
(Plan I)
0
1 km
A
B
1
2
3
Crowne Plaza
Restaurant
Le Bistrot de Marlène
Art
Podbabská
Horoměřická
DEJVICE
BUBENEČ
Korunovační
Milady
Horákové
Evropská
VOKOVICE
PRAŽSKÝ
HRAD
nábřeží
Edvarda
Křižovnická
STŘEŠOVICE
KARLŮV
MOST
Karmelitská
BŘEVNOV
Patočkova
BŘEVNOVSKÝ
KLÁŠTER
Újezd
Masarykovo
nábřeží
Pod stadiony
Rašínovo
nábřeží
Bělohorská
Prague Centre
(Plan II)
RUZYNĚ
Kukulova
MOTOL
Radlická
SMÍCHOV
KOŠÍŘE
Smíchovské
nádraží
Radlická
RADLICE
Jinonice
5
Bucharova
JINONICE
STODŮLKY
Nové Butovice
Hůrka
Jeremiášova
Hotel
Restaurant
HLUBOČEPY
4

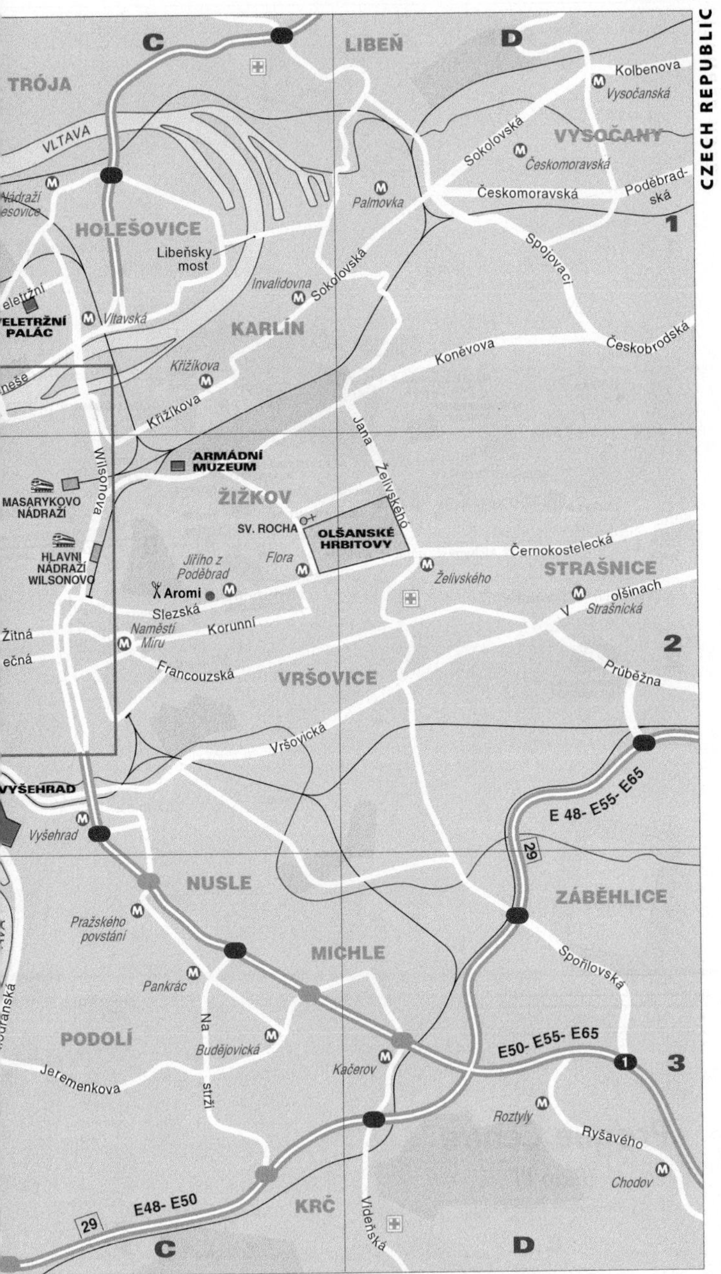
C
D
LIBEŇ
TRÓJA
VLTAVA
Kolbenova
Vysočanská
VYSOČANY
Sokolovská
Českomoravská
Českomoravská
Poděbradská
Palmovka
HOLEŠOVICE
Libeňsky most
1
Spojovací
Invalidovna
Sokolovská
Vltavská
VELETRŽNÍ PALÁC
KARLÍN
Českobrodská
Koněvova
Křižíkova
Křižíkova
Jana Želivského
Wilsonova
ARMÁDNÍ MUZEUM
ŽIŽKOV
MASARYKOVO NÁDRAŽÍ
SV. ROCHA
OLŠANSKÉ HRBITOVY
HLAVNÍ NÁDRAŽÍ WILSONOVO
Jiřího z Poděbrad
Flora
Želivského
Černokostelecká
STRAŠNICE
Aromi
Slezská
V olšinach
Strašnická
Náměstí Míru
Korunní
Žitná
2
Francouzská
VRŠOVICE
Průběžna
Vršovická
VYŠEHRAD
Vyšehrad
E 48- E55- E65
29
NUSLE
ZÁBĚHLICE
Pražského povstání
MICHLE
Spořilovská
Pankrác
Na strži
PODOLÍ
Budějovická
E50- E55- E65
1
3
Kačerov
Jeremenkova
Roztyly
Ryšavého
Chodov
E48- E50
29
KRČ
Vídeňská
C
D

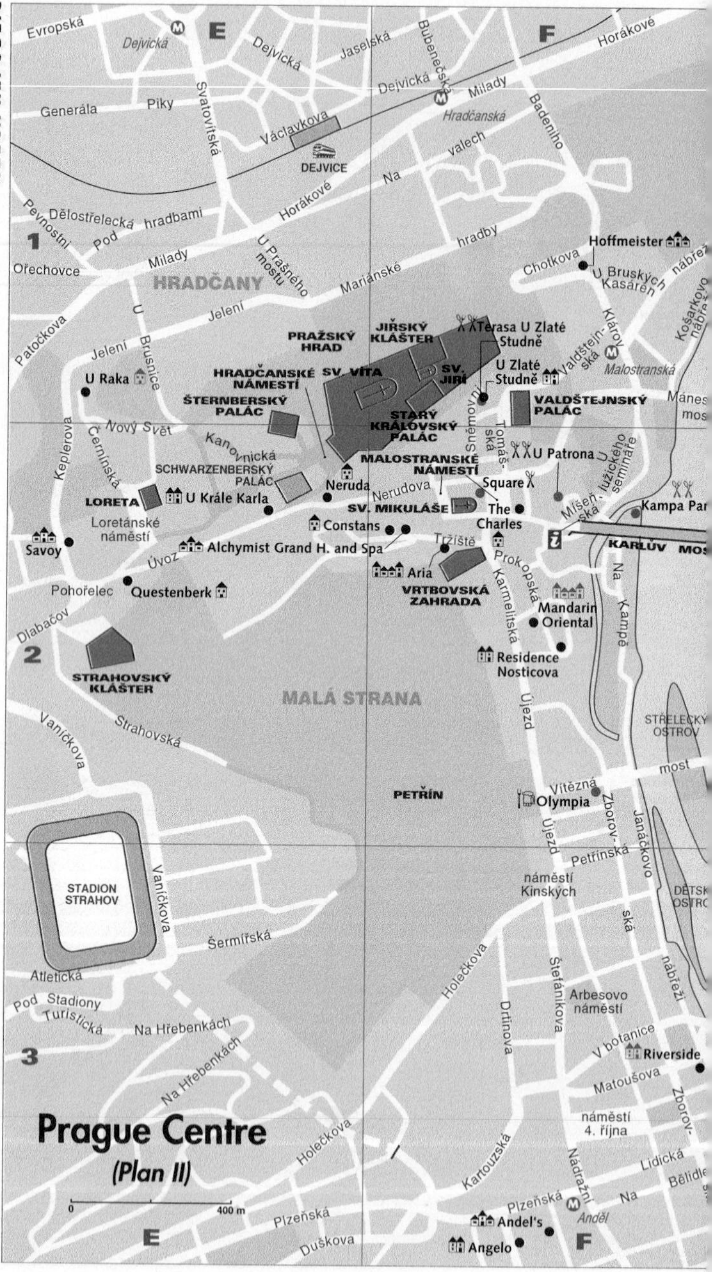

Prague Centre
(Plan II)

0 400 m

E
F
1
2
3
Evropská
Dejvická
Dejvická
Jaselská
Bubenečská
Horákové
Dejvická
Milady
Hradčanská
Generála
Piky
Svatovítská
Václavkova
DEJVICE
valech
Na
Badeniho
Horákové
Pevnostní
Dělostřelecká
Pod hradbami
Pod
Ořechovce
Milady
U Prašného mostu
hradby
Mariánské
HRADČANY
Chotkova
Hoffmeister
U Bruských Kasáren
nábřeží
Klárov
Košíkovo nábřeží
Patočkova
Jelení
Jelení
U Brusnice
PRAŽSKÝ HRAD
JIŘSKÝ KLÁŠTER
Terasa U Zlaté Studně
U Zlaté Studně
Valdštejnská
Malostranská
U Raka
HRADČANSKÉ NÁMĚSTÍ
SV. VÍTA
SV. JIŘÍ
ŠTERNBERSKÝ PALÁC
VALDŠTEJNSKÝ PALÁC
Mánesův most
Nový Svět
Keplerova
Černínská
Kanovnická
STARÝ KRÁLOVSKÝ PALÁC
Sněmovní
Tomášská
U Patrona
U Lužického semináře
SCHWARZENBERSKÝ PALÁC
MALOSTRANSKÉ NÁMĚSTÍ
Square
LORETA
U Krále Karla
Neruda
Nerudova
Míšeňská
Kampa Park
SV. MIKULÁŠE
The Charles
Loretánské náměstí
Constans
Savoy
Alchymist Grand H. and Spa
Úvoz
Tržiště
KARLŮV MOST
Prokopská
Aria
Na Kampě
Pohořelec
Questenberk
VRTBOVSKÁ ZAHRADA
Karmelitská
Mandarin Oriental
Dlabačov
Residence Nosticova
STRAHOVSKÝ KLÁŠTER
MALÁ STRANA
Újezd
STŘELECKÝ OSTROV
Vaníčkova
Strahovská
most
Vítězná
PETŘÍN
Olympia
Zborovská
Janáčkovo
Újezd
Petřínská
náměstí Kinských
DĚTSKÝ OSTROV
STADION STRAHOV
Vaníčkova
Šermířská
nábřeží
Holečkova
Atletická
Štefánikova
Arbesovo náměstí
Pod Stadiony
Turistická
Na Hřebenkách
Drtinova
V botanice
Riverside
Na Hřebenkách
Matoušova
Zborovská
náměstí 4. října
Holečkova
Kartouzská
Nádražní
Lidická
Na Bělidle
Plzeňská
Anděl
Plzeňská
Anděl's
Duškova
Angelo

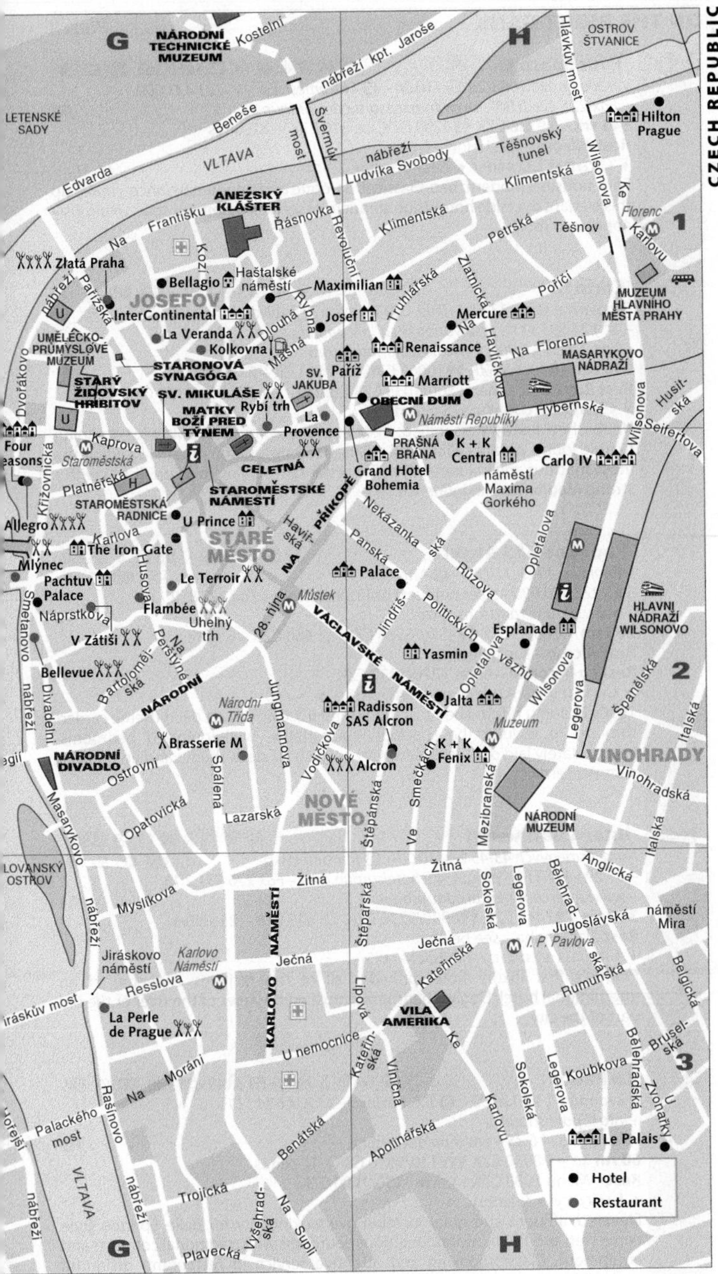

NÁRODNÍ TECHNICKÉ MUZEUM
LETENSKÉ SADY
VLTAVA
ANEŽSKÝ KLÁŠTER
JOSEFOV
UMĚLECKO-PRŮMYSLOVÉ MUZEUM
STARONOVÁ SYNAGÓGA
STARÝ ŽIDOVSKÝ HŘBITOV
SV. MIKULÁŠE
MATKY BOŽÍ PRED TÝNEM
STAROMĚSTSKÁ RADNICE
STAROMĚSTSKÉ NÁMĚSTÍ
CELETNÁ
STARÉ MĚSTO
OBECNÍ DUM
PRAŠNÁ BRÁNA
MUZEUM HLAVNÍHO MĚSTA PRAHY
MASARYKOVO NÁDRAŽÍ
HLAVNÍ NÁDRAŽÍ WILSONOVO
VÁCLAVSKÉ NÁMĚSTÍ
NA PŘÍKOPĚ
NÁRODNÍ
NÁRODNÍ DIVADLO
NOVÉ MĚSTO
NÁRODNÍ MUZEUM
VINOHRADY
KARLOVO NÁMĚSTÍ
VILA AMERIKA
OSTROV ŠTVANICE
Hilton Prague
Zlatá Praha
Bellagio
Maximilian
InterContinental
Josef
La Veranda
Kolkovna
Mercure
Renaissance
Paříž
Marriott
La Provence
Four Seasons
K + K Central
Carlo IV
Grand Hotel Bohemia
Allegro
U Prince
The Iron Gate
Mlýnec
Pachtuv Palace
Le Terroir
Palace
Flambée
V Zátiší
Esplanade
Yasmin
Bellevue
Jalta
Radisson SAS Alcron
Brasserie M
K + K Fenix
Alcron
La Perle de Prague
Le Palais
Hotel
Restaurant
G
H
1
2
3

ON THE RIGHT BANK

Plan II

Four Seasons

80 VISA

Veleslavínova 1098/2a ✉ *110 00 –* Ⓜ *Staroměstská –* ☎ *221 427 000 – Fax 221 426 0 00 – www.fourseasons.com/prague* **G2**

141 rm – †9230 CZK ††9790 CZK, ☕ 810 CZK – 20 suites

Rest *Allegro* – see below

♦ Grand Luxury ♦ Modern ♦

Four houses - modern, neo-Classical, Baroque and neo-Renaissance - make up this elegant riverside hotel. High standard of service. Basement spa. Luxuriously appointed rooms.

Carlo IV

rm 220 VISA

Senovážné Nám. 13 ✉ *110 00 –* Ⓜ *Náměsti Republiky – ☎ 224 593 111 – reservation@carloiv.boscolo.com – Fax 224 593 0 00 – www.boscolohotels.com* **H2**

150 rm – †10065 CZK ††10065 CZK, ☕ 700 CZK – 2 suites

Rest *Box Block* – Menu 560/1035 CZK (lunch) – Carte 1260/2155 CZK

♦ Grand Luxury ♦ Stylish ♦

Unabashed luxury personified: very impressive former bank with stunning marble lobby, ornate ceiling and pillars. Bedrooms in the original building the most spacious and luxurious. A stylish restaurant serving modern dishes with a strong Mediterranean influence.

Radisson SAS Alcron

rm 150 VISA

Štěpánská 40 ✉ *110 00 –* Ⓜ *Muzeum – ☎ 222 820 000 – sales.prague@radissonsas.com – Fax 222 820 1 00 – www.prague.radissonsas.com* **H2**

205 rm – †6580 CZK ††4570/6580 CZK, ☕ 660 CZK – 6 suites

Rest *Alcron* – see below

Rest *La Rotonde* – Carte 1270/1330 CZK

♦ Luxury ♦ Business ♦ Modern ♦

1930s building refurbished to a high standard. Original art deco theme carried through to include the spacious, comfortable, well-equipped bedrooms. Immaculately laid out restaurant with a stylish art deco theme and an outdoor summer terrace.

Inter-Continental

500 VISA

Nám. Curieových 43-45 ✉ *110 00 –* Ⓜ *Staroměstská – ☎ 296 631 111 – prague@ichotelsgroup.com – Fax 226 631 2 16 – www.intercontinental.com/prague* **G1**

349 rm – †7410 CZK ††6990/9230 CZK, ☕ 645 CZK – 23 suites

Rest Zlatá Praha – see below

♦ Grand Luxury ♦ Modern ♦

Prague's first luxury hotel provides all of the facilities expected of an international hotel. Elegant bedrooms, most enjoy views of the river or the old part of the city.

Le Palais

40 VISA

U Zvonařky 1 ✉ *120 00 –* Ⓜ *I. P. Pavlova – ☎ 234 634 111 – info@palaishotel.cz – Fax 234 634 6 35 – www.palaishotel.cz* **H3**

60 rm ☕ – †8950 CZK ††8110/9510 CZK – 12 suites

Rest – Menu 1080 CZK – Carte 1150/1600 CZK

♦ Luxury ♦ Classic ♦

Elevated, affluent and quiet location overlooking city for Belle Epoque style converted late 19C mansion. Luxurious bedrooms with traditional comforts and equipment. Classic cooking and attentive service in restaurant; delightful outlook from terrace.

Marriott

V Celnici 8 ✉ 110 00 – Ⓜ Náměsti Republiky – ✆ 222 888 888 – prague.marriott@marriott.cz – Fax 222 888 8 89 – www.marriott.com

258 rm – 7950 CZK 5970/7950 CZK, 625 CZK – 35 suites **H1**

Rest – Carte 645/1285 CZK

♦ Business ♦ Classic ♦

International hotel, opened in 1999. First-class conference and leisure facilities. Committed service and modern, smart bedrooms with all the latest facilities. Brasserie offers a wide selection of cuisine from American, French to traditional Czech.

Hilton Prague

Pobřežni 1 ✉ 186 00 – Ⓜ Florenc – ✆ 224 841 111 – sales.prague@hilton.com – Fax 224 842 3 78 – www.prague.hilton.com **H1**

761 rm – 5175/6990 CZK 5175/6990 CZK, 615 CZK – 27 suites

Rest *Czech House Grill & Rotisserie* – ✆ *224 842 700* – Menu 750 CZK (lunch) – Carte 940/1400 CZK

Rest *Café Bistro* – Menu 750 CZK (lunch) – Carte 940/1400 CZK

♦ Business ♦ Modern ♦

Expansive modern glass edifice by the river. Spectacular atrium befitting largest hotel in the country. Comprehensive facilities; well-equipped rooms with varied vistas. Relaxed rotisserie with wide range of global and Czech dishes. Informal Café Bistro.

Renaissance

V Celnici 7 ✉ 111 21 – Ⓜ Náměsti Republiky – ✆ 221 822 100 – renaissance.prague@renaissance.cz – Fax 221 822 2 00 – www.renaissancehotels.com

307 rm – 5250/6450 CZK 5250/6450 CZK, 625 CZK – 3 suites **H1**

Rest *Seven* – Carte 800/1720 CZK

Rest *U Korbele* – ✆ *221 822 433* – Carte 460/1140 CZK

♦ Business ♦ Modern ♦

World brand hotel in the heart of the City. Geared to the modern corporate traveller; well-equipped bedrooms, particularly those on the 'Renaissance Club' floor. Seven specialises in grills and seafood. Czech specialities in casual, relaxing U Korbele.

Palace

Panská 12 ✉ 111 21 – Ⓜ Můstek – ✆ 224 093 111 – info@palacehotel.cz – Fax 224 221 2 40 – www.palacehotel.cz **H2**

122 rm – 5315/10345 CZK 5650/10905 CZK – 2 suites

Rest *Gourmet Club* – *(dinner only)* Menu 1065/1175 CZK

♦ Traditional ♦ Classic ♦

Original Viennese Art Nouveau style façade dating back to 1906. Elegant interior; bedrooms combine period furniture with modern facilities and services. Classic club ambience and fine dining off broad global menu.

Paříž

U obecniho domu 1 ✉ 110 00 – Ⓜ Náměsti Republiky – ✆ 222 195 195 – booking@hotel-pariz.cz – Fax 224 225 4 75 – www.hotel-pariz.cz **H1**

84 rm – 9790 CZK 9790 CZK, 645 CZK – 2 suites

Rest *Sarah Bernhardt* – Menu 1170/1540 CZK

♦ Traditional ♦ Classic ♦

Culturally and historically, a landmark famed for its neo-Gothic, Art Nouveau architecture. Original staircase with preserved window panels. Sound-proofed rooms. Fine example of Art Nouveau in Sarah Bernhardt restaurant.

Jalta

Václavské Nám. 45 ✉ 110 00 – Ⓜ Muzeum – ✆ 222 822 111 – booking@hoteljalta.com – Fax 222 822 8 33 – www.hoteljalta.com **H2**

89 rm – 8390 CZK 8390 CZK – 5 suites

Rest *Hot* – Menu 675 CZK (lunch) – Carte 925/1595 CZK

♦ Traditional ♦ Classic ♦

Classic 1950s façade overlooking Wenceslas Square. Bedrooms recently modernised and soundproofed: they are now spacious, well equipped with a pleasant contemporary style. Stylish modern dining room with Asian/Mediterranean menus.

Grand Hotel Bohemia

Králodvorská 4 ✉ 110 00 – Ⓜ Náměsti Republiky – ☎ 234 608 111 – office@grandhotelbohemia.cz – Fax 222 329 5 45 – www.grandhotelbohemia.cz H1

78 rm – 5035/5595 CZK 5035/5595 CZK, ☕ 420 CZK

Rest – Carte 890/1360 CZK

◆ Traditional ◆ Classic ◆

Classic 1920s hotel, in an ideal location for tourists, with a splendid neo-Baroque ballroom. Comfortable bedrooms are generously proportioned and service professional. Large, classic restaurant with a menu of Czech/international dishes.

Mercure

Na Poříčí 7 ✉ 110 00 – Ⓜ Náměsti Republiky – ☎ 221 800 800 – h3440@accor.com – Fax 221 800 8 01 – www.accorhotels.com H1

173 rm – 4335/5565 CZK 4335/5565 CZK, ☕ 450 CZK – 1 suite

Rest *Felice* – Carte approx. 850 CZK

◆ Business ◆ Functional ◆

Modern hotel behind ornate 19C façade: many original features remain. Kafka worked here for seven years when insurance offices. Ask for more spacious deluxe room. Restaurant named after one of Kafka's lovers: modern Parisian brasserie; pleasant terrace.

Pachtuv Palace without rest

Karolíny Světlé 34 ✉ 110 00 – Ⓜ Staroměstská – ☎ 234 705 111 – reception@pachtuvpalace.com – Fax 234 705 1 12 – www.mamaisonresidences.com G2

18 rm – 9425/10900 CZK 12300/13800 CZK – 32 suites – 16500 CZK 20000 CZK, ☕ 725 CZK

◆ Traditional ◆ Classic ◆

17C residence with commanding views over the city. Large and luxurious bedrooms and suites blend antique furniture with modern accessories. Relaxing courtyard terrace.

Yasmin

Politických vězňu 12/913 ✉ 110 00 – Ⓜ Muzeum – ☎ 234 100 100 – info@hotel-yasmin.cz – Fax 234 110 1 01 – www.hotel-yasmin.cz F2

198 rm ☕ – 6000/7200 CZK 6000/7200 CZK

Rest – Carte 337/507 CZK

◆ Business ◆ Modern ◆

Modern and design-led centrally located hotel. Stylish lobby leads into winter garden and cool lounge. Modular bedrooms in soft shades of sage with black-tiled bathrooms. Colourful and casual dining room with vast Asian menu specialising in noodles.

Josef without rest

Rybná 20 ✉ 110 00 – Ⓜ Náměsti Republiky – ☎ 221 700 111 – reservation@hoteljosef.com – Fax 221 700 9 99 – www.hoteljosef.com G1

109 rm ☕ – 4170/5960 CZK 4170/10010 CZK

◆ Townhouse ◆ Stylish ◆

Stylish boutique hotel with light glass lobby, bar and breakfast room. Design-led bedrooms; deluxe rooms have ultra modern glass bathrooms.

Maximilian without rest

Haštalská 14 ✉ 110 00 – Ⓜ Náměsti Republiky – ☎ 225 303 111 – reservations@maximilianhotel.com – Fax 225 303 1 10 – www.maximilianhotel.com G1

70 rm ☕ – 3720/4560 CZK 3858/5540 CZK – 1 suite

◆ Business ◆ Classic ◆

Converted apartment block in quiet area near St Agnes Convent. Designer boutique style prevails. Glass and steel breakfast room. Basement Thai massage spa. Contemporary rooms.

K + K Central

Hybernská 10 ✉ 110 00 – Ⓜ Náměsti Republiky – ☎ 225 022 000 – hotel.central@kkhotels.cz – Fax 222 212 1 41 – www.kkhotels.com/central H2

125 rm – †7690/8250 CZK ††7690/8250 CZK – 1 suite

Rest – *(in bar)* Carte 440/710 CZK

♦ Business ♦ Modern ♦

Beautifully restored hotel; combination of elegant Art Nouveau and ultra modern décor. Glass and steel breakfast gallery in old theatre. Modish rooms. Light dishes in lounge.

U Prince

Staroměstské Nám. 29 ✉ 110 00 – Ⓜ Staroměstská – ☎ 224 213 807 – recepce@hoteluprince.cz – Fax 224 213 8 07 – www.hoteluprince.cz G2

23 rm – †4190/6990 CZK ††4490/6790 CZK – 1 suite

Rest – Carte 227/3119 CZK

♦ Traditional ♦ Classic ♦

Restored 17C town house on main square with atmospheric rooms blending with mod cons and antique furnishings. Roof terrace with marvellous city views. Choose the half-panelled bar-restaurant for international cooking or the brick vaulted cellars for seafood.

The Iron Gate

Michalská 19 ✉ 110 00 – Ⓜ Staroměstská – ☎ 225 777 777 – hotel@irongate.cz – Fax 225 777 7 78 – www.irongate.cz G2

13 rm – †4195/5595 CZK ††5315/6990 CZK – 30 suites – ††5595/27680 CZK

Rest *Zelezna Brata* – *(live gypsy music dinner only)* Menu 840/2240 CZK

♦ Traditional ♦ Classic ♦

Hidden away in Old Town's cobbled street maze. 14C origins; attractive central courtyard. Large rooms with antique furniture or painted beams; some duplex suites. Zelezna Brata in basement for Czech cuisine; gypsy music.

K + K Fenix

Ve Smečkách 30 ✉ 110 00 – Ⓜ Muzeum – ☎ 225 012 222 – hotel.fenix@kkhotels.cz – Fax 222 212 1 41 – www.kkhotels.com H2

128 rm – †7495 CZK ††8055 CZK

Rest – *(in bar)* Carte 450/840 CZK

♦ Business ♦ Modern ♦

Located off Wenceslas Square; up to date interior behind a classic façade. Bedrooms vary in size and shape but all are smart, clean and comfortable. Light dishes in lounge bar.

Esplanade

Washingtonova 1600-19 ✉ 110 00 – Ⓜ Muzeum – ☎ 224 501 111 – esplanade@esplanade.cz – Fax 224 229 3 06 – www.esplanade.cz H2

74 rm – †2490/5285 CZK ††2490/5565 CZK, 475 CZK

Rest – Menu 615 CZK – Carte 700/870 CZK

♦ Traditional ♦ Classic ♦

Charming and atmospheric; this Art Nouveau building is something of an architectural gem. Original features abound; bedrooms enjoy style and a timeless elegance. Menu of traditional Czech and French specialities offered in friendly surroundings.

Bellagio

U Milosrdných 2 ✉ 110 00 – Ⓜ Staroměstská – ☎ 221 778 999 – info@bellagiohotel.cz – Fax 221 778 9 00 – www.bellagiohotel.cz G1

46 rm – †4420/6490 CZK ††5035/6155 CZK – 1 suite

Rest *Isabella* – *(dinner only)* Carte 675/1225 CZK

♦ Business ♦ Stylish ♦

Quiet, converted apartment block near the river. Basement vaulted bar/breakfast room. Airy, attractive bedrooms, well equipped in warm colours. Impressive bathrooms. Restaurant is Mediterranean style.

CZECH REPUBLIC

XXXX **Allegro** – at Four Seasons H.

Veleslavínova 1098/2a ✉ 110 00 – Ⓜ Staroměstská – ✆ 221 426 880 – Fax 221 426 0 00 – www.fourseasons.com/prague **G2**

Rest – Menu 1200 CZK (lunch) – Carte 1645/1935 CZK

♦ Italian ♦ Formal ♦

Fine dining restaurant with lovely wood-panelled terrace and modern Czech art on the walls. Accomplished Italian cooking with originality and flair: truffle menu in season.

XXXX **Zlatá Praha** – at Inter-Continental H. < Prague,

Nám. Curieových 43-45 ✉ 110 00 – Ⓜ Staroměstská – ✆ 296 631 111 – prague@interconti.com – Fax 224 811 2 16 – www.zlatapraharestaurant.com **G1**

Rest – Carte 1175/2240 CZK

♦ Modern ♦ Formal ♦

Stunning views of the city skyline provide a backdrop to this elegant room. Modern gourmet cooking with fine wines on an extensive menu. Detailed service; piano accompaniment.

XXX **Alcron** – at Radisson SAS Alcron H.

Štěpánská 40 ✉ 110 00 – Ⓜ Muzeum – ✆ 222 820 038 – sales.prague@radissonsas.com – Fax 222 820 1 00 – www.prague.radissonsas.com closed Sunday **H2**

Rest – *(booking essential) (dinner only)* Menu 1700/2400 CZK – Carte approx. 1800 CZK

♦ Seafood ♦ Design ♦

An Art Deco mural after de Lempicka dominates this intimate, semi-circular restaurant. Creative and classic seafood served by friendly, professional staff.

XXX **Flambée**

Husova 5 ✉ 110 00 – Ⓜ Můstek – ✆ 224 248 512 – flambee@flambee.cz – Fax 224 248 5 13 – www.flambee.cz **G2**

Rest – Menu 255/615 CZK – Carte 225/475 CZK

Rest *Cafe Bistro 'F'* – ✆ *224 401 236* – Menu 255/615 CZK – Carte 225/475 CZK

♦ Traditional ♦ Formal ♦

Elegant fine dining in established cellar restaurant dating from 11C. Formal yet friendly service and well-judged classics - fine selection of clarets. Cafe Bistro 'F' - above the restaurant - is a little modern eatery serving simpler international dishes.

XXX **Bellevue** <

Smetanovo Nábřeží 18 ✉ 110 00 – Ⓜ Staroměstská – ✆ 222 221 443 – bellevue@zatisigroup.cz – Fax 222 220 4 53 – www.zatisigroup.cz – closed 24 December

Rest – Menu 1290/1590 CZK – Carte 1030/1770 CZK **G2**

♦ Traditional ♦ Formal ♦

Elegant 19C building, affording views of river and royal palace. Classic style and surroundings; serious and formal dining writ large as the nightly piano plays.

XXX **La Perle de Prague** < Prague, 25

Dancing House (7th floor), Rašínovo Nábřeží 80 ✉ 120 00 – Ⓜ Karlovo Náměstí – ✆ 219 841 60 – info@laperle.cz – Fax 219 841 79 – www.laperle.cz closed Sunday and lunch Monday **G3**

Rest – Menu 490/2500 CZK – Carte 990/1650 CZK

♦ French ♦ Fashionable ♦

Eye-catching riverside building: seventh floor restaurant has simply stunning views of city, river and castle. Comfortable, strikingly modern décor. French-inspired menu.

XX **Le Terroir**

Vejvodova 1 ✉ 110 00 – Ⓜ Můstek – ✆ 222 220 260 – rezervace@leterroir.cz – Fax 222 220 2 60 – www.leterroir.cz – closed 2-8 July **G2**

Rest – Menu 950/1150 CZK – Carte 920/1340 CZK

♦ Innovative ♦ Rustic ♦

Cobbled courtyard and steps descending past wine store to atmospheric vaulted 10C cellar. Personally run; superb wine list. Good value, accomplished, Pan-European cooking.

La Veranda

Elišky Krásnohorské 2/10 ✉ 110 00 – Ⓜ Staroměstská – ✆ 224 814 733 – office@laveranda.cz – Fax 224 814 5 96 – www.laveranda.cz **G1**

Rest – Menu 190/695 CZK – Carte 910/1375 CZK

♦ Innovative ♦ Design ♦

Stylish modern restaurant in the old Jewish district. Modern menu in keeping with the décor, fusing East and West to produce light dishes with interesting flavours.

V Zátiši

Liliová 1, Betlémské Nám. ✉ 110 00 – Ⓜ Můstek – ✆ 222 221 155 – vzatisi@zatisigroup.cz – Fax 222 220 6 29 – www.zatisigroup.cz closed 24 December **G2**

Rest – *(booking essential at dinner)* Menu 795/995 CZK – Carte 885/1585 CZK

♦ Modern ♦ Cosy ♦

Well run, slick and dependable restaurant offering modern, well-priced cuisine within a range of four rooms which are intimate in places, and more stylish in others.

Mlýnec

Charles Bridge,

Novotného Lávka 9 ✉ 110 00 – Ⓜ Staroměstská – ✆ 221 082 208 – mlynec@zatisigroup.cz – Fax 221 082 3 91 – www.zatisigroup.cz **G2**

Rest – Menu 445/1390 CZK – Carte 935/1285 CZK

♦ Modern ♦ Brasserie ♦

Spacious and contemporary; popular with tourists because of setting. Modern dishes combined with Czech classics. Terrace views of Charles Bridge on fine summer evenings.

Rybí trh

Týnský dvůr 5 ✉ 110 00 – Ⓜ Náměsti Republiky – ✆ 602 295 911 – info@rybitrh.cz – Fax 224 895 4 49 – www.rybitrh.cz **G1**

Rest – Menu 320/3500 CZK – Carte 730/2090 CZK

♦ Seafood ♦ Friendly ♦

Modern restaurant which lives up to its name - Fish Market - with fresh seafood on crushed ice before open-plan kitchen; fish tanks, adjacent wine shop and tasting cellar.

La Provence

Štupartská 9 ✉ 110 00 Praha – Ⓜ Náměsti Republiky – ✆ 296 826 155 – kontakt@laprovence.cz – Fax 224 819 5 70 – www.kampagroup.com **G1**

Rest – Menu 250/350 CZK (lunch) – Carte 655/1455 CZK

♦ French ♦ Brasserie ♦

Tucked down a central side street. Classic French brasserie with real 1920s feel: etched mirrors, tile mosaics, Gallic scenes. Menus, too, never stray from classics of France.

Brasserie M

Vladislavova 17 ✉ 110 00 – Ⓜ Národni Třída – ✆ 224 054 070 – info@brasseriem.cz – Fax 224 054 4 40 – www.brasseriem.cz closed dinner 24-26 December and Sunday dinner **G2**

Rest – Carte 345/1200 CZK

♦ French ♦ Bistro ♦

Central but away from touristy main streets. Big, high-ceilinged room with dominant open-plan kitchen and French accent to décor. Well-priced Gallic favourites on menu too.

Kolkovna

V Kolkovně 8 ✉ 110 00 – Ⓜ Staroměstská – ✆ 224 819 701 – info@kolkovna.cz – Fax 224 819 7 00 – www.kolkovna.cz **G1**

Rest – Menu 200/400 CZK – Carte 219/595 CZK

♦ Traditional ♦ Inn ♦

Atmospheric Czech Pilsner Urquell bar/restaurant: old pictures, tools and advertisements line green walls under vaulted ceilings. Huge traditional dishes and excellent beers.

CZECH REPUBLIC

ON THE LEFT BANK *Plan II*

Mandarin Oriental

Nebovidská 459/1 ✉ 118 00 – Ⓜ Malostranská – ✆ 233 088 888 – moprg-reservations@mohg.com – Fax 233 088 6 68 – www.mandarinoriental.com **F2**

77 rm – 10470 CZK 11070 CZK, ☕ 715 CZK – 22 suites

Rest *Essensia* – Carte 950/1425 CZK

◆ Luxury ◆ Stylish ◆

Housed within a 14C monastery, the hotel opened in 2006 and is more boutique in style than most in this group. Spa within the former chapel. Luxurious and sleek bedrooms. Vaulted, chic dining room with contemporary lighting; menu a blend of European and Asian.

Aria

Tržiště 9 ✉ 118 00 – Ⓜ Malostranská – ✆ 225 334 111 – stay@aria.cz – Fax 225 334 6 66 – www.aria.cz **F2**

43 rm ☕ – 6570/10065 CZK 6570/10065 CZK – 9 suites

Rest *Coda* – Menu 450/2100 CZK – Carte 950/1600 CZK

◆ Luxury ◆ Design ◆

Stylishly overlooking lovely castle gardens; boasts strong music orientation, including library and rooms themed individually to different music genres. Personable service. Choose from the menu in intimate Coda or eat on the stunning summer rooftop terrace.

Alchymist Grand H. and Spa

Tržiště 19 ✉ 118 00 – Ⓜ Malostranská – ✆ 257 286 011 – info@alchymisthotel.com – Fax 257 286 0 17 – www.alchymisthotel.com **F2**

38 rm ☕ – 8390/9370 CZK 8390/9370 CZK – 9 suites

Rest *Aquarius* – Carte 870/1260 CZK

◆ Luxury ◆ Classic ◆

Four 15C Renaissance and Baroque houses on UNESCO street. Sympathetically restored and offering sumptuous style. Beautiful spa; enchanting rooms with 16C-19C artefacts. Formal restaurant and café opening onto a courtyard.

Savoy

Keplerova 6 ✉ 118 00 – ✆ 224 302 430 – info@savoyhotel.cz – Fax 224 302 1 28 – www.savoyhotel.cz **E2**

60 rm ☕ – 10765 CZK 10765 CZK – 1 suite

Rest *Hradčany* – Menu 840 CZK

◆ Luxury ◆ Classic ◆

Timeless charm; popular with statesmen. Strength lies in its classically styled bedrooms, which are spacious, tasteful, well equipped and benefit from high levels of service. Bright formal dining room with glass ceiling and distant city view.

Andel's

Stroupeznického 21 ✉ 150 00 – Ⓜ Anděl – ✆ 296 889 688 – info@andelshotel.com – Fax 296 889 9 99 – www.andelshotel.com **F3**

257 rm ☕ – 6575 CZK 8250 CZK – 33 suites

Rest *Oscar's* – Carte 540/635 CZK

Rest *Nagoya* – *✆ 251 511 724 (closed Christmas-New Year and Sunday) (dinner only)* Menu 500 CZK (lunch) – Carte 500/1500 CZK

◆ Business ◆ Modern ◆

Stylish modern hotel with distinctively minimalist appeal; luxurious apartments in adjacent block. Conference and fitness centres. Well-equipped rooms with all mod cons. Informal dining in Oscar's brasserie; simple menu. Nagoya offers traditional Japanese dishes.

Hoffmeister rm 30 VISA AE

Pod Bruskou 7 ✉ 118 00 – Ⓜ Malostranská – ✆ 251 017 111 – hotel@hoffmeister.cz – Fax 251 017 1 20 – www.hoffmeister.cz **F1**

42 rm – 4475/5875 CZK 5035/7270 CZK – 5 suites

Rest *Ada* – Carte 1150/1510 CZK

♦ Traditional ♦ Classic ♦

Unprepossessing façade but inside full of artworks by Adolf Hoffmeister; son owns hotel. Eclectic range of bedrooms plus 15C steam room. Elegant restaurant with original cartoons. Attentive service; French and Italian influenced cooking.

Riverside without rest VISA AE

Janáčkovo Nábřeži 15 ✉ 150 00 – Ⓜ Anděl – ✆ 225 994 611 – reservation@riversideprague.com – Fax 225 994 6 22 – www.riversideprague.com **F3**

42 rm – 6850/13840 CZK 6850/13840 CZK, 700 CZK – 3 suites

♦ Business ♦ Modern ♦

An early 20C riverside façade conceals relaxing modern hotel with castle view. Efficient service. Very well-appointed bedrooms with luxurious bathrooms; many with views.

Residence Nosticova P VISA AE

Nosticova 1, Malá Strana ✉ 118 00 – Ⓜ Malostranská – ✆ 257 312 513 – info@nosticova.com – Fax 257 312 5 17 – www.nosticova.com **F2**

5 rm – 6435/7410 CZK 6435/7410 CZK, 420 CZK – 5 suites

Rest *Alchymist* – *✆ 257 312 518 (closed Monday November-March)* Carte 730/980 CZK

♦ Townhouse ♦ Classic ♦

Tastefully refurbished 17C town house in a quiet, cobbled side street. Stylish suites - all with their own kitchen - combine modern and antique furnishings and works of art.

U Zlaté Studně VISA AE

U Zlaté Studně 166/4 ✉ 118 00 – Ⓜ Malostranská – ✆ 257 011 213 – hotel@goldenwell.cz – Fax 257 533 3 20 – www.goldenwell.cz **F1**

18 rm – 4895/6850 CZK 4895/6850 CZK – 2 suites

Rest *Terasa U Zlaté Studně* – see below

♦ Historic ♦ Classic ♦

16C Renaissance building in quiet spot between the castle and Ladeburg Gardens. Inviting bedrooms - most boasting city views - are richly furnished but uncluttered.

U Krále Karla without rest VISA AE

Úvoz 4 ✉ 118 00 – ✆ 257 531 211 – ukrale@iol.cz – Fax 257 533 5 91 – www.romantichotels.cz **E2**

19 rm – 3400/5000 CZK 3900/7500 CZK

♦ Historic ♦ Classic ♦

Below the castle: rebuilt in 1639 into a Baroque house; the style of furniture endures. Bags of character: every bedroom features stained glass and a stencilled wood ceiling.

Angelo without rest 100 VISA AE

Radlicka 1g/3216 ✉ 150 00 – Ⓜ Anděl – ✆ 234 801 111 – info@angelohotel.com – Fax 234 809 9 98 – www.angelohotel.com **F3**

168 rm – 5200 CZK 5500 CZK

♦ Business ♦ Modern ♦

Behind its sister hotel, Andel's, this is a colourfully decorated and relaxed hotel. Spacious bedrooms, with showers and large beds; Executive rooms on the top two floors.

U Raka without rest P VISA AE

Černínská 10 ✉ 118 00 – ✆ 220 511 100 – info@romantikhotel-uraka.cz – Fax 233 358 0 41 – www.romantikhotel-uraka.cz **E1**

6 rm – 3200/4350 CZK 4350/6900 CZK

♦ Family ♦ Cosy ♦

Tucked away, two timbered cottages in a rustic Czech style creating a charming little hotel. Cosy, comfy and inviting. Clean-lined rooms in warm brick and wood.

CZECH REPUBLIC

Neruda

Nerudova 44 ✉ 118 00 – ✆ 257 535 557 – info@hotelneruda.cz
– Fax 257 531 4 92 – www.hotelneruda.eu **E2**
20 rm – 4335/5315 CZK 4615/5595 CZK
Rest – Menu 720 CZK (lunch) – Carte 720/870 CZK
◆ Business ◆ Modern ◆
Castle dominates views from rooftop terrace. Modern style complements 14C ceiling and architecture; poet Neruda's quotes decorate walls. Spacious, well sound-proofed rooms. Simple but attractive café/restaurant offering popular dishes.

The Charles without rest

Josefská 1 ✉ 118 00 – Ⓜ Malostranská – ✆ 257 532 913
– thecharles@bon.cz – Fax 257 532 9 10 **F2**
31 rm – 2240/4475 CZK 4195/5875 CZK
◆ Traditional ◆ Cosy ◆
Elegant and ideally situated little hotel. Spacious bedrooms decorated with stripped floorboards, hand-painted ceilings and Baroque style furnishings. Listed.

Questenberk without rest

Úvoz 15/155 ✉ 110 00 – ✆ 220 407 600 – hotel@questenberk.cz
– Fax 220 407 6 01 – www.questenberk.cz **E2**
30 rm – 3075/5315 CZK 3635/8110 CZK
◆ Historic ◆ Classic ◆
Converted 17C monastic hospital with ornate façade at the top of the Castle district. Arched corridors leading to sizeable bedrooms with good facilities overlooking the city.

Kampa Park

Charles Bridge,
Na Kampě 8b, Malá Strana ✉ 118 00 – Ⓜ Malostranská
– ✆ 296 826 102 – kontakt@kampapark.com – Fax 257 533 2 23
– www.kampagroup.com **F2**
Rest – *(booking essential at dinner)* Menu 840/1400 CZK – Carte 1205/1430 CZK
◆ Modern ◆ Fashionable ◆
Celebrity heavy; stunningly located at water's edge by Charles Bridge. Book for riverside table. Capacious interior; heated terraces: good view likely. Modern global menus.

Terasa U Zlaté Studně – at U Zlaté Studně H.

Prague,
U Zlaté Studně 4 ✉ 118 00 – Ⓜ Malostranská
– ✆ 257 011 213 – restaurant@zlatestudne.cz
– Fax 257 533 3 20
– www.terasauzlatestudne.cz **F1**
Rest – Menu 1120/2045 CZK (lunch) – Carte 1150/2210 CZK
◆ Modern ◆ Design ◆
Beautiful skyline views from a clean-lined top-floor restaurant and terrace, reached by its own lift. Affable staff; full-flavoured modern dishes.

U Patrona

Dražického Nám. 4 ✉ 118 00 – Ⓜ Malostranská
– ✆ 257 530 725 – upatrona@upatrona.cz – Fax 257 530 7 23
– www.upatrona.cz **F2**
Rest – Menu 1050/1100 CZK (dinner) – Carte 820/1340 CZK
◆ Traditional ◆ Cosy ◆
Charming period house near Charles Bridge. Small ground floor restaurant or larger upstairs room with window into kitchen. French-influenced classics and Czech specialities.

Square

Malostranské Nám. 5/28 ✉ 118 00 – Ⓜ Malostranská – ✆ 296 826 114 – kontakt@squarerestaurant.cz – Fax 257 532 1 07 – www.kampagroup.cz closed 24 December **F2**

Rest – Carte 600/950 CZK

◆ International ◆ Brasserie ◆

Simple modern eatery with contemporary décor in good position on a popular bustling square. Summer terrace and additional basement room. Menus have a global range.

Olympia

Vítězná 7 ✉ 110 00 – Ⓜ Národni Třída – ✆ 251 511 080 – info@olympia-restaurant.cz – Fax 251 511 0 79 – www.olympia-restaurant.cz **F2**

Rest – Carte 370/698 CZK

◆ Traditional ◆ Inn ◆

The menu of Czech specialities is a carnivore's delight, with generous portions and assured flavours. A relaxed and easy-going pub atmosphere pervades this converted bank.

ENVIRONS OF PRAGUE

Plan I

Crowne Plaza

rm 380

Koulova 15 ✉ 160 45 – ✆ 296 537 111 – hotel@crowneplaza.cz – Fax 296 537 5 35 – www.crowneplaza.cz closed 10-13 October **B1**

250 rm – †2520/4335 CZK ††2520/4335 CZK, ☕ 450 CZK – 4 suites

Rest – Menu 290 CZK (buffet lunch)/690 CZK

◆ Business ◆ Classic ◆

Stunning example of Socialist Realism architecture; built for Stalin in '50s but he never showed up! Softened interior retains grandeur. Refurbished, well-equipped bedrooms. Ornate decoration lends a period feel to the restaurant.

Art without rest

Nad Královskou oborou 53 ✉ 170 00 – Ⓜ Hradčanská – ✆ 233 101 331 – booking@arthotel.cz – Fax 233 101 3 11 – www.arthotel.cz **B1**

24 rm ☕ – †4475 CZK ††5035/6015 CZK

◆ Family ◆ Modern ◆

Stylish design in the shadow of Sparta Prague FC! Artists celebrated on each floor, including owner's father and grandfather. Sleek rooms: two attic suites with balconies.

Restaurant Le Bistrot de Marlène with rm

14

Hotel Villa Schwaiger, Schwaigerova 59/3, (Room reservations ✆ 233 320 271) ✉ 160 00 – Ⓜ Hradčanská – ✆ 224 921 853 – info@bistrotdemarlene.cz – Fax 233 320 2 72 – www.bistrotdemarlene.cz closed Saturday lunch and Sunday in winter **B1**

22 rm ☕ – †3480/4785 CZK ††3480/15950 CZK

Rest – Carte 1160/1678 CZK

◆ French ◆ Formal ◆

Well-renowned restaurant in a small residential villa. Dine in restaurant, Sunshine room, garden or terrace on accomplished, French based and original dishes. Comfy bedrooms.

Aromi

Mánesova 78/1442 ✉ 120 00 – Ⓜ Jiřiho z Poděbrad – ✆ 222 713 222 – info@aromi.cz – Fax 222 713 4 44 – www.aromi.cz closed 24-26 December **C2**

Rest – *(booking essential at dinner)* Menu 125 CZK (lunch) – Carte 530/1015 CZK

◆ Italian ◆ Rustic ◆

A couple of metro stops to the east, this buzzy restaurant is well worth the journey. Spacious interior with big, chunky wood tables. Great value, authentic Italian dishes.

DENMARK
DANMARK

PROFILE

◆ **AREA:**
43 069 km^2 (16 629 sq mi) excluding the Faroe Islands and Greenland.

◆ **POPULATION:**
5 432 000 inhabitants (est. 2005), density = 126 per km^2.

◆ **CAPITAL:**
Copenhagen (conurbation 1 426 000 inhabitants).

◆ **CURRENCY:**
Danish Krone (DKK) divided into 100 øre; rate of exchange: DKK 1 = € 0.13 = US$ 0.17 (Nov 2006).

◆ **GOVERNMENT:**
Constitutional parliamentary (single chamber) monarchy (since 1849). Member of European Union since 1973.

◆ **LANGUAGES:**
Danish; many Danes also understand and speak English.

◆ **SPECIFIC PUBLIC HOLIDAYS:**
Maundy Thursday (the day before Good Friday); Good Friday (Friday before Easter); Common Prayer Day (4th Friday after Easter); Constitution Day (5 June); Boxing Day (26 December).

◆ **LOCAL TIME:**
GMT + 1 hour in winter and 2 GMT + 2 hours in summer.

◆ **CLIMATE:**
Temperate northern maritime with cold winters and mild summers Copenhagen: January: 1°C, July: 18°C).

◆ **INTERNATIONAL DIALLING CODE:**
00 45 followed by full local number. Directory Enquiries: ✆ **118**; International Directory Enquiries: ✆ **113**.

◆ **EMERGENCY:**
Dial ✆ **112** for Police, Ambulance and Fire Brigade.

◆ **ELECTRICITY:**
220 volts AC, 50Hz; 2-pin round-shaped

FORMALITIES

Travellers from the European Union (EU), Switzerland, Norway, Iceland and the main countries of North and South America need a national identity card or passport (America: passport required) to visit Denmark for less than three months (tourism or business purpose). For visitors from other countries a visa may be required, in addition to a passport, especially for those wishing to stay for longer than three months. If you plan to visit Greenland or Faroe Islands while in Denmark, you must purchase a visa in advance in your own country. We advise you to check with your embassy before travelling.

MAJOR NEWSPAPERS

The main national daily Danish newspapers are Berlingske Tidende, Børsen, Politiken and Information.

The two largest tabloid newspapers are B.T. and Ekstrabladet. *The Copenhagen Post* is a weekly newspaper published in English.

USEFUL PHRASES

ENGLISH	DANISH
Yes	**Ja**
No	**Nej**
Good morning	**God morgen, God dag, Hej**
Goodbye	**Farvel**
Thank you	**Tak**
Excuse me	**Undskyld**
I don't understand	**Jeg forstår ikke**

HOTELS

→ CATEGORIES

From international luxury to cosy, family-run hotels and inns; castles and manor houses; bed & breakfast, farmhouse holidays, holiday cottages by the beach and in the country.

→ PRICE RANGE

The price is per room. There is little difference between the price of a single and a double room.
Between April and October it is advisable to book in advance. From November to March prices may be slightly lower, some hotels offer special cheap rates and a few may be closed. In Copenhagen hotel chains offer lower weekend rates in the low season.

→ TAX

Included in the room price.

→ CHECK OUT TIME

Usually between 10.30am and noon.

→ RESERVATIONS

By telephone or by Internet. A credit card number may be required.

→ TIP FOR LUGGAGE HANDLING

At the discretion of the customer (about Kr 10-15 per bag).

→ BREAKFAST

This can be included in the price of the room and is generally served between 7am and 10am. Most hotels offer a self-service buffet, including smørrebrød or something similar; generally it is possible to have breakfast served in the room.

Reception	**Reception**
Single room	**Erkeltvaerelse**
Double room	**Dobbeltvaerelse**
Bed	**Seng**
Bathroom	**Badevaerelse**
Shower	**Brusebad**

RESTAURANTS

In the last few years Copenhagen has developed into a foodies' paradise, even attracting diners from other countries. The locals dine out a lot and spend all evening at table for the pleasure of savouring the chefs' specialities. Many of the **restaurants** are very stylish, contemporary and minimalist in decor and design. The **brasseries** offer a more homely ambience. At lunchtime the choice is less varied as many of the restaurants, particularly the expensive ones with stars, are open for dinner only.

→ MEALS

Breakfast	**Morgenmad**	7am – 10am
Lunch	**Forkost**	12pm – 2-3pm
Dinner	**Middag, aftensmad**	6.30pm – 10pm

In the evening many restaurants offer **fixed priced set menus** without choice or **tasting menus** with a different glass of wine with each course. Lunch menus are mostly à la carte. Menus are usually printed in Danish and English. A fixed price menu is usually less expensive than a meal with the same number of courses selected from the à la carte menu. The Danish open sandwich, **smørrebrød**, is served mostly at lunch in specialist restaurants.

→ RESERVATIONS

It is essential to reserve in the evening, usually by phone, fax or Internet. For famous restaurants (including Michelin starred restaurants), it is advisable to book several days – or weeks in some instances – in advance. A credit card number or a phone number may be required as guarantee.

→ THE BILL

The bill (check) includes service charge and VAT. Tipping is optional but, if you are particularly pleased with the service, it is customary to round up the total to an appropriate figure.

Drink or aperitif	**Drink / drik / aperitif**
Appetizer Meal	**Måltid**
First course, starter	**Forret**
Main dish	**Hovedret**
Main dish of the day	**Dagens ret**
Dessert	**Dessert**
Water	**Vand**
Wine (red, white, rosé)	**Vin (rød, hvid, rosé)**
Beer, draught beer	**Øl, Fadøl**
Bread	**Brød**
Meat (medium, well done)	**Kød (medium, gennemstegt)**
Fish	**Fisk**
Salt/pepper	**Salt / Peber**
Cheese	**Ost**
Vegetables	**Grøntsager**
Hot/cold	**Varm / kold**
The bill (check)	**Regningen**

LOCAL CUISINE

The traditional feature of Danish culinary culture, the cold buffet *(det store kolde bord)*, is generally served at lunchtime in specialist restaurants. A great variety of hot and cold fish and meat dishes are presented, including the famous **smørrebrød**, an open sandwich of sliced buttered rye bread topped with fish (marinated herring), shellfish, liver pate *(leverpostej)*, meat balls *(frikadeller)*, usually accompanied by a glass of lager beer or a tot of aquavit.

At dinner the accent is on innovation. The modern chefs use only the best local and seasonal produce, combining the different elements with flair and originality to produce highly individual dishes. Seafood is always on the menu. Fusion gourmet restaurants offer dishes such as roasted zander served with lemongrass froth and parsnip crisps; Danish blue lobster with wild watercress; wild rabbit with allspice; marinated blueberries with blueberry sherbet. Less exotic dishes are breaded plaice and fish cakes. Classic lunchtime restaurants offer cold dishes such as **Christiansøsild**, herring marinated in herbs or spices and served on a slice of buttered wholemeal rye bread.

Danish **specialities** include smoked salmon and smoked eel, lobster, herring marinated with herbs or spices. Veal is very popular in summer, also veal sweetbreads. There is plenty of home-raised pork (sausages and bacon) and also game. Herbs, spices (carroway), rye bread and berries are frequent ingredients. The Danish have a reputation for their dairy produce, including a few well known cheeses: **Danish blue**, **Gammel Ole and Rygeost**. For dessert there are honey cakes and the more famous Danish pastries and chocolates; berries are served in tarts and brulées or made into sorbets.

DRINK

Denmark is famous for **lager** - Tuborg and Carlsberg. The Carlsberg Brewery, which has been in the same building since 1878 and is open to visitors, also produces 'real ale' in the semper Ardens range as well as the Jacobsen range. Wine is expensive, as it has to be imported, but wine lists are eclectic, offering a worldwide selection. Cocktails are also popular, particularly champagne cocktails. The traditional spirit is **aquavit**, which is often drunk as a chaser.

COPENHAGEN
KØBENHAVN

Population (est. 2005): 514 000 (conurbation 1 426 000) – Altitude: about 13 m above sea level

B. Pérousse / MICHELIN

Copenhagen covers the northeast coast of Sjaelland Island. It is a city of contrasts where tradition is preserved beside the ultramodern. The city is gracious, with red-brick walls and green copper roofs. The huge, busy harbour is a sign of economic importance but first impression is that of a friendly and dynamic city. The town carries its 800 years of history lightly and its architectural heritage is well preserved.

The Danish capital does not enjoy any expansive vistas; yet there is a sense of spaciousness created by impressive squares, parks, gardens and lakes.

The name København (port of merchants) evokes the commercial traditions of the city founded by the bishop Absalon in 1167. During the reign of Christian IV (1588-1648) the city enjoyed its golden age, with huge development, particularly in its architecture. Most beautiful monuments and the picturesque Christianshavn district date from this period. Since 2000, the refurbishment of the waterfront and docks is spurred on by Øresund Crossing, a combination of tunnel and bridge, carrying road and rail traffic between Copenhagen and Malmö in Sweden. Another stunning modern building is the 'Black Diamond' extension to the 18C Royal Library.

Famous writers such as Ludvig Holberg, Søren Kierkegård, Hans Christian Andersen and Karen Blixen lived in Copenhagen.

WHICH DISTRICT TO CHOOSE

Most **hotels** and **restaurants** are located in the Old Town and adjacent districts.

Copenhagen boasts an impressive range of restaurants. Alongside classic establishments with proud traditions you'll find a variety of restaurants offering some of the most original and innovative cooking in Europe.

The city also has a vibrant café culture with everything from coffee bars to brunch concepts; at the fusion cafés you can buy books, fashion items, ornaments or flowers, or even wash your clothes.

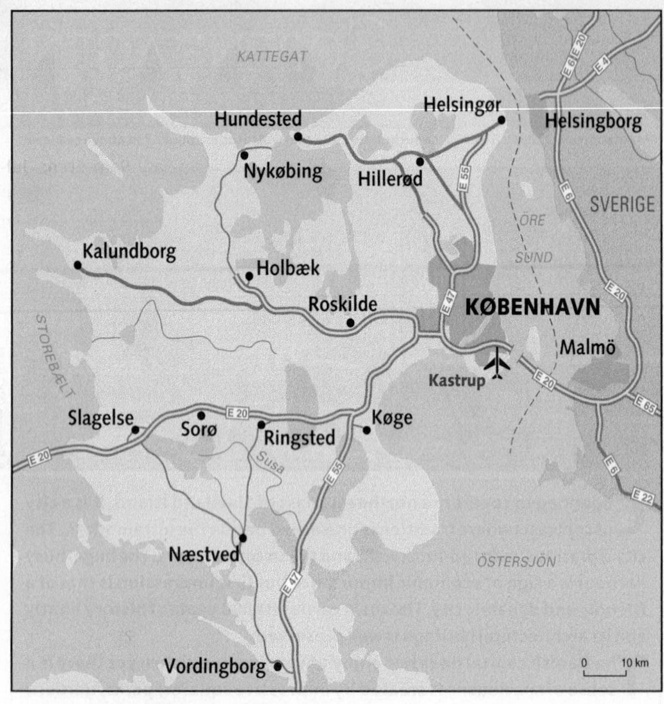

PRACTICAL INFORMATION

ARRIVAL – DEPARTURE

Copenhagen Airport – In Kastrup, about 9 km (5.5 mi) southeast of Copenhagen. ✆ 32 31 32 31, ✆ 32 31 23 60 (service information); www.cph.dk

From the airport to the city centre – By **train**: Airport City Express (13min) to Central Station every 20min. Single fare Kr27. By **bus** nos 9, 250S and 500S to city centre (30min). Fare Kr128.50. By **taxi**: Kr200.

Sea Services – **Car and passenger ferries** to Copenhagen from England, Norway, Sweden, Germany, the Netherlands, single and return fares. ✆ 08705 333 000 (8.30am-8pm, Sat 8.30am-5pm, Sun 10am-4pm); www.dfdsseaways.co.uk

Railway Station – **Hovedbanegård**, Bernstorffsgade. ✆ 70 13 14 15 (domestic), ✆ 70 13 14 16 (international); www.dsb.dk, www.rejseplanen.dk

Øresund Bridge – A combination of bridge and tunnel (10 miles/16km long) linking Copenhagen (via the airport) with Malmö in Sweden. Toll: Kr 225 (one way by car); Kr 73 (one way by train 35min).

TRANSPORT

→ METRO AND BUS

Tickets valid for metro, buses (Movia) and S-train are sold at Movia ticket offices and at DSB stations with ticket outlets. 24hr-ticket Kr110 valid for the entire Greater Copenhagen Region; 7-day Flexcard valid for selected zones; 10-journey punch cards (Klippekort) are valid for all zones. Discounts available for senior citizens and children under 16. The Metro and the S-trains link inner and outer Copenhagen (www.m.dk) (www.hur.dk) (www.dsb.dk/s-tog) (www.dsb.dk).

→ TAXIS

Vacant taxis carry a green light and a sign with the word FRI (free) on display. Credit cards are usually accepted; receipts given on request. Basic fare Kr19 (hailed), Kr32 (phone-booking); Kr10 pkm (6am-4pm) and Kr11 pkm (4pm-7am) and Kr13 Fri-Sat 11pm-7am; no need to tip in addition to the amount shown on the meter. ✆ 38 10 10 10 (Taxa Motor), ✆ 35 35 35 35 (Københavns Taxa), ✆ 70 25 25 25 (Codan Taxa). Taxi tours with foreign-language-speaking driver or guide can be arranged for a max of 4 persons at a fixed price. ✆ 38 10 10 10 (Taxa Motor), ✆ 35 35 35 35 (Taxa), ✆ 32 51 51 51 (Amager-Øbro Taxi).

→ COPENHAGEN CARD

Valid for unlimited transport by train, bus and metro, free entry to more than 60 museums and sights, as well as discounts on many attractions and on car rental throughout the Greater Copenhagen region. 24hr-card €29 (child €19); 72hr-card €58 (child €33) on sale at the airport, major railway stations and at tourist information offices throughout Denmark.

→ FREE CYCLES

Brightly painted bicycles, lined up in racks, are available to citizens and tourists for the deposit of a Dkr20 coin. The coin will release a cycle from a stand for an unlimited period and is retrieved when the cycle is returned to any of the 150 stands in the city.

USEFUL ADDRESSES

→ TOURIST INFORMATION

Copenhagen Right Now: Vesterbrogade 4A *Plan I* **B3**, ✆ 70 222 442. Open May-June, Mon-Sat, 9am-6pm; Jul-Aug, Mon-Sat 9am-8pm, Sun 10am-6pm; Jan-Apr and Sep-Dec, Mon-Fri 9am-4pm, Sat 9am-2pm (www.visitcopenhagen.com) (www.visitdenmark.com).

→ POST OFFICES

Opening times Mon-Sat 9/10am to 5/6pm (12/2pm Sat). Longer hours at the post office at the **Central Station**.

→ BANKS/CURRENCY EXCHANGE

Opening times Mon-Fri 10am-4pm (6pm Thurs). Exchange facilities available outside these hours in the centre of Copenhagen, at the Central Railway Station and at the Airport. ATMs available at most banks and at metro stations.

→ EMERGENCY

Dial ✆ **112** for Police, Fire Brigade, Ambulance.

BUSY PERIODS

It may be difficult to find a room at a reasonable price when special events are held in the city:

Copenhagen Fashion Fair Festival: February and mid August.

Copenhagen Jazz Festival: early July.

Copenhagen International Film Festival: August-September.

Christmas Market: mid November to December.

DIFFERENT FACETS OF THE CITY

It is possible to visit the main sights and museums in two to three days.

Museums and sights are usually open from 10/12am to 3/6pm. Many are closed on Monday.

OLD TOWN – **Slotsholmen**: Island surrounded by a canal on which stands **Christiansborg Slot**, fifth castle built on the site since 1167, housing the Danish Parliament *(Folketing)*, the Supreme Court and royal reception halls; **Marmorbroen**, rococo marble bridge as western entrance to castle courtyard. **Børsen** *Plan I* **C3**: Stock Exchange in the Dutch Renaissance style, founded by Christian IV in 1619. North of the island is a network of narrow streets and charming squares, mostly pedestrianised, lined with 18C terraced houses, cafés and boutiques, and bisected by **Strøget**, the main shopping street. **Vor Frue Kirke** *Plan I* **C2**: Neo-Classical cathedral designed in 1829 with sculptures by Thorwaldsen. Just north of the Old Town is **Rosenborg Slot** *Plan I* **C2**: Fine example of Dutch Renaissance style, built by Christian IV in 1633 as a summer pavilion, now housing the personal collections of the royal family.

NEW TOWN – **Kongens Nytorv** *Plan I* **C2**: the square, lined by impressive buildings, was the first feature of the New Town to be built. **Nyhavn** *Plan I* **D2**: 17C canal lined with warehouses and wharves, now restored or converted into restaurants, bars and cafés. **Amalienborg Palace** *Plan I* **D2**: Royal residence since 1794; changing of the guard daily at noon. **Marmorkirken** *Plan I* **D2**: 18C domed marble church, also called Frederiks Kirke.

MUSEUMS AND GALLERIES – **Nationalmuseet** *Plan I* **C3**: Denmark's history from prehistoric times to AD 1000. **Ny Carlsberg Glyptotek** *Plan I* **C3**: French art from 19C and 20C, Impressionist and Post-Impressionist works, sculptures by Degas and Rodin. **Statens Museum for Kunst** *Plan I* **C1**: Danish Fine Arts Museum displaying the royal art collections: foreign (20C French paintings) and Danish art (Edvard Munch). **Thorvaldsens Museum** *Plan I* **C3**: Memorial to Denmark's most famous sculptor, Bertel Thordvaldsen (1170-1844). **Hans Christian Andersen Museum** *Plan I* **D2**: The author's study and personal effects, photos, letters and a manuscript.

LOCAL COLOUR – **Tivoli Gardens** *Plan I* **B3**: one of the oldest and most prestigious amusement parks, lit at night by 1000 Venetian lanterns in the trees – carousels and crazy rides, concerts and restaurants; also site of the Copenhagen Christmas Market. **Den Lille Havfrue** *Plan I* **D1**: the Little Mermaid statue by Evard Eriksen perches on a rock gazing at the harbour entrance; behind her is the **Citadel of Kastellet**, an 18C fortification. **Waterfront**: experience the view from the water on the Movia waterbus or a guided harbour and canal cruise.

GOURMET TREATS

There are several excellent restaurants serving fish or seafood in the canal district near **Højbro Plads** *Plan I* **C2** and **Gammel Strand**. The place for the in-crowd is the **Kongens Nytorv** district : trendy cafés in the French or modern Scandinavia style. In **Nyhavn** *Plan I* **D2** popular restaurants and cafés, with tables on the waterside pavements in summer, have replaced the former sailors' taverns; many serve traditional Danish dishes, including the famous **smørrebrød**, but tend to charge for location as much as for food. The neighbouring streets offer better value. There are several good restaurants and cafés in **Gråbrødre Torv** *Plan I* **C2**. Ethnic restaurants are to be found in the **Vesterbro** district *Plan I* **A3**; **Nørrebro** *Plan I* **A1** will be more to the taste of those on a slim budget.

If you fancy real ale, try **Brewpub**, Copenhagen's new microbrewery, where there is new beer on draught every week.

SHOPPING

Stores are usually open from 9.30/10am to 5.30/7pm (Sat 9/10am-4pm) but they can stay open from 6am-8pm. Alcohol sales are forbidden after 8pm.

Strøget *Plan I* **C2** and **Købmagergade** are the two main shopping streets: for department stores (Magasin du Nord, Illum) **Strøget**; for fashion and knitwear **Kronprinsensgade**, **Adelgade** and **Ny Østergade**; for art, antiques and cutting edge design **Bredgade**; for avant-garde, underground and up-and-coming boutiques **Larsbjørnsstraede**; for sweaters **Nytorv**; for antiques **Kompagnistraede** *Plan I* **C3** and **Ravnsborggade** and neighbouring streets in the Nørrebro district.

The Danish flair for style is also on show at the **Danish Design Centre** (Dansk Design Center, H C Andersens Bld 27), the **Royal Copenhagen Welcome Centre** (Søndre Fasanvey 5), the **House of Amber** (6 Nygade and 34 Frederiksberggade) and various hand-made glass studios: **Glasseriet** (Jenagade 27); **Hagenglas** (Slotsgade 52E).

WHAT TO BUY – Royal Copenhagen porcelain, Holmegaard glassware, Georg Jensen silver, Bang & Olufsen stereo equipment, jewellery (amber), embroidery, linen, children's toys.

ENTERTAINMENT

Copenhagen This Week, published in English, is a good source of information on shopping, sightseeing, museums, music, theatre and films (www.ctw.dk).

CONCERT HALLS – Opera House. Tivoli Gardens Concert Hall *Plan I* **B3**. Black Diamond Radiohusets Koncertsal.

OTHER VENUES – Royal Danish Theatre Det Ny Teater *Plan I* **D2**. Dansescenen. Kanonhallen. Filmhuset. IMAX Tycho Brahe Planetarium.

NIGHTLIFE

Copenhagen This Week, published in English, prints a good selection. The most trendy bars and cafés are to be found in **Vesterbro** *Plan I* **A3** and **Nørrebro** *Plan I* **A1**, two districts which are transformed at night when DJ's change stylish brasseries into lively bars. There are also one or two night clubs round **Kongens Nytorv** *Plan I* **C2** and in the **Old Town**. For gambling there is the **Casino Copenhagen** (Amager Bld 70).

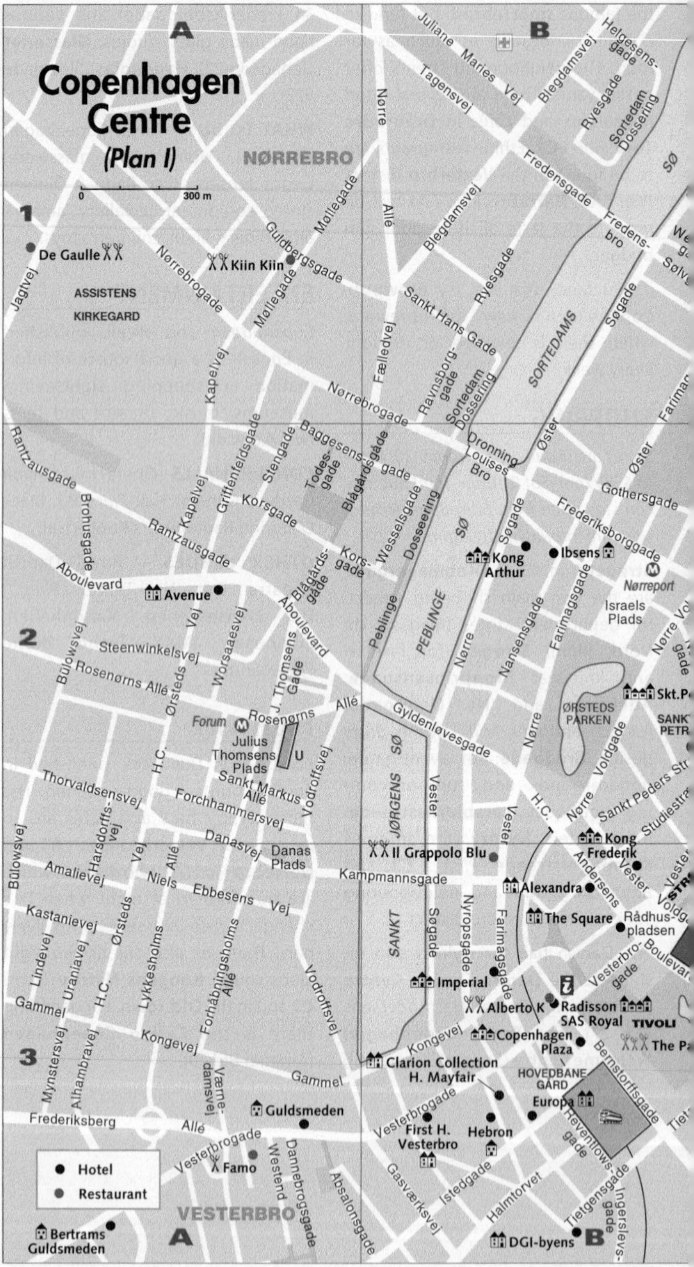

Copenhagen Centre
(Plan I)

0 300 m

A B
1 2 3

- ● Hotel
- ● Restaurant

NØRREBRO
VESTERBRO
ASSISTENS KIRKEGARD
PEBLINGE SØ
SORTEDAMS SØ
SANKT JØRGENS SØ
ØRSTEDS PARKEN
TIVOLI
HOVEDBANE GÅRD
Israels Plads
Julius Thomsens Plads
Danas Plads
Rådhuspladsen
Forum
Nørreport

De Gaulle
Kiin Kiin
Avenue
Kong Arthur
Ibsens
Skt. Pe
Kong Frederik
Il Grappolo Blu
Alexandra
The Square
Imperial
Alberto K
Radisson SAS Royal
Copenhagen Plaza
The Pa
Clarion Collection H. Mayfair
Europa
Hebron
First H. Vesterbro
Guldsmeden
Famo
Bertrams Guldsmeden
DGI-byens

Juliane Maries Vej
Tagensvej
Blegdamsvej
Helgesensgade
Ryesgade
Sortedam Dossering
Nørre Allé
Fredensgade
Fredensbro
Møllegade
Guldbergsgade
Nørrebrogade
Jagtvej
Sankt Hans Gade
Fælledvej
Ravnsborggade
Søgade
Kapelvej
Griffenfeldsgade
Stengade
Baggesensgade
Todesgade
Blågårdsgade
Dronning Louises Bro
Øster Farimagsgade
Gothersgade
Frederiksborggade
Rantzausgade
Brohusgade
Korsgade
Wesselsgade
Peblinge Dossering
Aboulevard
Nansensgade
Farimagsgade
Nørre Voldgade
Bülowsvej
Steenwinkelsvej
Rosenørns Allé
Ørsteds Vej
Worsaaesvej
J. Thomsens Gade
Gyldenløvesgade
H.C. Ørsteds Vej
Vodroffsvej
Thorvaldsensvej
Sankt Markus Allé
Forchhammersvej
Danasvej
Vester Søgade
Sankt Peders Stræde
Studiestræde
H.C. Andersens Boulevard
Harsdorffsvej
Amalievej
Niels Ebbesens Vej
Kampmannsgade
Nyropsgade
Vester Farimagsgade
Kastanievej
Lindevej
Uraniavej
Lykkesholms Allé
Forhåbningsholms Allé
Vesterbrogade
Gammel Kongevej
Mynstersvej
Alhambravej
Værnedamsvej
Frederiksberg Allé
Westend
Dannebrogsgade
Absalonsgade
Gasværksvej
Istedgade
Halmtorvet
Reventlowsgade
Tietgensgade
Ingerslevsgade
Bernstorffsgade

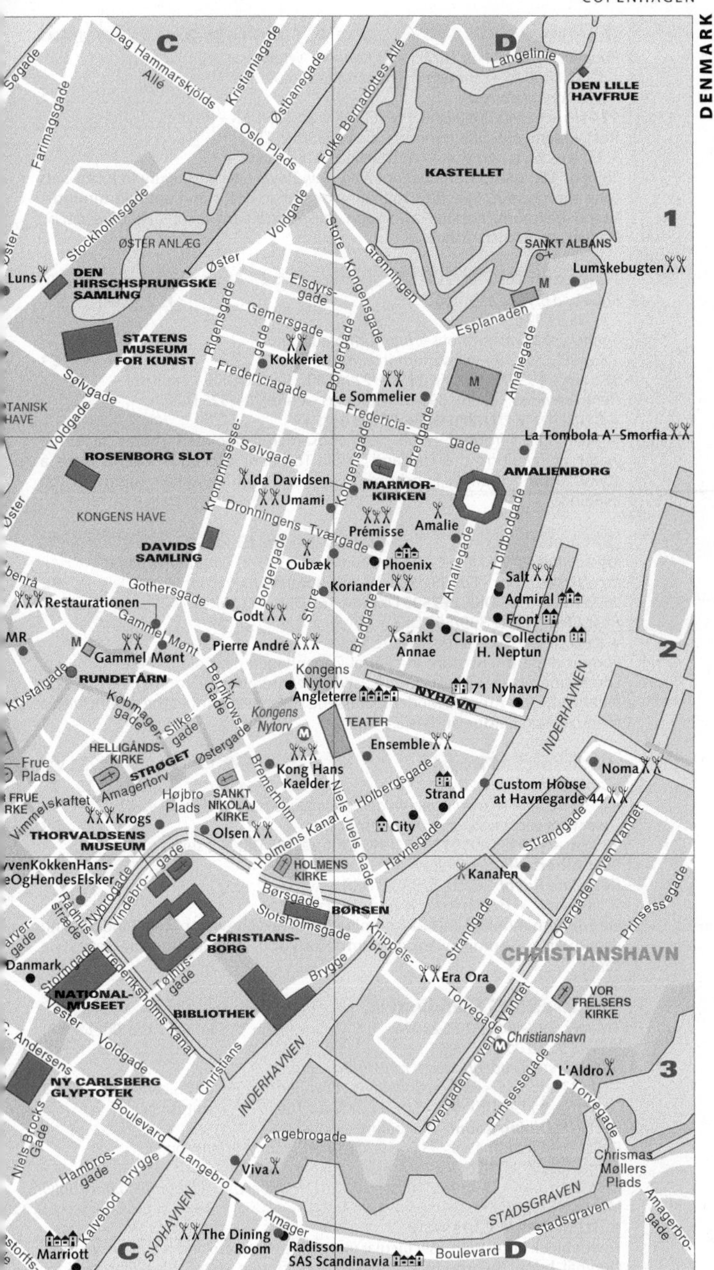
KASTELLET
DEN LILLE HAVFRUE
ØSTER ANLÆG
DEN HIRSCHSPRUNGSKE SAMLING
STATENS MUSEUM FOR KUNST
ROSENBORG SLOT
KONGENS HAVE
DAVIDS SAMLING
AMALIENBORG
MARMOR-KIRKEN
RUNDETÅRN
HELLIGÅNDS-KIRKE
STRØGET
SANKT NIKOLAJ KIRKE
THORVALDSENS MUSEUM
HOLMENS KIRKE
BØRSEN
CHRISTIANS-BORG
NATIONAL-MUSEET
BIBLIOTHEK
NY CARLSBERG GLYPTOTEK
CHRISTIANSHAVN
VOR FRELSERS KIRKE
NYHAVN
INDERHAVNEN
Lumskebugten
La Tombola A' Smorfia
Kokkeriet
Le Sommelier
Ida Davidsen
Umami
Prémisse
Amalie
Oubæk
Phoenix
Koriander
Salt
Admiral
Front
Restaurationen
Godt
Sankt Annae
Clarion Collection H. Neptun
Gammel Mønt
Pierre André
Angleterre
71 Nyhavn
Ensemble
Kong Hans Kaelder
Noma
Custom House at Havnegarde 44
Strand
Krogs
City
Olsen
Kanalen
Era Ora
L'Aldro
Viva
The Dining Room
Radisson SAS Scandinavia
Marriott
Danmark
Luns
STADSGRAVEN
SYDHAVNEN

DENMARK

Angleterre

Kongens Nytorv 34 ✉ 1022 K – Ⓜ Kongens Nytorv – ✆ 33 12 00 95 – remmen@remmen.dk – Fax 33 12 11 18 – www.dangleterre.dk **C2**

114 rm – 2340/2680 DKK 3760 DKK, ☕ 155 DKK – 9 suites

Rest – Menu 495 DKK (dinner) – Carte 535/685 DKK

◆ Grand Luxury ◆ Traditional ◆ Classic ◆

Elegant 18C grand hotel overlooking New Royal Square. Luxury in lobby sets tone throughout. Spacious rooms enjoy classic décor and antique furniture. Grand ballroom. Popular afternoon teas. Restaurant in marine blue décor; Danish and French dishes.

Copenhagen Marriott

Kalvebod Brygge 5 ✉ 1560 – ✆ 88 33 99 00 – mhrs.cphdk.reservations@marriotthotels.com – Fax 88 33 99 99 – www.marriott.com/cphdk **C3**

386 rm – 999/2299 DKK 999/2299 DKK, ☕ 150 DKK – 9 suites

Rest *Terraneo* – Menu 395 DKK (dinner) – Carte 205/525 DKK

◆ Luxury ◆ Business ◆ Modern ◆

Striking, glass-fronted hotel, its handsomely appointed rooms face the water or overlook the city and Tivoli. Top-floor executive rooms share a stylish private lounge. Lunchtime buffet and Mediterranean cuisine in the evening.

Skt.Petri

Krystalgade 22 ✉ 1172 K – Ⓜ Nørreport – ✆ 33 45 91 00 – reservation@hotelsktpetri.com – Fax 33 45 91 10 – www.hotelsktpetri.com **B2**

257 rm – 1995 DKK 2595 DKK, ☕ 165 DKK – 11 suites

Rest *Bleu* – Carte 335/565 DKK

◆ Luxury ◆ Business ◆ Design ◆

Former department store in central Copenhagen near old St Peter's Church. Large open-plan atrium. Bright, stylish contemporary rooms with design features by Per Arnoldi. Modern, brasserie style restaurant in the atrium with a menu mixing Europe and Asia.

Radisson SAS Royal

< Copenhagen,

Hammerichsgade 1 ✉ 1611 V – ✆ 33 42 60 00 – royal.copenhagen@radissonsas.com – Fax 33 42 61 00 – www.royal.copenhagen.radissonsas.com **B3**

258 rm – 1995 DKK 1495/1995 DKK, ☕ 165 DKK – 2 suites

Rest Alberto K – see below

Rest *Café Royal* – Carte 323/428 DKK

◆ Luxury ◆ Business ◆ Modern ◆

Large international hotel block dominating the skyline west of Tivoli and offering superb views. Scandinavian bedroom décor. Popular ground floor brasserie style café.

Radisson SAS Scandinavia

< Copenhagen,

Amager Boulevard 70 ✉ 2300 S – ✆ 33 96 50 00 – scandinavia.copenhagen@radissonsas.com – Fax 33 96 55 55 – www.scandinavia.copenhagen.radissonsas.com **C3**

538 rm – 1795 DKK 945/1795 DKK, ☕ 160 DKK – 4 suites

Rest *The Dining Room* – see below

Rest *Blue Elephant* – *✆ 33 96 59 70 (closed Sunday) (dinner only)* Menu 405/595 DKK

Rest *Kyoto* – *✆ 33 32 16 74 (closed 22-26 December and 1 January) (dinner only)* Menu 290/390 DKK

◆ Business ◆ Classic ◆

Tower block hotel with spectacular views. Shops, casino and bar in busy lobby. Original bright bedrooms themed in six different styles. Blue Elephant for authentic Thai cuisine. Kyoto for Japanese menu.

Imperial rm 200 VISA

Vester Farimagsgade 9 ✉ 1606 V – ✆ 33 12 80 00 – imperialhotel@arp-hansen.dk – Fax 33 93 80 03 – www.imperialhotel.dk **B3**

239 rm – 1695 DKK 1090/2040 DKK, 135 DKK – 1 suite

Rest *The Grill Room* – *(dinner only)* Menu 440 DKK – Carte 360/590 DKK

Rest *Imperial Brasserie* – *✆ 33 43 20 83* – Menu 280 DKK (dinner)

♦ Traditional ♦ Classic ♦

Large mid 20C hotel, renovated in 2006, on a wide city thoroughfare. Well serviced rooms range in size and are comfortable, stylish and elegantly decorated. Fine dining in attractive indoor "winter garden". Less formal dining in ground floor brasserie.

Copenhagen Plaza rm 25 VISA

Bernstorffsgade 4 ✉ 1577 V – ✆ 33 14 92 62 – copenhagenplaza@profilhotels.dk – Fax 33 93 93 62 – www.profilhotels.dk **B3**

87 rm – 2150 DKK 2150/2350 DKK, 145 DKK – 6 suites

Rest *Flora Danica* – Menu 295/595 DKK – Carte 275/475 DKK

♦ Traditional ♦ Cosy ♦

Venerable hotel commissioned in the early 20C by King Frederik VIII and overlooking Tivoli Gardens. Classically styled, cosy rooms and an atmospheric library bar. A modern, welcoming brasserie with a French-based menu.

Admiral 140 P VISA

Toldbodgade 24-28 ✉ 1253 – Ⓜ Kongens Nytorv – ✆ 33 74 14 14 – admiral@admiralhotel.dk – Fax 33 74 14 16 – www.admiralhotel.dk **D2**

366 rm – 1640 DKK 1640/2600 DKK, 120 DKK

Rest see ***Salt*** below

♦ Business ♦ Modern ♦

Converted 18C dockside warehouse with some rooms facing passing liners. Maritime theme throughout. Compact bedrooms complement the rustic charm.

Kong Arthur rm 50 P VISA

Nørre Søgade 11 ✉ 1370 K – Ⓜ Nørreport – ✆ 33 11 12 12 – hotel@kongarthur.dk – Fax 33 32 61 30 – www.kongarthur.dk **B2**

117 rm – 1570 DKK 1570/3070 DKK

Rest *Sticks 'n' Sushi* – *✆ 33 11 14 07* – Menu 168/265 DKK

♦ Traditional ♦ Family ♦ Classic ♦

Pleasant family run hotel on elegant late 19C residential avenue by Peblinge lake. Bedrooms divided between three different buildings. Sticks 'n' Sushi for Japanese dishes.

Kong Frederik rm 40 VISA

Vester Voldgade 25 ✉ 1552 V – ✆ 33 12 59 02 – remmen@remmen.dk – Fax 33 93 59 01 – www.remmen.dk **B3**

108 rm – 1300 DKK 1930 DKK, 135 DKK – 2 suites

Rest *Le Coq Rouge* – *✆ 33 42 48 48* – Menu 345 DKK (dinner) – Carte 319/595 DKK

♦ Traditional ♦ Classic ♦

Classic elegant old building in good location. Traditional style décor with dark wood panelling. Comfortable rooms with old-fashioned furniture. Atrium style banquet hall. Wood-panelled, atmospheric brasserie offering traditional Danish cooking.

Phoenix rm 90 VISA

Bredgade 37 ✉ 1260 K – Ⓜ Kongens Nytorv – ✆ 33 95 95 00 – phoenixcopenhagen@arp-hansen.dk – Fax 33 33 98 33 – www.phoenixcopenhagen.dk **D2**

210 rm – 1960 DKK 1450/2075 DKK, 135 DKK – 3 suites

Rest *Von Plessen* – *(closed Sunday and Monday) (dinner only)* Menu 255/525 DKK – Carte 385/405 DKK

♦ Traditional ♦ Classic ♦

Parts of this elegant hotel, located in the lively modern art and antiques district, date from the 17C. It features a grand marbled lobby and comfortable high ceilinged rooms. Elegant basement dining room with discreet décor in neutral tones.

Island
Kalvebod Brygge 53 ✉ 1560 – ✆ 33 38 96 00 – copenhagenisland@arp-hansen.dk – Fax 33 38 96 01 – www.copenhagenisland.dk
326 rm – †1525/1875 DKK ††1875/3375 DKK, ☕ 95 DKK
Rest *The Harbour* – Menu 330/380 DKK (dinner) – Carte 370/458 DKK
♦ Business ♦ Design ♦
A gleaming glass and steel structure on a man-made island in the harbour. Vast atrium with suspended walkways. Well-equipped bedrooms, some with balconies. Stylish multi-levelled lounge bar and restaurant with menu for all tastes.

The Square without rest
Rådhuspladsen 14 ✉ 1550 V – ✆ 33 38 12 00 – thesquare@arp-hansen.dk – Fax 33 38 12 01 – www.thesquare.dk **B3**
268 rm – †1890 DKK ††2390/3590 DKK, ☕ 95 DKK
♦ Business ♦ Design ♦
Ideally located hotel in Town Hall Square. Breakfast room on 6th floor with view of city roofs. Good sized modern bedrooms with square theme in décor and fabrics.

Front
Sankt Annae Plads 21 ✉ 1022 K – Ⓜ Kongens Nytorv – ✆ 33 13 34 00 – info@front.dk – Fax 33 11 77 07 – www.front.dk **D2**
131 rm – ††1670/2930 DKK, ☕ 145 DKK
Rest – Menu 275 DKK (dinner) – Carte 165/195 DKK
♦ Business ♦ Stylish ♦
Behind the understated façade lies a thoroughly modern and stylish hotel. All bedrooms boast plenty of mod cons and the best views are over the dockside. Equally stylish restaurant with a contemporary menu to match.

Strand without rest
Havnegade 37 ✉ 1058 K – Ⓜ Kongens Nytorv – ✆ 33 48 99 00 – copenhagenstrand@arp-hansen.dk – Fax 33 48 99 01 – www.copenhagenstrand.dk **D2**
172 rm ☕ – †1825 DKK ††990/1825 DKK – 2 suites
♦ Business ♦ Modern ♦
Modern warehouse conversion on waterfront and a useful central location. Comfortable and well-kept bedrooms with dark wood furniture and bright colours.

Avenue without rest
Åboulevard 29, Frederiksberg C ✉ 1960 – Ⓜ Forum – ✆ 35 37 31 11 – info@avenuehotel.dk – Fax 35 37 31 33 – www.avenuehotel.dk
closed 22 December-2 January **A2**
68 rm ☕ – †1175 DKK ††1125/1375 DKK
♦ Business ♦ Design ♦
Restored and refurbished in 2005, the hotel is housed within a building dating from 1898. The smart bedrooms are bright and crisp in style, well equipped and comfortable.

First H. Vesterbro
Vesterbrogade 23-29 ✉ 1620 V – ✆ 33 78 80 00 – reception.copenhagen@firsthotels.dk – Fax 33 78 80 80 – www.firsthotels.com **B3**
403 rm – †1745 DKK ††1145/1945 DKK, ☕ 125 DKK
Rest – *(closed Sunday) (dinner only)* Carte 80/200 DKK
♦ Business ♦ Modern ♦
Large modern hotel with metal and glass façade on busy avenue. All bedrooms have good modern facilities in a contemporary style; superior rooms are larger. Informal dining in front bar from international menu.

71 Nyhavn

Nyhavn 71 ✉ 1051 K – Ⓜ Kongens Nytorv – ☎ 33 43 62 00 – 71nyhavnhotel@arp-hansen.dk – Fax 33 43 62 01 – www.71nyhavnhotel.dk **D2**

142 rm – †1550 DKK ††1840/2420 DKK, ☕ 135 DKK – 8 suites – **Rest *Pakhus Kaelder*** – *(closed Sunday and Bank Holidays)* Menu 345/395 DKK (dinner)

♦ Business ♦ Stylish ♦

Charming converted warehouse by the canal. Interior features low ceilings with wooden beams throughout. Compact comfortable bedrooms, many with views of passing ships. Cellar restaurant with low wood-beamed ceiling. Interesting, seasonal menus.

Alexandra

H.C. Andersens Boulevard 8 ✉ 1553 V – ☎ 33 74 44 44 – reservations@hotel-alexandra.dk – Fax 33 74 44 88 – www.hotel-alexandra.dk

closed 24-27 December **B3**

61 rm ☕ – †1395 DKK ††1395/2095 DKK

Rest *Mühlhausen* – ☎ *33 74 44 66 (closed Sunday lunch)* Carte 328/355 DKK

♦ Traditional ♦ Classic ♦

Classic 19C hotel conveniently located for city centre. Some special design rooms feature Danish style furniture and fittings and an original painting in each. Banquettes and crisp linen in a stylish brasserie with a Mediterranean tone.

Clarion Collection H. Neptun

Sankt Annae Plads 18-20 ✉ 1250 K – Ⓜ Kongens Nytorv – ☎ 33 96 20 00 – cc.neptun@choice.dk – Fax 33 96 20 66 – www.choicehotels.dk

closed 22 December-3 January **D2**

133 rm – †1715 DKK ††1295/2300 DKK, ☕ 125 DKK

Rest *Gendarmen* – ☎ *33 93 66 55 (closed Sunday and Bank Holidays) (dinner only)* Carte 385/470 DKK

♦ Business ♦ Functional ♦

Converted from two characterful neighbouring houses in the popular Nyhavn district. Rooms are fitted with light wood furniture and offer good range of facilities. Rustic restaurant with traditional Danish menu; courtyard breakfast room.

Europa without rest

Colbjørnsensgade 5-11 ✉ 1652 V – ☎ 33 21 33 33 – co.europa@choice.dk – Fax 33 31 33 99 – www.choicehotels.dk **B3**

230 rm – †1545 DKK ††1595/1995 DKK, ☕ 95 DKK

♦ Chain hotel ♦ Modern ♦

Centrally located chain hotel fully renovated in 2002. Bedrooms are compact but tidy and decorated in a bright Nordic style. Comfortable breakfast room.

DGI-byen

Tietgensgade 65 ✉ 1704 V – ☎ 33 29 80 00 – info@dgi-byen.dk – Fax 33 29 80 80 – www.dgi-byen.dk

closed 22-27 December **B3**

104 rm ☕ – †1495 DKK ††1495 DKK

Rest *Vestauranten* – ☎ *33 29 80 30* – Menu 150/295 DKK

♦ Business ♦ Functional ♦

Turn of millennium hotel, part of huge, modern leisure complex with all the equipment. Minimalist bedrooms with simple, clean style and up-to-date facilities. Bright restaurant in original building offering a varied menu; pleasant terrace.

Clarion Collection H. Mayfair without rest

Helgolandsgade 3 ✉ 1653 V – ☎ 70 12 17 00 – cc.mayfair@choice.dk – Fax 33 23 96 86 – www.choicehotels.dk

closed 22 December-3 January **B3**

103 rm – †1595 DKK ††1595 DKK, ☕ 95 DKK – 3 suites

♦ Business ♦ Functional ♦

Large well run hotel usefully located near station. Interior décor and furniture in classic English style. Neat rooms, well equipped with mod cons. Relaxing bar.

City without rest — 20 VISA

Peder Skrams Gade 24 ✉ 1054 K – Ⓜ Kongens Nytorv – ☎ 33 13 06 66 – hotelcity@hotelcity.dk – Fax 33 13 06 67 – www.hotelcity.dk **D2**

81 rm – 1350 DKK 1350/1550 DKK

♦ Business ♦ Functional ♦

Usefully positioned, functional hotel between the city centre and docks. Simple and tidy Danish style interior décor with appropriate room facilities.

Danmark without rest — VISA

Vester Voldgade 89 ✉ 1552 V – ☎ 33 11 48 06 – hotel@hotel-danmark.dk – Fax 33 14 36 30 – www.hotel-danmark.dk **C3**

88 rm – 1360 DKK

♦ Business ♦ Classic ♦

Centrally located close to Tivoli Gardens, offers well kept functional rooms with traditional Scandinavian style décor. Newer rooms in older building are the best.

Bertrams Hotel Guldsmeden — VISA

Vesterbrogade 107 ✉ 1620 V – ☎ 33 25 04 05 – bertrams@hotelguldsmeden.dk – Fax 33 25 04 02 – www.hotelguldsmeden.dk **A3**

47 rm – 1495 DKK 1195/1895 DKK

Rest – *(closed Sunday and Bank Holidays) (dinner only)* Carte 211/218 DKK

♦ Family ♦ Personalised ♦

Opened in 2006 and sister hotel to Guldsmeden. It shares the same bright decor with most bedrooms looking out onto a courtyard. Four poster beds and balconies also available. Organic breakfasts and a warm, café style restaurant with set menu.

Ibsens — rm VISA

Vendersgade 23 ✉ 1363 K – Ⓜ Nørreport – ☎ 33 13 19 13 – hotel@ibsenshotel.dk – Fax 33 13 19 16 – www.ibsenshotel.dk **B2**

118 rm – 1270 DKK 1270/2320 DKK

Rest *La Rocca* – Menu 168/265 DKK – **Rest *Pintxos*** – Menu 168/265 DKK

♦ Business ♦ Classic ♦

Large characterful converted apartment block next to sister hotel Kong Arthur. Variety of neat rooms with good facilities. Superior top floor bedrooms. Modern La Rocca for formal Italian dining. Pintxos offers authentic Spanish tapas dinner menu.

Guldsmeden without rest — VISA

Vesterbrogade 66 ✉ 1620 V – ☎ 33 22 15 00 – carlton@hotelguldsmeden.dk – Fax 33 22 15 55 – www.hotelguldsmeden.dk **A3**

64 rm – 1395 DKK 1395/1595 DKK

♦ Family ♦ Personalised ♦

Family owned with a relaxing bohemian atmosphere. Extensive, mouthwatering organic breakfasts. Rooms are in a French colonial style: some are in annex, some with balconies.

Hebron without rest — 50 VISA

Helgolandsgade 4 ✉ 1653 V – ☎ 33 31 69 06 – info@hebron.dk – Fax 33 31 90 67 – www.hebron.dk

closed Christmas **B3**

93 rm – 1150 DKK 1550 DKK – 6 suites

♦ Traditional ♦ Functional ♦

When it opened in 1900 it was one of the biggest hotels in the city and some of the original features remain. Simple, clean and uncluttered bedrooms.

Prémisse — 16 VISA

Dronningens Tvaergade 2 ✉ 1302 K – Ⓜ Kongens Nytorv – ☎ 33 11 11 45 – mail@premisse.dk – Fax 33 11 11 68 – www.premisse.dk – closed Easter, 2 July-6 August, 23 December-3 January, Saturday lunch, Sunday and Bank Holidays

Rest – Menu 350/750 DKK – Carte 650/870 DKK **D2**

♦ Innovative ♦ Formal ♦

17C vaulted cellar restaurant further enhanced by modern décor. Wine cellar on view. Open-plan kitchen serving uncompromisingly adventurous menu with original flavours.

XXX ✿

Kong Hans Kaelder VISA MC AE D

Vingårdsstraede 6 ✉ 1070 K – Ⓜ Kongens Nytorv – ✆ 33 11 68 68 – kontakt@konghans.dk – Fax 33 32 67 68 – www.konghans.dk
closed 3 weeks in summer and last week December except 31 December **C2**

Rest – *(booking essential)* Carte approx. 790 DKK

Spec. Foie gras with rye bread, elderberries and mead. Fillet of Danish beef with broccoli and oxtail sauce. Apples and cowberries with salted caramel and apple sorbet.

♦ Modern ♦ Formal ♦

Discreetly located side street restaurant in vaulted Gothic cellar with wood flooring. Fine dining experience; classically based cooking. Friendly and dedicated service.

XXX

Restaurationen VISA MC AE D

Møntergade 19 ✉ 1116 K – Ⓜ Kongens Nytorv – ✆ 33 14 94 95 – Fax 33 14 85 30 – www.restaurationen.com – closed 1-9 April, 4-7 May, July-27 August, 22 December-8 January, Sunday and Monday **C2**

Rest – *(booking essential) (dinner only except Christmas) (set menu only)* Menu 660 DKK

♦ Classic ♦ Friendly ♦

A long standing and personally run restaurant. Accomplished classically based Danish cooking using well sourced ingredients, accompanied by a comprehensive wine list.

XXX

Pierre André VISA MC AE D

Ny Østergade 21 ✉ 1101 K – Ⓜ Kongens Nytorv – ✆ 33 16 17 19 – Fax 33 16 17 72 – www.pierreandre.dk
closed Easter, 3 weeks July-August, 24-26 December, 1 January, Sunday, Monday, Saturday lunch and Bank Holidays **C2**

Rest – *(booking essential)* Menu 395/780 DKK – Carte 530/755 DKK

♦ French ♦ Formal ♦

Elegant, comfortable dining room with stylish décor in an attractive old building. Full-flavoured cuisine on a classical French base. Efficient and attentive service.

XXX

Krogs AC VISA MC AE D

Gammel Strand 38 ✉ 1201 K – ✆ 33 15 89 15 – krogs@krogs.dk – Fax 33 15 83 19 – www.krogs.dk – closed 18-30 December and Sunday **C2**

Rest – *(booking essential) (dinner only)* Menu 565/1050 DKK – Carte 190/480 DKK

♦ Seafood ♦ Formal ♦

Characterful 18C house pleasantly located by canal. Classic room with high ceiling, well lit through large end window. Formal service; seafood dishes attractively presented.

XX ✿

Formel B (Jochumsen/Møller) AC ⇔30 VISA MC AE D

Vesterbrogade 182-184, Frederiksberg (via Vesterbrogade) ✉ 1800 C – ✆ 33 25 10 66 – info@formel-b.dk – www.formel-b.dk – closed 23-26 December and Sunday

Rest – *(booking essential) (dinner only)* Menu 700 DKK – Carte 650/1475 DKK

Spec. Turbot with pickled green tomato and caviar. Glazed lobster tart with baby vegetables. Chocolate fondant with panna cotta and vanilla ice cream.

♦ Innovative ♦ Neighbourhood ♦

Chic restaurant on the ground floor of an attractive period house. Sleek interior with sandstone and granite. Set menu: precise cooking with well chosen accompanying wines.

XX ✿

Ensemble (Schou/Egebol) VISA MC AE D

Tordenskjoldsgade 11 ✉ 1055 K – Ⓜ Kongens Nytorv – ✆ 33 11 33 52 – kontakt@restaurantensemble.dk – Fax 33 11 33 92 – www.restaurantensemble.dk –closed July, Christmas, Sun day and Monday **D2**

Rest – *(set menu only) (dinner only)* Menu 600 DKK

Spec. Codfish with oysters and wild mushrooms. Lobster with Jerusalem artichoke, lemon and watercress. Braised veal shank with truffle, celery and beetroot.

♦ Modern ♦ Formal ♦

Whites, greys and bright lighting add to the clean, fresh feel. Open-plan kitchen. Detailed and refined cooking from a set menu with attentive and courteous service.

XX ✿

Era Ora

Overgaden neden Vandet 33B ✉ 1414 K – Ⓜ Christianshavn – ✆ 32 54 06 93 – era-ora@era-ora.dk – Fax 32 96 02 09 – www.era-ora.dk
closed 1 day Easter, 24-26 December, 1 January and Sunday **D3**
Rest – *(booking essential at dinner) (set menu only)* Menu 325/990 DKK
Spec. Lime marinated halibut with green apple spiced with chilli. Duck orecchiette with rosemary. Sorbet of melon wth coconut sauce.
♦ Italian ♦ Formal ♦
Stylish, discreetly located canalside restaurant with an excellent overview of the best of Italian cuisine, by offering diners a large array of small dishes. Good wine list.

XX ✿✿

Noma (Redzepi)

⇔40 VISA MC AE

Strandgade 93 ✉ 1401 K – Ⓜ Christianshavn – ✆ 32 96 32 97 – noma@noma.dk – www.noma.dk – closed Easter, Sunday and lunch Monday and Saturday
Rest – Menu 298 DKK (lunch) – Carte 570/780 DKK **D2**
Spec. King crab and leeks with mussel jus. Musk ox with dark beer, wild herbs and beets. Sheep's yoghurt "in textures".
♦ Innovative ♦ Design ♦
Converted 19C harbour warehouse with designer fittings. Talented chefs producing original and innovative dishes with ingredients from Iceland, Greenland and the Faroe Islands.

XX ✿

MR (Refslund)

⇔25 VISA MC AE

Kultorvet 5 ✉ 1175 K – ✆ 33 91 09 49 – mr@mr-restaurant.dk – www.mr-restaurant.dk
closed 5-9 April, 1 week in summer, 21 December-2 January and Sunday
Rest – *(dinner only) (booking essential) (set menu only)* Menu 500/1000 DKK **C2**
Spec. Beetroot with goat's cheese and plums. Monkfish with pumpkin and marjoram. Chestnuts with apple, yoghurt and wheat syrup.
♦ Modern ♦ Fashionable ♦
18C three-storey town house on paved square. Stylish ground floor lounge with squashy sofas. First floor restaurant serves accomplished, innovative dishes. Knowledgeable service.

XX

Koriander

VISA MC AE

Store Kongensgade 34 ✉ 1264 K – Ⓜ Kongens Nytorv – ✆ 33 15 03 15 – mail@restaurantkoriander.dk – www.restaurantkoriander.dk
closed July and 1 week late December **C2**
Rest – *(dinner only)* Menu 485/1095 DKK – Carte 630/835 DKK
♦ Indian ♦ Exotic ♦
Charming both without and within: ornate décor that includes eye-catching lampshades, swags and curtains. Contemporary Indian cooking with subtle French influences.

XX

Kokkeriet

⇔18 VISA MC AE

Kronprinsessegade 64 ✉ 1306 K – ✆ 33 15 27 77 – info@kokkeriet.dk – Fax 33 15 27 75 – www.kokkeriet.dk
closed last 3 weeks July, 24-26 December, 1-8 January, Sunday, Monday and Bank Holidays **C1**
Rest – *(dinner only)* Menu 450/600 DKK – Carte 770/1020 DKK
♦ Modern ♦ Neighbourhood ♦
Smart, intimate restaurant with neighbourhood feel and stylish furnishings. Inventive modern menu offering 5-7 courses with wine to match. Enthusiastic service.

XX

Godt

VISA MC

Gothersgade 38 ✉ 1123 K – Ⓜ Kongens Nytorv – ✆ 33 15 21 22 – restaurant.godt@get2net.dk – www.restaurant-godt.dk
closed 11-19 February, 1-9 April, July-6 August, 14-22 October, 23 December-2 January, Sunday, Monday and Bank Holidays **C2**
Rest – *(booking essential) (set menu only) (dinner only)* Menu 480/640 DKK
♦ Classic ♦ Design ♦
Small, stylish modern two floor restaurant with grey décor, ceiling fans and old WWII shells as candle holders. Personally run. Classic fare in three, four or five courses.

XX **The Dining Room** – at Radisson SAS Scandinavia H.
25th Floor, Amager Boulevard 70 ✉ 23005 – ✆ 33 96 58 58 – info@thediningroom.dk – Fax 33 96 55 00 – www.thediningroom.dk
< Copenhagen, P VISA MC AE D
closed Sunday-Monday C3
Rest – *(dinner only)* Carte 395/700 DKK
◆ Modern ◆ Design ◆
Situated on the 25th floor of the hotel but run independently and providing diners with wonderful panoramic views of the city. Original and modern menu.

XX **De Gaulle**
VISA MC AE D
Kronborggade 3 ✉ 2200 – ✆ 35 85 58 66 – info@de-gaulle.dk – Fax 35 85 58 69 – www.de-gaulle.dk
closed 5-9 April, July, 23 December-2 January, Sunday, Monday and Bank Holidays A1
Rest – *(dinner only) (set menu only)* Menu 550/650 DKK
◆ French ◆ Friendly ◆
In the Nørrebro area, an intimate personally-run restaurant where young chef delivers some dishes to the table. Choice of 3-6 courses from set menu of modern French dishes.

XX **Kiin Kiin**
AC 16 VISA MC AE D
Guldbergsgade 21 ✉ 2200 – ✆ 35 35 75 55 – kiin@kiin.dk – Fax 35 35 75 59 – www.kiin.dk
closed Sunday A1
Rest – *(booking essential) (dinner only) (set menu only)* Menu 600 DKK
◆ Thai ◆ Exotic ◆
Within an apartment block but much thought has gone into the design and styling. Expect a weekly changing set menu of balanced, modern and flavoursome Thai cooking. Friendly and knowledgeable service.

XX **Umami**
AC VISA MC AE D
Store Kongensgade 59 ✉ 1264 – Ⓜ Kongens Nytorv – ✆ 33 38 75 00 – mail@restaurantumami.dk – Fax 33 38 75 15 – www.restaurantumami.dk
closed 24 December-3 January and lunch Saturday and Sunday C-D2
Rest – Menu 485/850 DKK – Carte 315/605 DKK
◆ Japanese ◆ Fashionable ◆
Elegant and contemporary with stylish wood tables and eating options on two floors: sushi bar, ancillary dining area or spacious main dining room. Modern Japanese dishes.

XX **Custom House at Havnegade 44**
< Harbour and Christianshavn, AC 26 VISA MC AE D
Havnegade 44 ✉ 1058 – Ⓜ Kongens Nytorv – ✆ 33 31 01 03 – info@customhouse.dk – Fax 33 31 01 29 – www.customhouse.dk
closed 24-26 December D2
Rest *Bacino* – *(closed Sunday)* Menu 311/577 DKK – Carte 255/544 DKK
Rest *Ebisu* – *(closed Sunday-Monday) (dinner only)* Menu 177/611 DKK – Carte 277/511 DKK
Rest *Bar and Grill* – Carte 244/866 DKK
◆ Modern ◆ Design ◆
Converted quayside customs building with harbour views and a choice of three restaurants. Bacino for Italian food. Ebisu is the first floor Japanese with a sushi counter. The busy Bar and Grill on the ground floor is the most informal.

XX **Alberto K** – at Radisson SAS Royal H.
< Copenhagen, AC P VISA MC AE D
Hammerichsgade 1 ✉ 1611 V – ✆ 33 42 60 00 – copenhagen@radissonsas.com – Fax 33 42 61 00
closed 22 December-8 January B3
Rest – *(dinner only)* Menu 560/670 DKK – Carte 555/675 DKK
◆ Italian influences ◆ Design ◆
Italian-influenced cuisine and terrific views are the attractions at this restaurant on the 20th floor of the Radisson SAS Royal Hotel. Open kitchen and a modern design; friendly service.

XX

Il Grappolo Blu

VISA MC AE ①

Vester Farimagsgade 35 ✉ 1606 V – ✆ 33 11 57 20 – ilgrappoloblu@ilgrappoloblu.com – Fax 33 12 57 20 – www.ilgrappoloblu.com

closed Easter, 5 weeks in summer, Christmas-New Year, Sunday, Monday and Bank Holidays **B3**

Rest – *(dinner only) (set menu only)* Menu 320/680 DKK

♦ Italian ♦ Friendly ♦

Behind the unpromising façade lies this friendly restaurant, personally run by the owner. Ornate wood panelling and carving. Authentic Italian dishes that just keep on coming.

XX

Frederiks Have

VISA MC AE ①

Smallegade 41/Virgina Vej, (West : 1 1/2 km via Gammel Kongevej) ✉ 2000 Frederiksberg – Ⓜ Frederiksberg – ✆ 38 88 33 35 – info@frederikshave.dk – Fax 38 88 33 37 – www.frederikshave.dk

closed Easter, 22 December-6 January and Sunday November-April

Rest – Menu 225/308 DKK – Carte 310/390 DKK

♦ Modern ♦ Neighbourhood ♦

Established restaurant in leafy residential district. Homely ambience and delightful terrace. Monthly menus offer traditional and modern Danish cooking.

XX

Gammel Mønt

VISA MC AE ①

Gammel Mønt 41 ✉ 1117 K – Ⓜ Kongens Nytorv – ✆ 33 15 10 60 – info@gammel-moent.dk – Fax 33 15 10 60 – www.gammel-moent.dk

closed Easter, 22 June-15 August, 22 December-8 January, Saturday, Sunday and Bank Holidays **C2**

Rest – *(lunch only)* Menu 275/650 DKK – Carte 245/495 DKK

♦ Traditional ♦ Cosy ♦

Half-timbered house from 1732 with striking red façade in smart commercial district. Traditional cuisine with seasonal variations and interesting range of herring dishes.

XX

Le Sommelier

VISA MC AE ①

Bredgade 63-65 ✉ 1260 K – ✆ 33 11 45 15 – mail@lesommelier.dk – Fax 33 11 59 79 – www.lesommelier.dk

closed 22 December-3 January **D1**

Rest – Menu 265/365 DKK – Carte 345/615 DKK

♦ French ♦ Brasserie ♦

Popular brasserie in the heart of the old town. The owners' passion for wine shows in posters, memorabilia and a good "by glass" list. Classic French cooking.

XX

Salt – at Admiral H.

P VISA MC AE ①

Toldbodgade 24-28 ✉ 1253 – Ⓜ Kongens Nytorv – ✆ 33 74 14 44 – info@saltrestaurant.dk – Fax 33 74 14 16 **D2**

Rest – Menu 345 DKK – Carte 350/432 DKK

♦ Modern ♦ Design ♦

Conran-designed restaurant in 18C warehouse; outdoor summer tables. Only sea salt is used. Danish buffet and modern a la carte at midday; more extensive modern dinner menu.

XX

La Tombola A'Smorfia

VISA MC AE ①

Toldbodgade 55 ✉ 1253 – ✆ 33 14 57 20 – info@latombola.dk – Fax 33 15 57 20 – www.latombola.dk

closed Christmas-New Year, Easter and Sunday lunch **D2**

Rest – Menu 188/406 DKK – Carte approx. 270 DKK

♦ Italian ♦ Brasserie ♦

Spacious and airy Italian brasserie, sister to Il Grappolo Blu. Decorated with tombola-themed numbers, with the chance to win your meal for free! Daily changing dishes with Neapolitan specialities.

Lumskebugten

Esplanaden 21 ✉ 1263 K – ✆ 33 15 60 29 – Fax 33 32 87 18 – www.lumskebugten.dk
closed 23 December-2 January, Sunday, Saturday lunch and Bank Holidays
Rest – Menu 375/455 DKK – Carte 455/700 DKK **D1**

◆ Traditional ◆ Cosy ◆

Mid 19C café-pavilion near quayside and Little Mermaid. Interesting 19C maritime memorabilia and old paintings. Good traditional cuisine. Possibility of dining on boat.

Oubaek

Store Kongensgade 52 ✉ 1264 – Ⓜ Kongens Nytorv – ✆ 33 32 32 09 – rasmus-oubaek@mail.dk – www.rasmusoubaek.dk
closed mid July-mid August, Christmas-New Year, Sunday and Monday **C-D2**
Rest – Menu 255/295 DKK – Carte 290/360 DKK

◆ Innovative ◆ Bistro ◆

Unpretentious restaurant with tables on mezzanine level above kitchen. Offers carefully prepared, classic and familiar bistro dishes at a competitive price. Informal and friendly service.

Olsen

Ved Stranden 18 ✉ 1061 – ✆ 33 14 64 00 – Fax 33 14 64 01 – www.restaurantolsen.com – closed 25 December, 1 January and Sunday
Rest – Menu 345 DKK (dinner) – Carte 255/405 DKK **C2**

◆ Modern ◆ Fashionable ◆

Centrally located restaurant boasts relaxing, though buzzy, vibe with terrace and canal views. Intimate, popular bar. Tightly packed dining tables: the place to be seen! Interesting seasonal menus with a Norwegian base.

TyvenKokkenHansKoneOgHendesElsker

Magstraede 16 ✉ 1204 K – ✆ 33 16 12 92 – post@tyven.dk 20
– www.tyven.dk – closed July, 23 December-3 January and Sunday **C3**
Rest – *(dinner only)* Menu 550/675 DKK – Carte 295/690 DKK

◆ Classic ◆ Rustic ◆

18C part timbered house in cobbled street. Named after the Peter Greenaway film. Set menu (5 courses) with small a la carte. French based dishes with Danish influence.

Kanalen

Christianshavn-Wilders Plads 1-3 ✉ 1403 K – Ⓜ Christianshavn – ✆ 32 95 13 30 – info@restaurant-kanalen.dk – Fax 32 95 13 38 – www.restaurant-kanalen.dk **D3**
closed 2-9 April, 23-30 December, Sunday and Bank Holidays
Rest – *(booking essential) (set menu only at dinner)* Menu 270/490 DKK – Carte lunch 290/358 DKK

◆ Modern ◆ Friendly ◆

Delightfully located former Harbour Police office on canalside. Simple elegant décor, informal yet personally run. Well balanced menu of modern Danish cooking.

Famo

Saxogade 3 ✉ 1662 – ✆ 33 23 22 50 – famo@mail.tele.dk – www.osteriafamo.dk – closed July, 24-27 December, 1-2 January, Saturday lunch and Sunday
Rest – *(booking essential) (set menu only)* Menu 250/350 DKK **A3**

◆ Italian ◆ Bistro ◆

Simple, personally run Italian eatery that feels like an osteria; opened in 2005. No written menus: owners propose the day's good value, authentic regional dishes. Chatty, attentive service completes the picture.

M/S Amerika

Dampfaergevej 8 (Pakhus 12, Amerikakaj) (via Folke Bernadottes Allée) ✉ 2100 K – ✆ 35 26 90 30 – info@msamerika.dk – Fax 35 26 91 30 – www.msamerika.dk
closed 24 December-2 January, Sunday and Bank Holidays
Rest – Menu 248/345 DKK – Carte 375/450 DKK

◆ Modern ◆ Brasserie ◆

Characterful 19C former warehouse in attractive quayside location with popular summer terrace. Lunch quite simple and traditional; more contemporary at dinner.

Fiasco

VISA MC AE D

Gammel Kongevej 176, Frederiksberg (via Gammel Kongevej) ✉ 1850 C – ✆ 33 31 74 87 – fiasco@tiscali.dk – Fax 33 31 74 87
closed July, Christmas-New Year, Sunday and Monday
Rest – *(dinner only) (set menu only)* Menu 245/355 DKK
♦ Italian ♦ Friendly ♦
Modern Italian restaurant to the west of the city centre. Bright room with fresh feel and large picture windows. Friendly young owners. Carefully prepared, authentic cuisine.

L'Altro

AC VISA MC AE D

Torvegade 62 ✉ 1400 K – Ⓜ Christianshavn – ✆ 32 54 54 06 – laltro@laltro.dk – Fax 32 54 54 06 – www.laltro.dk
closed 24-26 December, 1 January and Sunday **D3**
Rest – *(booking essential) (dinner only) (set menu only)* Menu 250/415 DKK
♦ Italian ♦ Intimate ♦
Little sister to Era Ora, well priced Tuscan and Umbrian home cooking is the feature here. Divided between the ground floor and a characterful wine cellar basement.

Viva

VISA MC AE D

Langebrogade Kaj 570 ✉ 1411 K – Ⓜ Christianshavn – ✆ 27 25 05 05 – viva@restaurantviva.dk – www.restaurantviva.dk
closed Christmas-New Year **C3**
Rest – Menu 345 DKK – Carte 350/500 DKK
♦ Modern ♦ Minimalist ♦
Converted German tug boat moored on the river; stylish minimalist interior and top deck terrace. Eclectic menu with strong Danish note at lunch.

Luns

VISA MC

Øster Farimagsgade 12 ✉ 2100 – ✆ 35 26 33 35 – www.restaurantluns.dk
closed mid July-mid August, Christmas, Sunday-Tuesday and Bank Holidays
Rest – *(booking essential) (dinner only)* Carte approx. 300 DKK **C1**
♦ Home cooking ♦ Rustic ♦
Opened in 2005: simple rustic neighbourhood eatery that's quickly become locally renowned. Owner cooks and serves set menus of good value rural French fare. You can eat from two to five courses in totally relaxed surroundings.

IN TIVOLI

The Paul (Cunningham)

AC 12 VISA MC AE D

Vesterbrogade 3 ✉ 1630 K – ✆ 33 75 07 75 – info@thepaul.dk – Fax 33 75 07 76 – www.thepaul.dk
closed mid September-mid November, Christmas Eve-mid April and Sunday **B3**
Rest – *(dinner only Wednesday-Saturday 15 November-22 December) (set menu only)* Menu 450/800 DKK
Spec. Pommes mousseline with caviar, quail egg, oyster and cucumber. Foie gras with lemon curd and meringue, pine infused olive oil. Blackened berries, chocolate, liquorice and black olive.
♦ Innovative ♦ Elegant ♦
Elegant glass-domed 20C structure by the lake in Tivoli Gardens. Open-plan kitchen with chef's table. Set menu (3-7 courses); original and precise cooking, attentive service.

SMØRREBRØD *The following list of simpler restaurants and cafés/bars specialize in Danish open sandwiches and are generally open from 10.00am to 4.00pm.*

Amalie

VISA MC AE

Amaliegade 11 ✉ 1256 K – Ⓜ Kongens Nytorv – ✆ 33 12 88 10 – jjmaltesen@mail.dk – Fax 33 12 88 10
closed Easter, July-August, Christmas-New Year, Sunday and Bank Holidays
Rest – *(booking essential) (lunch only)* Menu 188 DKK – Carte 188/274 DKK **D2**

◆ Traditional ◆ Friendly ◆

Located in a pretty 18C town house. Wood panelled walls and a clean, uncluttered style. Helpful service and ideal for those looking for an authentic, traditional Danish lunch.

Sankt Annae

VISA MC AE

Sankt Annae Plads 12 ✉ 1250 K – Ⓜ Kongens Nytorv – ✆ 33 12 54 97 – Fax 33 15 16 61 – www.restaurantsanktannae.dk **D2**
Rest – *(lunch only)* Carte 150/250 DKK

◆ Traditional ◆ Friendly ◆

Pretty terraced building in popular part of town. Simple décor with a rustic feel and counter next to kitchen. Typical menu of smørrebrød. Service prompt and efficient.

Ida Davidsen

VISA MC AE

Store Kongensgade 70 ✉ 1264 K – Ⓜ Kongens Nytorv – ✆ 33 91 36 55 – reservation@idadavidsen.dk – Fax 33 11 36 55 – www.idadavidsen.dk
closed July, 22 December-15 January, Saturday, Sunday and Bank Holidays
Rest – *(lunch only)* Carte 45/175 DKK **D2**

◆ Traditional ◆ Family ◆

Family run for five generations, this open sandwich bar on a busy city-centre street is almost a household name in Denmark. Offers a full range of typical smørrebrød.

ENVIRONS OF COPENHAGEN

at Nordhavn North : 3 km by Østbanegade and Road 2

Paustian at Bo Bech

AC P VISA MC

Kalkbraenderiløbskaj 2 ✉ 2100 – ✆ 39 18 55 01 – mail@bobech.net – www.bobech.net
closed 9-29 July, 23 December-6 January and Sunday
Rest – Menu 300/500 DKK – Carte 540/735 DKK

◆ Innovative ◆ Design ◆

Stylish quayside restaurant adjoining Paustian, a famous furniture store not far from city centre by train. Choice of menus offering original creations. Impressive wine list.

at Hellerup North : 7.5 km by Østbanegade and Road 2 - ✉ 2900 Hellerup

Hellerup Parkhotel

Lö ⇆rm SAT P VISA MC AE

Strandvejen 203 ✉ 2900 – ✆ 39 62 40 44 – info@hellerupparkhotel.dk – Fax 39 45 15 90 – www.hellerupparkhotel.dk
closed 23 December-2 January
71 rm ☕ – †1520 DKK ††1995/2995 DKK
Rest *Saison* – see below
Rest *Wine & Dine* – *✆ 39 62 27 67 (dinner only)* Carte 250/455 DKK

◆ Business ◆ Classic ◆

Attractive classic hotel located in affluent suburb north of the city. Rooms vary in size and colour décor but offer same good standard of facilities and level of comfort. Popular local Italian restaurant on side of hotel with terrace.

XX

Saison

Strandvejen 203 ✉ 2900 – ✆ 39 62 21 40 – saison@saison.dk – Fax 39 62 20 30 – www.saison.dk
closed 5-9 April, 3 weeks in summer, 23-26 December and Sunday
Rest – Menu 285/405 DKK – Carte dinner 425/485 DKK
♦ Modern ♦ Friendly ♦
Run separately from the hotel in which it is located. Enjoys a bright and airy feel with high ceiling and large windows. Carefully prepared cooking using quality ingredients.

at Skovshoved North : 10 km by Østbanegade and Road 2

Skovshoved

100 VISA AE
Strandvejen 267 ✉ 2920 K Charlottenlund – ✆ 39 64 00 28 – reception@skovshovedhotel.com – Fax 39 64 06 72 – www.skovshovedhotel.com
closed 24-25 December
20 rm – †1400 DKK ††1400/1600 DKK, ☕ 125 DKK – 2 suites
Rest – Menu 195/625 DKK – Carte 319/495 DKK
♦ Inn ♦ Cosy ♦
Set in a charming village, this inn dates from the 1660's and was fully refurbished in 2003. Cosy bedrooms, most with balconies looking out to sea. Welcoming atmosphere. Warm and inviting restaurant with pleasant terrace and a classic menu.

at Søllerød North : 20 km by Tagensvej (take the train to Holte then taxi) - ✉ 2840 Holte

XXX

Søllerød Kro

30 VISA AE
Søllerødvej 35 ✉ 2840 K – ✆ 45 80 25 05 – mail@soelleroed-kro.dk – Fax 45 80 22 70 – www.soelleroed-kro.dk – closed 1 week February, 1 week Easter, 2 weeks in summer, 1 week Christmas and Monday
Rest – Menu 350/555 DKK – Carte 580/1020 DKK
Spec. Foie gras torchon with preserved green strawberries and hazelnut. Roasted halibut and langoustine with sprouts, almonds and lemon. Valrhona chocolate dessert.
♦ Modern ♦ Inn ♦
Characterful 17C thatched inn with delightful courtyard terrace and stylish Danish rustic-bourgeois décor. Classically based cooking with modern notes and excellent wine list.

at Kastrup Airport Southeast : 10 km by Amager Boulevard

Hilton Copenhagen Airport

rm 450 VISA AE
Ellehammersvej 20, Kastrup ✉ 2770 – ✆ 32 50 15 01 – res_copenhagen-airport@hilton.com – Fax 32 52 85 28 – www.hilton.com
381 rm – †2395 DKK ††1295/2395 DKK, ☕ 160 DKK – 1 suite
Rest *Hamlet* – Menu 425 DKK (dinner) – Carte 395/485 DKK
Rest *Horizon* – ✆ 32 44 53 53 – Menu 195/495 DKK – Carte 265/385 DKK
♦ Business ♦ Modern ♦
Glass walkway leads from arrivals to this smart business hotel. Bright bedrooms with light, contemporary Scandinavian furnishings and modern facilities. Hamlet is a formal open-plan restaurant with eclectic menu. Relaxed dining in Horizon beneath vast atrium.

Quality Airport H. Dan

rest rm 60 VISA AE
Kastruplundgade 15, Kastrup (North : 2 ½ km by coastal rd) ✉ 2770 – ✆ 32 51 14 00 – q.dan@choice.dk – Fax 32 51 37 01 – www.choicehotels.dk – **227 rm** – ††1520 DKK, ☕ 95 DKK – 1 suite –
Rest – *(buffet dinner only)* Menu 65 DKK
♦ Business ♦ Functional ♦
Airport hotel not far from beach and countryside, popular with business travellers. All rooms with modern facilities; some with views of canal. Traditional Danish cuisine in the restaurant.

FINLAND
SUOMI

PROFILE

◆ **AREA:**
338 145 km^2
(130 558 sq mi).

◆ **POPULATION:**
5 225 000 inhabitants (est. 2005), density = 15 per km^2.

◆ **CAPITAL:**
Helsinki (conurbation 1 151 000 inhabitants).

◆ **CURRENCY:**
Euro (€); rate of exchange: € 1 = US$ 1.32 (Nov 2006).

◆ **GOVERNMENT:**
Parliamentary republic (since 1917). Member of European Union since 1995.

◆ **LANGUAGES:**
Finnish (a Finno-Ugric language related to Estonian) spoken by 92% of Finns, Swedish (6%) and Sami (some 7 000 native speakers). English is widely spoken.

◆ **SPECIFIC PUBLIC HOLIDAYS:**
Epiphany (6 January); Good Friday (Friday before Easter); Midsummer's Eve Day; Independence Day (6 December); Boxing Day (26 December).

LOCAL TIME:
GMT + 2 hours in winter and GMT + 3 hours in summer.

◆ **CLIMATE:**
Temperate continental with very cold winters and mild summers (Helsinki: January: -7°C, July: 17°C). Midnight sun: the sun never sets for several weeks around Midsummer in the north. Snow settles in early December to April in the south and centre of the country. Northern Lights

(*Aurora Borealis*) visible in the north on clear, dark nights; highest frequency in Feb-Mar and Sep-Oct.

◆ **INTERNATIONAL DIALLING CODE:**
00 358 followed by area code (Helsinki: 9) and then the local number.

EMERGENCY:
Fire Brigade, Ambulance, Police: ✆ **112**.

◆ **ELECTRICITY:**
220 volts AC, 50Hz; 2-pin round-shaped continental plugs.

FORMALITIES

Travellers from the European Union (EU), Switzerland, Iceland and the main countries of North and South America need a national identity card or passport (America: passport required) to visit Finland for less than three months (tourism or business purpose). For visitors from other countries a visa may be required, in addition to a passport, especially for those wishing to stay for longer than three months. If you plan to visit Russia while in Finland, you must purchase an appropriate visa in advance in your own country. We advise you to check with your embassy before travelling.

Nationals of EU or EEA countries require a national driving licence, other travellers should have an international driving licence. Third party insurance is compulsory and a green card is recommended. Laws on drink-driving are strictly enforced. Headlights should be switched on at all times. In winter, snow tyres are required from December to February and engine heaters recommended.

MAJOR NEWSPAPERS

The main national newspapers are: *Helsingin Sanomat* (Finnish), *Hufvudstadtsbladet* (Swedish), *Ilta-Sanomat*, *Iltalehti* and *Kauppalehti*.

USEFUL PHRASES

ENGLISH	**FINNISH**
Yes	**Kyllä**
No	**Ei**
Good morning	**Huomenta**
Goodbye	**Näkemiin**
Thank you	**Kiitos**
Please	**Olkaa hyvä**
Excuse me	**Anteeksi**
I don't understand	**En ymmärrä**

HOTELS

→ CATEGORIES

The standard of accommodation in Finland is very high from international luxury hotels, elegant manor house and spa hotels to reasonably priced establishments, comfortable motels, guesthouses and bed and breakfast accommodation in the countryside and wilderness lodges. A night in a snow hotel is a memorable experience. Several hotel chains operate throughout Finland.

→ PRICE RANGE

The price is per room and includes breakfast. Special rates are available during the holiday season. Most hotels have special weekend and summer offers. **Finncheque** and other hotel vouchers which offer special rates can be bought from travel agents.

→ TAX

Taxes and service are included in the hotel rate.

→ CHECK OUT TIME

Between 11am and noon.

→ RESERVATIONS

Bookings can be made by phone, on the Internet or via travel agencies.

→ TIPS FOR HANDLING LUGGAGE

Gratuities are not compulsory but a small tip is welcome.

→ BREAKFAST

Breakfast is a copious meal, a self-service buffet of porridge, cereals, pancakes, eggs, ham, sausage, yoghurt, jams and several types of bread.

Reception	**Vastaanotto**
Single room	**Yhden hengen huone**
Double room	**Kahden hengen huone**
Bed	**Vuode**
Bathroom	**Kylpyhuone**
Shower	**Suihku**

RESTAURANTS

The term **ravintola** is used for small intimate restaurants to grand establishments with music and dance floor. A **grilli** or **krouvi** is a small informal restaurant with a hearty menu. Other kinds of eating places include **kahvio** (self-service cafeteria), **kahvila** (café, snack-bar serving cakes, patisseries and light meals), **baari** (snack-bar offering light food and mild beer or coffee) and pubs (for meals with waitress-service). **Yökerho** are nightclubs in big hotels which also serve snacks.

→ MEALS

Breakfast	**Aamianen**	7/8am-10am
Lunch	**Lounas**	11am-1pm
Dinner	**Päivällinen**	7-8pm-10pm

Restaurants in Finland offer moderately priced set menus as well as a comprehensive à la carte menu. The menus include traditional Finnish dishes as well as classic international cuisine. The Finnish buffet **(seisova pöytä)** is a good lunch alternative. Menus in English are usually available in large towns.

→ RESERVATIONS

It is advisable to book in advance if you intend to visit a restaurant prized for its culinary expertise. Reservations should be made by telephone or by Internet. You will usually be asked for a credit card number as guarantee.

→ THE BILL

The bill (check) includes service and tax. If you are particularly pleased with the service you may wish to give an additional tip.

Appetizer	**Alkupala**
Meal	**Ateria**
Starter	**Alkuruoka**
Main dish	**Pääruoka**
Main dish of the day	**Päivän tarjous/annos**
Dessert	**Jälkiruoka**
Water/ mineral water (still, sparkling)	**Vesi/ kivennäisvesi (hiilihapoton/hiilihappoinen)**
Wine (red, white, rosé)	**Vïïni (punaviini, valkoviini, rosé)**
Beer	**Olut**
Bread	**Leipä**
Meat	**Liha**
Fish	**Kala**
Salt/pepper	**Suola/pippuri**
Cheese	**Juusto**
Vegetables	**Vihannes**
Hot/cold	**Kuuma/kylmä**
The bill (check) please	**Saisinko laskun**

LOCAL CUISINE

The culinary traditions of Finland reflect its location at the crossroads of Europe and Russia. The abundance and quality of fresh products from land and sea are outstanding and every season brings its own delicacies on offer at the many indoor and outdoor markets.

The Finnish **seisova pöytä** (buffet lunch) comprises a mouthwatering array of dishes: pickled and salted fish (herring, salmon), cold meats, sausages, salads, cheese and a variety of breads: whole wheat, white, black and rye. The dark sour rye **Ruisleipä** is a great favourite. **Rosolli** is a typical salad of beetroot, carrots, potatoes, cucumber, onion and apple.

Thick soups made with peas, fish, meat, mushrooms and summer vegetables are warming in the cold climate. Every region produces tasty sausages: salami sausage, **mustamakkara** (blood sausage from Tampere), **lenkkimakkara** (loop sausage), 'raisin' or 'onion' sausage from Turku. Finnish hors-d'œuvre include red Finnish caviar, white fish and herring roe and blini with sour cream and chopped onion; **graavilohi** (marinated or cold smoked fish).

The icy waters and rivers of Finland abound in very fine fish: salmon (lohi), burbot, lamprey, vendace, muikku (small fish related to salmon producing the best caviar), pike perch (kuha), perch (ahven), rainbow trout (kirjolohi). **Silakka** (Baltic herring) is pickled, fried, grilled or baked with potatoes and cheese sauce. The crayfish **(rapu)** season in August is a gastronomic highlight.

Among regional specialities are: **karjalanpaisti** (Karelian hotpot), **karjalanpiirakka** (Karelian pasties – a thin rye crust filled with rice), **kalakukko** (Karelian pasties filled with fish and fatty pork), lamb and cabbage stew, stuffed cabbage rolls, roast reindeer with cranberry sauce, sauteed reindeer **(poronkäristys)**, smoked reindeer **(savustettua poronlihaa)**, reindeer tongue **(poronkieli)**, meatballs **(lihapulla)**. Game is on the menu in season.

You can indulge in delicious pastries: **pikkupullat** (cardamom buns), **laskiaispulla** (buns filled with marzipan and cream especially during winter holidays), **korvapuusti** (cinnamon buns), **rahkapulla** (lemon and quark tarts), **tippaleipä** (pastry like brown crunchy spaghetti 1st May speciality), **pannukakku** (thick pancakes with jam), **torttu** (fruit tarts). **Mämmi** is a malt-flavoured pudding eaten at Easter.

The most popular cheeses (juusto) are **Finlandia** similar to Emmental, the Cheddar-like **juhlajuusto**, the blue-veined **aurajuusto**, the mild **Turunlinna**. **Uunijuusto** is a soft cheese baked in the oven. **Leipäjuusto** is a cheese bread which is warmed in the oven and eaten with cloudberry jam.

DRINK

Beer is the most popular drink: the secret of Finnish lager is the high quality water, good barley and a long brewing tradition. Koff and Lapinkulta and the malty sahti beer are worth tasting. Try the delicious fruit liqueurs: Lakka (cloudberry), Polar (cranberry), Mesimarja (Arctic raspberry).

The Finns are partial to a glass of schnapps. Mead and sparkling wine are drunk during carnival on 1 May in Vappu. Glögi, spicy mulled wine, is served at Christmas. Buttermilk is a popular drink with meals.

HELSINKI
HELSINGFORS

Population (est. 2005): 583 000 (conurbation 1 151 000) – Altitude: sea level

R. Mattès / MICHELIN

Helsinki 'Daughter of the Baltic' is located on a peninsula and is Europe's northernmost capital. The compact city has a unique character defined by its history and architectural heritage. Its formal neo-Classical showpieces, the imaginative volumes and decoration of the Art Nouveau period and the pure lines of modern architecture are set against a backdrop of sea and forest. It is a lively university town and a commercial centre with five busy harbours.

The city built in 16C by the King of Sweden was relocated to its present site by the sea in 1640. It was twice occupied by Russia in the 18C. It reverted to the Swedish kingdom from 1746 to 1809 but after the 1808-9 war, Finland broke with Sweden; after unification with Russia, it became an autonomous Grand Duchy while retaining the Swedish constitution and Lutheran religion. Helsinki became the capital in 1812 and prospered under the reign of Alexander II; by the end of the 19C it had become the cultural and political centre of Finland. Since 1917 it has been the capital of an independent state; it has acquired a new status for its bold, modern, post-war architectural achievements and as the Geneva of the North for hosting international conferences.

WHICH DISTRICT TO CHOOSE

Accommodation in Helsinki is of the highest standard with prestigious hotels in the city centre, near the railway station, in the Kamppi district *Plan I* **B2**, near the harbours; business hotels in Mannerheimintie *Plan I* **B1**, Pohjoisesplanadi *Plan I* **C2**, Kalastajatorpantie, Messuaukio Eteläranta; and friendly comfortable hotels in the Länsi-Pasila district.

Restaurants to suit all tastes are to be found in the city centre. There are restaurants in a pleasant setting on the islands. Restaurants with The Helsinki Menu sign offer high-quality Finnish dishes prepared with seasonal products.

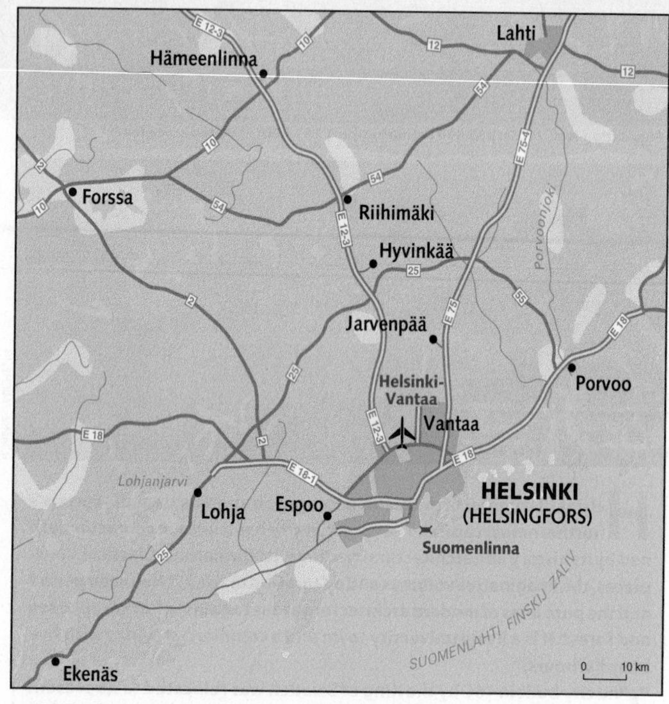

PRACTICAL INFORMATION

ARRIVAL – DEPARTURE

Helsinki-Vantaa Airport – 19 km (12 mi) north of the city. ✆ 0200 14636; www.ilmailulaitos.fi

From the airport to the city centre – By **taxi**: €30-35 or **shuttle minibus**: €20-55 (2-9 persons), time 20-30min. ✆ 0600 555 555; www.airporttaxi.fi; www.yellowline.fi. By **Finnair City Bus** (with request stops): every 20min, €5.20, time 30-40min. By **bus**: Lines 415, 451, 615 to Central Bus Station; time 40min, approx. €3.50.

→ MAIN STATIONS

Central Railway Station (Rautatieasema) *Plan I* **B2**. ✆ 0600 41 902 (daily 7am-10pm); www.vr.fi

Central Bus Station (Linja-autoasema) *Plan I* **B2**. ✆ 0200 4000; www.matkahuolto.fi

TRANSPORT

→ BUS, TRAM, METRO, TRAIN, FERRY

The public transport system is practical and efficient. Single tram ticket €1.80; single City ticket €2; Regional Travel card '2' €3.40. HKL tourist tickets *(matkakortti)* €5.40 (1 day), €10.80 (3 days), €16.20 (5 days). Single tickets are valid 1hr and transfers are allowed. Tickets can be purchased from the driver, ticket machines, R-kiosks, metro stations, ferry terminal. Prepaid tickets are slightly cheaper. Sightseeing Trams 3T, 3B hop-on hop-off. Helsinki

Card (24, 48, 72hr): approx. €25, 35, 45 gives unlimited transport, free entry to museums and various discounts.

→ TAXIS

Taxis can be hailed in the streets, at taxi stands, near stations and at the airport or can be ordered by phone. An average ride in the city is about €25 and there are evening, Sunday and luggage surcharges. Taxi Helsinki ✆ 09 700 700, 0100 0700; www.taxishelsinki.fi

USEFUL ADDRESSES

→ TOURIST OFFICE

Helsinki Tourist & Convention Bureau – Pohjoisesplanadi 19 *Plan I* **C2**. Open May-Sept, Mon-Fri 9am-8pm, Sat-Sun 9am-6pm; Oct-Apr, Mon-Fri 9am-6pm, Sat-Sun 10am-4pm. ✆ 09 169 3757; www.visithelsinki.fi

A smaller office is located at the Central Railway Station. From June to August 'Helsinki Helpers' in green overalls patrol the streets offering free advice and help to visitors.

→ BANKS / CURRENCY EXCHANGE

Banks open Mon-Fri 9.15am-4.15pm. ATMs are available all over the city. Credit cards are widely accepted. Exchange offices at the Central Railway Station and at the airport have longer opening hours.

→ POST OFFICES

Opening times Mon-Fri 9am-6pm. Post boxes are yellow. Main Post Offfice, Elielinaukio 2F *Plan I* **B1** open Mon-Fri 7am-9pm and Sat-Sun 10am-6pm. ✆ 0200 71000. Stamps are also available from book and paper shops, R-kiosks, stations and hotels.

→ PHARMACY

Look for the sign 'apteekki'. Opening times 9am-5.30pm. There is a 24hr pharmacy at Mannerheimintie 96 *Plan I* **B1**.

EXPLORING HELSINKI

VISITING

It is possible to visit sights and museums in Helsinki in two days.

Museums and other sights are usually open10-11am to 5-6pm; some close on Mondays.

Neo-Classical Helsinki – Imposing monumental ensemble: **Senaatintori** *Plan I* **C2**, a vast square (statue of Czar Alexander II) dominated by the domed **Tuomiokirkko**, with its stark interior; behind stands the delightful **Pyhän Kolminaisuuden kirkko (Orthodox church of Holy Trinity)**. Around the square are **Valtioneuvoston linna** (Senate House), the University and the domed library, **Yliopiston kirjasto**, and fine burghers' houses (**Sederholmin talo** *SE*). **Kauppatori** *Plan I* **C2**: In Market Square, the Empire frontage includes from east to west: **Presidentinlinna** (Presidential Palace), **Korkein Oikeus** (Supreme Court), **Kaupungintalo** (Town Hall). **Esplanadi** is lined with ornate neo-Renaissance buildings.

New City Centre – **Rautatieasema** (railway station) *Plan I* **B2** in Art Nouveau style. **Eduskuntatalo** (Parliament House) in red granite. **Finlandia-talo** (Finlandia Hall) *Plan I* **B1** in white marble. **Kansallisooppera** *Plan I* **A1** clad in Finnish granite and white ceramic tiles. **Temppeliaukion kirkko** *Plan I* **A2**: the circular Church in the rock combines ingenious engineering and architectural flair. The red-roofed

Suomen Kansallisteatteri *Plan I* **C2** in grey granite. The **Lasipalatsi** cultural centre *Plan I* **B2**.

Museums – Ateneum, The Museum of Finnish Art *Plan I* **B2**: excellent introduction to Finnish art (18C-1960s). **Kiasma**: housed in a striking building, the Museum of Contemporary Art presents an overview of contemporary trends. **Kansallismuseo** *Plan I* **B1**: interesting architectural style. Frescoes depicting the legends of the *Kalevala*. The museum presents the development of Finnish life from prehistory to the present. **Taideteollisuusmuseo** *Plan I* **C2**: Museum of Art and Design presents a survey of the famous names of Finnish design from 19C to the present day (Walter Jung, Alvar and Aino Aalto, Tapio Wirkkala). **Seurasaari**: open-air museum devoted to traditional ways of life.

Katajanokka *Plan I* **D2** – Art Nouveau buildings (Nos 1, 5 Luotsikatu). **Icebreaker fleet** and frontage of former naval headquarters. **Uspenskin katedraali**: 19C cathedral, evidence of the city's Russian heritage, ornate interior.

Suomenlinna *Plan I* **D3** – The Fortress built on a group of six islands is a World Heritage Site: museums, art exhibitions.

Views – Stroll along the waterfront, watch the activity in the harbour and enjoy the view of the rocky islands, of the ferries, Market Square and the two cathedrals as well as the lively atmosphere. View of the bay from the **Sibelius-monumentti** *Plan I* **A1**.

Boat trips – Excursions around offshore islands from Market Square *Plan I* **C2**, and to the original site of Helsinki and the archipelago departing from Pohjoisranta *Plan I* **D1** and Meritullintori *Plan I* **C2**.

SHOPPING

Shops usually open Mon-Fri 9/10am-5/6pm, Sat 9/10am-1/2pm. Shopping centres and department stores open Mon-Fri 9am-9pm, Sat 9am-6pm.

The main shopping streets are **Mannerheimintie** *Plan I* **B1**, **Aleksanterinkatu** *Plan I* **C2**, both sides of **Esplanadi** *Plan I* **C2**, **Fredrikinkatu** *Plan I* **B2** and **Bulevardi** *Plan I* **C2**. A new shopping gallery opened in 2006 (Kamppi) by the central bus station (Linja-autoasema). The main department stores and shopping centres are *Kämp Galleria* on Esplanadi, *Kluuvi, Kiseleff House* (handmade items) on Aleksanterinkatu; *Forum, Stockmann* and *Sokos* on Mannerheimintie, *Itäkeskus* (by metro going east). Visit *Design Forum*, Erottaja and along Esplanadi, the *Pentik* gift shop at Mannerheimintie 5 and *Arabia Factory Outlet*, Hämeentie 135A for stylish ceramics, gifts, interior decorations. Antique shops in **Kruununhaka** and **Ullanlinna** districts.

MARKETS – The Market Square on South Harbour for food, handicrafts, souvenirs – **Eteläsatama** *Plan I* **C2** daily 6.30am (10am Sun) to 6pm (4pm Sat-Sun). **Hakaniemi Market**, Siltasaarenkatu-Hakaniemenranta *Plan I* **C1** (Mon-Sat 6.30am-3pm, first Sun of each month 10am-4pm): fresh produce and baked goods; **Hakaniemi Hall**, Siltasaarenkatu-Hämeentie *Plan I* **C1** (Mon-Fri 8am-6pm, Sat 8am-4pm): 100 tiny shops selling delicacies, souvenirs, handicrafts, Finnish design. On the corner of Bulevardi and Hietalahdenkatu *Plan I* **B3** are held **Hietalahti Flea market** – Mon-Fri 8am-7pm (4pm Sat). **Hietalahti Antique and Art Hall** – Mon-Fri 10am-5pm (3pm Sat), Evening flea market – Jun-Aug, Mon-Fri 3.30pm-8pm. Sunday flea market – May-Sep, 10am-4pm.

WHAT TO BUY – Finnish design (jewellery, wood, glass and ceramic gifts), handicrafts, furs, smoked meats and fish.

ENTERTAINMENT

You should obtain a copy of *Helsinki this Week* to find out about events in the city. It is available free from hotels and Tourist Information Offices.

Finlandia-talo *Plan I* ***B1***: Finlandia Hall hosts concerts.

Kansallisooppera *Plan I* ***A1***: The National Opera presents classical and modern opera and ballet.

Suomen Kansallisteatteri *Plan I* ***C1***: The National Theatre presents plays in Finnish.

Kulttvuritalo: concerts.

Sibelius Academy of Music: classical music.

Kaupunginteatteri: The Municipal Theatre puts on plays, dance and musicals.

Svenska Teatern: plays, dance and musicals in Swedish.

Hartwall Arena, Olympiastadion, Helsinki Ice Hall: sporting events, pop concerts.

Kaapelitehdas *Plan I* ***A3***: The former Cable Factory is now a cultural centre.

NIGHTLIFE

Popular restaurants, pubs, bars and cafés are located on the sea-front, **Esplanadi**, at **Tennispalatsi** *Plan I* ***B2*** and **Lasipalatsi**. Helsinki has a fine café culture: *Café Engel*, Aleksanterinkatu 26; *Café Ekberg*, Bulevardi 9; *Café Strindberg* and *Café Esplanad*, Pohjoisesplanadi 33/37; *Café Ursula*, Ehrenströmintie 3. There are elegant cafés in museums (City museum, Kiasma) and hotels. Stylish places to visit are *Moskva Bar* and *Corona Baari* (no 11), *Helmi* (no 14), Eerikinkatu; *Bar 9*, Uudenmaankatu 9. For live music go to *Memphis*, Kluuvikatu 8; *Eats* and *On the Rocks*, Mikonkatu 15; *Tavastia Klubi* and *Semi Final*, Urho Kekkosenkatu 4/6; *Klaus Kurki Bar & Klubi*, Bulevardi 2; *Zetor*, Mannerheimintie 3-5. Trendy nightclubs include *Helsinki Club*, Yliopistonkatu 8; *Studio 51*, Fredrikinkatu 51-53; *La Tour Night Club Premier*, Mannerheimintie 5. Jazz fans will enjoy *Storyville Jazz Club*, Museokatu 8; *Umo Jazz House*, Pursimiehenkatu 6. The *Grand Casino Helsinki*, Mikonkatu 19 is the place for those who wish to try their luck.

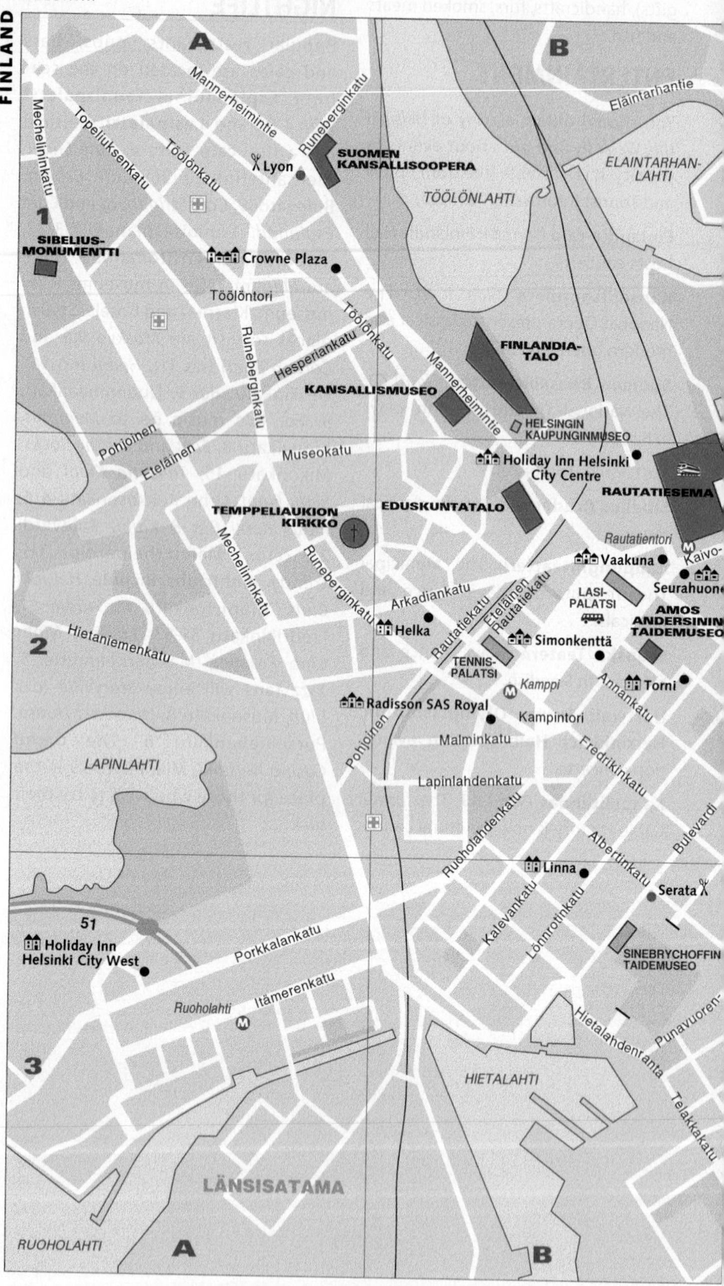
A
B
Mannerheimintie
Runeberginkatu
Eläintarhantie
Mechelininkatu
Topeliuksenkatu
Töölönkatu
Lyon
SUOMEN KANSALLISOOPERA
ELAINTARHAN-LAHTI
TÖÖLÖNLAHTI
1
SIBELIUS-MONUMENTTI
Crowne Plaza
Töölöntori
Töölönkatu
Hesperiankatu
FINLANDIA-TALO
KANSALLISMUSEO
Mannerheimintie
HELSINGIN KAUPUNGINMUSEO
Pohjoinen
Eteläinen
Museokatu
Holiday Inn Helsinki City Centre
RAUTATIESEMA
TEMPPELIAUKION KIRKKO
EDUSKUNTATALO
Mechelininkatu
Rautatientori
Vaakuna
Kaivo-
Runeberginkatu
Seurahuone
LASI-PALATSI
AMOS ANDERSININ TAIDEMUSEO
Arkadiankatu
Rautatiekatu
Eteläinen Rautatiekatu
Helka
2
Hietaniemenkatu
Simonkenttä
TENNIS-PALATSI
Kamppi
Annankatu
Torni
Radisson SAS Royal
Kampintori
Malminkatu
Pohjoinen
LAPINLAHTI
Fredrikinkatu
Lapinlahdenkatu
Ruoholahdenkatu
Bulevardi
Albertinkatu
Linna
Serata
51
Holiday Inn Helsinki City West
Porkkalankatu
Kalevankatu
Lönnrotinkatu
SINEBRYCHOFFIN TAIDEMUSEO
Ruoholahti
Itämerenkatu
Hietalahdenranta
Punavuoren-
3
HIETALAHTI
Telakkakatu
LÄNSISATAMA
RUOHOLAHTI
A
B

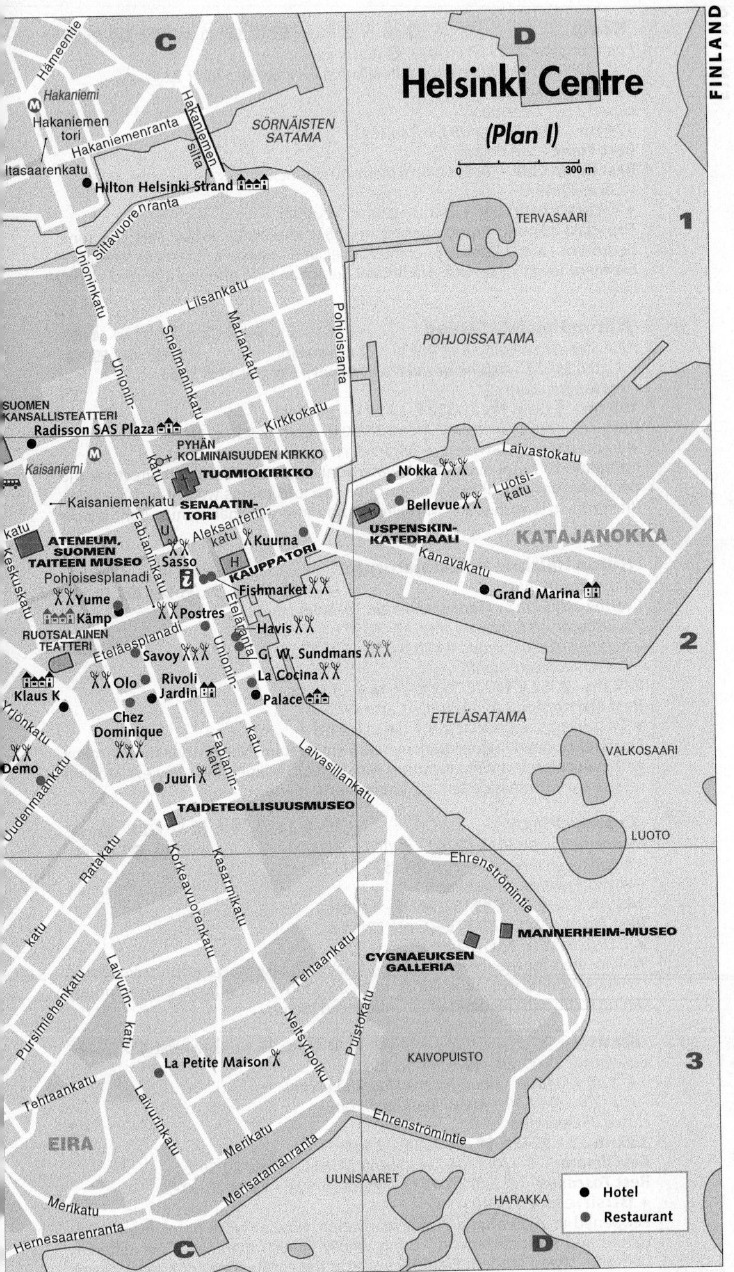
Helsinki Centre
(Plan I)
0
300 m
C
D
1
2
3
Hämeentie
Hakaniemi
Hakaniemen tori
Hakaniemenranta
Hakaniemen silta
Itasaarenkatu
SÖRNÄISTEN SATAMA
Hilton Helsinki Strand
Siltavuorenranta
TERVASAARI
Unioninkatu
Liisankatu
Mariankatu
Snellmaninkatu
Pohjoisranta
POHJOISSATAMA
Unionin-katu
Kirkkokatu
SUOMEN KANSALLISTEATTERI
Radisson SAS Plaza
PYHÄN KOLMINAISUUDEN KIRKKO
Kaisaniemi
TUOMIOKIRKKO
Nokka
Laivastokatu
Luotsi-katu
Bellevue
Kaisaniemenkatu
SENAATIN-TORI
USPENSKIN-KATEDRAALI
KATAJANOKKA
Aleksanterin-katu
Kuurna
ATENEUM, SUOMEN TAITEEN MUSEO
Sasso
KAUPPATORI
Kanavakatu
Keskuskatu
Fabianinkatu
Pohjoisesplanadi
Fishmarket
Grand Marina
Yume
Kämp
Postres
Eteläranta
Havis
RUOTSALAINEN TEATTERI
Eteläesplanadi
Savoy
G. W. Sundmans
Olo
Rivoli Jardin
La Cocina
Klaus K
Palace
Yrjönkatu
Chez Dominique
ETELÄSATAMA
VALKOSAARI
Demo
Uudenmaankatu
Fabianin-katu
Laivasillankatu
Juuri
TAIDETEOLLISUUSMUSEO
LUOTO
Ratakatu
Korkeavuorenkatu
Kasarmikatu
Ehrenströmintie
MANNERHEIM-MUSEO
CYGNAEUKSEN GALLERIA
Tehtaankatu
Laivurin-katu
Pursimiehenkatu
Neitsytpolku
Puistokatu
KAIVOPUISTO
La Petite Maison
Tehtaankatu
Laivurinkatu
EIRA
Merikatu
Merisatamanranta
UUNISAARET
HARAKKA
Hotel
Restaurant
Merikatu
Hernesaarenranta

FINLAND

Kämp

130 VISA AE

Pohjoisesplanadi 29 ✉ 00100 – Ⓜ Kaisaniemi – ✆ (09) 576 111 – hotelkamp@hotelkamp.fi – Fax (09) 576 11 22 – www.hotelkamp.fi

closed 23-27 December

C2

174 rm – 410 €, ☕ 29 € – 5 suites

Rest *Yume* – see below

Rest *Kämp Café* – *(buffet lunch)* Menu 30 € (lunch) – Carte 32/49 €

♦ Grand Luxury ♦ Business ♦ Stylish ♦

Top class historic hotel, opened in 1887. Impressive lobby sets the tone; bedrooms are extremely comfortable and boast a classical elegance. Excellent levels of service. Traditional European café offering assorted all day fare.

Hilton Helsinki Strand

180 VISA AE

John Stenbergin Ranta 4 ✉ 00530 – Ⓜ Hakaniemi – ✆ (09) 39 351 – helsinkistrand@hilton.com – Fax (09) 3935 32 55 – www.hilton.com

C1

185 rm – 352 € 222/352 €, ☕ 22 € – 7 suites

Rest – *(Sunday brunch only)* Menu 24/50 € – Carte 29/50 €

♦ Luxury ♦ Business ♦ Modern ♦

International hotel overlooking waterfront. Typically Finnish architecture and décor. Atrium style lobby. Comfortable spacious rooms with hi-tech facilities. Brasserie style restaurant with Finnish and international menus; light snacks served in Atrium.

Hilton Helsinki Kalastajatorppa

rm 550 VISA AE

Kalastajatorpantie 1 (Northwest : 5 km by Mannerheimintie, Tukholmankatu, Paciusgatan off Ramsaynranta) ✉ 00330 – ✆ (09) 45 811 – helsinkikalastajatorppa@hilton.com – Fax (09) 4581 22 11 – www.hilton.com/nordic

237 rm – 352 € 222/352 €, ☕ 15 € – 1 suite

Rest *Meritorppa* – *(dinner only)* Carte 29/50 €

♦ Business ♦ Luxury ♦ Functional ♦

Conference hotel in quiet park by sea, 5 km by tram. Nordic style rooms; many with balconies; Sea Wing for suites with hi-tech facilities and sea view. Modern restaurant with seaside terrace; international menu.

Crowne Plaza

550 VISA AE

Mannerheimintie 50 ✉ 00260 – ✆ (09) 2521 0000 – helsinki-cph@restel.fi – Fax (09) 2521 39 99 – www.crowneplaza-helsinki.fi

A1

345 rm ☕ – 287 € 157/287 € – 4 suites

Rest *Macu* – Menu 22/39 € – Carte 22/44 €

♦ Business ♦ Modern ♦

Well located for the Opera House and boasting lake views. Impressive leisure facilities. Rooms over nine floors: best are 'Club' on top floor. Contemporary dining room with Mediterranean influenced menus.

Klaus K

120 VISA AE

Bulevardi 2 ✉ 00120 – Ⓜ Rautatientori – ✆ (20) 7704 700 – klauskhotel@klauskhotel.com – Fax (20) 7704 7 30 – www.klauskhotel.com

closed 25 December

C2

135 rm ☕ – 248 € 268/298 € – 2 suites

Rest *Ilmatar* – ✆ *(20) 7704 714* – Menu 24/60 € – Carte 20/50 €

Rest *Toscanini* – ✆ *(20) 7704 713* – Menu 15/60 € – Carte 20/50 €

♦ Business ♦ Design ♦

Reopened in 2005 after a 2 year renovation. Now a stylish hotel, inspired by nature and mystical legends, using wholly Finnish materials. Four different bedroom styles. Modern Finnish cuisine in the earthy tones of Ilmatar. Rustic Tuscan fare in a trattoria setting in Toscanini.

Simonkenttä

Simonkatu 9 ✉ 00100 – Ⓜ Kamppi – ☎ (09) 68 380
– simonkentta@scandic-hotels.com – Fax (09) 683 81 11
– www.scandic-hotels.com
closed 22-27 December **B2**
357 rm – 227 € 145/247 € – 3 suites
Rest *Simonkatu* – *(closed Saturday lunch and Sunday)* Carte approx. 40 €
♦ Business ♦ Modern ♦
Ultra modern well-located hotel with imposing glazed façade. Stylish designer décor with colourful fabrics and parquet flooring in all rooms. Some rooms with a view. Stylish restaurant offers range of popular traditional dishes.

Holiday Inn Helsinki City Centre

Elielinaukio 5 ✉ 00100 – Ⓜ Rautatientori
– ☎ (09) 5425 5000 – helsinki.hihcc@restel.fi – Fax (09) 5425 52 99
– www.holidayinn.com/hihelsinkicc **B2**
174 rm – 245 € 245 €
Rest *Verde* – *(closed Saturday, Sunday and Bank Holiday lunch) (buffet lunch)* Menu 8 €
♦ Business ♦ Functional ♦
Modern city centre hotel near railway station, post office and all main shopping areas. Modern well-equipped bedrooms; good city view from 8th floor. Open style dining room serving popular menu using Finnish produce; lighter dishes available at lunchtime.

Seurahuone

Kaivokatu 12 ✉ 00100 – Ⓜ Kautatientori – ☎ (09) 69 141
– helsinki.seurahuone@restel.fi – Fax (09) 691 40 10
– www.hotelseurahuone.fi **B2**
118 rm – 245 € 159/400 €
Rest – *(closed Sunday)* Menu 45/65 € (lunch) – Carte 35/56 €
♦ Luxury ♦ Classic ♦
The hotel opened on this site in 1914 and was renovated in 2006. Spacious and smart bedrooms are classically decorated and respectful of the hotel's rich traditions. Dining room offers a traditional menu in elegant surroundings.

Holiday Inn Helsinki

Messuaukio 1 (near Pasila Railway Station)
(North : 4 km by Mannerheimintie, Nordenskiöldink,
Savonkatu off Ratapihantie) ✉ 00520 – ☎ (09) 150 900
– hi.reception@holidayinnhelsinki.fi – Fax (09) 150 9 01
– www.holidayinn.com
239 rm – 220 € 127/250 €, 15 € – 5 suites
Rest *Terra Nova* – Carte approx. 30 €
♦ Business ♦ Classic ♦
Purpose-built hotel in same building as congress centre; popular for conferences. Take breakfast in the winter garden style atrium. Spacious well-equipped rooms with warm décor. International menu for all tastes in the large restaurant.

Radisson SAS Royal

Runeberginkatu 2 ✉ 00100 – Ⓜ Kamppi – ☎ (20) 1234 701
– reservations.finland@radissonsas.com – Fax (20) 1234 7 02
– www.radissonsas.com
closed 5-9 April and 21-26 December **B2**
255 rm – 240 € 160/240 € – 7 suites
Rest – Carte 24/45 €
♦ Business ♦ Modern ♦
Usefully located purpose-built hotel offering easy transport links. Good-sized, well-maintained bedrooms and comprehensive conference facilities. Steaks and traditional cuisine feature in the restaurant.

FINLAND

Palace 350 VISA
Eteläranta 10 ✉ 00130 – Ⓜ Kaisaniemi – ✆ (09) 1345 6661 – palacehotel@palacekamp.fi – Fax (09) 654 7 86 – www.palacekamphotel.fi C2
37 rm – †262 € ††109/262 € – 2 suites – **Rest *La Cocina*** – see below
Rest *Palace Gourmet* – *✆ (09) 1345 6715 (closed Saturday and Sunday)*
Menu 41/65 € – Carte dinner 65/78 €
♦ Business ♦ Classic ♦
1950s hotel by harbour, occupying upper floors of building with street level reception. Spacious, comfortable rooms with modern facilities. Some with balconies and views. 10th-floor restaurant serves traditional Finnish cuisine with hint of France.

Radisson SAS Plaza 80 VISA
Mikonkatu 23 ✉ 00100 – Ⓜ Kaisaniemi – ✆ (20) 1234 703 – reservations.finland@radissonsas.com – Fax (20) 1234 7 04 – www.radissonsas.com C1-2
290 rm – †260 € ††170/260 € – 1 suite
Rest – Carte 23/52 €
♦ Business ♦ Functional ♦
Near the station, this sizeable modern business hotel maintains the reputation of this international group. Well-equipped rooms, in "Nordic", "Classic" or "Italian" style. Informal brasserie in a period townhouse; striking, painted windows.

Torni 35 VISA
Yrjönkatu 26 ✉ 00100 – Ⓜ Rautatientori – ✆ (20) 1234 604 – torni.helsinki@sokoshotels.fi – Fax (09) 4336 71 00 – www.sokoshotels.fi closed 21-28 December B2
146 rm – †243 € ††161/267 € – 6 suites
Rest – *(closed Sunday and Bank Holidays)* Menu 28/56 € – Carte 36/62 €
♦ Business ♦ Stylish ♦
Refurbished hotel in converted row of 1920s town houses in city centre. Rooms vary in size and are more Art Deco in style in the annexe. Choice of bars available. Inviting restaurant overlooking street offering a traditional menu.

Holiday Inn Helsinki City West VISA
Sulhasenkuja 3 ✉ 00180 – Ⓜ Ruoholahti – ✆ (09) 4152 1000 – helsinki.hihcw@restel.fi – Fax (09) 4152 12 99 – www.hi-helsinkiwest.fi A3
256 rm – †229 € ††130/229 €, 15 €
Rest – *(closed lunch Saturday and Sunday)* Menu 35/45 € (lunch) – Carte 32/48 €
♦ Business ♦ Modern ♦
Opened in 2005 and well located for the business parks west of the city. 9th floor Executive Rooms have king size beds and good views. Complimentary use of sauna. Huge ground floor bar and restaurant with global menus.

Vaakuna rm 20 VISA
Asema-aukio 2 ✉ 00100 – Ⓜ Rautatientori – ✆ (20) 1234 610 – vaakuna.helsinki@sokoshotels.fi – Fax (09) 4337 71 00 – www.sokoshotels.fi closed 5-8 April, 21-24 June and 22 December-1 January B2
258 rm – †225 € ††158/225 € – 12 suites
Rest – *(closed Saturday lunch and Sunday)* Menu 25 € (lunch) – Carte 37/43 €
♦ Business ♦ Classic ♦
Modern accommodation: spacious, colourful and well-appointed in this sizeable hotel, built for 1952 Olympics. Conveniently located for station. 10th-floor restaurant with views; lighter meals served in coffee shop.

Grand Marina 600 P VISA
Katajanokanlaitari 7 ✉ 00160 – ✆ (09) 16 661 – grandmarina@scandic-hotels.com – Fax (09) 664 7 64 – www.scandic-hotels.com D2
462 rm – †201 € ††114/420 € – **Rest *Makasiim*** – *(closed lunch Saturday and Sunday)* Menu 27/34 € (dinner) – Carte 34/40 €
♦ Business ♦ Functional ♦
Large harbourside hotel in converted warehouse opposite Marina Congress Centre. Practical rooms, functional fittings. Pub and coffee shop. Harbour views from roomy restaurant with Scandinavian cooking.

Rivoli Jardin without rest

Kasarmikatu 40 ✉ 00130 – Ⓜ Kaisaniemi – ✆ (09) 681 500 – rivoli.jardin@rivoli.fi – Fax (09) 656 9 88 – www.rivoli.fi – closed Christmas **C2**

55 rm – ††229/339 €

◆ Business ◆ Classic ◆

Well-run, traditional hotel close to city centre. Rooms are functional and comfortable, two on top floor have terrace. Winter garden style breakfast area.

Linna

Lönnrotinkatu 29 ✉ 00180 – Ⓜ Kamppi – ✆ (010) 3444 100 – linna@palacekamp.fi – Fax (010) 3444 1 01 – www.palacekamp.fi closed 5-10 April and 21 December-7 January **B3**

47 rm – †205 € ††205/390 € – 1 suite – **Rest** – *(closed 22 June-10 August, Saturday, Sunday and Bank Holidays) (dinner only)* Menu 49/68 € – Carte 37/52 €

◆ Business ◆ Modern ◆

An established local landmark, built in 1903, and a striking example of Finnish Art Nouveau. Renovated in 2005, it offers modern, well-equipped and quiet accommodation. Cosy 1st floor dining room with classic French cooking.

Pasila

Maistraatinportti 3 (North : 4 km by Mannerheimintie, Nordenskiöldink off Vetuvitie) ✉ 00240 – ✆ (20) 123 4613 – pasila.helsinki@sokoshotels.fi – Fax (09) 143 7 71 – www.sokoshotels.fi – closed 22 December-2 January

172 rm – †179 € ††179 € – 6 suites – **Rest *Sevilla*** – *(closed July)* Carte 18/25 €

◆ Business ◆ Modern ◆

Large, modern business hotel in tranquil district out of town, a short tram ride from city centre. Rooms feature contemporary local décor and furnishings. Informal Spanish-influenced restaurant; popular menu with grills.

Helka

Pohjoinen Rautatiekatu 23 ✉ 00100 – Ⓜ Kamppi – ✆ (09) 613 580 – reservations@helka.fi – Fax (09) 441 0 87 – www.helka.fi closed 22-27 December **B2**

150 rm – †132 € ††109/166 € – 7 suites

Rest *Helkan keittiö* – Menu 8/22 € (lunch) – Carte 23/36 €

◆ Family ◆ Functional ◆

A family-owned hotel offering affordable accommodation over five floors. The bedrooms were redecorated in 2005; if travelling alone ask for one of the larger single rooms. Clean, simple restaurant with a seasonal, contemporary Finnish menu.

Cumulus Olympia

Läntinen Brahenkatu 2 (North : 2 km by Siltasaarenkatu) ✉ 00510 – ✆ (09) 69 151 – olympia.cumulus@restel.fi – Fax (09) 691 52 19 – www.cumulus.fi closed 5-9 April and 17-26 December

101 rm – †173 € ††124/203 € – **Rest** – *(dinner only)* Carte 20/46 €

◆ Business ◆ Functional ◆

Situated in a residential area near the amusement park, 10 min. by tram from city centre. Modern bedrooms with standard décor and furnishings. Nightclub and Irish Pub. International menu in the restaurant.

Chez Dominique (Valimaki)

Rikhardinkatu 4 ✉ 00130 – Ⓜ Rautatientori – ✆ (09) 612 7393 – info@chezdominique.fi – Fax (09) 6124 42 20 – www.chezdominique.fi closed 3 weeks July, 1 week Christmas, Sunday and lunch Monday and Saturday **C2**

Rest – *(booking essential)* Menu 54 € (lunch) – Carte 84/101 €

Spec. Lobster poached in vanilla butter with avocado cannelloni. Baby lamb with eggplant lasagna and rosemary jus. Chocolate coulant with orange risotto and hazelnut.

◆ Inventive ◆ Elegant ◆

Relocated in November 2006 to new and very elegant surroundings. Sophisticated and comfortable room in black, white and red with on-view cellar. Highly accomplished Nordic and modern French cooking.

XXX

G. W. Sundmans

Eteläranta 16 (1st floor) ✉ 00130 – Ⓜ Kaisaniemi – ☎ (09) 622 6410 – myyntipalvelu@royalravintolat.com – Fax (09) 661 3 31 – www.royalravintolat.com/sundmans
closed Easter, Christmas, Saturday lunch and Sunday **C2**

Rest – Menu 45/66 € – Carte 67/78 €

Rest Krog (ground floor) – Menu 40/47 € (dinner) – Carte 29/49 €

Spec. Vendace roe with whitefish mousse and small potato pancakes. Cep and praline coated fillet of deer with peppery game sauce. Buckthorn berry soufflé with orange sorbet.

♦ Traditional ♦ Formal ♦

19C sea captain's Empire style mansion opposite harbour. Five classically decorated dining rooms with view. Elegant tables. Classically-based cuisine. Informal ground floor Krog restaurant features local seafood and traditional dishes.

XXX

Savoy

Eteläesplanadi 14 (8th floor) ✉ 00130 – Ⓜ Kaisaniemi – ☎ (09) 684 4020 – kai.kallio@royalravintolat.com – Fax (09) 628 7 15 – www.royalravintolat.com
closed 6-9 April, 23 June, Christmas, Saturday and Sunday **C2**

Rest – Menu 56/108 € – Carte dinner 72/87 €

♦ Traditional ♦ Formal ♦

Panoramic restaurant in city centre with typical Finnish design dating from 1937. Classic traditional menu of local specialities. Ask for a table in the conservatory.

XXX

Nokka

Kanavaranta 7F ✉ 00160 – ☎ (09) 687 7330 – Fax (09) 6877 33 30 – www.royalravintolat.com
closed 6-9 April, 23-24 June, 6 December, Christmas-7 January, Saturday lunch and Sunday **D2**

Rest – *(booking essential)* Menu 44/68 € – Carte dinner 38/63 €

♦ Modern ♦ Design ♦

Converted warehouse divided into two striking rooms; glazed wine cellar; waterfront terrace. Watch the chefs prepare appealing, modern Finnish cuisine. Good service.

XX

La Cocina – at Palace H.

Helsinki Harbour,

Eteläranta 10, (1st floor) ✉ 00130 Helsinki – Ⓜ Kaisaniemi – ☎ (09) 1345 6749 – sami.rekola@palace.fi – Fax (09) 1345 67 50 – www.palace.fi
closed 23 December-9 January, July, Saturday lunch and Sunday **C2**

Rest – *(dinner only except in December)* Menu 49/65 € – Carte 38/55 €

♦ Spanish ♦ Minimalist ♦

Fashionable restaurant with stylish bar. Trendy, vivid art on walls; pleasant harbour views. Spanish music blends perfectly with the earthy, powerful and authentic Basque dishes on offer, all presented with finesse.

XX

Olo

Kasarmikatu 44 ✉ 00130 – Ⓜ Kaisaneimi – ☎ (09) 665 565 – info@olo-restaurant.com – Fax (09) 665 5 75 – www.olo-restaurant.com
closed first week January, Easter, July, Saturday and Sunday **C2**

Rest – Menu 20/59 € – Carte 37/49 €

♦ Contemporary ♦ Design ♦

Opened in 2006 and the new place to be seen. Comfortable, well-organised restaurant with a discreet atmosphere. Contemporary Finnish cuisine using good quality ingredients.

XX

Sasso

Pohjoisesplanadi 17 ✉ 00170 Helsinki – Ⓜ Kaisaniemi – ☎ (09) 1345 6240 – tables@palacekamp.fi – Fax (09) 1345 62 42 – www.palacekamp.fi
closed Sunday and Bank Holidays **C2**

Rest – Carte 32/49 €

♦ Italian ♦ Fashionable ♦

Spacious, open-plan restaurant near market place and harbour. Stylish bar and lounge open all day. Shimmering fabrics typical of smart, contemporary interior with earthy and olive hues. Northern Italian dishes using top Finnish ingredients.

XX

Havis

Eteläranta 16 ✉ 00130 – ✆ (09) 6869 5660 – nina.koiranen@royalravintolat.com – Fax (09) 6869 56 56 – www.royalravintolat.com/havis
closed 6-9 April, 23 December-1 January, Sunday October-April and lunch Saturday and Sunday C2
Rest – Menu 29/58 € – Carte dinner 36/68 €
♦ Seafood ♦ Formal ♦
Divided into two contrasting styles of room: one classic and ornate, the other more lively with views into the kitchen. Same menu throughout features carefully prepared seafood.

XX

Yume – at Kämp H.

Kluuvikatu 2 ✉ 00100 – Ⓜ Kaisaniemi – ✆ (09) 576 117 18 – sales@palacekamp.fi – Fax (09) 576 115 15 – www.palacekamp.fi
closed 6-9 April, 22-27 June, 16 July-5 August, 22 December-8 January and Sunday C2
Rest – *(dinner only)* Carte 35/56 €
♦ Japanese ♦ Formal ♦
Both the menu and the décor change with the seasons at this smart Japanese restaurant. Located within the Kämp Hotel but with its own street entrance. Conscientious service.

XX ✿

Demo (Tuominen/ Aura)

Uudenmaankatu 11 ✉ 00120 Helsinki – Ⓜ Rautatientori – ✆ (09) 228 90840 – demo@restaurantdemo.fi – Fax (09) 228 9 08 41 – www.restaurantdemo.fi
closed 2 weeks Christmas and New Year, Sunday, Monday and Bank Holidays
Rest – *(booking essential) (dinner only)* Menu 48/52 € – Carte 44/52 € C2
Spec. Slightly smoked tuna with wasabi mayonnaise. Elk shoulder with wild mushrooms, elk sausage and blackcurrant sauce. Lime soufflé and sorbet.
♦ Contemporary ♦ Trendy ♦
Locally renowned restaurant run by talented young team. A compact interior houses trendy red fabric and chrome chairs with a warm candle-lit atmosphere. Modern, seasonal dishes with Gallic overtones, freshly prepared using local produce.

XX

Postres

Eteläesplanadi 8 ✉ 00130 – Ⓜ Kaisaniemi – ✆ (09) 663 300 – info@postres.fi – Fax 663 3 01 – www.postres.fi
closed 1-30 July, 23 December-8 January, Sunday and Monday lunch C2
Rest – Menu 22/59 €
♦ Modern ♦ Design ♦
Opened by a keen young team in 2006. Bright and inviting dining room divided into two. Friendly service pitched just right; good quality cooking with desserts a speciality.

XX

FishMarket

Pohjoisesplanadi 17 ✉ 00170 Helsinki – Ⓜ Kaisaniemi – ✆ (09) 1345 6220 – sales@palacekamp.fi – Fax (09) 1345 62 22 – www.palacekamp.fi
closed Sunday, Monday in July and Bank Holidays C2
Rest – *(dinner only)* Carte 40/53 €
♦ Seafood ♦ Design ♦
Basement restaurant on the market place with appealing shellfish bar. Bright white décor complemented by attentive, friendly service. Seafood menus change seasonally, highlighted by original combinations.

XX

Bellevue

Rahapajankatu 3 ✉ 00160 – Ⓜ Kaisaniemi – ✆ (09) 179 560 – info@restaurantbellevue.com – Fax (09) 636 9 85 – www.restaurantbellevue.com
closed 23 December-1 January, lunch in July, Saturday lunch May-August and Sunday D2
Rest – Menu 17/59 € – Carte 38/69 €
♦ Russian ♦ Cosy ♦
Opened in 1917 in a period townhouse and claims to be the oldest outside Russia. Fairly sombre traditionally styled décor and cosy, intimate atmosphere. Menu features Russian delicacies.

FINLAND

Lyon

Mannerheimintie 56 ✉ 00260 – ✆ (09) 408 131 – ravintola.lyon@kolumbus.fi – Fax (09) 422 0 74 – www.ravintolalyon.fi
restricted opening in summer and closed July, Sunday, Monday and Saturday lunch and Bank Holidays A1
Rest – Menu 34/62 € – Carte 46/64 €
♦ French ♦ Bistro ♦
Traditional, well-established restaurant near the Opera. Menu has varied choice: seasonal, vegetarian or Helsinki, as well as the main à la carte serving French-style dishes.

La Petite Maison

Huvilakatu 28A ✉ 00150 – Ⓜ Eiran Sai Raala – ✆ (09) 270 1704 – sales@henrix.fi – Fax (09) 6842 56 66 – www.henrix.fi
closed 25 December, Sunday and Bank Holidays C3
Rest – *(booking essential) (dinner only)* Carte 63/89 €
♦ French ♦ Cosy ♦
Cosy restaurant popular with local clientele in a quiet street known for its Art Deco architecture. Traditional décor with strong French note in the classic fare. Reasonably priced wine list.

Serata

Bulevardi 32 ✉ 00120 – Ⓜ Kamppi Kampen – ✆ (09) 680 1365 – serata@serata.net – www.serata.net
closed 22 December-7 January, Easter, 9-28 July, Sunday, Monday dinner, Saturday lunch and Bank Holidays B3
Rest – *(booking essential)* Menu 30/42 € – Carte 31/48 €
♦ Italian ♦ Friendly ♦
Warm and relaxed corner restaurant with a convivial atmosphere. Open kitchen with some counter seating. Authentic Italian cooking with good value set menus including wine.

Juuri

Korkeavuorenkatu 27 ✉ 00130 – ✆ (09) 635 732 – ravintola@juuri.fi – Fax (09) 635 7 32 – www.juuri.fi
closed 24-26 December C2
Rest – Carte approx. 28 €
♦ Finnish ♦ Bistro ♦
Close to the Design museum, a bistro with lots of wood brightened by large windows. The kitchen is keen to promote traditional Finnish home and country cooking. Starters served in tapas style.

Kuurna

Meritullinkatu 6 ✉ 00170 – Ⓜ Kaisaniemi – ✆ (09) 670 849 – info@kuurna.fi – www.kuurna.fi
closed 22 June-July, 25 December-7 January, Sunday and Monday C2
Rest – *(booking essential) (dinner only)* Menu 29/45 €
♦ Finnish ♦ Cosy ♦
Small and intimate restaurant with vaulted ceiling seating just 20. Always busy, creating plenty of noise. Traditional Finnish home cooking with blackboard supplements.

at Helsinki-Vantaa Airport North : 19 km by A 137

Vantaa

15 280
Hertaksentie 2 (near Tikkurila Railway Station) ✉ 00420 – ✆ (20) 1234 618 – hotelvantaa@sokoshotels.fi – Fax (09) 8578 55 55 – www.sokoshotels.fi
closed 23-27 December
265 rm – †173 € ††196/270 €
Rest ***Vantaa*** – Carte 20/43 €
♦ Business ♦ Functional ♦
Beside the railway station and convenient for the airport (bus number 61). Busy, corporate hotel with well-equipped rooms in a Scandinavian style. Rooms in the new wing are best.

FRANCE

PROFILE

◆ **Area:**
551 500 km² (212 934 sq mi).

◆ **Population:**
60 656 000 inhabitants (est. 2005), density = 110 per km².

◆ **Capital:**
Paris (conurbation 9 928 000 inhabitants).

◆ **Currency:**
Euro (€); rate of exchange: € 1 = US$ 1.17 (Nov 2005).

◆ **Government:**
Parliamentary republic (since 1946). Member of European Union since 1957 (one of the 6 founding countries).

◆ **Language:**
French.

◆ **Specific public holidays:**
Victory Day 1945 (8 May), Bastille Day-National Day (14 July), Armistice Day 1918 (11 November).

◆ **Local Time:**
GMT + 1 hour in winter and GMT + 2 hours in summer.

◆ **Climate:**
Temperate with cool winters and warm summers (Paris: January: 3°C, July: 20°C). Mediterranean climate in the south (mild winters, hot and sunny summers, occasional strong wind called the mistral).

◆ **International dialling Code:**
00 33 followed by regional code without the initial **0** and then the local number.

◆ **Emergency:**
Police: ✆ **17**; Ambulance: ✆ **15**; Fire Brigade: ✆ **18**.

◆ **Electricity:**
220 volts AC, 50Hz. 2-pin round-shaped continental plugs.

FORMALITIES

Travellers from the European Union (EU), Switzerland, Iceland and the main countries of North and South America need a national identity card or passport (America: passport required) to visit France for less than three months (tourism or business purpose). For visitors from other countries a visa may be required, in addition to a passport, especially for those wishing to stay for longer than three months. We advise you to check with your embassy before travelling.

Nationals of EU member countries require a valid national driving licence. Nationals of non-EU countries should obtain an international driving licence. Insurance cover is compulsory and although it is no longer a legal requirement in France, it is advisable to have an international insurance certificate (Green Card).

MAJOR NEWSPAPERS

The national daily papers with widest distribution are *Le Monde*, *Le Figaro* and *Libération*. *Le Parisien* covers Paris and the surrounding regions. *Ouest-France* (all of northwest France, including Brittany, Normandy and the Loire region) is the main regional daily. Weekly papers: *Le Point*, *L'Express*, *Le Nouvel Observateur*.

USEFUL PHRASES

ENGLISH	FRENCH
Yes	**Oui**
No	**Non**
Good morning	**Bonjour**
Goodbye	**Au revoir**
Thank you	**Merci**
Please	**S'il vous plaît**
Excuse me	**Excusez-moi**
I don't understand	**Je ne comprends pas**

HOTELS

→ CATEGORIES

Accommodation ranges from the most prestigious hotels to simple guesthouses, and include comfortable hotels for family and business travellers.

→ PRICE RANGE

The price is per room. There is no great difference between the charge for single and double rooms.

→ TAX

Included in the room rate.

→ CHECK OUT TIME

Usually between 11am and noon.

→ RESERVATIONS

By telephone or by Internet; a credit card number is required.

→ TIP FOR LUGGAGE HANDLING

At the discretion of the client (about €1 per item).

→ BREAKFAST

It is often not included in the room rate and is usually served from 7am to 10am. Most hotels offer a self-service buffet, but you may ask for continental breakfast to be served in the room.

Reception	**Réception**
Single room	**Chambre simple**
Double room	**Chambre double**
Bed	**Lit**
Bathroom	**Salle de bains**
Shower	**Douche**

RESTAURANTS

France is home to every imaginable type of restaurant, whether Michelin starred establishments or neighbourhood eateries where one can enjoy a delicious meal in pleasant surroundings. **Brasseries** serve hearty, traditional and regional fare such as seafood, cassoulet, choucroute and pigs' trotters. **Bistros** are small eating-places with no frills serving simple dishes in a cheerful atmosphere. A **bouchon** is a typical small establishment in Lyon and the **Winstub** is a winebar in Alsace .

Breakfast	**Petit-déjeuner**	7-10am
Lunch	**Déjeuner**	12.30-2pm
Dinner	**Dîner**	7.30-10pm; some places close later

Restaurants offer both a fixed menu (starter, main course and dessert) or a menu à la carte.

→ RESERVATIONS

Reservations can be made by phone. Some places may require a credit card number as guarantee. In the case of Michelin starred or other famous restaurants, it is advisable to book several days, or even weeks, in advance.

→ THE BILL

The bill (check) includes a service charge and VAT. However, if you are particularly happy with the service it is usual to leave a tip at your discretion (often 5% of the bill).

Aperitif	**Apéritif**
Meal	**Repas**
First course, starter	**Entrée**
Main dish	**Plat principal**
Main dish of the day	**Plat du jour**
Dessert	**Dessert**
Mineral water/ sparkling water	**Eau minérale/gazeuse**
Wine (rosé, red, white)	**Vin (rosé, rouge, blanc)**
Beer	**Bière**
Bread	**Pain**
Meat (medium, rare, blue)	**Viande (à point, saignant, bleu)**
Fish	**Poisson**
Salt/pepper	**Sel/poivre**
Cheese	**Fromages**
Vegetables	**Légumes**
Hot/cold	**Chaud/froid**
The bill (check) please	**L'addition s'il vous plaît**

LOCAL CUISINE

France is the land of good food and good living and each region takes great pride in its specialities. Some of the most famous dishes rely on **foie gras** and **seafood.** Of course the celebrated **cheeses** of France are an important part of the culinary experience. It is possible to give only an introduction to the delicious fare to savour in the country. In Paris you can sample the cuisine of all the regions of France.

→ Starters

A meal typically begins with soup or consommé: velouté d'asperges/de champignons (cream of asparagus/mushroom), soupe de poireaux-pommes de terre (leek and potato soup), soupe/gratinée à l'oignon (onion soup), bisque de homard (cream of lobster), garbure (a thick cabbage soup), cotriade (Breton fish soup). A tasty starter or light meal may consist of salade niçoise (tomatoes, anchovies, tuna, olives), salade lyonnaise (green salad with cubed bacon and soft-cooked eggs), salade cauchoise (celery, potatoes, ham). You can also choose a flamiche (leek quiche), a ficelle (ham pancake with mushroom sauce), **quiche lorraine** (ham and cheese flan), flammeküche (thin-crusted savoury tart covered with cream, onions and bacon), pissaladière (Provençal quiche with onions, tomatoes, anchovies) or tapenade (black olives, capers, anchovies). A seafood platter is a glorious dish – oysters, shrimps, prawns, clams, etc.

→ Main courses

Meat and fish courses are accompanied by seasonal vegetables or served with gratin dauphinois (potatoes, eggs and milk) or gratin savoyard (potatoes, eggs and stock). **Bouillabaisse** is the famous fish stew from Marseilles made with several types of fish and seasoned with saffron, garlic, fennel and herbs. A speciality from Nîmes is **brandade**, a creamy blend of cod mashed with olive oil, milk and garlic cloves. From Brittany come homard à l'armoricaine (lobster with tomatoes, Cayenne pepper, white wine, cognac and herbs), moules à la crème (mussels with cream) and brochet au beurre blanc (shad or pike with Nantes-style butter sauce). Shrimps and cockles are delicious when cooked fresh from the sea in Normandy, which is also well known for its sole dieppoise (sole in a creamy sauce). Loup grillé au fenouil or au sarment de vigne (seabass grilled with fennel or baked on a fire with vine twigs) are popular dishes in Provence and on the Riviera.

Other favourite regional specialities are: **choucroute** (cabbage, potatoes, pork, sausage and ham) and baeckeoffe (lamb, beef, pork, vegetables, white wine) from Alsace; **cassoulet** (bean stew, goose or duck pieces, pork) from Toulouse or Castelnaudary; tripes à la mode de Caen (tripe cooked with carrots, celery, herbs, calf's foot); canard au sang (pressed duck) from Rouen; sauce meurette (wine sauce) from Burgundy to accompany poached eggs. Also worth a mention are potée (thick cabbage stew with pork, bacon, turnips or with Morteau or Montbéliard sausage) from Auvergne or Franche-Comté; aligot (a creamy blend of fresh Tomme cheese and mashed potato seasoned with garlic) from Chaudes-Aigues; tripoux (stuffed tripe) from Aurillac; poulet basquaise (chicken with tomatoes, peppers and black olives).

→ Cheeses

France produces an amazing variety of cheeses with a delicate or pungent flavour. The **cheese platter** is an essential part of a French meal. There are soft, bloomy-rind cheeses such as Brie de Meaux, Brie de Melun, Camembert, Chaource; washed-rind cheeses – Livarot, Pont L'Évêque, Maroilles, Époisses, Reblochon, Munster, Vacherin; natural-rind cheeses – Saint-Marcellin, Cendrés de Bourgogne, de l'Orléanais, de Champagne. Most hard cheeses – Cantal, Beaufort, Comté, Emmental – are non-pasteurized. Some blue cheeses have a natural rind, or no rind at all; varieties include Bleu de Bresse, Fourme d'Ambert, Roquefort (ewe milk), Bleu d'Auvergne, Bleu des Causses.

Goat cheese is made in many regions, especially Touraine (Sainte-Maure, Valençay), Poitou (Chabichou, Bougon), Berry (Crottin de Chavignol), Quercy (Rocamadour), Haute Provence (Banon) and the Cévennes (Picodon).

They can be enjoyed soft (frais) or cured (sec) ; the textures vary greatly according to the time of aging. The best known cheeses made from ewe milk, besides Roquefort, are Corsican cheeses and Ossau-Iraty made in the Pyrenees.

→ Desserts

To round off a meal, the choice of **desserts** is mouth-watering. Besides a platter of fresh fruit, fruit salad or fruit stewed in red wine, there are all sorts of delicious cakes. One traditional favourite is **tarte Tatin** (caramelised upside-down apple tart); others are the **baba au rhum** (sponge cake soaked in rum syrup) and the **Paris-Brest** (a praline cream pastry). Of course, the regions all have their dessert specialities, too: gâteau aux noix (walnut cake) from Grenoble, far (baked custard) from Brittany, gâteau basque (chewy sweet cake filled with pastry cream), gâteau de Savoie (a fluffy bundt cake), pain d'épice (gingerbread) from Dijon, clafoutis (oven-baked fruit and custard tart) from Auvergne and Limousin, and Kougelhopf (a sweet crown-shaped yeast cake) from Alsace. Cream caramel, crème brûlée and île flottante (soft meringue with custard sauce) are popular in nearly every region of France.

WINE

Touring the wine-growing regions of France ranks among the great attractions of the country. Wine is the perfect complement to French culinary delights. A 'terroir' is a group of vineyards (or even vines) from the same region, belonging to a specified appellation, and sharing the same type of soil, weather conditions, grapes and wine making savoir-faire, which contribute to give its specific personality to the wine.

→ Burgundy

Red Burgundy is made of one grape, Pinot noir. The Burgundy area comprises Côte de Nuits, which boasts outstanding full-bodied wines – Gevrey-Chambertin, Chambolle-Musigny, Vosne-Romanée – and Côte de Beaune which also produces very attractive wines – Aloxe-Corton, Savigny-lès-Beaune, Chorey-lès-Beaune, Pommard, Volnay. Some of the famous white wines of the region are Chablis, Meursault, Puligny-Montrachet and Chassagne-Montrachet. The Côte Châlonnaise has some well-known names – Rully, Mercurey, Givry, Montagny while the Mâconnais produces Pouilly-Fuissé, St-Vérand and Mâcon Villages.

→ Beaujolais

Beaujolais is preferably drunk young but the best vintages, which include Fleurie, Morgon and Moulin-à-Vent, gain greater depth with age.

→ Bordeaux

Red Bordeaux are made from several grapes: Cabernet-Sauvignon, Cabernet Franc, Petit Verdot... This famous wine-producing area yields superb clarets: St-Estèphe, Pauillac, Pomerol, St-Émilion, St-Julien, Margaux and pleasant dry white wines – Graves, Entre-deux-Mers.

→ Rhône-Valley

The elegant wines of Côte-Rôtie, Hermitage, Châteauneuf-du-Pape, Gigondas and Condrieu are among the best of Côtes du Rhône, made with Syrah, Grenache, Viognier grapes.

→ Loire Valley

Loire wines – Muscadet, Anjou, Saumur, Touraine – are made from Muscadet, Chenin blanc, Cabernet Franc while the delicious Sancerre and flinty Pouilly-Fumé are made from Sauvignon blanc and Pinot Noir.

→ Alsace

The fragrant wines of Alsace are Riesling, Gewurztraminer, Tokay-Pinot-Gris and Sylvaner.

→ Champagne

Champagne, which is known as the 'nectar of the gods' and the 'wine of kings', brings a festive note to any occasion. The most celebrated champagnes are from the Côte des Blancs (Épernay, Ay, Chouilly terroirs). Only the best years are labelled with the vintage year.

→ Other sparkling wines

There are also some excellent sparkling wines such as Crémant de Bourgogne, Crémant d'Alsace, Crémant de Loire, Blanquette de Limoux and Clairette de Die.

→ Dessert wines

The best dessert wines are Sauternes (especially Château d'Yquem, a pure nectar and in a class of its own), Monbazillac, Muscat de Beaumes-de-Venise and Muscat de Rivesaltes. Banyuls and Maury are also delicious and accompany chocolate particularly well.

Beyond these famous wines, there are a multitude of regional wines available everywhere you travel in France (Languedoc-Roussillon, Provence, Jura, South-West…) and we hope this brief introduction will whet your appetite.

Population (est. 2005): 2 107 000 (conurbation 9 928 000) - Altitude: 60 m

J. Guillard/SCOPE

The architectural harmony of Paris is striking with its wide avenues lined with elegant 19C buildings, its mediaeval centre and Renaissance and Classical additions which have been remodelled over the centuries. From its origins as the small Gallo-Roman settlement known as Lutetia, Paris grew along the banks of the Seine. The splendid monuments, Notre-Dame, the Louvre, the Place de la Concorde, the Eiffel Tower, with the book stalls, cafés, art galleries and smart shops lining the banks are best admired on a leisurely boat trip by day or when lit up at night. For typically Parisian scenes, explore the maze of alleyways leading to the boulevards and watch the world go by as you savour an espresso or a cool beer at a café terrace where waiters wear the traditional long, white aprons and black waistcoats.

Paris is known as the City of Light. It has a reputation for elegance owing to its fashion designers, perfumers and jewellers and it is a vibrant artistic and intellectual capital with many theatres, concert halls, music halls, museums and bookshops. Its numerous attractions make it an ever popular tourist destination.

WHICH DISTRICT TO CHOOSE

It is useful to understand the layout of the city to avoid confusion over the names of the districts (quartiers) and the 20 arrondissements. The right bank takes in the north and west while the left bank comprises the south. The Île de la Cité *Plan V* **T2** is the nucleus around which the city grew and the oldest quarters around this site are the 1st, 2nd, 3rd, 4th arrondissements on the right bank and 5th, 6th on the left bank *(see the Plan I)*.

Accommodation is plentiful in Paris. Prestigious **hotels** with luxurious amenities are located in the fashionable districts – 1st, 2nd and 8th arrondissements – in the city centre and there are business and moderately

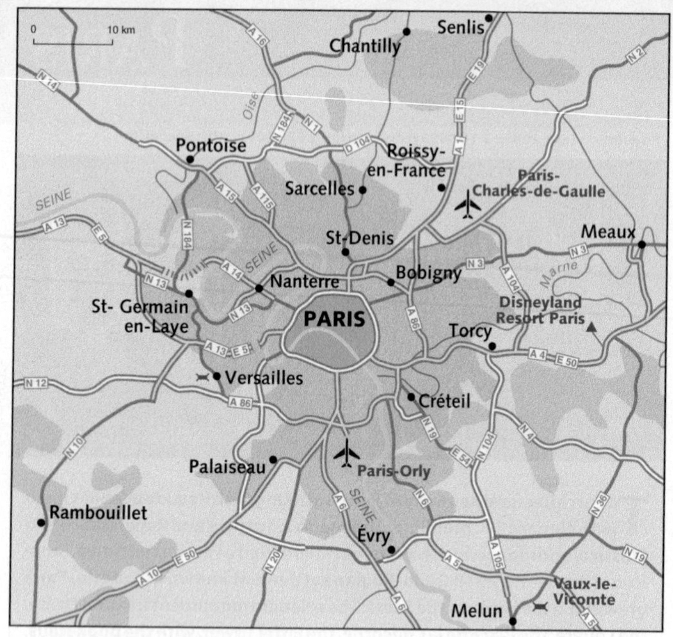

priced hotels in the 5th, 6th, 7th, 14th, 15th arrondissements. Charming small establishments are also to be found in various districts such as the Marais *Plan VII* **X1** and Saint-Germain-des-Prés *Plan V* **S2**.

The city takes great pride in the quality of food available in establishments of all kinds from the simple bistro to the gastronomic temples. You will find the finest **restaurants** in the 1st, 2nd, 5th, 6th, 8th, 16th and 17th arrondissements and excellent restaurants at reasonable prices in the 7th, 14th and 17th arrondissements. There are also cafés, bistros, crêperies, brasseries, tables d'hôte, winebars, tearooms and ethnic eateries for you to enjoy all over the city.

PRACTICAL INFORMATION

ARRIVAL – DEPARTURE

Roissy-Charles-de-Gaulle Airport – 23 km (14 mi) northeast of Paris. ✆ 01 48 62 22 80; www.adp.fr

Orly Airport – 14 km (9 mi) south of Paris. ✆ 01 49 75 15 15; www.adp.fr

From Roissy airport to Paris – By **taxi**: about €50 (+ €1 per item of luggage), time 30min-1hr according to the time of day and the traffic. By **RER**: via Gare du Nord, Châtelet-Les-Halles, Luxembourg and Port-Royal to the city centre, €8, 10. By **Air France bus**: to Montparnasse or Porte Maillot/Arc de Triomphe every 15min and to Gare de Lyon or Montparnasse every 30min. Fares €12 one-way, €18 round trip.

From Orly airport to Paris – By **taxi**: about €30, time 20-45min depending on the traffic. By **Orlyval shuttle-train** from the airport to Antony connecting with the RER and to other stations in Paris: €7.20-€9.10. By **Orly bus** to Denfert-Rochereau €6.00 or **Air France bus** to Invalides or Montparnasse, every 15min, €8 one way, €12 round trip.

Main Stations – **Gare de Lyon** *Plan I* **C2**: trains from southeast France, Italy, Switzerland. **Gare d'Austerlitz** *Plan I* **C3**: trains from southwest France and Spain. **Gare du Nord** *Plan I* **C1**: trains from the United Kingdom, Belgium, The Netherlands. **Gare de l'Est**: trains from Germany.

TRANSPORT

→ TAXIS

Taxis may be hailed in the streets, at taxi ranks or called by phone. Average trip: €15-25 during the day and €20-30 at night. For a tip, add up to 10% although this is not compulsory. *Taxis Bleus* ✆ 0891 70 10 10; *Alpha Taxis* ✆ 01 45 85 85 85.

→ BUS AND METRO

Paris has an excellent and inexpensive public transport system. Fares: €1.40 single ticket; €10.90 carnet (book of 10 tickets). **Paris Visite**: €8.35 (1-day pass 3 zones) to €53.35 (5-day pass 8 zones). **Mobilis** is a one-day pass giving unlimited travel in zones selected: €5.50 (Zones 1-2) to €18.70 (Zones 1-8). The weekly or monthly **Carte Orange** is valid from the first of the month or Mon-Sun and offers an advantageous rate; photograph required.

USEFUL ADDRESSES

→ TOURIST INFORMATION

Office du tourisme et des congrès de Paris, 25-27 Rue des Pyramides *Plan III* **K3**. ✆ 08 92 68 30 00. Open 9am-8pm; Nov-Mar, Sun and holidays 11am-6pm. Closed 1 May. www.parisinfo.com

There are also welcome points at **Gare de Lyon**, **Gare du Nord**, **Tour Eiffel**, **Opéra** (11 Rue Scribe), **Montmartre** (21 Place du Tertre) and **Carrousel du Louvre** (99 Rue de Rivoli).

→ POST OFFICES

Open Mon Fri, 8am-7pm; Sat 8am-noon. The main post office at 52 Rue du Louvre opens 24 hours 7 days a week.

→ BANKS/CURRENCY EXCHANGE

Open Mon-Fri, 4.30pm. Some branches open Sat mornings. Credit cards may be used to withdraw cash from ATMs which require a PIN. Bureaux de change have high charges.

→ EMERGENCY

Medical assistance (SAMU): ✆ **15**, police: ✆ **17**, Fire Brigade: ✆ **18**.

BUSY PERIODS

It may be difficult to find a room or prices may go up when certain events are held in the city:

Salon de l'Agriculture: late February-March.

Foire de Paris: May.

Mondial de l'Automobile: late September-October – every other year (next: 2008).

DIFFERENT FACETS OF THE CITY

It is possible to visit the main sights and museums in Paris in four to five days. *Museums and other sights are usually open from 10am to 6pm. Most close on Tuesdays.*

ROMANTIC CITY – A tour in a **bateau-mouche** on the Seine to admire the splendid cityscape. Take the lift to the top of the **Tour Eiffel** *Plan IV* **O1**. Walk down the **Champs-Élysées** *Plan II* **G3** to the **Arc de Triomphe** *Plan II* **F2**, then explore **Montmartre** *Plan VIII* **AA1** for one of the finest vistas in Paris.

HISTORIC CITY – Walk round the **Île de la Cité** and visit **Notre-Dame de Paris** *Plan V* **U2**. Then cross to the right bank of the Seine past the **Hôtel de Ville** *Plan V* **U1** and on to the **Marais** *Plan VII* **X1**, the oldest quarter with its splendid mansions.

ARTISTIC CITY – A visit to the **Musée du Louvre** *Plan V* **S1** is a must for art lovers, then explore the gardens of the **Palais Royal** *Plan III* **K3** behind the **Comédie Française**. The Musée d'Art Moderne at **Centre Georges-Pompidou** *Plan V* **U1** in the Beaubourg district is of interest for those keen on modern architecture and contemporary art.

LOCAL COLOUR – To capture the flavour of life in the city, spend some time on the left bank where the intellectuals frequent the cafés of the **Quartier Latin** *Plan V* **T2** and the Sorbonne, the **Quartier Saint-Germain-des-Prés** *Plan IV* **S2** where the major publishers are located. The trendy places for the young are near the Bastille and beyond towards **Oberkampf**. To go back in time visit the charming **galleries and arcades**: Passage des Panoramas *Plan III* **L2**, Passage de Choiseul *Plan III* **K3**, Passage Colbert *Plan III* **K3**, Passage Véro-Dodat *Plan III* **L3**, Passage Vivienne *Plan III* **L3**.

GREEN CITY – The **Jardin des Tuileries** *Plan III* **J3**, **Jardin du Luxembourg** *Plan IV* **S3**, **Buttes-Chaumont** *Plan I* **D1**, **Parc Monceau** *Plan II* **G1** and **Parc André-Citroën** *Plan I* **A3** are havens in central Paris. The **Bois de Boulogne** *Plan I* **A2** and **Bois de Vincennes** *Plan I* **D3** are on the outskirts.

MARKETS – The colourful and lively scene of **open-air markets** is a delight: Marché d'Aligre (near Gare de Lyon) *Plan I* **D2**, Rue Cler *Plan IV* **P2**, Rue de Levis *Plan II* **H1**, Rue Montorgueil *Plan I* **C2**, Boulevard Raspail *Plan VI* **W1**, Rue de Buci *Plan V* **S2**. The **flea markets** at Porte de Clignancourt *Plan I* **C1** and Porte de Vanves *Plan I* **A3** are famous for antiques. Also of interest are: the **flower markets** at Place Louis-Lépine *Plan V* **T1**, Place de la Madeleine *Plan III* **J2** and Place des Ternes *Plan III* **F1**; the **Bird Market**, Place Louis-Lépine *Plan V* **T1**; the **Stamp Market**, Carré Marigny *Plan II* **H3**.

VISITING

Notre-Dame de Paris *Plan V* **U2** – One of the major Gothic cathedrals in France. Nearby is the **Sainte-Chapelle**, a masterpiece of Gothic architecture celebrated for its pure lines and its sumptuous stained glass windows.

Tour Eiffel *Plan IV* **O1** – The soaring tower, which is the symbol of Paris, is a daring architectural achievement. The nightly illumination turns it into a sparkling jewel.

Musée du Louvre *Plan IV* **S1** – One of the world's greatest museums displaying masterpieces: *Mona Lisa*, The *Winged Victory of Samothrace, Venus de Milo* among others. The glass pyramid by Pei is remarkable.

Butte Montmartre and Basilique du Sacré-Cœur *Plan VIII* **AA1** – A Romano-Byzantine basilica crowns the heights of Montmartre. From the terrace and from the dome one can enjoy the best views of the city. Do not miss the bustling Place du Tertre where artists offer their paintings or portraits.

Musée National d'Art moderne *Plan V* **U1** – Housed in **Centre Georges-Pompidou**, the museum traces the evolution of art from fauvism and cubism to contemporary trends.

Musée d'Orsay *Plan V* **R1** – Collection of 19C art including many Impressionist works.

Place des Vosges *Plan VII* **X2** – A wonderful, shady square, the oldest in Paris (17C), at the heart of the Marais district. Nearby is the fine **Place des Victoires** dominated by a statue of Louis XIV.

Château de Versailles – *20 km-12.5 mi southwest.* A glorious monument to the French monarchy combining a splendid palace and harmonious gardens.

Disneyland Resort – *30 km-19 mi east.* A world of fun at Disneyland in Europe.

Viewpoints – **Sacré Cœur** *Plan VIII* **AA1**; **Tour Eiffel** *Plan IV* **O1**; **Tour Montparnasse** *Plan VI* **V1**; **Arc de Triomphe** *Plan II* **F2**; **Notre-Dame** towers.

Vistas – From the Rond-Point on the Champs-Élysées *Plan II* **F2** (Arc de Triomphe, Champs-Élysées, Place de la Concorde); from the obelisk on Place de la Concorde *Plan III* **J2** (Madeleine church, Place de la Concorde, Palais Bourbon); from the terrace of the Palais de Chaillot *Plan IV* **N1** (Trocadéro, Eiffel Tower, École Militaire); from Pont Alexandre-III *Plan IV* **Q1** (Invalides, Grand and Petit-Palais).

GOURMET TREATS

The centre of the capital city offers an enticing array of shops selling treats both savoury and sweet. Enjoy the scent and texture of a golden brown **baguette**; have the most typical of Parisian sandwiches, the "**jambon beurre**", made with fresh bread, ham and butter, available at all of the good bakeries (*Kayser*, 8 Rue Monge, to name but one) and in some bistros, cafés and brasseries.

Tasty delights spill out of the cornucopia of Place de la Madeleine, in shops whose names evoke the pleasures of the palate. *Fauchon, Hédiard, La Maison de la Truffe*, and the tea room *Ladurée* (around the corner at 16 Rue Royale) are among the most famous. Another charming tea room, *Angélina* (226 Rue de Rivoli), is known for serving the creamiest **hot chocolate** in town.

Near the Place des Victoires, in the beautiful covered passage Galerie Vivienne, *Legrand* sweet shop also offers a selection of 3 500 vintage **wines**, which you can enjoy with an assortment of cold meats. A different atmosphere prevails at *Père Louis* (38 Rue Monsieur-le-Prince), an authentic wine bar with wine casks for tables, and a friendly, relaxed ambience.

In the St-Germain-des-Prés neighbourhood, the *Pierre Hermé* pastry shop (72 Rue Bonaparte) is the place to go for chewy **macaroons**. Although the shop is unpretentious, it is a local favourite and known around the world. The nearby *Poilâne* bakery (8 Rue du Cherche-Midi) is famous as well for its shortbread biscuits (**sablés**) and many different varieties of **bread**. It is also well worth looking in at the *Fromagerie 31* (64 Rue de Seine), to take advantage of the tasting area and admire the tempting display of **cheeses** from all over France.

End your epicurean adventures on a note of freshness and colour on the island of Saint Louis, with a visit to the famous **ice cream** maker *Berthillon* (Rue St-Louis-en-l'Île). There is a flavour to please everyone, including exotic litchi, thyme or gingerbread.

SHOPPING

Department stores – Boulevard Haussmann *Plan III* **K2** *(Galeries Lafayette, Printemps)*, Rue de Rivoli *Plan V* **U1** *(Samaritaine, Bazar de l'Hôtel de Ville)*, Rue de Sèvres *Plan IV* **Q3** (the elegant *Bon Marché*).

Luxury and designer shops – Rue du Faubourg-St-Honoré *Plan II* **G2**, Rue de la Paix **T2** Rue Royale *Plan III* **J3**, Avenue Montaigne *Plan II* **G3** Place des Victoires *Plan I* **C2**. Famous jewellers' shops are to be found in Place Vendôme *Plan III* **K3**.

Boutiques – Rue des Francs-Bourgeois *Plan VII* **X1**, Forum des Halles *Plan V* **T1**, Rue Étienne-Marcel *Plan I* **C2**, Rue Montorgueil *Plan I* **C2**.

Antiques – Louvre des Antiquaires *Plan IV* **S1**, Village Suisse (Avenue de La Motte-Picquet), Carré Rive Gauche, Village St-Paul *Plan VII* **X2**, flea market, Porte de Clignancourt (Sat, Sun).

Art galleries – The Marais and Bastille districts, Avenue Matignon *Plan II* **H3**, the area around Rue de Seine to St-Germain-des-Prés.

Gourmet shops *(see more addresses in Gourmet Treats chapter)* – Fine foods and wines: *Hédiard* (No 21) and *Fauchon* (No 26) Place de la Madeleine. Chocolates: *La Maison du Chocolat*, 225 Rue du Faubourg-St-Honoré; *La Fontaine de Chocolat*, 201 Rue St-Honoré; *Christian-Constant*, 37 Rue d'Assas; *Jean-Paul Hévin*, 3 Rue Vavin; *Debauve et Gallais*, 30 Rue des Saints-Pères; *Michel Chaudun*, 149 Rue de l'Université; *Richart*, 238 Boulevard St-Germain. Cheeses: *Androuet*, 83 Rue St-Dominique; *Barthélemy*, 151 Rue de Grenelle; *Fil'O Fromage*, 4 Rue Poirier-de-Narçay; *La Ferme La Fontaine*, 75 Rue La Fontaine. Fine wines: *Les Caprices de l'Instant*, 12 Rue Jacques-Cœur; *Les Caves Taillevent*, 199 Rue du Faubourg-St-Honoré. Caviar: *Petrossian*, 18 Boulevard de Latour-Maubourg. Jams: *Furet*, 63 Rue de Chabrol.

ENTERTAINMENT

Several weekly publications (available at news-stands) publish entertainment listings – exhibitions, shows, festivals, concerts and theatres. The best known ones are *Pariscope*, *L'Officiel des Spectacles* and *Zurban*.

Theatre tickets can be bought at the kiosk at Place de la Madeleine Plan III **J2**.

Opera and dance – Opéra Bastille *Plan VII* **Y2**, Palais Garnier *Plan III* **K2**, Théâtre de la Ville *Plan VIII* **Z2**.

Classical and contemporary concerts – Théâtre du Châtelet *Plan V* **T1**, Cité de la Musique *Plan I* **D1**, Salle Pleyel *Plan II* **G2**, Salle Gaveau *Plan II* **H2**, Théâtre des Champs-Élysées *Plan II* **G3**.

Theatre – Comédie Française *Plan III* **K3**, Théâtre National de Chaillot *Plan IV* **N1**, Théâtre du Rond-Point *Plan II* **H3**, Odéon Théâtre de l'Europe *Plan IV* **S2**, Théâtre Marigny *Plan II* **H3**, Théâtre des Variétés *Plan III* **L2**.

Cabarets and revues – Lido *Plan II* **G2**, Moulin-Rouge *Plan VIII* **Z2**, Folies-Bergère *Plan III* **L2**, Crazy-Horse *Plan II* **F3**.

Variety shows – Olympia *Plan III* **K2**, Zénith *Plan I* **D1**, Palais Omnisports de Bercy *Plan I* **D3**, Casino de Paris *Plan III* **K1**, La Cigale *Plan VIII* **AA2**, Le Bataclan *Plan VII* **Y1**.

NIGHTLIFE

There is a profusion of bars and cafés to choose from when **going out for a drink or for the evening**, in particular in the districts of St-Germain-des-Prés, Bastille, Montparnasse, Pigalle. Some famous names are: *Café de Flore, Les Deux Magots, Brasserie Lipp* (Boulevard St-Germain), *La Coupole, La Rotonde, Le Dôme, Le Sélect* (Boulevard du Montparnasse), *Bar Hemingway* at the Ritz, 15 Place Vendôme, *Bar de l'hôtel Costes*, 239 Rue St-Honoré.

Hit the high spots of Paris in the bustling districts of: **St-Germain-des-Prés**, **Montparnasse, Pigalle**, **Bastille**, **Oberkampf** and **République** where discotheques and nightclubs are legion: *Les Bains-Douches*, 7 Rue du Bourg-l'Abbé; *Le Balajo*, 9 Rue de Lappe; *La Locomotive*, 90 Boulevard de Clichy; *Le Queen*, 102 Avenue des Champs-Élysées; *La Rive Gauche*, 1 Rue du Sabot, *Le Batofar*, Quai François-Mauriac.

If you are a jazz fan, some jazz clubs are veritable institutions: *Caveau de la Huchette*, 5 Rue de la Huchette, *Le Duc des Lombards*, 42 Rue des Lombards, *Petit Journal Montparnasse*, 13 Rue du Commandant-Mouchotte, *LeBilboquet*, 13 Rue Saint-Benoît, *Jazz Club Lionel Hampton* at Méridien Etoile, 81 Rue Gouvion-Saint-Cyr, *Le Petit Opportun*, 15 Rue des Lavandières.

HOTEL – ALPHABETIC LIST

RESTAURANTS – ALPHABETIC LIST

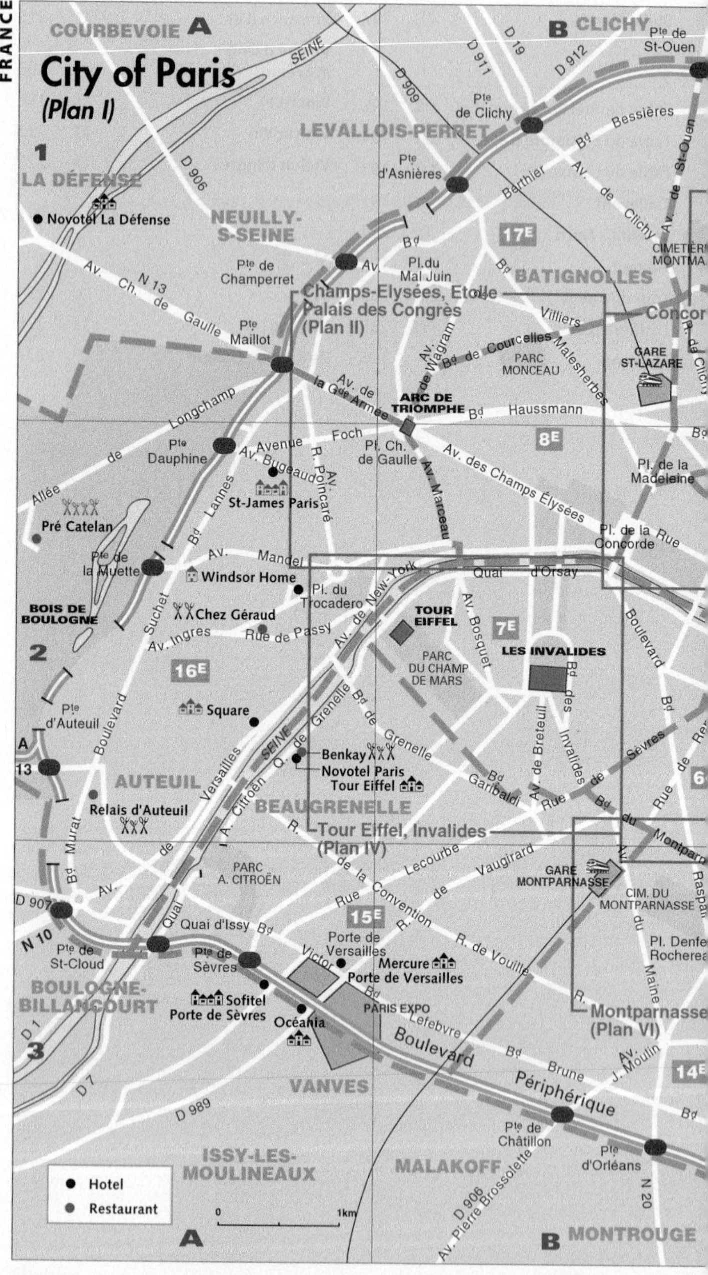
City of Paris
(Plan I)
COURBEVOIE
A
B
CLICHY
Pte de St-Ouen
LA DÉFENSE
Novotel La Défense
NEUILLY-S-SEINE
LEVALLOIS-PERRET
Pte de Clichy
Pte d'Asnières
Pte de Champerret
Pte Maillot
Champs-Elysées, Etoile
Palais des Congrès
(Plan II)
17E
BATIGNOLLES
PARC MONCEAU
GARE ST-LAZARE
ARC DE TRIOMPHE
8E
Pl. Ch. de Gaulle
Pl. de la Madeleine
Pl. de la Concorde
Pte Dauphine
St-James Paris
Pré Catelan
Pte de la Muette
Windsor Home
Pl. du Trocadero
Chez Géraud
BOIS DE BOULOGNE
16E
TOUR EIFFEL
PARC DU CHAMP DE MARS
7E
LES INVALIDES
Square
Pte d'Auteuil
Benkay
Novotel Paris Tour Eiffel
AUTEUIL
Relais d'Auteuil
BEAUGRENELLE
Tour Eiffel, Invalides
(Plan IV)
PARC A. CITROËN
GARE MONTPARNASSE
CIM. DU MONTPARNASSE
15E
Porte de Versailles
Mercure Porte de Versailles
Pte de St-Cloud
Pte de Sèvres
BOULOGNE-BILLANCOURT
Sofitel Porte de Sèvres
Océania
PARIS EXPO
Montparnasse
(Plan VI)
14E
Boulevard Périphérique
VANVES
Pte de Châtillon
Pte d'Orléans
ISSY-LES-MOULINEAUX
MALAKOFF
MONTROUGE
Hotel
Restaurant
0
1km
1
2
3

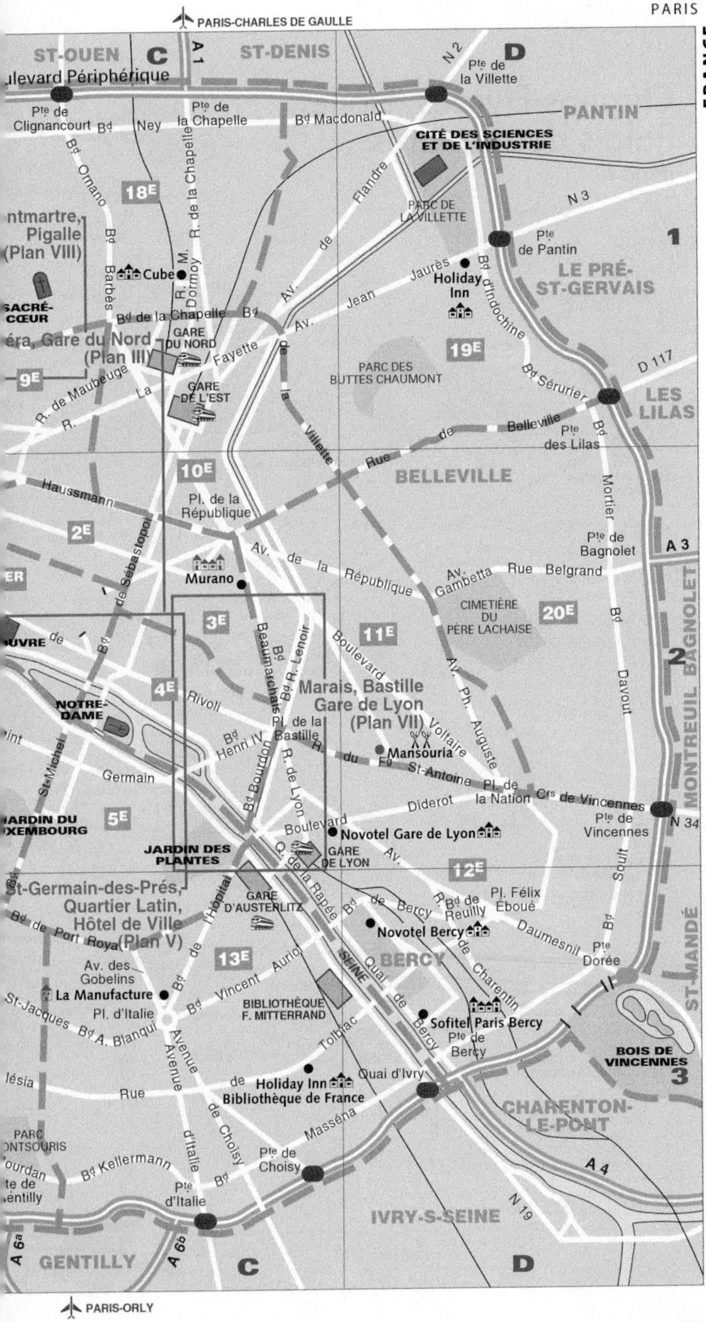

PARIS-CHARLES DE GAULLE

ST-OUEN
C
A 1
ST-DENIS
N 2
D
Boulevard Périphérique
Pte de Clignancourt
Bd Ney
Pte de la Chapelle
Bd Macdonald
Pte de la Villette
PANTIN
CITÉ DES SCIENCES ET DE L'INDUSTRIE
Bd Ornano
18E
R. de la Chapelle
Av. de Flandre
PARC DE LA VILLETTE
N 3
Montmartre, Pigalle (Plan VIII)
Bd Barbès
Cube
R. M. Dormoy
Pte de Pantin
1
LE PRÉ-ST-GERVAIS
SACRÉ-CŒUR
Av. Jean Jaurès
Holiday Inn
Bd d'Indochine
Bd de la Chapelle
Bd de la Villette
GARE DU NORD
Opéra, Gare du Nord (Plan III)
R. La Fayette
19E
9E
R. de Maubeuge
GARE DE L'EST
PARC DES BUTTES CHAUMONT
D 117
Bd Sérurier
LES LILAS
Rue de Belleville
Pte des Lilas
10E
BELLEVILLE
Bd Haussmann
Pl. de la République
Bd Mortier
2E
Pte de Bagnolet
A 3
Av. de la République
Av. Gambetta
Rue Belgrand
Murano
Bd de Sébastopol
CIMETIÈRE DU PÈRE LACHAISE
20E
3E
11E
LOUVRE
Bd Beaumarchais
Bd R. Lenoir
Boulevard Voltaire
2
MONTREUIL BAGNOLET
Bd Davout
4E
Rivoli
Marais, Bastille Gare de Lyon (Plan VII)
NOTRE-DAME
Pl. de la Bastille
Bd Henri IV
Mansouria
Av. Ph. Auguste
R. du Fg St-Antoine
Bd St-Michel
Bd St-Germain
Bd Bourdon
R. de Lyon
Pl. de la Nation
Crs de Vincennes
Diderot
Pte de Vincennes
N 34
JARDIN DU LUXEMBOURG
5E
Boulevard Diderot
Novotel Gare de Lyon
Bd Soult
JARDIN DES PLANTES
GARE DE LYON
Av.
12E
St-Germain-des-Prés, Quartier Latin, Hôtel de Ville (Plan V)
GARE D'AUSTERLITZ
Q. de la Rapée
Bd de Bercy
Bd de Reuilly
Pl. Félix Éboué
Bd de Port Royal
Bd de l'Hôpital
Novotel Bercy
Daumesnil
Pte Dorée
ST-MANDÉ
13E
BERCY
SEINE
R. de Charenton
Av. des Gobelins
Bd Vincent Auriol
Quai de Bercy
La Manufacture
BIBLIOTHÈQUE F. MITTERRAND
Pl. d'Italie
Sofitel Paris Bercy
Bd St-Jacques
Bd A. Blanqui
Pte de Bercy
BOIS DE VINCENNES
Tolbiac
3
Rue d'Alésia
Avenue d'Italie
Rue de Tolbiac
Holiday Inn Bibliothèque de France
Quai d'Ivry
Av. de Choisy
CHARENTON-LE-PONT
PARC MONTSOURIS
Bd Masséna
Pte de Choisy
Bd Jourdan
Bd Kellermann
A 4
Pte de Gentilly
Pte d'Italie
N 19
IVRY-S-SEINE
A 6a
A 6b
GENTILLY
C
D

PARIS-ORLY

Champs-Élysées, Étoile, Palais des Congrès
(Plan II)

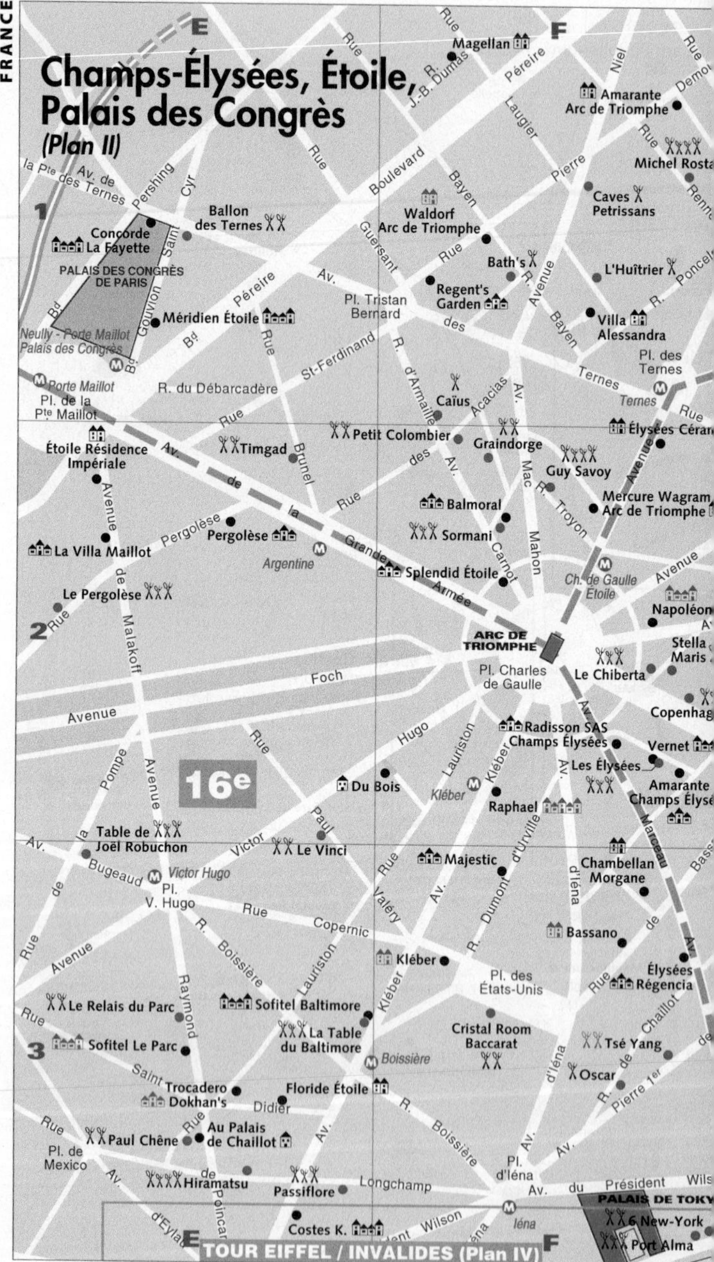

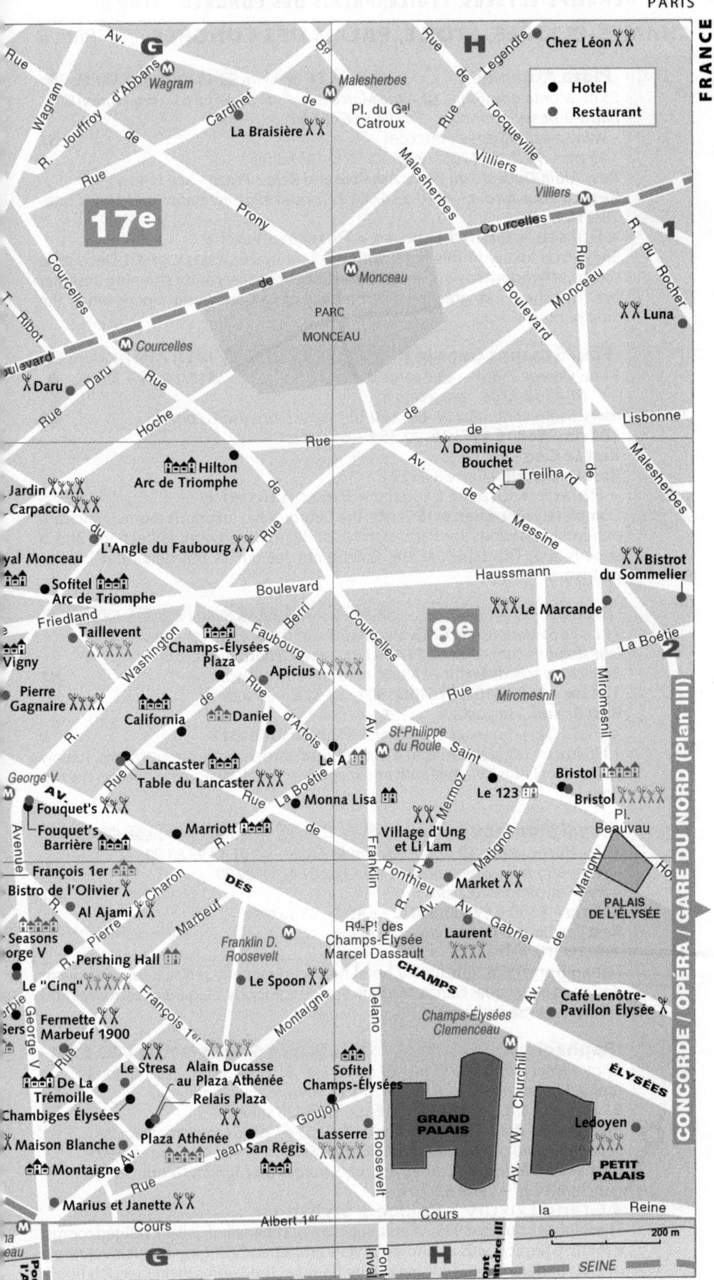

Hotel
Restaurant
17e
8e
PARC MONCEAU
Chez Léon
La Braisière
Luna
Daru
Hilton Arc de Triomphe
Dominique Bouchet
Jardin
Carpaccio
L'Angle du Faubourg
Bistrot du Sommelier
Sofitel Arc de Triomphe
Le Marcande
Taillevent
Champs-Élysées Plaza
Apicius
Vigny
Pierre Gagnaire
California
Daniel
Lancaster
Table du Lancaster
Le A
Le 123
Bristol
Fouquet's
Fouquet's Barrière
Monna Lisa
Marriott
Village d'Ung et Li Lam
François 1er
Bistro de l'Olivier
Al Ajami
Market
PALAIS DE L'ÉLYSÉE
Pershing Hall
Laurent
Le "Cinq"
Le Spoon
Café Lenôtre-Pavillon Elysée
Fermette Marbeuf 1900
Le Stresa
Alain Ducasse au Plaza Athénée
Relais Plaza
De La Trémoille
Chambiges Élysées
Sofitel Champs-Élysées
GRAND PALAIS
PETIT PALAIS
Ledoyen
Maison Blanche
Plaza Athénée
San Régis
Lasserre
Montaigne
Marius et Janette
SEINE
200 m
CONCORDE / OPÉRA / GARE DU NORD (Plan III)

CHAMPS-ÉLYSÉES, ÉTOILE, PALAIS DES CONGRÈS *Plan II*

Plaza Athénée
rm 20/60 VISA MC AE

25 av. Montaigne (8th) – Alma Marceau – 01 53 67 66 65 – reservation@plaza-athenee-paris.com – Fax 01 53 67 66 66 – www.plaza-athenee-paris.com **G3**

145 rm – 575 € 705/790 €, 35 € – 43 suites

Rest *Alain Ducasse au Plaza Athénée* and ***Relais Plaza*** – see below

Rest *La Cour Jardin* – *01 53 67 66 02 (closed mid-September-mid-May)* Carte 78/114 €

♦ Palace ♦ Grand Luxury ♦ Personalised ♦

Enjoy true luxury in this hotel with its comfortable, Classic or Art Deco-style rooms, afternoon teas with music in the Gobelins gallery and a stunning designer bar. The charming, greenery-filled terrace of La Cour Jardin opens when the weather turns nice.

Four Seasons George V
rm rm 30/240 VISA MC AE

31 av. George V (8th) – George V – 01 49 52 70 00 – par.lecinq@fourseasons.com – Fax 01 49 52 70 10 – www.fourseasons.com **G3**

184 rm – 680 € 710 €, 35 € – 61 suites

Rest *Le Cinq* – see below

Rest *La Galerie* – Carte 84/129 €

♦ Palace ♦ Grand Luxury ♦ Personalised ♦

Completely renovated in 18C style, the George V has luxurious rooms, which are extremely spacious by Paris standards. Beautiful artwork collections and a superb spa. The tables at the Galerie are set out in the delightful interior courtyard.

Bristol
30/100 VISA MC AE

112 r. Fg St-Honoré (8th) – Miromesnil – 01 53 43 43 00 – resa@lebristolparis.com – Fax 01 53 43 43 01 – www.lebristolparis.com
Reopening scheduled for 22 March on completion of work **H2**

124 rm – 590/610 € 640/1130 €, 51 € – 38 suites

Rest *Bristol* – see below

♦ Palace ♦ Grand Luxury ♦ Personalised ♦

1925 luxury hotel set around a magnificent garden. Sumptuous rooms, mainly Louis XV or Louis XVI-style with an exceptional "boat" swimming pool on the top floor.

Royal Monceau
15/200 VISA MC AE

37 av. Hoche (8th) – Charles de Gaulle-Etoile – 01 42 99 88 00 – reservations@royalmonceau.com – Fax 01 42 99 89 90 – www.royalmonceau.com **G2**

203 rm – 560 € 660/890 €, 45 € – 38 suites

Rest *Jardin* and ***Carpaccio*** – see below

♦ Luxury ♦ Palace ♦ Classical ♦

Dating from 1928, this luxury hotel has been recently renovated, with decor designed by Jacques Garcia. Magnificent lounge lobby, elegant guestrooms and a fitness centre with pool.

Raphael
rm 10/70 VISA MC AE

17 av. Kléber (16th) 75116 – Kléber – 01 53 64 32 00 – reservation@raphael-hotel.com – Fax 01 53 64 32 01 – www.raphael-hotel.com **F2**

61 rm – 335/475 € 335/570 €, 37 € – 25 suites

Rest *Jardins Plein Ciel* – (7th floor), *01 53 64 32 30 (open from May to September and closed Saturday lunch and Sunday)* Menu 70 € (lunch)/90 €

Rest *Salle à Manger* – *(closed August, Saturday and Sunday)* Menu 50 € bi (lunch)/60 € bi – Carte 62/76 €

♦ Grand Luxury ♦ Palace ♦ Stylish ♦

The Raphael, built in 1925, offers a superb wood-panelled gallery, refined rooms, a rooftop terrace with a panoramic view and a trendy English bar. A lovely view of Paris and traditional cuisine can be found at the Jardins Plein Ciel (7th floor). Superb dining room in Grand Hotel style.

Sofitel Le Parc — 40/250 VISA AE

55 av. R. Poincaré (16th) ✉ 75116 – Ⓜ Victor Hugo – ✆ 01 44 05 66 66 – h2797@accor.com – Fax 01 44 05 66 00 **E3**

116 rm – †210/580 € ††230/580 €, ☕ 26 € – 5 suites

Rest *Relais du Parc* – see below

◆ Grand Luxury ◆ Modern ◆

The rooms are elegant and pleasingly British in atmosphere. All are well equipped (with wifi) and distributed around a garden terrace. Part of the bar decor is by Arman.

Fouquet's Barrière — VISA AE

46 av. Georges V (8th) – Ⓜ George V – ✆ 01 40 69 60 00 – hotelfouquets@lucienbarriere.com – Fax 01 40 69 60 05 – www.fouquets-barriere.com **G2**

91 rm – †690 € ††690 €, ☕ 30 € – 15 suites

Rest *Fouquet's* – see below

Rest *Le Diane* – Menu 165 € – Carte 71/146 €

◆ Grand Luxury ◆ Modern ◆

True luxury in this hotel, the latest offering by the Barrière group. Covering an area of 16 000m², the hotel offers a spa, a garden and state-of-the-art technology. Decor by Garcia.

Hilton Arc de Triomphe — rm 15/800 VISA AE

51 r. Courcelles (8th) – Ⓜ Courcelles – ✆ 01 58 36 67 00 – info_adt@hilton.com – Fax 01 58 36 67 77 – www.arcdetriompheparis.hilton.com **G2**

438 rm – †290/680 € ††290/730 €, ☕ 30 € – 25 suites

Rest *Safran* – ✆ 01 58 36 67 96 – Carte 35/63 €

◆ Luxury ◆ Chain hotel ◆ Personalised ◆

This new hotel, inspired by the liners of the 1930s, has successfully created their luxurious and refined atmosphere. Elegant Art Deco rooms designed by Jacques Garcia, patio with a fountain, fitness centre etc. At the Safran the food reflects current tastes, influenced by the flavours and scents of Asia.

Lancaster — VISA AE

7 r. Berri (8th) – Ⓜ George V – ✆ 01 40 76 40 76 – reservations@hotel-lancaster.fr – Fax 01 40 76 40 00 – www.hotel-lancaster.fr **G2**

46 rm – †310 € ††410/590 €, ☕ 32 € – 11 suites

Rest *Table du Lancaster* – see below

◆ Luxury ◆ Classical ◆

Boris Pastoukhoff paid for his lodging in this hotel with his paintings, adding richly to this old townhouse's elegant decor. The hotel's discreet luxury was loved by Marlene Dietrich.

Sofitel Baltimore — 15/50 VISA AE

88 bis av. Kléber (16th) ✉ 75116 – Ⓜ Boissière – ✆ 01 44 34 54 54 – h2789-re@accor.com – Fax 01 44 34 54 44 – www.baltimore-sofitel-paris.com **E3**

102 rm – †405/505 € ††490/1035 €, ☕ 25 €

Rest *Table du Baltimore* – see below

◆ Luxury ◆ Modern ◆

Simple furniture, trendy fabrics, old photos of the city of Baltimore: the contemporary decor of the rooms contrasts with the architecture of this 19C building.

Vernet — VISA AE

25 r. Vernet (8th) – Ⓜ Charles de Gaulle-Etoile – ✆ 01 44 31 98 00 – reservations@hotelvernet.com – Fax 01 44 31 85 69 – www.hotelvernet.com **F2**

42 rm – †430/470 € ††550/630 €, ☕ 35 € – 9 suites

Rest *Les Élysées* – see below

◆ Luxury ◆ Classical ◆

A fine building dating from the 1920s, with a dressed-stone façade and wrought-iron balconies. Empire- or Louis XVI-style rooms. Fashionable bar and grill.

Costes K. without rest

81 av. Kléber (16th) ✉ 75116 – Ⓜ Trocadéro – ☎ 01 44 05 75 75 – resak@hotelcostesk.com – Fax 01 44 05 74 74 **E3**

83 rm – †300 € ††350/550 €, ☕ 20 €

◆ Luxury ◆ Modern ◆

This hotel by Ricardo Bofill is ultra-modern. It invites you to enjoy the discreet calm of its vast rooms with their pure lines, laid out around a Japanese-style patio.

San Régis

12 r. J. Goujon (8th) – Ⓜ Champs-Elysées Clemenceau – ☎ 01 44 95 16 16 – message@hotel-sanregis.fr – Fax 01 45 61 05 48 – www.hotel-sanregis.fr **G3**

33 rm – †330 € ††435/715 €, ☕ 32 € – 11 suites

Rest – *(closed August and Sunday)* Menu 40 € (lunch) – Carte 44/69 €

◆ Luxury ◆ Personalised ◆

This 1857 townhouse has been remodelled with taste. A fine staircase adorned with stained glass and statues leads to delightful guestrooms furnished with a diverse range of furniture. The exquisitely appointed restaurant of the San Régis is set in the subdued atmosphere of a luxurious private reading room.

Sofitel Arc de Triomphe

rm rm 6/60

14 r. Beaujon (8th) – Ⓜ Charles de Gaulle-Etoile – ☎ 01 53 89 50 50 – h1296@accor.com – Fax 01 53 89 50 51 – www.arcdetriomphe-sofitel-paris.com **G2**

128 rm – †230/400 € ††230/610 €, ☕ 27 € – 6 suites

Rest *Clovis* – *☎ 01 53 89 50 53 (Closed 29 July-28 August, 23 December-1st January, Saturday, Sunday and public holidays)* Menu 39 € (lunch)/70 € – Carte 55/96 €

◆ Luxury ◆ Chain hotel ◆ Personalised ◆

Typical late-19C Parisian building, with 18C-inspired decoration but fitted up to 21C standards. Elegant rooms. Try and book the amazing "Concept Room". Classical decor with a modern touch (beige and brown shades), attentive, cheerful service, refined cuisine: the gourmets in the area have made it their "local".

Méridien Étoile

rm rm 10/800

81 bd Gouvion St-Cyr (17th) – Ⓜ Neuilly-Porte Maillot – ☎ 01 40 68 34 34 – guest.etoile@lemeridien.com – Fax 01 40 68 31 31 – www.lemeriden.com/etoile **E1**

1008 rm – †225/450 € ††225/450 €, ☕ 25 € – 17 suites

Rest *L'Orenoc* – *☎ 01 40 68 30 40 (closed 24 July-24 August, 24-31 December, Sunday and Monday)* Menu 38 € – Carte 56/74 €

Rest *La Terrasse du Jazz* – *☎ 01 40 68 30 85 (closed Easter holidays, 1st-23 July, Friday and Saturday) (lunch only)* Menu 40 €

◆ Business ◆ Chain hotel ◆ Modern ◆

Facilities at this huge hotel include a jazz club, bar, boutiques and an impressive conference centre. Black granite and shades of beige predominate in the contemporary-style guestrooms. The Orenoc reflects current tastes in food, and has warm, colonial-style decor. A simple menu and buffets are on offer at La Terrasse.

Concorde La Fayette

rm 10/1200

3 pl. Gén. Koenig (17th) – Ⓜ Porte Maillot – ☎ 01 40 68 50 68 – booking@concorde-hotels.com – Fax 01 40 68 50 43 – www.concorde-lafayette.com **E1**

931 rm – †160/450 € ††160/450 €, ☕ 25 € – 19 suites

Rest *La Fayette* – ☎ 01 40 68 51 19 – Menu 38/71 € bi – Carte 47/72 €

◆ Business ◆ Modern ◆

This 33-floor tower, part of the city's convention centre, offers wonderful views of Paris from most of its spacious and comfortable rooms, as well as from the panoramic bar. Buffet meals are served in the La Fayette restaurant.

De Vigny

9 r. Balzac (8th) – George V – 01 42 99 80 80 – reservation@hoteldevigny.com – Fax 01 42 99 80 40 – www.hoteldevigny.com **G2**

26 rm – 290/395 € 320/440 €, 28 € – 11 suites

Rest *Baretto* – *(closed 14 to 20 August)* Menu 50/110 € bi – Carte 51/74 €

♦ Luxury ♦ Personalised ♦

A discreet hotel close to the Champs-Elysées with refined bedrooms with personalised touches including four-poster beds. Cosy lounge with attractive fireplace. The Baretto serves traditional cuisine in a stylish, low-key atmosphere and Art Deco setting.

Champs-Élysées Plaza without rest

35 r. Berri (8th) – George V – 01 53 53 20 20 – info@champselyseesplaza.com – Fax 01 53 53 20 21 – www.champselyseesplaza.com **G2**

32 rm – 390/890 € 390/890 €, 22 € – 11 suites

♦ Luxury ♦ Personalised ♦

The spacious and elegant rooms of this opulent (and completely non-smoking) hotel near the Champs-Élysées all have fireplaces and Art Deco-style bathrooms.

Marriott

12/220

70 av. Champs Élysées (8th) – Franklin D. Roosevelt – 01 53 93 55 00 – mhrs.pardt.ays@marriotthotels.com – Fax 01 53 93 55 01 – www.parismarriott.com **G2**

174 rm – 395/565 € 395/565 €, 29 € – 18 suites

Rest *Sur les Champs* – 01 53 93 55 44 *(closed Saturday lunch and Sunday lunch)* Menu 39 € – Carte 37/68 €

♦ Chain hotel ♦ Business ♦ Modern ♦

Enjoy American efficiency and cocoon-like comfort in this smart hotel. Most of the bedrooms overlook the Champs-Élysées. Cross the impressive atrium to find yourself in this "Sur les Champs" where the decor (lampposts and frescoes) brings back memories of an imagined Paris of old.

Napoléon

8/80

40 av. Friedland (8th) – Charles de Gaulle-Etoile – 01 56 68 43 21 – napoleon@hotelnapoleon.com – Fax 01 56 68 44 40 – www.hotelnapoleonparis.com **F2**

101 rm – 440/590 € 440/590 €, 26 €

Rest – *(closed August, dinner, Saturday and Sunday)* Carte 49/76 €

♦ Luxury ♦ Retro ♦

A stone's throw from Place de l'Étoile and the Arc de Triomphe, this hotel-museum honours the emperor's memory via autographs, figurines and paintings from the period. Elegant guestrooms in Directoire or Empire style. Traditional menu served in the cosy, subdued atmosphere (fine wood panels) of this restaurant.

California

20/100

16 r. Berri (8th) – George V – 01 43 59 93 00 – cal@hroy.com – Fax 01 45 61 03 62 – www.hotel-california-paris.com **G2**

162 rm – 415/440 € 415/440 €, 30 € – 12 suites – **Rest** – *(closed August, Saturday and Sunday) (lunch only)* Menu 39/55 € – Carte 39/47 €

♦ Luxury ♦ Classical ♦

Several thousand paintings adorn the walls of this old luxury hotel dating from the 1920s. The collection of 200 whiskies in the piano-bar is equally impressive! The restaurant room has a stunning patio-terrace extension (fountain, mosaics, and greenery).

De La Trémoille

8/20

14 r. Trémoille (8th) – Alma Marceau – 01 56 52 14 00 – reservation@hotel-tremoille.com – Fax 01 40 70 01 08 – www.hotel-tremoille.com **G3**

88 rm – 325/460 € 380/540 €, 24 € – 5 suites – **Rest *Senso*** – *(closed August, Saturday lunchtime and Sunday)* Menu 39 € bi (lunch) – Carte 46/69 €

♦ Luxury ♦ Modern ♦

The hotel has been successfully refurbished with contemporary decor combining the old and the ultra-modern, the latest high-tech equipment, and marble bathrooms with Portuguese tiles. An elegant dining room with a cosy atmosphere; cuisine in keeping with current taste.

Trocadero Dokhan's without rest

117 r. Lauriston (16th) ✉ 75116 – Ⓜ Trocadéro – ✆ 01 53 65 66 99 – welcome@dokhans.com – Fax 01 53 65 66 88 – www.dokhans.com

E3

45 rm – †430/510 € ††430/560 €, ☕ 25 € – 4 suites

◆ Townhouse ◆ Personalised ◆

One cannot help but be charmed by this elegant townhouse (1910) with its Palladian architecture and neo-Classical decor. 18C celadon wood panels in the lounge.

De Sers &rm rm 12/25

41 av. Pierre 1er de Serbie (8th) – Ⓜ George V – ✆ 01 53 23 75 75 – contact@hoteldesers.com – Fax 01 53 23 75 76 – www.hoteldesers.com

G3

45 rm – †480/550 € ††480/650 €, ☕ 29 € – 6 suites

Rest – *(closed August and Sunday)* Carte 40/160 €

◆ Luxury ◆ Modern ◆

Successfully refurbished late-19C townhouse. While the hall has kept its original character, the rooms are thoroughly modern. The food reflects current tastes and is served in a designer dining room or, in summer, on the pleasant terrace.

Montaigne without rest

6 av. Montaigne (8th) – Ⓜ Alma Marceau – ✆ 01 47 20 30 50 – contact@hotel-montaigne.com – Fax 01 47 20 94 12 – www.hotel-montaigne.com

G3

29 rm – †200/300 € ††300/450 €, ☕ 20 €

◆ Family ◆ Luxury ◆ Personalised ◆

The wrought-iron grilles, beautiful flower-decked façade and graciously cosy interior all contribute to the Hotel Montaigne's appeal. The avenue is lined by haute couture fashion designers.

La Villa Maillot without rest 15

143 av. Malakoff (16th) ✉ 75116 – Ⓜ Porte Maillot – ✆ 01 53 64 52 52 – resa@lavillamaillot.fr – Fax 01 45 00 60 61 – www.lavillamaillot.fr

E2

39 rm – †260/340 € ††290/390 €, ☕ 26 € – 3 suites

◆ Business ◆ Modern ◆

A step away from Porte Maillot. Soft colours, a high level of comfort and good soundproofing in the rooms. Glassed-in space for breakfasts, opening onto the greenery.

François 1er without rest 15

7 r. Magellan (8th) – Ⓜ George V – ✆ 01 47 23 44 04 – hotel@hotel-francois1er.fr – Fax 01 47 23 93 43 – www.the-paris-hotel.com

G3

40 rm – †300/780 € ††350/1000 €, ☕ 22 € – 2 suites

◆ Luxury ◆ Personalised ◆

Carrara marble, mouldings, curios, antique furniture and a plethora of paintings make up the luxurious decor created by French architect Pierre-Yves Rochon. Substantial buffet-style breakfast.

Daniel &rm rm

8 r. Frédéric Bastiat (8th) – Ⓜ St-Philippe du Roule – ✆ 01 42 56 17 00 – danielparis@relaischateaux.com – Fax 01 42 56 17 01 – www.hoteldanielparis.com

G2

22 rm – †320/450 € ††380/450 €, ☕ 30 € – 4 suites

Rest – *(closed 26 July-24 August, Saturday and Sunday)* Menu 80 € – Carte 45/67 €

◆ Luxury ◆ Personalised ◆

This hotel likes travel! Furniture and objects brought back from all over the world combined with toile de Jouy create a refined and welcoming decor for Parisian globetrotters.

Sofitel Champs-Élysées &rm rm 15/150

8 r. J. Goujon (8th) – Ⓜ Champs-Elysées Clemenceau – ✆ 01 40 74 64 64 – h1184-re@accor.com – Fax 01 40 74 79 66 – www.sofitel-champselysees-paris.com VISA MC AE D G-H3

42 rm – †365/430 € ††480/600 €, ☕ 25 € – 2 suites

Rest *Les Signatures* – *✆ 01 40 74 64 94 (closed 30 July-19 August, 24 December-1st January, Saturday and Sunday) (lunch only)* Menu 48 €

♦ Chain hotel ♦ Luxury ♦ Personalised ♦

A Second Empire building shared with the Press Club de France. The rooms have a contemporary new look and are equipped with state-of-the-art facilities. Business centre. Simple decor and lovely terrace at Les Signatures, a restaurant which is frequented by those working in the press.

Majestic without rest VISA MC AE D

29 r. Dumont d'Urville (16th) ✉ 75116 – Ⓜ Kléber – ✆ 01 45 00 83 70 – management@majestic-hotel.com – Fax 01 45 00 29 48 – www.majestic-hotel.com F3

27 rm – †260 € ††360 €, ☕ 18 € – 3 suites

♦ Traditional ♦ Classic ♦

A step away from the Champs-Elysées, this discreet building dating from the 1960s has quiet rooms, with an 'old-money' comfort, well-proportioned and impeccably well-maintained.

Splendid Étoile rm rm 20 VISA MC AE D

1bis av. Carnot (17th) – Ⓜ Charles de Gaulle-Etoile – ✆ 01 45 72 72 00 – hotel@hsplendid.com – Fax 01 45 72 72 01 – www.hsplendid.com F2

50 rm – †270 € ††270 €, ☕ 19 € – 7 suites

Rest *Le Pré Carré* – *(closed Saturday lunch and Sunday)* Menu 34 € (dinner) – Carte 34/69 €

♦ Traditional ♦ Classical ♦

Beautiful classical façade with wrought-iron balconies. Spacious rooms full of character, embellished with Louis XV furnishings; some look out onto the Arc de Triomphe.

Pergolèse without rest VISA MC AE D

3 r. Pergolèse (16th) ✉ 75116 – Ⓜ Argentine – ✆ 01 53 64 04 04 – hotel@pergolese.com – Fax 01 53 64 04 40 – www.hotelpergolese.com E2

40 rm – †190/300 € ††220/456 €, ☕ 18 €

♦ Business ♦ Design ♦

Restrained 16th arrondissement chic on the outside hides a successful designer interior combining mahogany, glass bricks, chrome and bright colours. Breakfast facing a pleasant patio.

Radisson SAS Champs Élysées &rm rm

78 av. Marceau (8th) – Ⓜ Charles de Gaulle-Etoile – ✆ 01 53 23 43 43 – reservations.paris@radissonsas.com – Fax 01 53 23 43 44 – www.paris.radissonsas.com VISA MC AE D F2

46 rm – †280/550 € ††280/650 €, ☕ 26 €

Rest *La Place* – *(closed 29 July-20 August, 25 December-2 January, Saturday and Sunday)* Carte 57/72 €

♦ Chain hotel ♦ Luxury ♦ Modern ♦

A new hotel occupying the former headquarters of Louis Vuitton. Restful, contemporary rooms, high-tech equipment (plasma TVs) and excellent soundproofing. Customers can sit in the bar, or on the terrace in summer. Short menu with a Provençal flavour.

Élysées Régencia without rest 20 VISA MC AE D

41 av. Marceau (16th) ✉ 75116 – Ⓜ George V – ✆ 01 47 20 42 65 – info@regencia.com – Fax 01 49 52 03 42 – www.regencia.com F3

43 rm – †170/310 € ††190/330 €, ☕ 18 €

♦ Traditional ♦ Personalised ♦

Three styles of rooms are offered behind this gracious facade: Louis XVI, Napoleon "just-home-from-Egypt" and contemporary. Elegant lounge, bar and library.

FRANCE

Regent's Garden without rest

6 r. P. Demours (17th) – Ⓜ Ternes – ✆ 01 45 74 07 30 – Fax 01 40 55 01 42 – www.bestwestern-regents.com **F1**

40 rm – †109/279 € ††109/279 €, ☕ 13 €

◆ Traditional ◆ Personalised ◆

Attractive, elegant townhouse commissioned by Napoleon III for his doctor. Vast period rooms, some giving onto the garden, which is very pleasant in summer.

Balmoral without rest

6 r. Gén. Lanrezac (17th) – Ⓜ Charles de Gaulle-Etoile – ✆ 01 43 80 30 50 – hotel@hotelbalmoral.fr – Fax 01 43 80 51 56 – www.hotel-balmoral.com **F2**

57 rm – †125/135 € ††145/175 €, ☕ 10 €

◆ Traditional ◆ Personalised ◆

A personalised welcome and calm atmosphere characterise this old hotel (1911) a stone's throw from the Étoile. Brightly coloured bedrooms, and elegant wood panelling in the lounge.

Pershing Hall

49 r. P. Charron (8th) – Ⓜ George V – ✆ 01 58 36 58 00 – info@pershinghall.com – Fax 01 58 36 58 01 – www.pershinghall.com **G3**

20 rm – †336/420 € ††336/420 €, ☕ 26 € – 6 suites

Rest – Carte 55/87 €

◆ Luxury ◆ Modern ◆

Once the home of General Pershing, then a veterans club and finally a charming hotel designed by Andrée Putman. Chic interior, original and enchanting hanging garden. Behind the curtain of glass beads, the decor is trendy and the cuisine very fashionable. Lounge parties.

Chambiges Élysées without rest

8 r. Chambiges (8th) – Ⓜ Alma Marceau – ✆ 01 44 31 83 83 – reservation@hotelchambiges.com – Fax 01 40 70 95 51 – www.hotelchambiges.com **G3**

26 rm ☕ – †265/340 € ††265/340 € – 8 suites

◆ Luxury ◆ Personalised ◆

Wood panelling, select drapes and fabrics, period furniture; a romantic, cosy atmosphere reigns in this fully renovated hotel. Comfy rooms and a pretty interior garden.

Le A without rest

4 r. Artois (8th) – Ⓜ St-Philippe du Roule – ✆ 01 42 56 99 99 – hotel-le-a@wanadoo.fr – Fax 01 42 56 99 90 – www.paris-hotel-a.com **G-H2**

16 rm – †345/472 € ††345/472 €, ☕ 23 € – 10 suites

◆ Luxury ◆ Modern ◆

F. Hybert, a visual artist, and F. Méchiche, an interior designer, masterminded this trendy hotel (or museum, perhaps?) in black and white. Relaxing lounge-library and bar-lounge.

Kléber without rest

7 r. Belloy ✉ 75116 – Ⓜ Boissière – ✆ 01 47 23 80 22 – kleberhotel@wanadoo.fr – Fax 01 49 52 07 20 – www.kleberhotel.com **F3**

23 rm – †129/199 € ††139/299 €, ☕ 14 € – 1 suite

◆ Traditional ◆ Classic ◆

The sitting rooms of this 1853 hotel have Louis XV style furniture, original frescoes and old paintings. Exposed stonework and parquet floors in the rooms.

Bassano without rest

15 r. Bassano (16th) ✉ 75116 – Ⓜ George V – ✆ 01 47 23 78 23 – info@hotel-bassano.com – Fax 01 47 20 41 22 – www.hotel-bassano.com **F3**

28 rm – †150/260 € ††170/280 €, ☕ 18 € – 3 suites

◆ Family ◆ Personalised ◆

Cosy atmosphere, wrought-iron furniture, sunny fabrics (it feels like being at a friend's home in Provence, but is only a few hundred metres from the Champs-Elysées).

Monna Lisa

97 r. La Boétie (8th) – Ⓜ St-Philippe du Roule – ✆ 01 56 43 38 38 – contact@hotelmonnalisa.com – Fax 01 45 62 39 90 **G-H2**
22 rm – 🛉170/220 € 🛉🛉180/235 €, ☕ 17 €
Rest *Caffe Ristretto* – *(closed Saturday and Sunday)* Carte 44/65 €
♦ Luxury ♦ Minimalist ♦
This fine hotel built in 1860 is a showpiece for audacious Italian design. Larger rooms on the street side. The Caffe Ristretto offers a delicious journey through the specialities of the Italian peninsula in a wonderfully modern setting.

Waldorf Arc de Triomphe without rest

36 r. Pierre Demours, (17th) – Ⓜ Ternes – ✆ 01 47 64 67 67 – arc@hotelswaldorfparis.com – Fax 01 40 53 91 34 – www.hotelswaldorfparis.com **F1**
45 rm – 🛉340/430 € 🛉🛉370/460 €, ☕ 20 €
♦ Business ♦ Design ♦
Guestrooms attractively refurbished in an elegant contemporary style, good fitness centre, and a small pool with sauna and hammam. Rest and relaxation guaranteed after a hard day's work or sightseeing!

Amarante Arc de Triomphe without rest

25 rue Th. de Banville, (17th) – Ⓜ Pereire – ✆ 01 47 63 76 69 – amarante-arcdetriomphe@jjwhotels.com – Fax 01 43 80 63 96 – www.jjwhotels.com 25 **F1**
50 rm – 🛉160/240 € 🛉🛉180/280 €, ☕ 22 €
♦ Chain hotel ♦ Classic ♦
This hotel has Directoire-style rooms which are popular with its business clientele. Attic-type rooms on the top floor, with some rooms opening onto the patio.

Étoile Résidence Impériale without rest

155 av. de Malakoff (16th) ✉ 75116 – Ⓜ Porte Maillot – ✆ 01 45 00 23 45 – res.imperiale@wanadoo.fr – Fax 01 45 01 88 82 – www.bestwestern-etoile-imperiale.com **E2**
37 rm – 🛉129/219 € 🛉🛉149/249 €, ☕ 14 €
♦ Traditional ♦ Personalised ♦
Recently-renovated and well-soundproofed hotel, with theme rooms (Africa, Asia, etc.). Some have retained their exposed beams, while others (ground floor) open onto the patio.

Villa Alessandra without rest

9 pl. Boulnois (17th) – Ⓜ Ternes – ✆ 01 56 33 24 24 – alessandra@leshoteldeparis.com – Fax 01 56 33 24 30 – www.leshotelsdeparis.com 15 **F1**
49 rm – 🛉244/289 € 🛉🛉314/483 €, ☕ 20 €
♦ Business ♦ Functional ♦
This Ternes quarter hotel is on a delightful quiet little square and is appreciated for its calm. Colours of southern France in the rooms, with wrought-iron beds and painted wood furniture.

Élysées Céramic without rest

34 av. Wagram (8th) – Ⓜ Ternes – ✆ 01 42 27 20 30 – info@elysees-ceramic.com – Fax 01 46 22 95 83 – www.elysees-ceramic.com **F2**
57 rm – 🛉175/185 € 🛉🛉200/210 €, ☕ 10 €
♦ Family ♦ Retro ♦
The Art Nouveau façade (1904), with its glazed stoneware, is an architectural gem. The interior lives up to the same standard, with furniture and decor inspired by the same style. A few rooms with balconies.

Mercure Wagram Arc de Triomphe without rest

3 r. Brey (17th) – Ⓜ Charles de Gaulle-Etoile – ✆ 01 56 68 00 01 – h2053@accor.com – Fax 01 56 68 00 02 – www.mercure.com **F2**
43 rm – 🛉120/230 € 🛉🛉120/240 €, ☕ 14 €
♦ Business ♦ Functional ♦
This new Mercure between Étoile and Ternes offers a warm welcome and cosy little rooms with pale wood panels and pretty fabrics that create a marine atmosphere.

Chambellan Morgane without rest
6 r. Keppler (16th) ✉ 75116 – Ⓜ George V – ✆ 01 47 20 35 72 – chambellan-morgane@wanadoo.fr – Fax 01 47 20 95 69 **F3**
20 rm – 156/175 € 156/175 €, ☕ 12 €
♦ Family ♦ Personalised ♦
Small hotel with character, with rooms decorated in Provence colours and all enhanced by the quiet atmosphere. Pleasant Louis XVI lounge decorated with painted wood panels.

Floride Étoile without rest
14 r. St-Didier (16th) ✉ 75116 – Ⓜ Boissière – ✆ 01 47 27 23 36 – floride.etoile@wanadoo.fr – Fax 01 47 27 82 87 – www.floride-paris-hotel.com **E3**
63 rm – 120/225 € 145/225 €, ☕ 14 €
♦ Traditional ♦ Functional ♦
A stone's throw from Trocadéro. The renovated rooms are comfortable; those on the courtyard side are smaller but more tranquil. Stylishly furnished lounge decorated with flowers.

Magellan without rest
17 r. J. B. Dumas (17th) – Ⓜ Porte de Champerret – ✆ 01 45 72 44 51 – paris@hotelmagellan.com – Fax 01 40 68 90 36 – www.hotelmagellan.com **F1**
72 rm – 136 € 142 €, ☕ 13 €
♦ Business ♦ Design ♦
Large, functional rooms in a beautiful building dating from 1900. The small pavilion at the far end of the garden is used as a breakfast room in summer. Art Deco-style lounge.

Le 123 without rest
123 r. fg. St-Honoré (8th) – Ⓜ St-Philippe du Roule – ✆ 01 53 89 01 23 – hotel.le123@astotel.com – Fax 01 45 61 09 07 – www.astotel.com **H2**
41 rm – 250/420 € 298/468 €, ☕ 22 €
♦ Luxury ♦ Personalised ♦
Contemporary decor and a mix of styles, materials and colours. The personalised rooms, which are decorated with fashion sketches, are extremely appealing.

Du Bois without rest
11 r. Dôme (16th) ✉ 75116 – Ⓜ Kléber – ✆ 01 45 00 31 96 – reservations@hoteldubois.com – Fax 01 45 00 90 05 – www.hoteldubois.com **E-F2**
41 rm – 120/185 € 145/215 €, ☕ 14 €
♦ Traditional ♦ Cosy ♦
This cosy hotel is in the most Montmartre-type street in the whole 16th district, where Baudelaire passed away. Charming and bright rooms. Georgian-style lounge.

Au Palais de Chaillot without rest
35 av. R. Poincaré (16th) ✉ 75116 – Ⓜ Trocadéro – ✆ 01 53 70 09 09 – palaisdechaillot-hotel@magic.fr – Fax 01 53 70 09 08 – www.hotel-palaisdechaillot.com **E3**
28 rm – 110 € 125/145 €, ☕ 9 €
♦ Family ♦ Classic ♦
Beautiful location near Trocadéro for this hotel renovated in the colours of southern France. Rooms are small but fresh and practical. Breakfast-room furnished in cane.

Le "Cinq" – Hôtel Four Seasons George V 8/20
31 av. George V (8th) – Ⓜ George V – ✆ 01 49 52 71 54 – par.lecinq@fourseasons.com – Fax 01 49 52 71 81 – www.fourseasons.com **G3**
Rest – Menu 75 € (lunch), 110/220 € – Carte 130/288 €
Spec. Tarte d'artichaut et de truffe noire. Fricassée de langoustines, lasagne au vieux parmesan. Côte de veau de lait fermier aux câpres de Pantelleria.
♦ Innovative ♦ Luxury ♦
Superb dining room - a majestic reference to the Grand Trianon - opening onto a delightful garden inside. Refined atmosphere and classic cuisine created with great talent.

XXXXX ✿✿✿ **Ledoyen** 10/20 VISA AE

Carré des Champs-Elysées (1st floor) (8th) – Ⓜ Champs Elysées Clemenceau – ✆ 01 53 05 10 01 – pavillon.ledoyen@ledoyen.com – Fax 01 47 42 55 01 – www.ledoyen.com

closed 28 July-26 August, Monday lunchtime, Saturday and Sunday **H3**

Rest – Menu 85 € (lunch), 198/284 € bi – Carte 148/244 €

Spec. Grosses langoustines bretonnes, émulsion d'agrumes. Blanc de turbot de ligne braisé, pommes rattes truffées. Ris de veau en brochette de bois de citronnelle, jus d'herbes.

♦ Innovative ♦ Luxury ♦

A neo-Classical lodge built on the Champs-Elysées in 1848. Magnificent Napoleon III-style decor, view of the gardens designed by Hittorff and delicious from land and sea cuisine.

XXXXX ✿✿✿ **Alain Ducasse au Plaza Athénée** – Hôtel Plaza Athénée

25 av. Montaigne (8th) – Ⓜ Alma Marceau – ✆ 01 53 67 65 00 – adpa@alain-ducasse.com – Fax 01 53 67 65 12 – www.alain-ducasse.com VISA AE

closed 13 July - 21 August, 21 - 31 Dec, Monday lunch, Tuesday lunch, Wednesday lunch, Saturday and Sunday **G3**

Rest – Menu 220/320 € – Carte 180/325 €

Spec. Caviar osciètre d'Iran, langoustines rafraîchies, nage réduite, bouillon parfumé. Volaille de Bresse, sauce albuféra aux truffes d'Alba (15 October-31 December). Fraises des bois en coupe glacée, sablé coco.

♦ Innovative ♦ Luxury ♦

The sumptuous regency decor has been enhanced in "design and organza"; creative menus ideated by a talented team coached by A. Ducasse. 1001 selected wines available!

XXXXX ✿✿ **Le Bristol** – Hôtel Bristol VISA AE

112 r. Fg St-Honoré (8th) – Ⓜ Miromesnil – ✆ 01 53 43 43 00 – resa@lebristolparis.com – Fax 01 53 43 43 01 – www.lebristolparis.com **H2**

Rest – Menu 90 € (lunch)/190 € – Carte 118/207 €

Spec. Macaroni farcis, truffe, artichaut et foie gras, gratinés au parmesan. Anguille des Sargasses sautée meunière. Poularde de Bresse cuite en vessie aux écrevisses.

♦ Contemporary ♦ Luxury ♦

The winter dining room resembles a small theatre, given its oval shape and splendid wood panels. The summer dining room opens widely onto the hotel's magnificent garden.

XXXXX ✿✿ **Taillevent** 5/25 VISA AE

15 r. Lamennais (8th) – Ⓜ Charles de Gaulle-Etoile – ✆ 01 44 95 15 01 – mail@taillevent.com – Fax 01 42 25 95 18 – www.taillevent.com

closed 28 July - 27 August, Saturday, Sunday and bank holidays **G2**

Rest – *(number of covers limited, pre-book)* Menu 70 € (lunch), 140/190 € – Carte 124/198 €

Spec. Rémoulade de tourteau à l'aneth. Selle d'agneau princier en rognonnade. Tarte inversée au chocolat et au café.

♦ Contemporary ♦ Luxury ♦

The Duke of Morny's former 19C town house has become a historical icon of the best French gastronomy. Exquisite cuisine and sumptuous wine list.

XXXXX ✿✿ **Apicius** (Vigato) 10/25 VISA AE

20 r. Artois (8th) – Ⓜ St-Philippe du Roule – ✆ 01 43 80 19 66 – restaurant-apicius@wanadoo.fr – Fax 01 44 40 09 57

closed August, Saturday and Sunday **G2**

Rest – Menu 140/150 € – Carte 79/156 €

Spec. Compote de cèpes frais et grillés, sabayon à la truffe blanche d'Alba (October-December). Milieu de gros turbot rôti, jus tranché aux épices. Soufflé au chocolat noir et chantilly sans sucre.

♦ Innovative ♦ Elegant ♦

This elegant restaurant, in a town house, is adorned with 19C Flemish paintings and 17C Indian sculptures. Up-to-date cuisine and superb wine list.

FRANCE

Lasserre
6/40 VISA

17 av. F.-D.-Roosevelt (8th) – Franklin D. Roosevelt – 01 43 59 53 43 – lasserre@lasserre.fr – Fax 01 45 63 72 23 – www.restaurant-lasserre.com
closed Aug, Sat lunchtime, Mon lunchtime, Tues lunchtime, Weds lunchtime and Sun **H3**

Rest – Menu 75 € (lunch)/185 € – Carte 122/206 €
Spec. Macaroni aux truffes noires et foie gras. Selle d'agneau de lait au serpolet et artichauts poivrades. Tarte soufflée au chocolat.

♦ Traditional ♦ Luxury ♦

For Parisian gourmets, this is an institution. The neo-classical dining hall's ceiling, decorated with a saraband of dancing females opens astonishingly. Superb wine list.

Guy Savoy
15 VISA

18 r. Troyon (17th) – Charles de Gaulle-Etoile – 01 43 80 40 61 – reserv@guysavoy.com – Fax 01 46 22 43 09 – www.guysavoy.com
closed Aug., 24 Dec. - 2 Jan., Sat. lunch, Sun. and Mon. **F2**

Rest – Menu 230/285 € – Carte 112/223 €
Spec. Soupe d'artichaut à la truffe noire, brioche feuilletée aux champignons et truffes. "Côte" de gros turbot à l'œuf en salade et soupe. Ris de veau rissolés, "petits chaussons" de pommes de terre et truffes.

♦ Inventive ♦ Trendy ♦

Glass work, leather and Wenge, works of the great names of contemporary art, African sculptures and inventive cuisine make this "the auberge of the 21C" par excellence.

Michel Rostang
6/20 VISA

20 r. Rennequin (17th) – Ternes – 01 47 63 40 77 – rostang@relaischateaux.com – Fax 01 47 63 82 75 – www.michelrostang.com
closed 1 - 21 Aug, Mon lunchtime, Sat lunchtime and Sun **F1**

Rest – Menu 70 € (lunch), 175 € – Carte 124/202 €
Spec. "Menu truffes" (15 December to 15 March). Foie gras chaud de canard rôti d'une fine croûte de sésame dorée. Canette au sang servie saignante en deux services.

♦ Contemporary ♦ Friendly ♦

Woodwork, Robj statuettes, works by Lalique and Art Deco stained-glass combine to create a luxurious and original setting. Fine cuisine and a splendid wine list.

Pierre Gagnaire
VISA

6 r. Balzac (8th) – George V – 01 58 36 12 50 – p.gagnaire@wanadoo.fr – Fax 01 58 36 12 51
closed 21 July - 20 August, 22 December - 6 January, Sunday lunchtime and Saturday **G2**

Rest – Menu 95 € (weekday lunch)/245 € – Carte 231/332 €
Spec. Langoustines de quatre façons. Pièce d'agneau de Lozère. Grand dessert Pierre Gagnaire.

♦ Innovative ♦ Trendy ♦

The sober and chic contemporary decor (light wood panelling, modern art) takes backstage to the unbridled, enchanting tones of the jazzman. Music, maestro!

Hiramatsu
(lunch) VISA

52 r. Longchamp (16th) 75116 – Trocadéro – 01 56 81 08 80 – paris@hiramatsu.co.jp – Fax 01 56 81 08 81 – www.hiramatsu.co.jp
closed 28 July - 26 August, 29 December - 6 January, Saturday and Sunday

Rest – *(number of covers limited, pre-book)* Menu 48 € (lunch), 95/130 € – Carte 103/140 € **E3**
Spec. Foie gras de canard aux choux frisés, jus de truffe. Feuilleté de homard au parfum de truffe, jus d'estragon. Fines lamelles d'agneau, compotée d'oignons blancs, jus de truffe.

♦ Innovative ♦ Fashionable ♦

Hiramatsu's team have moved from the 4th to the 16th district in Paris. New decor and inventive cuisine, as skilful as before. High-class Japanese gastronomy!

XXXX ✿

Le Jardin – Hôtel Royal Monceau

37 av. Hoche (8th) – Ⓜ Charles de Gaulle-Etoile – ✆ 01 42 99 98 70 – lejardin@royalmonceau.com – Fax 01 42 99 89 94 – www.royalmonceau.com
closed Aug., Mon. lunchtime, Sat. and Sun. **G2**

Rest – Menu 59 € (lunch), 95/125 € – Carte 86/126 €

Spec. Langoustines rôties, confit d'oignons doux, râpée de truffe noire. Bar de ligne étuvé aux palourdes. Suprêmes de palombe dorés, foie gras.

♦ Contemporary ♦ Romantic ♦

This place evokes an elegant Napoleon-style marquee and serves subtle Mediterranean cuisine. The terrace and garden have also been remodelled.

XXXX ✿

Laurent

6/60

41 av. Gabriel (8th) – Ⓜ Champs Elysées Clemenceau – ✆ 01 42 25 00 39 – info@le-laurent.com – Fax 01 45 62 45 21 – www.le-laurent.com
closed Sat. lunchtime, Sun. and public holidays **H3**

Rest – Menu 75/160 € – Carte 132/213 €

Spec. Araignée de mer dans ses sucs en gelée, crème de fenouil. Grosses langoustines "tandoori" poêlées, copeaux d'avocat à l'huile d'amande. Flanchet de veau braisé, blettes à la moelle et au jus.

♦ Contemporary ♦ Luxury ♦

This pavilion with its antique inspiration was built by Hittorff, offering elegant outside tables and a cuisine based on the great traditions. A little bit of paradise in the Champs-Élysées gardens.

XXX ✿

La Table du Lancaster – Hôtel Lancaster

15

7 r. Berri (8th) – Ⓜ George V – ✆ 01 40 76 40 18 – restaurant@hotel-lancaster.fr – Fax 01 40 76 40 00 – www.hotel-lancaster.fr – closed August –
Rest – Menu 60 € (weekday lunch)/120 € – Carte 75/135 € **G2**

Spec. Cuisses de grenouilles sautées au satay. Langouste grillée indonésienne (Spring-Summer). Grillon de ris de veau, pissalat d'anchois.

♦ Contemporary ♦ Friendly ♦

Clever and inventive food supervised by Michel Troisgros and a pleasant, contemporary setting (Chinese touches) opening onto the garden: a real Table for the Lancaster.

XXX ✿✿

La Table de Joël Robuchon

16 av. Bugeaud (16th) ✉ 75116 – Ⓜ Victor Hugo – ✆ 01 56 28 16 16 – latabledejoelrobuchon@wanadoo.fr – Fax 01 56 28 16 78 **E3**

Rest – Menu 55 € bi (lunch)/150 € – Carte 55/152 €

Spec. Œuf mollet et friand au caviar oscietre. Caille farcie de foie gras et caramélisée avec pomme purée truffée. Chocolat sensation.

♦ Innovative ♦ Trendy ♦

You are sure to enjoy your meal here, with tapas-style snacks and classic dishes, subtly updated by Joël Robuchon, in an elegant setting.

XXX

Maison Blanche

15 av. Montaigne (7th floor) (8th) ✉ 75008 – Ⓜ Alma Marceau – ✆ 01 47 23 55 99 – info@maison-blanche.fr – Fax 01 47 20 09 56 – www.maison-blanche.fr
closed Sat. lunchtime and Sun. lunchtime– **Rest** – Carte 74/133 € **G3**

♦ Inventive ♦ Trendy ♦

On the roof of the Théatre des Champs-Élysées, a loft-duplex design with an immense glass canopy facing the golden dome of the Invalides. A Languedoc-inspired cuisine.

XXX ✿✿

Les Élysées – Hôtel Vernet

25 r. Vernet (8th) – Ⓜ Charles de Gaulle-Etoile – ✆ 01 44 31 98 98 – reservations@hotelvernet.com – Fax 01 44 31 85 69 – www.hotelvernet.com
closed 28 July - 27 Aug., Mon. lunch, Sat. and Sun. **F2**

Rest – Menu 59 € (lunch), 94/130 € – Carte 89/142 €

Spec. Tranche d'aubergine potagère, copeaux de foie gras, sorbet tomate. Homard bleu cuit sur sel aux aromates, jus au naturel, fenouil, artichaut, gnocchi. Epaule d'agneau de Lozère fondante à l'orientale, gratin de tomate, figue.

♦ Contemporary ♦ Friendly ♦

An inventive and masterly cuisine of subtle flavours, to savour in Eiffel's splendid Belle Époque conservatory that bathes the dining room in a soft light.

XXX **Fouquet's** ⌂ 10/80 VISA MC AE

99 av. Champs-Elysées (8th) – Ⓜ George V – ☎ 01 47 23 50 00 – fouquets@lucienbarriere.com – Fax 01 47 23 60 02 – www.lucienbarriere.com **G2**

Rest – Menu 78/110 € bi – Carte 72/128 €

♦ Traditional ♦ Fashionable ♦

This rather famous establishment that has just celebrated its 100th anniversary was the headquarters for bi-plane aces before becoming the HQ for stars of the 7th art such as Raimu, Guitry and Pagnol.

XXX ✿ **Carpaccio** – Hôtel Royal Monceau AC 6/15 VISA MC

37 av. Hoche (8th) – Ⓜ Charles de Gaulle-Etoile – ☎ 01 42 99 98 90 – ilcarpaccio@royalmonceau.com – Fax 01 42 99 89 94

closed August **G2**

Rest – Carte 68/122 €

Spec. Carpaccio de filet de bœuf. Risotto au safran et poêlée de champignons de saison. Foie de veau à la vénitienne.

♦ Italian ♦ Romantic ♦

Cross the hall of the Hôtel Royal Monceau to eat in the pleasant Venetian decor among Murano glass chandeliers. Tasty Italian cuisine.

XXX ✿ **La Table du Baltimore** – Hôtel Sofitel Baltimore AC

1 r. Léo Delibes (16th) ✉ 75016 – Ⓜ Boissière VISA MC AE

– ☎ 01 44 34 54 34 – h2789-fb@accor.com – Fax 01 44 34 54 44 – www.sofitel.com

closed 28 July - 27 August, Saturday and Sunday **E3**

Rest – Menu 48 € bi (lunch), 50/95 € bi – Carte 46/64 €

Spec. Tourteau éffiloché au parfum d'aneth. Saint-Jacques cuites au plat, bouillon à la citronnelle (season). Chocolat en ganache moelleuse.

♦ Contemporary ♦ Friendly ♦

Antique woodwork, modern furnishings, warm colours and a collection of drawings all combine to create the subtle decor of this restaurant. Fine up-to-date cuisine.

XXX **Sormani** AC 5/15 VISA MC AE

4 r. Gén. Lanrezac (17th) – Ⓜ Charles de Gaulle-Etoile – ☎ 01 43 80 13 91 – sasormani@wanadoo.fr – Fax 01 40 55 07 37

closed 4 - 20 Aug., Sat., Sun. and bank holidays **F2**

Rest – Menu 44 € (lunch), 75/150 € bi – Carte 53/176 €

♦ Italian ♦ Formal ♦

Latin charm predominates in this restaurant near the Place de l'Etoile, with its new decor (red tones and Murano-glass chandeliers), dolce vita atmosphere and carefully-prepared Italian cuisine.

XXX ✿ **Le Pergolèse** (Gaborieau) AC VISA MC AE

40 r. Pergolèse (16th) ✉ 75116 – Ⓜ Porte Maillot – ☎ 01 45 00 21 40 – le-pergolese@wanadoo.fr – Fax 01 45 00 81 31 – www.lepergolese.com

closed 4 - 26 Aug., Sat. and Sun. **E2**

Rest – Menu 30 € (lunch), 38/80 € – Carte 68/124 €

Spec. Ravioli de langoustines en duxelles, émulsion de crustacés au foie gras. Aiguillette de Saint-Pierre meuniére, cannelloni aux multi-saveurs (winter). Double côte de veau rôtie en cocotte.

♦ Contemporary ♦ Fashionable ♦

Yellow wall hangings, pale wood panels and surprising sculptures in play among the mirrors, and forming an elegant decor a step away from the select Avenue Foch. Careful classic cuisine.

XXX ✿ **Le Chiberta** AC 15 VISA MC AE

3 r. Arsène-Houssaye (8th) – Ⓜ Charles de Gaulle-Etoile – ☎ 01 53 53 42 00 – chiberta@guysavoy.com – Fax 01 45 62 85 08 – www.lechiberta.com

closed 1 - 21 Aug., Sat. lunchtime and Sun. **F2**

Rest – Menu 60/100 € – Carte 77/98 €

Spec. Crême de carottes citronnelle-gingembre, langoustines éclatées. Tronçon de turbot cuit sur l'arête, ratte du Touquet. Saveur praliné-citron vert.

♦ Innovative ♦ Design ♦

The Chiberta has been refreshed with decor by J.-M. Wilmotte (dark shades and unusual "bottle" walls) and inventive cuisine supervised by Guy Savoy.

XXX

Le Marcande

52 r. Miromesnil (8th) – Ⓜ Miromesnil – ✆ 01 42 65 19 14
– info@marcande.com
– Fax 01 42 65 76 85 – www.marcande.com
closed 6- 20 Aug, 24 Dec - 2 Jan, Friday evening from October - April , Sat except in the evening from May - 30 Sept. and Sun **H2**

Rest – Menu 40/91 € bi – Carte 44/86 €

♦ Traditional ♦ Intimate ♦

Discreet restaurant frequented by a business clientele. Contemporary dining room facing a pleasant patio with tables outside, which is itself very popular in sunny weather.

XXX ✿

Copenhague

142 av. Champs-Elysées (1st floor) (8th)
– Ⓜ George V – ✆ 01 44 13 86 26
– floradanica@wanadoo.fr – Fax 01 44 13 89 44
– www.restaurantfloradanica.com
closed 28 July - 20 Aug., Sat., Sun. and bank holidays **F2**

Rest – Menu 55 € (lunch), 73/115 € – Carte 79/114 €

Rest *Flora Danica* – Menu 35 € – Carte 40/82 €

Spec. Foie gras poché à la bière. Dos de cabillaud demi-sel au bouillon mousseux de palourdes. Noisettes de renne légèrement fumées et rôties, sauce venaison.

♦ Danish ♦ Design ♦

Scandinavian cuisine, elegant Danish design, view of the Champs-Elysées and a terrace facing a lovely garden characterise this restaurant located in the Maison du Danemark. At the Flora Danica, salmon takes place of honour in the shop and on the menu.

XXX ✿

Passiflore (Durand)

33 r. Longchamp (16th) ✉ 75016 – Ⓜ Trocadéro – ✆ 01 47 04 96 81
– passiflore@club-internet.fr – Fax 01 47 04 32 27
– www.restaurantpassiflore.com
closed 14 July - 20 Aug., Sat. lunch and Sun. **E3**

Rest – Menu 35 € (lunch)/54 € (dinner) – Carte 63/95 €

Spec. Ravioles de homard. Tête de veau aux huitres (October-April). Tournedos de pied de cochon.

♦ Contemporary ♦ Fashionable ♦

An unassumingly elegant decor of ethnic inspiration (cameo of yellow and woodwork) and a classic, personalised cuisine combine to rejoice the taste buds of Parisian society.

XXX

Port Alma

10 av. New York (16th) ✉ 75116 – Ⓜ Alma Marceau
– ✆ 01 47 23 75 11 – restaurantportalma@wanadoo.fr
– Fax 01 47 20 42 92
closed 24 Dec. - 2 Jan., and Sun. **F3**

Rest – Menu 29 € (lunch)/39 € – Carte 28/105 €

♦ Seafood ♦ Friendly ♦

On the quays of the Seine, a dining room and veranda with blue beams, where seafood is the star. Fresh ingredients and smiling welcome.

XX

Cristal Room Baccarat

11 pl. des Etats-Unis (16th) ✉ 75116 – Ⓜ Boissière – ✆ 01 40 22 11 10
– cristalroom@baccarat.fr – Fax 01 40 22 11 99
closed Sun. **F3**

Rest – *(pre-book)* Menu 120 € – Carte 55/117 €

♦ Innovative ♦ Design ♦

This mansion was used by M-L de Noailles and now belongs to Baccarat. It offers a Starck decor and modern dishes at V.I.P. prices. Beauty can be far from reasonable!

Relais du Parc – Hôtel Sofitel Le Parc
59 av. R. Poincaré (16th) ✉ 75116 – Ⓜ Victor Hugo – ✆ 01 44 05 66 10 – le.relaisduparc@accor.com – Fax 01 44 05 66 39 – www.sofitel.com
closed 7 - 25 August, 22 December - 5 January, Saturday lunchtime from 15 September to 6 May, Sunday and Monday **E3**
Rest – Carte 65/83 €
Spec. Coquillettes aux truffes, jambon, jus d'un rôti. Jarret de veau fondant, os à moelle, gnocchi de pomme de terre (Winter). Baudroie piquée de chorizo, légumes de couscous, condiments, pois chiches, harissa.
♦ Contemporary ♦ Design ♦
The ground floor of this appealing Belle Époque town house was given designer touches by P. Jouin. Seasonal classic cuisine.

Tsé Yang
25 av. Pierre 1er de Serbie(16th) ✉ 75116 – Ⓜ Iéna – ✆ 01 47 20 70 22 – Fax 01 47 20 75 34 – www.tseyang.fr **F3**
Rest – Menu 49/59 € – Carte 37/66 €
♦ Chinese ♦ Exotic ♦
Two architects-cum-interior designers have revamped the decor in this temple of traditional Chinese cuisine, with its predominance of black decor, gilded coffered ceilings and attractive table layout.

Le Spoon
14 r. Marignan (8th) – Ⓜ Franklin D. Roosevelt – ✆ 01 40 76 34 44 – spoonfood@hotelmarignan.fr – Fax 01 40 76 34 37 – www.spoon.tm.fr
closed 28 July - 27 Aug., 22 Dec. - 2 Jan., Sat. and Sun. **G3**
Rest – Menu 45 € (lunch)/85 € – Carte 49/79 €
♦ Fusion ♦ Design ♦
Elegant contemporary decor, opening widely onto the kitchens. Take the time to discover the menu and its long list of dishes from the four corners of the world. A globetrotting experience!

Relais Plaza – Hôtel Plaza Athénée
25 av. Montaigne (8th) – Ⓜ Alma Marceau – ✆ 01 53 67 64 00 – reservation@plaza-athenee-paris.com – Fax 01 53 67 66 66 – www.plaza-athenee-paris.com
closed 25 July - 25 August **G3**
Rest – Menu 50 € – Carte 63/143 €
♦ Contemporary ♦ Friendly ♦
The chic, intimate "local" for the nearby fashion houses. A subtle renovation has restored its lustre to the original art deco setting. Classic, refined cuisine.

Fermette Marbeuf 1900
5 r. Marbeuf (8th) – Ⓜ Alma Marceau – ✆ 01 53 23 08 00 – fermettemarbeuf@blanc.net – Fax 01 53 23 08 09 – www.fermettemarbeuf.com **G3**
Rest – Menu 25 € (weekday lunch)/30 € – Carte 31/65 €
♦ Traditional ♦ Retro ♦
One must reserve one's table to enjoy the Art Nouveau of this glass dining hall dating back to 1898 and discovered by chance in the course of renovation. Classical cuisine.

Marius et Janette
4 av. George-V (8th) – Ⓜ Alma Marceau – ✆ 01 47 23 41 88 – Fax 01 47 23 07 19 **G3**
Rest – Menu 46 € bi (lunch)/48 € – Carte 60/140 €
♦ Seafood ♦ Bistro ♦
The sign refers to Marseille's Estaque quarter and Robert Guédiguian's films. Elegant "yacht"-style decor, pleasant outside dining area on the avenue, and the taste of the sea on your plate.

Stella Maris (Yoshino)
4 r. Arsène Houssaye (8th) – Ⓜ Charles de Gaulle-Etoile – ✆ 01 42 89 16 22 – stella.maris.paris@wanadoo.fr – Fax 01 42 89 16 01 – www.stellamaris.com
closed 10 - 20 August, Saturday lunch, Sunday and lunch on public holidays **F2**
Rest – Menu 43 € (lunch), 85/130 € – Carte 100/140 €
Spec. Fondant de foie gras de canard et carotte (March to September). Saumon mi-cuit à l'émulsion de citron confit. Tourte de pigeon (Autumn).
♦ Contemporary ♦ Design ♦
Classic cuisine with a modern touch in keeping with the pleasant, refined decor of this restaurant near the Arc de Triomphe. Charming reception.

Timgad
21 r. Brunel (17th) – Ⓜ Argentine – ✆ 01 45 74 23 70 – contact@timgad.fr – Fax 01 40 68 76 46 – www.timgad.fr **E2**
Rest – Menu 45/60 € bi – Carte 38/71 €
♦ Moroccan ♦ Friendly ♦
Delve into the past splendour of the city of Timgad: the elegant Moresque decor of the rooms was carried out by Moroccan stucco-workers. Fragrant Maghreb cuisine.

Le Stresa
7 r. Chambiges (8th) ✉ 75008 – Ⓜ Alma Marceau – ✆ 01 47 23 51 62
closed 1 - 8 May, Aug, 20 Dec - 3 Jan, Sat and Sun **G3**
Rest – *(pre-book)* Carte 56/105 €
♦ Italian ♦ Family ♦
Triangle d'Or trattoria frequented by a very jet-set clientele. Paintings by Buffet, compressed sculptural art by César...artists also appreciate the Italian cuisine here.

Bistrot du Sommelier 10/12
97 bd Haussmann (8th) – Ⓜ St-Augustin – ✆ 01 42 65 24 85 – bistrot-du-sommelier@noos.fr – Fax 01 53 75 23 23 – www.bistrotdusommelier.com
closed 28 July - 26 Aug., 22 Dec. - 2 Jan., Sat. and Sun. **H2**
Rest – Menu 39 € (lunch), 60 € bi/100 € bi – Carte 46/68 €
♦ Contemporary ♦ Bistro ♦
This bistrot of free-flowing Bacchanalian pleasure belongs to P. Faure-Brac, honoured as the 1992 World's Best Cellarman. How justly Rabelais wrote his praises of the bottle divine!

Graindorge
15 r. Arc de Triomphe (17th) – Ⓜ Charles de Gaulle-Etoile – ✆ 01 47 54 00 28 – le.graindorge@wanadoo.fr – Fax 01 47 54 00 28
closed 1 - 15 Aug., Sat. lunch and Sun. **F2**
Rest – Menu 28 € (weekday lunch)/32 € – Carte 43/56 €
♦ Belgian ♦ Retro ♦
Here, you can choose between beer and wine plus generous Flemish cuisine and appealing market dishes in an attractive Art Deco setting.

L'Angle du Faubourg
195 r. Fg St-Honoré (8th) – Ⓜ Ternes – ✆ 01 40 74 20 20 – angledufaubourg@cavestaillevent.com – Fax 01 40 74 20 21 – www.angledufaubourg.com
closed 28 July - 27 Aug., Sat., Sun. and bank holidays **G2**
Rest – Menu 35/70 € (dinner) – Carte 45/71 €
Spec. Étrilles farcies en gelée. Foie de canard poêlé au banyuls. Macaron aux fruits de saison.
♦ Contemporary ♦ Friendly ♦
On the corner of Rues du Faubourg-St-Honoré and Balzac. This modern bistrot has modernised classic cuisine in a simple décor.

FRANCE

XX ✿ **La Braisière** (Faussat) AC VISA MC AE D

54 r. Cardinet (17th) – M Malesherbes – ✆ 01 47 63 40 37 – labraisiere@free.fr – Fax 01 47 63 04 76

closed Aug., 1 - 8 Jan., Sat. lunchtime and Sun. **G1**

Rest – Menu 33 € (lunch) – Carte 50/58 €

Spec. Gâteau de pommes de terre au foie gras. Gibiers (October-January) . Tarte mirliton aux fruits de saison.

♦ South-West of France specialities ♦ Friendly ♦

Comfortable restaurant in soothing pastel colours. The menu has an appealing hint of the Southwest although it changes according to the market produce available and the mood of the chef.

XX **Paul Chêne** AC (dinner) VISA MC AE D

123 r. Lauriston (16th) ✉ 75116 – M Trocadéro – ✆ 01 47 27 63 17 – Fax 01 47 27 53 18

closed Easter holidays, August, 24 - 31 December, Saturday and Sunday

Rest – Menu 38/48 € – Carte 42/75 € **E3**

♦ Traditional ♦ Bistro ♦

This address has kept its 1950s soul: an old zinc counter, comfortable bench seats, tables crowded up together...an animated ambiance. Traditional dishes including the famous fish, merlan en colère.

XX **Market** AC VISA MC AE

15 av. Matignon (8th) – M Franklin D. Roosevelt – ✆ 01 56 43 40 90 – prmarketsa@aol.com – Fax 01 43 59 10 87 – www.jeangeorges.com

Rest – Menu 43 € (lunch), 55/85 € – Carte 48/82 € **H3**

♦ Fusion ♦ Design ♦

A trendy establishment with a prestigious location. Wood and marble decor, including African masks in niches. Mixed cuisine (French, Italian and Asian).

XX **Le Vinci** AC (dinner) VISA MC AE

23 r. P. Valéry (16th) ✉ 75116 – M Victor Hugo – ✆ 01 45 01 68 18 – levinci@wanadoo.fr – Fax 01 45 01 60 37

closed 28 July - 22 Aug, Sat and Sun **E2-3**

Rest – Carte 47/63 €

♦ Italian ♦ Friendly ♦

Tasty Italian cuisine, pleasant colourful interior and friendly service: a highly-prized establishment a step away from the chic shopping in Avenue Victor-Hugo.

XX **6 New-York** AC VISA MC AE D

6 av. New-York (16th) ✉ 75016 – M Alma Marceau – ✆ 01 40 70 03 30 – 6newyork@wanadoo.fr – Fax 01 40 70 04 77

closed Aug., Sat. lunchtime and Sun. **F3**

Rest – Menu 30 € – Carte 48/58 €

♦ Innovative ♦ Design ♦

The sign gives you a clue to the address but does not tell you that this stylish bistro prepares dishes perfectly suited to its modern and refined setting.

XX **Ballon des Ternes** 15 VISA MC AE

103 av. Ternes (17th) – M Porte Maillot – ✆ 01 45 74 17 98 – leballondesternes@fr.oleane.com – Fax 01 45 72 18 84

closed 1 - 21 Aug. – **Rest** – Carte 36/63 € **E1**

♦ Brasserie ♦ Retro ♦

No, you have not drunk too many "doubles"! The table set upside down on the ceiling is part of the pleasant 1900 decor of this brasserie next to the Parliament Building.

XX **Village d'Ung et Li Lam** AC VISA MC AE D

10 r. J. Mermoz (8th) – M Franklin D. Roosevelt – ✆ 01 42 25 99 79 – Fax 01 42 25 12 06

closed Sat. lunchtime and Sun. lunchtime **H2**

Rest – Menu 35 € – Carte 25/40 €

♦ Thai ♦ Exotic ♦

Ung and Li welcome you in a very original Asian setting: suspended aquariums and a flooring of glass-and-sand tiles. Sino-Thai cuisine.

Al Ajami

AC VISA MC ①

58 r. François 1er (8th) – M George V – ✆ 01 42 25 38 44 – ajami@free.fr – Fax 01 42 25 38 39 – www.ajami.com **G3**

Rest – Menu 24 € (weekdays)/41 € – Carte 29/52 €

♦ Lebanese ♦ Exotic ♦

This is the embassy of traditional Lebanese cuisine. From father to son, the food has been lovingly prepared here since 1920. Near East decor, family ambiance and a clientele of regulars.

Chez Léon

15 VISA MC AE

32 r. Legendre (17th) – M Villiers – ✆ 01 42 27 06 82 – chezleon32@wanadoo.fr – Fax 01 46 22 63 67

closed 30 July - 24 August, 24 - 31 December, Saturday and Sunday **H1**

Rest – Menu 26 € – Carte 28/52 €

♦ Traditional ♦ Bistro ♦

The bistro has for long been the favourite haunt of discerning Batignolles diners. Traditional dishes are served in three rooms, one upstairs.

Dominique Bouchet

AC 10/12 VISA MC AE

11 r. Treilhard (8th) – M Miromesnil – ✆ 01 45 61 09 46 – dominiquebouchet@yahoo.fr – Fax 01 42 89 11 14 – www.dominique-bouchet.com

closed August, February school holidays, Saturday, Sunday and public holidays **H2**

Rest – Menu 90 € – Carte 55/87 €

Spec. Escargots petits-gris, tarte aux olives. Encornets poêlés, picadillos et chorizo. Gigot d'agneau de sept heures à la cuillère.

♦ Traditional ♦ Design ♦

Pleasant break between Monceau Park and St Augustin church, with an elegant decor that combines walls with light stonework and modern furniture. Traditional cuisine.

Café Lenôtre-Pavillon Elysée

AC 20/80 P VISA MC AE ①

10 Champs-Elysées (8th) – M Champs Elysées Clemenceau – ✆ 01 42 65 85 10 – Fax 01 42 65 76 23 – www.lenotre.fr

closed 1 - 20 Aug., 1 - 7 Feb., Monday evening in winter and Sun. evening **H3**

Rest – Carte 42/65 €

♦ Brasserie ♦ Trendy ♦

This elegant building erected for the 1900 World Exhibition has been renovated and houses a shop, a catering school and a modern restaurant.

Caïus

AC VISA MC AE

6 r. Armaillé (17th) – M Charles de Gaulle-Etoile – ✆ 01 42 27 19 20 – Fax 01 40 55 00 93 **F1**

Rest – Menu 38 €

♦ Home cooking ♦ Trendy ♦

Warm wood panelling, bench seats and coffee-and-spice theme photos make up the decor of this smart bistro serving tasty dishes with market produce and personal touches.

Bath's

AC VISA MC AE

25 r. Bayen, (17th) – M Ternes – ✆ 01 45 74 74 74 – contact@baths.fr – Fax 01 45 74 71 15 – www.baths.fr

Closed August, Sunday and public holidays **F1**

Rest – Menu 25 € (lunch) – Carte 40/60 €

Spec. Cassolette d'œuf brouillés. Tatin de pied de porc. Riz au lait.

♦ Contemporary ♦ Design ♦

The owner's own sculptures as well as contemporary paintings decorate the modern restaurant where orange and black predominate. Delicious food.

FRANCE

Caves Petrissans
VISA AE

30bis av. Niel (17th) – Pereire – 01 42 27 52 03 – cavespetrissans@noos.fr – Fax 01 40 54 87 56
closed 28 July - 27 Aug., Sat., Sun. and Bank Holidays **F1**
Rest – *(pre-book)* Menu 34 € – Carte 38/55 €
♦ Traditional ♦ Bistro ♦
Céline, Abel Gance, Roland Dorgelès loved to visit these cellars more than a hundred years old, both a wine shop and a restaurant. Good, bistro-style cooking.

Daru
A/C (dinner) VISA AE

19 r. Daru (8th) – Courcelles – 01 42 27 23 60 – restaurant.daru@orange.fr – Fax 01 47 54 08 14 – www.daru.fr
closed Aug. and Sun. **G1**
Rest – Menu 34 € (lunch) – Carte 45/70 €
♦ Russian ♦ Formal ♦
Founded in 1918, Daru was Paris' first Russian foods shop. Today it is still a treat for gourmets with its zakouskis, blinis and caviars, offered in a red-and-black decor.

L'Huîtrier
A/C VISA AE

16 r. Saussier-Leroy (17th) – Ternes – 01 40 54 83 44 – Fax 01 40 54 83 86
closed Sunday from June to August, Sunday dinner in September and Monday **F1**
Rest – Carte 29/69 €
♦ Seafood ♦ Bistro ♦
As you enter, the oyster bar will make your mouth water. Then, you can also choose to eat other seafood, elbow to elbow, in a soberly-modern dining room.

Oscar
VISA AE

6 r. Chaillot (16th) 75016 – Iéna – 01 47 20 26 92 – Fax 01 47 20 27 93
closed 6 - 19 Aug., Sat. lunchtime and Sun. **F3**
Rest – Menu 21 € – Carte 30/46 €
♦ Traditional ♦ Bistro ♦
This bistro, with a discreet facade, tables close together and a blackboard with daily specials, does not need to advertise to attract a clientele from well beyond the area.

Bistro de l'Olivier
A/C VISA AE

13 r. Quentin Bauchart (8th) – George V – 01 47 20 78 63 – Fax 01 47 20 74 58
closed August, Sat. lunchtime and Sun. lunchtime **G3**
Rest – *(number of covers limited, pre-book)* Menu 34 € – Carte 65/75 €
♦ Mediterranean ♦ Family ♦
Provençal fabrics and paintings recalling southern France brighten the very warm dining room of this restaurant near Avenue George V. Mediterranean cuisine.

CONCORDE, OPÉRA, BOURSE, GARE DU NORD *Plan III*

Meurice
rm A/C rm 40/70 VISA AE

228 r. Rivoli (1st) – Tuileries – 01 44 58 10 10 – reservations@lemeurice.com – Fax 01 44 58 10 15 – www.lemeurice.com **J3**
137 rm – 520/610 € 620/725 €, 48 € - 23 suites
Rest *Le Meurice* – see below
Rest *Le Jardin d'Hiver* – 01 44 58 10 44 – Menu 45 € – Carte 64/87 €
♦ Palace ♦ Grand Luxury ♦ Historic ♦
One of the first luxury hotels, built in 1817 and later converted into a grand hotel in 1907. Sumptuous rooms and a superb suite on the top floor with a breathtaking, panoramic view of Paris. Very beautiful Art Nouveau glass roof and seventy exotic plants at the Jardin d'Hiver.

Ritz 30/80 VISA MC AE

15 pl. Vendôme (1st) – Opéra – 01 43 16 30 30 – resa@ritzparis.com – Fax 01 43 16 36 68 – www.ritzparis.com K3

106 rm – 710/810 € 710/810 €, 44 € – 56 suites

Rest *L'Espadon* – see below

Rest *Bar Vendôme* – *01 43 16 33 63* – Carte 74/130 €

♦ Grand Luxury ♦ Palace ♦ Stylish ♦

In 1898, César Ritz opened the "perfect hotel" of his dreams, boasting Rudolph Valentino, Proust, Hemingway and Coco Chanel among its guests. Incomparable refinement. Superb pool. A chic interior and superb terrace can be found at the Bar Vendôme, which turns into a tearoom in the afternoon.

Crillon rm 30/60 VISA MC AE

10 pl. Concorde (8th) – Concorde – 01 44 71 15 00 – crillon@crillon.com – Fax 01 44 71 15 02 – www.crillon.com J3

119 rm – 615/1160 € 615/1160 €, 47 € – 28 suites

Rest *Les Ambassadeurs* – see below

Rest *L'Obélisque* – *01 44 71 15 15* – Menu 50/89 € bi

♦ Grand Luxury ♦ Palace ♦ Personalised ♦

This 18C townhouse has kept its sumptuous, decorative features. The bedrooms, decorated with wood-furnishings, are magnificent. A French style luxury hotel through-and-through. Dining room ornamented with wood panels, mirrors and engraved glass, where the number of square feet is almost lower than the number of diners. Not so surprising, given the tasty and carefully-prepared cuisine!

Park Hyatt rm 15/50 VISA MC AE

5 r. Paix, (2th) – Opéra – 01 58 71 12 34 – vendome@hyattintl.com – Fax 01 58 71 12 35 – www.paris.vendome.hyatt.com K3

143 rm – 580/650 € 690/760 €, 44 € – 35 suites

Rest *Les Orchidées* – *01 58 71 10 61* – Carte 78/144 €

Rest *Le Pur' Grill* – *01 58 71 10 60* – Carte 83/146 €

♦ Grand Luxury ♦ Modern ♦

Contemporary decor by Ed Tuttle, a collection of modern art, spa and high-tech equipment; a new lease of life for this group of five Haussmann buildings transformed into an ultra-modern luxury hotel. Cuisine in keeping with current tastes, to be savoured below Les Orchidées' glass roof at lunchtime or in the evening in the cosy atmosphere of the Pur' Grill.

Intercontinental Le Grand Hôtel 20/120 P VISA MC AE

2 r. Scribe (9th) – Opéra – 01 40 07 32 32 – legrand.reservations@ichotelsgroup.com – Fax 01 42 66 12 51 – www.paris.intercontinental.com K2

450 rm – 335/650 € 335/650 €, 35 € – 28 suites

Rest *Café de la Paix* – see below

♦ Grand Luxury ♦ Personalised ♦

This famous luxury hotel, opened in 1862, reopened after full renovations in 2003. It offers modern comforts, but its French Second Empire spirit has been judiciously preserved.

The Westin Paris rm rm 15/350 VISA MC AE

3 r. Castiglione (1st) – Tuileries – 01 44 77 11 11 – reservation.01729@starwoodhotels.com – Fax 01 44 77 14 60 – www.westin.com/paris J3

409 rm – 249/730 € 249/730 €, 31 € – 29 suites

Rest *Le First* – *01 44 77 10 40* – Carte 44/86 €

Rest *Terrasse Fleurie* – *01 44 77 10 40 (open mid May-late September)* Carte 44/86 €

♦ Luxury ♦ Traditional ♦ Stylish ♦

A splendid hotel built in 1878, with decor in the guestrooms (some with views of the Tuileries) imitating the artistic styles of the 19C. Sumptuous Napoleon III lounges. Chic and convivial atmosphere at Le First. The courtyard of the Terrasse Fleurie is secluded from the hustle and bustle of Paris.

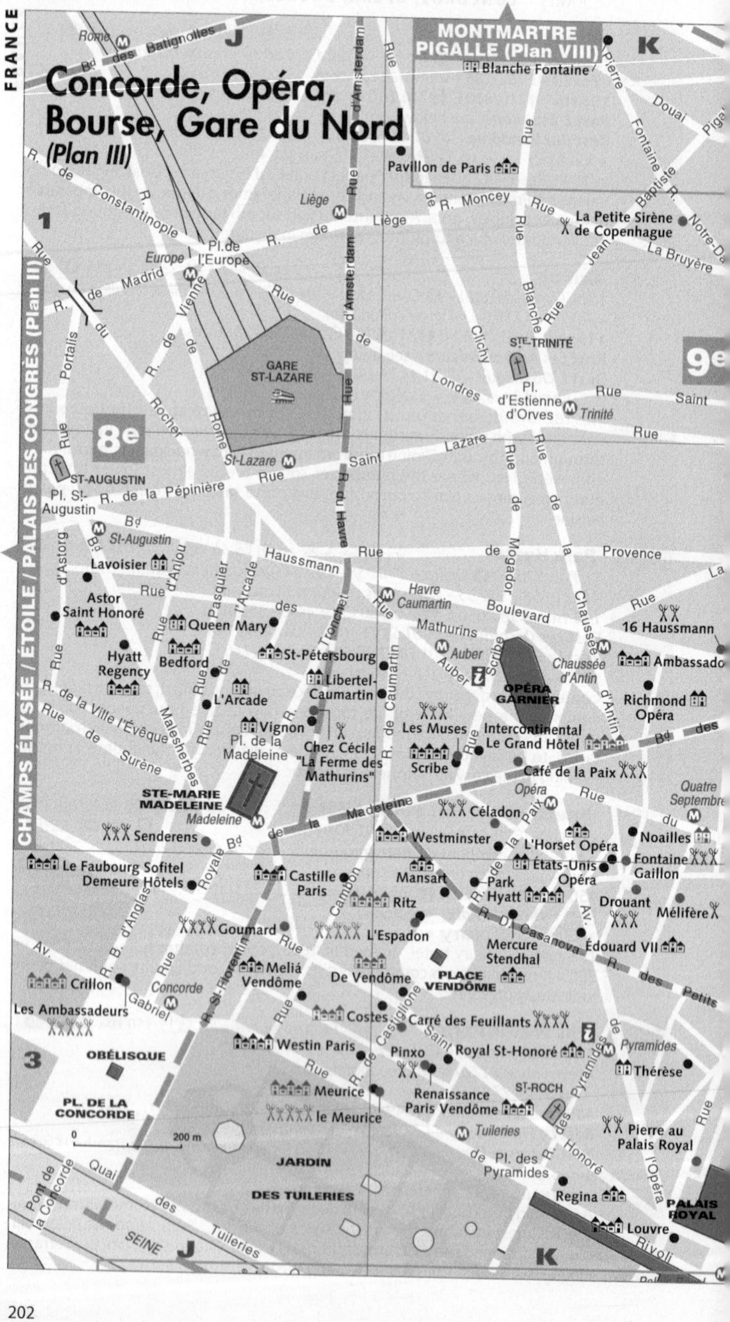

Concorde, Opéra, Bourse, Gare du Nord
(Plan III)

MONTMARTRE PIGALLE (Plan VIII)
CHAMPS ÉLYSÉE / ÉTOILE / PALAIS DES CONGRÈS (Plan II)

J
K
1
3
8e
9e

Rome
Bd des Batignolles
R. de Constantinople
R. de Madrid
Pl. de l'Europe
Europe
R. de Liège
Liège
Rue d'Amsterdam
Rue de Londres
R. de Rome
R. de Vienne
R. du Rocher
Rue Portalis
R. Moncey
Rue Blanche
Rue de Clichy
Rue Jean Baptiste
Rue Fontaine
Rue Pierre
Douai
Pigalle
La Bruyère
Notre-Dame
GARE ST-LAZARE
St-Lazare
Rue Saint Lazare
Rue de la Pépinière
ST-AUGUSTIN
Pl. St-Augustin
St-Augustin
Bd Haussmann
Rue de Provence
Rue de Mogador
Rue de la Chaussée d'Antin
R. du Havre
Havre Caumartin
Rue des Mathurins
Boulevard Haussmann
Rue Auber
Auber
Rue Scribe
Chaussée d'Antin
OPÉRA GARNIER
STE-TRINITÉ
Pl. d'Estienne d'Orves
Trinité
Rue Saint
Bd d'Astorg
Rue d'Anjou
Rue Pasquier
Rue de l'Arcade
Rue Tronchet
R. de Caumartin
R. de la Ville l'Évêque
Rue de Surène
Malesherbes
Pl. de la Madeleine
STE-MARIE MADELEINE
Madeleine
Bd de la Madeleine
Bd des Capucines
Rue du Quatre Septembre
Quatre Septembre
Opéra
Rue de la Paix
Bd Royale
R. B. d'Anglas
Av. Gabriel
Rue Concorde
Concorde
R. St-Florentin
Rue Cambon
Rue St-Honoré
R. D. Casanova
R. des Petits Champs
Av. de l'Opéra
PLACE VENDÔME
R. de Castiglione
Saint Honoré
Pyramides
R. des Pyramides
Pl. des Pyramides
ST-ROCH
Tuileries
Rue de Rivoli
OBÉLISQUE
PL. DE LA CONCORDE
JARDIN DES TUILERIES
Quai des Tuileries
SEINE
Pont de la Concorde
PALAIS ROYAL
Palais Royal
0 — 200 m

Blanche Fontaine
Pavillon de Paris
La Petite Sirène de Copenhague
Lavoisier
Astor Saint Honoré
Hyatt Regency
Queen Mary
Bedford
St-Pétersbourg
L'Arcade
Libertel-Caumartin
Vignon
Chez Cécile "La Ferme des Mathurins"
Les Muses
Scribe
Intercontinental Le Grand Hôtel
Café de la Paix
16 Haussmann
Ambassador
Richmond Opéra
Senderens
Céladon
Westminster
L'Horset Opéra
Noailles
Le Faubourg Sofitel Demeure Hôtels
Castille Paris
Mansart
États-Unis Opéra
Fontaine Gaillon
Park Hyatt
Ritz
Drouant
Mélifère
Goumard
L'Espadon
Mercure Stendhal
Édouard VII
Crillon
Les Ambassadeurs
Meliá Vendôme
De Vendôme
Costes
Carré des Feuillants
Westin Paris
Pinxo
Royal St-Honoré
Thérèse
Meurice
le Meurice
Renaissance Paris Vendôme
Pierre au Palais Royal
Regina
Louvre

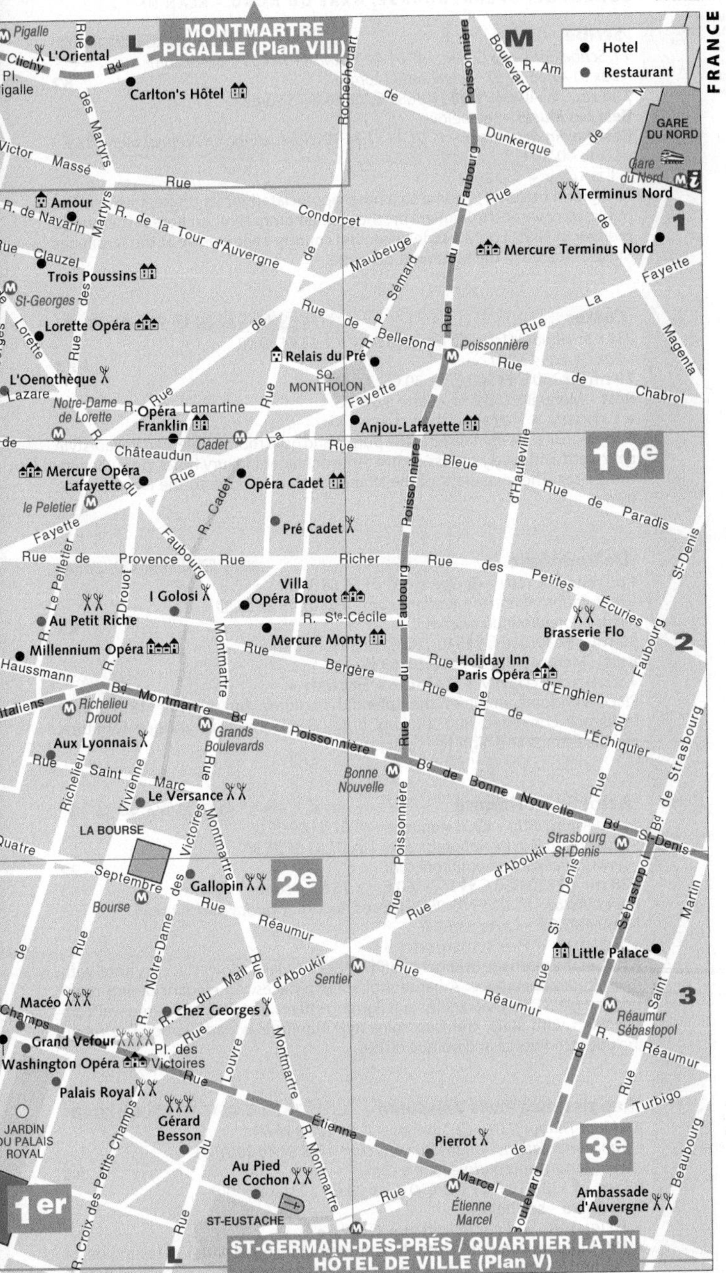
MONTMARTRE
PIGALLE (Plan VIII)
Hotel
Restaurant
GARE DU NORD
L'Oriental
Carlton's Hôtel
Amour
Trois Poussins
Lorette Opéra
L'Oenothèque
Opéra Franklin
Relais du Pré
Anjou-Lafayette
Terminus Nord
Mercure Terminus Nord
Mercure Opéra Lafayette
Opéra Cadet
Pré Cadet
I Golosi
Villa Opéra Drouot
Au Petit Riche
Mercure Monty
Millennium Opéra
Brasserie Flo
Holiday Inn Paris Opéra
Aux Lyonnais
Le Versance
LA BOURSE
Gallopin
Little Palace
Macéo
Chez Georges
Grand Vefour
Washington Opéra
Palais Royal
Gérard Besson
JARDIN DU PALAIS ROYAL
Pierrot
Au Pied de Cochon
ST-EUSTACHE
Ambassade d'Auvergne
10e
2e
3e
1er
1
2
3
ST-GERMAIN-DES-PRÉS / QUARTIER LATIN
HÔTEL DE VILLE (Plan V)

FRANCE

Scribe

rm 20/150 VISA

1 r. Scribe (9th) – Opéra – 01 44 71 24 24 – h0663@accor.com – Fax 01 42 65 39 97 – www.sofitel.com

K2

208 rm – 540/685 € 540/685 €, 28 € – 5 suites

Rest *Les Muses* – see below

Rest *Jardin des Muses* – *01 44 71 24 19 (closed dinner in August)* Menu 32 € – Carte 40/50 €

♦ Luxury ♦ Cosy ♦

This grand building is home to a hotel appreciated for its discreet luxury. The public discovered the Lumière brothers' cinematographic art here at their world premier in 1895. English-style decor and country-style cuisine at the Jardin des Muses, located in the basement of Scribe.

Costes

rm VISA

239 r. St-Honoré (1st) – Concorde – 01 42 44 50 00 – Fax 01 42 44 50 01

J-K3

79 rm – 350 € 500 €, 30 € – 3 suites

Rest – Menu 80/150 € bi – Carte 52/88 €

♦ Luxury ♦ Personalised ♦

Napoleon III style revitalised in the purple and gold rooms. Splendid Italian-style courtyard and lovely fitness centre. An extravagant luxury hotel, popular with the jet-set. The restaurant of the Hôtel Costes is a shrine to the latest lounge trend.

De Vendôme

rm VISA

1 pl. Vendôme (1st) – Opéra – 01 55 04 55 00 – reservations@hoteldevendome.com – Fax 01 49 27 97 89 – www.hoteldevendome.com

K3

19 rm – 430/660 € 510/780 €, 30 € – 10 suites

Rest – Menu 40/80 € – Carte 51/63 €

♦ Grand Luxury ♦ Palace ♦ Stylish ♦

Place Vendôme provides the splendid backdrop for this fine 18C private residence converted into a luxury hotel. Bedrooms with antique furniture, marble fittings and high-tech equipment.

Astor Saint Honoré

rm 12/30 VISA

11 r. d'Astorg (8th) – St-Augustin – 01 53 05 05 05 – reservation@astor.3ahotels.com – Fax 01 53 05 05 30 – www.hotel-astorsainthonore.com

J2

128 rm – 290/350 € 350/460 €, 25 € – 4 suites

Rest *L'Astor* – *01 53 05 05 20 (closed August, Saturday and Sunday)* Menu 48/76 € – Carte 53/67 €

♦ Luxury ♦ Personalised ♦

A successful marriage of Regency and Art Deco styles endows this cosy hotel with its unique appearance. A handful of small terraces. An elegant dining room under a glass roof that creates soft lighting effects. The sand-coloured walls are sprinkled with stars, the Directoire-style furniture is dark wood. The menu includes traditional and unique dishes.

Renaissance Paris Vendôme

VISA

4 r. Mont Thabor (1st) – Tuileries – 01 40 20 20 00 – francereservations@marriotthotels.com – Fax 01 40 20 20 01 – www.renaissanceparisvendome.com

K3

85 rm – 330/610 € 330/610 €, 29 € – 12 suites

Rest *Pinxo* – see below

♦ Business ♦ Traditional ♦ Cosy ♦

A 19C building converted into this contemporary hotel with interesting decor from the 1930s to 1950s. Honey and chocolate tones and wood predominate in the high-tech bedrooms. Attractive Chinese bar.

Castille Paris

33 r. Cambon (1st) – Ⓜ Madeleine – ✆ 01 44 58 44 58 – reservations@castille.com – Fax 01 44 58 44 00 – www.castille.com J3

86 rm – 🛉380/780 € 🛉🛉380/780 €, ☕ 28 € – 21 suites

Rest *Il Cortile* – ✆ 01 44 58 45 67 (closed August, 24-30 December, Saturday and Sunday) Menu 48 € (lunch)/95 € – Carte 55/82 €

♦ Luxury ♦ Traditional ♦ Personalised ♦

Delightful Venetian-inspired decor in the Opéra wing; redesigned black and white chic in the Rivoli wing in reverence to nearby Chanel. The villa d'Este-style dining room, the feverish activity of the piano brigade and the very fine patio-terrace embellished with azulejos create a pretty setting devoted to Italian cuisine.

Louvre

pl. A. Malraux (1st) – Ⓜ Palais Royal Musée du Louvre – ✆ 01 44 58 38 38 – hoteldulouvre@hoteldulouvre.com – Fax 01 44 58 38 01 – www.hoteldulouvre.com K3

132 rm – 🛉215/550 € 🛉🛉215/550 €, ☕ 21 € – 45 suites

Rest *Brasserie Le Louvre* – ✆ 01 42 96 27 98 – Menu 35/38 € – Carte 45/68 €

♦ Luxury ♦ Traditional ♦ Historic ♦

One of the first great Parisian hotels, where the painter Pissarro stayed. Some rooms offer a unique view of the Avenue de l'Opéra and the 'Palais Garnier' (Paris Opera House). The Brasserie Le Louvre is traditional both in its 1900s decor and in its cuisine.

Westminster

13 r. Paix (2nd) – Ⓜ Opéra – ✆ 01 42 61 57 46 – resa.westminster@warwickhotels.com – Fax 01 42 60 30 66 – www.hotelwestminster.com K2

80 rm – 🛉280/630 € 🛉🛉280/630 €, ☕ 28 € – 21 suites

Rest *Céladon* – see below

Rest *Petit Céladon* – ✆ 01 47 03 40 42 (closed August) (week-ends only) Menu 51 € bi

♦ Luxury ♦ Cosy ♦

In was in 1846 that this elegant hotel took the name of its most loyal guest, the Duke of Westminster. Sumptuous rooms, luxurious apartments. The hall is redecorated every season. The Céladon becomes the Petit Céladon at the weekend, with a simplified menu and more relaxed service.

Millennium Opéra

12 bd Haussmann (9th) – Ⓜ Richelieu Drouot – ✆ 01 49 49 16 00 – opera@mill-cop.com – Fax 01 49 49 17 00 – www.millenniumhotels.com L2

157 rm – 🛉400/900 € 🛉🛉400/900 €, ☕ 25 € – 6 suites

Rest *Brasserie Haussmann* – ✆ 01 49 49 16 64 – Carte 28/50 €

♦ Luxury ♦ Business ♦ Modern ♦

This 1927 hotel has lost none of its period lustre. Tastefully appointed rooms with Art Deco furniture. Modern facilities. Carefully renovated with modern decor, and typical brasserie fare at the Brasserie Haussmann.

Ambassador

16 bd Haussmann (9th) – Ⓜ Richelieu Drouot – ✆ 01 44 83 40 40 – ambass@concorde-hotels.com – Fax 01 44 83 40 57 – www.hotelambassador-paris.com K2

290 rm – 🛉360/500 € 🛉🛉360/500 €, ☕ 24 € – 4 suites

Rest *16 Haussmann* – see below

♦ Luxury ♦ Business ♦ Classic ♦

Painted wood panels, crystal chandeliers, antique furniture and decorative objects in this elegant hotel dating from the 1920s. The renovated rooms (2nd and 3rd floors) offer a simple, contemporary decor; the others have a more classical style.

FRANCE

Hyatt Regency rm rm 10/20 VISA
24 bd Malhesherbes, (8th) – Ⓜ *Madeleine* – ✆ *01 55 27 12 34*
– *madeleine@hyattintl.com* – *Fax 01 55 27 12 35*
– *www.paris.madeleine.hyatt.com* J2
86 rm – 🚹290/465 € 🚹🚹350/525 €, ☕ 28 €
Rest *Café M* – *(closed Monday dinner, Saturday and Sunday)* Menu 50 € (lunch) – Carte 52/64 €
♦ Luxury ♦ Chain hotel ♦ Modern ♦
Restrained, warm and highly contemporary best describes the Hyatt Regency's decor. Lobby-lounge with an Eiffel-designed glass roof, attractive personalised guestrooms, sauna and hammam. Tasty modern cuisine or brunch (weekends) – either is a good excuse to home in on Café M.

Bedford rm 15/50 VISA
17 r. de l'Arcade (8th) – Ⓜ *Madeleine* – ✆ *01 44 94 77 77*
– *reservation@hotel-bedford.com* – *Fax 01 44 94 77 97*
– *www.hotel-bedford.com* J2
135 rm – 🚹165 € 🚹🚹210 €, ☕ 15 € – 10 suites
Rest – *(closed 30 July-26 August, Saturday and Sunday) (lunch only)* Menu 41 € – Carte 55/72 €
♦ Luxury ♦ Personalised ♦
This hotel, built in 1860 in the elegant Madeleine district, offers guests tastefully decorated rooms of varying size. 1900s-style decor with an abundance of decorative, stucco motifs and a lovely cupola. The restaurant room is the Bedford's real jewel.

Royal St-Honoré without rest VISA
221 r. St-Honoré (1st) – Ⓜ *Tuileries* – ✆ *01 42 60 32 79* – *rsh@hroy.com*
– *Fax 01 42 60 47 44* – *www.hotel-royal-st-honore.com* K3
67 rm – 🚹320/370 € 🚹🚹370/420 €, ☕ 21 € – 5 suites
♦ Business ♦ Traditional ♦ Classical ♦
An affluent-looking 19C building on the site of the former Hôtel de Noailles. Elegant and refined guestrooms, with Louis XVI decor in the breakfast room and cosy bar.

Villa Opéra Drouot without rest VISA
2 r. Geoffroy Marie (9th) – Ⓜ *Grands Boulevards* – ✆ *01 48 00 08 08*
– *drouot@leshotelsdeparis.com* – *Fax 01 48 00 80 60* L2
29 rm – 🚹199/289 € 🚹🚹235/298 €, ☕ 20 €
♦ Business ♦ Stylish ♦
A surprising and subtle blend of Baroque decor and the latest in elegant comfort in these rooms embellished with wall hangings, velvets, silks and wood panelling.

Regina rm 20/60 VISA
2 pl. Pyramides (1st) – Ⓜ *Tuileries* – ✆ *01 42 60 31 10* – *reservation@regina-hotel.com* – *Fax 01 40 15 95 16* – *www.regina-hotel.com* K3
107 rm – 🚹350/420 € 🚹🚹420/480 €, ☕ 30 € – 13 suites
Rest – Menu 25 € (weekdays) – Carte 30/50 €
♦ Traditional ♦ Business ♦ Personalised ♦
The superb Art Nouveau reception of this 1900 hotel has been preserved. The rooms, rich in antique furniture, are quieter on the patio side; some offer views of the Eiffel Tower. Dining room with a pretty "Majorelle" fireplace and a courtyard-terrace that is very popular in summer.

Meliá Vendôme without rest 20 VISA
8 r. Cambon (1st) – Ⓜ *Concorde* – ✆ *01 44 77 54 00*
– *melia.vendome@solmelia.com* – *Fax 01 44 77 54 01*
– *www.solmelia.com* J3
83 rm – 🚹335 € 🚹🚹335 €, ☕ 25 €
♦ Business ♦ Traditional ♦ Functional ♦
Smart, restrained decor in tones of red and gold. Bedrooms with period furniture, elegant lounge with a Belle Époque glass roof, chic bar and attractive breakfast area.

Édouard VII AC rm SAT 15/25 VISA MC AE

39 av. Opéra (2nd) – Ⓜ Opéra – ✆ 01 42 61 56 90
– info@edouard7hotel.com
– Fax 01 42 61 47 73 – www.edouard7hotel.com **K3**

64 rm – 405/495 € 445/595 €, 23 € – 4 suites

Rest *Angl'Opéra* – *✆ 01 42 61 86 25 (closed 12 to 20 August, Saturday and Sunday)* Carte 43/47 €

♦ Luxury ♦ Modern ♦

Edward VII, Prince of Wales liked to stay here on his trips through Paris. Spacious, luxurious rooms. Dark wood panelling and stained glass decorate the bar. The contemporary and welcoming Angl' Opéra restaurant surprises the taste buds with its fusion food.

Mercure Terminus Nord without rest AC SAT

12 bd Denain (10th) – Ⓜ Gare du Nord 30/130 VISA MC AE
– ✆ 01 42 80 20 00 – h2761@accor.com
– Fax 01 42 80 63 89 – www.mercure.com **M1**

236 rm – 105/235 € 120/250 €, 14 €

♦ Chain hotel ♦ Business ♦ Cosy ♦

Thanks to skilful renovation, this hotel built in 1865 has recovered its former glory. Art Nouveau stained glass, "British" decor and a cosy atmosphere give it the air of a beautiful Victorian home.

Holiday Inn Paris Opéra rm AC rm SAT

38 r. Échiquier (10th) – Ⓜ Bonne Nouvelle 45 VISA MC AE
– ✆ 01 42 46 92 75 – information@hi-parisopera.com – Fax 01 42 47 03 97
– www.holiday-inn.com/paris-opera **M2**

92 rm – 155/205 € 255/309 €, 20 €

Rest – Menu 22 € (lunch)/39 € – Carte 36/48 €

♦ Chain hotel ♦ Business ♦ Retro ♦

A step away from the Grands Boulevards and their string of theatres and brasseries. This hotel offers large rooms decorated in the style of the Belle Époque. The dining room is an authentic gem from the year 1900: mosaics, glass roof, woodwork and fine Art Nouveau furniture.

Pavillon de Paris without rest AC SAT P VISA MC AE

7 r. Parme (9th) – Ⓜ Liège – ✆ 01 55 31 60 00 – mail@pavillondeparis.com
– Fax 01 55 31 60 01 – www.pavillondeparis.com **K1**

30 rm – 215/240 € 270/296 €, 16 €

♦ Business ♦ Minimalist ♦

Contemporary decor with a Zen twist, and sophisticated technology (Internet access via the TV, fax and answering machine) characterise the rooms in this hotel with its restrained luxury.

Washington Opéra without rest AC SAT VISA MC AE

50 r. de Richelieu (1st) – Ⓜ Palais Royal – ✆ 01 42 96 68 06
– hotel@washingtonopera.com – Fax 01 40 15 01 12
– www.washingtonopera.com **L3**

36 rm – 195/245 € 215/275 €, 15 €

♦ Traditional ♦ Luxury ♦ Classical ♦

Former townhouse of the Marquise de Pompadour. Directoire or 'Gustavian'-style rooms. The 6th floor terrace offers beautiful views over the gardens of the Palais-Royal.

Mercure Stendhal without rest AC SAT VISA MC AE

22 r. D. Casanova (2nd) – Ⓜ Opéra – ✆ 01 44 58 52 52 – h1610@accor.com
– Fax 01 44 58 52 00 – www.mercure.com **K3**

20 rm – 215/345 € 215/345 €, 17 €

♦ Luxury ♦ Modern ♦

On the trail of the famous writer, stay in the "Red and Black" suite of this stylish residence. Smart, personalised rooms and snug lounge-bar with fireplace.

FRANCE

Mansart without rest
5 r. Capucines (1st) – Ⓜ Opéra – ✆ 01 42 61 50 28 – mansart@espritfrance.com – Fax 01 49 27 97 44 – www.esprit-de-france.com **K3**
57 rm – 130/325 € 150/325 €, 12 €
♦ Business ♦ Traditional ♦ Functional ♦
Close to Place Vendôme, this hotel pays homage to Mansart, architect to Louis XIV. Classic rooms furnished in Empire or Directoire style. A more modern lobby-lounge.

L'Horset Opéra without rest
18 r. d'Antin (2nd) – Ⓜ Opéra – ✆ 01 44 71 87 00 – lopera@paris-hotels-charm.com – Fax 01 42 66 55 54 – www.paris-hotels-charm.com
54 rm – 180/245 € 200/275 € **K2**
♦ Luxury ♦ Cosy ♦
Colourful wall hangings, warm wood panelling and fine furnishings add style to the rooms of this traditional hotel a short distance from the Opera House. Cosy atmosphere in the lounge.

Mercure Opéra Lafayette without rest
49 r. Lafayette (9th) – Ⓜ Le Peletier – ✆ 01 42 85 05 44 – h2802-gm@accor.com – Fax 01 49 95 06 60 **L2**
94 rm – 99/199 € 109/214 €, 14 € – 7 suites
♦ Traditional ♦ Business ♦ Cosy ♦
This hotel has embraced contemporary design without sacrificing any of its inherent elegance with the emphasis on refined decor in the refurbished bedrooms. Winter garden-style breakfast room. Wellness centre.

St-Pétersbourg without rest
25
33 r. Caumartin (9th) – Ⓜ Havre Caumartin – ✆ 01 42 66 60 38 – info@hotelpeters.com – Fax 01 42 66 53 54 – www.hotelsaintpetersbourg.com **J2**
100 rm – 149/175 € 189/221 €
♦ Traditional ♦ Business ♦ Classic ♦
The Louis XVI-style rooms are often spacious and face the courtyard. Comfortable lounge, lit by coloured glass.

Lorette Opéra without rest
36 r. Notre-Dame de Lorette, (9th) – Ⓜ St-Georges – ✆ 01 42 85 18 81 – hotel.lorette@astotel.com – Fax 01 42 81 32 19 – www.asthotel.com
84 rm – 115/210 € 185/210 €, 11 € **L1**
♦ Business ♦ Modern ♦
The decor in this completely renovated hotel is a harmonious mix of dressed stone and contemporary touches. Large, pleasant rooms with a modern, refined feel.

Le Faubourg Sofitel Demeure Hôtels
rm
15 r. Boissy d'Anglas (8th) – Ⓜ Concorde – ✆ 01 44 94 14 14 – h1295@accor.com – Fax 01 44 94 14 28 – www.sofitelfaubourg.com **J3**
163 rm – 395/558 € 530/714 €, 28 € – 7 suites
Rest *Café Faubourg* – ✆ *01 44 94 14 24 (closed 1st-20 August, Saturday and Sunday)* Carte 51/62 €
♦ Chain hotel ♦ Luxury ♦ Modern ♦
This Sofitel is housed in two buildings, one 18C, the other 19C. Rooms with high-tech facilities; a 1930s bar; plus a lounge with a glass roof. Trendy decor, relaxing interior garden and modern cuisine at the Café Faubourg.

Richmond Opéra without rest
11 r. Helder (9th) – Ⓜ Chaussée d'Antin – ✆ 01 47 70 53 20 – paris@richmond-hotel.com – Fax 01 48 00 02 10 **K2**
59 rm – 134/149 € 154/225 €, 10 €
♦ Traditional ♦ Business ♦ Classic ♦
The spacious, elegant rooms almost all give onto the courtyard. The lounge is rather grandly decorated in the Empire style.

L'Arcade without rest 12/25 VISA MC AE

7-9 r. Arcade (8th) – Ⓜ Madeleine – ✆ 01 53 30 60 00 – reservation@hotel-arcade.com – Fax 01 40 07 03 07 – www.hotel-arcade.com **J2**

41 rm – 146/180 € 188/234 €, 11 €

◆ Luxury ◆ Personalised ◆

The marble and wood panels in the hall and lounges, and the soft colours and carefully-chosen furniture in the rooms, all contribute to the charm of this elegant and discreet hotel near the Madeleine.

Lavoisier without rest VISA MC AE

21 r. Lavoisier (8th) – Ⓜ St-Augustin – ✆ 01 53 30 06 06 – info@hotellavoisier.com – Fax 01 53 30 23 00 – www.hotellavoisier.com **J2**

27 rm – 179/270 € 179/270 €, 14 € – 3 suites

◆ Luxury ◆ Modern ◆

Contemporary rooms, cosy little library-cum-lounge also serving as a bar, and a vaulted breakfast room are the hallmarks of this hotel in the St-Augustin district.

Opéra Cadet without rest 50 VISA MC AE

24 r. Cadet (9th) – Ⓜ Cadet – ✆ 01 53 34 50 50 – infos@operacadet.com – Fax 01 53 34 50 60 – www.operacadet.com **L2**

85 rm – 120/169 € 133/195 €

◆ Business ◆ Modern ◆

Leave your car in the garage, settle into this contemporary-style hotel and get to know the capital on foot. Choose a room facing the garden for more peace and quiet.

Little Palace rm rm VISA MC AE

4 r. Salomon de Caus (3rd) – Ⓜ Réaumur Sébastopol – ✆ 01 42 72 08 15 – info@littlepalacehotel.com – Fax 01 42 72 45 81 – www.littlepalacehotel.com **M3**

49 rm – 148/168 € 165/185 €, 13 € – 4 suites

Rest – *(closed 29 July-28 August, dinner Friday, Saturday and Sunday)* Carte 28/40 €

◆ Family ◆ Traditional ◆ Modern ◆

This 1900s building on a charming small square has had a face-lift. It has pretty, modern rooms, with the best on the 5th and 6th floors offering a balcony and view of Paris. Lovely brown, sculpted wood panelling, light tones and minimalist furniture can be found in the restaurant.

Queen Mary without rest VISA MC AE

9 r. Greffulhe (8th) – Ⓜ Madeleine – ✆ 01 42 66 40 50 – reservations@hotelqueenmary.com – Fax 01 42 66 94 92 – www.hotelqueenmary.com **J2**

36 rm – 165/215 € 189/349 €, 18 €

◆ Family ◆ Personalised ◆

A refined establishment with a "British" feel to it, where a welcome gift of a carafe of sherry awaits you. Attentive service, pleasant patio, charming breakfast room and hushed bedrooms.

Vignon without rest VISA MC AE

23 r. Vignon (8th) – Ⓜ Madeleine – ✆ 01 47 42 93 00 – reservation@hotelvignon.com – Fax 01 47 42 04 60 – www.levignon.com **J2**

28 rm – 260/390 € 260/390 €, 20 €

◆ Chain hotel ◆ Personalised ◆

A friendly, discreet hotel just a few steps away from Place de la Madeleine. Cosy rooms – those on the top floor have just been refurbished in a distinctly contemporary style.

États-Unis Opéra without rest 25 VISA MC AE

16 r. d'Antin (2nd) – Ⓜ Opéra – ✆ 01 42 65 05 05 – us-opera@wanadoo.fr – Fax 01 42 65 93 70 – www.hotel-paris-opera.com **K3**

45 rm – 100/180 € 140/240 €, 11 €

◆ Traditional ◆ Classical ◆

This hotel in a 1930s building offers modern, comfortable, recently renovated rooms. Breakfast is served in the inviting English-style bar.

FRANCE

Noailles without rest
9 r. Michodière (2nd) – Ⓜ Quatre Septembre – ✆ 01 47 42 92 90 – goldentulip.denoailles@wanadoo.fr – Fax 01 49 24 92 71 – www.hoteldenoailles.com
59 rm – 🛉180/240 € 🛉🛉180/330 €, ☕ 15 € – 2 suites **K2**
♦ Traditional ♦ Modern ♦
Staunch contemporary elegance behind a pretty old façade. Minimalist decor in the rooms, most of which open onto a patio-terrace. Fashionable lounge (jazz on Thursdays).

Thérèse without rest
5-7 r. Thérèse (1st) – Ⓜ Pyramides – ✆ 01 42 96 10 01 – info@hoteltherese.com – Fax 01 42 96 15 22 – www.hoteltherese.com
43 rm – 🛉145/158 € 🛉🛉145/306 €, ☕ 13 € **K3**
♦ Traditional ♦ Business ♦ Personalised ♦
The charm of this hotel lies in its refined contemporary decor of paintings, attractive fabrics and pastel shades. Vaulted breakfast room occupying the former cellars.

Opéra Franklin without rest
19 r. Buffault (9th) – Ⓜ Cadet – ✆ 01 42 80 27 27 – info@operafranklin.com – Fax 01 48 78 13 04 – www.operafranklin.com
67 rm – 🛉139/163 € 🛉🛉152/176 €, ☕ 13 € **L1**
♦ Family ♦ Traditional ♦ Historic ♦
In a quiet street, this hotel's rooms have elegant furnishings recalling Napoleonic-era military campaigns. Unusual naive trompe-l'oeil at the front desk.

Libertel-Caumartin without rest
27 r. Caumartin (9th) – Ⓜ Havre Caumartin – ✆ 01 47 42 95 95 – hotel.caumartin@astotel.com – Fax 01 47 42 88 19 – www.astotel.com
40 rm – 🛉155/210 € 🛉🛉165/210 €, ☕ 14 € **J2**
♦ Chain hotel ♦ Business ♦ Modern ♦
Prettily-decorated contemporary rooms furnished in pale wood. Pleasant breakfast room decorated with colourful paintings.

Anjou-Lafayette without rest
4 r. Riboutté (9th) – Ⓜ Cadet – ✆ 01 42 46 83 44 – hotel.anjou.lafayette@wanadoo.fr – Fax 01 48 00 08 97 – www.hotelanjoulafayette.com
39 rm – 🛉98/150 € 🛉🛉118/170 €, ☕ 11.50 € **M1**
♦ Business ♦ Modern ♦
Near the leafy Square Montholon with its Second Empire wrought-iron gates, comfortable, soundproofed and totally renovated contemporary rooms.

Trois Poussins without rest
15 r. Clauzel (9th) – Ⓜ St-Georges – ✆ 01 53 32 81 81 – h3p@les3poussins.com – Fax 01 53 32 81 82 – www.les3poussins.com
40 rm – 🛉110/139 € 🛉🛉119/154 €, ☕ 10 € **L1**
♦ Traditional ♦ Business ♦ Cosy ♦
Elegant rooms offering several levels of comfort. View of Paris from the top floors. Prettily vaulted breakfast room. Small courtyard-terrace.

Mercure Monty without rest
5 r. Montyon (9th) – Ⓜ Grands Boulevards – ✆ 01 47 70 26 10 – hotel@mercuremonty.com – Fax 01 42 46 55 10 – www.mercure.com
69 rm – 🛉75/215 € 🛉🛉90/230 €, ☕ 13 € **L2**
♦ Chain hotel ♦ Business ♦ Functional ♦
Beautiful façade dating from the 1930s, Art Deco setting at the front desk, and the hotel chain's standard equipment characterise this Mercure located in view of the Folies Bergère.

Amour rm VISA AE

8 r. Navarin (9th) – Ⓜ Pigalle – ☎ 01 48 78 31 80 – Fax 01 48 74 14 09 L1

20 rm – †90 € ††120 €, ☕ 10 €

Rest – Carte 20/40 €

◆ Design ◆ Personalised ◆

This lovely hotel run by graphic designer André and friends has a fun and trendy atmosphere. Each bedroom is adorned with the work of a contemporary artist.

Relais du Pré without rest VISA AE

16 r. P. Sémard (9th) – Ⓜ Poissonnière – ☎ 01 42 85 19 59 – relais@duprehotels.com – Fax 01 42 85 70 59 – www.leshotelsdupre.com L-M1

34 rm – †85/90 € ††98/105 €, ☕ 10 €

◆ Business ◆ Modern ◆

Near two other older hotels in the same chain, this one offers the same rooms - modern and neat as a pin. Contemporary, rather cosy bar and lounge.

Le Meurice – Hôtel Le Meurice 25/120 VISA AE

228 r. Rivoli (1st) – Ⓜ Tuileries – ☎ 01 44 58 10 55 – restaurant@lemeurice.com – Fax 01 44 58 10 76 – www.lemeurice.com

closed 28 July - 26 August, 19 February - 4 March, Saturday and Sunday J-K3

Rest – Menu 75 € (lunch), 170/190 € – Carte 164/262 €

Spec. Vapeur de Saint-Jacques aux truffes, nage de corail de homard (autumn-winter). Noix de ris de veau rôtie (autumn-winter). Fraises soufflées, crème normande vanillée au "caviar" de fruits (summer).

◆ Inventive ◆ Luxury ◆

The Grand Siècle style dining hall has clearly drawn its inspiration from the Versailles chateau; the cuisine is exceptional and up-to-date - a palace for gourmets!

Les Ambassadeurs – Hôtel Crillon 12/40 VISA AE

10 pl. Concorde (8th) – Ⓜ Concorde – ☎ 01 44 71 16 16 – restaurants@crillon.com – Fax 01 44 71 15 02 – www.crillon.com

closed August, 1 - 8 January, Sunday and Monday J3

Rest – Menu 75 € (weekday lunch)/200 € – Carte 154/255 €

Spec. Blanc à manger d'œuf, truffe noire (January-March). Pigeonneau désossé, foie gras, jus à l'olive. Comme un vacherin, au parfum de saison.

◆ Innovative ◆ Luxury ◆

This splendid dining hall where gold and marble is reflected in immense mirrors, is in effect the ballroom of an 18C mansion. The cuisine is distinctive.

L'Espadon – Hôtel Ritz 15/300 VISA AE

15 pl. Vendôme (1st) – Ⓜ Opéra – ☎ 01 43 16 30 80 – food-bev@ritzparis.com – Fax 01 43 16 33 75 – www.ritzparis.com K3

Rest – Menu 75 € (lunch), 145/265 € bi – Carte 121/221 €

Spec. Araignée de mer, riviera de mangue au jus d'agrumes. Turbot en tronçon rôti à la fleur de sel. Rosette d'agneau en écrin d'herbes, pommes soufflées.

◆ Traditional ◆ Luxury ◆

Dining room weighted in gold and drapery, a dazzling decor reminiscent of its famous guests and a pleasant terrace in a flower garden. The Ritz in all its splendour!

Le Grand Vefour 2/20 VISA AE

17 r. Beaujolais (1st) – Ⓜ Palais Royal – ☎ 01 42 96 56 27 – grand.vefour@wanadoo.fr – Fax 01 42 86 80 71 – www.grand-vefour.com

closed 14 - 22 Apr, 30 July - 27 Aug, 24 Dec - 1 Jan, Fri evening, Sat and Sun L3

Rest – Menu 78 € (lunch)/256 € – Carte 177/207 €

Spec. Ravioles de foie gras à l'émulsion de crème truffée. Pigeon Prince Rainier III. Tourte d'artichaut et légumes confits.

◆ Innovative ◆ Romantic ◆

In the gardens of the Palais-Royal, sumptuous Directoire period dining rooms decorated with splendid "pictures under glass". The inspired and inventive cuisine is worthy of this historic monument.

XXXX ✿✿

Carré des Feuillants (Dutournier)

AC ⊕6/44 VISA MC AE DC

14 r. Castiglione (1st) – Ⓜ Tuileries – ☎ 01 42 86 82 82 – carre.des.feuillants@wanadoo.fr – Fax 01 42 86 07 71 – www.carredesfeuillants.fr
closed Aug., Sat. and Sun. **K3**

Rest – Menu 65 € (lunch)/165 € – Carte 127/158 €

Spec. Homard bleu en feuille de riz (autumn-winter). Tendron de veau de lait dans son jus truffé (spring-summer). Ravioles de mangue aux fruits de la passion.

♦ Traditional ♦ Cosy ♦

This restaurant, on the site of the former Feuillants convent, has a decisively modern setting. Up-to-date cuisine with Gascony touches and superb wine list.

XXXX ✿

Goumard

AC ⊕4/18 VISA MC AE DC

9 r. Duphot (1st) – Ⓜ Madeleine – ☎ 01 42 60 36 07 – goumard.philippe@wanadoo.fr – Fax 01 42 60 04 54 – www.goumard.com **J3**

Rest – Menu 46/60 € bi (lunch) – Carte 67/142 €

Spec. Tranches de tomate, balsamique blanc et crevettes tigrées au romarain (June to October). Aiguillette de Saint-Pierre doré (June to September). Homard bleu rôti.

♦ Seafood ♦ Formal ♦

Small, intimate dining rooms in art deco style, enhanced by ocean scenes. The toilets, vestige of the original Majorelle decor, are well worth a visit. Delicious seafood cuisine.

XXX ✿✿

Senderens

AC ⊕8/20 VISA MC AE DC

9 pl. Madeleine (8th) – Ⓜ Madeleine – ☎ 01 42 65 22 90 – restaurant@senderens.fr – Fax 01 42 65 06 23 – www.senderens.fr **J2**

Rest – Carte 73/91 €

Spec. Homard bleu et mangue en salade au basilic. Canard "Apicius" rôti au miel et aux épices. Coulant de samana, cerises amarena.

♦ Inventive ♦ Design ♦

Contemporary furnishings and Art Nouveau wood panels by Majorelle are artfully combined in this luxurious and ever-lively brasserie. Innovative cuisine; sublime blend of dishes and wines.

XXX ✿

Le Céladon – Hôtel Westminster

AC ⊕15/40 VISA MC AE DC

15 r. Daunou (2nd) – Ⓜ Opéra – ☎ 01 47 03 40 42 – christophemoisand@leceladon.com – Fax 01 42 61 33 78 – www.leceladon.com
closed Aug., Sat. and Sun. **K2**

Rest – Menu 48 € (lunch), 72 € bi/110 € – Carte 82/111 €

Spec. Pâté froid de lapin de garenne (15 September-15 January). Langoustines bretonnes en tempura au carry. Veau fermier, ris confit, onglet grillé.

♦ Innovative ♦ Romantic ♦

Delightful dining rooms with a high-class decor: Regency-style furniture, "celadon" green walls and a collection of Chinese porcelain. Cooking suited to current tastes.

XXX ✿

Gérard Besson

AC VISA MC AE DC

5 r. Coq Héron (1st) – Ⓜ Louvre Rivoli – ☎ 01 42 33 14 74 – gerard.besson4@libertysurf.fr – Fax 01 42 33 85 71 – www.gerardbesson.com
closed 13 July - 19 August, Mon lunchtime, Sat lunchtime and Sun. **L3**

Rest – Menu 56 € (lunch), 105/125 € – Carte 100/157 €

Spec. Fricassée de homard "Georges Garin". Gibier (October-mid December). Fenouil confit aux épices.

♦ Traditional ♦ Formal ♦

Elegant, low-key restaurant near the Halles decorated in beige tones with still-life paintings and Jouy prints. Subtly reinterpreted classic cuisine.

XXX

Café de la Paix – Intercontinental Le Grand Hôtel

AC ⊕10/450 VISA MC AE DC

12 bd Capucines (9th) – Ⓜ Opéra – ☎ 01 40 07 36 36 – legrand.reservations@ichotelsgroup.com – Fax 01 40 07 36 13 – www.paris.intercontinental.com **K2**

Rest – Menu 45 € (lunch)/85 € – Carte 50/106 €

♦ Traditional ♦ Brasserie ♦

This famous luxury brasserie, open from 7am to midnight, has been successfully renovated. Fine murals, wood-panelling and French Second Empire-inspired furniture.

XXX

Les Muses – Hôtel Scribe

1 r. Scribe (9th) – Ⓜ Opéra – ✆ 01 44 71 24 26 – h0663-re@accor.com – Fax 01 44 71 24 64

closed August, Saturday, Sunday and Bank Holidays **K2**

Rest – Menu 45 € (lunch), 75/95 € – Carte approx. 80 €

Spec. Foie gras de canard rôti. Filet de bar de ligne poêlé au beurre demi-sel. Agneau de Lozère tout simplement rôti.

♦ Contemporary ♦ Formal ♦

The dining hall, embellished by frescoes and canvasses evoking the 19C opera quarter, is located in the basement of the hotel. Enticing traditional menus.

XXX

Drouant

2/25

pl. Gaillon (2nd) – Ⓜ 4 Septembre – ✆ 01 42 65 15 16 – reservations@drouant.com – Fax 01 49 24 02 15 – www.drouant.com **K3**

Rest – Menu 42 € (weekday lunch)/52 € – Carte approx. 70 €

♦ Contemporary ♦ Trendy ♦

Small Art Deco dining rooms around a majestic staircase by Ruhlmann. The Louis XVI lounge on the first floor is where the Goncourt literary jury has chosen the prize-winner since 31 October 1914.

XXX

Fontaine Gaillon

12/40

Pl. Gaillon (2nd) – Ⓜ Quatre Septembre – ✆ 01 47 42 63 22 – Fax 01 47 42 82 84 – www.la-semaine-gaillon.com – closed 4 - 26 Aug., Sat. and Sun. **K2-3**

Rest – Menu 38 € (lunch) – Carte 47/66 €

♦ Seafood ♦ Cosy ♦

Elegant dining room in a 17C town house. Terrace set up around a fountain. Fish and seafood dishes and wine selection supervised by Gérard Depardieu.

XXX

Macéo

10/40

15 r. Petits-Champs (1st) – Ⓜ Bourse – ✆ 01 42 97 53 85 – info@maceorestaurant.com – Fax 01 47 03 36 93 – www.maceorestaurant.com

closed Aug., Sat. lunchtime and Sun. **L3**

Rest – Menu 30/36 € – Carte 46/61 €

♦ Innovative ♦ Friendly ♦

A surprising blend of French Second Empire decor and contemporary furniture. Up-to-date cuisine, a vegetarian menu and international wine list. Friendly lounge-bar.

XX

Pierre au Palais Royal

10 r. Richelieu (1st) – Ⓜ Palais Royal – ✆ 01 42 96 09 17 – pierreaupalaisroyal@wanadoo.fr – Fax 01 42 96 26 40

closed 5-26 August, Sat. lunchtime, Sun. and Bank Holidays **K3**

Rest – Menu 38 €

♦ Traditional ♦ Neighbourhood ♦

Sober and pleasant decor in aubergine shades with prints of the neighbouring Palais-Royal. Well-laid tables. Cuisine based on seasonal market produce.

XX

Palais Royal

110 Galerie de Valois (1st) – Ⓜ Bourse – ✆ 01 40 20 00 27 – palaisrest@aol.com – Fax 01 40 20 00 82 – www.restaurantdupalaisroyal.com

closed 20 Dec. - 10 Jan. and Sun. **L3**

Rest – Carte 36/64 €

♦ Traditional ♦ Retro ♦

Beneath the windows of Colette's apartment, an Art Deco-style restaurant and an idyllic terrace, opening onto the Palais-Royal garden.

XX

16 Haussmann – Hôtel Ambassador

16 bd Haussmann (9th) – Ⓜ Richelieu Drouot – ✆ 01 48 00 06 38 – 16haussmann@concorde-hotels.com – Fax 01 44 83 40 57 – www.hotelambassador-paris.com

closed 4 - 25 August, Saturday lunch and Sunday **K2**

Rest – Menu 32 € (dinner)/41 € – Carte 52/60 €

♦ Contemporary ♦ Design ♦

Contemporary Paris blue, golden yellow, reddish-brown wood, red seats by Starck and large bay windows opening onto the boulevard, the street life adding to the decor.

FRANCE

XX

Au Petit Riche

AC ⌂6/50 VISA MC AE ①

25 r. Le Peletier (9th) – Ⓜ Richelieu Drouot – ✆ 01 47 70 68 68 – aupetitriche@wanadoo.fr – Fax 01 48 24 10 79 – www.aupetitriche.com

closed Sun. **L2**

Rest – Menu 27/35 € bi – Carte 30/56 €

♦ Traditional ♦ Brasserie ♦

Gracious lounge-dining rooms dating from the late 19C, decorated with mirrors and hat-boxes. Perhaps you will be seated at Chevalier's or Mistinguett's favourite table.

XX

Gallopin

AC ⌂8 VISA MC AE ①

40 r. N.-D.-des-Victoires (2nd) – Ⓜ Bourse – ✆ 01 42 36 45 38 – administration@brasseriegallopin.com – Fax 01 42 36 10 32 – www.brasseriegallopin.com **L3**

Rest – Menu 28/34 € bi – Carte 28/73 €

♦ Brasserie ♦ Retro ♦

Arletty, Raimu and the exaggerated Victorian decor have brought fame to this brasserie situated opposite the Palais Brongniart. An attractive glass roof in the back room.

XX

Luna

AC VISA MC AE

69 r. Rocher (8th) – Ⓜ Villiers – ✆ 01 42 93 77 61 – laluna75008@yahoo.fr – Fax 01 40 08 02 44

closed 1 - 22 Aug. and Sun. *Plan II* **H1**

Rest – Carte 67/100 €

♦ Seafood ♦ Friendly ♦

Restrained Art Deco setting and fine cuisine based on fish delivered fresh daily from Atlantic coast waters. And the rum baba cakes for dessert will leave you agog...!

XX

Au Pied de Cochon

AC VISA MC AE ①

(24 hr service) 6 r. Coquillière (1st) – Ⓜ Châtelet-Les Halles – ✆ 01 40 13 77 00 – de.pied-de-cochon@blanc.net – Fax 01 40 13 77 09 – www.pieddecochon.com **L3**

Rest – Menu 24 € – Carte 30/65 €

♦ Brasserie ♦ Retro ♦

Pigs trotters are the speciality of this renowned brasserie that has been opened late into the night since it opened in 1946. Original murals and central lights with fruit designs.

XX

Ambassade d'Auvergne

AC ⌂10/40 VISA MC AE

22 r. du Grenier St-Lazare (3rd) – Ⓜ Rambuteau – ✆ 01 42 72 31 22 – info@ambassade-auvergne.com – Fax 01 42 78 85 47 – www.ambassade-auvergne.com **M3**

Rest – Menu 28 € – Carte 30/45 €

♦ Traditional ♦ Friendly ♦

True ambassadors of a province rich in flavours and traditions: Auvergne-style furniture and setting offering products, recipes and wines of the region.

XX

Brasserie Flo

AC (dinner) VISA MC AE ①

7 cour Petites-Écuries (10th) – Ⓜ Château d'Eau – ✆ 01 47 70 13 59 – Fax 01 42 47 00 80 – www.floparis.com **M2**

Rest – Menu 21/31 € – Carte 28/80 €

♦ Brasserie ♦ Retro ♦

In the heart of the picturesque Petites-Écuries courtyard. The beautiful decor of dark wood panels, coloured glass and painted panels recals the Alsace of the early 20C.

XX

Terminus Nord

AC ⌂6/12 VISA MC ①

23 r. Dunkerque (10th) – Ⓜ Gare du Nord – ✆ 01 42 85 05 15 – Fax 01 40 16 13 98 – www.terminusnord.com **M1**

Rest – Menu 31 € – Carte 29/69 €

♦ Traditional ♦ Brasserie ♦

High ceilings, frescos, posters and sculptures in the mirrors of this brasserie that mixes Art Deco and Art Nouveau. Cosmopolitan clientele.

XX **Pinxo** – Hôtel Renaissance Paris Vendôme
9 r. Alger (1st) – Ⓜ Tuileries – ✆ 01 40 20 72 00 – Fax 01 40 20 72 02 – www.pinxo.fr
closed Aug. K3
Rest – Menu 32 € bi (weekday lunch) – Carte 37/58 €
♦ Innovative ♦ Fashionable ♦
A restaurant with refined furniture, black and white shades, an open kitchen and sober but stylish decoration, serving tasty dishes à la Dutournier.

XX **Le Versance**
16 r. Faydeau, (2nd) – Ⓜ Bourse – ✆ 01 45 08 00 08 – contact@leversance.fr – Fax 01 45 08 47 99 – www.leversance.fr
closed August, Saturday lunch, Sunday and Monday L2
Rest – Menu 38 € bi – Carte 40/71 €
♦ Contemporary ♦ Fashionable ♦
Old (wooden beams, stained glass) meets new (designer furniture) in this refined restaurant decorated in grey and white. Modern cuisine created by the globetrotting chef. Smoking lounge.

X **Chez Georges**
1 r. Mail (2nd) – Ⓜ Bourse – ✆ 01 42 60 07 11
closed August, Saturday and Sunday L3
Rest – Carte 42/65 €
♦ Traditional ♦ Retro ♦
The Sentier "institution". This typical Parisian bistro has conserved its original decor : bar, seats, stucco and mirrors ; bathe in the Paris of the 1900's.

X **Aux Lyonnais**
32 r. St-Marc (2nd) – Ⓜ Richelieu Drouot – ✆ 01 42 96 65 04 – auxlyonnais@online.fr – Fax 01 42 97 42 95
closed 22 July - 21 Aug., 23 Dec. - 2 Jan., Sat. lunchtime, Sun. and Mon.
Rest – *(pre-book)* Menu 30 € – Carte 40/52 € L2
♦ Lyonnais cuisine ♦ Bistro ♦
This bistro founded in 1890 proposes delicious Lyonnais recipes, intelligently brought up to date. A deliciously "retro" setting: bar counter, bench seating, bevelled mirrors and mouldings.

X **La Petite Sirène de Copenhague**
47 r. N.-D. de Lorette (9th) – Ⓜ St-Georges – ✆ 01 45 26 66 66
closed 29 July - 27 Aug, 24 Dec - 2 Jan, Sat lunchtime, Sun and Mon K1
Rest – *(pre-book)* Menu 28 € (lunch)/32 € – Carte 48/64 €
♦ Danish ♦ Friendly ♦
One dines here in sober elegance - whitewashed walls, subdued lighting in the Danish style accompany the classical recipes of Andersen's homeland. A warm, attentive welcome.

X **L'Oenothèque**
20 r. St-Lazare (9th) – Ⓜ Notre Dame de Lorette – ✆ 01 48 78 08 76 – Fax 01 40 16 10 27
closed 1 - 8 May, 13 Aug - 12 Sept, 25 Dec - 1 Jan, Sat and Sun L1
Rest – Carte 29/50 €
♦ Traditional ♦ Bistro ♦
Neighbourhood establishment combining a simple restaurant with a wine shop. Nice selection of wines to accompany the market-based cuisine on the chalkboard.

X **I Golosi**
6 r. Grange Batelière (9th) – Ⓜ Richelieu Drouot – ✆ 01 48 24 18 63 – i.golosi@wanadoo.fr – Fax 01 45 23 18 96
closed 5 - 20 Aug., Sat. evening and Sun. L2
Rest – Carte 25/48 €
♦ Italian ♦ Minimalist ♦
On the 1st floor, Italian designer decor with a minimalism made up for by the joviality of the service. Café, shop and little spot for tasting things on the ground floor. Italian cuisine.

FRANCE

Pré Cadet

10 r. Saulnier (9th) – Ⓜ Cadet – ✆ 01 48 24 99 64 – Fax 01 47 70 55 96
closed 1 - 8 May, 1 - 21 Aug., 22 Dec - 1 Jan, Sat. lunch and Sun. **L2**
Rest – *(number of covers limited, pre-book)* Menu 30 € – Carte 34/47 €
◆ Traditional ◆ Friendly ◆
Pleasant and convivial, this restaurant near the "Folies" owes its success to its old-fashioned dishes such as veal brawn, a house speciality. Very good coffee list.

Pierrot

18 r. Etienne Marcel (2nd) – Ⓜ Etienne Marcel – ✆ 01 45 08 00 10 – Fax 01 42 77 35 92
closed 30 July-19 August and Sunday **M3**
Rest – Menu 40/50 € – Carte 33/50 €
◆ Traditional ◆ Bistro ◆
Right in the lively Sentier district, this friendly bistro offers a discovery tour of all the savours and specialities of the Aveyron. Small summer terrace on the pavement.

Mellifère

8 r. Monsigny, (2nd) – Ⓜ Quatre Septembre – ✆ 01 42 61 21 71 – mellifere@free.fr – Fax 01 42 61 31 71
closed Sat. lunchtime, Mon. evening and Sun. **K3**
Rest – Menu 30 € (lunch)/34 € – Carte approx. 43 €
◆ Traditional ◆ Bistro ◆
A colony of bees frequents this beehive that is as busy as the neighbouring Théâtre des Bouffes Parisiens. Bistrot cuisine and Basque dishes.

Chez Cécile la Ferme des Mathurins

17 r. Vignon(8th) – Ⓜ Madeleine – ✆ 01 42 66 46 39 – cecile@chezcecile.com – www.chezcecile.com
closed August and Sunday **J2**
Rest – Menu 33 € (lunch)/36 €
◆ Traditional ◆ Bistro ◆
Generous portions of fine, traditional cuisine are served in this authentic Parisian bistro, which has a loyal clientele. Lively atmosphere and often fully booked.

TOUR EIFFEL, INVALIDES *Plan IV*

Mercure Paris Suffren Tour Eiffel

30/100
20 r. Jean Rey (15th) – Ⓜ Bir-Hakeim – ✆ 01 45 78 50 00 – h2175@accor.com – Fax 01 45 78 91 42 – www.mercure.com **N2**
405 rm – 🚹150/300 € 🚹🚹165/415 €, ☕ 21 €
Rest – Carte 30/38 €
◆ Business ◆ Chain hotel ◆ Functional ◆
A complete, careful renovation has been carried out in this perfectly soundproofed hotel, and the new decor has a "nature and garden" theme. Some rooms have a view of the Eiffel Tower. A dining room opening directly onto a pleasant terrace surrounded by trees and greenery.

Mercure Tour Eiffel without rest

25/40
64 bd Grenelle (15th) – Ⓜ Dupleix – ✆ 01 45 78 90 90 – hotel@mercuretoureiffel.com – Fax 01 45 78 95 55 – www.mercuretoureiffel.com **N-O3**
77 rm – 🚹190/300 € 🚹🚹190/330 €, ☕ 19 €
◆ Chain hotel ◆ Business ◆ Functional ◆
The main building houses rooms designed to the standards of the chain. Those in the new wing are more comfortable and have many little extras.

Bourgogne et Montana without rest

3 r. Bourgogne (7th) – Ⓜ Assemblée Nationale – ☎ 01 45 51 20 22 – bmontana@bourgogne-montana.com – Fax 01 45 56 11 98 – www.bourgogne-montana.com **Q1**

28 rm – 🚹160/175 € 🚹🚹185/335 €, ☕ 15 € – 4 suites

♦ Traditional ♦ Business ♦ Classic ♦

Elegance and beauty fill every room of this discreet 18C hotel. The top floor rooms offer superb views over the "Palais-Bourbon" (French Parliament buildings).

Tourville without rest

16 av. Tourville (7th) – Ⓜ Ecole Militaire – ☎ 01 47 05 62 62 – hotel@tourville.com – Fax 01 47 05 43 90 – www.hoteltourville.com **P2**

30 rm – 🚹150/170 € 🚹🚹195/330 €, ☕ 18 €

♦ Business ♦ Traditional ♦ Cosy ♦

Sharp colours, pleasant combination of modern and period furniture and paintings create the decor of the elegant rooms. Lounge decorated by the David Hicks studio. Excellent service.

Eiffel Park Hôtel without rest

17bis r. Amélie (7th) – Ⓜ La Tour Maubourg – ☎ 01 45 55 10 01 – reservation@eiffelpark.com – Fax 01 47 05 28 68 – www.eiffelpark.com **P1**

36 rm – 🚹130/165 € 🚹🚹135/185 €, ☕ 12 €

♦ Traditional ♦ Family ♦ Personalised ♦

The furniture, painted in old-fashioned style, and the Indian and Chinese objects, create an exotic atmosphere in this hotel. Summer terrace and cosy lounge with a fireplace. Attentive service.

Walt without rest

37 av. La Motte Picquet (7th) – Ⓜ Ecole Militaire – ☎ 01 45 51 55 83 – lewalt@inwoodhotel.com – Fax 01 47 05 77 59 – www.lewaltparis.com **P2**

25 rm – 🚹260/310 € 🚹🚹280/330 €, ☕ 13 €

♦ Business ♦ Luxury ♦ Modern ♦

This new hotel near the École Militaire offers original rooms with modern furniture and an imposing Renaissance-style portrait at the head of each bed.

Les Jardins d'Eiffel without rest

8 r. Amélie (7th) – Ⓜ La Tour Maubourg – ☎ 01 47 05 46 21 – paris@hoteljardinseiffel.com – Fax 01 45 55 28 08 – www.hoteljardinseiffel.com **P1**

81 rm – 🚹165/185 € 🚹🚹165/185 €, ☕ 14 €

♦ Family ♦ Traditional ♦ Functional ♦

The two buildings of the hotel, in a quiet street, are linked by a patio where breakfast is served in summer. Gaily-coloured rooms; some with a balcony.

Relais Bosquet without rest

19 r. Champ-de-Mars (7th) – Ⓜ Ecole Militaire – ☎ 01 47 05 25 45 – hotel@relaisbosquet.com – Fax 01 45 55 08 24 – www.hotelrelaisbosquet.com **P2**

40 rm – 🚹108/155 € 🚹🚹125/175 €, ☕ 13 €

♦ Traditional ♦ Business ♦ Classic ♦

This discreet hotel has a prettily-furnished Directoire-style interior. Renovated rooms, all decorated with the same attention to detail, with thoughtful little touches.

Tour Eiffel Invalides without rest

35 bd La Tour Maubourg (7th) – Ⓜ La Tour Maubourg – ☎ 01 45 56 10 78 – invalides@my-paris-hotel.com – Fax 01 47 05 65 08 – www.my-paris-hotel.com **P1**

30 rm – 🚹89/209 € 🚹🚹99/309 €, ☕ 13 €

♦ Traditional ♦ Family ♦ Cosy ♦

Predominant red brick and white decor, Louis XVI-style furniture, and reproductions of Impressionist paintings characterise the rooms in this 19C building.

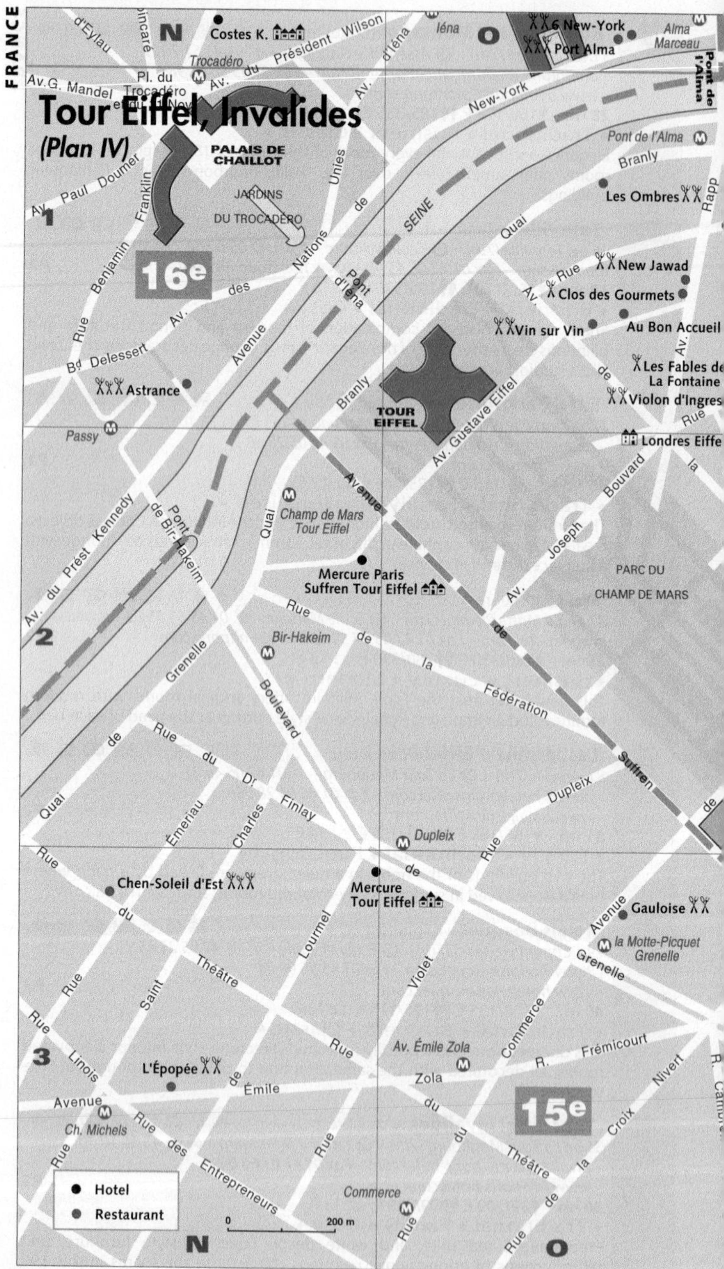
Tour Eiffel, Invalides
(Plan IV)
N
O
1
2
3
16e
15e
Costes K.
6 New-York
Port Alma
Les Ombres
New Jawad
Clos des Gourmets
Vin sur Vin
Au Bon Accueil
Les Fables de La Fontaine
Violon d'Ingres
Londres Eiffel
Astrance
Mercure Paris Suffren Tour Eiffel
Chen-Soleil d'Est
Mercure Tour Eiffel
Gauloise
L'Épopée
PALAIS DE CHAILLOT
JARDINS DU TROCADÉRO
TOUR EIFFEL
PARC DU CHAMP DE MARS
SEINE
Iéna
Alma Marceau
Trocadéro
Pont de l'Alma
Passy
Champ de Mars Tour Eiffel
Bir-Hakeim
Dupleix
la Motte-Picquet Grenelle
Av. Émile Zola
Ch. Michels
Commerce
Hotel
Restaurant
0
200 m

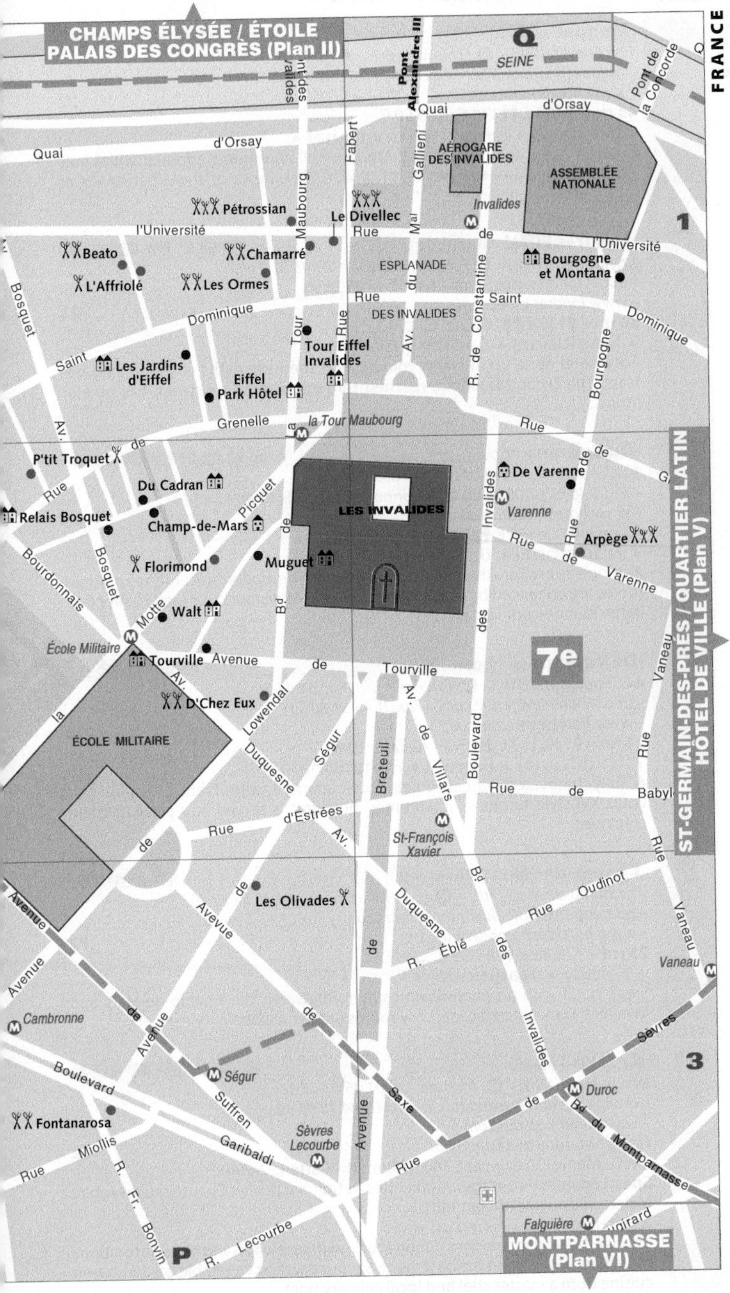

CHAMPS ÉLYSÉE / ÉTOILE PALAIS DES CONGRÈS (Plan II)

Q

SEINE

Pont des Invalides

Pont Alexandre III

Pont de la Concorde

Quai d'Orsay

Quai d'Orsay

AÉROGARE DES INVALIDES

ASSEMBLÉE NATIONALE

1

Pétrossian

Le Divellec

Invalides

Rue de l'Université

Beato

Chamarré

L'Affriolé

Les Ormes

ESPLANADE DES INVALIDES

Bourgogne et Montana

Rue Saint Dominique

Rue Maubourg

Rue Fabert

Av. du Mal Gallieni

R. de Constantine

Rue de Bourgogne

Av. Bosquet

Les Jardins d'Eiffel

Tour Eiffel Invalides

Eiffel Park Hôtel

Rue de Grenelle

La Tour Maubourg

P'tit Troquet

Du Cadran

Relais Bosquet

Champ-de-Mars

Rue Picquet

LES INVALIDES

De Varenne

Varenne

Rue de Varenne

Arpège

Florimond

Muguet

Bd de la Tour Maubourg

Bd des Invalides

Walt

Bourdonnais

Av. de la Motte Picquet

École Militaire

Tourville

Avenue de Tourville

D'Chez Eux

7e

ÉCOLE MILITAIRE

Av. Lowendal

Av. Duquesne

Av. de Ségur

Av. de Breteuil

Av. de Villars

Boulevard des Invalides

Rue Vaneau

Rue de Babylone

ST-GERMAIN-DES-PRES / QUARTIER LATIN HÔTEL DE VILLE (Plan V)

Rue d'Estrées

St-François Xavier

Les Olivades

Rue Oudinot

R. Éblé

Vaneau

Avenue de Suffren

Avenue de Saxe

Cambronne

Ségur

Rue de Sèvres

Duroc

Bd du Montparnasse

3

Boulevard Garibaldi

Fontanarosa

Rue Miollis

R. Fr. Bonvin

Sèvres Lecourbe

R. Lecourbe

P

Falguière

Vaugirard

MONTPARNASSE (Plan VI)

Muguet without rest
11 r. Chevert (7th) – Ⓜ Ecole Militaire – ✆ 01 47 05 05 93
– muguet@wanadoo.fr – Fax 01 45 50 25 37
– www.hotelmuguet.com **P2**
43 rm – 🚹100 € 🚹🚹130 €, ☕ 9.50 €
◆ Business ◆ Family ◆ Functional ◆
Hotel nestling in a quiet street. Modern hall and rooms adorned with Louis Philippe-style furniture (seven of which offer views of the Eiffel tower or Invalides).

Londres Eiffel without rest
1 r. Augereau (7th) – Ⓜ Ecole Militaire – ✆ 01 45 51 63 02
– info@londres-eiffel.com – Fax 01 47 05 28 96
– www.londres-eiffel.com **O2**
30 rm – 🚹130 € 🚹🚹165/205 €, ☕ 12 €
◆ Traditional ◆ Family ◆ Cosy ◆
Cosy hotel done up in warm colours near the leafy paths of the Champ-de-Mars. The second building, reached through a small courtyard, has quieter rooms.

Du Cadran without rest
10 r. Champ-de-Mars (7th) – Ⓜ Ecole Militaire
– ✆ 01 40 62 67 00 – info@cadranhotel.com – Fax 01 40 62 67 13
– www.hotelducadran.com **P2**
42 rm – 🚹125/165 € 🚹🚹135/178 €, ☕ 10 €
◆ Traditional ◆ Business ◆ Modern ◆
A stone's throw from the lively rue Cler market. The modern, recently refurbished rooms are enhanced by a number of Louis XVI-style touches. Fine 17C fireplace in the lounge-cum-library.

De Varenne without rest
44 r. Bourgogne (7th) – Ⓜ Varenne – ✆ 01 45 51 45 55
– info@hoteldevarenne.com – Fax 01 45 51 86 63
– www.hoteldevarenne.com **Q2**
24 rm – 🚹130/150 € 🚹🚹150/170 €, ☕ 10 €
◆ Traditional ◆ Family ◆ Functional ◆
A fully renovated, rather quiet hotel adorned with French Empire and Louis XVI-style furniture. In summer, breakfast is served in a small, verdant courtyard.

Champ-de-Mars without rest
7 r. Champ-de-Mars (7th) – Ⓜ Ecole Militaire – ✆ 01 45 51 52 30
– reservation@hotelduchampdemars.com – Fax 01 45 51 64 36
– www.hotelduchampdemars.com **P2**
25 rm – 🚹79/85 € 🚹🚹85/89 €, ☕ 7 €
◆ Family ◆ Traditional ◆ Cosy ◆
Small hotel with an English atmosphere, between the Champ-de-Mars and Invalides. Dark green façade, cosy rooms and neat Liberty-style decor.

Arpège (Passard) 8/14
84 r. Varenne (7th) – Ⓜ Varenne – ✆ 01 45 51 47 33
– arpege.passard@wanadoo.fr – Fax 01 44 18 98 39
– www.alain-passard.com
closed Saturday and Sunday **Q2**
Rest – Menu 130 € (lunch)/340 € (dinner) – Carte 122/294 €
Spec. Légumes du potager. Aiguillettes de homard des îles Chausey au savagnin. Millefeuille au miel du jardin.
◆ Innovative ◆ Formal ◆
Choose the elegant modern dining room, with rare wood and glass decorations by Lalique, rather than the basement. Savour dazzling vegetable garden-based cuisine from a master chef and local culinary poet.

Le Divellec

107 r. Université (7th) – Ⓜ Invalides – ✆ 01 45 51 91 96 – ledivellec@noos.fr – Fax 01 45 51 31 75
closed 27 July - 27 August, Saturday and Sunday **P-Q1**
Rest – Menu 55 € (lunch)/70 € – Carte 105/175 €
Spec. Homard bleu à la presse avec son corail. Blanc de turbot braisé aux truffes. Risotto de langoustines aux asperges vertes.
♦ Seafood ♦ Formal ♦
A nautical chic setting with waves on frosted glass, a lobster tank, and a blue and white colour scheme. Amazing seafood cuisine using only the freshest produce directly from the Atlantic.

Astrance (Barbot)

4 r. Beethoven (16th) ✉ 75016 – Ⓜ Passy – ✆ 01 40 50 84 40
closed 1 - 6 March, August, autumn half-term holidays, Saturday, Sunday and Monday **N1**
Rest – *(number of covers limited, pre-book)* Menu 70 € (lunch), 170/270 € bi
Spec. Galette de champignons de Paris, foie gras mariné au verjus, citron confit. Endive caramélisée, beurre de spéculoos, condiment banane. Selle d'agneau grillée, aubergine laquée au miso.
♦ Contemporary ♦ Fashionable ♦
The Astrance (from the Latin Aster, a star-like flower) boasts delicious, inventive cuisine, a surprise evening menu, choice wines and attractive modern decor.

Pétrossian

144 r. Université (7th) – Ⓜ Invalides – ✆ 01 44 11 32 32 – Fax 01 44 11 32 35
closed August, Sunday and Monday **P1**
Rest – Menu 35 € (weekday lunch), 45/250 € – Carte 56/149 €
♦ Seafood ♦ Formal ♦
The Petrossians have treated Parisians to caviar from the Caspian sea since 1920. On the upper floor of the shop, elegant restaurant room and inventive cuisine.

Chen-Soleil d'Est

4/14

15 r. Théâtre (15th) – Ⓜ Charles Michels – ✆ 01 45 79 34 34 – Fax 01 45 79 07 53
closed August and Sunday **N3**
Rest – Menu 40 € (weekday lunch), 75/160 € – Carte 55/225 €
♦ Chinese ♦ Exotic ♦
Delve softly beneath the buildings overlooking the Seine to discover an authentic little corner of Asia; steamed 'wok' cuisine. Furnishings have been imported from China.

Les Ombres

Paris,

27 quai Branly(7th) – Ⓜ Alma Marceau – ✆ 01 47 53 68 00 – Fax 01 47 53 68 18 – www.lesombres.fr **O1**
Rest – Menu 35 € (lunch)/95 € – Carte 57/95 €
♦ Contemporary ♦ Fashionable ♦
This restaurant enjoys fine views of the Eiffel Tower and its nocturnal illuminations from the roof-terrace of the Musée du Quai Branly. Contemporary dining.

Le Chamarré

13 bd La Tour Maubourg (7th) – Ⓜ Invalides – ✆ 01 47 05 50 18 – chantallaval@wanadoo.fr – Fax 01 47 05 91 21 – www.lechamarre.com
closed Saturday lunchtime and Sunday **P1**
Rest – Menu 40 € (lunch), 65/150 € – Carte 75/89 €
Spec. Poulpe aux deux saveurs. Cochon de lait fermier. Savarin punché au rhum.
♦ French-Mauritian cuisine ♦ Friendly ♦
Elegantly modern decor (exotic woodwork), friendly environment and a delightful cuisine combining French and Mauritius specialities (one of the chefs is from the island).

FRANCE

XX ✿ **Les Ormes** (Molé) VISA MC AE D

22 r. Surcouf (7th) – Ⓜ La Tour Maubourg – ✆ 01 45 51 46 93 – molestephane@noos.fr – Fax 01 45 50 30 11

closed 1 to 15 August, 7 to 14 January, Sunday and Monday **P1**

Rest – Menu 38 € (weekday lunch), 49/65 €

Spec. Foie gras d'oie en brioche. Jarret de veau, gnocchi de pomme de terre. Lièvre à la royale (mid October-mid December).

♦ Contemporary ♦ Cosy ♦

Goodbye Bellecour, hello Les Ormes! Stéphane Molé has left the 16th arrondissement to take over this restaurant near Invalides. Elegant setting. Traditional cuisine.

XX ✿ **Vin sur Vin** A/C VISA MC

20 r. de Monttessuy (7th) – Ⓜ Pont de l'Alma – ✆ 01 47 05 14 20

closed 29 April-8 May, 28 July-27 August, 22 December-6 january, Mon except in the evening from Sept. to Easter, Sat lunchtime and Sun **O1**

Rest – *(number of covers limited, pre-book)* Carte 65/89 €

Spec. Saint-Jacques d'Erquy (October to March). Canard sauvage (season). Assiette de légumes de saison.

♦ Traditional ♦ Cosy ♦

Warm welcome, elegant decor, delicious traditional dishes and extensive wine list (600 wines) - full marks for this restaurant close to the Eiffel Tower!

XX ✿ **Violon d'Ingres** (Constant) A/C VISA MC AE D

135 r. St-Dominique (7th) – Ⓜ Ecole Militaire – ✆ 01 45 55 15 05 – violondingres@wanadoo.fr – Fax 01 45 55 48 42 – www.leviolondingres.com

closed 30 July-22 August, 1 to 7 January, Sun. and Mon. **O1**

Rest – Menu 45/60 €

Spec. Millefeuille de langue et foie gras façon Lucullus. Pithiviers de gibier à plume (season). Volaille des Landes rôtie à la broche.

♦ Contemporary ♦ Fashionable ♦

Wood-furnishings enliven the atmosphere of this dining room which is an elegant meeting point for gourmets attracted by the very individual cuisine of the master chef.

XX ✿ **Auguste** (Orieux) A/C VISA MC AE D

54 r. Bourgogne – Ⓜ Varenne – ✆ 01 45 51 61 09 – Fax 01 45 51 27 34 – www.restaurantauguste.fr

closed August, Saturday and Sunday **CY**

Rest – Menu 35 € (lunch) – Carte 49/67 €

Spec. Fine gelée iodée aux huîtres creuses et bulots. Noix de ris de veau au vin jaune. Soufflé au chocolat pur Caraïbes.

♦ Contemporary ♦ Design ♦

This restaurant, at the heart of the ministerial district, has a new decor of modern paintings, designer furniture and muted lighting. The excellent cuisine has a loyal following.

XX **New Jawad** A/C VISA MC AE D

12 av. Rapp (7th) – Ⓜ Ecole Militaire – ✆ 01 47 05 91 37 – Fax 01 45 50 31 27 **O1**

Rest – Menu 16/40 € – Carte 21/42 €

♦ Indian-Pakistani cuisine ♦ Friendly ♦

Pakistani and Indian specialities, attentive service and a cosy setting characterise this restaurant in the immediate vicinity of the Pont de l'Alma.

XX **Beato** A/C VISA MC AE

8 r. Malar (7th) – Ⓜ Invalides – ✆ 01 47 05 94 27 – beato.rest@wanadoo.fr – Fax 01 45 55 64 41

closed 15 July - 15 Aug, 24 Dec - 1 Jan, and Sunday **P1**

Rest – Menu 27 € (lunch) – Carte 40/65 €

♦ Italian ♦ Friendly ♦

This chic restaurant has a bourgeois Italian decor with frescoes, Pompeii columns and neo-classical seats. Dishes from Milan, Rome and other Italian regions.

XX **D'Chez Eux**

2 av. Lowendal (7th) – Ⓜ Ecole Militaire – ✆ 01 47 05 52 55 – contact@chezeux.com – Fax 01 45 55 60 74 – www.chezeux.com

closed 29 July-27 August and Sunday **P2**

Rest – Carte 46/73 €

♦ De Terroir ♦

The regulars adore the hearty Auvergne and South-western style dishes and the "provincial auberge" atmosphere, with its diamond tablecloths and waiters in smocks.

XX **La Gauloise**

16

59 av. La Motte-Piquet (15th) – Ⓜ La Motte Picquet Grenelle – ✆ 01 47 34 11 64 – Fax 01 40 61 09 70 **O3**

Rest – Carte 32/50 €

♦ Brasserie ♦

This 1900 brasserie must have seen many celebrities pass through, judging from the signed photos on the walls. A pleasant, kerbside terrace.

XX **Fontanarosa**

28 bd Garibaldi (15th) – Ⓜ Cambronne – ✆ 01 45 66 97 84 – contact@fontanarosa-ristorante.eu – Fax 01 47 83 96 30 – www.fontanarosa-ristorante.eu **P3**

Rest – Menu 21 € (weekday lunch)/30 € – Carte 31/69 €

♦ Italian ♦

On the boulevard bearing the name of a famous Italian politician, this trattoria with a pink façade stands out prominently. Sardinian cuisine.

XX **L'Épopée**

89 av. É. Zola (15th) – Ⓜ Charles Michels – ✆ 01 45 77 71 37 – Fax 01 45 77 71 37

closed 22 July - 22 Aug., Sat. lunchtime and Sun. **N3**

Rest – Menu 34/40 €

♦ Traditional ♦

Far from aspiring to epic growth, this small restaurant prefers to be user-friendly. Regulars come back for its excellent wine list and traditional cuisine.

X **Au Bon Accueil**

14 r. Monttessuy (7th) – Ⓜ Pont de l'Alma – ✆ 01 47 05 46 11 – Fax 01 45 56 15 80

closed 4 to 19 August, Saturday and Sunday. **O1**

Rest – Menu 27 € (lunch)/31 € – Carte 34/69 €

♦ Bistro ♦

Beneath the shadow of the Eiffel Tower, this modern restaurant and small adjacent room offer delightfully up-to-date menus pleasantly reflecting the change of seasons.

X **Les Olivades**

41 av. Ségur (7th) – Ⓜ Ségur – ✆ 01 47 83 70 09 – Fax 01 42 73 04 75

closed August, lunch Saturday, lunch Monday and Sunday **P3**

Rest – Menu 25 € (weekday lunch), 40/60 € – Carte 40/67 €

♦ Provence cuisine ♦

A restaurant where olive oil flows freely, with appetising dishes based on Provençal cuisine. Simple, pleasant decor in pastel shades, with modern paintings and rustic furniture.

X **Clos des Gourmets**

16 av. Rapp (7th) – Ⓜ Alma Marceau – ✆ 01 45 51 75 61 – Fax 01 47 05 74 20 – www.closdesgourmets.fr

closed 10 - 25 Aug., Sun. and Mon. **O1**

Rest – Menu 29 € (weekday lunch)/35 €

♦ A la mode ♦

Many regulars love this discreet restaurant, which has just been redecorated in warm colours. The menu varies according to market availability of produce.

Les Fables de La Fontaine

131 r. St-Dominique(7th) – Ecole Militaire – 01 44 18 37 55 **O1**
Rest – Menu 32 € (lunch)/42 €
Spec. Menu du marché.
♦ Seafood ♦ Bistro ♦
This pocket-sized bistro and summer terrace pays full homage to the sea in its concise but astute menu. Good selection of wines by the glass. Decor featuring benches, tiling and varying shades of brown.

Florimond

19 av. La Motte-Picquet (7th) – Ecole Militaire – 01 45 55 40 38 – Fax 01 45 55 40 38
closed 30 April-5 May, 30 July-18 August, 23 December-6 January, Saturday and Sunday **P2**
Rest – Menu 21 € (lunch)/36 € – Carte 36/53 €
♦ Traditional ♦
Sun-drenched colours and woodwork decorate this pocket restaurant (for non-smokers) named after Monet's gardener in Giverny. The cuisine is redolent of market freshness.

P'tit Troquet

28 r. l'Exposition (7th) – Ecole Militaire – 01 47 05 80 39 – Fax 01 47 05 80 39
closed 1 to 28 August, lunch Saturday, lunch Monday and Sunday **P2**
Rest – *(number of covers limited, pre-book)* Menu 30 € – Carte approx. 36 €
♦ Traditional ♦ Retro ♦
This bistro is certainly small! But it has so much going for it, with its stylish setting enlivened by old "advertisements", its friendly atmosphere and its tasty market cuisine.

L'Affriolé

17 r. Malar (7th) – Invalides – 01 44 18 31 33
closed 30 July-20 August, Sunday and Monday **P1**
Rest – Menu 29 € (lunch)/34 €
♦ A la mode ♦ Bistro ♦
This bistro's chef prepares seasonal dishes with fresh market produce, which are announced as daily specials on a blackboard or in a set menu that changes every month.

SAINT-GERMAIN DES PRES, QUARTIER LATIN, HOTEL DE VILLE

Plan V

Lutétia

10/180 rm

45 bd Raspail (6th) – Sèvres Babylone – 01 49 54 46 46 – lutetia-paris@lutetia-paris.com – Fax 01 49 54 46 00 – www.lutetia-paris.com **R2**
220 rm – 230/950 € 230/950 €, 25 € – 11 suites
Rest *Paris* – see below
Rest *Brasserie Lutétia* – *01 49 54 46 76* – Menu 42/60 € – Carte 53/70 €
♦ Palace ♦ Historic ♦
Built in 1910, this famous luxury hotel on the Left Bank has lost none of its sparkle: "retro" elegance, Lalique lamps, sculptures by César, Arman, etc. Refurbished rooms. Paris' most chic come to the Brasserie Lutétia for its fine seafood menu.

Victoria Palace without rest

20

6 r. Blaise-Desgoffe (6th) – St-Placide – 01 45 49 70 00 – info@victoriapalace.com – Fax 01 45 49 23 75 – www.victoriapalace.com **R3**
62 rm – 320/382 € 320/610 €, 18 €
♦ Luxury ♦ Historic ♦
Small luxury hotel with undeniable charm: toiles de Jouy, Louis XVI-style furniture and marble bathrooms in the rooms. Paintings, red velvet and porcelain in the lounges.

Pont Royal without rest

7 r. Montalembert (7th) – Ⓜ Rue du Bac – ✆ 01 42 84 70 00 – hpr@hroy.com – Fax 01 42 84 71 00 – www.hotel-pont-royal.com **R1**

65 rm – 390/450 € 390/450 €, ☕ 26 € – 10 suites

♦ Luxury ♦ Stylish ♦

Bold colours and mahogany walls adorn the bedrooms; the romance of the salad days of St-Germain-des-Prés with all the comfort of an elegant "literary hotel"!

Duc de Saint-Simon without rest

14 r. St-Simon (7th) – Ⓜ Rue du Bac – ✆ 01 44 39 20 20 – duc.de.saint.simon@wanadoo.fr – Fax 01 45 48 68 25 – www.hotelducdesaintsimon.com **R1**

34 rm – 220 € 375 €, ☕ 15 €

♦ Luxury ♦ Business ♦ Stylish ♦

Cheerful colours, wood panelling, antique furniture and objects. The atmosphere here is that of a beautiful house of olden times, with the additional appeal of a friendly welcome and peaceful surroundings.

Montalembert

rm 20

3 r. Montalembert (7th) – Ⓜ Rue du Bac – ✆ 01 45 49 68 68 – welcome@montalembert.com – Fax 01 45 49 69 49 – www.montalembert.com **R1**

56 rm – 199/350 € 199/450 €, ☕ 20 € – 8 suites

Rest – Carte 32/71 €

♦ Luxury ♦ Modern ♦

Dark wood, leather, glass and steel, with tobacco, plum and lilac-coloured decor. The rooms combine all the components of contemporary style. Designer dining room, terrace protected by a boxwood partition, and cuisine for appetites large and small!

K+K Hotel Cayré without rest

4 bd Raspail (7th) – Ⓜ Rue du Bac – ✆ 01 45 44 38 88 – reservations@kkhotels.fr – Fax 01 45 44 98 13 – www.kkhotels.com/cayre **R1-2**

125 rm – 310/401 € 338/650 €, ☕ 24 €

♦ Luxury ♦ Business ♦ Modern ♦

The discreet Haussmann façade contrasts with the elegant designer rooms within. Fitness centre (with sauna), elegant lounge and bar serving simple bistro-style dishes.

D'Aubusson without rest

15/35

33 r. Dauphine (6th) – Ⓜ Odéon – ✆ 01 43 29 43 43 – reservations@hoteldaubusson.com – Fax 01 43 29 12 62 – www.hoteldaubusson.com

49 rm – 295/465 € 295/465 €, ☕ 23 € **T2**

♦ Luxury ♦ Traditional ♦ Historic ♦

A 17C townhouse with character, offering elegant rooms with Versailles parquet, Aubusson tapestries and jazz evenings at the Café Laurent on weekends.

Relais Christine without rest

20

3 r. Christine (6th) – Ⓜ St-Michel – ✆ 01 40 51 60 80 – contact@relais-christine.com – Fax 01 40 51 60 81 – www.relais-christine.com **T2**

35 rm – 360 € 410 €, ☕ 25 €

♦ Luxury ♦ Traditional ♦ Historic ♦

Beautiful townhouse built on the site of a 13C convent (the breakfast room occupies the former vaulted kitchen). Pretty, well-kept rooms with a personal touch.

Bel Ami St-Germain-des-Prés without rest

10/30

7 r. St-Benoit (6th) – Ⓜ St-Germain des Prés – ✆ 01 42 61 53 53 – contact@hotel-bel-ami.com – Fax 01 49 27 09 33 – www.hotel-bel-ami.com **S2**

115 rm – 270/540 € 270/540 €, ☕ 23 €

♦ Business ♦ Luxury ♦ Design ♦

Attractive 19C building near Café Flore and Les Deux Magots. A distinctly contemporary setting and "zen" decor with high-tech facilities; a designer look and very trendy.

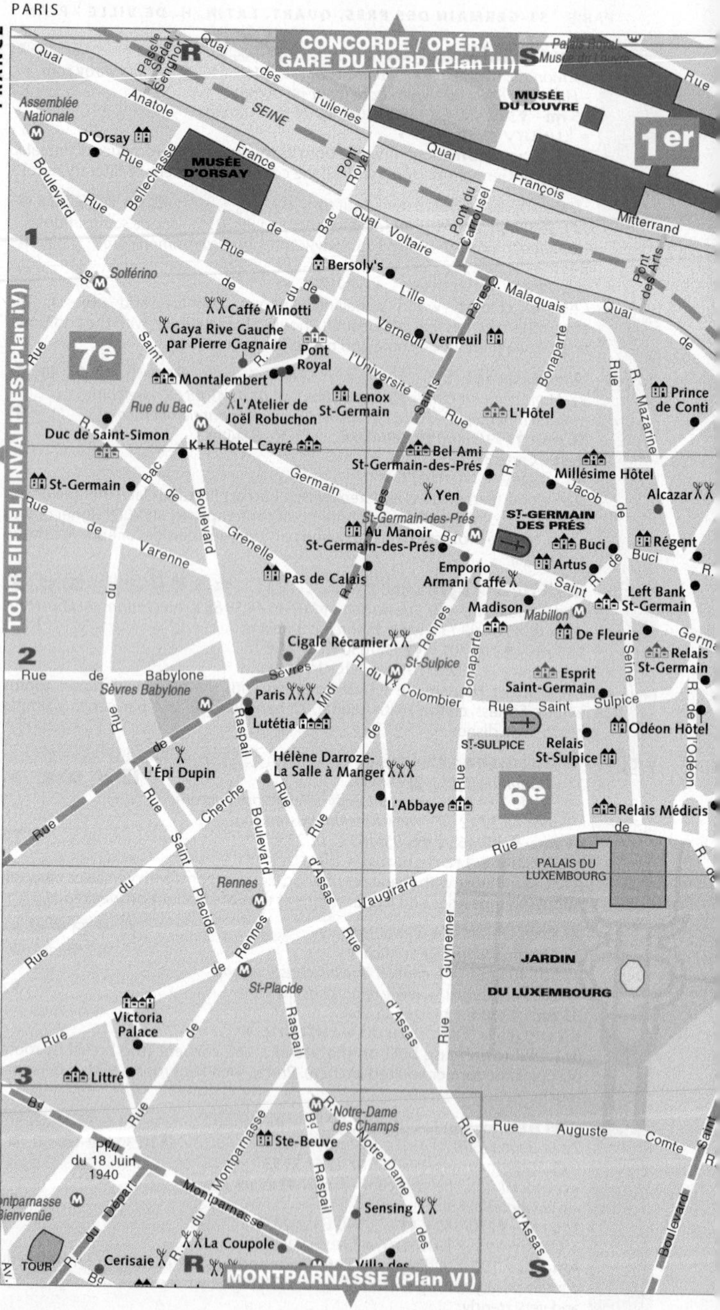

CONCORDE / OPÉRA
GARE DU NORD (Plan III)

TOUR EIFFEL/ INVALIDES (Plan IV)

MONTPARNASSE (Plan VI)

1er
7e
6e

1
2
3

Quai Anatole France
Quai des Tuileries
SEINE
Passle L. Sedar Senghor
Palais Royal Musée du Louvre
MUSÉE DU LOUVRE
Quai François Mitterrand
Pont Royal
Pont du Carrousel
Pont des Arts
Quai Voltaire
Q. Malaquais
Quai de Conti
Assemblée Nationale
MUSÉE D'ORSAY
Solférino
Rue du Bac
Rue de Lille
Rue de Verneuil
Rue de l'Université
Rue de Bellechasse
Boulevard Saint-Germain
Rue de Grenelle
Rue de Varenne
Rue du Bac
Rue des Saints-Pères
Rue Bonaparte
Rue Jacob
Rue de Seine
R. Mazarine
Rue de Buci
St-Germain-des-Prés
ST-GERMAIN DES PRÉS
Mabillon
Rue de Rennes
St-Sulpice
R. du Vx Colombier
Rue Saint Sulpice
ST-SULPICE
R. de l'Odéon
Rue de Babylone
Sèvres Babylone
Rue de Sèvres
R. du Midi
Boulevard Raspail
Rue du Cherche Midi
Rue Saint Placide
Rue d'Assas
Rue de Vaugirard
Rue Guynemer
Rennes
Rue de Rennes
St-Placide
PALAIS DU LUXEMBOURG
JARDIN DU LUXEMBOURG
Rue Auguste Comte
Boulevard Saint Michel
R. Notre-Dame des Champs
Bd Raspail
Bd du Montparnasse
Pl. du 18 Juin 1940
Rue du Départ
Montparnasse Bienvenüe
TOUR
Av.
R. du Montparnasse
R
S

D'Orsay
Caffé Minotti
Gaya Rive Gauche par Pierre Gagnaire
Montalembert
Pont Royal
Bersoly's
Verneuil
L'Atelier de Joël Robuchon
Lenox St-Germain
Duc de Saint-Simon
K+K Hotel Cayré
St-Germain
L'Hôtel
Prince de Conti
Bel Ami St-Germain-des-Prés
Millésime Hôtel
Alcazar
Yen
Au Manoir St-Germain-des-Prés
Emporio Armani Caffé
Buci
Artus
Régent
Pas de Calais
Madison
Left Bank St-Germain
De Fleurie
Relais St-Germain
Cigale Récamier
Esprit Saint-Germain
Paris
Lutétia
Odéon Hôtel
Relais St-Sulpice
Hélène Darroze-La Salle à Manger
L'Épi Dupin
L'Abbaye
Relais Médicis
Victoria Palace
Littré
Ste-Beuve
Sensing
La Coupole
Cerisaie
Villa des

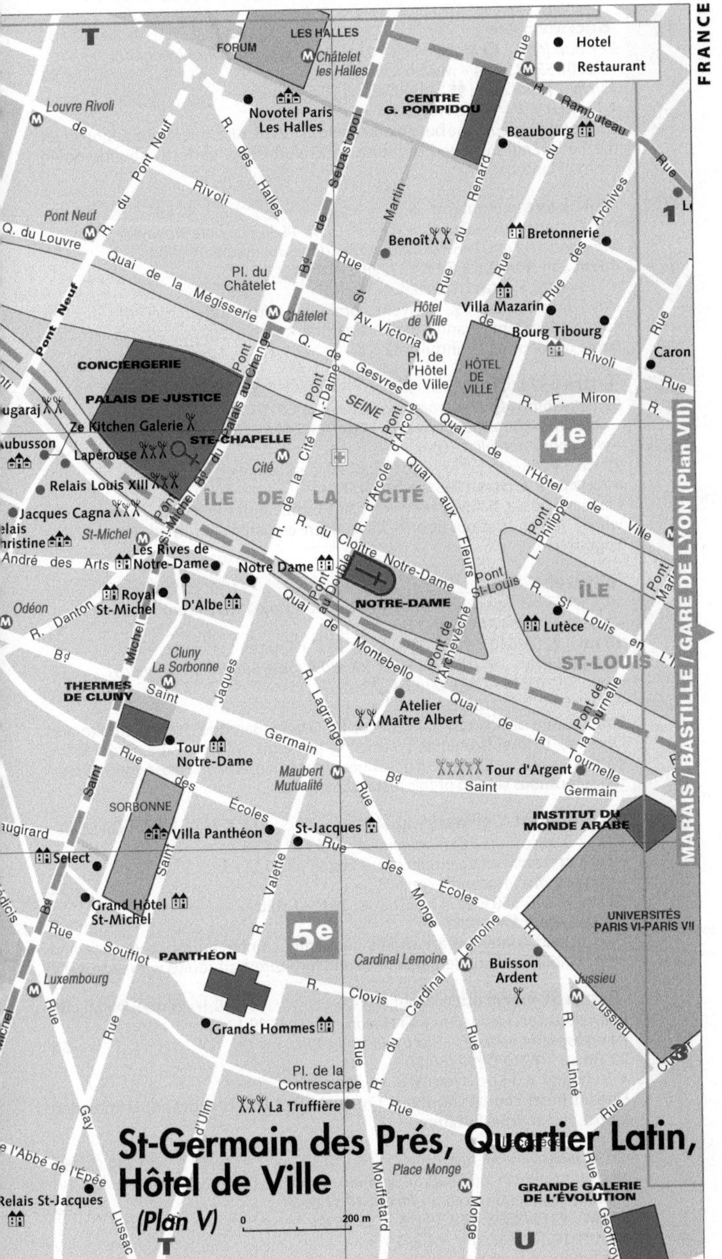

St-Germain des Prés, Quartier Latin, Hôtel de Ville
(Plan V)

Buci without rest VISA

22 r. Buci (6th) – Mabillon – 01 55 42 74 74 – hotelbuci@wanadoo.fr – Fax 01 55 42 74 44 – www.bucihotel.com **S2**

21 rm – 190/230 € 215/400 €, 18 € – 3 suites

◆ Luxury ◆ Personalised ◆

The hotel overlooks the busy market held in this picturesque street. Canopies on the beds, English period furniture and refurbished, perfectly soundproofed rooms. Piano-bar.

L'Abbaye without rest VISA

10 r. Cassette (6th) – St-Sulpice – 01 45 44 38 11 – hotel.abbaye@wanadoo.fr – Fax 01 45 48 07 86 – www.hotel-abbaye.com **S2**

40 rm – 211/228 € 211/228 € – 4 suites

◆ Luxury ◆ Traditional ◆ Stylish ◆

Hotel in a former 18C convent combining old-world charm with modern comfort. Pleasant veranda, duplex apartment with a terrace, and stylish rooms. Some overlook a delightful patio.

Littré without rest 8/20 VISA

9 r. Littré (6th) – Montparnasse Bienvenüe – 01 53 63 07 07 – hotellittre@hotellittreparis.com – Fax 01 45 44 88 13 – www.paris-hotel-littre.com **R3**

79 rm – 265/315 € 315/350 €, 20 € – 11 suites

◆ Luxury ◆ Business ◆ Stylish ◆

Classic building, halfway between Saint-Germain-des-Prés and Montparnasse, whose rather spacious rooms have been elegantly furnished. Comfortable English bar.

L'Hôtel VISA

– St-Germain des Prés – 01 44 41 99 00 – stay@l-hotel.com – Fax 01 43 25 64 81 – www.l-hotel.com **S1**

16 rm – 255/640 € 255/640 €, 18 € – 4 suites

Rest *Le Bélier* – *, 01 44 41 99 01 (closed August, Sunday and Monday)*
Menu 50/70 € bi – Carte 60/66 €

◆ Luxury ◆ Personalised ◆

Lofty atrium and extravagant decor by Garcia (Baroque, French Empire and Oriental). L'Hôtel is unique, combining nostalgia with pleasure. Oscar Wilde passed away here. Green and gold hues with old lanterns and glasswork make up the sumptuous setting of this restaurant.

Esprit Saint-Germain without rest VISA

22 r. St-Sulpice (6th) – Mabillon – 01 53 10 55 55 – contact@espritsaintgermain.com – Fax 01 53 10 55 56 – www.espritsaintgermain.com **S2**

31 rm – 310/550 € 310/550 €, 26 € – 1 suite

◆ Luxury ◆ Design ◆

Elegant and contemporary rooms pleasantly combining red, chocolate and beige colours with modern paintings and furniture; bathrooms with slate walls.

Relais St-Germain without rest VISA

9 carrefour de l'Odéon (6th) – Odéon – 01 43 29 12 05 – hotelrsg@wanadoo.fr – Fax 01 46 33 45 30 **S2**

22 rm – 210 € 275/420 €

◆ Luxury ◆ Traditional ◆ Historic ◆

Elegant hotel comprising three 17C buildings. Polished beams, shimmering fabrics and antique furniture.

Madison without rest VISA

143 bd St-Germain (6th) – St-Germain des Prés – 01 40 51 60 00 – resa@hotel-madison.com – Fax 01 40 51 60 01 **S2**

54 rm – 162/350 € 220/415 €, 15 €

◆ Luxury ◆ Family ◆ Cosy ◆

This hotel was popular with Albert Camus. Some of its elegant rooms offer views of the church of St-Germain-des Prés. Attractive Louis Philippe lounge.

Relais Médicis without rest
23 r. Racine (6th) – Odéon – 01 43 26 00 60 – reservation@relaismedicis.com – Fax 01 40 46 83 39 – www.relaismedicis.com S2
16 rm – 142/172 € 148/258 €
♦ Traditional ♦ Family ♦ Stylish ♦
A hint of Provence enhances the rooms of this hotel near the Odeon theatre; those overlooking the patio are quieter. Interesting antique furniture.

Villa Panthéon without rest
41 r. Ecoles (5th) – Maubert Mutualité – 01 53 10 95 95 – pantheon@leshotelsdeparis.com – Fax 01 53 10 95 96 – www.villa-pantheon.com T2
59 rm – 260/310 € 260/710 €, 25 €
♦ Townhouse ♦ Traditional ♦ Stylish ♦
The reception, rooms and bar (good selection of whiskies) have a British feel, with parquet floors, colourful hangings, exotic wood furniture and Liberty-style lights.

Left Bank St-Germain without rest
9 r. Ancienne Comédie (6th) – Odéon – 01 43 54 01 70 – lb@paris-hotels-charm.com – Fax 01 43 26 17 14 – www.paris-hotels-charm.com S2
31 rm – 150/230 € 160/250 €
♦ Traditional ♦ Family ♦ Classic ♦
Damask, toile de Jouy, Louis XIII period furniture and half-timbered walls create the decor in this 17C building. Some rooms offer views over Notre-Dame.

Millésime Hôtel without rest
15 r. Jacob (6th) – St-Germain des Prés – 01 44 07 97 97 – reservation@millesimehotel.com – Fax 01 46 34 55 97 – www.millesimehotel.com S2
22 rm – 190/210 € 190/375 €, 16 €
♦ Traditional ♦ Family ♦ Cosy ♦
Colours of the South and select furniture and fabrics create a warm atmosphere in the splendid rooms of this recently refurbished hotel. Superb 17C staircase.

Novotel Paris Les Halles
rm 15/80
8 pl. M.-de-Navarre (1st) – Châtelet Les Halles – 01 42 21 31 31 – h0785@accor.com – Fax 01 40 26 05 79 – www.novotelparisleshalles.com T1
280 rm – 179/330 € 199/350 €, 17 € – 5 suites
Rest – Carte 24/36 €
♦ Business ♦ Chain hotel ♦ Functional ♦
The main selling points of this modern hotel near the St Eustache church and opposite the Forum des Halles are its good meeting facilities and renovated minimalist-style rooms. When the restaurant is closed you can eat in the bar (traditional cuisine and grilled meat).

Bourg Tibourg without rest
19 r. Bourg Tibourg (4th) – Hôtel de Ville – 01 42 78 47 39 – hotel@bourgtibourg.com – Fax 01 40 29 07 00 – www.hotelbourgtibourg.com U1
30 rm – 160 € 220/250 €, 14 €
♦ Luxury ♦ Family ♦ Personalised ♦
The pleasant rooms in this charming hotel are decorated in a variety of styles (neo-Gothic, Baroque or Oriental). A little gem at the heart of the Marais quarter.

Les Rives de Notre-Dame without rest
15 quai St-Michel (5th) – St-Michel – 01 43 54 81 16 – hotel@rivesdenotredame.com – Fax 01 43 26 27 09 – www.rivesdenotredame.com T2
10 rm – 130/243 € 130/550 €, 14 €
♦ Traditional ♦ Family ♦ Classic ♦
Splendidly preserved 16C residence with spacious Provençal-style rooms all overlooking the Seine and Notre-Dame. Penthouse.

Royal St-Michel without rest

3 bd St-Michel (5th) – Ⓜ St-Michel – ✆ 01 44 07 06 06 – hotelroyalsaintmichel@wanadoo.fr – Fax 01 44 07 36 25 – www.hotelroyalsaintmichel.com

39 rm – †180/240 € ††195/290 €, ☕ 18 € T2

♦ Family ♦ Traditional ♦ Modern ♦

On the Boulevard St Michel, opposite the fountain of the same name, take in the Latin quarter atmosphere around this hotel, which houses modern and renovated rooms.

Au Manoir St-Germain-des-Prés without rest

153 bd St-Germain (6th) – Ⓜ St-Germain des Prés – ✆ 01 42 22 21 65 – reservation@hotelaumanoir.com – Fax 01 45 48 22 25 – www.paris-hotels-charm.com

33 rm ☕ – †150/190 € ††160/270 € S2

♦ Traditional ♦ Stylish ♦

Elegant hotel, opposite the Flore and Deux Magots (famous St-Germain-des Prés cafés), with period furniture, murals, wood panelling and toile de Jouy prints.

Grands Hommes without rest

17 pl. Panthéon (5th) – Ⓜ Luxembourg – ✆ 01 46 34 19 60 – reservation@hoteldesgrandshommes.com – Fax 01 43 26 67 32 – www.hoteldesgrandshommes.com

31 rm – †185/215 € ††195/255 €, ☕ 12 € T3

♦ Traditional ♦ Historic ♦

Facing the Panthéon, a pleasant hotel renovated in Directoire style (antique furnishings). Over half the rooms overlook the last resting place of the "great men of France".

Villa Mazarin without rest

6 r. des Archives, (4th) – Ⓜ Hôtel de Ville – ✆ 01 53 01 90 90 – resa@villamalraux.com – Fax 01 53 01 90 91 – www.villamalraux.com

26 rm – †130/400 € ††130/400 €, ☕ 12 € U1

♦ Business ♦ Design ♦

With its high-tech equipment (wi-fi, flatscreen TVs) and mix of modern and period furniture, this comfortable hotel near the Hôtel de Ville combines tradition and modernity.

Tour Notre-Dame without rest

20 r. Sommerard (5trh) – Ⓜ Cluny la Sorbonne – ✆ 01 43 54 47 60 – tour-notre-dame@magic.fr – Fax 01 43 26 42 34 – www.la-tour-notre-dame.com

48 rm – †129/176 € ††139/190 €, ☕ 12 € T2

♦ Traditional ♦ Family ♦ Stylish ♦

This hotel is very well situated, almost adjoining the Cluny museum. Comfortable, recently-renovated rooms. Those at the back are quieter.

Relais St-Sulpice without rest

3 r. Garancière (6th) – Ⓜ St-Sulpice – ✆ 01 46 33 99 00 – relaisstsulpice@wanadoo.fr – Fax 01 46 33 00 10 – www.relais-saint-sulpice.com

20

26 rm – †175/210 € ††175/210 €, ☕ 12 € S2

♦ Traditional ♦ Personalised ♦

Appealing hotel with 19C facade housing exotically decorated rooms, combining both African and Asian styles. Those at the back are very quiet.

Grand Hôtel St-Michel without rest

19 r. Cujas (5th) – Ⓜ Luxembourg – ✆ 01 46 33 33 02 – grand.hotel.st.michel@wanadoo.fr – Fax 01 40 46 96 33 – www.grand-hotel-st-michel.com

40 rm – †105/130 € ††140/170 €, ☕ 12 € – 5 suites T3

♦ Family ♦ Traditional ♦ Classic ♦

This renovated Haussmann-period building offers luxurious rooms with painted furniture. Napoleon III-style lounge; breakfast is served in a vaulted room.

De Fleurie without rest
32 r. Grégoire de Tours (6th) – Ⓜ Odéon – ✆ 01 53 73 70 00 – bonjour@hotel-de-fleurie.fr – Fax 01 53 73 70 20 – www.hotel-de-fleurie.fr **S2**
29 rm – 🚹135/150 € 🚹🚹170/190 €, ☕ 12 €
♦ Family ♦ Functional ♦
Stylish 18C façade adorned with statues in niches. Elegant rooms with soft tones, enhanced by woodwork. Choose the quieter rooms overlooking the courtyard.

Notre Dame without rest
1 quai St-Michel (5th) – Ⓜ St-Michel – ✆ 01 43 54 20 43 – hotel.denotredame@libertysurf.fr – Fax 01 43 26 61 75 **T2**
26 rm – 🚹150 € 🚹🚹199 €, ☕ 7 €
♦ Traditional ♦ Family ♦ Cosy ♦
The cosy little rooms in this hotel have all been refurbished and are air-conditioned and well appointed. Most rooms have a view over Notre-Dame cathedral.

Relais St-Jacques without rest
3 r. Abbé de l'Épée (5th) – Ⓜ Luxembourg – ✆ 01 53 73 26 00 – nevers.luxembourg@wanadoo.fr – Fax 01 43 26 17 81 – www.paris-hotal-saintjacques.com **T3**
22 rm – 🚹170/255 € 🚹🚹170/480 €, ☕ 17 €
♦ Traditional ♦ Family ♦ Stylish ♦
Rooms of various styles (Directoire, Louis Philippe, etc.), a glass-roofed breakfast room, Louis XV lounge and 1920s bar, make this a stylish hotchpotch hotel!

Artus without rest
34 r. de Buci(6th) – Ⓜ Mabillon – ✆ 01 43 29 07 20 – info@artushotel.com – Fax 01 43 29 67 44 – www.artushotel.com **S2**
27 rm ☕ – 🚹235/410 € 🚹🚹245/410 €
♦ Traditional ♦ Design ♦
Contemporary yet intimate, with modern bedrooms ornamented with antiques, an attractive vaulted cellar, designer bar, and paintings from nearby galleries on display.

Prince de Conti without rest
8 r. Guénégaud (6th) – Ⓜ Odéon – ✆ 01 44 07 30 40 – princedeconti@wanadoo.fr – Fax 01 44 07 36 34 – www.prince-de-conti.com **S1**
26 rm – 🚹165/280 € 🚹🚹165/280 €, ☕ 13 €
♦ Traditional ♦ Family ♦ Stylish ♦
This 18C building adjoining the Hotel de la Monnaie has a charming lounge full of interesting features; refined bedrooms; and a bright duplex decorated with precious objects.

Odéon Hôtel without rest
3 r. Odéon (6th) – Ⓜ Odéon – ✆ 01 43 25 90 67 – odeon@odeonhotel.fr – Fax 01 43 25 55 98 – www.odeonhotel.fr **S2**
33 rm – 🚹130/170 € 🚹🚹180/270 €, ☕ 12 €
♦ Family ♦ Classic ♦
The façade, stone walls and exposed beams bear witness to the age of this building (17C). Personalised guestrooms, some with views of the Eiffel Tower.

Régent without rest
61 r. Dauphine (6th) – Ⓜ Odéon – ✆ 01 46 34 59 80 – hotel.leregent@wanadoo.fr – Fax 01 40 51 05 07 – www.regent-paris-hotel.com **S2**
24 rm – 🚹170 € 🚹🚹238 €, ☕ 14 €
♦ Traditional ♦ Family ♦ Classic ♦
Tall façade dating from 1769. The rooms are cosy and well equipped. Breakfast room with exposed stone walls, located in the basement.

Verneuil without rest

8 r. de Verneuil (7th) – Ⓜ Rue du Bac – ✆ 01 42 60 82 14 – info@hotelverneuil.com – Fax 01 42 61 40 38 – www.hotelverneuil.com **S1**

26 rm – †136 € ††163/210 €, ☕ 13 €

♦ Traditional ♦ Family ♦ Classic ♦

Old building on the Left Bank, decorated in the style of a private house. Elegant rooms with prints on the walls. N°5 bis, the house with graffiti on it, was where singer Serge Gainsbourg lived.

Lenox Saint-Germain without rest

9 r. Université (7th) – Ⓜ St-Germain des Prés – ✆ 01 42 96 10 95 – hotel@lenoxsaintgermain.com – Fax 01 42 61 52 83 – www.lenoxsaintgermain.com **R-S1**

32 rm – †125/170 € ††125/192 €, ☕ 14 € – 2 suites

♦ Traditional ♦ Business ♦ Functional ♦

Rooms are a little on the small side, but attractively decorated and with an air of tasteful luxury. "Egyptian" frescos adorn the breakfast room. Art deco-style bar.

D'Orsay without rest

5/12

93 r. Lille (7th) – Ⓜ Solférino – ✆ 01 47 05 85 54 – orsay@espritfrance.com – Fax 01 45 55 51 16 – www.esprit-de-france.com **R1**

41 rm – †133/152 € ††175/330 €, ☕ 11 €

♦ Traditional ♦ Business ♦ Modern ♦

The hotel occupies two handsome, late-18C buildings that have been painstakingly renovated. Attractive individualised rooms and welcoming lounge overlooking a charming, green patio.

St-Germain without rest

88 r. Bac (7th) – Ⓜ Rue du Bac – ✆ 01 49 54 70 00 – info@hotel-saint-germain.fr – Fax 01 45 48 26 89 – www.hotel-saint-germain.fr **R2**

29 rm – †150/210 € ††150/230 €, ☕ 12 €

♦ Traditional ♦ Family ♦ Functional ♦

Empire, Louis-Philippe, high-tech design, antique objects, contemporary paintings - the charm of variety. Comfortable library, patio pleasant in summer.

Pas de Calais without rest

59 r. Saints-Pères (6th) – Ⓜ St-Germain des Prés – ✆ 01 45 48 78 74 – infos@hotelpasdecalais.com – Fax 01 45 44 94 57 – www.hotelpasdecalais.com **R2**

38 rm – †125/145 € ††145/165 €, ☕ 12 €

♦ Traditional ♦ Family ♦ Functional ♦

This discreet hotel, along a busy street, offers stylish, gradually renovated rooms with personal touches. Exposed beams on the top floor.

Select without rest

1 pl. Sorbonne (5th) – Ⓜ Cluny la Sorbonne – ✆ 01 46 34 14 80 – info@selecthotel.fr – Fax 01 46 34 51 79 – www.selecthotel.fr **T3**

67 rm – †129/225 € ††129/241 €, ☕ 6 €

♦ Traditional ♦ Family ♦ Functional ♦

Staunchly contemporary hotel in the heart of the student quarter of Paris. Bar and lounges disposed around a patio with a cactus garden. Some rooms offer views over the rooftops.

D'Albe without rest

1 r. Harpe (5th) – Ⓜ St-Michel – ✆ 01 46 34 09 70 – albehotel@wanadoo.fr – Fax 01 40 46 85 70 – www.albehotel.com **T2**

45 rm – †135/140 € ††160/215 €, ☕ 13 €

♦ Traditional ♦ Family ♦ Functional ♦

Attractive, modern hotel with smallish, yet nicely-arranged and cheerful rooms. With the Latin quarter and the Île de la Cité close by, Paris is at your doorstep!

Bretonnerie without rest — SAT VISA MC

22 r. Ste-Croix-de-la-Bretonnerie (4th) – Ⓜ Hôtel de Ville – ✆ 01 48 87 77 63 – hotel@bretonnerie.com – Fax 01 42 77 26 78 — U1

29 rm – 🚹116/180 € 🚹🚹116/180 €, ☕ 9.50 €

♦ Traditional ♦ Family ♦ Stylish ♦

Some of the rooms in this elegant 17C mansion in the Marais include four-poster beds and exposed beams. Vaulted ceiling in the breakfast room.

Beaubourg without rest — AC SAT VISA MC AE D

11 r. S. Le Franc (4th) – Ⓜ Rambuteau – ✆ 01 42 74 34 24 – htlbeaubourg@hotellerie.net – Fax 01 42 78 68 11 – www.htlbeaubourg.com — U1

28 rm – 🚹115/140 € 🚹🚹125/140 €, ☕ 8 €

♦ Traditional ♦ Business ♦ Classic ♦

Nestled in a tiny street behind the Georges-Pompidou Centre. Some of the friendly, well-soundproofed rooms have exposed stone walls and wooden beams.

Lutèce without rest — AC SAT VISA MC AE

65 r. St-Louis-en-l'Ile (4th) – Ⓜ Pont Marie – ✆ 01 43 26 23 52 – hotel.lutece@free.fr – Fax 01 43 29 60 25 – www.hoteldelutece.com — U2

23 rm – 🚹150 € 🚹🚹195 €, ☕ 12 €

♦ Traditional ♦ Family ♦ Retro ♦

The rustic charm of this mansion on the Ile St-Louis is particularly popular with American visitors. Modernised guestrooms with a country feel, plus attractive old woodwork in the lounge.

Bersoly's without rest — AC SAT VISA MC AE D

28 r. Lille (7th) – Ⓜ Musée d'Orsay – ✆ 01 42 60 73 79 – hotelbersolys@wanadoo.fr – Fax 01 49 27 05 55 – www.bersolyshotel.com closed Aug. — R-S1

16 rm – 🚹86/100 € 🚹🚹100/145 €, ☕ 10 €

♦ Traditional ♦ Business ♦ Personalised ♦

Impressionist nights in this 17C building in which each room honours an artist whose works are displayed in the nearby Musée d'Orsay (Renoir, Gauguin, etc.).

St-Jacques without rest — VISA MC AE D

35 r. Ecoles (5th) – Ⓜ Maubert Mutualité – ✆ 01 44 07 45 45 – hotelsaintjacques@wanadoo.fr – Fax 01 43 25 65 50 – www.paris-hotel-stjacques.com — T2

38 rm – 🚹58/88 € 🚹🚹100/130 €, ☕ 9 €

♦ Traditional ♦ Family ♦ Stylish ♦

Modern comfort allies with old-style charm in the rooms of this hotel. Library with 18C and 19C works. Breakfast room with Roaring Twenties cabaret-style decor.

XXXXX ✿

Tour d'Argent — < Notre - Dame, AC ⇔15/55 VISA MC AE D

15 quai Tournelle (5th) – Ⓜ Maubert Mutualité – ✆ 01 43 54 23 31 – resa@latourdargent.com – Fax 01 44 07 12 04 – www.latourdargent.com closed 31 July-4 September and Monday — U2

Rest – Menu 70 € (lunch), 200 € bi/230 € bi – Carte 132/427 € ✿

Spec. Caneton "Tour d'Argent". Noisette d'agneau des Tournelles. Poire "Vie parisienne".

♦ Traditional ♦ Luxury ♦

The open-air dining room offers a splendid view of Notre-Dame. Exceptional wine-cellar, renowned Challans duck and celebrated clientele dating back to the 16C. Mythical!

XXX ✿ **Jacques Cagna** (dinner)

14 r. Grands Augustins (6th) – Ⓜ St-Michel – ✆ 01 43 26 49 39 – jacquescagna@hotmail.com – Fax 01 43 54 54 48 – www.jacques-cagna.com
closed 27 July - 24 Aug., Sat. lunchtime, Mon. lunchtime and Sun. **T2**
Rest – Menu 45 € (lunch)/100 € – Carte 81/199 €
Spec. Foie gras de canard poêlé aux fruits de saison caramélisés. Noix de ris de veau en croûte de sel. Gibier (season).
◆ Traditional ◆ Rustic ◆
Located in one of the oldest homes in the old Paris, the comfortable dining hall is embellished by massive rafters, 16C woodwork and Flemish paintings. Refined cuisine.

XXX ✿ **Paris** – Hôtel Lutetia 15/40

45 bd Raspail (6th) – Ⓜ Sèvres Babylone – ✆ 01 49 54 46 90 – lutetia-paris@lutetia-paris.com – Fax 01 49 54 46 00 – www.lutetia-paris.com
closed Aug., Sat., Sun. and bank holidays **R2**
Rest – Menu 55 € bi (lunch), 75/135 € – Carte 94/107 €
Spec. Saint-Jacques marinées au caviar d'esturgeon blanc (October to April). Homard cuit en carapace (June to November). Agneau de lait des Pyrénées (January to May).
◆ Traditional ◆ Retro ◆
In keeping with the style of the hotel, the Sonia Rykiel art deco dining room is a recreation of one of the lounges from the ship The Normandy. Versatile contemporary cuisine.

XXX ✿✿ **Relais Louis XIII** (Martinez) 12/20

8 r. Grands Augustins (6th) – Ⓜ Odéon – ✆ 01 43 26 75 96 – contact@relaislouis13.com – Fax 01 44 07 07 80 – www.relaislouis13.com
closed 1 to 10 May, 29 July-20 August, 22 December - 3 January, Sunday and Monday.
Rest – Menu 50 € (lunch), 75/100 € – Carte 110/126 € **T2**
Spec. Ravioli de homard, foie gras et crème de cèpes. Coffre de canard rôti entier, cuisse confite. Millefeuille, crème légère à la vanille bourbon.
◆ Traditional ◆ Cosy ◆
The building dates from the 16C and there are three Louis XIII-style dining rooms with balustrades, tapestries and open stonework. The cuisine is subtle and up-to-date.

XXX ✿✿ **Hélène Darroze-La Salle à Manger**

4 r. d'Assas – Ⓜ Sèvres Babylone – ✆ 01 42 22 00 11 – reservation@helenedarroze.com – Fax 01 42 22 25 40 **R2**
Rest – *(1st floor) (closed lunch from 22 July-27 August, Monday except dinner from 22 July-27 August and Sunday)* Menu 72 € (lunch), 175/235 € – Carte 92/192 €
Rest *Salon* – *(closed 22 July -27 August, Sunday and Monday)* Menu 45/88 € – Carte 59/105 €
Rest *Le Boudoir* – *(closed 22 July-27 August, Sunday and Monday)* Carte 81/127 €
Spec. Foie gras de canard des Landes grillé au feu de bois. Cochon de lait de race basque sous toutes ses formes (May-October). Chocolat, coriandre, chicorée et vanille bourbon.
◆ South-West of France specialities ◆ Cosy ◆
Close to the Bon Marché, the decor is modern and rich in colour; here one can enjoy delicious cuisine and the fine wines of the south-west. On the ground floor of the restaurant, Hélène Darroze presides over the Salon and serves tapas and small dishes with a rustic flavour of the Landes.

XXX **Lapérouse** 2/50

51 quai Grands Augustins (6th) – Ⓜ St-Michel – ✆ 01 43 26 68 04 – restaurantlaperouse@wanadoo.fr – Fax 01 43 26 99 39
closed August, Saturday lunch and Sunday **T2**
Rest – Menu 45 € bi (lunch), 95/120 € – Carte 72/97 €
◆ Traditional ◆ Retro ◆
Founded in 1766, the Tout-Paris used to come here in the 19C and it is reputed for its small discreet salons. The restaurant has had a new lick of paint, but the spirit remains.

XXX

La Truffière

AC VISA MC AE

4 r. Blainville (5th) – Ⓜ Place Monge – ✆ 01 46 33 29 82
– restaurant.latruffiere@wanadoo.fr – Fax 01 46 33 64 74
– www.latruffiere.com
closed 23-30 December, Sunday and Monday **T3**

Rest – Menu 20 € (weekday lunch), 55/92 € – Carte 70/132 €

♦ Innovative ♦ Cosy ♦

A 17C house with two dining rooms. One is rustic with exposed beams and the other is vaulted. Traditional cuisine from south-west France and fine wine selection.

XX

Cigale Récamier

AC VISA MC

4 r. Récamier (7th) – Ⓜ Sèvres Babylone – ✆ 01 45 48 86 58
closed Sunday **R2**

Rest – Carte 38/48 €

♦ Traditional ♦ Friendly ♦

A literary establishment where writers and editors often meet up. Original menu with soufflés and sweet and savoury dishes renewed every month. Pleasant peaceful terrace.

XX

Caffé Minotti

(dinner) VISA MC AE

33 r. Verneuil (7th) – Ⓜ Rue du Bac – ✆ 01 42 60 04 04 – caffeminotti@wanadoo.fr – Fax 01 42 60 04 05
closed 29 July-22 August, 23 December-2 January, Sunday and Monday **R1**

Rest – Menu 39 € – Carte 43/69 €

♦ Italian ♦ Design ♦

Caffé with simple modern-style decor (unusual red chandelier in Murano glass), offering a full taste of Italy, minus the Vespa fumes!

XX ✿

Benoît

AC 10/20 VISA MC AE

20 r. St-Martin (4th) – Ⓜ Châtelet-Les Halles – ✆ 01 42 72 25 76
– restaurant.benoit@wanadoo.fr – Fax 01 42 72 45 68
– www.alain-ducasse.com
closed 21 July-20 August and 22 December-1 January **U1**

Rest – Menu 38 € (lunch) – Carte 54/83 €

Spec. Tête de veau sauce ravigote. Escargots en coquille aux fines herbes. Cassoulet maison.

♦ Traditional ♦ Retro ♦

Spurn the fast-food restaurants of this area! Instead, try this lively, traditional bistro, run by the same family since 1912, and taste their carefully prepared "old-style" cuisine.

XX

Yugaraj

AC VISA MC AE

14 r. Dauphine (6th) – Ⓜ Odéon – ✆ 01 43 26 44 91 – contact@yugaraj.com
– Fax 01 46 33 50 77
closed August, Thu lunchtime and Mon **T1**

Rest – Menu 30 € – Carte 37/60 €

♦ Indian ♦ Exotic ♦

Wood panelling, ornamental panels, silks and ancient works of art give an almost museum-style air to this highly acclaimed Indian restaurant with its very well researched menu.

XX

Atelier Maître Albert

AC VISA MC AE

1 r. Maître Albert (5th) – Ⓜ Maubert Mutualité – ✆ 01 56 81 30 01
– ateliermaitrealbert@guysavoy.com – Fax 01 53 10 83 23
– www.ateliermaitrealbert.com
closed 1 to 15 August, Christmas school holidays, Sat lunchtime and Sun lunchtime **U2**

Rest – Menu 28 € (weekday lunch) – Carte 39/51 €

♦ Meat specialities ♦ Bistro ♦

Guy Savoy has a winning team, serving carefully-prepared dishes in a sober modern setting that also includes a huge medieval fireplace, a rotisserie (meat on the spit) and exposed beams.

Alcazar

10/42 VISA

62 r. Mazarine (6th) – Odéon – 01 53 10 19 99
– contact@alcazar.fr
– Fax 01 53 10 23 23 – www.alcazar.fr **S2**

Rest – Menu 30 € bi (weekday lunch)/40 € – Carte 36/59 €

♦ Fusion ♦ Trendy ♦

J.-M. Rivière's frilly cabaret has been transformed into a huge, trendy, designer restaurant. The cooking ranges are visible from the tables, and the cuisine is contemporary.

L'Atelier de Joël Robuchon

VISA

7 r. de Montalembert (7th) – Rue du Bac
– 01 42 22 56 56 – latelierdejoelrobuchon@wanadoo.fr
– Fax 01 42 22 97 91
Open from 11.30 am to 3.30 pm and from 6.30 pm to midnight. Reservations only for certain services: please enquire **R1**

Rest – Menu 110 € – Carte 52/93 €

Spec. Langoustine en papillote croustillante au basilic. Caille farcie de foie gras et caramélisée, pomme-purée truffée. Merlan frit colbert, beurre aux herbes.

♦ Innovative ♦ Design ♦

An original concept in a chic decor designed by Rochon: no tables, just high stools in a row facing the counter where you can sample a selection of the fine, modern dishes, tapas style. Car parking service at lunchtime and on Saturday and Sunday evenings.

Yen

VISA

22 r. St-Benoît (6th) – St-Germain des Prés
– 01 45 44 11 18 – restau.yen@wanadoo.fr
– Fax 01 45 44 19 48
closed Sunday **S2**

Rest – Menu 55 € (dinner) – Carte 39/59 €

♦ Japanese ♦ Minimalist ♦

Two dining rooms with highly refined Japanese decor, the one on the first floor is slightly warmer in style. Pride of place on the menu for the chef's speciality : soba (buckwheat noodles).

Gaya Rive Gauche par Pierre Gagnaire

15/20 VISA

44 r. du Bac (7th) – Rue du Bac
– 01 45 44 73 73 – p.gagnaire@wanadoo.fr
– Fax 01 45 44 73 73
– www.pierre-gagnaire.com
closed 21 July - 20 August, 22 December-6 January, Saturday lunch and Sunday **R1**

Rest – Carte 58/97 €

♦ Contemporary ♦ Design ♦

A clientele that is very "Left Bank" frequents this fish and seafood restaurant. Nautical Decoration with a colour scheme and a dinner service signed Jean Cocteau.

L'Épi Dupin

VISA

11 r. Dupin (6th) – Sèvres Babylone – 01 42 22 64 56
– lepidupin@wanadoo.fr
– Fax 01 42 22 30 42
closed August, Mon. lunchtime, Sat. and Sun. **R2**

Rest – *(number of covers limited, pre-book)* Menu 32 €

♦ Innovative ♦ Friendly ♦

Beams and stonework for character, closely-packed tables for conviviality and delicious cuisine to delight the palate; this pocket-handkerchief-sized restaurant has captivated people in the Bon Marché area.

Buisson Ardent

25 r. Jussieu (5th) – Ⓜ Jussieu – ☎ 01 43 54 93 02 – info@lebuissonardent.fr – Fax 01 46 33 34 77 – www.lebuissonardent.fr
closed Aug., Sat. lunchtime and Sun. **U3**
Rest – Menu 29/45 €
◆ Traditional ◆ Bistro ◆
A childlike atmosphere characterises this small restaurant frequented at midday by Jussieu university students. Original frescoes dating back to 1923. Traditional cuisine.

Emporio Armani Caffé

149 bd St-Germain (6th) – Ⓜ St-Germain des Prés – ☎ 01 45 48 62 15 – Fax 01 45 48 53 17
closed Sun. **S2**
Rest – Carte 47/80 €
◆ Italian ◆ Fashionable ◆
Stylish, comfortable and attractively-redecorated Italian-style "caffé", on the first floor of this renowned designer's boutique. Trendy clientele and Italian cuisine.

Ze Kitchen Galerie

4 r. Grands Augustins (6th) – Ⓜ St-Michel – ☎ 01 44 32 00 32 – zekitchen.galerie@wanadoo.fr – Fax 01 44 32 00 33
closed Sat. lunchtime and Sun. **T1-2**
Rest – Menu 34 € (lunch), 50/70 € – Carte 52/55 €
◆ Fusion ◆ Design ◆
Ze Kitchen is "ze" hip place to be on the Left Bank. Works of art by modern artists, designer furniture and trendy cuisine prepared in front of your eyes.

MONTPARNASSE-DENFERT *Plan VI*

Méridien Montparnasse

19 r. Cdt-Mouchotte (14th) – Ⓜ Montparnasse Bienvenüe – ☎ 01 44 36 44 36 – meridien.montparnasse@lemeridien.com – Fax 01 44 36 49 00 – www.montparnasse.lemeridien.com 25/2000 **V1**
918 rm – 🚹205/410 € 🚹🚹205/410 €, ☕ 25 € – 35 suites
Rest *Montparnasse 25* – see below
Rest *Justine* – *☎ 01 44 36 44 00* – Menu 39/56 € bi – Carte 41/58 €
◆ Chain hotel ◆ Business ◆
Most of the rooms in this glass-and-concrete building have been redone; they are large and very modern. Beautiful view of the capital from the top floors. At Justine's, winter garden decor, green terrace and buffet menus.

Concorde Montparnasse

40 r. Cdt Mouchotte (14th) – Ⓜ Gaîté – ☎ 01 56 54 84 00 – montparnasse@concorde-hotels.com – Fax 01 56 54 84 84 – www.concorde-hotels.com 80 **V1**
354 rm – 🚹350 € 🚹🚹350 €, ☕ 15 €
Rest – *(closed 15 July-15 August)* Menu 34 € – Carte 37/49 €
◆ Chain hotel ◆ Business ◆
This completely new hotel, set on the Place de Catalogne, has many advantages: calm and refined rooms, interior garden, fitness centre, and bar. This restaurant, with rare wood and coloured fabrics, offers buffets and à la carte dishes.

L'Aiglon without rest

232 bd Raspail (14th) – Ⓜ Raspail – ☎ 01 43 20 82 42 – aiglon@espritfrance.com – Fax 01 43 20 98 72 – www.aiglon.com **W1**
38 rm – 🚹92/153 € 🚹🚹118/153 €, ☕ 9.50 € – 9 suites
◆ Traditional ◆ Classic ◆
The discreet façade of this hotel conceals a modern, plum-coloured interior. The guestrooms, sometimes a little on the small side, are gradually being renovated and have effective double-glazing.

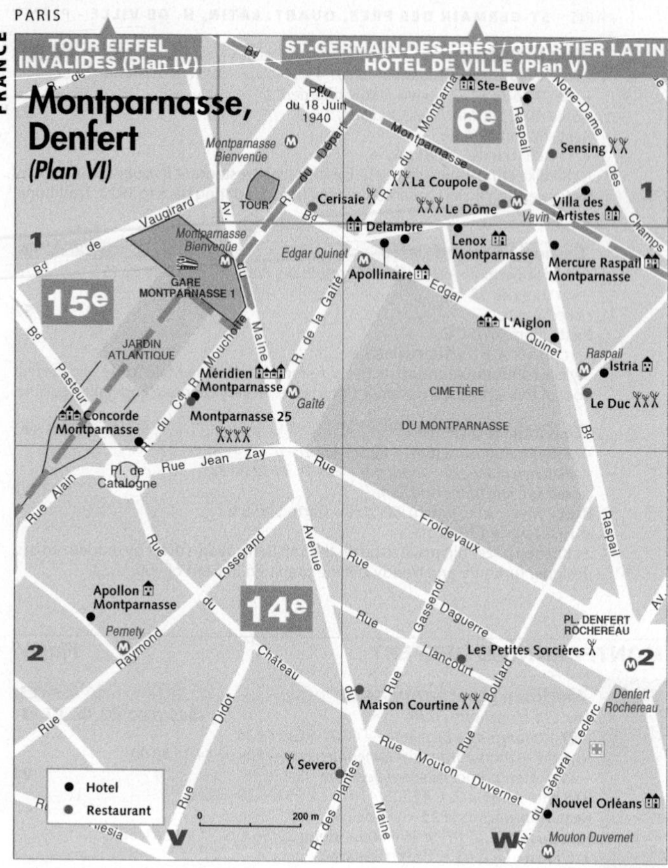

Ste-Beuve without rest

9 r. Ste-Beuve (6th) – Ⓜ Notre-Dame des Champs – ✆ 01 45 48 20 07 – saintebeuve@wanadoo.fr – Fax 01 45 48 67 52 – www.parishotelcharme.com **W1**

22 rm – †138/288 € ††138/288 €, ☕ 15 €

♦ Family ♦ Traditional ♦ Cosy ♦

This establishment resembles a private house: cosy atmosphere, soft sofas and glowing fire. The rooms are a tasteful blend of old-fashioned and contemporary styles.

Villa des Artistes without rest

9 r. Grande Chaumière (6th) – Ⓜ Vavin – ✆ 01 43 26 60 86 – hotel@villa-artistes.com – Fax 01 43 54 73 70 – www.villa-artistes.com **W1**

59 rm – †105 € ††132/184 €, ☕ 14 €

♦ Family ♦ Traditional ♦ Stylish ♦

The name pays tribute to the artists who embellished the history of the Montparnasse district. Pleasant rooms, most overlooking the courtyard. Glass-roofed breakfast room.

Lenox Montparnasse without rest

15 r. Delambre (14th) – Ⓜ Vavin – ✆ 01 43 35 34 50 – hotel@lenoxmontparnasse.com – Fax 01 43 20 46 64 – www.hotellenox.com **W1**

52 rm – 🚹165 € 🚹🚹165/260 €, ☕ 16 €

◆ Traditional ◆ Cosy ◆

Establishment frequented by elegant people, many from the fashion world. Period rooms, charming bathrooms, pleasant suites on the 6th floor. Nice bar and lounges.

Nouvel Orléans without rest

25 av. Gén. Leclerc (14th) – Ⓜ Mouton Duvernet – ✆ 01 43 27 80 20 – nouvelorleans@aol.com – Fax 01 43 35 36 57 – www.hotelnouvelorleans.com **W2**

46 rm – 🚹90/155 € 🚹🚹90/155 €, ☕ 10 €

◆ Traditional ◆ Modern ◆

The name comes from the Porte d'Orléans, 800 m away. In this entirely renovated hotel, modern furniture and warm colourful materials decorate the rooms.

Delambre without rest

35 r. Delambre (14th) – Ⓜ Edgar Quinet – ✆ 01 43 20 66 31 – delambre@club-internet.fr – Fax 01 45 38 91 76 – www.hoteldelambre.com **W1**

30 rm – 🚹85/115 € 🚹🚹85/160 €, ☕ 9 €

◆ Traditional ◆ Modern ◆

André Breton stayed over in this hotel located in a quiet street close to the Gare Montparnasse railway station. The decor is modern; the rooms are simple but bright and many are spacious.

Mercure Raspail Montparnasse without rest

207 bd Raspail (14th) – Ⓜ Vavin – ✆ 01 43 20 62 94 – h0351@accor.com – Fax 01 43 27 39 69 – www.mercure.com **W1**

63 rm – 🚹110/210 € 🚹🚹115/215 €, ☕ 14.50 €

◆ Chain hotel ◆ Business ◆ Functional ◆

Enjoy an overnight stay in this Haussmann building near the famous Montparnasse brasseries. Modern rooms with contemporary, light wood furniture.

Apollinaire without rest

39 r. Delambre (14th) – Ⓜ Edgar Quinet – ✆ 01 43 35 18 40 – infos@hotel-apollinaire.com – Fax 01 43 35 30 71 – www.hotel-apollinaire.com **W1**

36 rm – 🚹95/110 € 🚹🚹110/135 €, ☕ 7.50 €

◆ Traditional ◆ Functional ◆

The hotel is named after the poet who was a friend of the writers and artists living in Montparnasse. The colourful rooms are well-kept and functional. Comfortable lounge.

Istria without rest

29 r. Campagne Première (14th) – Ⓜ Raspail – ✆ 01 43 20 91 82 – hotel.istria@wanadoo.fr – Fax 01 43 22 48 45 **W1**

26 rm – 🚹80/170 € 🚹🚹85/180 €, ☕ 10 €

◆ Traditional ◆ Functional ◆

Aragon immortalised this hotel in "Il ne m'est Paris que d'Elsa". Small, simple bedrooms, a pleasant lounge and a breakfast room in a pretty vaulted cellar.

Apollon Montparnasse without rest

91 r. Ouest (14th) – Ⓜ Pernety – ✆ 01 43 95 62 00 – apollonm@wanadoo.fr – Fax 01 43 95 62 10 – www.apollon-montparnasse.com **V2**

33 rm – 🚹71/82 € 🚹🚹86/89 €, ☕ 8.50 €

◆ Traditional ◆ Functional ◆

Near Montparnasse station and the Air France airport shuttle, a courteous welcome and stylish rooms are the main assets of this hotel on a rather quiet street.

XXXX ✿

Montparnasse 25 – Hôtel Méridien Montparnasse

19 r. Cdt Mouchotte (14th) – Ⓜ Montparnasse Bienvenüe – ✆ 01 44 36 44 25 – meridien.montparnasse@lemeridien.com – Fax 01 44 36 49 03 – www.montparnasse.lemeridien.com

closed 7-15 April, 7 July - 2 September, Saturday, Sunday and public holidays **W1**

Rest – Menu 49 € (weekday lunch), 60/110 € – Carte 91/109 €

Spec. Langoustines à l'huile de vanille (spring). Sole, filets en bourride au vin du Jura et cèpes (autumn). Ris de veau rôti au comté.

♦ Contemporary ♦ Formal ♦

The modern setting based around black lacquer may surprise you, but this restaurant turns out to be comfortable and warm. Fashionable cuisine, superb cheese boards.

XXX ✿

Le Duc

243 bd Raspail (14th) – Ⓜ Raspail – ✆ 01 43 20 96 30 – Fax 01 43 20 46 73

closed 31 July - 22 August, 24 December - 2 January, Saturday lunchtime, Sunday and Monday **W1**

Rest – Menu 46 € (lunch) – Carte 48/138 €

Spec. Poissons crus. Langoustines rôties au gingembre. Homard à l'orange.

♦ Seafood ♦ Retro ♦

Fish and seafood cuisine - a blend of quality and simplicity - served in a comfortable yacht cabin with mahogany panelling, wall lights with a marine theme and gleaming brasses.

XXX

Le Dôme

108 bd Montparnasse (14th) – Ⓜ Vavin – ✆ 01 43 35 25 81 – Fax 01 42 79 01 19

closed Sunday and Monday in August **W1**

Rest – Carte 51/119 €

♦ Seafood ♦ Retro ♦

One of the temples to the literary and artistic bohemian lifestyle of the Twenties has been turned into a stylish and trendy Left-Bank brasserie, with a preserved Art Deco feel. Fish and seafood.

XX ✿

Maison Courtine (Charles)

157 av. Maine (14th) – Ⓜ Mouton Duvernet – ✆ 01 45 43 08 04 – yves.charles@wanadoo.fr – Fax 01 45 45 91 35

closed 3 - 27 August, 24 December - 3 January, Monday lunchtime, Saturday lunchtime and Sunday **W2**

Rest – Menu 38/43 €

Spec. Escalopes de foie gras de canard poêlées aux raisins. Canard sauvage rôti entier au poivre long (October-February). Médaillon de veau de lait et lentilles blondes de la Planèze.

♦ Traditional ♦ Cosy ♦

Here one can enjoy a culinary Tour de France; the bright coloured interiors are modern and the furnishing is in the Louis-Philippe style. An assiduously frequented establishment.

XX

Sensing

19 r Bréa(6th) – Ⓜ Vavin – ✆ 01 43 27 08 80 – sensing@orange.fr – Fax 01 43 26 99 27

closed 29 July - 27 August, Monday lunchtime and Sunday **W1**

Rest – Menu 55 € (lunch), 95/140 €

♦ Contemporary ♦

A concise, refined and contemporary menu based around high-quality ingredients and a mix of designer and Rococo decor provide Guy Martin's restaurant with its unique personality.

ACQUA PANNA
FROM THE HILLS OF TUSCANY
ACQUA
PANNA
Acqua
Oligominerale
S.PELLEGRINO
NATURAL MINERAL WATER
FRESCOBALDI
FRESCOBALDI

La Coupole

102 bd Montparnasse (14th) – Ⓜ Vavin – ✆ 01 43 20 14 20 – jtosi@groupeflo.fr – Fax 01 43 35 46 14 – www.flobrasseries.com **W1**

Rest – Menu 24/31 € – Carte 30/75 €

◆ Brasserie ◆ Retro ◆

The spirit of Montparnasse lives on in this immense Art Deco brasserie, first opened in 1927. The 32 pillars are decorated with masterpieces by artists of that period. A lively atmosphere.

Les Petites Sorcières

12 r. Liancourt (14th) – Ⓜ Denfert Rochereau – ✆ 01 43 21 95 68 – Fax 01 43 21 95 68

closed 13 July - 16 August, Monday lunchtime, Saturday lunchtime and Sunday **W2**

Rest – Menu 33 € – Carte 30/39 €

◆ Contemporary ◆ Cosy ◆

A meeting place for many a "Parisian Witch" - they meet on gourmet sabbaths, leave many objects and speed off on their broomsticks.

Cerisaie

70 bd E. Quinet (14th) – Ⓜ Edgar Quinet – ✆ 01 43 20 98 98 – Fax 01 43 20 98 98

closed 14 July - 20 August, 23 December - 6 January, Saturday and Sunday **V1**

Rest – *(pre-book)* Menu 31 € – Carte 31/37 €

◆ South-West of France specialities ◆ Bistro ◆

A tiny restaurant in the heart of the Breton quarter. Every day, the owner marks the carefully-prepared dishes of the southwest on a blackboard.

Severo

8 r. Plantes (14th) – Ⓜ Mouton Duvernet – ✆ 01 45 40 40 91

closed 23 July - 22 Aug, 23 Dec - 2 Jan, 5 - 13 Feb, Sat evening and Sun **V2**

Rest – Carte 28/46 €

◆ Meat specialities ◆ Bistro ◆

Products of Auvergne (meat, delicatessen) take centre stage on the daily slate menu of this lively bistro. The wine list is enticingly selective.

MARAIS-BASTILLE-GARE DE LYON — *Plan VII*

Pavillon de la Reine without rest — 25

28 pl. Vosges (3rd) – Ⓜ Bastille – ✆ 01 40 29 19 19 – contact@pavillon-de-la-reine.com – Fax 01 40 29 19 20 **Y2**

41 rm – †360 € ††415 €, ☕ 25 € – 15 suites

◆ Luxury ◆ Historic ◆

Behind one of the 36 brick houses lining the Place des Vosges stand two buildings, one dating from the 17C, housing refined guest rooms on the courtyard or (private) garden side.

Villa Beaumarchais without rest — 15

5 r. Arquebusiers (3rd) – Ⓜ Chemin Vert – ✆ 01 40 29 14 00 – beaumarchais@leshotelsdeparis.com – Fax 01 40 29 14 01 **X-Y1**

50 rm – †380 € ††480 €, ☕ 26 €

◆ Luxury ◆ Stylish ◆

Set back from the hustle and bustle of the boulevard Beaumarchais. Refined rooms graced with gold-leafed furniture; all rooms overlook a pretty winter garden.

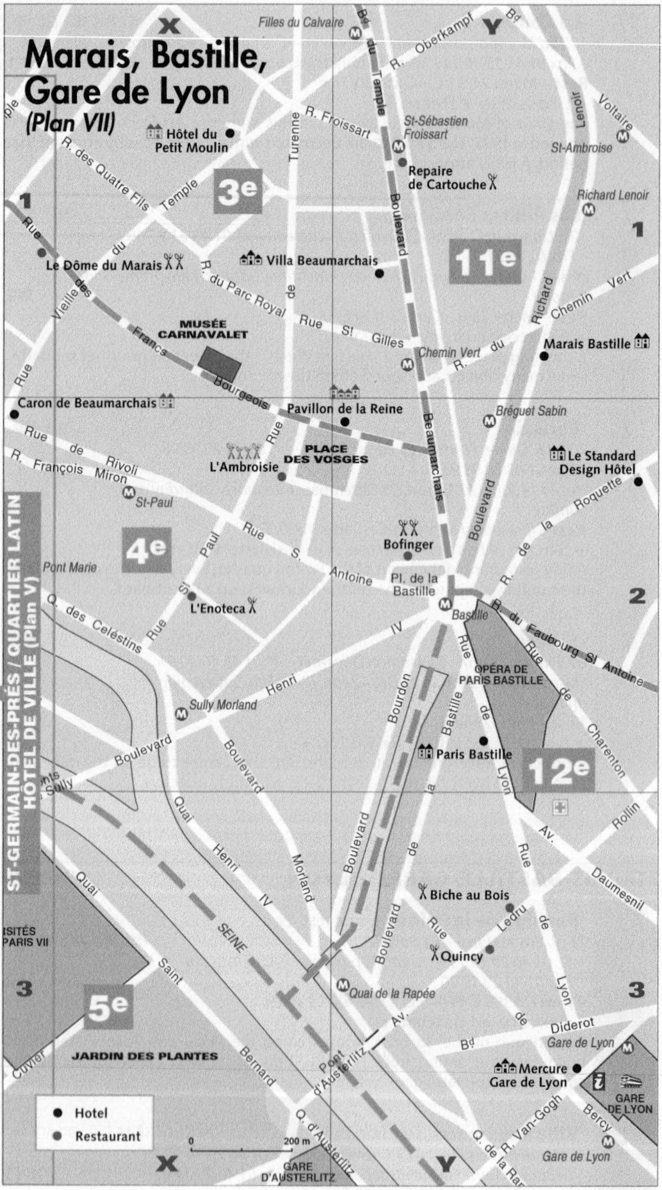

Marais, Bastille, Gare de Lyon
(Plan VII)

X
Y
1
2
3
3e
4e
5e
11e
12e
Filles du Calvaire
Bd du Temple
R. Oberkampf
Bd Voltaire
R. Froissart
St-Sébastien Froissart
Lenoir
St-Ambroise
Hôtel du Petit Moulin
R. des Quatre Fils
Temple
Turenne
Repaire de Cartouche
Richard Lenoir
Rue Vieille du Temple
Le Dôme du Marais
Villa Beaumarchais
R. du Parc Royal
Rue de Turenne
Rue St Gilles
Boulevard Beaumarchais
Boulevard Richard
Chemin Vert
R. du Chemin Vert
MUSÉE CARNAVALET
Rue des Francs Bourgeois
Marais Bastille
Caron de Beaumarchais
Pavillon de la Reine
Bréguet Sabin
Rue de Rivoli
R. François Miron
L'Ambroisie
PLACE DES VOSGES
Le Standard Design Hôtel
St-Paul
R. de la Roquette
Bofinger
Rue St. Antoine
Rue St Paul
Pont Marie
Pl. de la Bastille
Bastille
L'Enoteca
Q. des Célestins
Bd Henri IV
R. du Faubourg St Antoine
OPÉRA DE PARIS BASTILLE
Rue de Charenton
Rue de Lyon
Sully Morland
Boulevard Bourdon
Boulevard de la Bastille
Paris Bastille
Pont de Sully
Quai Henri IV
Boulevard Morland
Av. Rollin
Av. Daumesnil
Rue Ledru
Biche au Bois
Quincy
SEINE
Quai Saint Bernard
Quai de la Rapée
Rue de Lyon
Bd Diderot
Gare de Lyon
Mercure Gare de Lyon
GARE DE LYON
R. Van-Gogh
Bercy
Q. de la Rapée
Cuvier
JARDIN DES PLANTES
Pont d'Austerlitz
Q. d'Austerlitz
GARE D'AUSTERLITZ
…RSITÉS PARIS VII
ST-GERMAIN-DES-PRÉS / QUARTIER LATIN HÔTEL DE VILLE (Plan V)

● Hotel
● Restaurant

0 200 m

Mercure Gare de Lyon without rest

2 pl. Louis Armand (12th) 15/90 VISA AE
– Ⓜ Gare de Lyon – ✆ 01 43 44 84 84
– h2217@accor.com – Fax 01 43 47 41 94 – www.mercure.com **Y3**

315 rm – 87/247 € 99/257 €, 15 €

◆ Chain hotel ◆ Functional ◆

The modern architecture of this hotel contrasts with the nearby belfry of the Gare de Lyon. The bedrooms are furnished in ceruse wood and have the benefit of good soundproofing. Wine bar.

Du Petit Moulin without rest

26 r. du Poitou (3rd) – Ⓜ St-Sébastien Froissart
– ✆ 01 42 74 10 10 – contact@hoteldupetitmoulin.com
– Fax 01 42 74 10 97 – www.hoteldupetitmoulin.com **X1**

17 rm – 350 € 350 €, 15 €

◆ Traditional ◆ Design ◆

For this hotel in the Marais, Christian Lacroix has designed a unique and refined decor, playing on the contrasts between traditional and modern. Each room has a different design. Cosy bar.

Caron de Beaumarchais without rest

12 r. Vieille-du-Temple (4th) – Ⓜ Hôtel de Ville
– ✆ 01 42 72 34 12 – hotel@carondebeaumarchais.com
– Fax 01 42 72 34 63 – www.carondebeaumarchais.com **X2**

19 rm – 125/162 € 125/162 €, 12 €

◆ Traditional ◆ Business ◆ Historic ◆

Figaro's creator lived on this historic Marais street, and the stylish decoration in this charming hotel pays a faithful tribute to him. Small, comfortable rooms.

Le Standard Design Hôtel without rest

29 r. des Taillandiers (11th) – Ⓜ Bastille – ✆ 01 48 05 30 97
– reservation@standard-hotel.com – Fax 01 47 00 29 26
– www.standard-hotel.com **Y2**

34 rm – 90/120 € 130/165 €, 10 €

◆ Traditional ◆ Cosy ◆ Design ◆

A resolutely contemporary interior in black and white, with touches of colour in the bedrooms. A trendy and unique hotel embellished with numerous designer objects.

Paris Bastille without rest

67 r. Lyon (12th) – Ⓜ Bastille – ✆ 01 40 01 07 17
– infosbastille@wanadoo.fr – Fax 01 40 01 07 27
– www.hotelparisbastille.com **Y2**

37 rm – 159/240 € 168/240 €, 12 €

◆ Business ◆ Functional ◆

Up-to-date comfort, modern furnishings and carefully chosen colour schemes characterise the rooms in this hotel facing the Opéra.

Marais Bastille without rest

36 bd Richard Lenoir (11th) – Ⓜ Bréguet Sabin – ✆ 01 48 05 75 00
– maraisbastille@wanadoo.fr – Fax 01 43 57 42 85
– www.bestwestern.com/fr/maraisbastille **Y1**

36 rm – 145 € 145 €, 10 €

◆ Chain hotel ◆ Classical ◆

The hotel runs along the boulevard which has covered the Canal St-Martin since 1860. Comfortable, spacious and modern bedrooms embellished with oak and cherry wood furniture.

FRANCE

L'Ambroisie (Pacaud)
9 pl. des Vosges (4th) – St-Paul – 01 42 78 51 45
closed 31 July - 26 August, February holidays, Sunday and Monday **X2**
Rest – Carte 185/272 €
Spec. Feuillantine de langoustines aux graines de sésame, sauce curry. Navarin de homard et pommes de terre fondantes au romarin. Tarte fine sablée au chocolat, glace vanille.
♦ Contemporary ♦ Luxury ♦
Under the arcades of the Place des Vosges, a royal decor and a subtle cuisine, close to perfection. Was not ambrosia the food of the Greek Gods?

Bofinger
15/30 (dinner)
5 r. Bastille (4th) – Bastille – 01 42 72 87 82 – eberne@groupeflo.fr – Fax 01 42 72 97 68 – www.bofingerparis.com **Y2**
Rest – Menu 24 € (weekday lunch)/31 € – Carte 28/68 €
♦ Brasserie ♦ Retro ♦
The famous clients and remarkable decor make this brasserie created in 1864 an unforgettable location. The interior boasts a finely worked cupola, and a room on the first floor decorated by Hansi.

Le Dôme du Marais
53bis r. Francs-Bourgeois (4th) – Rambuteau – 01 42 74 54 17 – ledomedumarais@hotmail.com – Fax 01 42 77 78 17
closed 1 - 4 May, 8 - 31 August, Sunday and Monday **X1**
Rest – Menu 23 € (weekday lunch), 35/100 € bi – Carte 42/56 €
♦ Contemporary ♦ Friendly ♦
Tables are laid under the pretty dome in the old sales room of the Crédit Municipal and in a second winter garden dining room. Modern cuisine.

Quincy
28 av. Ledru-Rollin (12th) – Gare de Lyon – 01 46 28 46 76 – Fax 01 46 28 46 76 – www.lequincy.fr
closed 12 August - 12 September, Saturday, Sunday and Monday **Y3**
Rest – Menu 50/70 € – Carte 46/71 €
♦ Traditional ♦ Rustic ♦
A warm atmosphere in this rustic bistrot where you are served a hearty cuisine that like "Bobosse", the jovial owner, is not lacking in character.

L'Enoteca
25 r. Charles V (4th) – St-Paul – 01 42 78 91 44 – enoteca@enoteca.fr – Fax 01 44 59 31 72
closed 11 - 20 August **X2**
Rest – *(pre-book)* Carte 26/46 €
♦ Italian ♦ Friendly ♦
A 16C building housing a restaurant whose superb wine list of about 500 Italian wines is its main asset. Italian dishes and very lively atmosphere.

Repaire de Cartouche
99 r. Amelot (11th) – St-Sébastien Froissart – 01 47 00 25 86 – Fax 01 43 38 85 91
closed August, February Holidays, one week in May, Sunday and Monday **Y1**
Rest – Menu 16 € (weekday lunch)/25 € – Carte 33/52 €
♦ Traditional ♦ Friendly ♦
Cartouche, the impetuous yet honourable bandit, took refuge here between two bad adventures; the restaurant murals recall his epic life. Attractive wine list.

Biche au Bois
45 av. Ledru-Rollin (12th) – Gare de Lyon – 01 43 43 34 38
closed 22 July - 22 August, 24 December-2 January, lunch Monday, Saturday and Sunday **Y3**
Rest – Menu 24 € – Carte approx. 30 €
♦ Classic ♦ Rustic ♦
Restaurant with a simple decor and a noisy, smoky atmosphere, but there is attentive service and the generous traditional cuisine favours game in season.

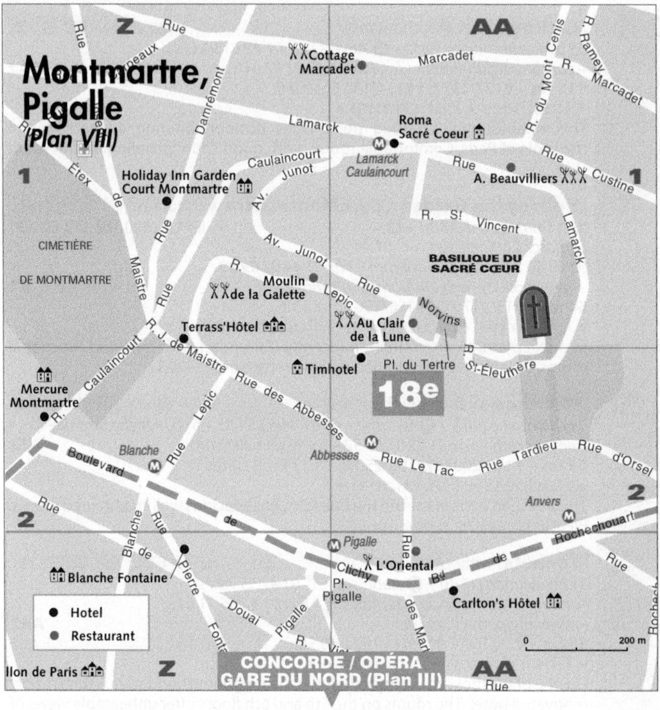

Montmartre, Pigalle *(Plan VIII)*

● Hotel
● Restaurant

CONCORDE / OPÉRA GARE DU NORD (Plan III)

MONTMARTRE, PIGALLE *Plan VIII*

Terrass'Hôtel AC rm 25/100 VISA MC AE

12 r. J. de Maistre (18th) – Place de Clichy – 01 46 06 72 85 – reservation@terrass-hotel.com – Fax 01 42 52 29 11 – www.terrass-hotel.com **Z1**

85 rm – 260/290 € 295/340 €, 19 € – 15 suites

Rest *Terrasse* – *01 44 92 34 00 (closed August and dinner Sunday)* Menu 29 € (lunch)/55 € bi – Carte 43/64 €

◆ Traditional ◆ Family ◆ Modern ◆

At the foot of Sacré-Cœur basilica, stunning views over Paris from the upper floor rooms on the street side. Neat and warm interior; lounge with a fine fireplace. Refined contemporary decor (shades of beige, grey and black) and an area specially dedicated to wine.

Mercure Montmartre without rest AC 20/70 VISA MC AE

1 r. Caulaincourt (18th) – Place de Clichy – 01 44 69 70 70 – h0373@accor.com – Fax 01 44 69 70 71 – www.mercure.com **Z2**

305 rm – 141/198 € 151/216 €, 14 €

◆ Chain hotel ◆ Business ◆ Functional ◆

The hotel is not far from the famous Moulin Rouge. Opt for one of the rooms on the top three floors so as to fully enjoy the view over the Paris rooftops.

Carlton's Hôtel without rest
55 bd Rochechouart (9th) – Ⓜ Anvers – ☎ 01 42 81 91 00 – carltons@club-internet.fr – Fax 01 42 81 97 04 **AA2**
111 rm – 🚹127/137 € 🚹🚹134/180 €, ☕ 9 €
◆ Business ◆ Functional ◆
This establishment's strong point is its position offering a panorama of the roofs of Paris. Comfortable rooms, with good soundproofing on the street side.

Holiday Inn Garden Court Montmartre without rest
23 r. Damrémont (18th) – Ⓜ Lamarck Caulaincourt – ☎ 01 44 92 33 40 – hiparmm@aol.com – Fax 01 44 92 09 30 – www.holiday-inn.com/parismontmartre **Z1**
20
54 rm – 🚹130/170 € 🚹🚹150/190 €, ☕ 13 €
◆ Chain hotel ◆ Business ◆ Functional ◆
In a steep Montmartre street, a recently-built hotel with cool and functional rooms. Breakfast room adorned with a pretty trompe-l'œil.

Blanche Fontaine without rest
34 r. Fontaine (9th) – Ⓜ Blanche – ☎ 01 44 63 54 95 – tryp.blanche.fontaine@solmelia.com – Fax 01 42 81 05 52 – www.solmelia.com **Z2**
65 rm – 🚹140/200 € 🚹🚹190/250 €, ☕ 17 € – 5 suites
◆ Business ◆ Functional ◆
This hotel, an oasis of calm in the busy city, has spacious well-maintained rooms. Pleasant breakfast room.

Timhôtel without rest
11 r. Ravignan (18th) – Ⓜ Abbesses – ☎ 01 42 55 74 79 – montmartre.manager@timhotel.fr – Fax 01 42 55 71 01 – www.my-paris-hotel.com **AA2**
59 rm – 🚹75/160 € 🚹🚹75/160 €, ☕ 8.50 €
◆ Chain hotel ◆ Functional ◆
On one of the most charming squares in the neighbourhood stands this smartly renovated hotel. The rooms on the 5th and 6th floors offer unbeatable views of the capital.

Roma Sacré Cœur without rest
101 r. Caulaincourt (18th) – Ⓜ Lamarck Caulaincourt – ☎ 01 42 62 02 02 – hotel.roma@wanadoo.fr – Fax 01 42 54 34 92 – www.hotelroma.com **AA1**
57 rm – 🚹75/95 € 🚹🚹85/110 €, ☕ 7.50 €
◆ Traditional ◆ Family ◆ Classic ◆
Here one finds all the charm of Montmartre – a front garden, side stairways and the Sacré-Cœur above. Vivid colours enliven the renovated rooms.

A Beauvilliers
10/15
52 r. Lamarck (18th) – Ⓜ Lamarck Caulaincourt – ☎ 01 42 55 05 42 – www.abeauvilliers.com
closed Sunday and Monday **AA1**
Rest – Menu 35 € (lunch), 45/63 € – Carte 61/74 €
◆ Traditional ◆ Romantic ◆
There is change in the air at this Montmartre institution: delicious contemporary cuisine with a personal touch and an elegant decor. Pleasant terrace for fine weather.

Cottage Marcadet
151bis r. Marcadet (18th) – Ⓜ Lamarck Caulaincourt – ☎ 01 42 57 71 22 – contact@cottagemarcadet.com – www.cottagemarcadet.com
closed August and Sun **AA1**
Rest – Menu 35/100 € – Carte 57/89 €
◆ Traditional ◆ Retro ◆
An intimate ambiance awaits you in this classic dining room with comfortable Louis XVI furnishings. Carefully-prepared traditional cuisine.

Moulin de la Galette

83 r. Lepic (18th) – Ⓜ Abbesses – ✆ 01 46 06 84 77 – moulindelagalette@yahoo.fr – Fax 01 46 06 84 78 **Z1**

Rest – Menu 33 € bi/60 € – Carte 38/57 €

♦ Traditional ♦ Retro ♦

A windmill since 1622, then a popular dance hall painted by Renoir and Toulouse-Lautrec, this place is now a pleasant restaurant with a charming terrace.

Au Clair de la Lune

9 r. Poulbot (18th) – Ⓜ Abbesses – ✆ 01 42 58 97 03 – Fax 01 42 55 64 74 closed 19 Aug - 16 Sept., Mon lunchtime and Sun . **AA1**

Rest – Menu 30 € – Carte 37/67 €

♦ Traditional ♦ Rustic ♦

Friend Pierrot opens the door to his tavern to you, just behind Place du Tertre. Convivial atmosphere with murals representing the old Montmartre as a backdrop.

L'Oriental

76 r. Martyrs (18th) – Ⓜ Pigalle – ✆ 01 42 64 39 80 – Fax 01 42 64 39 80 – www.loriental-restaurant.com **AA2**

Rest – Menu 14.50 € bi (weekday lunch)/34 € – Carte 27/39 €

♦ Moroccan ♦ Exotic ♦

Very warm welcome and a pretty Near East setting (tables decorated with Moroccan enameled tiles, and Arab architectural details) in this North African restaurant in the heart of Pigalle's cosmopolitan animation.

OUTSIDE CENTRAL AREA *Plan I*

Murano

13 bd Temple (3rd) – Ⓜ Filles du Calvaire – ✆ 01 42 71 20 00 – paris@muranoresort.com – Fax 01 42 71 21 01 – www.muranoresort.com **C2**

42 rm – †350 € ††400/650 €, ☕ 28 € – 9 suites

Rest – Menu 30 € (weekday lunch) – Carte 43/81 €

♦ Grand Luxury ♦ Design ♦

The Murano is a new trendy hotel that stands out from the others with its immaculate designer decor, play of colours, high-tech equipment, pop-art bar (150 types of vodka), etc. The restaurant has a colourful contemporary style, international food and a D.J. at the decks.

St-James Paris

rm 25

43 av. Bugeaud (16th) ✉ 75116 – Ⓜ Porte Dauphine – ✆ 01 44 05 81 81 – contact@saint-james-paris.com – Fax 01 44 05 81 82 – www.saint-james-paris.com **A2**

38 rm – †370 € ††480 €, ☕ 28 € – 10 suites

Rest – *(closed Saturday, Sunday and Bank Holidays) (residents only)* Menu 48 €

♦ Grand Luxury ♦ Personalised ♦

Beautiful private townhouse built in 1892 by Mrs. Thiers, in the heart of a shady garden. Majestic staircase, spacious rooms and a bar-library with the atmosphere of an English club.

Sofitel Paris Bercy

rm rm 250

1 r. Libourne (12th) – Ⓜ Cour St-Emilion – ✆ 01 44 67 34 00 – h2192@accor.com – Fax 01 44 67 34 01 – www.sofitel-paris-bercy.com **D3**

376 rm – †380 € ††380 €, ☕ 25 € – 10 suites

Rest *Café Ké* – *(closed Saturday and Sunday)* Menu 33 € – Carte 40/61 €

♦ Chain hotel ♦ Functional ♦

A beautiful glass façade, contemporary interior in shades of brown, beige and blue, and modern facilities. Some of the rooms enjoy views across Paris. The Café Ké with its new decor makes for a pleasant stop in the middle of Bercy "village"; modern cuisine.

FRANCE

Sofitel Porte de Sèvres

8 r. L. Armand (15th) – Ⓜ *Balard*
– ✆ 01 40 60 30 30 – h0572@accor.com
– Fax 01 40 60 30 00
– www.accorhotels.com/sofitel_paris_porte_de_sevres.htm **A3**
608 rm – †310/390 € ††310/390 €, ☕ 25 € – 12 suites
Rest *Brasserie* – *✆ 01 40 60 33 77 (closed Saturday lunch and Sunday lunch)* Menu 26 € – Carte 30/58 €

♦ Business ♦ Chain hotel ♦ Functional ♦

Opposite the heliport, this hotel offers soundproofed rooms, some of which have been refurbished in an elegantly modern style. The upper floors have a lovely view over western Paris. Brasserie with a setting from the Roaring Twenties: Mosaics, cupola, benches, etc..

Square

3 r. Boulainvilliers (16th) ✉ 75016
– Ⓜ Mirabeau – ✆ 01 44 14 91 90
– hotel.square@wanadoo.fr – Fax 01 44 14 91 99 **A2**
22 rm – †270/350 € ††270/350 €, ☕ 20 € – 2 suites
Rest *Zébra Square* – *✆ 01 44 14 91 91* – Menu 33 € bi – Carte 33/56 €

♦ Luxury ♦ Business ♦ Design ♦

A jewel of contemporary architecture across from the Maison de la Radio. Curves, colours, high-tech facilities and abstract paintings: a hymn to modern art! Trendy decor with striped theme in the restaurant, a cellar-library and contemporary cuisine on the menu.

Holiday Inn

216 av. J. Jaurès (19th) – Ⓜ Porte de Pantin
– ✆ 01 44 84 18 18 – hilavillette@alliance-hospitality.com
– Fax 01 44 84 18 20 – www.holidayinn-parisvillette.com **D1**
182 rm – †205/400 € ††250/480 €, ☕ 17 €
Rest – *(closed Saturday, Sunday and Banks Holidays)* Menu 26 € (lunch)/27 € – Carte 21/50 €

♦ Business ♦ Chain hotel ♦ Functional ♦

Modern construction across from the Cité de la Musique. Spacious and soundproofed rooms, offering modern comfort. Métro station a few metres away. Simple brasserie-style restaurant and small terrace protected from the street by a curtain of plants.

Kube without rest

1 passage Ruelle (18th) – Ⓜ La Chapelle
– ✆ 01 42 05 20 00 – paris@kubehotel.com
– Fax 01 42 05 21 01 – www.kubehotel.com **C1**
41 rm – †250 € ††300/750 €, ☕ 25 €

♦ Business ♦ Design ♦

The 19C façade belies the firmly designer, high-tech interior of this hotel. The bar – built entirely with ice (-5°C) – makes for an unusual and unforgettable experience.

Océania without rest

52 r. Oradour sur Glane(15th)
– Ⓜ Porte de Versailles – ✆ 01 56 09 09 09
– oceania.paris@oceaniahotels.com – Fax 01 56 09 09 19
– www.oceaniahotels.com **A3**
232 rm – †160/270 € ††175/285 €, ☕ 15 € – 18 suites

♦ Business ♦ Modern ♦

Modern comfort in an elegant, contemporary setting. This new hotel also offers well-equipped bedrooms, a relaxation centre offering a full range of facilities, and an exotic terrace-garden.

Mercure Porte de Versailles without rest
69 bd Victor (15th) – Ⓜ Porte de Versailles
– ✆ 01 44 19 03 03 – h1131@accor.com
– Fax 01 48 28 22 11
– www.accorhotels.com/mercure_paris_porte_de_versailles.htm **A3**
91 rm – 90/275 € 105/290 €, 16 €
◆ Chain hotel ◆ Business ◆ Functional ◆
A hotel in a 1970s building opposite the Parc des Expositions exhibition centre. Opt for one of the renovated rooms; the others are functional but plain.

Novotel Bercy
85 r. Bercy (12th) – Ⓜ Bercy – ✆ 01 43 42 30 00 – h0935@accor.com
– Fax 01 43 45 30 60 **D3**
151 rm – 130/195 € 130/203 €, 14 €
Rest – Carte 23/37 €
◆ Grand Luxury ◆ Functional ◆
The bright rooms in this Novotel are decorated in the chain's new "Novation" style. The nearby Parc de Bercy occupies the site of an old wine depot. In good weather, the dining room veranda and terrace are in great demand.

Novotel Gare de Lyon
2 r. Hector Malo (12th) – Ⓜ Gare de Lyon
– ✆ 01 44 67 60 00 – h1735@accor.com
– Fax 01 44 67 60 60 – www.novotel.com **D2**
253 rm – 185/236 € 195/250 €, 14 €
Rest – *(dinner only Saturday and Sunday)* Carte 18/36 €
◆ Chain hotel ◆ Functional ◆
This modern hotel overlooking a tranquil square offers comfortable, typical Novotel-style guestrooms; those on the sixth floor have a terrace. 24-hour swimming pool and well-designed children's area. Coté Jardin: traditional cuisine in a contemporary restaurant.

Novotel Paris Tour Eiffel
61 quai Grenelle (15th) – Ⓜ Charles Michels
– ✆ 01 40 58 20 00 – h3546@accor.com – Fax 01 40 58 24 44
– www.novotel.com **A2**
752 rm – 260/350 € 290/380 €, 20 € – 12 suites
Rest ***Café Lenôtre*** – *✆ 01 40 58 20 75* – Carte 29/46 €
◆ Chain hotel ◆ Business ◆ Functional ◆
This fully renovated hotel offers comfortable modern rooms (wood, light shades). Most of them overlook the Seine. High-tech conference centre. The Tour Eiffel Café offers a pleasant, refined decor, modern cuisine and a delicatessen area.

Holiday Inn Bibliothèque de France without rest
21 r. Tolbiac (13th)
– Ⓜ Bibliothèque F. Mitterrand – ✆ 01 45 84 61 61 – hibdf@wanadoo.fr
– Fax 01 45 84 43 38
– www.holiday-inn.com/paris-tolbiac **C3**
71 rm – 87/187 € 127/187 €, 13 €
◆ Chain hotel ◆ Functional ◆
In a busy street 20m from the métro station, this hotel offers comfortable, well-kept rooms with double glazing. Simple dishes available in the evening.

Windsor Home without rest
3 r. Vital (16 th) ✉ 75016 – Ⓜ La Muette – ✆ 01 45 04 49 49 – whparis@wanadoo.fr – Fax 01 45 04 59 50 **A2**
8 rm – 110/150 € 120/160 €, 11 €
◆ Traditional ◆ Cosy ◆
This charming, hundred-year-old residence with a garden in front is decorated like a private house: old furniture, mouldings, light colours and contemporary touches.

La Manufacture without rest

8 r. Philippe de Champagne (13th) ✉ 75013 – Ⓜ Place d'Italie – ✆ 01 45 35 45 25 – lamanufacture.paris@wanadoo.fr – Fax 01 45 35 45 40 – www.hotel-la-manufacture.com **C3**

56 rm – 120/230 € 120/230 €, 10 €

♦ Traditional ♦

Friendly service and elegant decor are the main features of this well-maintained hotel. Guestrooms somewhat on the small side. Breakfast room with a Provençal atmosphere.

Pré Catelan

rte Suresnes (In the Bois de Boulogne) (16th) ✉ 75016 – ✆ 01 44 14 41 14 – leprecatelan-restaurant@lenotre.fr – Fax 01 45 24 43 25 – www.lenotre.fr closed 28 Oct - 6 Nov, 17 Feb - 11 Mar, Sun except lunch from May to October and Mon **A2**

Rest – Menu 75 € (weekday lunch), 140/180 € – Carte 151/200 €

Spec. La tomate. La langoustine. Le café "expresso".

♦ Innovative ♦ Luxury ♦

Elegant Napoleon III pavilion is in the centre of the wood, near the unusual Shakespeare theatre. Caran d'Ache decor, refreshing terrace and creative cuisine.

Grande Cascade

6/47

allée de Longchamp (opposite the hippodrome)(16th) ✉ 75016 – ✆ 01 45 27 33 51 – contact@lagrandecascade.fr – Fax 01 42 88 99 06 – www.lagrandecascade.fr closed February holidays

Rest – Menu 70/165 € – Carte 130/170 €

Spec. Fleurs de courgette ivres de girolles, coques et couteaux (15 June-15 September). Homard de Nouvelle-Ecosse façon newburg (June-September). Pomme de ris de veau cuite lentement, olives, câpres et croutons frits.

♦ Traditional ♦ Retro ♦

A Parisian paradise at the foot of the Grande Cascade (10m!) in the Bois de Boulogne. Delicately distinctive cuisine served in the 1850 pavilion or on the splendid terrace.

Benkay – Novotel Paris Tour Eiffel

6/32

61 quai Grenelle (4th floor)(15th) – Ⓜ Bir-Hakeim – ✆ 01 40 58 21 26 – h3546@accor.com – Fax 01 40 58 21 30 – www.novotel.com **A2**

Rest – Menu 30 € (lunch), 75/125 € – Carte 42/131 €

♦ Japanese ♦ Exotic ♦

On the top floor of a small building, a restaurant with a fine view of the River Seine. Sober decor (wood and marble), a sushi and teppanyaki bar.

Relais d'Auteuil (Pignol)

31 bd Murat (16th) ✉ 75016 – Ⓜ Michel Ange Molitor – ✆ 01 46 51 09 54 – pignol.p@wanadoo.fr – Fax 01 40 71 05 03 closed August, Christmas Holidays, Monday lunch, Saturday lunch and Sunday **A2**

Rest – Menu 55 € (lunch), 118/148 € – Carte 110/164 €

Spec. Amandine de foie gras. Grosse sole de ligne. Côte de veau de lait.

♦ Contemporary ♦ Fashionable ♦

A pleasant setting that combines a touch of the modern with stylish furnishings. As for the menus, refinement of taste vies with culinary virtuosity. An exceptional wine list.

Chez Géraud

31 r. Vital (16th) ✉ 75016 – Ⓜ La Muette – ✆ 01 45 20 33 00 – Fax 01 45 20 46 60 closed 28 July-28 August, 25 December-2 January, Saturday and Sunday **A2**

Rest – Menu 30 € – Carte 50/72 €

♦ Traditional ♦ Bistro ♦

The facade and then the inside mural, both in Longwy faience, draw the eye. Chic bistrot setting with a cuisine that favours game in season.

Mansouria

11 r. Faidherbe (11th) – Ⓜ Faidherbe Chaligny – ✆ 01 43 71 00 16 – Fax 01 40 24 21 97
closed 13 - 19 Aug., Mon. lunchtime, Tues. lunchtime and Sun. **D2**
Rest – Menu 30/46 € bi – Carte 31/50 €
♦ Moroccan ♦ Exotic ♦
Kept by a former ethnologist, well-known in Paris in the field of Moroccan food. The delicate, aromatic dishes are prepared by women and served in a Moorish decor.

LA DÉFENSE

Plan I

Sofitel Grande Arche rm rm 10/100

11 av. Arche ✉ 92081 – ✆ 01 47 17 50 00 – h3013@accor.com – Fax 01 47 17 55 66 – www.sofitel.com
352 rm – 355/435 € 408/500 €, 25 € – 16 suites
Rest *Avant Seine* – *✆ 01 47 17 59 99 (closed 4-26 August, 22 December-1st January, Friday dinner, Saturday, Sunday and public holidays)* Carte 50/50 €
♦ Chain hotel ♦ Luxury ♦ Stylish ♦
Beautiful architecture, resembling a ship's hull, a combination of glass and ochre stonework. Spacious, elegant rooms, lounges and very well-equipped auditorium (with simultaneous translation booths). The Avant Seine offers you quality designer décor and spit-roast dishes.

Renaissance rm rm 160

60 Jardin de Valmy (on the circular road, exit La Défense 7) ✉ 92918 – ✆ 01 41 97 50 50 – rhi.parld.exec.sec@renaissancehotels.com – Fax 01 41 97 51 51 – www.renaissancehotels.com/parld
324 rm – 210/260 € 210/260 €, 24 € – 3 suites
Rest – *(closed Saturday lunch and Sunday lunch)* Menu 29 € (lunch)/43 € bi – Carte 35/52 €
♦ Chain hotel ♦ Luxury ♦ Cosy ♦
At the foot of the Carrare marble Grande Arche, this contemporary hotel has well-equipped rooms, with refined decoration. Good fitness facilities. In the restaurant, all-wood features with a "retro" brasserie atmosphere and a view of the gardens of Valmy.

Hilton La Défense rm rm 5/60

2 pl. Défense ✉ 92053 – ✆ 01 46 92 10 10 – parldhirm@hilton.com – Fax 01 46 92 10 50 – www.hilton.com
139 rm – 190/560 € 190/560 €, 26 € – 9 suites
Rest *Les Communautés* – *✆ 01 46 92 10 30 (closed 10-20 August, Saturday and Sunday)* Menu 57 € – Carte 56/71 €
Rest *L'Échiquier* – *✆ 01 46 92 10 35* – Menu 32 € (lunch) – Carte 36/58 €
♦ Chain hotel ♦ Business ♦ Modern ♦
The completely refurbished hotel is situated within the CNIT complex. The welcoming designer rooms cater particularly to a business clientele. Les Communautés restaurant offers modern cuisine and a fine view. The Échiquier offers a traditional menu.

Sofitel Centre rm 10/80

34 cours Michelet ✉ 92060 Puteaux – ✆ 01 47 76 44 43 – h0912@accor.com – Fax 01 47 76 72 10 – http://sofitel-paris-ladefense-centre.com
150 rm – 365 € 425 €, 25 € – 1 suite
Rest *La Tavola* – *✆ 01 47 76 72 30 (closed 13 July-21 August, 21 December-2 January, Saturday, Sunday and public holidays) (lunch only)* Menu 58/75 € – Carte approx. 70 €
Rest *L'Italian Lounge* – *✆ 01 47 76 72 40 (closed Friday evening, Sunday lunchtime, Saturday and public holidays)* Menu 41/64 €
♦ Chain hotel ♦ Business ♦ Design ♦
The scalloped façade of this hotel stands out amid the skyscrapers of La Défense. Spacious, well-equipped rooms, which have been refurbished in a more trendy style. Italian cuisine served in a modern setting. A relaxed atmosphere pervades the Italian Lounge.

FRANCE

Novotel La Défense 130

2 bd Neuilly – ✆ 01 41 45 23 23 – h0747@accor.com – Fax 01 41 45 23 24 – www.novotel.com VISA AE A1

280 rm – 105/320 € 105/450 €, 15 €

Rest – Menu 19/30 € – Carte 18/31 €

♦ Chain hotel ♦ Business ♦ Classic ♦

Sculpture and architecture: La Défense, a veritable open-air museum, is right at the foot of this hotel. Practical rooms, some overlooking Paris. The bar has a trendy new decor. Contemporary decor in the dining room, which also has a buffet area.

PARIS AIRPORTS

Orly

Hilton Orly rm 10/280 P VISA AE

✉ 94544 – ✆ 01 45 12 45 12 – rm.orly@hilton.com – Fax 01 45 12 45 00 – www.hilton.com

351 rm – 99/215 € 114/230 €, 19 €

Rest – Menu 35 € (weekdays) – Carte 30/44 €

♦ Chain hotel ♦ Business ♦ Functional ♦

The designer interior, discreet yet elegant bedrooms and state-of-the-art business facilities in this 1960s hotel make it a popular choice for corporate clients. Modern decor, brasserie-style dishes or buffet option at this restaurant.

Mercure rm 15/40 P VISA AE

✉ 94547 – ✆ 01 49 75 15 50 – h1246@accor.com – Fax 01 49 75 15 51

192 rm – 145 € 155 €, 13.50 €

Rest – Menu 24 € – Carte approx. 32 €

♦ Chain hotel ♦ Business ♦ Functional ♦

Convenient for travellers in need of a full-service hotel when they are between flights. Well-kept rooms. Trendy bistro setting, brasserie-style dishes and Mercure wine list.

Roissy-en-France

Z. I. Paris Nord II

Hyatt Regency rm rm 300

351 av. de la Pie – ✆ 01 48 17 12 34 – cdg@hyattintl.com – Fax 01 48 17 17 17 – www.paris.charlesdegaulle.hyatt.com P VISA AE

376 rm – 145/365 € 145/365 €, 26 € – 12 suites

Rest – Menu 46/65 € – Carte 51/68 €

♦ Chain hotel ♦ Business ♦ Modern ♦

Spectacular, contemporary architecture in a good location close to the airport. Large, stylish bedrooms equipped with ultra-modern facilities for its predominantly corporate guests. The Hyatt Regency dining area has a large glass-roof; buffets or classical menu.

à l'aérogare nº 2

Sheraton rm rm 2/65 P VISA AE

– ✆ 01 49 19 70 70 – Fax 01 49 19 70 71 – www.sheraton.com/parisairport

254 rm – 239/599 € 239/599 €, 30 €

Rest *Les Étoiles* – *✆ 01 41 84 64 54 (closed 21 July-26 August, Saturday, Sunday and public holidays)* Menu 57 € – Carte 77/88 €

Rest *Les Saisons* – Menu 47 € – Carte approx. 51 €

♦ Chain hotel ♦ Business ♦ Modern ♦

Leave your plane or train and take a trip on this "luxury liner" with its futuristic architecture. Decor by Andrée Putman, a view of the runways, absolute quiet and refined rooms. Les Étoiles offers modern cuisine and beautiful contemporary setting. Brasserie dishes at Les Saisons.

à Roissypole

Hilton

– ✆ 01 49 19 77 77 – cdghitwsal@hilton.com – Fax 01 49 19 77 78
385 rm – 149/509 € 149/509 €, 24 €
Rest *Le Gourmet* – ✆ 01 49 19 77 95 (closed July-August, 23-31 December, Saturday, Sunday and public holidays) Menu 47 €
Rest *Les Aviateurs* – ✆ 01 49 19 77 95 – Carte 30/60 €
♦ Chain hotel ♦ Business ♦ Modern ♦
Daring architecture, space and light are the main features of this hotel. Its ultra-modern facilities make it an ideal place in which to work and relax. Modern food is to be found at Le Gourmet. Côté Aviateurs, small choice of brasserie dishes.

Sofitel

West central zone – ✆ 01 49 19 29 29 – h0577@accor.com – Fax 01 49 19 29 00 – www.sofitel.com
344 rm – 275/555 € 320/640 €, 25 € – 4 suites
Rest *L'Escale* – Carte 25/72 €
♦ Chain hotel ♦ Business ♦ Modern ♦
A personal welcome, comfortable atmosphere, conference rooms, an elegant bar and well-looked-after rooms are the advantages of this hotel between two airport terminals. A restaurant with a nautical flavour and seafood. A pleasant port of call dedicated to the sea.

à Roissy-Ville

Courtyard by Marriott

allée du Verger – ✆ 01 34 38 53 53 – alexander.krips@courtyard.com – Fax 01 34 38 53 54
300 rm – 119/300 € 119/300 €, 20 € – 4 suites
Rest – Menu 35 € – Carte 32/54 €
♦ Business ♦ Modern ♦
Behind its colonnaded white façade, this establishment has modern facilities perfectly in tune with the requirements of businessmen transiting through Paris. Themed brasserie menu served in a large and carefully decorated dining room.

Millennium

allée du Verger – ✆ 01 34 29 33 33 – sales.cdg@mill-cop.com – Fax 01 34 29 03 05 – www.millenniumhotels.com
239 rm – 95/280 € 95/280 €, 20 €
Rest – Carte approx. 30 €
♦ Business ♦ Modern ♦
Bar, Irish pub, fitness centre, attractive swimming pool, conference rooms, and spacious bedrooms with one floor specially equipped for businessmen: a hotel with good facilities. International cuisine and brasserie buffet or fast food served at the bar.

Dorint by Novotel

– ✆ 01 30 18 20 00 – h5418@accor.com – Fax 01 34 29 95 60
288 rm – 185/485 € 190/495 €, 17 € – 1 suite
Rest – Menu 23 € – Carte 19/36 €
♦ Chain hotel ♦ Business ♦ Modern ♦
The latest arrival in the hotel zone at Roissy offers impressive services: extensive seminar facilities, kids' corner and comprehensive wellness centre. Lenôtre brasserie dishes available twenty-four hours a day at Novotel Café and Côté Jardin.

FRANCE

Country Inn and Suites

rm 15/95 P VISA MC AE

allée du Verger – ✆ 01 30 18 21 00
– info.paris@rezidorcountryinn.com – Fax 01 30 18 20 18
– www.countryinns.com/parisfra_cdg
180 rm – 135/400 € 135/400 €, 16 €
Rest – *(closed Sunday lunch and Saturday)* Carte 25/46 €

◆ Business ◆ Modern ◆

The former Château de Roissy, burnt down during the Revolution, provided the model for this hexagonal building with an interior garden. English-style bar. This restaurant offers a tasty combination of French and American dishes.

Mercure

rm 30/90 P VISA MC AE

allée des Vergers – ✆ 01 34 29 40 00 – h1245@accor.com – Fax 01 34 29 00 18
– www.mercure.com
203 rm – 120/180 € 130/190 €, 13 €
Rest – Menu 23 € – Carte 27/43 €

◆ Chain hotel ◆ Business ◆ Modern ◆

This hotel has a meticulous decor comprising Provençal style in the hall, old-fashioned zinc in the bar and spacious rooms in light wood. Traditional menu offered in a dining room adorned with a bakery and bread-themed gallery.

LYONS
LYON

Population (est. 2005): 468 000 (conurbation 1 449 000) – Altitude: 175m

DIAF / PHOTONONSTOP

Its favourable location at the confluence of two great waterways, the Rivers Saône and Rhône, gives Lyons, France's second city, a unique character. It is an industrial city specialising in metalworking and chemistry. It is also a university town and a world famous centre in the field of medicine. Its cuisine is renowned and it has a well-deserved reputation as one of the gastronomic centres in France. The city is a popular tourist destination.

Lyons has always been a prosperous city. Trade flourished during the Roman Empire and the Renaissance. The city took full advantage of its geographical situation as it lies on the road to Italy, between Central and Eastern France, and midway between northern France and the southern provinces. Christianity took hold in the 2C and several martyrs were put to death. In the Middle Ages, Lyons came under royal rule and the workers rebelled against the elected consuls. From the end of the 15C the city prospered with the organisation of fairs and the development of the banking sector. Artists, poets, writers and printers gave impetus to its social, intellectual and cultural life. In the 16C silk weaving was the major activity.

The spirit of the local people is embodied by the puppets, Guignol, his wife Madelon and his sparring partner Gnafron; the puppet shows are a Lyons tradition.

WHICH DISTRICT TO CHOOSE

The **city centre** from Place Bellecour to Place des Terreaux *Plan II* **F2** and the **old town** are the areas to choose for luxury accommodation. There are chain hotels around La Part-Dieu and Perrache stations and comfortable establishments in Rue Victor-Hugo *Plan II* **F3**, Rue de la Charité *Plan II* **F3**, along the quays near Place Bellecour and near the Opera *Plan II* **F1**.

It is unusual not to eat well in Lyons. The famous establishments in the city centre, in the old town and on the outskirts are the places to visit for

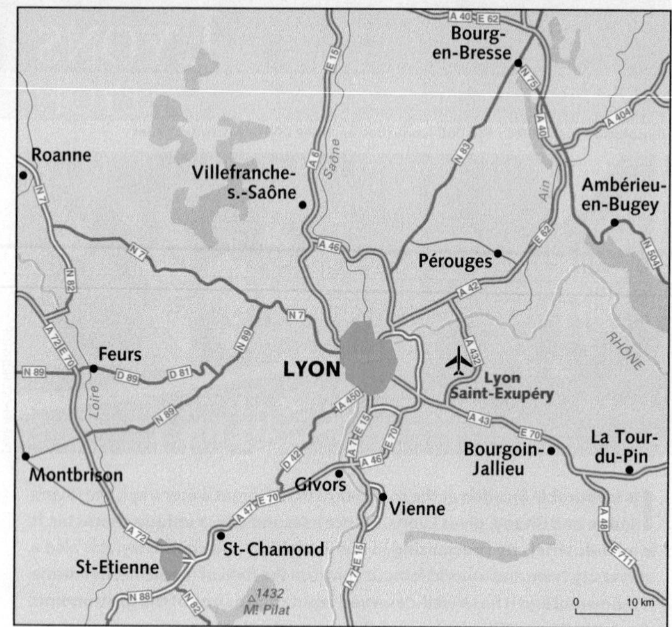

a gastronomic experience. A meal at one of the typical '**bouchons**' is a must to enjoy the hearty local specialities. **Brasseries** are also favourite haunts.

When going out **for a drink or for the evening**, make for the terraces lining Rue Ste-Catherine *Plan II* **F1**.

PRACTICAL INFORMATION

ARRIVAL – DEPARTURE

Lyon-Saint-Exupéry Airport – 27km (12mi) east of the city centre. ✆ 0826 800 826; www.lyon.aeroport.fr

From the airport to the city centre – By **express bus**: time: 20 min; fare €8.40 single, €14.90 return trip. ✆ 04 72 68 17. By **taxi**: approx. €36-40 (€50-55 between 7pm to 7am and Sun). GIE Aéroport ✆ 04 72 22 70 90.

Main Stations – La Part-Dieu Station *Plan II* **H3**: TGV high-speed trains; **Lyon-Perrache** *Plan II* **E3** TGV high-speed trains and regional destinations.

TRANSPORT

→ BUS, METRO, TRAM AND FUNICULAR

The 'Liberty' ticket (€4.30) is valid for 1 day for travel on the city's public transport network. A single ticket costs €1.50 and a book of 10 tickets €12.20.

→ TAXIS

Allow €10-15 for a short journey. Some taxis accept payment by credit card. Tips are not compulsory. *Espace Taxi* ✆ 04 78 27 31 31; *Lyon International Taxi* ✆ 04 78 88 16 16; *Allo Taxi* ✆ 04 78 28 23 23; *Taxi Lyonnais* ✆ 04 78 26 81 81.

USEFUL ADDRESSES

→ TOURIST OFFICE

Place Bellecour *Plan II* **F2**. ✆ 04 72 77 69 69; www.lyon-france.com; open 9am-7pm daily.

→ POST OFFICES

Opening times Mon-Fri 8am-noon and 2pm-6pm.

→ BANKS/CURRENCY EXCHANGE

Banks open Mon-Fri, 9am-noon and 2-5pm. There are cash dispensers (ATM), which require a PIN number, all over the city. Credit cards are widely accepted. Bureaux de change often charge high commissions.

→ EMERGENCY

Police ✆ **17,** Fire Brigade ✆ **18,** Medical assistance ✆ **15**.

EXPLORING LYONS

It is possible to visit the main sights and museums in two days.

Museums and other sights are usually open from 9-10am to 5.30-6pm. Some close on Mondays or Tuesdays and at lunchtime.

VISITING

Tour of the town centre (Péninsule) – The core of the city: from the shady Place Bellecour *Plan II* **F2** along Rue de la République to Place des Terreaux *Plan II* **F1**. Do not miss the **Musée des Tissus** devoted to the weaver's art and silk production in Lyons.

Musée des Beaux-Arts *Plan II* **F1** – Housed in Palais St-Pierre, the museum presents an excellent survey of art through the centuries.

Château Lumière *Plan I* **C2** – An elegant mansion, the former residence of the Lumière brothers: Institut Lumière, exhibition, performances.

Musée d'Art Contemporain *Plan III* **H1** – A display of modern art in a striking building.

Musée de l'Automobile Henri-Malartre – *At La Rochetaillée-sur-Saône.* A remarkable collection of vintage and racing cars, cycles, motor cycles and public transport vehicles.

Fourvière heights *Plan II* **E2** – **Basilique Notre-Dame**, Tour Métallique, archaeological site, museums, Roman theatres, aqueducts, mausoleums. Viewpoints from esplanade and observatory.

Tour of Old Lyons *Plan II* **E2** – Explore the St-Jean, St-Paul and St-Georges districts: the **'traboules' passageways**, squares and courtyards, fountains, **15-17C period mansions**, 12C church – Place St-Jean, Rue St-Jean, Rue des Trois-Maries, Place du Gouvernement, Place du Change, Rue Lainerie, Rue Juiverie, Rue du Bœuf, Place de la Trinité, Rue St-Georges, Montée du Gourguillon.

Tour of Croix-Rousse district *Plan II* **F1** – The **'traboules'**, the silk trade workshops (Maison des Canuts), Cour des Voraces, Amphithéâtre des Trois Gaules, Fresque des Lyonnais, Gros Caillou. View from Place Rouville.

Boat trips – On the Rhône and Saône from Quai des Célestins *Plan II* **F2**.

SHOPPING

Shops and malls usually open Mon-Fri, 9am-6.30pm, Sat 9am-5pm; many are open until 9pm on Thur and 7.30pm on Fri.

Le **Carré d'Or** between Place Bellecour *Plan II* **F2** and Place des Cordeliers is the area for **luxury and designer shops** (local designers Nathalie Chiaze, Max Chaoul, Azuleros). If you are keen on **antiques**, explore the **Quartier Auguste Comte** (Rue Auguste Comte *Plan II* **F3**, Rue de la Charité *Plan II* **F3**) and *Cité des Antiquaires*, 117 Boulevard Stalingrad. **Old-fashioned shops** (knives, hats etc.) are to be found in the arcade, **Le Passage de l'Argue**, between Rue de la République *Plan II* **F2** and Rue Édouard-Herriot *Plan II* **F1**. The pedestrian avenue running from Rue Victor-Hugo to Rue de la République is also worth a visit for **clothes and other goods**.

L'Atelier de Soierie, 33 Rue Romarin (silk and velvet fabric); *Chez Disagn' Cardelli*, 6 Rue St-Jean (music boxes, masks and puppets); *Bonnard*, 36 Rue Granette; *Reynon*, 13 Rue des Archers; *Pignol*, 8 Place Bellecour (Lyonnais specialities). *Voisin*, 28 Rue de la République (chocolates, candied fruit, confectionery).

MARKETS – **Marché de la Création**, Quai Romain Rolland *Plan II* **F2** (Sun 6am-1pm) – paintings, sculpture jewellery; **Marché de l'Artisanat**, Quai Fulchiron *Plan II* **E3** (Sun 7am-1pm) – crafts. **Puces du Canal**, 1 Rue du Canal *Plan I* **B1** (Thu-Sat 8am-noon, Sun 6am-1pm) – antiques. **Book sellers**, Quai de la Pêcherie *Plan II* **F2** (daily 9am-9pm). **Stamp market**, Place Bellecour *Plan II* **F2** (Sun). There are also traditional markets: **Halles de Lyon**, 102 Cours Lafayette *Plan III* **G3** (regional products and small taverns), Boulevard de la Croix-Rousse *Plan II* **F1** (Tue-Sun mornings), Quai St Antoine-Célestins *Plan II* **F2** (Tue-Sun mornings).

WHAT TO BUY – Silk goods, marionnettes and music boxes, fine foods, confectionery (coussins, cocons, quenelles, palets d'or).

ENTERTAINMENT

For listings of shows and entertainment consult *Lyon Poche*; www.lyonpoche.com

Opéra National de Lyon *Plan II* **F2**: opera, ballet, classical, jazz and world music.

Auditorium-Orchestre National de Lyon *Plan II* **F2**: concerts.

Théâtre National Populaire *Plan I* **C1**: contemporary plays.

Maison de la Danse *Plan I* **C2**: classical and modern dance.

Halle Tony-Garnier *Plan II* **B2**: shows and events.

Le Guignol de Lyon *Plan II* **F2**: shows for children and adults.

Au Pied dans l'Plat *Plan II* **E2**: cabaret.

NIGHTLIFE

Rue Ste-Catherine *Plan II* **F1** and **Rue Mercière** *Plan II* **F2** are particularly lively in the evenings. Jazz lovers should visit *Hot Club*, 26 Rue Lanterne, *Bar de la Tour Rose*, 22 Rue du Bœuf. *Le Cintra*, 43 Rue de la Bourse, is a smart piano-bar. Popular venues for dancing are *BC Blues*, 25 Place Carnot, *Fish Club*, 21 Quai Victor-Augagneur. *Ninkasi Ale House*, 267 Rue Marcel-Mérieux, is a trendy place with a micro-brewery, café, DJ evenings. Or while away the evening at *Casino Le Pharaon*, 70 Quai Charles-de-Gaulle or *Casino Le Lyon Vert*, 200 Avenue du Casino, La Tour-de-Salvagny.

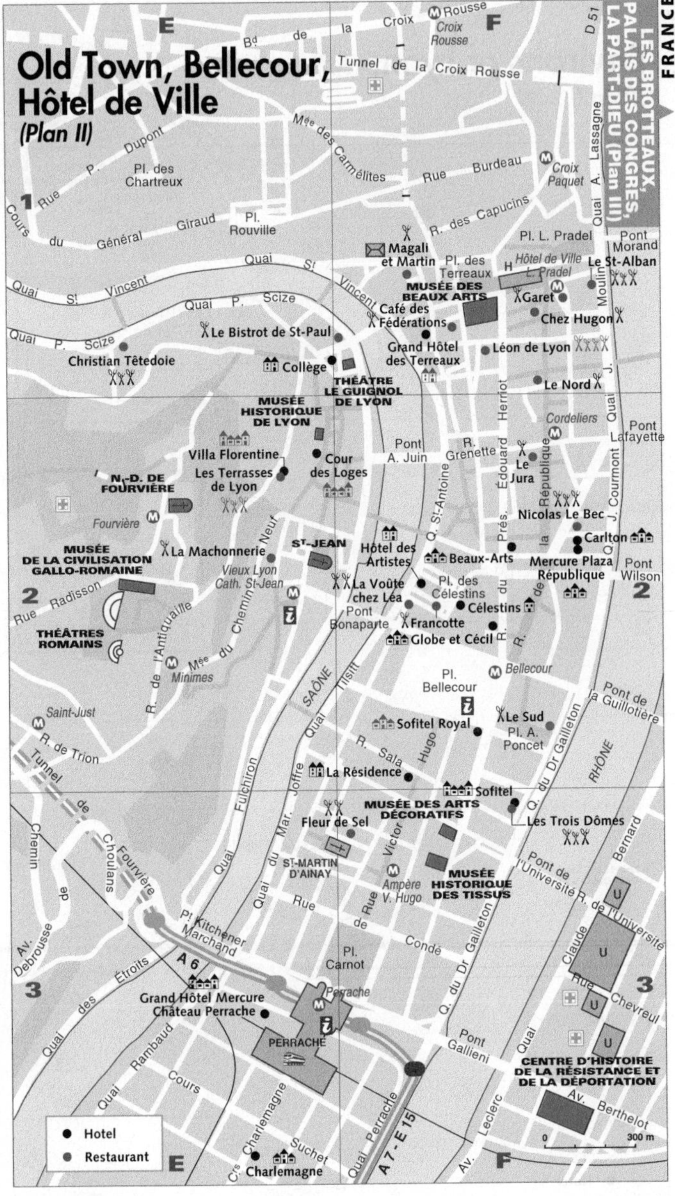
Old Town, Bellecour, Hôtel de Ville
(Plan II)
LES BROTTEAUX, PALAIS DES CONGRES, LA PART-DIEU (Plan III)
MUSÉE DES BEAUX ARTS
THÉATRE LE GUIGNOL DE LYON
MUSÉE HISTORIQUE DE LYON
N.-D. DE FOURVIÈRE
MUSÉE DE LA CIVILISATION GALLO-ROMAINE
THÉÂTRES ROMAINS
ST-JEAN
MUSÉE DES ARTS DÉCORATIFS
MUSÉE HISTORIQUE DES TISSUS
CENTRE D'HISTOIRE DE LA RÉSISTANCE ET DE LA DÉPORTATION
PERRACHE
Magali et Martin
Le St-Alban
Garet
Chez Hugon
Café des Fédérations
Le Bistrot de St-Paul
Grand Hôtel des Terreaux
Léon de Lyon
Christian Têtedoie
Collège
Le Nord
Villa Florentine
Cour des Loges
Les Terrasses de Lyon
Le Jura
Nicolas Le Bec
Carlton
La Machonnerie
Hôtel des Artistes
Beaux-Arts
Mercure Plaza République
La Voûte chez Léa
Célestins
Francotte
Globe et Cécil
Le Sud
Sofitel Royal
La Résidence
Sofitel
Les Trois Dômes
Fleur de Sel
Grand Hôtel Mercure Château Perrache
Charlemagne
Hotel
Restaurant
0
300 m

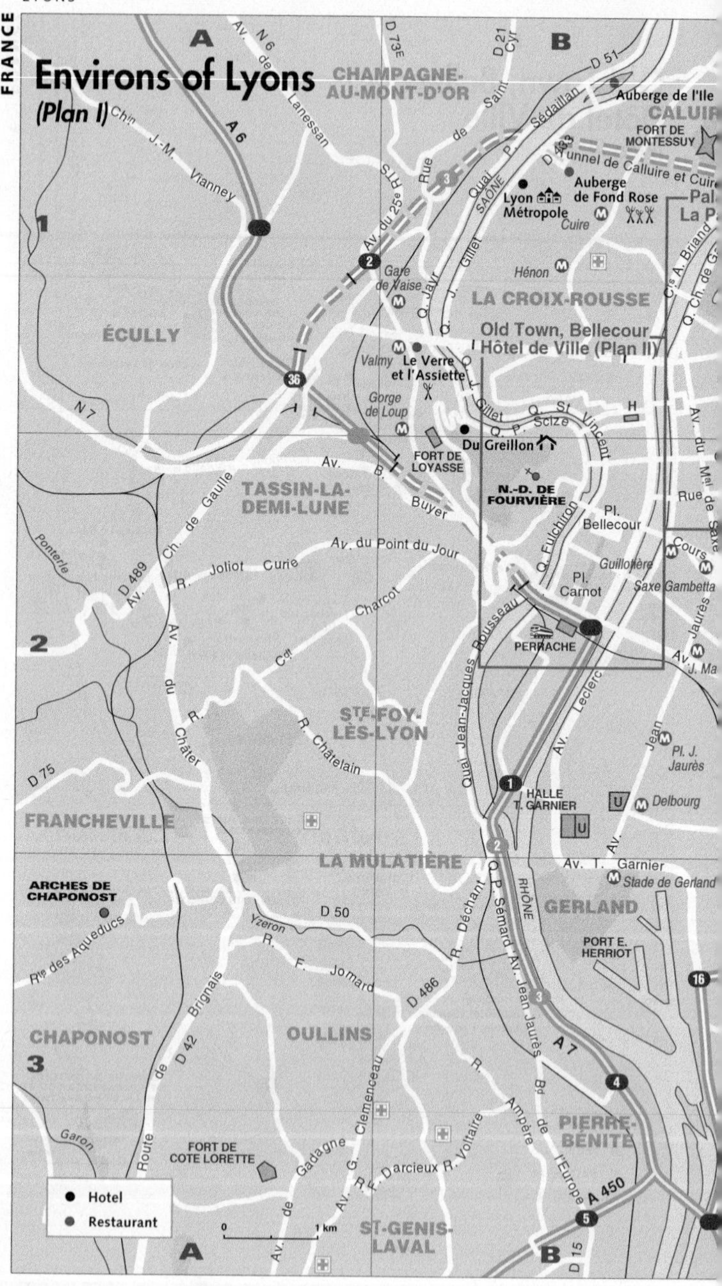
Environs of Lyons
(Plan I)
Hotel
Restaurant
ÉCULLY
TASSIN-LA-DEMI-LUNE
CHAMPAGNE-AU-MONT-D'OR
LA CROIX-ROUSSE
Old Town, Bellecour
Hôtel de Ville (Plan II)
STE-FOY-LÈS-LYON
FRANCHEVILLE
LA MULATIÈRE
ARCHES DE CHAPONOST
CHAPONOST
OULLINS
GERLAND
PIERRE-BÉNITE
ST-GENIS-LAVAL
FORT DE COTE LORETTE
FORT DE LOYASSE
N.-D. DE FOURVIÈRE
PERRACHE
HALLE T. GARNIER
PORT E. HERRIOT
FORT DE MONTESSUY
CALUIRE
Auberge de l'Ile
Auberge de Fond Rose
Lyon Métropole
Le Verre et l'Assiette
Du Greillon
Gare de Vaise
Valmy
Gorge de Loup
Cuire
Hénon
Pl. Bellecour
Pl. Carnot
Guillotière
Saxe Gambetta
Pl. J. Jaurès
Delbourg
Stade de Gerland
Tunnel de Calluire et Cuire
SAÔNE
RHÔNE
A6
A7
A 450
N 6
N 7
D 489
D 75
D 50
D 42
D 486
D 15
D 51
D 433
D 73E
D 21
0
1 km
A
B
1
2
3

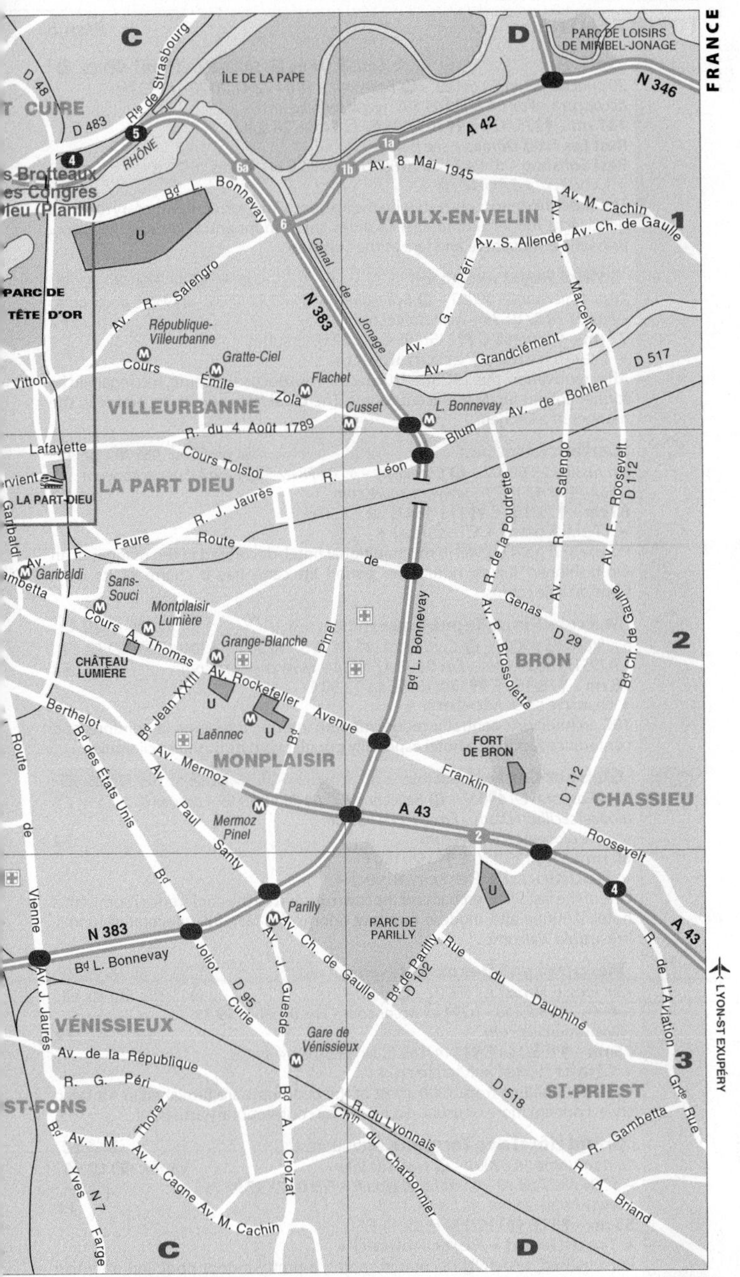
C
D
1
2
3
PARC DE LOISIRS DE MIRIBEL-JONAGE
ÎLE DE LA PAPE
N 346
A 42
Rte de Strasbourg
D 48
CUIRE
D 483
RHÔNE
Av. 8 Mai 1945
Av. M. Cachin
VAULX-EN-VELIN
Av. Ch. de Gaulle
Av. S. Allende
Bd L. Bonnevay
Canal de Jonage
N 383
Av. R. Salengro
PARC DE TÊTE D'OR
République-Villeurbanne
Gratte-Ciel
Cours Émile Zola
Flachet
Av. G. Péri
Av. P. Marcelin
Av. Grandclément
D 517
Vitton
VILLEURBANNE
Cusset
L. Bonnevay
Av. de Bohlen
R. du 4 Août 1789
Blum
Lafayette
Cours Tolstoï
R. Léon
LA PART DIEU
LA PART-DIEU
R. J. Jaurès
Av. F. Faure
Route de Genas
Garibaldi
Gambetta
Sans-Souci
Montplaisir Lumière
Cours A. Thomas
CHÂTEAU LUMIÈRE
Grange-Blanche
Pinel
Bd L. Bonnevay
R. de la Poudrette
Av. R. Salengo
Av. F. Roosevelt
D 112
Av. P. Brossolette
D 29
BRON
Bd Ch. de Gaulle
Av. Rockefeller
Avenue Franklin Roosevelt
Bd Jean XXIII
Laënnec
U
MONPLAISIR
FORT DE BRON
CHASSIEU
Berthelot
Bd des États Unis
Av. Mermoz
Av. Paul Santy
Mermoz Pinel
A 43
Route de Vienne
Bd I. Joliot Curie
D 95
Parilly
PARC DE PARILLY
Av. Ch. de Gaulle
Bd de Parilly
D 102
Rue du Dauphiné
R. de l'Aviation
N 383
Bd L. Bonnevay
Av. J. Jaurès
Av. J. Guesde
VÉNISSIEUX
Gare de Vénissieux
Av. de la République
R. G. Péri
D 518
ST-PRIEST
Grde Rue
ST-FONS
Thorez
Av. M.
Bd Yves Farge
N 7
Av. J. Cagne
Av. M. Cachin
Bd A. Croizat
R. du Lyonnais
Chin du Charbonnier
R. Gambetta
R. A. Briand
LYON-ST EXUPÉRY

FRANCE

TOWN CENTRE

Plan II

Sofitel rm rm 10/200 VISA AE

20 quai Gailleton ✉ 69002 – Ⓜ Bellecour – ✆ 04 72 41 20 20 – h0553@accor.com – Fax 04 72 40 05 50 – www.sofitel.com **F3**

137 rm – †275/420 € ††305/495 €, ☕ 24 € – 28 suites

Rest *Les Trois Dômes* – see below

Rest *Sofishop* – *✆ 04 72 41 20 80* – Menu 26 € bi – Carte 26/77 €

◆ Luxury ◆ Modern ◆

The cuboid exterior contrasts with the luxurious interior: contemporary rooms in good taste, modern conference facilities, smart shops and a hair-dressing salon. Brasserie atmosphere and fare at the Sofishop.

Sofitel Royal without rest VISA AE

20 pl. Bellecour ✉ 69002 – Ⓜ Bellecour – ✆ 04 78 37 57 31 – h2952@accor.com – Fax 04 78 37 01 36 – www.sofitel.com **F2**

77 rm – †180/465 € ††215/465 €, ☕ 22 € – 3 suites

◆ Traditional ◆ Personalised ◆

After renovation, this 19C hotel run by the Paul Bocuse Institute, has regained its former splendour. Magnificent rooms. The breakfast room is decorated in the manner of a kitchen.

Carlton without rest VISA AE

4 r. Jussieu ✉ 69002 – Ⓜ Cordeliers – ✆ 04 78 42 56 51 – h2950@accor.com – Fax 04 78 42 10 71 – www.mercure.com **F2**

83 rm – †79/156 € ††113/164 €, ☕ 12.50 €

◆ Traditional ◆ Classical ◆

Purple and gold prevail in this traditional hotel, decorated in the manner of an old-fashioned luxury hotel. The period lift cage has a charm of its own. Comfortable rooms.

Mercure Plaza République without rest

5 r. Stella ✉ 69002 – Ⓜ Cordeliers – ✆ 04 78 37 50 50 10/15 VISA AE

– h2951@accor.com – Fax 04 78 42 33 34 – www.mercure.com **F2**

78 rm – †78/150 € ††120/158 €, ☕ 12.50 €

◆ Business ◆ Modern ◆

19C architecture, central location, modern interior, full range of comforts and conference facilities: a hotel especially popular with its business clientele.

Globe et Cécil without rest 40 VISA AE

21 r. Gasparin ✉ 69002 – Ⓜ Bellecour – ✆ 04 78 42 58 95 – accueil@globeetcecilhotel.com – Fax 04 72 41 99 06 – www.globeetcecilhotel.com **F2**

60 rm ☕ – †125/130 € ††155/160 €

◆ Traditional ◆ Personalised ◆

One of the last silk-merchants of the town decorated the conference room of this hotel. Antique and modern furniture adorns the tastefully decorated rooms. Irresistible welcome.

Mercure Lyon Beaux-Arts without rest

75 r. Prés. E. Herriot ✉ 69002 – Ⓜ Cordeliers 15 VISA AE

– ✆ 04 78 38 09 50 – h2949@accor.com – Fax 04 78 42 19 19 – www.mercure.com **F2**

75 rm – †106/144 € ††114/160 €, ☕ 12.50 € – 4 suites

◆ Chain hotel ◆ Modern ◆

Beautiful building from 1900, most of the bedrooms are furnished in Art Deco style. Four are more unusual, decorated by contemporary artists.

Grand Hôtel des Terreaux without rest

16 r. Lanterne ✉ 69001 – Ⓜ Hôtel de Ville VISA AE

– ✆ 04 78 27 04 10 – ght@hotel-lyon.fr – Fax 04 78 27 97 75 – www.hotel-lyon.fr **F1**

53 rm – †85 € ††115/130 €, ☕ 11 €

◆ Traditional ◆ Personalised ◆

Personalised, tastefully decorated rooms, a pretty indoor pool and attentive service ensure that guests can relax to the full in this former 19C post house.

FRANCE

La Résidence without rest

18 r. V. Hugo ✉ 69002 – Ⓜ Bellecour – ☎ 04 78 42 63 28 – hotel-la-residence@wanadoo.fr – Fax 04 78 42 85 76 – www.hotel-la-residence.com F2

67 rm – 🚹75 € 🚹🚹75 €, ☕ 7 €

◆ Business ◆ Functional ◆

In a pedestrian street near Bellecour square, this hotel provides rooms and a lounge in a 1970s style. A few rooms are more elegant and graced with wainscoting.

Des Artistes without rest

8 r. G. André ✉ 69002 – Ⓜ Cordeliers – ☎ 04 78 42 04 88 – hartiste@club-internet.fr – Fax 04 78 42 93 76 – www.hoteldesartistes.fr F2

45 rm – 🚹80/138 € 🚹🚹90/144 €, ☕ 9 €

◆ Traditional ◆ Personalised ◆

The hotel is named after the "artistes" of the neighbouring Célestins theatre. Stylish rooms; a Cocteau style fresco adorns the breakfast room.

Célestins without rest

4 r. Archers ✉ 69002 – Ⓜ Guillotière – ☎ 04 72 56 08 98 – info@hotel-celestins.com – Fax 04 72 56 08 65 – www.hotelcelestins.com F2

20 rm – 🚹60/75 € 🚹🚹65/85 €, ☕ 8 €

◆ Functional ◆

Hotel occupying several floors in a residential building. Light rooms with simple furnishings; those at the front have a view over the Fourvière hillside.

Léon de Lyon (Lacombe)

1 r. Pleney ✉ 69001 – Ⓜ Hôtel de ville – ☎ 04 72 10 11 12 – leon@relaischateaux.com – Fax 04 72 10 11 13 – www.leondelyon.com

Closed 8-16 April, 29 July-27 August, Sunday and Monday F1

Rest – Menu 59 € (lunch), 118/150 € – Carte 96/118 €

Spec. Cochon fermier du Cantal, foie gras et oignons confits. Traditionnelle quenelle de brochet lyonnaise "revue et corrigée". Cinq petits desserts sur le thème de la praline de Saint-Genix.

◆ Formal ◆

The great Lyon tradition for food is alive and well in these wood-panelled dining rooms, decorated with paintings in honour of the kitchen apprentice. Splendid!

Les Trois Dômes – Hôtel Sofitel ≤ Lyon,

20 quai Gailleton (8th floor) ✉ 69002 – Ⓜ Bellecour – ☎ 04 72 41 20 97 – reservation@les-3-domes.com – Fax 04 72 40 05 50 – www.les-trois-domes.com

closed 13-17 July, 21 July-22 August, 17-26 February, Sunday and Monday F3

Rest – Menu 51 € (weekday lunch), 73/126 € bi – Carte 81/102 €

Spec. Millefeuille de crabe et avocat. Homard de Nouvelle-Ecosse à la verveine. Volaille de Bresse.

◆ Traditional ◆ Formal ◆

This restaurant offers a fine panoramic view from the top floor of the Sofitel hotel, where you can also enjoy delicious cuisine with regional touches.

Nicolas Le Bec

14 r. Grolée ✉ 69002 – Ⓜ Cordeliers – ☎ 04 78 42 15 00 – restaurant@nicolaslebec.com – Fax 04 72 40 98 97 – www.nicolaslebec.com

closed 1st-21 August, 1st-8 January, Sunday and Monday F2

Rest – Menu 48 € (weekday lunch), 98/138 € – Carte 81/136 €

Spec. Foie gras de canard à l'hibiscus. Pigeonneau à la royale (autumn). Caramel mou au beurre demi-sel.

◆ Design ◆

Restaurant in a modern setting decorated in shades of caramel and chocolate, serving refined and inventive cuisine. Top-notch French wine list.

FRANCE

XXX **Le St-Alban** A/C VISA MC

2 quai J. Moulin ✉ 69001 – Ⓜ Hôtel de ville – ✆ 04 78 30 14 89 – Fax 04 72 00 88 82
closed 25 July-25 August, 1st-10 January, Saturday lunch and Sunday **F1**
Rest – Menu 36/66 € – Carte 50/63 €
♦ Traditional ♦ Formal ♦
Silk squares depicting Lyon monuments enliven the chic interior of this vaulted dining room near the opera house. Classical cuisine with a contemporary touch.

XX **Fleur de Sel** VISA MC

3 r. Remparts d'Ainay ✉ 69002 – Ⓜ Ampère Victor Hugo – ✆ 04 78 37 40 37 – Fax 04 78 37 26 37
closed 14-20 May, August, 1st-6 January, Sunday and Monday **F3**
Rest – Menu 19/29 € – Carte 20/37 €
♦ Contemporary ♦ Cosy ♦
The light gently filters through the green and yellow curtains of this vast dining area. Well-spaced tables and modern seating. Personalised cooking, inspired by the flavours of Provence.

XX **La Voûte - Chez Léa** A/C VISA MC AE

11 pl. A. Gourju ✉ 69002 – Ⓜ Bellecour – ✆ 04 78 42 01 33 – Fax 04 78 37 36 41
closed Sun. **F2**
Rest – Menu 18 € (weekday lunch), 28/40 € – Carte 31/44 €
♦ Friendly ♦
This restaurant serves meals very much in line with the Lyon gastronomic tradition. Featuring three dining areas, recently redecorated.

X **Le Nord** A/C VISA MC AE

18 r. Neuve ✉ 69002 – Ⓜ Hôtel de ville – ✆ 04 72 10 69 69 – commercial@brasseries-bocuse.com – Fax 04 72 10 69 68 – www.bocuse.fr **F1**
Rest – Menu 22 € (weekdays)/27 € – Carte 25/49 €
♦ Traditional ♦ Brasserie ♦
"The North" is proud of its speciality - Alsatian choucroute from eastern France. Authentic 1900s brasserie decor: wine-coloured banquettes, colourful tile floors, wood panelling and globe lamps.

X **Le Sud** A/C VISA MC AE

11 pl. Antonin Poncet ✉ 69002 – Ⓜ Bellecour – ✆ 04 72 77 80 00 – Fax 04 72 77 80 01 – www.bocuse.fr **F2**
Rest – Menu 22 € (weekdays)/27 € – Carte 27/48 €
♦ Traditional ♦ Brasserie ♦
"The South" is another of chef Paul Bocuse's cardinal points, this one specialising in "sunny cuisine", in a bright and youthful ambience. Almost like being there...

X **Francotte** A/C VISA MC AE

8 pl. des Célestins ✉ 69002 – Ⓜ Bellecour – ✆ 04 78 37 38 64 – infos@francotte.fr – Fax 04 78 38 20 35 – www.francotte.fr
Closed 31 July-15 August, Sunday and Monday **F2**
Rest – Menu 22/31 € – Carte 27/44 €
♦ Brasserie ♦ Neighbourhood ♦
This restaurant next to the Célestins theatre in a bistro setting serves brasserie-style cuisine. Breakfasts served in the morning; tea room in the afternoon.

BOUCHONS *Regional wine tasting and local cuisine in a typical Lyonnais atmosphere*

X **Daniel et Denise** A/C VISA MC AE

156 r. Créqui ✉ 69003 – Ⓜ Place Guichard – ✆ 04 78 60 66 53 – Fax 04 78 60 66 53 – Closed August, 23 December-3 January, Saturday, Sunday and public holidays – **Rest** *– Carte 27/36 €* *Plan III* **G3**
♦ Lyons cuisine ♦ Bistro ♦
The former delicatessen provides an attractive setting – smooth, time-worn surfaces, old posters and photographs, chequered tablecloths. Generous helpings of tasty Lyon specialities.

Garet

A/C VISA MC AE

7 r. Garet ✉ 69001 – Ⓜ Hôtel de ville – ☎ 04 78 28 16 94 – legaret@wanadoo.fr – Fax 04 72 00 06 84

closed 1st-8 May, 20 July-19 August, 18-24 February, Saturday and Sunday

Rest – *(pre-book)* Menu 18 € (lunch)/22 € – Carte 19/35 € **F1**

♦ Lyons cuisine ♦ Bistro ♦

Locals in shirtsleeves, coveralls, or business suits mingle here to enjoy the traditional dishes ... and never count the calories!

Chez Hugon

VISA MC

12 r. Pizay ✉ 69001 – Ⓜ Hôtel de ville – ☎ 04 78 28 10 94 – Fax 04 78 28 10 94

Closed August, Saturday and Sunday **F1**

Rest – *(pre-book)* Menu 23/33 €

♦ Lyons cuisine ♦ Bistro ♦

You can watch the chef stirring the blanquette de veau in this warm and lively "bouchon". Plenty of good cheer for all!

Café des Fédérations

A/C VISA MC

8 r. Major Martin ✉ 69001 – Ⓜ Hôtel de ville – ☎ 04 78 28 26 00 – yr@lesfedeslyon.com – Fax 04 72 07 74 52 – www.lesfedeslyon.com

closed 23 December-2 January, 21 July-20 August, Saturday and Sunday **F1**

Rest – *(pre-book)* Menu 20 € (lunch)/24 €

♦ Lyons cuisine ♦ Bistro ♦

Checked tablecloths, tables and guests close together, giant sausages hanging above the counter and copious regional cooking: a genuine "bouchon" for sure!

Le Jura

VISA MC

25 r. Tupin ✉ 69002 – Ⓜ Cordeliers – ☎ 04 78 42 20 57

closed August, Monday from September to May, Saturday from May to September and Sunday **F2**

Rest – *(pre-book)* Menu 20 € – Carte 28/32 €

♦ Lyons cuisine ♦ Bistro ♦

Do not be misled by the sign: this is an authentic "bouchon", the 1930s setting scrupulously preserved, serving typical dishes of Lyon.

OLD TOWN *Plan II*

Villa Florentine

< Lyon, A/C 20 P VISA MC AE

25 montée St-Barthélémy ✉ 69005 – Ⓜ Fourvière – ☎ 04 72 56 56 56 – florentine@relaischateaux.com – Fax 04 72 40 90 56 – www.villaflorentine.com **E2**

20 rm – †155/430 € ††155/430 €, ☐ 22 € – 8 suites

Rest ***Les Terrasses de Lyon*** – see below

♦ Luxury ♦ Personalised ♦

On the Fourvière hill, this Renaissance-inspired abode commands a matchless view of the town. The interior sports an elegant blend of old and new.

Cour des Loges

A/C rm 15/40 VISA MC AE

6 r. Boeuf ✉ 69005 – Ⓜ Vieux Lyon Cathédrale Saint Jean – ☎ 04 72 77 44 44 – contact@courdesloges.com – Fax 04 72 40 93 61 – www.courdesloges.com **E2**

52 rm – †240/290 € ††240/290 €, ☐ 27 € – 10 suites

Rest ***Les Loges*** – *(open October-April) (dinner only)* Menu 55/80 € – Carte 69/82 €

♦ Luxury ♦ Personalised ♦

The astonishing decoration of a group of 14C and 18C houses set around a splendid galleried courtyard was designed by contemporary designers and artists. At Les Loges, in the winter, creative cuisine and decor with a personal touch.

FRANCE

Collège without rest

5 pl. St-Paul ✉ 69005 – Ⓜ Vieux Lyon Cathédrale Saint Jean – ☎ 04 72 10 05 05 – contact@college-hotel.com – Fax 04 78 27 98 84 – www.college-hotel.com

39 rm – 105/125 € 125/140 €, ☕ 11 € **E1**

♦ Business ♦ Minimalist ♦

Take a trip down memory lane: old-fashioned school desks, a pommel horse and geography maps. The rooms are white, resolutely modern, with balcony or terrace.

Les Terrasses de Lyon – Hôtel Villa Florentine

25 montée St-Barthélémy ✉ 69005 – Ⓜ Fourvière – ☎ 04 72 56 56 56 – lesterrassesdelyon@villaflorentine.com – Fax 04 72 40 90 56 – www.villaflorentine.com **E2**

Rest – Menu 45 € (weekday lunch except Monday)/98 € – Carte 64/87 €

Spec. Médaillon de homard breton poêlé. Saint-Pierre cuit au sautoir. Côte de veau de lait poêlée, timbale de macaroni.

♦ Contemporary ♦ Formal ♦

Choose between the former nuns' dining hall, stunning glass roof and panoramic terrace: three elegant settings offering lovely, modern food.

Christian Têtedoie

54 quai Pierre Scize ✉ 69005 – ☎ 04 78 29 40 10 – restaurant@tetedoie.com – Fax 04 72 07 05 65 – www.tetedoie.com – closed 29 July-19 August, 18-24 February, Monday lunch, Saturday lunch and Sunday **E1**

Rest – Menu 44/110 € bi – Carte 62/74 €

Spec. Cromesquis de foie gras au jus de viande. Pigeonnneau rôti aux raisins confits. Gâteau de févettes à la sarriette.

♦ Traditional ♦ Formal ♦

Behind this elegant façade is a dining room with modern decor in subtle yellow tones. Some tables have a view of the Saône River. Contemporary cuisine and wine display cabinet.

La Machonnerie

36 r. Tramassac ✉ 69005 – Ⓜ Ampère Victor Hugo – ☎ 04 78 42 24 62 – felix@lamachonnerie.com – Fax 04 72 40 23 32 – www.lamachonnerie.com Closed 15-30 July, Sunday and lunch except Saturday **E2**

Rest – *(pre-book)* Menu 20/43 € bi – Carte 26/47 €

♦ Lyons cuisine ♦ Rustic ♦

The tradition of the Lyon "mâchon" has been respected in this restaurant: informal service, a friendly atmosphere and authentic cuisine.

Le Bistrot de St-Paul

2 quai Bondy ✉ 69005 – Ⓜ Vieux Lyon Cathédrale Saint Jean – ☎ 04 78 28 63 19 – Fax 04 78 28 63 19

Closed 1st-6 May, August, Saturday lunch and Sunday **F1**

Rest – Menu 13 € (weekday lunch), 19/29 € – Carte 29/34 €

♦ South-western France ♦

Cassoulet, duck breast, Bordeaux and Cahors wines, etc.: the essence of south-west France in this friendly bistro on an embankment of the Saône.

PERRACHE

Plan II

Grand Hôtel Mercure Château Perrache

12 cours Verdun ✉ 69002 – Ⓜ Perrache 10/200 *– ☎ 04 72 77 15 00 – h1292@accor.com – Fax 04 78 37 06 56 – www.mercure.com* **E3**

111 rm – 142/185 € 157/197 €, ☕ 13.50 € – 2 suites

Rest ***Les Belles Saisons*** – *(closed 31 July-21 August and lunch Saturday)* Menu 33 €

♦ Traditional ♦ Art Deco ♦

This hotel built in 1900 has partially conserved its Art Nouveau style: intricate wood carving in the lobby and period furniture in some of the rooms and suites. The full effect of the Majorelle style is reflected in the superb restaurant, Les Belles Saisons.

Charlemagne rm 10/120 VISA AE

23 Cours Charlemagne ✉ 69002 – Perrache – ✆ 04 72 77 70 00 – charlemagne@hotel-lyon.fr – Fax 04 78 42 94 84 – www.charlemagne-hotel.fr **E3**

116 rm – 80/155 € 85/170 €, 10 €

Rest – *(closed 29 July-27 August, Saturday and Sunday)* Menu 22 € – Carte approx. 27 €

♦ Business ♦ Modern ♦

Two buildings, home to renovated, comfortable and tastefully appointed rooms; a business centre; winter-garden style breakfast room. Modern restaurant with a pleasant terrace in summer and unpretentious fare.

LES BROTTEAUX - LA PART-DIEU *Plan III*

Hilton rm rm 10/280 VISA AE

70 quai Ch. de Gaulle ✉ 69006 – ✆ 04 78 17 50 50 – rm-lyon@hilton.com – Fax 04 78 17 52 52 – www.hilton.com **H1**

198 rm – 107/422 € 107/422 €, 23 €

Rest *Blue Elephant* – *✆ 04 78 17 50 00 (closed 20 July-20 August, Saturday lunch and Sunday)* Menu 28 € (lunch), 42/55 € – Carte 29/44 €

Rest *Brasserie* – *✆ 04 78 17 51 00* – Menu 22 € (lunch)/29 € bi – Carte 36/51 €

♦ Chain hotel ♦ Modern ♦

This impressive modern hotel built in brick and glass is equipped with a comprehensive business centre. Fully equipped bedrooms and apartments facing the Tête d'Or park or the Rhône. Thai specialities and decor at the Blue Elephant. Traditional food is to be found at the Brasserie.

Radisson SAS < Lyon and Rhône valley, rm 10/120 VISA AE

129 r. Servient (32nd floor) ✉ 69003 – Part Dieu – ✆ 04 78 63 55 00 – info.lyon@radissonsas.com – Fax 04 78 63 55 20 **H3**

245 rm – 120/250 € 120/270 €, 20 €

Rest *L'Arc-en-Ciel* – *(closed 15 to 25 July, Saturday lunch and Sunday)* Menu 40/57 € – Carte 63/81 €

Rest *Bistrot de la Tour* – (ground floor) *(closed Sunday lunch and Saturday)* Menu 19 € – Carte 26/47 €

♦ Business ♦ Functional ♦

At the top of the "pencil" (100m high), interior layout inspired by the houses of old Lyons: interior courtyards and superimposed galleries. Exceptional view from some rooms. You are guaranteed a view at the Arc-en-Ciel, located on the 32nd floor of the tower! The Bistrot is situated on the ground floor.

La Reine Astrid rm VISA AE

✉ 69006 – Foch – ✆ 04 72 82 18 00 – infora@warwickhotels.com – Fax 04 78 93 80 06 – www.warwickastrid.com **G2**

11 rm – 215 € 215 € – 77 suites – 265/460 €, 18 €

Rest *Le Lounge* – Menu 25 € – Carte 35/55 €

♦Business♦

The proportions of these rooms are such that they are really suites. View of the Tête d'Or park or the private garden. Space, elegance and high-quality fixtures and fittings.

Novotel La Part-Dieu rm rm 15/70 VISA AE

47 bd Vivier-Merle ✉ 69003 – Part Dieu – ✆ 04 72 13 51 51 – h0735@accor.com – Fax 04 72 13 51 99 – www.novotel.com **H3**

124 rm – 115/150 € 123/150 €, 13 €

Rest – *(closed Friday dinner, Saturday and Sunday)* Menu 24 € – Carte 24/36 €

♦ Business ♦ Functional ♦

Two minutes from the railway station. The rooms are being progressively revamped in line with latest Novotel standards. Lounge-bar with an Internet area. This Novotel restaurant is practical for business travellers with a train to catch or between meetings.

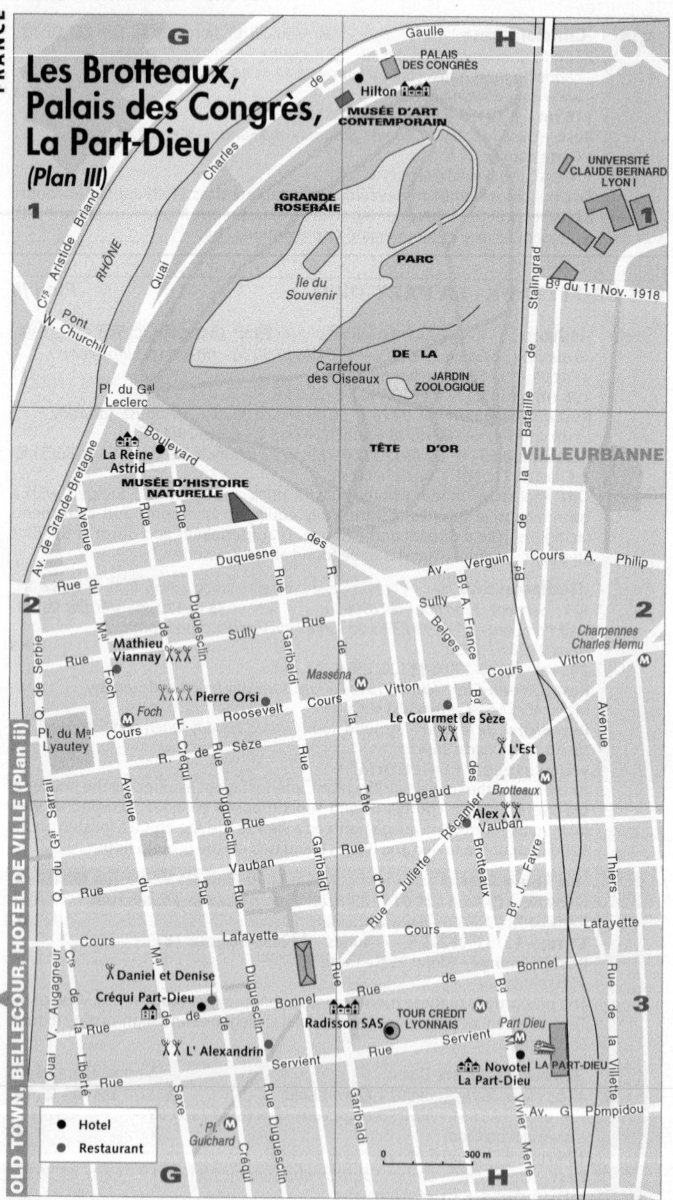

Les Brotteaux, Palais des Congrès, La Part-Dieu
(Plan III)
PALAIS DES CONGRÈS
Hilton
MUSÉE D'ART CONTEMPORAIN
UNIVERSITÉ CLAUDE BERNARD LYON I
GRANDE ROSERAIE
Île du Souvenir
PARC DE LA TÊTE D'OR
Carrefour des Oiseaux
JARDIN ZOOLOGIQUE
RHÔNE
Pl. du Gal Leclerc
La Reine Astrid
MUSÉE D'HISTOIRE NATURELLE
VILLEURBANNE
Charpennes Charles Hernu
Mathieu Viannay
Pierre Orsi
Masséna
Foch
Pl. du Mal Lyautey
Le Gourmet de Sèze
L'Est
Brotteaux
Alex
Daniel et Denise
Créqui Part-Dieu
L' Alexandrin
Radisson SAS
TOUR CRÉDIT LYONNAIS
Part Dieu
Novotel La Part-Dieu
LA PART-DIEU
Pl. Guichard
Hotel
Restaurant
0 300 m
OLD TOWN, BELLECOUR, HOTEL DE VILLE (Plan ii)

Créqui Part-Dieu

37 r. Bonnel ✉ 69003 – Ⓜ Place Guichard – ✆ 04 78 60 20 47 – inforesa@hotel-crequi.com – Fax 04 78 62 21 12 **G3**

46 rm – 🛉70/147 € 🛉🛉80/157 €, ☕ 11.50 € – 3 suites

Rest – *(closed 31 July-21 August, Saturday and Sunday out of season)* Menu 30 € – Carte 26/41 €

♦ Business ♦ Functional ♦

The establishment is located opposite the law court district. The renovated rooms are decorated in warm tones; those in the new wing are particularly modern in style.

Pierre Orsi

3 pl. Kléber ✉ 69006 – Ⓜ Masséna – ✆ 04 78 89 57 68 – orsi@relaischateaux.com – Fax 04 72 44 93 34 – www.pierreorsi.com

closed Sunday and Monday except public holidays **G2**

Rest – Menu 60 € (weekday lunch), 85/115 € – Carte 68/105 €

Spec. Ravioles de foie gras de canard au jus de porto et truffes. Homard acadien en carapace. Pigeonneau en cocotte aux gousses d'ail confites.

♦ Traditional ♦ Formal ♦

This old building is home to an elegant restaurant and rose garden terrace. Fine cuisine from Lyon and a 200-year old vaulted cellar.

Mathieu Viannay

47 av. Foch ✉ 69006 – Ⓜ Foch – ✆ 04 78 89 55 19 – Fax 04 78 89 08 39

closed 30 July-26 August, 25 February-2 March, Saturday and Sunday **G2**

Rest – Menu 33 € (lunch), 49/85 € – Carte 59/78 €

Spec. Fricassée d'ormeaux et pignons de pin, émulsion de champignons (October-May). Fricassée de homard et ris de veau de lait du Limousin, tombée de petites feuilles. Madeleines tièdes au miel, glace au fromage blanc.

♦ Contemporary ♦ Fashionable ♦

Resolutely modern dining room, with parquet flooring, colourful seating and an original chandelier created by the Lyon designer, Alain Vavro. Delicious contemporary cuisine.

L'Alexandrin (Alexanian)

83 r. Moncey ✉ 69003 – Ⓜ Place Guichard – ✆ 04 72 61 15 69 – lalexandrin@lalexandrin.com – Fax 04 78 62 75 57 – www.lalexandrin.com

Closed 17-21 May, 28 July-22 August, 1st-5 November, 23 December-3 January, Saturday lunch from May to August, Sunday, Monday and public holidays **G3**

Rest – Menu 38 € (weekday lunch), 60/80 €

Spec. Cocotte de légumes. Mousseline de brochet en quenelle. Aubergine à l'épaule d'agneau confite, riz pilaw à l'arménienne (summer).

♦ Traditional ♦ Cosy ♦

Modern, chic decor with friendly service, a good selection of Côtes-du-Rhône wines and original cuisine that gives a new lease of life to traditional recipes. Popular with Lyon's jet set.

Le Gourmet de Sèze (Mariller)

129 r. Sèze ✉ 69006 – Ⓜ Masséna – ✆ 04 78 24 23 42 – legourmetdeseze@wanadoo.fr – Fax 04 78 24 66 81

Closed 20 July-21 August, 1st-3 January, 24 February-3 March, Sunday, Monday and public holidays **H2**

Rest – *(number of covers limited, pre-book)* Menu 37/64 €

Spec. Croustillants de pieds de cochon. Saint-Jacques d'Erquy (October-April). Grand dessert.

♦ Traditional ♦ Cosy ♦

Smart, small restaurant and classical cooking intelligently brought up-to-date : the gourmets of the Rue de Sèze are not the only ones to be beguiled.

FRANCE

XX **Alex**

44 bd Brotteaux ✉ 69006 – Ⓜ Brotteaux – ✆ 04 78 52 30 11 – chez.alex@club-internet.fr – Fax 04 78 52 34 16
closed August, Saturday lunch in July, Sunday and Monday **H3**
Rest – Menu 22 € (weekday lunch), 26/55 € – Carte approx. 51 €
◆ Innovative ◆ Design ◆
Restaurant in a smart, refined setting boldly allying colours, designer furniture and contemporary artworks. Fine cuisine for the modern palate.

X **L'Est**

Gare des Brotteaux, 14 pl. J. Ferry ✉ 69006 – Ⓜ Brotteaux – ✆ 04 37 24 25 26 – Fax 04 37 24 25 25 – www.bocuse.fr **H2**
Rest – Menu 22 € (weekdays)/27 € – Carte 27/50 €
◆ Bistro ◆ Fashionable ◆
Old station converted into a trendy brasserie. Model trains and cooking from the continents: gourmet globe-trotters, all aboard!

AROUND LYONS *Plan I*

Lyon Métropole rm 10/200

85 quai J. Gillet ✉ 69004 – ✆ 04 72 10 44 44 – metropole@lyonmetropole-concorde.com – Fax 04 72 10 44 42 – www.lyonmetropole-concorde.com **B1**
118 rm – †160/250 € ††160/250 €, ☕ 23 €
Rest ***Brasserie Lyon Plage*** – ✆ 04 72 10 44 30 – Menu 25 € – Carte 33/49 €
◆ Business ◆ Modern ◆
This 1980s hotel, reflected in the Olympic swimming pool, offers a superb spa, fitness facilities, tennis and squash courts, as well as golf practice areas. Modern rooms. A blue interior and terrace by the water at the Brasserie Lyon Plage.

Du Greillon without rest

12 montée du Greillon ✉ 69009 Lyon – ✆ 06 08 22 26 33 – contact@legreillon.com – Fax 04 72 29 10 97 – www.legreillon.com **B1**
closed 1st-12 August and 18-24 February
5 rm ☕ – †78/92 € ††85/100 €
◆ Personalised ◆
The former property of sculptor J. Chinard has been turned into a guesthouse. Pretty rooms, old furniture and ornaments, gorgeous garden and superb view of the Saône and Croix-Rousse.

XXX **Auberge de Fond Rose** (Vignat)

23 quai G. Clemenceau ✉ 69300 – ✆ 04 78 29 34 61 – contact@aubergedefondrose.com – Fax 04 72 00 28 67 – www.aubergedefondrose.com
Closed 15 February-11 March, Sunday dinner and Monday except public holidays **B1**
Rest – Menu 38 € bi (weekday lunch), 51/78 € – Carte 69/79 €
Spec. Mesclun de langoustines aux céréales et citron confit. Féra du lac Léman au caviar d'aubergine. Suprême de pigeonneau cuit dans la rôtissoire, jus aux olives.
◆ Traditional ◆ Formal ◆
This grand 1920s house is surrounded by a shady garden with flowers. Dining area with fireplace and peaceful terrace, serving good traditional cuisine.

XX **Auberge de l'Ile** (Ansanay-Alex) (dinner)

sur l'Ile Barbe (On Barbe Island) ✉ 69009 – ✆ 04 78 83 99 49 – info@aubergedelile.com – Fax 04 78 47 80 46 – www.aubergedelile.com
closed Sunday and Monday **B1**
Rest – Menu 60 € (weekday lunch), 90/120 €
Spec. Gelée d'écrevisses et pêches blanches, lait d'amandes frappé (spring). Bar en écaille de cèpes, sabayon au jus de cèpes (autumn). Glace réglisse, cornet de pain d'épice.
◆ Contemporary ◆ Friendly ◆
This charming restaurant is set in a 17C building on an island in the middle of the Saône River. Refined, modern cuisine is served in the characterful (non-smoking) dining area.

Le Verre et l'Assiette

20 Grande rue de Vaise ✉ 69009 – ✆ 04 78 83 32 25
– leverreetlassiette@free.fr
– Fax 04 37 46 09 34
Closed 28 July-19 August, dinner except Thursday and Friday, Saturday, Sunday and public holidays **B1**
Rest – Menu 21/31 €
♦ Bistro ♦ Classic ♦
In a lively street in Vaise, this small, attractive bistro serves standard dishes with exotic touches in a contemporary atmosphere with a décor combining wood and leather.

Magali et Martin

11 rue des Augustins ✉ 69001 – Ⓜ Place des Terreaux – ✆ 04 72 00 88 01
closed 6-26 August, 24 December-6 January, Sunday lunch and Saturday **F1**
Rest – Menu 17 € – Carte 22/35 €
♦ Contemporary ♦ Friendly ♦
Magali is in charge of welcoming guests and advising them on their choice of wine. Martin for his part is responsible for the tasty cuisine inspired by local market produce. A winning duet!

Collonges-au-Mont-d'Or

Paul Bocuse

Pont de Collonges (North: 12 km on the banks of the Saône (D 433, D 51)) ✉ 69660 – ✆ 04 72 42 90 90
– paul.bocuse@bocuse.fr – Fax 04 72 27 85 87
– www.bocuse.fr
Rest – Menu 115/195 € – Carte 98/157 €
Spec. Soupe aux truffes noires VGE. Rouget barbet en écailles de pommes de terre. Volaille de Bresse en vessie "Mère Fillioux".
♦ Traditional ♦ Formal ♦
The colourful and elegant Paul Bocuse restaurant serves historic dishes to an international clientele. Paintings of the great chefs adorn the courtyard.

Charbonnières-les-Bains

Le Pavillon de la Rotonde

10/30

au Casino Le Lyon Vert
– ✆ 04 78 87 79 79 – contact@pavillon-rotonde.com
– Fax 04 78 87 79 78 – www.pavillon-rotonde.com
closed 22 July-23 August
16 rm – †295 € ††525 €, ☕ 24 €
Rest ***La Rotonde*** – see below
♦ Luxury ♦ Design ♦
A stone's throw from the casino, a luxurious hotel with contemporary decor and discreet Art Deco touches. Spacious rooms with terrace giving onto the gardens. Heated indoor swimming pool and spa.

La Rotonde

au Casino Le Lyon Vert ✉ 69890 La Tour de Salvagny – ✆ 04 78 87 00 97
– restaurant-rotonde@g-partouche.fr – Fax 04 78 87 81 39
– www.restaurant-rotonde.com
closed 22 July-23 August, Sunday and Monday
Rest – Menu 40 € (weekday lunch), 85/140 € – Carte 93/164 €
Spec. Il était une fois... quatre foies pressés. Tajine de homard entier aux petits farcis. Cannelloni de chocolat amer à la glace de crème brûlée.
♦ Innovative ♦ Formal ♦
A renowned gourmet restaurant on the first floor of the famous casino, under the sign of Lady Luck since 1882. An elegant Art Deco-style dining room enlivened with superb flower arrangements, opening onto the gardens.

STRASBOURG

STRASBOURG

Population (est. 2004) : 273 100 (conurbation 427 300) – Altitude: 143m

R. Mattès / MICHELIN

Strasbourg's favourable location as a major communications hub linking the Mediterranean with the Rhineland, Central Europe, the North Sea and the Baltic, has shaped its character. It is an outgoing city as befits its role as the seat of the Council of Europe and other European institutions. Visitors will be charmed by the attractive historic district with its elegant old houses and mansions surrounded by the canal and the River Ill. Strasbourg is also famous as a gastronomic centre.

From its beginnings as a small Roman town, it rapidly became a prosperous city and a meeting-point of different peoples. It remained a free city within the Holy Roman Empire but was annexed to France in 1681. It is famous for the Strasbourg Oaths of 842; this is considered to be the oldest document in a Romance language which was to evolve into modern French. Strasbourg has suffered a varied fate during the wars but now the institutions set up in the city champion reconciliation and human rights. Its famous sons inlude Frédéric de Dietrich, the mayor who commissioned the French national anthem, La Marseillaise; Gustave Doré, the caricaturist and illustrator; Jean Arp, the avant-garde painter.

WHICH DISTRICT TO CHOOSE

In the old city, you will find elegant **accommodation** in period houses and mansions which have been turned into hotels in the cathedral area *Plan II* **G2** and in the Petite France *Plan II* **F2**. There are comfortable modern, business hotels near the Palais de l'Europe *Plan I* **C1** and Palais des Droits de l'Homme *Plan I* **D1**.

There are highly-prized **restaurants** around the cathedral, in the Petite France district and on the outskirts of the city *(see listings in the guide)* and numerous excellent establishments along the canal and river banks. To sample the hearty Alsatian cuisine – Baeckeoffe, flammekueche, pot-au-feu with bacon and sausages, potato pancakes, quenelles – and delightful Alsatian wines – Riesling, Sylvaner, Muscat, Pinot Blanc, Gewurztraminer – beers and fruit-flavoured liqueurs in the convivial atmosphere of the typical **Winstubs** (wine bars), large **brasseries** and **bierstubs**, try *Maison Kammerzell*, 16 Place de la Cathédrale, *La Maison des Tanneurs*, 42 Rue du Bain-aux-Plantes, *À l'Ancienne Douane*, 6 Rue de la Douane, *Le Clou*, 3 Rue du Chaudron, *Gurtlerhorf*, 13 Place de la Cathédrale. Tea rooms and cake shops serve delicious cakes such as kougelhopf.

PRACTICAL INFORMATION

ARRIVAL – DEPARTURE

Strasbourg-Entzheim International Airport – 12 km (7.5 mi) from the city centre. ✆ 03 88 64 67 67; www.strasbourg.aeroport.fr

From the airport to the city centre – By **train** to Central Station: from Entzheim Station (5min on foot from airport) regular services, time: 15min. €5 single. By **taxi**: about €30. By **shuttle bus** and **tram**: bus to Baggersee (Tram Line A), every 20min, time: 12min; fare €5, 10 single, €9.50 round trip.

Railway Station – Central Station *Plan II* **E1**: good train service to many European destinations and major cities in France.

TRANSPORT

→ BUS AND TRAM

Tickets are valid for the whole transport network. €1.30 single. Tour-Pass gives unlimited travel for 24hr: €3.50. Family Pass: €4.50

→ TAXIS

Taxis can be hailed at taxi ranks at the Central railway station and at Place de l'Homme-de-Fer *Plan II* **F1**. Allow €10-15 for a short journey. Payment by credit card is accep-

ted and tipping is not expected. *France Taxis* ✆ 03 88 22 19 19; *Taxi 13* ✆ 03 88 36 13 13. The base fare is €1.20/km during the day, €1.80/km at night and weekends. There is an extra charge of €0.50 per item of luggage.

USEFUL ADDRESSES

→ TOURIST OFFICES

17 Place de la Cathédrale *Plan II* **G2** ✆ 03 88 52 28 28; Place de la Gare *Plan II* **E1** ✆ 03 88 32 51 49; Pont de l'Europe ✆ 03 88 61 39 23; www.ot-strasbourg.fr; open 9am-7pm daily.

→ POST OFFICES

Opening times Mon-Fri 8am-7pm, Sat 8am-noon. Some branches close between noon and 2pm and may finish for the day at 4pm.

→ BANKS/CURRENCY EXCHANGE

Banks open Mon-Fri, 9am-noon and 2-5pm. There are cash dispensers all over the city. Credit cards are widely accepted. Bureaux de change often charge high commissions.

→ EMERGENCY

Police: ✆ **17**, Fire Brigade: ✆ **18**, Medical services: ✆ **15**.

EXPLORING STRASBOURG

It is possible to visit the main sights and museums in two days.

Museums and other sights are usually open from 9-10am to 6-7pm. Some close on Mondays or Tuesdays and at lunchtime.

VISITING

Cathédrale Notre-Dame *Plan II* **G2** – A splendid Gothic cathedral with a Romanesque east end: facade, steeple, astronomical clock. Spectacular view from platform. Proceed to the **cathedral museum** and then to the fine 18C **Palais Rohan**, which houses the **Musée des Arts décoratifs** (arts and crafts from Strasbourg and Eastern France).

Musée des Beaux-Arts *Plan II* **G2** – An interesting collection of paintings from the Middle Ages to the 18C.

Musée alsacien *Plan II* **G2** – A museum dedicated to the history and traditions of Alsace is housed in three 16-17C houses.

Musée d'Art moderne et contemporain *Plan II* **E2** – A collection of modern art (works by Arp) presented in a striking building.

Tour of the old city *Plan II* **G2** – The area around the cathedral boasts charming squares.

Petite France *Plan II* **F2** – A medieval quarter by the canal with typical old houses, in particular in Rue du Bain-aux-Plantes.

Boat trips – On the Ill from the quay near the Palais Rohan *Plan II* **G2**.

Views from Quai de la Petite-France *Plan II* **F2**, Barrage Vauban *Plan II* **E2**, Pont St-Martin *Plan II* **F2**.

SHOPPING

Shops usually open Mon-Fri, 9am-8pm, Sat 9am-7pm; department stores open 10am-7pm.

The main commercial centre is at **Place des Halles** *Plan II* **F1** with 120 shops. For **designer shops** visit **Rue des Orfèvres** *Plan II* **G2** and **Rue de la Mésange** *Plan II* **G1**. Smart outlets are to be found in **Rue des Hallebardes** *Plan II* **G2** and **Rue du Vieux-Marché** *Plan II* **F1**. *Galeries Lafayette* is at Rue du 22 Novembre, *Printemps* at 1-5 Rue de la Haute-Montée and *FNAC* at Place Kléber. You will find Alsatian costumes at *Maison du Costume Alsacien*,

11b Quai de Turckheim, Christmas decorations at *Un Noël en Alsace*, 10 Rue des Dentelles, English and American books at *The Bookwork*, 3 Rue de Pâques. Visit *Edouard Artzner*, 7 Rue de la Mésange and *Souvenirs et Foie Gras d'Alsace*, 7 Rue d'Austerlitz for foie gras and other delicacies. Au *Millésime Sárl*, 7 Rue du Temple Neuf are suppliers of fine wines. For traditional products go to *Dietrich d'Obernai*, 4 Rue Merdère, *La Cure Gourmande*, 5 Rue Merdère, *Biscuiterie St-Thomas*, 9 Rue des Serruriers, and *Vitrines d'Alsace*, 18 Place de la Cathédrale.

WHAT TO BUY – Christmas decorations, loden coats, Alsatian wines and fruit liqueurs, foie gras, biscuits, chocolates.

MARKETS – There is a **flea market** in Rue du Vieil-Hôpital *Plan II* **G2** and Place de la Grande-Boucherie (Wed, Sat, 9am-6pm); a **book market**, Place and Rue Gutenberg *Plan II* **G2** (Wed, Sat 6am-6pm). **Traditional markets** are held at Place de Broglie *Plan II* **G1** and Quai de Turckheim *Plan II* **E2** (Wed, Fri 7am-1pm), Boulevard de la Marne *Plan I* **D2** (Tue, Sat 7am-1pm) and Rue de Zurich *Plan II* **H2** (Wed) as well as a **farmers' market** at Place du Marché-aux-Poissons *Plan II* **G2** (Sat 7am-1pm). There is also a **Christmas market** (Christkindelsmärkt).

ENTERTAINMENT

National Theatre of Strasbourg *Plan II* **G1**: contemporary works.

Palais de la Musique et des Congrès *Plan I* **C1.**

Opéra National du Rhin *Plan II* **G1**: opera, chamber music, dance, concerts.

La Laiterie *Plan I* **A3**: 'New Music' venue.

La Choucrouterie *Plan II* **F2**: Cabaret-theatre.

NIGHTLIFE

There are plenty of lively places to visit in the historic centre and on the river banks when going out **for a drink or for the evening**: *Les 3 Brasseurs*, 22 Rue des Veaux; *Les Aviateurs*, 12 Rue des Sœurs; *L'Opéra-Café*, Place Broglie; *Bar des Glacières*, 5 Rue des Moulins; *Key West*, 9 Quai des Pêcheurs.

The area around the cathedral, the covered markets and the districts of St-Étienne, Krutenau, Petite France come to life in the evening. *Le Chalet*, 376 Route de la Wantzenau, is a giant complex with restaurants, bars and discos. The disco *Le Retro* is at 24 Place des Halles. For a smart venue, choose *Le Bateau Ivre*, Quai des Alpes, a bar-disco in a huge barge. You can also venture further afield to try your luck at *Casino de Niederbronn*, 10 Place des Thermes.

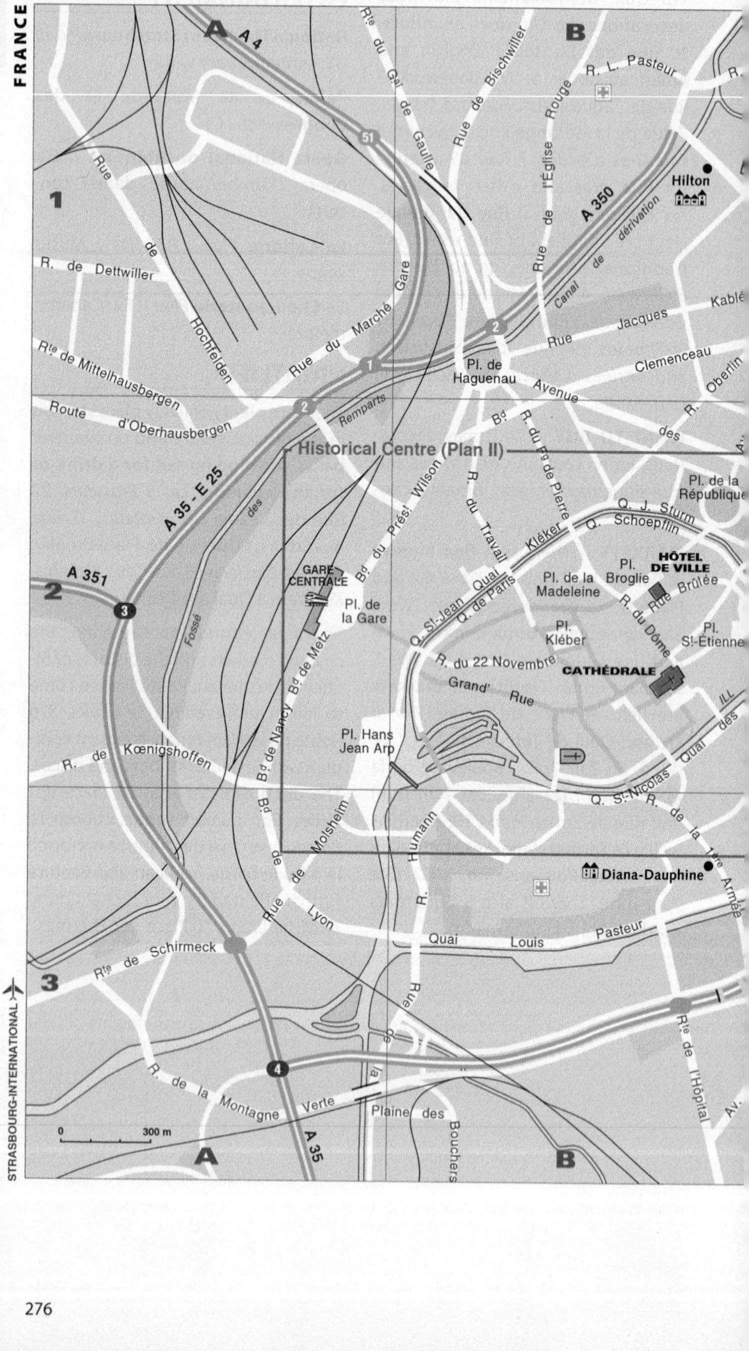

Historical Centre (Plan II)

A 4
Rte du Gal de Gaulle
Rue de Bischwiller
R. L. Pasteur
Rue de l'Église Rouge
Hilton
A 350
Canal de dérivation
Rue de Hochfelden
R. de Dettwiller
Rue du Marché Gare
Rte de Mittelhausbergen
Route d'Oberhausbergen
Remparts
Rue Jacques Kablé
Avenue Clemenceau
Pl. de Haguenau
Bd
R. Oberlin
R. des
R. du Fg de Pierre
R. du Travail
Bd du Prést Wilson
A 35 - E 25
Fossé des
A 351
GARE CENTRALE
Pl. de la Gare
Bd de Metz
Bd de Nancy
Pl. de la République
Q. J. Sturm
Q. Schoepflin
Quai Kléber
Q. St-Jean
Q. de Paris
Pl. de la Madeleine
Pl. Broglie
HÔTEL DE VILLE
Rue Brûlée
R. du Dôme
Pl. Kléber
Pl. St-Étienne
R. du 22 Novembre
CATHÉDRALE
Grand' Rue
ILL
Quai des
Pl. Hans Jean Arp
R. de Kœnigshoffen
Q. St-Nicolas
R. de la 1ère Armée
Bd de Molsheim
R. Humann
Diana-Dauphine
Rue de Lyon
Quai Louis Pasteur
Rte de Schirmeck
Rue de la Plaine des Bouchers
Rte de l'Hôpital
R. de la Montagne Verte
A 35
Av.
0 300 m
STRASBOURG-INTERNATIONAL

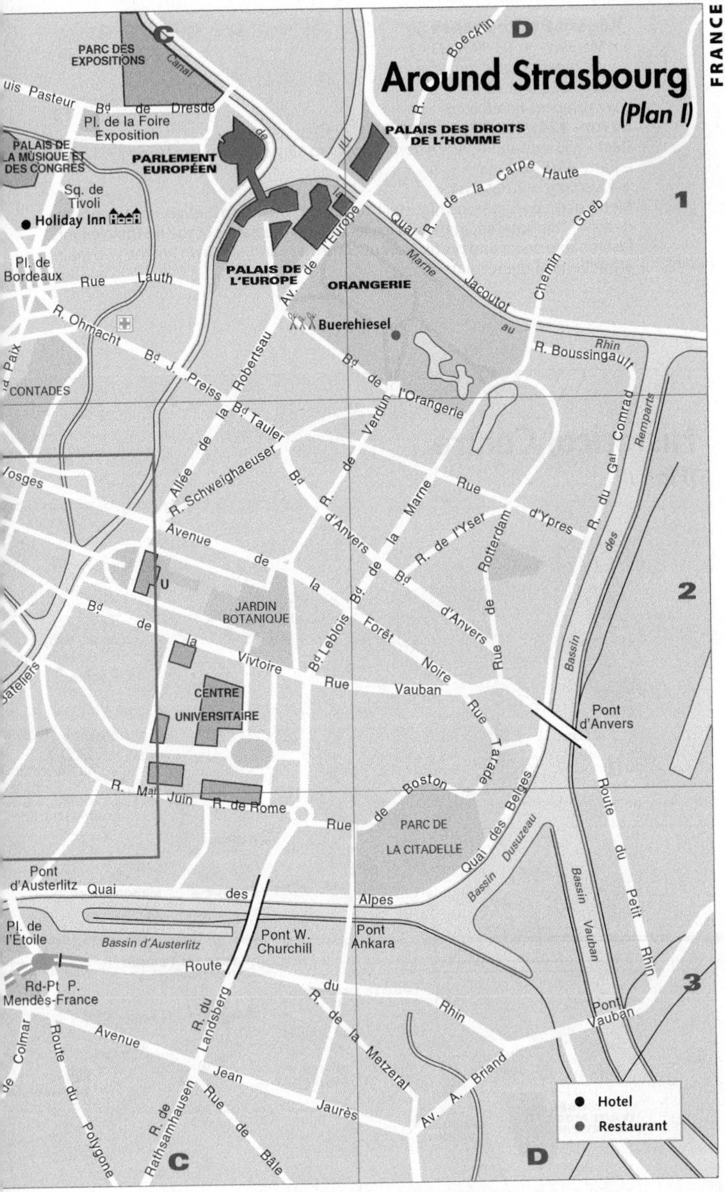

Around Strasbourg
(Plan I)

C
D
1
2
3

PARC DES EXPOSITIONS
Canal
Louis Pasteur
Bd de Dresde
Pl. de la Foire Exposition
PALAIS DE LA MUSIQUE ET DES CONGRÈS
PARLEMENT EUROPÉEN
Sq. de Tivoli
Holiday Inn
Pl. de Bordeaux
Rue Lauth
PALAIS DE L'EUROPE
PALAIS DES DROITS DE L'HOMME
ORANGERIE
Buerehiesel
Boecklin
R. de la Carpe Haute
Chemin Goeb
Quai Jacoutot
Marne
au Rhin
ILL
Av. de l'Europe
R. Ohmacht
Bd J. Preiss
Allée de la Robertsau
CONTADES
de la Paix
Bd Tauler
R. Schweighaeuser
Bd de l'Orangerie
R. Boussingault
R. du Gal Comrad
Remparts
Bd d'Anvers
R. de Verdun
Rue d'Ypres
R. de l'Yser
R. de la Marne
Rue de Rotterdam
Vosges
Avenue de la Forêt Noire
U
JARDIN BOTANIQUE
Bd de la Victoire
Bd Leblois
Bassin des Remparts
Rue Vauban
Pont d'Anvers
Ateliers
CENTRE UNIVERSITAIRE
Rue Tarade
R. Mal Juin
R. de Rome
Rue de Boston
PARC DE LA CITADELLE
Quai des Belges
Bassin Dusuzeau
Route du Petit Rhin
Pont d'Austerlitz
Quai des Alpes
Pl. de l'Étoile
Bassin d'Austerlitz
Pont W. Churchill
Pont Ankara
Bassin Vauban
Route du Rhin
Rd-Pt P. Mendès-France
R. du Landsberg
R. de la Metzeral
Pont Vauban
Avenue Jean Jaurès
Av. A. Briand
de Colmar
Route du Polygone
R. de Rathsamhausen
Rue de Bâle

● Hotel
● Restaurant

Régent Petite France

30/80

5 r. Moulins – 03 88 76 43 43
– rpf@regent-hotels.com
– Fax 03 88 76 43 76
– www.regent-hotels.com

VISA

F2

60 rm – 245/365 € 265/385 €, 20 € – 6 suites
Rest – *(closed Sunday, lunch from October to May and Monday)* Menu 37/62 € – Carte 49/52 €

♦ Luxury ♦ Design ♦

Metal, glass, designer and high-tech furnishings make up the very contemporary decor of this hotel set in the old ice factory on the banks of the Ill. The elegant, fashionable decor and pretty view over the river and old town are the two main attractions of the restaurant.

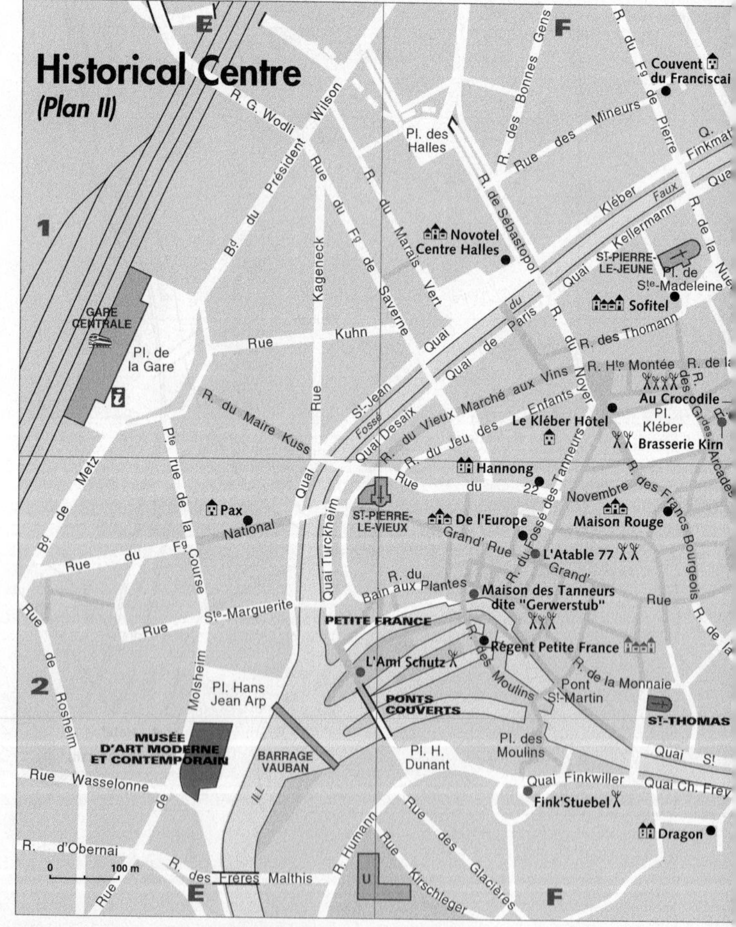

Hilton 25/350 VISA

av. Herrenschmidt – ✆ *03 88 37 10 10*
– info@hilton-strasbourg.com
– Fax 03 88 36 83 27 – www.hilton-strasbourg.com *Plan I* **B1**

237 rm – 150/240 € 150/240 €, 23 € – 6 suites

Rest *La Table du Chef* – ✆ *03 88 37 41 42 (closed July-August, Saturday, Sunday and Bank Holidays) (lunch only)* Menu 34 €

Rest *Le Jardin du Tivoli* – ✆ *03 88 35 72 61* – Menu 29/32 €

♦ Chain hotel ♦ Business ♦ Modern ♦

This glass and steel hotel boasts carefully renovated rooms. Lobby with shops, a multimedia centre and bars. La Table du Chef offers a British ambience: traditional food at lunchtime and wine bar in the evening. A fine terrace is to be found at the Jardin du Tivoli (buffets).

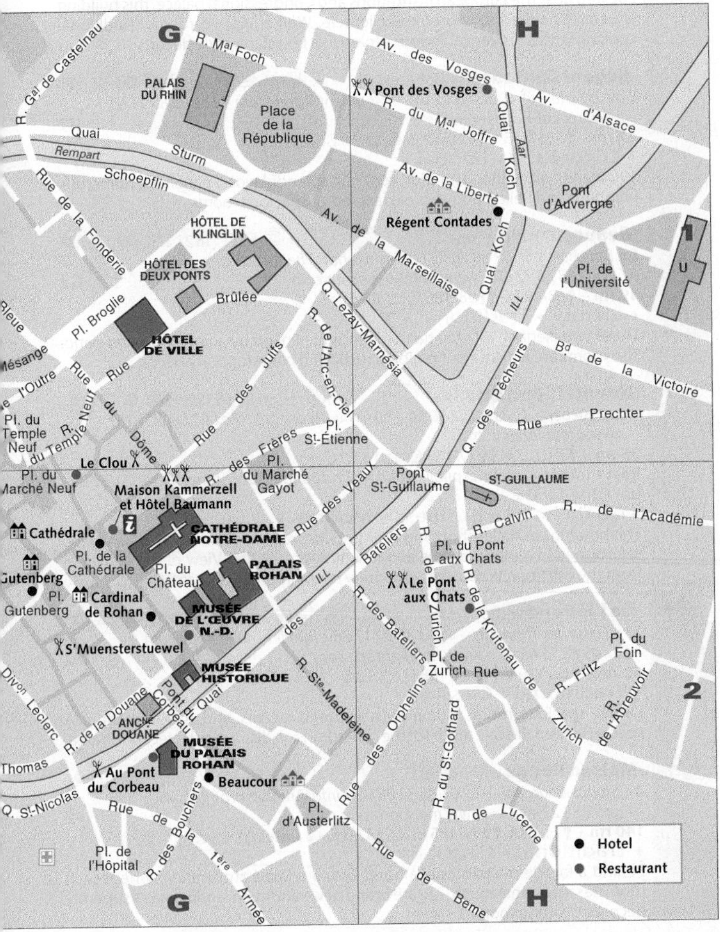

G
H
R. Mal Foch
Av. des Vosges
R. Gal de Castelnau
PALAIS DU RHIN
Place de la République
Pont des Vosges
R. du Mal Joffre
Av. d'Alsace
Quai Sturm
Rempart
Schoepflin
Quai Koch
Aar
Av. de la Liberté
Pont d'Auvergne
Régent Contades
Rue de la Fonderie
HÔTEL DE KLINGLIN
Av. de la Marseillaise
HÔTEL DES DEUX PONTS
Brûlée
Pl. de l'Université
Pl. Broglie
HÔTEL DE VILLE
Q. Lezay-Marnésia
R. de l'Arc-en-Ciel
Rue des Juifs
Bd de la Victoire
Q. des Pêcheurs
Rue Prechter
Rue du Dôme
Rue des Frères
Pl. St-Étienne
Pl. du Temple Neuf
R. du Temple Neuf
Le Clou
Pl. du Marché Neuf
Maison Kammerzell et Hôtel Baumann
Pl. du Marché Gayot
Rue des Veaux
Pont St-Guillaume
ST-GUILLAUME
R. de l'Académie
R. Calvin
Cathédrale
CATHÉDRALE NOTRE-DAME
Pl. de la Cathédrale
Pl. du Château
PALAIS ROHAN
Bateliers
Pl. du Pont aux Chats
Le Pont aux Chats
Gutenberg
Pl. Gutenberg
Cardinal de Rohan
MUSÉE DE L'ŒUVRE N.-D.
R. de Zurich
R. de la Krutenau
R. des Bateliers
S'Muensterstuewel
MUSÉE HISTORIQUE
Pl. de Zurich
Rue de Zurich
Pl. du Foin
R. Fritz
R. de l'Abreuvoir
2
R. Ste-Madeleine
Pont du Corbeau
Quai des Bateliers
R. de la Douane
ANCne DOUANE
MUSÉE DU PALAIS ROHAN
Rue des Orphelins
R. du St-Gothard
Au Pont du Corbeau
Beaucour
Q. St-Nicolas
Rue de la 1ère Armée
Pl. d'Austerlitz
R. de Lucerne
R. des Bouchers
Pl. de l'Hôpital
Rue de Berne
Hotel
Restaurant

FRANCE

Sofitel rm 100 VISA

pl. St-Pierre-le-Jeune – ✆ 03 88 15 49 00 – h0568@accor.com – Fax 03 88 15 49 99 – www.sofitel-strasbourg.com **F1**

155 rm – 195/255 € 250/295 €, 22 €

Rest – *(closed Sunday)* Menu 29 € (weekday lunch) – Carte 44/51 €

♦ Chain hotel ♦ Business ♦ Modern ♦

The first Sofitel built in France (1964) still provides modern comfort and many services. Lobby leading onto patio. Cosy rooms. Restaurant with discreet wood panelling and contemporary cuisine with a regional touch.

Holiday Inn rm rm 300 VISA

20 pl. Bordeaux – ✆ 03 88 37 80 00 – histrasbourg@alliance-hospitality.com – Fax 03 88 37 07 04 – www.holidayinn-strasbourg.com *Plan I* **C1**

170 rm – 100/210 € 100/235 €, 17 €

Rest – *(closed Saturday lunch and Sunday lunch)* Menu 26 € – Carte 24/36 €

♦ Business ♦ Chain hotel ♦ Modern ♦

Located near the European institutions and Congressional palace, this building is perfectly suited to a business clientele. Well-equipped rooms. Traditional cooking with a Provençal flavour served in a Louisiana-style decor.

Régent Contades without rest 15 VISA

8 av. Liberté – ✆ 03 88 15 05 05 – rc@regent-hotels.com – Fax 03 88 15 05 15 – www.regent-hotels.com **H1**

47 rm – 185/235 € 205/255 €, 18 €

♦ Luxury ♦ Traditional ♦

19C manor with refined interior: cosy bar, splendid wood panelling, numerous paintings and Belle-Epoque breakfast room. Spacious rooms.

Beaucour without rest 25 VISA

5 r. Bouchers – ✆ 03 88 76 72 00 – info@hotel-beaucour.com – Fax 03 88 76 72 60 – www.hotel-beaucour.com **G2**

49 rm – 68/121 € 98/186 €, 12 €

♦ Luxury ♦ Traditional ♦

These two elegant 18C Alsatian buildings are linked by a flower-decked patio. The rooms are a mixture of regional rustic and contemporary decor.

Novotel Centre Halles rm rm 15/80 VISA

4 quai Kléber – ✆ 03 88 21 50 50 – h0439@accor.com – Fax 03 88 21 50 51 – www.accorhotels.com **F1**

96 rm – 79/157 € 79/167 €, 14.50 €

Rest – *(closed lunchtime public holidays and Sunday lunchtime)* Menu 20/32 € bi – Carte 16/33 €

♦ Chain hotel ♦ Business ♦ Modern ♦

This hotel, in Les Halles shopping mall, provides rooms, most of which have been refurbished in a modern style and new fitness facilities. View of the cathedral from the 8th floor. Warm, contemporary decor in the restaurant.

De l'Europe without rest 30 VISA

38 r. Fossé des Tanneurs – ✆ 03 88 32 17 88 – info@hotel-europe.com – Fax 03 88 75 65 45 – www.hotel-europe.com **F2**

61 rm – 62/136 € 114/188 €, 12 €

♦ Traditional ♦ Classic ♦

Rather spacious rooms, some with exposed beams and half-timbering. A spectacular small-scale model of the cathedral is on display in the reception area.

Maison Rouge without rest 15/30 VISA

4 r. Francs-Bourgeois – ✆ 03 88 32 08 60 – info@maison-rouge.com – Fax 03 88 22 43 73 – www.maison-rouge.com **F2**

140 rm – 71/83 € 99/175 €, 13.50 € – 2 suites

♦ Traditional ♦ Classic ♦

Behind a façade of red stone, a hotel with a refined atmosphere where each room has a personal touch – 22 are brand new - and each landing has a superbly decorated sitting room.

Cathédrale without rest SAT VISA MC AE
12, pl. Cathedrale – ✆ 03 88 22 12 12 – reserv@hotel-cathedrale.fr – Fax 03 88 23 28 00 – www.hotel-cathedrale.fr **G2**
47 rm – †55/140 € ††55/150 €, ☕ 10 €
◆ Family ◆ Classic ◆
This century-old residence enjoys an ideal location opposite the cathedral, visible from the breakfast room and some of the comfortable rooms. Religious architecture-inspired decor in some rooms.

Hannong without rest A/C SAT 20/40 VISA MC AE
15, r. 22 Novembre – ✆ 03 88 32 16 22 – info@hotel-hannong.com – Fax 03 88 22 63 87 – www.hotel-hannong.com
Closed 2-6 January **F2**
72 rm – †78/182 € ††99/182 €, ☕ 14 €
◆ Family ◆ Classic ◆
The fresco in the elegant Horn living room recalls the history of this hotel built in 1920 on the site of the old Hannong (18C) pottery works. Parquet floors and warm colours in the rooms.

Diana-Dauphine without rest A/C SAT VISA MC AE
30 r. 1e Armée – ✆ 03 88 36 26 61 – info@hotel-diana-dauphine.com – Fax 03 88 35 50 07 – www.hotel-diana-dauphine.com *Plan I* **B3**
45 rm – †90/135 € ††90/135 €, ☕ 10 €
◆ Modern ◆
The tram passes in front of this hotel, leading you quickly to the old town. Rooms with beautiful Louis XV and Louis XVI furniture; renovated bathrooms. Well-prepared breakfast.

Dragon without rest SAT VISA MC AE
2 r. Ecarlate – ✆ 03 88 35 79 80 – hotel@dragon.fr – Fax 03 88 25 78 95 – www.dragon.fr **F2**
32 rm – †69/109 € ††84/119 €, ☕ 11 €
◆ Business ◆ Modern ◆
17C building around a small quiet courtyard with a clearly contemporary feel. Shades of grey, designer furniture, rooms in a pared-down style and art exhibitions.

Cardinal de Rohan without rest A/C SAT VISA MC AE
17 r. Maroquin – ✆ 03 88 32 85 11 – info@hotel-rohan.com – Fax 03 88 75 65 37 – www.hotel-rohan.com **G2**
36 rm – †65/125 € ††65/135 €, ☕ 10.50 €
◆ Traditional ◆ Classic ◆
Hotel near the cathedral in the pedestrian part of town, providing comfortable soudproofed rooms furnished in different styles (Louis XV, Louis XVI or rustic). Cosy lounges.

Gutenberg without rest SAT VISA MC
31 r. Serruriers – ✆ 03 88 32 17 15 – hotel.gutenberg@wanadoo.fr – Fax 03 88 75 76 67 – www.hotel-gutenberg.com **G2**
42 rm – †59/68 € ††78/88 €, ☕ 9 €
◆ Traditional ◆ Classic ◆
This building dating back to 1745 is home to rather spacious and comfortable rooms. Those on the top floor are somewhat smaller. Breakfast room under a glass roof.

Couvent du Franciscain without rest A/C SAT 15 P VISA MC AE
18 r. Fg de Pierre – ✆ 03 88 32 93 93 – info@hotel-franciscain.com – Fax 03 88 75 68 46 – www.hotel-franciscain.com **F1**
43 rm – †38/39 € ††66/70 €, ☕ 9 €
◆ Traditional ◆ Functional ◆
Two buildings nestled at the far end of a cul-de-sac. Opt for the rooms in the new wing. Breakfast served in a basement room brightened by an amusing mural.

Le Kléber Hôtel without rest

29 pl. Kléber – ✆ 03 88 32 09 53 – hotel-kleber-strasbourg@wanadoo.fr – Fax 03 88 32 50 41 – www.hotel-kleber.com F1

30 rm – 🚹45/67 € 🚹🚹62/75 €, ☕ 7.50 €

◆ Traditional ◆ Personalised ◆

"Meringue", "Cherry Plum" and "Cinnamon" are just a few of the names of the personalised rooms of this hotel. Contemporary decor with a cake theme.

Pax

24 r. Fg National – ✆ 03 88 32 14 54 – info@paxhotel.com – Fax 03 88 32 01 16 – www.paxhotel.com

Closed 24 December-7 January E2

106 rm – 🚹56/71 € 🚹🚹71 €, ☕ 8 €

Rest – Menu 18/24 € – Carte 22/45 €

◆ Traditional ◆ Functional ◆

This hotel is on a street reserved for Strasbourg tramway traffic. Simply furnished rooms. On fine days, dining is outside on the pretty terrace-patio under the Virginia creeper. Regional cuisine.

Au Crocodile (Jung)

10 r. Outre – ✆ 03 88 32 13 02 – info@au-crocodile.com – Fax 03 88 75 72 01 – www.au-crocodile.com

Closed 8-31 July, 24 December-8 January, Sunday except December and Monday F1

Rest – Menu 58 € (lunch), 87/127 € – Carte 87/121 €

Spec. Sandre et laitance de carpe au beurre fumé, ventrèche et asperges rissolées. Foie de canard en croûte de sel, légumes en baeckeoffa. Fruits tropicaux et sorbet lychee à l'écume d'orange.

◆ Alsatian cuisine ◆ Formal ◆

Splendid wood panelling, classical paintings and the famous crocodile brought back from the Egyptian campaign by an Alsatian captain: The decor is as refined as the cuisine.

Buerehiesel

set in the Orangery Park – ✆ 03 88 45 56 65 – westermann@buerehiesel.fr – Fax 03 88 61 32 00 – www.buerehiesel.com

Closed 30 July-23 August, 31 December-17 January, Sunday dinner, Tuesday dinner and lunch weekdays *Plan I* D1

Rest – Menu 32 € (lunch)/60 €

◆ Contemporary ◆ Romantic ◆

The authentic, half-timbered farmhouse, restored in 1904, and its modern glass roof nestle under the foliage of the Orangery Park. Eric Westermann has replaced his father Antoine as chef.

Maison Kammerzell et Hôtel Baumann with rm

16 pl. Cathédrale – ✆ 03 88 32 42 14 – info@maison-kammerzell.com – Fax 03 88 23 03 92 – www.maison-kammerzell.com 80/100

Closed 18 February-8 March G2

9 rm – 🚹69/73 € 🚹🚹97/117 €, ☕ 10 €

Rest – Menu 30/45 € – Carte 27/57 €

◆ Alsatian cuisine ◆ Retro ◆

With its murals, stained-glass windows, wood carvings and Gothic vaulting, this 16C Strasbourg institution resembles a museum. Regional dishes.

Maison des Tanneurs dite "Gerwerstub"

42 r. Bain aux Plantes – ✆ 03 88 32 79 70 – maison.des.tanneurs@wanadoo.fr – Fax 03 88 22 17 26

Closed 31 July-13 August, 30 December-23 January, Sunday and Monday F2

Rest – Menu 24 € (lunch)/30 € – Carte 36/63 €

◆ Alsatian cuisine ◆ Rustic ◆

Ideally located by the Ill, this typical Alsatian house in La Petite France district is the place to go to if you love choucroute.

XX

L'Atable 77

AC VISA MC AE

77 Grand'Rue – ✆ 03 88 32 23 37 – latable77@free.fr – Fax 03 88 32 50 24 – www.latable77.com
Closed 13-21 May, 22 July-15 August, 21 January-4 February, Sunday, Monday and lunch on public holidays **F2**
Rest – Menu 30/75 € bi
♦ Contemporary ♦ Trendy ♦
Deliberately pared-down contemporary decor, with fine design features and painting exhibitions. Appetising modern dishes served in this attractive restaurant.

XX ✿

Serge and Co (Burckel)

AC VISA MC AE

14 r. Pompiers ✉ 67300 Schiltigheim – ✆ 03 88 18 96 19 – serge.burckel@wanadoo.fr – Fax 03 88 83 41 99 – www.serge-and-co.com
closed Saturday lunch, Sunday dinner and Monday **BS**
Rest – Menu 28 € (weekday lunch), 48/88 €
Spec. Thon rouge mariné. Grenouilles "clin d'œil aux escargots". "Cigare" au chocolat.
♦ Innovative ♦ Trendy ♦
The chef, Serge, is back home after a long trip through Asia and America. Appetising cuisine, inspired by his travels, served in a pleasant, contemporary restaurant.

XX

Pont des Vosges

VISA MC AE

15 quai Koch – ✆ 03 88 36 47 75 – pontdesvosges@noos.fr – Fax 03 88 25 16 85
closed Sunday **H1**
Rest – Carte 32/53 €
♦ Brasserie ♦ Retro ♦
Located on the ground floor of an old building, this semi-circular restaurant boasts a mix of retro and modern decor. Brasserie-style menu.

XX

Brasserie Kirn

AC VISA MC AE

6/8 r. de l'Outre – ✆ 03 88 52 03 03 – brasserie@kirn.fr – Fax 03 88 52 01 00 – www.brasserie-kirn.fr
closed Sunday evening **F1**
Rest – Menu 17 € (weekday lunch)/30 €
♦ Brasserie ♦ Retro ♦
This former butcher's shop contains a large 1900s-style dining room lit by a beautiful central cupola and decorated with stained glass windows. Brasserie dishes.

XX

Le Pont aux Chats

VISA MC AE

42, r. Krutenau – ✆ 03 88 24 08 77 – Fax 03 88 24 08 77
Closed 1st-20 August, 11-24 February, Sunday dinner except from April to September and December, Saturday lunch and Wednesday **H2**
Rest – Carte 42/50 €
♦ Contemporary ♦ Trendy ♦
This small restaurant on the right bank successfully marries contemporary furnishings with old half-timbering. Delightful terrace nestled in the interior courtyard. Innovative cuisine.

WINSTUBS *Regional specialities and wine tasting in a typical alsatian atmosphere*

X

L'Ami Schutz

VISA MC AE

1 r. Ponts Couverts – ✆ 03 88 32 76 98 – info@ami-schutz.com – Fax 03 88 32 38 40 – www.ami-schutz.com
Closed Christmas holidays **E-F2**
Rest – Menu 23/47 € bi – Carte 31/55 €
♦ Alsatian cuisine ♦ Inn ♦
Between the meanders of the Ill, a typical "winstub" extended by a terrace shaded by lime trees. Charming dining area with a warm atmosphere and beautiful old wood panelling.

Le Clou

AC VISA MC AE

3 r. Chaudron – ✆ 03 88 32 11 67 – Fax 03 88 21 06 43
closed Wednesday lunchtime, Sunday and public holidays **G1-2**
Rest – Menu 25/30 € – Carte 25/52 €
♦ Alsatian cuisine ♦ Inn ♦
Traditional decor and a friendly atmosphere characterise this winstub situated near the cathedral, frequented by passing celebrities whose photos are displayed.

Au Pont du Corbeau

AC VISA MC

21 quai St-Nicolas – ✆ 03 88 35 60 68 – corbeau@reperes.com – Fax 03 88 25 72 45
Closed 28 July-26 August, February half-term holidays, Sunday lunch and Saturday except in December **G2**
Rest – Carte 24/38 €
♦ Alsatian cuisine ♦ Inn ♦
On the banks of the Ill, next to the Alsatian Museum (folk art), a house with its original decoration inspired by the regional Renaissance style. Regional specialities.

Fink'Stuebel

rm VISA MC

26 r. Finkwiller – ✆ 03 88 25 07 57 – finkstuebel@noos.fr – Fax 03 88 36 48 82 – http://finkstuebel.free.fr
closed 10-25 August, Sunday and Monday **F2**
Rest – Carte 29/55 €
♦ Alsatian cuisine ♦ Family ♦
Half timbering, bare parquet floor, painted wood, regional furniture and floral tablecloths: this place is the epitome of the traditional winstub. Regional cooking ; foie gras has pride of place.

S'Muensterstuewel

AC VISA

8 pl. Marché au Cochons de Lait – ✆ 03 88 32 17 63 – muensterstuewel@wanadoo.fr – Fax 03 88 21 96 02
Closed 29 April-13 May, 25 August-2 September, 27 October-4 November, 1st-7 January, Saturday and Sunday **G2**
Rest – Menu 30 € (weekday lunch)/45 € bi – Carte 35/55 €
♦ Alsatian cuisine ♦ Rustic ♦
A former butcher's shop in the pure winstub style brightened by beautiful rustic furniture. In summer, dine at the terrace bordering the touristy small square.

Toulouse

TOULOUSE

Population (est. 2004): 390 350 (conurbation 761 100) – Altitude: 146m

J. Sierpinski/TOP

Toulouse is a pleasant university town, known as the 'ville rose' or pink city. The historic city is bounded on three sides by the Canal du Midi, the Canal de Brienne and the Garonne. The squares and gardens and the cultural and leisure amenities add to its charm.

Over the centuries the city has been the focus of diverse influences, as it is linked to the Mediterranean via the low Lauraguais Pass and with the Atlantic via the Garonne, while the valleys running down from the Pyrenees keep it in touch with Spain. Great movements of populations since Roman times have left their mark. Toulouse has a stormy history; it was the capital of the Visigoths in the 5C and then came under the rule of the Franks. From the 9C to the 13C it was the fief of the Counts of Toulouse and it became part of the French kingdom in the 13C. Europe's oldest literary society to celebrate the 'Langue d'oc', the language of southern France, was founded here in 1323. In the 16C the city flourished as the cultivation of woad, which yielded a blue-black colour for use in dyestuff, boomed. It is now a major industrial centre dominated by the aeronautical and other high-tech industries.

WHICH DISTRICT TO CHOOSE

There are elegant **hotels** around Place du Capitole *Plan II* **E1**, Place Wilson *Plan II* **F1** and Avenue Jean-Jaurès. For comfortable accommodation at reasonable rates look near the Matabiau station and in the Pont-Neuf area. You will find modern business hotels near the Centre des Congrès *Plan I* **C2**.

The southwest is famous for its hearty fare: cassoulet, sausages, foie gras, confits, ham, salami, bouillinade to list but a few of its specialities. **Restaurants** with a gastronomic reputation are to be found around Place du Capitole, near Place St-Sernin as well as in the environs of the city *(see listings in the guide)*. There are brasseries, bistros and other charming establishments in the old town and along the quays.

If you prefer a light meal with a glass of wine try *Au Père Louis*, 45 Rue des Tourneurs; *Le Petit Bacchus*, 16 Rue Pharaon. For a quick bite, go to *L'Autre Salon de Thé*, 45 Rue des Tourneurs, for pastries to *Jean Chiche*, 3 Rue St-Pantaléon.

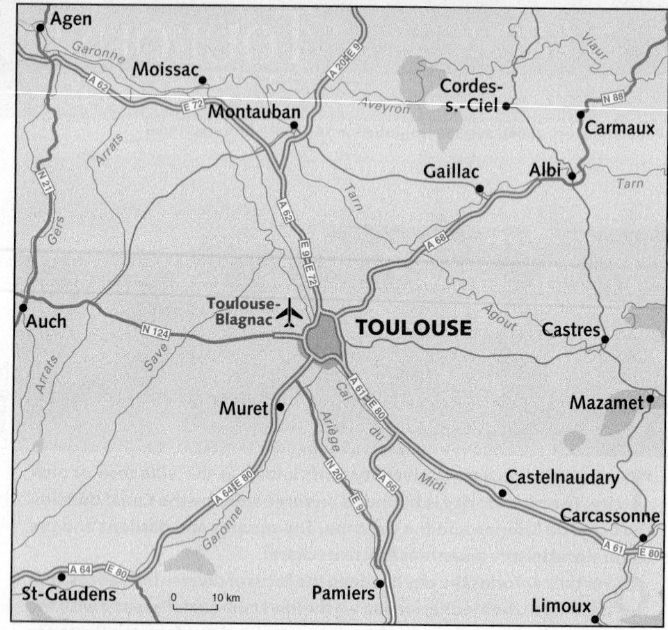

PRACTICAL INFORMATION

ARRIVAL – DEPARTURE

Toulouse-Blagnac Airport – 7 km (4 mi) from the city centre. ✆ 0825 38 00 00; www.toulouse.aeroport.fr

From the airport to the city centre – By **express bus**: to the city centre Gare Matabiau SNCF terminus, time: 20min; €4.00 single, €6.00 return trip. By **taxi**: approx. €25. *Taxi aéroport* ✆ 05 61 30 02 54, 06 09 30 84 35.

Main Station – Gare **Matabiau** SNCF *Plan II* **F1**: High-speed trains to Paris and the regions of France.

TRANSPORT

→ BUS AND METRO

A red ticket €1.30 one trip allows you to travel anywhere on the network for 1hr. A round trip ticket €2.40, a Day ticket €4 and 10-12 trip tickets are also available. Information: Tisseo-Connex, 9 rue Michel-Labrousse. ✆ 05 61 41 70 70; www.tisseo.fr

→ TAXIS

There are taxi stands around the main squares and at the Station. Allow €10-15 for a short journey. Tips are not compulsory. *Taxi Radio Toulousain* ✆ 05 61 42 38 38; *Association Taxis* ✆ 05 61 35 89 00, 06 09 33 25 83, *Capitole Taxi* ✆ 05 34 25 02 50.

USEFUL ADDRESSES

→ TOURIST OFFICE

Donjon du Capitole *Plan II* **E1**. ✆ 05 61 11 02 22; www.ot-toulouse.fr

→ POST OFFICES

Main Post Offfice, 9 Rue Lafayette. Open Mon-Fri 8am-7pm, Sat 8am-noon. Other post offices close noon-2pm and in the afternoon at 4pm.

→ BANKS/CURRENCY EXCHANGE

Banks open Mon-Fri, 9am-noon and 2-5pm. Branches at the airport open 7am-7pm on weekdays. There are cash dispensers (ATM), which require a PIN number, all over the city.

→ EMERGENCY

Police: ✆ **17**, Fire Brigade: ✆ **18**, First Aid: ✆ **15**.

It is possible to visit the main sights and museums in two days.

VISITING

Basilique St-Sernin *Plan II* **E1** – A great Romanesque pilgrimage church (12C) – octagonal bell-tower.

Les Jacobins *Plan II* **E2** – An architectural masterpiece with ribbed vaulting, 'palm-tree' pillars and radiating arches (13C).

Cathédrale St-Étienne *Plan II* **F2** – An interesting building with an unusual plan – vast 12C hall and Gothic chancel.

Musée des Augustins *Plan II* **E2** – A splendid collection of Romanesque sculpture and French paintings.

Hôtel d'Assezat *Plan II* **E2** – The magnificent mansion is home to the Bemberg Foundation – paintings and works of art from the Renaissance to the 20C.

Musée St-Raymond *Plan II* **E1** – Interesting collections of archaeology and ancient art.

Cité de l'Espace *Plan I* **D3** – Interactive presentation of the evolution of the universe and space travel.

Boat trips – On the Garonne from Quai de la Daurade *Plan II* **E2**.

Views from Quai de la Daurade *Plan II* **E2**, Pont St-Michel *Plan II* **E3**, Rue de Metz (near Musée des Augustins) *Plan II* **E2**.

SHOPPING

The main shopping streets (*Plan II* **E2-F2**) are **Rue de l'Alsace-Lorraine**, **Rue Croix-Baragnon**, **Rue St-Antoine-du-T.**, **Rue Boulbonne**, **Rue des Arts** and the pedestrian sections of **Rue St-Rome**, **Rue des Filatiers**, **Rue Baronie** and **Rue de la Pomme**.

Specialist shops include *Atelier du Chocolat de Bayonne*, 1 Rue du Rempart Villeneuve; *Olivier Confiseur-Chocolatier*, 20 Rue Lafayette; – fine chocolates; *Busquets*, 10 Rue Rémusat – regional specialities and wines from the southwest; *La Maison de la Violette*, Boulevard de Bonrepos-Canal du Midi, *Violette & Pastels*, 10 Rue St-Pantaléon – confectionery, liqueurs, cosmetics.

WHAT TO BUY – Foie gras, cassoulet, confits, candied violets and other violet-based products, wine and liqueurs; chocolates (*capitouls* – almonds in dark chocolate, *Clémence Isaure* – Armagnac-soaked grapes in dark chocolate, *brindilles* – nougatine in chocolate praline, *Péché du Diable* – dark chocolate ganache with orange peel and ginger).

MARKETS (*Plan II* **E1 à E3**) – **Flea markets**: L'**Inquet**, around Basilique St-Sernin (Sun mornings); Allée Jules-Guesde (first weekend of each month). **Farmers markets** are held around Église St-Aubin (Sun mornings), Place du Capitole (organic products, Sun mornings) and Place du Salin (foie gras, etc. Wed-Fri, Nov-Mar).

ENTERTAINMENT

Théâtre du Capitole *Plan II* **E2**: opera, operetta. **Théâtre de la Cité**: music, theatre, entertainment. **Théâtre Garonne** 6 Av Château d'Eau: plays. **Auditorium St-Pierre-des-Cuisines** 12, place Saint-Pierre: music, plays. **Café-Théâtre des 3T**: shows. **Halle aux Grains**, Place Dupuy *Plan II* **F2**: pop and classical concerts. **Zénith**, 11 Avenue Raymond-Badiou *Plan I* **B2**: rock concerts, variety acts, musical comedies.

NIGHTLIFE

The café terraces lining **Place du Capitole** *(Le Bibent, Le Café des Arcades, Brasserie de l'Opéra, Mon Caf)* are ideal places to visit when going out **for a drink or for the evening**.

For a lively scene with music and dancing explore the **areas around Place du Capitole**, **Place St-Georges**, **Place St-Pierre** and just off **Rue St-Rome** and **Rue des Filatiers**. *Bar La Loupiote*, 39 Rue Réclusane; *Bar One*, 27 Boulevard de Strasbourg; *La Bodega Bodega*, 1 Rue Gabriel-Péri; *Monsieur Carnaval*, 34 Rue Bayard; *La Tantina de Bourgos*, 27 Rue de la Garonette are very popular. Also worth a visit are *Disco Cockpit*, 1 Rue du Puits-Vert; *Disco La Strada*, 4 Rue Gabriel-Péri; *Le New Shangai*, 12 Rue de la Pomme.

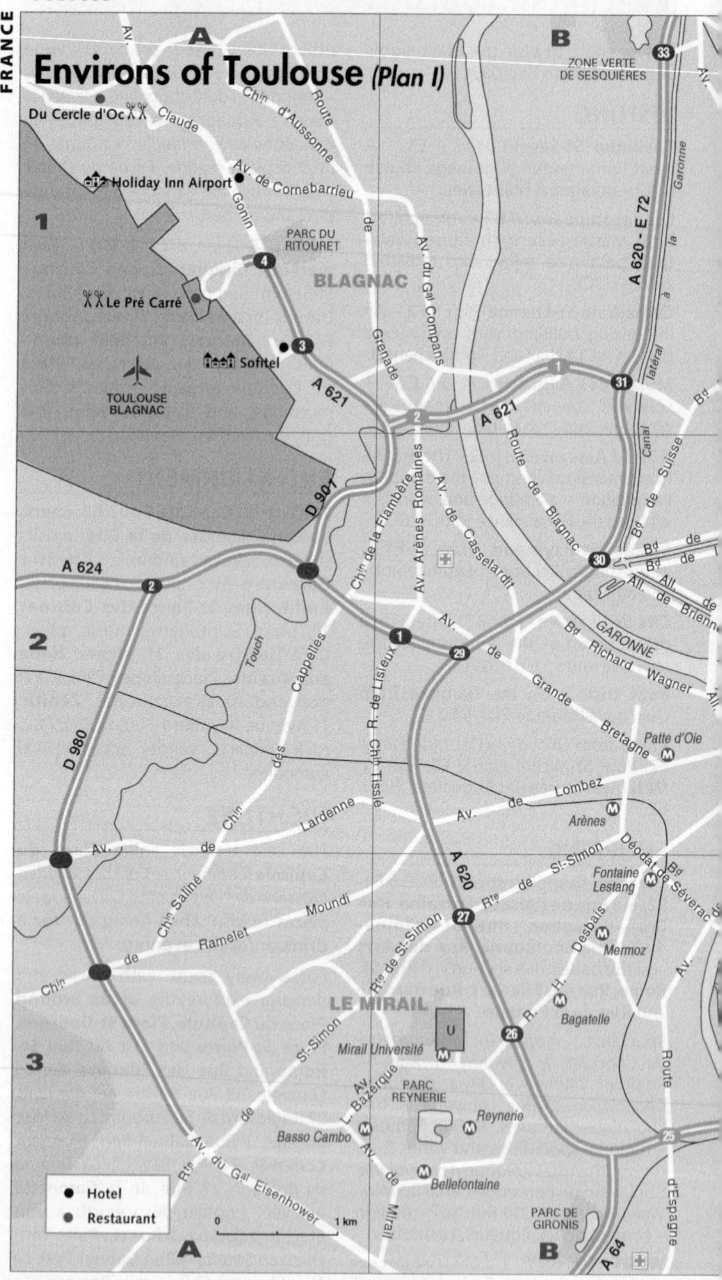
Environs of Toulouse (Plan I)
Du Cercle d'Oc
Holiday Inn Airport
Le Pré Carré
Sofitel
TOULOUSE BLAGNAC
PARC DU RITOURET
BLAGNAC
ZONE VERTE DE SESQUIÈRES
LE MIRAIL
Mirail Université
PARC REYNERIE
Reynerie
Basso Cambo
Bellefontaine
Bagatelle
Mermoz
Fontaine Lestang
Arènes
Patte d'Oie
PARC DE GIRONIS
GARONNE
A 621
A 624
A 620 - E 72
A 620
A 64
D 901
D 980
Hotel
Restaurant
0
1 km

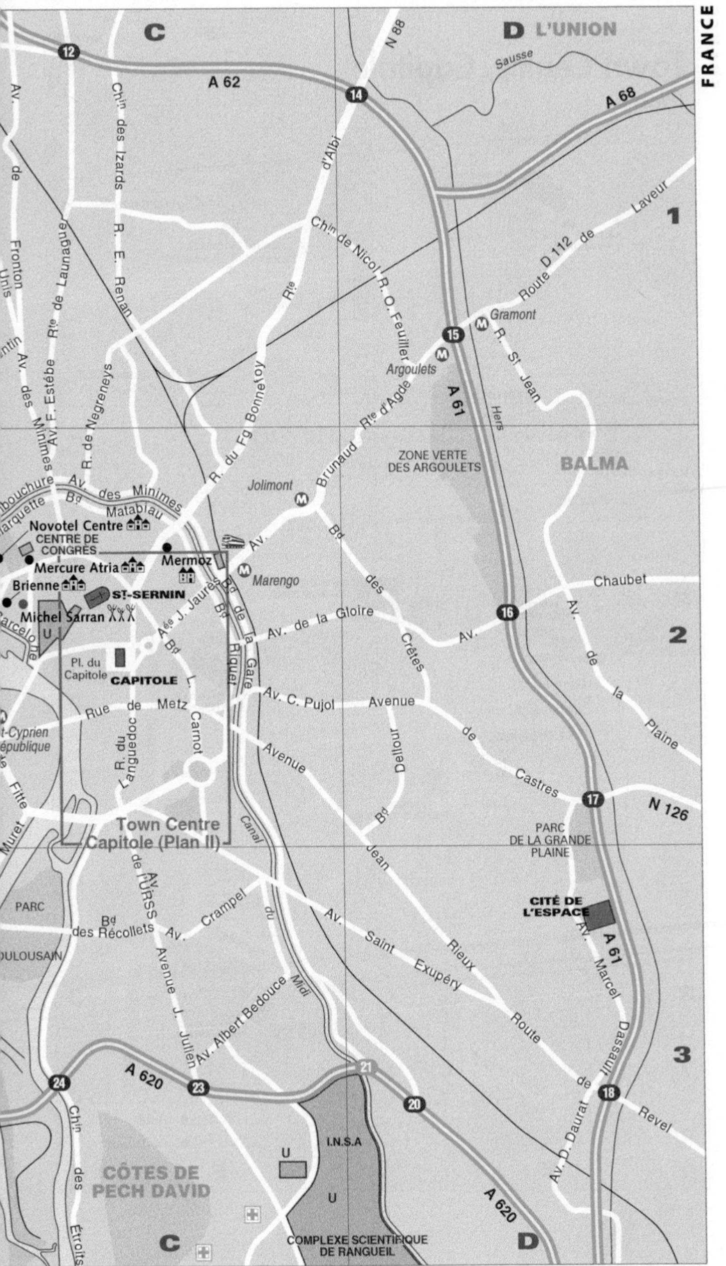
C
D
L'UNION
A 62
A 68
N 88
Sausse
Rte d'Albi
Chin de Nicol
R. O. Feuiller
Route D 112 de Laveur
Gramont
R. St Jean
Argoulets
Rte d'Agde
A 61
Hers
ZONE VERTE DES ARGOULETS
BALMA
Jolimont
Brunaud
R. du Fg Bonnefoy
R. de Negreneys
Chin des Izards
R. E. Renan
Rte de Launaguet
Av. F. Estèbe
Av. des Minimes
Av. de Fronton
Bd Matabiau
Novotel Centre
CENTRE DE CONGRES
Mercure Atria
Mermoz
Brienne
ST-SERNIN
Michel Sarran
Marengo
Bd des Crêtes
Chaubet
Av. de la Gloire
Av. de la Plaine
Pl. du Capitole
CAPITOLE
Bd de la Gare
Riquet
Av. C. Pujol
Avenue de Castres
Rue de Metz
R. du Languedoc
Carnot
Dellour
N 126
PARC DE LA GRANDE PLAINE
Town Centre Capitole (Plan II)
Canal du Midi
Avenue Jean Rieux
CITÉ DE L'ESPACE
Av. de l'URSS
Av. Crampel
Bd des Récollets
PARC
Av. Saint Exupéry
Av. Marcel Dassault
Avenue J. Julien
Av. Albert Bedouce
Route de Revel
A 620
Av. D. Daurat
Chin des Étroits
CÔTES DE PECH DAVID
I.N.S.A
COMPLEXE SCIENTIFIQUE DE RANGUEIL
1
2
3

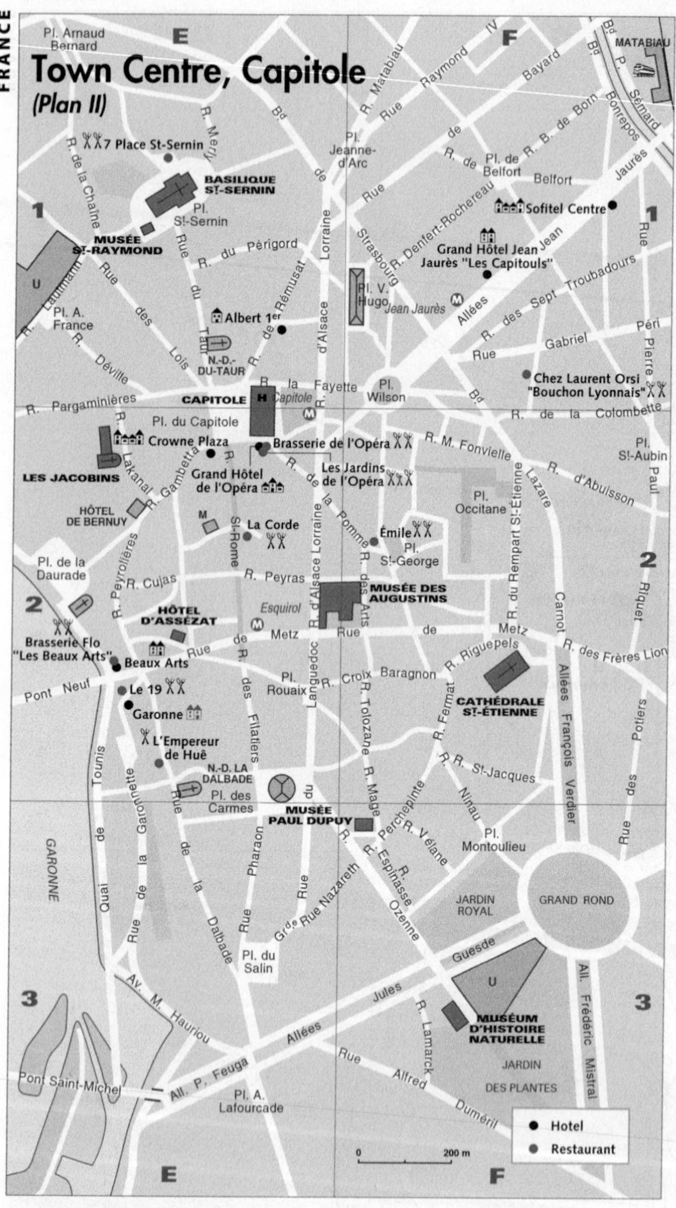
Town Centre, Capitole
(Plan II)
7 Place St-Sernin
BASILIQUE ST-SERNIN
MUSÉE ST-RAYMOND
Pl. St-Sernin
Albert 1er
N.-D.-DU-TAUR
CAPITOLE
Pl. du Capitole
Crowne Plaza
Brasserie de l'Opéra
Grand Hôtel de l'Opéra
Les Jardins de l'Opéra
LES JACOBINS
HÔTEL DE BERNUY
La Corde
Émile
MUSÉE DES AUGUSTINS
HÔTEL D'ASSÉZAT
Brasserie Flo "Les Beaux Arts"
Beaux Arts
Le 19
Garonne
L'Empereur de Huê
N.-D. LA DALBADE
MUSÉE PAUL DUPUY
CATHÉDRALE ST-ÉTIENNE
Sofitel Centre
Grand Hôtel Jean Jaurès "Les Capitouls"
Chez Laurent Orsi "Bouchon Lyonnais"
MATABIAU
GRAND ROND
JARDIN ROYAL
MUSÉUM D'HISTOIRE NATURELLE
JARDIN DES PLANTES
GARONNE
Pont Neuf
Pont Saint-Michel
Hotel
Restaurant
200 m

TOWN CENTRE *Plan II*

Sofitel Centre

84 allées J. Jaurès – ☎ 05 61 10 23 10 – h1091@accor.com – Fax 05 61 10 23 20 – www.sofitel-toulouse-centre.com **F1**

119 rm – 🚹290 € 🚹🚹330 €, ☕ 22 € – 14 suites

Rest *S W Café* – Carte 32/58 €

♦ Luxury ♦ Chain hotel ♦ Classical ♦

The hotel occupies an imposing red-brick and glass building. Discreetly luxurious rooms, with good soundproofing. Business centre and good seminar facilities. At SW Café, you will find a contemporary setting and recipes combining regional products and international spices.

Crowne Plaza

7 pl. Capitole – ☎ 05 61 61 19 19 – hicptoulouse@alliance-hospitality.com – Fax 05 61 23 79 96 – www.crowne-plaza-toulouse.com **E2**

162 rm – 🚹270/570 € 🚹🚹270/570 €, ☕ 22 € – 3 suites

Rest – *(closed August)* Menu 25/60 € bi – Carte 47/64 €

♦ Business ♦ Chain hotel ♦ Classical ♦

This luxury hotel enjoys a prestigious location on the famous Place du Capitole. Spacious, comfortable rooms, some of which look out onto the town hall. An intimate atmosphere in the dining room opening onto a pleasant interior courtyard.

Grand Hôtel de l'Opéra without rest

1 pl. Capitole – ☎ 05 61 21 82 66 – contact@grand-hotel-opera.com – Fax 05 61 23 41 04 – www.grand-hotel-opera.com **E2**

49 rm – 🚹180/470 € 🚹🚹380/470 €, ☕ 22 €

♦ Luxury ♦ Cosy ♦

This hotel in a 17C convent has an air of serenity and charm. Beautiful rooms with wood panels and velvet. Pleasant bar lounge and attractive vaulted reception hall.

Brienne without rest

20 bd Mar. Leclerc – ☎ 05 61 23 60 60 – brienne@hoteldebrienne.com – Fax 05 61 23 18 94 – www.hoteldebrienne.com *Plan I* **C2**

70 rm – 🚹68/92 € 🚹🚹68/92 €, ☕ 10 € – 1 suite

♦ Chain hotel ♦ Classical ♦

Colourful and impeccably maintained rooms, numerous work and leisure areas (bar-library, patio): very popular with a business clientele.

Mercure Atria

8 espl. Compans Caffarelli – ☎ 05 61 11 09 09 – h1585@accor.com – Fax 05 61 23 14 12 – www.mercure.com *Plan I* **C2**

134 rm – 🚹121/139 € 🚹🚹131/149 €, ☕ 14 € – 2 suites

Rest – Carte 21/38 €

♦ Chain hotel ♦ Modern ♦

Modern comfortable furnishings, decorative wood panels and warm colours in rooms that have been recently refurbished in line with the chain's new look. Vast business area. The restaurant dining room offers a soothing view of the public park, and another, busier one of the work in the kitchen.

Novotel Centre

5 pl. A. Jourdain – ☎ 05 61 21 74 74 – h0906@accor.com – Fax 05 61 22 81 22 – www.novotel.com *Plan I* **C2**

135 rm – 🚹99/140 € 🚹🚹99/185 €, ☕ 13 € – 2 suites

Rest – Carte 21/33 €

♦ Chain hotel ♦ Modern ♦

This regional-style building adjacent to a Japanese garden and large park has spacious rooms renovated in a contemporary spirit, some with a terrace. A festival of colours in this dining room opening onto the greenery. Traditional and local cuisine.

FRANCE

Garonne without rest

22 descente de la Halle aux Poissons – ✆ 05 34 31 94 80 – contact@hotelgaronne.com – Fax 05 34 31 94 81 – www.hotelsdecharmetoulouse.com **E2**

14 rm – 160/180 € 180/260 €, 20 €

◆ Traditional ◆ Modern ◆

An old building in one of the Old Town's narrow streets. A fine contemporary interior: stained-oak parquet flooring, design furniture, silk draperies and the odd Japanese touch.

Beaux Arts without rest

1 pl. Pont-Neuf – ✆ 05 34 45 42 42 – contact@hoteldesbeauxarts.com – Fax 05 34 45 42 43 – www.hoteldesbeauxarts.com **E2**

20 rm – 103 € 175/220 €, 16 €

◆ Business ◆ Modern ◆

Tastefully done 18C establishment with cosy refined rooms, most with a view of the Garonne. Number 42 enjoys the additional benefit of a mini-terrace.

Les Capitouls without rest

29 allées J. Jaurès – ✆ 05 34 41 31 21 – info@hotel-capitouls.com – Fax 05 61 63 15 17 – www.bestwestern-capitouls.com **F1**

53 rm – 126/176 € 138/230 €, 13.50 € – 1 suite

◆ Chain hotel ◆ Classical ◆

Just at the metro station, this former private residence has a distinctive foyer with red brick vaulting. The rooms have access to Wifi.

Mermoz without rest

50 r. Matabiau – ✆ 05 61 63 04 04 – reservation@hotel-mermoz.com – Fax 05 61 63 15 64 *Plan I* **C2**

52 rm – 120 € 120 €, 12 €

◆ Family ◆ Art Deco ◆

This hotel's spare decor recalls the Aeropostale's heroic pilots. Bright, candy-coloured rooms. Flower-decked glassed-in area or tree-shaded outside tables for breakfast.

Albert 1er without rest

8 r. Rivals – ✆ 05 61 21 17 91 – toulouse@hotel-albert1.com – Fax 05 61 21 09 64 – www.hotel-albert1.com **E1**

48 rm – 55/91 € 65/91 €, 10 €

◆ Family ◆ Functional ◆

A very practical base for discovering the "pink city" by foot. Ask for one of the refurbished rooms, or one at the rear for peace and quiet.

Les Jardins de l'Opéra

1 pl. Capitole – ✆ 05 61 23 07 76 – contact@lesjardinsdelopera.com – Fax 05 61 23 63 00 – www.lesjardinsdelopera.com

closed August, 1st-8 January, Sunday and Monday **E2**

Rest – Menu 42 € bi (weekday lunch), 70/90 € – Carte approx. 92 €

◆ Innovative ◆ Modern ◆

The elegant lounges under a vast glass roof are decorated in Florentine style and separated by a fountain dedicated to Neptune. The cuisine is inventively reinterpreted.

Michel Sarran

21 bd A. Duportal – ✆ 05 61 12 32 32 – restaurant@michel-sarran.com – Fax 05 61 12 32 33 – www.michel-sarran.com

Closed 28 July-28 August, 1st-8 January, Wednesday lunch, Saturday and Sunday *Plan I* **C2**

Rest – *(pre-book)* Menu 45 € bi (weekday lunch), 85/150 € bi – Carte 87/132 €

Spec. Yaourt fermier à la truffe du Périgord, tartine et confit de porto. Saint-Pierre en croûte de champignons, crème d'oseille. Pigeon fermier en kadaïf, cuisses confites à l'encre de seiche.

◆ Innovative ◆ Fashionable ◆

This charming large 19C residence invites gourmets to enjoy savoury cuisine of southern specialities in purposely minimalist decor.

XX

7 Place St-Sernin

6/50 VISA AE

7 pl. St-Sernin – ✆ 05 62 30 05 30 – restaurant.le.7.saint.sernin@wanadoo.fr – Fax 05 62 30 04 06

Closed Saturday and Sunday **E1**

Rest – Menu 24 € bi (lunch), 34/60 € bi – Carte 45/59 €

♦ Contemporary ♦ Fashionable ♦

This restaurant set in a typical Toulouse house boasts flamboyant colours and is elegantly arranged and brightened with contemporary paintings. Modern dishes.

XX

Brasserie Flo " Les Beaux Arts"

VISA AE

1 quai Daurade – ✆ 05 61 21 12 12 – s.giroussens@groupeflo.fr – Fax 05 61 21 14 80 – www.brasserie-lesbeauxarts.com **E2**

Rest – Menu 30 € – Carte 27/58 €

♦ Brasserie ♦ Retro ♦

This brasserie at the Garonne's edge was once frequented by Ingres, Matisse and Bourdelle, and is appreciated by the locals. Pretty retro decor. Highly varied menu.

XX

Le 19

6/12 VISA

19 descente de la Halle aux Poissons – ✆ 05 34 31 94 84 – contact@restaurantle19.com – Fax 05 34 31 94 85 – www.restaurantle19.com

Closed 12-20 August, 23 December-8 January, Monday lunch, Saturday lunch and Sunday **E2**

Rest – Menu 28 € (lunch), 35/60 € bi (b.i.) – Carte 44/54 €

♦ Contemporary ♦ Trendy ♦

Welcoming dining rooms, one with a superb 16C rib vaulted ceiling, an open wine cellar and smoking room in a resolutely modern style. Dishes with an international flavour.

XX

Chez Laurent Orsi "Bouchon Lyonnais"

VISA AE

13, r. Industrie – ✆ 05 61 62 97 43 – orsi.le-bouchon-lyonnais@wanadoo.fr – Fax 05 61 63 00 71 – www.le-bouchon-lyonnais.com

closed Saturday lunch and Sunday **F1**

Rest – Menu 20/33 € – Carte 33/52 €

♦ Lyonnais cuisine ♦ Brasserie ♦

A large bistro whose imitation leather benches, end-to-end tables and mirrors are reminiscent of the brasseries of the 1930s. The menu oscillates between southwest France and Lyon.

XX

Émile

VISA AE

13 pl. St-Georges – ✆ 05 61 21 05 56 – restaurant-emile@wanadoo.fr – Fax 05 61 21 42 26 – www.restaurant-emile.com

Closed 23 December-7 January, Monday except dinner from May to September and Sunday **F2**

Rest – Menu 18 € (lunch), 35/48 € – Carte 35/62 €

♦ Contemporary ♦ Friendly ♦

This restaurant created in the 1940s is prized for its wonderful wine list and cuisine of hearty local food and fish. The outside dining area is invaded in summer.

XX

Brasserie de l'Opéra

20/60 VISA AE

1 pl. Capitole – ✆ 05 61 21 37 03 – Fax 05 62 27 16 49

closed Sunday **E2**

Rest – Menu 16/25 € – Carte 29/46 €

♦ Brasserie ♦ Retro ♦

Chic 1930s style brasserie where you meet everyone in Toulouse, along with stars who leave their photo to mark their visit. The veranda is turned into an outside dining area in fine weather.

La Corde
AC 6/25 VISA MC AE

4 r. Chalande – ✆ 05 61 29 09 43 – Fax 05 61 29 09 43 – www.lacorde.com
closed Monday lunch, Saturday lunch and Sunday **E2**
Rest – Menu 20 € (weekday lunch), 30/100 € bi – Carte 45/94 €
♦ Contemporary ♦ Formal ♦
This impressive 15C tower, all that remains of a mansion that used to belong to prominent families of Toulouse, is home to the city's oldest restaurant (1881). Updated regional dishes

L'Empereur de Huê
AC VISA MC

17 r. Couteliers – ✆ 05 61 53 55 72 – Fax 05 61 53 55 72
– www.empereurdehue.com **E2**
Rest – *(closed Tuesday) (dinner only) (pre-book)* Menu 33 € (weekdays)
– Carte 39/46 €
♦ Vietnamese ♦ Exotic ♦
If the decor of this family restaurant is contemporary, the cooking holds on to its Vietnamese roots.

BLAGNAC *Plan I*

Sofitel
rm 90/90 VISA MC AE

2 av. Didier Daurat (dir. airport (exit n° 3)) – ✆ 05 34 56 11 11 – h0565@accor.com – Fax 05 61 30 02 43 **A1**
100 rm – †230/290 € ††230/290 €, ☐ 22 €
Rest *Caouec* – *(closed Saturday, Sunday and Bank Holidays)* Carte 42/60 €
♦ Chain hotel ♦ Business ♦ Modern ♦
This hotel built in the 1970s is being treated to a total facelift: new trendy public areas and many of the rooms made over in the same spirit. Free shuttle to the airport. The Caouec offers traditional cuisine and some specialities of southwest France.

Holiday Inn Airport
rm AC rm 15/150 P VISA MC AE

pl. Révolution – ✆ 05 34 36 00 20 – tlsap@ichotelsgroup.com – Fax 05 34 36 00 30
– www.toulouseairport.holiday-inn.com **A1**
150 rm – †135/260 € ††135/260 €, ☐ 20 €
Rest – Menu 22/35 €
♦ Chain hotel ♦ Business ♦ Modern ♦
Both peaceful and warm shades adorn the rooms decorated with modern furniture. A well-appointed seminar area. A shuttle links the hotel to the airport. A pleasant brasserie-style restaurant decorated with frescoes depicting olive trees.

Du Cercle d'Oc
AC 10/20 P VISA MC AE

6 pl. M. Dassault – ✆ 05 62 74 71 71 – cercledoc@wanadoo.fr
– Fax 05 62 74 71 72
closed 1st-19 August, 25 December-1st January, Saturday and Sunday **A1**
Rest – Menu 34 € bi (weekday lunch), 50 € bi/58 € bi
♦ Contemporary ♦ Fashionable ♦
This pretty 18C farm is an island of greenery in the middle of a shopping area. English club atmosphere in the lounge and elegant dining room. Pleasant terrace.

Le Pré Carré
AC 25 VISA MC AE

Toulouse-Blagnac airport, (2nd flour) – ✆ 05 61 16 70 40 – Fax 05 61 16 70 50
closed 15 July-19 August, Saturday and Sunday **A1**
Rest – Menu 42 € – Carte approx. 58 €
♦ Contemporary ♦ Brasserie ♦
Pleasant airport restaurant facing the runways, inside a brasserie. Design decor in red tones and wood furnishings.

GERMANY
DEUTSCHLAND

PROFILE

◆ **Area:**
356 733 km² (137 735 sq mi).

◆ **Population:**
82 431 000 inhabitants (est. 2005), density = 231 per km².

◆ **Capital:**
Berlin (conurbation 3 761 000 inhabitants).

◆ **Currency:**
Euro (€); rate of exchange: € 1 = US$ 1.32 (Nov 2006).

◆ **Government:**
Parliamentary federal republic, comprising 16 states (Länder) since 1990. Member of European Union since 1957 (one of the 6 founding countries).

◆ **Language:**
German.

◆ **Specific public holidays:**
Epiphany (6 January – in Baden-Württemberg, Bayern and Sachsen-Anhalt only); Good Friday (Friday before Easter); Corpus Christi (in Baden-Württemberg, Bayern, Hessen, Nordrhein-Westfalen, Rheinland-Pfalz, Saarland, Sachsen, Thüringen and those communities with a predominantly Roman Catholic population only); Day of German Unity (3 October); Reformation Day (31 October – in new Federal States only); 26 December.

◆ **Local Time:**
GMT + 1 hour in winter and GMT + 2 hours in summer.

◆ **Climate:**
Temperate continental, with cold winters and warm summers (Berlin: January: 0°C, July: 20°C).

◆ **International dialling Code:**
00 49 followed by area code and then the local number. International directory enquiries ✆ **11 834**.

◆ **Emergency:**
Police: ✆ **110**; Fire Brigade: ✆ **112**.

◆ **Electricity:**
220 volts AC, 50HZ; 2-pin round-shaped continental plugs.

FORMALITIES

Travellers from the European Union (EU), Switzerland, Iceland and the main countries of North and South America need a national identity card or passport (America: passport required) to visit Germany for less than three months (tourism or business purpose). For visitors from other countries a visa may be required, in addition to a passport, especially for those wishing to stay for longer than three months. We advise you to check with your embassy before travelling.

A valid national or international driving licence is required. Valid insurance cover is compulsory. To hire a car the driver must be over 23 and have held a driving licence for more than one year.

MAJOR NEWSPAPERS

Die Welt, Frankfurter Allgemeine Zeitung, Frankfurter Rundschau and *Süddeutsche Zeitung* are distributed nationally; Regional newpapers: in Berlin: *Berliner Morgenpost, Tagesspiegel, Berliner Zeitung, taz, BZ*; in Frankfurt: *Frankfurter Neue Presse*; in Hamburg: *Hamburger Morgenpost, Hamburger Abendblatt*; in Munich: *Münchner Merkur, AZ*.

USEFUL PHRASES

ENGLISH	GERMAN
Yes	**Ja**
No	**Nein**
Good morning	**Guten Tag**
Goodbye	**Auf Wiedersehen**
Thank you	**Danke**
Please	**Bitte**
Excuse me	**Entschuldigung**
I don't understand	**Ich verstehe nicht**

HOTELS

→ CATEGORIES

Accommodation ranges from luxurious 5-star international hotels, via smaller, family-run guesthouses to bed-and-breakfast establishments. The German Hotel Reservation Service (HRS) makes reservations in all hotels, inns and pensions – www.hrs.de

→ PRICE RANGE

The price is per room. In summer hotels in Berlin and Frankfurt may offer cheaper rates.

→ TAX

Included in the room price.

→ CHECK OUT TIME

Usually between 11am and noon.

→ RESERVATIONS

By telephone or by Internet; a credit card number may be required.

→ TIP FOR LUGGAGE HANDLING

At the discretion of the customer (about €1 per bag).

→ BREAKFAST

Breakfast is usually included in the price of the room and is served between 7am and 10am. Most hotels offer a buffet meal but usually it is possible to have continental breakfast served in the room.

Reception	**Rezeption**
Single room	**Einzelzimmer**
Double room	**Doppelzimmer**
Bed	**Bett**
Bathroom	**Badezimmer**
Shower	**Dusche**

RESTAURANTS

Restaurants serve lunch from noon to 2pm and dinner from 7pm to 10pm, although some restaurants continue to serve after 10pm.

Besides the traditional **restaurants** there are small fast-food concerns (**Imbiss)** in towns, at the roadside and on motorways, and which are good for a light lunch of grilled sausage *(Bratwurst)* with potato salad or chips.

Breakfast	**Frühstück**	7am – 10am
Lunch	**Mittagessen**	12 noon – 2pm
Dinner	**Abendessen**	7pm – 10pm

Restaurants offer fixed price menus (starter, main course and dessert) or à la carte. A fixed price menu is usually less expensive than the same dishes chosen à la carte. Menus are printed in German and sometimes in English.

→ RESERVATIONS

Reservations are usually made by phone. For famous restaurants (including Michelin starred restaurants), it is advisable to book several days – in some instances weeks – in advance. A credit card number or a phone number may be required to guarantee the booking.

→ THE BILL

The bill (check) includes service charge and VAT. It is customary to leave a tip of about 5-10% of the total bill.

Drink or aperitif	**Getränk oder Aperitif**
Appetizer	**kleine Vorspeise**
Meal	**Mahlzeit**
Starter	**Vorspeise**
Main dish	**Hauptgericht**
Main dish of the day	**Tagesgericht**
Dessert	**Nachspeise**
Water, mineral water	**Wasser, Wasser mit Kohlensäure**
Wine (red, white, rosé)	**Wein (rot, weiss, rosé)**
Beer	**Bier**
Bread	**Brot**
Meat	**Fleisch**
Fish	**Fisch**
Salt/pepper	**Salz/Pfeffer**
Cheese	**Käse**
Vegetables	**Gemüse**
Hot/cold	**heiss/kalt**
The bill (check) please	**Die Rechnung, bitte**

LOCAL CUISINE

German food is more varied and better balanced than is generally supposed, and the composition and presentation of meals are in themselves original.

Breakfast includes cold meats and cheese with some of Germany's 300 varieties of breads and rolls, and often a soft-boiled egg. Lunch usually begins with soup, followed by a fish or meat main course always accompanied by a salad (lettuce, cucumber, shredded cabbage). For the evening meal, there will be a choice of cold meats (**Aufschnitt**), delicatessen and cheeses, with a selection of different types of bread and/or rolls.

Certain dishes are served all over the country: the most popular are **Wiener Schnitzel** (veal cutlet fried in bread crumbs), **Eisbein** (salted knuckle or shin of pork), **Sauerbraten** (beef in a brown sauce) and **Gulasch** (either in the form of soup or as a stew).

Certain specialities are regional: in Hessen and Westphalia you may find **Töttchen** (ragout of brains and calf's head, cooked with herbs). Lower Saxony and Schleswig-Holstein are known for **Aalsuppe** (sweet-and-sour soup, made of eels, prunes, pears, vegetables, bacon and seasoning) and **Labskaus** (a favourite sailor's dish of beef, pork and salted herrings with potatoes and beetroot, the whole topped with gherkins and fried egg). The specialities in Bavaria and Franconia include **Leberknödel** (large dumplings of liver, bread and chopped onion, served in a clear soup), **Leberkäs** (minced beef, pork and liver, cooked as a galantine), **Knödel** (dumplings of potato or soaked bread), **Haxen** (veal or pork trotters), **Schlachtschüssel** (breast of pork, liver sausage and black pudding, served with pickled cabbage and dumplings) and **Rostbratwürste** (small sausages grilled over beechwood charcoal).

➜ DRINK

The national beverage is **beer**, of which the Germans are justifiably proud. There are nearly 1,200 breweries in Germany, still brewing in accordance with a purity law *(Reinheitsgebot)* decreed in 1516 which forbids the use of anything but barley, hops and plain water, although nowadays yeast may be added.

German vineyards produce a great variety of wine from a wide range of grapes – as the visitor may discover in most bars and restaurants, sampling them by the glass *(offene Weine)*. Notable among the **white wines** (80% of production) are the vigorous Rieslings of the Middle Rhein and those of the Mosel, Saar and Ruhr rivers, aromatic and refreshing; the high quality, delicate wines of the Rheingau; full-bodied and elegant Nahe wines; the potent wines of Franconia, verging sometimes on the bitter; and the many and varied wines of Baden and Württemberg. Among the **red wines**, particularly choice examples come from Rheinhessen and Württemberg, not forgetting the vigorous, well-balanced reds of the Palatinate and, above all, the wines of the Ahr, paradise of the Spätburgunder. **Sekt**, German sparkling wine is popular for special occasions. Germany also bottles a good range of mineral waters.

In Germany the favourite spirit, for an after-dinner drink, is **Schnapps**, the generic term for all spirits, whether they are clear or coloured, bitter or sweet; generally they are clear. In the northern and eastern part of Germany Schnapps is mostly distilled from grain, such as Doppelkorn (corn spirit); in the south, however, fruits from the orchards of the Rhine Valley and the Lake Constance area are distilled to obtain fruit-flavoured spirits, and the berries from the Black Forest are used to create fine, scented spirits, such as Kirschwasser (cherry brandy).

BERLIN

BERLIN

Population: 3 373 000 (conurbation 3 761 000) – Altitude: 40m

N. Hautemanière / SCOPE

Berlin, once symbol of two opposing ideologies, is a modern metropolis with a lively economic and cultural life. It owes its dynamism to the fact that for 30 years both Federal Republic and former East Germany made the city a showcase for their respective ways of life.

Berlin was first mentioned in 1244 and in 1359 joined the Hanseatic League. In 1871 the city became the German Empire's capital. Industrialisation began in the early 19C and by 1929 it was the largest commercial city in continental Europe. The Allies (France, UK, USA, USSR) administered Berlin after 1945. During the 1950s the disparity in the standard of living between East and West Berlin caused important immigration to the West.

In August 1961 the crossing points were closed and the wall was built. West Berlin became an enclave in East Germany, linked to West Germany by a road, a rail and an air corridor. In 1990 the wall was demolished and the city and the country reunified.

During division period, West Berlin was embellished with the work of famous architects such Le Corbusier and provided with many cultural facilities to keep the town alive: numerous first-class museums, universities, concert and opera halls, Schiller Theatre and Kulturforum. The city has had a great reputation for music, maintained in the post-war years especially by H. von Karajan.

WHICH DISTRICT TO CHOOSE

Berlin offers a great selection of **hotels** in all categories. Most of the established hotels are located in the western part of the city near Kurfürstendamm *Plan III* **K2**. Several new hotels have been opened in the last 10 years, mostly in the eastern part of the city – near Sony Center, Unter den Linden *Plan II* **G1** and Gendarmenmarkt *Plan II* **G2**.

The best cooking in the city is usually found in the grand hotels but there are a good many interesting **restaurants** in the town centre, which is also a focal point for shopping and sightseeing. Many of these restaurants are located near Gendarmenmarkt, Unter den Linden and Brandenburger Tor *Plan II* **F1**. In the last few

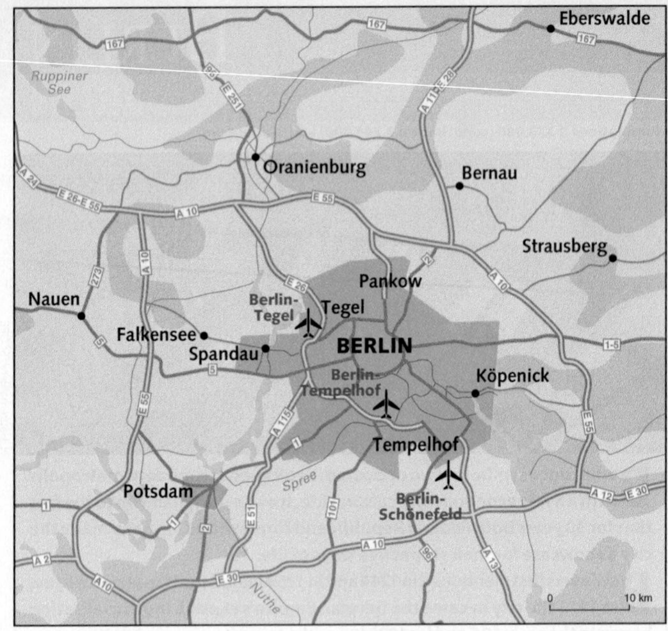

years several small restaurants have been opened in the Kreuzberg district *Plan I* **C3** offering a casual atmosphere and good value. An interesting selection of cosy restaurants also exists in the western part of the city not far from Kurfürstendamm and Europacenter *Plan III* **K2**.

PRACTICAL INFORMATION

ARRIVAL – DEPARTURE

Berlin-Tegel Airport (TXL) about 12 km (8 mi) northwest of the city centre – **Transport to the city centre**: by **taxi** (€18), by **U-Bahn** and **S-Bahn** trains.

Berlin-Tempelhof Airport (THF) about 7 km (4 mi) south of the city centre – **Transport to the city centre**: by **U-Bahn** train.

Berlin-Schönefeld Airport (SXF) about 21 km (13 mi) southeast of the city centre – **Transport to the city centre**: by **S-Bahn** trains; by **taxi** to the Zoo station (approx. €30-35).

Buses operate between Tegel Airport and Schönefeld Airport every 30min. ✆ 01 805 000 186.

Railway Stations – **Hauptbahnhof** (Lehrter Bahnhof) ✆ (030) 2 97 10 55; **Bahnhof Zoo-logischer Garten** (Bahnhof Zoo) in Charlottenburg for trains to the west, ✆ (030) 19 44 9; **Spandau Station** for trains to the north; **Wannsee Station** for trains to the south and west; **Ostbahnhof** for trains to the east; **Bahnhof Lichtenberg** for regional trains and trains to the north.

TRANSPORT

→ BUSES, TRAMS AND METRO

Buses operate between 4.30am and 1am (entrance is at the front - exit in the middle); the metro (**U-Bahn**) operates between 4am and midnight/1am; **S-Bahn** trains run every 10min.

Berlin and its environs (eg Potsdam) are divided into 3 fare zones; Zone AB for journeys within the city. Tickets are available in all U-Bahn and S-Bahn stations, at yellow and orange ticket vending machines, on trams and from bus drivers; the ticket must be punched in the red box on the bus or in front of the escalators. Normal fare €2.10 (valid 2hr); short journey *(Kurzstreckentarif)* €1.20 valid for 3 U-Bahn or S-Bahn stations and for 6 bus stations without changing line; weekly pass *(Wochenkarte)* €25.40; day ticket €5.80; group day ticket (2 adult and up to 3 children) €14.80 – day cards are valid from the time of punching until 3am next morning.

Buses, **trams** and **metro** are controlled by the **BGV** (Berliner Verkehrs-Betriebe); ✆ (030) 1 94 49 (Mon-Fri 6am-11pm); the **S-Bahn** and the region round Berlin are controlled by the **VBB** (Verkehrsverbund Berlin-Brandenburg) in conjunction with the BGV, ✆ (030) 25 41 41 41 (Mon-Fri 8am-8pm, Sat-Sun 9am-6pm). Information available at the BGV-Pavilion in Hardenbergplatz (Bahnhof Zoo) (6.30am-8.30pm) and at many U-Bahn and S-Bahn stations.

The **Berlin–Potsdam Welcome Card** €22 (valid 3 days) for an adult with up to three children (under 14yrs) on the entire VBB network; it also gives discounts for selected theatres, museums, attractions and city tours. The card is available at public transport ticket desks, in many hotels and at the information offices of the Berlin Tourismus Marketing.

Bus number 100, which shuttles between Bahnhof Zoo and Alexanderplatz, connecting the two city centres, passes many of Berlin's sights.

→ TAXIS

There are taxi ranks dispersed all over the western part of Berlin, in particular at the **Zoo Station** (Hardenbergplatz in Charlottenburg) and at **Savignyplatz** (in Charlottenburg too); in the east the taxi ranks are concentrated in **Alexanderplatz**, at the entrance to the S-Bahn station, in front of the Palasthotel, on **Unter den Linden**, to the south of the **Weidendammerbrücke**, in **Rosenthaler Platz** and near the **Volksbühne**. Basic fare €2.50; many taxis accept credit cards. ✆ (0800) 026 10 26; www.funktaxi-berlin.de

USEFUL ADDRESSES

→ TOURIST INFORMATION

Berlin Tourismus Marketing: Mon-Fri 8am-7pm, Sat-Sun 9am-6pm; ✆ (030) 25 00 25. **Brandenburg Gate** *Plan II* ***F1***, south wing: 9.30am-6pm. **Hauptbahnhof** *Plan II* ***F1***, (entrance nord) Mon-Sat 10am-8pm, Sun 10am-6pm. **Reichstag**. *Plan II* ***F1***, (pavillon) 8.30am-8pm, www.berlin-tourist.information.de.

→ POST OFFICES

Mon-Fri 8am-6pm, Sat 8am-12 noon. **Post-Office 120**, Zoologischer Garten Station: Mon-Sat 9am-8pm; **Post-Office 519**, Tegel Airport, Main Hall: Mon-Fri 8am-8pm, Sat 8-1am (Deutsche Post AG ✆ (01802) 33 33).

→ BANKS/CURRENCY EXCHANGE

Mon-Fri 8.30am-12.30pm and 2-4pm (sometimes later); closed Sat-Sun and public holidays. Foreign exchange offices generally offer better rates than banks and some are open until late in the evening and at the weekend.

➜ **EMERGENCY**

Police : ✆ **110**; Fire Brigade: ✆ **112**.

BUSY PERIODS

It may be difficult to find a room at a reasonable price (except during weekends) when special events are held in the city as hotel prices may be raised substantially:

Berlin Fair: January.

Berlinale: February – International Film Festival.

Internationale Tourismus-Börse (ITB): March – International Tourism Fair.

Internationale Funkausstellung: September – International Consumer Electronics trade fair.

Jazz Festival: November.

EXPLORING BERLIN

DIFFERENT FACETS OF THE CITY

It is possible to visit the main museums and sights of Berlin in four to five days.

Museums and sights are usually open from 10am to 5pm. Most close on Mondays and public holidays.

Bus number 100 which shuttles between Bahnhof Zoo and Alexanderplatz, connecting the two city centres, passes by many of Berlin's sights.

HISTORIC CENTRE – **Brandenburg Gate** *Plan II* **F1**. Once part of the wall dividing the city but now restored to its role as triumphal arch. **Unter den Linden** *Plan II* **G1**. Famous avenue 'under the lime trees'. **Gendarmenmarkt** *Plan II* **G2**. The most beautiful square in Berlin, bordered by the **Schauspielhaus** and two 18C churches – **Deutscher Dom** and **Französischer Dom** – which now house museums. **Zeughaus** *Plan II* **H1**. Baroque edifice housing the German Historical Museum.

MUSEUM SELECTION – **Gemäldegalerie** *Plan II* **F2**. Comprehensive collection of European painting from 13C to 18C. **Neue Nationalgalerie.** 20C paintings and sculpture housed in a steel and glass structure by Mies van der Rohe. **Pergamonmuseum** *Plan II* **G1**. Greek and Roman Antiquities, Middle Eastern antiquities and Islamic Art. **Egyptian Museum** *Plan III* **I1**. Collections from the time of the Pharaohs, including the bust of Queen Nefertiti. **Museum of Ethnography**. **Alte Nationalgalerie** *Plan II* **H1**. 19C paintings and sculptures. **Bode-Museum** *Plan II* **G1**. Sculpture and numismatic collections. **Altes Museum** *Plan II* **H1**. Antique jewellery (Hildesheimer Silberfund) and Greek and Roman antiquities. **Deutsches Historisches Museum** *Plan II* **H1**. German Historical Museum. **Kunstgewerbemuseum** *Plan II* **F2**. Museum of decorative art. **Museum Haus am Checkpoint Charlie** *Plan II* **G2**. Berlin Wall Museum illustrating the construction of the Berlin Wall and attempts to climb over it.

CHARLOTTENBURG – **Schloss Charlottenburg** *Plan III* **I1**. Royal summer residence named after Sophie-Charlotte, wife of Frederick I, and its English landscaped garden. **Kaiser-Wilhelm-Gedächtniskirche** *Plan III* **K2**. Ruined neo-Romanesque church preserved as a reminder of the horrors of conflict. **Kurfürstendamm**. The prestigious Ku'damm, the centre of Berlin cosmopolitan life (cafés, restaurants, theatres, cinemas, galleries and fashion boutiques).

OUTDOOR BERLIN – **Boat trips**. Through the **historic centre** (1hr) beginning in the Nikolaiviertel *Plan II* **H1**; through the **inner city** on the Spree and the Landwehr canals (3hr 30min) beginning at the Jannowitzbrücke and Schlossbrücke; on the **Havel** from Wannsee to Potsdam/Lange Brücke (1hr 15min); ✆ (030) 5 36 36 00.

GOURMET TREATS

A great variety of international cuisine is on offer together with traditional Brandenburger specialities such as **Eisbein** (pig's knuckles with sauerkraut and pease-pudding). Berliners call a tankard of lager beer a **Berliner Molle**; a light beer with a dash of raspberry syrup or woodruff is a **Berliner Weisse mit Schuss**. In summer the **beer** tastes better in a beer garden. For **Kaffee und Kuchen** (coffee and cake) try one of the cafés in the Kurfürstendamm or Unter den Linden; the **Tele-Café** (Panoramastrasse 1) in the Television Tower (200m/640ft) turns on its axis every 30min and offers a fine view.

SHOPPING

Shops are usually open from 9am/10am to 6.30pm/8pm. They are closed on Sunday.

Good shopping streets are **Tauentzienstrasse/Kurfürstendamm** *Plan III* **K2** and the **Potsdamer Platz Arkaden** *Plan II* **G2**. Berlin's most famous **department stores** are the *KaDeWe* (Tauentzienstrasse 221), a gigantic selection in a luxurious setting, and *Galeries Lafayette* (Friedrichstrasse 207), a reasonably priced shop in an amazing architectural setting. **Exclusive shops** are located in **Fasanenstrasse** *Plan III* **K2** and **Friedrichstrasse** *Plan II* **G1**. **Off-beat shops** are to be found in **Kreuzberg** *Plan I* **C3** and **Prenzlauer Berg** *Plan I* **D1**. *Hackesche Höfe* (Rosenthalerstrasse/Sophienstrasse) is a special shopping address, offering 8 floors of arcades, fashion boutiques, antiques shops, restaurants and bars, a cinema and even a cabaret (www.hackesche-hoefe.com).

For **antiques** the best streets are around **Eisenacher Strasse/Kalckreuthstrasse** and **Keithstrasse**, in **Fasanenstrasse**, around **Bleibtreustrasse**, **Pestalozzistrasse**, and **Knesebeckstrasse** and under the arches of the S-Bahn in **Friedrichstrasse**.

MARKETS – There is a twice-weekly market in **Winterfeldplatz** *Plan III* **L3** (Wed and Sat 8am-1pm) and a **Turkish** weekly market in **Maybachufer** *Plan I* **D3** (Tue and Fri noon-6.30pm). The Great Berlin **flea and art** market is held in **Charlottenburg** (Strasse des 17 Juni – Sat-Sun 11am-5pm). There are other flea markets in **Wilmersdorf** (Fehrbelliner Platz – Sat-Sun 7am-4pm). Berlin **art and nostalgia** market in **Museumsinsel** *Plan II* **H1** (Sat-Sun 11am-5pm).

WHAT TO BUY – Porcelain, crystal glass, fashion, music recordings, children's toys, Cold War souvenirs (Red Army clothes and symbols etc.).

ENTERTAINMENT

Zitty and *Tip*, published fortnightly and the *Berlin-Programm*, published monthly, provide information on events of all kinds. Berlin's major dailies have a weekly insert featuring a calendar of events. Tickets are available up to 3 weeks before the performance at *Berlin Tourismus Marketing*. The numerous theatre box offices are the best place to buy tickets when in town.

Deutsche Oper Berlin *Plan III* **I1** – Charlottenburg Opera House rebuilt after the war.

Staatsoper Unter den Linden *Plan II* **G1** – The oldest and most magnificent opera house in Berlin.

Komische Oper *Plan II* **G1** – Theatre founded in 1947.

Theater des Westens *Plan III* **K2** – Musical productions.

Konzerthaus Berlin *Plan II* **G1** – Berlin's most beautiful concert hall.

Philharmonie und Kammermusiksaal *Plan II* **F2** – Home of the Berlin Philharmonic Orchestra.

Berliner Ensemble *Plan II* **G1** – Home base of the company founded by Bertolt Brecht who staged the *Threepenny Opera* here in 1928.

Deutsches Theater *Plan II* **G1** – With 3 stages and repertory ranging from classical to contemporary.

Friedrichstadtpalast *Plan II* **G1** – The most important revue theatre in Europe.

Wintergarten Variété *Plan II* **F2** – Variety, acrobats, magicians and illusionists.

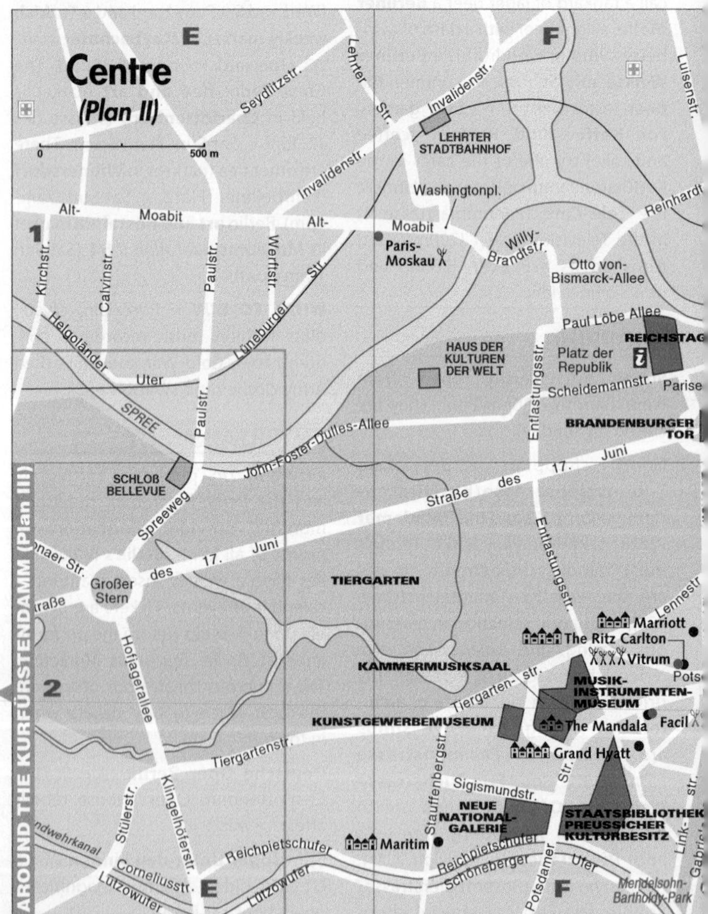

NIGHTLIFE

Berlin's night-life has a great reputation with countless bars, discotheques, pubs and clubs of all styles. All the 'in' shops sell magazines, such as *030*, which publishes information about all the latest trends and clubs. The night-life on the **Kreuzberg Hill** has a cosmopolitan, anti-establishment flavour but many other districts have plenty going on. *Dorian Gray*, Marlene-Dietrich-Platz 4, Mitte provides 3 floors of music and partying. *Knaack Klub Berlin*, Greifswalder Strasse 224, **Prenzlauer Berg**, for every type of music and karaoke. In **Charlottenburg** for a traditional atmosphere try *Schwarzes Café*, Kantstrasse 148; *Zillemarket*, Bleibtreustrasse 48a or *Hardtke*, Meineckestrasse 27. In **Schöneberg** *Slumberland*, Goltzstrasse 24, plays reggae. In **Tiergarten** try the elegant cocktails served at the very long bar in *Bar am Lützowplatz*, Lützowplatz 7. German's most modern casino is the *Spielbank Berlin*, Marlene-Dietrich-Platz 1, Mitte.

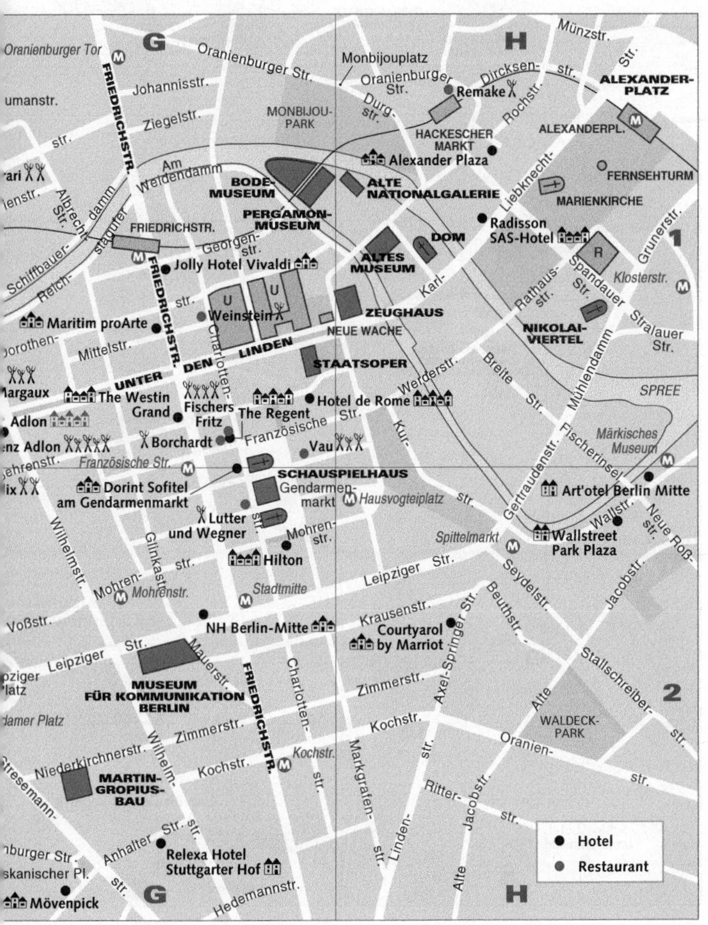

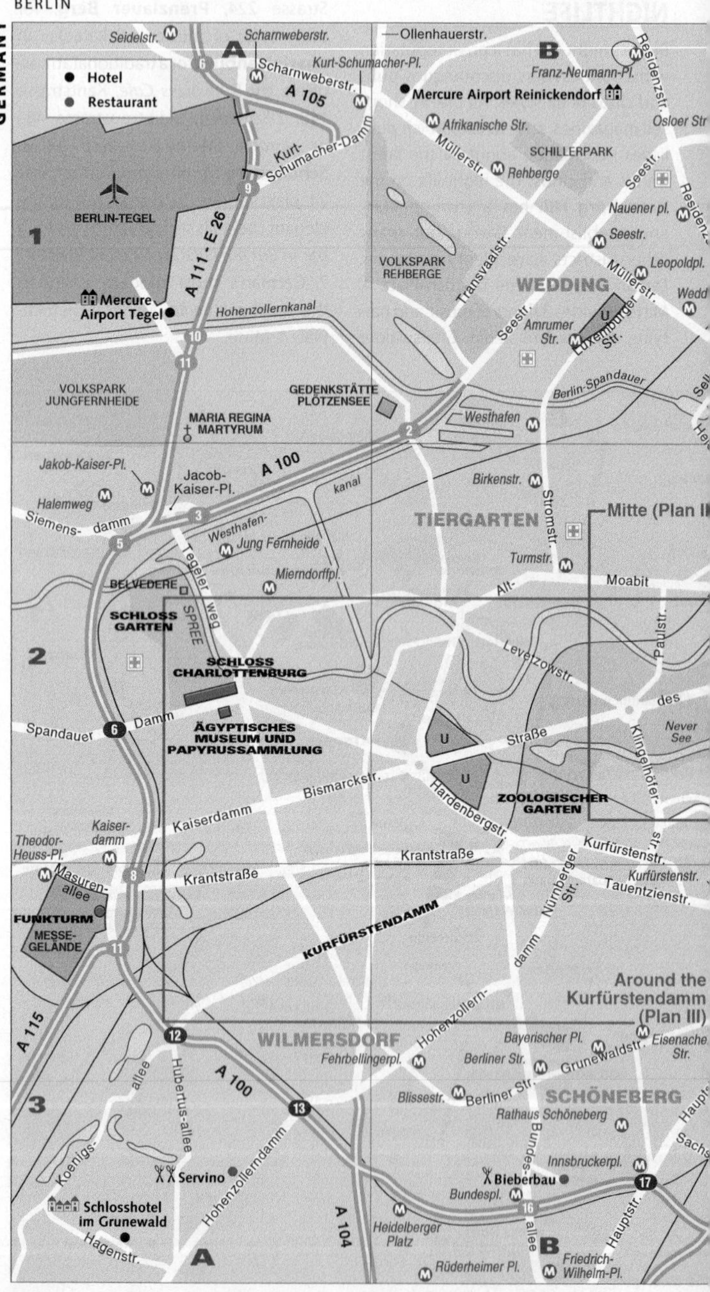
Hotel
Restaurant
Seidelstr.
Scharnweberstr.
Ollenhauerstr.
Kurt-Schumacher-Pl.
Scharnweberstr.
A 105
Franz-Neumann-Pl.
Mercure Airport Reinickendorf
Residenzstr.
Osloer Str
Afrikanische Str.
Müllerstr.
Rehberge
SCHILLERPARK
Kurt-Schumacher-Damm
BERLIN-TEGEL
A 111 - E 26
Seestr.
Nauener pl.
Seestr.
Residenz
Transvaalstr.
VOLKSPARK REHBERGE
Müllerstr.
Leopoldpl.
WEDDING
Wedd
Mercure Airport Tegel
Hohenzollernkanal
Seestr.
Amrumer Str.
Luxemburger Str.
VOLKSPARK JUNGFERNHEIDE
GEDENKSTÄTTE PLÖTZENSEE
Berlin-Spandauer
MARIA REGINA MARTYRUM
Westhafen
A 100
Jakob-Kaiser-Pl.
Jacob-Kaiser-Pl.
Halemweg
kanal
Birkenstr.
Siemens- damm
TIERGARTEN
Stromstr.
Mitte (Plan I
Westhafen-
Jung Fernheide
Tegeler weg
Turmstr.
Mierndorffpl.
BELVEDERE
Alt-
Moabit
SCHLOSS GARTEN
SPREE
Paulstr.
SCHLOSS CHARLOTTENBURG
Levetzowstr.
des
Spandauer Damm
ÄGYPTISCHES MUSEUM UND PAPYRUSSAMMLUNG
Straße
Never See
Klingelhöfer-str.
Bismarckstr.
Hardenbergstr.
ZOOLOGISCHER GARTEN
Kaiserdamm
Theodor-Heuss-Pl.
Kaiser-damm
Krantstraße
Kurfürstenstr.
Masurenallee
Krantstraße
Kurfürstenstr.
Tauentzienstr.
Nürnberger Str.
FUNKTURM
MESSE-GELÄNDE
KURFÜRSTENDAMM
A 115
Hohenzollern-damm
Around the Kurfürstendamm (Plan III)
WILMERSDORF
Bayerischer Pl.
Eisenacher Str.
Fehrbellingerpl.
Berliner Str.
Grunewaldstr.
A 100
allee
Hubertus-allee
Blissestr.
Berliner Str.
SCHÖNEBERG
Rathaus Schöneberg
Hauptstr.
Koenigs-
Hohenzollerndamm
Sachs
Servino
Innsbruckerpl.
Bieberbau
Bundes-allee
Bundespl.
Schlosshotel im Grunewald
A 104
Heidelberger Platz
Hauptstr.
Hagenstr.
A
B
Rüderheimer Pl.
Friedrich-Wilhelm-Pl.
1
2
3

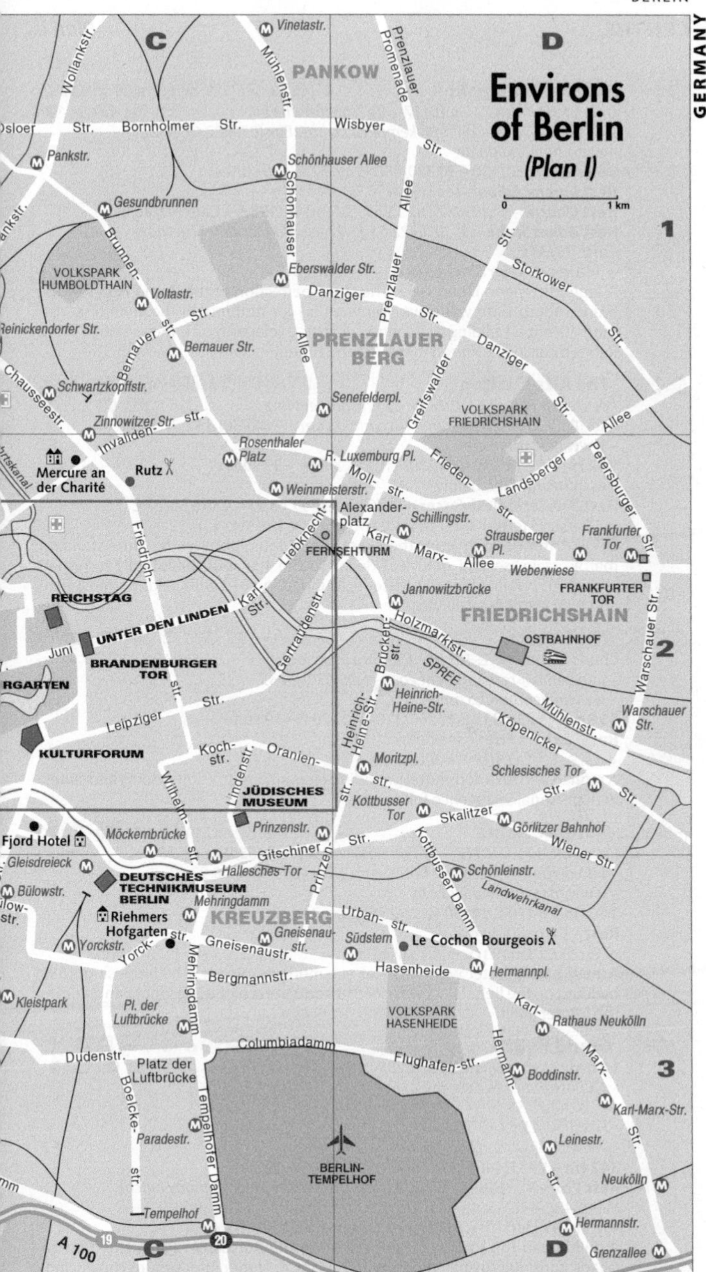
Environs of Berlin
(Plan I)
0
1 km
C
D
1
2
3
PANKOW
PRENZLAUER BERG
FRIEDRICHSHAIN
KREUZBERG
VOLKSPARK HUMBOLDTHAIN
VOLKSPARK FRIEDRICHSHAIN
VOLKSPARK HASENHEIDE
Vinetastr.
Pankstr.
Gesundbrunnen
Schönhauser Allee
Eberswalder Str.
Voltastr.
Bernauer Str.
Schwartzkopffstr.
Senefelderpl.
Zinnowitzer Str.
Rosenthaler Platz
R. Luxemburg Pl.
Weinmeisterstr.
Alexanderplatz
Schillingstr.
Strausberger Pl.
Frankfurter Tor
Weberwiese
Jannowitzbrücke
Heinrich-Heine-Str.
Warschauer Str.
Moritzpl.
Schlesisches Tor
Kottbusser Tor
Görlitzer Bahnhof
Prinzenstr.
Möckernbrücke
Gleisdreieck
Bülowstr.
Mehringdamm
Gneisenaustr.
Südstern
Hermannpl.
Schönleinstr.
Yorckstr.
Kleistpark
Pl. der Luftbrücke
Rathaus Neukölln
Boddinstr.
Karl-Marx-Str.
Leinestr.
Neukölln
Hermannstr.
Grenzallee
Paradestr.
Tempelhof
Wollankstr.
Mühlenstr.
Prenzlauer Promenade
Bornholmer Str.
Wisbyer Str.
Schönhauser Allee
Prenzlauer Allee
Storkower Str.
Danziger Str.
Brunnenstr.
Bernauer Str.
Reinickendorfer Str.
Chausseestr.
Invalidenstr.
Greifswalder Str.
Friedenstr.
Landsberger Allee
Petersburger Str.
Mollstr.
Karl-Marx-Allee
Liebknechtstr.
Karl-Str.
Friedrichstr.
Gertraudenstr.
Holzmarktstr.
Brückenstr.
SPREE
Mühlenstr.
Köpenicker Str.
Warschauer Str.
Leipziger Str.
Kochstr.
Oranienstr.
Lindenstr.
Wilhelmstr.
Skalitzer Str.
Wiener Str.
Gitschiner Str.
Hallesches Tor
Prinzenstr.
Kottbusser Damm
Landwehrkanal
Urbanstr.
Gneisenaustr.
Yorckstr.
Bergmannstr.
Hasenheide
Karl-Marx-Str.
Hermannstr.
Mehringdamm
Columbiadamm
Flughafenstr.
Dudenstr.
Boelckestr.
Tempelhofer Damm
A 100
19
20
FERNSEHTURM
REICHSTAG
UNTER DEN LINDEN
BRANDENBURGER TOR
Juni
RGARTEN
KULTURFORUM
JÜDISCHES MUSEUM
DEUTSCHES TECHNIKMUSEUM BERLIN
OSTBAHNHOF
FRANKFURTER TOR
BERLIN-TEMPELHOF
Platz der Luftbrücke
Mercure an der Charité
Rutz
Fjord Hotel
Riehmers Hofgarten
Le Cochon Bourgeois

CENTRE

Plan II

Adlon Kempinski

Unter den Linden 77 ✉ 10117 – Ⓜ Französische Str.
– ✆ (030) 2 26 10 – adlon@kempinski.com – Fax (030) 22 61 22 22
– www.hotel-adlon.de **G1**

385 rm – 380/490 € 380/490 €, ☕ 32 € – 29 suites

Rest *Lorenz Adlon* – see below

Rest *Quarré* – *✆ (030) 22 61 15 55* – Menu 46/108 € – Carte 42/86 €

Rest *Adlon Stube* – *✆ (030) 22 61 11 27 (closed Monday - Tuesday)*
Carte 25/34 €

♦ Palace ♦ Grand Luxury ♦ Classic ♦

A legend came to life in 1997. The sheer perfection of the Grand Hotel by the Brandenburg Gate will leave you wanting for nothing. In the style of earlier magnificent buildings. Quarré: classic, elegant. Terrace with view. Refined cuisine is offered in the Adlon Stube.

The Ritz-Carlton

Potsdamer Platz 3 ✉ 10785 – Ⓜ Potsdamer Platz
– ✆ (030) 33 77 77 – berlin@ritzcarlton.com – Fax (030) 3 37 77 55 55
– www.ritzcarlton.com **F2**

302 rm – 250/330 € 280/410 €, ☕ 29 € – 32 suites

Rest *Vitrum* – see below

Rest *Brasserie Desbrosses* – *✆ (030) 3 37 77 63 41* – Carte 30/57 €

♦ Chain hotel ♦ Grand Luxury ♦ Classic ♦

Elegant throughout: from the most sumptuous lobby with a free-standing marble staircase and gold leaf décor to the spacious, beautifully furnished rooms. An original French brasserie, founded in 1875 with a light atmosphere and typical meals available.

The Regent

Charlottenstr. 49 ✉ 10117 – Ⓜ Französische Str. – ✆ (030) 2 03 38
– info.berlin@rezidorregent.com – Fax (030) 20 33 61 19
– www.regenthotels.com **G1**

195 rm – 230/335 € 260/370 €, ☕ 29 € – 39 suites

Rest *Fischers Fritz* – see below

♦ Grand Luxury ♦ Classic ♦

A refined and luxurious hotel providing elegant and spacious rooms and suites, with personalised service for guests.

Hotel de Rome

Behrenstr. 17 ✉ 10117 – Ⓜ Französische Str. – ✆ (030) 4 60 60 90
– info.derome@roccofortehotels.com – Fax (030) 4 60 60 92 00
– www.roccofortehotels.com **G1**

146 rm – 420 € 450 €, ☕ 25 € – 9 suites

Rest – Carte 30/42 €

♦ Grand Luxury ♦ Classic ♦

A new luxury hotel with classical yet modern interior. This imposing 1889 building on the Bebelplatz was once headquarters of the Dresdner Bank. Pool in the former vault.

Grand Hyatt

Marlene-Dietrich Platz 2 ✉ 10785
– Ⓜ Potsdamer Platz
– ✆ (030) 25 53 12 34 – berlin@hyatt.de
– Fax (030) 25 53 12 35
– www.berlin.grand.hyatt.com **F2**

342 rm – 235/440 € 265/480 €, ☕ 27 € – 12 suites

Rest *Vox* – *✆ (030) 25 53 17 72 (closed Saturday lunch, Sunday lunch)*
Menu 42/54 € – Carte 43/56 €

♦ Chain hotel ♦ Grand Luxury ♦ Design ♦

A building in the shape of a trapezium on the Potsdamer Platz. The modern façade continues inside: rooms with puristic designer interiors are convincing. Vox offers an Asian atmosphere.

Marriott

rm 420 VISA

Inge-Beisheim-Platz 1 ✉ 10785 – Ⓜ Potsdamer Platz – ☎ (030) 22 00 00 – berlin@marriotthotels.com – Fax (030) 2 20 00 10 00 – www.berlinmarriott.com **F2**

379 rm – 179/259 € 179/259 €, 23 € – **Rest** – Carte 24/52 €

◆ Chain hotel ◆ Luxury ◆ Modern ◆

A modern business hotel with spacious atrium style lobby and comfortable rooms with American cherry wooden furnishings. Bistro style restaurant with open kitchen and large window façade.

Hilton

rm 330 VISA

Mohrenstr. 30 ✉ 10117 – Ⓜ Stadtmitte – ☎ (030) 2 02 30 – info.berlin@hilton.com – Fax (030) 20 23 42 69 – www.hilton.de **G2**

589 rm – 139/299 € 139/329 €, 23 € – 14 suites

Rest *Fellini* – *(closed 2 weeks early January, 3 weeks July - August) (dinner only)* Carte 30/40 €

Rest *Mark Brandenburg* – Carte 28/40 €

Rest *Trader Vic's* – *(dinner only)* Carte 31/46 €

◆ Chain hotel ◆ Functional ◆

Look forward to the spacious lobby, modern health facilities and the views of the Gendarmenmarkt from some of the rooms in this grand hotel. Fellini – Italian cuisine. Mark Brandenburg offers regional style. Polynesian cuisine served.

Radisson SAS-Hotel

rm 220 VISA

Karl-Liebknecht-Str. 3 ✉ 10178 – Ⓜ Alexanderplatz – ☎ (030) 23 82 80 – info.berlin@radissonsas.com – Fax (030) 2 38 28 10 – www.berlin.radissonsas.com **H1**

427 rm – 140/380 € 140/380 €, 22 €

Rest *HEat* – Menu 32/46 € – Carte 28/57 €

Rest *Noodle Kitchen* – *(dinner only)* Menu 28/38 € – Carte 28/41 €

◆ Chain hotel ◆ Business ◆ Stylish ◆

In the sleek atrium lobby is a 25-meter high cylindrical aquarium. Clean lines define the décor of the rooms. International cuisine in a modern bistro atmosphere. Noodle Kitchen with southeast Asian cuisine.

Maritim

1200 VISA

Stauffenbergstr. 26 ✉ 10785 – Ⓜ Mendelssohn-Bartholdy-Park – ☎ (030) 2 06 50 – info.ber@maritim.de – Fax (030) 20 65 10 10 – www.maritim.de **F2**

505 rm – 139/289 € 160/310 €, 22 €

Rest *Grandrestaurant M* – Menu 51/72 € – Carte 31/62 €

◆ Chain hotel ◆ Modern ◆

An exclusive, elegant lobby, refined rooms equipped with the most modern technology, and many options for special events. The presidential suite is an impressive 350 sq.m. A 1920s style restaurant.

The Westin Grand

rm 200 VISA

Freidrichstr. 158 ✉ 10117 – Ⓜ Französische Str. – ☎ (030) 2 02 70 – info@westin-grand.com – Fax (030) 20 27 33 62 – www.westin.com/berlin **G1**

358 rm – 129/435 € 129/435 €, 25 € – 18 suites

Rest *Friedrichs* – Carte 32/59 € – **Rest *Stammhaus*** – Carte 23/35 €

◆ Chain hotel ◆ Luxury ◆ Classic ◆

This hotel with the 30m high glass roof in the heart of the historical town is impressive. The hotel radiates elegance and nostalgic charm. Elegant ambience in the Friedrichs. Regional Berlin specialities are served in the Stammhaus. Lobster House with small fish counter.

The Mandala

20 VISA

Potsdamer Str. 3 ✉ 10785 – Ⓜ Potsdamer Platz – ☎ (030) 5 90 05 00 00 – welcome@themandala.de – Fax (030) 5 90 05 05 00 – www.themandala.de **F2**

166 rm – 180/370 € 205/395 €, 22 € – 17 suites – **Rest *Facil*** – see below

◆ Business ◆ Stylish ◆

An impressive location on Potsdamer Platz, opposite the Sony-Center, offering spacious, modern rooms with good technical facilities.

GERMANY

Mövenpick
rm 175 VISA

Schönebergerstr. 3 ✉ 10963 – ✆ (030) 23 00 60 – hotel.berlin@moevenpick.com – Fax (030) 23 00 61 99 – www.moevenpick-berlin.com **G2**

243 rm – †150/190 € ††170/210 €, ☕ 17 €

Rest – Carte 24/36 €

◆ Chain hotel ◆ Modern ◆

Formerly a Siemens building, now listed, providing a mixture of modern design and historical touches to create an unusual interior. Restaurant with glass-covered interior courtyard.

Maritim proArte
rm 600 VISA

Friedrichstr. 151 ✉ 10117 – Ⓜ Friedrichstr. – ✆ (030) 2 03 35 – info.bpa@maritim.de – Fax (030) 20 33 42 09 – www.maritim.de **G1**

403 rm – †137/263 € ††154/282 €, ☕ 20 €

Rest ***Atelier*** – *(dinner only)* Menu 49 €

Rest ***Bistro media*** – *(lunch only)* Carte 22/32 €

◆ Chain hotel ◆ Business ◆ Modern ◆

An avant-garde hotel near the lime tree-lined Pracht blvd. Providing well-appointed rooms with Jungen Wilden art on display. A modern designer style restaurant.

Jolly Hotel Vivaldi
rm 60 VISA

Friedrichstr. 96 ✉ 10117 – Ⓜ Friedrichstr. – ✆ (030) 2 06 26 60 – vivaldi.jhb@jollyhotels.de – Fax (030) 2 06 26 69 99 – www.jollyhotels.de **G1**

254 rm – †160/210 € ††180/230 €, ☕ 19 €

Rest – Carte 36/43 €

◆ Business ◆ Stylish ◆

When entering this modern, well-run hotel you will notice the spacious hall. High-quality wooden furniture and agreeable colours make the rooms a pleasant place to stay. Light, open-plan restaurant with Italian cuisine.

Dorint Sofitel am Gendarmenmarkt
rm 80 VISA

Charlottenstr. 50 ✉ 10117 – Ⓜ Französische Str. – ✆ (030) 20 37 50 – h5342@accor.com – Fax (030) 20 37 51 00 – www.sofitel.com **G1-2**

92 rm – †240/255 € ††270/285 €, ☕ 23 €

Rest ***Aigner*** – *✆ (030) 2 03 75 18 50* – Carte 30/47 €

◆ Chain hotel ◆ Business ◆ Design ◆

The hotel is directly opposite the French cathedral at the Gendarmenmarkt and has modern, designer rooms and a recreation area on the top floor. The Aigner was built from original parts of a Viennese coffeehouse.

Courtyard by Marriott
120 VISA

Axel-Springer-Str. 55 ✉ 10117 – Ⓜ Spittelmarkt – ✆ (030) 8 00 92 80 – berlin.mitte@coutyard.com – Fax (030) 80 09 28 10 00 – www.courtyard.com/bermt **H2**

267 rm – †99/189 € ††99/189 €, ☕ 16 € – 4 suites

Rest – Carte 19/26 €

◆ Chain hotel ◆ Business ◆ Functional ◆

A centrally located business hotel providing homely, well-equipped rooms with functional furnishings. A Mediterranean bistro style restaurant with bar.

Alexander Plaza
rm 70 VISA

Rosenstr. 1 ✉ 10178 – Ⓜ Alexanderplatz – ✆ (030) 24 00 10 – info@hotel-alexander-plaza.de – Fax (030) 24 00 17 77 – www.hotel-alexander-plaza.de **H1**

92 rm – †115/170 € ††125/180 €, ☕ 17 €

Rest – *(closed Sunday) (dinner only)* Carte 26/34 €

◆ Business ◆ Functional ◆

Between the Marienkirche and the market, this restored old building provides modern rooms and apartments with small kitchen facilities. International dishes are served in the restaurant with conservatory.

NH Berlin-Mitte rm 150 VISA AE

Leipziger Str. 106 ✉ 10117 – Ⓜ Stadtmitte – ✆ (030) 20 37 60 – nhberlinmitte@nh-hotels.com – Fax (030) 20 37 66 00 – www.nh-hotels.com **G2**

392 rm – †99/246 € ††99/246 €, ☕ 18 € – **Rest** – Carte 22/41 €

♦ Chain hotel ♦ Functional ♦

This residence with its spacious hall and rooms, which are modern, functional and comfortable, is well situated in the centre of Berlin. Leisure area on the 8th floor. The bistro-style restaurant is open to the lobby.

Wallstreet Park Plaza rm 20 P VISA AE

Wallstr. 23 ✉ 10179 – Ⓜ Spittelmarkt – ✆ (030) 8 47 11 70 – wppinfo@pphe.de – Fax (030) 8 47 11 77 77 – www.wallstreetparkplaza.com **H2**

167 rm – †99/190 € ††109/220 €, ☕ 15 €

Rest – *(closed Sunday) (dinner only)* Carte 24/41 €

♦ Townhouse ♦ Design ♦

Behind the classical townhouse facade is modern design. Copper, gold and silver underline the money-theme. Rooms with original dollar-note-motifs.

relexa Hotel Stuttgarter Hof rm 160 VISA AE

Anhalter Str. 8 ✉ 10963 – Ⓜ Kochstr. – ✆ (030) 26 48 30 – berlin@relexa-hotel.de – Fax (030) 26 48 39 00 – www.relexa-hotels.de **G2**

206 rm ☕ – †95/160 € ††105/185 € – 10 suites – **Rest** – Carte 28/34 €

♦ Business ♦ Functional ♦

This hotel has a large reception area and provides rooms with light beech wood furniture and warm décor. A charming restaurant.

Art'otel Berlin Mitte rm rm 35 VISA AE

Wallstr. 70 ✉ 10179 – Ⓜ Märkisches Museum – ✆ (030) 24 06 20 – aobminfo@artotels.de – Fax (030) 24 06 22 22 – www.artotels.com **H2**

109 rm – †130/180 € ††160/210 €, ☕ 14 € – **Rest** – *(dinner only)* Carte 25/36 €

♦ Business ♦ Design ♦

Listed building on the Mark Brandenburg bank that is an interesting link with the modern architecture of the hotel. Exclusively designed interior.

Mercure an der Charité rm 85 VISA AE

Invalidenstr. 38 ✉ 10115 – Ⓜ Zinnowitzer Str. – ✆ (030) 30 82 60 – h5341@accor.com – Fax (030) 30 82 61 00 – www.mercure.com Plan I **C2**

246 rm – †72/179 € ††72/189 €, ☕ 14 € – **Rest** – Carte 19/29 €

♦ Chain hotel ♦ Functional ♦

Next to the National History Museum. Modern hotel especially designed for business guests. Large postcards decorate the passageways and rooms.

Fjord Hotel without rest P VISA AE

Bissingzeile 13 ✉ 10785 – Ⓜ Mendelssohn-Bartholdy-Park – ✆ (030) 25 47 20 – rezeption@fjordhotelberlin.de – Fax (030) 25 47 21 11 – www.fjordhotelberlin.de – closed 23 - 26 December Plan I **C2**

57 rm ☕ – †80/99 € ††100/119 €

♦ Business ♦ Functional ♦

Hotel on the octagonal Leipziger Platz. Welcoming light rooms of standard design with cherry coloured furnishings. In fine weather breakfast is served on the roof terrace!

Riehmers Hofgarten rest VISA

Yorckstr. 83 ✉ 10965 – Ⓜ Mehringdamm – ✆ (030) 78 09 88 00 – info@riehmers-hofgarten.de – Fax (030) 78 09 88 08 – www.riehmers-hofgarten.de Plan I **C3**

23 rm ☕ – †98/125 € ††125/165 €

Rest *e.t.a. hoffmann* – ✆ *(030) 78 09 88 09 (closed Tuesday) (dinner only)* Menu 29/42 € – Carte 33/43 €

♦ Townhouse ♦ Functional ♦

This old town house provides spacious rooms with high ceilings, with simple, modern rooms. International cuisine is served in this welcoming restaurant. A pretty courtyard terrace.

Lorenz Adlon – Hotel Adlon Kempinski

Unter den Linden 77 ✉ 10117 – Ⓜ Französische Str. – ✆ (030) 22 61 19 60 – adlon@kempinski.com – Fax (030) 22 61 22 22 – www.hotel-adlon.de closed mid July - mid August and Sunday - Monday **G1**

Rest – *(dinner only)* Menu 115/160 € – Carte 70/108 €

Spec. Perlgraupenkaviar mit gebratenem Hummermedaillon. Périgord Trüffel im Ochsenschwanz-Kartoffelmantel gebacken mit Trüffelnage. Caneton à la presse mit Pommes Maximes und Sauce Rouennaise.

♦ French ♦ Formal ♦

Stylish ambience and perfect service at this establishment with lovely views of the Brandenburg Gate. Exquisite classical cuisine.

Fischers Fritz – Hotel The Regent

Charlottenstr. 49 ✉ 10117 – Ⓜ Französische Str. – ✆ (030) 2 03 36363 – fischersfritz.berlin@rezidorregent.com – Fax (030) 20 33 61 19 – www.fischersfritzberlin.com **G1**

Rest – Menu 30 € (lunch)/125 € – Carte 77/88 €

Spec. Geröstetes und Tatar von Langostinos mit Vanillegurken. Tournedos vom Polarsaibling mit grünen Erbsen und Blutwurst. Charlotte von süßem Ananas-Sauerkraut mit Wassereis von weissen Pfirsichen.

♦ Seafood ♦ Formal ♦

The stylish restaurant in The Regent serves creative cuisine with classical foundations. Service is friendly and professional.

Vitrum – Hotel The Ritz Carlton

Potsdamer Platz 3 ✉ 10785 – Ⓜ Potsdamer Platz – ✆ (030) 3 37 77 63 40 – ccr.berlin@ritzcarlton.com – Fax (030) 3 37 77 53 41 – www.restaurant-vitrum.de closed 2 weeks January, 3 weeks August and Sunday - Monday **F2**

Rest – *(dinner only) (booking advisable)* Menu 58 € (veg.)/98 € – Carte 58/71 €

Spec. Thunfisch mit Limonen-Currymarinade und Spargel-Melonensalat. Heilbutt im Pergament gegart mit Safranrisotto. Ziegenkäse-Espuma mit Bronzefenchelparfait.

♦ Contemporary ♦ Formal ♦

The traditional grand hotel restaurant offers luxurious ambience. Lavish and creative cuisine.

Margaux (Hoffmann)

Unter den Linden 78 (entrance Wilhelmstraße) ✉ 10117 – Ⓜ Französische Str. – ✆ (030) 22 65 26 11 – hoffmann@margaux-berlin.de – Fax (030) 22 65 26 12 – www.margaux-berlin.de closed Sunday **G1**

Rest – *(Monday - Thursday dinner only)* Menu 35 € (lunch)/120 € – Carte 66/86 €

Spec. Marinierte Entenstopfleber. Gedämpfter Glattbutt mit geliertem Badoit-Mineralwasser und geeisten Olivenöl. Poulet de Bresse à la Barigoule.

♦ Contemporary ♦ Fashionable ♦

Close to the Brandenburg Gate is this modern restaurant with a somewhat hidden entrance. Michael Hoffmann calls his creative cuisine "Cuisine Avantgarde Classique".

FACIL – Hotel The Mandala

Potsdamer Str. 3 (5th floor) ✉ 10785 – Ⓜ Potsdamer Platz – ✆ (030) 5 90 05 12 34 – welcome@facil.de – Fax (030) 5 90 05 05 00 – www.facil.de closed 1 - 21 January, 21 July - 5 August and Saturday - Sunday **F2**

Rest – *(booking advisable)* Menu 39 € (lunch)/100 € – Carte 69/78 €

Spec. Felsenoktopus gegrillt mit Tomaten-Chorizomarmelade und Holzkohleöl. Jakobsmuschel mit Spanferkeleisbein und Banyulsbutter. Karamellisierte Schmandtarte mit Vierfruchtsorbet, Erdnuss-Meersalz und Mango-Litschiragout.

♦ French ♦ Design ♦

Clean, minimalist design and interesting creative cuisine are characteristic of this restaurant on Potsdamer Platz. The glass ceiling and large windows onto the courtyard can be opened.

XXX ✿

VAU (Kleeberg)

Jägerstr. 54 ✉ 10117 – Ⓜ Französische Str. – ☎ (030) 2 02 97 30 – restaurant@vau-berlin.de – Fax (030) 20 29 73 11 – www.vau-berlin.de
closed Sunday **G1**

Rest – Menu 36 € (lunch)/100 € – Carte 68/78 €

Spec. Jakobsmuscheln mit gebackener Zucchiniblüte und warmem Safrangelee. Doppelkotelett vom Iberico-Schwein mit Aprikosen und Erbsen. "Tirami in VAU" mit Mokkasorbet und gefüllten Datteln.

♦ Contemporary ♦ Fashionable ♦

Modern design sets the scene in this restaurant on the Gendarmenmarkt. Creative cuisine with classical roots. Lovely inner courtyard terrace. Bar in the basement.

XX

Ferrari

Rheinhardtstr. 33 ✉ 10117 – Ⓜ Friedrichstr. – ☎ (030) 27 58 26 08 – info@ferrari-ristorante.de – Fax (030) 27 58 26 10 – www.ferrari-ristorante.de
closed Saturday lunch, Sunday **G1**

Rest – Menu 52/82 € (dinner) – Carte 37/46 €

♦ Italian ♦ Friendly ♦

Restaurant with Mediterranean, elegant atmosphere and friendly service. North Italian cuisine.

XX

Felix

Behrenstr. 72 ✉ 10117 – Ⓜ Französische Str. – ☎ (030) 2 06 28 60 – info@felixrestaurant.de – Fax (030) 20 62 86 11 – www.felixrestaurant.de
closed Sunday - Tuesday **G2**

Rest – *(dinner only) (booking advisable)* Carte 38/58 €

♦ International ♦ Trendy ♦

A club-restaurant on two levels, near the Brandenburg Gate in the Hotel Adlon complex. Nightclub after 23:00.

X

Rutz

Chausseestr. 8 ✉ 10115 – Ⓜ Oranienburger Tor – ☎ (030) 24 62 87 60 – info@rutz-weinbar.de – Fax (030) 24 62 87 61 – www.rutz-weinbar.de
closed Sunday *Plan I* **C2**

Rest – *(dinner only)* Menu 43/56 € – Carte 43/48 €

♦ Contemporary ♦ Trendy ♦

A minimalist modern restaurant on the first floor, serving Mediterranean creative cuisine. Enjoy the courtyard in summer. A lovely wine bar on the ground floor, decorated with wine bottles.

X

Remake

Große Hamburger Str. 32 ✉ 10115 – ☎ (030) 20 05 41 02 – restaurantremake@aol.com – Fax (030) 97 89 48 60 – www.restaurant-remake.de
closed Sunday – **Rest** – *(dinner only)* Menu 45/63 € – Carte 35/45 € **H1**

♦ Contemporary ♦ Fashionable ♦

Casual atmosphere and modern décor await guests in this theme restaurant offering creative cuisine.

X

Paris-Moskau

Alt-Moabit 141 ✉ 10557 – ☎ (030) 3 94 20 81 – restaurant@paris-moskau.de – Fax (030) 3 94 26 02 – www.paris-moskau.de
closed Saturday lunch, Sunday lunch **F1**

Rest – *(booking advisable)* Menu 58/70 € – Carte 33/46 €

♦ International ♦ Rustic ♦

Not far from the Lehrt train station is this old timber-framed hotel in the former border region. Timeless interiors and international cuisine.

X

Borchardt

Französische Str. 47 ✉ 10117 – Ⓜ Französische Str. – ☎ (030) 81 88 62 62 – Fax (030) 81 88 62 49 **G1**

Rest – Carte 30/46 €

♦ International ♦ Trendy ♦

Columns with gold-plated chapters and stucco ceilings impress guests. It is no wonder at this fine address. Here you have to "see and be seen"! Courtyard terrace.

Weinstein

Mittelstr. 1 ✉ 10117 – Ⓜ Friedrichstr. – ✆ (030) 20 64 96 69
– weinstein-mitte@gmx.de – Fax (030) 20 64 96 99
closed 2 weeks July - August and Saturday lunch, Sunday, Bank Holidays lunch **G1**
Rest – Menu 29/41 €
◆ Mediterranean ◆ Bistro ◆
This restaurant is centrally located and its interior combines an exclusive Paris bistro ambiance with a hint of Art Deco. The cuisine has a strong Mediterranean flavour.

Lutter und Wegner

Charlottenstr. 56 ✉ 10117 – Ⓜ Französische Str. – ✆ (030) 2 02 95 40
– info@l-w-berlin.de – Fax (030) 20 29 54 25 – www.l-w-berlin.de **G2**
Rest – Carte 30/45 €
◆ Austrian ◆ Wine bar ◆
The writer and composer E.T.A. Hoffman once lived in this building. Three large columns painted by contemporary artists set the motto: Wine, women and song. Cosy wine bar.

Le Cochon Bourgeois

Fichtestr. 24 ✉ 10967 – Ⓜ Südstern – ✆ (030) 6 93 01 01 – Fax (030) 6 94 34 80
– www.le-cochon.de
closed 1 week early January and Sunday - Monday *Plan I* **D3**
Rest – *(dinner only)* Menu 37/48 € – Carte 32/44 €
◆ French ◆ Cosy ◆
With a character all its own: cosy rustic décor forms the backdrop for the French cuisine served here.

AROUND THE KURFÜRSTENDAMM *Plan III*

Palace

350

Budapester Str. 45 ✉ 10787 – Ⓜ Zoologischer Garten – ✆ (030) 2 50 20
– hotel@palace.de – Fax (030) 25 02 11 19 – www.palace.de **K2**
282 rm – †232/510 € ††232/510 €, ☕ 24 € – 19 suites
Rest *First Floor* – see below
◆ Grand Luxury ◆ Classic ◆
Guests at this private hotel enjoy modern, smart rooms with extensive technical facilities, luxurious suites and an elegant Mediterranean 800 m2 spa area.

Grand Hotel Esplanade

rm 260

Lützowufer 15 ✉ 10785 – ✆ (030) 25 47 80
– info@esplanade.de – Fax (030) 2 54 78 82 22 – www.esplanade.de **L2**
385 rm – †230/280 € ††255/305 €, ☕ 20 € – 23 suites
Rest *Vivo* – *(closed July and Sunday - Monday) (dinner only)* Carte 32/48 €
Rest *Eckkneipe* – Carte 17/38 €
◆ Grand Luxury ◆ Modern ◆
A fine example of modern design, this grand hotel also displays Jungen Wilden art. Ideal for conference guests. Vivo serves cuisine with Asian inspiration. Down-to-earth Berlin fare served in this rustic pub.

Concorde

rm 280

Augsburger Str. 41 ✉ 10789 – Ⓜ Kurfürstendamm – ✆ (030) 8 00 99 90
– info-berlin@concorde-hotels.com – Fax (030) 80 09 99 99
– www.hotelconcordeberlin.com **K2**
311 rm – †230/425 € ††230/425 €, ☕ 21 € – 22 suites
Rest *Le Faubourg* – ✆ (030) 80 09 99 77 00 – Carte 31/60 €
◆ Business ◆ Luxury ◆ Fashionable ◆
This centrally located hotel offers generous, modern rooms with state-of-the-art facilities. Most suites have lovely views. VIP lounge. Le Faubourg: a bright restaurant with pictures by well-known artists.

InterContinental

Budapester Str. 2 ✉ 10787 – ✆ (030) 2 60 20
– berlin@ichotelsgroup.com – Fax (030) 26 02 26 00
– www.berlin.intercontinental.com **L2**

rm 860

584 rm – 130/320 € 130/320 €, 24 € – 42 suites
Rest *Hugos* – see below
Rest *L.A. Cafe* – *✆ (030) 26 02 12 50* – Carte 33/58 €

◆ Chain hotel ◆ Luxury ◆ Classic ◆

An impressive hotel, from the conference facilities to the spacious and luxurious Vitality Club. Rooms are tastefully elegant or simple and modern. The L.A. Café offers international as well as Chinese cuisine.

Swissôtel

220

Augsburger Str. 44 ✉ 10789 – Ⓜ Kurfürstendamm – ✆ (030) 22 01 00 – berlin@swissotel.com – Fax (030) 2 20 10 22 22 – www.swissotel-berlin.com **K2**

316 rm – 160/290 € 180/310 €, 21 €
Rest *44* – see below

◆ Luxury ◆ Modern ◆

As cosmopolitan and international as Berlin itself is this modern, luxurious hotel with a glass facade: spacious atrium hall as well as rooms with contemporary technology and comfort.

Dorint Sofitel Schweizerhof

rm 500

Budapester Str. 25 ✉ 10787
– ✆ (030) 2 69 60 – h5347@accor.com – Fax (030) 26 96 10 00
– www.schweizerhof.com **L2**

384 rm – 185/235 € 210/245 €, 20 € – 10 suites
Rest – Menu 29/42 € – Carte 31/38 €

◆ Chain hotel ◆ Business ◆ Design ◆

The bright and spacious lobby greets guests at this business-oriented hotel. Impressive rooms with modern technology. Bistro style restaurant.

Steigenberger

rm 300

Los-Angeles-Platz 1 ✉ 10789 – Ⓜ Augsburger Str. – ✆ (030) 2 12 70
– berlin@steigenberger.de – Fax (030) 2 12 71 17
– www.berlin.steigenberger.de **K2**

397 rm – 199/395 € 199/395 €, 22 € – 11 suites
Rest *Berliner Stube* – Menu 23/27 € – Carte 22/34 €

◆ Business ◆ Classic ◆

A spacious lobby with a modern design welcomes you to this city hotel with functional guest rooms. The executive floor (6th floor) affords privacy with its Club Lounge. Rustic flair in the Berliner Stube.

Kempinski Hotel Bristol

rm 300

Kurfürstendamm 27 ✉ 10719 – Ⓜ Uhlandstr.
– ✆ (030) 88 43 40 – reservations.bristol@kempinski.com – Fax (030) 8 83 60 75
– www.kempinski.com **K2**

301 rm – 295/355 € 420/480 €, 23 € – 22 suites
Rest *Kempinski Grill* – *(closed 4 weeks July - August)* Menu 69 € – Carte 41/68 €

◆ Luxury ◆ Classic ◆

A red carpet leads directly from the renowned Kudamm to the elegant luxury hotel built in the 1950's. Distinguished guests such as John F. Kennedy or Sophia Loren have stayed here. Legendary Kempinski Grill with a classical setting.

Brandenburger Hof

rm 30

Eislebener Str. 14 ✉ 10789 – Ⓜ Augsburger Str. – ✆ (030) 21 40 50
– info@brandenburger-hof.com – Fax (030) 21 40 51 00
– www.brandenburger-hof.com **K3**

72 rm – 185/285 € 270/325 € – 8 suites
Rest *Die Quadriga* – see below
Rest *Quadriga-Lounge* – *✆ (030) 21 40 56 51* – Menu 24/90 € – Carte 29/42 €

◆ Traditional ◆ Design ◆

Elegant décor elements in this city palace from the Victorian and Edwardian eras are blended with the tasteful modern design of the guest rooms. Pure elegance: the Quadriga Lounge extending into the Bar area.

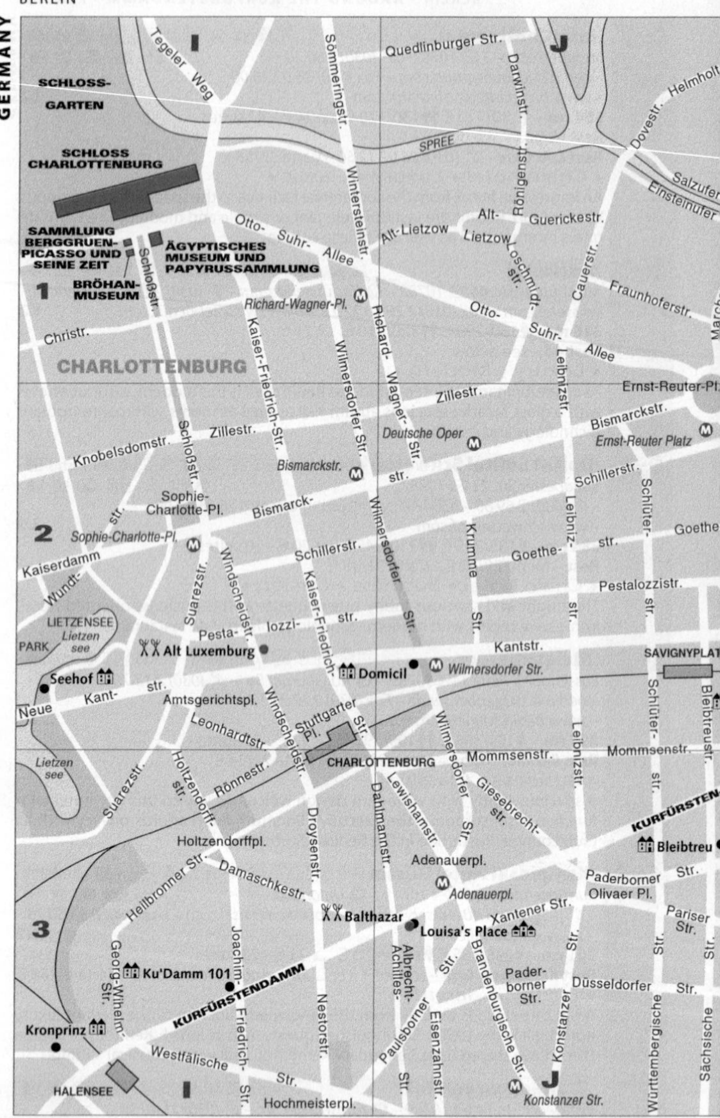

Louisa's Place

Kurfürstendamm 160 ✉ 10709 – Ⓜ Adenauerplatz – ✆ (030) 63 10 30 – info@louisas-place.de – Fax (030) 63 10 31 00 – www.louisas-place.de **J3**

47 suites – †135/255 € ††155/295 €, ☕ 20 €

Rest Balthazar – see below

◆ Business ◆ Personalised ◆

Tasteful, spacious suites with kitchens and friendly service in this exclusive hotel. Also features a stylish breakfast room and library.

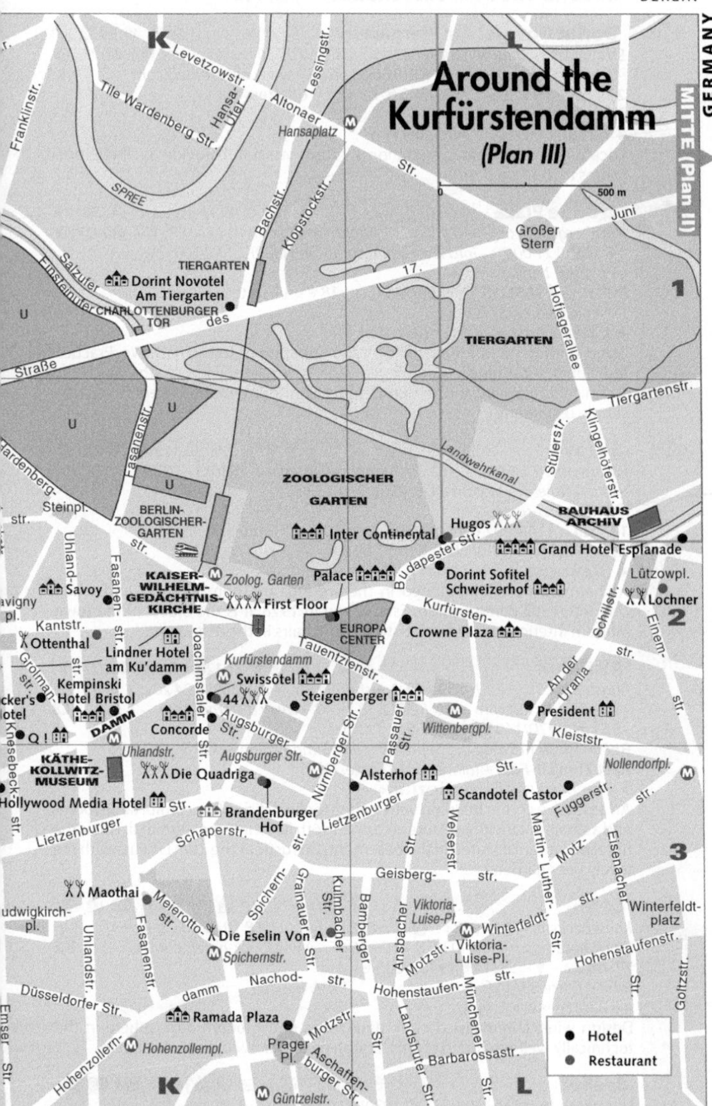

Ramada Plaza

rm 70

Pragerstr. 12 ✉ 10779 – Güntzelstr. – ☎ (030) 2 36 25 00 – berlin.plaza@ramada-treff.de – Fax (030) 2 36 25 05 50 – www.ramada-plaza-berlin.de **K3**

184 rm – 139/189 € 139/189 €, 18 € – 60 suites – **Rest** – Carte 26/33 €

◆ Chain hotel ◆ Modern ◆

A business hotel providing elegant rooms and suites with American cherry wood furnishings and the latest technical facilities. With executive suites on the sixth floor. A classic style restaurant.

Dorint Novotel Am Tiergarten

300 VISA

Straße des 17. Juni 106 ✉ 10623 – ☏ (030) 60 03 50 – h3649@accor.com – Fax (030) 60 03 56 66 – www.accorhotels.com **K1**

274 rm – 95/395 € 95/395 €, 17 € – 6 suites

Rest – Carte 29/44 €

◆ Chain hotel ◆ Modern ◆

Located near the Tiergarten station, this business hotel provides well-equipped rooms in modern design.

Crowne Plaza

rm 350 VISA

Nürnberger Str. 65 ✉ 10787 – Ⓜ Wittenbergplatz – ☏ (030) 21 00 70 – info@cp-berlin.com – Fax (030) 2 13 20 09 – www.cp-berlin.com **L2**

423 rm – 108/215 € 108/215 €, 18 € – 11 suites

Rest – Carte 25/37 €

◆ Chain hotel ◆ Functional ◆

Good starting point for a stroll over the Kudamm or to the KaDeWe. Practical, individual furnishings. Conference area, complete with all the necessary technical equipment and new Conference Centre. International repertoire in the simple restaurant.

Savoy

rm rm 40 VISA

Fasanenstr. 9 ✉ 10623 – Ⓜ Zoologischer Garten – ☏ (030) 31 10 30 – info@hotel-savoy.com – Fax (030) 31 10 33 33 – www.hotel-savoy.com **K2**

125 rm – 142/292 € 152/295 €, 19 € – 18 suites

Rest – Menu 13 € (lunch) – Carte 31/39 €

◆ Business ◆ Modern ◆

A charming hotel, mentioned in the writings of Thomas Mann, and where celebrities still come and go. Established in 1928, it is the oldest in the town. Modern interior with red upholstered armchairs in the restaurant.

Alsterhof

rm 120 VISA

Augsburger Str. 5 ✉ 10789 – Ⓜ Augsburger Str. – ☏ (030) 21 24 20 – info@alsterhof.com – Fax (030) 2 18 39 49 – www.alsterhof.com **L3**

195 rm – 70/140 € 80/160 €, 16 €

Rest – *(closed 15 May - 15 September and Sunday dinner)* Carte 27/34 €

Rest *Zum Lit-Fass* – *(dinner only)* Carte 22/31 €

◆ Business ◆ Functional ◆

An attractive corner building with a glass roof pavilion. Very comfortable rooms and a small, but inviting leisure area on the 6th floor. Internet terminal. This is the hotel restaurant, located in the basement. Go rustic at the Zum Lit-Fass with the lovely beer garden.

Q!

rm 15 VISA

Knesebeckstr. 67 ✉ 10623 – Ⓜ Uhlandstr. – ☏ (030) 8 10 06 60 – q-berlin@loock-hotels.com – Fax (030) 8 10 06 66 66 – www.loock-hotels.com **K2**

77 rm – 159/217 € 179/235 €

Rest – Carte 33/44 €

◆ Business ◆ Stylish ◆

Design wins: Minimalist design, dark tones and modern atmosphere in the technically well-equipped rooms. Stylish restaurant with Euro-Asian fare.

Seehof

rm 30 VISA

Lietzensee-Ufer 11 ✉ 14057 – ☏ (030) 32 00 20 – info@hotel-seehof-berlin.de – Fax (030) 32 00 22 51 – www.hotel-seehof-berlin.de **I2**

75 rm – 98/225 € 105/275 €

Rest – Menu 33/38 € – Carte 28/37 €

◆ Business ◆ Classic ◆

This hotel is located on the green shores of Lake Lietzen and features refined and elegant guest rooms, some furnished with period furniture. Convenient travel distance to the trade fair centre. Restaurant with classic ambience and beautiful terrace overlooking the lake.

President rm 70 VISA

An der Urania 16 ✉ 10787 – Ⓜ Wittenbergplatz – ✆ (030) 21 90 30 – info@president.bestwestern.de – Fax (030) 2 18 61 20 – www.president.bestwestern.de **L2**

178 rm – 🚹99/145 € 🚹🚹110/175 €, ☕ 14 € – 3 suites

Rest – Carte 29/37 €

◆ Business ◆ Functional ◆

Choose from functional Economy and Business rooms with Internet access or Club rooms with extra large desks and comfortable leather armchairs. Wicker chairs and contemporary design in the restaurant.

Lindner Hotel am Ku'damm rm

Kurfürstendamm 24 ✉ 10719 – Ⓜ Kurfürstendamm – ✆ (030) 81 82 50 – info.berlin@lindner.de – Fax (030) 8 18 25 11 88 – www.lindner.de 140 VISA **K2**

146 rm – 🚹159/299 € 🚹🚹189/329 €, ☕ 17 €

Rest – Carte 23/35 €

◆ Chain hotel ◆ Modern ◆

Located on a lively shopping promenade in the heart of the city, this hotel is sophisticated, modern and elegant. En-suite bathrooms. Restaurant serving international cuisine.

Hollywood Media Hotel without rest 90

Kurfürstendamm 202 ✉ 10719 – Ⓜ Uhlandstr. – ✆ (030) 88 91 00 – info@filmhotel.de – Fax (030) 88 91 02 80 – www.filmhotel.de VISA **K3**

182 rm ☕ – 🚹118/190 € 🚹🚹139/211 € – 12 suites

◆ Business ◆ Modern ◆

This residence is devoted to the world of film. The tasteful, contemporary rooms are decorated with numerous film posters and photos of stars. The hotel has its own small cinema.

Domicil rm 50 VISA

Kantstr. 111a ✉ 10627 – Ⓜ Wilmersdorfer Str. – ✆ (030) 32 90 30 – info@hotel-domicil-berlin.de – Fax (030) 32 90 32 99 – www.hotel-domicil-berlin.de **J2**

70 rm ☕ – 🚹118/163 € 🚹🚹154/204 € – 3 suites

Rest – Menu 31 € – Carte 23/36 €

◆ Business ◆ Modern ◆

In this hotel high above the city you will stay in attractive rooms in Italian style, in which the highlights are contemporary art and Tuscan fabrics. Rooftop restaurant with a roof garden. Cuisine with international influences.

Hecker's Hotel rm rm 25 P VISA

Grolmanstr. 35 ✉ 10623 – Ⓜ Uhlandstr. – ✆ (030) 8 89 00 – info@heckers-hotel.de – Fax (030) 8 89 02 60 – www.heckers-hotel.de **K2**

69 rm – 🚹120/250 € 🚹🚹140/330 €, ☕ 16 €

Rest *Cassambalis* – *✆ (030) 8 85 47 47 (closed Sunday lunch)* Carte 31/42 €

◆ Business ◆ Design ◆

A hotel which values individuality and service. The rooms, some cosy and functional, some in modern designer style or tastefully fitted out as themed rooms. Mediterranean flair on offer in the Cassambalis.

Bleibtreu rm VISA

Bleibtreustr. 31 ✉ 10707 – Ⓜ Uhlandstr. – ✆ (030) 88 47 40 – info@bleibtreu.com – Fax (030) 88 47 44 44 – www.bleibtreu.com **J3**

60 rm – 🚹122/222 € 🚹🚹132/232 €, ☕ 15 €

Rest – Carte 29/36 €

◆ Business ◆ Design ◆

Restored Gründerzeit town house. From the bedrooms to the bathrooms, Italian and German manufacturers have made the modern furniture especially for the hotel. The chic, bistro-style restaurant is open to the lobby.

GERMANY

Ku' Damm 101 without rest 60
Kurfürstendamm 101 ✉ 10711 – ☎ (030) 5 20 05 50 – info@kudamm101.com – Fax (030) 5 20 05 55 55 – www.kudamm101.com I3
170 rm – †101/161 € ††118/178 €, ☕ 14 €
♦ Business ♦ Design ♦
Deliberately understated designer style. Rooms with modern colour schemes, large windows and modern facilities. The breakfast room on the seventh floor offers a view over the town.

Kronprinz without rest 25
Kronprinzendamm 1 ✉ 10711 – ☎ (030) 89 60 30 – reception@kronprinz-hotel.de – Fax (030) 8 93 12 15 – www.kronprinz-hotel.de I3
76 rm ☕ – †115/185 € ††145/205 €
♦ Traditional ♦ Cosy ♦
A late 19th century building is home to light, homely rooms and a charming "Romantic room". Convention centre within walking distance. Terrace shaded by chestnut trees.

Scandotel Castor without rest
Fuggerstr. 8 ✉ 10777 – Ⓜ Nollendorfplatz – ☎ (030) 21 30 30 – scandotel@t-online.de – Fax (030) 21 30 31 60 – www.scandotel-castor.de L3
78 rm ☕ – †90/107 € ††100/135 €
♦ Business ♦ Functional ♦
Whether you want to visit the Ku'damm or KaDeWe, the cinema or pub: this contemporary hotel with its functionally furnished rooms and full technical facilities is close to it all!

First Floor – Hotel Palace
Budapester Str. 45 ✉ 10787 – Ⓜ Zoologischer Garten – ☎ (030) 25 02 10 20 – hotel@palace.de – Fax (030) 25 02 11 19 – www.firstfloor.palace.de
closed 16 July - 12 August and Sunday - Monday K2
Rest – Menu 39 € (lunch)/105 € – Carte 59/75 €
Spec. Carpaccio vom Pulpo mit Olivenvinaigrette und weißem Tomatenmousse. Kabeljau mit Pak-Choi und Jakobsmuschel im Zitronengrassud pochiert. Kalbskotelette mit glaciertem Kalbsbries und Spitzmorcheln.
♦ French ♦ Formal ♦
The luxuriously decorated, classical interior of this restaurant is a fitting setting for Matthias Buchholz's French cuisine. The wine list includes a number of rarities.

Hugos – Hotel InterContinental ≤ Berlin,
Budapester Str. 2, (14th floor) ✉ 10787 – ☎ (030) 26 02 12 63 – mail@hugos-restaurant.de – Fax (030) 26 02 12 39 – www.hugos-restaurant.de
closed 2 weeks January, 4 weeks July - August and Sunday L2
Rest – *(dinner only)* Menu 80/127 € – Carte 70/80 €
Spec. Seesaibling mit Gartengurken und Wasabivinaigrette. Gebratener Loup de mer mit Karotten in Orangen-Kaffeesud und Estragonpistou. Lauwarmer Kuchen von weißer Schokolade mit Zitronen-Olivenöl und Himbeersorbet.
♦ French ♦ Design ♦
From the modern-elegant restaurant on the 14th floor of the InterContinental guests enjoy fantastic views over the city. Classical cuisine with creative touches.

Die Quadriga – Hotel Brandenburger Hof
Eislebener Str. 14 ✉ 10789 – Ⓜ Augsburger Str. – ☎ (030) 21 40 56 51 – info@brandenburger-hof.com – Fax (030) 21 40 51 00 – www.brandenburger-hof.com
closed 1 - 14 January, 16 July - 19 August and Saturday lunch, Sunday - Monday lunch K3
Rest – Menu 55/110 € – Carte 63/81 €
Spec. Bretonischer Hummer mit Estragonöl und schwarzen Oliven. Lammrücken mit Lavendel und Fenchelrisotto. Törtchen von Schokolade und Chili mit Tahiti-Vanille.
♦ French ♦ Formal ♦
Classical creative cuisine is served in two tasteful Art Deco style salons, decorated in blue tones or with modern red pictures. Courtyard views.

44 – Hotel Swissôtel

Augsburger Str. 44 ✉ 10789 – Ⓤ Kurfürstendamm – ☎ (030) 2 20 10 22 88 – berlin@swissotel.com – Fax (030) 2 20 10 22 22 – www.swissotel-berlin.com closed Sunday **K2**

Rest – Menu 21 € (lunch)/88 € – Carte 47/78 €

Spec. Linsenravioli mit Sauerkraut, Schweinebauch und Estragonsenf. Rinderfilet in Olivenöl gebraten mit Artischocken à la Barigoule und Banyuljus. Aprikosenpudding mit Himbeeren und Passionsfrucht.

♦ Innovative ♦ Fashionable ♦

A simple, elegant restaurant with large window front on the Ku'damm. Creative cuisine by Tim Raue is guided by themes of tradition and evolution.

Alt Luxemburg

Windscheidstr. 31 ✉ 10627 – Ⓤ Wilmersdorfer Str. – ☎ (030) 3 23 87 30 – info@altluxemburg.de – Fax (030) 3 27 40 03 – www.altluxemburg.de closed Sunday **I2**

Rest – *(dinner only) (booking advisable)* Menu 64/70 € – Carte 47/56 €

♦ French ♦ Family ♦

Beautiful, cheery colours define the ambiance of this restaurant, under the management of the Wannemacher family since 1982. In this restaurant, tradition is maintained and classic cuisine is enjoyed.

Balthazar – Hotel Luisa's Place

Kurfürstendamm 160 ✉ 10709 – Ⓤ Adenauerplatz – ☎ (030) 89 04 91 87 – info@balthazar-restaurant.de – Fax (030) 89 04 91 89 – www.balthazar-restaurant.de **J3**

Rest – Menu 38 € (dinner) – Carte 28/41 €

♦ International ♦ Friendly ♦

This restaurant on the Ku'damm features a modern-minimalist interior and serves a predominantly international menu. Terrace at the front.

Lochner

Lützowplatz 5 ✉ 10785 – Ⓤ Nollendorfplatz – ☎ (030) 23 00 52 20 – info@lochner-restaurant.de – Fax (030) 23 00 40 21 – www.lochner-restaurant.de closed 1 week early August and Monday **L2**

Rest – *(dinner only)* Menu 58 € – Carte 37/50 €

♦ International ♦ Friendly ♦

A pleasant, bright atmosphere and subdued décor in this restaurant serving international cuisine. Small terrace in front.

Maothai

Meierottostr. 1 ✉ 10719 – Ⓤ Spichernstr. – ☎ (030) 8 83 28 23 – maothaiaf@aol.com – Fax (030) 88 67 56 58 – www.maothai-am-fasanenplatz.de

Rest – *(Monday - Friday dinner only)* Carte 20/48 € **K3**

♦ Thai ♦ Exotic ♦

An intimate, candle-lit atmosphere in this restaurant near the Fasanen square, serving Thai cuisine. Charming terrace dining area.

Bieberbau

Durlacher Str. 15 ✉ 10715 – Ⓤ Bundesplatz – ☎ (030) 8 53 23 90 – webmaster@bieberbau-berlin.de – Fax (030) 81 00 68 65 – www.bieberbau-berlin.de closed Sunday - Monday *Plan I* **B3**

Rest – *(dinner only) (booking advisable)* Menu 30/49 €

♦ International ♦ Cosy ♦

The ambience of this restaurant is characterised by half timbering, panelling and stucco. Youthful, friendly service and set menu dining.

Die Eselin von A.

Kulmbacher Str. 15 ✉ 10777 – Ⓤ Spichernstr. – ☎ (030) 2 14 12 84 – info@die-eselin-von-a.de – Fax (030) 21 47 69 48 – www.die-eselin-von-a.de closed 1 - 18 January, 2 weeks end July - early August **K3**

Rest – *(dinner only)* Carte 29/41 €

♦ International ♦ Bistro ♦

A favourite of many long-time guests due to its wonderful service, relaxing atmosphere and modern, international cuisine made from fresh ingredients.

GERMANY

Ottenthal

Kantstr. 153 ✉ 10623 – Ⓜ Uhlandstr. – ☎ (030) 3 13 31 62 – restaurant@ottenthal.com – Fax (030) 3 13 37 32 – www.ottenthal.com **K2**

Rest – *(dinner only) (booking advisable)* Carte 25/40 €

♦ Austrian ♦ Bistro ♦

This restaurant is named after a wine estate in Austria. Serving food from that country, and featuring décor inspired by the old church.

ENVIRONS OF BERLIN

at Berlin-Grunewald *Plan I*

Schlosshotel im Grunewald

Brahmsstr. 10 ✉ 14193 – ☎ (030) 89 58 40 – info@schlosshotelberlin.com – Fax (030) 89 58 48 00 – www.schlosshotelberlin.com 40 **A3**

54 rm – †225/265 € ††245/285 €, ☕ 23 € – 12 suites

Rest – *(lunch only, Tuesday - Wednesday also dinner)* Carte 49/69 €

Rest *Vivaldi* – *(closed 1 - 17 January and Tuesday - Wednesday) (dinner only)* Menu 85/98 € – Carte 55/76 €

♦ Castle ♦ Luxury ♦ Design ♦

This beautiful hotel in an exclusive area boasts lavish and unique interiors, under the design decoration of Karl Lagerfeld. In Vivaldi: the most elegant atmosphere and classical cuisine with a creative touch.

Servino

Flinsberger Platz 8 ✉ 14193 – ☎ (030) 89 73 86 28 – servino@servino.de – Fax (030) 89 73 86 28 – www.servio.de

closed Sunday - Tuesday **A3**

Rest – *(dinner only)* Menu 30/65 € – Carte 23/31 €

♦ International ♦ Friendly ♦

Peter Frühsammer serves international cuisine in this villa that is part of the Grunewald Tennis Club. The terrace affords a view of the courts. At midday, a small club menu is offered.

at Berlin-Tegel (Airport) *Plan I*

Mercure Airport

Gotthardstr. 96 ✉ 13403 – ☎ (030) 49 88 40 – h5348@accor.com – Fax (030) 49 88 45 55 – www.mercure.de 70 **B1**

303 rm – †59/119 € ††59/128 €, ☕ 13 € – **Rest** – Carte 20/33 €

♦ Chain hotel ♦ Functional ♦

The bus for Tegel airport stops on the doorstep. There are also good connections to the extensive transport system. Rooms are furnished in functional and contemporary style. Restaurant serving international cuisine.

Sorat Hotel Humboldt-Mühle

An der Mühle 5, (by Seidelstraße A 1) ✉ 13507 – ☎ (030) 43 90 40 – humboldt-muehle@sorat-hotels.com – Fax (030) 43 90 44 44 – www.sorat-hotels.com 50

120 rm ☕ – †113/183 € ††138/208 € – **Rest** – Menu 20 € – Carte 32/50 €

♦ Chain hotel ♦ Functional ♦

The rooms of this distinctive hotel are shared over the former grain silo, a modern building with glass façade and a villa. Cross a narrow bridge over the Tegelersee side canal to get to the restaurant.

Mercure Airport

Kurt-Schumacher-Damm 202 (by airport approach) ✉ 13405 – Ⓜ Kurt-Schumacher-Platz – ☎ (030) 4 10 60 – h0791@accor.com – Fax (030) 4 10 67 00 – www.mercure.com 150 **A1**

186 rm – †55/145 € ††55/145 €, ☕ 14 € – **Rest** – Carte 24/36 €

♦ Chain hotel ♦ Functional ♦

Following renovation in 2006, this functional hotel, with a new, modern design and located near the Tegel Airport, is ideal for business guests.

FRANKFURT

FRANKFURT AM MAIN

Population: 649 000 (conurbation 1 489 000) – Altitude: 40m

ALLOVER:COLORISE

Frankfurt is set on the banks of the River Main at the crossing point of Germany's north-south and east-west roads. It is the commercial capital of Germany and a truly cosmopolitan city with a rich tradition.

The city centre is Cathedral Hill (Domhügel), once the site of Roman fortifications and a Carolingian palace; the election of the Holy Roman Emperors first took place in the cathedral in 1356. Germany's first freely elected parliament met in Frankfurt in 1848 in St Paul's Church.

In the 16C the city was granted the right to mint money leading to a flourishing money market and foundation of the stock exchange. In the 18C the economy was dominated by German banks, which in the 19C acquired a worldwide reputation thanks to financiers such as Rothschild (1744-1812). Frankfurt is now home to the Federal Bank and the European Central Bank. Modern high-rise office blocks in the commercial district – the German Manhattan – dwarf the medieval historic centre.

Frankfurt is the birthplace of J. W. von Goethe, who described his native town in his memoirs; here he wrote several great works as Die Leiden des jungen Werthers (1744), written in one month. The university founded in 1914, research institutes, the opera, theatres and museums have made the city the scientific and cultural metropolis of the Hessen Land.

WHICH DISTRICT TO CHOOSE

Most **hotels** and **restaurants** are in the city centre, around the railway station *Plan III* **H2** and near the exhibition centre *Plan III* **G2**. There are also several attractive small restaurants in the Westend *Plan III* **H1** and in side-streets of the Fressgass (Eatery Alley) *Plan II* **F2** as well as near the opera house *Plan II* **E2** and the stock exchange. Round the station there are cafés, cabarets, bars and various exotic places. Popular with tourists and local people are the **Äppelwoilokale** in the Sachsenhausen district *Plan II* **F2**; they have a casual and lively atmosphere where you can try *Handkäs' mit Musik* (a small yellow cheese with vinegar, oil and onions), *Frankfurter Grüne Sauce* (a herb sauce) and – of course – *Apfelwein.*

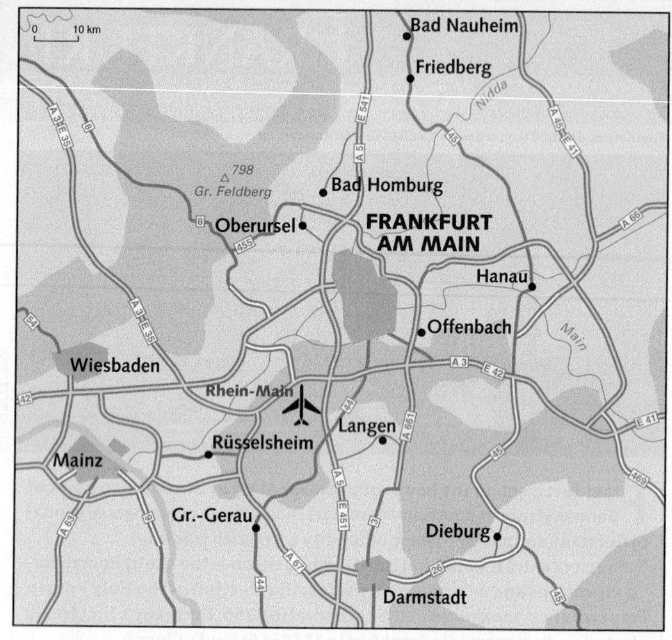

PRACTICAL INFORMATION

ARRIVAL – DEPARTURE

Frankfurt Airport, about 9 km (5 mi) southwest of the city centre, ✆ (01805) 372 46 36.

From the airport to the city centre – By **taxi**: approx. €20-25. By **train**: the S-Bahn trains S8 and S9 leave every 15min for Frankfurt Station in the city centre (journey time: 11min; ticket tariff is rate 4).

By rail – There are regular national and international train services from **Frankfurt Station**.

TRANSPORT

METRO, BUSES AND TRAMS

Normal fare is €2.10 (between 9am and 4pm); day ticket €4.90, group day ticket (max 5 people) €8 (valid until the last ride of the day). Tickets are available at vending machines and from bus drivers but **not** on tramcars, the U-Bahn and S-Bahn. Local public transport within the city of Frankfurt is managed by the **VGF** (Verkehrsgesellschaft Frankfurt am Main); ✆ (069) 1 94 49 (Mon-Thu 8am-5pm, Fri 8am-1pm); buses, trams, the U-Bahn (metro) and S-Bahn and regional trains in the greater Frankfurt region are managed by the **RMV** (Rhein-Main-Verkehrsbund); ✆ (01805) 76 84 63 (daily 6am-12pm). Information on the traffic island of the Hauptwache (Mon-Fri 9am-8pm, Sat 9am-4pm); also at Konstablerwache, Passage B level and other U-Bahn and S-Bahn stations. www.rmv.de; www.vgt-ffm.de

→ **FRANKFURT CARD**

The **Frankfurt Card** is valid for the RMV network within city limits, including the airport, and also discounts at 15 museums and other attractions; also 25-30% for selected boat rides. The card is available in many travel agencies, at tourist information offices and in both terminals at the airport. 1-day ticket €8; 2-day ticket €12.

→ **TAXIS**

Taxis are cream-coloured, numerous and relatively cheap. They can be hailed in the street, hired at taxi ranks and called by telephone. The initial charge is €2 (€1.60 per km); night rate €2.50 (€1.70 per km). ✆ (069) 25 00 01 (Taxi Zentrale).

USEFUL ADDRESSES

→ **TOURIST INFORMATION**

Tourismus + Congress GmbH; Mon-Fri 8.30am-5pm; ✆ (069) 21 23 88 00. **Railway Station Entrance Hall** *Plan III* **H1**; Mon-Fri 8am-9pm, Sat-Sun 9am-6pm; ✆ (069) 21 23 88 49. **Römer** *Plan II* **E1**, Römerberg 27; Mon-Fri 9.30am-5.30pm, Sat-Sun 9.30am-4pm. www.frankfurt-tourismus.de

→ **POST OFFICES**

Mon-Fri 8am-6pm, Sat 8am-12 noon. **Zeil Post Office**: Mon-Fri 9.30am-8pm, Sat 9am-4pm; **Railway Station**: Mon-Fri 7am-7.30pm, Sat 8am-4pm; **Airport**: daily 7am-9pm.

→ **BANKS**

Mon-Fri, 8.30am-12.30pm and 2-4pm (sometimes later); closed Sat-Sun and public holidays.

→ **EMERGENCY**

Police ✆ **110**; Fire Brigade ✆ **112**.

BUSY PERIODS

It may be difficult to find a room at a reasonable price (except during weekends) when special events are held in the city as hotel prices may be raised substantially:

Frankfurt International Fair: February and August.

Dippemess: end March to early April and September – Pottery fair.

Mainfest: end July to early August – Festival of the river Main.

Apfelwein Festival: early August – Apple wine festival on the Römerberg.

Museumsuferfest: August – Museum Embankment Festival of art and culture beside the river.

International Motor Show: September (alternate years) – 10 days with cars in the limelight.

Buchmesse: October – Frankfurt Book Fair, one of the biggest in the world.

Traditional Christmas Market: late November to 22 December.

EXPLORING FRANKFURT

It is possible to visit the main sights and museums in two days.

Museums and sights are usually open between 10am and 5pm. Most are closed on Mondays and public holidays.

VISITING

Dom *Plan II* **F1** – Gothic Cathedral (13C-15C), where the emperors were crowned.

Goethe-Haus und Goethe-Museum *Plan II* **E1** – Goethe's birthplace and adjoining art gallery of his era.

Städtisches Kunstinstitut und Städtische Galerie *Plan II* **E2** – Art Museum displaying an important collection of works by Old Masters, 18C German works and German Expressionists.

Zoo *Plan I* **D2** – One of the leading zoos in Europe, famous for its rare species, living in their natural habitat.

Palmengarten *Plan III* **G1** – The Tropical Gardens are a lush oasis of calm in the heart of the city with plants from nearly every climatic region.

SHOPPING

Shops are usually open from 9am/10am to 6.30pm/8pm. They are closed on Sunday.

In Frankfurt the main street for **shops and department stores** is **Zeil**, including among others the passage called *les facettes*. Nearby are the more **exclusive shops** in the streets around the **Grosse Bockenheimer Strasse** *Plan II* **E1** and **Goethestrasse. Schillerstrasse** has upmarket shops selling porcelain and household goods. There are interesting shops in Schweizer Strasse in **Sachsenhausen** *Plan II* **F2** and in Leipziger Strasse in **Bockenheim** *Plan I* **A1**.

Most **art galleries** are concentrated in **Braubachstrasse** *Plan II* **F1**, although they are to be found throughout the city; the **antique dealers** have settled in Pfarrgasse in the **cathedral (Dom) district**.

MARKETS – The **flea market** is always held **along the Main** on Sat 9am-2pm. Other markets are a **farmers' market** in **Konstablerwache** every Thu and Sat; in Berger Strasse, **Bornheim**, Wed 7am-6pm, Sat 8am-4pm and at the Südbahnhof in **Sachsenhausen** (South Bank) Fri 8am-6pm.

ENTERTAINMENT

Journal Frankfurt (in newsagents), *Fritz* (no charge) and *Welcome to Frankfurt* (in German) provide information on all events. Ticket sales (only on location) at the Tourismus + Congress GmbH.

Oper und Ballett Frankfurt *Plan II* **E1** – Daring staging and modern choreography under the direction of William Forsythe have earned the ensemble admiration and fame. www.oper-frankfurt.de

Alte Oper Frankfurt *Plan II* **E1** – Concert and conference centre opened in 1981 in the Old Opera House. www.alte-oper-frankfurt.de

Jahrhunderthalle Hoechst, Pfaffenwiese – Venue for classical concerts and other entertainment events.

Schauspiel Frankfurt *Plan II* **E2** – Home of the Schauspielhaus (Theatre), the Kammerspiele (Chamber Theatre), opera and ballet.

Die Komödie *Plan II* **E2** – Comedies and variety theatre.

Künstlerhaus Mousonturm *Plan I* **D2** – Cultural Centre, in converted soap factory, offering professional free theatre and also a stage for various local and guest ensembles. www.mousonturm.de

Schirn Kunsthalle *Plan II* **F1** – Prestigious art gallery.

NIGHTLIFE

The main centre for nightlife is around **Frankfurt Station**, where there is a selection of cabarets, bars, cafés and restaurants, and other exotic places.

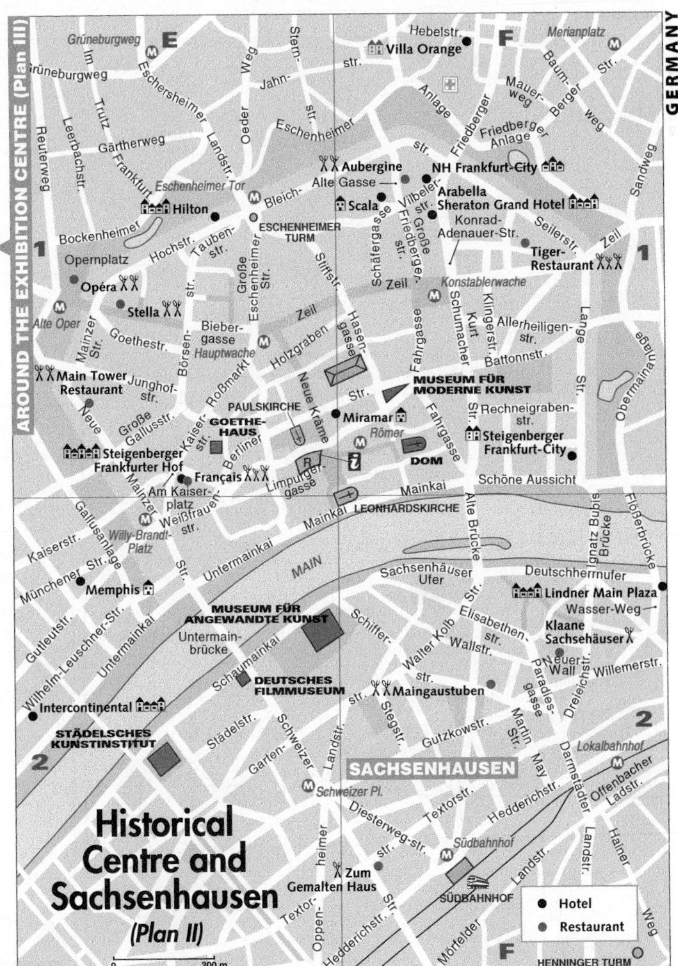

HISTORICAL CENTRE AND SACHSENHAUSEN — *Plan II*

Steigenberger Frankfurter Hof

Am Kaiserplatz ✉ 60311 – Ⓜ Willy-Brandt-Platz — 300 VISA
– ☎ (069) 2 15 02 – frankfurter-hof@steigenberger.de – Fax (069) 21 59 00
– www.frankfurter-hof.steigenberger.de **E1**

321 rm – 🚹249/619 € 🚹🚹299/669 €, ☕ 27 € – 20 suites – **Rest Français** – see below – **Rest *Oscar's*** – *☎ (069) 21 51 50 (closed Sunday lunch) (booking advisable)* Menu 29 € – Carte 32/49 € – **Rest *Iroha*** – *☎ (069) 21 99 49 30 (closed Sunday and Bank Holidays except during exhibitions)* Menu 25/120 € (dinner) – Carte 53/68 €

♦ Grand Luxury ♦ Business ♦ Classic ♦

This grand hotel from 1876 is the traditional home of Steigenberger. An opulent, historically listed building with luxurious interior. Exclusive suites. Beauty and massage treatments. Oscar's: A bistro. Iroha brings you the Far East.

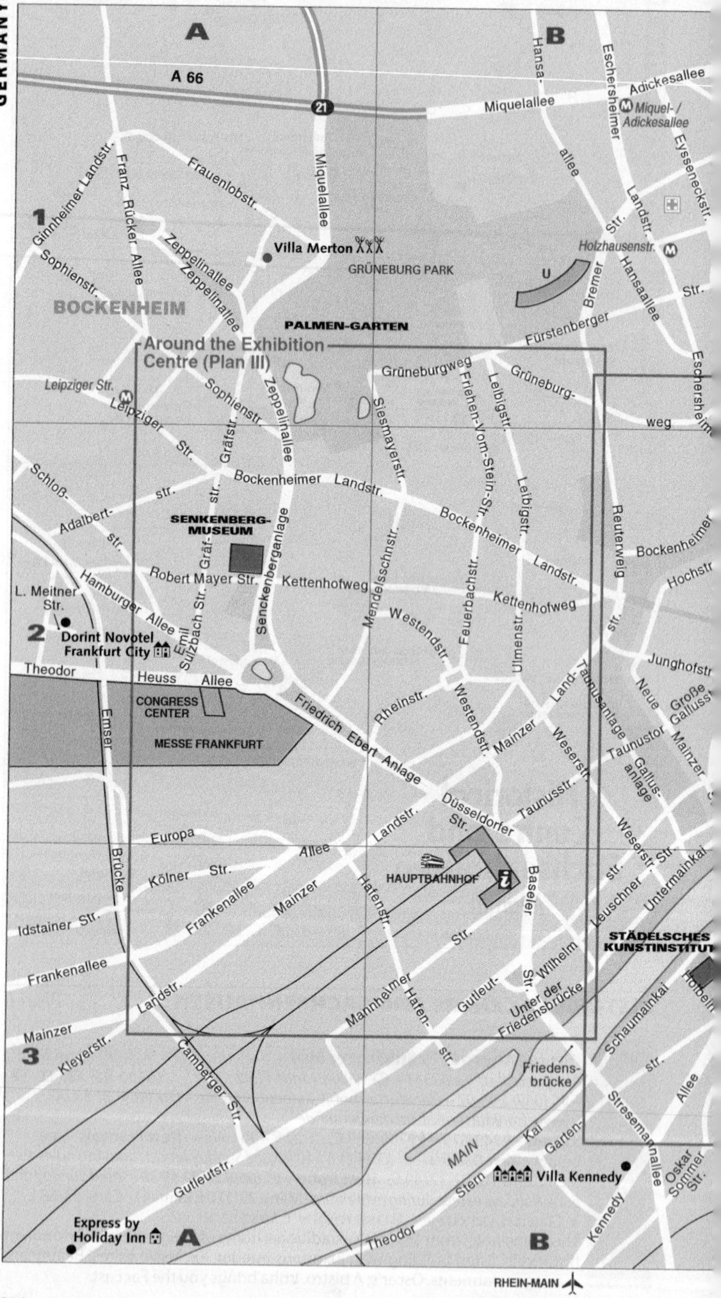

A
B
A 66
21
Miquelallee
Adickesallee
Miquel- / Adickesallee
Hansa-
allee
Eschersheimer
Landstr.
Eyssenecksr.
Frauenlobstr.
Ginnheimer Landstr.
Franz Rücker Allee
1
Villa Merton
GRÜNEBURG PARK
Holzhausenstr.
U
Bremer
Str.
Hansaallee
Sophienstr.
Zeppelinallee
Zeppelinallee
BOCKENHEIM
PALMEN-GARTEN
Fürstenberger
Around the Exhibition Centre (Plan III)
Grüneburgweg
Grüneburg-
weg
Frieden-Vom-Stein-Str.
Leibigstr.
Eschersheim
Leipziger Str.
Leipziger
Str.
Sophienstr.
Zeppelinallee
Siesmayerstr.
Gräfstr.
Schloß-
str.
Bockenheimer Landstr.
Adalbert-
str.
SENKENBERG-MUSEUM
Gräf-
str.
Senckenberganlage
Mendelsschnstr.
Bockenheimer
Landstr.
Reuterweg
Bockenheimer
Leibigstr.
Hochstr.
Hamburger Allee
Robert Mayer Str.
Kettenhofweg
Kettenhofweg
L. Meitner Str.
Emil Sulzbach Str.
Westendstr.
Feuerbachstr.
Ulmenstr.
str.
2
Dorint Novotel Frankfurt City
Junghofstr.
Theodor
Heuss
Allee
Land-
Taunusanlage
Neue
Große Gallusstr.
Emser
CONGRESS CENTER
Friedrich Ebert Anlage
Rheinstr.
Westendstr.
Mainzer
Weserstr.
Taunustor
Mainzer
MESSE FRANKFURT
Gallus-
anlage
Taunusstr.
Düsseldorfer
Str.
Europa
Landstr.
Allee
Brücke
Weserstr.
Kölner
Str.
Baseler
HAUPTBAHNHOF
str.
Str.
Frankenallee
Mainzer
Hafenstr.
Untermainkai
Idstainer Str.
Str.
Leuschner
STÄDELSCHES KUNSTINSTITUT
Frankenallee
Str.
Wilhelm
Landstr.
Mannheimer
Hafen-
Gutleut-
Unter der Friedensbrücke
Holbein
Mainzer
Schaumainkai
3
Kleyerstr.
Camberger Str.
str.
Friedens-
brücke
str.
Allee
Stresemannallee
Kai
Garten-
MAIN
Gutleutstr.
Villa Kennedy
Oskar Sommer Str.
Stern
Kennedy
Express by Holiday Inn
A
Theodor
B
RHEIN-MAIN

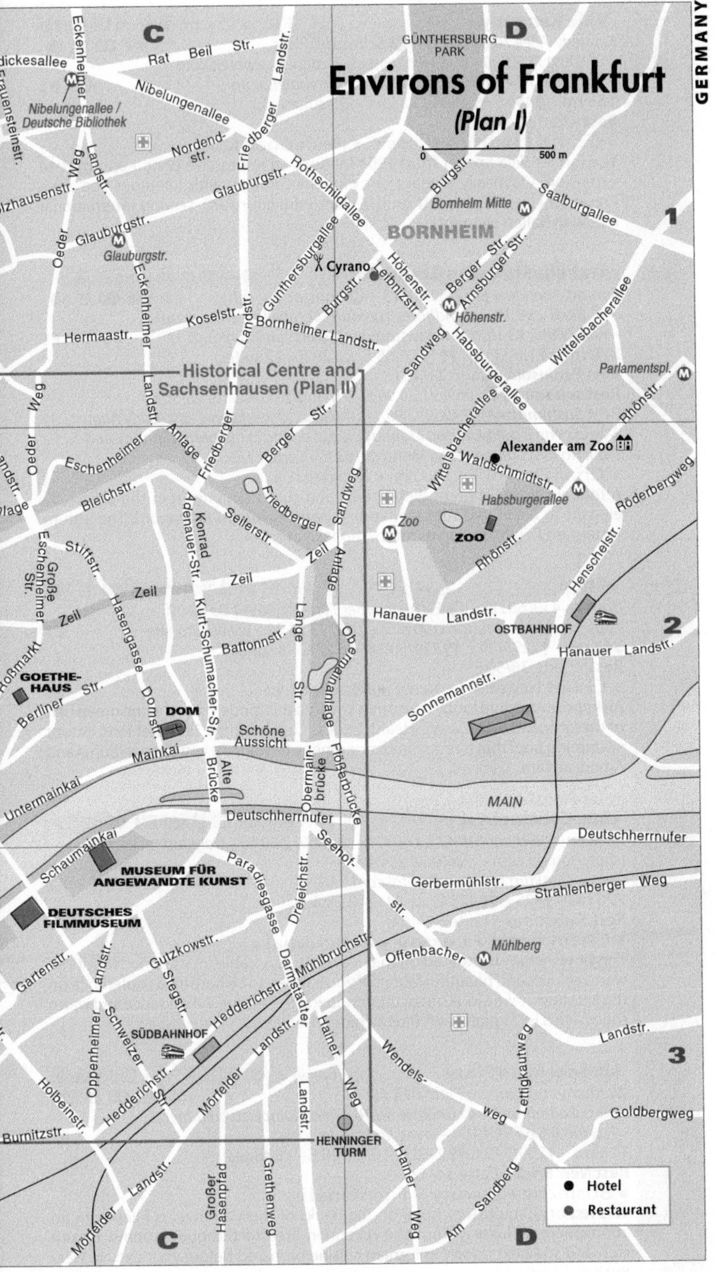

Environs of Frankfurt
(Plan I)
0
500 m
Hotel
Restaurant
GÜNTHERSBURG PARK
BORNHEIM
Cyrano
Alexander am Zoo
Historical Centre and Sachsenhausen (Plan II)
GOETHE-HAUS
DOM
ZOO
OSTBAHNHOF
MAIN
MUSEUM FÜR ANGEWANDTE KUNST
DEUTSCHES FILMMUSEUM
SÜDBAHNHOF
HENNINGER TURM
Nibelungenallee / Deutsche Bibliothek
Glauburgstr.
Bornhelm Mitte
Höhenstr.
Parlamentspl.
Habsburgerallee
Zoo
Mühlberg

GERMANY

Villa Kennedy

Kennedy-Allee 70 ✉ 60596 – Ⓜ Schweizer Platz – ✆ (069) 71 71 20 – info.villakennedy@roccofortehotels.com – Fax (069) 7 17 12 24 30 – www.roccofortehotels.com

rm – rm – 180 – VISA – AE

Plan I **B3**

163 rm – †440 € ††490 €, ☕ 26 € – 22 suites

Rest – Carte 44/73 €

♦ Grand Luxury ♦ Classic ♦ Fashionable ♦

The former Villa Speyer from 1904 features an impressive period-appropriate extension. Classically elegant yet modern complex with luxurious spa area. President suite. Restaurant on the wonderful courtyard, serving international fare with Italian elements.

ArabellaSheraton Grand Hotel

Konrad-Adenauer Str. 7 ✉ 60313 – Ⓜ Konstablerwache – ✆ (069) 2 98 10 – grandhotel.frankfurt@arabellasheraton.com – Fax (069) 2 98 18 10 – www.starwoodhotels.com/frankfurt

rm – 280 – VISA – AE

F1

378 rm – †155/335 € ††175/365 €, ☕ 28 € – 12 suites

Rest *Peninsula* – Carte 31/45 €

Rest *san san* – , ✆ *(069) 91 39 90 50* – Menu 16 € – Carte 25/36 €

Rest *Sushimoto* – , ✆ *(069) 2 98 11 87 (closed 2 weeks end July - early August, 2 weeks end December and Monday except during exhibitions) (Sunday and Bank Holidays dinner only)* Menu 40/82 € – Carte 27/56 €

♦ Chain hotel ♦ Luxury ♦ Modern ♦

A modern establishment with rooms and suites ranging from the classically elegant to Asian and Arabian. Roman baths Balneum Romanum. The atrium restaurant Peninsula serves international cuisine.

Hilton

rm – 280 – VISA – AE

Hochstr. 4 ✉ 60313 – Ⓜ Eschenheimer Tor – ✆ (069) 1 33 80 00 – sales.frankfurt@hilton.com – Fax (069) 13 38 20 – www.hilton.de

E1

342 rm – †229/489 € ††229/539 €, ☕ 27 € – 3 suites

Rest – Carte 36/50 €

♦ Chain hotel ♦ Luxury ♦ Modern ♦

An imposing atrium lobby welcomes you into this modern hotel in the green belt of the city centre. The Wave-Health Fitness Club houses a 25-meter long indoor swimming pool that is registered monument. Restaurant with international and American fare.

InterContinental

rm – 400 – VISA – AE

Wilhelm-Leuschner-Str. 43 ✉ 60329 – ✆ (069) 2 60 50 – frankfurt@ichotelsgroup.com – Fax (069) 25 24 67 – www.frankfurt.intercontinental.com

E2

770 rm – †425 € ††425 €, ☕ 24 € – 35 suites

Rest *Signatures* – Carte 31/46 €

♦ Chain hotel ♦ Luxury ♦ Functional ♦

This hotel, which is situated on the river Main, is notable for its period furniture, warm colours and beautiful fabrics. If you happen to be here for a conference on the 21st floor, take a look out of the window at the skyline. All elegance and warm tones – this is "Signatures ". Plus a chic conservatory.

Lindner Main Plaza

Skyline, – rm – 60

Walther-von-Cronberg Platz 1 ✉ 60594 – Ⓜ Lokalbahnhof – ✆ (069) 66 40 10 – info.mainplaza@lindner.de – Fax (069) 6 64 01 40 04 – www.lindner.de

VISA – AE

F2

118 rm – †239/349 € ††239/349 €, ☕ 20 € – 15 suites

Rest *New Brick* – Carte 34/42 €

♦ Business ♦ Luxury ♦ Fashionable ♦

This red brick multistory hotel on the banks of the Main river is filled with an atmosphere of luxury, from the reception area to the guest rooms. Health club and spa next door. Californian cuisine prepared before your eyes in New Brick.

Holiday Inn City-South

Mailänder Str. 1, (by Darmstädter Landstr. C 3)
60598 – (069) 6 80 20 – info.hi-frankfurt-citysouth@queensgruppe.de – Fax (069) 6 80 23 33 – www.frankfurt-citysouth-holiday-inn.de
435 rm – 180/390 € 200/410 €, 19 € – **Rest** – Carte 27/45 €
♦ Chain hotel ♦ Functional ♦
Newly furnished rooms await you in the hotel opposite the Henninger tower. The rooms on the 25th floor offer breathtaking views of the city. Elegant hotel restaurant "Le Chef" with international dishes.

NH Frankfurt-City

Vilbelerstr. 2 60313 – Konstablerwache – (069) 9 28 85 90 – nhfrankfurtcity@nh-hotels.com – Fax (069) 9 28 85 91 00 – www.nh-hotels.com **F1**
256 rm – 169 € 191 €, 22 € – 8 suites – **Rest** – Carte 23/34 €
♦ Chain hotel ♦ Functional ♦
Centrally located, this well run hotel is right on the pedestrian zone of town. Providing modern comfortable rooms with all mod cons. Restaurant on the first floor with a large buffet.

Villa Orange without rest

Hebelstr. 1 60318 – (069) 40 58 40 – contact@villa-orange.de – Fax (069) 40 58 41 00 – www.villa-orange.de **F1**
38 rm – 125/145 € 145/155 €
♦ Business ♦ Personalised ♦
A friendly establishment with bright orange façade is home to homely, comfortable rooms. Charming bathrooms with free-standing tubs.

Steigenberger Frankfurt-City

Lange Str. 5 60311 – (069) 21 93 00 – frankfurt-city@steigenberger.de – Fax (069) 21 93 05 99 – www.frankfurt-city.steigenberger.de **F1**
149 rm – 140/261 € 170/296 €, 16 € – **Rest** – Carte 22/48 €
♦ Business ♦ Functional ♦
This hotel, a favourite of business travellers, offers elegant, homelike guest rooms in a casual Italian style with a view of the city skyline. Restaurant with an open kitchen and international specialities.

Alexander am Zoo without rest

Waldschmidtstr. 59 60316 – Habsburgerallee – (069) 94 96 00 – info@alexanderamzoo.de – Fax (069) 94 96 07 20 – www.alexanderamzoo.de *Plan I* **D2**
66 rm – 130 € 155 € – 9 suites
♦ Business ♦ Modern ♦
A modern angular facade with equally modern, elegant rooms. Spend your leisure time during meetings and conferences on the terraces, admiring the views of the city.

Memphis without rest

Münchener Str. 15 60329 – Willy-Brandt-Platz – (069) 2 42 60 90 – memphis-hotel@t-online.de – Fax (069) 24 26 09 99 – www.memphis-hotel.de **E2**
42 rm – 65/140 € 75/170 €
♦ Business ♦ Design ♦
In the city centre, in the heart of a lively arts scene is this charming hotel, which features modern, rooms with an attractive colour scheme. Quiet rooms facing the inner courtyard.

Miramar without rest

Berliner Str. 31 60311 – (069) 9 20 39 70 – info@miramar-frankfurt.de – Fax (069) 92 03 97 69 – www.miramar-frankfurt.de
closed 23 - 31 December – **39 rm** – 92/130 € 105/150 € **E-F1**
♦ Business ♦ Functional ♦
Located between the Zeil and the Römer this hotel offers comfortable, cheerful rooms with dark grained root wood furniture – functional fittings include internet access.

GERMANY

Scala without rest

Schäfergasse 31 ✉ 60313 – Ⓜ Konstablerwache – ✆ (069) 1 38 11 10 – info@scala.bestwestern.de – Fax (069) 13 81 11 38 – www.scala.bestwestern.de **F1**

40 rm – †95/139 € ††118/159 €, ☕ 12 €

◆ Business ◆ Functional ◆

Are you looking for accommodation in the city centre? This hotel has modern style – refined and technologically up-to-date. Reception area with 24-hour beverage service.

Tiger-Restaurant

Heiligkreuzgasse 20 ✉ 60313 – Ⓜ Konstablerwache – ✆ (069) 92 00 22 25 – info@tigerpalast.de – Fax (069) 92 00 22 17 – www.tigerpalast.de closed 18 - 20 February, 22 July - 21 August, 25 - 31 December and Sunday - Monday **F1**

Rest – *(dinner only) (booking essential)* Menu 68/110 € – Carte 66/80 €

Rest *Palast-Bistrot* – *✆ (069) 92 00 22 92 (closed 18 - 20 February, 22 July - 21 August and Monday) (dinner only)* Carte 40/55 €

Spec. Gelierte Rinderconsommé mit Flusskrebsen und Kartoffel-Wasabi-Salat. Glasierte Brust und Croustade von der Taube mit Erbsen-Minzpüree. Fourme d'Ambert mit Honig-Lavendel-Krokant und mariniertem Radicchio Treviso.

◆ French ◆ Fashionable ◆

In the same building as the Varieté-Theater is this modern basement restaurant serving classical cuisine with Mediterranean influences. Good selection of French wines. An historic brick-vaulted ceiling in this bistro style restaurant.

Français – Hotel Steigenberger Frankfurter Hof

Am Kaiserplatz ✉ 60311 – Ⓜ Willy-Brand-Platz – ✆ (069) 21 51 38 – frankfurter-hof@steigenberger.de – Fax (069) 21 59 00 – www.frankfurter-hof.steigenberger.de closed 1 week January, 2 weeks by Easter, 3 weeks July - August and Saturday - Sunday except during exhibitions **E1**

Rest – Menu 35 € (lunch)/112 € (dinner) – Carte 56/74 €

◆ French ◆ Elegant ◆

Take your seat in classical elegant atmosphere and attractive tables. "Français Light" - a smaller lunch menu.

Opéra

Opernplatz 1 (level 3) ✉ 60313 – Ⓜ Alte Oper – ✆ (069) 1 34 02 15 – info@opera-restauration.de – Fax (069) 1 34 02 39 – www.opera-restauration.de

Rest – Menu 32 € – Carte 35/52 € **E1**

◆ International ◆ Formal ◆

A restaurant in the former foyer of the Alte Oper, with impressive ceiling paintings and original Art Nouveau chandeliers. Terrace with pretty views. Saturday morning tea and Sunday brunch.

Aubergine

Alte Gasse 14 ✉ 60313 – Ⓜ Konstablerwache – ✆ (069) 9 20 07 80 – info@aubergine-frankfurt.de – Fax (069) 9 20 07 86 – www.aubergine-frankfurt.de closed 3 weeks July - August and Saturday lunch, Sunday **F1**

Rest – *(booking advisable)* Menu 28 € (lunch)/66 € (dinner) – Carte 44/57 €

◆ International ◆ Cosy ◆

Enjoy Italian-inspired cuisine on Versace china in this historic townhouse with its red sandstone walls. Large selection of Tuscan wines.

Maingaustuben

Schifferstr. 38 ✉ 60594 – ✆ (069) 61 07 52 – maingau@t-online.de – Fax (069) 61 99 53 72 – www.maingau.de closed 2 weeks end July - early August and Saturday lunch, Sunday dinner - Monday **F2**

Rest – Menu 15 € (lunch)/64 € (dinner) – Carte 28/42 €

◆ International ◆ Friendly ◆

Refined décor and stylish ambiance characterize this restaurant, which offers both international and classic cuisine. A smaller version of the regular menu is available at midday.

XX **Stella** VISA MC AE

Große Bockenheimer Str. 52, (Gallerie Fressgass) ✉ 60313 – Ⓜ Alte Oper – ✆ (069) 90 50 12 71 – info@stella-ffm.de – Fax (069) 90 50 16 69 – www.stella-ffm.de

closed Sunday, except during exhibitions **E1**

Rest – Menu 25 € (lunch)/69 € (dinner) – Carte 47/53 €

Rest *La Trattoria* – – Menu 69/95 €

♦ Italian ♦ Fashionable ♦

The Stella family serves Italian fare and good Tuscan wines in their bright and welcoming restaurant. Outside seating in the glass-covered passage. This long-standing resto is now located on the first floor of the building.

XX **Main Tower Restaurant** ≤ Frankfurt, VISA AE

Neue Mainzer Str. 52 , (53th floor, charge) ✉ 60311 – Ⓜ Alte Oper – ✆ (069) 36 50 47 77 – maintower.restaurant@compass-group.de – Fax (069) 36 50 48 71 – www.maintower-restaurant.de

closed Sunday - Monday **E1**

Rest – *(dinner only) (booking essential)* Menu 57/98 €

♦ Contemporary ♦ Trendy ♦

Two hundred meters over the city, a sleek, modern ambiance and a breathtaking view await you. Creative cuisine is served – there are 3 set menus to choose from. Bar.

X **Cyrano** VISA MC AE

Leibnizstr. 13 ✉ 60385 – Ⓜ Höhenstr. – ✆ (069) 43 05 59 64 – info@cyrano-restaurant.de – Fax (069) 43 05 59 65 – www.cyrano-restaurant.de

closed 24 December - 8 January *Plan I* **D1**

Rest – *(dinner only)* Menu 55 € – Carte 39/51 €

♦ Contemporary ♦ Minimalist ♦

A restaurant with a sleek, modern atmosphere, where refined, creative cuisine is served by friendly staff on beautifully set tables.

X **Klaane Sachsehäuser**

Neuer Wall 11 ✉ 60594 – ✆ (069) 61 59 83 – klaanesachse@web.de – Fax (069) 62 21 41 – www.klaanesachsehaeuser.de

closed 22 December - 3 January and Sunday **F2**

Rest – *(open from 4pm)* Carte 12/22 €

♦ Regional ♦ Rustic ♦

The home-brewed "Stöffche" and good Frankfurt food have been served in this traditional pub since 1876. And no one ever has to sit alone!

X **Zum gemalten Haus** VISA MC

Schweizer Str. 67 ✉ 60594 – Ⓜ Schweizer Platz – ✆ (069) 61 45 59 – Fax (069) 6 03 14 57 – www.zumgemaltenhaus.de

closed 17 July - 7 August and Monday **F2**

Rest – Carte 13/20 €

♦ Regional ♦ Rustic ♦

Huddle up, talk shop and chat in the midst of these wall murals and mementoes from bygone days. The main thing is the "Bembel" is always full!

WESTEND, EXHIBITION-CENTRE AND STATION *Plan III*

Hessischer Hof AC ⇔rm SAT 120 P VISA MC AE

Friedrich-Ebert-Anlage 40 ✉ 60325 – ✆ (069) 7 54 00 – info@hessischer-hof.de – Fax (069) 75 40 29 24 – www.hessischer-hof.de **G2**

117 rm – †224/539 € ††270/539 €, ☕ 21 € – 3 suites

Rest – Menu 29 € (lunch)/60 € (dinner) – Carte 49/61 €

♦ Luxury ♦ Traditional ♦ Classic ♦

Exclusive antiques that once belonged to the Prince of Hesse make a stay here memorable. The elegant, luxurious rooms and attentive service appeal to the most discerning guest. Sèvres porcelain and trompe l'oeil paintings create a classical atmosphere in the restaurant.

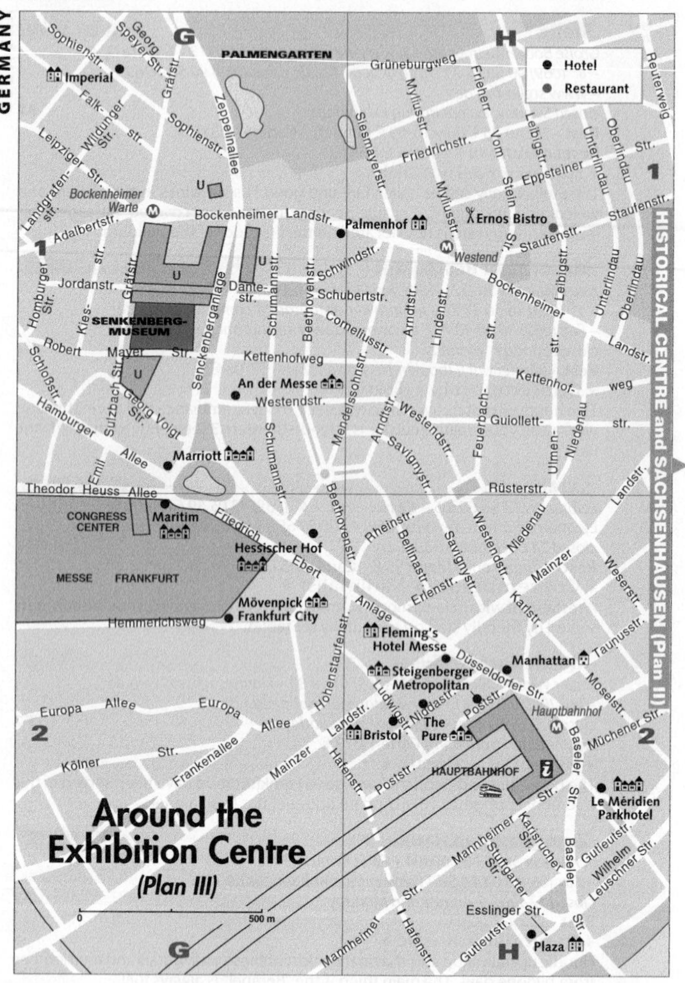

Le Méridien Parkhotel 180

Wiesenhüttenplatz 28 ✉ 60329 – Ⓜ Hauptbahnhof
– ✆ (069) 2 69 70 – info.frankfurt@lemeridien.com
– Fax (069) 2 69 78 84
– www.frankfurt.lemeridien.com **H2**

297 rm – 350/390 € 360/420 €, 21 €

Rest – Menu 35 € – Carte 28/49 €

♦ Chain hotel ♦ Luxury ♦ Design ♦

An historical town house with sandstone façade and a modern extension. Well-appointed rooms and technically well-equipped rooms available. Art nouveau style. A light, bistro-style restaurant: Le Parc.

Marriott Frankfurt, rm 600

Hamburger Allee 2 ✉ 60486 – ✆ (069) 7 95 50 – info.frankfurt@marriotthotels.com – Fax (069) 79 55 24 32 – www.frankfurt-marriott.com **G1**

588 rm – 139 € 139 €, 23 € – 11 suites

Rest – Menu 29 € – Carte 25/33 €

♦ Chain hotel ♦ Luxury ♦ Modern ♦

Situated opposite the trade fair centre, this hotel offers you classic, elegant rooms equipped with the latest technology and top-quality private baths. All rooms are on the upper floors and have a view. This beautifully designed brasserie serves French cuisine.

Maritim rm 250

Theodor-Heuss-Allee 3 ✉ 60486 – ✆ (069) 7 57 80 – info.fra@maritim.de – Fax (069) 75 78 10 00 – www.maritim.de **G2**

543 rm – 240/490 € 285/535 €, 25 € – 24 suites

Rest *Classico* – Carte 36/57 €

Rest *SushiSho* – *(closed Saturday - Sunday, except during exhibitions)* Menu 30 € (dinner) – Carte 32/50 €

♦ Chain hotel ♦ Business ♦ Modern ♦

Located at the exhibition centre, next to the Festhalle, this hotel offers fantastic views from the upper floors. Modern rooms. The elegant Classico offers international cuisine. Japanese cuisine features in SushiSho, which opens onto the lobby.

Radisson SAS rm 350

Franklinstr. 65 (by Theodor Heuss Allee A2) ✉ 60486 – ✆ (069) 7 70 15 50 – info.frankfurt@radissonsas.com – Fax (069) 77 01 55 10 – www.frankfurt.radissonsas.com

440 rm – 185 € 185 €, 24 € – 10 suites

Rest – Carte 29/44 €

♦ Business ♦ Chain hotel ♦ Design ♦

The designer rooms of this cylindrical hotel are named At Home, Chic, Fashion and Fresh. Tasteful and with good facilities. Lovely view from the upper floors. Mediterranean fare at Restaurant Gaia - seafood at the Coast Brasserie & Oyster Bar.

Steigenberger Metropolitan rm rm 220

Poststr. 6 ✉ 60329 – Ⓜ Hauptbahnhof – ✆ (069) 5 06 07 00 – metropolitan@steigenberger.de – Fax (069) 5 06 07 05 55 – www.metropolitan.steigenberger.de **H2**

131 rm – 220/445 € 245/445 €, 21 € – 3 suites

Rest – Carte 20/28 €

Rest *Fine Dining* – ✆ *(069) 5 06 07 03 00 (closed Saturday lunch, Sunday lunch)* Carte 40/52 €

♦ Chain hotel ♦ Modern ♦

Behind the beautiful façade of this 19C town palace guests find a successful combination of functionality, modernity and elegance. The Brasserie M. restaurant offers modern style. Classical Fine Dining.

An der Messe without rest

Westendstr. 104 ✉ 60325 – ✆ (069) 74 79 79 – hotel.an.der.messe@web.de – Fax (069) 74 83 49 – www.hotel-an-der-messe.de **G1**

45 rm – 130/295 € 155/330 €

♦ Business ♦ Personalised ♦

Individually designed rooms ranging from rustic-style to elegant, as well as a few interesting theme rooms set this hotel apart. Located near the trade fair centre.

The Pure without rest

Niddastr. 86 ✉ 60329 – Ⓜ Hauptbahnhof – ✆ (069) 7 10 45 70 – info@the-pure.de – Fax (069) 7 10 45 71 77 – www.the-pure.de **H2**

50 rm – 160 € 190 €

♦ Business ♦ Design ♦

Minimalist, modern elegance. The interior of this hotel is exclusively in white. Close to the railway station. Dark furnishings create an interesting contrast.

GERMANY

Mövenpick Frankfurt City

Den Haager Str. 5 ✉ 60327 – ✆ (069) 7 88 07 50 – hotel.frankfurt.city@moevenpick.com – Fax (069) 7 88 07 58 88 – www.moevenpick-frankfurt-city.com G2

288 rm – †120/167 € ††140/187 €, ☐ 18 €

Rest – Carte 28/39 €

♦ Chain hotel ♦ Business ♦ Fashionable ♦

Located directly next to the exhibition centre is this business hotel with conspicuous red-green facade. The rooms feature clean, modern and functional design. Fitness area with roof terrace. Bistro-style restaurant with international menu.

Imperial

Sophienstr. 40 ✉ 60487 – Ⓜ Leipziger Str. – ✆ (069) 7 93 00 30 – info@imperial.bestwestern.de – Fax (069) 79 30 03 88 – www.imperial.bestwestern.de closed 22 December - 2 January G1

68 rm ☐ – †130 € ††160 € – **Rest** – *(dinner only)* Carte 16/28 €

♦ Business ♦ Functional ♦

Mahogany furnishings and bold coloured décor in this comfortable, homely hotel. Peaceful rooms available towards the back. Restaurant with an international menu.

Fleming's Hotel Messe

Mainzer Landstr. 87 ✉ 60329 – Ⓜ Hauptbahnhof – ✆ (069) 8080800 – frankfurt-messe@fleming-hotels.com – Fax (069) 8 08 08 04 99 – www.flemings-hotel.com H2

96 rm – †69/301 € ††69/331 €, ☐ 14 € – **Rest** – Carte 17/40 €

♦ Business ♦ Modern ♦

A business hotel in the centre of town with modern, functional rooms equipped with the latest technology. Bistro style restaurant with international cuisine.

Dorint Novotel Frankfurt City

Lise-Meitner-Str. 2 ✉ 60486 – ✆ (069) 79 30 30 – h1049@accor.com – Fax (069) 79 30 39 30 – www.novotel.com *Plan I* A2

235 rm – †130/185 € ††145/200 €, ☐ 16 € – **Rest** – Carte 24/33 €

♦ Chain hotel ♦ Functional ♦

Located in the industry district, across from the trade fair centre, this hotel features modern, functional guest rooms and a wide range of options for meetings and conferences. Small fitness room available.

Bristol

Ludwigstr. 15 ✉ 60327 – Ⓜ Hauptbahnhof – ✆ (069) 24 23 90 – info@bristol-hotel.de – Fax (069) 25 15 39 – www.bristol-hotel.de H2

145 rm ☐ – †90/120 € ††140 € – **Rest** – *(residents only)*

♦ Business ♦ Modern ♦

Very close to the main railway station and inner city is this contemporary hotel with modern, functional décor. Summer lounge. Bar and reception with 24 hour service.

Plaza without rest

Esslinger Str. 8 ✉ 60329 – ✆ (069) 2 71 37 80 – info@plaza-frankfurt.bestwestern.de – Fax (069) 23 76 50 – www.plaza-frankfurt.bestwestern.de H2

45 rm – †95/117 € ††118/145 €, ☐ 12 €

♦ Business ♦ Modern ♦

This hotel, in a quiet side street near the train station, offers functional, modern, light-toned beech furnishings and friendly, warm fabrics and colours.

Palmenhof without rest

Bockenheimer Landstr. 89 ✉ 60325 – Ⓜ Westend – ✆ (069) 7 53 00 60 – info@palmenhof.com – Fax (069) 75 30 06 66 – www.palmenhof.com closed 23 December - 2 January G1

46 rm – †110/125 € ††150/170 €, ☐ 15 €

♦ Business ♦ Classic ♦

This hotel in the financial district features individually decorated rooms, some with beautiful secretary desks and most with brass beds.

Express by Holiday Inn without rest 35
Gutleutstr. 296 ✉ 60327 – ✆ (069) 50 69 60 – express.frankfurtmesse@ichotelsgroup.com – Fax (069) 50 69 61 00 – www.hiexpress.com Plan I **A3**
175 rm – 99 € 99 €
◆ Chain hotel ◆ Functional ◆
Ideal for business travellers, this modern well-equipped hotel is conveniently located near the exhibition centre and the local station.

Manhattan without rest
Düsseldorfer Str. 10 ✉ 60329 – ✆ (069) 2 69 59 70 – manhattan-hotel@t-online.de – Fax (069) 2 69 59 77 77 – www.manhattan-hotel.com **H2**
60 rm – 80/110 € 95/130 €
◆ Business ◆ Modern ◆
The modern design of the hotel extends from the lobby to the chic guest rooms that have a Manhattan-style ambiance. Trade fairs, banks, art and culture are just a short walk away.

Villa Merton 40
Am Leonhardsbrunnen 12 ✉ 60487 – ✆ (069) 70 30 33 – jp@kofler-company.de – Fax (069) 7 07 38 20 – www.kofler-company.de
closed 23 December - 10 January and Saturday - Sunday Plan I **A1**
Rest – *(booking advisable)* Menu 30 € (lunch)/110 € – Carte 58/71 €
Spec. Andalusische Tomate mit sautiertem Rochenflügel und Basilikumöl. Tafelspitz rosa gebraten mit Morcheln und grünem Spargel. Vanille und Roibusch mit Rhabarber und Mara de Bois.
◆ Contemporary ◆ Formal ◆
A villa built for the entrepreneur Richard Merton is home to this elegant restaurant in the diplomatic quarter. Creative cuisine with classical roots. A more modest lunch menu.

Ernos Bistro
Liebigstr. 15 ✉ 60323 – Ⓜ Westend – ✆ (069) 72 19 97 – Fax (069) 17 38 38
closed Christmas - early January, 3 weeks July - August and Saturday - Sunday, Bank Holidays **H1**
Rest – *(booking advisable)* Menu 36 € (lunch)/105 € – Carte 60/84 €
Spec. Foie Gras d'oie Maison mit Sauternes-Gelee. Rouget Barbet auf schwarzem Risotto mit Pulpo-Carpaccio und Gemüsevinaigrette. Kalbsfilet mit Pfifferlingen und Zwiebelconfit.
◆ French ◆ Bistro ◆
This restaurant in Westend appeals because of its cosy, charming bistro atmosphere. Impressive French cuisine by Valéry Mathis and attentive service.

ENVIRONS OF FRANKFURT *Plan I*

at Frankfurt-Fechenheim by Hanauer Landstr. D 2

Silk (Lohninger)
Carl-Benz-Str. 21 ✉ 60386 – ✆ (069) 90 02 00 – reservierung@cocoonclub.net – Fax (069) 90 02 02 90 – www.cocoonclub.net
closed 1 - 10 January, August and Sunday - Monday
Rest – *(dinner only)* Menu 76 €
Rest *Micro* – *(dinner only)* Menu 49 € – Carte 35/52 €
Spec. Ein-Stunden-Bio-Ei, Frankfurter Grüne Sauce und La Ratte-Kartoffel. Schwarzfussschwein mit Trüffel und Wildkräutersalat. Geeiste Marille.
◆ Innovative ◆ Trendy ◆
The restaurant in the futuristic Cocoon-Club represents a completely new concept: guests "bed down" in the white couches where creative cuisine is served in bowls. Micro features an open kitchen serving fusion cuisine. The disco is next door.

GERMANY

at Frankfurt-Rödelheim by Theodor Heuss Allee A 2

Osteria Enoteca

Arnoldshainer Str. 2, (corner of Lorscher Straße) ✉ 60489 – ✆ (069) 7 89 22 16 – Fax (069) 7 89 22 16 – www.osteria-enoteca.de
closed 22 December - 5 January and Saturday lunch, Sunday, Bank Holidays
Rest – Menu 58/108 € – Carte 49/55 €
Spec. Etui von Sardellen, Auberginen und Apfel mit Olivenkrokant. Gebratene Langostinos, Granità von Zitrusfrüchten und Cornetto mit Stopfleberpaté. Geschmorte Kalbsbrust mit Maispolenta.
◆ Italian ◆ Friendly ◆
Restaurant with attentive, friendly service serving creative Italian cuisine. Light décor and some modern, colourful artworks contribute to the atmosphere.

at the Rhein-Main Airport by Kennedy Allee B 3

Sheraton Frankfurt Hotel & Towers

Hugo-Eckener-Ring 15 , (terminal 1)
✉ 60549 Frankfurt – ✆ (069) 6 97 70 – reservationsfrankfurt@sheraton.com – Fax (069) 69 77 22 09 – www.sheraton.com/frankfurt
700 VISA MC AE
1006 rm – †249/485 € ††274/507 €, ☐ 24 € – 21 suites
Rest *Flavors* – ✆ (069) 69771246 – Carte 38/70 €
Rest *Taverne* – ✆ *(069) 69771259 (closed Saturday - Sunday)* Carte 34/51 €
◆ Chain hotel ◆ Business ◆ Modern ◆
This hotel with an imposing lobby is located directly opposite Terminal 1. Fitness centre, sauna and massage service. Modern ambience and good choice of international cuisine in the Flavors. Rural charm in the Taverne.

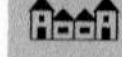

Kempinski Hotel Gravenbruch

(heated)
Graf zu Ysenburg und Büdingen-Platz 1 ✉ 63263 – ✆ (069) 38 98 80 – reservations.gravenbruch@kempinski.com – Fax (069) 38 98 89 00 – www.kempinski-frankfurt.com
rm 180 VISA MC AE
283 rm – †132/165 € ††132/165 €, ☐ 23 € – 15 suites
Rest – Carte 31/44 €
Rest *L'Olivo* – *(closed Saturday - Sunday) (dinner only)* Carte 25/32 €
◆ Chain hotel ◆ Classic ◆
A former estate in the midst of an attractive, small park, rooms in classic style and luxurious suites. Leisure area with beauty farm, hairdresser and cosmetics studio. A fine restaurant with garden views. L'Olivo is in the Italian style.

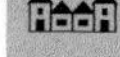

Steigenberger Airport

rm 270
Unterschweinstiege 16 ✉ 60549 Frankfurt – ✆ (069) 6 97 50 – info@airporthotel.steigenberger.de – Fax (069) 69 75 25 05 – www.airporthotel.steigenberger.de
VISA MC AE
573 rm – †120/219 € ††140/239 €, ☐ 21 € – 10 suites
Rest *Unterschweinstiege* – Carte 32/50 €
Rest *Faces* – *(closed by Easter, 4 weeks July - early August, 22 December - 6 January and Sunday - Monday) (dinner only)* Menu 42 € – Carte 48/66 €
◆ Chain hotel ◆ Modern ◆
A spacious, elegant reception area with pale marble décor leads you to comfortable guest rooms, some with designer baths. Recreation area on the top floor boasts a stunning view. A cosy atmosphere in the historic Unterschweinstiege restaurant. A fine bistro atmosphere.

InterCityHotel Frankfurt Airport

rm 150
Cargo City Süd ✉ 60549 Frankfurt – ✆ (069) 69 70 99 – frankfurt-airport@intercityhotel.de – Fax (069) 69 70 94 44 – www.frankfurt-airport.intercityhotel.de
P VISA MC AE
360 rm – †68/239 € ††88/299 €, ☐ 16 €
Rest – Carte 24/33 €
◆ Chain hotel ◆ Functional ◆
Convenient Autobahn access and an airport location – with shuttle service to the terminals – as well as functional, up-to-date guest rooms highlight this hotel. Modern restaurant with international cuisine and buffet.

HAMBURG

HAMBURG

Population: 1 750 000 (conurbation 2 290 000) – Altitude: at sea level

Comnet/COLORISE

Hamburg, the second largest city in Germany after Berlin, is one of the most important ports in Europe. Its old title of 'Free and Hanseatic Town' and its status as a 'City State' (Stadtstaat) testify to its eminence and influence over the centuries.

Each year, in May, there is an anniversary celebration in the port of Hamburg (Hafengeburtstag), commemorating the concession granted by Frederick Barbarossa in 1189 of the right to free navigation on the lower Elbe. The exercise of this right, menaced by piracy and the feudal pretensions of neighbouring states, especially Denmark, demanded a continual watch by the city fathers until the 17C.

As a port Hamburg enjoys a large recreational lake, the Alster, at its centre and the Speicherstadt district contains one of the largest former warehouse complexes.

Hamburg is the birthplace of Johannes Brahms, where he composed many of his works, and has a strong musical tradition.

WHICH DISTRICT TO CHOOSE

The highest concentration of **hotels** and **restaurants** is to be found around the Binnenalster and the Aussenalster *Plan I* **C2**. Hamburg is well-known for its good fish restaurants located in the harbour district *Plan I* **B3**; here you will find eel in all its forms as well as the famous *Labskaus*, a local dish of herring, beetroot, salt meat and pickled gherkins. The numerous scenic restaurants recently opened by the harbour offer a great view of the passing shipping. The Altona *Plan I* **B3** and Eppendorf *Plan I* **C1** districts are also known for very good restaurants but some of the best restaurants are out of town along the Elbe.

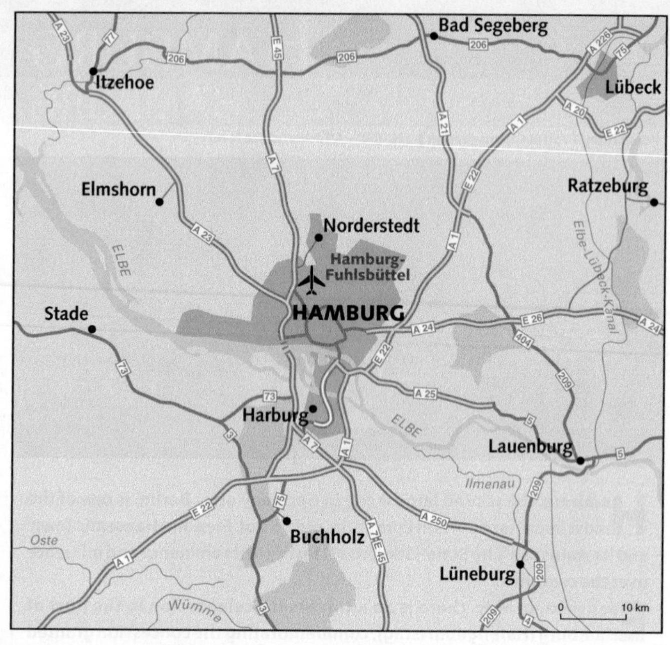

PRACTICAL INFORMATION

ARRIVAL – DEPARTURE

Hamburg Airport about 15 km (10 mi) from the city centre. ✆ (040) 5 07 50; info@ham.airport.de; www.ham.airport.de

From the airport to the city centre – By **taxi**: approx. €17-20 (20min). By **public transport**: Airport buses leave for Hamburg Hauptbahnhof every 15-20min and Altona Station every 30min (journey time for both: 30min).

Railway Stations – Hauptbahnhof Nord and Hauptbahnhof Süd for international and national services. ✆ (0900) 150 70 90 (€1.99 per min) (24hr).

River Boat and Ferry Stations – Tours of Hamburg Harbour depart from the Landungsbrücken 1-9 in St Pauli (every 20min) Mon-Sun 10am-5pm. Tours of the Alster, Fleet and canal depart from Jungfernstieg.

TRANSPORT

♦ METRO AND BUSES

All buses and underground trains are controlled by the **HVV** (Hamburger Verkehrsverbund); the lines reach into the surrounding region of Schleswig-Holstein. Tickets are available from vending machines and from bus drivers. Single ticket for rides into the town centre from €1.10; 1-day ticket €5.80; 3-day ticket €14.40; group day ticket for up to 5 people €8.10 (the 2 latter tickets are valid from 9am until the last ride). Information available at many V- and S-Bahn stations and at the HVV office at the Railway Station (Hauptbahnhof), Mon-Fri 6am-10pm, Sat-Sun 7am-9pm; ✆ (040) 1 94 49 (24hrs) – www.hvv.de

The **Hamburg Card** is valid for the **HVV** network, free entrance to 11 state-run museums, discounts on other activities and on tours on water and on land. The card is available at the Tourist Information Offices, at vending machines, in many hotels and travel agents and in the HVV Customer Offices. Single person €7.80; group card for up to 5 people €11.20 (both are valid on the date of issue and from 6pm onward on the previous day); 3 day card €17.40.

➜ TAXIS

Taxis are cream-coloured. They can be hailed in the street, hired at taxi ranks and called by telephone. Initial charge €2.10 (€1.60 per km for first 11km, €1.28 per km thereafter). *Taxi Hamburg* ✆ 040 66 66 66, www.taxihamburg.de

USEFUL ADDRESSES

➜ TOURIST INFORMATION

Hamburg Tourismus GmbH, daily 8am-8pm; ✆ 40 30 05 13 00. **Main Railway Station** (Hauptbahnhof) *Plan II* **H2**; daily 8am-9pm. **Harbour**, *Plan I* **C3,** St Pauli Landungsbrücken (between piers 4 and 5) daily 8am-6pm – **Airport Office**, Terminal 1 and 2 arrival – area daily 5.30am-11pm – info@hamburg-tourismus.de; www.hamburg-tourismus.de

➜ POST OFFICES

Mon-Fri 8am-6pm, Sat 8am-12 noon. **Railway Station**, Hachmannplatz: Mon-Fri 8am-8pm, Sat 8.30-12am.

➜ BANKS

Mon-Fri 8.30am-12.30pm and 2-4pm (sometimes later); closed Sat-Sun and public holidays.

➜ EMERGENCY

Police ✆ **110**; Fire Brigade ✆ **112**.

BUSY PERIODS

It may be difficult to find a room at a reasonable price when special events are held in the city as hotel prices may be raised substantially:

Volksfest Dom: mid March to mid April, mid July to end August, early Nov to Dec – Folk festival near the cathedral with the biggest funfair in north Germany.

Hafengeburtstag: mid May – Harbour anniversary.

Hamburger Ballet-Tage: July – Ballet days.

Alstervergnügen: end of August – Alster Fair offering art, culture and fun around the Inner Alster.

Hamburg Christmas Market: late November to 23 December – Traditional Christmas market in the city centre and Town Hall Square.

EXPLORING HAMBURG

It is possible to visit the main sights and museums in two days.

Museums and sights are usually open between 9am/10am and 5pm/6pm (some later on Thursday). Most are closed on Mondays and public holidays.

VISITING

Views of Hamburg – Take a boat trip around the Harbour *(Hafenrundfahrt)* from the quayside in St Pauli. Take a boat trip on the **Aussenalster** *Plan I* **C2.** Make a circuit by road of the **Alster** *Plan II* **E3.**

Hauptkirche St Michaelis *Plan II* **E3** – A fine brick-built church (1762) in the Baroque tradition with a tower, known locally as *Michel* which is the emblem of the city; view from the platform of the town centre and the river.

Hamburger Kunsthalle *Plan II* **H2** – Fine Art Museum housing one of the largest art collections in Germany.

Altonaer Museum in Hamburg – Norddeutsches Landesmuseum *Plan III* **I1** – Art, culture and daily life in Schleswig-Holstein including an exceptional collection of **ships' figureheads** from 18C-19C.

SHOPPING

Shops are usually open between 9am/10am and 6.30pm/8pm. They are closed on Sunday.

The wealth of pedestrianised areas and old-established stores makes Hamburg a shoppers' paradise. **Jungfernstieg**, **Mönckebergstrasse** *Plan II* **G2** and **Spitalerstrasse** are the big shopping streets with department stores. The many shopping arcades in the inner city are especially attractive, with over 300 speciality stores and boutiques. **Exclusive stores** can be found in **Neuer Wall** *Plan II* **F3**. The shopping streets between **Neuer Wall** and **Colonnaden** *Plan II* **F2** are lined with luxurious arcades.

For **antiques** try the **Quartier Satin** in ABC-Strasse *Plan II* **F2** and the **Antik-Center** of the market hall in Klosterwall *Plan II* **H3**.

MARKETS – Hamburg's most famous market is the **fish market** (Sun 5am (7am winter) to 10am). **Weekly markets** are held in all districts of the city. Particularly recommended is the especially beautiful market held on the covered central strip of the elevated train at the U-bahn station Eppendorfer Baum (Mon-Fri). Regular **flea markets** are held on Saturdays in Barmbek (Hellbrockstrasse – 7am-5pm) and in Eppendorf (Nedderfeld/Parkhaus – 4.30-7.30pm). For information about more spontaneous flea markets in Hamburg consult the *Menschen & Märkte* brochure.

WHAT TO BUY – *Harry's Hamburger Hafenbasar*, Balduinstrasse 18 St Pauli, for worldly souvenirs.

ENTERTAINMENT

Prinz, published every 2 weeks, *Szene Hamburg*, published every 4 weeks, and the *Hamburger Vorschau* (available at the Tourist Information Offices) provide information on events of all sorts. Tickets for select events are on sale at the Tourist Information Office.

Hamburgische Staatsoper *Plan II* **F2** – Opera and ballet – www.hamburgische-staatsoper.de; www.hamburgballett.de

Allee-Theater *Plan III* **J1** – Hamburg chamber opera and children's theatre – www.theater-fuer-kinder.de

Neue Flora *Plan III* **I1** – Musicals.

Operettenhaus *Plan II* **F2** – Musicals.

Musikhalle *Plan II* **E2** – Baroque concert hall at the centre of the musical life of Hamburg, where all three Hamburg orchestras play.

NIGHTLIFE

The famous nightclub district is **Sankt Pauli** *Plan III* **J1** with cabarets, bars and various exotic places. In the side streets flanking the **Reeperbahn** and the **Grosse Freiheit**, bars, discotheques, exotic restaurants, clubs and the Eros Centre function day and night in the gaudy illumination of multicoloured neon signs.

CENTRE

Plan II

Raffles Hotel Vier Jahreszeiten

Binnenalster, rm 110 VISA AE

Neuer Jungfernstieg 9 ✉ 20354 – Ⓜ Jungfernstieg – ✆ (040) 3 49 40 – hamburg@raffles.com – Fax (040) 34 94 26 00 – www.raffles-hvj.de

F2

157 rm – 220/315 € 270/385 €, 24 € – 17 suites

Rest *Haerlin* – see below

Rest *Doc Cheng's* – *✆ (040) 3 49 43 33 (closed Saturday lunch, Sunday) (July - August dinner only)* Carte 38/48 €

Rest *Jahreszeiten Grill* – *✆ (040) 34 94 33 12* – Carte 39/67 €

♦ Grand Luxury ♦ Traditional ♦ Classic ♦

This establishment on the Binnenalster is the epitome of a grand hotel: incomparable service, classically luxurious ambience and exclusive Amrita Spa. The lounge is extremely stylish. Eurasian cuisine is served in Doc Cheng's. The Grill serves international specialities.

Park Hyatt

rm 120 VISA AE

Bugenhagenstr. 8 ✉ 20095 – Ⓜ Mönckebergstr. – ✆ (040) 33 32 12 34 – hamburg@hyatt.de – Fax (040) 33 32 12 35 – www.hamburg.park.hyatt.com

H2

252 rm – 185/325 € 210/350 €, 28 € – 21 suites

Rest *Apples* – *✆ (040) 33 32 15 11* – Carte 31/58 €

♦ Chain hotel ♦ Grand Luxury ♦ Stylish ♦

This historic brick-built, former office building opens up a world of simple elegance with high quality fabrics, Canadian cherry and bathrooms by Philipp Starcke. Stylish contemporary decoration gives "Apples" its unmistakable charm.

Atlantic Kempinski

Außenalster, rm 220 VISA AE

An der Alster 72 ✉ 20099 – ✆ (040) 2 88 80 – hotel.atlantic@kempinski.com – Fax (040) 24 71 29 – www.kempinski.atlantic.de

H1

252 rm – 230/430 € 270/470 €, 28 € – 13 suites

Rest – *(closed Sunday lunch)* Carte 50/71 €

♦ Grand Luxury ♦ Traditional ♦ Classic ♦

The "Weisse Riese" has been a renowned meeting point for society since 1909. The rooms have high stucco ceilings and period furniture; some rooms with a view of the Alster. This restaurant boasts a tastefully elegant atmosphere and an indoor terrace.

Le Royal Méridien

rm 220 VISA AE

An der Alster 52 ✉ 20099 – ✆ (040) 2 10 00 – info.lrmhamburg@lemeridien.com – Fax (040) 21 00 11 11 – www.hamburg.lemeridien.com

H1

284 rm – 169/399 € 189/419 €, 24 € – 19 suites

Rest – Menu 55 € (dinner) – Carte 34/52 €

♦ Chain hotel ♦ Luxury ♦ Modern ♦

A touch of exclusivity will follow you from the spacious hall through to the "Art + Tech Design" rooms equipped with the most modern facilities. The restaurant Le Ciel, on the 9th floor, offers a fantastic view over the Aussenalster.

Grand Elysée

rm 750 VISA AE

Rothenbaumchaussee 10 ✉ 20148 – ✆ (040) 41 41 20 – info@elysee.de – Fax (040) 41 41 27 33 – www.elysee.de

F1

511 rm – 139 € 159 €, 18 € – 11 suites

Rest *Piazza Romana* – *✆ (040) 41 41 27 34* – Carte 31/44 €

Rest *Brasserie* – *✆ (040) 41 41 27 24* – Carte 24/29 €

♦ Luxury ♦ Classic ♦

Classic elegance and spacious, comfortable rooms await you. The spirit of the boulevard pervades the palatial hall with café. The Piazza Romana serves Italian cuisine in a Mediterranean ambience. Parisian flair in the Brasserie.

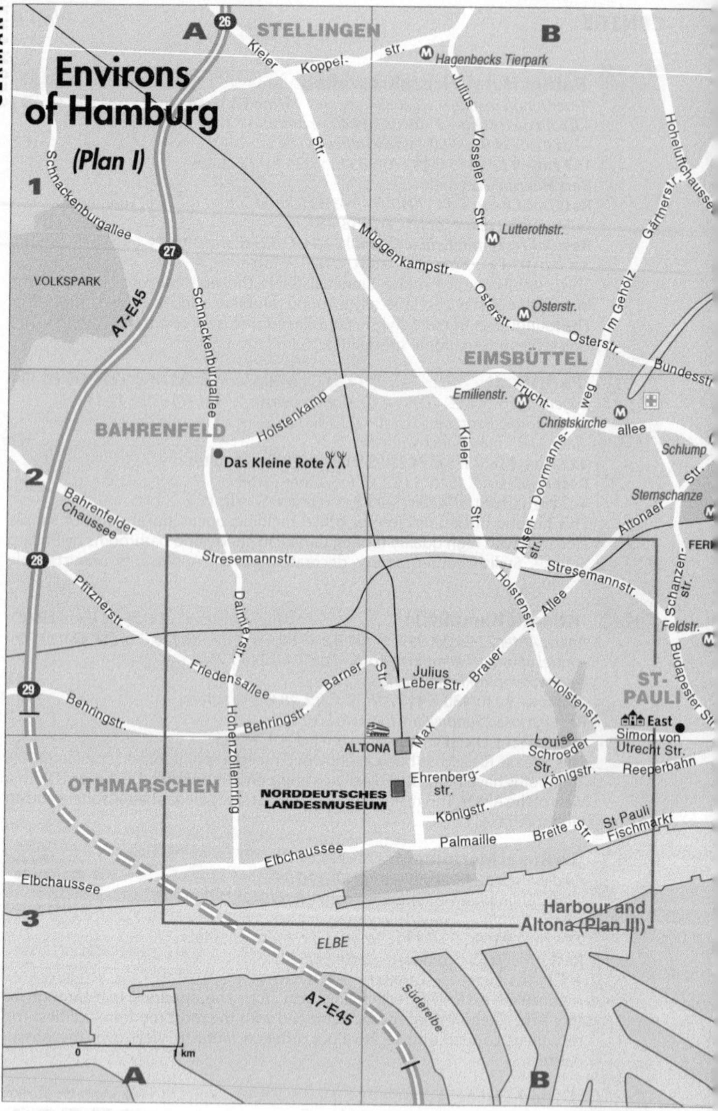

Environs of Hamburg
(Plan I)

A
B
1
2
3
STELLINGEN
Kieler Koppel-str.
Hagenbecks Tierpark
Julius Vosseler Str.
Str.
Hoheluftchaussee
Gärtnerstr.
Lutterothstr.
Müggenkampstr.
Osterstr.
Osterstr.
Osterstr.
Im Gehölz
Bundesstr.
EIMSBÜTTEL
Emilienstr.
Frucht-allee
Christskirche
Doormanns-weg
Schlump
Sternschanze
Altonaer Str.
Schnackenburgallee
VOLKSPARK
A7-E45
Schnackenburgallee
Holstenkamp
BAHRENFELD
Das Kleine Rote
Kieler Str.
Alsen-str.
Bahrenfelder Chaussee
Stresemannstr.
Stresemannstr.
Pfitznerstr.
Daimlerstr.
Holstenstr.
Max Brauer Allee
Schanzen-str.
Feldstr.
FERN
Budapester Str.
Friedensallee
Barner Str.
Julius Leber Str.
ST-PAULI
Holstenstr.
Behringstr.
Behringstr.
Hohenzollernring
ALTONA
East
Louise Schroeder Str.
Simon von Utrecht Str.
Reeperbahn
OTHMARSCHEN
NORDDEUTSCHES LANDESMUSEUM
Ehrenberg-str.
Königstr.
Königstr.
Palmaille
Breite Str.
St Pauli Fischmarkt
Elbchaussee
Elbchaussee
Harbour and Altona (Plan III)
ELBE
Süderelbe
A7-E45
0
1 km
26
27
28
29

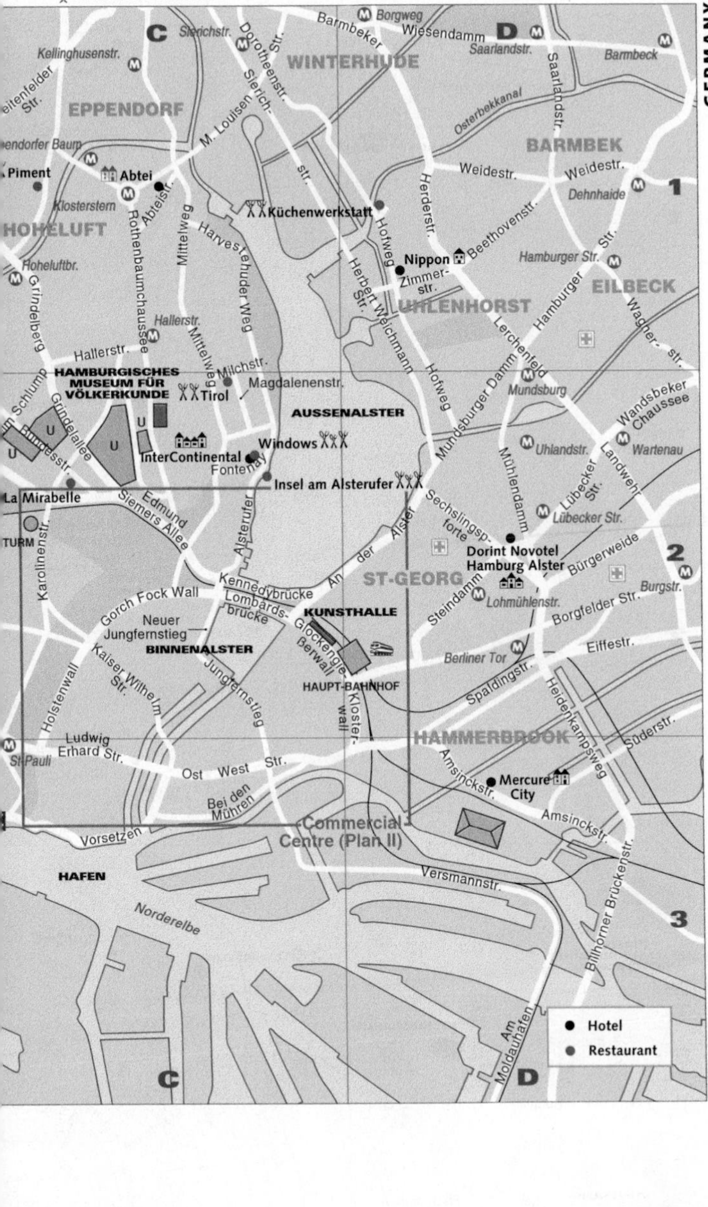

C
D
WINTERHUDE
EPPENDORF
BARMBEK
HOHELUFT
UHLENHORST
EILBECK
ST-GEORG
HAMMERBROOK
HAFEN
AUSSENALSTER
BINNENALSTER
KUNSTHALLE
HAUPT-BAHNHOF
HAMBURGISCHES MUSEUM FÜR VÖLKERKUNDE
Commercial Centre (Plan II)

Piment
Abtei
Küchenwerkstatt
Nippon
Tirol
Windows
InterContinental
Fontenay
Insel am Alsterufer
La Mirabelle
Dorint Novotel Hamburg Alster
Mercure City

Borgweg
Barmbeker Str.
Wiesendamm
Saarlandstr.
Barmbeck
Sierichstr.
Dorotheenstr.
Kellinghusenstr.
Sierich-str.
M. Louisen Str.
Osterbekkanal
Eppendorfer Baum
Klosterstern
Abteistr.
Rothenbaumchaussee
Mittelweg
Harvestehuder Weg
Weidestr.
Dehnhaide
Hofweg
Herderstr.
Beethovenstr.
Hamburger Str.
Zimmerstr.
Herbert Weichmann Str.
Hoheluftbr.
Grindelberg
Hallerstr.
Milchstr.
Magdalenenstr.
Lerchenfeld
Mundsburger Damm
Mundsburg
Wagnerstr.
Wandsbeker Chaussee
Grindelallee
Bundesstr.
Uhlandstr.
Wartenau
Mühlendamm
Lübecker Str.
Landwehr
Edmund Siemers Allee
Alsterufer
An der Alster
Sechslingspforte
TURM
Karolinenstr.
Kennedybrücke
Lombardsbrücke
Gorch Fock Wall
Neuer Jungfernstieg
Steindamm
Lohmühlenstr.
Bürgerweide
Burgstr.
Borgfelder Str.
Glockengießerwall
Eiffestr.
Berliner Tor
Kaiser Wilhelm Str.
Holstenwall
Jungfernstieg
Klosterwall
Spaldingstr.
Heidenkampsweg
Süderstr.
St. Pauli
Ludwig Erhard Str.
Ost West Str.
Bei den Mühren
Amsinckstr.
Vorsetzen
Versmannstr.
Norderelbe
Billhorner Brückenstr.
Am Moldauhafen
1
2
3

● Hotel
● Restaurant

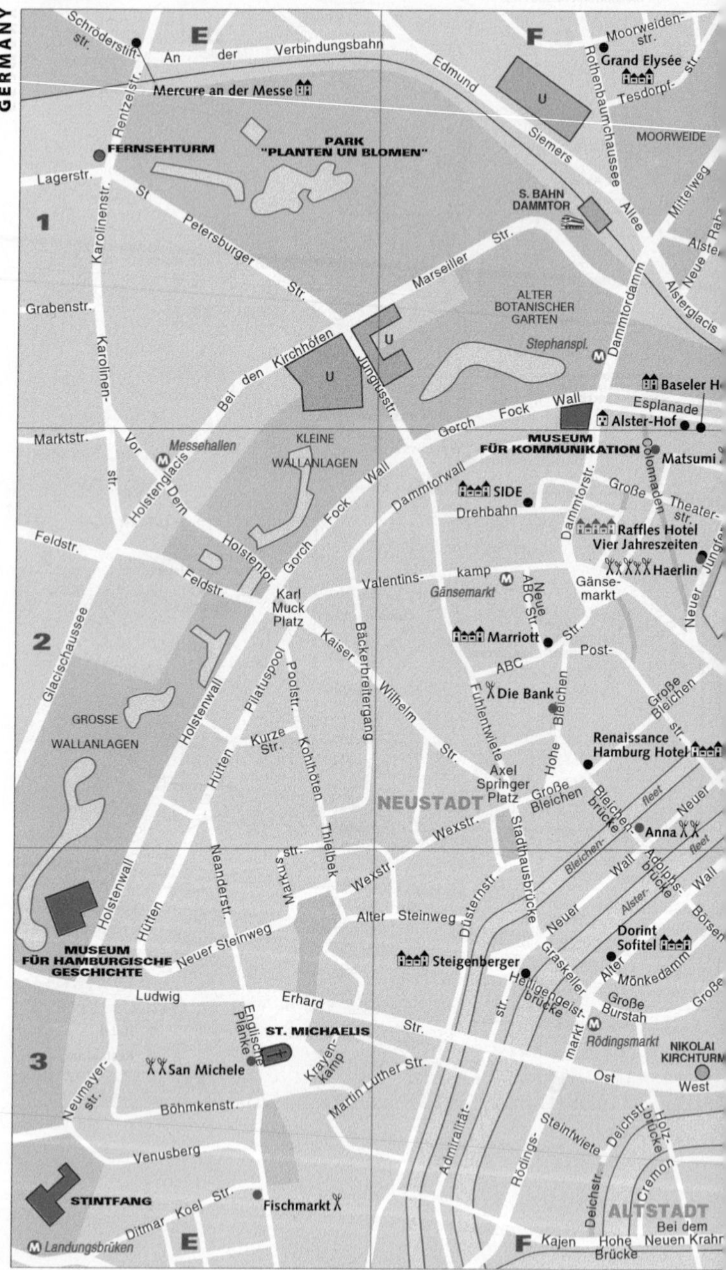
E
F
1
2
3
Schröderstift-str.
An der Verbindungsbahn
Mercure an der Messe
Rentzelstr.
FERNSEHTURM
PARK "PLANTEN UN BLOMEN"
Lagerstr.
St Petersburger Str.
Karolinenstr.
Grabenstr.
Karolinen-
Marseiller Str.
Bei den Kirchhöfen
Jungiusstr.
U
Edmund Siemers Allee
Moorweiden-str.
Grand Elysée
Rothenbaumchaussee
Tesdorpf-str.
MOORWEIDE
S. BAHN DAMMTOR
Mittelweg
Alsterglacis
ALTER BOTANISCHER GARTEN
Stephanspl.
Dammtordamm
Baseler H
Esplanade
Alster-Hof
Gorch Fock Wall
MUSEUM FÜR KOMMUNIKATION
Colonnaden
Matsumi
Marktstr.
Vor Dem Holstentor
Messehallen
KLEINE WALLANLAGEN
Holstenglacis
str.
Dammtorwall
SIDE
Drehbahn
Dammtorstr.
Große Theater-str.
Raffles Hotel Vier Jahreszeiten
Haerlin
Feldstr.
Valentins-kamp
Gänsemarkt
Neue ABC Str.
Gänse-markt
Karl Muck Platz
Kaiser Wilhelm Str.
Bäckerbreitergang
Marriott
Post-str.
Glacischaussee
Holstenwall
Pilatuspool
Poolstr.
ABC
Fuhlentwiete
Die Bank
Hohe Bleichen
Große Bleichen
GROSSE WALLANLAGEN
Kurze Str.
Kohlhöfen
Hütten
Renaissance Hamburg Hotel
Axel Springer Platz
NEUSTADT
Bleichen-brücke
Bleichen-fleet
Neuer Wall
Anna
Wexstr.
Thielbek
Markus str.
Neanderstr.
Stadthausbrücke
Düsternstr.
Adolphs-brücke
Alster-fleet
Börsen
Alter Steinweg
Neuer Steinweg
Dorint Sofitel
MUSEUM FÜR HAMBURGISCHE GESCHICHTE
Steigenberger
Heiligengeist-brücke
Graskeller
Alter Mönkedamm
Große Burstah
Ludwig Erhard Str.
Englische Planke
ST. MICHAELIS
Rödingsmarkt
NIKOLAI KIRCHTURM
Ost West
San Michele
Krayen-kamp
Martin Luther Str.
Neumayer-str.
Böhmkenstr.
Admiralität-str.
Steinwiete
Deichstr.
Holz-brücke
Venusberg
Rödings-
Cremon
STINTFANG
Fischmarkt
Ditmar Koel Str.
ALTSTADT
Bei dem Neuen Krahn
Landungsbrüken
Kajen
Hohe Brücke

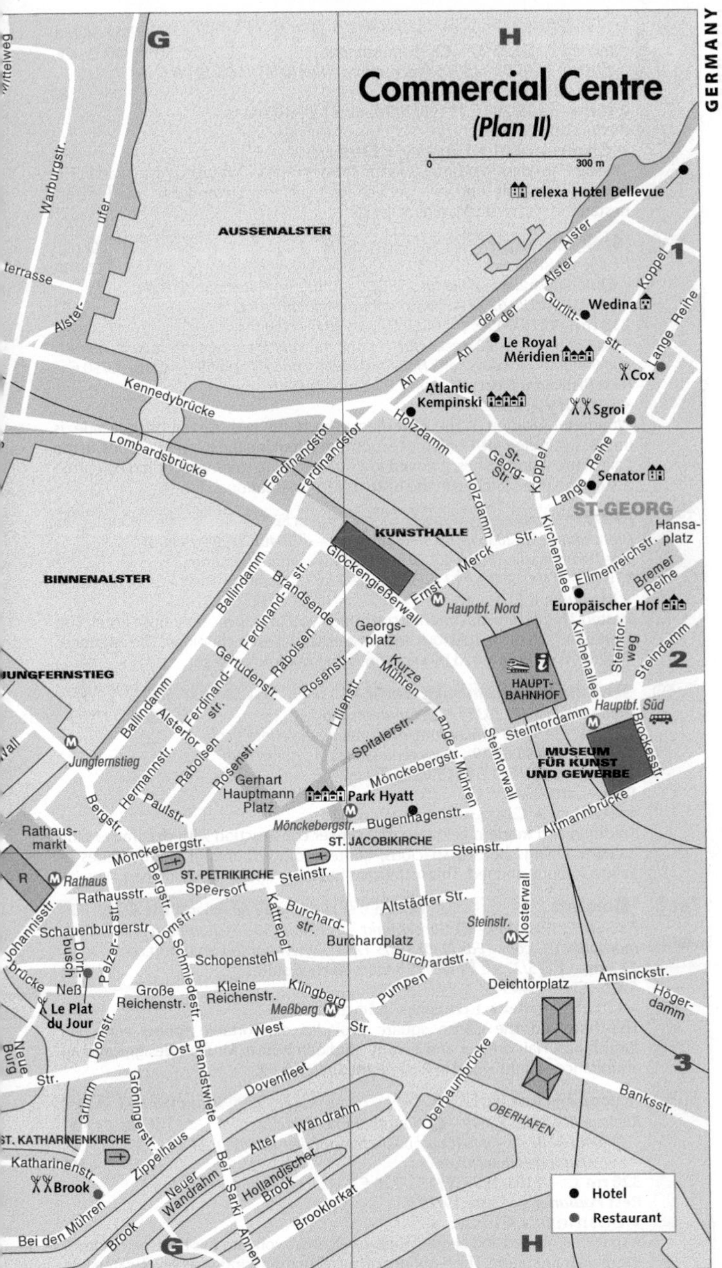
Commercial Centre
(Plan II)
0
300 m
relexa Hotel Bellevue
AUSSENALSTER
BINNENALSTER
JUNGFERNSTIEG
KUNSTHALLE
ST-GEORG
Wedina
Le Royal Méridien
Atlantic Kempinski
Cox
Sgroi
Senator
Europäischer Hof
HAUPT-BAHNHOF
MUSEUM FÜR KUNST UND GEWERBE
Park Hyatt
ST. JACOBIKIRCHE
ST. PETRIKIRCHE
ST. KATHARINENKIRCHE
Le Plat du Jour
Brook
OBERHAFEN
Hotel
Restaurant

Dorint Sofitel

250

Alter Wall 40 ✉ 20457 – Ⓜ Rödingsmarkt
– ✆ (040) 36 95 00 – h5395@accor.com – Fax (040) 36 95 10 00
– www.sofitel.com **F3**
241 rm – 🛉195/290 € 🛉🛉195/290 €, ☕ 21 € – 10 suites
Rest – Carte 35/54 €

♦ Chain hotel ♦ Luxury ♦ Design ♦

This modern designer hotel is in the former post office on an Alster canal. The interior is marble and exposed concrete, elegant wood and modern art. Restaurant with a sleek, minimalist style.

Steigenberger

rm 180

Heiligengeistbrücke 4 ✉ 20459
– Ⓜ Rödingsmarkt – ✆ (040) 36 80 60 – hamburg@steigenberger.de
– Fax (040) 36 80 67 77 – www.hamburg.steigenberger.de **F3**
233 rm – 🛉175/245 € 🛉🛉195/265 €, ☕ 20 € – 6 suites
Rest *Calla* – *(closed 2 weeks end December - early January, 4 weeks July - August and Sunday - Monday, Bank Holidays) (dinner only)* Menu 59 € – Carte 39/50 €
Rest *Bistro am Fleet* – Menu 27 € – Carte 24/37 €

♦ Luxury ♦ Classic ♦

Wonderful location at the Alsterfleet. The hotel, with its red brick facade, is impressively elegant. Conference rooms overlooking the town's rooftops. In the Calla: Euro-Asian dishes, enjoyed as you watch the steamers gliding by on the Alster. The open kitchen in the Bistro offers international dishes.

SIDE

rm 160

Drehbahn 49 ✉ 20354 – Ⓜ Stephansplatz – ✆ (040) 30 99 90 – info@side-hamburg.de – Fax (040) 30 99 93 99 – www.side-hamburg.de **F2**
178 rm – 🛉190/290 € 🛉🛉215/315 €, ☕ 23 € – 10 suites – **Rest** – Carte 30/62 €

♦ Luxury ♦ Design ♦

Matteo Thun's unusual interior surrounds you in this recently built hotel. The rooms and suites are spacious and contain the latest technology. The interior of "Fusion" is distinguished by clean lines and minimalist décor.

Renaissance Hamburg Hotel

rm 120

Große Bleichen ✉ 20354 – Ⓜ Jungfernstieg
– ✆ (040) 34 91 80 – rhi.hamrn.info@renaissancehotels.com
– Fax (040) 34 91 89 19 – www.renaissance-hamburg.com **F2**
205 rm – 🛉139/169 € 🛉🛉139/169 €, ☕ 20 €
Rest – Carte 29/42 €

♦ Luxury ♦ Classic ♦

Tradition and modern elegance: the clinker construction with decorative blue balcony railings houses spacious, contemporary rooms in warm shades of yellow, orange and red. This restaurant has a bar and an open kitchen.

Marriott

rm 160

ABC-Str. 52 ✉ 20354 – Ⓜ Gänsemarkt – ✆ (040) 3 50 50 – hamburg.marriott@marriotthotels.com – Fax (040) 35 05 17 77 – www.hamburgmarriott.com
277 rm – 🛉175/225 € 🛉🛉175/225 €, ☕ 23 € – 5 suites **F2**
Rest – Carte 29/43 €

♦ Chain hotel ♦ Luxury ♦ Modern ♦

This hotel on the Gänse square provides comfortable rooms with fine furnishings. Hair dresser and beauty studio in house. Modern designs and an abundance of light wood in Restaurant Speicher 52.

Europäischer Hof

rest rm 200

Kirchenallee 45 ✉ 20099 – Ⓜ Hauptbahnhof Süd
– ✆ (040) 24 82 48 – info@europaeischer-hof.de – Fax (040) 24 82 47 99
– www.europaeischer-hof.de **H2**
320 rm ☕ – 🛉105/180 € 🛉🛉135/220 €
Rest *Paulaner's* – Carte 19/29 €

♦ Business ♦ Classic ♦

A spacious, refined and elegant lobby welcomes you into this hotel across from the main train station. The highlight of the recreation area is a six-level waterslide down to the swimming pool. Paulaner's: rustic and relaxed.

Dorint Novotel Hamburg Alster 120 VISA
Lübecker Str. 3 ✉ 22087 – Ⓜ Lübecker Str.
– ✆ (040) 39 19 00 – h3737@accor.com – Fax (040) 39 19 02 72
– www.novotel.com *Plan I* **D2**
210 rm – ♦79/209 € ♦♦79/209 €, 17 €
Rest – Carte 29/47 €
♦ Chain hotel ♦ Modern ♦
A modern hotel providing well-equipped rooms in comfortable, modern style. Conferences facilities available. Restaurant accessed from the hotel lobby.

relexa Hotel Bellevue rm 45 VISA
An der Alster 14 ✉ 20099 – ✆ (040) 28 44 40 – hamburg@relexa-hotel.de
– Fax (040) 28 44 42 22 – www.relexa-hotels.de **H1**
85 rm – ♦75/110 € ♦♦105/145 €
Rest – Carte 27/32 €
♦ Business ♦ Functional ♦
Classical white hotel building. The rooms are pretty - some in the main building have pretty views of the Alster, while those in the St. Georg building are smaller single rooms. Lunch restaurant on the Außenalster. Dinner in the basement with tasteful, cosy atmosphere.

Mercure an der Messe rm 70 VISA
Schröderstiftstr. 3 ✉ 20146 – ✆ (040) 45 06 90 – h5394@accor.com
– Fax (040) 4 50 69 10 00 – www.mercure.com **E1**
180 rm – ♦89/255 € ♦♦89/255 €, 14 €
Rest – *(closed Sunday dinner)* Carte 24/32 €
♦ Business ♦ Functional ♦
Business hotel next door to the exhibition centre and a few minutes' walk from the TV tower. Rooms with a modern design and functional equipment.

Mercure City rm 60 VISA
Amsinckstr. 53 ✉ 20097 – ✆ (040) 23 63 80 – h1163@accor.com
– Fax (040) 23 42 30 – www.mercure.com *Plan I* **D3**
187 rm – ♦85/210 € ♦♦85/210 €, 17 €
Rest – Carte 24/37 €
♦ Chain hotel ♦ Functional ♦
Modern functional rooms in this inner city hotel, ideal for business guests.

Senator without rest VISA
Lange Reihe 18 ✉ 20099 – Ⓜ Hauptbahnhof Nord – ✆ (040) 24 12 03
– info@hotel-senator-hamburg.de – Fax (040) 2 80 37 17
– www.hotel-senator-hamburg.de **H2**
56 rm – ♦99/179 € ♦♦99/179 €
♦ Business ♦ Functional ♦
Pale wood and pastel tones create a harmonious atmosphere in the rooms, some of which have a waterbed for a perfect night's sleep.

Baseler Hof rm 120 VISA
Esplanade 11 ✉ 20354 – Ⓜ Stephansplatz – ✆ (040) 35 90 60
– info@baselerhof.de – Fax (040) 35 90 69 18 – www.baselerhof.de **F1**
168 rm – ♦89/119 € ♦♦119/139 €
Rest *Kleinhuis* – ✆ *(040) 35 33 99* – Carte 25/32 €
♦ Traditional ♦ Functional ♦
This hotel is located between the Außenalster and the Botanical Gardens, and is a member of the Association of Christian Hotels. A range of rooms, some with rattan furniture. The Kleinhuis is a nice bistro-style restaurant.

Wedina without rest VISA
Gurlittstr. 23 ✉ 20099 – ✆ (040) 2 80 89 00 – info@wedina.de
– Fax (040) 2 80 38 94 – www.wedina.de **H1**
59 rm – ♦88/145 € ♦♦108/165 €
♦ Family ♦ Cosy ♦
The different buildings which make up this hotel are aglow in Bauhaus colours. The interior is also attractively designed featuring natural materials.

GERMANY

Alster-Hof without rest

Esplanade 12 ✉ 20354 – Ⓜ Stephansplatz – ✆ (040) 35 00 70
– info@alster-hof.de – Fax (040) 35 00 75 14 – www.alster-hof.de
closed 23 December - 2 January **F1**
113 rm – †81/96 € ††105/131 €
◆ Traditional ◆ Functional ◆
This centrally located hotel provides functional rooms with a refined atmosphere.

Haerlin – Hotel Vier Jahreszeiten

< Binnenalster,

Neuer Jungfernstieg 9 ✉ 20354 – Ⓜ Jungfernstieg – ✆ (040) 34 94 33 10
– hamburg@raffles.com – Fax (040) 34 94 26 08 – www.raffles-hvj.de
closed 27 December - 8 January, 2 weeks March, 4 weeks July - August and Sunday - Monday **F2**
Rest – *(dinner only)* Menu 69/98 € – Carte 64/75 €
Spec. Mosaik von der Gänsestopfleber und Trüffel. Lammrücken auf zwei Arten zubereitet. Krosse Vierländer Ente aus dem Rohr (2 people).
◆ French ◆ Formal ◆
In a stylishly elegant restaurant setting enjoy elaborate and excellent classical cuisine. The friendly and outstandingly professional service is perfect.

Insel am Alsterufer

40

Alsterufer 35 , (1st floor) ✉ 20354 – ✆ (040) 4 50 18 50 – info@insel-am-alsterufer.de – Fax (040) 45 01 85 11 – www.insel-am-alsterufer.de
closed September - May Sunday, June - August Sunday dinner *Plan I* **C2**
Rest – Menu 20 € (lunch) – Carte 40/55 €
◆ French ◆ Trendy ◆
The white façade of this villa is beautifully lit up at night. An elegant Mediterranean style interior with warm décor, serving classic dishes.

Sgroi

Lange Reihe 40 ✉ 20099 – ✆ (040) 28 00 39 30 – Fax (040) 28 00 39 31
– www.sgroi.de
closed Saturday lunch, Sunday - Monday **H1**
Rest – Menu 58/72 € – Carte 54/59 €
Spec. Quetschkartoffeln mit mariniertem Kabeljau und Rucola. Ravioli von Jakobsmuscheln mit Ingwer und Zitrone. Gebratenes Rotbarbenfilet mit Auberginenpüree und geschmorten Tomaten.
◆ Italian ◆ Minimalist ◆
Straight up and down - the interiors of this modern restaurant reflect the no-nonsense Italian cuisine prepared from excellent produce.

Anna

Bleichenbrücke 2 ✉ 20354 – Ⓜ Rathaus – ✆ (040) 36 70 14
– Fax (040) 37 50 07 36
closed Sunday, Bank Holidays **F2**
Rest – Carte 36/43 €
◆ International ◆ Friendly ◆
The restaurant features Feng Shui design and spans two floors. It offers a wide range of international cuisine. Beautiful terrace overlooking the Fleet.

San Michele

Englische Planke 8 ✉ 20459 – Ⓜ Landungsbrücken – ✆ (040) 37 11 27
– info@san-michele.de – Fax (040) 37 81 21 – www.san-michele.de
closed Monday **E3**
Rest – Carte 36/56 €
◆ Italian ◆ Friendly ◆
The "most Italian of all Italians" is directly opposite the "Michel"! Enjoy traditional Neapolitan cuisine in a cheerful Mediterranean ambience. Small bistro on the ground floor.

XX

Brook

AE

Bei den Mühren 91 ✉ 20457 – ✆ (040) 37 50 31 28 – Fax (040) 37 50 31 27 – www.restaurant-brook.de
closed Sunday **G3**
Rest – Menu 29 € – Carte 31/43 €
◆ Contemporary ◆ Minimalist ◆
A modern restaurant with friendly service and good international cuisine. In the evening you have views of the illuminated old warehouse district.

X

Die Bank

VISA AE

Hohe Bleichen 17 ✉ 20354 – Ⓜ Gänsemarkt – ✆ (040) 2 38 00 30 – info@diebank-brasserie.de – Fax (040) 23 80 03 33 – www.diebank-brasserie.de
closed Sunday and Bank Holidays **F2**
Rest – Carte 33/58 €
◆ International ◆ Brasserie ◆
The imposing tellers' hall on the first floor of this former bank is now home to this trendy restaurant. A variety of Mediterranean and classical dishes with Asian influences.

X

La Mirabelle

VISA MC AE

Bundesstr. 15 ✉ 20146 – ✆ (040) 4 10 75 85 – Fax (040) 4 10 75 85 – www.la-mirabelle-hamburg.de
closed Sunday *Plan I* **C2**
Rest – *(dinner only)* Menu 36 € – Carte 34/47 €
◆ French ◆ Bistro ◆
Small, friendly restaurant with relaxed atmosphere and a touch of France. The chef personally recommends the specialities of the day to his guests.

X

Fischmarkt

VISA MC AE

Ditmar-Koel-Str. 1 ✉ 20459 – Ⓜ Landungsbrücken – ✆ (040) 36 38 09 – Fax (040) 36 21 91 – www.restaurant-fischmarkt.de
closed Saturday lunch **E3**
Rest – *(booking advisable)* Menu 28/45 € – Carte 29/43 €
◆ Seafood ◆ Bistro ◆
Close to the harbour, this fine restaurant with Mediterranean décor and a bistro atmosphere with open kitchen serves many fish specialities.

X

Le Plat du Jour

VISA MC AE

Dornbusch 4 ✉ 20095 – Ⓜ Rathaus – ✆ (040) 32 14 14 – Fax (040) 32 52 63 93
closed Sunday, Bank Holidays, July - August Saturday - Sunday **G3**
Rest – *(booking advisable)* Menu 26 € (dinner) – Carte 27/32 €
◆ French ◆ Bistro ◆
A pleasant French style bistro with wooden seats, black and white photos on the walls. Good value for money.

X

Cox

AE

Lange Reihe 68 ✉ 20099 – ✆ (040) 24 94 22 – info@restaurant-cox.de – Fax (040) 28 05 09 02 – www.restaurant-cox.de
closed Saturday lunch, Sunday lunch **H1**
Rest – Carte 25/35 €
◆ Modern ◆ Bistro ◆
Diners are served international cuisine with a Mediterranean touch in this charming, warm bistro near the city's principal theatre.

X

Matsumi

VISA MC AE

Colonnaden 96 (1st floor) ✉ 20354 – Ⓜ Stephansplatz – ✆ (040) 34 31 25 – Fax (040) 34 42 19 – www.matsumi.de
closed Sunday, Bank Holidays lunch **F2**
Rest – Menu 50 € (dinner) – Carte 22/43 €
◆ Japanese ◆ Minimalist ◆
You will find this classic Japanese restaurant in the pedestrian zone. The authentic fare is served at the table, at the sushi bar or in the tatami rooms (for groups).

GERMANY

NORTH OF THE CENTRE *Plan I*

InterContinental
< Hamburg and Alster, rm
Fontenay 10 ✉ 20354 – ☎ (040) 4 14 20 300 P VISA MO AE
– hamburg@interconti.com – Fax (040) 41 42 22 99
– www.hamburg.intercontinental.com **C2**
281 rm – †185/260 € ††185/260 €, ☕ 21 € – 12 suites
Rest Windows – see below
Rest *Signatures* – Carte 35/44 €
♦ Chain hotel ♦ Luxury ♦ Functional ♦
This hotel located on the Alster will charm guests thanks to its extravagant appearance, international flair and contemporary, functional rooms. Pleasantly bright: the conservatory restaurant. International cuisine.

Abtei
rest VISA MO AE
Abteistr. 14 ✉ 20149 – ☎ (040) 44 29 05 – abtei@relaischateaux.com
– Fax (040) 44 98 20 – www.abtei-hotel.de
closed 24 - 26 December **C1**
11 rm ☕ – †145/200 € ††180/240 €
Rest – *(closed Sunday - Monday) (dinner only) (booking essential)* Menu 60/90 € – Carte 56/74 €
Spec. Marinierte Gänseleber mit Apfelconfit und Brioche. Lammrücken im Brotmantel mit gefüllter Paprika. Schokoladenvariation.
♦ Townhouse ♦ Personalised ♦
An extremely pleasant, gorgeous establishment in a quiet and elegant residential area. Charming private atmosphere and very tasteful, individually decorated rooms. This restaurant with refined salon has an intimate ambience.

Nippon
rm 20 VISA MO AE
Hofweg 75 ✉ 22085 – ☎ (040) 2 27 11 40 – reservations@nipponhotel.de
– Fax (040) 22 71 14 90 – www.nipponhotel.de
closed 23 December - 1 January **D1**
42 rm – †98/121 € ††116/150 €, ☕ 11 €
Rest – *(closed Monday) (dinner only)* Carte 26/38 €
♦ Business ♦ Minimalist ♦
Furnished in a modern, purist Japanese style with light colours and clear shapes: tatami floors, shoji walls and futons. A Japanese restaurant and sushi bar.

XXX

Windows – Hotel InterContinental
< Hamburg and Alster, rm
Fontenay 10 ✉ 20354 – ☎ (040) 41422531 P VISA MO AE
– hamburg@interconti.com – Fax (040) 41 42 22 99
– www.hamburg.intercontinental.com
closed 1 - 21 January, 12 July - 22 August and Sunday - Monday **C2**
Rest – *(dinner only)* Carte 51/66 €
♦ Classic ♦ Formal ♦
This 9th floor restaurant charms with elegant ambience and an incomparable view. French cuisine.

XX

Piment (Nouri)
VISA MO AE
Lehmweg 29 ✉ 20251 – ☎ (040) 42 93 77 88 – info@restaurant-piment.de
– Fax (040) 42 93 77 89
closed 5 - 17 March, 2 weeks July - August and Sunday **C1**
Rest – *(dinner only)* Menu 52/78 € – Carte 55/61 €
Spec. Unsere Gänsestopfleber. Geschmorte Ochsenschulter mit Schalotten gratiniert. Topfenknödel mit zweierlei Apfel.
♦ Contemporary ♦ Friendly ♦
This cosy restaurant is housed in a lovely Art Nouveau building. Chef Wahabi Nouri adds North African elements to his classical cuisine.

XX

Poletto

Eppendorfer Landstr. 145, (by Breitenfelder Str. C 1) ✉ 20251 – ✆ (040) 4 80 21 59 – Fax (040) 41 40 69 93 – www.poletto.de
closed 2 weeks July - August and Saturday lunch, Sunday - Monday
Rest – *(booking advisable)* Menu 49 € (lunch)/72 € – Carte 65/74 €
Spec. Tatar von Thunfisch mit Römersalat-Vinaigrette. Steinbutt an der Gräte mit Räucheraal und altem Balsamico. Das Beste von Lamm mit gratinierter Auberginentarte.

♦ Italian influences ♦ Friendly ♦

A restaurant decorated in pleasant light tones, run by chef Cornelia Poletto and her husband. Italian cuisine showing Mediterranean influences.

XX

Allegria

Hudtwalckerstr. 13, (by Sierichstr. C 1) ✉ 22299 – ✆ (040) 46 07 28 28 – info@allegria-restaurant.de – Fax (040) 46 07 26 07 – www.allegria-restaurant.de
closed Monday
Rest – *(weekdays dinner only)* Menu 48 € – Carte 29/47 €

♦ International ♦ Fashionable ♦

Directly adjacent to the Winterhuder Fährhaus-Theater, you'll dine in a modern, bright restaurant with international cuisine. Friendly service managed by the hostess.

XX

Küchenwerkstatt

Hans-Henny-Jahnn-Weg 1, (entrance by Hofweg) ✉ 22085 – ✆ (040) 22 92 75 88 – mail@kuechenwerkstatt-hamburg.de – Fax (040) 22 92 75 99 – www.kuechenwerkstatt-hamburg.de
closed 2 weeks early January, 2 weeks July - August and Sunday - Monday
Rest – Menu 21 € (lunch)/69 € (dinner) **D1**

♦ Contemporary ♦ Trendy ♦

The former ferry terminal has been attractively decorated in simple modern style. Creative cuisine on classical foundations - more modest lunch menu.

XX

Tirol

VISA MC AE

Milchstr. 19 ✉ 20148 – ✆ (040) 44 60 82 – Fax (040) 44 80 93 27
closed Sunday **C2**
Rest – Carte 28/46 €

♦ Austrian ♦ Cosy ♦

For anyone who is homesick for Austria! Austrian specialties are served in the cosy, rustic atmosphere of this restaurant.

HARBOUR AND ALTONA *Plan III*

East

100 VISA MC AE

Simon-von-Utrecht-Str. 31 ✉ 20359 – Ⓜ St. Pauli – ✆ (040) 30 99 30 – info@east-hamburg.de – Fax (040) 30 99 32 00 – www.east-hamburg.de Plan I **B2**
125 rm – †155/175 € ††175/195 €, ☕ 14 € – 3 suites
Rest – Carte 34/42 €

♦ Business ♦ Design ♦

In a former iron smelting factory, stands this stunning designer hotel providing rather modern rooms with all mod cons and large bar area on the 2nd floor. Restaurant with brick vaulted ceiling in a converted factory shop.

InterCityHotel Hamburg Altona

rm 60 VISA MC AE

Paul-Nevermann-Platz 17 ✉ 22765 – ✆ (040) 38 03 40 – hamburg-altona@intercityhotel.de – Fax (040) 38 03 49 99 – www.hamburg-altona.intercityhotel.de **I1**
133 rm – †122/132 € ††144/154 €, ☕ 13 €
Rest – Carte 23/28 €

♦ Chain hotel ♦ Functional ♦

Right by the ICE-train station, this hotel provides modern, spaciously furnished rooms. The use of local transport is included in the room price. Bistro style restaurant.

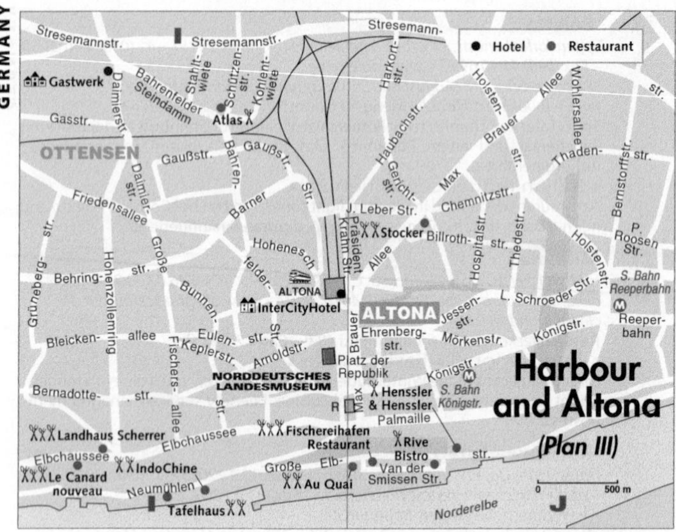

Landhaus Scherrer

Elbchaussee 130 ✉ 22763 – ✆ (040) 8 80 13 25 – info@landhausscherrer.de – Fax (040) 8 80 62 60 – www.landhausscherrer.de

closed Easter, Whitsun and Sunday I1

Rest – Menu 79/108 € – Carte 51/90 €

Rest *Bistro* – Menu 28 € – Carte 35/41 €

Spec. Gepökelter Kalbskopf mit Kardamomjus und gewürztem Bulgur. Forellenstör mit Wok-Gemüse und Tandoori-Aroma. Steinbutt an der Gräte gebraten.

♦ French ♦ Formal ♦

This 1827 country house has an appealing, elegant and classical interior. French cuisine. Of note is the wine cellar. Pleasant, friendly Bistro with light wood panelling.

Le Canard nouveau (Güngörmüs)

Elbchaussee 139 ✉ 22763 – ✆ (040) 88 12 95 31 – info@lecanard-hamburg.de – Fax (040) 88 12 95 33 – www.lecanard-hamburg.de

closed Monday, Saturday lunch, Sunday lunch, Bank Holidays I1

Rest – Menu 24 € (lunch)/90 € – Carte 42/50 €

Spec. Variation vom Thunfisch mit Pepperonata. Rehmedaillon mit Foie gras und Selleriecreme. Schokoladenkuchen mit Mango.

♦ International ♦ Fashionable ♦

Set above the Elbe is this semi-circular restaurant with a modern, chic atmosphere and windowed façade affording harbour views. Classic dishes, with an additional, simpler and inexpensive lunch menu.

Fischereihafen Restaurant

Große Elbstr. 143 ✉ 22767 – ✆ (040) 38 18 16 – info@fischereihafenrestaurant.de – Fax (040) 3 89 30 21 – www.fischereihafenrestaurant.de J1

Rest – *(booking advisable)* Menu 19 € (lunch) – Carte 26/58 €

♦ Seafood ♦ Formal ♦

This classic restaurant is a Hamburg institution serving regional cuisine and featuring fish dishes. Terrace overlooking the Elbe.

XX

Au Quai

Große Elbstr. 145 b ✉ 22767 – ✆ (040) 38 03 77 30 – info@au-quai.com – Fax (040) 38 03 77 32 – www.au-quai.com
closed 1 - 7 January and Sunday **J1**
Rest – Menu 18 € (lunch) – Carte 36/46 €
♦ Modern ♦ Trendy ♦
This popular establishment is situated close to the harbour and has a terrace facing the water. The modern interior is complemented by designer items and holographs.

XX

IndoChine

Neumühlen 11 ✉ 22763 – ✆ (040) 39 80 78 80 – info@indochine.de – Fax (040) 39 80 78 82 – www.indochine.de **I1**
Rest – Carte 31/52 €
♦ Asian ♦ Trendy ♦
A fantastic view from this modern, elegant restaurant situated on the 2nd and 3rd floors. Cambodian, Laotian, Vietnamese cuisine. Riverside terrace, IceBar and PianoBeach.

XX

Tafelhaus

Neumühlen 17 ✉ 22763 – ✆ (040) 89 27 60 – anfrage@tafelhaus.de – Fax (040) 8 99 33 24 – www.tafelhaus.de
closed Saturday lunch, Sunday **I1**
Rest – Menu 37 € (lunch)/85 € – Carte 57/75 €
Spec. Hummercocktail. Wolfsbarsch mit gegrilltem Gemüse und Sherry-Walnussvinaigrette. Gegrillte Taube mit orientalischen Gewürzen und Joghurt-Minzdip.
♦ Modern ♦ Fashionable ♦
Behind the glass façade of this office building is a modern-minimalist restaurant with views of the Elbe. French influences in creative cuisine. Terrace facing the Elbe.

XX

Stocker

Max-Brauer-Allee 80 ✉ 22765 – ✆ (040) 38 61 50 56 – info@restaurant-stocker.de – Fax (040) 38 61 50 58 – www.restaurant-stocker.de
closed 2 weeks early January and Saturday lunch, Sunday - Monday **J1**
Rest – Menu 18 € (lunch)/65 € (dinner) – Carte 32/43 €
♦ Austrian ♦ Friendly ♦
Playful frescoes and stucco ornamentation are the backdrop for the Austrian cuisine of this restaurant, which also offers typical Viennese dishes.

X

Henssler Henssler

Große Elbstr. 160 ✉ 22767 – Ⓜ Königstr. – ✆ (040) 38 69 90 00 – Fax (040) 38 69 90 55 – www.hensslerhenssler.de
closed 2 weeks Christmas - early January, 4 weeks July - August and Sunday, Bank Holidays **J1**
Rest – Carte 31/39 €
♦ Japanese ♦ Minimalist ♦
Very modern, deliberately simple restaurant in an old fishmonger's: Japanese-inspired interior, sushi bar and Japanese cuisine with Californian highlights.

X

Rive Bistro

Van-der-Smissen Str. 1, (Cruise-Centre) ✉ 22767 – Ⓜ Königstr. – ✆ (040) 3 80 59 19 – info@rive.de – Fax (040) 3 89 47 75 – www.rive.de **J1**
Rest – *(booking advisable)* Carte 28/41 €
♦ International ♦ Fashionable ♦
Directly on the harbour, close to the Fischmarkt is this modern restaurant. The international menu has a strong emphasis on fish dishes. Fresh oysters at the bar.

ELBE-WESTERN DISTRICTS *Plan III*

Louis C. Jacob
port and Elbe River, ½ rm 120 VISA

Elbchaussee 401, (by Elbchaussee A 3)
22609 – (040) 82 25 50 – jacob@hotel-jacob.de
– Fax (040) 82 25 54 44
– www.hotel-jacob.de
85 rm – 195/245 € 245/475 €, 24 € – 8 suites
Rest *Weinwirtschaft Kleines Jacob* – see below
Rest – *(closed 1 - 19 January) (booking advisable)* Menu 59 € (lunch)/98 € (dinner) – Carte 67/88 €
Spec. Sautierte Jakobsmuscheln mit Rotwein-Apfeljus und Couscous. Geschmorte Rinderschulter mit Baroloessig-Jus und kleinen Zwiebeln. Coulant von der Bitterschokolade mit Crème Chantilly und Lakritzeis demi-sel.
♦ Luxury ♦ Traditional ♦ Personalised ♦
This elegant hotel overlooking the Elbe offers first-class service. Modern and classical elements are carefully combined in the guest rooms. Impressive French cuisine in a stylish restaurant. Fabulous terrace shaded by lime trees.

Gastwerk
½ rm 100 P VISA

Beim Alten Gaswerk 3, (corner of Daimlerstraße) 22761
– (040) 89 06 20 – info@gastwerk-hotel.de
– Fax (040) 8 90 62 20
– www.gastwerk-hotel.de I1
141 rm – 131/162 € 131/162 €, 17 € – 3 suites
Rest – *(closed Saturday lunch, Sunday lunch)* Carte 40/50 €
♦ Business ♦ Stylish ♦
From the gasworks to a guest work: the impressive industrial memorial has been turned into a loft-style designer hotel with spacious rooms, natural materials and lots of tasteful details. A modern restaurant serving Italian cuisine.

Landhaus Flottbek
30 P

Baron-Voght-Str. 179, (by Stresemannstr. A 2) 22607
– (040) 8 22 74 10 – info@landhaus-flottbek.de
– Fax (040) 82 27 41 51 – www.landhaus-flottbek.de
25 rm – 90/120 € 105/150 €, 13 €
Rest – *(closed Saturday lunch, Sunday lunch)* Carte 29/43 €
♦ Family ♦ Cosy ♦
A group of 18C farmhouses with a beautiful garden. The lovely, individually furnished, country-style rooms are rustic and elegant. This restaurant, situated in former stables, has lots of atmosphere.

Süllberg-Seven Seas (Hauser) with rm

Süllbergsterrasse 12, (by Elbchaussee A 3) 100 VISA
22587 – (040) 8 66 25 20
– info@suellberg-hamburg.de
– Fax (040) 86 62 52 13 – www.suellberg-hamburg.de
11 rm – 130/160 € 160/190 €, 16 €
Rest – *(closed 3 - 23 January and Monday - Tuesday) (weekdays dinner only)* Menu 56/98 € – Carte 52/73 €
Rest *Bistro* – Carte 28/43 €
Spec. Geräucherte Bresse Taube mit Sauce Périgourdine und Wildkräutersalat. Gebratener Loup de mer mit Gambaravioli und Curry-Auberginenkaviar. Filet und Involtini vom Milchkalb mit glacierten Perlzwiebeln.
♦ French ♦ Formal ♦
The majestically impressive Sullberg ensemble, built in Wilhelminian style, looks down over the Elbe. The centrepiece is the gourmet restaurant Seven Seas, with fine views and a new bar. The Bistro: light, friendly and with a modern style.

Das Kleine Rote (Hinz)

Holstenkamp 71 ✉ 22525 – ✆ (040) 89 72 68 13 – das-kleine-rote@web.de – Fax (040) 89 72 68 14 – www.das-kleine-rote.de
closed Saturday lunch, Sunday - Monday — *Plan I* **A2**
Rest – *(booking advisable)* Menu 34 € (lunch)/74 € – Carte 47/64 €
Spec. Tatar vom Wolfbarsch mit Gurken und gebackenen Austern. Rücken und Schulter vom Rind mit Blumenkohl. Knuspriger Blätterteig mit Vanillecreme und Himbeersorbet.

♦ Contemporary ♦ Friendly ♦

The small red building with modern ambience is home to classical cuisine with creative elements. Atmospheric lighting in the evening. Pretty garden.

Atlas

Schützenstr. 9a, (entrance Phoenixhof) ✉ 22761 – ✆ (040) 8 51 78 10 – atlas@atlas.at – Fax (040) 8 51 78 11 – www.atlas.at
closed Saturday lunch — **I1**
Rest – Menu 16 € (lunch)/28 € (dinner) – Carte 27/39 €

♦ International ♦ Bistro ♦

A former fish smokery which has been converted into a well-run restaurant with a modern and simple bistro style. Behind the building there is a small, ivy-covered terrace.

Weinwirtschaft Kleines Jacob – Hotel Louis C. Jacob

Elbchaussee 404, (by Elbchaussee A 3) ✉ 22609 – ✆ (040) 82 25 55 10 – kleines-jacob@hotel-jacob.de – Fax (040) 82 25 54 44 – www.hotel-jacob.de
closed 4 weeks July - August and Tuesday
Rest – *(weekdays dinner only)* Carte 24/38 €

♦ International ♦ Cosy ♦

This cosy restaurant opposite the Louis C. Jacob Hotel features attractive décor in the style of a wine tavern. Mediterranean cuisine.

AT THE AIRPORT

Courtyard by Marriott

Flughafenstr. 47 ✉ 22415 – ✆ (040) 53 10 20 – service@airporthh.com – Fax (040) 53 10 22 22 – www.courtyard.com/hamcy
159 rm – 🚹105/199 € 🚹🚹105/199 €, ☕ 17 €
Rest – Carte 27/50 €

♦ Business ♦ Functional ♦

A country-house hotel just 500 m from the airport. Impressive combination of well judged colours and functional décor. A classic restaurant serving international specialities.

MUNICH
MÜNCHEN

Population: 1 205 000 (conurbation 1 656 000) – Altitude: 520m

AGE Carlos/HOA QUI

The Bavarian capital, third largest and one of the most important German towns, lies on River Isar's banks, not far north of the Alps. It is a renowned cultural centre (over 40 theatres, an academy of fine arts, one of Europe's largest film studios, dozens of museums, 10 university colleges) and the most flourishing economic zone in southern Germany. Its commercial influence has increased enormously in recent years, through the rising of high-tech industries allied to the production of motor vehicles (BMW), locomotives, rubber, chemicals and electronics (Siemens).

The choice of Munich as seat of the European Patents Office since 1980 recognises the city's illustrious scientific past, resounding with such famous names as Fraunhofer, Liebig, Ohm and Sauerbruch.

Among writers working in Munich were T. Mann, F. Wedekind and L. Thoma. It is however in the absurd logic of the stand-up comedian K. Valentine that Munich's spirit most popularly expresses itself. With the foundation of the review Jugend (1896) the city became the centre of the Jugendstil movement; and later, one of the Mecca of modern art.

Munich's cultural wealth, its special atmosphere – blend of gaiety, tolerance and respect for tradition – and the beauty of the surrounding countryside have combined to make it one of the most attractive German cities.

WHICH DISTRICT TO CHOOSE

The greatest concentration of **hotels** is in the immediate neighbourhood of the station. Many of the hotels and restaurants are located in the city centre – near Stachus, Marienplatz, Maximilianstrasse and Frauenkirche. A number of characterful **restaurants** and **inns** are located around the Viktualienmarkt but the best restaurants in Munich are to be found in the city centre and in the Bogenhausen and Schwabing districts. Munich is known for its solid regional cooking and especially for its attractive, lively **brewery-inns** where locals and visitors meet over

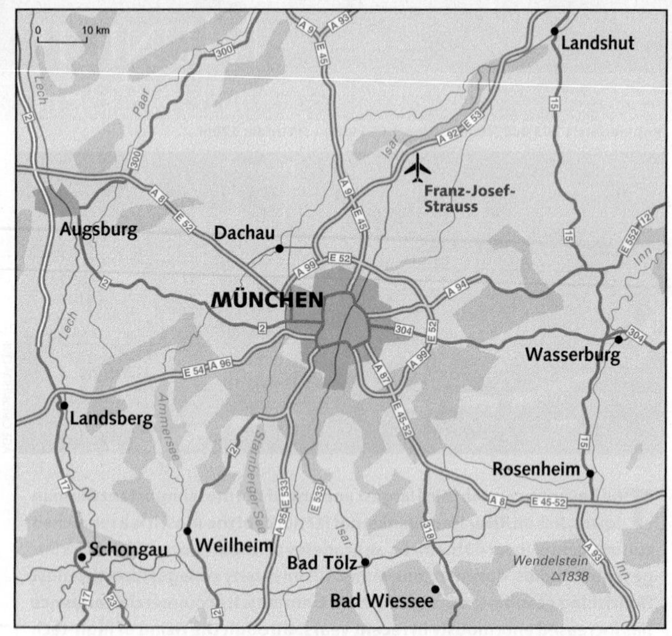

a tankard of the typical Bavarian *Weissbier* and a portion of the famous *Weisswurst* (local sausage). In recent decades so many small intimate **Italian restaurants** have appeared on the scene that Munich has been dubbed "the northernmost city of Italy".

PRACTICAL INFORMATION

ARRIVAL – DEPARTURE

Airport Franz-Josef Strauss about 28 km (17,5 mi) northeast of the city centre. ✆ (089) 9 75 00; info@munich-airport.de; www.munich-airport.de

From the airport to the city centre – By **taxi**: approx. €56. By rapid transit **train** (Line 8) to Railway Station every 20min.

Railway Station – Hauptbahnhof for international routes and trains. ✆ (0900) 150 70 90 (24hr - €1.99 per min); www.bahn.de

TRANSPORT

→ METRO, BUS AND TRAM

Munich and its surroundings are divided into four ring-shaped price zones. Underground trains (U-Bahn), trams (Straßenbahn) and buses are controlled by the local transport and fare association **MVV** (Münchner Verkehrs- und Tarifverbund); ✆ (089) 41 42 43 44. 9am-6pm and Marienplatz mezzanine level, Mon-Fri 9am-8pm, Sat 9am-4pm. Tickets on sale at any underground or railway station, from ticket machines or bus drivers and on trams. Tickets for the central zone (Münchner Innenraum), including Munich city centre: single ticket €2.20, 10-trip ticket *(10er Streifenkarte)* €10.50 (in Munich city centre two strips on this ticket must be validated), 1-day ticket €4.80. 1-day 'Partner' ticket €8.50. There is a 3-day ticket: €11.80 for 1 person, €20 for 'Partner' ticket.

→ MÜNCHEN WELCOME CARD

The **München Welcome Card** is valid for use on public transport in Munich city centre and for discounts of up to 50% for more than 30 sights, museums, castles and palaces, city tours and bicycle hire; 1-day single €6.50; 3-day single €16; 3-day Partner (2 adults and up to 3 children under 18yrs) €23.50.

→ TAXIS

Taxis are cream-coloured and numerous. They can be hailed in the street, hired at taxi ranks and called by telephone. Initial charge €2.90 (€1.60 per km for first 5km, €1.40 per km for next 5km, €1.25 per km thereafter). *Taxi München* ✆ (089) 2 16 10; www.taxi-muenchen-online.de

USEFUL ADDRESSES

→ TOURIST INFORMATION

Railway Station; *Plan II* **F2**, Mon-Sat 9am-8pm, Sun 10am-6pm; ✆ (089) 23 39 65 00. **Neues Rathaus**, *Plan II* **G2**, Marienplatz; Mon-Fri 10am-8pm, Sat 10am-4pm, ✆ (089) 23 39 65 00, www.muenchen.de

→ POST OFFICES

Mon-Fri 8am-6pm, Sat 8am-12 noon. **Railway Station** (Postfiliale 32), Bahnhofsplatz: Mon-Fri 7.30am-8pm, Sat 9am-4pm. **Airport** (Postfiliale 24), central area, level 3 in McPaper: Mon-Sun 7.30am-9pm.

→ BANKS

Mon-Fri 8.30am-12.30pm and 2-4pm (sometimes later); closed Sat-Sun and public holidays.

→ EMERGENCY

Police ✆ **110**; Fire Brigade ✆ **112**.

BUSY PERIODS

It may be difficult to find a room at a reasonable price when special events are held in the city as hotel prices may be raised substantially:

Starkbierzeit: March – Festival of strong beers.

Fasching: Carnival is celebrated just before Lent.

Auer Dult: late April to early May, late July and mid October – antiques market.

TollWood Sommerfestival: mid June to mid July.

Opernfestspiele: July – Opera festival.

Feast of the Assumption: 15 August – the Blessed Virgin Mary is the patron of Munich.

Oktoberfest: late September to early October (16 days) – Beer festival.

Christkindlmarket: December.

EXPLORING MUNICH

DIFFERENT FACETS OF THE CITY

It is possible to visit the main sights and museums in two to three days.

Museums and sights are usually open between 9am or 10am and 5pm (later on Thursday). Most are closed on Mondays or Tuesdays and public holidays.

OLD TOWN – **Marienplatz** *Plan II* **G2**. The heart of Munich where the carillon plays three times a day. **Frauenkirche** A hall church with twin onion domes housing the cenotaph of Emperor

Ludwig of Bavaria; good view of Munich from the top of the South Tower (lift). **Theatinerkirche** *Plan II* **G1**. 17C Baroque church with a rococo façade.

ROYAL MUNICH – Residenz *Plan II* **G1**. Former royal palace of the Wittelsbach family, comprising the **Schatzkammer** (Treasury) and the state rooms, a very rich example of interior design. **Nymphenburg**, once the summer residence of the Bavarian sovereigns set in a formal park. **Englischer Garten** *Plan I* **C2**. One of the largest and most beautiful town parks, laid out by Prince Elector Karl Theodor in 1789.

ART COLLECTIONS – Deutsches Museum *Plan II* **H3**. History of science and technology from the beginning of time to the present. **Alte Pinakothek** *Plan I* **B2**. Outstanding works by European painters from 14C to 18C collected by the rulers of Bavaria. **Neue Pinakothek**. 19C art. **Pinakothek der Moderne** *Plan I* **F1**. Modern and contemporary painting and sculpture, jewellery, design, graphic art and the architectural museum collection. **Bayerisches Nationalmuseum** *Plan I* **C2**. Bavarian arts and crafts. **Städtische Galerie im Lenbachhaus** *Plan II* **E1**. The Lenbach Collections are housed in a Florentine villa, devoted mainly to 19C Munich painters but including the avant-garde *Blaue Reiter* works of art.

GOURMET TREATS

Each year five million hectolitres (110 000 000 gallons) of **beer** are brewed in Munich. To sample the locals' favourite drink, visit one of the beer cellars or taverns; in fine weather it tastes best in one of the beer gardens, where you can take your own food. The best-known of the famous beer halls is the *Hofbräuhaus Plan II* **H2**; in the huge vaulted ground-floor Bierschwemme, the rowdiest part of the house, the servers deliver fistfuls of tankards to the tables, while odours of strong tobacco mingle with those of sausages and beer. The arrival of the month of May is celebrated by the drinking of Maibock. Local specialities to sample with the beer are white sausages *(Weisswurst)*, roast knuckle of pork *(Schweinshaxe)* and a meat and offal pâté *(Leberkäs)* which can be bought in slices, hot, from most butchers any time after 11am. Other accompaniments for beer are white radishes *(Radi)*, pretzels and small salt rolls *(Munich Salzstangen)*. A favourite offering at the beer festivals is small fish grilled on a skewer *(Steckerlfisch)*.

SHOPPING

Shops are usually open from 9am/10am to 6.30pm/8pm. They are closed on Sundays.

The **Old Town** has numerous shopping arcades which cater for all budgets. *Beck am Rathauseck* and other department stores are located between **Marienplatz** *Plan II* **G2** and **Stachus** *Plan II* **F2**. **Exclusive boutiques** are to be found in **Residenzstrasse**, **Brienner Strasse** and of course **Maximilianstrasse** *Plan II* **H2**. There is also the *Fünf Höfen* shopping centre in stylish **Theatinerstrasse** *Plan II* **G1**. Another good shopping district is **Schwabing** (on and to the west of Leopoldstrasse) *Plan I* **B1**.

Munich covers the whole range of antiques from elegant, exclusive antique dealers' establishments to inexpensive bric-à-brac shops. **Schwabing** boasts a wealth of antique shops in the area around Amalien-, Türken-, Barer-, Kurfürsten- and Hohenzollernstrasse, as does the city centre around Lenbach- and Promenadenplatz.

MARKETS – **Flea markets** are held in Arnulfstrasse by the old container depot (Fri-Sat 7am-6pm) and in Kunstpark Ost behind the Ostbahnhof (Fri 9am-6pm, Sat 7am-6pm). The best market in town is, as it has always been, the **Viktualienmarket** *Plan II* **G2**; small permanent markets are held in Elisabethplatz in **Schwabing** and in Wiener Platz in **Haidhausen**.

WHAT TO BUY – Beer mugs, traditional Bavarian clothes.

ENTERTAINMENT

Prinz and *Münchner* are local newspapers, available from news kiosks, which publish details of events.

Tickets can be booked in advance at the tourist information point in the Neues Rathaus or at the ticket booths.

Nationaltheater *Plan II* **G2** – The main stage venue for the Bavarian State Opera, which also offers ballet performances as part of its programme. From time to time they perform in the rococo treasure, the Cuvilliés-Theater and the Prinzregententheater – www.staatstheater.bayern.de

Staatstheater am Gärtnerplatz *Plan II* **G3** – Opera evenings and also operettas, ballet and musicals – www.staatstheater.bayern.de

Deutsches Theater *Plan II* **F2** – Musical and operettas, in which the Paris Lido also makes an appearance during its tour – www.deutsches-theater.de

Philharmonie im Gasteig *Plan I* **C3** – Modern cultural centre and base of the Munich Philharmonic Orchestra – www.muenchnerphilharmoniker.de

Herkulessaal der Residenz *Plan II* **G1** – Classical music in a classical setting.

Prinzregententheater *Plan I* **C3** – Magnificent concert hall in a converted 1900 theatre – www.prinzregententheater.de

Müncher Kammerspiele-Schauspielhaus *Plan II* **H2** – The famous company offers superb spoken theatre – www.muenchner-kammerspiele.de

Residenztheater and the **Altes Residenztheater (Cuvilliés-Theater)** *Plan II* **G2** – The home of the Bayrisches Staatsschauspiel.

Münchner Volkstheater *Plan II* **F1** – High quality popular theatre, a cut above farce – www.muenchner-volkstheatre.de

Muffathalle *Plan I* **C3** – Another place to experience the multicultural scene offering concerts, theatre and dance.

NIGHTLIFE

Kunstpark Ost (Grafinger Strasse 6 - by the Ostbahnhof) has over 30 bars, clubs and restaurants, where people party through the night every weekend from about 11pm onwards. **Nachtwerk** (Landsberger Strasse 185 - continuation of Bayerstrasse, towards Ammersee) is a warehouse converted into a discotheque for young people.

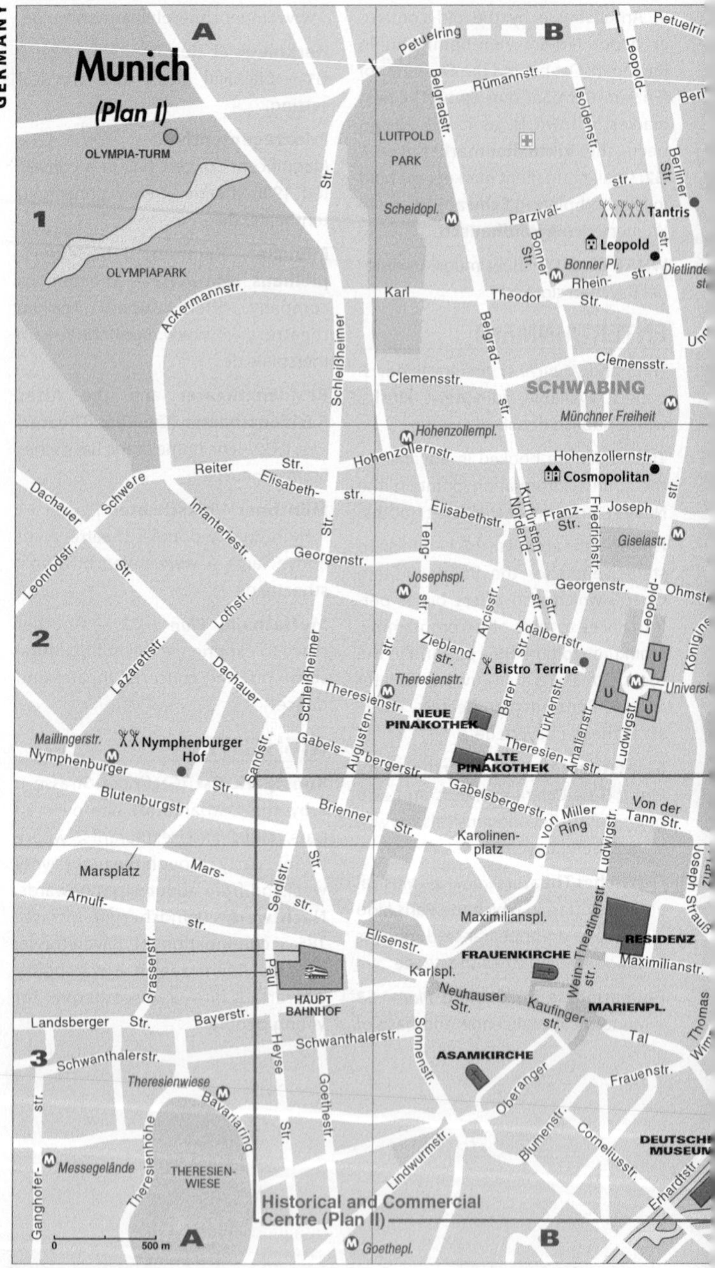
Munich
(Plan I)
A
B
1
2
3
OLYMPIA-TURM
OLYMPIAPARK
LUITPOLD PARK
Scheidopl.
Petuelring
Rümannstr.
Belgradstr.
Isoldenstr.
Leopold-
Berliner Str.
Parzival- str.
Tantris
Leopold
Bonner Str.
Bonner Pl.
Rhein- str.
Dietlinde
Karl Theodor Str.
Ackermannstr.
Schleißheimer Str.
Belgrad- str.
Clemensstr.
SCHWABING
Münchner Freiheit
Hohenzollernpl.
Hohenzollernstr.
Cosmopolitan
Schwere Reiter Str.
Elisabeth- str.
Elisabethstr.
Dachauer Str.
Infanteriestr.
Teng- str.
Kurfürsten- Nordend- str.
Franz- Joseph Str.
Friedrichstr.
Giselastr.
Leonrodstr.
Georgenstr.
Josephspl.
Ohmstr.
Lothstr.
Arcisstr.
Adalbertstr.
Ziebland- str.
Bistro Terrine
Lazarettstr.
Theresienstr.
Barer Str.
Türkenstr.
Amalienstr.
Ludwigstr.
Universität
NEUE PINAKOTHEK
ALTE PINAKOTHEK
Maillingerstr.
Nymphenburger Hof
Nymphenburger Str.
Sandstr.
Gabels- bergerstr.
Augusten-
Blutenburgstr.
Gabelsbergerstr.
Brienner Str.
O. von Miller Ring
Von der Tann Str.
Karolinenplatz
Marsplatz
Mars- str.
Seidlstr.
Arnulf- str.
Maximilianspl.
Elisenstr.
RESIDENZ
Joseph Str.
FRAUENKIRCHE
Karlspl.
Maximilianstr.
Paul Heyse Str.
HAUPT BAHNHOF
Grasserstr.
Neuhauser Str.
Kaufinger- str.
Wein- Theatinerstr.
MARIENPL.
Landsberger Str.
Bayerstr.
Schwanthalerstr.
Sonnenstr.
Tal
ASAMKIRCHE
Theresienwiese
Bavariaring
Oberanger
Frauenstr.
Goethestr.
Lindwurmstr.
Blumenstr.
Corneliusstr.
DEUTSCHES MUSEUM
Messegelände
Theresienhöhe
THERESIEN- WIESE
Ganghofer- str.
Erhardtstr.
Historical and Commercial Centre (Plan II)
0
500 m
Goethepl.

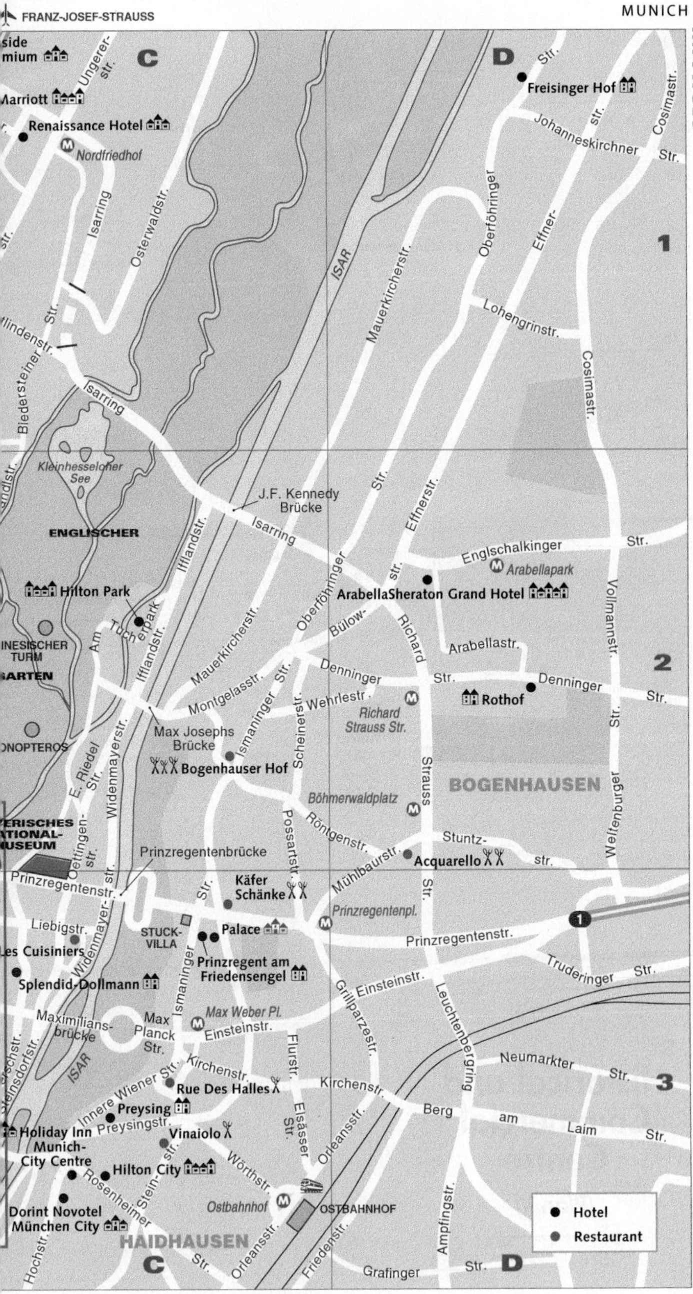

FRANZ-JOSEF-STRAUSS

C
D
1
2
3

Freisinger Hof
Marriott
Renaissance Hotel
Nordfriedhof
Johanneskirchner Str.
Cosimastr.
Isarring
Osterwaldstr.
Oberföhringer
Effner-
ISAR
Mauerkircherstr.
Lohengrinstr.
Biedersteiner Str.
Isarring
Kleinhesseloher See
J.F. Kennedy Brücke
ENGLISCHER
Effnerstr.
Englschalkinger Str.
Arabellapark
ArabellaSheraton Grand Hotel
Hilton Park
Am Tucherpark
Ifflandstr.
Mauerkircherstr.
Oberföhringer Str.
Bülow-
Richard Strauss Str.
Arabellastr.
Vollmannstr.
Denninger Str.
Wehrlestr.
Richard Strauss Str.
Rothof
Montgelasstr.
Ismaninger Str.
Scheinerstr.
Max Josephs Brücke
Bogenhauser Hof
BOGENHAUSEN
Böhmerwaldplatz
Wolfenburger
E. Riedel Str.
Widenmayerstr.
Oettingenstr.
Possartstr.
Röntgenstr.
Mühlbaurstr.
Stuntzstr.
Acquarello
Prinzregentenbrücke
Prinzregentenstr.
Käfer Schänke
Prinzregentenpl.
Liebigstr.
STUCK-VILLA
Palace
Prinzregentenstr.
Truderinger Str.
Les Cuisiniers
Prinzregent am Friedensengel
Splendid-Dollmann
Einsteinstr.
Grillparzerstr.
Leuchtenbergring
Maximiliansbrücke
Max Planck Str.
Max Weber Pl.
Einsteinstr.
Flurstr.
Kirchenstr.
Neumarkter Str.
Innere Wiener Str.
Rue Des Halles
Kirchenstr.
Berg am Laim Str.
Preysing
Preysingstr.
Holiday Inn Munich-City Centre
Vinaiolo
Elsässer Str.
Orleansstr.
Wörthstr.
Hilton City
Steinstr.
Rosenheimer Str.
Ostbahnhof
OSTBAHNHOF
Dorint Novotel München City
Ampfingstr.
HAIDHAUSEN
Hochstr.
Orleansstr.
Friedenstr.
Grafinger Str.

● Hotel
● Restaurant

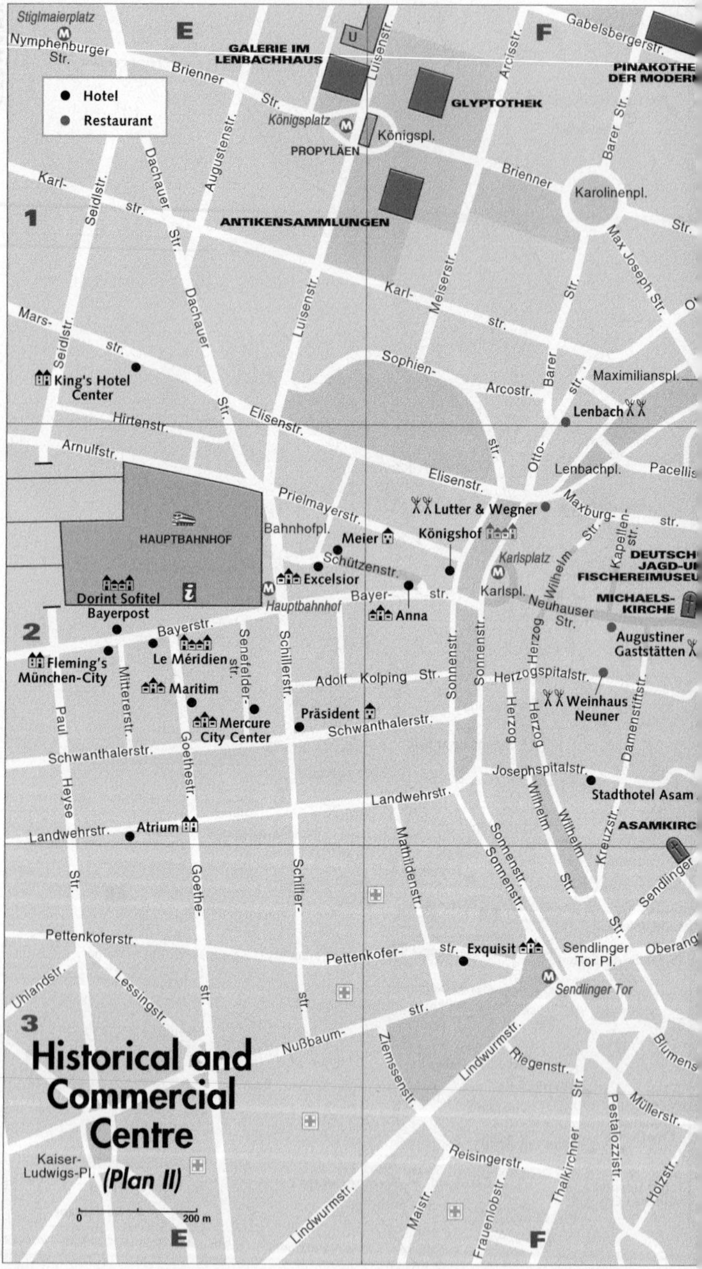

Historical and Commercial Centre (Plan II)

- Hotel
- Restaurant

E
F
1
2
3

Stiglmaierplatz
Nymphenburger Str.
Brienner Str.
GALERIE IM LENBACHHAUS
Luisenstr.
Arcisstr.
Gabelsbergerstr.
PINAKOTHEK DER MODERNE
GLYPTOTHEK
Königsplatz
Königspl.
PROPYLÄEN
Barer Str.
Karolinenpl.
Karl-str.
Seidlstr.
Dachauer Str.
Augustenstr.
ANTIKENSAMMLUNGEN
Max Joseph Str.
Meiserstr.
Mars-str.
King's Hotel Center
Sophien-str.
Arcostr.
Maximilianspl.
Lenbach
Hirtenstr.
Elisenstr.
Arnulfstr.
Otto-str.
Lenbachpl.
Pacellistr.
Prielmayerstr.
Lutter & Wegner
Maxburg-str.
HAUPTBAHNHOF
Bahnhofpl.
Meier
Königshof
Kapellenstr.
DEUTSCHES JAGD-UND FISCHEREIMUSEUM
Schützenstr.
Karlsplatz
Excelsior
Karlspl.
Wilhelm
Dorint Sofitel Bayerpost
Hauptbahnhof
Bayer-str.
Anna
Neuhauser Str.
MICHAELS-KIRCHE
Augustiner Gaststätten
Bayerstr.
Senefelder-str.
Schillerstr.
Le Méridien
Fleming's München-City
Mitterer str.
Maritim
Adolf Kolping Str.
Sonnenstr.
Herzog
Herzogspitalstr.
Weinhaus Neuner
Präsident
Mercure City Center
Schwanthalerstr.
Damenstiftstr.
Paul Heyse Str.
Goethestr.
Josephspitalstr.
Stadthotel Asam
Landwehrstr.
ASAMKIRCHE
Atrium
Mathildenstr.
Wilhelm Str.
Kreuzstr.
Goethe-str.
Schiller-str.
Sendlinger Str.
Pettenkoferstr.
Pettenkofer-str.
Exquisit
Sendlinger Tor Pl.
Oberanger
Uhlandstr.
Lessingstr.
Sendlinger Tor
Nußbaum-str.
Ziemssenstr.
Lindwurmstr.
Riegenstr.
Blumenstr.
Thalkirchner Str.
Pestalozzistr.
Müllerstr.
Kaiser-Ludwigs-Pl.
Reisingerstr.
Holzstr.
Maistr.
Frauenlobstr.
0 200 m

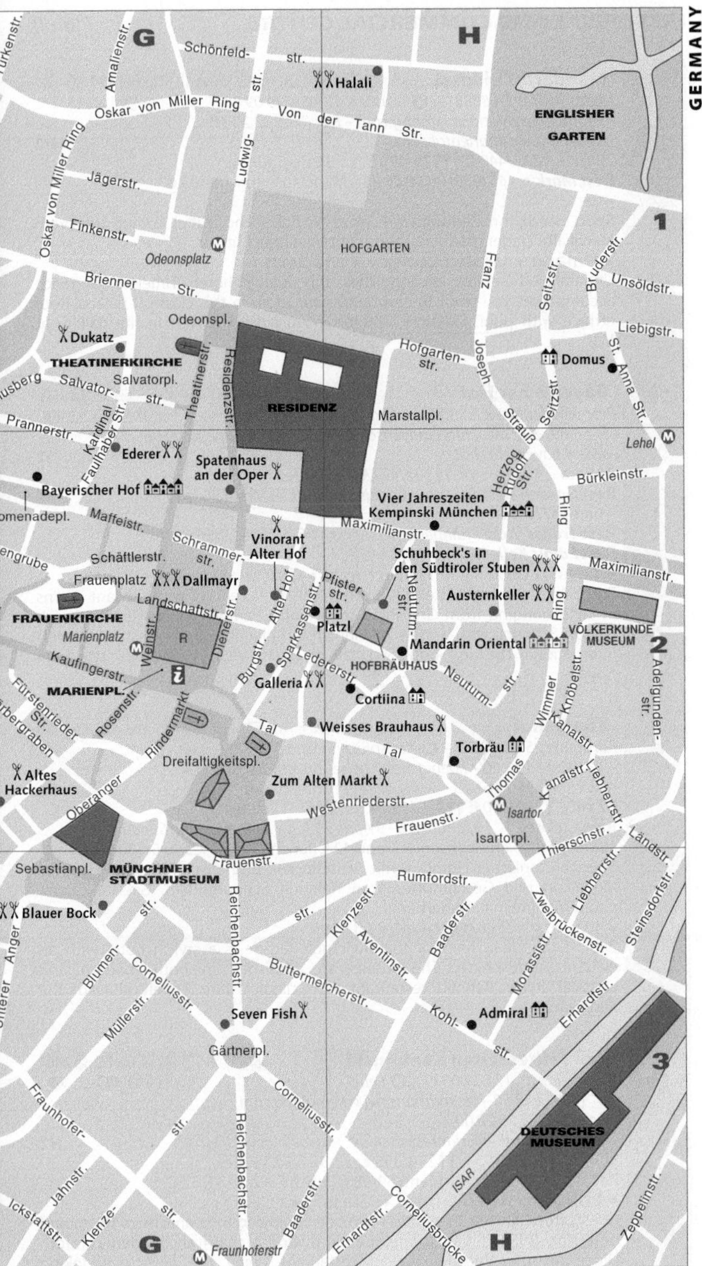

G
H
Schönfeld-str.
Halali
ENGLISHER GARTEN
Oskar von Miller Ring
Von der Tann Str.
Ludwig-str.
Amalienstr.
Oskar von Miller Ring
Jägerstr.
Finkenstr.
Odeonsplatz
HOFGARTEN
Brienner Str.
Franz Joseph Strauß Ring
Seitzstr.
Bruderstr.
Unsöldstr.
Liebigstr.
Odeonspl.
Dukatz
THEATINERKIRCHE
Hofgarten-str.
Domus
St. Anna Str.
Salvator-str.
Salvatorpl.
Theatinerstr.
Residenzstr.
RESIDENZ
Marstallpl.
Prannerstr.
Kardinal Faulhaber Str.
Ederer
Lehel
Spatenhaus an der Oper
Herzog Rudolf Str.
Bürkleinstr.
Bayerischer Hof
Vier Jahreszeiten Kempinski München
Promenadepl.
Maffeistr.
Maximilianstr.
Vinorant Alter Hof
Schrammer-str.
Schäftlerstr.
Schuhbeck's in den Südtiroler Stuben
Maximilianstr.
Frauenplatz
Dallmayr
Pfister-str.
Alter Hof
Sparkassenstr.
Neuturm-str.
Austernkeller
Landschaftstr.
Platzl
FRAUENKIRCHE
Marienplatz
R
Weinstr.
Dienerstr.
VÖLKERKUNDE MUSEUM
Mandarin Oriental
1
2
3
Kaufingerstr.
Burgstr.
Ledererstr.
HOFBRÄUHAUS
Neuturm-str.
Adelgunden-str.
Galleria
MARIENPL.
Rosenstr.
Fürstenrieder Str.
Färbergraben
Cortiina
Knöbelstr.
Wimmer
Tal
Weisses Brauhaus
Kanalstr.
Rindermarkt
Torbräu
Dreifaltigkeitspl.
Altes Hackerhaus
Oberanger
Zum Alten Markt
Thomas
Westenriederstr.
Isartor
Liebherrstr.
Frauenstr.
Isartorpl.
Thierschstr.
Ländstr.
Sebastianpl.
MÜNCHNER STADTMUSEUM
Frauenstr.
Rumfordstr.
Blauer Bock
Reichenbachstr.
Klenzestr.
Baaderstr.
Zweibrückenstr.
Liebherrstr.
Steinsdorfstr.
Unterer Anger
Blumen-str.
Corneliusstr.
Aventinstr.
Buttermelcherstr.
Morassistr.
Erhardtstr.
Müllerstr.
Seven Fish
Kohl-str.
Admiral
Gärtnerpl.
Fraunhofer-str.
Corneliusstr.
DEUTSCHES MUSEUM
Reichenbachstr.
ISAR
Jahnstr.
Ickstattstr.
Klenze-str.
Baaderstr.
Erhardtstr.
Corneliusbrücke
Zeppelinstr.
Fraunhoferstr

HISTORICAL AND COMMERCIAL CENTRE *Plan II*

Mandarin Oriental
(heated) VISA

Neuturmstr. 1 ✉ 80331 – Ⓜ Isartor – ✆ (089) 29 09 80
– momuc-reservations@mohg.com – Fax (089) 22 25 39
– www.mandarinoriental.com **H2**

73 rm – †325/440 € ††375/490 €, ☕ 32 € – 6 suites
Rest *Mark's* – *✆ (089) 29 09 88 75* – Menu 40 € (lunch)/105 €
– Carte 65/80 €
Spec. Essenz vom Perlhuhn mit Gänsestopfleber und Trüffel. Komposition vom Milchkalb. Ziegenfrischkäseragout mit Tomatenchutney.

♦ Palace ♦ Grand Luxury ♦ Modern ♦

Unparalleled service distinguishes this luxury hotel. Timeless elegance accompanies you from the lobby to your room in this classical palace. Roof terrace with pool. Classical Mediterranean cuisine served in the gallery at Mark's.

Bayerischer Hof
rm 850 VISA

Promenadeplatz 2 ✉ 80333 – Ⓜ Marienplatz
– ✆ (089) 2 12 00 – info@bayerischerhof.de – Fax (089) 2 12 09 06
– www.bayerischerhof.de **G2**

395 rm – †223/454 € ††302/477 € – 15 suites
Rest *Garden-Restaurant* – *(booking advisable)* Menu 36 € (lunch)
– Carte 47/59 €
Rest *Trader Vic's* – *(dinner only)* Menu 44 € – Carte 29/56 €
Rest *Palais Keller* – Carte 18/35 €

♦ Grand Luxury ♦ Traditional ♦ Classic ♦

Privately run Grand Hotel dating from the 19th century with elegant rooms in styles ranging from Graf Pilati to Colonial. Pamper yourself in the lavish spa on 3 floors, with a view of Munich. An elegant garden restaurant with international cuisine. South Sea flair in Trader Vic's. A Bavarian style beer house.

Königshof
rm 80 VISA

Karlsplatz 25 ✉ 80335 – Ⓜ Karlsplatz (Stachus)
– ✆ (089) 55 13 60 – koenigshof@geisel-privathotels.de
– Fax (089) 55 13 61 13 – www.geisel-privathotels.de **F2**

87 rm – †230/350 € ††290/450 €, ☕ 22 € – 11 suites
Rest – *(closed 1 - 14 January, 6 - 9 April, 29 July - 28 August and Sunday - Monday) (booking advisable)* Menu 42 € (lunch)/118 € – Carte 58/80 €
Spec. Bretonischer Hummer mit Artischocken und Mispeln in zwei Gängen. Medaillon und Geschmortes vom Reh mit Schupfnudeln. Geeiste Champagnerpraline mit Rhabarber.

♦ Luxury ♦ Traditional ♦ Classic ♦

Behind the clean lines of the building's facade is a stylish hotel with an elegant atmosphere. The rooms are furnished in both modern and classical styles. Refined restaurant with classical fare. Lovely view of the Karlsplatz.

Vier Jahreszeiten Kempinski
rm 230 VISA

Maximilianstr. 17 ✉ 80539 – Ⓜ Lehel
– ✆ (089) 2 12 50 – reservations.nvj@kempinski.com
– Fax (089) 21 25 20 00
– www.kempinski-vierjahreszeiten.de **H2**

308 rm – †230/395 € ††230/395 €, ☕ 32 € – 27 suites
Rest *Vue Maximilian* – Menu 59/98 € (lunch) – Carte 41/62 €

♦ Luxury ♦ Traditional ♦ Classic ♦

Guests from all over the world have been enjoying the panache of this grand hotel since 1858. Elegant rooms combine historical charm and modern comfort. Diners in the Vue Maximilian restaurant enjoy the view overlooking Maximilianstrasse.

Dorint Sofitel Bayerpost

rm 450

Bayerstr. 12 ✉ 80335 – Ⓜ Hauptbahnhof – ✆ (089) 59 94 80 – h5413@accor.com – Fax (089) 5 99 48 10 00 – www.sofitel.com **E2**

396 rm – 165/375 € 165/375 €, 22 € – 26 suites
Rest – *(dinner only)* Carte 38/51 €
Rest *Suzie W.* – *(lunch only)* Carte 29/36 €

♦ Chain hotel ♦ Luxury ♦ Design ♦

Behind the sandstone facade of a former post office lies a modern hotel featuring avant-garde design throughout - dark colours and subdued lighting. The restaurant offers an international menu.

Hilton Park

rm 690

Am Tucherpark 7 ✉ 80538 – ✆ (089) 3 84 50 – info.munich@hilton.com – Fax (089) 38 45 25 88 – www.hilton.de *Plan I* **C2**

479 rm – 119/403 € 144/429 €, 23 € – 3 suites
Rest – Carte 25/37 €
Rest *Tivoli & Club* – Carte 27/43 €

♦ Chain hotel ♦ Luxury ♦ Modern ♦

This hotel offers an attractive location at the English Garden and provides contemporary, technologically equipped rooms. Business and executive rooms also available. The bistro-style main restaurant offers international cuisine and a buffet.

Le Méridien

rm 160

Bayerstr. 41 ✉ 80335 – Ⓜ Hauptbahnhof – ✆ (089) 2 42 20 – info.muenchen@lemeridien.com – Fax (089) 24 22 11 11 – www.munich.lemeridien.com **E2**

381 rm – 175/435 € 175/435 €, 22 € – 9 suites
Rest – Carte 34/46 €

♦ Chain hotel ♦ Luxury ♦ Design ♦

Simple elegance is evident throughout - clean lines and exquisite materials. Lovely views from the restaurant of the pretty, plant-filled courtyard.

Excelsior

rm 25

Schützenstr. 11 ✉ 80335 – Ⓜ Hauptbahnhof – ✆ (089) 55 13 70 – excelsior@geisel-privathotels.de – Fax (089) 55 13 71 21 – www.geisel-privathotels.de **E2**

113 rm – 155/280 € 200/280 €, 18 €
Rest *Geisel's Vinothek* – *(closed Saturday lunch)* Carte 31/38 €

♦ Business ♦ Classic ♦

Perhaps the elegant yet rustic ambience of the foyer and the rooms explain the feeling that, amid the pulsing life of the city centre, you are in a quiet country house. Rustic, country vinotheque with painted cross-vaults.

Maritim

rm 250

Goethestr. 7 ✉ 80336 – Ⓜ Hauptbahnhof – ✆ (089) 55 23 50 – info.mun@maritim.de – Fax (089) 55 23 59 00 – www.maritim.de **E2**

339 rm – 193 € 218 €, 20 € – 6 suites
Rest – Carte 26/35 €

♦ Business ♦ Functional ♦

Enjoy pleasant comfort in the tastefully elegant rooms in this hotel, which is close to the Deutsches Theater, the "Stachus" and the "Theresienwiese". The grill-room and bistro restaurants serve international cuisine.

Exquisit

25

Pettenkoferstr. 3 ✉ 80336 – Ⓜ Sendlinger Tor – ✆ (089) 5 51 99 00 – info@hotel-exquisit.com – Fax (089) 55 19 94 99 – www.hotel-exquisit.com **F3**

50 rm – 135 € 170 € – 5 suites
Rest – *(closed Saturday - Sunday) (lunch only)* Carte 18/30 €

♦ Business ♦ Classic ♦

This hotel offers attentive service and is located near the Sendlinger Tor. It combines classical style and quality furnishings. Not far from the Sendlinger gate, this hotel provides stylish mahogany furnished rooms. Fine, comfortable suites also available.

GERMANY

Anna

Schützenstr. 1 ✉ 80335 – Ⓜ Karlsplatz (Stachus)
– ✆ (089) 59 99 40 – anna@geisel-privathotels.de – Fax (089) 59 99 43 33
– www.geisel-privathotel.de **F2**

73 rm – 170/215 € 190/235 €

Rest – Carte 28/32 €

◆ Business ◆ Modern ◆

This trend-setting hotel on the outskirts of Munich's old city, directly at Stachus. The very comfortable guest rooms feature modern design and the latest technology. Contemporary bistro-like restaurant with a sushi bar.

Mercure City Center

Senefelder Str. 9 ✉ 80336 – Ⓜ Hauptbahnhof – ✆ (089) 55 13 20
– h0878@accor.com – Fax (089) 59 64 44 – www.mercure.com **E2**

167 rm – 99/425 € 99/489 €, 15 €

Rest – Carte 29/43 €

◆ Chain hotel ◆ Functional ◆

Modern style and warm tones accompany the guest from the reception through to the well-equipped rooms of this hotel located close to the main railway station. Opening off the lobby, the restaurant features international fare.

Platzl

Sparkassenstr. 10 ✉ 80331 – Ⓜ Marienplatz – ✆ (089) 23 70 30 – info@platzl.de
– Fax (089) 23 70 38 00 – www.platzl.de **G2**

167 rm – 119/164 € 185/236 €

Rest *Pfistermühle* – (closed Sunday) Carte 27/43 €

Rest *Ayingers* – Carte 19/33 €

◆ Traditional ◆ Cosy ◆

In the middle of the old town. The new rooms beautifully combine the classical and modern. Health and fitness area in the style of Ludwig II's "Moorish Kiosk". Old Munich flair under the vaults of the Pfistermühle. Ayingers: tasteful tavern style.

Stadthotel Asam without rest

Josephspitalstr. 3 ✉ 80331 – Ⓜ Sendlinger Tor
– ✆ (089) 2 30 97 00 – info@hotel-asam.de – Fax (089) 23 09 70 97
– www.hotel-asam.de
closed Christmas **F2**

25 rm – 137/154 € 167/184 €, 16 € – 8 suites

◆ Business ◆ Personalised ◆

A small hotel with a touch of luxury in the City Centre. The rooms are stylish and tasteful with very carefully chosen details.

Cortiina without rest

Ledererstr. 8 ✉ 80331 – Ⓜ Isartor – ✆ (089) 2 42 24 90 – info@cortiina.com
– Fax (089) 2 42 24 91 00 – www.cortiina.com **H2**

39 rm – 126/176 € 186 €

◆ Business ◆ Modern ◆

The rooms all have a modern style with clean lines and parquet floors. State of the art technical equipment. Nice bar with a small menu.

Torbräu

Tal 41 ✉ 80331 – Ⓜ Isartor – ✆ (089) 24 23 40 – info@torbraeu.de
– Fax (089) 24 23 42 35 – www.torbraeu.de **H2**

92 rm – 144/258 € 180/342 € – 3 suites

Rest *La Famiglia* – ✆ (089) 22 80 75 33 – Carte 34/44 €

◆ Traditional ◆ Classic ◆

Built in the 15C, this hotel must be the oldest in the city. Pleasant spacious rooms, all with air conditioning. Tuscan flair and Italian cuisine in the terracotta-tiled "La Famiglia".

Admiral without rest
Kohlstr. 9 ✉ 80469 – Ⓜ Isartor – ✆ (089) 21 63 50 – info@hotel-admiral.de – Fax (089) 29 36 74 – www.hotel-admiral.de **H3**
33 rm – 170 € 200 €
◆ Business ◆ Functional ◆
Just a few minutes by foot from the City Centre this hotel has functional rooms, some of which are extremely quiet. In fine weather you can enjoy breakfast in the small garden.

King's Hotel Center without rest
Marsstr. 15 ✉ 80335 – ✆ (089) 51 55 30 – center@kingshotels.de – Fax (089) 51 55 33 00 – www.kingshotels.de **E1**
90 rm – 99/130 € 130 €, 12 €
◆ Business ◆ Classic ◆
Centrally located hotel with inviting wooden lobby and comfortable rooms with four-poster beds.

Atrium without rest
Landwehrstr. 59 ✉ 80336 – Ⓜ Theresienwiese – ✆ (089) 51 41 90 – info@atrium-hotel.de – Fax (089) 53 50 66 – www.atrium-hotel.de **E2**
162 rm – 129/149 € 159 €
◆ Business ◆ Functional ◆
Marble and mirrors welcome you into the lobby of this modern hotel. The rooms are furnished in natural wood with modern technical facilities. Lovely, small, leafy courtyard.

Splendid-Dollmann without rest
Thierschstr. 49 ✉ 80538 – Ⓜ Lehel – ✆ (089) 23 80 80 – splendid-muc@t-online.de – Fax (089) 23 80 83 65 – www.hotel-splendid-dollmann.de *Plan I* **C3**
36 rm – 120/150 € 150/190 €, 13 €
◆ Traditional ◆ Personalised ◆
A 19C middle-class house with a stylish lobby, presented as a library; individually decorated rooms, some with antiques, and a pretty breakfast room with arched ceiling.

Domus
St-Anna-Str.31 ✉ 80538 – Ⓜ Lehel – ✆ (089) 2 17 77 30 – reservation@domus-hotel.de – Fax (089) 2 28 53 59 – www.domus-hotel.de
closed Christmas **H1**
45 rm – 109/120 € 135/150 €
Rest ***facile*** – *(closed Saturday lunch, Sunday and Bank Holidays)* Carte 26/34 €
◆ Business ◆ Functional ◆
Embedded between the Maximilianstrasse and Prinzregentenstrasse, this tastefully furnished establishment is ideal as a base from which to explore the town's art, culture and shopping. Modern atmosphere and Italian cuisine served.

Fleming's München-City
Bayerstr. 47 ✉ 80335 – Ⓜ Hauptbahnhof – ✆ (089) 4 44 46 60 – muenchen-city@flemings-hotels.com – Fax (089) 4 44 46 69 99 – www.flemings-hotels.com **E2**
112 rm – 108/335 € 133/335 €
Rest – Carte 19/35 €
◆ Business ◆ Fashionable ◆
Centrally located near the main railway station, this hotel offers functional, modern rooms. Bistro-style restaurant with bar and delicatessen.

Präsident without rest
Schwanthalerstr. 20 ✉ 80336 – Ⓜ Hauptbahnhof – ✆ (089) 5 49 00 60 – hotel.praesident@t-online.de – Fax (089) 54 90 06 28 – www.hotel-praesident.de **E2**
42 rm – 75/159 € 95/191 €
◆ Business ◆ Functional ◆
The location of this fairly central hotel is ideal for theatre-goers and is diagonally opposite the Deutsche Theater. Contemporary rooms with light-coloured wooden furniture.

Meier without rest

Schützenstr. 12 ✉ 80335 – Ⓜ Hauptbahnhof – ☎ (089) 5 49 03 40 – info@hotel-meier.de – Fax (089) 5 49 03 43 40 – www.hotel-meier.de

closed 23 - 27 December **E2**

50 rm – ♦75/88 € ♦♦95/116 €

♦ Business ♦ Functional ♦

At the end of the 1990s the Etagenhotel was renovated and it now offers its visitors uniform, functional rooms.

Schuhbeck's in den Südtiroler Stuben 60

Platzl 6 ✉ 80331 – Ⓜ Isartor – ☎ (089) 2 16 69 00 – info@schuhbeck.de – Fax (089) 21 66 90 25 – www.schubeck.de

closed 2 weeks early January and Sunday - Monday lunch, Bank Holidays **H2**

Rest – Menu 73/113 €

Spec. Knuspriger Saibling mit Kartoffel-Gurkengemüse. Blutwurst-Gänseleberravioli mit Apfelmeerrettich und Schalotten. Allerhand vom Lamm mit Artischocken-Kartoffelgröstl.

♦ Contemporary ♦ Rustic ♦

A combination of the elegant and rustic. Fine regional cuisine. Alfons Schuhbeck's gastronomic empire now includes a wine bistro.

Dallmayr

Dienerstr. 14, (1st floor) ✉ 80331 – Ⓜ Marienplatz – ☎ (089) 2 13 51 00 – gastro@dallmayr.de – Fax (089) 2 13 54 43 – www.dallmayr.de

closed 3 weeks July - August and Sunday - Monday, Bank Holidays **G2**

Rest – *(booking advisable)* Menu 49 € (lunch)/109 € (dinner) – Carte 55/92 €

♦ Contemporary ♦ Friendly ♦

The restaurant run by the well-known delicatessen which has in the past supplied crowned heads has made the freshness and naturalness of its products into a philosophy.

G

Geyerstr. 52, (by Lindwurmstr. A 3 and Kapuzinerstr.) ✉ 80469 – ☎ (089) 74 74 79 99 – info@g-munich.de – Fax (089) 74 74 79 29 – www.g-munich.de

closed 23 December - 14 January, 6 - 9 April and Sunday - Monday

Rest – *(dinner only) (booking advisable)* Menu 100 €

♦ Modern ♦ Fashionable ♦

A modern-minimalist ambience is the setting for creative Mediterranean cuisine. Six course menu for 100 Euros. Stylish lounge with elegant leather cushions.

Lutter & Wegner

Lenbachplatz 8 ✉ 80333 – Ⓜ Karlsplatz (Stachus) – ☎ (089) 5 45 94 90 – info@l-w-muenchen.de – Fax (089) 54 59 49 30 – www.l-w-muenchen.de

closed Sunday and Bank Holidays **F2**

Rest – *(dinner only)* Carte 32/46 €

Rest *Weinstube* – Menu 35 € (dinner) – Carte 27/43 €

♦ International ♦ Friendly ♦

The Munich House of Artists is the perfect setting for this restaurant with modern interior. The menu is international in flavour. Lovely terrace. A winebar with lovely painted vaulted ceiling.

Blauer Bock

Sebastiansplatz 9 ✉ 80331 – Ⓜ Marienplatz – ☎ (089) 45 22 23 33 – mail@restaurant-blauerbock.de – Fax (089) 45 22 23 30 – www.restaurant-blauerbock.de

closed July - September Saturday dinner - Sunday and Bank Holidays **G3**

Rest – Menu 26 € (lunch)/50 € (dinner) – Carte 49/60 €

♦ International ♦ Minimalist ♦

Just a few steps from the Viktualienmarkt is this modern restaurant. The ambience is simple, with warm tones. International cuisine with French roots.

Halali

Schönfeldstr. 22 ✉ 80539 – Ⓜ Odeonsplatz – ✆ (089) 28 59 09 – halali-muenchen@t-online.de – Fax (089) 28 27 86 – www.halali-muenchen.de

closed 3 weeks August and Saturday lunch, Sunday, Bank Holidays **H1**

Rest – *(booking advisable)* Menu 22 € (lunch) – Carte 34/47 €

♦ International ♦ Cosy ♦

A historic 19th century guest house with a cosy, rustic-style restaurant, a favourite of many long-time guests.

Ederer

Kardinal-Faulhaber-Str. 10 ✉ 80333 – Ⓜ Odeonsplatz – ✆ (089) 24 23 13 10 – restaurant-ederer@t-online.de – Fax (089) 24 23 13 12 – www.restaurant-ederer.de

closed 1 week Christmas and Sunday, Bank Holidays **G2**

Rest – *(booking advisable)* Menu 35 € (lunch)/65 € (dinner) – Carte 38/71 €

♦ Contemporary ♦ Fashionable ♦

A chic location for this restaurant with modern, stylish atmosphere. International cuisine. Nice inner courtyard dining.

Austernkeller

Stollbergstr. 11 ✉ 80539 – Ⓜ Isartor – ✆ (089) 29 87 87 – Fax (089) 22 31 66 – www.austernkeller.de **H2**

Rest – *(dinner only) (booking advisable)* Carte 31/42 €

♦ Seafood ♦ Cosy ♦

If your taste is for crustaceans and freshly-caught fruits de mer, try this listed cellar vault decorated with porcelain plates.

Nymphenburger Hof

Nymphenburger Str. 24 ✉ 80335 – Ⓜ Maillingerstr. – ✆ (089) 1 23 38 30 – Fax (089) 1 23 38 52 – www.nymphenburgerhof.de

closed 24 December - 5 January and Saturday lunch, Sunday, Bank Holidays *Plan I* **A2**

Rest – *(booking advisable)* Menu 22 € (lunch) – Carte 31/47 €

♦ International ♦ Friendly ♦

Bright, informal restaurant with lots of flowers and a lovely terrace in front of the building. Cuisine is international with Austrian highlights.

Lenbach

Ottostr. 6 ✉ 80333 – Ⓜ Karlsplatz (Stachus) – ✆ (089) 5 49 13 00 – info@lenbach.de – Fax (089) 54 91 30 75 – www.lenbach.de

closed Sunday and Bank Holidays **F1**

Rest – Menu 64 € (dinner) – Carte 32/43 €

♦ Modern ♦ Trendy ♦

The Lenbach Palais houses trend-setting gastronomy in a 2200-square meter space that was designed by Sir Terence Conran. The restaurant is a blend of modern and historic. Sushi bar.

Galleria

Sparkassenstr. 11, (corner of Ledererstraße) ✉ 80331 – Ⓜ Marienplatz – ✆ (089) 29 79 95 – ristorantegalleria@yahoo.de – Fax (089) 2 91 36 53

closed Sunday **G2**

Rest – *(booking advisable)* Menu 24 € (lunch)/54 € (dinner) – Carte 36/41 €

♦ Italian ♦ Rustic ♦

A small, cosy restaurant in the inner city with Italian cuisine. Temporary art displays in the dining area.

Weinhaus Neuner

Herzogspitalstr. 8 ✉ 80331 – Ⓜ Karlsplatz (Stachus) – ✆ (089) 2 60 39 54 – info@weinhaus-neuner.de – Fax (089) 26 69 33 – www.weinhaus-neuner.de

closed Sunday and Bank Holidays **F2**

Rest – Menu 19 € (lunch)/40 € – Carte 29/36 €

♦ International ♦ Rustic ♦

As the "oldest wine bar" in Munich, this building dating back to 1852 stands out with its cross-shaped vaults and lovely wall paintings. International cuisine.

XX

Les Cuisiniers

Reitmorstr. 21 ✉ 80538 – Ⓜ Lehel – ✆ (089) 23 70 98 90 – Fax (089) 23 70 98 91 – www.lescuisiniers.de
closed Saturday lunch, Sunday - Monday lunch *Plan I* **C3**
Rest – Menu 36 € – Carte 29/35 €
♦ Mediterranean ♦ Bistro ♦
Light and friendly décor in this bistro-style restaurant - modern pictures adorn the walls. An uncomplicated Mediterranean menu.

X

Seven Fish

Gärtnerplatz 6 ✉ 80469 – Ⓜ Fraunhoferstr. – ✆ (089) 23 00 02 19 – info@seven-fish.de – Fax (089) 48 95 21 81 – www.sevenfish.de **G3**
Rest – Menu 40 € – Carte 32/44 €
♦ Seafood ♦ Friendly ♦
Creative fish dishes prepared from quality produce and served by friendly staff in a modern atmosphere. A selection of Greek wines. More modest menu at lunch.

X

Vinorant Alter Hof

Alter Hof 3 ✉ 80331 – Ⓜ Marienplatz – ✆ (089) 24 24 37 33 – mail@alter-hof-muenchen.de – Fax (089) 24 24 37 34 – www.alter-hof-muenchen.de
closed Sunday and Bank Holidays dinner **G2**
Rest – Carte 23/29 €
♦ Regional ♦ Rustic ♦
At the former Wittelsbach residence, one of the oldest buildings in Munich, guests dine in two halls with attractive vaulted ceilings and simple modern decoration. Downstairs there is a vinotheque and bar.

X

Dukatz

Salvatorplatz 1 ✉ 80333 – Ⓜ Odeonsplatz – ✆ (089) 2 91 96 00 – info@dukatz.de – Fax (089) 29 19 60 28 – www.dukatz.de
closed Sunday dinner **G1**
Rest – *(booking advisable)* Carte 21/44 €
♦ International ♦ Fashionable ♦
At the Literaturhaus, a former market hall dating from 1870, international cuisine is served on two levels beneath a fine cross-vault.

X

Zum Alten Markt

Dreifaltigkeitsplatz 3 ✉ 80331 – Ⓜ Marienplatz – ✆ (089) 29 99 95 – lehner.gastro@zumaltenmarkt.de – Fax (089) 2 28 50 76 – www.zumaltenmarkt.de
closed Sunday and Bank Holidays **G2**
Rest – Carte 22/36 €
♦ Regional ♦ Cosy ♦
With lavish wood panelling in the style of a South Tyrolean councillor's office, part of which is authentic and over 400 years old, this establishment on the Viktualienmarkt has a very cosy atmosphere.

X

Spatenhaus an der Oper

Residenzstr. 12 ✉ 80333 – Ⓜ Marienplatz – ✆ (089) 2 90 70 60 – spatenhaus@kuffler.de – Fax (089) 2 91 30 54 – www.kuffler.de **G2**
Rest – Carte 31/41 €
♦ Bavarian specialities ♦ Cosy ♦
This town house, over 100 years old, houses a lovely rustic restaurant. The different rooms on the 1st floor are particularly cosy.

X

Weisses Brauhaus

30 VISA

Tal 7 ✉ 80331 – Ⓜ Isartor – ✆ (089) 2 90 13 80 – info@weisses-brauhaus.de – Fax (089) 29 01 38 15 – www.weisses-brauhaus.de **G2**
Rest – Carte 18/32 €
♦ Bavarian specialities ♦ Inn ♦
This house in the Old Town, built around 1900, has a fine façade and cosy furnishings. The restaurant serves authentic regional specialities.

Augustiner Gaststätten

VISA

Neuhauser Str. 27 ✉ 80331 – Ⓜ Karlsplatz (Stachus)
– ✆ (089) 23 18 32 57
– mail@augustiner-restaurant.com – Fax (089) 2 60 53 79
– www.augustiner-restaurant.com **F2**

Rest – Carte 15/29 €

♦ Bavarian specialities ♦ Inn ♦

Until 1885, beer was still brewed in the Augustinians' "headquarters" on the Neuhauser Strasse. An arcaded garden and a "Muschelsaal" are among the monuments of Munich's Art Nouveau period. Lovely beer garden.

Altes Hackerhaus

AC VISA AE

Sendlinger Str. 14 ✉ 80331 – Ⓜ Marienplatz – ✆ (089) 2 60 50 26
– hackerhaus@aol.com – Fax (089) 2 60 50 27
– www.hackerhaus.de **G2**

Rest – Carte 17/37 €

♦ Bavarian specialities ♦ Inn ♦

The lovingly decorated rooms of this inn are really cosy with their rustic panelling and sturdy seating. Extremely pretty inner courtyard terrace. Good home cooking.

ENVIRONS *Plan I*

ArabellaSheraton Grand Hotel

AC ⇆rm SAT 650 VISA AE

Arabellastr. 6 ✉ 81925
– Ⓜ Arabellapark – ✆ (089) 9 26 40
– grandhotel.muenchen@arabellasheraton.com
– Fax (089) 92 64 86 99 – www.sheraton.com/grandmunich **D2**

643 rm – 🚹115/445 € 🚹🚹140/470 €, ☕ 23 € – 14 suites

Rest – *(closed Sunday) (lunch only)* Menu 26 € – Carte 28/34 €

Rest *Die Ente vom Lehel* – *(closed August and Sunday - Monday) (dinner only)* Carte 38/48 €

Rest *Paulaner's* – *(closed Saturday lunch, Sunday and Bank Holidays lunch)* Carte 19/33 €

♦ Chain hotel ♦ Grand Luxury ♦ Modern ♦

An impressive lobby greets you at this luxurious hotel. Guests in the Towers rooms on the top four floors have their own lounge. Large meeting space. A lively atmosphere welcomes you in the elegant Ente vom Lehel, which is open to the foyer.

Marriott

AC ⇆rm SAT 300 VISA AE

Berliner Str. 93 ✉ 80805 – Ⓜ Nordfriedhof – ✆ (089) 36 00 20
– muenchen.marriott@marriotthotels.com – Fax (089) 36 00 22 00
– www.marriott.com/mucno **C1**

348 rm – 🚹169 € 🚹🚹169 €, ☕ 22 € – 14 suites

Rest – Carte 29/40 €

♦ Luxury ♦ Traditional ♦ Functional ♦

An establishment in the grand hotel style, with a modern conference floor. The recently renovated rooms are comfortably decorated in floral fabrics. An "American-style" with a lovely large buffet and a show kitchen.

Hilton City

AC ⇆rm SAT 200 VISA AE

Rosenheimer Str. 15 ✉ 81667 – ✆ (089) 4 80 40 – info.munich@hilton.com
– Fax (089) 48 04 48 04 – www.hilton.de **C3**

480 rm – 🚹119/403 € 🚹🚹144/429 € – 3 suites

Rest – Carte 26/37 €

♦ Chain hotel ♦ Functional ♦

This hotel is next to the Philharmonic Orchestra centre and the Gasteig Cultural Centre. With its modern, functional rooms, it is tailored primarily to the needs of the business traveller. Executive Floor. Rustic-style restaurant serving regional and international cuisine.

GERMANY

Palace
rm 20 VISA

Trogerstr. 21 ✉ 81675 – Ⓜ Prinzregentenplatz – ✆ (089) 41 97 10 – palace@kuffler.de – Fax (089) 41 97 18 19 – www.muenchenpalace.de **C3**

74 rm – †155/180 € ††200/230 €, ☕ 18 € – 3 suites

Rest – Carte 32/41 €

♦ Luxury ♦ Traditional ♦ Personalised ♦

Friendly staff provides attentive service in this hotel, providing tastefully furnished, Louis XVI-style rooms. Beautiful garden and roof terrace. Stylish dining in the intimate ambience of the timelessly elegant Palace.

Innside Premium
rm 80 VISA

Mies-van-der-Rohe-Str. 10 ✉ 80807 – ✆ (089) 35 40 80 – muenchen.schwabing@innside.de – Fax (089) 35 40 82 99 – www.innside.de **C1**

160 rm – †119/185 € ††149/195 €, ☕ 16 €

Rest – *(closed Saturday lunch, Sunday lunch)* Carte 30/38 €

♦ Business ♦ Functional ♦

A modern building with a glass façade and contemporary design interior, with well-equipped rooms. Bistro style restaurant with interesting lighting. International cuisine served.

Renaissance Hotel
rm 30 VISA

Theodor-Dombart-Str. 4, (corner of Berliner Straße) ✉ 80805 – Ⓜ Nordfriedhof – ✆ (089) 36 09 90 – rhi.mucbr.night.audit@renaissancehotels.com – Fax (089) 3 60 99 65 00 – www.marriott.com/mucbr **C1**

261 rm – †155/179 € ††155/179 €, ☕ 19 € – 40 suites

Rest – Carte 20/34 €

♦ Chain hotel ♦ Modern ♦

Close to the English Garden. Comfortable rooms and elegant suites offer a high level of quality. Relax in the "Oasis of Rest". Modern Bistro in Mediterranean colours. International cuisine with the emphasis on the Mediterranean area.

Dorint Novotel München City
rm 120 VISA

Hochstr. 11 ✉ 81669 – ✆ (089) 66 10 70 – h3280@accor.com – Fax (089) 66 10 79 99 – www.novotel.com **C3**

307 rm – †112/172 € ††135/195 €, ☕ 17 €

Rest – Carte 24/42 €

♦ Chain hotel ♦ Modern ♦

The well-equipped rooms of this business hotel are presented in pleasant tones and with smart design, some with a lovely view of the inner city. Light, contemporary restaurant.

Holiday Inn Munich - City Centre
rm 350 VISA

Hochstr. 3 ✉ 81669 – ✆ (089) 4 80 30 – muchb@ichotelsgroup.com – Fax (089) 4 48 82 77 – www.holidayinn.de **C3**

582 rm – †185 € ††185 €, ☕ 19 €

Rest – Menu 29 €

♦ Chain hotel ♦ Functional ♦

A modern, renovated hotel designed for business guests attending meetings and events, with comfortable, functional rooms and a 2,100 square metre conference area. A colourful, Mediterranean-style bistro with a rustic-style pub.

Cosmopolitan without rest
VISA

Hohenzollernstr. 5 ✉ 80801 – Ⓜ Münchner Freiheit – ✆ (089) 38 38 10 – cosmo@cosmopolitan-hotel.de – Fax (089) 38 38 11 11 – www.cosmopolitan-hotel.de **B2**

71 rm ☕ – †115/170 € ††125/180 €

♦ Business ♦ Modern ♦

Two annexed houses in the heart of Schwabing provide modern rooms with functional furnishings and modern, technical equipment.

Prinzregent am Friedensengel without rest 35

Ismaninger Str. 42 ✉ 81675 – Ⓜ Prinzregentenplatz – ✆ (089) 41 60 50 – friedensengel@prinzregent.de – Fax (089) 41 60 54 66 – www.prinzregent.de

closed 23 December - 8 January **C3**

65 rm – 130/205 € 150/225 €

◆ Traditional ◆ Cosy ◆

After a night in an Alpine natural-wood bed, breakfast can be eaten amid fine wainscoting or in the winter garden, followed by only five minutes' walk to the Englischer Garten.

Freisinger Hof 20

Oberföhringer Str. 189 ✉ 81925 – ✆ (089) 95 23 02 – freisinger.hof@t-online.de – Fax (089) 9 57 85 16 – www.freisinger-hof.de **D1**

51 rm – 115/135 € 145/150 €

Rest – Carte 27/43 €

◆ Personalised ◆ Cosy ◆

This old tavern from 1875 has been extended with a hotel annex. Look forward to good, homely country-style rooms. A cosy rustic setting for regional cuisine. Lovely garden.

Preysing without rest 20

Preysingstr. 1 ✉ 81667 – ✆ (089) 45 84 50 – info@hotel-preysing.de – Fax (089) 45 84 54 44 – www.hotel-preysing.de

closed 24 December - 6 January **C3**

62 rm – 130/200 € 180/250 € – 5 suites

◆ Family ◆ Functional ◆

The attention to detail in these rooms furnished in modern pale wood furniture makes them comfortable and welcoming. Attractive also is the bright breakfast room with a generous buffet.

Rothof without rest

Denninger Str. 114 ✉ 81925 – Ⓜ Richard-Strauss-Str. – ✆ (089) 9 10 09 50 – reservierung@rothof-muc.de – Fax (089) 91 50 66 – www.hotel-rothof.de

closed 21 December - 7 January **D2**

37 rm – 125/145 € 162/212 €

◆ Family ◆ Functional ◆

The well-run hotel offers light, spacious and friendly rooms with large windows and modern facilities - some well-located rooms at the rear.

Leopold 20

Leopoldstr. 119 ✉ 80804 – Ⓜ Dietlindenstr. – ✆ (089) 36 04 30 – hotel-leopold@t-online.de – Fax (089) 36 04 31 50 – www.hotel-leopold.de

closed 23 - 28 December **B1**

65 rm – 105/148 € 128/185 €

Rest – Carte 20/29 €

◆ Family ◆ Classic ◆

Hotel rich in tradition, family-run, with a wide range of rooms furnished in different styles. Ask for a room with a view of the idyllic garden.

Tantris

Johann-Fichte-Str. 7 ✉ 80805 – Ⓜ Dietlindenstr. – ✆ (089) 3 61 95 90 – info@tantris.de – Fax (089) 36 19 59 22 – www.tantris.de

closed 1 - 9 January and Sunday - Monday, Bank Holidays **B1**

Rest – *(booking advisable)* Menu 60 € (lunch)/135 € – Carte 69/93 €

Spec. Rotbarbenfilet mit Saubohnenravioli und Curryfond. Lauwarmer Räucheraal auf Chiligurken. Medaillon vom Rehrücken mit eingelegten Balsamicokirschen und Kartoffel-Grießknödel.

◆ French ◆ Retro ◆

Hans Haas is responsible for classical cuisine with creative touches, served in the atmospheric, modern-elegant ambience of this red and white restaurant.

XXX

Bogenhauser Hof

40 VISA MC AE

Ismaninger Str. 85 ✉ 81675 – ✆ (089) 98 55 86
– info@bogenhauser-hof.de
– Fax (089) 9 81 02 21 – www.bogenhauser-hof.de
closed 24 December - 7 January and Sunday, Bank Holidays **C2**
Rest – *(booking advisable)* Menu 50 € – Carte 43/67 €

♦ International ♦ Rustic ♦

This hunting lodge dating from 1825 is a classic of Munich gastronomy. Superior classical cuisine, which can also be enjoyed in the idyllic summer garden.

XX ✿

Acquarello

MC AE

Mühlbaurstr. 36 ✉ 81677 – Ⓜ Böhmerwaldplatz
– ✆ (089) 4 70 48 48 – info@acquarello.com
– Fax (089) 47 64 64 – www.acquarello.com **D2**
closed 1 - 4 January and Saturday lunch, Sunday, Bank Holidays lunch
Rest – Menu 29 € (lunch)/79 € – Carte 49/65 €
Spec. Vitello Tonnato. Feigentortelli mit Gänseleber und Cassissauce. Taubenbrust mit Petersilienfarce und schwarzer Nusssauce.

♦ Italian ♦ Friendly ♦

Italian cuisine in a Mediterranean setting - prepared by Waldemar Gollan with creativity and finesse. Lovely large wall paintings decorate the restaurant.

XX

Käfer Schänke

45 VISA MC AE

Prinzregentenstr. 73 ✉ 81675 – Ⓜ Prinzregentenplatz – ✆ (089) 4 16 82 47
– kaeferschaenke@feinkost-kaefer.de
– Fax (089) 4 16 86 23
– www.feinkost-kaefer.de
closed Sunday and Bank Holidays **C3**
Rest – *(booking essential)* Carte 39/57 €

♦ International ♦ Cosy ♦

The restaurant is comfortable, and the small rooms have been lovingly decorated, from the "Cutlery Parlour" to the "Tobacco Parlour".

X ✿

Acetaia

VISA MC AE

Nymphenburger Str. 215, (A 2) ✉ 80639 – ✆ (089) 13 92 90 77
– info@restaurant-acetaia.de – Fax (089) 13 92 90 78
– www.restaurant-acetaia.de
closed Saturday lunch
Rest – Menu 24 € (lunch)/69 € – Carte 39/44 €
Spec. Pecorino-Ravioli mit Majoran und Aceto Balsamico. Seewolf mit Tomaten und Venusmuscheln. Schokoladenterrine mit Kakao-Aprikosen.

♦ Italian ♦ Cosy ♦

Comfortably elegant décor with chandeliers, mosaic floors and cabinets decorated with wine bottles. Italian and Mediterranean dishes.

X

Terrine

VISA MC AE

Amalienstr. 89 , (Amalien-Passage) ✉ 80799
– Ⓜ Universität – ✆ (089) 28 17 80
– geniessen@terrine.de – Fax (089) 2 80 93 16 – www.terrine.de
closed Sunday - Monday lunch, Saturday lunch **B2**
Rest – Menu 56/74 € (dinner) – Carte 29 €

♦ Seasonal cuisine ♦ Bistro ♦

Creative cuisine in an intimate ambience at this Art Nouveau restaurant adorned with lamps. At lunch an inexpensive à la carte menu.

X

Rue Des Halles

VISA MC

Steinstr. 18 ✉ 81667 – Ⓜ Max Weber Platz – ✆ (089) 48 56 75
– Fax (089) 44 45 10 76
closed Saturday lunch, Sunday lunch **C3**
Rest – *(booking advisable)* Menu 19 € (lunch)/52 € – Carte 28/35 €

♦ French ♦ Bistro ♦

Experience the typically French flair of this bistro-style townhouse restaurant. The menu includes both classical and French regional dishes.

Vinaiolo

Steinstr. 42 ✉ 81667 – Ⓜ Ostbahnhof – ✆ (089) 48 95 03 56 – Fax (089) 48 06 80 11 – www.vinaiolo.de
closed Saturday lunch C3
Rest – Menu 44 € (lunch) – Carte 38/42 €
♦ Italian ♦ Bistro ♦
A restaurant styled as a colonial warehouse. The wines are displayed in cabinets from the former apothecary, which are still the originals. Italian cuisine.

AT THE EXHIBITION CENTRE

NH Dornach

Einsteinring 20, (Industrialpark-East) ✉ 85609 – ✆ (089) 9 40 09 60 – nhmuenchendornach@nh-hotels.com – Fax (089) 9 40 09 61 00 – www.nh-hotels.com
222 rm – †70/160 € ††70/160 €, ☕ 18 €
Rest – Carte 27/38 €
♦ Chain hotel ♦ Functional ♦
This hotel has been especially designed for business travellers, offering modern functional rooms at a location close to the exhibition centre. This modern restaurant opens onto the hall. Large glass façade.

Innside Premium

Humboldtstr. 12, (Industrialpark-West) ✉ 85609 – ✆ (089) 94 00 50 – muenchen@innside.de – Fax (089) 94 00 52 99 – www.innside.de
closed 24 December - 1 January
134 rm – †146/166 € ††160/180 €, ☕ 16 €
Rest – *(closed Saturday lunch, Sunday lunch)* Carte 21/35 €
♦ Business ♦ Modern ♦
Interestingly designed rooms with unusual features - free-standing glass showers for instance. Be inspired by the original art works. Bistro-style restaurant with international cuisine.

Schreiberhof

Erdinger Str. 2 ✉ 85609 – ✆ (089) 90 00 60 – info@schreiberhof.de – Fax (089) 90 00 64 59 – www.schreiberhof.de
87 rm ☕ – †78/173 € ††88/183 €
Rest *Alte Gaststube* – Carte 25/39 €
♦ Family ♦ Classic ♦
An upgraded former hotel with spacious, contemporary, functional rooms. The light-filled conservatory is available for meetings. Delicious international and regional dishes are served in the cosy Alte Gaststube.

Prinzregent an der Messe

Riemer Str. 350 ✉ 81829 – ✆ (089) 94 53 90 – messe@prinzregent.de – Fax (089) 94 53 95 66 – www.prinzregent.de
91 rm ☕ – †130 € ††150 € – 4 suites
Rest – Carte 28/45 €
♦ Traditional ♦ Classic ♦
18C building extended with a modern annexe. Together they offer traditionally furnished, cosy rooms and a leisure centre. Close to the exhibition centre. The cosy restaurant is located in the historical part of the building.

Dorint Novotel München Messe

Willy-Brandt-Platz 1 ✉ 81829 – ✆ (089) 99 40 00 – h5563@accor.com – Fax (089) 99 40 01 00 – www.novotel.com
278 rm – †85/135 € ††105/155 €, ☕ 17 €
Rest – Menu 25 € – Carte 26/37 €
♦ Chain hotel ♦ Business ♦ Modern ♦
Located in the former airport grounds next to the conference centre, this hotel features modern décor from the spacious lobby to the rooms. Light, friendly restaurant with glass frontage.

GERMANY

AT THE AIRPORT

Kempinski Airport München

Terminalstraße Mitte 20 ✉ 85356 Munich
– ✆ (089) 9 78 20 – info@kempinski-airport.de – Fax (089) 97 82 26 10
– www.kempinski-airport.de

389 rm – 180/405 € 180/405 €, 26 € – 46 suites
Rest – Carte 27/52 €
Rest *Safran* – *(closed Sunday - Monday) (dinner only)* Menu 40/59 €
– Carte 27/58 €

♦ Business ♦ Functional ♦

The huge glass atrium stands out as a pinnacle of modern hotel architecture, with 18m-high palms soaring upwards. Completely up-to-date technical facilities in the conference area. Thai and Mediterranean cuisine served.

GREECE
ELLÁDA

PROFILE

- **Area:**
131 944 km^2 (50 944 sq mi).
- **Population:**
10 668 000 inhabitants (est. 2005), density = 81 per km^2.
- **Capital:**
Athens (conurbation 3 368 000 inhabitants).
- **Currency:**
Euro (€); rate of exchange: € 1 = US$ 1.32 (Nov 2006).
- **Government:**
Parliamentary republic (since 1974). Member of European Union since 1981.
- **Language:**
Greek.
- **Specific public holidays:**
Epiphany (6 January); Orthodox Shrove Monday (late February-March); Independence Day (25 March); Orthodox Good Friday (Friday before Easter); Orthodox Easter Monday; Day of the Holy Spirit (late May-June); Ochi Day (28 October); Boxing Day (26 December).
- **Local Time:**
GMT + 2 hours in winter and GMT + 3 hours in summer.
- **Climate:**
Temperate Mediterranean, with mild winters and hot, sunny summers (Athens: January: 10°C, July: 27°C).

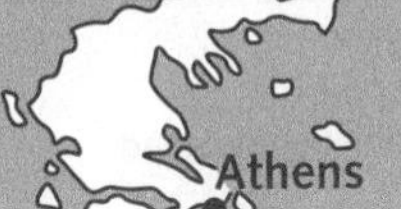

- **International dialling code:**
00 30 followed by local number.
- **Emergency:**
General Police: ✆ **100**, Tourist Police: ✆ **171**, Ambulance: ✆ **166.**
- **Electricity:**
220 volts AC, 50Hz; 2-pin round-shaped continental plugs.

FORMALITIES

Travellers from the European Union (EU), Switzerland, Iceland and the main countries of North and South America need a national identity card or passport (America: passport required) to visit Greece for less than three months (tourism or business purpose). For visitors from other countries a visa may be required, in addition to a passport, especially for those wishing to stay for longer than three months. We advise you to check with your embassy before travelling.

A valid national driving licence is sufficient for citizens of EU member countries and for US drivers for up to 3 months but an international driving licence is necessary for other drivers. Fully comprehensive insurance cover (Green Card) is compulsory.

MAJOR NEWSPAPERS

The main national newspapers are: *Eleftherotipia, Ethnos, Kathimerini* (Greek, English), *Ta Nea, To Vima, Adesmeytos Typos. Athens News* is the main English language paper in the capital.

USEFUL PHRASES

ENGLISH	GREEK
Yes	**Né**
No	**Óhi**
Good morning	**Kaliméra**
Goodbye	**Andío**
Thank you	**Efharistó**
Please	**Parakaló**
Excuse me	**Signómi**
I don't understand	**Then katalavéno**

HOTELS

→ CATEGORIES

Greece has a well-developed tourist infrastructure offering everything from luxury hotels to rooms in private houses (**thomátia**). Establishments approved by the GNTO (EOT) display a blue and yellow plaque – details from local tourist offices. Outside large towns and resorts, it is common to take a room in a private house, especially on the Aegean Islands. It is advisable to seek accommodation through the local tourist office.

→ PRICE RANGE

The price is quoted per room. Prices vary according to category and are often reduced by half out of season.

→ TAX

Prices include taxes and service charges.

→ CHECK OUT TIME

Usually between 10.30am and noon.

→ RESERVATIONS

By telephone or by Internet. Credit card details may be requested. It is advisable to reserve a room well in advance in high season, especially in areas popular with tourists.

→ TIP FOR LUGGAGE HANDLING

At the discretion of the customer.

→ BREAKFAST

It is not normally included in the price of the room. It is served between 7.30am and 10am and most hotels offer a buffet. Some budget hotels do not serve breakfast but there are usually cafés nearby.

Reception	**Resepsió**
Single room	**Monóklino thomátio**
Double room	**Thíklino thomátio**
Bed	**Kreváti**
Bathroom	**Bánio**
Shower	**Doús**

RESTAURANTS

There are five types of establishments to be found in Greece. Restaurants **(estiatória)** offer a smart décor and excellent service and serve both Greek and international cuisine. **Tavernas** are popular restaurants serving traditional fare. **Ouzería** and **mezedopolia** are different from tavernas because their menus feature mezédes (small dishes) instead of cooked or meat dishes. **Psistariá** (steakhouses) are small, inexpensive eateries, offering souvlákia (skewers) and grilled meats served with chips and a tomato salad. **Kafenía**, Greek cafés, also serve a variety of mezédes. Cafeterias serving breakfast and simple meals are numerous. For desserts go to a **zaharoplastío** (patisserie).

→ MEALS

Breakfast	**Proïnó**	7am – 10am
Lunch	**Mesimerianó**	12.30pm – 2.30pm
Dinner	**Thípno**	7-8pm – 10-11pm sometimes later

→ RESERVATIONS

It is generally a good idea to book in advance if you wish to visit a smart or popular restaurant.

→ THE BILL

The bill (check) includes service charge and tax but it is customary to leave a tip.

Appetizer	**Mezéthes**
Meal	**Yévma**
First course	**Orektiká**
Main dish	**Kírio pyáto**
Dessert	**Gliká, epithórpio**
Water/mineral water (still, sparkling)	**Neró/metalikó neró (apló, aerioúko)**
Wine (red, white, rosé)	**Krasí (kókino, áspro, rosé)**
Beer	**Bíra**
Bread	**Psomí**
Meat	**Kréas**
Fish	**Psári**
Salt/pepper	**Aláti/pipéri**
Cheese	**Tirí**
Vegetables	**Lahaniká**
Hot/cold	**Zestó/krío**
The bill (check) please	**To logariasmó, parakaló**

LOCAL CUISINE

Greek fare is simple but full of flavour. A Greek menu comprises numerous side dishes and starters, which tend to be served all at once (be sure to ask if you want them served one after another). Most dishes are prepared in advance and often served lukewarm. The words **tis oras** next to a dish on the menu mean that it will be freshly cooked (ie while you wait).

Aperitifs are usually accompanied by **mezedes** which include vine leaves stuffed with meat and rice **(dolmáthes)**, spit-roasted offal sausages **(kokorétsi)**, aubergine purée with black olives **(melidzánasalata)**, yoghurt with chopped cucumber and garlic **(tzatzíki)**, fish roe puréed with breadcrumbs or potatoes **(taramosaláta)**, rice with tomatoes **(piláfi)**, stuffed tomatoes, peppers and aubergines **(gemistá)**. **Moussaká** is a traditional dish of minced lamb and aubergine with a béchamel sauce. **Psarosoúpa** is a fish soup and **soupa avgolémono** is a broth with rice, egg and lemon. **Mayerítsa** is an offal soup served at Easter. For fish **(psári)** dishes, the fish is weighed before cooking and priced per pound and is served boiled (vrastó), fried or grilled (psitó). Prawns (garídes), sole (glóssa), swordfish (ksifías), squid (kalamári), octopus (oktapódi) and sardines (sardéles) are the staple seafood dishes.

Meat – mutton and lamb (arní, arnáki), minced beef (biftéki), pork (hirinó), chicken (kotópoulo), veal (moshári) – can be roasted, grilled (skára), boiled or braised (stifádo). **Soutzoukákia** are meatballs in tomato sauce and **souvlákia** are beef, mutton or goat meat on a skewer served with tomatoes and onions. Vegetables are often stuffed or fried. Cucumbers (angouria), beans (fasolakia), courgettes (kolokinthákia), aubergines (melidzánes), potatoes (patátes) are plentiful. **Thomátes gemistés** (tomatoes with rice), **thomatosalata** (tomato salad) are delicious. The classic Greek salad, **saláta horiatikí**, composed of tomatoes, cucumber, oregano, onions, olives, green peppers and féta cheese, is usually served with pitta bread. Other tasty snacks are **spanakópita** (spinach in filo pastry) and **tirópita** (cheese in filo pastry).

The Greeks are very fond of cheese. The best known are goat's or sheep's milk cheese **(féta)**, a type of Gruyère (graviéra) and a mild cheese similar to Cheddar (kasséri). Kefalotíri is a sweeter version of Parmesan.

Meals often end with fresh fruit. Desserts tend to be eaten separately, often as an afternoon snack. These include millefeuilles with walnuts or almonds and cinnamon **(baklavá)**; rolls of thread-like pastry with honey and walnuts or almonds **(kadaïfi)**, mini doughnuts with honey and sesame or cinnamon **(loukoumádes)**, flaky pastry turnover with cream and cinnamon **(bougátsa)**, rice cake **(rizógalo)** and almond and sesame paste **(halvá)**. To accompany these, try Greek coffee **(Elinikós kafés)** which has a strong aromatic flavour. You should let the grounds settle and then only drink about half the cup. Ask for **skéto** (without sugar), **métrio** (slightly sweet), **glikó** (sweet). Greek coffee is always served with a glass of water.

DRINK

Oúzo is the national drink; aniseed-flavoured, it is either consumed neat or diluted with water. The best-known Greek wine is **retsína**, a white wine to which pine resin has been added as a preservative. Among the unresinated wines (aretsínato), some are reputed: the full-bodied red from Náoussa in Macedonia, the fruity reds from Neméa in the Argolid, the scented rosé from Aráhova near Delphi, the well-rounded dry white wines of Hymettos and Palíni in Attica, the sparkling dry white wine of Zítsa in Epirós, the white wines of Chalcidice, and the popular white wines of Achaia (Demestica, Santa Laura, Santa Helena). In the islands there are the generous reds and rosés from Crete, dry whites from Lindos in Rhodes, the heady and scented wines from the Cyclades, particularly Náxos and Santoríni, and from the Ionian Islands: Zákynthos (Verdéa, Delizia), Kephalloniá (fruity and musky Róbola) and Lévkas (Santa Maura).
Samian wine can be drunk as a liqueur. Métaxa is the brand name of Greek brandy. Cretan **rakí** is a fruit brandy, and **mastíka** a sweet liqueur flavoured with mastic gum.

ATHENS
ATHÍNA

Population (est. 2005): 732 000 (conurbation 3 368 000) – Altitude: 156m

R. Mattès / MICHELIN

Athens spreads out over eight hills and plains planted with vines and olive trees. The attractive site, the brilliant light, the beauty of the Ancient monuments, the quality of the museums and the unique landscape of indented coastline, beaches and mountains of its environs, all contribute to the fascination of Athens, the city of Athena and the cradle of Western civilization. It is, however, a modern metropolis which has been greatly enhanced by recent improvements in the infrastructure. The verve of the Athenians is reflected in the ebullient way of life and the sense of enjoyment and revelry which characterises the city.

The city has a long history with the first settlement dating back to the Neolithic age. In 5C BC, the 'Golden Age of Pericles', its civilisation was at its zenith and its ideas and values have proved to be seminal influences which have enriched western culture. Athens also has many Roman, Byzantine and neo-Classical remains; certain districts, such as the old Bazaar, have a strong and enticing oriental flavour and remarkable monuments of the Ottoman period have been preserved.

WHICH DISTRICT TO CHOOSE

The luxury and design-oriented boutique **hotels** in Athens are located around Síntagma Square *Plan I* **C2** and Odós Panepistimiou. For comfortable mid-range hotels look around Omonia Square *Plan I* **B2**; hotels near the Acropolis and Philoppapos Hill have a good location and great views. The Plaka *Plan I* **B3** has many budget hotels.

The elegant district of Kolonaki *Plan I* **C2** bounded by Síntagma Square and Vassilisis Sofias Avenue abounds in fashionable cafés and luxury **restaurants**. You will find cafés, traditional tavernas and first class restaurants around Varnava Square *Plan I* **D3** in the fashionable Metz neighbourhood. In the narrow alleys of Plaka *Plan I* **B3**, Monastiraki *Plan I* **A3**, Psiri there is a multitude of cafés, restaurants and ouzeries with a great atmosphere. Kyfissiá on the outskirts has some excellent restaurants.

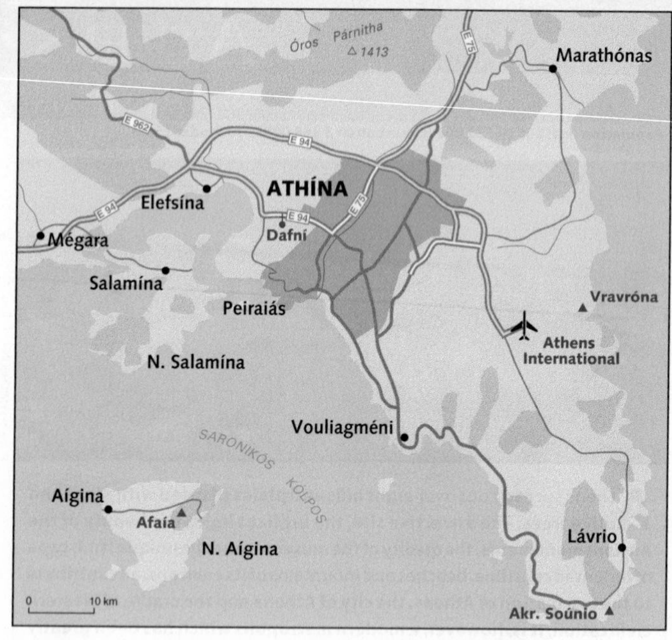

PRACTICAL INFORMATION

ARRIVAL – DEPARTURE

Athens International Airport 'Eleftherios Venizelos' – 33 km (20 mi) east of the city centre. ✆ 210 3530000; www.aia.gr

From the airport to the city centre – By **taxi**: about €20-25 (airport surcharge €3, surcharge for baggage over 10kg €0.30). SATA ✆ 210 5239524, 5221123, 5227986; sataxi@freemail.gr. By **metro**: Line 3 to Monastiraki. Time: 27min. Fare: €6 single (€10 for 2-3 people), €10 round trip (within 48hr). By **express bus**: Line E95 to Síntagma Square 24hr a day, every 10-30min, time: 70-80min, fare: €2.90. By **rail**: to Larissis Station, 6.50am-9.05pm, time: 30min; fare: €6. Express buses also run to the outlying districts and to Piraeus.

Railway stations – **Larissis Station** (Athens Central Railway Station), 31 Odós Deligiani for northern and eastern Greece. ✆ 210 5297777. **Peloponnese Station** *Plan I* **A1**, 3 Odós Sidirodromon for the south-west of the country. ✆ 210 51 31601; www.ose.gr

TRANSPORT

→ METRO, BUS AND TROLLEY BUSES

Athens has an excellent, integrated public transport network. Buses and trolley-buses: €0.70 single (carnets of 10 available); metro and ISAB (subway)

€0.70 single. A day ticket €2.80 valid 24hr gives unlimited travel on the whole network. Remember to validate your ticket. Tickets can be bought from newsstands, OASA booths and kiosks and at metro or subway stations. www.oasa.gr

→ TAXIS

Taxis (yellow vehicles with an illuminated sign when free) can be hailed in the street or ordered by phone. Minimum fare: €2.50, €0.85 pick-up charge, €0.30-0.56 per km and luggage surcharge €0.30. There is also a night rate. *Radio Taxis Ikaros* ✆ 210 515 2800; *Express* ✆ 210 994 3000; *Kosmos* ✆ 210 1300.

USEFUL ADDRESSES

→ TOURIST INFORMATION

Greek National Tourism Organisation (EOT), 26A Amalia St *Plan I* **C3**, ✆ 210 3310392, 210 3310716, 210 3310640; info@gnto.gr, www.gnto.gr; Airport Information Centre, ✆ 210 3530445-448; venizelos@gnto.gr

→ POST OFFICES

Opening times Mon-Fri, 7.30am-2pm. The branches at Mitropoleos St *Plan I* **B2**, 100 Aeolou St open Mon-Fri 7.30am-8pm, Sat 7.30am-2pm, Sun 9am-1pm. The branch at Mitropoleos Square has similar opening hours but is closed on Sunday.

→ BANKS/CURRENCY EXCHANGE

Banks open Mon-Thu 8am-2pm, Fri 8am-1.30pm. There are ATMs and exchange offices all over the city. You can also change money at the post office.

→ EMERGENCY

Police : ✆ **100**; Tourist Police: ✆ **171**; Medical emergencies: ✆ **166**; Fire Brigade: ✆ **199**.

BUSY PERIODS

It may be difficult to find a room when special events are held in the city:

Athens Festival – June to September.

EXPLORING ATHENS

It is possible to visit the main sights and museums in three days.

Classical sights and the national museum are open 8am-7pm. Other sights and museums open 9am to 4-5pm. Some may be closed on Tuesdays or Thursdays and Sundays.

VISITING

Acropolí *Plan I* **B3** – The upper town crowning the summit of a steep rock platform epitomises Greek civilisation. Pass the Odeon of Herodes Atticus **(Odío Iródou Atikoú)** and Temple of Athena Nike **(Naos Athinás Níkis)** on the way to the monumental entrance **(Propílea)**. The Parthenon **(Parthenónas)** – splendid Doric temple, dedicated to Athena (pediments, fluted columns, frieze, metopes). Elegant Erechtheum **(Eréthio)** – Caryatid Porch with noble statues dressed in pleated tunics. **Acropolis Museum** – Classical statues, Parthenon pediments, caryatids. **Théatro Dioníssou** – Splendid views.

Thissío *Plan I* **A3** – **Theseion**: 5C BC Doric temple. From the **Hephaisteion**: views of the agora, the Monastiráki district and the Acropolis. **Arhéa Agorá**, the centre of Athenian public life in Antiquity: **Stoa of the Giants, Stoa Atálou.**

Lófos Filopápou *Plan I* **A3** – Cave dwellings, Philopappos monument and theatre. Spectacular views of the Acropolis, Athens, Hymettos and the Attica plain.

Ethnikó Arheologikó Moussío *Plan I* **B2** – Fabulous collection of treasures from Greece's main archaeological sites.

Moussío Benáki *Plan I* **C2** – Ancient Greek and Byzantine art and costumes.

Moussío Kikladikís Téhnis *Plan I* **D2** – The Museum of Cycladic Art presents a superb private collection illustrating the development of Greek art over a period of 3 000 years – magnificent collection of Cycladic marble figurines.

Vizandinó Moussío *Plan I* **D2** – The Byzantine Museum displays a rich collection of icons. Reconstructions of two early churches.

Pláka *Plan I* **B3** – Picturesque narrow streets and alleys, squares and terraces – shops, tavernas famous for the nightlife. **Mikrí Mitrópoli** – 12C Byzantine church. **Romaikí Agorá** (Roman Forum). **Aérides** (Tower of the Winds) – carved winged figures of the winds. **Píli Adrianoú** (Hadrian's Arch). **Naós Olímbiou Diós** (Olympieion) – huge Corinthian marble columns.

Platía Sindágmatos *Plan I* **C2** – Elegant Síntagma Square lined with famous buildings. Parliament **(Voulí)** on the east side: Changing of the guard. **Ethnikós Kípos** (National Garden), **Zápio** (Zappeion Park). Walk up Odós El. Venizélou (Panepistimíou) past **Schliemann's House**, the Cathedral **Ágios Dionisis Areopagitis**, **Panepistímio** (University), **Akadimía** (Academy) and **Ethnikí Vivliothíki** (National Library).

Views – **Lycabettos** *Plan I* **D1** – Exceptional view of the Acropolis, the whole city and of the sea beyond; from rooftop bar of Hilton Hotel (opposite Megalis Tou Genous Scholi Square). From the terrace of the Pnyx **(Pnílka)** *Plan I* **A3** – view of the Acropolis.

Kessarianí Monastery and **Mount Hymettos** – *9km-5.5mi E.* 11C monastery in a beautiful setting. Continue through the pine woods past 11C Asteri Monastery for fine views of Athens and the Saronic Gulf as far as the Peloponnese to the west, and of the Attic peninsula (Mesógia), its eastern shore and Euboia to the east.

Apollo Coast to Cape Sounion – *65km-41mi round trip.* An unforgettable excursion along the coast road past elegant resorts and beaches (Glyfáda, Voúla, Vouliagméni, Lagoníssi, Anávissos) to Soúnio (view of the cape) and Akri Soúnio (Temple of Poseidon).

Daphní and **Elefsina** – *Around 90km-56mi.* 11C domed Byzantine church – superb mosaics. The Sanctuary at Eleusis was one of the great shrines in Antiquity – acropolis, temples, museum.

SHOPPING

In summer shops are usually open 8am-1.30pm and 5.30pm-8.30pm. They close on Sun and at 2.30pm on Mon, Wed, Sat. In winter they open 9am-5pm on Mon, Wed, 10am-7pm on Tue, Thu, Fri, 8.30am-3.30pm Sat. Department stores in **Odós Patission** *Plan I* **B2** and **Eolou** open 8.30am-8pm weekdays (3pm Sat).

Fashionable shops featuring Greek and international designers line **Odós Ermou** *Plan I* **A2**. For that special gift visit the jewellery shops around Síntagma Square, in **Letka St** *Plan I* **C2** which connects **Perikleous St** and **Kolokotroni St** and nearby arcades. The elegant districts of **Kolonáki**, **Kyfissia** and **Glyfada** boast luxury shops for fashion, jewellery, antiques. Browse along **Odós Panepistimiou** linking Síntagma and Omónia Squares. The streets around **Omónia** are full of small shops. For handicrafts, souvenirs, leather goods and antiques explore the colourful **Plaka**, **Monastiraki**, **Psiri** districts.

MARKETS – The **flea market** in Monastiraki is an amazing experience. The shops are open all week but it is at weekends that it is particularly busy.

WHAT TO BUY – Jewellery, Kastoria furs, crafts, ceramics, pottery, wool and cotton garments, carpets and rugs, embroidery, embroidered tapestries, cushions and bags, leather goods.

ENTERTAINMENT

For information on cultural events consult *Athens News* on sale at central kiosks or visit www.cultureguide.gr; *Time Out Athens* is another useful source of information.

National Opera House *Plan I* **B3** – Opera, ballet and music in two auditoria (Olympia, Acropol).

Odeon of Herodes Atticus *Plan I* **B3** – Opera, ballet, concerts, traditional dance and Classical tragedies during Athens Festival.

Dora Stratou Theatre *Plan I* **B3** – Traditional dance. Performances at **Philopappos Theatre** during festival.

Athens Concert Hall *Plan I* **D2** – Concerts, opera, ballet.

Likavitós *Plan I* **C1** – Folk dancing.

NIGHTLIFE

Explore the streets around **Síntagma Square** for restaurants, bars clubs and disco bars. The lively venues in **Plaka**, **Monastiraki**, **Psiri**, **Gazi**, **Thissio** (Irakleidon St *Plan I* **A3**) are open late into the night. Some tavernas have live bouzouki music. A young crowd flocks to establishments in **Exarchia Square** and the streets up to Streffi Hill. There are smart clubs with dancing in **Kolonaki**, along **Singrou** and **Poseidonos Avenues** leading to the elegant south coast resorts of **Glyfada**, **Voula** and **Vougliameni**. Casinos on Mount Parnitha and at Loutraki are frequented by a fashionable clientele.

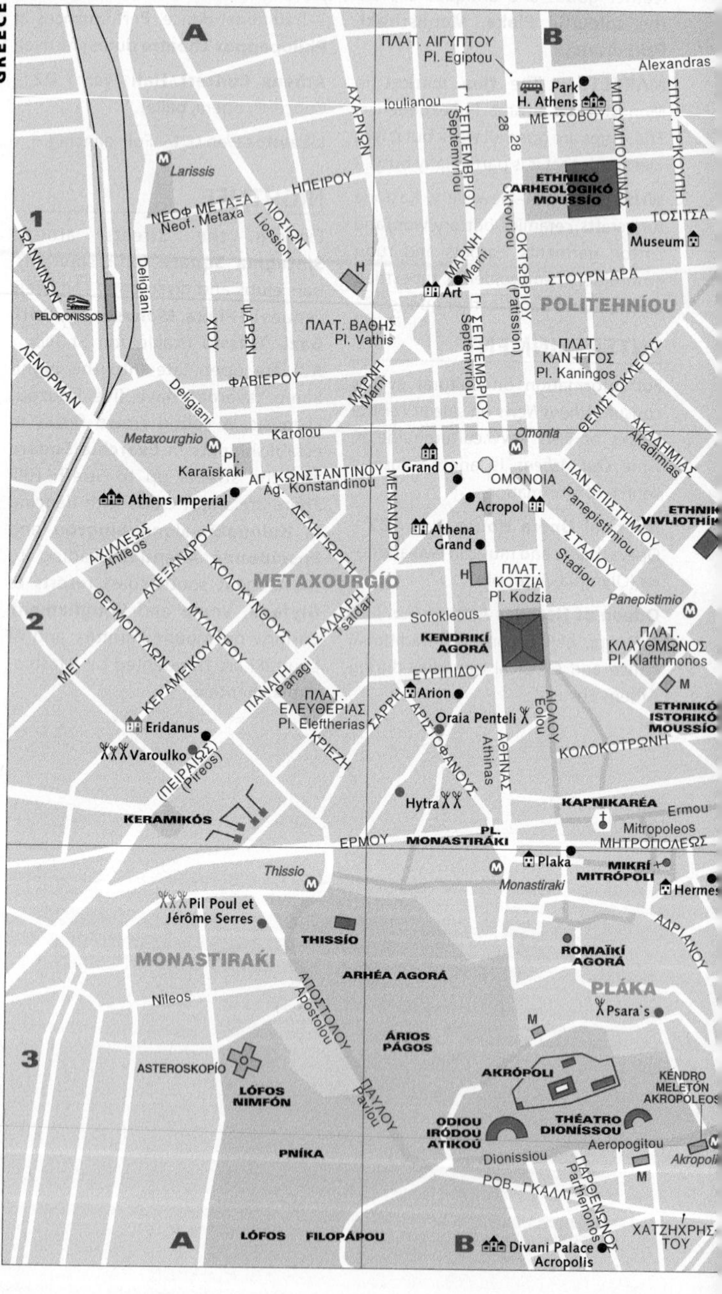

A
B
ΠΛΑΤ. ΑΙΓΥΠΤΟΥ
Pl. Egiptou
Alexandras
Park
H. Athens
Ioulianou
ΜΕΤΣΟΒΟΥ
ΑΧΑΡΝΩΝ
Γ' ΣΕΠΤΕΜΒΡΙΟΥ
Septemvriou
28
28
ΜΠΟΥΜΠΟΥΛΙΝΑΣ
ΣΠΥΡ. ΤΡΙΚΟΥΠΗ
Larissis
ΗΠΕΙΡΟΥ
ETHNIKÓ
ARHEOLOGIKÓ
MOUSSÍO
Oktovriou
1
ΝΕΟΦ ΜΕΤΑΞΑ
Neof. Metaxa
ΛΙΟΣΙΩΝ
Liossion
ΤΟΣΙΤΣΑ
Museum
ΙΩΑΝΝΙΝΩΝ
Deligiani
H
ΜΑΡΝΗ
Marni
ΟΚΤΩΒΡΙΟΥ
(Patission)
ΣΤΟΥΡΝ ΑΡΑ
Art
POLITEHNÍOU
PELOPONISSOS
ΧΙΟΥ
ΨΑΡΩΝ
ΠΛΑΤ. ΒΑΘΗΣ
Pl. Vathis
Γ' ΣΕΠΤΕΜΒΡΙΟΥ
Septemvriou
ΠΛΑΤ.
ΚΑΝ ΙΓΓΟΣ
Pl. Kaningos
ΘΕΜΙΣΤΟΚΛΕΟΥΣ
ΛΕΝΟΡΜΑΝ
ΦΑΒΙΕΡΟΥ
ΜΑΡΝΗ
Marni
Deligiani
ΑΚΑΔΗΜΙΑΣ
Akadimias
Metaxourghio
Karolou
Omonia
Pl.
Karaïskaki
Grand O`
ΟΜΟΝΟΙΑ
ΑΓ. ΚΩΝΣΤΑΝΤΙΝΟΥ
Ág. Konstandinou
ΜΕΝΑΝΔΡΟΥ
ΠΑΝ ΕΠΙΣΤΗΜΙΟΥ
Panepistimiou
Athens Imperial
Acropol
ETHNIKÍ
VIVLIOTHÍKI
ΔΕΛΗΓΙΩΡΓΗ
Athena
Grand
ΑΧΙΛΛΕΩΣ
Ahileos
ΑΛΕΞΑΝΔΡΟΥ
ΚΟΛΟΚΥΝΘΟΥΣ
ΣΤΑΔΙΟΥ
Stadiou
H
ΠΛΑΤ.
ΚΟΤΖΙΑ
Pl. Kodzia
METAXOURGÍO
ΘΕΡΜΟΠΥΛΩΝ
ΜΥΛΛΕΡΟΥ
ΤΣΑΛΔΑΡΗ
Tsaldari
Panepistimio
2
Sofokleous
KENDRIKÍ
AGORÁ
ΠΛΑΤ.
ΚΛΑΥΘΜΩΝΟΣ
Pl. Klafthmonos
ΜΕΓ.
ΚΕΡΑΜΕΙΚΟΥ
ΠΑΝΑΓΗ
Panagi
ΕΥΡΙΠΙΔΟΥ
M
ΠΛΑΤ.
ΕΛΕΥΘΕΡΙΑΣ
Pl. Eleftherias
ΣΑΡΡΗ
Arion
ΑΙΟΛΟΥ
Eolou
ETHNIKÓ
ISTORIKÓ
MOUSSÍO
Eridanus
Oraia Penteli
ΑΡΙΣΤΟΦΑΝΟΥΣ
ΚΡΙΕΖΗ
Athinas
ΑΘΗΝΑΣ
ΚΟΛΟΚΟΤΡΩΝΗ
Varoulko
(ΠΕΙΡΑΙΩΣ)
(Pireos)
KAPNIKARÉA
Hytra
Ermou
KERAMIKÓS
Mitropoleos
PL.
ΕΡΜΟΥ
MONASTIRÁKI
ΜΗΤΡΟΠΟΛΕΩΣ
Plaka
MIKRÍ
MITRÓPOLI
Thissio
Monastiraki
Hermes
Pil Poul et
Jérôme Serres
ΑΔΡΙΑΝΟΥ
THISSÍO
ROMAÏKÍ
AGORÁ
MONASTIRÁKI
ARHÉA AGORÁ
PLÁKA
ΑΠΟΣΤΟΛΟΥ
Apostolou
Nileos
Psara`s
M
ÁRIOS
PÁGOS
3
ASTEROSKOPÍO
AKRÓPOLI
KÉNDRO
MELETÓN
AKROPOLEOS
LÓFOS
NIMFÓN
ΠΑΥΛΟΥ
Pavlou
ODIOU
IRÓDOU
ATIKOÚ
THÉATRO
DIONÍSSOU
Aeropogitou
Akropoli
PNÍKA
Dionissiou
ΡΟΒ. ΓΚΑΛΛΙ
ΠΑΡΘΕΝΩΝΟΣ
Parthenonos
M
ΧΑΤΖΗΧΡΗΣ-
ΤΟΥ
A
LÓFOS
FILOPÁPOU
B
Divani Palace
Acropolis

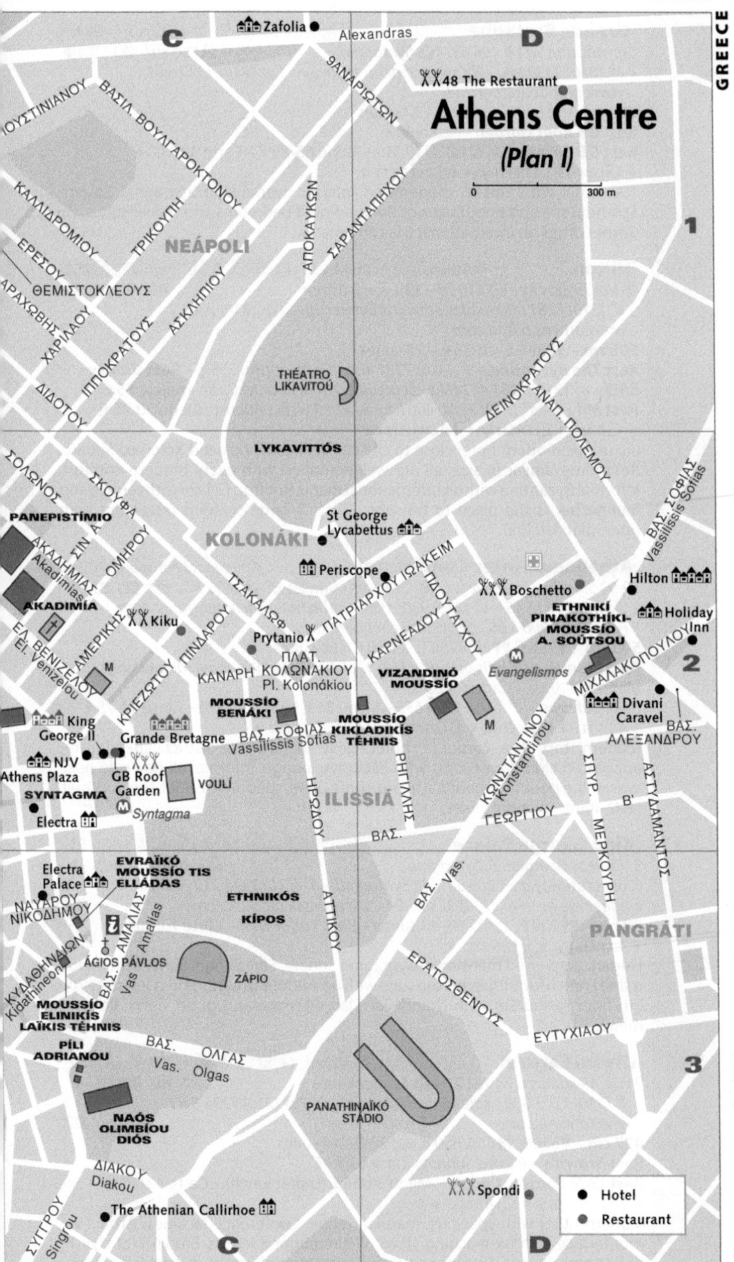
Athens Centre
(Plan I)
0
300 m
C
D
1
2
3
Zafolia
Alexandras
48 The Restaurant
NEÁPOLI
THÉATRO LIKAVITOÚ
LYKAVITTÓS
PANEPISTÍMIO
AKADIMÍA
KOLONÁKI
St George Lycabettus
Periscope
Kiku
Prytanio
Boschetto
Hilton
Holiday Inn
ETHNIKÍ PINAKOTHÍKI-MOUSSÍO A. SOÚTSOU
Evangelismos
Divani Caravel
VIZANDINÓ MOUSSÍO
MOUSSÍO BENÁKI
MOUSSÍO KIKLADIKÍS TÉHNIS
Pl. Kolonákiou
Vassilissis Sofias
King George II
Grande Bretagne
NJV Athens Plaza
GB Roof Garden
VOULÍ
SYNTAGMA
Syntagma
Electra
ILISSIÁ
Electra Palace
EVRAÏKÓ MOUSSÍO TIS ELLÁDAS
ETHNIKÓS KÍPOS
PANGRÁTI
ÁGIOS PÁVLOS
ZÁPIO
MOUSSÍO ELINIKÍS LAÏKIS TÉHNIS
PÍLI ADRIANOU
Vas. Olgas
NAÓS OLIMBÍOU DIÓS
PANATHINAÏKÓ STÁDIO
Diakou
The Athenian Callirhoe
Singrou
Spondi
Hotel
Restaurant

Grande Bretagne < Athens, rm
Constitution Sq ✉ 105 63 – Ⓜ Syntagma 380 VISA MC AE
– ☎ (210) 3330 000 – info@grandebretagne.gr – Fax (210) 3220 8 01
– www.grandebretagne.gr **C2**
284 rm – 600 €, ☕ 29 € – 37 suites
Rest *GB Roof Garden* – see below
Rest *GB Corner* – *☎ (210) 3330 750* – Menu 65/89 € – Carte 39/108 €
♦ Grand Luxury ♦ Modern ♦
19C hotel with classic, modernised interior overlooking Syntagma Square. Splendid spa and pool. Luxuriously-appointed bedrooms and corner suites. GB Corner offers an international à la carte menu.

Hilton < Athens and Acropolis, rm 2000
46 Vas. Sofias Ave ✉ 115 28 – Ⓜ Evangelismos VISA MC AE
– ☎ (210) 7281 000 – sales.athens@hilton.com – Fax (210) 7281 2 41
– www.athens.hilton.com **D2**
505 rm – 349 €, ☕ 33 € – 18 suites
Rest *The Byzantine* – *☎ (210) 7281 400* – Carte approx. 55 € – **Rest *Galaxy BBQ*** – *☎ (210) 7281 402 (May-September) (dinner only)* Carte approx. 55 €
Rest *Milo's* – *☎ (210) 7244 400 (closed last 3 weeks August)* Menu 20/40 €
♦ Grand Luxury ♦ Modern ♦
Luxurious modern hotel close to city centre, near shops and Kolonaki Square. Bedrooms similar in size; all are well-equipped with every modern comfort. Informal Byzantine with an international menu. Rooftop Galaxy with terrace and lounge/bar is the place to be seen. Milo's is large seafood restaurant with open-plan kitchen.

Athenaeum Inter-Continental < Athens and Acropolis,
89-93 Singrou (Southwest : 2 ¾ km) ✉ 117 45 – ☎ (210) 9206 000 – attha.hotel@ichotelsgroup.com – Fax (210) 9206 5 06 – www.intercontinental.com rm 2000 VISA MC AE
543 rm – 256 € 200/256 €, ☕ 30 € – 60 suites
Rest *Première (9th floor)* – *☎ (210) 9206 981 (closed Sunday) (dinner only)* Menu 57/102 € – Carte 63/85 €
Rest *Cafezoe* – *☎ (210) 9206 655* – Menu 36 € (buffet lunch) – Carte 34/75 €
♦ Grand Luxury ♦ Business ♦ Modern ♦
Modern, top class corporate hotel, close to business district. Luxuriously-appointed club floor rooms with exclusive lounge. Informal all day café near swimming pool; international menu, some Greek specialities. Roof-top gourmet restaurant; splendid views.

King George Palace rm
3 Vasileos Georgiou A, Syntagma (Constitution) Sq ✉ 105 64 – Ⓜ Syntagma – ☎ (210) 3222 210 – info@kinggeorge.gr – Fax (210) 3250 5 04 – www.classicalhotels.com 410 VISA MC AE **C2**
89 rm – 220 €, ☕ 32 € – 13 suites – **Rest *Tudor Hall*** – Carte 73/90 €
♦ Luxury ♦ Classic ♦
Elegant converted mansion in Syntagma Square. Stylish bedrooms with hand-made French furniture; rooftop suite with own pool and panoramic views. Stylish 7th floor restaurant with chandeliers, large terrace and good views. Eclectic menu.

Divani Caravel < Athens, 1000
2 Vas. Alexandrou ✉ 161 21 – Ⓜ Evangelismos VISA MC AE
– ☎ (210) 7207 000 – sales@divanicaravel.gr – Fax (210) 7236 6 83
– www.divanis.com **D2**
427 rm – 570 € 550/650 €, ☕ 27 € – 44 suites
Rest *Brown's* – *(closed Sunday)* Carte 63/89 €
Rest *Café Constantinople* – Menu 31/35 € (buffet lunch) – Carte 43/70 €
♦ Business ♦ Classic ♦
Modern hotel with spacious, marbled lobby. Conference facilities. Attractive roof terrace with far-reaching views. Well-equipped rooms. Brown's for stylish dining and elegant cigar lounge. Café Constantinople open all day for local and international dishes.

Metropolitan

385 Singrou (Southwest : 7 km) ✉ 175 64 – ✆ (210) 9471 000 – metropolitan@chandris.gr – Fax (210) 9471 0 10 – www.chandris.gr
362 rm – ††600 €, ☕ 21 € – 12 suites
Rest *Trocadero* – Menu 25 € (buffet lunch Monday-Friday)
♦ Business ♦ Modern ♦
Striking, modern corporate hotel with easy access into and out of the city. Spacious, comfortable rooms with state-of-the-art facilities. Popular for business conventions. International or Italian fare can be taken overlooking the garden or beside the pool.

Ledra Marriott

115 Singrou (Southwest : 3 km) ✉ 117 45 – ✆ (210) 9300 000 – mhrs.athgr.exec.asst@marriott.com – Fax (210) 9559 1 53 – www.marriott.com
300 rm – †230 € ††185/230 €, ☕ 23 € – 14 suites
Rest *Kona Kai* – *(dinner only)* Menu 43/65 € – Carte 26/45 €
Rest *Zephyros* – Carte 26/35 €
♦ Business ♦ Modern ♦
Commercial hotel with panoramic views from rooftop terrace. Executive rooms have exclusive lounge and high-tech extras. Ornate Kona Kai for authentic Thai and Polynesian dishes. Zephyros on 1st floor for traditional and international buffet.

Athens Imperial

Karaiskaki Sq ✉ 104 37 – Ⓜ Metaxourghio – ✆ (210) 5201 600 – sales_ai@classicalhotels.gr – Fax (210) 5225 5 21 – www.classicalhotels.com **A2**
236 rm ☕ – ††165 € – 24 suites
Rest – Carte 30/45 €
♦ Business ♦ Modern ♦
Modern hotel, its impressive atrium boasting an opulent lounge and bar. Lovely rooftop decked pool area with superb views to Acropolis. Mod cons match smart, stylish rooms. Views over the square from restaurant; Mediterranean food served.

St George Lycabettus

< Athens,
2 Kleomenous ✉ 106 75 – ✆ (210) 7290 711 – sales@sglycabettus.gr – Fax (210) 7290 4 39 – www.sglycabettus.gr **C2**
148 rm – †393 € ††382/393 €, ☕ 27 € – 6 suites
Rest *Le Grand Balcon* – *(closed Sunday and Monday) (dinner only)* Carte 37/56 €
Rest *Frame* – Carte 37/56 €
♦ Business ♦ Classic ♦
Elevated position on Lycabettus Hill. Greek artwork and artifacts throughout. Roof-top pool. South-facing rooms with balconies, view of Acropolis and Athens skyline. Le Grand Balcon roof-top restaurant for international menu. All day Frame for Greek dishes.

Electra Palace

18-20 Nikodimou St ✉ 105 57 – Ⓜ Syntagma – ✆ (210) 3370 000 – salesepath@electrahotels.gr – Fax (210) 3241 8 75 – www.electrahotels.gr **C3**
145 rm ☕ – †240 € ††190/342 € – 10 suites – **Rest** – Carte 24/39 €
♦ Business ♦ Modern ♦
Modern interior behind a classical façade in Plaka. Ultramodern bedrooms and suites with classical décor; some with view of the Acropolis. Ground-floor restaurant opened in 2005: American buffet breakfast; à la carte lunch and dinner.

NJV Athens Plaza

2 Vas. Georgiou A, Syntagma Sq ✉ 105 64 – Ⓜ Syntagma – ✆ (210) 3352 400 – sales_njv@grecotel.gr – Fax (210) 3235 8 56 – www.grecotel.gr **C2**
159 rm – †440 € ††440 €, ☕ 25 € – 23 suites
Rest *The Parliament* – Carte 63/94 €
♦ Business ♦ Modern ♦
Modern hotel handy for the shopping and business districts. Local stone adorns the contemporary lobby and bar. Boldly decorated, hi-tech bedrooms and luxurious suites. Modern menu of international dishes on first floor.

GREECE

Stratos Vassilikos 180 VISA

Mihalakopoulou 114 (via Mihalakopoulou, past Holiday Inn) ✉ 115 27 – Ⓜ Megaro Moussikis – ✆ (210) 7706 611 – stratos-vassilikos@airotel.gr – Fax (210) 7708 1 37 – www.airotel.gr

82 rm – 142 € – 6 suites

Rest – Carte approx. 40 €

♦ Business ♦ Modern ♦

Elegant, modern hotel with an interesting décor, set away from the city centre. Spacious well-furnished bedrooms, some with balconies. Riva restaurant in the atrium for lunch or formal dinner.

Park H. Athens < Athens, rm 700

10 Alexandras Ave ✉ 106 82 – Ⓜ Victoria VISA

– ✆ (210) 8894 500 – sales@athensparkhotel.gr – Fax (210) 8238 4 20 – www.athensparkhotel.gr **B1**

140 rm – 175 € – 10 suites

Rest *Alexandra's* – Carte 18/40 € – **Rest *Park Café*** – Carte 18/40 €

Rest *St'Astra* – *(closed Sunday)* Carte 50/100 €

♦ Business ♦ Traditional ♦ Classic ♦

Modern, family-owned hotel between the archaeological museum and Pedio Areos Park. Smartly fitted rooms, suites with spa baths. Dine in Alexandra's with piano accompaniment. All day Park Café for a light meal. Enjoy view from St'Astra by rooftop pool and French menu.

Zafolia < Athens, rm 200 VISA

87-89 Alexandras Ave ✉ 114 74 – ✆ (210) 6449 002 – info@zafoliahotel.gr – Fax (210) 6442 0 42 – www.zafoliahotel.gr **C1**

185 rm – 173 € 162/180 € – 7 suites

Rest – Menu 23/42 €

♦ Business ♦ Modern ♦

Privately-owned, commercial hotel on east side of city. Well-equipped rooms with modern amenities, some with private balcony. Excellent views from rooftop bar and pool. Shop-fitted mezzanine level restaurant. Greek and international menu.

Holiday Inn < rm 650 VISA

50 Mihalakopoulou ✉ 115 28 – Ⓜ Megaro Moussikis – ✆ (210) 7278 000 – info@hiathens.com – Fax (210) 7278 6 00 – www.hiathens.com **D2**

192 rm – 520 € 450/1000 €, 22 €

Rest – Carte 25/55 €

♦ Chain hotel ♦ Business ♦ Modern ♦

Modern corporate hotel with extensive state-of-the-art conference facilities. All bedrooms are aimed at the commercial traveller. Plaza Restaurant offers international menu; light meals in summer in poolside roof garden commanding far-reaching city views.

Holiday Suites without rest VISA

4 Arnis St (by Mihalakopoulou) ✉ 115 28 – Ⓜ Megaro Moussikis – ✆ (210) 7278 500 – info@holiday-suites.com – Fax (210) 7278 6 00 – www.holiday-suites.com

34 rm – 550 € 520/550 €, 18 €

Rest *Holiday Inn* – see below

♦ Business ♦ Modern ♦

Converted apartments in quiet residential area. Spacious rooms each with kitchenette and work area, superbly equipped with CD/DVD/fax. Breakfast here or at Holiday Inn.

Divani Palace Acropolis rm 300 VISA

19-25 Parthenonos ✉ 117 42 – Ⓜ Akropolis – ✆ (210) 9280 100 – divanis@divaniacropolis.gr – Fax (210) 9214 9 93 – www.divaniacropolis.gr **B3**

242 rm – 285 € 240/285 €, 27 € – 8 suites

Rest *Aspassia* – Menu 36 € – Carte 36/60 € – **Rest *Roof Garden*** – Carte 42/55 €

♦ Traditional ♦ Classic ♦

Near the Parthenon yet fairly quiet with parts of Themistocles' wall in the basement. Particularly comfortable suites. Aspassia for formal meals. Roof Garden for barbecue buffet with live music.

The Athenian Callirhoe without rest

32 Kallirois Ave and Petmeza ✉ 117 43 100 VISA

– ✆ (210) 9215 353 – hotel@tac.gr – Fax (210) 9215 3 42 – www.tac.gr

84 rm – 160 € 160/400 € **C3**

◆ Business ◆ Stylish ◆

A bright, contemporary boutique hotel with subtle Art Deco styling. City views from the rooftop terrace and balconies of the smartly fitted executive rooms.

Eridanus without rest 60 VISA

78 Pireaus Ave, Keramikos ✉ 104 35 – Ⓜ Thissio – ✆ (210) 5205 360 – eridanus@eridanus.gr – Fax (210) 5200 5 50 – www.eridanus.gr **A2**

38 rm – 185/380 €

◆ Business ◆ Stylish ◆

Contemporary design hotel on a busy main road. Luxurious bedrooms with high-tech equipment and hydro massage showers; some with views of the Acropolis.

Athena Grand 30 VISA

65 Athens St ✉ 105 52 – Ⓜ Omonia – ✆ (210) 3250 900 – athenagrand@grecotel.gr – Fax (210) 3743 6 43 – www.grecotel.gr **B2**

70 rm – 550 €, 25 € – 6 suites

Rest *Meat Me* – Carte 19/37 €

◆ Business ◆ Modern ◆

Totally renovated city centre hotel. Relax in lounge with squashy sofas; take breakfast at marble tables. Individually designed rooms are well equipped. Taverna-style restaurant serves Greek meze dishes; terrace for alfresco dining.

Alexandros 220 VISA

8 Timoleontos Vassou St (via Vas. Sofias off Soutsou D.) ✉ 115 21 – Ⓜ Megaro Moussikis – ✆ (210) 6430 464 – alexandros@airotel.gr – Fax (210) 6441 0 84 – www.airotel.gr

89 rm – 128 €

Rest *Don Giovanni* – Carte 20/32 €

◆ Business ◆ Design ◆

A relaxed, commercial hotel off a very busy avenue in residential area. Simple accommodation is offered in comfortably appointed bedrooms. Don Giovanni is an elegant little restaurant with marble décor offering international/ Mediterranean cuisine with some Greek specialities.

Electra 60 VISA

5 Ermou ✉ 105 63 – Ⓜ Syntagma – ✆ (210) 3378 000 – saleselath@electrahotels.gr – Fax (210) 3220 3 10 – www.electrahotels.gr **C2**

106 rm – 220 € 312 € – 3 suites

Rest – Carte 18/31 €

◆ Business ◆ Modern ◆

Popular tourist hotel within the lively pedestrianised shopping area. Sound-proofed bedrooms are thoughtfully equipped and well maintained, some have spa baths.

Art 40 VISA

27 Marni St ✉ 104 32 – Ⓜ Omonia – ✆ (210) 5240 501 – info@arthotelathens.gr – Fax (210) 5243 3 84 – www.arthotelathens.gr **B1**

30 rm – 105 € 85/150 €

Rest – *(room service only)* Menu 30/60 €

◆ Family ◆ Personalised ◆

The name's the clue: artwork in all areas of this family-owned 21C boutique hotel behind a classic 1930s façade on busy central street. Simply furnished, unfussy bedrooms.

GREECE

Periscope without rest — AC SAT VISA AE

22 Haritos St, Kolonaki ✉ 106 75 – Ⓜ Evangelismos – ✆ (210) 7297 200 – info@periscope.gr – Fax (210) 7297 2 06 – www.periscope.gr **D2**

21 rm ☕ – 🚹195 € 🚹🚹270/450 €

♦ Business ♦ Modern ♦

Minimalism in an area renowned for its smartness; trendy bar has plasma screens and reconditioned Mini Cooper seats! Uniquely-styled rooms boast balconies and enlarged Athenian images on ceiling.

Grand O' — AC SAT VISA AE

2 Pireos, Omonia Sq ✉ 105 52 – Ⓜ Omonia – ✆ (210) 5235 230 – Fax (210) 5234 9 55 – www.classicalhotels.com **B2**

115 rm ☕ – 🚹🚹380/700 €

Rest – Carte approx. 30 €

♦ Business ♦ Modern ♦

Beyond the bronze sculptured door and impressive marbled lobby is a bright and up-to-date hotel. Many of the interior-designed bedrooms overlook the bustling square. Appealing, modern first floor restaurant with international menu.

Acropol — AC SAT 350 VISA AE

1 Pireos, Omonia Sq ✉ 105 52 – Ⓜ Omonia – ✆ (210) 5282 100 – Fax (210) 5231 3 61 – www.classicalhotels.com **B2**

167 rm ☕ – 🚹🚹380/700 €

Rest – Carte approx. 22 €

♦ Business ♦ Modern ♦

Sister hotel to Omonia, blending modern and classic styling. Soundproofed bedrooms and suites offer sanctuary from the hustle and bustle of the city centre below. Spacious Acropol restaurant with extensive international menu or lighter snacks in bar.

Hermes without rest — AC SAT VISA AE

19 Apollonos St ✉ 105 57 – Ⓜ Syntagma – ✆ (210) 3235 514 – hermes@tourhotel.gr – Fax (210) 3211 8 00 – www.hermeshotel.gr **B3**

45 rm ☕ – 🚹120 € 🚹🚹95/135 €

♦ Family ♦ Modern ♦

Small modern hotel, refurbished in 2005, in Plaka near the shops. Stylish lobby and breakfast room. Bedrooms have balcony or terrace and all mod cons.

Arion without rest — AC SAT VISA AE

18 Aglou Dimitriou St ✉ 105 54 – Ⓜ Monastiraki – ✆ (210) 3240 415 – arion@tourhotel.gr – Fax (210) 3222 4 19 – www.arionhotel.gr **B2**

51 rm ☕ – 🚹100 € 🚹🚹80/125 €

♦ Family ♦ Modern ♦

Opened in 2005, a sensibly priced tourist hotel in lively part of city. Roof-top terrace with superb views. Compact, impressive rooms - ask for one that overlooks Acropolis.

Plaka without rest — < Athens, AC SAT VISA AE

7 Kapnikareas and Mitropoleos St ✉ 105 56 – Ⓜ Monastiraki – ✆ (210) 3222 096 – plaka@tourhotel.gr – Fax (210) 3211 8 00 – www.plakahotel.gr **B3**

67 rm ☕ – 🚹145 € 🚹🚹95/145 €

♦ Traditional ♦ Family ♦

Privately owned hotel among shops and tavernas, with a rooftop bar overlooking the old town. Spotless, sensibly priced modern rooms; ask for one with a view of the Acropolis.

Museum without rest ⁂80

16 Bouboulinas St ✉ 106 82 – Ⓜ Victoria – ☎ (210) 3805 611 – museum@hotelsofathens.com – Fax (210) 3800 5 07 – www.hotelsofathens.com **B1**

93 rm – 80 € 75/160 €

◆ Family ◆ Functional ◆

Overlooking the National Archaeological Museum and offering comfy facilities; extension rooms are more stylish and modern. Other rooms all benefit from balcony views.

Spondi

5 Pyronos, off Varnava Sq, Pangrati ✉ 116 36 – ☎ (210) 7564 021 – spond@relaischateaux.com – Fax (210) 7567 0 21 – www.spondi.gr closed 1 week Easter and 10-16 August **D3**

Rest – Menu 95/122 € – Carte 76/114 €

Spec. Frog's legs with peanut crust, celery purée with coconut milk and salad leaves. Sea bass in walnut crust with rocket and botargo. Apple millefeuille with bourbon vanilla infusion.

◆ French ◆ Formal ◆

Attractive converted villa creating an intimate atmosphere in its elegant rooms and external courtyard and terraces. Outstanding modern French cooking.

Pil Poul et Jérôme Serres < Acropolis,

51 Apostolou Pavlou, Thissio ✉ 118 51 – Ⓜ Thissio – ☎ (210) 342 36 65 – jerome.serres@pilpoul.gr – Fax (210) 341 30 46 – www.pilpoul.gr **A3**
closed 5 days at Easter, 15-20 August, 25-26 December, 1-2 January and Sunday 30 September-1 May

Rest – *(dinner only)* Menu 62/84 € – Carte 64/80 €

Spec. 'Forgotten vegetables', artichoke mousse, truffle sauce. Monkfish, ouzo bonbon, hazelnut risotto. Pineapple with bergamot ice cream.

◆ French ◆ Elegant ◆

Opened in 2006 on the first floor of a restored former hat maker's mansion in a lively part of the city. Superb Acropolis views from the rooftop terrace. Classic French cuisine in a modern idiom.

GB Roof Garden – Grande Bretagne H. < Athens and Acropolis,

Constitution Sq ✉ 105 63 – Ⓜ Syntagma – ☎ (210) 3330 000 – info@grandebretagne.gr – Fax (210) 3228 0 34 **C2**

Rest – *(dinner only)* Menu 55/65 € – Carte 52/70 €

◆ Mediterranean ◆ Formal ◆

The full length windows make the most of the spectacular views. Plush and very comfortable roof-top dining room with lively bar. Elegantly dressed tables and formal service.

Varoulko (Lefteris)

80 Pireaus Ave, Keramikos ✉ 104 35 – Ⓜ Thissio – ☎ (210) 5228 400 – info@varoulko.gr – Fax (210) 5228 8 00 – www.varoulko.gr closed Sunday **A2**

Rest – *(booking essential) (dinner only)* Menu 55 € – Carte 50/60 €

Spec. Cuttlefish ink soup with grouper. Noodles with seafood. John Dory with lentils.

◆ Seafood ◆ Fashionable ◆

Modern, stylish restaurant in converted house with roof terrace and view of the Acropolis. À la carte and tasting menu of finest local seafood. Accomplished cooking.

Boschetto

Evangelismou, off Vas. Sofias & Gennadiou St. ✉ 106 76 – Ⓜ Evangelismos – ☎ (210) 7210 893 – info@boschetto.gr – Fax (210) 7223 5 98 – www.boschetto.gr closed 1 week August **D2**

Rest – Carte 48/75 €

◆ Italian ◆ Formal ◆

Attractive summer house secluded within the neatly trimmed hedge of this small city park. Polished service of an elaborate international menu with strong Italian influences.

XX

48 The Restaurant

48 Armatolon and Klefton ✉ 114 71 – Ⓜ Ambelokipi – ✆ (210) 6411 082 – 48_ilta@otenet.gr – Fax 6462 1 82 – www.48therestaurant.com
closed June-1 September and Sunday **D1**
Rest – *(dinner only)* Menu 48 € – Carte 53/76 €
◆ Inventive ◆ Design ◆
Trendy, atmospheric restaurant where minimalism holds sway, underpinned by modern art on the walls. Dishes, accordingly, are an evolving, modish reworking of Greek classics.

XX

Hytra

Navarhou Apostoli 7, Psirri ✉ 105 54 – Ⓜ Monastiraki – ✆ (210) 3316 767 – Fax (210) 3316 7 67
closed Easter-October and Sunday **B2**
Rest – *(dinner only)* Menu 37/45 € – Carte 39/45 €
◆ Inventive ◆ Trendy ◆
Refurbished, vibrant modern restaurant in trendy Psirri. Modish Greek menus, innovative in places; reworking of Greek classics. Friendly, knowledgeable service.

XX

Kiku

12 Dimokritou St, Kolonaki ✉ 106 73 – Ⓜ Syntagma – ✆ (210) 3647 033 – athenskiku@yahoo.gr – Fax (210) 3626 2 39 – www.kiku.com
closed 4 days Easter, July-3 September, 25 December and Sunday **C2**
Rest – Menu 30/80 € – Carte 33/54 €
◆ Japanese ◆ Minimalist ◆
Authentic Japanese restaurant hidden away in a quiet side street. Clean, crisp, minimalist interior and large sushi counter with mood changing lighting.

XX

Luna Rossa

213 Sokratous, Kallithea (Southwest : 4 km) ✉ 176 74 – ✆ (210) 9423 777 – info@lunarossa.gr – Fax (210) 9328 1 46 – www.lunarossa.gr
closed 3 days Easter, August and Sunday dinner
Rest – *(lunch by arrangement)* Menu 40/60 € (lunch) – Carte 46/93 €
◆ Italian ◆ Family ◆
Delightful and intimate converted house which still feels like a family home. Divided into four dining rooms and small terrace. Authentic Italian cooking with Roman base.

X

Psara's

16 Erehtheos and Erotokritou St, Plaka ✉ 105 56 – Ⓜ Monastiraki – ✆ (210) 3218 733 – Fax (210) 3218 7 34 **B3**
Rest – Menu 15/40 € – Carte 19/31 €
◆ Traditional ◆ Rustic ◆
Just below the Acropolis; has been a taverna since 1898. Refurbished rustic style within two yellow-washed houses with terrace. Fresh ingredients enhance classic taverna menus.

X

Prytanio

7 Milioni St, Kolonaki ✉ 106 73 – ✆ (210) 3643 353 – info@prytaneion.gr – Fax (210) 8082 5 77 – www.prytaneion.gr **C2**
Rest – Carte 21/63 €
◆ Mediterranean ◆ Bistro ◆
Watch the fashionable shoppers go by from a table on the terrace or choose the more intimate interior or the garden. Pleasant service and modern Mediterranean-influenced menu.

X

Oraia Penteli

Iroon Sq, Psirri ✉ 105 54 – Ⓜ Monastiraki – ✆ (210) 3218 627 – Fax (210) 3218 6 27 **B2**
Rest – Carte 12/31 €
◆ Traditional ◆ Rustic ◆
Historic building in the centre of Psirri converted into café-restaurant preparing traditional Greek recipes; live Greek music mid-week evenings and weekend afternoons.

ENVIRONS OF ATHENS

at Kifissia Northeast : 15 km by Vas. Sofias

Pentelikon AC ⇆rm 350 P VISA MO AE

66 Diligianni St, Kefalari (off Harilaou Trikoupi, follow signs to Politia) ⊠ 145 62 – M Kifissia – ☏ (210) 6230 650 – pentilik@otenet.gr – Fax (210) 8019 2 23 – www.pentelikon.gr

94 rm – †380 € ††315/380 €, 26 € – 7 suites

Rest *Vardis* – see below

Rest *La Terrasse* – Carte 40/58 €

♦ Grand Luxury ♦ Traditional ♦ Classic ♦

Imposing late 19C mansion in affluent residential suburb. Opulence and antiques throughout. Most charming and tranquil rooms overlook the gardens. Traditional service. Conservatory restaurant with a Mediterranean theme offering full range of dishes.

Theoxenia Palace AC ⇆rm 350 VISA MO AE

2 Filadelfeos St ⊠ 145 62 – M Kifissia – ☏ (210) 6233 622 – reservations@theoxeniapalace.com – Fax (210) 6231 6 75 – www.theoxeniapalace.com

69 rm – †345 € ††370 € – 2 suites

Rest – Carte 36/47 €

♦ Business ♦ Modern ♦

Renovated 1920s hotel with imposing façade. Spacious well-equipped rooms. Good leisure and large conference/banqueting facilities. Informal dining room.

Theoxenia House without rest AC 80 VISA MO AE

42 Charilaou Trikoupi St and 9 Pentelis St ⊠ 145 62 – M Kifissia – ☏ (210) 6233 622 – reservations@theoxeniapalace.com – Fax (210) 6231 6 75 – www.theoxeniapalace.com

11 rm – ††380 € – 1 suite

♦ Business ♦ Modern ♦

Stylish house in pleasant suburb converted to provide very large, well-equipped rooms, each with lounge area and cooking facilities, plus full use of Theoxenia Palace hotel.

The Kefalari Suites without rest AC ⇆ VISA MO AE

1 Pentelis and Kolokotroni St, Kefalari ⊠ 145 62 – M Kifissia – ☏ (210) 6233 333 – info@kefalarisuites.gr – Fax (210) 6233 3 30 – www.kefalarisuites.gr

2 rm – ††200 € – 11 suites – †250 € ††250 €

♦ Townhouse ♦ Stylish ♦

Early 20C villa set in a smart, quiet suburb; stylish, airy, thoughtfully appointed rooms, each on a subtle, imaginative theme, most with lounge and veranda. Rooftop spa bath.

Semiramis AC ⇆rm 160 VISA MO AE

48 Charilaou Trikoupi St, Kefalari ⊠ 145 62 – M Kifissia – ☏ (210) 6284 400 – info@semiramisathens.com – Fax (210) 6284 4 99 – www.semiramisathens.com

50 rm – ††265 € – 1 suite

Rest – Carte 30/50 €

♦ Business ♦ Modern ♦

Striking 1930s conversion accentuated by lime green balconies, boldly hued public areas and organic shaped pool. Rooms with no numbers on the doors and stunning interiors. Dine on soft seats at a mix of tables; Greek dishes meet mainstream Med style.

GREECE

Twenty One

21 Kolokotroni and Mykonou St, Kefalari ✉ 145 62 – Ⓜ Kifissia – ✆ (210) 6233 521 – info@twentyone.gr – Fax (210) 6233 8 21 – www.twentyone.gr

21 rm – 190/290 €

Rest – Carte 26/36 €

◆ Business ◆ Modern ◆

Converted slate grey 19C former watermill in pleasant suburb. Flowing minimalistic interior. Standard rooms are well designed, some with balconies; five trendy loft suites. Informal dining room and expansive terrace; simple international menus.

Vardis – at Pentelikon H.

66 Diligianni St, Kefalari (off Harilaou Trikoupi, follow signs to Politia) ✉ 145 62 – Ⓜ Kifissia – ✆ (210) 6230 660 – vardis@hotelpentelikon.gr – Fax (210) 8019 2 23 – www.hotelpentelikon.gr

closed 2 weeks August, 25 December, 1 January and Sunday

Rest – *(booking essential) (dinner only)* Carte 60/90 €

◆ French ◆ Formal ◆

Elegant, ornately decorated restaurant with extensive terrace. Fine table settings. Formal and polished service of elaborate classic French/ Mediterranean-influenced cuisine.

at Ekali Northeast : 20 km by Vas. Sofias

Life Gallery

103 Thisseos Ave ✉ 145 78 – ✆ (210) 6260 400 – info-lifegallery@bluegr.com – Fax (210) 6229 3 53 – www.bluegr.com

30 rm – 270 € 690/990 €

Rest – *(closed Sunday and Monday dinner) (residents only Sunday and Monday)* Carte 35/73 €

◆ Luxury ◆ Stylish ◆

Strikingly smart 'glass cube' with discreet yet eye-catchingly contemporary décor at every turn: don't miss the modern library. Sleek, stylish bedrooms all boast balconies. Bright, spacious restaurant with capacious outdoor terrace. Mediterranean-influenced menus.

at Athens International Airport East : 35 km by Vas. Sofias

Sofitel Athens Airport

✉ 190 19 – Ⓜ Airport – ✆ (210) 3544 000 – h3167@accor.com – Fax (210) 3544 4 44 – www.sofitel.com

332 rm – 373 €, 22 € – 13 suites

Rest *Karavi* – *(dinner only)* Menu 35 € – Carte 61/100 €

Rest *Mesoghaia* – *✆ (210) 3544 920 (closed Saturday and Sunday lunch)* Menu 28 € – Carte 31/67 €

◆ Business ◆ Modern ◆

First hotel at the new airport. Modern and very well equipped from comfy library bar to exclusive leisure club. Spacious rooms and impressive bathrooms. French menus on the 9th floor in Karavi. Informal brightly decorated Mediterranean-themed Mesoghaia.

at Vouliagmeni South : 18 km by Singrou

Astir Palace - The Westin

40 Apollonos St ✉ 166 71 – ✆ (210) 8902 000 – reservation@astir.gr – Fax (210) 8962 5 82 – www.astir-palace.com

153 rm – 480 € – 9 suites

Rest *Sao* – Menu 50 €

Rest *Kymata* – Carte 35/60 €

◆ Luxury ◆ Modern ◆

Recently transformed vast 75 acre resort complex on its own peninsula. Supremely comfortable hotel with private beaches and extensive facilities. Delightful bedrooms. Fusion cooking in Sao with its own terrace. All day dining in Kymata with a Mediterranean menu.

Astir Palace - Arion

550 P VISA AE

40 Apollonos St ✉ 166 71 – ✆ (210) 8902 000 – reservation@astir.gr – Fax (210) 8962 5 82 – www.astir-palace.com

107 rm – 420 € – 16 suites

Rest *Alia* – Carte 30/50 €

Rest *Grill Room* – Carte approx. 50 €

◆ Luxury ◆ Modern ◆

Next door to the Westin and sharing many of the wide-ranging facilities. Bedrooms are large, contemporary in style and most have balconies. Relaxed sophistication and a Mediterranean menu at Alia. International cuisine and local seafood in the Grill Room.

Divani Apollon Palace

Saronic Gulf, rm 1200 VISA AE

10 Ag. Nikolaou and Iliou St (Kavouri) off Athinas ✉ 166 71 – ✆ (210) 8911 100 – divanis@divaniapollon.gr – Fax (210) 9658 0 10 – www.divanis.com

286 rm – 720 € 620/740 €

Rest *Mythos* – *(closed Sunday) (dinner only)* Carte 58/89 €

Rest *Anemos* – Carte 45/67 €

◆ Luxury ◆ Modern ◆

Modern hotel in fashionable resort. Poolside lounge. Spa and thalassotherapy centre. Every bedroom boasts balcony overlooking the Saronic Gulf. Small private beach. Dine in Mythos on the beach with local dishes. Anemos is modern with global fare.

The Margi

500 VISA AE

11 Litous St, off Athinas by Apollonos ✉ 166 71 – ✆ (210) 8929 000 – sales@themargi.gr – Fax (210) 8929 1 43 – www.themargi.gr

88 rm – 210 € 210/280 €

Rest – Carte 30/59 €

◆ Business ◆ Stylish ◆

A stylish hotel that combines contemporary elegance with a colonial feel. Breakfast can be taken on the poolside terrace. Bedrooms have antique pieces and smart marble bathrooms. Informal restaurant with its eclectic menu is popular with the 'in crowd'.

Ithaki

Bay, P VISA AE

28 Apollonos St ✉ 166 71 – ✆ (210) 8963 747 – ithaki@enternet.gr – Fax (210) 8963 7 72 – www.ithakirestaurantbar.gr

closed 2 days Easter

Rest – Carte 53/76 €

◆ Seafood ◆ Formal ◆

A long standing but revitalised restaurant with a truly stunning terrace. Open and spacious dining room with on-view wine cellar. Classical cooking with local seafood a speciality.

at Kalamaki Southwest : 14 km by Singrou

Akrotiri

P VISA AE

Vas. Georgiou B5, Agios Kosmas, Elliniko ✉ 167 77 – ✆ (210) 9859 147 – akrotiri@enternet.gr – Fax (210) 9859 1 49 – www.akrotirilounge.gr

Rest – *(dinner only)* Menu 50/75 € – Carte 49/64 €

◆ French ◆ Fashionable ◆

A seaside restaurant combining simplicity and luxury. Candlelit dinners on the pool terrace; DJ music. Menu of good quality international cuisine with French influence.

HUNGARY
MAGYARORSZÁG

PROFILE

- **Area:** 93 032 km^2 (35 920 sq mi).
- **Population:** 10 007 000 inhabitants (est. 2005), density = 108 per km^2.
- **Capital:** Budapest (conurbation 2 232 000 inhabitants).
- **Currency:** Forint (Ft or HUF); rate of exchange: HUF 100 = € 0.39 = US$ 0.51 (Nov 2006).
- **Government:** Parliamentary republic (since 1989). Member of European Union since 2004.
- **Language:** Hungarian; many Hungarians also speak English and German.
- **Specific public holidays:** 1848 Revolution Day (15 March); National Day-St. Stephen Day (20 August); Republic Day-1956 Uprising Remembrance Day (23 October); All Saints' Day (1 November); Boxing Day (25-26 December).
- **Local time:** GMT + 1 hour in winter and GMT + 2 hours in summer.
- **Climate:** Temperate continental with cold winters and warm summers (Budapest: January: -1°C, July: 22°C).
- **International dialling Code:** **00 36** followed by area code (1 for Budapest) and local number. International enquiries: ✆ **199.**
- **Emergency:** Central emergency line: ✆ **112**; Ambulance: ✆ **104**, Fire Brigade: ✆ **105**, Police: ✆ **107**, Roadside breakdown service: ✆ **188**.
- **Electricity:** 220 volts, 50 Hz; 2-pin round-shaped continental plugs.

FORMALITIES

Travellers from the European Union (EU), Switzerland, Iceland and the main countries of North and South America need a national identity card or passport (America: passport required) to visit Hungary for less than three months (tourism or business purpose). For visitors from other countries a visa may be required, in addition to a passport, especially for those wishing to stay for longer than three months. We advise you to check with your embassy before travelling.

A valid driving licence is essential. The larger car rental companies require that the driver is at least 18 years old with at least one year's driving experience.

MAJOR NEWSPAPERS

The main dailies are *Magyar Nemzet, Népszabadság* and *Magyar Hirlap*. The *Budapest Sun*, the *Budapest Business Journal* and the *Hungarian Quarterly* are printed in English.

USEFUL PHRASES

ENGLISH	**HUNGARIAN**
Yes	**Igen**
No	**Nem**
Good morning	**Jó**
Goodbye	**Viszlàt**
Thank you	**Köszönöm**
Please	**Kérem**
Excuse me	**Bocsánat**
I don't understand	**Nem értem**

HOTELS

→ CATEGORIES

In Budapest accommodation ranges from luxurious 5-star international hotels, to smaller, family-run guesthouses and paying-guest rooms.

→ PRICE RANGE

The price is per room. There is little difference between the price of a single and a double room.

Budapest is a popular resort throughout the year and it is therefore advisable to book in advance. However some hotel chains offer lower weekend rates in low season.

→ TAX

Included in the room price.

→ CHECK OUT TIME

Usually between 10am and noon.

→ RESERVATIONS

By telephone or by Internet. A credit card number may be required.

→ TIP FOR LUGGAGE HANDLING

At the discretion of the customer (about Ft 500 per bag).

→ BREAKFAST

It is often not included in the price of the room and is generally served between 7am and 10am. Most hotels offer a self-service buffet but it is usually possible in the more expensive hotels to have continental breakfast served in the room.

Reception	**Recepció**
Single room	**Egyágyas szoba**
Double room	**Kétágyas szoba**
Bed	**Ágy**
Bathroom	**Fürdö szoba**
Shower	**Tusoló**

RESTAURANTS

Most **restaurants (étterem)** are in the traditional Hungarian style, sometimes with live gypsy music; most are also privately owned and reflect the philosophy of the chef/patron. There are also Italian, French and other ethnic restaurants.

→ MEALS

Breakfast	**Reggeli**	7am – 10am
Lunch	**Ebéd**	12.30pm – 2-3pm
Dinner	**Vacsora**	6.30pm – 10-11pm

A traditional Hungarian menu does not list starters but they are offered in most restaurants. The majority of menus are à la carte but there are some fixed price menus.

→ RESERVATIONS

Reservations are usually made by phone, fax or Internet. For famous restaurants, it is advisable to book several days in advance. A credit card number or a phone number may be required as guarantee.

→ THE BILL

The bill (check) includes VAT but no service charge. Tipping is optional but, if you are particularly pleased with the service, it is customary to round up to an appropriate figure (10%).

Drink or aperitif	**Rövid ital**
Appetizer	**Étel**
First course, starter	**Elöétel**
Main dish	**Föétel**
Main dish of the day	**Napi ajánlat**
Dessert	**Desszert**
Water	**Víz**
Wine (red, white, rosé)	**Bor (vörös, fehér, rosé)**
Beer, draught beer	**Sör, csapolt sör**
Bread	**Kenyér**
Meat	**Hús**
Fish	**Hal**
Salt/pepper	**Só / Bors**
Cheese	**Sajt**
Vegetables	**Zöldség**
Hot/cold	**Forró / hideg**
The bill (check) please	**A számlát, kérem**

LOCAL CUISINE

Hungarian chefs are versatile and inventive, making good use of local seasonal produce. Many of the dishes are nourishing and hearty – and portions are generous – but not all are flavoured with **paprika**, although the red powder, hot *(csípõs)* or sweet *(édesnemes)*, is much in evidence and on sale in all tourist haunts. Other flavourings are herbs and pickles.

There is little saltwater fish but plenty of freshwater **pike-perch (fogas)** from Lake Balaton and also **trout (pisztráng). Halászlé** is a fish soup made of a mixture of sea and freshwater fish poached with tomatoes, green peppers and paprika. The best known dish is probably **goulash (gulyás)**, a thick soup of beef, onions and potatoes, usually served as a main course; other favourite soup ingredients are beans, dumplings and cabbage. In summer there are cold fruit soups. Menus offer beef and pork, chicken and turkey, goose and game in season, but lamb is rare. The accent of paprika is stronger in dishes such as **töltött káposzta**, stuffed cabbage, and **pörkölt**, meat and onion stew, which is known as **paprikás**, when thickened with flour and sour cream. **Lecsó** is a sauce of onions, tomatoes and stewed peppers, served with meat. Some ingredients – beef and salmon – may be served tartar style. Garlic sausage, salami and goose liver are served as starters, as are smoked fish, ham and goose. Cheeses are made from cow's and ewe's milk; curd cheese is a particular favourite.

Pancakes *(palacsinta)*, dumplings and strudels appear frequently, as savoury (herb dumplings, spinach strudel) or sweet dishes. The wide choice of desserts includes such peaks of Hungarian gastronomy as Gundel pancakes, filled with a walnut mixture and served with hot chocolate sauce; golden dumplings, flavoured with ground walnuts and served with vanilla custard; Somlói galuska, layers of sponge cake and custard, smothered in walnuts, sultanas, chocolate sauce, rum syrup and whipped cream; Eszterházy cake made with ground walnuts, layered with a cream filling and white chocolate coating; Vargabéles, a soft sweet sponge cake made with curd cheese and flavoured with vanilla and raisins; strudels filled with apple, plums or cherries.

DRINK

Hungary has 22 wine regions producing both red and white wine. Best known among the reds is the dark and spicy-flavoured **Egri Bikavér** (Bull's Blood of Eger); there are also distinctive reds from **Villány** and **Szekszárd** and **Kéknyelű**. Among the whites **Olaszrizling** (Italian Riesling), with the taste of bitter almonds, is recommended with fish, **Hárslevelü** with poultry and dry **Furmint** with desserts; the Eger district also produces reputed white wines. The wines from the Tokaj region have the highest alcohol, sugar and acid content of any wines in Hungary. The non-*aszú* Tokaji wines generally have a hard, acidic character, with strong body and bouquet. Bottles bearing the words *édes or félszáraz* cater to the local taste for sweet red and white wine.

The most famous Hungarian wine is the dessert wine, **Tokaji aszú**. The grapes are grown on the south and southwest facing slopes of the foothills of the Zemplén range; the volcanic soil is rich in nutrients. In autumn while the grapes are maturing there is often a period of perhaps one week during which a mild, sunny and dry spell takes over from the otherwise drizzly, damp weather. This favours the development of the Botrytis fungus, which causes the 'noble rot' which makes Tokaji aszú so distinctive. Aszú wines are prepared by adding grapes with the famed 'noble rot' to the wine base; the number of baskets *(puttonyok)* of grapes added is signified in the type of wine – ranging from 3-6 puttonyos. Among speciality wines, the dry and sweet **Szamorodni** wines deserve special mention; they are produced by adding small quantities of *aszú* grapes.

Beer is sold by the half-litre *(korsó)* or a smaller glass *(pohár)*. As well as local brands such as Dreher and Borsodi, bars may also offer the products of German, Austrian, Czech or even Belgian breweries.

Hungary produces its own **brandy (pálinka)**; pear brandy *(körtepálinka)*, apricot brandy *(barackpálinka)* and the plum brandy *(szilvapálinka)* of Szatmár are drunk as aperitifs. **Unicum**, a dark brown herb liqueur with a bitter flavour, is a unique Hungarian aperitif to be drunk sparingly.

BUDAPEST

BUDAPEST

Population (est. 2005): 1 702 000 (conurbation 2 232 000) – Altitude: 102m

R. Mattès/MICHELIN

The Hungarian capital on the River Danube was formed in 1873 by the merger of three towns: Buda, Pest and Òbuda (Old Buda), whose Roman remains are still visible.

Budapest has a continental climate, with cold winters and warm summers. It is a lively, friendly city which has succeeded in integrating modern innovations and architecture with a rich historical heritage, and now offers a wealth of entertainment and cultural activities for visitors. An excellent but inexpensive public transport system of buses, trolleybuses, trams and underground lines covers the city.

Buda and Pest are linked by bridges; the most famous of which are Chain Bridge (Széchenyi Lánchíd), guarded by huge stone lions, and Liberty Bridge (Szabadsághíd), a fine metal structure built at the end of the 19C. The city's golden age was in the 19C which has left a rich legacy of Art Nouveau buildings. Passenger craft provide regular trips on the Danube to see the sights, particularly when they are flood-lit at night, or 20km up stream to Szentendre.

Budapest is a great place for 'taking the waters'; the thermal springs developed into a national institution under the Turkish occupation; some Turkish baths are still in use in their original state; the warm open air baths are popular in winter; there are also modern spa hotels and medical treatment centres.

WHICH DISTRICT TO CHOOSE

The majority of **hotels**, particularly the group hotels and the smaller privately owned ones, are in the commercial district *Plan II* **E2** in Pest on the east bank of the Danube. The castle district *Plan II* **D1** on the west bank of the Danube also has a few hotels.

Restaurants are distributed on the same pattern as the hotels, being mostly in the commercial district *Plan II* **E2** and **F2** in Pest, with a few

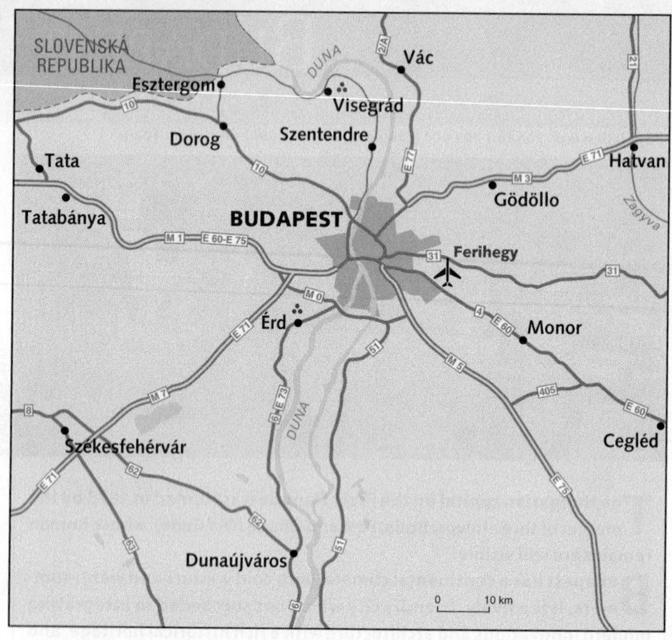

up near the Castle *Plan II* **D1**. There are also some in the Városliget, the City Park next to Heroes Square *Plan I* **B1**. The floating restaurants moored along the east bank of the Danube provide a splendid view at night of the Castle and the flood-lit bridges.

PRACTICAL INFORMATION

ARRIVAL – DEPARTURE

Ferihegy Budapest National Airport – About 24 km (15 mi) southeast of the city centre. ✆ 296 9696; flight information ✆ 296 7000.

From the airport to the city centre – By **airport minibus** to individual hotels. Return fare Ft 3 900. ✆ 296 8555. By **taxi**: 45min-Ft 4 000 to Pest, 1hr 15min-Ft 5 000 to Buda. By **public transport – bus** (20min), BKV Busz (Reptér Busz) which stops between the terminals and **metro** (blue line – 35mins). Fares Ft 190.

Railway Stations – **Eastern Station** (Keleti pályaudvar) *Plan I* **B2**. ✆ 413 4610. **Western Station** (Nyugati Pályaudvar) *Plan I* **A1**. ✆ 349 8503. **Southern Station** (Déli pályaudvar) *Plan II* **C2**. ✆ 375 6593, 461 5400 (domestic services), 461 5500 (international services); www.elvira.hu

River Station – Belgrád Rakpart; **Hydrofoil service** to Budapest from Bratislava (3hr 30min – 6hr) and Vienna (4hr-6hrs 30min) April-October. Ft 19 977.50 (€79). ✆ 318 6042, 484 4000; (passnave@mahartpassnave.hu)

TRANSPORT

→ METRO, TRAM, TROLLEYBUS AND BUS

The extensive public transport network is composed of three metro lines (M1 yellow, M2 red and M3 blue)

intersecting at Deák tér, trams, trolleybuses and buses. Tickets must be purchased in advance and validated in the ticket stampers at the start of the journey; spot checks are made. Tickets are available from metro stations, ticket machines, tobacconists and newsagents. Single Ft 230; different cheaper ticket types are available at metro stations Tourist pass (3 days) Ft 3 100 (see also Budapest Card). ✆ 461 6688 (www.bkv.hu).

→ TAXIS

Authorised taxis display a yellow taxi sign and yellow number plates. It is best to order one through hotel reception (less expensive) or take one waiting outside a hotel. Unauthorised taxis can be very expensive. Maximum basic charge Ft 300 (day), Ft 420 (night); Ft 240 per km (day), Ft 336 per km (night). The larger companies have lower charges. A tip of 10% is generally acceptable. ✆ 233 3333 (Budataxi), 211 1111 (Citytaxi), 222 2222 (Fõtaxi).

→ BUDAPEST CARD

Includes unlimited travel on public transport, free or reduced price admission to 60 museums and sights, cultural and folklore programmes, discounts in some shops, restaurants and thermal baths, discounts on car hire. 48hr-card Ft 6 450; 72hr-card Ft 7 950. On sale at the airport, in Tourist Offices and in some hotels.

USEFUL ADDRESSES

→ TOURIST INFORMATION

Tourinform Main Office, Sütõ u.2, Deák Tér. ✆ 438 8080. Open 8am-8pm. **Buda Castle**, Szentháromság tér (Budai Vár) *Plan II* **D1**. ✆ 488 0474/5. Open mid-Jun to mid-Sep 9am-8pm, otherwise 10am-7pm (Nov-Mar Mon-Fri 10am-7pm, Sat-Sun 10am-4pm). **Western Railway Station** (Nyugati Pályaudvar) *Plan I* **A1**. ✆ 302 8580. Open mid-Jun to mid-Sep 9am-7pm, otherwise Mon-Fri 9am-6pm, Sat-Sun 9am-3pm. **Ferihegy Airport**, Terminals 2A and 2B. ✆ 438 8080, 488 4661. Open 8am-11pm. **Tourinform Hotline** ✆ (06 80) 630 800; from abroad ✆ (0036 30) 30 30 600; hungary@tourinform.hu; info@budapestinfo.hu; www.hungarytourism.hu; www.budapestinfo.hu

→ POST OFFICES

Opening times Mon-Fri 8am-6pm, Sat, 8am-1pm. Longer opening hours at Teréz körút 51, Mon-Sat 7am-8pm, Sun 8am-6pm and at the **Eastern Railway Station**, Baross tér, Mon-Fri 7am-9pm, Sat 8am-2pm.

→ BANKS/CURRENCY EXCHANGE

Opening times Mon-Thurs 8.30am to 3pm, Fri 8am-1pm. There are ATMs at most banks and many currency exchange machines.

→ EMERGENCY

Central emergency line ✆ **112**; Ambulance ✆ **104**; Fire Brigade ✆ **105**; Police ✆ **107**; Roadside breakdown service ✆ **188**.

BUSY PERIODS

It may be difficult to find a room at a reasonable price when special events are held in the city:

Budapest Spring Festival: 13 March-1 April – music, opera, ballet and folklore performances.

Budapest Búcsú: 23-24 June – rock and pop music festival celebrating the departure of the Soviet army.

Sziget Festival: 8-15 August – 8-day multicultural popular music festival on Hajógyári Island.

St Stephens' Day: August 20th – 3 day festival of events and fireworks to commemorate the first King of Hungary.

Formula 1 Grand Prix: 3-5 August.

Budapest International Wine and Champagne Festival: 5-9 September.

Budapest Christmas Fair: December.

EXPLORING BUDAPEST

DIFFERENT FACETS OF THE CITY

It is possible to visit the main sights and some museums in three days.

Museums and sights are usually open from 10am to 6pm. Most museums are closed on Monday.

CASTLE HILL – **Budavári Palota** *Plan II* **D2**: the Royal Castle *(funicular railway from Chain Bridge)* is the former royal residence, built in Classical and Baroque style. **Mátyás Templom** *Plan II* **D1**: 13C Gothic church with glazed tile roof. **Várnegyed** *Plan II* **D2**: charming old streets lined with medieval houses, Baroque mansions, small interior courtyards and other interesting buildings; in summer, horse-drawn carriage rides.

MUSEUMS AND GALLERIES – **BUDA**: **Magyar Nemzeti Galéria** *Plan II* **D2**: Hungarian art with medieval sculpture; 19C and 20C paintings and sculptures. **Budapesti Történeti Múzeum** *Plan II* **D2**: History of Budapest from the Magyar period. **PEST**: **Szépművészeti Múzeum** *Plan I* **B1**: National Museum of Fine Arts (gallery of Old Masters, paintings from the Spanish School, drawing and print room). **Magyar Nemzeti Múzeum** *Plan II* **F3**: Hungarian National Museum tracing the country's history from prehistoric times to the 1848 revolution. **Iparművészeti Múzeum** *Plan I* **B2**: Museum of Applied Arts, housed in an Art Nouveau building; reconstructions of Hungarian and European interiors.

PEST – **Országház** *Plan II* **E1**: the Parliament with its pinnacle turrets, arcades and flying buttresses fronting the river, displays St Stephen's crown. **Szent István Bazilika**: immense domed basilica dedicated to the first king of Hungary. **Magyar Állami Operaház** *Plan II* **F1**: impressive Opera House with richly-decorated interior. **Dohány Utcai Zsinagóga** *Plan II* **F2**: Great Synagogue in Byzantine-Moorish style with beautiful interior decoration. **Vásárcsarnok** *Plan II* **F3**: Central Market, an attractive metal structure full of stalls selling fresh food – meat, fish, vegetables, fruit; also linen and crafts *(upper gallery)*.

CITY OF BATHS – Budapest has some 50 thermal baths *(fürdő)*, fed by over 80 active thermal springs and wells. **Király** *Plan I* **A1**, **Rácz** and **Rudas** *Plan II* **E3** are Turkish baths preserved in their original state. The **Gellért Baths** *Plan II* **E3** opened in 1918; the pool, built in the former greenhouse, is renowned for its mosaics, columns and balconies. **Széchenyi Baths** *Plan I* **B1** are housed in a huge neo-Classical building with domes, pediments, statues and a late 19C interior; floating chessboards in the open-air pool. **Danubius Health Spa and Resort Margitsziget** *Plan I* **A1** part of a luxury modern hotel on Margaret Island.

OUTDOOR BUDAPEST – **Hősök tere and Városliget** *Plan I* **B1**: Heroes Square, marked by the Millennium Monument, a column symbolising 1 000 years of Hungarian history, leads into City Park; zoo, circus and amusement park. **MargitSziget** *Plan I* **A1**: a green island of tranquillity; lawns, flower beds, trees, walks, play areas, sports grounds, swimming pools, pump rooms and hotels. **Gyermekvasút**: the Children's (Pioneers') Train, staffed by children, runs mainly through woods (12km/7.5miles) in the Buda Hills; from Janós-Hegy Tokaji station a path leads up to a viewing tower with a magnificent panorama *(From near Hotel Budapest take the rack railway to the top of Mount Széchenyi; walk to the Children's Train Station)*.

GOURMET TREATS

The cafés and tea rooms of Budapest offer a great array of **pastries** and **cakes** – strudels, sponges and layer cakes, chocolate confections and a variety of ice creams. Drinks range from **coffee** (introduced by the Turks), **hot chocolate** and **tea** to freshly pressed **fruit juices** – orange, peach. For refreshment and shade in summer or warmth and shelter in winter, take a seat in a café/tea house: *Gerbeaud Plan II* **E2**; *Zsolnay* in the Béke Hotel *Plan II* **F1**; *Hauer*, Rákóczi Ut; *Mozart*, Erzsébet Bld; *Gellért Hotel Plan II* **E3**.

SHOPPING

Stores are usually open from Mon-Fri 10am to 6pm (7pm Thurs), Sat 9am-1pm; food stores 7am-6pm. Large shopping centres are open daily, 9/10am to 9pm.

The main shopping area is **Váci utca** *Plan II* **E2**, a pedestrianised street, which links **Vörösmarty Square** *Plan II* **E2** and **Fövám Tér** and is lined, above and below ground, with fashion boutiques, indoor and pavement cafés, jewellers shops, bookstores and street vendors; also some of the side streets, such as **Párizsi Udvar** (the Paris Arcade is worth seeing if only for its architecture) and **Kígyó ut**. For Hungarian folk art try *Folkart Centrum*, Váci utca 58. *The House of Hungarian Wines*, Szentháromság tér, on Castle Hill, offers wine tasting and a detailed display about Hungarian wine.

WHAT TO BUY – Herend porcelain, Zsolnay porcelain, leather goods, embroidery and lace, Tokaj (Tokaij) and other Hungarian wines, paprika, salami, palinka, goose liver, Szamos marzipan, dried fruit, pasta in fancy shapes.

ENTERTAINMENT

Budapest City Guide, published in English and German by the Budapest Tourist Office, is a good source of information about cultural events in Budapest.

CONCERT HALLS – **Hungarian State Opera House** *Plan II* **F1**: opera and ballet. **Academy of Music** *Plan II* **E2**. **Budai Vigadó** *Plan II* **D1**: Hungarian State Folk Ensemble.

THEATRES – **National Theatre** *Plan II* **E2**. **Vigszínház Comedy Theatre** *Plan I* **A1**. **Katona József** *Plan II* **E2**. **International Buda Stage (IBS). Merlin International Theatre** *Plan II* **F2**.

OTHER VENUES – **Várszínház** *Plan II* **D2**. **The National Dance Theatre. Contemporary Dance Theatre Society** *Plan I* **A2**.

NIGHTLIFE

Budapest City Guide, published by the Budapest Tourist Office, lists places for music and dancing. There are a number of addresses in the side streets around **Kálvin tér.** *Plan II* **F3** and also in the side streets off **Andrássy út**. between the Opera and the Octagon *Plan II* **F1**.

PEST

Plan II

Four Seasons Gresham Palace

Roosevelt tér 5-6 ✉ 1051 – Ⓜ Vörösmarty tér – ✆ 268 6000 – budapest.reservations@fourseasons.com – Fax 268 50 00 – www.fourseasons.com/budapest **E2**

90

179 rm – ††81020 HUF, ☕ 6330 HUF

Rest *Páva* – *(closed Sunday) (dinner only)* Carte 10890/17470 HUF

Rest *Gresham Kávénáz* – *✆ 268 5110* – Carte 8100/10890 HUF

♦ Grand Luxury ♦ Business ♦ Classic ♦

Art Nouveau palace on the Danube converted into an elegant, modern hotel with excellent service; stunning atrium. Riverside Páva restaurant and terrace offers a menu of seasonal Italian-influenced dishes with modish twist. Kávénáz is coffee house renowned for traditional dishes - and its cakes.

New York Palace

120

Erzébet Krt 9-11 ✉ 1073 – Ⓜ Blaha Tér – ✆ 886 6111 – info@newyorkboscolo.com – Fax 886 61 99 – www.boscolohotels.com *Plan 1* **B 2**

108 rm – †113930 HUF ††63290/113930 HUF, ☕ 6330 HUF – 4 suites

Rest *Deep Water* – *✆ 886 6166* – Menu 7595/15190 HUF – Carte 7595/17215 HUF

Rest *New York Cafe* – Menu 4050/11140 HUF – Carte 4050/11140 HUF

♦ Grand Luxury ♦ Classic ♦

This stunning 1894 former insurance company building opened as a hotel in 2006. Sympathetic renovation has created impressive levels of comfort. Deep Water is for fine dining with wood panelling and formal table settings. The New York Cafe is rightly celebrated for its striking baroque style and long history.

Kempinski H. Corvinus

rm 450

Erzsébet tér 7-8 ✉ 1051 – Ⓜ Deák tér – ✆ 429 3777 – hotel.corvinus@kempinski.com – Fax 429 47 77 – www.kempinski-budapest.com **E2**

337 rm – ††80760 HUF, ☕ 7595 HUF – 28 suites

Rest *Ristorante Giardino* – *(dinner only)* Carte 8600/11600 HUF

Rest *Bistro Jardin* – *(buffet lunch)* Menu 6950/7950 HUF – Carte 8600/11600 HUF

♦ Grand Luxury ♦ Business ♦ Modern ♦

Modern hotel in the heart of the city. Spa boasts panoply of up-to-date treatments. Rooms provide top class comforts and facilities. Italian Ristorante Giardino. Bistro Jardin buffet restaurant.

Corinthia Grand H. Royal

rm 400

Erzsébet krt 43-49 ✉ 1073 – Ⓜ Oktogon – ✆ 479 4000 – royal@corinthia.hu – Fax 479 43 33 – www.corinthia.hu *Plan I* **B2**

383 rm – ††88610 HUF, ☕ 5570 HUF – 31 suites

Rest *Brasserie Royale* – Carte approx. 8000 HUF

Rest *Rickshaw* – *(dinner only)* Carte approx. 6750 HUF

♦ Grand Luxury ♦ Business ♦ Modern ♦

Early 20C grand hotel with impressive atrium. Well appointed bedrooms - particularly Executive - with modern décor in warm colours. Brasserie Royale for pleasant atrium dining. Far Eastern dishes and sushi bar in Rickshaw.

Le Meridien

rm 200

Erzsébet tér 9-10 ✉ 1051 – Ⓜ Deák tér – ✆ 429 5500 – sales@le-meridien.hu – Fax 429 55 55 – www.budapest.lemeridien.com **E2**

203 rm – ††101010 HUF, ☕ 6330 HUF – 15 suites

Rest *Le Bourbon* – Menu 5900/12000 HUF – Carte 5600/8000 HUF

♦ Business ♦ Modern ♦

Top class hotel, ideally located for both business and leisure. Classically furnished, very comfortable bedrooms and particularly smart bathrooms. Atrium styled restaurant with Art Deco glass dome and impressive French-influenced desserts.

Sofitel Budapest

Roosevelt tér 2 ✉ *1051* – Ⓜ *Vörösmarty tér* – ✆ *266 1234* – *h3229-re@accor.com* – *Fax 235 91 01* – *www.sofitel-budapest.com*

VISA MC AE D

E2

328 rm – †50875 HUF ††35750/50875 HUF, ☕ 6600 HUF – 23 suites

Rest *Paris Budapest Café* – Menu 4300/5000 HUF – Carte 6450/9900 HUF

♦ Business ♦ Modern ♦

Modern hotel near Chain Bridge. 'Bibliotheque' and coffee lounge; bi-plane suspended from roof. Comfortable, well-equipped rooms. Café has Hungarian edge to menus: Paris meets Budapest in retro décor.

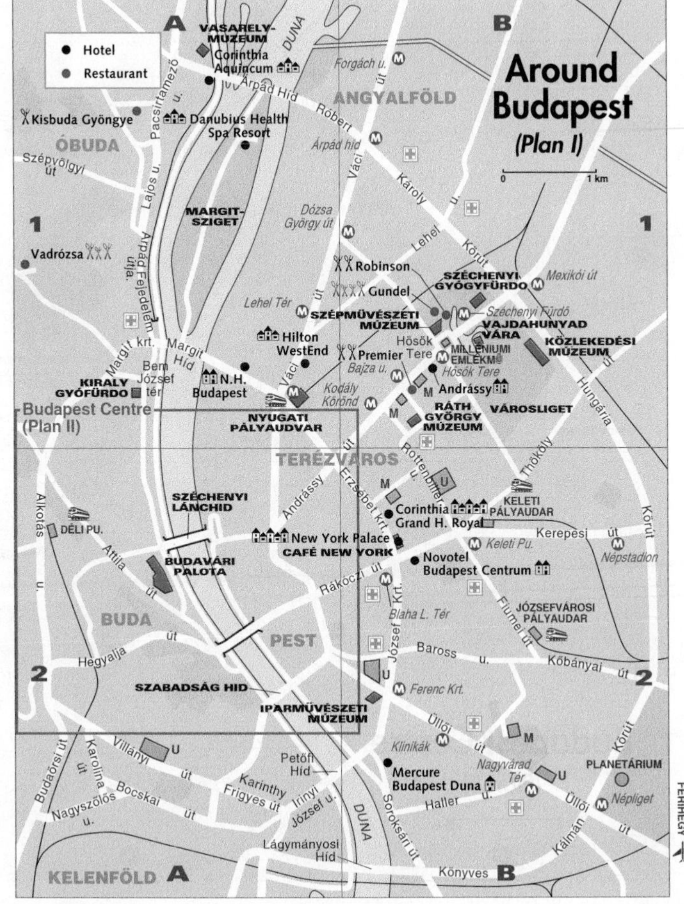

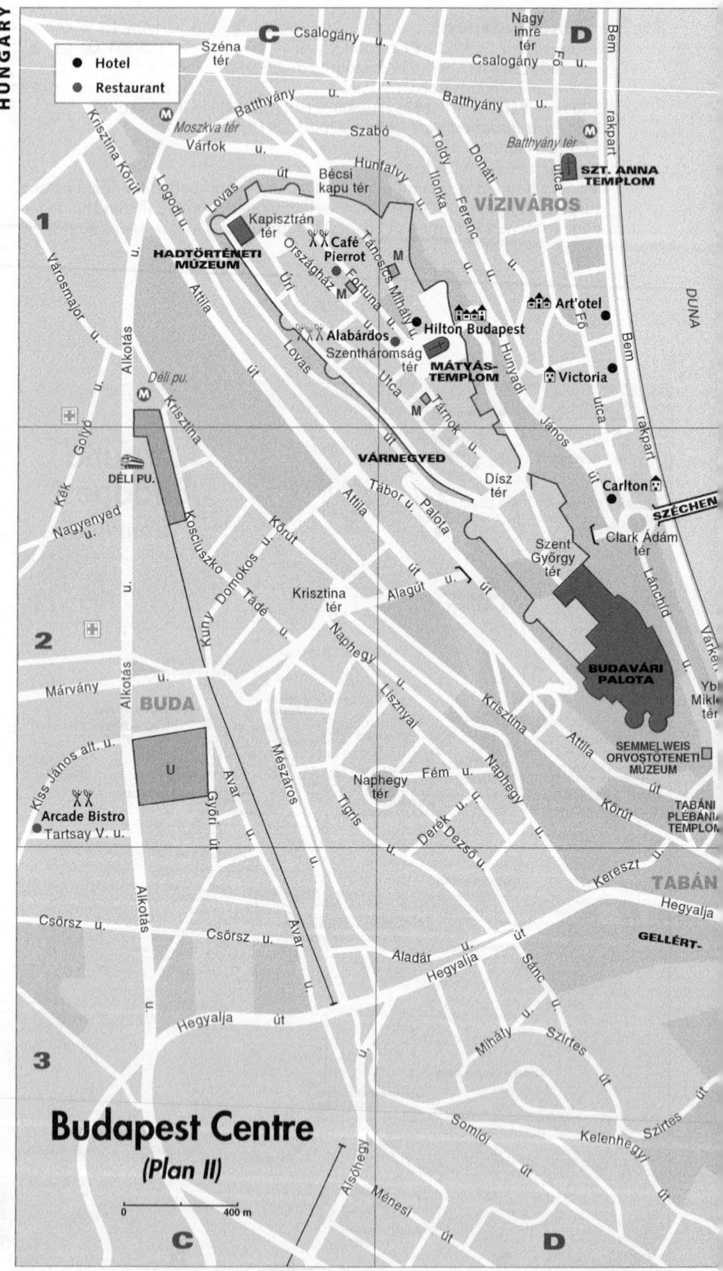
Budapest Centre
(Plan II)
Hotel
Restaurant
0
400 m
C
D
1
2
3
HADTÖRTÉNETI MÚZEUM
SZT. ANNA TEMPLOM
MÁTYÁS-TEMPLOM
BUDAVÁRI PALOTA
SEMMELWEIS ORVOSTÖTENETI MÚZEUM
TABÁNI PLÉBÁNIA TEMPLOM
VÍZIVÁROS
VÁRNEGYED
BUDA
TABÁN
GELLÉRT-
DUNA
Café Pierrot
Alabárdos
Arcade Bistro
Hilton Budapest
Art'otel
Victoria
Carlton
DÉLI PU.
Déli pu.
Széna tér
Moszkva tér
Batthyány tér
Nagy imre tér
Kapisztrán tér
Bécsi kapu tér
Szentháromság tér
Dísz tér
Szent György tér
Clark Ádám tér
Krisztina tér
Naphegy tér
Csalogány u.
Batthyány u.
Szabó
Várfok u.
Hunfalvy u.
Lovas út
Logodi u.
Krisztina körút
Városmajor u.
Országház
Úri
Fortuna
Táncsics Mihály u.
Toldy Ferenc u.
Ilonka
Donáti u.
Fő utca
Bem rakpart
Hunyadi János út
Attila út
Alkotás u.
Golyó u.
Kék
Nagyenyed u.
Kosciuszko Tádé u.
Kuny Domokos u.
Tábor u.
Palota
Tárnok u.
Alagút u.
Lánchíd
Naphegy u.
Lisznyai u.
Márvány u.
Mészáros u.
Avar u.
Győri út
Kiss János alt. u.
Tartsay V. u.
Fém u.
Tigris u.
Derék u.
Dezső u.
Kereszt u.
Hegyalja út
Csörsz u.
Aladár u.
Sánc u.
Mihály u.
Szirtes út
Somlói út
Kelenhegyi út
Alsóhegy u.
Ménesi út
SZÉCHENY
M
U

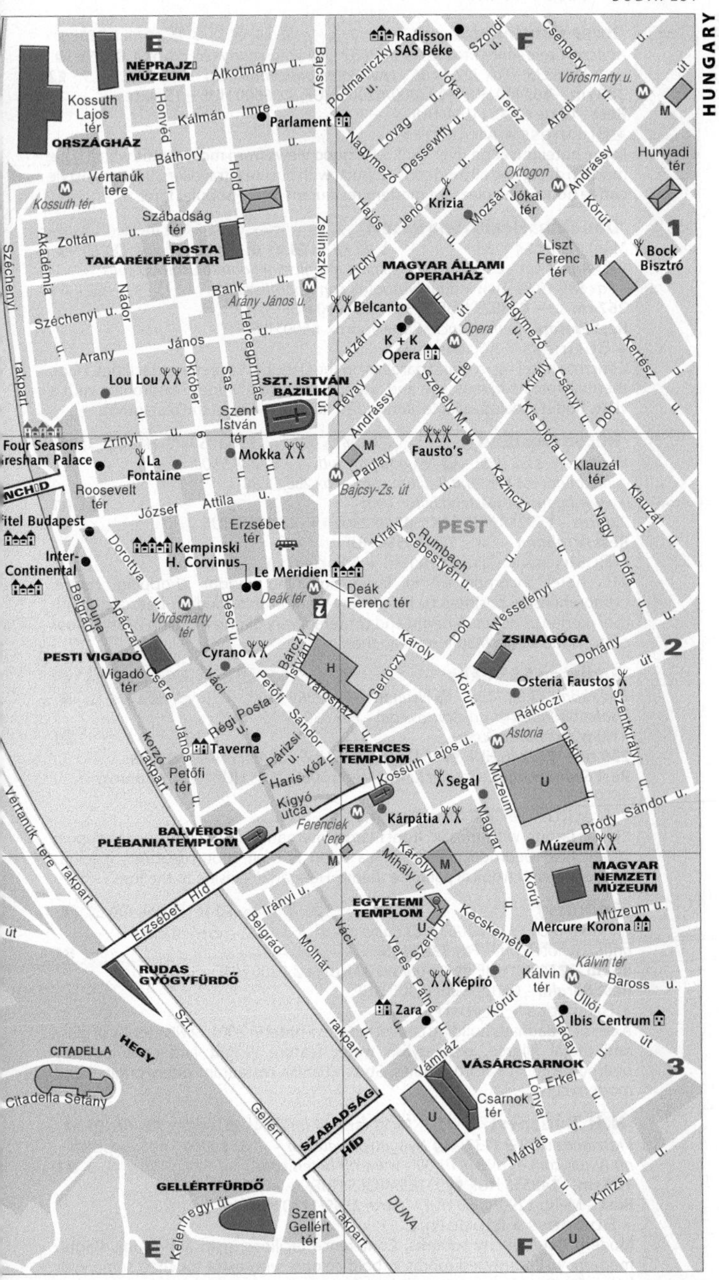

NÉPRAJZI MÚZEUM
Kossuth Lajos tér
ORSZÁGHÁZ
Parlament
Radisson SAS Béke
Vértanúk tere
Kossuth tér
Szabadság tér
POSTA TAKARÉKPÉNZTAR
MAGYAR ÁLLAMI OPERAHÁZ
Belcanto
K + K Opera
Krizia
Oktogon
Jókai tér
Liszt Ferenc tér
Hunyadi tér
Bock Bisztró
Lou Lou
SZT. ISTVÁN BAZILIKA
Szent István tér
Mokka
Fausto's
Four Seasons Gresham Palace
La Fontaine
Roosevelt tér
Erzsébet tér
Kempinski H. Corvinus
Le Meridien
Inter-Continental
Deák tér
Deák Ferenc tér
Vörösmarty tér
PEST
Klauzál tér
ZSINAGÓGA
Osteria Faustos
PESTI VIGADÓ
Vigadó tér
Cyrano
Taverna
Petőfi tér
FERENCES TEMPLOM
Segal
Astoria
Kárpátia
Ferenciek tere
BALVÉROSI PLÉBANIATEMPLOM
Múzeum
MAGYAR NEMZETI MÚZEUM
EGYETEMI TEMPLOM
Mercure Korona
Erzsébet Híd
RUDAS GYÓGYFÜRDŐ
Képíró
Kálvin tér
Ibis Centrum
Zara
VÁSÁRCSARNOK
Csarnok tér
CITADELLA
Citadella Sétány
HEGY
SZABADSÁG HÍD
GELLÉRTFÜRDŐ
Szent Gellért tér
DUNA

Inter-Continental

Apáczai Csere János útca 12-14 ✉ 1052 – Ⓜ Vörösmarty tér – ✆ 327 6333 – Fax 327 64 66 – www.intercontinental.com **E2**

383 rm – †62400 HUF ††33800/62400 HUF, ☕ 6600 HUF – 15 suites

Rest – Carte 6700/11000 HUF

♦ Business ♦ Modern ♦

Large hotel tower on river bank with good views from most rooms which have modern décor and all mod cons. Popular with business travellers. Viennese-style coffee house. The pleasant modern restaurant offers popular fare.

Danubius Health Spa Resort

(heated)

Margitsziget ✉ 1138 – Ⓜ Árpád híd – ✆ 889 4700 – resind@margitsziget.danubiusgroup.com – Fax 889 49 88 – www.danubiushotels.com/margitsziget *Plan I* **A1**

267 rm ☕ – †33925 HUF ††34940/38990 HUF

Rest *Platan* – *(buffet lunch)* Carte approx. 6500 HUF

♦ Business ♦ Modern ♦

Concrete hotel set in island gardens on the Danube. Conference facilities. Huge thermal spa: heat, massage and water treatments. Modern bedrooms with a view. Buffet meals available alongside à la carte menu in the restaurant.

Hilton WestEnd

Váci útca 1-3 ✉ 1062 – Ⓜ Nyugati pályaudvar – ✆ 288 5500 – info.budapest-westend@hilton.com – Fax 288 55 88 – www.budapest-westend.hilton.com *Plan I* **A1**

230 rm – †59240 HUF ††43545/98230 HUF, ☕ 6835 HUF

Rest *Arrabona* – Carte 7200/9550 HUF

♦ Business ♦ Chain hotel ♦ Modern ♦

21C hotel incorporated in large adjoining indoor shopping centre. Comprehensive business facilities. Very comfortable modern bedrooms with roof garden as bonus. A bright and contemporary dining room on the first floor of the hotel with a Mediterranean theme.

Radisson SAS Béke

Teréz körút 43 ✉ 1138 – Ⓜ Nyugati tér – ✆ 889 3900 – sales.budapest@radissonsas.com – Fax 889 39 15 – www.radissonsas.com **F1**

239 rm – †52940 HUF ††26470/105875 HUF, ☕ 4305 HUF – 8 suites

Rest *Szondi Lugas* – *(buffet lunch)* Menu 5065/7595 HUF – Carte approx. 6500 HUF

♦ Traditional ♦ Functional ♦

Classic façade with mosaic fronts large international hotel in busy shopping street. Rear bedrooms quieter. Tea salon is their proud feature. Spacious restaurant with tropical paradise theme; Hungarian cuisine to the fore.

Andrássy

Andrássy útca 111 ✉ 1063 – Ⓜ Bajza u. – ✆ 462 2100 – reservation@andrassyhotel.com – Fax 322 94 45 *Plan I* **B1**

65 rm – †44800 HUF ††39500/52700 HUF, ☕ 5300 HUF – 5 suites

Rest *Baraka* – Carte 7900/11300 HUF

♦ Business ♦ Stylish ♦

A classical Bauhaus building converted into a hotel in 2001. Stylish lobby of glass and metal filigree, plus stylish water feature. Bright and contemporary bedrooms, most with balconies. Stylish Baraka restaurant offers original and modern cuisine.

N. H. Budapest

Vigszinház u. 3 ✉ 1137 – Ⓜ Nyugati pályaudvar – ✆ 814 0000 – nhbudapest@nh-hotels.com – Fax 814 01 00 – www.nh-hotels.com *Plan I* **A1**

160 rm – †48355 HUF ††33165/48355 HUF, ☕ 4050 HUF

Rest – Menu 3290/4560 HUF – Carte 3595/7270 HUF

♦ Business ♦ Modern ♦

Modern hotel in city suburbs. Conference facilities; gym and sauna. Bright, modern, well-furnished rooms in bold colours with extra touches; some with balconies. Simple restaurant; dishes show modern Hungarian style.

Parlament without rest 70 VISA

Kálmán Imre U. 19 ✉ 1054 – ✆ 3746000
– reservation@parlament-hotel.hu
– Fax 3 73 08 43 – www.parlament-hotel.hu **E1**
65 rm – ♦43040 HUF ♦♦40500/45570 HUF
♦ Business ♦ Design ♦
Stylish modern interior contrasts with the classic 19C exterior. Open plan atrium with display of famous Hungarians. Identical bedrooms have a clean and crisp design.

K + K Opera rm 80 VISA

Révay utca 24 ✉ 1065 – Ⓜ Opera – ✆ 269 0222
– kk.hotel.opera@kkhotels.hu
– Fax 269 02 30 – www.kkhotels.com **F1**
203 rm – ♦61265 HUF ♦♦61265 HUF – 2 suites
Rest – *(dinner only)* Carte approx. 6000 HUF
♦ Business ♦ Modern ♦
Well run hotel in quiet street of business district near opera. Stylish modern interior design. Good size rooms smartly furnished and well equipped. Informal dining in bar with bright modern décor and pale wood furniture; bistro-style menu.

Zara VISA

Só U. 6 ✉ 1056 – ✆ 5770700 – info@zarahotels.com – Fax 5 77 07 10
– www.zarahotels.com **F3**
74 rm – ♦31390 HUF ♦♦29870/53160 HUF
Rest – Carte 3850/5250 HUF
♦ Townhouse ♦ Modern ♦
Adjacent to the river and the main shopping street, this purpose-built hotel opened in 2006. Mirrored glass façade; compact but comfortable bedrooms with modern fabrics. Atrium bar and a simple dining room with an easy menu.

Mercure Korona rm 100 VISA

Kecskeméti útca 14 ✉ 1053 – Ⓜ Kálvin tér – ✆ 486 8800
– h1765@accor.com – Fax 318 38 67
– www.mercure.com **F3**
412 rm – ♦40505 HUF ♦♦32910/40505 HUF, 4305 HUF – 8 suites
Rest – Menu 6330 HUF – Carte 5825/8100 HUF
♦ Business ♦ Chain hotel ♦ Modern ♦
Well-equipped modern business hotel close to Hungarian National Museum. Contemporary rooms with all mod cons. Coffee bar and modish lounge. Buzzy restaurant above lobby; informal, modern with original lighting and contemporary local menus.

Novotel Budapest Centrum rm 350 VISA

Rákóczi útca 43-45 ✉ 1088 – Ⓜ Blaha tér
– ✆ 477 5300 – h3560@accor.com – Fax 477 53 53
– www.novotel-bud-centrum.hu *Plan I* **B2**
227 rm – ♦41770 HUF ♦♦32910/41770 HUF, 4305 HUF
Rest *Palace Garden Brasserie* – ✆ 477 5400 – Menu 5315/7090 HUF
♦ Business ♦ Chain hotel ♦ Functional ♦
Early 20C Art Deco hotel with extensions, in the business district. Conference facilities; basement leisure club. Spacious, well-fitted and modern bedrooms. The ornate, classic Palace restaurant serves an international menu.

Ibis Centrum without rest VISA

Raday útca 6 ✉ 1092 – Ⓜ Kálvin tér – ✆ 456 4100 – h2078@accor.com
– Fax 456 41 16 – www.ibis-centrum.com **F3**
126 rm – ♦19745 HUF ♦♦16455/19745 HUF, 2025 HUF
♦ Business ♦ Chain hotel ♦ Functional ♦
Modern hotel well located for city and national museum. Good functional accommodation with all necessary facilities. Lounge, small bar, bright breakfast room and roof garden.

HUNGARY

Mercure Budapest Duna without rest

Soroksári útca 12 ✉ 1095 – ✆ 455 8300 50 VISA MC AE

– h2025@accor.com – Fax 455 83 85 – www.mercure.com *Plan I* **B2**

130 rm – †26585 HUF ††21520/45570 HUF, ☕ 3040 HUF

♦ Business ♦ Chain hotel ♦ Functional ♦

Modern hotel catering well for business people and tourists, close to river and city. Fair-sized bedrooms offer simple but modern comforts and reasonable level of mod cons.

Gundel 60 P VISA MC AE

Állatkerti útca 2 ✉ 1146 – Ⓜ Hösök tere – ✆ 468 4040 – info@gundel.hu – Fax 363 19 17 – www.gundel.hu

closed 24 December *Plan I* **B1**

Rest – *(booking essential)* Menu 3300/11890 HUF – Carte 6320/14720 HUF

Rest *1894* – *(closed Sunday) (dinner only)* Menu 6500/9000 HUF – Carte 4000/8350 HUF

♦ Traditional ♦ Elegant ♦

Hungary's best known restaurant, an elegant classic. Spacious main room with walnut panelling and ornate ceiling. Traditional cuisine. Summer terrace. Live music at dinner.

Fausto's VISA MC AE

Székely Mihaly U.2 ✉ 1061 – Ⓜ Opera – ✆ 8776210 – www.fausto.hu

closed Easter, 1 May, 23 October, 25 December, Saturday lunch and Sunday **F1/2**

Rest – Menu 12000/14000 HUF – Carte 6500/12300 HUF

♦ Italian ♦ Design ♦

Relocated here in 2006. Discreet façade; sophisticated interior divided into two. Husband and wife team deliver accomplished Italian cooking with superb ingredients.

Lou Lou VISA MC AE

Vigyázó Ferenc Útca 4 ✉ 1051 – ✆ 3124505 – loulou@loulourestaurant.com – Fax 4 72 05 95 – www.loulourestaurant.com

closed Saturday lunch, Sunday and Bank Holidays **E 1**

Rest – Menu 8000 HUF (lunch) – Carte 9200/12500 HUF

♦ Innovative ♦ Fashionable ♦

Relaunched with considerable style and panache, with chocolate coloured walls and vaulted ceiling. Original and cutting-edge cuisine with vivid flavours. The place to be seen.

Premier VISA MC AE

Andrássy útca 101 ✉ 1062 – Ⓜ Bajza u. – ✆ 342 1768 – info@premier-restaurant.hu – Fax 322 16 39 – www.premier-restaurant.hu

closed 24 December and Sunday October-April *Plan I* **B1**

Rest – Carte 4600/9900 HUF

♦ Traditional ♦ Intimate ♦

Early 20C Art Nouveau villa with three basement rooms and a pleasant outdoor terrace. Attentive service. Traditional or global dishes; look out too for specials on offer.

Robinson VISA MC AE

Városligeti tó ✉ 1146 – Ⓜ Széchenyi Fürdö – ✆ 422 0222 – robinson@axelero.hu – Fax 422 00 72 – www.restaurantguide.hu/robinson

closed 24-26 December *Plan I* **B1**

Rest – Carte 4500/7000 HUF

♦ Traditional ♦ Friendly ♦

Pavilion on tiny island in park; plenty of ducks to watch in lake with fountains. Spacious conservatory with terrace. Extensive menu of traditional and modern fare. Guitar music at dinner.

XX **Mokka**

Sas u. 4 ✉ 1051 – Ⓜ Bajcsy-Zs. út – ✆ 328 0081 – mokkar@mokkarestaurant.hu – Fax 328 00 82 – www.mokkarestaurant.hu **E2**

Rest – *(booking essential)* Carte 5640/14760 HUF

◆ Innovative ◆ Trendy ◆

Trendy, warm and buzzy destination close to the Basilica; booking essential. Decorated with Moroccan lighting and North African artefacts. Totally eclectic menus (French, Asian, African) bursting with spices, exotic combinations and originality.

XX **Kárpátia**

⇔35

Ferenciek tere 7-8 ✉ 1053 – Ⓜ Ferenciek tere – ✆ 317 3596 – restaurant@karpatia.hu – Fax 318 05 91 – www.karpatia.hu

closed 24 December **F2**

Rest – Carte 6300/11400 HUF

◆ Traditional ◆ Rustic ◆

One of the city's oldest restaurants with characterful vaulted Gothic-style interior, beautifully painted walls and works of art. Extensive menu of good traditional cuisine.

XX **Cyrano**

⇔30

Kristóf tér 7-8 ✉ 1052 – Ⓜ Vörösmarty tér – ✆ 266 4747 – cyrano@citynet.hu – Fax 266 68 18 **E2**

Rest – Carte 5170/9070 HUF

◆ Contemporary ◆ Trendy ◆

Popular informal restaurant just off main shopping street with unusual dramatic modern designer-style décor. Serves selection of good modern European and Hungarian food.

XX **Képiró**

Képiró u. 3 ✉ 1053 – Ⓜ Kálvin tér – ✆ 266 0430 – info@kepirorestaurant.com – Fax 266 04 25 – www.kepirorestaurant.com

closed 24-27 December **F3**

Rest – Carte 4200/9900 HUF

◆ Innovative ◆ Friendly ◆

Glass-fronted restaurant, in narrow street near city centre, divided by central bar. Approachable and friendly serice. Modern-style cooking with eclectic, seasonal menus.

XX **Múzeum**

Múzeum körút 12 ✉ 1088 – Ⓜ Astoria – ✆ 338 4221 – muzeum11@axelero.hu – Fax 338 42 21 – www.muzeumkavehaz.hu

closed Sunday and Bank Holidays **F2**

Rest – Carte 6500/13970 HUF

◆ Traditional ◆ Brasserie ◆

Founded in 1885, next to National Museum. High ceilings, tiled walls and large windows. Formally-attired staff serve large portions of traditional Hungarian cooking.

XX **Belcanto**

⇔35

Dalszínház útca 8 ✉ 1062 – Ⓜ Opera – ✆ 269 2786 – restaurant@belcanto.hu – Fax 311 95 47 – www.belcanto.hu

closed 24 December **F1**

Rest – *(booking essential)* Menu 7595/30380 HUF – Carte 7595/12660 HUF

◆ Traditional ◆ Musical ◆

Next to the opera and famous for classical and operatic evening recitals, including impromptu performances by waiters! Atmosphere is lively and enjoyable. Hungarian food.

HUNGARY

Segal

Magyar útca 12-14 ✉ 1053 – Ⓜ Astoria – ☎ 3280774
closed 24-25 December and Sunday **F2**
Rest – *(booking essential) (dinner only)* Carte 5300/9800 HUF
♦ Asian influences ♦ Fashionable ♦
Modern restaurant with simple décor and original style; quieter tables on mezzanine floor. Modern, eclectic dishes showing French and Asian influences; blackboard specials.

Krizia

Mozsár útca 12 ✉ 1066 – Ⓜ Oktogon – ☎ 331 8711
– ristorante.krizia@axelero.hu
– Fax 331 87 11 – www.ristorantekrizia.hu
closed 15 July-7 August, 24-26 December, 1-10 January and Sunday **F1**
Rest – Menu 2600 HUF (lunch) – Carte 3700/8200 HUF
♦ Italian ♦ Cosy ♦
A pleasant intimate atmosphere with candlelight and friendly service. Carefully-prepared Italian cooking with the menu supplemented by regularly changing specials.

Bock Bisztró

Erzsébet Krt 43-49 ✉ 1073 – Ⓜ Oktogon – ☎ 321 0340 – bockbisztro@axelero.hu – Fax 321 03 40
closed Sunday and Bank Holidays **F1**
Rest – Carte 4450/7750 HUF
♦ Traditional ♦ Bistro ♦
Run independently of Corinthia Grand Hotel Royal, this is a serious wine establishment with over 50 by the glass; you can just walk in and buy. Stylish décor with Art Deco lighting, though the feel is informal bistro. Classic local recipes with a 21C lift, though tapas and cheese/ham plates are available too.

La Fontaine

Mérleg útca 10 ✉ 1051 – Ⓜ Bajcsy-Zs. út – ☎ 317 3715 – restaurant@lafontaine.hu – Fax 318 85 62 – www.lafontaine.hu
closed 1 week in spring, 2 weeks late July, 1 week Christmas and Sunday **E2**
Rest – *(dinner only)* Carte 7970/11470 HUF
♦ French ♦ Friendly ♦
Authentic Gallic charm, run by gregarious young owner. High ceiling adds to the airy feel. Traditional French menu with blackboard specials, all described with enthusiasm.

Osteria Fausto's

Dohàny U.5 ✉ 1072 – Ⓜ Astoria – ☎ 2696806 – faustos@fausto.hu
– Fax 2 69 68 06 – www.fausto.hu
closed Easter, 1 May, 23 October, 25 December and Sunday **F 2**
Rest – Menu 3000/13000 HUF – Carte 5300/9000 HUF
♦ Italian ♦ Bistro ♦
Now that Fausto's has moved to its new address, the owners have turned this location into a much more informal and flexible affair. Simple, rustic Italian food is the attraction.

BUDA

Plan II

Hilton Budapest

← Danube and Pest, rm 650
Hess András tér 1-3 ✉ 1014 – Ⓜ Batthyány tér
– ☎ 889 6600 – info.budapest@hilton.com – Fax 889 66 44
– www.budapest.hilton.com **D1**
299 rm – †49510 HUF ††49510/77535 HUF – 23 suites
Rest *Dominican* – *(pianist)* Menu 12000 HUF – Carte 6900/25600 HUF
Rest *Corvina* – Carte approx. 7500 HUF
♦ Traditional ♦ Classic ♦
Large hotel in historic castle district with stunning views. Remains of 13C Dominican church and cellars. Classic rooms. Dominican is fine dining room with superb views. Informal Corvina with traditional Hungarian menu.

Corinthia Aquincum

Arpád Fejedelem útca 94 ✉ *1036 – Ⓜ Árpád híd – ✆ 436 4100 – info@aqu.hu – Fax 436 41 22 – www.corinthian.hu* Plan I **A1**

300 rm – 63290 HUF 63290 HUF – 8 suites

Rest *Apicius* – Carte 4025/10430 HUF

♦ Business ♦ Modern ♦

Modern hotel on west bank, north of centre with own comprehensive thermal spa and therapy centre. Executive level rooms are best; worth the short trip from the city. Apicius restaurant with smart modern décor in warm tones and a pleasant atmosphere.

Art'otel

Bem Rakpart 16-19 ✉ *1011 – Ⓜ Batthyány tér – ✆ 487 9487 – budapest@artotel.hu – Fax 487 94 88 – www.artotels.com* **D1**

156 rm – 62785 HUF 32660/62785 HUF, 3040 HUF – 9 suites

Rest *Chelsea* – Carte approx. 7600 HUF

♦ Business ♦ Design ♦

Half new building, half converted baroque houses. Stylish and original interior in cool shades and clean lines. Features over 600 pieces of original art by Donald Sultan. Bright dining room with vaulted ceiling topped with glass and modern artwork.

Uhu Villa

Keselyü l/a (Northwest : 8 km by Szilágyi Erzsébet fasor) ✉ *1025 – ✆ 275 1002 – uhuvilla@uhuvilla.hu – Fax 398 05 71 – www.uhuvilla.hu*

13 rm – 24910 HUF 18685/31140 HUF, 4400 HUF – 1 suite

Rest – *(dinner only)* Carte 5900/12300 HUF

♦ Traditional ♦ Cosy ♦

Friendly, discreet, personally-styled early 20C villa with gardens in peaceful Buda Hills. Smart, contemporary bedrooms with neat décor, some with balconies. Restaurant with terrace and view serving Italian dishes; Hungarian and Italian wine list.

Carlton without rest

Apor Péter útca 3 ✉ *1011 – Ⓜ Batthyány tér – ✆ 224 0999 – carltonhotel@t-online.hu – Fax 224 09 90 – www.carltonhotel.hu* **D2**

95 rm – 24050 HUF 22785/27850 HUF

♦ Traditional ♦ Classic ♦

Usefully-located hotel on Buda side of river, offering straightforward accommodation for the cost-conscious traveller. Rooms are functional and comfortable. Small bar.

Victoria without rest

Danube and Pest,

Bem Rakpart 11 ✉ *1011 – Ⓜ Batthyány tér – ✆ 457 8080 – victoria@victoria.hu – Fax 457 80 88 – www.victoria.hu* **D1**

27 rm – 29620 HUF 24305/31140 HUF

♦ Traditional ♦ Functional ♦

Family-run hotel, popular with tourists, in a row of town houses just below the castle. Rooms are spacious, equipped with good range of facilities and all offer fine views.

Vadrózsa

Pentelei Molnár útca 15 (via Rómer Flóris útca) ✉ *1025 – ✆ 326 5817 – vadrozsa@hungary.net – Fax 326 58 09 – www.vadrozsa.hu*

closed 24-26 December Plan I **A1**

Rest – Menu 12500/16700 HUF – Carte 6980/9620 HUF

♦ Traditional ♦ Formal ♦

Pleasant villa just out of town. Elegant dining room with wood panelling. Display of raw ingredients presented with the menu. Attractive summer terrace. Detailed service.

Alabárdos

Országház útca 2 ✉ 1014 – Ⓜ Moszkva tér – ✆ 356 0851 – alabardos@t-online.hu – Fax 214 38 14 – www.alabardos.hu
closed Sunday **D1**

Rest – *(dinner only and Saturday lunch) (booking essential)* Carte 8100/10890 HUF

◆ Traditional ◆ Formal ◆

Well-run restaurant in vaulted Gothic interior of characterful 17C building with covered courtyard in castle square. Extensive menu of good traditional Hungarian classics.

Café Pierrot

Fortuna u. 14 ✉ 1014 – Ⓜ Moszkva tér – ✆ 375 6971 – info@pierrot.hu – Fax 375 69 71 – www.pierrot.hu
closed 24 December **C1**

Rest – Menu 3500 HUF (lunch) – Carte 4370/8970 HUF

◆ Modern ◆ Friendly ◆

Eye-catching exterior will make you stop and look; trees in pots, twinkling fairy lights. Inside is tasteful Pierrot clown theming with some original artwork by local artists. Hungarian base underpins dishes skilfully concocted with Gallic finesse.

Arcade Bistro

Kiss Janos Alt u. 38 ✉ 1126 – Ⓜ Déli pu. – ✆ 225 1969 – arcade@freestart.hu – Fax 225 19 68 – www.arcadebistro.hu
closed 24-26 December, 1 January and Sunday **C2-3**

Rest – *(booking essential)* Carte 3360/7480 HUF

◆ Traditional ◆ Bistro ◆

Small and friendly local restaurant in drab residential area, with central column water feature and colourful modern art décor. Traditional Hungarian cooking.

Kisbuda Gyöngye

Kenyeres útca 34 ✉ 1034 – Ⓜ Árpád híd – ✆ 368 9246 – gyongye@remiz.hu – Fax 368 92 27 – www.remiz.hu
closed 24 December and Sunday *Plan I* **A1**

Rest – *(booking essential music at dinner)* Carte 5840/9140 HUF

◆ Traditional ◆ Cosy ◆

A genuine neighbourhood restaurant in a residential street. Wood panelling created by old wardrobes. Attentive service. Good choice menu; international and authentic food.

Náncsi Néni

Ördögárok útca 80, Hüvösvölgy (Northwest : 10 km by Szilágyi Erzsébetfasor) ✉ 1029 – ✆ 397 2742 – info@nancsineni.hu – Fax 397 27 42 – www.nancsineni.hu
closed dinner 24 and 31 December

Rest – Carte 3190/6650 HUF

◆ Home cooking ◆ Bistro ◆

Interior similar to a Swiss chalet with gingham tablecloths, convivial atmosphere and large terrace. Well-priced home-style Hungarian cooking. Worth the drive from the city.

Republic of IRELAND
ÉIRE

PROFILE

- **Area:**
70 284 km^2
(27 137 sq mi).
- **Population:**
4 016 000 inhabitants (est. 2005), density = 57 per km^2.
- **Capital:**
Dublin (population 1 004 614).
- **Currency:**
Euro (€); rate of exchange: € 1 = US$ 1.32 (Nov 2006).
- **Government:**
Parliamentary republic (since 1921). Member of European Union since 1973.
- **Languages:**
Irish and English.
- **Specific public holidays:**
St. Patrick's Day (17 March); Good Friday (Friday before Easter); May Bank Holiday (first Monday in May); June Bank Holiday (first Monday in June); August Bank Holiday (first Monday in August); October Bank Holiday (last Monday in October); St. Stephens Day (26 December).
- **Local Time:**
GMT in winter and GMT + 1 hour in summer.
- **Climate:**
Temperate maritime, with cool winters and mild summers, fairly high rainfall (Dublin : January: 5°C, July: 15°C).
- **International dialling Code:**
00 353 followed

by area code and then the local number.
- **Emergency:**
✆ **999** for all emergency services – Fire Brigade, Police, Ambulance, Mountain, Cave, Coastguard and Sea rescue.
- **Electricity:**
230 volts AC, 50Hz; 3 pin flat or 2-pin round-shaped wall sockets are standard.

FORMALITIES

Travellers from the European Union (EU), Switzerland, Iceland and the main countries of North and South America need a national identity card or passport (except for British nationals travelling from the UK; America: passport required) to visit Ireland for less than three months (tourism or business purpose). For visitors from other countries a visa may be required, in addition to a passport, especially for those wishing to stay for longer than three months. We advise you to check with your embassy before travelling.

Nationals of EU countries require a valid national driving licence; nationals of non-EU countries require an International Driving Licence. Third party insurance is essential. Drivers must be at least 21 or 25 to hire a vehicle.

MAJOR NEWSPAPERS

The main daily newspapers in the Irish Republic are *The Irish Times*, *The Independent* and *The Examiner.* Additionally Dublin has three local newspapers: *Northside People, Southside People* and *Fingal Independent.*

SMOKING-NO SMOKING

The laws in the Republic of Ireland prohibit smoking in all restaurants, bars and in the public areas of hotels. Some hotel bedrooms are still available for smokers.

HOTELS

→ CATEGORIES

Accommodation ranges from luxurious 5-star international hotels, via smaller, family-run guesthouses to bed and breakfast establishments.

→ PRICE RANGE

The price is per room. There is little difference between the price of a single and a double room.

Between April and October it is advisable to book in advance. From November to March prices may be slightly lower, some hotels offer special cheap rates and some may be closed.

→ TAX

Included in the room price.

→ CHECK OUT TIME

Usually between 11am and noon.

→ RESERVATIONS

By telephone or by Internet. A credit card number may be required.

→ TIP FOR LUGGAGE HANDLING

At the discretion of the customer (about €1 per bag).

→ BREAKFAST

It is usually included in the price of the room and is generally served between 7.30am and 9.30am. Most hotels offer a full cooked breakfast as well as a continental breakfast and usually it is possible to have continental breakfast served in the room.

RESTAURANTS

Besides the more formal **restaurants** there are **brasseries, bistros** and pubs, which serve simpler fare, and cafés and fast-food outlets, where one can eat quickly and cheaply.

Breakfast	7.30am – 9.30am
Lunch	12.30pm – 2.30pm
Dinner	7pm – 10-11pm

Restaurants in Ireland offer fixed price menus (starter, main course and dessert) and à la carte. Menus are written in English. A fixed price menu is usually cheaper than the same dishes chosen à la carte.

→ RESERVATIONS

Reservations are usually made by phone, fax or via the Internet. For famous restaurants (including Michelin starred restaurants), it is advisable to book several days – in some instances weeks – in advance.

A credit card number or a phone number may be required to guarantee the booking.

→ THE BILL

The bill (check) includes VAT. Tipping is at the client's discretion but, if you are particularly pleased with the service, it is customary to add 10% or to round up the total to an appropriate figure.

LOCAL CUISINE

Ireland is a sociable and hospitable country where the people readily gather in a bar or round a table. There are two culinary traditions: the formal meals served in town and country mansions, and the simple dishes of earlier centuries. As Ireland is an agricultural country, there is an abundance of fresh produce: fruit and vegetables, meat and dairy products and a wide variety of fresh and saltwater fish. The Irish have a great way with the potato, which was introduced at the end of the 16C and became a staple of the national diet.

The traditional cooked breakfast, known as the Irish Fry, consists of some or all of the following: egg, bacon, sausage, black pudding, potato cakes, mushrooms and tomatoes; it is sometimes served as the evening meal. Other breakfast dishes are kippers, kedgeree and smoked salmon omelette.

Salmon, farmed or wild, is rarely off the menu, which may also include trout. Near the coast the menus might feature **shellfish**: crab, lobster, scallops, mussels, Dublin Bay prawns and Galway Bay oysters. From the local fishing grounds come black sole (known also as Dover sole), lemon sole, plaice, monkfish, turbot, brill, John Dory, cod, hake, haddock, mackerel and herring.

Prime **beef** is raised on the lush grass of the lowlands and **lamb** on the uplands; **pigs** are raised everywhere. Chicken is common; duck appears more rarely. There is also game in season.

The most popular traditional dishes are **Irish stew** (neck of mutton layered in a pot with potatoes, onions and herbs); **Colcannon** (mashed potatoes, onions, parsnips and white cabbage, mixed with butter and cream); **champ** (a simpler dish of potatoes mashed with butter and vegetables such as chopped chives, parsley, spring onions, shallots, cabbage, nettles or peas). Nettles are also made into soup. Seaweed is also a culinary ingredient; traditionally it was used to thicken soups and stews: **carrageen** is still used to make a dessert with a delicate flavour and **dulse** is made into a sweet (candy).

The country produces excellent milk and cream, which is served as whipped cream or made into ice cream, a popular dessert, into butter and into a wide variety of **cheeses** – **Cashel Blue** (a soft creamy, blue-veined cow's milk cheese); **Cooleeny** (a Camembert-type soft cheese); **Milleens** (a distinctive spicy cheese, which is washed with salt water as it matures); **Gubbeen** (a soft surface-ripening cheese).

Many different breads and cakes are baked for breakfast and tea. The most well-known is **soda bread**, made of white or brown flour and buttermilk. **Barm brack** is a rich fruit cake made with yeast.

DRINK

Stout or porter, made by Guinness or Murphys is the traditional thirst-quencher in Ireland but the drinking of ales (bitter) and lagers is not uncommon. Black Velvet is a mixture of stout and champagne.

Although there are now only three distilleries in Ireland, there are many different brands of whiskey; their distinctive flavours arise from subtle variations in the production process, in which the spirit is triple distilled. **The Flag** is a patriotic drink, a mixture of crème de menthe, tequila and Southern Comfort representing the green, white and orange of the Republican tricolour.

Irish coffee is a delicious creation, consisting of a measure of whiskey, brown sugar and very hot black coffee mixed in a heated glass and topped with a layer of fresh cream.

DUBLIN

BAILE ÁTHA CLIATH

Population (2002): 495 101 (conurbation 1 004 614) - Altitude: sea level

Ph. Bénet, R. Holzbachova / MICHELIN

Dublin's 'fair city', the capital of Ireland, bestrides the River Liffey and looks seawards to its port and the broad water of Dublin Bay. The Vikings settled on both banks of the Liffey; the Anglo-Normans sited their castle on the mound on the south side. In the relative peace of the Georgian era, after centuries of conflict, the city expanded: public bodies put up handsome buildings; men of property commissioned fine mansions. Under the Wide Streets Commissioners (1758) Dublin developed into an elegant city; the Liffey was embanked between quays and spanned by several bridges. The 19C brought stagnation and the 20C the destruction caused by the Easter Rising and the Civil War; most of it has, however, been made good, and Dublin can claim to be the finest Georgian city in the British Isles.

Something like a third of Ireland's population lives in the greater Dublin area and a disproportionate amount of the country's business is conducted there. The economic success of the 'Celtic tiger' period has resulted in much modernisation and improvement as well as the building of many houses in the suburbs and adjacent towns and villages. The increasingly cosmopolitan life of street, café, restaurant and bar coupled with the city's Georgian architectural heritage make Dublin an attractive destination for a weekend or longer.

WHICH DISTRICT TO CHOOSE

The greatest concentration of **hotels** is in the city centre and the districts south of the Grand Canal; there are also a few near the airport. *Plan II* **F1**; guesthouses cluster south of the Grand Canal; there are B&B addresses in most districts and near the airport. Many of the **restaurants** are also found in the city centre and the districts south of the Grand Canal. In Dublin there seems to be a pub in every street, with many of the more popular places in **Temple Bar** *Plan II* **E2**.

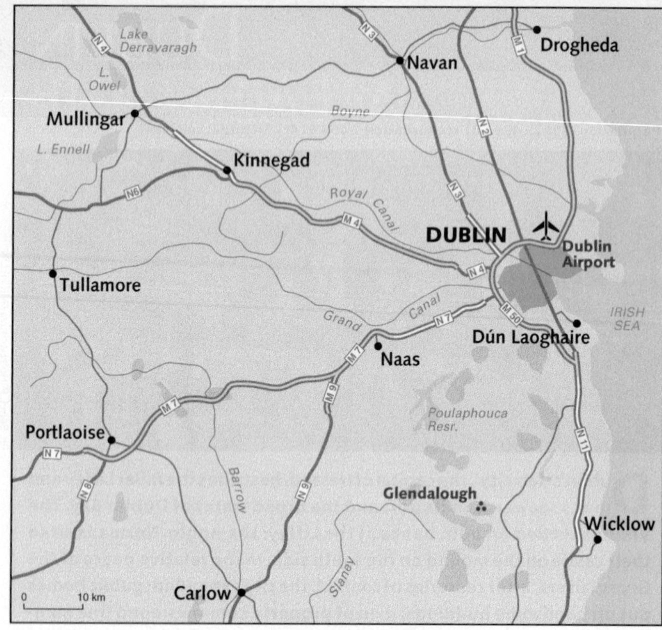

PRACTICAL INFORMATION

ARRIVAL – DEPARTURE

Dublin Airport – About 12 km (7.5 mi) north of the city centre, ✆ 01 814 1111.

From the airport to the city centre – By **taxi**: the cost is approx. €20, including one piece of luggage; €0.50 extra for each additional piece of luggage. By **coach**: Air Coach (30mins) between Dublin Airport and the city centre, every 15min during daytime (24hrs/24 service), stopping at major hotels as far south as Stillorgan; €7, return €12. ✆ 01 844 7118; www.aircoach.ie. By **bus**: Air Link No 747 from Dublin Airport to the bus station *(Busáras)*, €5, return €9; and Air Link No 748 from Dublin Airport via city centre to Heuston Railway Station, €5.50; ✆ 01 873 4222 (Mon-Sat 9am-7pm); info@dublinbus.ie; www.dublinbus.ie

By sea – There are regular ferry services to and from two terminals – Dublin Port and Dún Laoghaire.

TRANSPORT

→ TAXIS

Taxis can be hailed in the street but the best way is to request them at a taxi rank. Tariff calculated at approx. €0.15 pkm (approx. €0.20 Sundays, public holidays and at night 10pm-8am).

→ BUSES

The bus network covers the whole city from the Central Bus Station *(Busáras)* in Store Street *Plan II* **F1**; any bus bearing the direction An Lár is going to the city centre. The price of a single ticket varies according to the number of stages from €0.90 to €1.65. Dublin Rambler 1-day bus ticket €5; 3-day €10, 5-day €15.50, 7-day €19; 1-day Family ticket €8; 5 1-day €17, 6 5-day €75. ✆ 01 873 4222 (Mon-Sat 9am-7pm); ✆01 703

3028 (ticket sales); info@dublinbus.ie; www.dublinbus.ie

➜ TRAMS

The two LUAS tram routes are the Green Line from St Stephen's Green to Sandyford and the Red Line from Connolly Station to Tallaght; Mon-Fri 5.30am-0.30am, every 5 mins (less frequently outside the rush hour and not so early and late at the weekend). Fares vary according to zones from €1.30 to €3.80; 7-day ticket from €10; 30-day ticket from €40; tickets can be bought from ticket vending machines at Luas stops or, more cheaply, from selected retailers. ✆ 1800 300 604; www.luas.ie

➜ DART

The **Dublin Area Rapid Transport (DART)** operates a rail service along the coast (40 km – 25 mi) from Howth in the north to Bray in the south. It serves three stations in central Dublin – Connolly *Plan II* **F1**, Tara Street *Plan II* **F2** and Pearse. Trains daily between 6am (9am Sun) and 11.45pm every 5-10min during peak times and every 15min off-peak. Tickets available at any station: All-day rail ticket (according to distance) up to €2.15; all-day rail and bus ticket €7.20. ✆ 01 814 1062 or 01 836 6222 (passenger information); www.aerdart.ie

➜ DUBLIN PASS

Free entry to over 30 tourist attractions, free transport with AirCoach from Dublin Airport to the city centre and discounts on purchases and admissions; 1-day €29 (child €17), 2-day €49 (child €29), 3-day €59 (child €34), 6-day €89 (child €44); available at Tourist Information Offices; www.dublinpass.com

USEFUL ADDRESSES

➜ TOURIST OFFICES

Dublin Tourism Centre – Suffolk Street *Plan II* **D2** (Mon-Fri, 9am-5.30 (7pm July and August), Sun and public hols (10.30am-3pm); O'Connell Street *Plan II* **E1** (Mon-Sat; closed bank hols); Dublin Airport, Arrivals Hall (daily). ✆ 1850 230 330 (Mon-Fri 8am-11pm, Sat 9am-6pm), Reservations ✆ 1800 668 668; information@dublintourism.ie; www.visitdublin.com

➜ BANKS/CURRENCY EXCHANGE

The major banks are to be found in the town centre and at the railway stations, Mon-Fri, 8.30am-4.30pm (closed at lunchtime); some larger banks are open on Sat morning. Bank cash machines (ATMs) are open 24hrs (pin number required).

➜ POST OFFICES

O' Connell Street *Plan II* **E1**, Suffolk Street *Plan II* **D2**. Opening times: Mon-Sat 8am-5pm.

➜ EMERGENCY

✆ **999** for Fire Brigade, Police, Ambulance, Mountain, Cave, Coastguard and Sea rescue.

BUSY PERIODS

It may be difficult to find a room at a reasonable price when special events are held in the city:

St Patrick's Day: 17 March – Patron saint of Ireland's feast day with processions.

Bloomsday: 16 June – Annual celebration of James Joyce's great novel *Ulysses* reading, re-enactments, music, theatre, street theatre.

Dublin Horse Show: August – International equestrian and social event of the year with team jumping competitions held at the Royal Dublin Society ground in Ballsbridge.

All Ireland Hurling Finals: September – Annual national hurling championships at Croke Park.

All Ireland Football Finals: September – Annual national Gaelic Football championship finals at Croke Park.

Dublin Theatre Festival: September – Best of world theatre and new productions from all the major Irish companies.

DIFFERENT FACETS OF THE CITY

There is time to visit the main sights and museums in two to three days.

Usual opening times 10am-5pm but closed on Mondays and public holidays.

TRINITY COLLEGE – The **Long Room** in the **Old Library** housing the **Book of Kells** and other illuminated medieval manuscripts, as well as a medieval Irish Harp.

OLD DUBLIN – **Dublin Castle** *Plan II* **D2**; formerly the centre of British rule in Ireland: State Appartments, Throne Room, Wedgwood Room, St Patrick's Hall, Church of the Most Holy Trinity. **Christ Church Cathedral**; Romanesque/Early English building, largely rebuilt in the 19C by George Scott: Romanesque south door, brass eagle lectern, Strongbow monument, 12C crypt. **St Patrick's Cathedral** *Plan II* **D3**; Early-English building: tomb of Jonathan Swift, Dean of the cathedral and author of *Gulliver's Travels*, banners of the knights of the Order of St Patrick, the door of the old Chapter House with the hole through which the Earl of Kildare 'chanced his arm'.

GEORGIAN DUBLIN – **Marsh's Library** *Plan II* **D3**; 18C library with 'cages' where precious books can be consulted behind locked wire screens. **Liffey Bridge** *Plan II* **E2**; cast-iron footbridge (1816) better known as the Ha'penny Bridge owing to the original ½d toll. **Bank of Ireland**; formerly the Irish Parliament containing the original House of Lords and a display about banking. **Newman House** *Plan II* **E3**; two 18C houses, the smaller by Richard Castle with many original features and plasterwork by the Lafranchini brothers, the larger with rococo plasterwork by Richard West. **Custom House** *Plan II* **F1**; 18C masterpiece designed by James Gandon; the ceremonial vestibules behind the south portico contain a **Visitor Centre** illustrating the work of the government offices which have occupied the building **Number Twenty-Nine** *Plan II* **F3**; vivid picture of 18C life in Dublin; some original furniture. **Marino Casino** *Plan I* **B1**; charming Palladian villa designed by Sir William Chambers.

MUSEUMS AND GALLERIES – **Chester Beatty Library** *Plan II* **D2**; beautiful display of Islamic, Far Eastern and European manuscripts and artworks collected by Sir Alfred Chester Beatty (1875-1968). **National Museum** (Kildare Street) *Plan II* **E3**; outstanding collection of work by Irish artists (Jack B Yeats) as well as by British and other European painters. **National Museum** (Collins Barracks); decorative arts, folk life, history and geology. **National Gallery** *Plan II* **F3**; **Kilmainham Gaol Museum** *Plan I* **A1**; Irish struggle for political independence: souvenirs.

OUTDOOR DUBLIN – **Phoenix Park** *Plan I* **A1**; the largest urban park in Europe was enclosed in 1662 by the Duke of Ormond: herd of fallow deer, Wellington Monument, Papal Cross (1979), Visitor, Zoological Gardens, official residence of the President of Ireland. **National Botanic Gardens** *Plan I* **A1**; 20 000 species growing beside the Tolka River: rose garden, peat garden, bog garden, Victorian glasshouses.

SHOPPING

The smartest shopping district is **Grafton Street** *Plan II* **E2** and its side streets; the **Powerscourt Centre** comprises a complex of individual boutiques housed in the stables, yard and rooms of an elegant Georgian mansion with decorative plasterwork; **Nassau Street** *Plan II* **E2** contains several shops selling a range of Irish goods from high fashion to modest souvenirs: clothing, craftwork, pottery, Irish music and instruments, family crests; **Dawson Street** is home to the major book shops. **Temple Bar** offers an eclectic mix of individual little shops and outdoor stalls. The north bank of the Liffey has its own shopping district centred on **O'Connell Street** *Plan II* **E1** and the side streets to the west – Henry Street and Abbey Street. Cobblestones in **Smithfield Village** *Plan II* **C1** offers examples of Irish craftsmanship. **Francis Street** *Plan II* **C2** is a good place to buy **antiques**.

MARKETS – Lovers of markets should visit the **Temple Bar Market** (Sat morning) in Meeting House Square which sells local produce – cheeses, sauces, bread, chocolates, vegetables, drink, pizzas, pies and sausages; **Moore Street Market** (Mon-Sat) *Plan II* **E1**; the Dublin Corporation **Fruit and Vegetable Market** (Sat morning) under a cast-iron roof in **Mary's Lane** *Plan II* **D1**.

WHAT TO BUY – Food (smoked salmon, cheeses), alcohol (whiskey, Guinness and liqueurs), perfumes and soaps, fashion (linen, lace, Donegal tweed and chunky Aran sweaters), linen napkins and tablecloths, crystal from Waterford and other factories, hand-blown glass, porcelain from Belleek, Irish Dresden figures, Celtic inspired jewellery, silverware, hand-turned wooden bowls, bog wood sculptures, musical instruments, CDs of Irish music.

ENTERTAINMENT

Abbey Theatre *Plan II* **E2**: a proud symbol of Irish culture performing plays by Ireland's best-known authors (Shaw, Synge, Yeats, O'Casey) and lesser known playwrights; also experimental Peacock Theatre.

Gate Theatre *Plan II* **E1**: another Dublin institution founded in the 1920s, which includes non-Irish works in its repertoire.

Olympia Theatre *Plan II* **D2** and **Gaiety Theatre** *Plan II* **E3**: opera and musicals.

National Concert Hall *Plan II* **E3**: concerts and recitals.

Bank of Ireland Arts Centre *Plan II* **E2**: evening and lunchtime musical recitals, exhibitions, theatre, poetry readings.

Jurys Irish Cabaret *Plan III* **J1**: 2000 shows a year incorporating music, singing and dancing in both modern and traditional styles (also facilities for a drink and a meal).

Burlington Cabaret *Plan III* **H1**: cabaret venue which describes itself as "a celebration of everything Irish in comedy, music, song and dance".

NIGHTLIFE

The *Event Guide*, published weekly, lists the major entertainments; available free of charge from record shops (www.eventguide.ie). The most central district for night-life is **Temple Bar** *Plan II* **E2**, a medieval network of narrow streets, alleys and courts on the south bank of the Liffey, where traditional pubs and restaurants alternate with ethnic restaurants, alternative shops and hotels. Most of the larger nightclubs are south of the Liffey. Good places include *D Basement* (Fleet Street); *Gaiety Theatre* (South King Street); *The International Bar* (23 Wicklow Street) cosy little bar where assorted blues bands alternate with theatre and comedy club; *O'Donoghue's* (14-15 Merrion Row) where *The Dubliners* came roaring on the music scene in 1962 – traditional Irish music; *Brazen Head* (20 Lower Bridge Street) which claims to be the oldest pub in Dublin – music; *Café Bewley* (Grafton Street) Art deco décor with Café Cabaret in the evening; *Mitchell & Son* (21 Kildare Street) celebrated for its famous 'Green Spot' whiskey, rare malts, spirits and vast range of wines.

IRELAND

CENTRAL DUBLIN

Plan II

The Merrion

50 VISA AE

Upper Merrion St ✉ D2 – ✆ (01) 603 0600 – info@merrionhotel.com – Fax (01) 603 07 00 – www.merrionhotel.com **F3**

133 rm – 450 € 565 €, 27 € – 10 suites

Rest *The Cellar* and ***The Cellar Bar*** – see below

♦ Grand Luxury ♦ Classic ♦

Classic hotel in series of elegantly restored Georgian town houses; many of the individually designed grand rooms overlook pleasant gardens. Irish art in opulent lounges.

The Westin

250 VISA AE

College Green, Westmoreland St ✉ D2 – ✆ (01) 645 1000 – reservations.dublin@westin.com – Fax (01) 645 12 34 – www.westin.com/dublin **E2**

150 rm – 519 € 519 €, 26 € – 13 suites – **Rest *The Exchange*** – *(closed Saturday lunch and Sunday dinner)* Carte 39/58 €

Rest *The Mint* – Carte 26/60 €

♦ Luxury ♦ Modern ♦

Immaculately kept and consummately run hotel in a useful central location. Smart, uniform interiors and an ornate period banking hall. Excellent bedrooms with marvellous beds. Elegant, Art Deco 1920s-style dining in Exchange. More informal fare at The Mint.

The Westbury

220 VISA AE

Grafton St ✉ D2 – ✆ (01) 679 1122 – westbury@jurysdoyle.com – Fax (01) 679 70 78 – www.jurysdoyle.com **E2**

197 rm – 401 € 441 €, 22 € – 8 suites

Rest *Russell Room* – Menu 35/60 € – Carte 42/55 €

Rest *The Sandbank* – *(closed Sunday and Bank Holidays)* Carte 26/42 €

♦ Luxury ♦ Modern ♦

Imposing marble foyer and stairs lead to lounge famous for afternoon teas. Stylish Mandarin bar. Luxurious bedrooms offer every conceivable facility. Russell Room has distinctive, formal feel. Informal, bistro-style Sandbank.

Conrad Dublin

370 VISA AE

Earlsfort Terrace ✉ D2 – ✆ (01) 602 8900 – dublininfo@conradhotels.com – Fax (01) 676 54 24 – www.conradhotels.com **E3**

192 rm – 470 € 485/670 €, 25 €

Rest *Alex* – Menu 30/40 € – Carte 36/58 €

♦ Luxury ♦ Modern ♦

Smart, business oriented international hotel opposite the National Concert Hall. Popular, pub-style bar. Spacious rooms with bright, modern décor and comprehensive facilities. Modern, bright and airy restaurant offers seafood specialities.

The Clarence

60 P VISA AE

6-8 Wellington Quay ✉ D2 – ✆ (01) 407 0800 – reservations@theclarence.ie – Fax (01) 407 08 20 – www.theclarence.ie

closed 24-27 December **D2**

43 rm – 350 € 350 €, 28 € – 5 suites – **Rest *The Tea Room*** – see below

♦ Luxury ♦ Design ♦

Discreet, stylish former warehouse overlooking river boasting 21C interior design. Small panelled library. Modern, distinctive rooms: quietest face courtyard on fourth floor.

The Fitzwilliam

80 VISA AE

St Stephen's Green ✉ D2 – ✆ (01) 478 7000 – enq@fitzwilliamhotel.com – Fax (01) 478 78 78 – www.fitzwilliamhotel.com **E3**

136 rm – 220/400 € 220/400 €, 19 € – 3 suites

Rest *Thornton's* – see below – **Rest *Citron*** – Carte 25/50 €

♦ Business ♦ Modern ♦

Rewardingly overlooks the Green and boasts a bright contemporary interior. Spacious, finely appointed rooms offer understated elegance. Largest hotel roof garden in Europe. Very trendy, informal brasserie.

Brooks

50

Drury St ✉ D2 – ✆ (01) 670 4000 – sales@brookshotel.ie – Fax (01) 670 44 55 – www.brookshotel.ie **E2**

98 rm – 240/320 € 450/700 €

Rest *Francesca's* – *(dinner only)* Carte 23/42 €

◆ Business ◆ Stylish ◆

Commercial hotel in modish, boutique, Irish town house style. Smart lounges and stylish rooms exude contemporary panache. Extras in top range rooms, at a supplement. Fine dining with open kitchen for chef-watching.

Stephen's Green

50

Cuffe St, off St Stephen's Green ✉ D2 – ✆ (01) 607 3600 – info@ocallaghanhotels.com – Fax (01) 478 14 44 – www.ocallaghanhotels.com

closed 25-27 December **E3**

64 rm – 325 € 325 €, 14 € – 11 suites

Rest *The Pie Dish* – *(closed lunch Saturday and Sunday)* Carte 35/60 €

◆ Business ◆ Modern ◆

This smart modern hotel housed in an originally Georgian property frequented by business clients; popular Magic Glass bar. Bright bedrooms offer a good range of facilities. Bright and breezy bistro restaurant.

The Morrison

240

Lower Ormond Quay, ✉ D1 – ✆ (01) 887 2400 – reservations@morrisonhotel.ie – Fax (01) 874 40 39 – www.morrisonhotel.ie

closed 24-27 December **D2**

135 rm – 340 € 340 €, 22 € – 3 suites

Rest *Halo* – *(bar lunch Saturday and Sunday)* Carte 33/46 €

◆ Luxury ◆ Design ◆

Modern riverside hotel with ultra-contemporary interior by acclaimed fashion designer John Rocha. New rooms are particularly stylish. Relaxed dining room concentrates on Irish produce in modish and home-cooked blend of dishes.

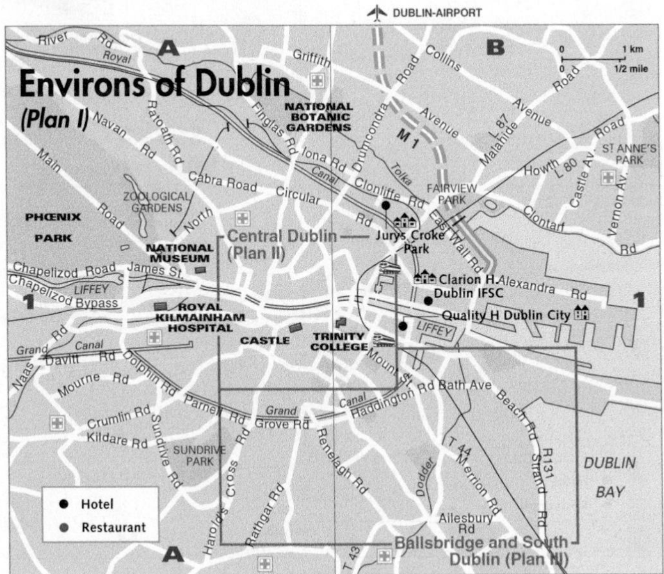

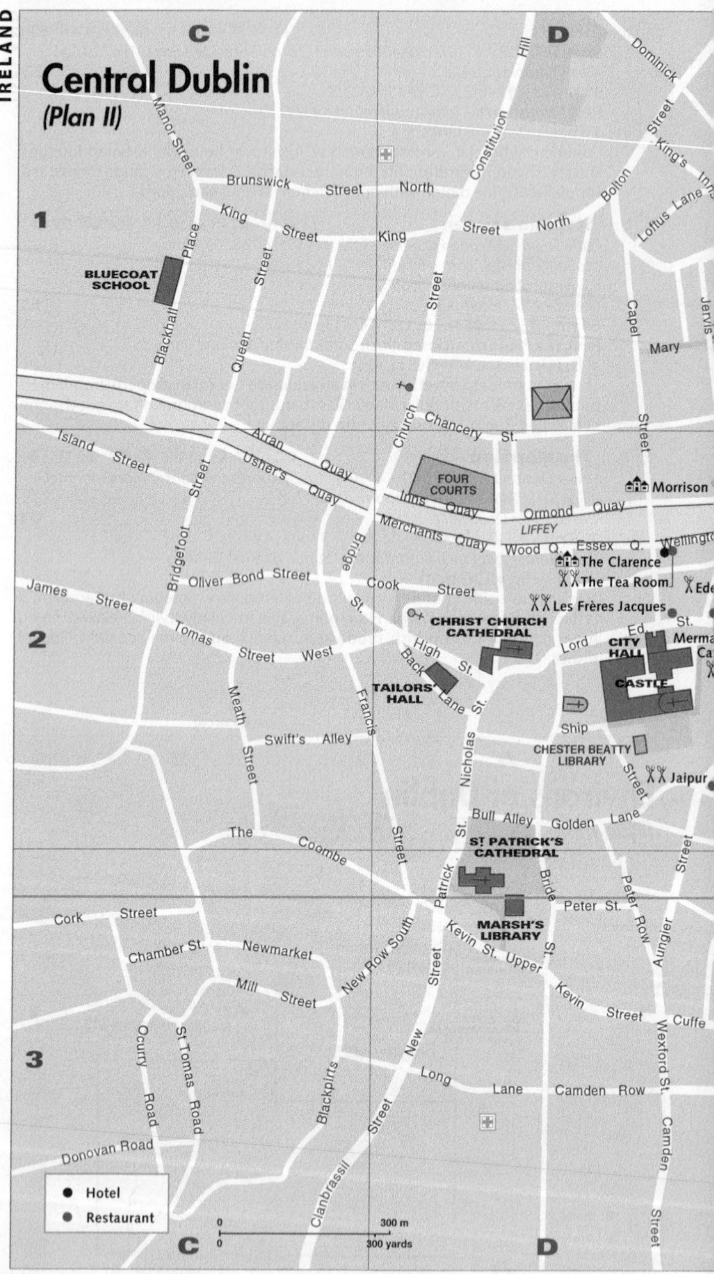
Central Dublin
(Plan II)
C
D
1
2
3
BLUECOAT SCHOOL
FOUR COURTS
LIFFEY
The Clarence
The Tea Room
Les Frères Jacques
Morrison
CHRIST CHURCH CATHEDRAL
TAILORS' HALL
CITY HALL
CASTLE
CHESTER BEATTY LIBRARY
Jaipur
ST PATRICK'S CATHEDRAL
MARSH'S LIBRARY
Manor Street
Brunswick Street North
King Street North
Constitution Hill
Dominick Street
King's Inns
Bolton Street
Loftus Lane
Blackhall Place
Queen Street
Church Street
Capel Street
Jervis
Mary
Chancery St.
Arran Quay
Usher's Quay
Island Street
Inns Quay
Ormond Quay
Merchants Quay
Wood Q.
Essex Q.
Wellington
Bridgefoot Street
Bridge St.
Oliver Bond Street
Cook Street
James Street
Tomas Street West
High St.
Back Lane
Lord Ed. St.
Francis Street
Meath Street
Swift's Alley
Nicholas St.
Ship Street
Bull Alley
Golden Lane
The Coombe
Patrick St.
Bride St.
Peter St.
Peter Row
Aungier Street
Cork Street
Chamber St.
Newmarket
Mill Street
New Row South
Kevin St. Upper
Kevin Street
Cuffe
Wexford St.
Ocurry Road
St Tomas Road
Blackpirts
New Street
Long Lane
Camden Row
Camden Street
Donovan Road
Clanbrassil Street
Hotel
Restaurant
0
300 m
300 yards

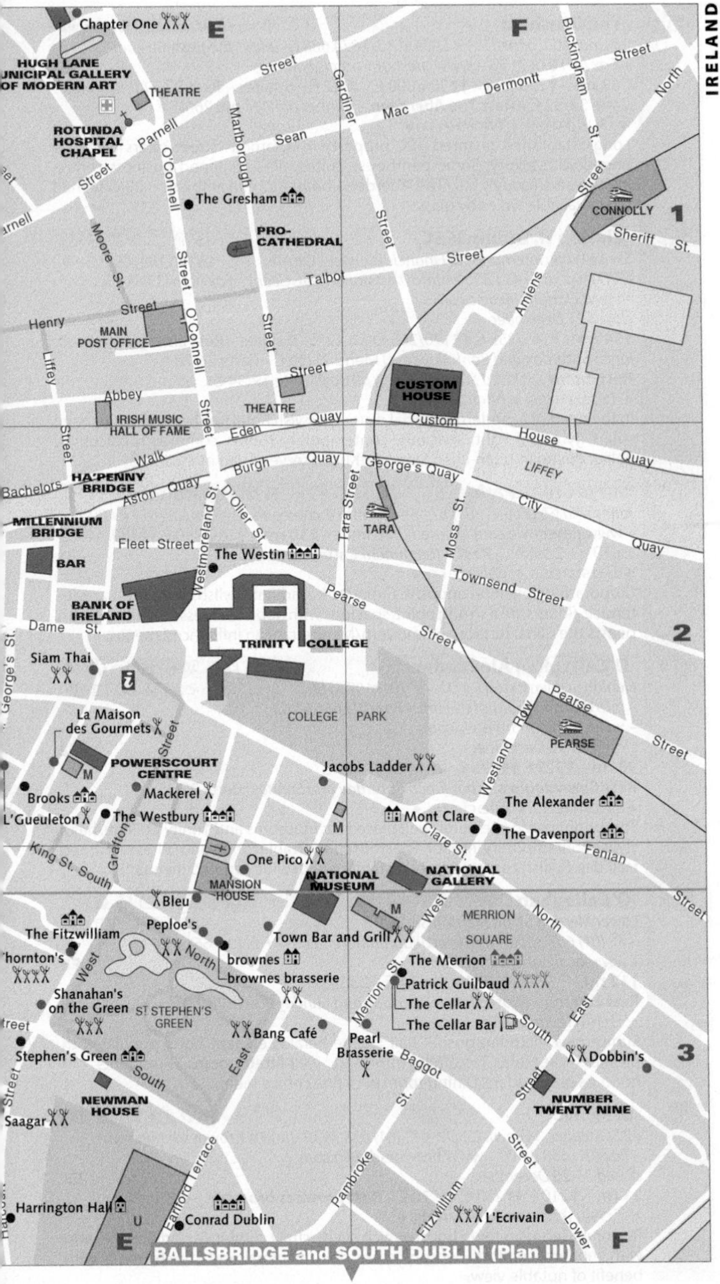
Chapter One
HUGH LANE MUNICIPAL GALLERY OF MODERN ART
THEATRE
ROTUNDA HOSPITAL CHAPEL
Parnell Street
Sean Mac Dermott Street
Buckingham St.
North Strand
O'Connell Street
Marlborough Street
Gardiner Street
The Gresham
PRO-CATHEDRAL
CONNOLLY
Sheriff St.
Moore St.
Talbot Street
Amiens Street
Henry Street
MAIN POST OFFICE
Liffey Street
Abbey Street
THEATRE
CUSTOM HOUSE
IRISH MUSIC HALL OF FAME
Eden Quay
Custom House Quay
Bachelors Walk
HA'PENNY BRIDGE
Aston Quay
Burgh Quay
George's Quay
LIFFEY
City Quay
MILLENNIUM BRIDGE
D'Olier St.
Westmoreland St.
Tara Street
TARA
Moss St.
Fleet Street
The Westin
BAR
Townsend Street
BANK OF IRELAND
Pearse Street
Dame St.
TRINITY COLLEGE
George's St.
Siam Thai
COLLEGE PARK
La Maison des Gourmets
Grafton Street
PEARSE
Westland Row
POWERSCOURT CENTRE
Jacobs Ladder
Brooks
Mackerel
The Alexander
L'Gueuleton
The Westbury
Mont Clare
The Davenport
Clare St.
Fenian Street
King St. South
One Pico
NATIONAL MUSEUM
NATIONAL GALLERY
MANSION HOUSE
Bleu
MERRION SQUARE
Merrion Square North
Merrion Square West
Peploe's
The Fitzwilliam
Town Bar and Grill
Thornton's
St. Stephen's Green North
browns
browns brasserie
The Merrion
Patrick Guilbaud
Shanahan's on the Green
ST STEPHEN'S GREEN
The Cellar
The Cellar Bar
Merrion St.
Merrion Square South
Merrion Square East
Bang Café
Pearl Brasserie
Baggot St.
Stephen's Green
Dobbin's
St. Stephen's Green South
St. Stephen's Green East
NUMBER TWENTY NINE
NEWMAN HOUSE
Saagar
Pembroke St.
Fitzwilliam Street Lower
Earlsfort Terrace
Harrington Hall
Conrad Dublin
L'Ecrivain
BALLSBRIDGE and SOUTH DUBLIN (Plan III)
E
F
1
2
3

IRELAND

The Gresham

23 Upper O'Connell St ✉ D1 – ✆ (01) 874 6881 – info@thegresham.com – Fax (01) 878 71 75 – www.gresham-hotels.com **E1**

283 rm – 🚹200/506 € 🚹🚹506/600 €, ☕ 22 € – 6 suites – **Rest** ***23*** – *(dinner only)* Carte 33/52 € – **Rest** ***The Aberdeen*** – *(dinner only)* Menu 26/45 €

♦ Business ♦ Modern ♦

Long-established restored 19C property in a famous street offers elegance tinged with luxury. Some penthouse suites. Well-equipped business centre, lounge and Toddy's bar. The Aberdeen boasts formal ambience. 23 is named after available wines by glass.

Clarion H. Dublin IFSC

Excise Walk, International Financial Services Centre, ✉ D1 – ✆ (01) 433 8800 – info@clarionhotelifsc.com – Fax (01) 433 88 11 – www.clarionhotelifsc.com

closed 25 December *Plan I* **B1**

154 rm – 🚹165/255 € 🚹🚹170/265 €, ☕ 22 € – 9 suites – **Rest** ***Sinergie*** – *(closed lunch Saturday and Bank Holidays)* Menu 21/30 € – Carte 23/28 €

Rest ***Kudos*** – *(closed Sunday) (open all day)* Carte 19/34 €

♦ Business ♦ Modern ♦

In the heart of a modern financial district, a swish hotel for the business person; smart gym and light, spacious, contemporary rooms, some with balconies. Italian dining in clean-lined Sinergie. Kudos serves Asian menus.

Jurys Croke Park

Jones's Rd ✉ D3 – ✆ (01) 871 4444 – info@crokepark.ie – Fax (01) 871 44 00 – www.jurysdoyle.com – closed Christmas – **230 rm** – 🚹189/440 € 🚹🚹189/440 €, ☕ 19 € – 2 suites – **Rest** – *(bar lunch)* Carte /dinner 30/41 € *Plan I* **B1**

♦ Business ♦ Modern ♦

Corporate styled hotel opposite Croke Park Stadium. Stylish 'Side Line' bar with terrace. Rooms are a strong point: spacious with good business amenities. Bistro boasts the Canal terrace and modern/Mediterranean influenced menus.

O'Callaghan Alexander

Fienian St, Merrion Sq ✉ D2 – ✆ (01) 607 3700 – info@ocallaghanhotels.com – Fax (01) 661 56 63 – www.ocallaghanhotels.com

closed 24-26 December **F2**

98 rm – 🚹325 € 🚹🚹325 €, ☕ 14 € – 4 suites

Rest ***Caravaggio's*** – *(bar lunch Saturday and Sunday)* Carte 25/35 €

♦ Business ♦ Modern ♦

This bright corporate hotel, well placed for museums and Trinity College, has a stylish contemporary interior. Spacious comfortable rooms and suites with good facilities. Stylish contemporary restaurant with wide-ranging menus.

O'Callaghan Davenport

Lower Merrion St, off Merrion Sq ✉ D2 – ✆ (01) 607 3500 – info@ocallaghanhotels.com – Fax (01) 661 56 63 – www.ocallaghanhotels.com **F2**

112 rm – 🚹371 € 🚹🚹371 €, ☕ 14 € – 2 suites

Rest ***Lanyon*** – *(closed lunch Saturday and Sunday)* Carte 35/60 €

♦ Business ♦ Modern ♦

Sumptuous Victorian gospel hall façade heralds elegant hotel popular with business clientele. Tastefully furnished, well-fitted rooms. Presidents bar honours past leaders. Dining room with fine choice menu.

brownes

22 St Stephen's Green, ✉ D2 – ✆ (01) 638 3939 – info@brownesdublin.com – Fax (01) 638 39 00 – www.brownesdublin.com

closed 25-26 December **E3**

11 rm – 🚹210 € 🚹🚹280 €, ☕ 20 € – **Rest** ***brownes brasserie*** – see below

♦ Townhouse ♦ Stylish ♦

Restored Georgian town house which successfully combines traditional charm with modern comfort. Bedrooms are bold, minimal and stylish, some with benefit of notable view.

O'Callaghan Mont Clare AC 120 VISA MC AE
Lower Merrion St, off Merrion Sq ✉ D2 – ☎ (01) 607 3800 – info@ocallaghanhotels.com – Fax (01) 661 56 63 – www.ocallaghanhotels.com
closed 24-26 December **F2**
74 rm – †253 € ††253 €, ☕ 14 €
Rest *Goldsmiths* – *(dinner only)* Carte 30/40 €
♦ Business ♦ Modern ♦
Classic property with elegant panelled reception and tasteful comfortable rooms at heart of Georgian Dublin. Corporate suites available. Traditional pub style Gallery bar. Informal restaurant with tried-and-tested menus.

Quality H.Dublin City AC rest 50 VISA MC AE
Sir John Rogerson's Quay, Cardiff Lane, ✉ D2 – ☎ (01) 643 9500 – info@qualityhoteldublin.com – Fax (01) 643 95 10 – www.qualityhoteldublin.com
closed 23-27 December *Plan I* **B1**
211 rm – †229 € ††229 €, ☕ 14 €
Rest – *(bar lunch)* Carte /dinner 35€ and 32/43 €
♦ Business ♦ Modern ♦
Based in 'new generation' quayside area. Sleek Vertigo bar named after U2 song. Impressive health club with large pool. Spacious, modern rooms, 48 boasting balconies. Irish and European mix of dishes in open plan restaurant.

Harrington Hall without rest P VISA MC AE
70 Harcourt St ✉ D2 – ☎ (01) 475 3497 – harringtonhall@eircom.net – Fax (01) 475 45 44 – www.harringtonhall.com **E3**
28 rm ☕ – †110/140 € ††188/230 €
♦ Townhouse ♦ Classic ♦
Two usefully located mid-terrace Georgian town houses. Friendly and well-run. Bright, spacious, superior bedrooms with co-ordinated décor. Welcoming guest lounge.

Kilronan House without rest VISA MC AE
70 Adelaide Rd ✉ D2 – ☎ (01) 475 5266 – info@dublinn.com – Fax (01) 478 28 41 – www.dublinn.com *Plan III* **G1**
12 rm ☕ – †55/120 € ††120/170 €
♦ Traditional ♦ Classic ♦
In the heart of Georgian Dublin, a good value, well-kept town house run by knowledgeable, friendly couple. Individually styled rooms; sustaining breakfasts.

Patrick Guilbaud AC 25 VISA MC AE
21 Upper Merrion St ✉ D2 – ☎ (01) 676 4192 – restaurantpatrickguilbaud@eircom.net – Fax (01) 661 00 52 – www.restaurantpatrickguilbaud.ie
closed 17 March, 25-26 December, Good Friday, Sunday and Monday **F3**
Rest – Menu 48 € (lunch) – Carte 88/115 €
Spec. Lobster ravioli in coconut scented cream. Veal sweetbread in liquorice with parsnip sauce. Assiette of chocolate.
♦ Contemporary ♦ Formal ♦
Top class restaurant run by consummate professional offering accomplished Irish-influenced dishes in elegant Georgian town house. Contemporary Irish art collection.

Thornton's – at The Fitzwilliam H. AC P VISA MC AE
St Stephen's Green ✉ D2 – ☎ (01) 478 7008 – thorntonsrestaurant@eircom.net – Fax (01) 478 70 09 – www.thorntonsrestaurant.com
closed 2 weeks Christmas, Sunday and Monday **E3**
Rest – Menu 30/40 € (lunch) – Carte 91/104 €
Spec. Sautéed prawns with prawn bisque, truffle sabayon. Suckling pig with trotter, glazed turnip and poitin sauce. Orange and chocolate soufflé with raspberry sauce.
♦ Modern ♦ Formal ♦
Second floor style, offering interesting culinary ideas drawing on Irish and French influences; fine views too. Good value lunches. Walls hung with chef's striking photos.

IRELAND

XXX **Shanahan's on the Green** AC VISA MC AE D

119 St Stephen's Green ✉ D2 – ✆ (01) 407 0939
– sales@shanahans.ie
– Fax (01) 407 09 40
– www.shanahans.ie
closed Christmas-New Year **E3**

Rest – *(booking essential) (dinner only and Friday lunch)* Menu 45 € (lunch) – Carte 76/105 €

♦ Beef specialities ♦ Formal ♦

Sumptuous Georgian town house; upper floor window tables survey the Green. Supreme comfort enhances your enjoyment of strong seafood dishes and choice cuts of Irish beef.

XXX ✿ **L'Ecrivain** (Clarke) AC 20 VISA MC AE

109A Lower Baggot Street ✉ D2 – ✆ (01) 661 1919
– enquiries@lecrivain.com
– Fax (01) 661 06 17 – www.lecrivain.com
closed 23 December-4 January, Easter, Saturday lunch, Sunday and Bank Holidays **F3**

Rest – *(booking essential)* Menu 45/75 € – Carte dinner 75/93 €

Spec. Dublin Bay prawn plate. Roast quail with white onion cream and braised leg. Lobster with cauliflower purée and spiced cauliflower beignets.

♦ Contemporary ♦ Formal ♦

Robust, well prepared, modern Irish menus with emphasis on fish and game. Well established, with business clientele at lunch. Attentive service from well-versed team.

XXX ✿ **Chapter One** (Lewis) AC 14 VISA MC

The Dublin Writers Museum, 18-19 Parnell Sq ✉ D1
– ✆ (01) 873 2266 – info@chapteronerestaurant.com
– Fax (01) 873 23 30
– www.chapteronerestaurant.com
closed first 2 weeks August, 24 December-8 January, Sunday, Monday and Bank Holidays **E1**

Rest – Menu 34 € (lunch) – Carte dinner 50/60 €

Spec. Pithivier of wild mushrooms, pancetta and foie gras, celeriac purée. John Dory with broccoli purée, mussels and tomato confit. Chocolate millefeuille with banana mousse and coffee coulis.

♦ Modern ♦ Formal ♦

In basement of historic building, once home to whiskey baron. Comfy restaurant with Irish art on walls. Interesting menu skilfully prepared with refined and original edge.

XX **The Tea Room** – at The Clarence H. VISA MC AE D

6-8 Wellington Quay ✉ D2 – ✆ (01) 407 0813 – tearoom@theclarence.ie
– Fax (01) 407 08 26 – www.theclarence.ie
closed 24-26 December and Saturday lunch **D2**

Rest – *(booking essential)* Menu 24/29 € (lunch) – Carte 37/65 €

♦ Modern ♦ Fashionable ♦

Spacious elegant ground floor room with soaring coved ceiling and stylish contemporary décor offers interesting modern Irish dishes with hint of continental influence.

XX **brownes brasserie** – at brownes H. AC 35 VISA MC AE D

22 St Stephen's Green ✉ D2 – ✆ (01) 638 3939 – info@brownesdublin.ie
– Fax (01) 638 39 00 – www.brownesdublin.com
closed Saturday lunch **E3**

Rest – *(booking essential)* Carte 39/57 €

♦ Modern ♦ Brasserie ♦

Smart, characterful with a Belle Époque feel. On the ground floor of the eponymous Georgian town house, in central location, with interesting and appealing classic dishes.

XX **The Cellar** - at The Merrion H.

Upper Merrion St ✉ D2 - ☏ (01) 603 0630 - Fax (01) 603 07 00 - www.merrionhotel.com
closed Saturday lunch **F3**
Rest - Menu 25 € (lunch) - Carte dinner 26/54 €
♦ Mediterranean ♦ Formal ♦
Smart open-plan basement restaurant with informal ambience offering well-prepared formal style fare crossing Irish with Mediterranean influences. Good value lunch menu.

XX **One Pico**

5-6 Molesworth Pl ✉ D2 - ☏ (01) 676 0300 - eamonnoreilly@ireland.com - Fax (01) 676 04 11 - www.onepico.com
closed 25 December-4 January and Sunday **E3**
Rest - Menu 25/35 € - Carte 40/55 €
♦ Modern ♦ Fashionable ♦
Wide-ranging cuisine, classic and traditional by turns, always with an original, eclectic edge. Décor and service share a pleasant formality, crisp, modern and stylish.

XX **Rhodes D7**

The Capel Buildings, Mary's Abbey, ✉ D7 - ☏ (01) 804 4444 - info@rhodesd7.com - Fax (01) 804 44 47 - www.rhodesd7.com
closed dinner Sunday and Monday - **Rest** - Carte 32/47 € Plan III **J1**
♦ Modern ♦ Brasserie ♦
Cavernous restaurant: take your pick from four dining areas. Bright, warm décor incorporating bold, colourful paintings accompanies classic Rhodes menus given an Irish twist.

XX **Les Frères Jacques**

74 Dame St ✉ D2 - ☏ (01) 679 4555 - info@lesfreresjacques.com - Fax (01) 679 47 25 - www.lesfreresjacques.com
closed 24 December-3 January, Saturday lunch, Sunday and Bank Holidays
Rest - Menu 22/36 € - Carte 42/66 € **D2**
♦ French ♦ Bistro ♦
Smart and well established, offering well prepared, classic French cuisine with fresh fish and seafood a speciality, served by efficient French staff. Warm, modern décor.

XX **Peploe's**

16 St Stephen's Green ✉ D2 - ☏ (01) 676 3144 - reservations@peploes.com - Fax (01) 676 31 54 - www.peploes.com
closed 24-28 December - **Rest** - Carte 31/48 € **E3**
♦ Mediterranean ♦ Fashionable ♦
Fashionable restaurant - a former bank vault - by the Green. Irish wall mural, Italian leather chairs, suede banquettes. Original dishes with pronounced Mediterranean accents.

XX **Town Bar and Grill**

21 Kildare St ✉ D2 - ☏ (01) 662 4724 - reservations@townbarandgrill.com - Fax (01) 662 38 57 - www.townbarandgrill.com **E3**
Rest - Menu 26 € (lunch) - Carte dinner 40/63 €
♦ Italian influences ♦ Rustic ♦
Located in wine merchant's old cellars: brick pillars divide a large space; fresh flowers and candles add a personal touch. Italian flair in bold cooking with innovative edge.

XX **Saagar**

16 Harcourt St ✉ D2 - ☏ (01) 475 5060 - info@saagarindianrestaurants.com - Fax (01) 475 11 51 - www.saagarindianrestaurants.com
closed 23-25 December and Sunday **E3**
Rest - Menu 13/25 € - Carte 14/33 €
♦ Indian ♦ Friendly ♦
Well-run restaurant serving subtly toned, freshly prepared Indian fare in basement of Georgian terraced house. Attentive service. Ring bell at foot of stairs to enter.

XX **Dobbin's**

15 Stephen's Lane, off Lower Mount St ✉ D2 – ✆ (01) 661 9536 – dobbinsbistro@mail.com – Fax (01) 661 33 31

closed 1 week Christmas-New Year, Saturday lunch, Sunday dinner and Bank Holidays **F3**

Rest – *(booking essential)* Menu 25/35 € – Carte 25/54 €

♦ Traditional ♦ Retro ♦

In the unlikely setting of a former Nissen hut, and now with contemporary styling, this popular restaurant, something of a local landmark, offers good food to suit all tastes.

XX **Jacobs Ladder**

4-5 Nassau St ✉ D2 – ✆ (01) 670 3865 – dining@jacobsladder.ie – Fax (01) 670 38 68 – www.jacobsladder.ie

closed 2 weeks Christmas, 1 week August, 17 March, Sunday, Monday and Bank Holidays **E2**

Rest – *(booking essential)* Menu 40 € (dinner) – Carte 48/58 €

♦ Modern ♦ Fashionable ♦

Up a narrow staircase, this popular small first floor restaurant with unfussy modern décor and a good view offers modern Irish fare and very personable service.

XX **Siam Thai**

14-15 Andrew St ✉ D2 – ✆ (01) 677 3363 – siam@eircom.net – Fax (01) 670 76 44 – www.siamthai.ie

closed 25-26 December and lunch Saturday and Sunday **E2**

Rest – Menu 35 € – Carte 27/38 €

♦ Thai ♦ Exotic ♦

Invariably popular, centrally located restaurant with a warm, homely feel, embodied by woven Thai prints. Daily specials enhance Thai menus full of choice and originality.

XX **Jaipur**

41 South Great George's St ✉ D2 – ✆ (01) 677 0999 – dublin@jaipur.ie – Fax (01) 677 09 79 – www.jaipur.ie

closed 25-26 December **D2**

Rest – *(dinner only)* Menu 20 € – Carte 25/50 €

♦ Indian ♦ Minimalist ♦

Vivid modernity in the city centre; run by knowledgeable team. Immaculately laid, linen-clad tables. Interesting, freshly prepared Indian dishes using unique variations.

XX **Bang Café**

11 Merrion Row ✉ D2 – ✆ (01) 676 0898 – Fax (01) 676 08 99 – www.bangrestaurant.com

closed 1 week Christmas and Sunday **E3**

Rest – *(booking essential)* Carte 26/49 €

♦ Innovative ♦ Fashionable ♦

Stylish feel, closely set tables and an open kitchen lend a lively, contemporary air to this established three-tier favourite. Menus balance the classical and the creative.

X **Pearl Brasserie**

20 Merrion St Upper ✉ D2 – ✆ (01) 661 3572 – info@pearl-brasserie.com – Fax (01) 661 36 29

closed Bank Holidays and lunch Saturday-Monday **F3**

Rest – Menu 26 € (lunch) – Carte dinner 31/44 €

♦ French ♦ Brasserie ♦

A metal staircase leads down to this intimate, vaulted cellar brasserie and oyster bar. Franco-Irish dishes served at granite-topped tables. Amiable and helpful service.

Eden

Meeting House Sq, Temple Bar ✉ D2 – ✆ (01) 670 5372 – eden@edenrestaurant.ie – Fax (01) 670 33 30 – www.edenrestaurant.ie
closed 25 December-3 January and Bank Holidays **D2**
Rest – Menu 25 € (lunch) – Carte dinner 33/50 €
◆ Modern ◆ Minimalist ◆
Modern minimalist restaurant with open plan kitchen serves good robust food. Terrace overlooks theatre square, at the heart of a busy arty district. The place for pre-theatre.

Mermald Café

69-70 Dame St ✉ D2 – ✆ (01) 670 8236 – info@mermald.ie – Fax (01) 670 82 05 – www.mermaid.ie
closed 24-26 and 31 December, 1 January and Good Friday **D2**
Rest – *(booking essential) (Sunday brunch)* Menu 26 € (lunch) – Carte 32/46 €
◆ Modern ◆ Fashionable ◆
This informal restaurant with unfussy décor and bustling atmosphere offers an interesting and well cooked selection of robust modern dishes. Efficient service.

L'Gueleton

1 Fade St, ✉ D2 – ✆ (01) 675 3708
closed 25 December-1 January, Sunday and Bank Holidays **E2**
Rest – *(Bookings not accepted)* Carte 27/42 €
◆ French ◆ Bistro ◆
Busy, highly renowned recent arrival. Rustic style: mish-mash of roughed-up chairs and tables with candles or Parisian lamps. Authentic French country dishes full of flavour.

Bleu

Joshua House, Dawson St ✉ D2 – ✆ (01) 676 7015 – Fax (01) 676 70 27 – www.onepico.com **E3**
Rest – Carte 28/43 €
◆ Modern ◆ Fashionable ◆
Distinctive modern interior serves as chic background to this friendly all-day restaurant. Appealing and varied menu, well executed and very tasty. Good wine selection.

Mackerel

(first Floor) Bewley's Building, Grafton St, ✉ D2 – ✆ (01) 672 7719 – info@mackerel.ie
closed 25 December and Bank Holidays **E2**
Rest – Carte 25/47 €
◆ Seafood ◆ Fashionable ◆
Above famous 1920s coffee shop. Fossilised marble, purple chenille and deep blue gel as one. Seasonally changing, market-fresh seafood dishes: spicing and eclectic touches.

La Maison des Gourmets

15 Castlemarket ✉ D2 – ✆ (01) 672 7258 – Fax (01) 672 72 38
closed 25 December-2 January, Sunday and Bank Holidays **E2**
Rest – *(Booking not accepted) (lunch only)* Carte 20/25 €
◆ French ◆ Cosy ◆
Neat, refurbished eatery on first floor above an excellent French bakery. Extremely good value Gallic meals with simplicity the key. Get there early or be prepared to wait!

The Cellar Bar – at The Merrion H.

Upper Merrion St ✉ D2 – ✆ (01) 603 0600 – info@merrionhotel.com – Fax (01) 603 07 00 – www.merrionhotel.com
closed Sunday **F3**
Rest – *(carving lunch)* Carte 30/45 €
◆ Traditional ◆ Pub ◆
Characterful stone and brick bar-restaurant in the original vaulted cellars with large wood bar. Popular with Dublin's social set. Offers wholesome Irish pub lunch fare.

BALLSBRIDGE and SOUTH DUBLIN *Plan III*

Four Seasons 800

Simmonscourt Rd ✉ D4 – ✆ (01) 665 4000 – sales.dublin@fourseasons.com – Fax (01) 665 40 99 – www.fourseasons.com/dublin **J2**

157 rm – **†490 € ††645 €, ☕ 30 € – 40 suites**

Rest *Seasons* – Menu 35/45 € (lunch) – Carte 58/91 €

Rest *The Cafe* – Carte 34/48 €

♦ Grand Luxury ♦ Modern ♦

Every inch the epitome of international style - supremely comfortable rooms with every facility; richly furnished lounge; a warm mix of antiques, oils and soft piano études. Dining in Seasons guarantees luxury ingredients. Good choice menu in The Café.

The Berkeley Court 450

Lansdowne Rd ✉ D4 – ✆ (01) 665 3200 – berkeleycourt@jurysdoyle.com – Fax (01) 661 72 38 – www.jurysdoyle.com **J1**

182 rm – **†399 € ††399 €, ☕ 30 € – 4 suites**

Rest *Berkeley Room* – *(closed Sunday dinner)* Menu 40/50 €

Rest *Palm Court Café* – Menu 30 € (lunch) – Carte dinner 40/50 €

♦ Luxury ♦ Classic ♦

Luxurious international hotel in former botanical gardens two minutes from the home of Irish rugby. Large amount of repeat business. Solidly formal feel throughout. Berkeley Room for elegant fine dining. Breakfast buffets a feature of Palm Court Café.

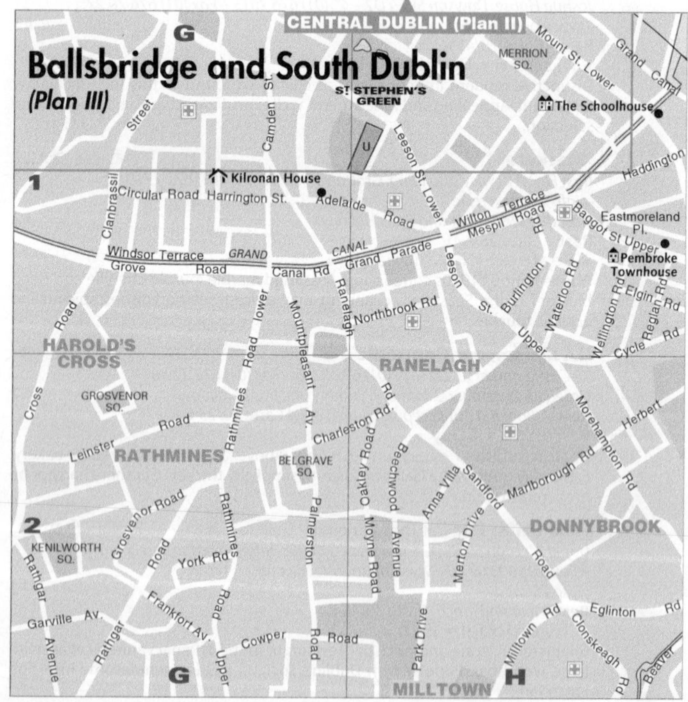

Herbert Park

100 VISA

D4 – (01) 667 2200 – reservations@herbertparkhotel.ie – Fax (01) 667 25 95 – www.herbertparkhotel.ie **J2**

151 rm – 240 € 375 €, 19 € – 2 suites

Rest *The Pavilon* – *(closed dinner Sunday and Monday)* Menu 26 € (lunch) – Carte dinner 35/65 €

◆ Business ◆ Modern ◆

Stylish contemporary hotel. Open, modern lobby and lounges. Excellent, well-designed rooms with tasteful décor: fifth floor Executive rooms boast several upgraded extras. French-windowed restaurant with alfresco potential; oyster/lobster specialities.

The Schoolhouse

VISA

2-8 Northumberland Rd D4 – (01) 667 5014 – reservations@schoolhousehotel.com – Fax (01) 667 50 15 – www.schoolhousehotel.com closed 24-26 December **H1**

31 rm – 165 € 199 €

Rest *Canteen* – *(brunch Saturday and Sunday)* Menu 24 € (lunch) – Carte 28/42 €

◆ Business ◆ Historic ◆

Spacious converted 19C schoolhouse, close to canal, boasts modernity and charm. Inkwell bar exudes a convivial atmosphere. Rooms contain locally crafted furniture. Old classroom now a large restaurant with beamed ceilings.

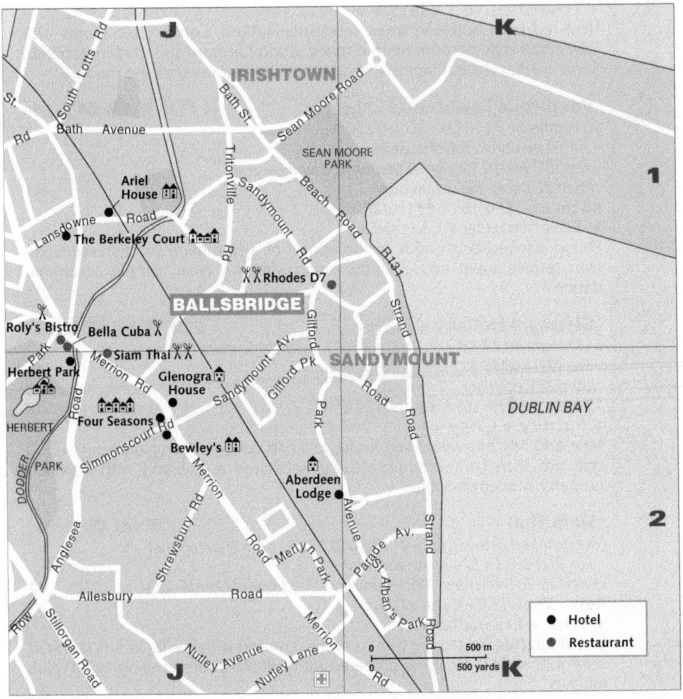

J
K
IRISHTOWN
SEAN MOORE PARK
BALLSBRIDGE
SANDYMOUNT
DUBLIN BAY
HERBERT PARK
Ariel House
The Berkeley Court
Rhodes D7
Roly's Bistro
Bella Cuba
Siam Thai
Herbert Park
Glenogra House
Four Seasons
Bewley's
Aberdeen Lodge
Hotel
Restaurant
500 m
500 yards

Ariel House without rest
50-54 Lansdowne Rd ✉ D4 – ✆ (01) 668 5512
– reservations@ariel-house.net
– Fax (01) 668 58 45 – www.ariel-house.net **J1**
37 rm – 79/109 € 89/200 €
◆ Business ◆ Classic ◆
Restored, listed Victorian mansion in smart suburb houses personally run, traditional small hotel. Rooms feature period décor and some antiques; comfy four poster rooms..

Bewley's rest 30
Merrion Rd ✉ D4 – ✆ (01) 668 1111
– bb@bewleyshotel.com
– Fax (01) 668 19 99 – www.bewleyshotels.com
closed 24-26 December **J2**
304 rm – 99/109 € 99/109 €, 11 €
Rest *O'Connells* – *✆ (01) 647 3400 (carvery lunch)* Menu 28/35 €
◆ Business ◆ Functional ◆
Huge hotel offers stylish modern accommodation behind sumptuous Victorian façade of former Masonic school. Location, facilities and value for money make this a good choice. Informal modern O'Connells restaurant, cleverly constructed with terrace in stairwell.

Aberdeen Lodge
53-55 Park Ave ✉ D4 – ✆ (01) 283 8155 – aberdeen@iol.ie
– Fax (01) 283 78 77
– www.halpinsprivatehotels.com **J2**
17 rm – 109 € 159 €
Rest – *(residents only) (light meals)* Carte 25/34 €
◆ Townhouse ◆ Classic ◆
Neat red brick house in smart residential suburb. Comfortable rooms with Edwardian style décor in neutral tones, wood furniture and modern facilities. Some garden views. Comfortable, traditionally decorated dining room.

Pembroke Townhouse without rest
90 Pembroke Rd ✉ D4 – ✆ (01) 660 0277
– info@pembroketownhouse.ie
– Fax (01) 660 02 91 – www.pembroketownhouse.ie
closed 22 December-3 January **H1**
48 rm – 90/165 € 130/230 €
◆ Townhouse ◆ Classic ◆
Period-inspired décor adds to the appeal of a sensitively modernised Georgian terrace town house in the smart suburbs. Neat, simple accommodation.

Glenogra House without rest
64 Merrion Rd ✉ D4 – ✆ (01) 668 3661 – info@glenogra.com
– Fax (01) 668 36 98 – www.glenogra.com
closed 23 December-10 January **J2**
13 rm – 79/109 € 109/129 €
◆ Family ◆ Cosy ◆
Neat and tidy bay-windowed house in smart suburb. Personally-run to good standard with bedrooms attractively decorated in keeping with a period property. Modern facilities.

Siam Thai
Sweepstake Centre ✉ D4 – ✆ (01) 660 1722 – siam@eircom.net
– Fax (01) 660 15 37 – www.siamthai.ie
closed 25-26 December, lunch Saturday, Sunday and Good Friday **J2**
Rest – Menu 35 € – Carte 27/38 €
◆ Thai ◆ Friendly ◆
Unerringly busy restaurant that combines comfort with liveliness. Efficient staff serve authentic Thai cuisine, prepared with skill and understanding. Good value lunches.

Roly's Bistro
AC 30 VISA MC AE

7 Ballsbridge Terrace ✉ D4 – ✆ (01) 668 2611 – ireland@rolysbistro.ie
– Fax (01) 660 33 42 – www.rolysbistro.ie
closed 25-27 December **J1**

Rest – *(booking essential)* Menu 20/45 € – Carte 41/49 €

♦ Traditional ♦ Bistro ♦

A Dublin institution: this roadside bistro is very busy and well run with a buzzy, fun atmosphere. Its two floors offer traditional Irish dishes and a very good value lunch.

Bella Cuba
AC VISA MC AE

11 Ballsbridge Terrace ✉ D4 – ✆ (01) 660 5539
– info@bella-cuba.com
– Fax (01) 660 55 39 – www.bella-cuba.com
closed lunch Saturday and Sunday **J1**

Rest – *(booking essential)* Menu 25 € (lunch) – Carte 41/49 €

♦ Cuban ♦ Family ♦

Family-owned restaurant with an intimate feel. Cuban memoirs on walls, fine choice of cigars. Authentic Cuban dishes, employing many of the island's culinary influences.

---

at DUBLIN AIRPORT

Crowne Plaza
AC SAT 1000 P VISA MC AE

Northwood Park, Santry Demesne, Santry (South : 3 1/4 km on R 132) ✉ D9
– ✆ (01) 862 8888 – info@crowneplazadublin.ie – Fax (01) 862 88 00
– www.cpdublin-airport.com

202 rm – †99/380 € ††99/380 €, ☕ 21 € – 2 suites

Rest *Touzai* – *(closed Saturday lunch) (buffet lunch)* Carte dinner 27/41 €

Rest *Cinnabar* – Carte 21/28 €

♦ Luxury ♦ Modern ♦

Next to Fingal Park, two miles from airport. Hotel has predominant Oriental style, extensive meeting facilities and modern, well-equipped rooms, some of Club standard. Cool, clear-linedTouzai for Asian specialities. Stylish Cinnabar has extensive menu range.

Hilton Dublin Airport
AC SAT 550 P VISA MC AE

Northern Cross, Malahide Rd ✉ D17 – ✆ (01) 866 1800
– reservations.dublinairport@hilton.com – Fax (01) 866 18 66
– www.hilton.com

162 rm – †119 € ††119 €, ☕ 20 € – 4 suites

Rest *Solas* – *(dinner only and Sunday lunch)* Carte /dinner approx. 40 €

♦ Business ♦ Modern ♦

Opened in 2005, just five minutes from the airport, adjacent to busy shopping centre. Modish feel throughout. State-of-the-art meeting facilities. Airy, well-equipped rooms. Spacious dining room serves tried-and-tested dishes with distinct Irish flavour.

Carlton Dublin Airport
AC SAT 450 P VISA MC AE

Old Airport Rd, Cloughran, (on R132 Santry Rd) – ✆ (01) 866 7500
– info@carltondublinairport.com – Fax (01) 862 31 14
– www.carltondublinairport.com
closed 3 days Christmas

99 rm – †225/420 € ††225/420 €, ☕ 14 € – 1 suite

Rest *Carlton Dublin Airport* – *(closed Sunday dinner and Monday) (dinner only and Sunday lunch)* Carte /dinner 34/47 €

♦ Business ♦ Modern ♦

Purpose-built hotel on edge of airport. State-of-the-art conference rooms. Impressive bedrooms, though many a touch compact, in warm colours with high level of facilities. Fine dining restaurant: worldwide cooking accompanied by excellent views.

Great Southern

450 VISA AE

– ✆ (01) 844 6000 – sales@dubairport-gsh.com – Fax (01) 844 60 01
– www.greatsouthernhotels.com
closed 25 December
227 rm – 139 € 149 €, 15 € – 2 suites
Rest *Potters* – *(closed Sunday and Monday) (dinner only)* Carte 34/54 €
Rest *O'Deas Bar* – *(carvery lunch)* Carte /dinner 23/37 €

♦ Business ♦ Modern ♦

Modern hotel catering for international and business travellers. Range of guest rooms, all spacious and smartly furnished with wood furniture and colourful fabrics. Potters has a spacious, formal feel. O'Deas Bar for intimate carvery menus.

ITALY
ITALIA

PROFILE

◆ **AREA:**
301 262 km² (116 317 sq mi).

◆ **POPULATION:**
58 103 000 inhabitants (est. 2005), density = 193 per km².

◆ **CAPITAL:**
Rome (conurbation 2 867 000 inhabitants).

◆ **CURRENCY:**
Euro (€); rate of exchange: € 1 = 1.32 US$ (Nov 2006).

◆ **GOVERNMENT:**
Parliamentary republic with two chambers (since 1946). Member of European Union since 1957 (one of the 6 founding countries).

◆ **LANGUAGE:**
Italian.

◆ **SPECIFIC PUBLIC HOLIDAYS:**
Epiphany (6 January); Liberation Day (25 April); Anniversary of the Republic (2 June); Immaculate Conception (8 December); St. Stephen's Day (26 December). Each town also celebrates the feast day of its patron saint (Rome: 29 June St. Peter, Milan: 7 December St. Ambrose, etc details from the local tourist offices).

◆ **LOCAL TIME:**
GMT + 1 hour in winter and GMT + 2 hours in summer.

◆ **CLIMATE:**
Temperate Mediterranean, with mild winters and hot, sunny summers (Rome: January: 8°C, July: 25°C).

◆ **INTERNATIONAL DIALLING CODE:**
00 39 followed by area or city code and then the local number.

◆ **EMERGENCY:**
Police: ✆ **112**; Fire Brigade: ✆ **115**; Health services: ✆ **118**.

◆ **ELECTRICITY:**
220 volts AC, 50Hz; 2-pin round-shaped continental plugs.

FORMALITIES

Travellers from the European Union (EU), Switzerland, Iceland and the main countries of North and South America need a national identity card or passport (America: passport required) to visit Italy for less than three months (tourism or business purpose). For visitors from other countries a visa may be required, in addition to a passport, especially for those wishing to stay for longer than three months. We advise you to check with your embassy before travelling.

A valid driving licence is essential. Third party insurance is the minimum cover required by Italian legislation but it is advisable to take out fully comprehensive cover (Green Card).

MAJOR NEWSPAPERS

The main Italian dailies are *Corriere della Sera* and *La Repubblica*, available throughout Italy. There are also many important local papers like *Il Messaggero* in Rome, *La Stampa* in Turin and *La Nazione* in Florence; the main economic newspaper is *Il Sole 24 Ore*. The *Osservatore Romano* is the official paper of the Vatican City.

SMOKING-NO SMOKING

The laws in Italy prohibit smoking in all restaurants, bars and in the public areas of hotels. Some hotel bedrooms are still available for smokers.

USEFUL PHRASES

ENGLISH	ITALIAN	ENGLISH	ITALIAN
Yes	**Si**	Thank you	**Grazie**
No	**No**	Please	**Per favore**
Good morning	**Buon giorno**	Excuse me	**Mi scusi**
Goodbye	**Arrivederci**	I don't understand	**Non capisco**

HOTELS

→ CATEGORIES

Major towns have **hotels** in all categories from luxury establishments to **guest-houses**. It is not always easy to find value for money accommodation in tourist centres and during the summer months prices may well go up. For regions and cities popular with tourists, it is advisable to book well in advance if you plan to go from April to October.

→ PRICE RANGE

Prices are quoted per room. In general from November to March (with the exception of the art cities such as Florence, Venice and Rome) prices are considerably lower and many hotels offer discounts or special weekend deals.

→ TAX

Included in the price of the room.

→ CHECK OUT TIME

Usually between 11am and noon.

→ RESERVATIONS

By telephone or by Internet. A credit card number may be required.

→ TIP FOR LUGGAGE HANDLING

At the discretion of the customer (about €1 per item).

→ BREAKFAST

It is often not included in the price of the room. It is served between 7am and 10am. Most hotels offer a self-service buffet but usually it is possible to have continental breakfast served in the room.

Reception	**Ufficio ricevimento**	Bed	**Letto**
Single room	**Camera singola**	Bathroom	**Bagno**
Double room	**Camera doppia**	Shower	**Doccia**

RESTAURANTS

Besides the traditional **restaurants** which offer elegant cuisine and service, there are various types of places to eat which serve simpler fare. A **trattoria** is a medium-priced, family-run establishment serving home-made dishes, a **taverna** is a more modest type of trattoria and an **osteria** is a local inn serving simple dishes in an informal atmosphere. A **locanda** usually serves local dishes. A **pizzeria** is the place to choose for a tasty, quick and reasonably priced meal; other dishes are often on offer. **Tavola calda** (hot table) is a cafeteria-style restaurant serving hot dishes and a **rosticceria** specialises in grilled meat, chicken and fish. **Enoteche** (wine bars) serve light starters and daily specials with a varied choice of wines by the glass or bottle.

Breakfast	**Colazione**	7am – 10am
Lunch	**Pranzo**	12.30pm – 2.30pm
Dinner	**Cena**	7.30-11pm sometimes later

Most restaurants offer a fixed price menu (*menù turistico* – a three or four course meal with limited choice), the speciality of the day or the more extensive à la carte menu.

→ RESERVATIONS

Reservations are usually made by phone. For famous restaurants (including Michelin starred restaurants), it is advisable to book several days, even weeks, in advance.

→ THE BILL

The bill (check) includes service and VAT (sales tax IVA). Bread and cover charges are usually included in the price but in some trattorie and pizzerie they are calculated separately.

Appetizer	**Antipasto**	Bread	**Pane**
Meal	**Pasto**	Meat (rare, medium well done)	**Carne (al sangue, a puntino, ben cotta)**
First course	**Primi piatti**	Fish	**Pesce**
Main dish	**Secondi piatti**	Salt/pepper	**Sale/pepe**
Main dish of the day	**Piatto del giorno**	Cheese	**Formaggio**
Dessert	**Dolce**	Vegetables	**Verdure**
Water/ sparkling/ mineral	**Acqua naturale/ gasata/minerale**	Hot/cold	**Caldo/freddo**
Wine (red, white, rosé)	**Vino (rosso, bianco, rosé)**	The bill (check) please	**Il conto per favore**
Beer	**Birra**		

LOCAL CUISINE

The gastronomic excellence of Italy rates among the pleasures of a visit to the country and the great variety of regional specialities never ceases to delight. The fertile land ensures a plentiful supply of fresh fruits and vegetables and the local markets are a riot of colour. The long coastline and many rivers provide fresh fish in abundance.

Popular dishes of **Piedmont** are fonduta (melted cheese with milk, eggs and white truffles when in season), agnolotti (ravioli), braised beef in Barolowine, boiled bee and bonèt (chocolate pudding). In **Lombardy**, polenta is a staple in country cooking; minestrone (soup of green vegetables and pasta), risotto and costoletta (breaded veal fillet) are all prepared with saffron *'alla milanese'*. Ossobuco (veal shank with marrow bone) and tortelli di zucca (pumpkin fritters), pizzoccheri (buckwheat tagliatelle), panettone (fruit cake with lemon peel), torrone (nougat) and mostarda (candied fruits in mustard) from Cremona are regional delicacies. Gorgonzola, Grana Padano and Taleggio are well-known cheeses.

The people of **Veneto** in the Po delta eat polenta, bigoli (a type of spaghetti), risi e bisi (rice and peas), risotto with chicory, fegato alla veneziana (calves' liver with onions) and excellent fish dishes including shellfish, eels, sardines in brine and spaghetti with squid ink. Pandoro, a star-shaped Christmas cake, is baked in Verona. Specialities of **Alto Adige** comprise canederli (dumplings), gröstl (meat and potato pie), smoked pork with sauerkraut and delicious pastries (Strüdel) while **Friuli** is famous for cialzons (ravioli), jòta (meat soup), prosciutto di San Daniele (raw ham), scampi, grancèvole (spider crabs), frico (fried cheese) and montasio cheese. **Liguria** enjoys pasta with pesto sauce, lasagne, pansotti (ravioli) with walnut sauce, cima (stuffed meat parcels), buridda and cappon magro (fish and vegetable salad).

Emilia-Romagna is renowned for Bologna salami and mortadella, Parma ham, pasta alla bolognese and Parmesan cheese, and, last but not least, the balsamic vinegar of Modena, aged in traditional oak and chestnut barrels. **Tuscany** is a gourmet heaven with soups (*pappa col promodoro*, ribollita), Florentine specialities: baccalà alla fiorentina (dried cod), bistecca (grilled steak), fagioli all'uccelletto (beans with quails) or 'al fiasco' (with oil, onions and herbs), as well as triglie (red mullet from Livorno), Sienese panforte and pecorino and caciotta cheeses. The glories of **Umbria** include black truffles (tartufo nero) and porchetta (roast suckling pig) while the **Marche** serve vincisgrassi (pasta with a meat and cream sauce), stringozzi (a type of pasta), stuffed olives, brodetto (fish soup) and stocco all'anconetana (dried cod).

Rome sets the standard in **Lazio**: pasta with tomatoes and red pepper *(all'amatriciana)* or eggs and guanciale (bacon) *(alla carbonara)* sauce, saltimbocca alla romana (veal fillet with ham, sage and Marsala), abbacchio al forno (roast lamb), lamb alla cacciatora (with anchovy sauce) and carciofi alla Guidia. In **Campania**, choose spaghetti with shellfish (alle vongole), costata alla pizzaiola (fillet steak with wild marjoram), mozzarella in carrozza (cheese savoury) and especially pizza and calzone (a folded pizza). Typical dishes of **Puglia** are orecchiette con cime di rapa (pasta with turnip tops), rice with mussels, capretto ripieno al forno (roast kid) and oysters from Taranto while in **Basilicata** you will find pasta alla potentina, lamb and mutton dishes and good cheeses (caciocavallo, scamorza, ricotta). In **Sicily** look out for pasta con le sarde (with sardines) or alla Norma (with aubergine, tomato, ricotta), swordfish dishes, couscous with a fish soup as well as cassata and cannoli (pastry with ricotta and candied fruit). **Sardinia** is famous for malloreddus (pasta shells with sausage and tomato), lobster soup and spit-roasted pork.

There is a good choice of desserts: cakes and tarts including zuppa inglese (a kind of trifle), tiramisu, zabaglione. Ice-cream (gelato) is a firm favourite with an amazing choice of flavours.

DRINK

Italy is one of the leading wine-producing countries in Europe. Vineyards grow all over the country and most regions have notable wines. Some establishments offer local wine, mostly drunk young, in carafes at moderate prices.

The most famous wines from **Piedmont** are Barolo, Barbaresco and Barbera and sweet dessert wine Moscato d'Asti. **Tuscany** produces the popular Chianti and good wines such as Brunello di Montalcino, Nobile di Montepulciano (reds), Vernaccia di San Gimignano (white) and Vin Santo (dessert wine). Lambrusco, a fruity, sparkling red wine, and white Albana are to be found in **Emilia-Romagna**.

Red wines from the Pinot, Cabernet, Merlot grapes and white wines such as Soave, Riesling, Sauvignon, Pinot Bianco and Chardonnay are very palatable and are produced in **Trentino-Alto Adige**, **Veneto** and **Friuli Venezia Giulia**. Valpolicella and Bardolino from the **Veneto**, the red wines of Valtellina and Pavia districts in **Lombardy** are pleasant wines. White wines from **Umbria** (Orvieto) and Marche (Verdicchio) and **Lazio** (Montefiascone, Castelli – Frascati) are deliciously fragrant. Wines produced from grapes grown in volcanic soil have a delicate, slightly sulphurous taste: Lacryma Christi, Fiano di Avellino, Greco di Tufo, and red Gragnano and Taurasi **(Campania)**, white wines of Etna and Lipari **(Sicily)**. Sicily is best known for Marsala, a dark, strong wine and Malvasia, a dessert wine.

The most popular aperitifs are vermouth (Martini, Americano) and Campari, bitter flavoured with orange peel and herbs, with ice and sparkling water.

ROME
ROMA

Population (est. 2005): 2 480 000 (conurbation 2 867 000) – Altitude: about 100m above sea level

J. Malburet / MICHELIN

Rome, the Eternal City built on seven hills, never fails to impress by the imposing remains of its ancient civilizations and its lively modern activity. No other city boasts such a wealth of Classical antiquities, Renaissance palaces and Baroque churches, all bathed in the soft, golden light for which Rome is famous. There is a profusion of domes, bell towers and fine palaces. Explore the older districts with ochre-coloured facades to catch a glimpse of small squares with a bustling market, or stairways descending to a fountain; go to the fashionable areas to admire the elegant shops, cafés and buildings but most of all take in the lively character of the people in daily life.

Two centuries of Etruscan settlement were followed by the Republican era when disputes among political rivals led to civil war, which was resolved by the rise of Julius Caesar. Augustus became the first Roman emperor and extended Rome's influence. His successors driven by their qualities and flaws, have all left their mark on the city. As Roman power waned, a new force, Christianity, began to emerge and was to spread its message throughout the world. The popes embellished the city during the Renaissance. Since Rome was proclaimed the capital of Italy in 1870, it has undergone widespread expansion into a sprawling modern city.

WHICH DISTRICT TO CHOOSE

For luxury **accommodation** choose the Via Veneto *Plan II* **G1** and the area around Villa Borghese *Plan II* **G1**. You will find comfortable **pensioni** and hotels in the historical centre with its many shops and tourist sights. Trastevere *Plan II* **E3** is an attractive area but it has limited accommodation. The Vatican *Plan III* **J2** and Prati districts, which are quieter, offer reasonably priced hotels. Via Cavour *Plan II* **H2** (near the Rione Monti district) between Stazione Termini and the Fori Imperiali has a good selection of mid-range hotels. There is a concentration of pensioni and smaller hotels in the area around Stazione Termini *Plan II* **H2**, which is well served by public transport. For your comfort, choose a hotel with air-conditioning during the summer.

There is an ample choice of **restaurants** to suit all tastes ranging from

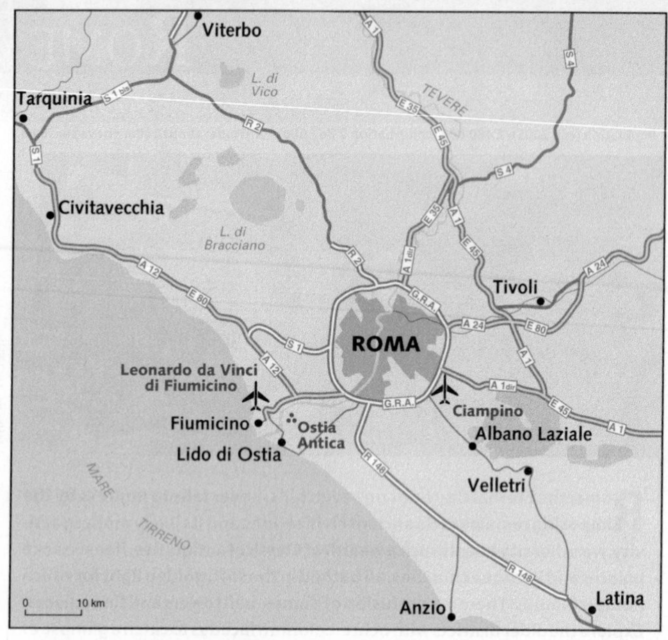

family-run **trattorias** or **osterias**, **pizzerias** to elegant establishments. The historical centre – Piazza Venezia *Plan II* **G3**, Piazza di Spagna *Plan II* **F1**, Piazza Navona *Plan II* **E2**, Corso Vittorio Emanuele II *Plan II* **F3**, Vatican City *Plan II* **J2** also offers a good selection of places serving excellent fare while the area around Stazione Termini *Plan II* **H2** has classic restaurants with good food and atmosphere. For simple, traditional cuisine go to Trastevere *Plan II* **E3**. Restaurants bearing a green logo 'Ristorante tipico' promote traditional Roman cuisine.

PRACTICAL INFORMATION

ARRIVAL – DEPARTURE

Leonardo da Vinci Airport at Fiumicino, 32 km (20 mi) southwest of Rome. ✆ 06 65 631; **Ciampino Airport**, 15 km (10 mi) southeast. ✆ 06 79 49 41.

From the airport to the city centre – By **taxi**: €35-40 (Fiumicino), €25 + additional charge for luggage, night runs and public holidays. By **train**: from Fiumicino Leonardo Express to Stazione Termini – every 30min; time: 32min; ✆ 06 65 951, 06 36 00 43 999; fares €9.50 (€11 on board); from the airport to Tiburtina Station every 15min, fare €5 and from Tiburtina to Roma Termini every 15min, journey time 40min, fare €5. From Ciampino Railway Station to Termini Station every 10-15min.

By **bus**. From Fiumicino to Stazione Termini every 2hrs, time 40min, fare €9; also to Cornelia metro station (line A), every hour, time 90min, fare €2.80. ✆ 06 65 95 86 46. From Ciampino to Ciampino **rail station** and Anagnina **metro** (line A), every 10-15min.

Main Stations – Stazione Termini or Tiburtina for mainline national and international services; both are linked to the city centre on Lines A and B. ✆ 8488 88 088; www.trenitalia.com

TRANSPORT

→ METRO, BUS AND TRAM

Tickets are available from metro stations, bus terminals, ticket machines, tobacconists, newsagents, cafés and tourist information centres. A single ticket costs €1; travelcards (1, 3, 7 days) are available (€4, €11, €16 respectively).

→ TAXIS

Taxis, which are white vehicles, bear an illuminated sign on the car roof. They may be hailed in the street, called by telephone, hired at taxi ranks. Minimum pick-up charge is €2.33 (extra charge for luggage and at night); mileage is charged at €0.78 km. An average taxi ride costs €10-15. Radio Taxis ✆ 06 35 70, 06 66 45, 06 88 22, 06 41 57, 06 55 51.

USEFUL ADDRESSES

→ TOURIST INFORMATION

APT (Azienda di Promozione Turistica), Via Parigi 11, 00185 Roma *Plan II* **H1** ✆ 06 48 89 91; at Fiumicino Airport ✆ 06 65 95 60 74; www.romaturismo.it; open 9am-6pm (2pm Sunday in winter).

Comune di Roma has information kiosks at Stazione Termini, Castel Sant'Angelo, Fontana di Trevi, Fori Imperiali, Piazza di Spagna, Piazza Navona, Santa Maria Maggiore, Via Nazionale, Piazza Sonnino in Trastevere, Piazza San Giovanni. Open 9am-6pm. www.comune.roma.it

→ POST OFFICES

Opening times Mon-Sat, 8am to 1.45pm.

→ BANKS / CURRENCY EXCHANGE

Open Mon-Fri, 8.30am to 1.30pm. Some branches open in the city centre and shopping centres on Saturday mornings.

→ EMERGENCY

✆ **118** for Ambulance, ✆ **115** for Fire Brigade and ✆ **113** for Police.

BUSY PERIODS

It may be difficult to find a room at a reasonable price (except during weekends) when special events are held in the city as hotel prices may be raised substantially:

Industrial and Commercial Fair: June

Tevere-Expo: June-July

Furniture and Design Show : June

Alta Moda a Roma: February, June

EXPLORING ROME

DIFFERENT FACETS OF THE CITY

It is possible to visit the main sights and museums in four to five days.

Museums and sights are usually open from 10am to 5pm. Some close on Mondays.

ANCIENT ROME – Campidoglio *Plan II* **G3**: **Piazza del Campidoglio**, palaces and gardens, views from Via del Campidoglio. **Terme di Caracalla** *Plan I* **C3**, baths decorated with marble, mosaics and statues. Ruins of the **Fori Imperiali** *Plan II* **G3** (Trajan's Column, markets, temples). The **Colosseum** *Plan II* **H3**, an amphitheatre for Roman spectacles, and **Arco di Constantino**. **Foro Romano** *Plan II* **G3** (basilicas, temples and arches). The **Palatino** *Plan II* **G3** and imperial residences (Domus Augustana, Casa di Livia). **Pantheon** *Plan II* **F2**. **Aula Ottagona** *Plan II* **H1**, **Ara Pacis Augustae** *Plan II* **F1**, **Area Sacra di Largo Argentina** *Plan II* **F3**.

CHRISTIAN ROME – Basilica di San Pietro *Plan III* **K2** (Sistine Chapel, Raphael Rooms, views from the dome); **Chiesa del Gesù** *Plan II* **H3**; **San Giovanni in Laterano** *Plan I* **C3**; **Santa Maria Maggiore** *Plan II* **H2**; **Santa Maria d'Aracoeli** *Plan II* **E3**; **San**

Paolo fuori le Mura *Plan I* **B3**; **San Luigi dei Francesi** *Plan II* **F2** (works by Caravaggio); **Sant'Andrea al Quirinale** *Plan II* **G2**; **San Carlo alle Quattro Fontane** *Plan II* **G2**; **Santa Cecilia in Trastevere** *Plan I* **B3** (*Last Judgement* by Cavallini); **San Clemente** *Plan II* **H3**; **Sant'Ignazio** *Plan II* **F2**; **San Lorenzo Fuori le Mura** *Plan I* **C2**; **Santa Maria degli Angeli** *Plan II* **H2**; **Santa Maria della Vittoria** *Plan II* **H1** (*Ecstasy of St Teresa* by Bernini); **Santa Susanna** *Plan II* **G1**; **Santa Maria in Cosmedin** *Plan I* **B3** *(Bocca della Verita)*; **Santa Maria in Trastevere** *Plan II* **E3**; **Santa Maria sopra Minerva** *Plan II* **F2**; **Santa Maria del Popolo** *Plan IV* **L2** (paintings by Caravaggio); **Sant'Andrea della Valle** *Plan II* **F3**; **Sant'Agostino** *Plan II* **F2** (*Madonna of the Pilgrims* by Caravaggio); **San Pietro in Vincoli** *Plan II* **H3** (*Moses* by Michelangelo); **Catacombs** *Plan I* **C3**.

PALACES AND MUSEUMS – **Palazzo Altemps**; **Castel Sant'Angelo** *Plan II* **E2**; **Villa Borghese** *Plan IV* **M2** (Galleria Borghese); Palazzo Barberini *Plan II* **G2**; Palazzo Senatorio; Palazzo dei Conservatori and Palazzo Nuovo *Plan II* **G3** (views); **Palazzo del Quirinale** *Plan II* **G2**; **Palazzo Farnese** *Plan II* **E3**; Palazzo della Cancelleria; **Villa Farnesina** *Plan I* **B2**; **Musei Vaticani** *Plan III* **J1**; **Musei Capitolini** *Plan II* **G3**; **Museo Nazionale di Villa Giulia** *Plan IV* **L2**; **Museo Nazionale Romano** (Palazzo Massimo alle Terme) *Plan II* **H1**; **Galleria Doria Pamphili** *Plan II* **F2**.

SQUARES, PARKS GARDENS – **Piazza San Pietro** *Plan III* **K2**; **Giardini Vaticani** *Plan II* **J2**; **Piazza di Spagna** *Plan II* **F1** (Spanish Steps); **Piazza Navona** *Plan II* **E2** (Fontana dei Fiumi); **Piazza del Popolo** *Plan II* **F1**; **Fontana di Trevi** *Plan II* **G2**; **Piazza dell'Esquilino** *Plan II* **H2** (views); **Orti Farnesiani** *Plan II* **E3** (views); **Pincio** *Plan II* **F1** (views); **Gianicolo** *Plan II* **E3** (views); **Borghese Gardens** *Plan IV* **M2**; **Monte Mario** *Plan I* **A1** (views); **Parco Savello** on the **Aventino** *Plan I* **B3** (views).

OUTSKIRTS – **Tivoli** (Villa Adriana, Villa d'Este); **Ostia Antica**; tour of the **Castelli Romani**.

GOURMET TREATS

To enjoy a refreshing **ice cream**, *granita* or *grattachecca*, take a break at *Il Gelato di San Crispino*, Via della Panetteria 42 and Via Acaia 56, *Giolitti*, Via Uffici del Vicario and Via Oceania 90, *Bar Cile*, Piazza Santiago del Cile, *Duse (Da Giovanni)*, Via Duse 1E, *Alberto Pica*, Via della Seggiola 12, *Santa Barbara*, Largo dei Librari 86, *Gelateria Tony*, Largo Nassiroli 15-17, *Chioschi Grattachecca*, Lungotevere Trastevere near Ponte Umberto, which are among the best in the city.

Chocoholics will enjoy *La Bottega del Cioccolato*, Via Leonina 82; *Dolce Idea* – Fabbrica di **Cioccolato** – Via San Francesco a Ripa 27. **Cheese** lovers should visit *Latticini Micocci*, Via Collina 14, *Cooperativa Agricola Stella*, Via Garigliano 68. For traditional Gentilini **biscuits** go to *Latteria Ugolini*, Via della Lungaretta 161. Some of the best **pasticcerias** are *Boccioni*, Via del Portico d'Ottavia 1, *La Dolceroma*, Via del Portico d'Ottavia 20b, *La Deliziosa*, Via Savelli 50, *Dolci Claudio Desideri*, Via Barrilli 66, *Cipriani*, Via C. Botta 21. Typical Roman cakes and pastries include *panpepato* with cystallised fruit and spices, *pangiallo* with walnuts and pine nuts, *torta di ricotta e visciole* (ricotta and sour cherry) and *bignè di San Giuseppe* (puff pastry with cream).

Antica Enoteca, Via della Croce 76b, sells **olive oil** and **wine**; *Enoteca Cavour*, Via Cavour 313, has fine wines, *Divinare*, Via Ostilia 4 for hams, cheese, fine wines. The shops in Via Natale del Grande, *Trimani*, Via Cernaia 37, *Andreoli*, Via del Pellegrino 116 and *Cambi*, Via del Leoncino 30 are also recommended.

SHOPPING

Stores are usually open from 10am to 1pm and from 4pm to 7pm in winter and 5pm to 8pm in summer. In the historic centre shops tend to stay open all day. Clothes stores are closed on Monday morning and food shops on Thursday afternoon. In Rome there are boutiques and small shops to suit all tastes and budgets but few department stores. Luxury stores line **Via Veneto** *Plan II* **G1** and you will find some of the best-known names of the world of fashion (Armani, Gucci, Prada, Valentino) in the area between **Via del Corso** *Plan II* **F2** and **Piazza di Spagna** *Plan II* **F1**, especially in **Via Frattina** *Plan II* **F2**, **Via del Babuino** *Plan II* **F1**, **Via Borgognona** *Plan II* **F1** (*Laura Biagiotti, Versace, Fendi* etc.), and **Via Bocca di Leone** *Plan II* **F1**. The famous jewellers *Bulgari* is located at the beginning of **Via dei Condotti** *Plan II* **F1** where *Raggi*, a popular shop selling striking jewellery, is also located. Antique and second-hand shops line **Via dei Coronari** *Plan II* **E2**. The shops in Via del Corso, **Via Nazionale** *Plan II* **G2**, **Via del Tritone** *Plan II* **G2** and **Via Cola di Rienzo** *Plan III* **K1** sell a variety of goods at reasonable prices.

For antique shops browse in the area of **Via dei Coronari** *Plan II* **E2** and Via del Babuino.

MARKETS – There is a long-standing flea market in **Via Portuense** (Sun, dawn to 2pm). Visit also **Borgo Parioli**, Via Tirso 14 *Plan IV* **N2**. Catacombe di Priscilla district (Sat-Sun, 9am to 8pm) is famous for antiques. Go to **Mercato di Via Sannio**, Via Sannio *Plan I* **C3**, San Giovanni in Laterano district (Mon-Sat, 10am-1pm) for new and second-hand clothes and shoes sold at factory prices and to *Testaccio*, Piazza di Testaccio *Plan I* **B3** (Mon-Sat) for quality goods. Visit **Mercato dell'Antiquariato**, Piazza Borghese *Plan II* **F2** for books and prints and in Piazza Verdi *Plan IV* **N1** for antiques, arts and crafts.

WHAT TO BUY – The latest fashions, leather goods, design and craft products, high-quality food products, antiques.

ENTERTAINMENT

For listings of venues and programmes see the brochure *L'Evento* published by the tourist office (in Italian, English). It is available from information points throughout the city. www.romaturismo.it

Auditorium Parco della Musica – Viale Pietro de Coubertin 15/30 *Plan I* **A1**.

Auditorium di Via della Conciliazione – Via della Conciliazione 4 (Vatican) *Plan III* **K2**.

Accademia Filarmonica Romana (Teatro Olimpico) – Piazza Gentile da Fabriano 17 *Plan I* **B1**.

Teatro dell'Opera – Piazza Beniamino Gigli 1 (S. Maria Maggiore) *Plan II* **H2**.

Teatro Eliseo – Via Nazionale 183 (Quirinal) *Plan II* **G2**.

Teatro Sistina – Via Sistina 129 (Piazza di Spagna) *Plan II* **F1**.

NIGHTLIFE

A visit to one of the atmospheric traditional Roman cafés should not be missed when **going out for a drink** or **for the evening**: *Caffè Capitolino*, Piazzale Cafarelli 4 for snacks, drinks, cocktails; *Ciampini*, Viale della Trinità dei Monti and Lucina 29; *Caffè Greco*, Via dei Condotti 86, the oldest literary café in Rome, *Doney*, Via Vittorio Veneto 145. Other pleasant venues include *Bar del Fico*, Piazza del Fico 26, *Vineria*, Piazza Campo dei Fiori, *Trimani*, Via Cernaia 37, *Antica Enoteca*, Via della Croce 76b, *Bar della Pace*, Via della Pace 5, *Bulzoni*, Viale Parioli 36, *Marco e Giancarlo*, Via Monte della Farina 38 and *Bar San Callisto*, Piazza San Callisto.

For **music and dancing**, Rome boasts trendy nightclubs, disco bars and bars with live bands. The district between **Piazza Campo dei Fiori** *Plan II* **E3** and **Piazza Navona** *Plan II* **E2** has a wide choice of pubs and bars, where students, tourists and the theatre crowd congregate. The bars and restaurants in **Trastevere** *Plan II* **E3**, which play live music, have a particular Roman character. The popular nightclubs are in the **Testaccio district** *Plan I* **B3** and in the nearby **Via di Libetta**.

Environs of Rome

(Plan I)

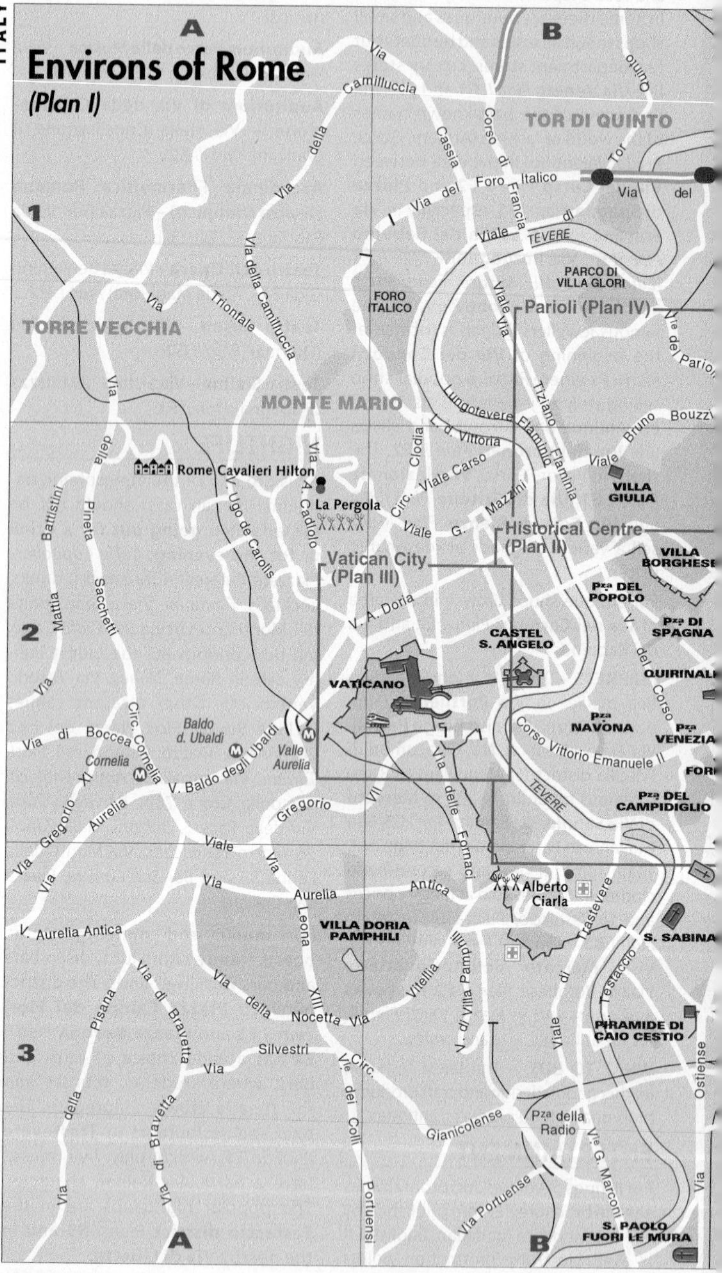

A
B
1
2
3
TORRE VECCHIA
MONTE MARIO
TOR DI QUINTO
FORO ITALICO
PARCO DI VILLA GLORI
Parioli (Plan IV)
Historical Centre (Plan II)
Vatican City (Plan III)
Rome Cavalieri Hilton
La Pergola
VILLA GIULIA
VILLA BORGHESE
Pza DEL POPOLO
Pza DI SPAGNA
CASTEL S. ANGELO
QUIRINALE
VATICANO
Pza NAVONA
Pza VENEZIA
FORI
Pza DEL CAMPIDIGLIO
Baldo d. Ubaldi
Valle Aurelia
Cornelia
Alberto Ciarla
VILLA DORIA PAMPHILI
S. SABINA
PIRAMIDE DI CAIO CESTIO
Pza della Radio
S. PAOLO FUORI LE MURA
TEVERE
Via della Camilluccia
Via Cassia
Corso di Francia
Via del Foro Italico
Viale di Tor di Quinto
Via Trionfale
Via della Pineta Sacchetti
Via Battistini
Via Mattia
V. Ugo de Carolis
Via A. Cadlolo
Circ. Clodia
Viale Carso
Viale G. Mazzini
Lungotevere Flaminio
L. d. Vittoria
Viale Tiziano
Via Flaminia
Viale Bruno Bouzzi
Vle del Parioli
V. A. Doria
V. del Corso
Corso Vittorio Emanuele II
Via di Boccea
Circ. Cornelia
V. Baldo degli Ubaldi
Via Gregorio XI
Via Aurelia
Viale Gregorio VII
Via delle Fornaci
Via Aurelia Antica
V. Aurelia Antica
Via Leone XIII
Via della Nocetta
Via Vitellia
V. di Villa Pamphili
Viale di Trastevere
Testaccio
Via Ostiense
Via di Bravetta
Via Pisana
Via Silvestri
Vle Circ. dei Colli Portuensi
Via della Bravetta
Gianicolense
Vle G. Marconi
Via Portuense

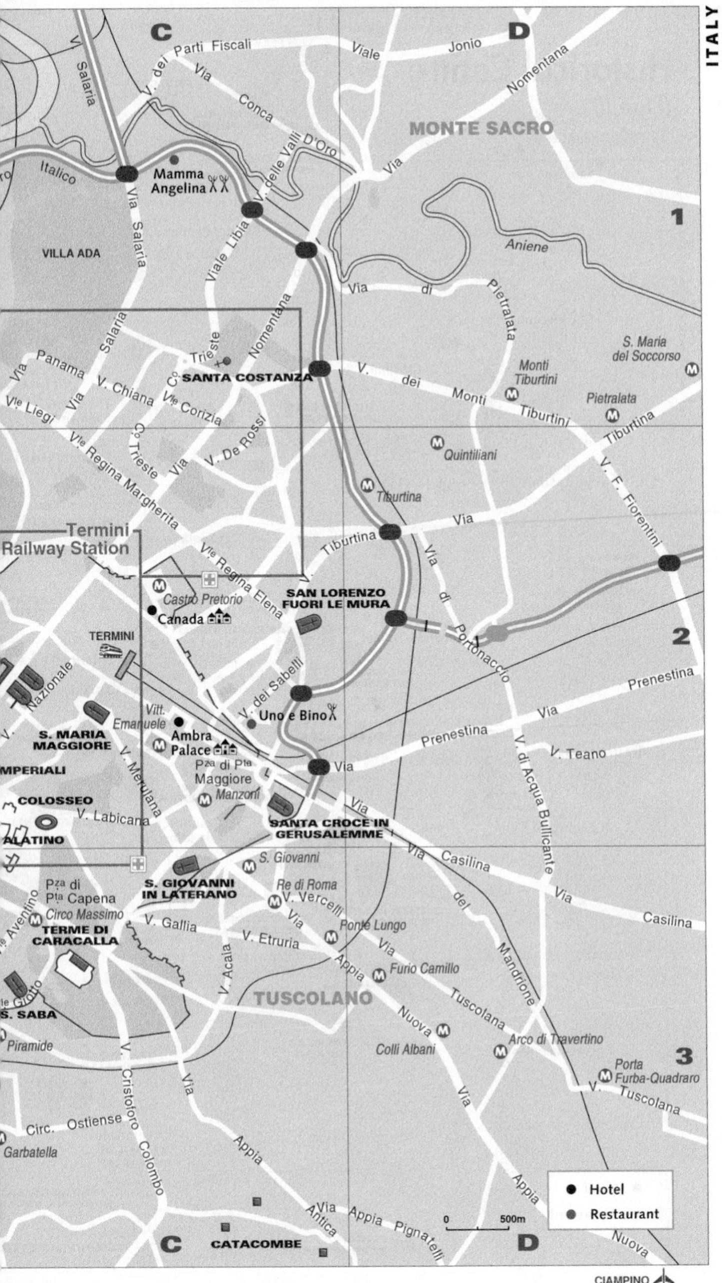
MONTE SACRO
VILLA ADA
Mamma Angelina
SANTA COSTANZA
Termini Railway Station
TERMINI
Castro Pretorio
Canada
SAN LORENZO FUORI LE MURA
Uno e Bino
S. MARIA MAGGIORE
Ambra Palace
Pza di Pta Maggiore
Manzoni
COLOSSEO
SANTA CROCE IN GERUSALEMME
S. GIOVANNI IN LATERANO
S. Giovanni
Re di Roma
Circo Massimo
TERME DI CARACALLA
Ponte Lungo
Furio Camillo
TUSCOLANO
S. SABA
Piramide
Colli Albani
Arco di Travertino
Porta Furba-Quadraro
Garbatella
CATACOMBE
Tiburtina
Quintiliani
Monti Tiburtini
Pietralata
S. Maria del Soccorso
Aniene
Hotel
Restaurant
0 500m
CIAMPINO
C
D
1
2
3

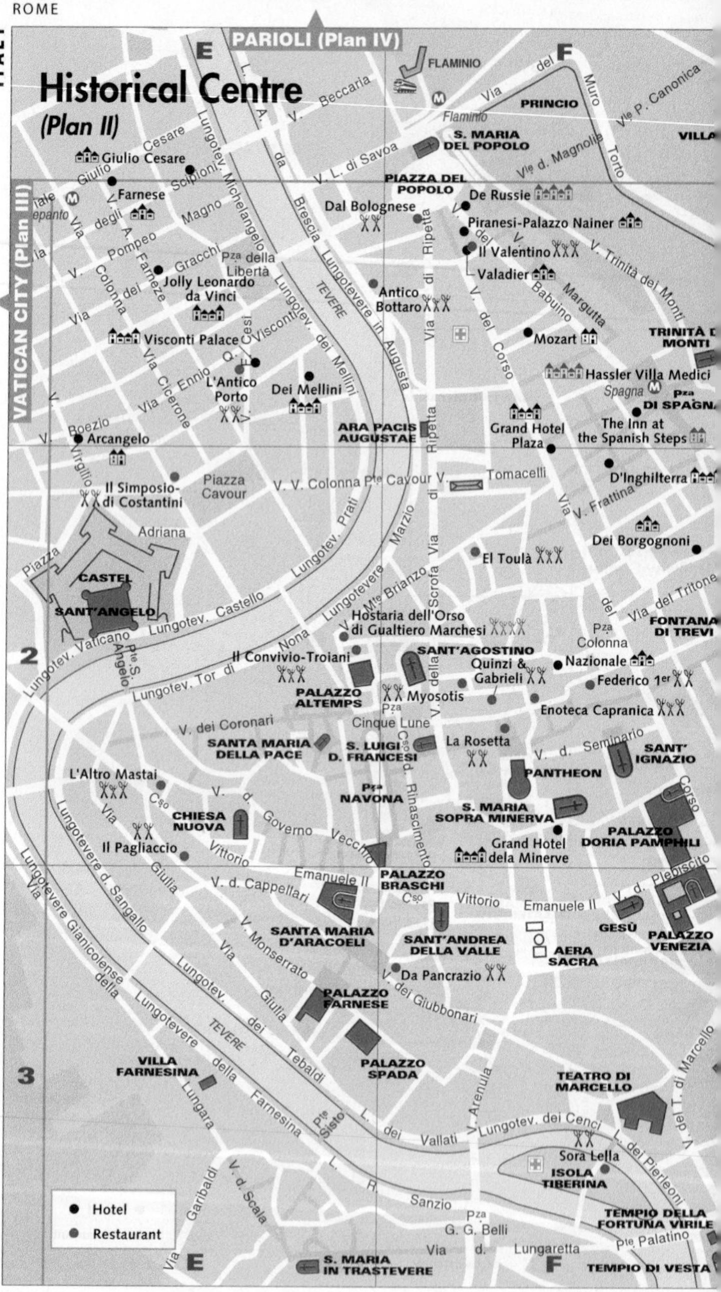

Historical Centre
(Plan II)

PARIOLI (Plan IV)
VATICAN CITY (Plan III)

FLAMINIO
PRINCIO
S. MARIA DEL POPOLO
PIAZZA DEL POPOLO
Giulio Cesare
Farnese
De Russie
Dal Bolognese
Piranesi-Palazzo Nainer
Il Valentino
Valadier
Jolly Leonardo da Vinci
Antico Bottaro
Visconti Palace
Mozart
TRINITÀ DEI MONTI
L'Antico Porto
Dei Mellini
Hassler Villa Medici
Arcangelo
ARA PACIS AUGUSTAE
Grand Hotel Plaza
The Inn at the Spanish Steps
Pza DI SPAGNA
Il Simposio-di Costantini
Piazza Cavour
D'Inghilterra
Dei Borgognoni
El Toulà
CASTEL SANT'ANGELO
Hostaria dell'Orso di Gualtiero Marchesi
FONTANA DI TREVI
Il Convivio-Troiani
SANT'AGOSTINO
Quinzi & Gabrieli
Nazionale
Federico 1er
PALAZZO ALTEMPS
Myosotis
Enoteca Capranica
SANTA MARIA DELLA PACE
S. LUIGI D. FRANCESI
La Rosetta
SANT' IGNAZIO
PANTHEON
L'Altro Mastai
Pza NAVONA
S. MARIA SOPRA MINERVA
CHIESA NUOVA
Il Pagliaccio
Grand Hotel dela Minerve
PALAZZO DORIA PAMPHILI
PALAZZO BRASCHI
SANTA MARIA D'ARACOELI
SANT'ANDREA DELLA VALLE
GESÙ
PALAZZO VENEZIA
AERA SACRA
Da Pancrazio
PALAZZO FARNESE
PALAZZO SPADA
VILLA FARNESINA
TEATRO DI MARCELLO
Sora Lella
ISOLA TIBERINA
TEMPIO DELLA FORTUNA VIRILE
S. MARIA IN TRASTEVERE
TEMPIO DI VESTA

● Hotel
● Restaurant

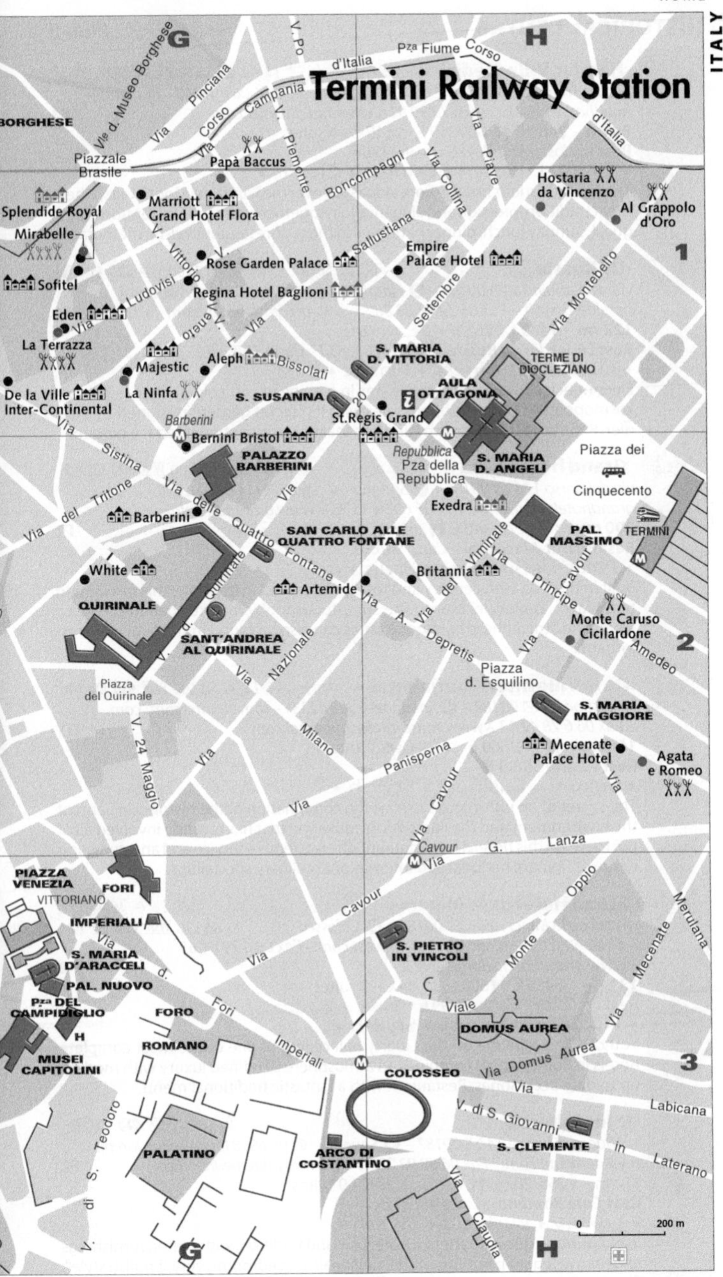
Termini Railway Station
BORGHESE
Piazzale Brasile
Papà Baccus
Marriott Grand Hotel Flora
Splendide Royal
Mirabelle
Sofitel
Rose Garden Palace
Regina Hotel Baglioni
Empire Palace Hotel
Hostaria da Vincenzo
Al Grappolo d'Oro
Eden
La Terrazza
Majestic
Aleph
La Ninfa
De la Ville Inter-Continental
S. MARIA D. VITTORIA
AULA OTTAGONA
TERME DI DIOCLEZIANO
S. SUSANNA
St.Regis Grand
Barberini
Bernini Bristol
Repubblica
Pza della Repubblica
S. MARIA D. ANGELI
Piazza dei Cinquecento
TERMINI
PALAZZO BARBERINI
Exedra
PAL. MASSIMO
Barberini
SAN CARLO ALLE QUATTRO FONTANE
White
Britannia
Artemide
QUIRINALE
Monte Caruso Cicilardone
SANT'ANDREA AL QUIRINALE
Piazza del Quirinale
Piazza d. Esquilino
S. MARIA MAGGIORE
Mecenate Palace Hotel
Agata e Romeo
Cavour
PIAZZA VENEZIA
VITTORIANO
FORI IMPERIALI
S. MARIA D'ARACŒLI
PAL. NUOVO
Pza DEL CAMPIDIGLIO
FORO ROMANO
MUSEI CAPITOLINI
S. PIETRO IN VINCOLI
DOMUS AUREA
COLOSSEO
PALATINO
ARCO DI COSTANTINO
S. CLEMENTE
Via Pinciana
Vle d. Museo Borghese
Corso d'Italia
Pza Fiume
Via Campania
V. Po
V. Piemonte
Via Boncompagni
Via Collina
Via Piave
Via Sallustiana
Via XX Settembre
Via Montebello
Via Vittorio Veneto
Via Ludovisi
Via V. E. Orlando
Via Bissolati
Via Sistina
Via del Tritone
Via delle Quattro Fontane
Via d. Quirinale
Via del Viminale
Via Principe Amedeo
Via Cavour
Via A. Depretis
Via Nazionale
Via Milano
V. 24 Maggio
Via Panisperna
Via G. Lanza
Via Cavour
Via Merulana
Via Mecenate
Via Monte Oppio
Viale Domus Aurea
Via d. Fori Imperiali
Via Labicana
V. di S. Giovanni in Laterano
Via Claudia
V. di S. Teodoro
0
200 m
G
H
1
2
3

HISTORICAL CENTRE

Plan II

Hassler Villa Medici

100 VISA

piazza Trinità dei Monti 6 ✉ 00187 – Ⓜ Spagna – ✆ 06 699340 – booking@hotelhassler.it – Fax 06 6 78 99 91 – www.hotelhassler.com **F1**

98 rm – 484 € 572/869 €, ☕ 45 € – 6 suites

Rest – *(closed Monday)* Carte 96/126 €

◆ Grand Luxury ◆ Business ◆ Classic ◆

The most luxurious hotel in Rome looks out over the Trinità dei Monti stairs, where great tradition, prestige and elegance join together with careful attention for the guest. Sunday lunch, dinner or brunch in the roof-restaurant will be memorable.

De Russie

rm 90 VISA

via del Babuino 9 ✉ 00187 – Ⓜ Flaminio – ✆ 06 328881 – reservations@hotelderussie.it – Fax 06 32 88 88 88 – www.roccofortehotels.com **F1**

122 rm – 480 € 650/910 €, ☕ 28 €

Rest *Le Jardin du Russie* – ✆ 06 32888870 – Carte 69/88 €

◆ Luxury ◆ Business ◆ Classic ◆

Elegant eclectic contemporary styles in a range of soft colours for a legendary cosmopolitan hotel, which emerges with its "secret garden" designed by Valadier. Refined restaurant with windows that open out onto the terrace garden.

Grand Hotel Plaza

rm 400 VISA

via del Corso 126 ✉ 00186 – Ⓜ Spagna – ✆ 06 69921111 – plaza@grandhotelplaza.com – Fax 06 69 94 15 75 – www.grandhotelplaza.com

200 rm ☕ – 220/340 € 265/450 € **F1**

Rest *Bistrot-Mascagni* – Carte 51/66 €

◆ Palace ◆ Business ◆ Stylish ◆

Built in the mid 19th century and totally redone in Liberty style, this fascinating hotel faces Trinitá dei Monti. The sumptuous lobby features beautiful stucco work. The atmosphere of bygone times can also be found in the evocative restaurant.

De la Ville Inter-Continental

100 VISA

via Sistina 69 ✉ 00187 – Ⓜ Spagna – ✆ 06 67331 – rome@interconti.com – Fax 06 6 78 42 13 – www.rome.intercontinental.com **G1**

168 rm – 399/660 €, ☕ 39 € – 24 suites

Rest – Carte 59/98 €

◆ Luxury ◆ Business ◆ Stylish ◆

The secret of an unforgettable stay: the combination of the historical charm of the environment and the successful renovation that has recently involved all of the rooms in this hotel. This restaurant offers attentive service and an interesting range of Roman, national and international culinary specialities.

Grand Hotel de la Minerve

rm 120 VISA

piazza della Minerva 69 ✉ 00186 – Ⓜ Colosseo – ✆ 06 695201 – minerva@hotel-invest.com – Fax 06 6 79 41 65 – www.grandhoteldelaminerve.it **F2**

131 rm – 385 € 600 €, ☕ 34 € – 3 suites

Rest *La Cesta* – Carte 55/99 €

◆ Luxury ◆ Business ◆ Stylish ◆

You can find Minerva on the Liberty hall ceiling of one of the most complete hotels in Rome, which combines an atmosphere of refined luxury with modern up to date accessories. Restaurant with a fantastic traditional menu.

D'Inghilterra

55 VISA

via Bocca di Leone 14 ✉ 00187 – Ⓜ Spagna – ✆ 06 699811 – reservation.hir@royaldemeure.com – Fax 06 69 92 22 43 – www.royaldemeure.com **F2**

88 rm – 256/287 € 462 €, ☕ 28 € – 9 suites

Rest *Cafè Romano* – Carte 45/70 €

◆ Luxury ◆ Business ◆ Stylish ◆

In old princely guest quarters, a hotel of grand tradition, with period furnishings and many elegant paintings inside; personalised bedrooms, very "English style". The totally renovated restaurant offers international fusion cuisine.

Dei Borgognoni without rest ⊠ 60 VISA MC AE ⓓ

via del Bufalo 126 ⊠ 00187 – Ⓜ Spagna – ☎ 06 69941505 – info@hotelborgognoni.it – Fax 06 69 94 15 01 – www.hotelborgognoni.it **F2**

51 rm – 200/247 € 260/325 €

◆ Traditional ◆ Business ◆ Modern ◆

In a 19th Century modernised building, a distinguished hotel with an elegant atmosphere, comfortable bedrooms and an unexpected green interior area.

Piranesi-Palazzo Nainer without rest 40 VISA MC AE ⓓ

via del Babuino 196 ⊠ 00187 – Ⓜ Flaminio – ☎ 06 328041 – info@hotelpiranesi.com – Fax 06 3 61 05 97 – www.hotelpiranesi.com **F1**

32 rm – 240 € 320 €

◆ Palace ◆ Business ◆ Classic ◆

A recently-opened hotel with a classic and elegant stylishness. The white marble of the interiors improves the light inside and sets off the lovely furnishings.

White without rest VISA MC AE ⓓ

via in Arcione 77 ⊠ 00187 – Ⓜ Barberini – ☎ 06 6991242 – white@travelroma.com – Fax 06 6 78 84 51 – www.travelroma.com **G2**

40 rm – 200/250 € 220/300 €

◆ Traditional ◆ Modern ◆

Next to the Trevi fountain and the Quirinale, a comfortable hotel with a modern interior and avant-garde installations ; light coloured wood furniture in the bedrooms.

Valadier rm 35 VISA MC AE ⓓ

via della Fontanella 15 ⊠ 00187 – Ⓜ Flaminio – ☎ 06 3611998 – info@hotelvaladier.com – Fax 06 3 20 15 58 – www.hotelvaladier.com **F1**

67 rm – 140/270 € 210/390 € – 7 suites

Rest *Il Valentino* – see below

Rest *Hi-Res* – *(dinner only)* Carte 72/93 €

◆ Traditional ◆ Modern ◆

Elegant hotel close to Piazza del Popolo; refined interior and great attention to detail, with a profusion of wood and also mirrors in the bedrooms; panoramic roof-garden.

Nazionale 800 VISA MC AE ⓓ

piazza Montecitorio 131 ⊠ 00186 – Ⓜ Spagna – ☎ 06 695001 – hotel@nazionaleroma.it – Fax 06 6 78 66 77 – www.nazionaleroma.it **F2**

95 rm – 280/340 € 340/530 € – 2 suites

Rest *31 Al Vicario* – *☎ 06 69925530 (closed 7 August-4 September and Sunday)* Carte 38/56 €

◆ Traditional ◆ Business ◆ Classic ◆

This classic well maintained hotel is the result of joining two distinct buildings in perfect harmony. It faces the square in Montecitorio. Guests will enjoy the traditional menu in this comfortable restaurant.

Barberini without rest VISA MC AE ⓓ

via Rasella 3 ⊠ 00187 – Ⓜ Barberini – ☎ 06 4814993 – info@hotelbarberini.com – Fax 06 4 81 52 11 – www.hotelbarberini.com **G2**

35 rm – 181/235 € 232/316 €, 28 €

◆ Traditional ◆ Classic ◆

Near the Palazzo of the same name, this elegant hotel is decorated with fine marble, stylish fabrics and wood fittings. The roof-garden is perfect for a breakfast with a view or an atmospheric evening aperitif.

The Inn at the Spanish Steps without rest VISA MC AE ⓓ

via dei Condotti 85 ⊠ 00187 – Ⓜ Spagna – ☎ 06 69925657 – spanishstep@tin.it – Fax 06 6 78 64 70 – www.atspanishsteps.com **F1**

24 rm – 400/850 €

◆ Inn ◆ Classic ◆

Situated in the same building that houses the celebrated Caffè Greco, this restaurant is an answer to the dreams of all those tourists desirous of experiencing the mythical "Roman Holidays".

ITALY

Mozart without rest
via dei Greci 23/B ✉ 00187 – Ⓜ Spagna – ✆ 06 36001915 – info@hotelmozart.com – Fax 06 36 00 17 35 – www.hotelmozart.com **F1**
56 rm – 🛉126/180 € 🛉🛉175/250 €
♦ Traditional ♦ Classic ♦
In a 19th century palazzo in the centre of the city, this restored hotel has elegant furnishings in the public areas and in the rooms; pretty terrace - solarium.

Hostaria dell'Orso di Gualtiero Marchesi
via dei Soldati 25/c ✉ 00186 – Ⓜ Spagna 12/28
– ✆ 06 68301192 – info@hdo.it – Fax 06 68 21 70 63 – www.hdo.it
closed 10-25 August and Sunday **E-F2**
Rest – *(dinner only)* Carte 60/98 €
♦ Contemporary ♦ Fashionable ♦
Return to the past splendor of worldly Rome. This stylishly decorated 15th century building features a restaurant, piano bar and disco.

Il Convivio-Troiani (Troiani) 16/24
Vicolo dei Soldati 31 ✉ 00186 – Ⓜ Spagna – ✆ 06 6869432 – info@ilconviviotroiani.com – Fax 06 6 86 94 32 – www.ilconviviotroiani.com
closed 9 to 15 August and Sunday **E2**
Rest – *(dinner only)* Carte 79/124 €
Spec. Fegato grasso d'anatra al torcione in crosta di fichi e pistacchi. Gnocchi di patate ripieni di broccoletti con salsa alla pescatora. Variazione di agnello da latte della campagna romana.
♦ Innovative ♦ Fashionable ♦
Hidden in the alleyways of the historic centre, this restaurant serves meat and fish dishes with an innovative, modern slant. The three dining rooms are simple yet elegant in style.

El Toulà 18
via della Lupa 29/b ✉ 00186 – Ⓜ Spagna – ✆ 06 6873498 – toula2@libero.it – Fax 06 6 87 11 15 – www.toula.it
closed August, 24 to 26 December, Saturday lunch, Sunday and Monday **F2**
Rest – Carte 53/107 €
♦ Contemporary ♦ Formal ♦
Traditional Venetian specialities have been given a modern twist in this old restaurant situated in the political heart of the city. Stylish, elegant dining rooms.

Antico Bottaro
Passeggiata di Ripetta 15 ✉ 00186 – Ⓜ Flaminio – ✆ 06 3236763 – anticobottaro@anticobottaro.it – Fax 06 3 23 67 63 – www.anticobottaro.it
closed 4 to 31 August and Wednesday **E-F1**
Rest – Carte 63/94 €
♦ Inventive ♦ Fashionable ♦
There has been a restaurant in this location for 130 years. The 17th century villa has been renovated and features pink stucco walls and terra cotta flooring.

L'Altro Mastai
via Giraud 53 ang. via dei Bianchi Nuovi ✉ 00186 – ✆ 06 68301296 – restaurant@laltromastai.it – Fax 06 6 86 13 03 – www.laltromastai.it
closed August, 1 week in January, Sunday and Monday **E2**
Rest – *(dinner only) (booking essential)* Carte 64/98 €
Spec. Ostriche in gelatina di sedano con mele candite e scaglie di gorgonzola (autumn-winter). Ravioli di coniglio e indivia con burro alle alici. Petto di piccione cotto nella cenere di quercia con salsa di peperoni e scorzanera.
♦ Inventive ♦ Fashionable ♦
This restaurant, opened towards the end of 2003, will come as a pleasant surprise to many and is destined to leave its mark on Rome's culinary history. The decor is discreet and the service courteous and efficient. Fine wine cellar.

XXX **Enoteca Capranica** AC 25 VISA MC AE

piazza Capranica 99/100 ✉ 00186 – Ⓜ Spagna – ✆ 06 69940992 – Fax 06 69 94 09 89 – www.enotecacapranica.it – closed Saturday lunch and Sunday

Rest – *(dinner only in August)* Carte 50/80 € **F2**

♦ Innovative ♦ Fashionable ♦

Near Montecitorio, a wine bar that has been changed into an exclusive elegant restaurant where one can sample traditional Mediterranean cuisine. Excellent cellar.

XXX **Il Valentino** – Hotel Valadier AC 15/20 VISA MC AE

via della Fontanella 14 ✉ 00187 – Ⓜ Flaminio – ✆ 06 3610880 – Fax 06 3 20 15 58 – www.ilvalentino.com **F1**

Rest – Carte 42/72 €

♦ Seafood ♦ Cosy ♦

Light wood panelling and a warm colour scheme are the key features of this stylish restaurant, which serves creative cuisine in an elegant atmosphere. Efficient service.

XXX **Alberto Ciarla** AC 18 VISA MC AE

piazza San Cosimato 40 ✉ 00153 – ✆ 06 5816068 – alberto@albertociarla.com – Fax 06 58 33 01 62 – www.albertociarla.com

closed 1 week in August, 1 week in January and Sunday *Plan I* **B3**

Rest – *(dinner only)* Carte 52/76 €

♦ Seafood ♦ Friendly ♦

Roman dishes have been added to traditional fish specialities (raw and cooked) in an elegant establishment in the heart of Trastevere. Good choice of wines.

XX **La Rosetta** AC VISA MC AE

via della Rosetta 9/8 ✉ 00186 – Ⓜ Spagna – ✆ 06 6861002 – larosetta@tin.it – Fax 06 68 21 51 16 – www.larosetta.com

closed 10 to 30 August and Sunday – **Rest** – Carte 72/147 € **F2**

♦ Seafood ♦ Formal ♦

Inviting display, at the entrance to the establishment, of fresh fish caught daily; the fact that the place is very popular does not detract from the carefully planned and pleasant atmosphere in the dining room.

XX **Dal Bolognese** AC VISA MC AE

piazza del Popolo 1/2 ✉ 00187 – Ⓜ Flaminio – ✆ 06 3611426 – dalbolognese@virgilio.it – Fax 06 3 22 27 99 – closed 5-25 August, Christmas, New Year and Monday **F1**

Rest – Carte 51/70 €

♦ Seafood ♦ Formal ♦

When sampling the traditional Emiliana cuisine it is impossible to ignore this historic reference point. Outdoor dining available on the piazza in summer months.

XX **Quinzi & Gabrieli** AC 20/25 VISA MC AE

via delle Coppelle 6 ✉ 00186 – Ⓜ Spagna – ✆ 06 6879389 – quinziegabrieli@tin.it – Fax 06 6 87 49 40 – www.quinziegabrieli.it – closed August **F2**

Rest – *(dinner only and Sunday lunch)* Carte 80/105 €

♦ Seafood ♦ Trendy ♦

All the scented fragrance and tastes of the sea without the movement of the city: this is the experience offered by an establishment of high standards, always crowded and fashionable.

XX **Il Pagliaccio** (Genovese) AC VISA MC AE

via dei Banchi Vecchi 129 ✉ 00186 – Ⓜ Spagna – ✆ 06 68809595 – info@ristoranteilpagliaccio.it – Fax 06 68 21 75 04 – www.ristoranteilpagliaccio.it closed 6-25 August, 9 to 17 January, Sunday, Monday and Tuesday lunch

Rest – Menu 48/70 € – Carte 60/83 € **E2**

Spec. Crema tiepida di cannelini, pomodorini e alici fritte in pastella. Candele al forno con cipolle rosse e asparagi selvaggi. Branzino in lardo di Colonnata con polpetta di coda di manzo.

♦ Inventive ♦ Formal ♦

"Youth" combined with a discreet elegance is the keynote of this restaurant; the small tables in two main rooms are soberly equipped and the cuisine offers creatively reinterpreted local dishes.

XX **Myosotis** AC 12 VISA MO AE

piazza delle Coppelle 49 ✉ 00186 – M Spagna – ☎ 06 6865554 – marsili@libero.it – Fax 06 6 86 55 54 – www.myosotis.it

closed 10 to 24 August, 2 to 9 January and Sunday **F2**

Rest – *(dinner only)* Carte 28/74 €

♦ Seafood ♦ Formal ♦

In a delightful alley between Piazza Navona and Montecitorio, a rustic yet distinctive restaurant, run by a family with vast experience in cuisine from land and sea.

XX **Sora Lella** AC VISA MO AE

via di Ponte Quattro Capi 16, Isola Tiberina ✉ 00186 – ☎ 06 6861601 – soralella@soralella.com – Fax 06 6 86 16 01 – www.soralella.com

closed 24 to 26 December and Sunday **F3**

Rest – Carte 55/82 €

♦ Roman specialities ♦ Family ♦

Son and grandchildren of the famous late ""Sora Lella"", perpetuate in a dignified way the tradition both in the warmth of the welcome and in the typical Roman elements of the offer.

XX **Federico I** AC 26 VISA MO AE

via della Colonna Antonina 48 ✉ 00186 – M Barberini – ☎ 06 6783717 – info@federicoprimo.com – Fax 06 6 78 78 18 – www.federicoprimo.com

closed 10-30 August, 24 December-1 January, and Sunday **F2**

Rest – Carte 68/86 €

♦ Seafood ♦ Formal ♦

A place not to be missed by fish lovers – the specialities of this well kept restaurant that, in summertime, invites one to enjoy the pleasure of outside dining.

XX **Da Pancrazio** 15/30 VISA MO AE

piazza del Biscione 92 ✉ 00186 – M Piazza del Popolo – ☎ 06 6861246 – dapancrazio@tin.it – Fax 06 97 84 02 35 – www.dapancrazio.com

closed 5-25 August, Christmas and Wednesday **F3**

Rest – Carte 37/52 €

♦ Roman ♦ Formal ♦

Experience two thousand years of history in this typical restaurant built over part of the ruins of Pompey's Theatre. Local cuisine is the speciality of this tavern-cum-museum.

TERMINI RAILWAY STATION *Plan II*

St. Regis Grand AC 300 VISA MO AE

via Vittorio Emanuele Orlando 3 ✉ 00185 – M Repubblica – ☎ 06 47091 – stregisgrandrome@stregis.com – Fax 06 47 09 28 31 – www.stregis.com/grandrome **H1**

157 rm – †320/785 € ††380/920 €, ☕ 43 € – 21 suites

Rest *Vivendo* – ☎ *06 47092736 (closed Saturday lunch and Sunday)* Carte 76/104 €

♦ Chain hotel ♦ Luxury ♦ Historic ♦

Frescoes, valuable furnishings and Empire-style antiques in the luxurious bedrooms and the magnificent lounges of a hotel restored to its original antique splendours (1894). The restaurant preserves a prestigious atmosphere from the past.

Eden AC 80 VISA MO AE

via Ludovisi 49 ✉ 00187 – M Barberini – ☎ 06 478121 – 1872.resevations@lemeridien.com – Fax 06 4 82 15 84 – www.lemeridien.com/eden **G1**

108 rm – †506/528 € ††748/858 €, ☕ 50 € – 13 suites

Rest *La Terrazza* – see below

♦ Palace ♦ Luxury ♦ Stylish ♦

Quality and simplicity in a large hotel where elegance and tone complement the warmth of the welcome. Service and bedrooms well suited to the most demanding clientele.

Exedra

120 VISA AE

piazza della Repubblica 47 ✉ 00185 – Ⓜ Repubblica – ✆ 06 48938020 – reservation@exedra.boscolo.com – Fax 06 48 93 80 00 – www.boscolo.com **H2**

238 rm – 660 €, 26 € – 5 suites

Rest *Tazio* – *✆ 06 489381* – Carte 76/103 €

◆ Luxury ◆ Chain hotel ◆ Classic ◆

This luxury hotel boasts spacious public lounges, comfortable guestrooms and state-of-the-art technology. The decor is tasteful and elegant, featuring a profusion of marble and inlaid wood. The Tazio restaurant is particularly suited to business lunches and dinners.

Sofitel

rm 45 VISA AE

via Lombardia 47 ✉ 00187 – Ⓜ Barberini – ✆ 06 478021 – prenotazioni.sofitelroma@accor-hotels.it – Fax 06 4 82 10 19 – www.sofitel.com **G1**

113 rm – 440 € 500 €

Rest – Carte 55/67 €

◆ Luxury ◆ Business ◆ Historic ◆

The neo-Classical style of the Imperial Roman period dominates in this hotel, with statues and sculptures dotted around the historic palazzo. Choose between the terrace bar with its views of Rome, and the cosy, British atmosphere in the bar. An elegant restaurant with vaulted ceilings, fashioned out of the former stables of the building.

Majestic

rm 150 VISA AE

via Vittorio Veneto 50 ✉ 00187 – Ⓜ Barberini – ✆ 06 421441 – info@hotelmajestic.com – Fax 06 4 88 09 84 – www.hotelmajestic.com **G1**

98 rm – 400/495 € 530/690 €, 40 € – 8 suites

Rest *La Ninfa* – see below

Rest *La Veranda* – *(closed January and Sunday)* Carte 48/66 €

◆ Luxury ◆ Traditional ◆ Classic ◆

Although space is limited in the hotel lobby, this is compensated for by the elegant lounge areas adorned with late-19C frescoes on the first floor. Splendid lift and charming guestrooms. Warm atmosphere, table linen and silverware in the refined dining room of "La Veranda" restaurant.

Regina Hotel Baglioni

rm 80 VISA AE

via Vittorio Veneto 72 ✉ 00187 – Ⓜ Barberini – ✆ 06 421111 – regina.roma@baglionihotels.com – Fax 06 42 01 21 30 – www.baglionihotels.com **G1**

143 rm – 290/410 € 420/470 €, 29 € – 6 suites

Rest – Carte 54/82 €

◆ Luxury ◆ Traditional ◆ Art Deco ◆

This building restructured in Art Nouveau style is home to an historic hotel with Art Deco interiors and excellent facilities. The attractive guestrooms are striking for their marble decor. Restaurant with warm, refined atmosphere; international cuisine.

Splendide Royal

50 VISA AE

porta Pinciana 14 ✉ 00187 – Ⓜ Barberini – ✆ 06 421689 – reservations@splendideroyal.com – Fax 06 42 16 88 00 – www.splendideroyal.com **G1**

69 rm – 300/450 € 400/680 €

Rest *Mirabelle* – see below

◆ Luxury ◆ Traditional ◆ Stylish ◆

Gilded stucco, damask fabrics and sumptuous antique furnishings contribute to the Roman Baroque style of this hotel, which is in sharp contrast to the contemporary trend for minimalist design.

Aleph

rm rm 60 P VISA AE

via San Basilio 15 ✉ 00187 – Ⓜ Barberini – ✆ 06 422901 – reservation@aleph.boscolo.com – Fax 06 42 29 00 00 – www.boscolohotels.com **G1**

96 rm – 250/400 € 300/600 €

Rest *Maremoto* – Carte 103/155 €

◆ Luxury ◆ Design ◆

One of a group of "designer hotels". The lobby design and colour scheme are incomparable, the room designs innovative. This prestigious hotel also has a fitness centre. A modern restaurant with minimalist decor.

ITALY

Bernini Bristol

rm 100 VISA

piazza Barberini 23 ✉ 00187 – Ⓜ Barberini – ✆ 06 488931 – reservationsbb@sinahotels.it – Fax 06 4 82 42 66 – www.berninibristol.com **G2**

127 rm – 445 € 566 €, 30 € – 9 suites

Rest *L'Olimpo* – ✆ *06 488933288* – Carte 84/128 €

♦ Traditional ♦ Business ♦ Classic ♦

The perfect combination of the refined fascination with the past and the advantages of modern hospitality await you inside one of the most elegant hotels of the capital. Roof-garden restaurant, with outdoor dining in the summer and a marvellous view of the Eternal City.

Marriott Grand Hotel Flora

rest rm 150

via Vittorio Veneto 191 ✉ 00187 – Ⓜ Spagna – ✆ 06 489929 VISA

– info@grandhotelflora.net – Fax 06 4 82 03 59 – www.hotelfloraroma.com

137 rm – 322 € 478 €, 30 € – 19 suites – **Rest** – Carte 42/82 € **G1**

♦ Luxury ♦ Business ♦ Classic ♦

After its total renovation, the hotel, at the end of Via Veneto, looks like a harmonious and functional building of simple and functional classical elegance, finished in a modern style. Warm parquet flooring and other wooden finishes in the elegant restaurant dining room.

Empire Palace Hotel

rm 160 VISA

via Aureliana 39 ✉ 00187 – Ⓜ Repubblica – ✆ 06 421281 – gold@empirepalacehotel.com – Fax 06 42 12 84 00 – www.empirepalacehotel.com

105 rm – 420 € 586 € – 5 suites

Rest *Aureliano* – *(closed Sunday)* Menu 25 € **H1**

♦ Palace ♦ Business ♦ Design ♦

Sophisticated combination of elements of the 19C building and contemporary design, with a collection of modern art in the public areas; simple, classic bedrooms. The dining room features cherry wood decor and pink and blue table lamps.

Rose Garden Palace

rm 50 VISA

via Boncompagni 19 ✉ 00187 – Ⓜ Barberini – ✆ 06 421741 – info@rosegardenpalace.com – Fax 06 4 81 56 08 **G1**

65 rm – 300 € 520 € – **Rest** – *(residents only)* Carte 45/67 €

♦ Business ♦ Design ♦

A modern, minimalist design in muted colours is the inspiration behind the furnishing of this hotel housed in an early-20C palazzo.

Mecenate Palace Hotel without rest

45 VISA

via Carlo Alberto 3 ✉ 00185 – Ⓜ Vittorio Emanuele – ✆ 06 44702024 – info@mecenatepalace.com – Fax 06 4 46 13 54 – www.mecenatepalace.com **H2**

72 rm – 155/330 € 200/390 €

♦ Business ♦ Classic ♦

The warm and elegant period-style interiors are in perfect keeping with the spirit of the 19C building which houses this new hotel. Fine views of Santa Maria Maggiore from the upper floors.

Artemide without rest

120 VISA

via Nazionale 22 ✉ 00184 – Ⓜ Repubblica – ✆ 06 489911 – info@hotelartemide.it – Fax 06 48 99 17 00 – www.hotelartemide.it **G-H2**

85 rm – 257/262 € 235/362 €

♦ Traditional ♦ Business ♦ Classic ♦

In a precious restored Art Nouveau building, a classically elegant hotel which satsifies all the requirements of modern hospitality; very well organised Conference areas.

Canada without rest

VISA

via Vicenza 58 ✉ 00185 – Ⓜ Castro Pretorio – ✆ 06 4457770 – info@hotelcanadaroma.com – Fax 06 4 45 07 49 – www.hotelcanadaroma.com

70 rm – 124/158 € 142/190 € *Plan I* **C2**

♦ Business ♦ Classic ♦

In period style building near the Termini railway station, a simple but elegant hotel, with period style furnishings; luxurious rooms: some with four poster beds available on request.

Ambra Palace without rest — 55 VISA MC AE

via Principe Amedeo 257 ✉ 00185 – Ⓜ Vittorio Emanuele – ✆ 06 492330 – booking@ambrapalacehotel.com – Fax 06 49 23 31 00 – www.ambrapalace.com — Plan I **C2**

78 rm – †210 € ††430 €

◆ Business ◆ Classic ◆

The building is mid-19C, the hotel is set up prevalently to meet the needs of the business visitor.

Britannia without rest — AC VISA MC AE

via Napoli 64 ✉ 00184 – Ⓜ Repubblica – ✆ 06 4883153 – info@hotelbritannia.it – Fax 06 48 98 63 16 – www.hotelbritannia.it — **H2**

33 rm – †140/190 € ††220/290 €

◆ Traditional ◆ Business ◆ Personalised ◆

This small hotel has reasonable facilities, comfortable guestrooms and an English-style bar. Marble decor, neo-Classical reproductions and attention to detail.

La Terrazza – Hotel Eden — AC 20 VISA MC AE

via Ludovisi 49 ✉ 00187 – Ⓜ Barberini – ✆ 06 47812752 – reservations@hotel-eden.it – Fax 06 4 81 44 73 – www.hotel-eden.it — **G1**

Rest – Carte 86/136 €

◆ Contemporary ◆ Fashionable ◆

The most striking feature of this modern, soberly elegant hall is the magnificent view of Rome it offers. Here, you are assured of a truly memorable evening.

Mirabelle – Hotel Splendide Royal — AC 20 VISA MC AE

Porta Pinciana 14 ✉ 00187 – Ⓜ Barberini – ✆ 06 42168838 – reservation@splendideroyal.com – Fax 06 42 16 88 70 – www.splendideroyal.com

Closed 8 to 18 January — **G1**

Rest – Carte 73/110 €

Spec. Astice al vapore con insalata e frutti di bosco. Pezzogna all'acqua pazza. Piccione disossato in crosta con salsa al tartufo.

◆ Mediterranean ◆ Fashionable ◆

On the seventh floor of the hotel, an elegant restaurant richly decorated with mirrors reflecting and highlighting the view on San Peter's basilica. Modern cuisine with Mediterranean roots.

Agata e Romeo (Parisella) — AC VISA MC AE

via Carlo Alberto 45 ✉ 00185 – Ⓜ Piazza Vittorio – ✆ 06 4466115 – ristorante@agataeromeo.it – Fax 06 4 46 58 42 – www.agataeromeo.it

closed 4 to 25 August, 1 to 13 January, Saturday, Sunday and Monday lunch

Rest – Carte 80/108 € — **H2**

Spec. Il gambero servito in cinque modi diversi (summer). Raviolini di caprino e asparagi selvatici (spring). Quattro modi di cucinare il baccalà islandese (autumn-winter).

◆ Roman ◆ Formal ◆

Small, elegant and well-maintained establishment, for two sorts of cuisine: one traditional, the other creative. The wines are among the best in Rome.

Al Grappolo d'Oro — AC 20 VISA MC AE

via Palestro 4/10 ✉ 00185 – Ⓜ Repubblica – ✆ 06 4941441 – info@algrappolodoro.it – Fax 06 4 45 23 50 – www.algrappolodoro.it

closed August, Saturday lunch and Sunday – **Rest** – Carte 36/48 € — **H1**

◆ Seafood ◆ Formal ◆

Not far from the Terme di Diocleziano, a classic restaurant, where recent work has improved and refined the building, and where there is a large menu of traditional dishes on offer.

La Ninfa – Hotel Majestic — AC 15/20 VISA MC AE

via Vittorio Veneto 50 ✉ 00187 – Ⓜ Barberini – ✆ 06 421441 — **G1**

Rest – Carte 46/66 €

◆ Mediterranean ◆ Formal ◆

Situated in the same building as the Hotel Majestic, this restaurant with its simple American-bar decor recalls the splendour of the "dolce vita" period. Flexible opening hours.

XX

Monte Caruso Cicilardone AC 15 VISA MC AE

via Farini 12 ✉ 00185 – Ⓜ Termini – ☎ 06 483549 – cicilardone@tiscali.it – www.montecaruso.com
closed August, Sunday and Monday lunch **H2**
Rest – Carte 34/47 €
◆ Regional ◆ Family ◆
The flavours of the South in a warm and welcoming family-run establishment, with a menu based on Lucanian specialities, achieved in a simple and genuine manner.

XX

Papà Baccus AC 20 VISA MC AE

via Toscana 32/36 ✉ 00187 – Ⓜ Barberini – ☎ 06 42742808 – papabaccus@papabaccus.com – Fax 06 42 01 00 05 – www.papabaccus.com
closed 15 days in August, Saturday lunch and Sunday **G1**
Rest – Carte 42/55 €
◆ Tuscany ◆ Formal ◆
This typical restaurant in the Via Veneto district is understandably popular given its delicious seafood cuisine and Tuscan specialities, which include Chianina beef and Cinta Senese pork.

XX

Hostaria da Vincenzo 20/30 VISA MC AE

via Castelfidardo 6 ✉ 00185 – Ⓜ Termini – ☎ 06 484596 – Fax 06 4 87 00 92
closed August and Sunday **H1**
Rest – Carte 24/41 €
◆ Seafood ◆ Friendly ◆
With its traditional, friendly atmosphere and typical regional and Italian dishes, this restaurant has a loyal following and is particularly popular with business clientele.

X

Uno e Bino AC 15/20 VISA MC

via Degli Equi 58 ✉ 00185 – Ⓜ Termini – ☎ 06 4460702
closed August and Monday *Plan I* **C2**
Rest – (dinner only) Carte 45/54 €
◆ Contemporary ◆ Bistro ◆
The fact that it is good value for money is the trump card of this quiet and attractive restaurant. The bistro-style decor creates a cordial and informal atmosphere.

ST-PETER'S BASILICA *Plan III*

Rome Cavalieri Hilton < city, AC

via Cadlolo 101 ✉ 00136 rm 2000 P VISA MC AE
– ☎ 06 35091 – sales.rome@hilton.com – Fax 06 35 09 22 41
– www.cavalieri-hilton.it *Plan I* **A2**
370 rm – †655/850 € ††710/905 €, ☕ 38 € – 25 suites
Rest *La Pergola* – see below
Rest *Il Giardino dell'Uliveto* – Carte 66/118 €
◆ Luxury ◆ Business ◆ Classic ◆
View high over the town, solarium terraces and park with swimming pool, art collection: only some of the advantages of a large hotel that always offers the best. Restaurant with an informal atmosphere by the edge of the swimming pool for dining with live music.

Dei Mellini without rest AC 70 VISA MC AE

via Muzio Clementi 81 ✉ 00193 – Ⓜ Piazza di Spagna – ☎ 06 324771 – info@hotelmellini.com
– Fax 06 32 47 78 01 – www.hotelmellini.com *Plan II* **E1**
67 rm ☕ – †255/275 € ††275/385 € – 13 suites
◆ Luxury ◆ Classic ◆
This hotel is on the right bank of the Tiber; the environment is soberly elegant, comfort is of the highest level and the rooms are large, modern and well equipped. There is a solarium-terrace.

Visconti Palace without rest 150 VISA

via Federico Cesi 37 ✉ 00193 – Ⓜ Lepanto – ✆ 06 3684 – info@viscontipalace.com – Fax 06 3 20 05 51 – www.viscontipalace.com Plan II **E1**

247 rm – ♦290 € ♦♦330/340 €

◆ Business ◆ Modern ◆

Occupying a large building dating from the 1970s, this hotel is ideal for tourists and business travellers alike. Facilities include a new, modern lobby, conference centre and well-appointed guestrooms.

Jolly Leonardo da Vinci rm 180 VISA

via dei Gracchi 324 ✉ 00192 – Ⓜ Lepanto – ✆ 06 328481 – roma_leonardodavinci@jollyhotels.com – Fax 06 3 61 01 38 – www.jollyhotels.com Plan II **E1**

244 rm – ♦195/235 € ♦♦225/265 €, 18 €

Rest – Carte 36/66 €

◆ Chain hotel ◆ Business ◆ Modern ◆

This hotel provides a high standard of comfort for business, conference and leisure visitors to the city. Elegant and spacious lobby and guestrooms. This restaurant features a classic style décor and menus adapted to every palate.

Giulio Cesare without rest 30 VISA

via degli Scipioni 287 ✉ 00192 – ✆ 06 3210751 – giulioce@uni.net – Fax 06 3 21 17 36 – www.hotelgiuliocesare.com Plan II **E1**

78 rm – ♦180/265 € ♦♦210/330 €

◆ Luxury ◆ Stylish ◆

This hotel, housed in a villa dating from 1906, has a simple, elegant feel both inside and out. Friendly service, tasteful Louis XVI furnishings and a small internal garden.

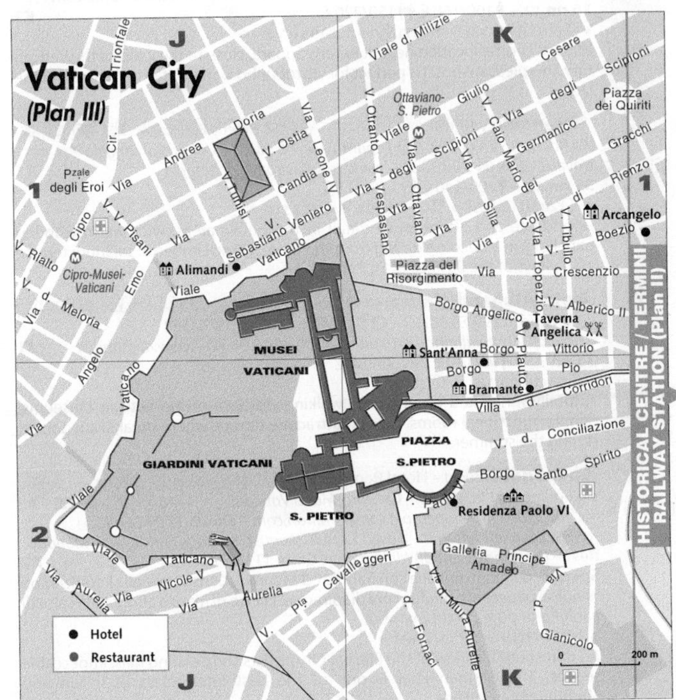

Farnese without rest
via Alessandro Farnese 30 ✉ 00192 – Ⓜ Lepanto – ✆ 06 3212553 – info@hotelfarnese.com – Fax 06 3 21 51 29 – www.hotelfarnese.com Plan II **E1**
23 rm – †170/230 € ††190/300 €
◆ Luxury ◆ Business ◆ Stylish ◆
A hotel in a restored Patrician villa in the quiet Prati district, conveniently situated 50 m. from the underground; elegant and well maintained period style interior.

Residenza Paolo VI without rest
via Paolo VI 29 ✉ 00193 – Ⓜ San Pietro – ✆ 06 684870 – info@residenzapaoloVI.com – Fax 06 6 86 74 28 – www.residenzapaoloVI.com
29 rm – †210/230 € ††270/290 € **K2**
◆ Luxury ◆ Stylish ◆
Located in a former monastery, with a terrace looking over San Pietro, giving one of the most exclusive and majestic views over the Eternal City, this hotel offers singular fascination and grace.

Sant'Anna without rest
Borgo Pio 133 ✉ 00193 – Ⓜ Ottaviano – ✆ 06 68801602 – santanna@travel.it – Fax 06 68 30 87 17 – www.hotelsantanna.com **K1-2**
20 rm – †100/150 € ††150/220 €
◆ Traditional ◆ Personalised ◆
Original trompe l'oeil murals and a pleasant interior courtyard in this small and welcoming hotel, situated in a 16th Century building a short distance away from St Peter's.

Bramante without rest
Vicolo delle Palline 24 ✉ 00193 – Ⓜ Ottaviano – ✆ 06 68806426 – hotelbramante@libero.it – Fax 06 68 13 33 39 – www.hotelbramante.com
16 rm – †100/160 € ††150/220 € **K2**
◆ Traditional ◆ Family ◆ Classic ◆
With its central location near St Peter's Square, close to the walls of the Vatican City, this pleasant hotel is perfect for visitors who want to stay in the heart of the city.

Arcangelo without rest ← St. Peter's Basilica,
via Boezio 15 ✉ 00192 – Ⓜ Lepanto – ✆ 06 6874143 – hotel.arcangelo@travel.it – Fax 06 6 89 30 50 – www.travel.it/roma/arcangelo **K1**
33 rm – †100/140 € ††170/211 €
◆ Traditional ◆ Business ◆ Classic ◆
Good taste and attention to detail in the public areas, with warm wooden panelling, in a building dating from the time of King Umberto; solarium terrace with views of the Basilica of St. Peter.

Hotel Alimandi Vaticano without rest
viale Vaticano 99 ✉ 00192 – Ⓜ Ottaviano – ✆ 06 39745562 – hotelali@hotelalimandie.191.it – Fax 06 39 73 01 32 – www.alimandi.it **J1**
35 rm – †90/120 € ††160/180 €
◆ Traditional ◆ Classic ◆
A totally renovated hotel within walking distance of the Vatican Museums. Simple, functional rooms, plus an attractive terrace where breakfast is served during the summer.

La Pergola (Beck) – Hotel Rome Cavalieri Hilton ← city,
via Cadlolo 101 ✉ 00136 – Ⓜ Cipro-Musei Vaticani ⇔18
– ✆ 06 35092152 – lapergola.rome@hilton.com – Fax 06 35 09 21 65 – www.cavalieri-hilton.it – closed 12 to 27 August, January, Sunday and Monday
Rest – *(booking essential) (dinner only)* Carte 111/171 € Plan I **A2**
Spec. Medaglioni di astice con fragole ed asparagi. Consommé alla liquirizia con ravioli ai peperoni e medaglioni di salmone. Filetto di manzo affogato in salsa di vaniglia su purea di topinambur.
◆ Inventive ◆ Formal ◆
An unforgettable view of the Eternal City and its surrounding hills. Impeccable service. The German chef is one of the best interpreters of Italian and Mediterranean cuisine.

Il Simposio-di Costantini

piazza Cavour 16 ✉ 00193 – Ⓜ Lepanto – ✆ 06 32111131 – Fax 06 3 21 15 02
closed August, Saturday lunch and Sunday – **Rest** – Carte 35/68 € *Plan II* **E2**

♦ Contemporary ♦ Wine bar ♦

Restaurant-wine bar where you can drink a glass of wine at the counter or in the elegant dining room and choose between hot and cold dishes; wide selection of cheeses.

Taverna Angelica

piazza Amerigo Capponi 6 ✉ 00193 – Ⓜ Ottaviano – ✆ 06 6874514 – www.tavernaangelica.it – closed 10 to 20 August and lunch except Sunday
Rest – *(Post theatre restaurant, open until late)* Carte 33/54 € **K1**

♦ Contemporary ♦ Trendy ♦

Expertly cooked dishes with an innovative flavour are the trademark of this modern restaurant, which is popular with theatre-goers.

L'Antico Porto

via Federico Cesi 36 ✉ 00193 – ✆ 06 3233661 – boombastik@alice.it – Fax 06 3 20 34 83 – www.ristorantelanticoporto.it
closed 3 weeks in August, Saturday lunch and Sunday *Plan II* **E1**
Rest – Carte 38/76 €

♦ Seafood ♦ Family ♦

The serious and friendly management decided to serve fish in this restaurant and the decision was a wise one. This restaurant is refined, classic and totally pleasing.

PARIOLI

Plan IV

Grand Hotel Parco dei Principi

(heated)

via Gerolamo Frescobaldi 5 ✉ 00198 – Ⓜ Veneto – ✆ 06 854421 – principi@parcodeiprincipi.com – Fax 06 8 84 51 04 – www.parcodeiprincipi.com 900 **M2**
180 rm – 350/450 € 450/550 € – 20 suites
Rest *Pauline Borghese* – Carte 60/80 €

♦ Luxury ♦ Business ♦ Classic ♦

Overlooking the Villa Borghese park, the hotel is a veritable sea of green tranquillity in the heart of Rome; warm and elegant interiors, attention to detail and careful service. Exclusive restaurant serving well-prepared, varied cuisine.

Aldrovandi Palace

300

via Ulisse Aldravandi 15 ✉ 00197 – ✆ 06 3223993 – hotel@aldrovandi.com – Fax 06 3 22 14 35 – www.aldrovandi.com **M2**
121 rm – 400 € 490/560 €, 30 € – 10 suites – **Rest *Baby*** – see below

♦ Luxury ♦ Stylish ♦

In an elegant building dating from the end of the 19th Century with view over the Villa Borghese, a small shaded park, with swimming pool, luxurious period style interiors and elegant sumptuous bedrooms.

Lord Byron

via De Notaris 5 ✉ 00197 – Ⓜ Flaminio – ✆ 06 3220404 – info@lordbyronhotel.com – Fax 06 3 22 04 05 – www.lordbyronhotel.com
32 rm – 275/400 € 330/540 € **L-M1**
Rest *Sapori del Lord Byron* – *(closed Sunday)* Carte 51/70 €

♦ Luxury ♦ Stylish ♦

More than a hotel, it is a residence for an exclusive stay: elegant and refined interiors, bedrooms which combine luxury and modern comfort, impeccable high quality service. This is a very refined dining room, perfect for intimate quiet diners.

The Duke Hotel

rm 80

via Archimede 69 ✉ 00197 – ✆ 06 367221 – theduke@thedukehotel.com – Fax 06 36 00 41 04 – www.thedukehotel.com **L1**
78 rm – 315/277 € 370/490 € – 7 suites – **Rest** – Menu 43 €

♦ Luxury ♦ Business ♦ Stylish ♦

The discreet, soft atmosphere of an elegant English club with the interiors decorated in new style, equipped with modern accessories; 5 o'clock tea is served in front of the fireplace.

ITALY

Mercure Roma Corso Trieste without rest
via Gradisca 29 ✉ 00198 – Ⓜ Bologna – ✆ 06 852021 – mercure.romatrieste@accor-hotels.it – Fax 06 8 41 24 44 – www.mercure.com **O1**
97 rm ☕ – †165/180 € ††185/200 €
◆ Chain hotel ◆ Business ◆ Modern ◆
This hotel is located in a neighbourhood that is almost entirely residential. There is a gym and a sunroom on the top floor.

Albani without rest
via Adda 45 ✉ 00198 – ✆ 06 84991 – info.rom@albanihotels.it – Fax 06 8 49 93 99 – www.albanihotels.com **N2**
154 rm ☕ – †190/210 € ††270/310 €
◆ Business ◆ Modern ◆
Facing the park of the ancient Villa Albani, not far from Via Veneto, a modern concept hotel; comfortable public areas, like the bright and large hall.

Claridge
viale Liegi 62 ✉ 00198 – ✆ 06 845441 – claridge@rhr.it – Fax 06 8 55 51 71 – www.rosciolihotels.com **M1**
93 rm ☕ – †156/205 € ††210/305 €
Rest – Carte 20/25 €
◆ Business ◆ Modern ◆
White predominates in the large, lightsome lobby, whereas the rooms are warmly coloured and enhanced by the attractive woodwork; many are with a balcony.

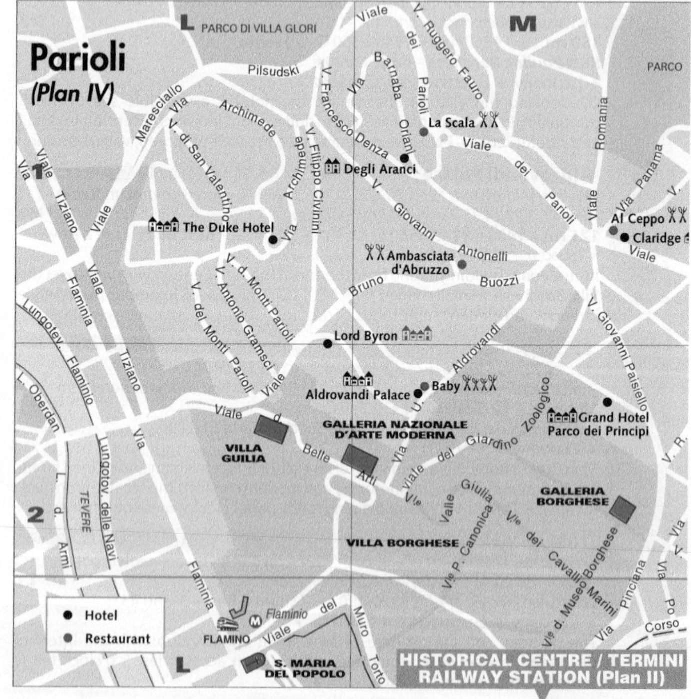

Degli Aranci

via Oriani 11 ✉ 00197 – Ⓜ Flaminio – ✆ 06 8070202 – info@hoteldegliaranci.com – Fax 06 8 07 07 04 **M1**

54 rm – 130/200 € 200/250 € – 2 suites – **Rest** – Menu 35/55 €

♦ Traditional ♦ Modern ♦

In the vicinity of Viale Parioli, in a green belt area which is rather quiet, there stands a luxury hotel, with pleasant well-cared-for public areas in period style; bedrooms with every comfort. Restaurant dining room with the windows overlooking the green garden.

Mercure Roma Piazza Bologna without rest

via Reggio Calabria 54 ✉ 00161 – Ⓜ Bologna – ✆ 06 440741 – mercurehotelsroma@accor-hotels.it – Fax 06 44 24 54 61 – www.accorhotels.com **O2**

113 rm – 180/195 € 215/245 €

♦ Chain hotel ♦ Modern ♦

This hotel is aimed primarily at business travellers, with all the comfort and services required by that clientele. The bedrooms are decorated in a modern style.

Fenix

viale Gorizia 5 ✉ 00198 – Ⓜ Bologna – ✆ 06 8540741 – info@fenixhotel.it – Fax 06 8 54 36 32 – www.fenixhotel.it **O1**

73 rm – 110/130 € 150/200 € – 8 suites

Rest – *(closed August, Saturday dinner and Sunday)* Carte 24/40 €

♦ Traditional ♦ Business ♦ Classic ♦

Near the park of Villa Torlonia, a hotel with public areas which are luxurious and well-maintained, tastefully furnished rooms and well refined; pleasant internal garden. Soft, elegant colours dominant the dining room of the restaurant.

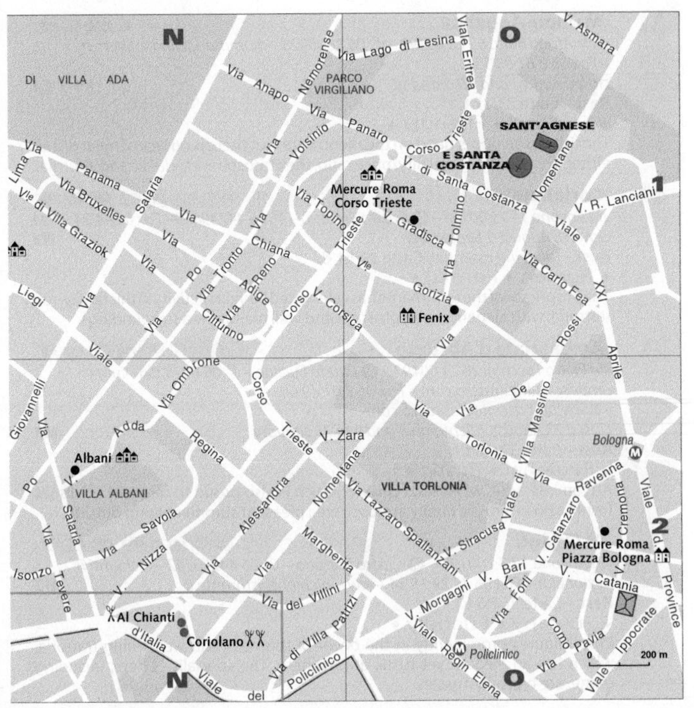

XXXX ✿

Baby – Hotel Aldrovandi Palace

via Ulisse Aldrovandi 15 ✉ 00197 – Ⓜ Flaminia – ✆ 06 3216126 – baby@aldrovandi.com – Fax 06 3 22 14 35 – www.aldrovandi.com
closed Monday **M2**
Rest – Carte 72/93 €
Spec. Ravioli di caciotta fresca e maggiorana con pomodorini vesuviani e basilico. Pesce di scoglio all'acqua pazza. Sfogliatella napoletana.
♦ Mediterranean ♦ Fashionable ♦
Housed in the deluxe Aldrovandi Palace hotel. Charming contemporary decor offering the sunny cuisine of the south. Products and revisited recipes of the Campanian region.

XX

Al Ceppo

via Panama 2 ✉ 00198 – ✆ 06 8551379 – info@ristorantealceppo.it – Fax 06 85 30 13 70 – www.ristorantealceppo.it
closed 8 to 24 August and Monday **M1**
Rest – Carte 47/62 €
♦ Mediterranean ♦ Rustic ♦
This friendly, much frequented family-managed restaurant is elegantly rustic in style. It offers specialities that adhere to traditional recipes but always with a touch of the modern.

XX

La Scala

viale dei Parioli 79/d ✉ 00197 – ✆ 06 8084463 – Fax 06 8 08 39 78
closed 6 to 21 August and Wednesday **M1**
Rest – Carte 31/45 €
♦ Roman ♦ Formal ♦
Managed by the same family for 30 years, this typical restaurant serves traditional Italian cuisine. The restaurant also operates as a pizzeria in the evenings.

XX

Mamma Angelina

viale Arrigo Boito 65 ✉ 00199 – ✆ 06 8608928 – mammangelina@libero.it – Fax 06 8 61 03 55
closed August and Wednesday *Plan I* **C1**
Rest – Carte 23/37 €
♦ Seafood ♦ Friendly ♦
The fish has an upper hand on the menu here, but there is no lack of meat dishes either. There is a good quality/price ratio; the atmosphere is classic and informal.

XX

Coriolano

via Ancona 14 ✉ 00198 – Ⓜ Castro Pretorio – ✆ 06 44249863 – Fax 06 44 24 97 24
closed 8 August-1 September **N2**
Rest – *(booking essential)* Carte 39/61 €
♦ Roman ♦ Formal ♦
The proprietor of the same name has celebrated 50 years activity in this family-run trattoria, with elegant tones, pleasant and well maintained surroundings.

XX

Ambasciata d'Abruzzo

via Pietro Tacchini 26 ✉ 00197 – Ⓜ Piazza Euclide – ✆ 06 8078256 – info@ambasciatadiabruzzo.com – Fax 06 8 07 49 64 – www.ambasciatadiabruzzo.com
closed 23 August-7 September and 9 to 23 January **M1**
Rest – Carte 32/48 €
♦ Regional ♦ Rustic ♦
An "ambassador" of Abruzzi cuisine, which is also proud to offer classic dishes from Lazio in a rustic family atmosphere ; pleasant summer eating outside.

X

Al Chianti

20/30

via Ancona 17 ✉ 00198 – Ⓜ Castro Pretorio – ✆ 06 44250242 – alchianti@nexianet.it – Fax 06 44 29 15 34 – www.alchiantiristorante.it **N2**
Rest – Carte 36/45 €
♦ Tuscany ♦ Friendly ♦
Wood figures prominently in the decor of this cosy and welcoming trattoria, which has an elegant yet rustic atmosphere. The specialities here, including game, are typically Tuscan.

MILAN
MILANO

Population (est. 2005): 1 216 000 (conurbation 3 798 000) – Altitude: 122m

AGE Cavalli/HOA QUI

Milan, which has a well-earned reputation for elegance, artistic flair, cultural tradition and gastronomic excellence, enjoys a lively social and political life. It offers a vibrant combination of old and new. It is famous for its historical monuments, outstanding museums, ultra-modern architecture and contemporary art. Although Milan is Italy's second city as regards population, politics and cultural heritage, it proudly claims to be the country's financial heartland owing to its commercial, industrial and banking activities.

Milan has a rich history from Roman occupation when it became the seat of the Western Empire at the end of the 3C. Emperor Constantine granted freedom of worship to Christians by the Edict of Milan (313) and St Ambrose became bishop in 375. Barbarian invasions in 5C and 6C were followed by the creation of the Lombard kingdom. After conquest by the Franks, Charlemagne became King of the Lombards in 774. In the 12C Milan joined the Lombard League against Emperor Frederic Barbarossa and gained independence. During the rule of the Visconti and the Sforza, the city flourished and attracted the geniuses of the time, Leonardo da Vinci and Bramante. Milan became the capital of the Cisalpine Republic in 1797, and later of the Kingdom of Italy (1805) and of the Venetian-Lombard Kingdom (1815).

WHICH DISTRICT TO CHOOSE

You will find a large selection of **hotels** in the luxury category near the Duomo in the historical centre *Plan II* **G2**, and hotels of a good standard near Stazione Centrale *Plan III* **M1**, near Piazza della Repubblica *Plan III* **M2**, in the Montenapoleone district, and in the business district around Corso Buenos Aires *Plan I* **C1**. There are moderately priced hotels in the university area *Plan II* **G2** and in the trade fair district around Viale Certosa *Plan I* **A1**. Business hotels are also to be found on the outskirts. Milan has many **restaurants** with a fine culinary tradition. The historical area abounds in luxury

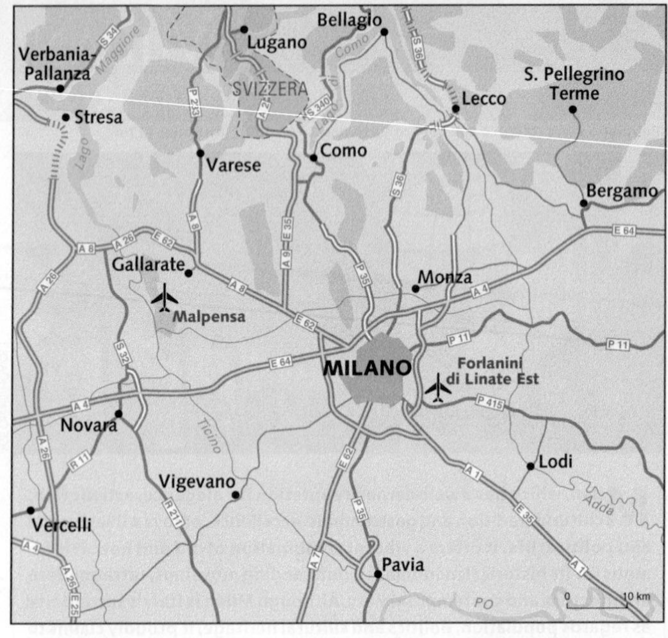

establishments near the Duomo *Plan II* **G2**, Via Manzoni *Plan II* **G1**, Piazza della Scala. For good food at reasonable prices look in the Romana-Vittoria area – Porta Romana *Plan I* **D3**, Viale Umbria, Corso Porta Vittoria *Plan II* **H2**. For typical restaurants with a pleasant ambience and trattorias serving seafood, visit the Navigli district – Piazza XXIV Maggio *Plan II* **F3**, Ripa di Porta Ticinese *Plan I* **B3**, Via Solari *Plan I* **B3**.

PRACTICAL INFORMATION

ARRIVAL – DEPARTURE

Malpensa Airport, 45 km (28 mi) northwest of the city centre. **Linate Airport**, 8 km (5 mi) east. ✆ 02 748 52200.

From the airport to the city centre – Taxis are rather expensive as **Malpensa** Airport is some distance from the city. A train connects Malpensa Airport with Stazione Cadorna (every 30min, time: 40min) which in turn connects to the metro system. Fare €9. Malpensa Express, ✆ 02 20 222. There is a shuttle bus service to Stazione Centrale (every 20min, time 45min/1hr depending on the traffic) costing €5.50 (one way). Malpensa Shuttle Express, ✆ 02 58 58 10 64; www.sea-aeroportimilano.it

From **Linate** Airport bus no 73 runs to Piazza San Babila metro station (every 10min, time 25min). Fare €1 (tickets on sale at newsstands). ✆ 800 016 857. There is also a STARFLY bus service to Stazione Centrale (every 30min, time

30min) which also stops at Stazione Lambrate. Fare €2.50. www.sea-aeroportimilano.it

Main station – International and inter-city train services operate from Stazione Centrale *Plan III* **M1**.

TRANSPORT

→ BUS AND METRO

There are three metro lines. Tickets are valid for 75min on the whole bus/metro network. A single ticket costs €1 (book of 10 tickets €9.20); a 1-day travel card costs €3, 2-day travel card €5.50. Tickets can be purchased at kiosks, bars, tobacconists and ticket machines.

→ TAXIS

Taxis, which are white vehicles and bear an illuminated sign, can be hired at a taxi stand or hailed in the street. The minimum pick-up charge is €3.10. There is a supplement of €3.10 at night and €1.55 on public holidays. An average taxi ride costs €10-15. *Radio Taxis* ✆ 02 4040, 02 8585, 02 8383.

USEFUL ADDRESSES

→ TOURIST OFFICE

Via Marconi, 1 – 20123 Milano *Plan II* **G2**. ✆ 02 72 52 43 01/2; www.milanoinfotourist.com

→ BANKS/CURRENCY EXCHANGE

The major banks and foreign exchange offices are to be found in the town centre and at the main railway stations. Banks open Mon-Fri, 8.30am-1.30pm and 3-4.30pm (some banks open on Saturday morning until 1.30pm); closed national holidays and 7 December (the town's patron Saint's Day). Bank cash machines (ATMs) are open 24hrs (pin number required).

→ EMERGENCY

Medical emergencies: ✆ **118**; Police: ✆ **113**.

→ CHEMIST / PHARMACY

The chemist in Galleria delle Partenze, Stazione Centrale *Plan III* **M1** is open 24 hours. ✆ 02 66 90 935.

BUSY PERIODS

It may be difficult to find a room when special events are held in the city:

Milano Internazionale Antiquariato – Antiques Fair: early May.

Naviglio Grande – Antiques Fair: late June.

International Furniture Fair – April.

Milanovendemoda – Fashion: late February (winter fashion), late Sept-early Oct (summer fashion).

MICAM – Footwear Fair: late March and late September.

Moda Prima – International knitwear market: early June. Fashion and accessories show: late November-early December.

Monza – Formula One race: September.

Smau – Electronic Fair: late October.

EXPLORING MILAN

In two days there is time to visit the main sights and museums.

Opening times are usually from 9.30-10am to 5-5.30pm but closed on Mondays and public holidays.

VISITING

Duomo *Plan II* **G2** – A Gothic marvel in white marble with belfries, gables, pinnacles, statues, rose windows and tracery. Do not miss a visit to the roof for stunning views and the cathedral museum. Then go through to the magnificent **Galleria Vittorio Emanuele**, with fine shops and some libraries.

Pinacoteca di Brera *Plan II* **G1** – A 17C palace houses masterpieces (*Dead Christ* by Mantegna, *Pietà* by Bellini, *Montefeltro altarpiece* by Piero della Francesca, *Marriage of the Virgin* by Raphael, *Meal at Emmaus* by Caravaggio) and 20C works by Italian Futurists.

Castello Sforzesco *Plan II* **F1** – The former residence of the Dukes of Milan – sculpture museum (*Rondanini Pietà* by Michaelangelo), picture gallery, archaeological museum and musical instruments.

Palazzo Bagatti Valsecchi *Plan II* **G2** – A Renaissance palace with opulent decor: frescoes, sculpture, paintings, furnishings.

Pinacoteca Ambrosiana *Plan II* **F2** – One of the oldest libraries in the world displays outstanding exhibits: drawings and *The Musician* by Leonardo da Vinci, cartoons by Raphael, *Basket of Fruit* by Caravaggio.

Museo della Scienza e della Tecnica Leonardo da Vinci *Plan II* **E2** – Models of Leonardo's inventions and displays tracing scientific advances through the ages.

Chiesa di Santa Maria delle Grazie *Plan II* **E2** – A 15-16C Renaissance church with an impressive dome by Bramante. Leonardo's *Last Supper* in the restored Cenacolo.

Galleria d'Arte Moderna *Plan II* **G2** – An interesting display of contemporary art by Italian and European artists. Marino Marini Museum.

Basilica di Sant'Ambrogio *Plan II* **E2** – A magnificent basilica, founded in 4C by St Ambrose, is in the Lombard-Romanesque (11-12C) – altar front, ambo, mosaics, portico by Bramante.

Monza *(21 km – 13 mi – NE of Milano)* – Attractive town famous for its cathedral (Iron Crown of the Kings of Lombardy in the treasury), and the royal villa Parco di Villa Reale with a vast park where the **Monza racing circuit** is.

GOURMET TREATS

If you fancy a snack or light meal, visit *Bar della Crocetta*, Corso di Porta Romana 67 and the tiny *Crota piemunteisa*, Piazza Cesare Beccaria 10. *Gattullo*, Piazza Porta Ludovica 2, is one of the best places for a freshly baked brioche and a cappuccino. *Taveggia*, Via Visconti di Modrone 2, serves dark and syrupy hot chocolate. *Cova*, Via Monte Napoleone 8, *Panerello*, Via Speronari and Corso di Porta Romana, *Cucci*, Corso di Porta Genova offer delicious pastries.

Gelateria Marghera, Via Marghera 33, *Umberto*, Piazza Cinque Giornate, *Il Massimo del Gelato*, Via Castelvetro 18, *Riva Reno*, Via Col di Lana 8 and *Ruggero*, Piazza Emilia 4 have an excellent selection of ice cream.

SHOPPING

Shops are open daily except Sun and Monday morning except Grocery shops, 9-9.30am to 12.30-1pm and from 3.30-4pm to 7.30-8pm.

For **luxury items** stroll through the fashionable districts – Corso Vittorio Emanuele II *Plan II* **G2**, Piazza San Babila *Plan II* **G1**, Corso Venezia *Plan II* **H1**, Via Monte Napoleone *Plan II* **G1**, Via Dante *Plan II* **F1**, Corso Vercelli *Plan I* **B2**, Corso Buenos Aires *Plan I* **C1** and Via della Spiga (where the couture houses are) *Plan II* **G1**. For **young fashions** browse in Corsa di Porta Ticinese and Via Torino *Plan II* **F2**. Lovers of **antiques** will find a profusion of shops in Corso Magenta *Plan II* **F2** and the narrow streets around Sant'Ambrogio *Plan II* **E2**, Via Lanzone *Plan II* **F2**, Via Caminadella *Plan II* **F3**, Via Santa Marta *Plan II* **F2**, Via Brera *Plan II* **F1** and environs and in Via Bagutta *Plan II* **G1**.

Peck and other shops in Via Spadari *Plan II* **F2**, Via Speronari *Plan II* **G2** and Via Cantù *Plan II* **F2** specialise in delicacies and fine foods.

MARKETS – In Piazza Diaz *Plan II* **G2**, (**old books** – every second Sun), in Via Armorari *Plan II* **F2** (**stamps and postcards** – Sun), in Piazza Gaspari (**objects** – Sat) and in Via Fiori Chiari *Plan II* **F1** (**antiques** – every third Sun). Popular **flea markets** are: Fiera di Senigallia, Piazza Stazione di Porta Genova *Plan II* **E3** (Sat), Mercato di San Donato (Metro San Donato, Sun).

WHAT TO BUY – Latest fashions, leather goods, shirts of the famous football teams Milan AC and Inter Milan, furniture and design.

ENTERTAINMENT

Consult the brochure *Milano Mese* which gives listings of entertainment and venues throughout the city. It is available from the tourist office. www.milanoturismo.com

La Scala *Plan II* **G1** – A world famous venue for opera and ballet. The season starts on St Ambrose Day (7 Dec).

Conservatorio *Plan II* **H2** – Chamber and orchestral music.

Auditorium di Milano *Plan I* **B3** – Classical, jazz and other types of music, literary evenings, events for children and audiences with famous artists.

Teatro Dal Verme *Plan II* **F1** – Plays.

Piccolo Teatro *Plan II* **F2** – Three theatres present drama.

NIGHTLIFE

Milan has lively cafés and bars for **going out for a drink** or **for the evening** in the historical centre and near the station. *Bar Magenta*, Via Carducci 13 is one of the famous bars in Milan and *Bar Basso*, Via Plinio 39 serves delicious cocktails. Other pleasant venues are *Moscatelli*, Corso Garibaldi, *Morigi*, Via Morigi, *Roïalto*, Via Piero della Francesca, *La Belle Aurore*, via Abamonti 1/Via Castel Morrone. *See Entertainment above.*

At night the liveliest part of the city is the picturesque **Brera** district *Plan II* **G1** where there are bars and nightclubs popular with artists. The **Navigli** and **Ticinese** areas and **Corso Como** *Plan III* **L1** are also well worth a visit.

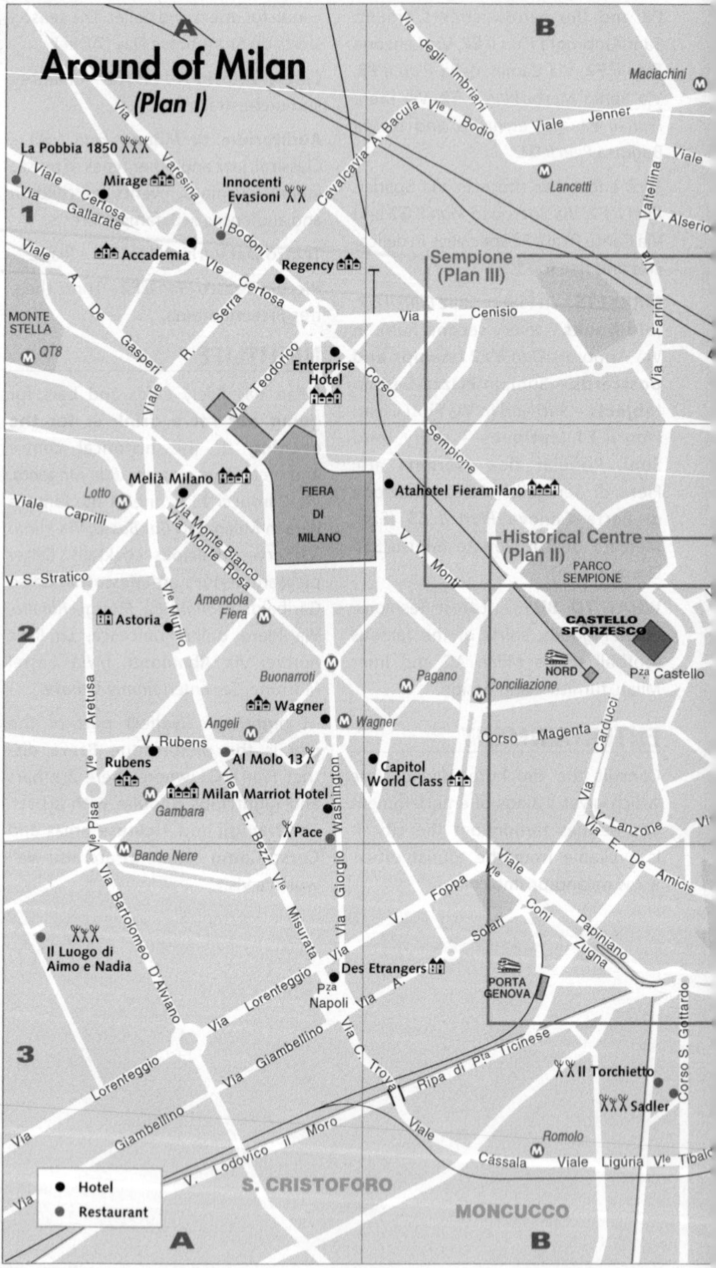

Around of Milan

(Plan I)

A

B

La Pobbia 1850

Mirage

Innocenti Evasioni

Accademia

Regency

Enterprise Hotel

Sempione (Plan III)

Melià Milano

FIERA DI MILANO

Atahotel Fieramilano

Historical Centre (Plan II)

PARCO SEMPIONE

CASTELLO SFORZESCO

Astoria

Wagner

Rubens

Al Molo 13

Capitol World Class

Milan Marriot Hotel

Pace

Il Luogo di Aimo e Nadia

Des Etrangers

PORTA GENOVA

Il Torchietto

Sadler

S. CRISTOFORO

MONCUCCO

Via degli Imbriani

Vle L. Bodio

Viale Jenner

Maciachini

Viale

Lancetti

Cavalcavia A. Bacula

Via Varesina

Viale Certosa

Via Gallarate

V. Bodoni

Vle Certosa

Viale A. De Gasperi

Viale R. Serra

MONTE STELLA

QT8

Via Teodorico

Via Cenisio

Corso Sempione

Via Valtellina

V. Alserio

Via Farini

Lotto

Viale Caprilli

Via Monte Bianco

Via Monte Rosa

V. V. Monti

V. S. Stratico

Vle Murillo

Amendola Fiera

Buonarroti

Pagano

Conciliazione

NORD

Pza Castello

Via Aretusa

Angeli

Wagner

V. Rubens

Corso Magenta

Via Carducci

Gambara

Vle E. Bezzi

Via Giorgio Washington

Vle Pisa

Bande Nere

V. Lanzone

Via E. De Amicis

Via Bartolomeo D'Alviano

Vle Misurata

V. Foppa

Viale Coni Zugna

Vle Papiniano

Via A. Solari

Via Lorenteggio

Pza Napoli

Via Lorenteggio

Via Giambellino

Via C. Troya

Ripa di Pta Ticinese

Corso S. Gottardo

Via Giambellino

V. Lodovico il Moro

Viale Cássala

Romolo

Viale Ligúria

Vle Tibald

Via

1

2

3

A

B

- Hotel
- Restaurant

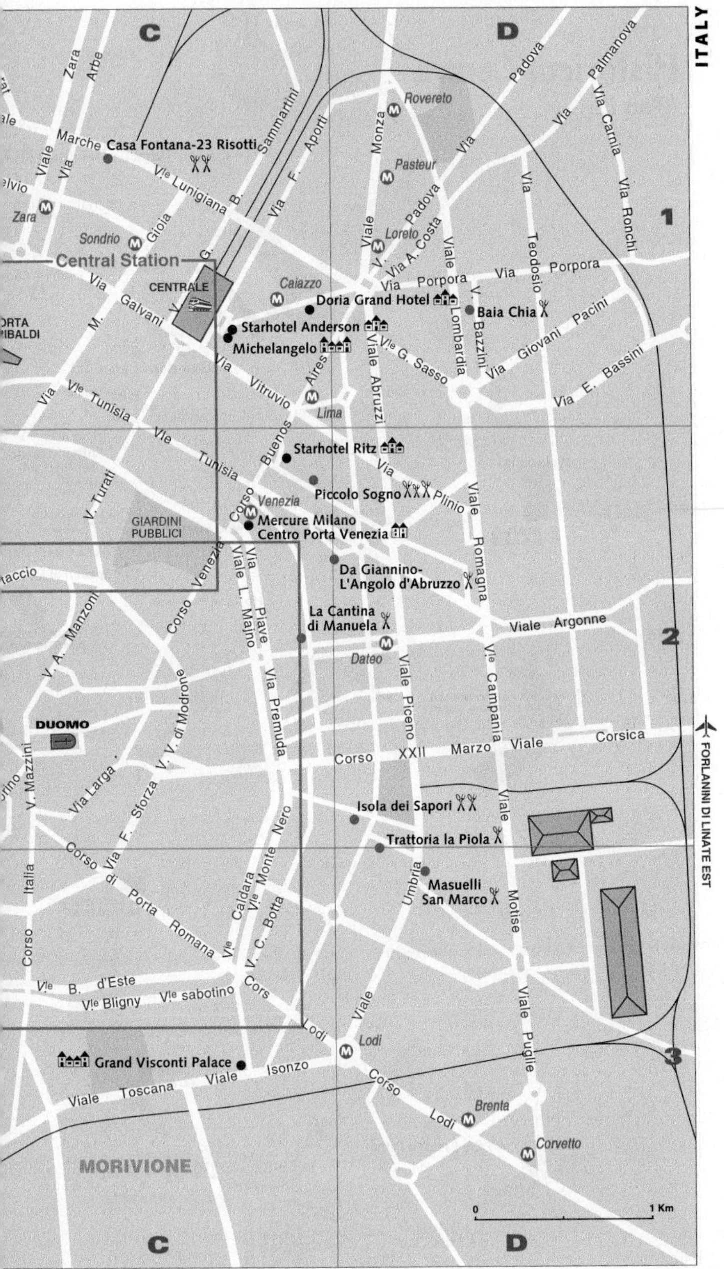
C
D
1
2
3
Casa Fontana-23 Risotti
Central Station
CENTRALE
Doria Grand Hotel
Baia Chia
Starhotel Anderson
Michelangelo
Starhotel Ritz
Piccolo Sogno
Mercure Milano
Centro Porta Venezia
Da Giannino-
L'Angolo d'Abruzzo
La Cantina
di Manuela
GIARDINI
PUBBLICI
DUOMO
Isola dei Sapori
Trattoria la Piola
Masuelli
San Marco
Grand Visconti Palace
MORIVIONE
FORLANINI DI LINATE EST
Rovereto
Pasteur
Loreto
Caiazzo
Lima
Venezia
Dateo
Lodi
Brenta
Corvetto
Sondrio
Zara
Viale Argonne
Corso XXII Marzo
Viale Corsica
Corso di Porta Romana
Viale Toscana
Viale Isonzo
Corso Lodi
0
1 Km

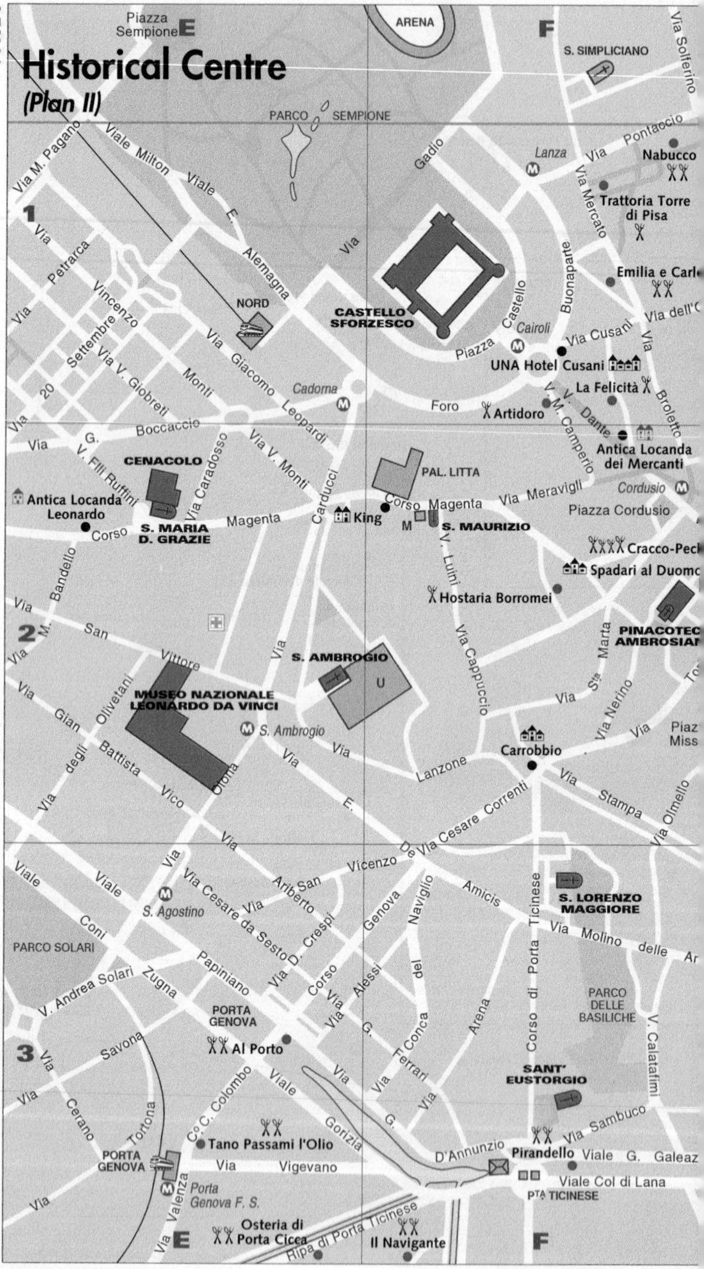
Historical Centre
(Plan II)
Piazza Sempione
E
F
ARENA
S. SIMPLICIANO
Via Solferino
PARCO SEMPIONE
Via M. Pagano
Viale Milton
Viale E. Alemagna
Via Gadio
Lanza
Via Pontaccio
Nabucco
Via Mercato
Trattoria Torre di Pisa
Via Buonaparte
Emilia e Carl
Via dell'
NORD
CASTELLO SFORZESCO
Piazza Castello
Cairoli
Via Cusani
UNA Hotel Cusani
Via Petrarca
Via Vincenzo
Via 20 Settembre
Via V. Giobreti
Via Monti
Via Giacomo Leopardi
Cadorna
Foro
Artidoro
La Felicità
V. M. Camperio
V. Dante
Broletto
Antica Locanda dei Mercanti
Via G. Boccaccio
V. Flli Ruffini
CENACOLO
Via Caradosso
Via V. Monti
Carducci
PAL. LITTA
Corso Magenta
Via Meravigli
Cordusio
Piazza Cordusio
Antica Locanda Leonardo
Corso
S. MARIA D. GRAZIE
Magenta
King
M
S. MAURIZIO
V. Luini
Cracco-Pecl
Spadari al Duomo
Via M. Bandello
Hostaria Borromei
Via San Vittore
S. AMBROGIO
U
Via Cappuccio
Via Sta Marta
PINACOTEC AMBROSIAN
MUSEO NAZIONALE LEONARDO DA VINCI
Via Olivetani
Via Gian Battista Vico
S. Ambrogio
Via Lanzone
Via Nerino
Carrobbio
Piaz Miss
Via degli
Via E. De Amicis
Via Cesare Correnti
Via Stampa
Via Olmetto
Via Ariberto
Via San Vicenzo
Viale Coni
Via S. Agostino
Via Cesare da Sesto
Via D. Crespi
Corso Genova
Via Naviglio
S. LORENZO MAGGIORE
Corso di Porta Ticinese
Via Molino delle Ar
PARCO SOLARI
V. Andrea Solari
Zugna
Papiniano
PORTA GENOVA
Al Porto
Via G. Alessi
Via del
Via Conca
Via Arena
PARCO DELLE BASILICHE
V. Calatafimi
Via Savona
Via Cerano
Via Tortona
Co C. Colombo
Viale Gorizia
Via G. Ferrari
SANT' EUSTORGIO
Via Sambuco
Tano Passami l'Olio
D'Annunzio
Pirandello
Viale G. Galeaz
PORTA GENOVA
Via Vigevano
Viale Col di Lana
PTA TICINESE
Porta Genova F. S.
Via Valenza
Osteria di Porta Cicca
Ripa di Porta Ticinese
Il Navigante
1
2
3

Flemish masters (Bruegel, Rubens, Hieronymus Bosch, Memling). **Musée d'Art Moderne**: Highlights of the 20C collections include Belgian paintings – works by Delvaux and Magritte – and sculpture by Belgian and international artists. **Musée du Cinquantenaire** *Plan II* **H2**: ethnographical and decorative art collections.

ART NOUVEAU CAPITAL – **Musée des Instruments de Musique** *Plan IV* **N2**: The Art Nouveau buildings of Old England house a prestigious collection of musical instruments – section devoted to Adolphe Sax, Brussels tavern piano, lutemaker's workshop. **Centre Belge de la Bande Dessinée** *Plan IV* **N1**. **Saint-Gilles district**, in particular **Musée Horta** *Plan III* **J2** and **Hotel Hannon** *Plan II* **F3**. **Maison Cauchie** *Plan II* **H2**. The squares around the **Quartier des Institutions Européennes** *Plan II* **G2**. Trail around the lakes at **Ixelles** *Plan III* **K1**.

LOCAL COLOUR – **Manneken Pis** *Plan IV* **M2**: the mascot of the city. **Underground Art** – 40 stations of the Brussels Metro decorated by famous Belgian artists (*L'Art dans le métro* brochure – in French – from tourist offices). Trail tracing buildings decorated with characters from comic strips (brochure from tourist offices). **Galeries Saint-Hubert** *Plan IV* **M1**: elegant covered arcade with shops, restaurants, tea shops, theatre and cinema.

Lively **markets** are great attractions at weekends: **Place du Grand Sablon** *Plan IV* **M3** and surrounding area; **Place du Jeu de Balle** (flea market) *Plan II* **E3**; **Gare du Midi** *Plan II* **E3**.

To enjoy Brussels-style **'zwanze'** (zwanzer, meaning joking in local dialect, a favourite pastime of the people of Brussels), listen to the people talking around you and try to join in, in particular in the cafés, boutiques and markets in the lower town.

OUTSKIRTS – **Basilique du Sacré-Cœur in Koekelberg** *Plan I* **A2**, in the Art Deco style. **Atomium in Heysel** *Plan I* **B1**: view from the top sphere at a height of 102m/332ft above ground level, a glittering steel structure consisting of nine spheres represents an iron crystal molecule expanded 165 billion times.

GOURMET TREATS

As you amble along the streets around the **Grand'Place** *Plan IV* **M2** or in the **quartier des Marolles** *Plan IV* **M3** treat yourself to **'caricoles'**, whelks cooked in a peppery broth, or a Belgian waffle, **gaufre de Bruxelles**, a crispy, light pastry, covered with whipped cream *(crème chantilly)*.

For a bag of thick, golden chips **(cornet de frites)** served with a variety of sauces, stop at one of the many popular chip shops. The *Maison Antoine*, place Jourdan 1, is one of the best in town.

To sample a thirst-quenching **Gueuze**, a spontaneously fermented regional beer, with a sharp, natural or fruity flavour, such as the delightful **Kriek** (with cherries), or a full-bodied abbey or Trappist beer, take a break in one of the typical **bars (estaminets), cafés, taverns** or **bistros** : *À la Mort Subite*, rue Montagne-Aux-Herbes-Potagères 7; *Au Roy d'Espagne*, Grand'Place 1; *Au Bon Vieux Temps*, rue du Marché-aux-Herbes 12; *L'Imaige de Nostre-Dame*, Impasse des Cadeaux 6; *La Bécasse*, rue Tabora 11; *Le Cirio*, rue de la Bourse 18.

Estaminets and **tavernes-restaurants** *(see listing in the Guide)* are open all day and serve **mussels** (mostly from Zeeland) tasting of the sea and presented in a traditional enamel pot, with a copious helping of chips.

ble (€6.70, €10.50, €4.00 respectively); www.stib.irisnet.be

→ TAXIS

Taxis bear an illuminated sign on the car roof. They may be hailed in the street, called by telephone, hired at taxi ranks. *Taxis Verts* ✆ 02 349 49 49; *Taxis Orange* ✆ 02 349 43 43; *Taxis Bleus* ✆ 02 268 00 00. Minimum pick-up charge is €2.40; a journey inside the urban centre (agglomeration) costs €1.23/km and €2.46 outside urban centre. It is customary to round up taxi fares. A night tariff (double the daytime tariff) is applicable from 10pm to 6am.

USEFUL ADDRESSES

→ TOURIST OFFICES

BI-TC (Bruxelles International – Tourisme & Congrès) *Plan IV* **M2**, Hôtel de Ville, Grand-Place, 1000 Bruxelles. ✆ 02 513 89 40. Open 9am-6pm (2pm Sunday in winter).

OPT (Office de Promotion du Tourisme Wallonie-Bruxelles) *Plan IV* **M2**, 63 rue du Marché-aux-Herbes, 1000 Bruxelles. ✆ 02 504 03 90. Open 9am-6pm (7pm July-August).

→ POST OFFICES

Opening times 9am to 4-5pm. The post office on the first floor of Centre Monnaie, Place de la Monnaie *Plan IV* **M1** is open on Friday evenings and Saturday mornings; the one at Gare du Midi is open from 7am to 11pm (7pm for financial operations).

→ BANKS/CURRENCY EXCHANGE

Banks open Monday to Friday, 9am-4pm. There are cash dispensers all over the city.

→ EMERGENCY

Dial ✆ **100** (✆ **112** if calling on a mobile phone) for Ambulance and Fire Brigade and ✆ **101** for Police and Gendarmerie.

BUSY PERIODS

It may be difficult to find a room at a reasonable price (except during weekends) when special events are held in the city:

Sea-Food Expo: end of April or early March.

Labelexpo: September – Stickers show.

Decosit: September – Tissues show.

European Summits: two times a year.

EXPLORING BRUSSELS

DIFFERENT FACETS OF THE CITY

It is possible to visit the main sights and museums in two to three days.

Museums and sights are usually open from 10am to 5pm. Some close on Mondays.

HISTORIC CITY – Grand'Place *Plan IV* **M2**: this splendid square is lined with the ornate Baroque facades of the guildhalls which were built in the 18C and restored in the 19C and are adorned with scrolled gables, sculptures, gilded motifs and flame ornaments. A stunning architectural ensemble at its best during the early morning flower market or floodlit at night. You may also include visits to the **Musée de la Brasserie** (No 10) and the **Musée du Cacao et du Chocolat** (No 13). **Cathédrale des Saints Michel-et-Gudule** *Plan IV* **N1**: a beautiful Gothic building with additions in various styles; wonderful stained glass windows and furnishings.

ARTISTIC CITY – Do not miss **Musées Royaux des Arts de Belgique** *Plan IV* **N2** including **Musée d'Art Ancien** with its outstanding collections of

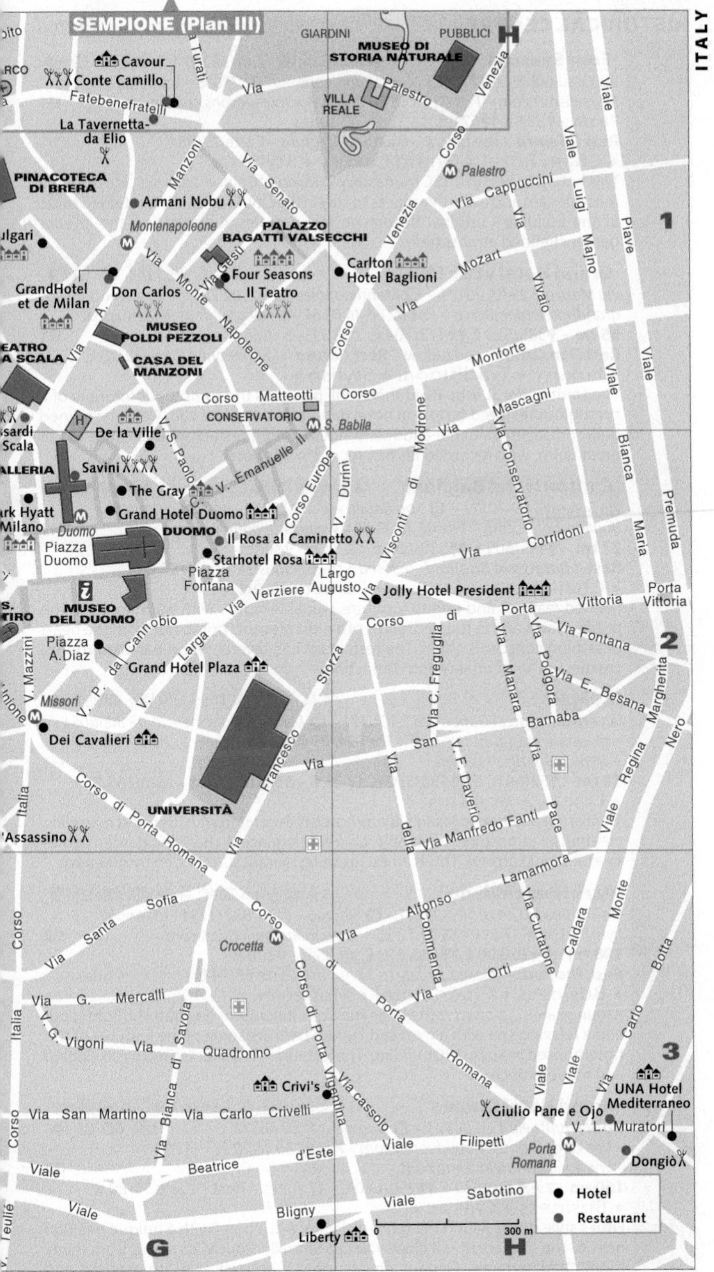
SEMPIONE (Plan III)
GIARDINI PUBBLICI
MUSEO DI STORIA NATURALE
VILLA REALE
Cavour
Conte Camillo
La Tavernetta-da Elio
PINACOTECA DI BRERA
Armani Nobu
Montenapoleone
PALAZZO BAGATTI VALSECCHI
Carlton Hotel Baglioni
Four Seasons
Il Teatro
GrandHotel et de Milan
Don Carlos
MUSEO POLDI PEZZOLI
CASA DEL MANZONI
CONSERVATORIO
S. Babila
De la Ville
Savini
The Gray
Grand Hotel Duomo
DUOMO
Piazza Duomo
Il Rosa al Caminetto
Starhotel Rosa
Piazza Fontana
Largo Augusto
Jolly Hotel President
MUSEO DEL DUOMO
Piazza A.Diaz
Grand Hotel Plaza
Missori
Dei Cavalieri
UNIVERSITÀ
Crocetta
Crivi's
Giulio Pane e Ojo
UNA Hotel Mediterraneo
Porta Romana
Dongiò
Liberty
Porta Vittoria
Palestro
Hotel
Restaurant
300 m
1
2
3
G
H

HISTORICAL CENTRE *Plan II*

Four Seasons

via Gesù 6/8 ✉ 20121 – Ⓜ Montenapoleone – ✆ 02 77088 – tes.milano@fourseasons.com – Fax 02 77 08 50 00 – www.fourseasons.com/milan **G1**

78 rm – †594 € ††671 €, ☕ 33 € – 25 suites

Rest *Il Teatro* – see below – **Rest *La Veranda*** – Carte 72/98 €

♦ Chain hotel ♦ Grand Luxury ♦ Stylish ♦

This hotel, housed in a 15C monastery in Milan's "Golden Triangle", is one of the most elegant and exclusive places to stay in the city. The hotel has retained some of the building's original decorative features. Restaurant facing the interior garden. Refined atmosphere.

Grand Hotel et de Milan

via Manzoni 29 ✉ 20121 – Ⓜ Montenapoleone – ✆ 02 723141 – reservations@grandhoteletdemilan.it – Fax 02 86 46 08 61 – www.grandhoteletdemilan.it **G1**

95 rm – †385/539 € ††473/704 €, ☕ 35 € – 8 suites

Rest *Don Carlos* – see below – **Rest *Caruso*** – *(dinner only)* Carte 42/75 €

♦ Luxury ♦ Traditional ♦ Stylish ♦

The spirit of Verdi, who lived there, still pervades the sumptuous interiors of a prestigious restored historical hotel dating from the late 19th Century; refined bedrooms with valuable antique furniture. Bright restaurant dedicated to the great tenor, who recorded his first record in this hotel.

Carlton Hotel Baglioni

via Senato 5 ✉ 20121 – Ⓜ San Babila – ✆ 02 77077 – carlton.milano@baglionihotels.com – Fax 02 78 33 00 – www.baglionihotels.com **H1**

87 rm – †495/605 € ††550/660 €, ☕ 33 € – 9 suites

Rest *Il Baretto al Baglioni* – *(closed 5 to 26 August)* Carte 70/90 €

♦ Chain hotel ♦ Luxury ♦ Personalised ♦

Refined features and period furniture, valuable fabrics with warm tones in the public rooms and in the bedrooms of a most elegant "bomboniera" in the heart of fashion conscious Milan. The restaurant has several, wood-panelled rooms, creating an air of quality and distinction.

Bulgari

via Privata Fratelli Gabba 7/B ✉ 20121 – Ⓜ Montenapoleone – ✆ 02 8058051 – milano@bulgarihotels.com – Fax 02 8 05 80 52 22 – www.bulgarihotels.com **G1**

58 rm – †520/610 € ††590/650 €, ☕ 28 € – 6 suites – **Rest** – Menu 65/85 €

♦ Luxury ♦ Stylish ♦

This recent addition to Milan's luxury hotels is decorated with the finest materials, creating an atmosphere of simple, discreet elegance. A charming garden comes as a pleasant surprise. This is an exclusive restaurant surrounded by greenery.

Park Hyatt Milano

via Tommaso Grossi 1 ✉ 20121 – Ⓜ Duomo – ✆ 02 88211234 – milano@hyattintl.com – Fax 02 88 21 12 35 – www.milan.park.hyatt.com **G2**

108 rm – †430/600 € ††480/650 €, ☕ 35 € – 9 suites

Rest *The Park* – *(closed 30 July to 27 August)* Carte 68/94 €

♦ Business ♦ Chain hotel ♦ Modern ♦

A lounge area crowned with a large cupola, public rooms decorated in light tones and a relaxing spa with a gym and Turkish bath are some of the features of this hotel housed in a late-19C building. The restaurant is characterised by an elegant and modern decor.

Grand Hotel Duomo

< Duomo, handy rm AC rm 100

via San Raffaele 1 ✉ 20121 – Ⓜ Duomo – ✆ 02 88331 – bookings@grandhotelduomo.com – Fax 02 86 46 20 27 – www.grandhotelduomo.com **G2**

160 rm ☕ – †230/530 € ††290/640 € – 17 suites – **Rest** – Carte 55/80 €

♦ Business ♦ Classic ♦

Fifties style décor within the refined elegance of a hotel with a unique position next to the Cathedral - so close you can virtually "touch" its spires from many rooms and terraces. Elegant dining room with exclusive atmosphere and windows facing over Piazza del Duomo.

Starhotel Rosa

130 VISA AE

via Pattari 5 ✉ 20122 – Ⓜ Duomo – ✆ 02 8831 – rosa.mi@starhotels.it – Fax 02 8 05 79 64 – www.starhotels.com **G2**

247 rm – ††385/495, € 19 – 2 suites

Rest *Il Rosa al Caminetto* – see below

◆ Business ◆ Classic ◆

Near to the Cathedral, a recently renovated hotel, which has a spacious and elegant ground floor, with marble and stuccoes, and functional bedrooms; fully equipped Conference Centre.

Grand Visconti Palace

rm rm 250 VISA AE

viale Isonzo 14 ✉ 20135 – Ⓜ Lodi T.I.B.B. – ✆ 02 540341 – info@grandviscontipalace.com – Fax 02 54 06 95 23 – www.grandviscontipalace.com *Plan I* **C3**

166 rm – †330/460 € ††400/530 € – 6 suites

Rest *Al Quinto Piano* – *(closed 4 to 28 August)* Carte 57/86 €

◆ Business ◆ Personalised ◆

This elegant hotel is housed in the extensive buildings of an old industrial mill. Facilities include conference rooms, a delightful garden and a first-class fitness centre. The restaurant, showing unmistakably on the fifth floor, is reminiscent of an attractively coloured candy-box.

Jolly Hotel President

rm rm 140 VISA AE

largo Augusto 10, ✉ 20122 – Ⓜ San Babila – ✆ 02 77461 – milano_president@jollyhotels.com – Fax 02 78 34 49 – www.jollyhotels.com **H2**

244 rm – †205/350 € ††240/390 € – 12 suites

Rest *Il Verziere* – Carte 40/55 €

◆ Business ◆ Classic ◆

In a central piazza, a large international hotel, with available conference equipment; spacious bedrooms, with adequate accessories for its class. An elegant and refined restaurant.

UNA Hotel Cusani

VISA AE

via Cusani 13 ✉ 20121 – Ⓜ Cairoli – ✆ 02 85601 – una.cusani@unahotels.it – Fax 02 8 69 36 01 – www.unahotels.it **F1**

87 rm – ††160/612 € – 5 suites

Rest – Carte 52/69 €

◆ Business ◆ Modern ◆

Privileged position, opposite the Castello Sforzesco, for a comfortable building, that has very spacious bedrooms available, with recent furnishings in mahogany and pastel colours. Small restaurant dining room; bright and refined.

De la Ville

rm rm 60 VISA AE

via Hoepli 6 ✉ 20121 – Ⓜ Duomo – ✆ 02 8791311 – reservationsdlv@sinahotels.it – Fax 02 86 66 09 – www.delavillemilano.com **G2**

109 rm – †374 € ††390 €

Rest *L'Opera* – *✆ 02 8051231 (closed Sunday)* Carte 40/60 €

◆ Luxury ◆ Cosy ◆

Warm atmosphere in the style of an elegant English lounge, with imaginative woodwork, velvets and carpets, inside a centrally situated hotel; elegant period style bedrooms. Classy atmosphere in the restaurant.

The Gray

VISA AE

via San Raffaele 6 ✉ 20121 – Ⓜ Duomo – ✆ 02 7208951 – info.thegray@sinahotels.it – Fax 02 86 65 26 – www.hotelgray.com **G2**

21 rm – †374 € ††550 €

Rest – Carte 50/72 €

◆ Luxury ◆ Stylish ◆

This establishment is characterised by elegance and style. All the rooms have something special in terms of interesting details and some offer a view of the Galleria. A pleasant and stylish restaurant.

ITALY

Spadari al Duomo AC ⊬rm VISA MC AE ①
via Spadari 11 ✉ 20123 – Ⓜ Duomo – ✆ 02 72002371 – reservation@spadarihotel.com – Fax 02 86 11 84 – www.spadarihotel.com
closed Christmas **F2**
40 rm ☕ – ♂228/278 € ♂♂238/308 € – **Rest** – *(light meals only)*
♦ Business ♦ Functional ♦
With its extensive collection of contemporary art, this small hotel combines comfort with a penchant for new and exciting forms of artistic expression.

Cavour AC ⊬ 🏛80 VISA MC AE ①
via Fatebenefratelli 21 ✉ 20121 – Ⓜ Turati – ✆ 02 620001 – booking@hotelcavour.it – Fax 02 6 59 22 63 – www.hotelcavour.it
Closed August **G1**
113 rm – ♂231 € ♂♂265 €, ☕ 21 €
Rest *Conte Camillo* – see below
♦ Business ♦ Functional ♦
This traditional, family-run hotel, situated near the city's main cultural sights, cafés and restaurants, offers its guests well-furnished, sound-proofed rooms and excellent service.

Dei Cavalieri AC ⊬rm 🏛250 VISA MC AE ①
piazza Missori 1 ✉ 20123 – Ⓜ Missori – ✆ 02 88571 – info@hoteldeicavalieri.com – Fax 02 8 85 72 41 – www.hoteldeicavalieri.com **G2**
177 rm ☕ – ♂369 € ♂♂399 € – **Rest** – Carte 54/68 €
♦ Traditional ♦ Functional ♦
This hotel, which celebrated 50 year's existence in 1999, does not have large public areas, but the practical bedroom area has been recently renovated; fine panoramic terrace. Restaurant with elegant, classical style interiors.

Grand Hotel Plaza without rest Fö AC 🏛100 VISA MC AE ①
piazza Diaz 3 ✉ 20123 – Ⓜ Duomo – ✆ 02 8555 – info@grandhotelplazamilano.it – Fax 02 86 72 40 – www.grandhotelplazamilano.it **G2**
136 rm ☕ – ♂210/315 € ♂♂265/370 €
♦ Business ♦ Traditional ♦ Classic ♦
A traditional hotel in the heart of the city, with large, tastefully furnished rooms, a lobby with a bar and piano, and a new fully-equipped gym.

Carrobbio without rest AC 🏛30 VISA MC AE ①
via Medici 3 ✉ 20123 – Ⓜ Duomo – ✆ 02 89010740 – info@hotelcarrobbiomilano.com – Fax 02 8 05 33 34 – www.hotelcarrobbiomilano.com
closed August and 22 December-6 January **F2**
56 rm ☕ – ♂185 € ♂♂436 €
♦ Business ♦ Classic ♦
This recently restored hotel is located in a central, but secluded area. Practical, good quality hotel, with well equipped rooms, recently refurbished.

Crivi's without rest AC 🏛120 🚗 VISA MC AE ①
corso Porta Vigentina 46 ✉ 20122 – Ⓜ Crocetta – ✆ 02 582891 – crivis@tin.it – Fax 02 58 31 81 82 – www.crivis.com
closed August and Christmas **G3**
86 rm ☕ – ♂121/180 € ♂♂166/260 €
♦ Business ♦ Functional ♦
In a convenient location near the metro, this comfortable hotel has pleasant public areas and traditionally furnished, reasonably comfortable and spacious guestrooms.

Liberty without rest AC VISA MC AE ①
viale Bligny 56 ✉ 20136 – ✆ 02 58318562 – reserve@hotelliberty-milano.com – Fax 02 58 31 90 61 – www.hotelliberty-milano.com
closed 24 July-20 August and Christmas **G3**
58 rm ☕ – ♂200/250 € ♂♂250/360 €
♦ Traditional ♦ Personalised ♦
Near to the Bocconi University, an elegant hotel, with public areas inspired by the style from which they take their name and some antique furniture; many bedrooms with hydromassage unit.

UNA Hotel Mediterraneo

via Muratori 14 ✉ 20135 – Ⓜ Porta Romana – ✆ 02 550071 – una.mediterraneo@unahotel.it – Fax 02 5 50 07 22 17 – www.unahotels.it

93 rm – ††105/404 € – **Rest** – *(residents only)* Carte 29/38 € **H3**

♦ Business ♦ Functional ♦

This business hotel, situated near the metro in the Porta Romana district, is modern in style, with functional, comfortable and sound-proofed guestrooms.

Antica Locanda dei Mercanti without rest

via San Tomaso 6 ✉ 20121 – Ⓜ Cordusio – ✆ 02 8054080 – locanda@locanda.it – Fax 02 8 05 40 90 – www.locanda.it **F2**

14 rm – †142 € ††162 €, 10 €

♦ Towhouse ♦ Family ♦ Personalised ♦

A small, cosy hotel, simple and elegant in style, and furnished with antique furniture. Many of the light and spacious guestrooms have a small terrace.

King without rest

corso Magenta 19 ✉ 20123 – Ⓜ Cadorna F.N.M. – ✆ 02 874432 – info@hotelkingmilano.com – Fax 02 89 01 07 98 – www.mokinba.it **F2**

48 rm – †100/220 € ††140/300 €

♦ Business ♦ Functional ♦

Housed in a six-storey building not far from the Duomo, this hotel has been renovated with opulent and elegant furnishings. The guestrooms, although not that spacious, are very comfortable.

Mercure Milano Centro Porta Venezia without rest

piazza Oberdan 12 ✉ 20129 – Ⓜ Porta Venezia 20 *– ✆ 02 29403907 – booking@hotelmercuremilanocentro.it – Fax 02 29 52 61 71 – www.mercure.com* *Plan I* **C2**

30 rm – †130/209 € ††249 €

♦ Chain hotel ♦ Business ♦

Close to the cultural centre of Milan. A renovated and refurbished building from the 19C, with elegant and comfortable bedrooms.

Cracco-Peck

via Victor Hugo 4 ✉ 20123 – Ⓜ Duomo – ✆ 02 876774 – cracco-peck@peck.it – Fax 02 86 10 40 – www.peck.it

closed 3 weeks in August, 22 December-10 January, Sunday and Saturday lunch. Also Saturday dinner from June to August **F2**

Rest – Carte 77/110 €

Spec. Tuorlo d'uovo marinato con spinaci, pinoli ed uvetta. Ravioli di maionese con grancevola. Rognone di vitello con ricci di mare e spugnole bianche.

♦ Inventive ♦ Fashionable ♦

A legendary name in Milanese gastronomy and a famous chef: a combination that guarantees success for a new restaurant. Classical elegance, perfect service, and the best cooking.

Il Teatro – Hotel Four Seasons

via Gesù 68 ✉ 20121 – Ⓜ Montenapoleone – ✆ 02 77081435 – milano@fourseasons.com – Fax 02 77 08 50 00 – www.fourseasons.com/milan

closed August and Sunday – **Rest** – *(dinner only)* Carte 64/112 € **G1**

♦ Contemporary ♦ Formal ♦

A very elegant and exclusive ambience in this restaurant among the stunning surroundings of the Four Seasons hotel. Creatively prepared cuisine.

Savini

Galleria Vittorio Emanuele II ✉ 20121 – Ⓜ Duomo – ✆ 02 72003433 – savini@thi.it – Fax 02 72 02 28 88 – www.thi.it

closed 6 to 27 August, 1 to 6 January and Sunday **G2**

Rest – Carte 60/84 € (+ 12 %)

♦ Milanese ♦ Formal ♦

Once a favourite meeting-place for Milan's intellectuals and socialites, this traditional restaurant combines the elegance of the past with the flavours of regional Lombard cuisine.

XXX

Don Carlos – Grand Hotel et de Milan

via Manzoni 29 ✉ 20121 – Ⓜ Montenapoleone – ☎ 02 72314640 – info@ristorantedoncarlos.it – Fax 02 86 46 08 61 – www.ristorantedoncarlos.it

closed August and Sunday **G1**

Rest – Carte 65/105 €

♦ Regional ♦ Cosy ♦

A charming restaurant with a quiet atmosphere and elegant decor, including wood panelling, red appliqué and pictures and photos dating from the time of Verdi. Fine seasonal and regional cuisine with a creative touch.

XXX

Conte Camillo – Hotel Cavour

via Fatebenefratelli 21 (Galleria di piazza Cavour) ✉ 20121 – Ⓜ Turati – ☎ 02 6570516 – booking@hotelcavour.it – Fax 02 6 59 22 63 – www.hotelcavour.it

closed August, Saturday and Sunday lunch **G1**

Rest – Carte 26/47 €

♦ Contemporary ♦ Formal ♦

Attentive service and a classic, elegant and welcoming dining room where you can sample traditional cuisine with a modern touch, original "thematic itineraries".

XXX ✿✿

Sadler

16

via Ettore Troilo 14 (angolo via Conchetta (moving to via Ascanio Sforza 77)) ✉ 20136 – Ⓜ Romolo – ☎ 02 58104451 – sadler@sadler.it – Fax 02 58 11 23 43 – www.sadler.it

closed 8 August-2 September, 1 to 12 January and Sunday Plan I **B3**

Rest – *(dinner only)* Carte 73/119 €

Spec. Tonno crudo del Mediterraneo ai sapori italiani (summer). Ravioli di coniglio con punte di asparagi e tartufo nero (spring). Padellata di crostacei con passatina di broccoletti, patate cristallo e trevisana saltata.

♦ Innovative ♦ Trendy ♦

Architectural and gastronomic rationalism abound in this elegant establishment with its modern design, by a famous name in the Milanese restaurant world; strictly creative cuisine.

XXX

Trussardi alla Scala

piazza della Scala 5 (Trussardi Palace) ✉ 20121 – Ⓜ Duomo – ☎ 02 80688201 – ristorante@trussardiallascala.com – Fax 02 80 68 82 87 – www.marinoallascala.com

closed 7 to 31 August, Saturday lunch and Sunday **G1**

Rest – Carte 60/80 €

♦ Innovative ♦ Trendy ♦

Tradition and innovation blend together in the carefully designed dining hall and in the dishes served in this elegant restaurant situated in the building next to the theatre that is the hallmark of Milan.

XX

Il Rosa al Caminetto – Starhotel Rosa

30

via Beccaria 4 ✉ 20122 – Ⓜ Duomo – ☎ 02 89095235 – info@ilrosa.it – Fax 02 89 01 68 93 – www.ilrosa.it **G2**

Rest – Carte 40/56 €

♦ Classic ♦ Friendly ♦

A premises of new management, characterized by a quick and careful service, proposing a regional and national menu, but at lunch time, it also server a rich buffet.

XX

Armani Nobu

30

via Pisoni 1 ✉ 20121 – Ⓜ Montenapoleone – ☎ 02 62312645 – Fax 02 62 31 26 74 – www.armaninobu.com

closed August, 25 December-7 January, and Sunday lunch **G1**

Rest – Carte 48/76 € (10 %)

♦ Japanese ♦ Fashionable ♦

An exotic union between fashion and gastronomy: Japanese "fusion" cuisine with South American influences in a simple, refined atmosphere inspired by Japanese design.

XX **Nabucco**

via Fiori Chiari 10 ✉ 20121 – Ⓜ Cairoli – ☎ 02 860663 – info@nabucco.it – Fax 02 8 36 10 14 – www.nabucco.it **F1**

Rest – Carte 49/67 € (10 %)

♦ Milanese ♦ Friendly ♦

Located in a typical alleyway in the Brera district with interesting inspired cuisine, both fish and meat dishes, evening meals by candlelight.

XX **L'Assassino**

via Amedei 8 (angolo via Cornaggia) ✉ 20123 – Ⓜ Missori – ☎ 02 8056144 – lambgori@tin.it – Fax 02 86 46 73 74 – www.ristorantelassassino.it

closed 2 to 17 August, 23 December-2 January and Monday **G2**

Rest – Carte 32/56 €

♦ Seafood ♦ Friendly ♦

This typical restaurant in the heart of the city is always busy, and is particularly popular with a business clientele. Traditional Italian menu featuring seafood and home-made pasta.

XX **Emilia e Carlo**

via Sacchi 8 ✉ 20121 – Ⓜ Lanza – ☎ 02 875948 – emiliaecarlosas@virgilio.it – Fax 02 86 21 00 – www.emiliaecarlo.it

closed Easter, August, Christmas, Saturday lunch and Sunday **F1**

Rest – Carte 48/58 €

♦ Innovative ♦ Cosy ♦

This imposing building that dates back to the very early 19C houses a Tuscan trattoria opened in 1966. Since then, the premises have been constantly renovated from year to year. Contemporary cuisine and a fine choice of wines.

XX **Al Porto**

piazzale Generale Cantore ✉ 20123 – Ⓜ Porta Genova – ☎ 02 89407425 – alportodimilano@acena.it – Fax 02 8 32 14 81

closed August, 24 December-3 January, Sunday and Monday lunch **E3**

Rest – Carte 45/65 €

♦ Seafood ♦ Retro ♦

There is a definite maritime flavour to this restaurant, which occupies the old 19C Porta Genova toll house. Always busy, Al Porto specialises exclusively in fish and seafood.

XX **Osteria di Porta Cicca**

ripa di Porta Ticinese 51 ✉ 20143 – Ⓜ Porta Genova – ☎ 02 8372763 – osteriadiportacicca@hotmail.com – Fax 02 8 37 27 63

closed Saturday lunch and Sunday – **Rest** – Carte 31/43 € **E3**

♦ Contemporary ♦ Cosy ♦

This well-established, popular restaurant on the Naviglio canal has simple decor and a pleasant, friendly atmosphere. Traditional cuisine with a modern twist.

XX **Tano Passami l'Olio**

via Villoresi 32/A ✉ 20143 – Ⓜ Porta Genova – ☎ 02 8394139 – info@tanopassamilolio.it – Fax 02 83 24 01 04 – www.tanopassamilolio.it

closed August, 24 December-6 January and Sunday **E3**

Rest – *(dinner only)* Carte 66/91 €

♦ Inventive ♦ Cosy ♦

The key features here are the soft lighting, romantic atmosphere and creative fish and meat dishes, flavoured with a choice of extra-virgin olive oils on display in the dining room. Smoking lounge with a sofa.

ITALY

XX

Il Torchietto

AC VISA MC AE D

via Ascanio Sforza 47 ✉ 20136 – Ⓜ Porta Genova – ✆ 02 8372910 – info@il.torchietto.com – Fax 02 8 37 20 00 – www.il-torchietto.com
closed August, 26 December-3 January, Saturday lunch and Monday *Plan I* **B3**
Rest – Carte 34/49 €
♦ Regional ♦ Friendly ♦
Specialising in regional cuisine using seasonal ingredients, with a particular emphasis on dishes from Mantua, this large, traditional trattoria is situated on the Naviglio Pavese canal.

XX

Il Navigante

AC VISA MC AE D

via Magolfa 14 ✉ 20143 – Ⓜ Porta Genova – ✆ 02 89406320 – info@navigante.it – Fax 02 89 42 08 97 – www.navigante.it
closed August, Sunday lunch and Monday **F3**
Rest – Carte 36/68 €
♦ Seafood ♦ Friendly ♦
On a road at the back of the waterway, live music every evening in an establishment, managed by an ex-ship's cook, with an unusual aquarium on the floor; seafood cuisine.

XX

Isola dei Sapori

AC ⇔16 VISA MC AE

via Anfossi 10 ✉ 20135 – Ⓜ Porta Romana – ✆ 02 54100708 – Fax 02 54 10 07 08
closed August, 23 December-3 January, Sunday and Monday lunch *Plan I* **D2**
Rest – Carte 31/44 €
♦ Sardinian ♦ Friendly ♦
Three young Sardinians have introduced a nautical note in the modern décor of this restaurant; the cuisine features fish specialities, prime quality ingredients and generous portions.

XX

Pirandello

AC VISA MC AE D

viale Gian Galeazzo 6 ✉ 20136 – ✆ 02 89402901 – Fax 02 89 40 29 01
closed 4 to 30 August, Saturday lunch and Sunday **F3**
Rest – Carte 39/52 €
♦ Sicilian ♦ Friendly ♦
The ambience and cuisine are certainly Sicilian. Aromatic seafood and local specialities are served in a choice of two dining rooms.

X

La Felicità

♿ AC VISA MC AE D

via Rovallo 3 ✉ 20121 – Ⓜ Cordusio – ✆ 02 865235 – fangleivalerio@hotmail.com – Fax 02 86 52 35 **F1**
Rest – Carte 21/28 €
♦ Chinese (Canton) ♦ Family ♦
This simple, well-run Chinese restaurant also serves Vietnamese, Thai and Korean cuisine. Elegant furnishings which are broadly Oriental in style.

X

Artidoro

AC ⇔10/30 VISA MC AE D

via Camperio 15 ✉ 20123 – Ⓜ Cairoli – ✆ 02 8057386 – info@artidoro.it – Fax 02 85 91 04 10 – www.artidoro.it
closed 6 to 19 August and Christmas **F1**
Rest – Carte 39/50 € 🍇
♦ Regional ♦ Friendly ♦
A modern style osteria run by a young team with international experience. Emilian cooking in the heart of the city. Dinner comes with a musical ambience.

X

La Tavernetta-da Elio

AC ⇔12 VISA MC AE

via Fatebenefratelli 30 ✉ 20121 – Ⓜ Montenapoleone – ✆ 02 653441 – ristorante@tavernetta.it – Fax 02 6 59 76 10 – www.tavernetta.it
closed August, 24 December-2 January, Saturday lunch, Sunday and Bank Holidays **G1**
Rest – Carte 33/45 €
♦ Tuscany ♦ Family ♦
Experience consolidated for over 40 years, a simple, lively and welcoming restaurant, frequented by regulars; classic dishes with Tuscan specialities.

Hostaria Borromei

20 VISA MC AE

via Borromei 4 ✉ 20123 – Ⓜ Cordusio – ✆ 02 86453760 – Fax 02 86 45 21 78
closed 8 to 31 August, 24 December-7 January, Saturday lunch and Sunday

F2

Rest – Carte 40/52 €

◆ Mantuan ◆ Family ◆

Housed in an 18C palazzo in the heart of the historic centre, this small restaurant serves traditional, regional cuisine, with the accent on dishes from Mantua. Outdoor dining in the courtyard in summer.

Trattoria Torre di Pisa

AC 12/28 VISA MC AE

via Fiori Chiari 21/5 ✉ 20121 – Ⓜ Lanza – ✆ 02 874877 – Fax 02 80 44 83 – www.trattoriatorredipisa.it
closed 3 weeks August, Saturday lunch

F1

Rest – Carte 40/49 €

◆ Tuscany ◆ Family ◆

A family-type Tuscan restaurant located at the heart of the characteristic quarter of Brera. Enjoy the cuisine of Dante's homeland at particularly attractive prices.

Masuelli San Marco

AC 14/16 VISA MC AE

viale Umbria 80 ✉ 20135 – Ⓜ Lodi T.I.B.B. – ✆ 02 55184138 – masuelli.trattoria@tin.it – Fax 02 54 12 45 12 – www.masuelli-trattoria.com
closed 3 weeks in August, 25 December-6 January, Sunday and Monday lunch

Plan I **D3**

Rest – Carte 31/42 €

◆ Milanese ◆ Friendly ◆

A rustic atmosphere with a luxurious feel in a typical trattoria, with the same management since 1921; cuisine strongly linked to traditional Lombardy and Piedmont recipes.

Trattoria la Piola

AC VISA MC AE

via Perugino 18 ✉ 20135 – ✆ 02 55195945 – info@lapiola.it – Fax 02 55 19 59 45 – www.lapiola.it
closed Easter, August, 24 December-2 January, Saturday lunch and Sunday

Plan I **D2**

Rest – Carte 35/57 €

◆ Seafood ◆ Rustic ◆

The freshness of the raw products is the strong point of this simple establishment, which, among its tasty seafood offerings includes particular raw specialities.

Dongiò

AC VISA MC AE

via Corio 3 ✉ 20135 – Ⓜ Porta Romana – ✆ 02 5511372 – Fax 02 5 51 03 71
closed August, Saturday lunch and Sunday

H3

Rest – Carte 21/35 €

◆ Regional ◆ Family ◆

A proper trattoria which you do not find many of, plain family-run management and environment; the specialities are fresh pasta, meats and Calabrese products.

Giulio Pane e Ojo

AC 30 VISA MC AE

via Muratori 10 ✉ 20135 – Ⓜ Porta Romana – ✆ 02 5456189 – info@giuliopaneojo.com – Fax 02 36 50 46 03 – www.giuliopaneojo.com
closed 24 December-1 January and Sunday

H3

Rest – Carte 27/35 €

◆ Roman ◆ Friendly ◆

This is a small and informal inn-type restaurant under youthful management and offering a typically Roman cuisine. Dinners are simple and economical but supper tables must be booked in advance.

CENTRAL STATION

Plan III

Principe di Savoia

1000 VISA

piazza della Repubblica 17 ✉ 20124 – Ⓜ Repubblica – ☎ 02 62301 – principe@hotelprincipedisavoia.com – Fax 02 6 59 58 38 – www.hotelprincipedisavoia.com **M2**

337 rm – †590/860 € ††660/930 €, ☕ 45 € – 64 suites

Rest *Acanto* – see below

◆ Palace ◆ Grand Luxury ◆ Stylish ◆

A sumptuous opulence reigns in the interiors of this veritable Aladdin's cave of antique furniture, where everything has been perfected to satisfy the most refined tastes. Regal suite with private swimming pool.

The Westin Palace

rm 250 VISA

piazza della Repubblica 20 ✉ 20124 – Ⓜ Repubblica – ☎ 02 63361 – palacemilan@westin.com – Fax 02 65 44 85 – www.westin.com **M2**

228 rm – †270/730 € ††270/850 €, ☕ 31 €

Rest *Casanova Grill* – Carte 67/84 €

◆ Grand Luxury ◆ Stylish ◆

A modern tower hides in its interior brocades, gilding, woodwork and precious detailing which furnish the sumptuous and opulent spaces in the style of a top class hotel. Well spaced tables, sofas, soft shades and plush atmosphere in the elegant restaurant.

Le Meridien Gallia

rm 500 VISA

piazza Duca d'Aosta 9 ✉ 20124 – Ⓜ Centrale F.S. – ☎ 02 67851 – reservations.gallia@lemeridien.com – Fax 02 6 69 89 42 – www.starwoodhotels.com **M1**

237 rm – †486/506 € ††580/590 €, ☕ 33 € – 13 suites

Rest – Carte 70/100 €

◆ Palace ◆ Classic ◆

Spacious public areas furnished in warm tones, elegant guestrooms, a beauty centre and gym are some of the features of this luxury hotel, which has long been a favourite with politicians and celebrities.

Michelangelo

rm 550 VISA

via Scarlatti 33 ang. piazza Luigi di Savoia ✉ 20124 – Ⓜ Centrale F.S. – ☎ 02 67551 – michelangelo@milanhotel.it – Fax 02 6 69 42 32 – www.milanhotel.it *Plan I* **C1**

305 rm ☕ – †170/280 € ††200/320 €

Rest – Carte 42/54 €

◆ Business ◆ Functional ◆

One of the more functional buildingsin the city with simple elegant, spacious bedrooms equipped in a modern manner; excellent Conference areas with modular and multi-purpose rooms. Restaurant dining room with refined atmosphere.

Jolly Hotel Touring

rm 120 VISA

via Tarchetti 2 ✉ 20121 – Ⓜ Repubblica – ☎ 02 63351 – milano_touring@jollyhotels.com – Fax 02 6 59 22 09 – www.jollyhotels.com **M2**

289 rm ☕ – †194/294 € ††234/334 €

Rest – Carte 38/50 €

◆ Chain hotel ◆ Functional ◆

Between Piazza della Repubblica and the gardens of via Palestro, a hotel of excellent standards, well suited to Conference work and group work; well maintained rooms, for the most part renovated.

Grand Hotel Verdi

25 VISA

via Melchiorre Gioia 6 ✉ 20124 – Ⓜ Gioia – ☎ 02 62371 – reservation.ver@framon-hotels.it – Fax 02 6 23 70 50 – www.framonhotels.it – closed 3 to 19 August **L1**

100 rm ☕ – †205/428 € ††246/476 € – 3 suites

Rest *L'Opera* *(closed Saturday-Sunday lunch)* – Carte 43/60 €

◆ Business ◆ Modern ◆

Antique red is the dominant colour of the interior of this hotel, with furnishings reminiscent of those in the La Scala Theatre. Spacious, comfortable and fully-equipped guestrooms.

Atahotel Executive without rest 800 VISA

viale Luigi Sturzo 45 ✉ 20154 – Ⓜ Garibaldi F.S. – ✆ 02 62941
– prenotazioni@hotel-executive.com
– Fax 02 29 01 02 38 – www.hotel-executive.com **L1**

414 rm – 🚹180/287 € 🚹🚹220/357 € – 6 suites

♦ Chain hotel ♦ Classic ♦

Situated opposite the Garibaldi railway station, this large hotel with its well-equipped conference centre is ideal for business clients and meetings. The guestrooms are attractive and comfortable.

Four Points Sheraton Milan Center rm 180 VISA

via Cardano 1 ✉ 20124 – Ⓜ Gioia
– ✆ 02 667461 – front.office@fourpointsmilano.it – Fax 02 66 10 43 35
– www.fourpointsmilano.it **M1**

254 rm – 🚹295 € 🚹🚹335 €, ☕ 20 € – 10 suites

Rest – Carte 30/63 €

♦ Chain hotel ♦ Modern ♦

Housed in a modern building in the centre of Milan, this hotel offers relaxing public areas furnished in a simple, elegant style, as well as pleasant and comfortable guestrooms. Large windows in the bright, refined restaurant dining room; tastefully furnished.

UNA Hotel Tocq rm 110 VISA

via A. De Tocqueville 7/D ✉ 20154 – Ⓜ Garibaldi F.S. – ✆ 02 62071 – una.tocq@unahotels.it – Fax 02 6 57 07 80 – www.unahotels.it **L1**

122 rm ☕ – 🚹🚹134/531 € – 13 suites

Rest – Carte 38/50 €

♦ Chain hotel ♦ Business ♦ Design ♦

Modern design is the key feature of this hotel, with its subtle, minimalist furnishings. Fully equipped with all the facilities expected of a contemporary hotel. Main dining room of the restaurant with summer colours and natural Danish oak parquet flooring.

Holiday Inn Milan Garibaldi Station rm rm 50 VISA

via Farini (angolo via Ugo Bassi) ✉ 20154
– Ⓜ Garibaldi F.S. – ✆ 02 6076801
– reservations@himilangaribaldi.com
– Fax 02 6 88 07 64 – www.himilangaribaldi.com **K1**

129 rm – 🚹99/349 € 🚹🚹129/399 €, ☕ 18 €

Rest – Carte 39/58 €

♦ Chain hotel ♦ Design ♦

The hotel has undergone a complete restructuring. It is bright and welcoming and particularly attractive thanks to its minimalist decor. The pleasant lunch-room has a glass cupola. This little restaurant features a "fusion" type cuisine.

Starhotel Ritz rm 180 VISA

via Spallanzani 40 ✉ 20129 – Ⓜ Lima – ✆ 02 2055 – ritz.mi@starhotels.it
– Fax 02 29 51 86 79 – www.starhotels.com *Plan I* **C2**

187 rm ☕ – 🚹🚹130/650 € – 6 suites

Rest – Carte 51/87 €

♦ Chain hotel ♦ Functional ♦

Central, yet peaceful, recently renovated hotel, which offers both large public areas and bedrooms with an excellent level of furnishings and comfort.

Starhotel Anderson rm rm 50 VISA

piazza Luigi di Savoia 20 ✉ 20124 – Ⓜ Centrale F.S. – ✆ 02 6690141
– anderson.mi@starhotels.it – Fax 02 6 69 03 31 – www.starhotels.com *Plan I* **C1**

106 rm ☕ – 🚹🚹100/600 €

Rest – Carte 33/43 €

♦ Chain hotel ♦ Traditional ♦ Classic ♦

There is a distinctly exclusive air to this hotel, which is decorated with elegant fabrics and traditional ethnic furnishings. The guestrooms here are modern, light and spacious.

ITALY

Jolly Hotel Machiavelli ♿ AC ⅟rm 🏢90 VISA MC AE ⓓ

via Lazzaretto 5 ✉ 20124 – Ⓜ Repubblica – ☎ 02 631141 – machiavelli@jollyhotels.com – Fax 02 6 59 98 00 **M2**

103 rm ☕ – 🚹324 € 🚹🚹374 €

Rest ***Caffè Niccolò*** – Carte 29/38 €

♦ Chain hotel ♦ Modern ♦

An airy and harmonious "open space", which encompasses all the public areas, is introduced to the new, modern and completely comfortable building; warm furnishings in the rooms. A sophisticated bistro-style setting in the restaurant; a wine-tasting corner.

Doria Grand Hotel ♿ AC ⅟rm ☎ 🏢120 VISA MC AE ⓓ

viale Andrea Doria 22 ✉ 20124 – Ⓜ Caiazzo – ☎ 02 67411411 – infodoriagrandhotel@adihotels.com – Fax 02 6 69 66 69 – www.adihotels.com

124 rm ☕ – 🚹110/265 € 🚹🚹140/360 € – 2 suites *Plan I* **C1**

Rest – *(closed 18 July-21 August and 24 December-6 January)* Carte 34/64 €

♦ Business ♦ Personalised ♦

A classical building with an elegant lobby furnished in early-20C style and large, comfortable guestrooms. Cultural and musical events are occasionally held in the spacious public areas.

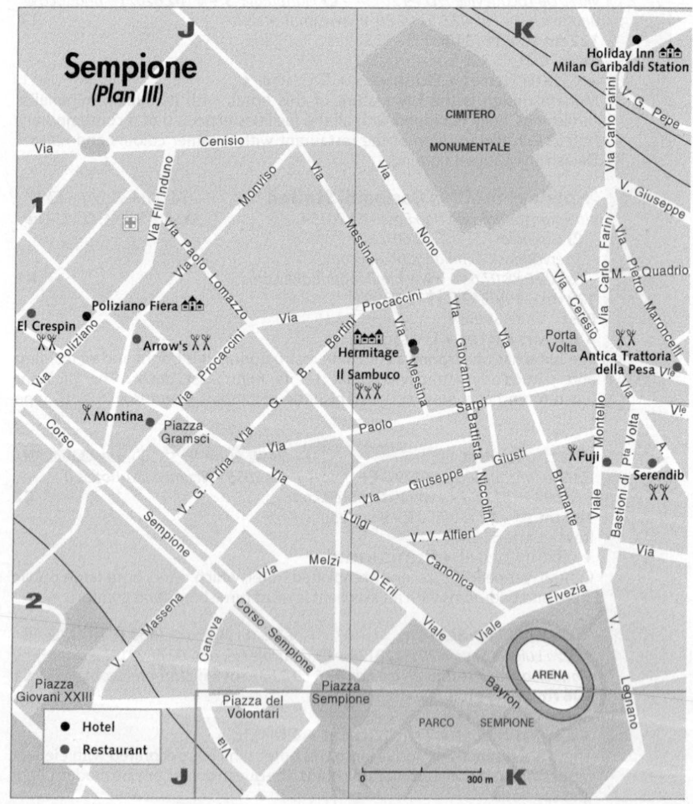

Manin rm 80 VISA

via Manin 7 ✉ 20121 – Ⓜ Palestro – ✆ 02 6596511 – info@hotelmanin.it – Fax 02 6 55 21 60 – www.hotelmanin.it

closed 3 to 26 August **M2**

118 rm – 🚹148/225 € 🚹🚹172/310 €

Rest *Il Bettolino* – *(closed Saturday)* Carte 33/44 €

◆ Business ◆ Classic ◆

A hotel in the busy cultural heart of the city, with large, simply furnished guestrooms. Charming decoration above the beds. Cosy and refined atmosphere in the pleasant warm-toned restaurant.

Sanpi without rest 30 VISA

via Lazzaro Palazzi 18 ✉ 20124 – Ⓜ Porta Venezia – ✆ 02 29513341 – info@hotelsanpimilano.it – Fax 02 29 40 24 51 – www.hotelsanpimilano.it

closed 24 December-2 January **M2**

79 rm – 🚹175/310 € 🚹🚹215/420 €

◆ Business ◆ Classic ◆

Comprising three buildings in the heart of the city, this quiet hotel has well-lit public areas and guestrooms decorated in pastel shades. There is a small garden in the internal courtyard.

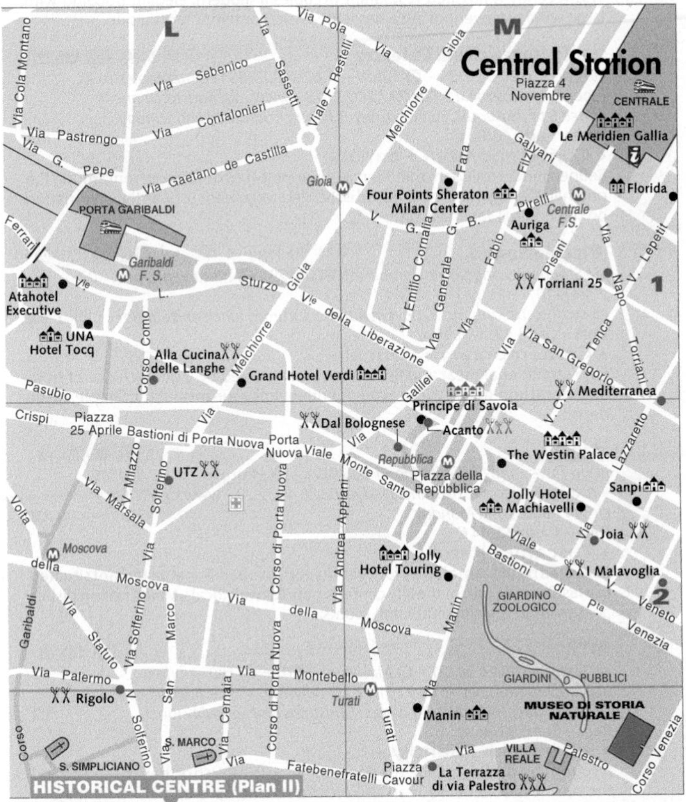

ITALY

Auriga without rest
via Giovanni Battista Pirelli 7 ✉ 20124 – Ⓜ Centrale F.S. – ✆ 02 66985851 – auriga@auriga-milano.com – Fax 02 66 98 06 98 – www.auriga-milano.com
closed 3 to 26 August and 21 December-7 January **M1**
52 rm – 105/210 € 160/300 €
♦ Business ♦ Personalised ♦
The mix of styles, unusual façade and bright colours of this hotel combine to create a striking exterior. Comfortable facilities and efficient service for tourists and business travellers alike.

Florida without rest
via Lepetit 33 ✉ 20124 – Ⓜ Centrale F.S. – ✆ 02 6705921 – info@hotelfloridamilan.com – Fax 02 6 69 28 67 – www.hotelfloridamilan.com
54 rm – 135 € 210 € – 1 suite **M1**
♦ Family ♦ Classic ♦
This modern hotel offers simple but spacious rooms furnished in a clean, geometrical style. A small office inside the hotel is available for business meetings.

Acanto – Hotel Principe di Savoia
piazza della Repubblica 17 ✉ 20124 – Ⓜ Repubblica – ✆ 02 62302026 – Fax 02 62 30 40 93 **M2**
Rest – Carte 81/98 €
♦ Innovative ♦ Formal ♦
This recently renovated restaurant occupies a modern, elegant building with large windows overlooking a garden. Classic, contemporary cuisine.

La Terrazza di via Palestro
via Palestro 2 ✉ 20121 – Ⓜ Turati – ✆ 02 76002186 – terrazzapalestro@esperiaristorazione.it – Fax 02 76 00 33 28 – www.esperiaristorazione.it
closed 8 to 28 August, 23 December-8 January, Saturday and Sunday
Rest – Carte 40/80 € **M2**
♦ Contemporary ♦ Formal ♦
Refined modern elegance and service in summer on the terrace; from among the original offerings, not to be missed is the Mediterranean sushi, an Italian variation on the original Japanese dish.

Piccolo Sogno
via Stoppani 5 angolo via Zambelletti ✉ 20129 – Ⓜ Porta Venezia – ✆ 02 20241210
closed 1 to 10 January, 20 days in August, Saturday lunch and Sunday *Plan I* **C2**
Rest – Carte 42/67 €
♦ Contemporary ♦ Formal ♦
Enjoy traditional meat and fish dishes accompanied by a good choice of both Italian and non-Italian wines in this friendly, family-run restaurant. Simple, rustic decor.

Rigolo
largo Treves ang. via Solferino 11 ✉ 20121 – Ⓜ Moscova – ✆ 02 804589 – ristorante.rigolo@tiscalinet.it – Fax 02 86 46 32 20 – www.rigolo.it
closed August and Monday **L2**
Rest – Carte 32/44 €
♦ Tuscany ♦ Retro ♦
Managed by the same family for over 40 years, this traditional restaurant situated in a fashionable part of the city centre is popular with locals. Meat and fish dishes are served in the elegant dining rooms.

UTZ
via Solferino 48 ✉ 20121 – Ⓜ Moscova – ✆ 02 6551180 – parla@utz-foodemotion.net – Fax 02 31 52 22 – www.utz-foodemotion.net
closed 10 days in August, 10 days at Christmas and Saturday lunch **L2**
Rest – Carte 32/45 €
♦ Inventive ♦ Friendly ♦
A young and dynamic place, the décor comes with a touch of Iberian folklore and the cuisine is eclectic. You can also order pizza and have brunch on Sunday.

XX

Alla Cucina delle Langhe

25 VISA AE

corso Como 6 ✉ 20154 – Ⓜ Garibaldi F.S. – ☎ 02 6554279 – Fax 02 29 00 68 59
closed August, Saturday in July and Sunday **L1**

Rest – Carte 38/58 €

♦ Regional ♦ Friendly ♦

The typical atmosphere of this beautiful trattoria is in keeping with the traditional Lombard and Piedmontese specialities served here. Comprehensive salad buffet.

XX

Dal Bolognese

20 VISA AE

piazza della Repubblica 13 ✉ 20124 – Ⓜ Repubblica – ☎ 02 62694843
– dalbolognese@virgilio.it – Fax 02 62 02 71 28 **M2**
closed August, New Year's day, Saturday lunch and Sunday

Rest – Carte 55/77 €

♦ Classic ♦ Friendly ♦

A place with a classical décor and an animated atmosphere. It is a bistro deluxe, offering traditional cuisine. In summer you'll enjoy the open-air terrace.

XX

Casa Fontana-23 Risotti

VISA AE

piazza Carbonari 5 ✉ 20125 – Ⓜ Sondrio – ☎ 02 6704710 – trattoria@23risotti.it – Fax 02 66 80 04 65 – www.23risotti.it
closed 9 to 12 April, 23 June-7 July, 1 to 6 January, Monday, Saturday lunch and Saturday dinner-Sunday in July *Plan I* **C1**

Rest – Carte 31/46 €

♦ Milanese ♦ Cosy ♦

Despite its location in the suburbs and the obligatory 25-minute wait for your food, this small, friendly restaurant is well worth a visit for its excellent risottos.

XX

Mediterranea

VISA AE

piazza Cincinnato 4 ✉ 20124 – Ⓜ Porta Venezia – ☎ 02 29522076
– ristmediterranea@fastwebnet.it – Fax 02 20 11 56
– www.ristorantemediterranea.it
closed 5 to 25 August, 30 December-10 January, Sunday and Monday lunch **M1-2**

Rest – Carte 40/63 €

♦ Seafood ♦ Formal ♦

The touch of "marine" style is given by a blue glass roof illuminated all along the establishment and by the crustacean tank; genuine tasty cuisine, fish only.

XX ✿

Joia (Leemann)

16/20 VISA AE

via Panfilo Castaldi 18 ✉ 20124 – Ⓜ Repubblica
– ☎ 02 29522124 – joia@joia.it
– Fax 02 2 04 92 44 – www.joia.it
closed 4 to 25 August, Saturday lunch and Sunday **M2**

Rest – Carte 58/90 €

Spec. Appunti di viaggio (spuma di parmigiano con degustazione di aceti). Prosperità (raviolo di melanzane e parmigiano). Conserva musicale (frutti di bosco).

♦ Inventive ♦ Minimalist ♦

The dark parquet flooring and skylights of the main dining hall must be admired before settling in to enjoy the pleasures of a creative "vegetarian concept" cuisine that includes some excellent fish dishes.

XX

Torriani 25

18 VISA AE

via Napo Torriani 25 ✉ 20124 – Ⓜ Centrale F.S.
– ☎ 02 67078183 – acena@torriani25.it – Fax 02 67 47 95 48
– www.torriani25.it
closed 9 to 26 August, Saturday lunch and Sunday **M1**

Rest – Carte 41/62 €

♦ Seafood ♦ Design ♦

This modern restaurant is decorated in warm colours, with plenty of natural light. Choose from a wide selection of fish - the house speciality - on display on the buffet in the dining room.

ITALY

XX

I Malavoglia

AC VISA MC AE

via Lecco 4 ✉ 20124 – Ⓜ Porta Venezia – ☎ 02 29531387 – www.ristorante-imalavoglia.com
closed Easter, 1 May, August, 24 December-4 January and Sunday **M2**
Rest – (dinner only) Carte 42/56 €
♦ Sicilian ♦ Family ♦
Since 1973 a husband and wife team, with him serving and her in the kitchen, have managed this pleasant establishment of luxurious good taste; Sicilian dishes and seafood, lightened in a modern variation.

XX

Antica Trattoria della Pesa

AC VISA MC AE

via Pasubio 10 ✉ 20154 – Ⓜ Garibaldi F.S. – ☎ 02 6555741 – Fax 02 29 01 51 57 – closed August and Sunday **K1**
Rest – Carte 50/60 €
♦ Milanese ♦ Rustic ♦
A delightfully old-time atmosphere remains in this Milanese trattoria that has entered into Italian history; the cuisine is consistently faithful to the Lombardian tradition. One of the rooms is dedicated to Ho Chi Min.

XX

Serendib

AC VISA MC

via Pontida 2 ✉ 20121 – Ⓜ Moscova – ☎ 02 6592139 – surange@email.it – Fax 02 6 59 21 39 – www.serendib.it
closed 10 to 20 August **K2**
Rest – *(dinner only)* Menu 14 /18 € – Carte 22/26 €
♦ Indian ♦ Friendly ♦
Loyal to the original both in the decoration and in the Indian and "Cingalese" cuisine, is a pleasant establishment which bears the old name of Sri Lanka ("to make people happy").

X

La Cantina di Manuela

AC VISA MC AE

via Poerio 3 ✉ 20129 – Ⓜ Porta Venezia – ☎ 02 76318892 – info@lacantinadimanuela.it – Fax 02 76 31 29 71 – www.lacantinadimanuela.it
closed Sunday *Plan I* **C2**
Rest – Carte 35/43 €
♦ Regional ♦ Wine bar ♦
Quality products and interesting wines in this informal restaurant; the various dishes, from cold meats and cheeses to the traditional menu, are highly appreciated.

X

Da Giannino-L'Angolo d'Abruzzo

AC VISA MC AE

via Pilo 20 ✉ 20129 – Ⓜ Porta Venezia – ☎ 02 29406526 – Fax 02 29 40 65 26
closed August and Monday *Plan I* **D2**
Rest – Carte 23/34 €
♦ Regional ♦ Friendly ♦
Visitors can expect a warm welcome in this simple and cheerful restaurant run by the same family for the past 35 years. The menus adhere strictly to the best of Abruzzi cuisine and prices are reasonable.

X

Baia Chia

AC 20/25 VISA MC

via Bazzini 37 ✉ 20131 – Ⓜ Piola – ☎ 02 2361131 – fabrizio.papetti@fastwebnet.it – Fax 02 2 36 11 31 – closed Easter, 3 weeks in August, 24 December-2 January, Sunday and Monday lunch *Plan I* **D1**
Rest – Carte 26/36 €
♦ Seafood ♦ Family ♦
This pleasant local establishment has been extended by the addition of a new family orientated room, where you can sample good fish cuisine and some tasty Sardinian specialities.

X

Fuji

AC VISA MC

viale Montello 9 ✉ 20154 – Ⓜ Moscova – ☎ 02 29008349 – Fax 02 29 00 35 92
closed Easter, 1 to 23 August, 24 December-2 January and Sunday **K2**
Rest – *(dinner only)* Carte 47/64 €
♦ Japanese ♦ Minimalist ♦
Jointly managed by its Italian and Japanese owners for the past 10 years, this simple Japanese restaurant has hit on a winning formula. The restaurant also has a sushi bar next door.

FIERA-SEMPIONE

Plan I

Hermitage

180 VISA

via Messina 10 ✉ 20154 – Ⓜ Garibaldi F.S. – ✆ 02 318170 – hermitage.res@monrifhotels.it – Fax 02 33 10 73 99 – www.monrifhotels.it
closed August *Plan III* **K1**
131 rm – 200/320 € 280/490 € – 12 suites
Rest *Il Sambuco* – see below
◆ Business ◆ Stylish ◆
Style and comfort are the trademarks of this hotel which combines the atmosphere of elegant period-style interiors with modern facilities; popular with models and other celebrities.

Melià Milano

rm 500 VISA

via Masaccio 19 ✉ 20149 – Ⓜ Lotto – ✆ 02 44406 – melia.milano@solmelia.com – Fax 02 44 40 66 00 – www.solmelia.com **A2**
288 rm – 439 € 489 €, 30 € – 6 suites
Rest *Alacena* – *(closed August)* Carte 59/115 €
◆ Chain hotel ◆ Modern ◆
A modern and very prestigious hotel, a triumph of marble and crystal chandeliers, with antique tapestries in the hall; Empire style bedrooms, with all comforts. An exclusive place to stay. Haute cuisine from Spain in this refined restaurant, the "Alacena".

Milan Marriott Hotel

rm 1300 VISA

via Washington 66 ✉ 20146 – Ⓜ Wagner – ✆ 02 4852020 – milan@marriothotels.com – Fax 02 4 81 89 25 – www.marriott.com **A2**
322 rm – 462 €, 22 €
Rest *La Brasserie de Milan* – ✆ 02 48522834 – Carte 35/68 €
◆ Chain hotel ◆ Modern ◆
Original contrast between the modern building and the imposing classic interiors of a hotel clearly geared towards Conference and Trade Fair business clientele; functional period style bedrooms. Restaurant dining room with the kitchen in full view; classical style.

Enterprise Hotel

rm 350 VISA

corso Sempione 91 ✉ 20154 – ✆ 02 318181 – info@enterprisehotel.com – Fax 02 31 81 88 11 – www.enterprisehotel.com **A1**
123 rm – 120/575 € 140/590 €
Rest *Sophia's* – Carte 49/64 €
◆ Business ◆ Design ◆
Attention to detail and design is evident in every aspect of this elegant modern hotel, from the marble and granite exterior to its bespoke furnishings and pleasing geometrical lines. A pleasant and original place for lunch and dinner.

Atahotel Fieramilano

rm rm 220 VISA

viale Boezio 20 ✉ 20145 – ✆ 02 336221 – prenotazioni@grandhotelfieramilano.com – Fax 02 31 41 19 – www.atahotels.it
closed August **B2**
236 rm – 250/270 € 330/350 € – 2 suites
Rest *Ambrosiano* – *(dinner only)* Carte 37/57 €
◆ Chain hotel ◆ Modern ◆
This tastefully furnished hotel opposite the Fiera Milano offers modern and comfortable rooms. In summer, breakfast is served in a gazebo in the garden. Quiet, elegant dining room.

Capitol World Class

70 VISA

via Cimarosa 6 ✉ 20144 – Ⓜ Pagano – ✆ 02 438591 – info@capitolmilano.com – Fax 02 4 69 47 24 – www.capitolmilano.com **B2**
66 rm – 165/275 € 225/420 € – **Rest** – Carte 46/63 €
◆ Business ◆ Personalised ◆
An elegant, modern hotel with warm, traditional touches both in its public areas and the fully equipped guestrooms, many of which overlook a peaceful internal courtyard.

ITALY

Wagner without rest

via Buonarroti 13 – Ⓜ Wagner – ✆ 02 463151 – wagner@roma-wagner.com – Fax 02 48 02 09 48 – www.roma-wagner.com

closed 12 to 9 August **A2**

48 rm – †119/219 € ††149/298 € – 1 suite

♦ Business ♦ Personalised ♦

Close to the eponymous metro station, this hotel has been completely renovated, with marble and modern accessories used to good effect.

Regency without rest

via Arimondi 12 ✉ 20155 – ✆ 02 39216021 – regency@regency-milano.com – Fax 02 39 21 77 34 – www.regency-milano.com

closed 5 to 25 August and 24 December-7 January **A1**

71 rm ☕ – †140/200 € ††180/300 € – 2 suites

♦ Traditional ♦ Personalised ♦

This charming mansion dating from the late 19C is built around a delightful courtyard. Stylish interior furnishings, including an elegant living room with a real open fire.

Poliziano Fiera without rest

via Poliziano 11 ✉ 20154 – ✆ 02 3191911 – info.hotelpolizianofiera@adihotels.com – Fax 02 3 19 19 31 – www.adihotels.com

closed 25 July-25 August and 18 December-7 January

100 rm ☕ – †102/297 € ††122/337 € – 2 suites

♦ Business ♦ Modern ♦

Friendly, attentive service and spacious guestrooms furnished in light green and sand-coloured tones compensate for the rather small public areas in this modern hotel.

Rubens

via Rubens 21 ✉ 20148 – Ⓜ Gambara – ✆ 02 40302 – rubens@antareshotels.com – Fax 02 48 19 31 14 – www.antareshotels.com

closed 3 to 19 August **A2**

87 rm ☕ – †140/225 € ††99/299 €

Rest – Carte 38/49 €

♦ Business ♦ Personalised ♦

The spacious, comfortable guestrooms in this elegant hotel are adorned with frescoes by contemporary artists and furnished in stylish purple and cobalt-blue tones.

Accademia

viale Certosa 68 ✉ 20155 – ✆ 02 39211122 – accademia@antareshotels.com – Fax 02 33 10 38 78 – www.antareshotels.com **A1**

67 rm ☕ – †105/230 € ††150/299 €

Rest – Carte 20/50 €

♦ Business ♦ Personalised ♦

A modern feel, new rooms with designer-style furnishings, and relaxing public areas are some of the features of this attractive, recently refurbished hotel.

Mirage

viale Certosa 104/106 ✉ 20156 – ✆ 02 39210471 – mirage@gruppomirage.it – Fax 02 39 21 05 89 – www.gruppomirage.it

closed 4 to 28 August and 23 December-2 January **A1**

86 rm ☕ – †115/198 € ††136/259 €

Rest – *(closed Friday and Saturday) (residents only)* Carte 37/47 €

♦ Business ♦ Functional ♦

Not far from the Trade Fair complex, this hotel offers simply furnished public areas and guestrooms renovated in classical style; the bathrooms are decorated with large tiles or mosaics.

Astoria without rest 50 VISA
viale Murillo 9 ✉ 20149 – Lotto – ☎ 02 40090095 – info@astoriahotelmilano.com – Fax 02 40 07 46 42 – www.astoriahotelmilano.com **A2**
68 rm – †90/200 € ††100/250 € – 1 suite
◆ Business ◆ Functional ◆
Along the ring-road, a recently renovated hotel, frequented by tourists and business clientele; modern furnished bedrooms with excellent soundproofing.

Des Etrangers without rest 80 VISA
via Sirte 9 ✉ 20146 – ☎ 02 48955325 – info@hde.it – Fax 02 48 95 53 59 – www.hoteldesetrangers.it **A3**
94 rm – †90/120 € ††140/180 €
◆ Family ◆ Classic ◆
This well-maintained hotel in a quiet street offers its guests functional and comfortable public areas and guestrooms, as well as convenient underground parking.

Antica Locanda Leonardo without rest
corso Magenta 78 ✉ 20123 – Conciliazione VISA
– ☎ 02 48014197 – info@anticalocandaleonardo.com – Fax 02 48 01 90 12 – www.anticalocandaleonardo.com
closed 5 to 25 August and 31 December-6 January *Plan II* **E2**
16 rm – †95/105 € ††150/215 €
◆ Inn ◆ Cosy ◆
The luxury atmosphere combines with the family-style welcome in a hotel which overlooks a small inner courtyard, in an ideal location near the place where Leonardo da Vinci's "Last Supper" is housed.

Il Luogo di Aimo e Nadia (Moroni) 12 VISA
via Montecuccoli 6 ✉ 20147 – Primaticcio – ☎ 02 416886 – info@aimoenadia.com – Fax 02 48 30 20 05 – www.aimoenadia.com
closed 1 to 10 January, 6 to 26 August, Saturday lunch and Sunday **A3**
Rest – Carte 80/136 €
Spec. Petto d'anatra affumicato all'anice stellato con insalata di mele annurche, spinaci e aceto balsamico tradizionale (spring-autumn). Cernia grigia con succo di melograno e tartufi di mare (summer-autumn). Cubo di granache di cioccolato al pepe verde con sorbetto di ananas e gelatina di fave di cacao e menta.
◆ Contemporary ◆ Formal ◆
A leading light of the city's culinary scene, this restaurant, with an impressive display of modern works of art, has cuisine memorable for its creativity.

La Pobbia 1850 12/20 VISA
via Gallarate 92 ✉ 20151 – ☎ 02 38006641 – lapobbia@lapobbia.com – Fax 02 38 00 07 24 – www.lapobbia.com
closed August and Sunday **A1**
Rest – Carte 48/75 €
◆ Milanese ◆ Formal ◆
The management in this historic restaurant has a lot of experience (since 1920). Rustic-elegant atmosphere featuring Lombard and international cuisine.

Il Sambuco – Hotel Hermitage VISA
via Messina 10 ✉ 20154 – Garibaldi F.S. – ☎ 02 33610333 – info@ilsambuco.it – Fax 02 33 61 18 50 – www.ilsambuco.it
closed Easter, 1 to 20 August, 25 December-3 January, Saturday lunch and Sunday *Plan III* **K1**
Rest – Carte 48/85 €
◆ Seafood ◆ Trendy ◆
Like the hotel of which it is a part, this restaurant is characterised by elegant decor and attentive service. The cuisine is renowned for its seafood specialities and, on Mondays, for its dishes of boiled meat.

ITALY

XX

Arrow's

15/18 VISA AE

via Mantegna 17/19 ✉ 20154 – ✆ 02 341533 – Fax 02 33 10 64 96
closed August, Sunday and Monday lunch Plan III **J1**
Rest – Carte 42/57 €
◆ Seafood ◆ Formal ◆
Packed, even at midday, mainly by business clients, with a more intimate atmosphere in the evening, an establishment near to corso Sempione; traditional fish cuisine.

XX

El Crespin

AC 20/30 VISA MC AE

via Castelvetro 18 ✉ 20154 – ✆ 02 33103004 – Fax 02 33 10 30 04 – www.pagine.gialle.it/elcrespin
closed August, 26 December-7 January, Saturday lunch and Sunday Plan III **J1**
Rest – Carte 39/53 €
◆ Seasonal cuisine ◆ Friendly ◆
The entrance of this restaurant is decorated with period photos, while the dining room is tastefully furnished in a simple, modern style. Both meat and fish dishes feature on the menu.

XX

Innocenti Evasioni

AC 14 VISA MC AE

via privata della Bindellina ✉ 20155 – ✆ 02 33001882 – ristorante@innocentievasioni.com – Fax 02 33 00 18 82 – www.innocentievasioni.com
closed 3 to 9 January, August and Sunday **A1**
Rest – (dinner only) Carte 37/47 €
◆ Contemporary ◆ Cosy ◆
From a hardly promising suburban alleyway you enter a pleasant fashionable establishment, with defused lighting and large windows overlooking a small garden; inspiration and creativity in the kitchen.

X

Trattoria Montina

AC VISA MC AE

via Procaccini 54 ✉ 20154 – Ⓜ Garibaldi F.S. – ✆ 02 3490498
closed August, 25 December-5 January, Sunday and Monday lunch Plan III **J2**
Rest – Carte 20/37 €
◆ Seasonal cuisine ◆ Friendly ◆
Nice bistro atmosphere, tables close together, defused lighting in the evening in an establishment managed by twin brothers; seasonal national and Milanese dishes.

X

Pace

AC VISA MC AE

via Washington 74 ✉ 20146 – Ⓜ Wagner – ✆ 02 43983058 – Fax 02 46 85 67
closed Easter, 1 to 24 August, 24 December-5 January, Saturday lunch and Wednesday **A2-3**
Rest – Carte 27/36 €
◆ Seasonal cuisine ◆ Rustic ◆
For over 30 years there has been a cordial welcome waiting for you in the simple but well-maintained environment of this family run trattoria ; traditional cuisine, with meat and fish dishes.

X

Al Molo 13

AC VISA MC AE

via Rubens 13 ✉ 20148 – Ⓜ De Angelis – ✆ 02 4042743 – info@molo13.it – Fax 02 40 07 26 16 – www.molo13.it
closed August, 31 December-9 January, Sunday and Monday lunch **A2**
Rest – Carte 31/57 €
◆ Seafood ◆ Rustic ◆
Typical Sardinian fish and seafood dishes are the specialities of this modern restaurant, which is especially busy in the evening. The two colourful dining rooms have been recently renovated.

LUXEMBOURG
LËTZEBUERG

PROFILE

◆ **Area:**
2 586 km² (998 sq mi).

◆ **Population:**
468 600 inhabitants (est. 2005) nearly 62% nationals, 38% resident foreigners (mostly Belgian, French, German, Italian and Portuguese). Density = 181 per km².

◆ **Capital:**
Luxembourg (conurbation 125 000 inhabitants).

◆ **Currency:**
Euro (€); rate of exchange: € 1 = US$ 1.32 (Nov 2006).

◆ **Government:**
Constitutional parliamentary monarchy (since 1868). Member of European Union since 1957 (one of the 6 founding countries).

◆ **Languages:**
The official language is Lëtzebuergesch, a variant of German, similar to the Frankish dialect of the Moselle valley; High German is used for general purposes and is the first language for teaching; French is the literary and administrative language.

◆ **Specific public holidays:**
Carnival (Late February-March); National Day (23 June); Luxembourg City Kermesse (early September, applies to the Luxembourg City only); St. Stephen's Day (26 December).

◆ **Local Time:**
GMT + 1 hour in winter and GMT + 2 hours in summer.

◆ **Climate:**
Temperate continental with cold winters

and mild summers (Luxembourg: January: 1°C, July: 17°C).

◆ **International dialling Code:**
00 352 (from USA: **011352**; from Japan: **001352**) followed by the local number of 5 or 6 or (exceptionally) 8 figures. Online telephone directory: www.editus.lu

◆ **Emergency numbers:**
Police : ✆ **113** ;
Medical Assistance : ✆ **112**.

◆ **Electricity:**
220 volts AC, 50Hz;

FORMALITIES

Travellers from the European Union (EU), Switzerland, Iceland and the main countries of North and South America need a national identity card or passport (America: passport required) to visit the Grand Duchy of Luxembourg for less than three months (tourism or business purpose). For visitors from other countries a visa may be required, in addition to a passport, especially for those wishing to stay for longer than three months. We advise you to check with your embassy before travelling.

An international driving licence is not required, only the traveller's own national driving licence.

MAJOR NEWSPAPERS

The daily press in Luxembourg reflects the multilingual population and is printed in Lëtzebuergesch, French and German. In some papers more than one language is used. Of the 6 major daily newspapers 4 are mainly in German (*Luxemburger Wort* and *Tageblatt* being the most important) and 2 are in French *(La Voix, Le Quotidien)*.

USEFUL PHRASES

ENGLISH	**FRENCH**
Yes	**Oui**
No	**Non**
Good morning	**Bonjour**
Goodbye	**Au revoir**
Thank you	**Merci**
Please	**S'il vous plaît**
Excuse me	**Excusez-moi**
I don't understand	**Je ne comprends pas**

HOTELS

→ CATEGORIES

Accommodation ranges from luxurious 5-star international hotels, via smaller, family-run guesthouses and bed and breakfast establishments. The Benelux star rating is conferred on the application of the owner.

→ PRICE RANGE

The price is per room. There is little difference between the price of a single and a double room.

Between April and October it is advisable to book in advance. From November to March prices may be slightly lower, some hotels offer special cheap rates and some may be closed. At the weekend out of season, chain hotels in the capital often offer reduced rates.

→ TAX

Included in the room price.

→ CHECKOUT TIME

Usually between 11am and noon.

→ RESERVATIONS

By telephone or by the Internet using a credit card.

→ TIPS FOR HANDLING LUGGAGE

At the discretion of the client (about €1 per suitcase).

→ BREAKFAST

Breakfast is usually included in the room price, although this may not be so in smaller hotels. Most hotels offer a self service buffet between 7am and 10am but it is often possible to order a continental breakfast in the bedroom.

Reception	**Reception**
Single room	**Chambre simple**

Double room	**Chambre double**
Bed	**Lit**
Bathroom	**Salle de bains**
Shower	**Douche**

→ RESTAURANTS

As well as the **traditional restaurants** there are **brasseries** which offer a main dish of the day, **bistros** and **cafés** which serve lighter meals. The **Winstub** is principally a wine bar which also serves food. In the commercial districts the **patisseries** serve breakfast as well as tea/coffee and pastries.

Breakfast	**Petit-déjeuner**	7-10am
Lunch	**Déjeuner**	12.30-2pm
Dinner	**Dîner**	7.30-10pm

***NB**: French speakers in Luxembourg usually say «déjeuner» for breakfast, «dîner» for the midday meal and «souper» for the evening meal.*

Restaurants in Luxembourg offer the choice of a menu (starter, main dish and dessert) or à la carte. Menus are usually printed in French and English and sometimes also in Lëtzebuergesch. A fixed-price menu (menu à prix fixe) is usually less expensive than the same number of dishes chosen à la carte.

With some fixed-price menus there is a food and wine suggestion, where the wine is served by the glass.

In some restaurants the lunchtime menu is shorter than the dinner menu or there may be two different menus: one for midday and one for the evening.

→ RESERVATIONS

Reservations can be made by telephone, Internet or fax. To book a table in a well known restaurant (those with Michelin stars) it is best to phone several days or even weeks in advance. A credit card number or a phone number may be required as a guarantee.

→ THE BILL

The bill (check) includes service charge and VAT. Tipping is optional but, if you are particularly pleased with the service, it is customary to round up the total to an appropriate figure – 10% in larger restaurants and the value of the small change elsewhere.

Drink or aperitif	**Apéritif**
Appetizer	**Mise en bouche**
Meal	**Repas**
Starter	**Entrée**
Main dish	**Plat principal**
Main dish of the day	**Plat du jour**
Dessert	**Dessert**
Water/ Sparkling water	**Eau/gazeuse**
Wine (red, white, rosé)	**Vin (rouge, blanc, rosé)**
Beer	**Bière**
Bread	**Pain**
Meat (medium, rare, blue)	**Viande (à point, saignant, bleu)**
Fish	**Poisson**
Salt/pepper	**Sel/poivre**

Cheese	**Fromage**
Vegetables	**Légumes**
Hot/cold	**Chaud/froid**
The bill (check) please	**L'addition s'il vous plaît**

LOCAL CUISINE

Luxembourg Grand Duchy's culinary traditions are similar to those of France, its regional specialities lending it a special distinction. Among the gastronomic specialities of the Grand Duchy are suckling pig in aspic, smoked and cured ham from the Ardennes, and other smoked meats. The national dish is **Judd mat Gaardebounen**, smoked neck of pork with broad beans, which makes a hearty meal in itself. Game and mushrooms from Ardennes are eaten in season. Freshwater fish is delicious fried (friture de la Moselle) or poached in Riesling. **Kachkéis** is a soft, cooked cheese. In September plum tart is eaten, and, in season, the little puff-pastry crowns known as Veianer Kränzercher.

DRINK

Although beer is the most popular drink, Luxembourg produces its own dry white wines, from the vineyards which carpet the slopes of the Moselle Valley – the more expensive Auxerrois, the less expensive Rivaner and Elbling, and Pinot Blanc, Pinot Gris, Riesling and Traminer. There are also a few rosé and sparkling wines (crémant). The liqueurs of Luxembourg – made with cherries (kirsch), plums (quetsch), blackcurrants, pears, elderberries and marc – have a good reputation.

LUXEMBOURG
LËTZEBUERG

Population (est. 2004): 77 400 (conurbation 125 000) – Altitude: 300m

SGM/COLORISE

Luxembourg is set high on a sandstone bluff or deep down in the bottom of the deep ravines created by two rivers – the Pétrusse and the Alzette – which divide the city into distinctive districts, linked by spectacular bridges spanning lush green valleys. The city squares, with their elegant facades painted in pastel colours, may suggest a theatrical backdrop but Luxembourg is a lively business centre with all the dignity of a capital city, despite its comparatively small size. In 1994 UNESCO World Heritage status was conferred on the Old Town and its extensive defences; floodlighting in the high season enhances the city and its setting.

Luxembourg first took its name in 963 as an autonomous earldom but, owing to its strategic position at one of the major European crossroads, it was a desirable prize; for four centuries the city was ruled successively by the Burgundians, Spanish, French and Austrians, until its independence was established by the Treaties of London in 1839 and 1867. In 1952 Luxembourg, the birthplace of Robert Schuman who was one of the fathers of EC, became the headquarters of the European Coal and Steel Community (ECSC) and is now the seat of many other European institutions, including the Council of Ministers of the European Union (for 3 months a year) and the General Secretariat of the European Parliament.

WHICH DISTRICT TO CHOOSE

The greatest concentration of **hotels** is near the railway station *Plan I* **B3**; it is not however difficult to find a room in the Old Town *Plan II* **C1**. There are also a few charming places to stay scattered on the outskirts of Luxembourg.

For a **restaurant** it is best to look in the Old town, especially in the pedestrian area bordered by Place d'Armes, Place Guillaume II and Rue Notre-Dame *Plan II* **C1**.

For a **drink only**, choose the shady terraces in Place d'Armes *Plan II* **C1** or try one of the many **brasseries** and **tavernes** in the town centre: eg *Brasserie Mansfeld*, 3 rue de la Tour Jacob *Plan I* **B2**, taverne *Wëlle Man*, 12 rue Wiltheim *Plan II* **D1**, etc.

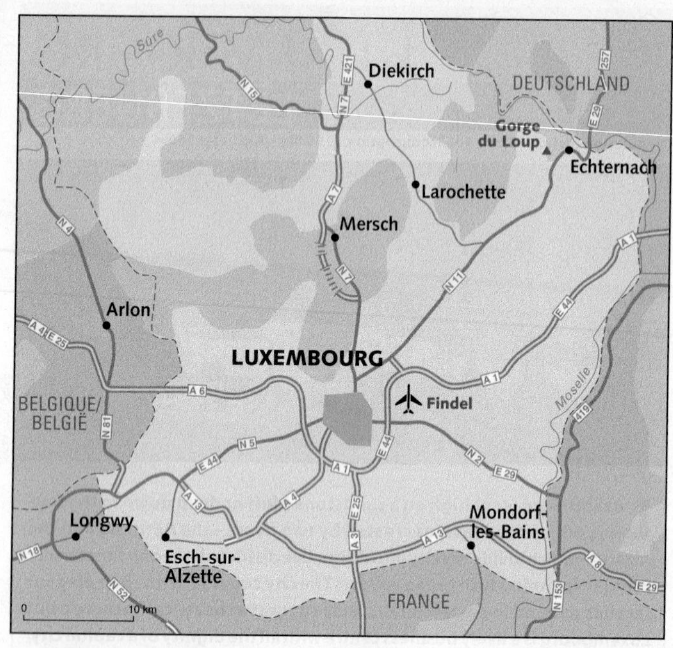

PRACTICAL INFORMATION

ARRIVAL – DEPARTURE

Luxembourg-Findel Airport – About 6 km (4 mi) NE of the city centre, ☎ 24 56 50 50.

From the airport to the city centre – By **taxi** the cost is about €25 including one piece of luggage; €0.75 extra for each additional piece. There is a **bus** service costing €1.20 for the ticket and €1.20 for bulky luggage.

Railway Station – There are regular train services from **Luxembourg Station** *Plan I* **B3** to Namur, Brussels and Liège (Belgium), to Trier (Germany) and to Metz (France); www.cfl.lu

TRANSPORT

→ BUS

Tickets can be purchased on the bus or at the bus station or at newsagents and tobacconists. A single short distance ticket (valid for 1hr) costs €1.50 (book of 10 tickets €10.00); a single network ticket (valid for 24 hrs) costs €5.00 (book of 5 tickets €20.00); www.autobus.lu

→ TAXIS

Taxis, which are distinguished by a yellow light, can be hired only at a taxi stand. The minimum pick up charge is €2, the cost calculated at €2.50 per km; at night the cost increases by between 10% and 35% of the daytime fare. *Colus Taxis* ☎ (352) 48 22 33; www.colux.lu

USEFUL ADDRESSES

→ TOURIST OFFICE

City Tourist Office, Place d'Armes, Luxembourg, ☎ 22 28 09 – Place de la Gare, Luxembourg. ☎ 42 82 82-20; www.lcto.lu; touristinfo@lcto.lu

→ **BANKS/CURRENCY EXCHANGE**

The major banks are to be found in the town centre *Plan II* **C1** and at the railway station *Plan I* **B3**, Mon-Fri, 8.30am-4.30pm (closed at lunchtime); some larger banks are open on Saturday morning. Bank cash machines (ATMs) are open 24hrs (pin number required).

→ **EMERGENCY**

Ambulance, Doctor, Dentist ✆ **112**; Police ✆ **113**; also ✆ **999**.

BUSY PERIODS

It may be difficult to find a room at a reasonable price when special events are held in the city as hotel prices may be raised substantially:

Emais'chen: Easter Monday – Traditional folk festival.

Printemps Musical-Festival de Luxembourg: March-May – Classic jazz festival.

April, June and October – Sessions of the Council of Ministers of the European Union.

National Day and the Eve of National Day: 22nd and 23rd June.

Schueberfouer: late August to mid-September – Large fair and market dating from 1340.

EXPLORING LUXEMBOURG

In one day there is time to visit the main sights and museums.

Opening times are usually from 10am-5pm but closed on Mondays and public holidays.

VISITING

Chemin de la Corniche *Plan II* **D1** – Called the most beautiful balcony in Europe for its splendid views of the the Alzette Gorge and the Plateau du Rham.

Le Bock *Plan II* **D1** – Site of ruined fortifications (10C-18C) with a view of the Plateau du Rham.

Casemates du Bock *Plan II* **D1** – Labyrinth of 17C-18C underground defences.

The Pétrusse and Alzette Valleys viewed from the top of the **citadel on the Plateau du St-Esprit** *Plan II* **D1**.

Pont Adolphe (1899-1903) and the Pétrusse Gorge viewed from **Place de la Constitution** *Plan II* **C1**.

Tour of the **Old Town** *Plan II* **C1** from Place d'Armes to **Le Bock** taking in the views listed above.

Musée national d'Histoire et d'Art *Plan II* **D1** – Gallo-Roman collection; Luxembourg Life section: decorative arts, folk art and tradition.

Pétrusse Express – Tour of the historic sights in the lower town and the Pétrusse Valley by motor train starting from Place de la Constitution *Plan II* **C1** (Mar-Oct).

Luxembourg City Tour – Tour of the main city sights by hop-on-hop-off open-top bus starting from Place de la Constitution or Place d'Armes *Plan II* **C1** (Mar-Oct).

SHOPPING

Shops are open daily except Sun, 9am-6pm (Mon 2-6pm) but may close for 1hr at midday; there are some shopping Sundays near Christmas.

The pedestrian streets around Place d'Armes (including **Grand-Rue**, **Rue des Capucins** and **Rue Chimay**) are particularly good for browsing and window-shopping. There are also many opportunities in the district near the railway station. There are a few luxury shops around Place d'Armes in the Old Town *Plan II* **C1**.

MARKETS – There is a **food and flower market** in Place Guillaume II in the Old Town, every Wed and Sat morning (Sat only in winter) and a **flea market** in Place d'Armes, every 2nd and 4th Saturday, mainly in the morning.

WHAT TO BUY – The local specialities are **porcelain** by Villeroy & Boch, **chocolate,** cakes and pastries (try one of the many tea rooms in the city, eg *la Maison Namur*, 27 rue des Capucins); excellent **Moselle wines** and **sparkling wines** (eg on the outskirts of the capital: *Caves vinicoles de Wormeldange*, 115 route du Vin at Wormeldange).

ENTERTAINMENT

Utopolis *Plan I* **B1** – Vast complex with a hi-tech cinema and a range of leisure facilities, including themed bars and restaurants, a 'Bistropolis' and a 'Coyote Café' as well as boutiques.

Conservatoire – Modern concert hall.

Salle de Concerts Grande–Duchesse Joséphine-Charlotte *Plan I* **B1** – Home of the Luxembourg Philharmonic Orchestra (Orchestre Philharmonique de Luxembourg).

Grand Théâtre de la Ville *Plan I* **A1** – Drama in different languages, opera and dance.

Théâtre des Capucines *Plan II* **C1** – Home productions and guest performances.

NIGHTLIFE

There are three sources for details of theatres, concerts, cinemas, shows and exhibitions – *Agenda Lux* (www.agendalux.lu) and *Rendez-vous Lëtzebuerg*, which are published monthly and are available free of charge from hotels and the Tourist Information Office; also *Vademecum*, a monthly listing of cultural events, available from the City Tourist Office in Place d'Armes.

At night the liveliest part of the city is the **Station district** *Plan I* **B3** where there are bars and night clubs. In the lower town – **Grund/Clausen** *Plan II* **D1** – there are bars and music cafés, which are popular with the locals; they have outdoor tables and live music – jazz and folk.

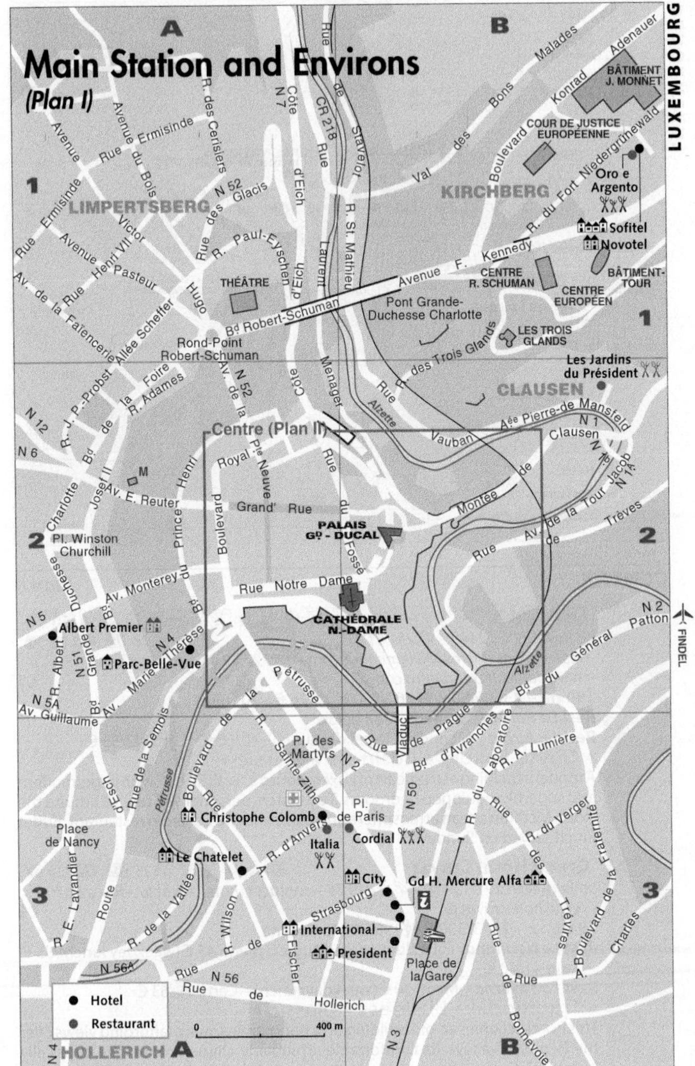
Main Station and Environs
(Plan I)
A
B
1
2
3
LIMPERTSBERG
KIRCHBERG
CLAUSEN
HOLLERICH
THÉÂTRE
Rond-Point Robert-Schuman
Bd Robert-Schuman
Avenue F. Kennedy
Pont Grande-Duchesse Charlotte
BÂTIMENT J. MONNET
COUR DE JUSTICE EUROPÉENNE
CENTRE R. SCHUMAN
CENTRE EUROPÉEN
BÂTIMENT-TOUR
LES TROIS GLANDS
Oro e Argento
Sofitel
Novotel
Les Jardins du Président
Centre (Plan II)
PALAIS Gd - DUCAL
CATHÉDRALE N.-DAME
Grand' Rue
Rue Notre Dame
Pl. Winston Churchill
Albert Premier
Parc-Belle-Vue
Pl. des Martyrs
Pl. de Paris
Christophe Colomb
Italia
Cordial
Le Chatelet
City
Gd H. Mercure Alfa
International
President
Place de la Gare
Place de Nancy
FINDEL
Hotel
Restaurant
0
400 m

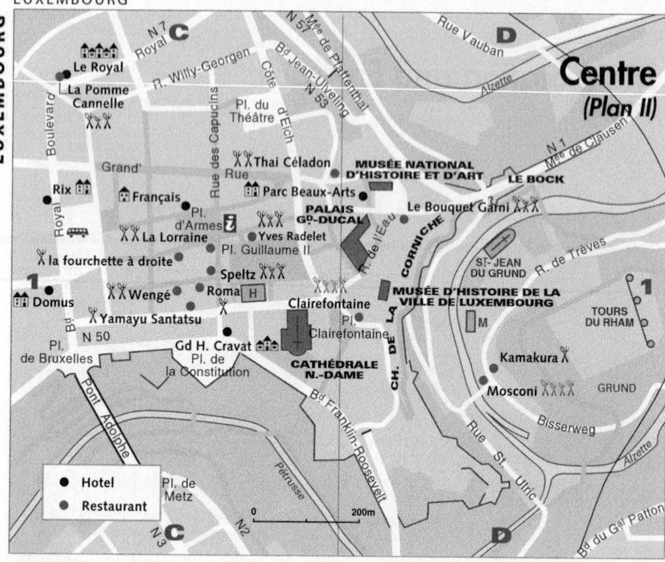

CENTRE

Plan II

Le Royal

bd Royal 12 ✉ 2449 – ☎ 241 61 61 – reservations@leroyalluxembourg.com – Fax 22 59 48 – www.leroyalluxembourg.com — C1

rest · 350 · VISA

190 rm – 360/490 € 360/490 €, 26 € – 20 suites

Rest *La Pomme Cannelle* – see below

Rest *Le Jardin* – Menu 28 € (weekday lunch), 40/60 € – Carte 42/55 €

◆ Grand Luxury ◆ Business ◆ Classic ◆

A modern building at the heart of Luxembourg's "Wall Street" with large, modern and superbly-equipped bedrooms. Top-notch, personalised service around the clock. Mediterranean atmosphere and cuisine in the Le Jardin restaurant. Buffet lunch served on Sundays.

Grand Hôtel Cravat

rest · 25 · VISA

bd Roosevelt 29 ✉ 2450 – ☎ 22 19 75 – contact@hotelcravat.lu – Fax 22 67 11 – www.hotelcravat.lu — C1

59 rm – 173/330 € 199/397 € – 1 suite

Rest *Le Normandy* – 1st floor *(closed August)* Menu 45 € (weekday lunch)/55 € – Carte 41/73 €

Rest *La Taverne* – Menu 30 € (weekday lunch) – Carte 28/63 €

◆ Traditional ◆ Business ◆ Classic ◆

This hotel occupies an old building on a panoramic square (affording views over the Pétrusse Valley). Its comfortable, irregularly shaped rooms are classically furnished. Gourmet restaurant at the Normandy (on the first floor). Regional cuisine served at the Taverne on the ground floor.

Parc Belair

300 · VISA

av. du X Septembre 111 ✉ 2551 (by N 5) – ☎ 442 32 31 – reservations@goeres-group.com – Fax 44 44 84 – www.goeres-group.com

52 rm – 250/310 € 270/330 € – 1 suite

Rest – *(closed Saturday lunch and Sunday lunch)* Carte 23/41 €

◆ Traditional ◆ Business ◆ Functional ◆

This luxury hotel on the edge of a park is appreciated by guests for its modern, comfortable rooms, including junior suites and rooms with themed decor. Pleasant lounge bar and lovely views.

Albert Premier without rest

r. Albert 1er 2a ✉ 1117 – ☎ 442 44 21
– info@albert1er.lu
– Fax 44 74 41 – www.albert1er.lu *Plan I* **A2**
14 rm – 🚹140/245 € 🚹🚹145/245 €, ☕ 15 €

♦ Luxury ♦ Business ♦ Stylish ♦

This hotel on the city's outskirts was formerly a grand residence. Guests are won over by its plush, English-style interior decor and cosy rooms.

Parc Beaux-Arts without rest

r. Sigefroi 1 ✉ 2536 – ☎ 268 67 61
– reservations@goeres-group.com
– Fax 26 86 76 36 – www.goeres-group.com **D1**
10 rm ☕ – 🚹330/395 € 🚹🚹350/415 €

♦ Luxury ♦ Modern ♦

This ancient building close to the history and art museum has been lovingly restored. Attractive parquet floors in the suites; those at the front offer views of the Palais Grand-Ducal.

Domus

av. Monterey 37 ✉ 2163 – ☎ 467 87 81
– info@domus.lu – Fax 46 78 79 – www.domus.lu
closed late December **C1**
38 rm – 🚹135/150 € 🚹🚹135/220 €, ☕ 18 €
Rest *Le Sot l'y laisse* – *☎ 467 87 88 (closed 1 week Easter, mid August-early September, late December, Saturday, Sunday and Bank Holidays)* Menu 15 € (weekday lunch) – Carte 36/58 €

♦ Business ♦ Modern ♦

A contemporary "apartment-hotel" with spacious, modern, meticulously kept rooms, almost all of which have fully equipped kitchenettes. Bright dining room with high-tech bistro-style furnishings and a summer restaurant in the garden.

Rix without rest

bd Royal 20 ✉ 2449 – ☎ 47 16 66 – rixhotel@pt.lu – Fax 22 75 35
– www.hotelrix.lu
closed 11-19 August and 22 December-6 January **C1**
20 rm ☕ – 🚹140/165 € 🚹🚹165/195 €

♦ Family ♦ Business ♦ Functional ♦

A pleasant family-run hotel offering sober, varied rooms. Impressive Classical-style breakfast room and priceless private parking.

Parc-Belle-Vue 350

av. Marie-Thérèse 5 ✉ 2132 – ☎ 456 14 11
– reservations@goeres-group.com
– Fax 456 14 12 20 – www.goeres-group.com *Plan I* **A2**
58 rm ☕ – 🚹130/160 € 🚹🚹145/175 €
Rest – *(closed Saturday lunch and Sunday lunch) (buffets)* Menu 19 € (weekday lunch) – Carte approx. 38 €

♦ Business ♦ Functional ♦

This hotel certainly lives up to its name with its park and fine views. The rooms in the new extension are the most comfortable but here the views are lacking. The restaurant and tavern serve buffet meals. Panoramic summer terrace.

Français 30

pl. d'Armes 14 ✉ 1136 – ☎ 47 45 34 – hfinfo@pt.lu – Fax 46 42 74
– www.hotelfrancais.lu **C1**
25 rm ☕ – 🚹95/99 € 🚹🚹120/150 €
Rest – Menu 12 € (weekday lunch), 20/45 € – Carte 28/60 €

♦ Family ♦ Business ♦ Functional ♦

Run by the same family since 1970, the Français overlooks the liveliest square in the city. Works of art are dotted about the public areas and the rooms are impeccably kept. Tavern-style restaurant serving classic-traditional cuisine.

XXXX ✿

Clairefontaine (Magnier) 4/20 P VISA MC AE

pl.de Clairefontaine 9 ✉ 1341 – ☎ 46 22 11 – clairefo@pt.lu – Fax 47 08 21 – www.restaurantclairefontaine.lu

closed 1 week Easter, 15 August-5 September, 22 December-3 January, Saturday, Sunday and Bank Holidays **C-D1**

Rest – Menu 50 € (weekday lunch), 74/93 € – Carte 64/99 €

Spec. Carpaccio et tartare de Saint-Jacques au céleri et truffe (October-March). Poularde de Bresse cuite en vessie, farce au foie gras et sauce Albufera. Sablé breton aux fraises, compote de rhubarbe, glace "Tagada".

♦ Innovative ♦ Formal ♦

In the old town, fronting a charming square close to the cathedral, this renowned restaurant is known for its ever-evolving cuisine, complementary, well-balanced cellar and quality service.

XXXX ✿✿

Mosconi 8/17 VISA MC AE

r. Münster 13 ✉ 2160 – ☎ 54 69 94 – mosconi@pt.lu – Fax 54 00 43 – www.mosconi.lu

closed 1 week Easter, 12 August-3 September, Christmas- NewYear, Saturday lunch, Sunday, Monday and Bank Holidays **D1**

Rest – Menu 34 € (weekday lunch), 50/98 € – Carte 64/93 €

Spec. Pâté de foie de poulet à la crème de truffes blanches. Risotto aux truffes blanches (October-December). Entrecôte de veau légèrement panée.

♦ Italian ♦ Cosy ♦

A smart house on the banks of the River Alzette serving fine Italian cuisine. A romantic setting where the emphasis is on discreet luxury. Attractive terrace by the water's edge and fine wine list.

XXX ✿

Le Bouquet Garni (Duhr) 4/30 VISA MC AE

r. Eau 32 ✉ 1449 – ☎ 26 20 06 20 – Fax 26 20 09 11 – www.thierryduhr.com

closed late August-early September, Christmas-New Year, Sunday, Monday and Bank Holidays **D1**

Rest – Menu 32 € (weekday lunch)/74 € – Carte 58/88 €

Spec. Mousseline de pomme de terre au caviar. Pied de cochon farçi de morilles et ris de veau (winter).

♦ Traditional ♦ Rustic ♦

An elegant, rustic-style restaurant housed in an 18C building in a street running alongside the Palais Grand-Ducal. Classic fare enlivened by modern touches and served meticulously.

XXX

Speltz 10/40 VISA MC AE

r. Chimay 8 (angle r. Louvigny) ✉ 1333 – ☎ 47 49 50 – info@restaurant-speltz.lu – Fax 47 46 77 – ww.restaurant-speltz.lu

closed 1-9 April, 29 July-15 August, 23 December-1 January, Sunday, Monday and Bank Holidays **C1**

Rest – Menu 45 € (weekday lunch), 35/112 € bi – Carte 62/76 €

♦ Contemporary ♦ Friendly ♦

Refined, contemporary cuisine served in two rooms with period furniture or, on sunny days, on the busy front terrace lining one of the city's pedestrian streets. Well-informed and informative sommelier.

XXX

La Pomme Cannelle – Hotel Le Royal 20/280 VISA MC AE

bd Royal 12 ✉ 2449 – ☎ 241 61 61 – catering@leroyalluxembourg.com – Fax 22 59 48 – www.leroyalluxembourg.com

closed first 3 weeks August, late December, Saturday and Sunday **C1**

Rest – Menu 28 € (weekday lunch), 39/68 € – Carte 36/55 €

♦ Contemporary ♦ Fashionable ♦

Highly original cuisine in which high-quality ingredients, wines and spices from the New World take pride of place. The chic, yet welcoming interior calls to mind exotic locations.

XXX **Yves Radelet** 15/30 VISA

r. Curé 20 ✉ 1368 – ✆ 22 26 18 – info@yvesradelet.lu – Fax 46 24 40 – www.yvesradelet.lu

closed late August-early September, Sunday and Monday **C1**

Rest – Menu 26 € (weekday lunch), 45/80 € – Carte approx. 55 €

♦ Contemporary ♦ Cosy ♦

You will be handed an appetising menu of classic dishes with a modern twist at this restaurant whose owner, who is also the chef, produces the cheeses, charcuterie and cured foods himself.

XX **La Lorraine** 80 VISA

pl. d'Armes 7 (1st floor) ✉ 1136 – ✆ 47 14 36 – lorraine@pt.lu – Fax 47 09 64 – ww.lorraine.lu

closed Sunday **C1**

Rest – Menu 39/52 € – Carte 60/70 €

Rest *Bistrot de La Lorraine* – ground floor – Menu 39 € – Carte 37/57 €

♦ Seafood ♦ Retro ♦

Two main types of cuisine are served in this fine edifice on the place d'Armes: local cuisine, with oysters (in season) on the bistro-style ground floor, and contemporary fare in an attractive Art Deco room on the first floor.

XX **Thai Céladon** 40/48 VISA

r. Nord 1 ✉ 2229 – ✆ 47 49 34 – Fax 37 91 73

closed Saturday lunch and Sunday **C1**

Rest – Menu 18 € (weekday lunch), 37/46 € – Carte 37/44 €

♦ Thai ♦ Exotic ♦

This central restaurant with two floors serves Thai cuisine and vegetarian dishes in a simple, contemporary ambience. It takes its name from a glaze used by Oriental potters.

X **Wengé** 20/30 VISA

r. Louvigny 15 ✉ 1946 – ✆ 26 20 10 58 – wenge@vo.lu – Fax 26 20 12 59 – www.wenge.lu

closed 9-16 April, 20 August-3 September, 1-8 January and Sunday **C1**

Rest – *(lunch only except Wednesday and Friday)* Menu 30 € (weekday lunch), 37/58 € – Carte 40/77 €

♦ Contemporary ♦ Fashionable ♦

Occupying the back of a pâtisserie-cum-delicatessen, this minimalist-style restaurant has a mezzanine and is adorned with Wengé panelling. Contemporary cuisine accompanied by fine wines.

X **Roma** 10/25 VISA

r. Louvigny 5 ✉ 1946 – ✆ 22 36 92 – Fax 22 04 96

closed Sunday dinner and Monday **C1**

Rest – Carte 31/57 €

♦ Italian ♦ Friendly ♦

One of the oldest "ristoranti" in Luxembourg. Relaxed atmosphere and decor to match the era. Two types of menu: classic and contemporary. Good choice of Italian wines.

X **La Fourchette à droite** 30/50 VISA

av. Monterey 5 ✉ 2163 – ✆ 22 13 60 – Fax 22 24 95

closed Saturday lunch **C1**

Rest – Menu 18 € (weekday lunch), 34/50 € – Carte 46/59 €

♦ Traditional ♦ Bistro ♦

Modern bistro set amid a variety of restaurants in a pedestrian area attracting a range of clients, including locals, tourists and workers. A second room upstairs.

X **Yamayu Santatsu** 5/8 VISA

r. Notre-Dame 26 ✉ 2240 – ✆ 46 12 49 – Fax 46 05 71

closed 1 week Easter, first 3 weeks August, late December-early January, Sunday lunch, Monday and Bank Holidays **C1**

Rest – Menu 14 € (weekday lunch)/28 € – Carte 18/43 €

♦ Japanese ♦ Minimalist ♦

Japanese restaurant in a minimalist setting about 200m/220yd from the cathedral. Typical and varied choice, including one fixed menu. You can see the sushi being made behind the counter in the restaurant.

Kamakura

r. Münster 4 ✉ 2160 – ✆ 47 06 04 – kamakura@pt.lu – Fax 46 73 30 – www.kamakura.lu

closed 31 March-11 April, 2 weeks August, Bank Holidays lunch, Saturday lunch and Sunday **D1**

Rest – Menu 12 € (weekday lunch), 28/51 € bi – Carte 33/51 €

♦ Japanese ♦ Exotic ♦

The Kamakura makes few concessions to the West with its minimalist ambience and design. Good sushi-bar and fixed menus which remain loyal to Japanese customs. A firm favourite.

MAIN STATION *Plan I*

President

pl. de la Gare 32 ✉ 1024 – ✆ 48 16 11 – info@president.lu – Fax 48 61 80 – www.president.lu **B3**

41 rm – 150/180 € 180/250 € – 1 suite

Rest *Les Jardins du President* – see below at environs of Luxembourg

♦ Traditional ♦ Business ♦ Classic ♦

The rooms at this attractive, discreetly luxurious hotel in front of the station are comfortable and frequently refurbished. Personalised service, neo-Classical lobby and an intimate ambience.

Mercure Grand Hotel Alfa

pl. de la Gare 16 ✉ 1616 – ✆ 490 01 11 – h2058@accor.com – Fax 49 00 09 – www.accorhotels.com **B3**

140 rm – 175/270 € 175/270 €, 18 € – 1 suite

Rest – Menu 20 € (weekday lunch) – Carte 31/57 €

♦ Chain hotel ♦ Business ♦ Modern ♦

This completely refurbished chain hotel is a useful address for rail travellers. Behind its imposing façade, typical of the 1930s, are pleasant rooms where a good night's sleep is guaranteed. The atmosphere of a Parisian-style brasserie reigns in the vast Art Deco restaurant.

International

pl. de la Gare 20 ✉ 1616 – ✆ 48 59 11 – info@hotelinter.lu – Fax 49 32 27 – www.hotelinter.lu **B3**

69 rm – 90/250 € 110/280 € – 1 suite

Rest *Am Inter* – *(closed 22 December-5 January and Saturday lunch)* Menu 20 € (weekday lunch), 30/40 € – Carte 32/62 €

♦ Family ♦ Business ♦ Classic ♦

Located opposite the railway station, this hotel is gradually being overhauled. Well-maintained rooms, the best being the new junior suites at the front. The restaurant occupies the corner of the building and the large bay windows allow light to flood in. Classic menu with substantial choice.

Le Châtelet without rest

bd de la Pétrusse 2 ✉ 2320 – ✆ 40 21 01 – contact@chatelet.lu – Fax 40 36 66 – www.chatelet.lu **A3**

39 rm – 95/114 € 108/130 €

♦ Family ♦ Business ♦ Classic ♦

Overlooking the Pétrusse Valley, this hotel is an amalgam of several houses, one of which is crowned by an imposing turret. White-leaded furniture and Oriental carpets in the largest rooms.

City without rest

r. Strasbourg 1 ✉ 2561 – ✆ 29 11 22 – mail@cityhotel.lu – Fax 29 11 33 – www.cityhotel.lu **B3**

35 rm – 90/135 € 124/185 €

♦ Family ♦ Business ♦ Classic ♦

This corner building dating from the inter-war period has fairly spacious rooms decorated in a style reminiscent of the 1980s, each with an individual feel.

Christophe Colomb without rest 25 VISA
r. Anvers 10 ✉ 1130 – ✆ 408 41 41 – mail@christophe-colomb.lu – Fax 40 84 08 – www.christophe-colomb.lu **A3**
24 rm – 80/160 € 90/170 €
◆ Family ◆ Business ◆ Modern ◆
Just 500m/550yd from the station, this pleasant small hotel is ideal for those arriving in the city by train. Standard, reasonably spacious rooms with modern furnishings.

Cordial 6/20 VISA
pl. de Paris 1 (1st floor) ✉ 2314 – ✆ 48 85 38 – Fax 48 85 38 – www.lecordial.lu
closed 9-15 April, 28 May-3 June, 6-26 August and Saturday **B3**
Rest – *(lunch only)* Menu 33 € (weekday lunch), 42/70 € – Carte 43/69 €
◆ French traditional ◆ Formal ◆
A large, comfortable restaurant with a conventional layout and elegant ambience. Classic culinary options including a combination of menus and daily specials.

Italia with rm rest VISA
r. Anvers 15 ✉ 1130 – ✆ 486 62 61 – italia@euro.lu – Fax 48 08 07 **A3**
20 rm – 70/80 € 80/90 € – **Rest** – Carte 35/53 €
◆ Italian ◆ Family ◆
A restaurant with classic set-up and a menu strong on Italian specialities and grilled meats. Terrace hidden at the rear. The best rooms are at the front.

ENVIRONS OF LUXEMBOURG *Plan I*

Sheraton Aérogolf 120 VISA
rte de Trèves 1 ✉ 2633 (Airport) – ✆ 34 05 71 – sheraton.luxembourg@sheraton.com – Fax 34 02 17 – www.sheraton.com
147 rm – 89/340 € 89/340 €, 20 € – 1 suite
Rest – *(open until 11 p.m.)* Carte 35/55 €
◆ Chain hotel ◆ Business ◆ Modern ◆
A full range of creature comforts, sophisticated luxury, triple glazing, views of the airport and impeccable service are the hallmarks of this recently renovated 1970s-built hotel. Bright, simple brasserie with an international menu and a summer terrace.

Hilton 360 VISA
r. Jean Engling 12 ✉ 1466 (Dommeldange) – ✆ 4 37 81 – hilton.luxembourg@hilton.com – Fax 43 60 95 – www.hilton.com
298 rm – 99/144 € 99/340 € – 39 suites
Rest – Menu 16 € (weekday lunch) – Carte 36/58 €
◆ Chain hotel ◆ Business ◆ Classic ◆
This luxury hotel situated on a wooded hillside in a valley has comfortable rooms, friendly service and a large conference centre. Modern bistro decor in the restaurant.

Sofitel Europe rm 75 VISA
r. Fort Niedergrünewald 6 (European Centre) ✉ 2015 (Kirchberg) – ✆ 43 77 61 – h1314@accor.com – Fax 42 50 91 **B1**
100 rm – 89/350 € 89/350 €, 20 € – 4 suites
Rest Oro e Argento – see below
Rest *Le Stübli* – *(closed July, Sunday and Monday)* Menu 25 € (weekday lunch) – Carte approx. 30 €
◆ Chain hotel ◆ Business ◆ Classic ◆
This bold, oval-shaped hotel with a central atrium is located at the heart of the European institutions district. Comfortable, spacious rooms with service to match. Regional cuisine served in a welcoming setting, where waiting staff are dressed in traditional attire.

Novotel 300 VISA
r. Fort Niedergrünewald 6 (European Centre) ✉ 2226 (Kirchberg) – ✆ 429 84 81 – Fax 43 86 58 – **260 rm** – 160/176 € 160/176 €, 15 € **B1**
Rest – *(open until midnight)* Menu 24 € (weekday lunch) – Carte 26/48 €
◆ Chain hotel ◆ Business ◆ Functional ◆
The Novotel is run by the same group as its neighbour, the Sofitel, and offers business customers a full range of seminar facilities as well as recently refurbished rooms. Brasserie-style restaurant with an international menu in line with the Novotel standard.

Ponte Vecchio without rest

r. Neudorf 271 ✉ 2221 (Neudorf) – ✆ 424 72 01 – vecchio@pt.lu – Fax 424 72 08 88 – www.vecchio.lu

45 rm – 90 € 108/115 €

◆ Traditional ◆ Business ◆ Functional ◆

This old brewery has been skilfully redeveloped into a series of impressive bedrooms (with and without kitchenettes) - including nine split-level - and public areas adorned with romantic Italianate frescoes.

Ibis

rm 60

rte de Trèves ✉ 2632 (Airport) – ✆ 43 88 01 – h0974@accor.com – Fax 43 88 02

167 rm – 60/85 € 65/85 €, 10 €

Rest – Carte approx. 25 €

◆ Chain hotel ◆ Business ◆ Functional ◆

A chain hotel with attractive lounge and dining areas plus a cheaper annexe for the budget-conscious. Although quite small, the bedrooms offer the level of comfort you would expect from the Ibis name. A glass rotunda provides the backdrop for the restaurant.

Oro e Argento – Hotel Sofitel Europe

20/35

r. Fort Niedergrünewald 6 (European Centre) ✉ 2015 (Kirchberg) – ✆ 43 77 61 – h1314@accor.com – Fax 42 50 91

closed August and Saturday **B1**

Rest – Carte 45/60 €

◆ Italian ◆ Cosy ◆

Part of a luxury hotel, this attractive Italian restaurant has a rich Venetian decor, intimate atmosphere and impeccable service. Contemporary Italian cuisine.

Hostellerie du Grünewald with rm

rest

rte d'Echternach 10 ✉ 1453 (Dommeldange) – ✆ 43 18 82 – hostgrun@pt.lu – Fax 42 06 46 – www.hotel-romantik.com

25 rm – 100/130 € 130/160 €

Rest – *(closed 29 July-15 August, 1-17 January, Saturday lunch, Sunday, Monday lunch and Bank Holidays)* Menu 52 € (weekday lunch), 63/90 € – Carte 55/74 €

◆ Traditional ◆ Cosy ◆

The ambience in this appealing hostelry is quiet and romantic - the central dining room is especially charming. Fine traditional cuisine and attentive service. A delightful, traditional-style hostelry with a hushed, romantic atmosphere.

Les Jardins du President – Hotel President with rm

rm

pl. Ste-Cunégonde 2 ✉ 1367 (Clausen) – ✆ 260 90 71 – jardins@president.lu – Fax 26 09 07 73 – www.president.lu

closed last week December- first week January, Saturday and Sunday **B2**

7 rm – 250/350 € 350/400 €

Rest – *(closed Saturday lunch and Sunday)* Menu 29 € (weekday lunch), 45/65 € – Carte 51/69 €

◆ Contemporary ◆ Fashionable ◆

An elegant restaurant set amid an oasis of greenery producing dishes with a modern touch. Well-informed sommelier. The terrace overlooks a garden and waterfall. Individually designed bedrooms.

Le Grimpereau

r. Cents 140 ✉ 1319 (Airport) – ✆ 43 67 87 – bridard@pt.lu – Fax 42 60 26 – www.legrimpereau.lu

closed 1 week Easter, first 3 weeks August, Saturday lunch, Sunday dinner and Monday

Rest – Menu 40 € (weekday lunch) – Carte 63/73 €

◆ Contemporary ◆ Rustic ◆

A villa reminiscent of a chalet is the setting for this simple and spacious neo-rustic restaurant with exposed beams and stone fireplace. Contemporary cuisine.

NETHERLANDS
NEDERLAND

PROFILE

◆ **Area:**
41 863 km^2
(16 163 sq mi).

◆ **Population:**
16 407 000 inhabitants (est. 2005), density = 392 per km^2.

◆ **Capital:**
Amsterdam (conurbation 1 193 000 inhabitants); The Hague is the seat of government and Parliament.

◆ **Currency:**
Euro (€); rate of exchange: € 1 = US$1.32 (Nov 2006).

◆ **Government:**
Constitutional parliamentary monarchy (since 1815). Member of European Union since 1957 (one of the 6 founding countries).

◆ **Language:**
Dutch; many Dutch people also speak English.

◆ **Specific public holidays:**
Good Friday (Friday before Easter); Queen's Day (30 April, 2006: 29 April); Liberation Day (5 May); Boxing Day (26 December).

◆ **Local Time:**
GMT + 1hour in winter and GMT + 2 hours in summer.

◆ **Climate:**
Temperate maritime with cool winters and mild summers (Amsterdam: January: 2°C, July: 17°C), rainfall evenly distributed throughout the year.

◆ **International dialling Code:**
00 31 followed by area code without the initial **0** and then the local number. International Directory enquiries: ✆ **06 0418**.

◆ **Emergency:**
Fire Brigade: ✆ **112**; Police, Ambulance, Roadside assistance: ✆ **0900 8418**.

◆ **Electricity:**
220 volts AC, 50Hz; 2-pin round-shaped continental plugs.

FORMALITIES

Travellers from the European Union (EU), Switzerland, Iceland and the main countries of North and South America need a national identity card or passport (America: passport required) to visit the Netherlands for less than three months (tourism or business purpose). For visitors from other countries a visa may be required, in addition to a passport, especially for those wishing to stay for longer than three months. We advise you to check with your embassy before travelling.

Nationals of EU member states require a valid national driving licence; nationals of non-EU countries require an international driving licence. Car hire is available in most major towns and resorts. The minimum age for the driver is 21-25, having held a valid licence for at least one year.

MAJOR NEWSPAPERS

The main national newspapers are: *de Telegraaf, NRC Handelsblad, Algemeen Dagblad, de Volkskrant* and *het Nederlands Dagblad*. The main dailies of Amsterdam, Den Haag and Rotterdam are respectively *Het Parool, de Haagsche Courant* and *het Rotterdams Dagblad. Het Financieele Dagblad* deals with financial matters.

USEFUL PHRASES

ENGLISH	**DUTCH**
Yes	**Ja**
No	**Nee**
Good morning	**Goedemorgen, Dag**
Goodbye	**Dag, Tot ziens**
Thank you	**Dank u, bedankt**
Please	**Alstublieft**
Excuse me	**Excuseer mij / Neemt U mij niet kwalijk**
I don't understand	**Ik begrijp het niet**

HOTELS

→ CATEGORIES

Accommodation ranges from luxurious 5-star international hotels, via simple hotels and smaller, family-run guesthouses and bed and breakfast establishments. There is also a wide range of rented accommodation – bungalows, log cabins, holiday cottages, flats and apartments. The Benelux star rating is conferred on the application of the owner.

→ PRICE RANGE

The price is per room. There is little difference between the price of a single and a double room. Between April and October it is advisable to book in advance. From November to March prices may be slightly lower, some hotels offer special cheap rates and some may be closed. In the major towns hotel chains may offer lower weekend rates in the low season.

→ TAX

Included in the room price.

→ CHECK OUT TIME

Usually between 11am and noon.

→ RESERVATIONS

By telephone or by Internet. A credit card number may be required.

→ TIP FOR LUGGAGE HANDLING

At the discretion of the customer (about €1 per bag).

→ BREAKFAST

It is often not included in the price of the room in the more expensive hotels and is generally served between 7am and 10am. Most hotels offer a self-service buffet but usually it is possible to have continental breakfast served in the room.

Reception	**Receptie**
Single room	**Eenpersoonskamer**
Double room	**Kamer met tweepersoonsbed / Kamer met twee bedden**
Bed	**Bed**
Bathroom	**Badkamer**
Shower	**Douche**

RESTAURANTS

Besides traditional **restaurants** there are **brasseries**, serving less formal meals. Asian cuisines are well represented: Chinese, Japanese, Indian and particularly the famous Indonesian *rijsttafel.*

Breakfast	**Het ontbijt**	7am – 10am
Lunch	**Middagmaal**	11am – 2-3pm
Dinner	**Avondeten**	5.30pm – 10pm

The more formal restaurants are usually open only in the evening and not at midday. Menus are usually printed in Dutch and sometimes in English. Some Dutch restaurants offer a 3-course tourist menu, which offers good value but not much choice. A fixed price menu is usually less expensive than a meal with the same number of courses selected from the à la carte menu. The restaurants of the Neerlands Dis chain, displaying a red, white and blue soup tureen emblem, offer a selection of traditional Dutch dishes. Restaurants displaying a blue wall plaque with a white fork offer a tourist menu at a reasonable price – a three course meal (starter, main course and dessert).

→ RESERVATIONS

Reservations are usually made by phone, fax or Internet. For famous restaurants (including Michelin starred restaurants), it is advisable to book several days – or weeks in some instances – in advance. A credit card number or a phone number may be required as guarantee.

→ THE BILL

The bill (check) includes service charge and VAT. Tipping is optional but, if you are particularly pleased with the service, it is customary to round up the total to an appropriate figure – 10% in larger restaurants and the value of the small change elsewhere.

Drink or aperitif	**Aperitief**
Appetizer	**Hapje**
Meal	**Maaltijd**
First course, starter	**Voorgerecht**
Main dish	**Hoofdgerecht**
Main dish of the day	**Dagschotel**
Dessert	**Nagerecht**
Water	**Water**
Wine (red, white, rosé)	**Wijn (rood, witte, rosé)**
Beer	**Bier, Pils**
Bread	**Brood**
Meat (rare, medium, well done)	**Vlees (rood, saignant, gaar)**

Fish	**Vis**
Salt/pepper	**Zout/peper**
Cheese	**Kaas**
Vegetables	**Groenten**
Hot/cold	**Heet/koud**
The bill (check) please	**De rekening alstublieft**

LOCAL CUISINE

The Netherlands is the world's third largest exporter of agricultural produce: dairy products from the famous black and white Friesian cattle, vegetables and flowers. This is reflected in the local cuisine. Breakfast is a generous meal consisting of cheese, cold meats, eggs and milk products, as well as cereal, different kinds of breads and pastries, and is accompanied by coffee, tea, hot chocolate and milk. Lunch is usually a cold snack with coffee: a shrimp or eel sandwich; soft bread rolls with various fillings *(broodje)* ; open sandwiches *(uitsmijter)* with butter, ham or roast beef and two fried eggs on top; deep-fried balls of spiced mince meat *(kroketten)*.

Dinner is a larger meal starting with soup, kippers (marinated, smoked herrings), a vegetable hors-d'œuvre, followed by a main dish of meat or fish and an abundance of fresh vegetables in gravy, salad with mayonnaise, finishing with dessert (ice-cream or pastries topped with whipped cream).

Fish soup is popular but two more unusual recipes are **Abraham's Mosterdsoep**, mustard soup, and **Erwten Soep**, split-pea soup cooked with pieces of sausage and bacon fat. Owing to their long coastline the Dutch catch a lot of fish: cod, haddock, herring, also oysters, mussels, crab and lobster. A favourite dish is **mussels** *(mosselen)* served with a white wine Hollandaise sauce and chives, or cooked with celery and onions in white wine and served with French fries *(patat)*. Their speciality is herring; **maatjesharing** is eaten raw with onions in early summer; for **Hollandse Nieuwe** the herrings are caught in the spring when their fat content is high, then gutted, salted, matured, filleted and preserved in brine.

Most menus will feature beef, veal and calves liver; **Friet met Zoervlies** is a dish of beef cooked in a sour vinegar and apple sauce and served with French fries. **Hutspot**, a traditional recipe from Leiden, is steak or brisket boiled with potatoes and carrots in milk and water. In spring asparagus (*asperge*) will be on the menu, often served with ham and butter.

Both fish and cheese are preserved by smoking; smoked eel *(gerookte paling)* is a delicacy on the coast.

Cheese is the staple ingredient of breakfast and cold meals. Creamy when fresh (*jonge*), it becomes dry and pungent when ripe *(oude)*: the cylindrical, flat **Gouda** and spherical **Edam** are both found in the picturesque market of Alkmaar; **Leyden** cheese *(Leidse kaas)* contains caraway seeds, while **Friesland** *(Friese kaas)* is flavoured with cloves.

For dessert there is fruit, particularly apples: **Appelbol**, a pastry ball filled with apples and raisins; **appelgebak**, apple and cinnamon pie; **Krudoorntjesbrij**, a gooseberry porridge made with gooseberries, milk, cream and sugar; **Haagse Bluf**, a blackcurrant fool. Other sweet dishes are syrup waffles *(siroopwafels)*, a speciality from Gouda; **Haagse Kakker**, bread pudding flavoured with cinnamon, raisins and almond paste; **Vlaai**, an open tart filled with apples, cherries or strawberries; **Bossche Bol**, a chocolate covered pastry; **Eierkoeken**, large soft pastries made of eggs; **Pannenkoeken**, sweet or spicy pancakes; **Oliebollen**, doughnuts filled with raisins, apple or custard. **Speculaas** are almond biscuits and **pepernoten** are a sort of ginger nut.

DRINK

Beer is the most popular drink. Among the popular brands are Amstel, Grolsch, Heineken and Oranjeboom. There are several smaller breweries: Gulpen, Bavaria, Drie Ringen Leeuw and Utrecht; La Trappe is brewed by Trappist monks. Belgian beers are also popular. There are also seasonal beers: **witbier**, brewed in summer, is served with a slice of lemon or lime, and **bockbier**, rich and fruity appears in autumn.

The only grape-growing area is round Maastricht where there are 12 vineyards, some of which organise tours. To try a local wine at dinner ask for Apostelhoeve for white wine and Thiessen for red. Advocaat is a famous brand of eggnog; in Groningen they drink **Hiet Beer**, another Dutch eggnog. In Noord-Brabant the local tipple is **Brandewijn**, brandy served with sugar.

The Dutch are famous for their **gin** (genever). Starting with distilling grain in about 1600, they narrowed down their production over the years to malt spirit. Finally they specialised in making genever, using the juice of juniper berries to give the spirit its particular flavour. Schiedam, with its five distilleries, is the centre of the industry. Each distillery has its own recipe, which is a closely-guarded secret. They produce young genever - **jong jenever** and old genever - **oude jenever**, the latter having a fuller flavour. **Kopstout** is a glass of beer with a genever chaser.

Amsterdam

AMSTERDAM

Population (est. 2005): 750 000 (conurbation 1 193 000) – Altitude: sea level

R. Mattès / MICHELIN

Amsterdam is a magnificent city dominated by water. It is divided into different districts by rivers and numerous canals. It is also famous for its architecture, particularly the stepped façades of its tall, narrow brick houses. The best way to explore the town is on foot, by bicycle or boat.

Apart from its international importance as a port, Amsterdam is a city of great cultural wealth, with prestigious museums and galleries, containing works by some of the great Dutch painters. The first written record of the city dates from 1275, when Count Floris V of Holland granted toll privileges to the herring-fishing village, situated on two dikes joined by a dam, at the mouth of the Amstel River.

In the late 16C a period of great affluence began with the arrival of diamond merchants from Antwerp and the Marranos, Jews from Spain and Portugal. In the 17C the Dutch began a period of overseas expansion, particularly in the Far East. The revival of economic activity in the early 20C is marked by the Amsterdam School of architecture, which favoured asymmetry, differences of level and curved walls. Amsterdam is now a major industrial city; its activities include medical technology, metals, printing, food and tourism. Despite the development of modern suburbs many people live in the numerous houseboats moored along the canals.

WHICH DISTRICT TO CHOOSE

Most **hotels** and **restaurants** are located within the great curve of the Singelgracht canal, although there are a few beyond this line.

The city offers various cuisines – traditional Dutch restaurants and **brasseries**, the famous Indonesian **rijsttafel** and other Asian restaurants. *See also Gourmet Treats chapter.*

ARRIVAL – DEPARTURE

Schiphol International Airport *Plan I* **A3** – About 18 km (11 mi) south-west of the city centre. ✆ 0900 724 474 65 (from inside The Netherlands); ✆ 0031 (0) 20 794 0800 (from outside the Netherlands); www.schiphol.com

From the airport to the city centre – By **train**: Suburban train (20min) to Amsterdam Central Station every 20min during daytime; €3.70 single, approx. €6.50 return. By **bus**: No 197 Connexion and No 370 Interliner (30min). ✆ 020 653 49 75. By **taxi**: 20min (1hr in the rush hour), approx. €40. ✆ 020 653 10 00. Airport shuttles and KLM shuttle are also available to reach the city centre.

Railway Station – Central Station *Plan II* **G1**: regular train services from major towns in the Netherlands, Belgium, France and Germany. ✆ 0900 202 11 63, 0900 92 92; www.ns.nl

Ferry Terminal – Regular ferries to **Amsterdam (IJmuiden)** from Newcastle in England; www.dfdsseaways.co.uk

TRANSPORT

→ TRAM, BUS AND METRO

Most of the trams and buses run from the Central Station. Tram tickets to be punched in the yellow machines; bus tickets to be shown to the driver; metro tickets to be punched in the machines near the platform steps. Tickets are sold at the main information office (opposite Central Railway Station), in ticket vending machine and in many tobacconists' shops. Prices vary according to the number of pricing zones crossed: 15-stripcard *(strippenkaart)*,

approx. €7.00 or 45-stripcard, approx. €20.00, valid throughout the country on buses, trams and metro; one-week pass: between €11 and €27 (according to pricing zones). **Circle-Tram 20** has a circular route (31 stops) which takes in most of the main sights, museums and large hotels in the city (9am-7pm every 10min). ✆ 0900 80 11, 0900 92 92; www.gvb.nl

→ BOAT

Canal Bus has 3 routes (green, red, blue) with 11 stops; day ticket; ✆ 020 626 55 74; www.canal.nl **Museum Boat** has a single route with 7 stops (10am-5pm); price according to length of journey. **Artis Express** runs regularly from Central Station to Nederlands Scheepvaartmuseum and Artis; ✆ 020 530 10 90; www.lovers.nl Several companies offer boat trips; most from opposite the Central Station. In fine weather the Canal Bike is a good way of touring the canals; 4 landing stages (start at one stage and finish at another). ✆ 020 626 55 74; www.canal.nl

→ TAXI

Taxis bear blue number plates and an illuminated sign on the roof. They may be called by telephone (✆ 020 677 77 77) or hired at taxi ranks – airport, railway stations, Dam Square; although they are not supposed to stop, they can also be hailed in the street. Pick-up charge €5.12; price per km €1.94; taxi fares are usually rounded up (5-10%); www.taxi.amsterdam.nl

→ TAXI-CYCLE

Wieler Taxi €2.50 + €1 per 3 min per person; ✆ 282 475 50.

→ I AMSTERDAM CARD

This card entitles the holder to free public transport, free admission to major museums, a canal cruise and 25% discounts in some restaurants; 24hr-card €33; 48hr-card €43; 72hr-card €53. Available from the Tourist Office; www.iamsterdam.nl

USEFUL ADDRESSES

→ TOURIST OFFICES

VVV Amsterdam: Stationsplein 10 *Plan II* **G1**; ✆ 020 201 88 00; open 9am-6pm (2pm Sunday in winter). **Central Station**, platform 2, Leidsestraat1; ✆ 020 551 25 25. **Schipol Airport**, Arrivals Hall 2 (daily 7am-10pm); ✆ 900 400 40 40; www.amsterdam.nl; www.visitamsterdam.nl; info@atcb.nl

→ POST OFFICES

Open Mon-Fri 8.30am-5pm, Sat 8.30am-12 noon. The Main Post Office (Hoofdpostkantoor PTT) is at Singel 250-256 *Plan II* **F1** (open Mon-Fri 8.30am-6pm (8pm Thurs), Sat 10am-1.30pm).

→ BANKS

Opening times generally are Mon-Fri 9am-4/5pm. Most banks have ATMs.

→ EMERGENCY

Phone ✆ **112** for Fire Brigade, Police, Ambulance.

BUSY PERIODS

It may be difficult to find a room at a reasonable price (except at weekends) during special events:

Carnival: February.

Nationaal Museumweekend: April (3rd weekend) – Free admission to all museums.

Koninginnedag: April 30 – Queen's Birthday celebrated by young people dressed in orange.

Holland Festival: June – Concerts, opera, ballet, theatre.

Vondelpark Openluchttheater: June-August – Open-air theatre – free concerts in Vondelpark.

Grachtenfestival: August – Classical concert in courtyards, private canal-side houses and on the canals.

Uitmarkt: late August (3 days) – Free concerts and info booths advertising the new cultural season.

Bloemencorso: September (1st Sat) – Floral procession from Aalsmeer to Amsterdam.

Jordaan Festival: September (3 days) – Crooners singing in Westerkerk.

Sinterklaas: December (3rd Sat before 5 Dec) – Official entry of Sinterklaas (St Nicolas) in Prins Hendrikkade.

EXPLORING AMSTERDAM

DIFFERENT FACETS OF THE CITY

It is possible to visit the main sights and museums in three to four days. **Museumjaarkaart** provides free admission to some 440 museums throughout the Netherlands for one year.

Museums and sights are usually open from 10am to 5pm. Some close on Mondays and public holidays.

OLD AMSTERDAM – Grachten *Plan II* **G2**: City centre canals, lined with beautiful 17C and 18C merchants houses, with brick façades and gables of various shapes and decoration, surmounted by carved pediments, some with a small sculptured stone which was the owner's emblem or the symbol of his trade. To the north (near the port) warehouses have characteristic wooden shutters. **Koninklijk Paleis** *Plan II* **F1**: The Royal Palace, formerly the town hall redesigned in 1808 by Louis Bonaparte. **Nieuwe Kerk** *Plan II* **F1**: The New Church (15C Gothic), setting for the coronations of Dutch sovereigns. **Begijnhof** *Plan II* **F2**: Former church of the Beguines, founded in 14C, set in a green meadow, surrounded by lovely sculptured 17C and 18C stone façades – one of the rare surviving church enclosures. **Bloemenmarkt** *Plan II* **F2**: Open-air flower stalls, supplied by barges on the Singel.

MUSEUMS AND GALLERIES – Rijksmuseum *Plan II* **F3**: The National museum, founded by Louis Bonaparte in 1808: exceptional collection of 15C and 17C paintings; sculpture and decorative arts, historical department, print collection, Asian arts section. **Van Gogh Museum** *Plan II* **F3**: Over 200 paintings and 600 drawings by Van Gogh (1853-90): Dutch and Provençal landscapes, peasant portraits, views of Paris and self-portraits. **Stedelijk Museum** *Plan II* **E3**: Municipal museum of modern art (1850 to the present day): Cézanne, Monet, Picasso, Léger, Malevitch, Chagall, Mondrian and Van Doesburg; recent trends in European and American Art. **Nederlands Scheepvaart Museum** *Plan II* **H2**: Maritime Museum in 17C maritime warehouse; exhibits on navigation, replica of 18C merchant ship.

WEST OF CENTRE – Anne Frank Huis *Plan II* **F1**: Narrow 17C house where Anne Frank and her family hid until deported to Auschwitz in 1944. **Westerkerk** *Plan II* **F1**: Stone church (1619-31) with original colours (restored) and bell-tower (85m/280ft) with remarkable carillon; wooden vaulted nave.

SOUTH EAST OF CENTRE – Museum Het Rembrandthuis *Plan II* **F3**: Rembrandt's House (in main street of old Jewish district); collection of his drawings. **Magere Brug** *Plan II* **G3**: Fragile 18C bridge spanning the Amstel. **Artis** *Plan II* **H2**: Zoo with 6000 animals; planetary show at Zeiss Planetarium.

GOURMET TREATS

Amsterdam is the city of a thousand **cafés** *(kroeg)*, renowned for serving drinks in their warm and friendly atmosphere; some *(eetcafé)* also serve snacks and simple meals. Coffee houses serving coffee are not to be confused with **coffeeshops**, which also serve drinks but whose main business is selling legal soft drugs. The area around **Leidseplein** *Plan II* **F3** and **Rembrandtplein** *Plan II* **G2** is particularly busy in the evenings; the latter is mainly known for its large terrace cafés, restaurants and discos – *Café Américain* (Leidsekade 97 and Leidseplein 26): Art Deco brasserie; *Café Dantzig* (Zwanenburgwal 15): terrace on the Amstel and separate reading area; *De Kroon* (Rembrandtplein 17): Amsterdam landmark with terrace overlooking the square; *De Prins* (Prinsengracht 124): pleasant place with a terrace near Anne Frank's House; *Winkel* (Noordermarkt 43) for breakfast and apple cake; *Het Blauwe Theehuis* (Vondelpark) for breakfast; *De Bakkerswinkel* (Warmoestraat 69) for traditional Dutch sandwiches, quiches and cakes; *Lunchcafé 404* (Singel 404) for excellent open sandwiches.

The **brown cafés**, so-called because of their nicotine-stained wooden interiors, are the most typically Dutch; they tend to be small and crowded. Most customers order beer or schnapps but coffee and hot chocolate are also served. The most authentic brown cafés are in the **city centre** and **Jordaan** *Plan II* **F1**. *Café Hoppe* (Spui 18-20): meeting place for writers and journalists, where customers spill out onto the pavement in summer; *De Admiraal* (Herengracht 563): makes its own gin in one of the city's oldest distilleries; *'t Papeneiland* (Prinsengracht 2): the most romantic with Delft tile decoration, old-fashioned stove and waterside location; *'t Smalle* (Egelantiersgracht 12): tiny café with terrace overlooking the canal.

The **proeflokalen**, tasting places set up in the 17C, still offer the chance to sample the product before buying – Dutch gin and other spirits, many of them distilled on the premises – *De Drie Fleschjes* (Gravenstraat 18), its walls lined with carafes of exotically named drinks; *Wynand Fockink* (Pijlsteeg 31) an attractive courtyard and wide selection of gin and other local spirits.

SHOPPING

Stores are usually open daily from 8.30/9am to 5.30/6pm but close on Monday mornings; Thursday is late-night shopping until 9pm. Supermarkets are open Mon-Sat 8am-8pm (Sat 6pm).

De Bijenkorf (Damrak 1): department store. *Magna Plaza Center* (Nieuwezijds Voorburgwal 182): up-market indoor shopping centre (40 shops). Metz & Co (corner of Keizersgracht and Leidsestraat): design, gifts etc. *Vroom and Dreesmann* (Kalverstraat 201): department store.

The **Museum District** *Plan II* **F3** for exclusive and trendy fashion stores, luxury shoe shops and jewellers, particularly in **P C Hooftstraat** and **Van Baerlestraat**; pedestrianised **Kalverstraat** and **Nieuwendijk** for more down-to-earth clothes shops.

10 **diamond factories** are open to the public; ask at the Tourist Information Centre.

For **antique shops** visit the main canal area (Singel, Herengracht,

Keizersgracht and Prinsengracht) and more especially in **Spiegelstraat**, **Nieuwe Spiegelstraat** and **Kerkstraat**.

MARKETS – The **markets** are a delight. **Albert Cuypmarkt** *Plan II* **F2** (Albert Cuypstraat): general goods (Mon-Sat). **Bloemenmarkt** *Plan II* **F2** (Singel between Muntplein and Koningsplein): flower market (Mon-Sat). **Antiques market** *Plan II* **G1** (Nieuwmarkt) (Sun; May-Sep). There are two **flea markets**: one outdoor *Plan II* **G2** (Waterlooplein) (Mon-Sat) and one indoor *Plan II* **E2** (Looiersgracht 38) (Sat-Sun).

WHAT TO BUY – Diamonds, Delft porcelain, Dutch cheese, Dutch gin and other spirits, cigars, clogs.

ENTERTAINMENT

Full listings of music, dance, theatre etc. are published in *Uitkrant* (www.uitkrant.nl) available from theatres, bookshops and cafés, and in *What's On in Amsterdam*, published in English every three weeks and available in tourist offices and some bookshops, and in *Day by Day*, published monthly.

Concertgebouw *Plan I* **B2** (Concertgebouwplein 2-6): home of the world-famous orchestra.

Beurs van Berlage *Plan II* **G1** (Damrak 213) for concerts by the Netherlands Philharmonic Orchestra and others.

Felix Meritis *Plan II* **F2** (Keizersgracht 324): classical concerts in a magnificent 18C auditorium. **Bimhuis** *Plan II* **H1** (Oude Schans 73) for jazz lovers.

Amsterdam ArenA *Plan I* **D3** (Huntum 2): performances by big international names.

Koninklijk Theater Carré *Plan II* **H3** (Amstel 115-125): musicals, variety, circus.

Muziektheater (Stopera) *Plan II* **G2** (Amstel 3): performances by the Nederlandse Opera, the Nationale Ballet and the Nederlands Dans Theater.

Stadsschouwburg *Plan II* **F3** (Leidsplein 26): neo-renaissance building hosting the City Theater; plays some international English-language productions.

NIGHTLIFE

What's On in Amsterdam gives full listings of music, dance, theatre, and other events (see above). Amsterdam has some of the best nightlife anywhere, including the *Holland Casino* (Max Euweplein 64) and **Walletjes** *Plan II* **G1**, the famous red-light district. Nightclubs operate from about midnight to 3 or 4am; admission €3-€20: *Escape* (Rembrandtplein 11) which is one of the largest clubs; *iT* (Amstelstraat 24), an extravagant venue with go-go girls, drag queens and special gay evenings; *Club II* (Oosterdokskade 3-5), great atmosphere and fabulous DJs; *Club Arena* (in Hotel Arena), popular with Amsterdammers.

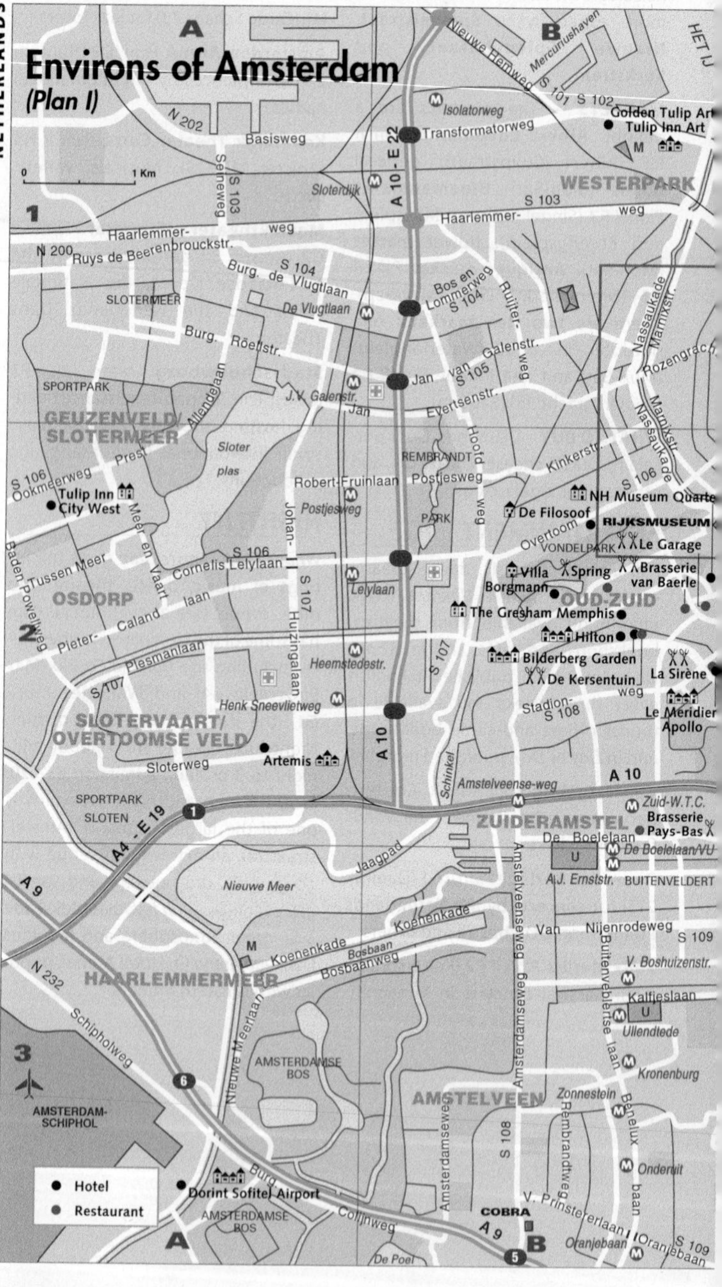

Environs of Amsterdam
(Plan I)

A
B
1
2
3
0 1 Km
Nieuwe Hemweg
Mercuriushaven
HET IJ
S 101
S 102
Isolatorweg
Golden Tulip Art
Tulip Inn Art
N 202
Basisweg
Transformatorweg
A 10 - E 22
Seineweg
S 103
Sloterdijk
WESTERPARK
Haarlemmer-
weg
Haarlemmer-
weg
S 103
N 200
Ruys de Beerenbrouckstr.
S 104
Burg. de Vlugtlaan
De Vlugtlaan
Bos en Lommerweg
S 104
SLOTERMEER
Ruijter-weg
Nassaukade
Marnixstr.
Burg. Röellstr.
Jan van Galenstr.
S 105
Rozengracht
SPORTPARK
Allendelaan
J.V. Galenstr.
Jan Evertsenstr.
GEUZENVELD/
SLOTERMEER
Sloter plas
Hoofd weg
Nassaukade
Marnixstr.
REMBRANDT
Kinkerstr.
Prest
S 106
Ookmeerweg
Robert-Fruinlaan
Postjesweg
S 106
Tulip Inn City West
Meer en Vaart
Johan-
Postjesweg
PARK
NH Museum Quarter
De Filosoof
RIJKSMUSEUM
Overtoom
VONDELPARK
Le Garage
Baden Powellweg
Tussen Meer
S 106
Cornelis Lelylaan
Lelylaan
Villa Borgmann
Spring
Brasserie van Baerle
OSDORP
laan
S 107
Huizingalaan
OUD-ZUID
The Gresham Memphis
Pieter-Caland
Hilton
Plesmanlaan
Heemstedestr.
S 107
Bilderberg Garden
De Kersentuin
La Sirène
S 107
Henk Sneevlietweg
Stadion-weg
S 108
Le Meridien Apollo
SLOTERVAART/
OVERTOOMSE VELD
Artemis
A 10
Sloterweg
Schinkel
Amstelveense-weg
A 10
SPORTPARK SLOTEN
1
A4 - E 19
ZUIDERAMSTEL
Zuid-W.T.C.
Brasserie Pays-Bas
Jaagpad
De Boelelaan
U
De Boelelaan/VU
A 9
Nieuwe Meer
A.J. Ernststr.
BUITENVELDERT
Koenenkade
Van Nijenrodeweg
S 109
M
Koenenkade
Bosbaan
Bosbaanweg
V. Boshuizenstr.
N 232
HAARLEMMERMEER
Amstelveenseweg
Buitenveldertse laan
Kalfjeslaan
U
Uilenstede
Schipholweg
Nieuwe Meerlaan
AMSTERDAMSE BOS
Kronenburg
6
AMSTELVEEN
Zonnestein
AMSTERDAM-SCHIPHOL
Rembrandtweg
Amsterdamseweg
S 108
Benelux baan
Onderuit
Hotel
Restaurant
Dorint Sofitel Airport
Burg. Colijnweg
AMSTERDAMSE BOS
V. Prinstererlaan
COBRA
A 9
S 109
Oranjebaan
Oranjebaan
De Poel
5

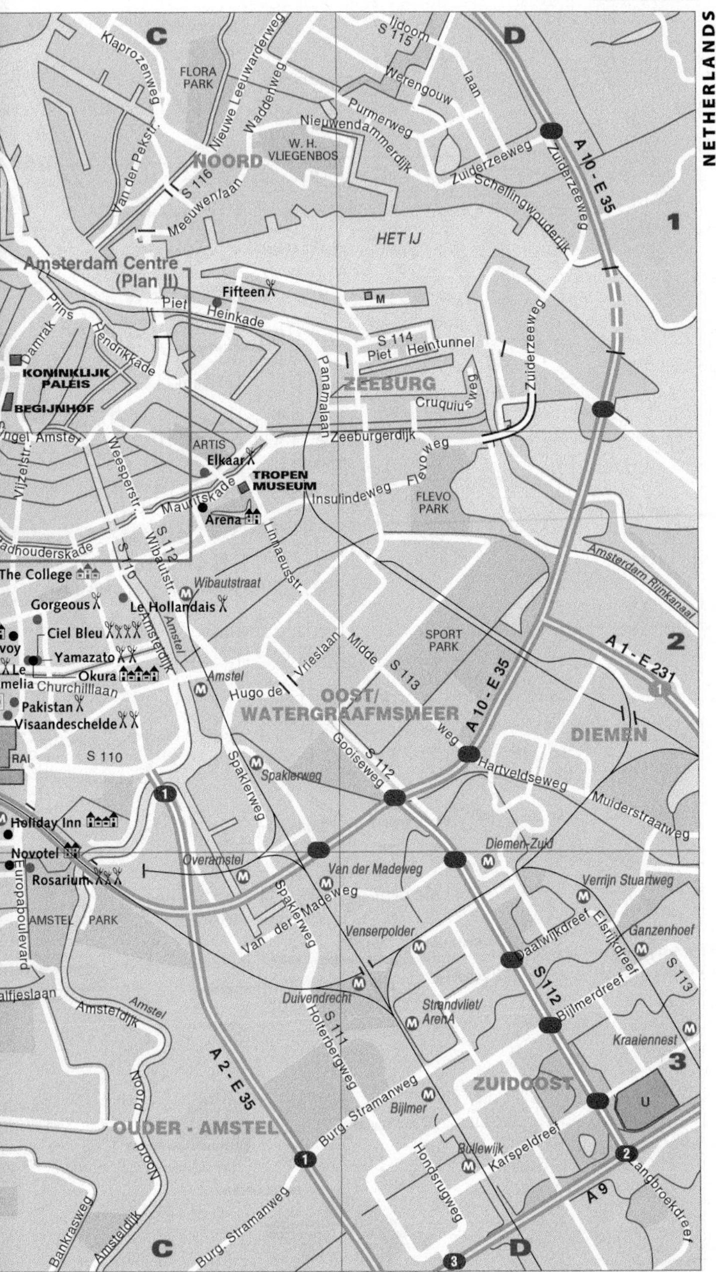
Amsterdam Centre (Plan II)
NOORD
HET IJ
ZEEBURG
OOST/WATERGRAAFSMEER
DIEMEN
ZUIDOOST
OUDER - AMSTEL
FLORA PARK
W. H. VLIEGENBOS
ARTIS
FLEVO PARK
SPORT PARK
AMSTEL PARK
KONINKLIJK PALEIS
BEGIJNHOF
TROPEN MUSEUM
Fifteen
Elkaar
Arena
The College
Gorgeous
Le Hollandais
Ciel Bleu
Yamazato
Okura
Pakistan
Visaandeschelde
Holiday Inn
Novotel
Rosarium
A 10 - E 35
A 1 - E 231
A 2 - E 35
A 9
Amsterdam Rijnkanaal
Wibautstraat
Spaklerweg
Overamstel
Van der Madeweg
Venserpolder
Duivendrecht
Strandvliet/ ArenA
Bijlmer
Bullewijk
Diemen-Zuid
Verrijn Stuartweg
Ganzenhoef
Kraaiennest
Klaprozenweg
Nieuwe Leeuwarderweg
Waddenweg
Nieuwendammerdijk
Purmerweg
Werengouw
IJdoorn
Zuiderzeeweg
Schellingwouderdijk
Van der Pekstr.
Meeuwenlaan
Piet Heinkade
Piet Heintunnel
Prins Hendrikkade
Damrak
Panamalaan
Cruquiusweg
Zeeburgerdijk
Flevoweg
Insulindeweg
Mauritskade
Weesperstr.
Wibautstr.
Linnaeusstr.
Singel
Amstel
Vijzelstr.
Stadhouderskade
Amsteldijk
Churchilllaan
Hugo de Vrieslaan
Middelweg
Gooiseweg
Hartveldseweg
Muiderstraatweg
Europaboulevard
Kalfjeslaan
Holterbergweg
Burg. Stramanweg
Hondsrugweg
Karspeldreef
Bijlmerdreef
Daalwijkdreef
Elsrijkdreef
Langbroekdreef
Bankrasweg
Noord
S 110
S 111
S 112
S 113
S 114
S 115
S 116
C
D
1
2
3

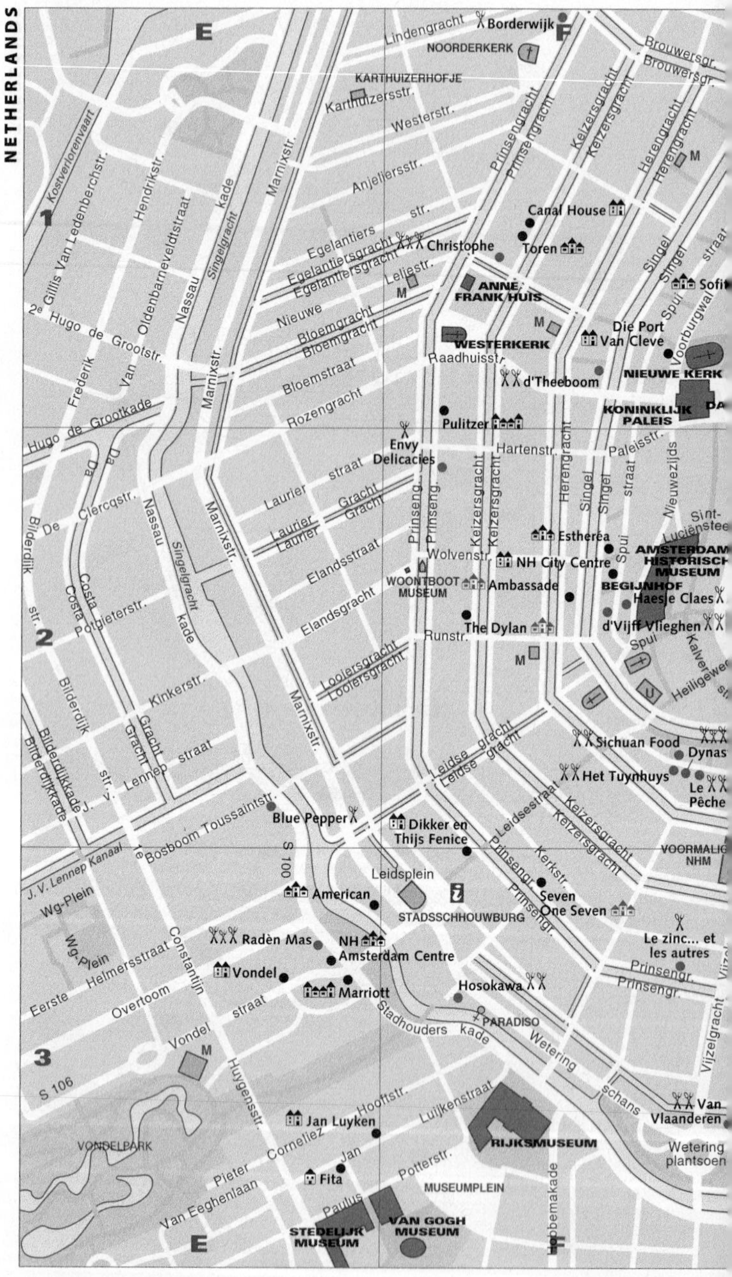

E
F
1
2
3
Borderwijk
NOORDERKERK
KARTHUIZERHOFJE
Canal House
Toren
Christophe
ANNE FRANK HUIS
WESTERKERK
Die Port Van Cleve
NIEUWE KERK
KONINKLIJK PALEIS
d'Theeboom
Pulitzer
Envy Delicacies
Estheréa
NH City Centre
AMSTERDAM HISTORISCH MUSEUM
WOONTBOOT MUSEUM
Ambassade
BEGIJNHOF
Haesje Claes
The Dylan
d'Vijff Vlieghen
Sichuan Food
Het Tuynhuys
Blue Pepper
Dikker en Thijs Fenice
Leidsplein
American
STADSSCHHOUWBURG
Seven One Seven
Le zinc... et les autres
Radèn Mas
NH Amsterdam Centre
Vondel
Marriott
Hosokawa
PARADISO
Van Vlaanderen
Jan Luyken
VONDELPARK
RIJKSMUSEUM
Fita
MUSEUMPLEIN
STEDELIJK MUSEUM
VAN GOGH MUSEUM
Wetering plantsoen
VOORMALIG NHM

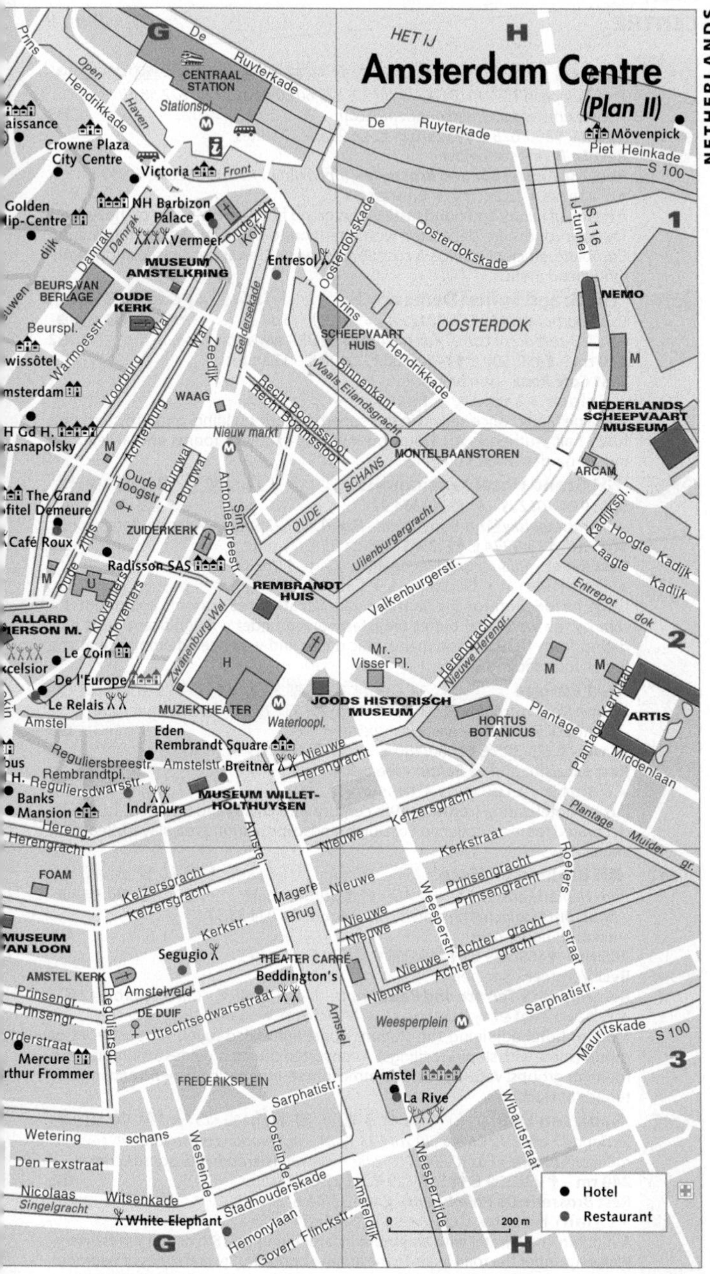

Amsterdam Centre
(Plan II)
HET IJ
CENTRAAL STATION
De Ruyterkade
Mövenpick
Piet Heinkade
Oosterdokskade
OOSTERDOK
NEMO
NEDERLANDS SCHEEPVAART MUSEUM
SCHEEPVAART HUIS
Prins Hendrikkade
MONTELBAANSTOREN
ARCAM
Crowne Plaza City Centre
Victoria
NH Barbizon Palace
Vermeer
Entresol
MUSEUM AMSTELKRING
BEURS VAN BERLAGE
OUDE KERK
Damrak
WAAG
Nieuw markt
Zeedijk
OUDE SCHANS
Uilenburgergracht
Valkenburgerstr.
ZUIDERKERK
The Grand
Café Roux
Radisson SAS
REMBRANDT HUIS
ALLARD PIERSON M.
Le Coin
De l'Europe
Le Relais
MUZIEKTHEATER
Waterloopl.
JOODS HISTORISCH MUSEUM
Mr. Visser Pl.
HORTUS BOTANICUS
ARTIS
Plantage Kerklaan
Plantage Middenlaan
Eden Rembrandt Square
Breitner
Indrapura
MUSEUM WILLET-HOLTHUYSEN
Rembrandtpl.
Reguliersbreestr.
Amstelstr.
Amstel
Herengracht
Keizersgracht
Prinsengracht
Magere Brug
THEATER CARRÉ
Beddington's
Segugio
AMSTEL KERK
Amstelveld
DE DUIF
Utrechtsedwarsstraat
FOAM
MUSEUM VAN LOON
Mercure
FREDERIKSPLEIN
Sarphatistr.
Weesperplein
Weesperstr.
Roeterstraat
Mauritskade
Amstel
La Rive
Wibautstraat
Weesperzijde
Stadhouderskade
White Elephant
Wetering schans
Den Texstraat
Westeinde
Oosteinde
Hemonylaan
Govert Flinckstr.
Amsteldijk
Singelgracht
Hotel
Restaurant
0
200 m
G
H
1
2
3

NETHERLANDS

CENTRE Plan II

Amstel 180 VISA

Prof. Tulpplein 1 ✉ 1018 GX – ✆ (0 20) 622 60 60 – Fax (0 20) 622 58 08 – www.amsterdam.intercontinental.com **H3**

62 rm – 390/625 € 325/625 €, 25 € – 17 suites

Rest *La Rive* – see below

Rest *The Amstel Bar and Brasserie* – *(open until 11.30 p.m.)* Carte 50/59 €

♦ Palace ♦ Luxury ♦ Classic ♦

A haven of luxury and good taste in this grand hotel on the banks of the Amstel. The vast rooms are decorated with attention to detail and stylish furnishings. Complete, efficient service. A cosy library-bar, with an appetising cosmopolitan-influenced menu.

The Grand Sofitel Demeure 300

O.Z. Voorburgwal 197 ✉ 1012 EX – ✆ (0 20) 555 31 11 – h2783-re@accor.com – Fax (0 20) 555 32 22 – www.thegrand.nl VISA **G2**

170 rm – 450/500 € 450/500 €, 28 € – 12 suites

Rest *Café Roux* – see below

♦ Palace ♦ Luxury ♦ Historic ♦

Maria de Medici once stayed in this superb historic building, once Amsterdam's town hall. Authentic Art Nouveau lounges, exquisite rooms and a beautiful indoor garden await you.

NH Grand Hotel Krasnapolsky 750

Dam 9 ✉ 1012 JS – ✆ (0 20) 554 91 11 – nhkrasnapolsky@nh-hotels.com – Fax (0 20) 622 86 07 – www.nh-hotels.com VISA **G2**

467 rm – 139/274 € 139/374 €, 25 € – 1 suite

Rest *Reflet* – *(dinner only)* Menu 38 € – Carte 43/58 €

♦ Traditional ♦ Business ♦ Classic ♦

Large, historic hotel on the Dam with various categories of rooms, apartments for rent by the week and buffet breakfast served under a magnificent glass roof dating from 1879. Classic menu, chic décor and well-heeled ambiance at the Reflet, founded in 1883.

De l'Europe 150 VISA

Nieuwe Doelenstraat 2 ✉ 1012 CP – ✆ (0 20) 531 17 77 – hotel@leurope.nl – Fax (0 20) 531 17 78 – www.leurope.nl **G2**

95 rm – 325/395 € 400/480 €, 25 € – 5 suites

Rest *Excelsior* and ***Le Relais*** – see below

♦ Palace ♦ Luxury ♦ Classic ♦

Luxury hotel dating from late 19th century with charm and tradition. Tastefully decorated rooms. A collection of Dutch landscape paintings displayed. Beautiful water views.

NH Barbizon Palace 300

Prins Hendrikkade 59 ✉ 1012 AD – ✆ (0 20) 556 45 64 – nhbarbizonpalace@nh-hotels.com – Fax (0 20) 624 33 53 – www.nh-hotels.com VISA **G1**

266 rm – 169/289 € 169/289 €, 24 € – 3 suites

Rest *Vermeer* – see below

Rest *Hudson's Terrace and Restaurant* – Menu 38/45 € – Carte approx. 42 €

♦ Chain hotel ♦ Business ♦ Modern ♦

Modern hotel adjoining the station. Huge, light-filled foyer, various types of rooms (some with sloping ceilings). A converted church provides a multipurpose room for groups. Vaguely nautical atmosphere, international menu and interior terrace at Hudson's.

Radisson SAS 180 VISA

Rusland 17 ✉ 1012 CK – ✆ (0 20) 623 12 31 – reservations.amsterdam@radissonsas.com – Fax (0 20) 520 82 00 – www.amsterdam.radissonsas.com **G2**

240 rm – 169/329 € 169/329 €, 22 € – 2 suites

Rest *Brasserie De Palmboom* – Carte 33/44 €

♦ Chain hotel ♦ Business ♦ Stylish ♦

A modern chain hotel with an atrium incorporating an 18th century presbytery. Walkway under the road leads to the annexe opposite. Several styles of bedroom available. International menu offered in two Scandinavian-inspired dining rooms.

NETHERLANDS

Marriott

Stadhouderskade 12 ⊠ 1054 ES – ✆ (0 20) 607 55 55 – amsterdam@marriott.com – Fax (0 20) 607 55 11 – www.amsterdammarriott.com **E3**

387 rm – 169/345 € 169/345 €, 25 € – 5 suites

Rest – *(closed Sunday and Monday) (dinner only until 11 p.m.)* Carte 36/77 €

♦ Chain hotel ♦ Business ♦ Cosy ♦

A high-class, American-style hotel on a major thoroughfare. The rooms are vast and well-equipped. A good seminar infrastructure and business centre. International menu served in the restaurant; grilled meats, salads and pizza in the brasserie.

Pulitzer

Prinsengracht 323 ⊠ 1016 GZ – ✆ (0 20) 523 52 35 – sales.amsterdam@starwoodhotels.com – Fax (0 20) 627 67 53 – www.luxurycollection.com/pulitzer **F1**

227 rm – 245/450 € 270/475 €, 25 € – 3 suites

Rest *Pulitzers* – Carte 44/61 €

♦ Chain hotel ♦ Luxury ♦ Historic ♦

25 admirably-restored 17th and 18th century houses, around a well-tended garden. Public areas filled with works of art; refined, individualized bedrooms. Modern restaurant with novel décor (amusing reference to the painter, Frans Hals). Intimate bar.

Renaissance

Kattengat 1 ⊠ 1012 SZ – ✆ (0 20) 621 22 23 – renaissance.amsterdam@renaissancehotels.com – Fax (0 20) 627 52 45 – www.renaissancehotels.com/amsrd **G1**

399 rm – 159/400 € 189/400 €, 25 € – 6 suites

Rest – *(closed Saturday and Sunday) (open until 11.30 p.m.)* Carte 28/44 €

♦ Traditional ♦ Business ♦ Classic ♦

Rooms, suites and junior suites with modern comfort and numerous services on offer. Excellent conference facilities beneath the dome of an old Lutheran church dating from 1671. Bar with an international menu; simplified dining in the "brown café".

Crowne Plaza City Centre

N.Z. Voorburgwal 5 ⊠ 1012 RC – ✆ (0 20) 620 05 00 – amsnl.reservations@ichotelsgroup.com – Fax (0 20) 620 11 73 – www.amsterdam-citycentre.crowneplaza.com **G1**

268 rm – 159/289 € 159/289 €, 22 € – 2 suites

Rest *Dorrius* – *(closed Sunday) (dinner only until 11 p.m.)* Menu 30/45 € – Carte 30/45 €

♦ Chain hotel ♦ Business ♦ Classic ♦

Chain hotel near the station. Functional bedrooms. Town roofscape view from the top-floor "lounge club". A restaurant featuring reconstructed 19th century décor. Classic menu accompanied by local dishes.

American

Leidsekade 97 ⊠ 1017 PN – ✆ (0 20) 556 30 00 – info@amsterdamamerican.com – Fax (0 20) 556 30 01 – www.amsterdamamerican.com **E3**

173 rm – 310 € 350 €, 21 € – 1 suite

Rest *Café Americain* – Carte 33/46 €

♦ Palace ♦ Business ♦ Art Deco ♦

Near a lively square, this hotel with its imposing historic façade is a local institution. Bedrooms are gradually being updated. Bar popular with artists and people watchers. Elegant vaulted Art Deco café. International menu; high tea served in the afternoon.

NETHERLANDS

The Dylan rm 70 VISA
Keizersgracht 384 ✉ 1016 GB – ✆ (0 20) 530 20 10 – hotel@dylanamsterdam.com – Fax (0 20) 530 20 30 – www.dylanamsterdam.com **F2**
38 rm – 260 € 420 €, 24 € – 3 suites
Rest – *(closed Saturday lunch and Sunday)* Menu 48 € (weekday lunch), 65/90 € – Carte 55/78 €
♦ Grand Luxury ♦ Design ♦
Order and beauty; luxury, peace and exquisite delight. Discover the harmony of this residence with a surprising oriental-style designer decor. Rooms with personal touches. Modern cuisine served within the old brick walls of a modernised former bakery.

Ambassade without rest VISA
Herengracht 341 ✉ 1016 AZ – ✆ (0 20) 555 02 22 – info@ambassade-hotel.nl – Fax (0 20) 555 02 77 – www.ambassade-hotel.nl **F2**
51 rm – 185 € 185/225 €, 16 € – 8 suites
♦ Family ♦ Luxury ♦ Stylish ♦
Beautiful and stylishly personalised rooms and suites spread over ten 17th century houses next to the canal. Modern art and interesting library. Float and massage centre.

Sofitel rm 55 VISA
N.Z. Voorburgwal 67 ✉ 1012 RE – ✆ (0 20) 627 59 00 – h1159@accor.com – Fax (0 20) 623 89 32 – www.sofitel.com **F1**
148 rm – 245/305 € 245/695 €, 22 €
Rest – Carte 32/50 €
♦ Chain hotel ♦ Traditional ♦ Classic ♦
Chain hotel near a main road, made up of three 17th to 19th century houses. Various types of bedrooms, including about ten modern junior suites. Orient-Express atmosphere and brasserie-style cuisine in the restaurant.

Seven One Seven without rest VISA
Prinsengracht 717 ✉ 1017 JW – ✆ (0 20) 427 07 17 – info@717hotel.nl – Fax (0 20) 423 07 17 – www.717hotel.nl **F3**
8 rm – 435 € 460/660 €
♦ Grand Luxury ♦ Traditional ♦ Classic ♦
Small, attractive 18th century house converted into an intimate and select place to stay. The guestrooms are veritable gems. Romantic lounges; leafy courtyard where breakfast is served in summer.

Victoria rm 150 VISA
Damrak 1 ✉ 1012 LG – ✆ (0 20) 623 42 55 – vhares@pphe.com – Fax (0 20) 625 29 97 – www.parkplaza.com **G1**
296 rm – 315 € 330 €, 20 € – 10 suites
Rest – *(open until 11 p.m.)* Carte 23/33 €
♦ Traditional ♦ Chain hotel ♦ Classic ♦
Classical luxury hotel (19th century) and its extension dating from the 1890s located close to the station. Domed vestibule with modern stained glass. Rooms gradually being reburbished. Tavern-restaurant with traditional menu.

Eden Rembrandt Square VISA
Amstelstraat 17 ✉ 1017 DA – ✆ (0 20) 890 47 47 – res.rembrandtsquare@edenhotelgroup.com – Fax (0 20) 890 47 40 – www.edenhotelgroup.com **G2**
165 rm – 175/265 € 195/305 €, 10 € – 1 suite
Rest *Flo* – *(closed Saturday lunch and Sunday lunch) (open until 11 p.m.)* Menu 23/28 € – Carte 30/62 €
♦ Chain hotel ♦ Functional ♦
Old hotel building with modernised interior, set on a lively square. High-tech bedrooms with contemporary minimalist décor. Classic-traditional cooking served in the atmosphere of a Parisian-style brasserie.

Banks Mansion without rest

Herengracht 519 ✉ 1017 BV – ✆ (0 20) 420 00 55 – desk@banksmansion.nl – Fax (0 20) 420 09 93 – www.banksmansion.nl **G2**

51 rm – ♦270/290 € ♦♦300/595 €

♦ Chain hotel ♦ Business ♦ Modern ♦

Building dating from 1923 whose interior combines the styles of Dutch architect Hendrik Petrus Berlage and American architect Frank Lloyd Wright. Modern rooms with retro touches. Attractive, intimate lounge.

Mövenpick rm 300 VISA

Piet Heinkade 11 ✉ 1019 BR – ✆ (0 20) 519 12 00 – hotel.amsterdam@moevenpick.com – Fax (0 20) 519 12 39 – www.moevenpick-amsterdam.com

407 rm – ♦150/325 € ♦♦150/325 €, ☕ 21 € – 1 suite **H1**

Rest – Carte 23/46 €

♦ Chain hotel ♦ Business ♦ Modern ♦

Modern chain hotel inaugurated in 2006 in a modern district. The rooms have panoramic views. Concert hall, jazz club and congress centre next door. Restaurant serving Asian cuisine: Chinese, Thai and Indonesian.

Estheréa without rest 36 VISA

Singel 305 ✉ 1012 WJ – ✆ (0 20) 624 51 46 – info@estherea.nl – Fax (0 20) 623 90 01 – www.estherea.nl **F2**

71 rm – ♦171/236 € ♦♦182/299 €, ☕ 14 €

♦ Family ♦ Traditional ♦ Personalised ♦

The same family have run this hotel since 1942 set in a row of old merchants' houses with refined, neoclassical communal areas, personalised rooms and characterful breakfast room.

Swissôtel rm VISA

Damrak 96 ✉ 1012 LP – ✆ (0 20) 522 30 00 – ask-us.amsterdam@swissotel.com – Fax (0 20) 522 32 23 – www.swissotel-amsterdam.com **G1**

109 rm – ♦350/490 € ♦♦350/520 €, ☕ 18 € – 5 suites

Rest – Carte 23/44 €

♦ Chain hotel ♦ Business ♦ Functional ♦

Renovated chain hotel in a centrally-located traditional-looking building. Modern public areas, functional bedrooms and good reception. Contemporary brasserie-restaurant. International menu.

Toren without rest VISA

Keizersgracht 164 ✉ 1015 CZ – ✆ (0 20) 622 60 33 – info@hoteltoren.nl – Fax (0 20) 626 97 05 – www.hoteltoren.nl **F1**

39 rm – ♦105/235 € ♦♦125/245 €, ☕ 12 € – 1 suite

♦ Traditional ♦ Classic ♦

Anne Frank's House is just 200 m away from this charming family hotel with spruce rooms in a classic style. Elegant breakfast room in front of an attractive bar.

NH Amsterdam Centre 200

Stadhouderskade 7 ✉ 1054 ES – ✆ (0 20) 685 13 51 – nhamsterdamcentre@nh-hotels.com – Fax (0 20) 685 16 11 – www.nh-hotels.com **E3**

228 rm – ♦100 € ♦♦100 €, ☕ 24 € – 2 suites

Rest *Bice* – *(closed Sunday) (dinner only)* Carte approx. 45 €

♦ Chain hotel ♦ Business ♦ Modern ♦

Renovated chain hotel built to host athletes attending the Amsterdam Olympic Games in 1928. Designer public areas. Large modern bedrooms. Italian menu, contemporary setting and view over the Leidseplein at the Bice restaurant.

Amsterdam VISA

Damrak 93 ✉ 1012 LP – ✆ (0 20) 555 06 66 – info@hotelamsterdam.nl – Fax (0 20) 620 47 16 – www.hotelamsterdam.nl **G1**

79 rm – ♦110/239 € ♦♦130/349 €, ☕ 12 €

Rest *De Roode Leeuw* – Menu 33 € – Carte 34/44 €

♦ Traditional ♦ Classic ♦

This traditional Amsterdam hotel is on a very central section of the busy Damstraat. Very comfortable rooms. Public car parks nearby. A brasserie offering traditional Dutch dishes in a modernised setting with red decor.

Die Port van Cleve rest 30

N.Z. Voorburgwal 178 ✉ 1012 SJ – ☎ (0 20) 624 48 60 – sales-marketing@dieportvancleve.com – Fax (0 20) 421 03 10 – www.dieportvancleve.com

119 rm – 210/295 € 235/350 €, 18 € – 1 suite **F1**

Rest – Carte 26/50 €

◆ Traditional ◆ Functional ◆

The first Dutch brewers started work in the 19th century behind the flamboyant façade of this building (1864). Tidy rooms. Dutch gin bar decorated with Delft china and panelling. Restaurant-grill with a tally of the number of steaks served since 1870.

Dikker en Thijs Fenice without rest

Prinsengracht 444 ✉ 1017 KE – ☎ (0 20) 620 12 12 – info@dtfh.nl – Fax (0 20) 625 89 86 – www.dtfh.nl **F2**

42 rm – 125/245 € 150/345 €

◆ Traditional ◆ Business ◆ Classic ◆

A building dating from 1921 on the corner of a shopping street, opposite the Princes Canal, where an assistant of Escoffier once owned a food shop. Large guestrooms, studio and penthouse.

Canal House without rest

Keizersgracht 148 ✉ 1015 CX – ☎ (0 20) 622 51 82 – info@canalhouse.nl – Fax (0 20) 624 13 17 – www.canalhouse.nl **F1**

26 rm – 120/190 € 140/190 €

◆ Traditional ◆ Classic ◆

A 17th century building that has retained all its character. The personalised guestrooms look out over the canal or garden. Period decoration and furniture of varying styles.

Golden Tulip-Centre without rest

Nieuwezijdskolk 19 ✉ 1012 PV – ☎ (020) 530 18 18 – infoamsterdam@goldentuliphotelinntel.com – Fax (020) 422 19 19 – www.goldentulipamsterdamcentre.com **G1**

239 rm – 119/350 € 119/350 €, 18 €

◆ Chain hotel ◆ Modern ◆

A modern glass-fronted establishment in the heart of the busy Nieuwe Zijde, the shopping area next to the station. Well sound-proofed rooms. Breakfast area entirely surrounded by glass.

NH City Centre

Spuistraat 288 ✉ 1012 VX – ☎ (0 20) 420 45 45 – nhcitycentre@nh.hotels.com – Fax (0 20) 420 43 00 – www.nh-hotels.com **F2**

209 rm – 89/219 € 89/219 €, 16 €

Rest – Carte 23/39 €

◆ Chain hotel ◆ Business ◆ Functional ◆

Slotted between the Singel canal and the Béguine convent, this hotel has neutral, contemporary-style bedrooms typical of the NH chain. Spacious and comfortable lounge. An informal restaurant-inn serving a small Italian-influenced menu.

Mercure Arthur Frommer without rest

Noorderstraat 46 ✉ 1017 TV – ☎ (0 20) 622 03 28 – h1032@accor.com – Fax (0 20) 620 32 08 – www.accorhotels.com **G3**

90 rm – 105/160 € 125/180 €, 15 €

◆ Traditional ◆ Classic ◆

A group of houses (including a former wool factory) in a quiet residential street, close to the Rijksmuseum. Public areas and bedrooms with Dutch decorative touches.

Le Coin without rest

Nieuwe Doelenstraat 5 ✉ 1012 CP – ☎ (0 20) 524 68 00 – lecoin@holding.uva.nl – Fax (0 20) 524 68 01 – www.lecoin.nl **G2**

42 rm – 110 € 130/145 €, 10 €

◆ Traditional ◆ Functional ◆

Seven houses next to the University of Amsterdam make up this hotel. Rooms of various shapes and sizes, but all decorated in a contemporary style and equipped with a kitchenette.

Albus Grand Hotel

Vijzelstraat 49 ✉ 1017 HE – ✆ (0 20) 530 62 00 – info@albusgrandhotel.com – Fax (0 20) 530 62 99 – www.albusgrandhotel.com **G2**

74 rm – 🚹180/220 € 🚹🚹180/240 €, ☕ 14 €

Rest – *(open until 11 p.m.)* Carte 16/42 €

◆ Business ◆ Functional ◆

This modern hotel located near the tram network fits in well with the style of the local urban area. Modern décor in communal areas. Rooms are gradually being renovated – those at the back are quieter. Chic bistro playing "lounge" music. International menu.

Vondel without rest

Vondelstraat 26 ✉ 1054 GE – ✆ (0 20) 612 01 20 – info@hotelvondel.com – Fax (0 20) 685 43 21 – www.hotelvondel.com **E3**

78 rm – 🚹90/320 € 🚹🚹99/499 €, ☕ 19 €

◆ Luxury ◆ Business ◆ Cosy ◆

Hotel occupying several late-19th century houses. Trendy communal areas in Italian designer style, works of modern art, contemporary bedrooms and ornamental garden.

Jan Luyken without rest

Jan Luykenstraat 58 ✉ 1071 CS – ✆ (0 20) 573 07 30 – jan-luyken@bilderberg.nl – Fax (0 20) 676 38 41 – www.janluyken.nl **E3**

62 rm – 🚹119/199 € 🚹🚹169/294 €, ☕ 18 €

◆ Family ◆ Business ◆ Classic ◆

Three 1900s houses make up this hotel with contemporary interior décor. Modern bedrooms, designer bar with a few period touches and small courtyard terrace.

Fita without rest

Jan Luykenstraat 37 ✉ 1071 CL – ✆ (0 20) 679 09 76 – info@fita.nl – Fax (0 20) 664 39 69 – www.hotelfita.com

closed 14-31 December and 1-15 January **E3**

16 rm ☕ – 🚹90/135 € 🚹🚹125/150 €

◆ Family ◆ Classic ◆

This typical family-run hotel has functional rooms in three different sizes with the added advantage of being near Amsterdam's most prestigious museums. Friendly welcome.

La Rive – Hotel Amstel

8/16

Prof. Tulpplein 1 ✉ 1018 GX – ✆ (0 20) 520 32 64 – evert.groot@ichotelsgroup.com – Fax (0 20) 520 32 66 – www.restaurantlarive.com

closed 30 July-20 August, 1-11 January, Saturday lunch and Sunday **H3**

Rest – Menu 48 € (weekday lunch), 85/189 € bi – Carte 78/110 €

Spec. Terrine van ham en ganzenlever, ossenstaartgelei met sichuanpeper. Cannelloni van pepers en wortelen met kreeft en thijmbouilon. Kaneelbladerdeeg met gebakken appel, vanilleparfait en karamelsaus met gezouten boter.

◆ Contemporary ◆ Formal ◆

A fine atmosphere with refined décor, a prestigious wine collection and high level of comfort characterize this gastronomic restaurant on the Amstel. Views of the river from the dining area at the front.

Excelsior – Hotel De l'Europe

4/80

Nieuwe Doelenstraat 2 ✉ 1012 CP – ✆ (0 20) 531 17 05 – hotel@leurope.nl – Fax (0 20) 531 17 78

closed 1-13 January, Saturday lunch and Sunday lunch **G2**

Rest – Menu 45 € (weekday lunch), 65/90 € – Carte 55/75 €

◆ Contemporary ◆ Formal ◆

Elegant restaurant serving modern cuisine in a one-hundred-year-old luxury hotel. Enjoy views of the Munttoren and busy boats on the Amstel from the attractive terrace. Knowledgeable sommelier.

XXXX ✿

Vermeer – Hotel NH Barbizon Palace

Prins Hendrikkade 59 ✉ 1012 AD – ✆ (0 20) 556 48 85 – vermeer@nh-hotels.com – Fax (0 20) 624 33 53 – www.restaurantvermeer.nl

closed 9 July-12 August, 24 December-7 January, Saturday lunch and Sunday

Rest – Menu 40 € (weekday lunch), 65/155 € bi – Carte approx. 80 € **G1**

Spec. Gepocheerde kreeft met amandelsoep (April-July). Groentencasserole en bouillon van kropsla en venkel. Mokkasoufflé, citroengras en karamel.

♦ Innovative ♦ Minimalist ♦

A large restaurant belonging to a luxurious hotel with a warm reception, good service and serving individualised cuisine in a refined classic atmosphere.

XXX

Christophe

Leliegracht 46 ✉ 1015 DH – ✆ (0 20) 625 08 07 – info@christophe.nl – Fax (0 20) 638 91 32 – www.christophe.nl

closed Sunday and Monday **F1**

Rest – *(dinner only)* Menu 45/65 € – Carte 51/87 €

♦ French traditional ♦ Trendy ♦

This low-key, refined restaurant in a traditional building on the banks of the canal Lys serves good classic to modern cuisine. Summer dining is better at the front dining area.

XXX

Dynasty

Reguliersdwarsstraat 30 ✉ 1017 BM – ✆ (0 20) 626 84 00 – Fax (0 20) 622 30 38

closed 27 December-30 January and Tuesday **F2**

Rest – *(dinner only)* Menu 36/58 € – Carte 32/61 €

♦ Chinese ♦ Exotic ♦

Stroll through the lively street before having a meal in this pleasant long-standing oriental restaurant. Walls decorated with photos of fruit taken by Hageman, a local food photographer.

XXX

Radèn Mas

Stadhouderskade 6 ✉ 1054 ES – ✆ (0 20) 685 40 41 – Fax (0 20) 685 39 81

closed 24 and 31 December **E3**

Rest – *(dinner only until 11 p.m.)* Menu 40/45 € – Carte 35/63 €

♦ Indonesian ♦ Exotic ♦

This Indonesian restaurant has worthily preserved the culinary heritage of the former Dutch colony. Several "rijsttafel" (rice table) set menus. Slightly fancy, upmarket setting.

XX

Café Roux – Hotel The Grand Sofitel Demeure

O.Z. Voorburgwal 197 ✉ 1012 EX – ✆ (0 20) 555 35 60 – h2783-fb@accor.com – Fax (0 20) 555 32 90 – www.thegrand.nl **G2**

Rest – Menu 33 € (weekday lunch)/39 € – Carte 39/55 €

♦ Contemporary ♦ Brasserie ♦

A painting by the Dutch artist Karen Appel adorns the vestibule of this beautiful Art Deco restaurant, part of a luxury hotel. Modern cuisine, good wine list and informed sommelier.

XX

d'Vijff Vlieghen

Spuistraat 294 (by Vlieghendesteeg 1) ✉ 1012 VX – ✆ (0 20) 530 40 60 – restaurant@d-vijffvlieghen.com – Fax (0 20) 623 64 04 – www.d-vijffvlieghen.nl

closed 24 December-2 January **F2**

Rest – *(dinner only)* Menu 33/51 € – Carte 38/54 €

♦ Dutch regional cuisine ♦ Rustic ♦

Modern cuisine prepared using typically Dutch produce and served in a restaurant taking up five 17th century townhouses. Maze of fully-renovated rustic dining rooms.

XX

Breitner

Amstel 212 ✉ 1017 AH – ✆ (0 20) 627 78 79 – info@restaurant-breitner.nl – Fax (0 20) 330 29 98 – www.restaurant-breitner.nl

closed last week July-first week August, last week December and Sunday

Rest – *(dinner only)* Menu 43/57 € – Carte 45/70 € **G2**

♦ Contemporary ♦ Cosy ♦

Creative and elaborate meals served in a modern setting, with views over the Amstel and drawbridges. Designer lighting and contemporary art in the dining room.

XX **Het Tuynhuys** ⊙45 VISA MC AE

Reguliersdwarsstraat 28 ✉ 1017 BM – ✆ (0 20) 627 66 03 – info@tuynhuys.nl – Fax (0 20) 423 59 97 – www.tuynhuys.nl
closed 31 December-2 January, Saturday lunch and Sunday lunch **F2**
Rest – Menu 30 € (weekday lunch), 33/53 € – Carte 44/67 €
♦ Contemporary ♦ Fashionable ♦
A Mediterranean-inspired menu in keeping with current taste is offered in this restaurant with a pleasant interior terrace. A contemporary dining room, decorated with azulejo tiles.

XX **Indrapura** AC ⊙30/86 VISA MC AE

Rembrandtplein 42 ✉ 1017 CV – ✆ (0 20) 623 73 29 – info@indrapura.nl – Fax (0 20) 624 90 78 – www.indrapura.nl
closed 31 December **G2**
Rest – *(dinner only)* Carte approx. 58 €
♦ Indonesian ♦ Exotic ♦
On a busy, crowded square. A good choice of reasonably-priced Indonesian dishes, including the famous "rijsttafel" (rice table). A mixed clientele, exotic atmosphere and weekend pianist.

XX **Van Vlaanderen** AC

Weteringschans 175 ✉ 1017 XD – ✆ (0 20) 622 82 92
closed first two weeks August, Sunday and Monday **F3**
Rest – *(dinner only) (booking essential)* Menu 43/50 € – Carte 53/64 €
♦ Contemporary ♦ Fashionable ♦
This restaurant stands out due to its bow windowed-frontage. Cordial reception, polished, neutral dining rooms on two levels, trendy atmosphere and copious modern cuisine. Reservations advised.

XX **Hosokawa** AC ⊙8/16 VISA MC AE

Max Euweplein 22 ✉ 1017 MB – ✆ (0 20) 638 80 86 – info@hosokawa.nl – Fax (0 20) 638 22 19 – www.hosokawa.nl
closed Sunday lunch **F3**
Rest – Menu 14 € (weekday lunch), 40/78 € – Carte 25/71 €
♦ Japanese ♦ Minimalist ♦
A sober, modern Japanese restaurant equipped with eight cooking tables, worth a detour to watch the entertaining show of food rotating past your eyes! At lunchtimes, only sushi is available.

XX **Le Pêcheur** VISA MC AE

Reguliersdwarsstraat 32 ✉ 1017 BM – ✆ (0 20) 624 31 21 – lepecheuramsterdam@hotmail.com – Fax (0 20) 624 31 21 – www.lepecheur.nl
closed Saturday lunch and Sunday **F2**
Rest – Menu 33 € (weekday lunch) – Carte 36/52 €
♦ Seafood ♦ Friendly ♦
Anchored in a small street of restaurants alongside the flower market, the Pêcheur serves classically-prepared fish and seafood dishes. Yellow-toned décor and hidden terrace.

XX **d' Theeboom** VISA MC AE

Singel 210 ✉ 1016 AB – ✆ (0 20) 623 84 20 – info@theeboom.com – Fax (0 20) 421 25 12 – www.theeboom.com
closed 24 December-5 January and Sunday **F1**
Rest – *(dinner only)* Menu 35/40 € – Carte approx. 45 €
♦ Contemporary ♦ Retro ♦
Former cheese warehouse from 1712 where updated traditional meals are served in a pleasant setting with yellow walls, panelling, modern china and huge chandeliers.

XX **Beddington's** VISA MC AE

Utrechtsedwarsstraat 141 ✉ 1017 WE – ✆ (0 20) 620 73 93 – Fax (0 20) 620 01 90
closed 16 July-7 August, 1-2 January, Sunday and Monday **G3**
Rest – *(dinner only)* Menu 45/52 €
♦ Contemporary ♦ Fashionable ♦
A British chef runs the open kitchen of this modern restaurant serving contemporary cuisine in her adopted home of Amsterdam. Black and white décor.

XX

Sichuan Food

AC ⌂10/25 VISA MC AE D

Reguliersdwarsstraat 35 ✉ 1017 BK – ☎ (0 20) 626 93 27 – Fax (0 20) 627 72 81
closed 31 December **F2**
Rest – *(dinner only)* Menu 31/43 € – Carte 36/55 €
♦ Chinese ♦ Exotic ♦
Small oriental restaurant with good local reputation situated in a lively area. Typical local Chinese restaurant décor. Peking Duck prepared and served in the dining room.

XX

Le Relais – Hotel de l'Europe

AC ⌂4/160 VISA MC AE D

Nieuwe Doelenstraat 2 ✉ 1012 CP – ☎ (0 20) 531 17 04 – hotel@leurope.nl – Fax (0 20) 531 17 78 – www.leurope.nl **G2**
Rest – *(open until 11 p.m.)* Menu 24 € (weekday lunch)/30 € – Carte approx. 37 €
♦ Brasserie ♦ Wine bar ♦
Small, stylish restaurant with bistro décor in a large hotel, with good service. Blackboard lunch menu, set menu and local specialities.

X

Bordewijk

AC VISA MC AE D

Noordermarkt 7 ✉ 1015 MV – ☎ (0 20) 624 38 99 – www.bordewijk.nl
closed mid July-mid August, 24 December-3 January and Monday **F1**
Rest – *(dinner only)* Menu 38/52 € – Carte 49/63 €
♦ Contemporary ♦ Minimalist ♦
Popular restaurant due to its modern menu with inventive touches and minimalist décor: bare floorboards, Formica tables and designer chairs. Noisy atmosphere when busy.

X

Entresol

AC VISA MC AE

Geldersekade 29 ✉ 1011 EJ – ☎ (0 20) 623 79 12 – entresol@chello.nl – www.entresol.nu
closed first 3 weeks August, Monday and Tuesday **G1**
Rest – *(dinner only)* Menu 34/44 € – Carte 40/48 €
♦ Contemporary ♦ Cosy ♦
Small modern restaurant in a narrow 17th century house. Intimate dining rooms on two levels, the one on the first floor features a Delft china fireplace.

X

Envy Delicacies

AC VISA MC AE

Prinsengracht 381 ✉ 1016 HL – ☎ (0 20) 344 64 07 – info@envy.nl – Fax (0 20) 344 64 05 – www.envy.nl **F2**
Rest – *(open until 11 p.m.)* Carte approx. 32 €
♦ Contemporary ♦ Minimalist ♦
Contemporary-style brasserie where guests eat on both sides of a long Wengé wood bar lit by modern globe-shaped lights or at one of the neighbouring tables. Open kitchen.

X

Segugio

AC ⌂7/10 VISA MC AE D

Utrechtsestraat 96 ✉ 1017 VS – ☎ (0 20) 330 15 03 – adriano@segugio.nl – Fax (0 20) 330 15 16 – www.segugio.nl
closed Sunday **G3**
Rest – *(dinner only until 11 p.m.)* Menu 38/53 € – Carte 47/64 €
♦ Italian ♦ Design ♦
This "ristorante" takes its name from a breed of gun dog, also used to search for truffles. Serves a good selection of regional wines.

X

Blue Pepper

⌂36 VISA MC AE D

Nassaukade 366h ✉ 1054 AB – ☎ (0 20) 489 70 39 – info@restaurantbluepepper.com – www.restaurantbluepepper.com **E2**
Rest – *(dinner only)* Menu 45/105 € bi – Carte approx. 47 €
♦ Indonesian ♦ Fashionable ♦
Soft lighting and a décor of blue monochrome and delicate floral touches make up the relaxing setting of the Blue Pepper. With fine Javanese meals served in attractive dishes.

Le zinc... et les autres

15/55 VISA AE

Prinsengracht 999 ✉ 1017 KM – ✆ (0 20) 622 90 44 – info@lezinc.nl – Fax (0 20) 639 02 70 – www.lezinc.nl
closed late July-beginning August, 27 December-1 January and Sunday
Rest – *(dinner only until 11 p.m.)* Menu 32/79 € bi – Carte 35/51 € **F3**

♦ Contemporary ♦ Rustic ♦

Former warehouse from the 17th century located off the tourist trail opposite the Prinsengracht. Superb zinc bar with rustic dining room above. Modern classic cuisine.

Haesje Claes

AC 15/100 VISA AE

Spuistraat 275 ✉ 1012 VR – ✆ (0 20) 624 99 98 – info@haesjeclaes.nl – Fax (0 20) 627 48 17 – www.haesjeclaes.nl
closed 30 April and 25, 26 and 31 December **F2**
Rest – Menu 20/29 € – Carte 25/42 €

♦ Dutch regional cuisine ♦ Rustic ♦

A popular restaurant reflecting the town's atmosphere. Simple and copious Dutch cuisine served in a cheerful setting. Historical museum nearby.

Fifteen

AC VISA AE

Jollemanhof 9 ✉ 1019 GW – ✆ (0 20) 509 50 11 – Fax (0 20) 509 50 19
closed 31 December-1 January *Plan I* **C1**
Rest – *(dinner only until 11 p.m.)* Menu 44 € – Carte 31/40 €

♦ Contemporary ♦ Fashionable ♦

Former warehouse where guests eat in the lively atmosphere of a large modern dining room partitioned by walls brightened with colourful graffiti. Mediterranean cuisine. Intimate lounge bar.

SOUTH and WEST QUARTERS *Plan I*

Okura

rm AC 1200 P VISA AE

Ferdinand Bolstraat 333 ✉ 1072 LH – ✆ (0 20) 678 71 11 – sales@okura.nl – Fax (0 20) 671 23 44 – www.okura.nl **C2**
300 rm – †260/350 € ††295/385 €, ☕ 28 € – 15 suites
Rest *Ciel Bleu* and ***Yamazato*** and ***Le Camelia*** – see below
Rest *Sazanka* – *(dinner only)* Menu 58/83 € – Carte 43/61 €

♦ Grand Luxury ♦ Business ♦ Modern ♦

Luxury Japanese-style hotel set in a modern tower block with 23 floors. Various types of rooms and suites, superb wellness centre and a full range of services offered. Large conference centre. Spectacular Japanese cuisine around cooking tables at the Sazanka.

Hilton

rm AC 550 P

Apollolaan 138 ✉ 1077 BG – ✆ (0 20) 710 60 00 – info.amsterdam@hilton.com – Fax (0 20) 710 60 80 – www.amsterdamhilton.com **B2**
267 rm – †205/430 € ††205/430 €, ☕ 25 € – 4 suites
Rest *Roberto's* – Carte 47/67 €

♦ Chain hotel ♦ Business ♦ Modern ♦

This modern and spacious hotel belonging to a chain has a terrace and garden with a water feature. Rooms and suites with superb views, one on a 1969 theme of 'John Lennon and Yoko Ono'. Italian menu served in a contemporary setting at Roberto's restaurant.

Le Meridien Apollo

AC 200 P VISA AE

Apollolaan 2 ✉ 1077 BA – ✆ (0 20) 673 59 22 – info.apollo@lemeridien.com – Fax (0 20) 570 57 44 – www.lemeridien.com **B2**
217 rm – †120/325 € ††120/325 €, ☕ 22 € – 2 suites
Rest *La Sirène* – see below

♦ Chain hotel ♦ Business ♦ Stylish ♦

An international chain hotel located at the intersection of five canals. Guestrooms designed with the business traveller in mind. Waterside bar, terrace and landing stage.

Bilderberg Garden

150

Dijsselhofplantsoen 7 ✉ 1077 BJ – ✆ (0 20) 570 56 00 – garden.reservations@bilderberg.nl – Fax (0 20) 570 56 54 – www.gardenhotel.nl **B2**

122 rm – †279/309 € ††279/309 €, ☕ 21 € – 2 suites

Rest ***De Kersentuin*** – see below

♦ Luxury ♦ Business ♦ Stylish ♦

Chain hotel offering accommodation in the business district to mainly corporate customers. Communal areas and guestrooms are gradually being updated.

Holiday Inn

rm 350

De Boelelaan 2 ✉ 1083 HJ – ✆ (0 20) 646 23 00 – vermont@diningcity.com – Fax (0 20) 517 27 64 – www.vermont.nl **C2**

256 rm – †135/295 € ††135/690 €, ☕ 20 € – 2 suites

Rest – *(open until 11 p.m.)* Menu 25 € (weekday lunch)/33 € – Carte 33/44 €

♦ Chain hotel ♦ Business ♦ Classic ♦

Chain hotel close to the RAI. Enjoy the discreet luxury and spaciousness of the communal areas and the comfortable guestrooms. Lounge-bar and restaurant in a modern setting evocative of New England. International and American cuisine.

Golden Tulip Art-Tulip Inn Art

120

Spaarndammerdijk 302 (Westerpark) ✉ 1013 ZX – ✆ (0 20) 410 96 70 – sales@westcordhotels.nl – Fax (0 20) 681 08 02 – www.westcordhotels.nl **B1**

187 rm – †89/205 € ††89/205 €, ☕ 15 € – 3 suites

Rest – Menu 20 € (weekday lunch), 25/33 € – Carte 31/52 €

♦ Chain hotel ♦ Business ♦ Stylish ♦

Near a slip road off the ring, a modern hotel with very contemporary guestrooms, available in two sizes. Exhibition of modern paintings in the public areas. Modern meals served in a trendy atmosphere; simpler set menu in the "eetcafé".

The College – Hotel school

60

Roelof Hartstraat 1 ✉ 1071 VE – ✆ (0 20) 571 15 11 – info@thecollegehotel.com – Fax (0 20) 571 15 13 – www.thecollegehotel.com **C2**

39 rm – †205 € ††235/285 €, ☕ 18 € – 1 suite

Rest – *(open until 11 p.m.)* Menu 26 € (weekday lunch), 39/51 €

♦ Grand Luxury ♦ Historic ♦ Design ♦

This hotel is located in a former 19th monastery, redecorated with refinement. Chic and fashionable lounge bar and rooms in the same style. Modern restaurant located in a former gym. Serves modern cuisine.

Tulip Inn City West

rm 70

Reimerswaalstraat 5 ✉ 1069 AE – ✆ (0 20) 410 80 00 – info@tiamsterdamcw.nl – Fax (0 20) 410 80 30 – www.tulipinnamsterdamwest.nl **A2**

162 rm – †65/170 € ††65/170 €, ☕ 14 €

Rest – *(dinner only except Friday, Saturday and Sunday) (open until 11 p.m.)* Menu 15 € (weekday lunch), 22/33 € – Carte approx. 30 €

♦ Chain hotel ♦ Business ♦ Classic ♦

In a quiet area, this chain hotel boasts large rooms and public areas. With nearby parking available. Traditional-classic menu presented on a blackboard in the restaurant.

Savoy without rest

Ferdinand Bolstraat 194 ✉ 1072 LW – ✆ (0 20) 644 74 45 – office@savoyamsterdam.nl – Fax (0 20) 644 89 89 – www.savoyamsterdam.nl **C2**

41 rm ☕ – †120/180 € ††130/190 €

♦ Traditional ♦ Business ♦ Functional ♦

The architectural style of this brick building dating from 1933 was inspired by the Amsterdam School. Functional comfort and sufficiently-large guestrooms. Bright public areas.

Novotel rm 210 VISA

Europaboulevard 10 ✉ 1083 AD – ☎ (0 20) 541 11 23 – h0515@accor.com – Fax (0 20) 646 28 23 – www.accorhotels.com

C3

611 rm – 165 € 185/399 €, 20 €

Rest – *(open until midnight)* Menu 20 € (weekday lunch) – Carte 19/42 €

♦ Chain hotel ♦ Business ♦ Functional ♦

Imposing hotel block, with one of the largest guest capacities in Benelux. Fully-renovated interior. Bright, modern and functional bedrooms. Functional tavern-restaurant serving traditional classic cuisine.

The Gresham Memphis without rest 40 VISA

De Lairessestraat 87 ✉ 1071 NX – ☎ (0 20) 673 31 41 – info@memphishotel.nl – Fax (0 20) 673 73 12 – www.memphishotel.nl

B2

74 rm – 170/245 € 205/345 €, 20 €

♦ Chain hotel ♦ Classic ♦

The tram line to the city centre runs in front of this ivy-covered hotel. Modern and intimate lounge bar with hushed atmosphere. Fresh bedrooms and pleasant breakfast area.

NH Museum Quarter without rest VISA

Hobbemakade 50 ✉ 1071 XL – ☎ (0 20) 573 82 00 – nhmuseumquarter@nh-hotels.com – Fax (0 20) 573 82 99 – www.nh-hotels.com

B-C2

163 rm – 135/250 € 135/250 €, 16 €

♦ Chain hotel ♦ Business ♦ Functional ♦

This chain hotel provides modern, standard guestrooms, the better ones located at the rear. Bright breakfast room facing the courtyard. Lounge-bar and modern dining room. Limited international menu.

Arena rest 120

's-Gravesandestraat 51 ✉ 1092 AA – ☎ (0 20) 850 24 00 – Fax (0 20) 850 24 15

C2

127 rm – 85/185 € 170/250 €, 13 €

Rest – *(open until 11 p.m.)* Menu 33/44 € – Carte 33/43 €

♦ Historic ♦ Retro ♦

Formerly an orphanage (1890), now an ultra-trendy hotel. Fantastic old staircase, designer bar and guestrooms of various styles and levels of comfort. Weekend nightclub (separate access). Designer setting and modern cuisine in the restaurant.

De Filosoof without rest 25 VISA

Anna van den Vondelstraat 6 ✉ 1054 GZ – ☎ (0 20) 683 30 13 – reservations@hotelfilosoof.nl – Fax (0 20) 685 37 50 – www.hotelfilosoof.nl

B2

38 rm – 95/135 € 105/265 €

♦ Family ♦ Personalised ♦

The originality of this hotel in a one-way street alongside the Vondelpark is in the decor of its rooms, based on cultural or philosophical themes. Garden.

Villa Borgmann without rest VISA

Koningslaan 48 ✉ 1075 AE – ☎ (0 20) 673 52 52 – info@hotel-borgmann.nl – Fax (0 20) 676 25 80 – www.hotel-borgmann.nl

B2

15 rm – 80/105 € 100/175 €

♦ Family ♦ Functional ♦

A Russian couple play host in this large red-brick 1900s villa in a quiet and safe diplomatic district near the Vondelpark. Easy car parking.

NETHERLANDS

XXXX ✿ **Ciel Bleu** – Hotel Okura (23rd floor) ≤ city, AC ⇔4/24 P VISA MC AE D
Ferdinand Bolstraat 333 ✉ 1072 LH – ✆ (0 20) 678 83 40 – restaurants@okura.nl – Fax (0 20) 678 77 88 – www.okura.nl
closed 3 weeks for building workers holidays and 1 week after Christmas
Rest – *(dinner only)* Menu 65/165 € bi – Carte 73/97 € C2
Spec. Tarbot met ganzenlever en truffel, kreeftbitterballetjes en parmezaanse kaas. Kalfsvlees met gerookte zwezerik, saus van cantharel. Parade van chocolade.
♦ Contemporary ♦ Formal ♦
At the top of a luxury international hotel, this restaurant with contemporary atmosphere has a wonderful view over the town. Creative cuisine that guests can watch on the video screens. Good wines.

XXX **Rosarium** ⇔4/250 P VISA MC AE D
Amstelpark 1 ✉ 1083 HZ – ✆ (0 20) 644 40 85 – info@rosarium.net – Fax (0 20) 646 60 04
closed Saturday lunch and Sunday C3
Rest – Menu 30 € (weekday lunch), 43/103 € bi – Carte approx. 48 €
♦ Contemporary ♦ Formal ♦
Modern restaurant on the edge of the Amstelpark, located in a modern circular building with two wings. Spacious and bright designer setting, wine bar and verdant terrace.

XX ✿ **Yamazato** – Hotel Okura AC ⇔4/40 P VISA MC AE D
Ferdinand Bolstraat 333 ✉ 1072 LH – ✆ (0 20) 678 83 51 – restaurants@okura.nl – Fax (0 20) 678 77 88 – www.okura.nl C2
Rest – Menu 49 € (weekday lunch), 65/90 € – Carte 38/105 €
Spec. Kani Salad (crab). Sushi Kaiseki (fish). Wagyu Rib Sumibi Yakz (beef).
♦ Japanese ♦ Minimalist ♦
A "zen" atmosphere and setting in this Japanese restaurant, where you can savour the whole range of traditional dishes. Friendly, kimono-clad waitresses; simplified menu at lunchtime.

XX **Visaandeschelde** AC (dinner) VISA MC AE D
Scheldeplein 4 ✉ 1078 GR – ✆ (0 20) 675 15 83 – info@visaandeschelde.nl – Fax (0 20) 471 46 53 – www.visaandeschelde.nl
closed 30 April, 24-26 and 31 December-1 January, Saturday lunch and Sunday lunch C2
Rest – *(open until 11 p.m.)* Menu 33 € (weekday lunch), 37/54 € – Carte 41/81 €
♦ Seafood ♦ Fashionable ♦
Opposite the RAI congress centre, this restaurant is popular with Amsterdammers for its dishes full of the flavours of the sea, contemporary brasserie décor and lively atmosphere.

XX **La Sirène** – Hotel Le Meridien Apollo ≤ AC ⇔10/50 P
Apollolaan 2 ✉ 1077 BA – ✆ (0 20) 570 57 24 – info.apollo@lemeridien.com – Fax (0 20) 570 57 44 – www.lemeridien.com B2
Rest – Menu 67 € (weekday lunch), 50/62 € bi – Carte 47/79 €
♦ Seafood ♦ Formal ♦
Cuisine which comes in with the tide, served either in the large, bright dining room with views over the point where five canals meet or on the panoramic waterside terrace.

XX **De Kersentuin** – Hotel Bilderberg Garden AC ⇔10/100 P VISA MC AE D
Dijsselhofplantsoen 7 ✉ 1077 BJ – ✆ (0 20) 570 56 00 – garden.reservation@bilderberg.nl – Fax (0 20) 570 56 54 – www.dekersentuin.nl
closed Saturday lunch and Sunday B2
Rest – Menu 25 € (weekday lunch), 40/48 € – Carte 43/61 €
♦ Contemporary ♦ Brasserie ♦
Modern meals served in a dining room of similar décor: unpolished floor, large bay windows, open kitchens and brown and orange tones. Sheltered pavement terrace.

Le Camelia – Hotel Okura AC 50/100 P VISA MC AE
Ferdinand Bolstraat 333 ✉ 1072 LH – ✆ (0 20) 678 74 50 – restaurant@okura.nl – Fax (0 20) 678 77 88 – www.okura.nl C2
Rest – *(open until 11 p.m.)* Menu 33 € – Carte 36/43 €
♦ Contemporary ♦ Brasserie ♦
Parisian-inspired brasserie on the ground floor of a prestigious Japanese hotel. Modern menu and interior décor with light Art Deco touches.

Le Garage AC 20/80 (dinner) VISA MC AE
Ruysdaelstraat 54 ✉ 1071 XE – ✆ (0 20) 679 71 76 – info@restaurantlegarage.nl – Fax (0 20) 662 22 49 – www.restaurantlegarage.nl
closed Easter, Whitsun, first 2 weeks August, 24-26 and 31 December-1 January, Saturday lunch and Sunday lunch B-C2
Rest – *(booking essential)* Menu 30 € (weekday lunch), 33/50 € – Carte 37/73 €
♦ Brasserie ♦ Trendy ♦
An artistic and cosmopolitan atmosphere in this modern brasserie in an unusual setting where as well as coming for the food, guests come to see and be seen.

Brasserie van Baerle 4/45 VISA MC AE
Van Baerlestraat 158 ✉ 1071 BG – ✆ (0 20) 679 15 32 – info@brasserievanbaerle.nl – Fax (0 20) 671 71 96 – www.brasserievanbaerle.nl
closed 25-26 and 31 December dinner-1 January B2
Rest – *(open until 11 p.m.)* Menu 33/39 € – Carte 42/60 €
♦ Contemporary ♦ Retro ♦
This retro brasserie attracts regular customers, predominantly from the local area because of its attractive menu, delicious steak tartare and well-matched wines. Courtyard terrace.

Le Hollandais AC 4/14 VISA MC AE
Amsteldijk 41 ✉ 1074 HV – ✆ (0 20) 679 12 48 – info@lehollandais.nl – www.lehollandais.nl
closed 3 weeks August and Sunday C2
Rest – *(dinner only)* Menu 32/45 € – Carte approx. 45 €
♦ French traditional ♦ Trendy ♦
Endearing little local eatery serving classic French cuisine in a pared-down setting. Bistro dining room with covered tables and 1970s-style chairs.

Gorgeous 25/42 VISA MC AE
2[de] v.d. Helststraat 16 ✉ 1072 PD – ✆ (0 20) 379 14 00 – info@gorgeousrestaurant.nl – www.gorgeousrestaurant.nl
closed 24 July-7 August, 24 December-8 January, Sunday and Monday
Rest – *(dinner only)* Menu 33/58 € – Carte 28/54 € C2
♦ Contemporary ♦ Bistro ♦
Located in a working class district, not far from the Sarphati Park, this bistro can be spotted by its ornate tiled façade. Modernised interior. Menu read aloud.

Pakistan VISA MC AE
Scheldestraat 100 ✉ 1078 GP – ✆ (0 20) 675 39 76 – Fax (0 20) 675 39 76 C2
Rest – *(dinner only until 11 p.m.)* Menu 20/45 € – Carte 26/45 €
♦ Indian ♦ Family ♦
An authentic Pakistani restaurant with exotic, generous menus, located not far from the RAI congress centre. Beef dishes instead of pork.

White Elephant 12/24 VISA MC AE
Van Woustraat 3 ✉ 1074 AA – ✆ (0 20) 679 55 56 – info@whiteelephant.nl – Fax (0 20) 679 55 58 – www.whiteelephant.nl G3
closed Monday
Rest – Menu 34/58 € – Carte 31/52 €
♦ Fashionable ♦ Thai ♦
Thai restaurant with typical décor: panelling, orchids and a traditional hut reconstructed in the dining room. Authentic cuisine and pleasant servers in traditional Thai dress.

Spring

4/14 VISA

Willemsparkweg 177 ✉ 1071 GZ – ✆ (0 20) 675 44 21
– info@restaurantspring.nl – Fax (0 20) 676 94 14
– www.restaurantspring.nl
closed 25-26 and 31 December-1 January, Saturday lunch and Sunday **B2**
Rest – Menu 30 € (weekday lunch), 35/64 € bi – Carte 45/58 €

◆ Contemporary ◆ Cosy ◆

Designer dining room decorated with paintings by Amsterdam artist Jeroen Krabbé. A long central bench seat divides the room in two. Lunchtime set menu; a la carte in the evening.

Brasserie Pays-Bas

20/40 VISA

Gustav Mahlerplein 14 ✉ 1082 MA – ✆ (0 20) 642 06 73
– info@brasseriepaysbas.nl – Fax (0 20) 642 22 27
– www.brasseriepaysbas.nl
closed 31 July-15 August, Saturday lunch and Sunday **B2**
Rest – Menu 35 € (weekday lunch) – Carte 36/55 €

◆ French traditional ◆ Design ◆

Recently-opened designer restaurant in a business district, where the corporate clientele from local offices flock at lunchtime. French classics and a la carte brasserie dishes.

Elkaar

10/15 VISA

Alexanderplein 6 ✉ 1018 CG – ✆ (0 20) 330 75 59 – Fax (0 20) 423 44 78
– www.etenbijelkaar.nl
closed 30 April, 31 December-1 January and Saturday lunch **C2**
Rest – Menu 33/38 € – Carte 35/46 €

◆ Contemporary ◆ Bistro ◆

Warm contemporary bistro set in a smart house situated between the zoo and the Tropenmuseum. Softly-lit dining room; pavement-terrace open on fine days.

AT SCHIPHOL AIRPORT *Plan I*

Sheraton Airport

rm 500 VISA

Schiphol bd 101 ✉ 1118 BG Schiphol
– ✆ (0 20) 316 43 00
– sales.amsterdam@starwoodhotels.com
– Fax (0 20) 316 43 00 – www.sheraton.com/amsterdamair
400 rm – †165/395 € ††190/420 €, ☕ 25 € – 6 suites
Rest *Voyager* – *(open until 11 p.m.)* Menu 40 € (weekday lunch) – Carte 43/82 €

◆ Chain hotel ◆ Business ◆ Modern ◆

Modern hotel complex near the airport, designed for a globe-trotting business clientèle. Guestrooms offer every comfort. Fine atrium. Full service. Modern brasserie with a star-decorated ceiling. International menu and buffets.

Dorint Sofitel Airport

rm 620 VISA

Stationsplein Zuid-West 951 (Schiphol-Oost)
✉ 1117 CE Schiphol – ✆ (0 20) 540 07 77
– H5332.FB1@accor.com
– Fax (0 20) 540 07 00 – www.dsaa.nl **A3**
429 rm – †99/229 € ††99/229 €, ☕ 22 € – 11 suites
Rest *Nadar* – *(closed Saturday lunch and Sunday lunch)* Menu 25 € (weekday lunch), 33/65 € bi – Carte 31/50 €

◆ Chain hotel ◆ Luxury ◆ Modern ◆

Between the airport and the woods of Amsterdam, this modern hotel-congress centre has several executive rooms and an English-style pub open all day long. This modern restaurant owes its name to an aerostat pilot. Large terrace.

Hilton Schiphol

Schiphol Bd 701 ✉ 1118 ZK Schiphol – ✆ (0 20) 710 40 00 – Fax (0 20) 710 40 80 – www.hilton.com

278 rm – †135/345 € ††150/360 €, ☕ 25 € – 2 suites

Rest ***East West*** – *(closed mid July-August and Friday, Saturday, Sunday) (dinner only)* Carte 40/71 €

◆ Chain hotel ◆ Business ◆ Functional ◆

A chain hotel, located near the airport and popular with business clientele. Modern, well-equipped guestrooms and meeting rooms. Meals combining Asian and Western flavours at the East West restaurant (Japanese cooking table during the week).

Radisson SAS Airport

Boeing Avenue 2 (South : 4 km by N 201 at Rijk) ✉ 1119 PB Schiphol – ✆ (0 20) 655 31 31 – reservations.amsterdam.airport@radissonsas.com – Fax (0 20) 655 31 00 – www.amsterdam.airport.radissonsas.com

277 rm – †95/299 € ††95/399 €, ☕ 19 € – 2 suites

Rest – Menu 26 € – Carte 30/48 €

◆ Chain hotel ◆ Business ◆ Functional ◆

This hotel is ideal for business trips. It is spacious, close to the airport and motorway, with a convivial bar, meeting rooms and modern guestrooms which want for nothing. The restaurant menu offers international cuisine, dominated by Mediterranean dishes.

Courtyard by Marriott-Amsterdam Airport

Kruisweg 1401 ✉ 2131 MD Hoofddorp – ✆ (0 23) 556 90 00 – jo-habets@courtyard.com – Fax (0 23) 556 90 09

148 rm – †99/175 € ††99/223 €, ☕ 16 €

Rest – Menu 20 € (weekday lunch) – Carte 22/38 €

◆ Chain hotel ◆ Business ◆ Modern ◆

A modern-style business hotel next to a wooded area and lake. Spacious and contemporary guestrooms with king-size beds. Designer fireside lounge. Brasserie in a modern setting serving intercontinental cuisine and pizzas.

Schiphol A 4

Rijksweg A 4 n' 3 (South : 4 km, direction Amsterdam, Den Ruygen Hoek) ✉ 2132 MA Hoofddorp – ✆ (0 252) 67 53 35 – info@schiphol.valk.nl – Fax (0 252) 62 92 45 – www.hotelschiphol.valk.nl

429 rm – †50/140 € ††60/160 €, ☕ 15 € – 2 suites

Rest – *(open until 11 p.m.)* Menu 13 € (weekday lunch), 18/35 € bi – Carte 21/49 €

◆ Chain hotel ◆ Business ◆ Functional ◆

Various categories of bedroom as well as huge conference facilities in this vast establishment typical of the Van der Valk hotel chain. Updated classic interior décor. Large restaurant with international menu.

Artemis

John M. Keynesplein 2 (exit ① Sloten) ✉ 1066 EP – ✆ (0 20) 718 90 00 – sales-marketing@aconplazahotels.com – Fax (0 20) 718 90 01 – www.artemisamsterdam.com **A2**

256 rm – †270/365 € ††270/365 €, ☕ 18 €

Rest – *(open until 11 p.m.)* Carte 33/46 €

◆ Luxury ◆ Design ◆

This modern building of original design in the business district features Dutch designer-style décor. There is an art gallery for exploring the subject in more detail. A large restaurant with ultra-modern décor and a big waterside terrace. Contemporary menu.

XX **De Herbergh** with rm — rest 20/50 P VISA MC AE

Sloterweg 259 ✉ 1171 CP Badhoevedorp – ☎ (0 20) 659 26 00 – info@herbergh.nl – Fax (0 20) 659 83 90 – www.herbergh.nl

24 rm – †80/111 € ††85/120 €, ☕ 11 €

Rest – Menu 28 € (weekday lunch)/38 €

♦ Contemporary ♦ Cosy ♦

Hundred-year-old auberge with cosy dining room and hidden, tree-lined terrace. The best rooms are upstairs. Small executive seminars are catered for.

XX **Marktzicht** — 8/25 VISA MC AE

Marktplein 31 ✉ 2132 DA Hoofddorp – ☎ (0 23) 561 24 11 – keesplasmeijer@planet.nl – Fax (0 23) 563 72 91 – www.restaurant-marktzicht.nl

closed Sunday and Bank Holidays

Rest – Menu 31 € (weekday lunch)/39 € – Carte 41/57 €

♦ Contemporary ♦ Rustic ♦

An old 19th century inn on the Markt, built when the polder on which the airport stands was erected. Nostalgic atmosphere, modern menu and terrace to the front.

THE HAGUE

DEN HAAG - 'SGRAVENHAGE

Population (est. 2005): 468 500 – Altitude: 3m

E. Valenne / GEOSTORY PICTURES

Although the capital of the country is Amsterdam, The Hague is its seat of government and Parliament. This coastal town is a pleasant and quiet residential community, with many squares, parks and several canals. It sprawls over a large area with a relatively small population, so earning the title of 'biggest village in Europe'. It is marked by an aristocratic charm and is considered the most worldly and elegant town in the Netherlands. It also boasts some important modern architecture – Lucent Danstheater by R. Koolhaas and the Transport and Planning ministry by H. Hertzberger. The development between the Binnenhof and the station has involved famous international architects such as R. Meier.

Until the 13C The Hague was a hunting lodge for Count Floris IV of Holland. In the 17C it became the seat of the States General of the United Provinces, then of the government. In 1806 Amsterdam became the capital of the country but The Hague has kept its diplomatic status, with many foreign embassies. In 1899 and 1907 it was the location for peace conferences and it is now the seat of the International Court of Justice, the Permanent Court of Arbitration and the Academy of International Law.

The philosopher Spinoza (1632-77) lived in The Hague. Between 1870 and 1890 a group of painters in The Hague tried to renew painting, notably the art of landscapes.

WHICH DISTRICT TO CHOOSE

Most of the **hotels** cluster round the Binnenhof *Plan II* **F2.** Others are by the sea at Scheveningen *Plan I* **B1** or a few miles from the centre at Leidschendam (6 km east), Rijswijk (5 km south), Voorburg (5 km east) and Wassenaar (11 km northeast). As The Hague is not only a diplomatic but also an administrative and commercial centre, the hotels are mostly modern and business-oriented but there are one or two good 19C hotels.

The pattern of **restaurants** is similar, some in the city centre and others in the suburbs.

For a **drink only**, try one of the places near the Binnenhof, in the Dag Groenmarkt or in Hoogstraat.

ARRIVAL – DEPARTURE

→ ROTTERDAM

Airport – About 16 km (10 mi) southeast of The Hague. ✆ 010 446 34 44; www.rotterdam-airport.nl

From the airport to the city centre – By **taxi** (15min), about €45; ✆ 010 262 04 06. By **Rotterdam Airport Shuttle** (45min) to Central Station. By **train** (30min) to Central Station and Hollands Spoor Station.

Railway Station – Regular train services to **The Hague Central Station** *Plan I* **C2** from Utrecht and to **Hollands Spoor Station** from Amsterdam and Rotterdam; also from Belgium, France and Germany; www.ns.nl

TRANSPORT

→ BUS AND TRAM

Single tickets can be purchased from the bus driver but saver tickets must be bought in advance from the tourist information office, post offices, most tobacconists, newsagents and hotels. 15-stripcard *(strippenkaart)*, €6.70 or 45-stripcard, €19.80, valid throughout the country on buses, trams and metro; 1-day pass €5.90-€7.90 according to the zone; ✆ 070 384 86 66; www.htm.net

TAXIS

Taxis bear blue number plates and an illuminated sign on the roof. They may be called by telephone or hired at taxi ranks at the railway stations and throughout the city; although they are not supposed to stop, they can also be hailed in the street. Pick-up charge €2.80; price per km €1.94; taxi fares are usually rounded up (5-10%). ✆ 070 390 77 22; 070 317 88 77 (ATC Taxi); www.atc-taxi.nl

→ BICYCLES

Bicycles can be hired at the railway stations and from Du Nord Rijwielen (Keizerstraat 27-29).

USEFUL ADDRESSES

→ TOURIST OFFICES

Tourist Office (VVV), Hofweg 1 *Plan I* **C2**; Mon-Fri 10am-6pm, Sat 10am-5pm, Sun 11am-4pm; ✆ 0900 340 35 05. City Mondial, Wagenstraat 193, The Hague; Tues-Sat 10am-5pm; ✆ 070 402 33 36; info@vvvdenhaag.nl; www.citylnndial.nl; www.denhaag.com. **Tourist Office (VVV)**, Gevers Deynootweg 1134, Palace Promenade shopping centre, Scheveningen; Apr-Sep Mon-Fri 9.30am-5.30pm, Sat 10-5pm, Sun 11-4pm; ✆ 0900 340 35 05; vvvscheveningen@spdh.net

→ POST OFFICES

Post Offices are open Mon-Fri 9am-5pm (8pm Thurs; 4pm Sat). Longer opening hours are available at some large city branches (also Sat 8.30-noon).

→ BANKS/CURRENCY EXCHANGE

Opening times are Mon-Fri 9am-4pm. Longer opening hours are available at some large city banks (Thurs 9am-9pm and Sat Morning); all close on public holidays. Bank cash machines (ATMs) are open 24hrs (pin number required).

→ EMERGENCY

Phone ✆ **112** for the Emergency services. Tourist Assistance Service (TAS) ✆ **070 310 32 74** (daily 9am-9pm).

BUSY PERIODS

It may be difficult to find a room at a reasonable price (except at weekends) during special events:

Herring Festival: May-June – Auction of the first batch of new Dutch herring.

Vliegerfeest: early June – Kite Flying Festival on the beach.

Pasar Malam Besar: June – Indonesian market with stalls, theatre performances, lectures and music in the Malieveld.

North Sea Jazz Festival: July (2nd weekend) – Jazz and blues.

Holland Dance Festival: Oct-Nov (17 days) – In alternate years – 60 performances in 7 locations; also dance parade through the Hague.

CaDance Festival: Oct-Nov (17 days) – In alternate years at the Theater aan het Spui.

Prinsjesdag: September (3rd Tuesday) – State Opening of Parliament by the Queen who arrives in a golden coach.

EXPLORING THE HAGUE

In two days there is time to visit the main sights and museums.

Opening times are usually from 10/11am-4/5pm but closed on Mondays and public holidays.

VISITING

Mauritshuis *Plan II* **F2** – Royal Picture Gallery: Holbein the Younger (16C), Rubens, David Teniers, Rembrandt, Vermeer.

Haags Gemeentemuseum *Plan III* **G3** – Municipal Museum (1935): decorative arts and 19C and 20C sculpture and painting; works by Mondrian and artists from the De Stijl movement.

Scheveningen *Plan I* **B1** – Lively fishing port *(full-day fishing trips)* and elegant seaside resort with a popular long, wide stretch of fine sand, backed by the Strandweg, the main thoroughfare.

SHOPPING

The Hague is best known for its many antique shops and commercial art galleries; the Tourist Information Centre (VVV) publishes brochures full of useful shopping suggestions. In The Hague late-night shopping until 9pm is on Thursdays. In addition to the big city centre department stores and chain stores – *Maison de Bonneterie* (Gravenstraat 2), *De Bijenkorf* (Wagenstraat 32), *V&D* (Grote Marktstraat 50), *Hema* (Grote Marktstraat 57) – there are lots of excellent small shops in the streets and squares around the palaces. Indoor shopping is available at the stylish **Passage** (Hofweg 5-7/ Buitenhof 4-5) and at the **Babylon shopping centre** next to the Central Station *Plan I* **C2**.

MARKETS – The Hague has excellent markets: **general goods markets** in Herman Costerstraat (Mon, Wed, Fri and Sat) *Plan I* **B2** and in Markthof (daily except Sun) *Plan I* **B3**; **farmers' market** by the Grote Kerk (Wed); **art and antiques market** in Lange Voorhout *Plan II* **F2** (May-Sept Thurs and Sun) also in the Plein (Oct-Apr Thurs).

In **Scheveningen** late-night shopping is on Friday. The best places to shop are **Palace Promenade** (open daily 10am-10pm) *Plan III* **G1**, **Gevers Deynootplein** and the **Boulevard (Strandweg)**.

WHAT TO BUY – The local **specialities** are Delft porcelain, Hollandsche Waaren, art and antiques, cigars, clogs, fashion, design, books.

ENTERTAINMENT

Dr Anton Philipszaal (Spuiplein 150) for classical music.

Circustheater (Circusstraat 4) for classical music and musicals.

't Paard (Prinsegracht 12) for pop, rock and blues.

Koninklijke Schouwburg (Korte Voorhout 3).

Lucent Danstheater (Spuiplein 152), home of the world-famous **Nederlands Dans Theater.**

Nederlands Congres Centrum (Churchillplein 10).

Theater aan het Spui (Spui 187).

Diligentia (Lange Voorhout 5).

NIGHTLIFE

The place to be is **Schevening's Boulevard** *Plan III* **G1**, crowded and boisterous with street cafés, restaurants, bars and discos; also the *Holland Casino*.

CENTRE

Plan II

Le Méridien Hotel des Indes

A/C rm 100 P VISA AE

Lange Voorhout 54 ✉ 2514 EG – ✆ (0 70) 361 23 45 – info@desindes.nl – Fax (0 70) 361 23 50 – www.desindes.nl **F1**

92 rm – 345 € 395 €, 25 €

Rest – Menu 43/91 € bi – Carte 33/65 €

♦ Palace ♦ Business ♦ Historic ♦

This 1858 mansion, located in the institutional district, has recently been fully renovated by the architect Jacques Garcia. Every comfort in a refined and modern atmosphere. Restaurant for food-lovers, well known for its "High Tea" and "Afternoon Tea".

Crowne Plaza Promenade

rm A/C 425 P VISA AE

van Stolkweg 1 ✉ 2585 JL – ✆ (0 70) 352 51 61 – info@crowneplazadenhaag.nl – Fax (0 70) 354 10 46 – www.crowneplazadenhaag.nl Plan III **H2**

93 rm – 295 € 310 €, 23 € – 1 suite

Rest *Brasserie Promenade* – Menu 30 € (weekday lunch), 35/40 € – Carte 44/56 €

♦ Chain hotel ♦ Luxury ♦ Modern ♦

Big chain hotel, lining the interior ring road, opposite a vast park. Rooms with modern comfort, modern painting collection and sharp service. Relaxed brasserie offering a simple meal.

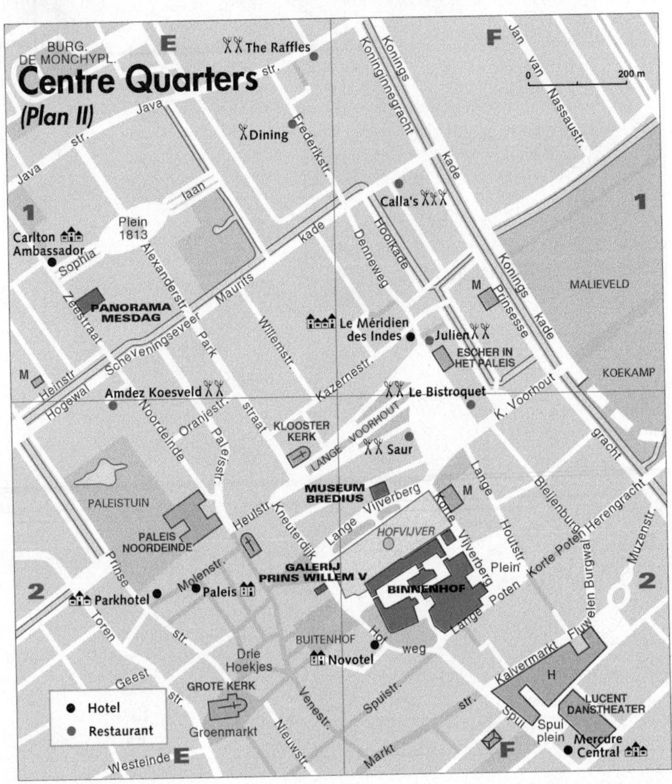

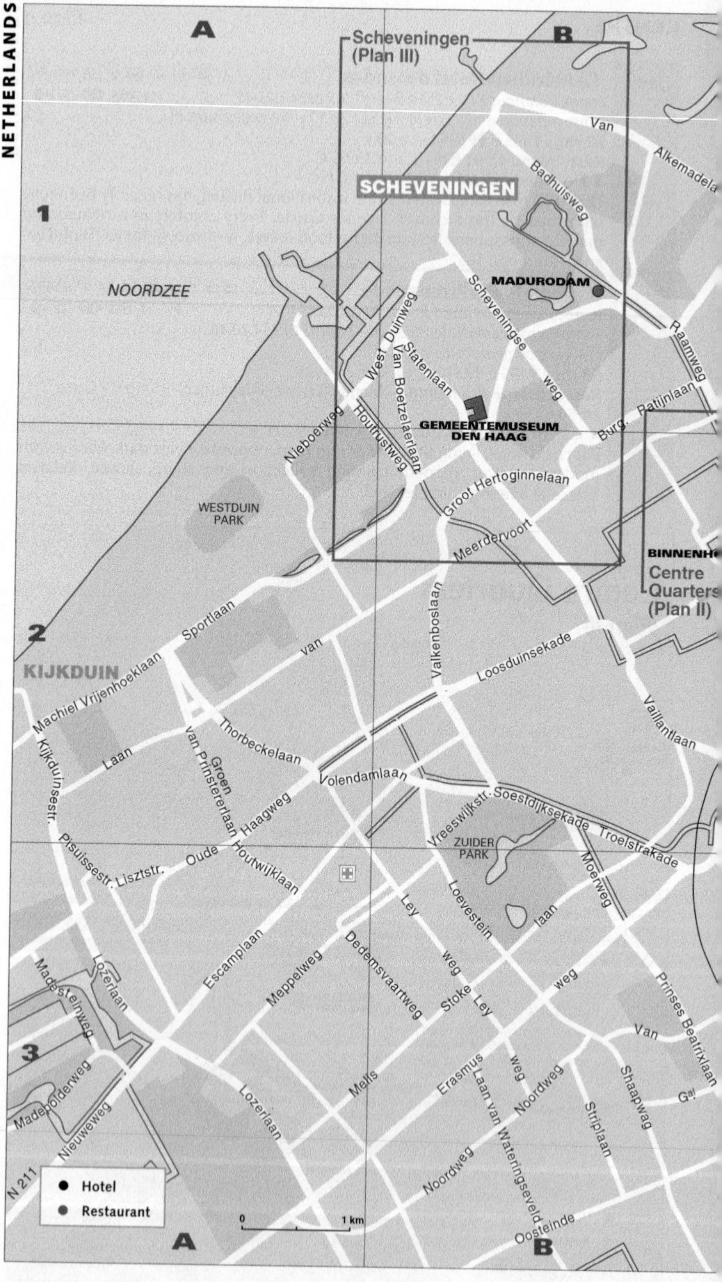

A
B
Scheveningen (Plan III)
Van Alkemadelaan
SCHEVENINGEN
Badhuisweg
1
NOORDZEE
MADURODAM
Scheveningseweg
Raamweg
West Duinweg
Van Boetzelaerlaan
Statenlaan
Burg. Patijnlaan
GEMEENTEMUSEUM DEN HAAG
Nieboerweg
Houtrustweg
Groot Hertoginnelaan
WESTDUIN PARK
Meerdervoort
BINNENH
Centre Quarters (Plan II)
Sportlaan
2
KIJKDUIN
Valkenboslaan
Machiel Vrijenhoeklaan
van Laan
Loosduinsekade
Vaillantlaan
Thorbeckelaan
Kijkduinsestr.
Groen van Prinstererlaan
Volendamlaan
Haagweg
Vreeswijkstr.
Soestdijksekade
Troelstrakade
ZUIDER PARK
Pisuissestr.
Lisztstr.
Oude Houtwijklaan
Moerweg
Ley
Loevesteinlaan
Escamplaan
Meppelweg
Dedemsvaartweg
weg
Madesteinweg
Lozerlaan
Stoke Ley weg
Prinses Beatrixlaan
Van Gal
3
Madepolderweg
Melis
Erasmusweg
Laan van Wateringseveld
Noordweg
Striplaan
Shaapweg
Nieuweweg
N 211
Hotel
Restaurant
0
1 km
Oosteinde

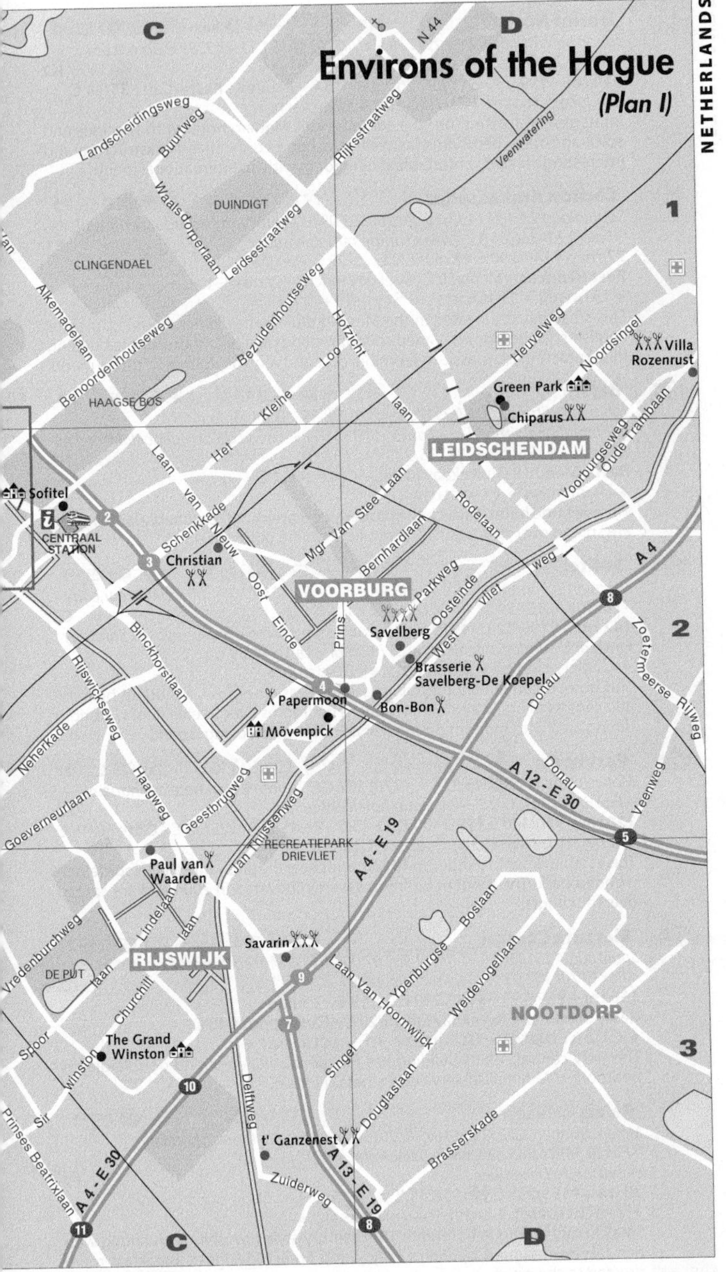
Environs of the Hague
(Plan I)
C
D
1
2
3
Landscheidingsweg
Buurtweg
Waalsdorperlaan
DUINDIGT
Leidsestraatweg
Rijksstraatweg
N 44
Veenwatering
CLINGENDAEL
Alkemadelaan
Benoordenhoutseweg
Bezuidenhoutseweg
HAAGSE BOS
Hofzicht
Loo
Kleine
laan
Het
Laan
van
Nieuw
Oost
Einde
Heuvelweg
Noordsingel
Villa Rozenrust
Green Park
Chiparus
LEIDSCHENDAM
Voorburgseweg
Oude Trambaan
Rodelaan
Mgr Van Stee Laan
Bernhardlaan
Sofitel
CENTRAAL STATION
Schenkkade
Christian
VOORBURG
Parkweg
Oosteinde
West
Vliet
weg
A 4
Savelberg
Brasserie Savelberg-De Koepel
Papermoon
Bon-Bon
Mövenpick
Prins
Donau
Zoetermeerse Rijweg
Binckhorstlaan
Rijswijckseweg
Neherkade
Haagweg
Geestbrugweg
Jan Thijssenweg
A 12 - E 30
Veenweg
RECREATIEPARK DRIEVLIET
A 4 - E 19
Goeverneurlaan
Paul van Waarden
Lindelaan
laan
Vredenburchweg
RIJSWIJK
Savarin
Laan Van Hoornwijck
Ypenburgse Boslaan
Weidevogellaan
NOOTDORP
DE PUT
laan
Churchill
Spoor
The Grand Winston
Winston
Sir
Singel
Douglaslaan
Delftweg
Brasserskade
t' Ganzenest
Prinses Beatrixlaan
A 4 - E 30
A 13 - E 19
Zuiderweg
2
3
4
5
7
8
9
10
11

Dorint Novotel 2000

Johan de Wittlaan 42 2517 JR – (0 70) 416 91 11 – h5389@accor.com – Fax (0 70) 416 91 00 – www.novotel.com *Plan III* **H2**

214 rm – 99/250 € 119/265 €, 18 € – 2 suites – **Rest** – Carte 35/44 €

♦ Chain hotel ♦ Business ♦ Modern ♦

Strategically situated "on" the congress hall. Modern hotel, with spacious and spick-and-span bedrooms, as well as a huge conference infrastructure and interesting views. Comfortable dining room with an international menu.

Carlton Ambassador 160

Sophialaan 2 2514 JP – (0 70) 363 03 63 – info@ambassador.carlton.nl – Fax (0 70) 360 05 35 – www.carlton.nl/ambassador **E1**

77 rm – 140/290 € 160/320 €, 22 € – 1 suite

Rest *Henricus* – Menu 30 € (weekday lunch) – Carte 41/49 €

♦ Luxury ♦ Business ♦ Stylish ♦

This small palace, located in the Mesdag diplomatic district, houses Dutch or English-style bedrooms. Varied soundproofing quality, but the whole building has character. Neo-classic style dining room and very cosy lounge. Modern menu.

Bel Air 250 P

Johan de Wittlaan 30 2517 JR – (0 70) 352 53 54 – info@goldentulipbelairhotel.nl – Fax (0 70) 352 53 85 – www.goldentulipbelairhotel.nl *Plan III* **H3**

324 rm – 135/205 € 135/275 €, 18 €

Rest – Menu 18 € (weekday lunch) – Carte 34/54 €

♦ Business ♦ Functional ♦

This is a huge hotel in which the properly equipped and reasonably large rooms are spread over nine floors. The public areas are quite spacious.

Sofitel rm 150 P

Koningin Julianaplein 35 2595 AA – (0 70) 381 49 01 – h0755@accor.com – Fax (0 70) 382 59 27 *Plan I* **C2**

142 rm – 199/320 € 199/320 €, 23 € – 1 suite – **Rest** – *(closed Saturday lunch and Sunday lunch)* Menu 37/82 € bi – Carte 44/59 €

♦ Chain hotel ♦ Business ♦ Modern ♦

This hotel is convenient for train passengers, as it occupies a modern building adjacent to the railway station. Modern bedrooms over twelve floors. A bright dining area with modern designer style décor overlooking a park.

Parkhotel 200

Molenstraat 53 2513 BJ – (0 70) 362 43 71 – info@parkhoteldenhaag.nl – Fax (0 70) 361 45 25 – www.parkhoteldenhaag.nl **E2**

120 rm – 80/140 € 95/400 €, 15 € – **Rest** – Menu 25/38 € – Carte 30/45 €

♦ Traditional ♦ Business ♦ Classic ♦

This establishment, founded in 1912, stands near the pleasant Paleis Noordeinde wooded park. The modern bedrooms were renovated in 2004 and are spread over four floors.

Mercure Central 135

Spui 180 2511 BW – (0 70) 363 67 00 – h1317@accor.com – Fax (0 70) 363 93 98 – www.mercure.nl **F2**

156 rm – 89/190 € 89/280 €, 19 € – 3 suites

Rest – Menu 17 € (weekday lunch)/20 € – Carte approx. 40 €

♦ Chain hotel ♦ Business ♦ Functional ♦

This very central, 1980s building has functional, well-kept and double-glazed bedrooms. "Minimalist" service. Business clientèle.

Paleis without rest

Molenstraat 26 2513 BL – (0 70) 362 46 21 – info@paleishotel.nl – Fax (0 70) 361 45 33 – www.paleishotel.nl
closed 22-26 December **E2**

20 rm – 185/235 € 195/245 €, 15 €

♦ Traditional ♦ Business ♦ Classic ♦

Small luxury boutique hotel with 18th century-style furnishings and hung with rich fabrics designed by Pierre Frey, a top French designer. Breakfast room dressed to the nines.

Novotel 100 VISA
Hofweg 5 ✉ 2511 AA – ✆ (0 70) 364 88 46 – h1180@accor.com – Fax (0 70) 356 28 89 – www.novotel.com **F2**
106 rm – †80/170 € ††90/235 €, ☕ 16 €
Rest – *(open until 11 p.m.)* Carte 29/36 €
◆ Chain hotel ◆ Business ◆ Functional ◆
This chain hotel opposite the Binnenhof used to be a cinema; it now houses a shopping mall. Modern bedrooms which were refurbished in 2004. A large restaurant in a former cinema.

XXX ✿ **Calla's** (van der Kleijn) VISA
Laan van Roos en Doorn 51a ✉ 2514 BC – ✆ (0 70) 345 58 66 – info@restaurantcallas.nl – Fax (0 70) 345 57 10 – www.restaurantcallas.nl closed 22 July-14 August, 22-30 December, 1-4 January, Saturday lunch, Sunday and Monday **F1**
Rest – Menu 38 € (weekday lunch), 70/133 € bi – Carte 77/94 €
Spec. Salade van noordzeekrab met avocado, parfait van ganzenlever. Met aardappel en knoflook gesouffleerde tarbot (July-January). Gegratineerde flensjes met seizoensfruit en vanilleroomijs.
◆ Innovative ◆ Fashionable ◆
A former warehouse, now home to a restaurant with minimalist décor in striking white. Lounge and open kitchen on the ground floor. Standard modern cuisine served.

XX **Le Bistroquet** VISA
Lange Voorhout 98 ✉ 2514 EJ – ✆ (0 70) 360 11 70 – info@bistroquet.nl – Fax (0 70) 360 55 30 – www.bistroquet.nl closed 24 December-1 January, Saturday lunch and Sunday **F1-2**
Rest – Menu 30 € (weekday lunch), 39/72 € bi – Carte 49/67 €
◆ Contemporary ◆ Retro ◆
This small friendly bistro, located in the diplomatic-parliament district, has an intimate atmosphere, nostalgic for the 1920s. Modern menu.

XX **Saur** 6/20 VISA
Lange Voorhout 47 ✉ 2514 EC – ✆ (0 70) 346 25 65 – info@saur.nl – Fax (0 70) 326 13 13 – www.saur.nl closed 1 January, Saturday lunch and Sunday **F2**
Rest – Menu 38 € (weekday lunch)/45 € – Carte 41/83 €
◆ Seafood ◆ Brasserie ◆
Fish, lobster and shellfish look forward to being savoured in this long-standing Hague restaurant. Chic modern brasserie atmosphere. Oyster bar.

XX **Julien** 4/45 VISA
Vos in Tuinstraat 2a ✉ 2514 BX – ✆ (0 70) 365 86 02 – info@julien.nl – Fax (0 70) 365 31 47 – www.julien.nl closed Sunday and Bank Holidays **F1**
Rest – Menu 33 € (weekday lunch), 38/55 € – Carte 50/64 €
◆ Traditional ◆ Retro ◆
This restaurant will delight Art Nouveau enthusiasts. Hushed dining rooms, mezzanine and bar with a 1900s atmosphere. Classic cooking enjoyed by politicians and the Dutch Royal Family.

XX **Rousseau** 10/50 VISA
Van Boetzelaerlaan 134 ✉ 2581 AX – ✆ (0 70) 355 47 43 – info@restaurantrousseau.com – www.restaurantrousseau.com closed 29 July-20 August, 23 December-2 January, 17-26 February, Saturday lunch, Sunday and Monday *Plan III* **G3**
Rest – Menu 25 € (weekday lunch), 30/84 € bi – Carte 48/70 €
◆ Contemporary ◆ Family ◆
The spirit of Douanier Rousseau, the landlord's namesake, lives on these premises. A fine wall painting in his hand decorates the dining room. Well thought out seasonal menu.

NETHERLANDS

XX **The Raffles** AC VISA MC AE ①

Javastraat 63 ✉ 2585 AG – ✆ (0 70) 345 85 87 – info@restaurantraffles.com – Fax (0 70) 356 00 84 – www.restaurantraffles.com

closed late July-early August, 1 week February, Sunday and Monday **E1**

Rest – *(dinner only)* Menu 37/45 € – Carte 33/50 €

♦ Indonesian ♦ Friendly ♦

Located on the fittingly-named Javastraat, restaurant serving flavoursome and authentic Indonesian cooking, served in an appropriate setting.

XX **Christian** ⌂ ◌4/12 VISA MC AE

Laan van Nieuw Oost Indië 1f ✉ 2593 BH – ✆ (0 70) 383 88 56 – info@restaurantchristian.nl – Fax (0 70) 385 59 32 – www.restaurantchristian.nl

closed last week July-first 2 weeks August, 26 December-3 January, Tuesday, Wednesday and Saturday lunch *Plan I* **C2**

Rest – Menu 29 € (weekday lunch), 35/73 € – Carte approx. 50 €

♦ Contemporary ♦ Cosy ♦

Modern cuisine served in this restaurant, whose new interior décor is dominated by the colour orange. Chef's table for 8 to 10 guests to the rear; courtyard terrace.

XX **Amdez Koesveld** ⌂ ◌16/40 VISA MC AE ①

Maziestraat 10 ✉ 2514 GT – ✆ (0 70) 360 27 23 – info@restaurantkoesveld.nl – www.restaurantkoesveld.nl

closed Monday and Tuesday **E1**

Rest – *(dinner only)* Menu 40/43 € – Carte 35/49 €

♦ Contemporary ♦ Friendly ♦

Small restaurant located between the Panorama Mesgag and Paleis Noordeinde. Cooking suited to current tastes with dishes inspired by the south of France served in generous portions.

X **Shirasagi** ⌂ ◌35 VISA MC AE ①

Stadhouderslaan 76 R ✉ 2517 JA – ✆ (0 70) 346 47 00 – shirasagi@planet.nl – Fax (0 70) 346 26 01 – www.shirasagi.nl

closed 31 December-3 January and Sunday *Plan III* **G3**

Rest – Menu 20 € (weekday lunch), 38/60 € – Carte 20/58 €

♦ Japanese ♦ Minimalist ♦

Japanese restaurant located away from the town centre in an attractive old house opposite the municipal museum. Cooking tables, sushi bar, open kitchens and inviting rear terrace.

X **Dining** ⌂ AC ◌20 VISA MC AE ①

Frederikstraat 54 ✉ 2514 LL – ✆ (0 70) 312 24 77 – info@diningrestaurant.nl – Fax (0 70) 345 64 76 – www.diningrestaurant.nl

closed 23 July-5 August, Sunday and Monday **E1**

Rest – Menu 23 € (weekday lunch), 33/65 € bi – Carte 37/56 €

♦ Contemporary ♦ Bistro ♦

Contemporary restaurant associated with an interior decoration shop. Open kitchen and small terrace. A simpler choice of food is served at lunchtime.

SCHEVENINGEN *Plan III*

Kurhaus < Spa Lá ⅏ & rm AC ⇜ ▣ 🏛600 P VISA MC AE ①

Gevers Deynootplein 30 ✉ 2586 CK – ✆ (0 70) 416 26 36 – info@kurhaus.nl – Fax (0 70) 416 26 46 – www.kurhaus.nl **G1**

245 rm – †275/350 € ††300/375 €, ☕ 23 € – 10 suites

Rest *Kandinsky* – see below

Rest *Kurzaal* – Menu 20 € (weekday lunch), 25/42 €

♦ Palace ♦ Business ♦ Modern ♦

This magnificent beachside palace houses an outstanding concert room, dating from the end of the 19th century, converted into a restaurant. Refined rooms with modern comfort. Large modern menu offered under the superb dome of the Kurzaal.

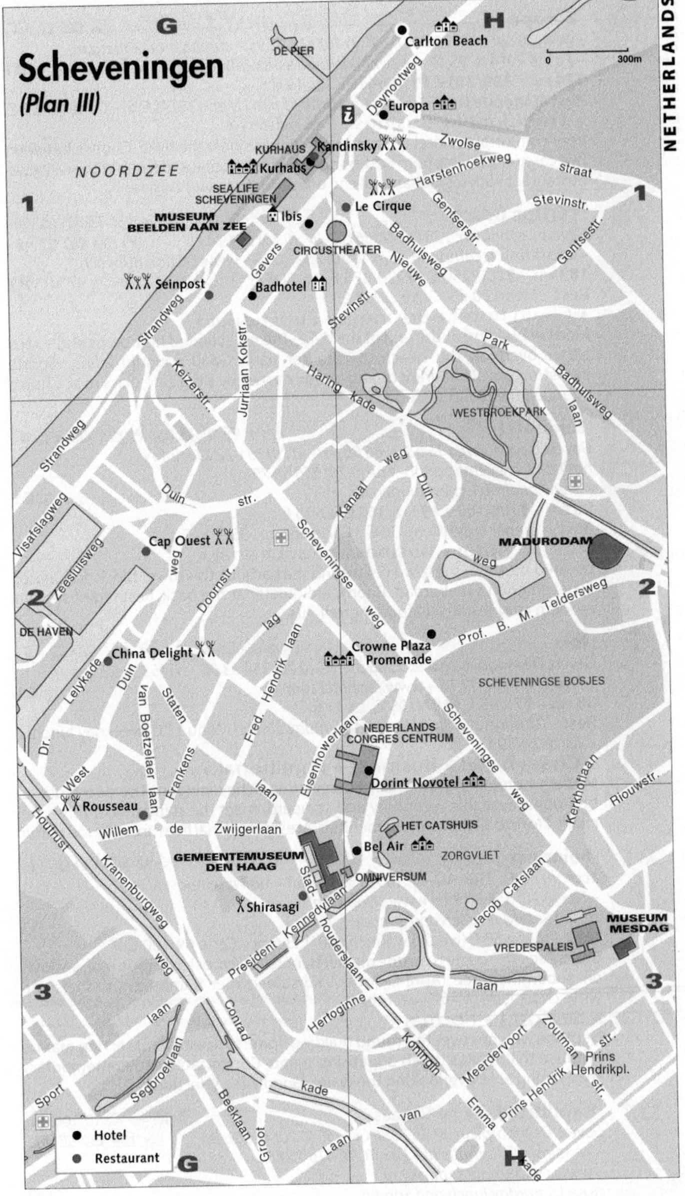
Scheveningen
(Plan III)
G
H
1
2
3
0
300m
DE PIER
Carlton Beach
Devnootweg
Europa
Zwolse
straat
KURHAUS
Kandinsky
Kurhaus
NOORDZEE
Harstenhoekweg
SEA LIFE SCHEVENINGEN
Le Cirque
Stevinstr.
MUSEUM BEELDEN AAN ZEE
Ibis
Gentserstr.
Gentsestr.
CIRCUSTHEATER
Badhuisweg
Nieuwe
Gevers
Seinpost
Badhotel
Stevinstr.
Strandweg
Jurriaan Kokstr.
Keizerstr.
Park
Haring
kade
Badhuisweg
laan
WESTBROEKPARK
Strandweg
Duin
str.
weg
Kanaal
Duin
Visafslagweg
Zeesluisweg
Cap Ouest
weg
Scheveningse
MADURODAM
weg
Doornstr.
weg
DE HAVEN
lag
Prof. B. M. Teldersweg
Crowne Plaza Promenade
China Delight
Fred. Hendrik laan
Lelykade
Duin
Staten
van Boetzelaer laan
SCHEVENINGSE BOSJES
Dr.
Frankens
NEDERLANDS CONGRES CENTRUM
Eisenhowerlaan
Scheveningse
West
laan
Dorint Novotel
weg
Kerkhoflaan
Riouwstr.
Rousseau
Houtrust
Willem de Zwijgerlaan
HET CATSHUIS
Kranenburgweg
GEMEENTEMUSEUM DEN HAAG
Bel Air
ZORGVLIET
Stad-
OMNIVERSUM
Shirasagi
President Kennedylaan
houderslaan
Jacob Catslaan
MUSEUM MESDAG
VREDESPALEIS
weg
laan
laan
Conrad
Hertoginne
Koningin
Meerdervoort
Zoutman
str.
Prins Hendrikpl.
Segbroeklaan
Sport
kade
Beeklaan
Prins Hendrik
str.
Emma
van
Groot
Laan
kade
Hotel
Restaurant

NETHERLANDS

Europa

rest 460

Zwolsestraat 2 ✉ 2587 VJ – ✆ (0 70) 416 95 95 – europa@bilderberg.nl – Fax (0 70) 416 95 55 – www.bilderberg-europa-hotel.nl **H1**

174 rm – 99/210 € 129/425 €, 19 €

Rest *Mangerie Oxo* – *(dinner only until 11 p.m.)* Menu 35/71 € bi – Carte 40/52 €

♦ Traditional ♦ Business ♦ Modern ♦

Very comfortable hotel adjacent to crossroads near the dyke. Choose between five categories of modern bedroom, all with a balcony and some with sea views. Restaurant with fashionable décor, offering up-to-date cuisine.

Carlton Beach

rm 250

Gevers Deynootweg 201 ✉ 2586 HZ – ✆ (0 70) 354 14 14 – info@beach.carlton.nl – Fax (0 70) 352 00 20 – www.carlton.nl/beach **H1**

183 rm – 200/250 € 220/375 €, 21 €

Rest – Menu 30 € – Carte 23/37 €

♦ Chain hotel ♦ Business ♦ Functional ♦

Modern building at the end of the dyke. The redecorated bedrooms and suites either overlook the beach, or the car park. Good soundproofing. Sports infrastructure. Restaurant dining room covered by a delicate glass roof. Choice of grilled meat and seafood.

Badhotel

100

Gevers Deynootweg 15 ✉ 2586 BB – ✆ (0 70) 351 22 21 – info@badhotelscheveningen.nl – Fax (0 70) 355 58 70 – www.badhotelscheveningen.nl **G1**

90 rm – 108/160 € 118/160 €, 15 €

Rest – *(dinner only)* Menu 30 € – Carte approx. 35 €

♦ Chain hotel ♦ Business ♦ Functional ♦

Located between the town centre and the harbour, this tower block dominates Scheveningen's main road. Rooms are quieter at the back. Restaurant serving modern cuisine with seafood ingredients.

Ibis

40

Gevers Deynootweg 63 ✉ 2586 BJ – ✆ (0 70) 354 33 00 – h1153@accor.com – Fax (0 70) 352 39 16 – www.ibishotel.com **G1**

88 rm – 75/85 € 97/105 €, 11 €

Rest – *(closed Saturday dinner and Sunday dinner)* Menu 13 € (weekday lunch) – Carte 21/39 €

♦ Chain hotel ♦ Business ♦ Functional ♦

Modern hotel lining the main boulevard in Scheveningen. The two types of bedrooms available (economy and standard) meet the standards of this hotel chain. Close to all the resort's amenities. A restaurant that lives up to the Ibis name.

Seinpost

Zeekant 60 ✉ 2586 AD – ✆ (0 70) 355 52 50 – mail@seinpost.nl – Fax (0 70) 355 50 93 – www.seinpost.nl

closed Saturday lunch and Sunday **G1**

Rest – Menu 50 € (weekday lunch), 60/133 € bi – Carte 69/100 €

Spec. Zeeuwse oesters op drie manieren bereid. Geroosterde rode mul, ansjovis en auberginepuree (April-October). Korstdeeg met frambozen, roomijs van witte chocolade (May-September).

♦ Seafood ♦ Formal ♦

Neptune watches over this round building home to a restaurant serving marine produce that makes up an appetising menu. Comfortable and contemporary style dining area overlooking the water. Good wine selection.

Kandinsky – Hotel Kurhaus

10/100

Gevers Deynootplein 30 ✉ 2586 CK – ✆ (0 70) 416 26 36 – kandinsky@kurhaus.nl – Fax (0 70) 416 26 46 – www.restaurantkandinsky.nl

closed Saturday lunch and Sunday **G1**

Rest – Menu 33 € (weekday lunch), 48/93 € bi – Carte 53/83 €

♦ French traditional ♦ Formal ♦

An elegant, modern restaurant in the resort's flagship hotel. A comfortable dining area with beige décor. Traditional and modern blend of cuisine.

Le Cirque (Kranenborg) 8/20 VISA AE
Circusplein 50 ✉ 2586 CZ – ✆ (0 70) 416 76 76
– info@restaurantlecirque.com – Fax (0 70) 416 75 37
– www.restaurantlecirque.com
closed 22 January-6 February, Monday and Tuesday H1
Rest – *(dinner only except Saturday and Sunday)* Menu 55/165 € bi – Carte 56/85 €
Spec. Bonbons van koolrabi, gelei van zeewater en citroen. Zonnevis krokant, selderie, limoen en mierikswortel, karamel van soja. T-bone van ree met müsli, parmentier van witloof en bietenjus (May-March).
◆ Innovative ◆ Design ◆
A designer restaurant next to the Circustheater. Veranda and rear dining area with red and black décor contrasts. Classic and creative cuisine served. Very popular pre-theatre menu.

Cap Ouest VISA AE
Schokkerweg 37 ✉ 2583 BH – ✆ (0 70) 306 09 35
– info@capouest.nl – Fax (0 70) 350 84 54
– www.capouest.nl
closed 31 December-4 January, Saturday lunch and Sunday lunch G2
Rest – Menu 25 € (weekday lunch), 43/95 € bi – Carte 43/67 €
◆ Seafood ◆ Formal ◆
This house, overlooking quays, offers predominantly fish and seafood dishes. Its modern dining room offers views of the fishing and yachting harbours.

China Delight 40/150 VISA
Dr Lelykade 116 ✉ 2583 CN – ✆ (0 70) 355 54 50 – info@chinadelight.nl
– Fax (0 70) 354 66 52 – www.chinadelight.nl
closed Monday G2
Rest – *(dinner only)* Carte 26/34 €
◆ Chinese ◆ Exotic ◆
Large Chinese restaurant, occupying a former warehouse near a dock. Its "delightful" menu takes you towards Beijing and the Sichuan region. Glossy decorations, just like the duck.

ENVIRONS *Plan I*

The Grand Winston 200 VISA AE
Generaal Eisenhowerplein 1 ✉ 2288 AE Rijswijk
– ✆ (0 70) 414 15 00 – info@grandwinston.nl – Fax (0 70) 414 15 10
– www.grandwinston.nl C3
245 rm – †109/198 € ††109/234 € – 7 suites
Rest *The Grand* – 2nd floor *(closed Sunday and Monday) (dinner only)* Menu 48/75 € – Carte 56/114 €
Rest *The Grand Canteen* – *(open until 11 p.m.)* Menu 21 € (weekday lunch) – Carte 33/43 €
◆ Chain hotel ◆ Business ◆ Design ◆
A designer hotel next to the Rijswijk station with Winston Churchill watching over the lobby! Rooms in two modern blocks. Futuristic décor, modern seafood menu and attractive selection of wines at The Grand. New-style canteen with a varied menu.

Green Park 250 VISA AE
Weigelia 22 ✉ 2262 AB Leidschendam
– ✆ (0 70) 320 92 80 – info@greenpark.nl
– Fax (0 70) 327 49 07 – www.greenpark.nl D1
92 rm – †60/169 € ††75/184 €, 16 € – 4 suites
Rest *Chiparus* – see below
◆ Chain hotel ◆ Business ◆ Modern ◆
Great lakeside chain hotel, built on piles. Rooms equipped with modern comfort and set around a bright atrium. Thoughtful service.

NETHERLANDS

Mövenpick
Stationsplein 8 ✉ 2275 AZ Voorburg – ✆ (0 70) 337 37 37 – hotel.voorburg@moevenpick.com – Fax (0 70) 337 37 00 – www.moevenpick-voorburg.com

VISA MC AE 180

125 rm – 128/145 € 148/165 €, 15 €

C2

Rest – Menu 21 € – Carte 18/35 €

◆ Chain hotel ◆ Business ◆ Modern ◆

Modern-style chain hotel, housing functional and correctly-sized bedrooms that are as well kept as they are soundproofed. Attractive, designer-style bar. Lots to choose from when you are hungry: buffets, grilled meat, pasta or wok-cooked dishes.

Savelberg with rm
Oosteinde 14 ✉ 2271 EH Voorburg – ✆ (0 70) 387 20 81 – info@restauranthotelsavelberg.nl – Fax (0 70) 387 77 15 – www.restauranthotelsavelberg.nl

4/44 P VISA MC AE

closed 27 December-8 January

14 rm – 150/215 € 150/350 €, 16 €

D2

Rest – *(closed Saturday lunch, Sunday and Monday)* Menu 47 € (weekday lunch), 65/140 € bi – Carte 65/92 €

Spec. Salade van kreeft. Gegrilde tarbot met asperges (summer). Lamsvlees (spring).

◆ Traditional ◆ Formal ◆

A luxurious 17th century residence which is a real treat for the eyes! Classic menu, huge wine list, with terrace overlooking a park; personalised rooms.

Villa Rozenrust
Veursestraatweg 104 ✉ 2265 CG Leidschendam – ✆ (0 70) 327 74 60 – villarozenrust@planet.nl – Fax (0 70) 327 50 62 – www.villa-rozenrust.nl

24/80 P VISA MC AE

closed Tuesday and Wednesday

D1

Rest – *(dinner only)* Menu 50 € – Carte 53/73 €

◆ Traditional ◆ Formal ◆

A lovely old villa with a romantic atmosphere, serving modern cuisine with creative touches and featuring a summer dining area outdoors.

Savarin
Laan van Hoornwijck 29 ✉ 2289 DG Rijswijk – ✆ (0 70) 307 20 50 – info@savarin.nl – Fax (0 70) 307 20 55 – www.savarin.nl

4/150 P VISA MC AE

closed 1 January, Saturday lunch and Sunday lunch

C3

Rest – Menu 32 € (weekday lunch), 38/77 € bi – Carte approx. 42 €

◆ Innovative ◆ Formal ◆

Former farm dating from 1916 where inventive cuisine is served in a part-designer, part-rustic style dining room. Summer terrace and modern meeting areas.

Chiparus – Hotel Green Park
Weigelia 22 ✉ 2262 AB Leidschendam – ✆ (0 70) 320 92 80 – info@greenpark.nl – Fax (0 70) 327 49 07 – www.greenpark.nl

10/250 VISA MC AE

closed Sunday

D1

Rest – Menu 28 € (weekday lunch), 33/49 € bi – Carte 41/50 €

◆ Contemporary ◆ Design ◆

This restaurant, named after a 20th century Romanian sculptor, offers a dining room with a water view. Modern Mediterranean cuisine. Lakeside terrace.

t' Ganzenest
Delftweg 58 (near A 13-E 19, exit ⑧ Rijswijk-Zuid) ✉ 2289 AL Rijswijk – ✆ (0 70) 414 06 42 – info@ganzenest.nl – Fax (0 70) 414 07 05 – www.ganzenest.nl

8/24 P VISA MC AE

closed late July-early August, first week January, Sunday and Monday

Rest – *(dinner only)* Menu 32/104 € bi – Carte 48/70 €

C3

◆ Contemporary ◆ Friendly ◆

This welcoming "Goose Nest" (Ganzenest) occupies a small farmhouse on a golf course. Dashing interior decoration, enticing up-to-date menu and delightful terrace.

Paul van Waarden

10/18 VISA MC AE

Tollensstraat 10 ✉ 2282 BM Rijswijk – ✆ (0 70) 414 08 12 – info@paulvanwaarden.nl – Fax (0 70) 414 03 91 – www.paulvanwaarden.nl
closed 2 weeks July, 27 December-8 January, Sunday and Monday **C3**

Rest – Menu 33/75 € bi – Carte 51/70 €

Spec. Vier bereidingen van vier verschillende soorten lever. Krokant gebakken kabeljauw, erwtensoep met gerookte paling (21 September-21 March). Tarte tatin van rabarber met gemberroomijs.

♦ Contemporary ♦ Friendly ♦

Paul van Waarden hosts you in one of the series of rooms which make up the restaurant, designed in the style of a modern brasserie. Modern cuisine. Walled terrace.

Brasserie Savelberg-De Koepel

10/16 VISA MC AE

Oosteinde 1 ✉ 2271 EA Voorburg – ✆ (0 70) 369 35 72 – Fax (0 70) 369 32 14 – www.brasseriedekoepel.nl
closed 28 December-5 January **D2**

Rest – *(dinner only except Sunday) (open until 11 p.m.)* Menu 30/49 € bi – Carte approx. 38 €

♦ French traditional ♦ Brasserie ♦

Upmarket brasserie in a huge building in the shape of a rotunda, topped by a pretty cupola. A summer terrace and a pleasant park for after-dinner walks.

Bon-Bon

A/C VISA MC AE

Kerkstraat 52 ✉ 2271 CT Voorburg – ✆ (0 70) 386 29 00 – info@bon-bon.nl – Fax (0 70) 386 55 92 – www.bon-bon.nl
closed 29 July-20 August, Saturday lunch, Sunday lunch and Monday **D2**

Rest – Menu 30 € (weekday lunch), 32/70 € bi – Carte 37/67 €

♦ Contemporary ♦ Bistro ♦

Two 17th century houses host this warm, modern brasserie-type restaurant, with its red benches, light-grey walls, closely-placed tables and set of mirrors. Enclosed terrace.

Papermoon

A/C VISA MC

Herenstraat 175 ✉ 2271 CE Voorburg – ✆ (0 70) 387 31 61 – info@papermoon.nl – Fax (0 70) 387 75 20
closed 31 December-1 January and Monday **C2**

Rest – *(dinner only)* Menu 29/65 € bi – Carte approx. 40 €

♦ Contemporary ♦ Bistro ♦

An appealing modern menu with several set menus at this friendly restaurant where the dining room has a refined atmosphere.

ROTTERDAM

ROTTERDAM

Population (est. 2005): 601 000 (conurbation 3 340 000) – Altitude: sea level

M. Gotin/SCOPE

Rotterdam, the Netherlands' second most populated city, is one of the world's largest ports, located on the Nieuwe Maas which flows into the North Sea, and near the mouth of two important rivers – the Rhine and the Maas – leading to the industrial areas inland. The city of Rotterdam sprawls over both banks of the river and is linked by tunnels, bridges and the metro.

Rotterdam has been improving its port since it was first developed in the late 16C. From 1866 to 1872 the Nieuwe Waterweg (New Waterway) leading to the sea was excavated; several man-made harbours were built in the late 19C. Rotterdam was largely destroyed during the Second World War but has been entirely rebuilt and has a great deal of important modern architecture. Many new buildings erected during the 1980s and 90s have made radical changes to the city's skyline and earned Rotterdam the nick-name of Manhattan on the Maas. The latest project is the development of the Kop van Zuid on the south side of the Nieuwe Maas – the creation of a second centre for Rotterdam by around 2010. In 1996 the two halves were linked by Erasmusbrug (Erasmus Bridge).

Rotterdam is the birth place (1469) of the great humanist Erasmus, Geert Geertsz. He travelled widely in Europe and died in Basle in 1536 but he is honoured in the name of the university in his native city.

WHICH DISTRICT TO CHOOSE

The greatest concentration of **hotels** is in the city centre between the railway station *Plan II* **E1** and the Nieuwe Maas *Plan II* **F2**; as the city was rebuilt after the war, the hotels are modern buildings. There are also a few more traditional hotels on the outskirts.

Most **restaurants** are in the city centre, although a few are attached to the hotels in the suburbs.

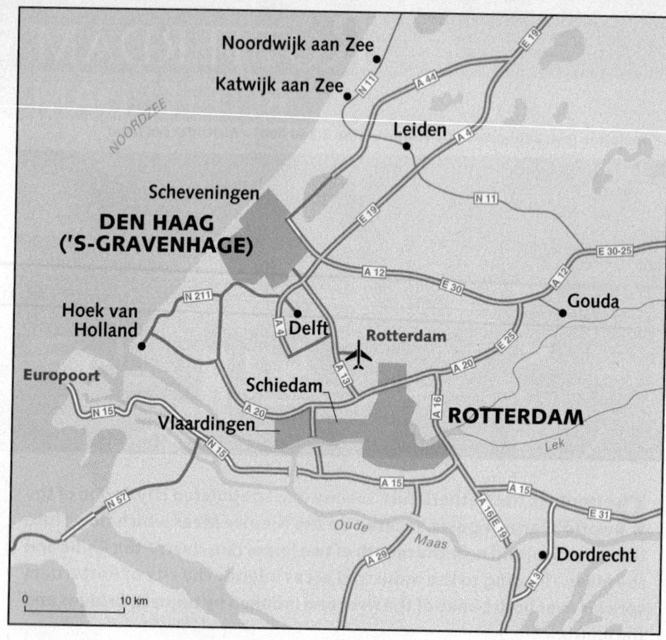

PRACTICAL INFORMATION

ARRIVAL – DEPARTURE

ROTTERDAM

➜ **Airport** – About 6km (4 miles) northwest of city centre. ✆ 010 446 34 44; www.rotterdam-airport.nl

From the airport to the city centre – By **taxi** (15min), €20-€23, ✆ 0102 62 04 06 (Rotterdam Airport Taxi). By **shuttle bus** No 33 and No 43 (20min) to Central Railway Station every 10min, single €2.70; ✆ 0900 92 92; www.9292ov.nl; www.ret.nl

Railway Station – Regular train services to the **Centraal Station** *Plan II* **E1** from the major towns in the Netherlands, Belgium, France and Germany; www.ns.nl

Ferry Terminal – Regular ferry services from England: Harwich (www.stenaline.co.uk) and Hull (www.poferries.com).

TRANSPORT

➜ BUSES

The extensive network (RET) consists of metro, bus and train services. ✆ 0900 92 92. Tickets on sale at the service point in front of the railway station or at Coolsingel 141; 1-hour ticket €2.70; 2-strip, 3-strip, 8-strip, 15-strip and 45-strip tickets at €1.60, €2.40, €6.40, €6.80 and €20.10; 1-day, 2-day and 3-day tickets, €6.40, €9.60 and €12.80. In summer the tourist tram, No 10, serves the main sights. ✆ 0800 60 61; www.ret.rotterdam.nl

→ TAXIS

Taxis bear blue number plates and an illuminated sign on the roof. They may be called by telephone or hired at taxi ranks – airport, railway stations; although they are not supposed to stop, they can also be hailed in the street. Pick-up charge €2.00; price per km €1.50; taxi fares are usually rounded up (5-10%). ✆ 462 60 60 (Rotterdam Taxi Centre).

→ BICYCLES

Bicycles can be hired at the cycle shop at the station; €6.50 per day, €32.50 per week. ✆ 010 412 62 20.

→ ROTTERDAM CARD

Rotterdam card provides unlimited use of the transport network and free admission to most attractions; 24hr-card €25 and 72hr-card €49.50.

USEFUL ADDRESSES

→ TOURIST OFFICES

VVV Rotterdam – Coolsingel 67 *Plan II* **E1**; Open Mon-Sat 9.30am-6pm (9pm Fri, 5pm Sat), ✆ 010 403 40 65, 010 414 0000. Coolsingel 197, ✆ 010 489 77 77. Rotterdam Airport Info Desk, Airportplein 60, ✆ 010 446 34 44; www.vvv.rotterdam.nl; www.rotterdam.info; www.gorotterdam.com; www.rotterdam-Airport.nl

→ POST OFFICES

Post Offices are open Mon-Fri 8.30am-5pm. Longer opening hours (also Saturday 8.30-noon) are available at some large city branches.

→ BANKS/CURRENCY EXCHANGE

Opening times are Mon-Fri 9am-4pm. Longer opening hours (Thurs 9am-9pm and Sat morning) are available at some large city banks. All close on public holidays. Bank cash machines (ATMs) are open 24hrs (pin number required).

→ EMERGENCY

Phone ✆ **112** for the emergency services; Police ✆ **0900 88 44**.

BUSY PERIODS

It may be difficult to find a room at a reasonable price (except at weekends) during special events:

International Film Festival: January – 12-day film festival.

Dunya Festival: early June – Multicultural event.

Carnival Street Parade: July – Tropical-style summer event.

FFWD Dance Parade: August – huge techno, hip-hop and big-beat event.

Wereldhavenfestival: early September – Discover the port of Rotterdam.

September in Rotterdam: September – Arts and cultural event.

EXPLORING ROTTERDAM

In two days there is time to visit the main sights and museums.

Rotterdam Welcome Card offers €100 worth of benefits.

Opening times are usually from 10/11am-4/5pm but closed on Mondays and public holidays.

VISITING

Museum Boijmans Van Beuningen *Plan II* **E2** – Fine Arts Museum: rich collection of antiques, modern and contemporary works of art, engravings, decorative arts section (17C glassware and earthenware).

Maritiem Museum Rotterdam *Plan II* **F2** – History of the port of Rotterdam.

Nederlands Architectuurinstituut *Plan II* **E2** – Complex, consisting of four buildings, each in its own style serving a different function: offices and library on Dutch and foreign architecture; auditorium, exhibition wing; collection wing.

Oude Haven *Plan II* **F2** – Rotterdam's first harbour (1325), now a pleasant place for a stroll or for admiring the **Witte Huis**, a 19C office block and the only remnant of the pre-war period; the old Dutch commercial sailing ships of the Inland Waterways Museum *(Openlucht Binnenvaart Museuum)*, and the impressive cable-stayed **Willemsbrug** spanning the Nieuwe Maas. A few steps north is **Overblaak**, cube-shaped apartments spanning the road near the **Blaak Station**, both impressive examples of modern architecture. A few steps south west is **Boompjes**, "little trees", a 17C double row of lime trees, now a modern boulevard with three tower blocks, **Boompjestorens**.

Euromast *Plan II* **E3** – Tower built in 1960 with a viewing platform: remarkable view of the port and city.

Port *Plan II* **E2** – Boat trip along the Nieuwe Maas (River Meuse) to Eemhaven and Botlek: harbours, docks, quay, **Europoort** and **Maasvlakte** facilities.

Molens van Kinderdijk *(30 km – 19 mi – east of Rotterdam)* – Series of 19 windmills used until 1950 to drain the Alblasserwaard, on the banks of the canal amid meadows and reeds (windmill festivals July and August, Saturday afternoons).

SHOPPING

Shops are usually open from Mon-Sat (in town centre also Sun 12-5pm).

The Tourist Information Centre (VVV) sells a guide to some of the more interesting shopping areas.

There are many shopping centres: the *Lijnbaan Plan II* **E2**, Europe's first pedestrian area; the *Beurstraverse* one of the city's architectural highlights; the *Plaza Plan II* **E1**, opposite the railway station (Centraal Station); and the *Zuiderboulevard Plan I* **C3**. The *Vrij Entrepot* is a new shopping area in the **Kop van Zuid district** *Plan I* **C2**. The area in and around the former warehouse **De Vijf Werelddelen** (late-night shopping on Fridays until 9pm) has all kinds of shops and numerous restaurants and bars. The many commercial art galleries are centred around **Witte de Withstraat** *Plan II* **E2**, the cultural hub of Rotterdam.

MARKETS – **Centrummarkt** (Tues and Sat) in the Binnenrotteterrein; **antiques market** (Sun) on Schiedamsdijk *Plan II* **F2**; **Markt Zuid** (Wed and Sat) in the Afrikaanderplein *Plan I* **C2**; **Markt West** (Thurs and Sat) in Grote Visserijplein *Plan I* **B2** for wide variety of exotic foreign products.

WHAT TO BUY – The local **specialities** are Delft porcelain, Dutch cheese, cigars, Dutch gin and spirits, clogs.

ENTERTAINMENT

R'Uit Magazine gives a full summary of all exhibitions, dance and theatre performances, concerts and other events; published monthly and available free of charge from the tourist information offices or other outlets.

Schouwburg *Plan II* **E2** (Schouwburgplein 25) – Dance, theatre, drama.

Luxor Theatre *Plan I* **C2** (Posthumalaan 125) – Great variety of events.

NIGHTLIFE

Rotterdam's reputation for clubbing attracts fans from all over the Netherlands and abroad: *Off Corso* (Kruiskade 22); *Now-Wow* (Maashaven); *Las Palmas* (Wilhelminakade 66).

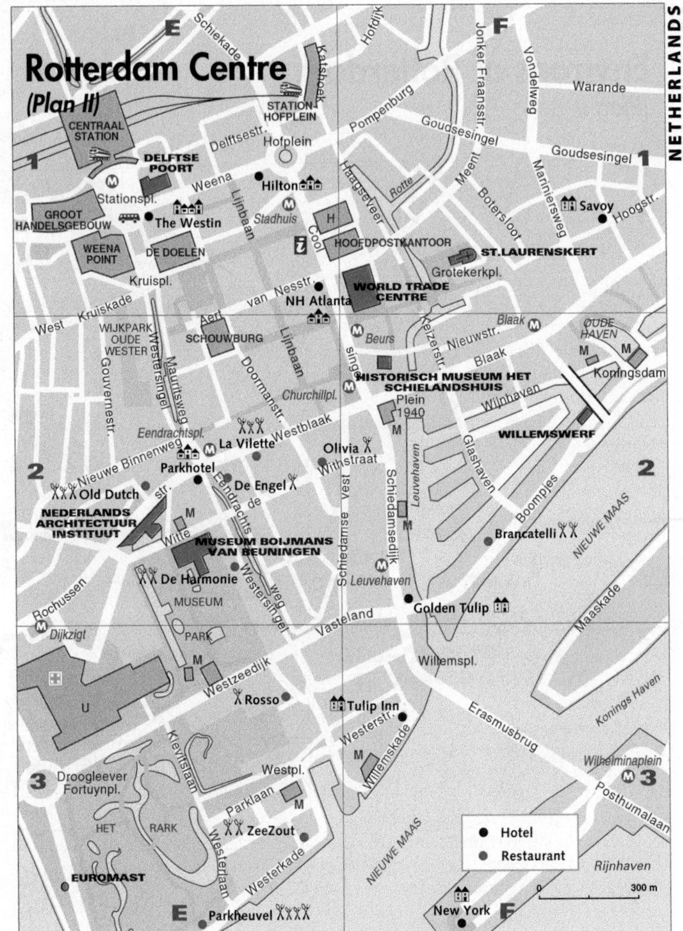
Rotterdam Centre
(Plan II)
CENTRAAL STATION
DELFTSE POORT
GROOT HANDELSGEBOUW
WEENA POINT
DE DOELEN
STATION HOFPLEIN
Hofplein
Hilton
The Westin
Stadhuis
HOOFDPOSTKANTOOR
ST.LAURENSKERT
Grotekerkpl.
WORLD TRADE CENTRE
NH Atlanta
WIJKPARK OUDE WESTER
SCHOUWBURG
Beurs
HISTORISCH MUSEUM HET SCHIELANDSHUIS
Plein 1940
Churchillpl.
Eendrachtspl.
La Vilette
Olivia
Parkhotel
Old Dutch
De Engel
NEDERLANDS ARCHITECTUUR INSTITUUT
MUSEUM BOIJMANS VAN BEUNINGEN
De Harmonie
MUSEUM PARK
WILLEMSWERF
Brancatelli
Leuvehaven
Golden Tulip
Dijkzigt
Willemspl.
Rosso
Tulip Inn
Erasmusbrug
Droogleever Fortuynpl.
HET PARK
ZeeZout
EUROMAST
Parkheuvel
New York
Savoy
OUDE HAVEN
Koningsdam
NIEUWE MAAS
Maaskade
Konings Haven
Wilhelminaplein
Rijnhaven
Posthumalaan
Schiekade
Katshoek
Hofdijk
Jonker Fraansstr.
Vondelweg
Warande
Pompenburg
Goudsesingel
Delftsestr.
Weena
Stationspl.
Lijnbaan
Coolsingel
Haagseveer
Rotte
Meent
Botersloot
Mariniersweg
Hoogstr.
Kruispl.
West Kruiskade
van Nesstr.
Aert van Nesstr.
Westersingel
Mauritsweg
Gouvernestr.
Doormanstr.
Westblaak
Blaak
Nieuwstr.
Keizerstr.
Wijnhaven
Glashaven
Boompjes
Nieuwe Binnenweg
Witte de Withstraat
Eendrachtsweg
Schiedamse vest
Schiedamsedijk
Rochussenstr.
Vasteland
Westzeedijk
Kievitslaan
Westerstr.
Willemskade
Westpl.
Parklaan
Westerlaan
Westerkade
Hotel
Restaurant
300 m
E
F
1
2
3

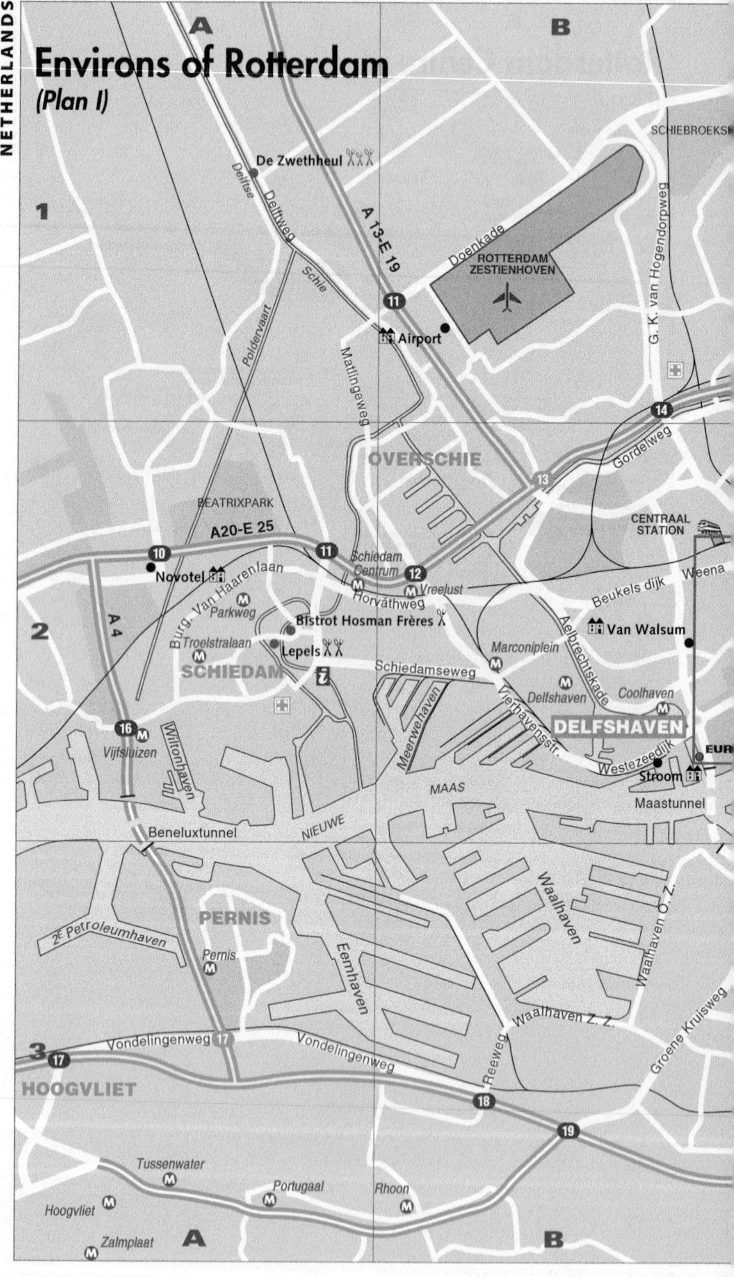
Environs of Rotterdam
(Plan I)
A
B
1
2
3
De Zwethheul
Delftse
Delftweg
Schie
A 13-E 19
Doenkade
ROTTERDAM ZESTIENHOVEN
SCHIEBROEKS
G. K. van Hogendorpweg
Airport
Poldervaart
Matlingeweg
OVERSCHIE
Gordelweg
BEATRIXPARK
A20-E 25
CENTRAAL STATION
Schiedam Centrum
Novotel
Burg. Van Haarenlaan
Parkweg
Vreelust
Horváthweg
Weena
Beukels dijk
A 4
Bistrot Hosman Frères
Van Walsum
Troelstralaan
Lepels
Aelbrechtskade
SCHIEDAM
Schiedamseweg
Marconiplein
Delfshaven
Coolhaven
Vierhavensstr.
Meerwehaven
DELFSHAVEN
Vijfsluizen
Wiltonhaven
Westezeedijk
Stroom
MAAS
Maastunnel
Beneluxtunnel
NIEUWE
Waalhaven
PERNIS
Waalhaven O. Z.
2E Petroleumhaven
Pernis
Eemhaven
Waalhaven Z. Z.
Groene Kruisweg
Vondelingenweg
Reeweg
HOOGVLIET
Tussenwater
Portugaal
Rhoon
Hoogvliet
Zalmplaat

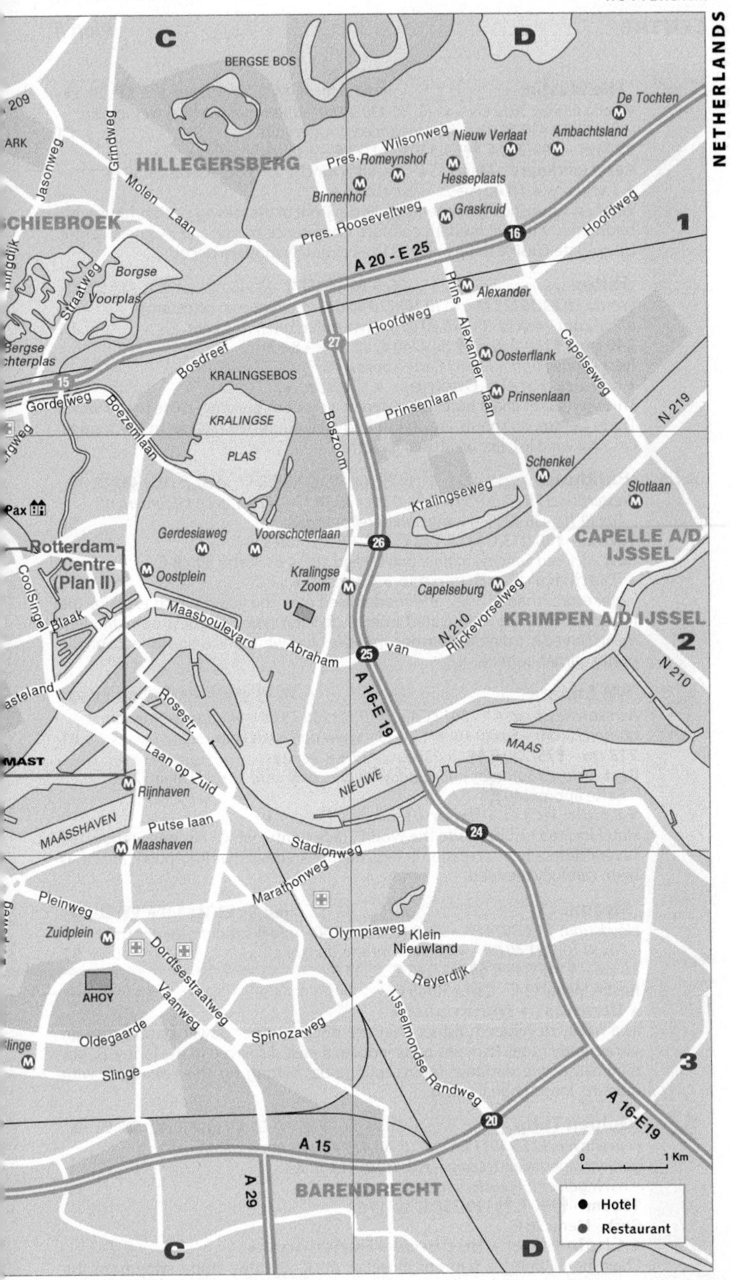

C
D
BERGSE BOS
HILLEGERSBERG
SCHIEBROEK
Grindweg
Jasonweg
Molen
Laan
Borgse
Straatweg
Voorplas
Bergse
Achterplas
De Tochten
Nieuw Verlaat
Ambachtsland
Wilsonweg
Pres.
Romeynshof
Hesseplaats
Binnenhof
Pres. Rooseveltweg
Graskruid
16
Hoofdweg
1
A 20 - E 25
Prins
Alexander
Alexander
laan
Oosterflank
Prinsenlaan
Capelseweg
N 219
Hoofdweg
27
Bosdreef
KRALINGSEBOS
KRALINGSE
PLAS
Boszoom
15
Gordelweg
Boezemlaan
Prinsenlaan
Schenkel
Slotlaan
Kralingseweg
Pax
Gerdesiaweg
Voorschoterlaan
26
CAPELLE A/D
IJSSEL
Rotterdam-
Centre
(Plan II)
Oostplein
Kralingse
Zoom
Capelseburg
Rijckevorselweg
KRIMPEN A/D IJSSEL
Coolsingel
Blaak
Maasboulevard
U
Abraham
25
van
N 210
2
N 210
Roseestr.
A 16-E 19
MAAS
MAST
Laan op Zuid
Rijnhaven
NIEUWE
MAASHAVEN
Putse laan
Maashaven
Stadionweg
24
Marathonweg
Pleinweg
Zuidplein
Olympiaweg
Klein
Nieuwland
Dordtsestraatweg
AHOY
Vaanweg
Reyerdijk
Oldegaarde
Spinozaweg
IJsselmondse Randweg
Slinge
3
A 16-E19
20
A 15
A 29
BARENDRECHT
0
1 Km
Hotel
Restaurant
C
D

CENTRE

Plan II

The Westin

Weena 686 ✉ 3012 CN – ✆ (0 10) 430 20 00 – rotterdam.westin@westin.com – Fax (0 10) 430 20 01 – www.westin.com/rotterdam **E1**

227 rm – 99/300 € 99/330 €, 23 € – 4 suites

Rest *Lighthouse* – Menu 25 € (weekday lunch), 22/37 € – Carte 28/59 €

♦ Luxury ♦ Business ♦ Stylish ♦

This new futuristic skyscraper, standing in front of the railway station, houses big bedrooms, with full modern comfort. Conference rooms and business centre. Up-to-date cuisine to be enjoyed in a resolutely modern decor.

Hilton

Weena 10 ✉ 3012 CM – ✆ (0 10) 710 80 00 – reservations.rotterdam@hilton.com – Fax (0 10) 710 80 00 – www.rotterdam.hilton.com **E1**

246 rm – 150/240 € 150/240 €, 23 € – 8 suites

Rest – *(open until 11 p.m.)* Carte approx. 45 €

♦ Chain hotel ♦ Business ♦ Classic ♦

This up-market chain hotel is housed in a modern building, close to the World Trade Centre. Its rooms are stylish and well equipped. Snacks in the lounge. Original wine list, like an artist's "palette".

Parkhotel

Westersingel 70 ✉ 3015 LB – ✆ (0 10) 436 36 11 – parkhotel@bilderberg.nl – Fax (0 10) 436 42 12 – www.parkhotelrotterdam.nl **E2**

187 rm – 80/213 € 80/213 €, 21 € – 2 suites

Rest – *(closed Sunday) (dinner only)* Menu 28/34 € – Carte 30/48 €

♦ Traditional ♦ Business ♦ Classic ♦

Hotel established in 1922 and modernised over the years, which explains the mixed architecture. Renovated interior. Several types of guestroom. Modern meals served in a dining room decorated in blue, white and beige tones or on the pretty garden terrace.

NH Atlanta

Aert van Nesstraat 4 ✉ 3012 CA – ✆ (0 10) 206 78 00 – nhatlantarotterdam@nh-hotels.com – Fax (0 10) 411 74 23 – www.nh-hotels.com **E1**

213 rm – 75/220 € 75/220 €, 17 € – 2 suites

Rest – *(closed Saturday and Sunday) (dinner only until 11 p.m.)* Menu 26 € – Carte approx. 40 €

♦ Chain hotel ♦ Business ♦ Art Deco ♦

Hotel located just opposite the World Trade Centre which has been renovated several times since its creation in 1930 but the Art deco style in its public areas has been carefully retained.

Stroom

Lloydstraat 1 ✉ 3024 EA – ✆ (0 10) 221 40 60 – info@stroomrotterdam.nl – Fax (0 10) 221 40 61 – www.stroomrotterdam.nl *Plan I* **B2**

18 rm – 145/345 € 145/345 €, 11 €

Rest – Menu 33 € – Carte 30/45 €

♦ Business ♦ Minimalist ♦

In a newly-developed district near the docks, former power station now an ultra-trendy hotel. Remains of its industrial past displayed in the lobby. Bright minimalist-style designer rooms.Lounge-bar setting for this restaurant with modern, international menu.

Golden Tulip

Leuvehaven 80 ✉ 3011 EA – ✆ (0 10) 413 41 39 – inforotterdam@goldentuliphotelinntel.com – Fax (0 10) 413 32 22 – www.goldentuliprotterdamcentre.com **F2**

150 rm – 190 € 190/350 €, 19 €

Rest – Menu 26 €

♦ Chain hotel ♦ Business ♦ Functional ♦

Chain hotel, lining a harbour museum dock, just one stride away from the majestic Erasmus Bridge (Erasmusbrug). Top-floor pool and panoramic bar.

Savoy without rest 60 VISA

Hoogstraat 81 ✉ 3011 PJ – ✆ (0 10) 413 92 80 – info.savoy@ edenhotelgroup.com – Fax (0 10) 404 57 12 – www.edenhotelgroup.com **F1**

94 rm – 80/205 € 80/205 €, 17 €

♦ Traditional ♦ Business ♦ Classic ♦

A short distance away from the famous "cube houses" designed by Blom, a pleasant hotel with rooms over seven storeys. Free internet access on the ground floor.

New York 100 VISA

Koninginnenhofd 1 (Wilhelminapier) ✉ 3072 AD – ✆ (0 10) 439 05 00 – info@ hotelnewyork.nl – Fax (0 10) 484 27 01 – www.hotelnewyork.nl **F3**

72 rm – 98/220 € 98/220 €, 12 €

Rest – *(open until midnight)* Menu 23 € – Carte 21/49 €

♦ Traditional ♦ Business ♦ Personalised ♦

Former headquarters of the Holland-America shipping line, converted into a hotel, with character. Original, customized bedrooms with views of the port, town or river. Spacious dining room adorned with "bistro"-type furniture.

Pax without rest 80 VISA

Schiekade 658 ✉ 3032 AK – ✆ (0 10) 466 33 44 – pax@bestwestern.nl – Fax (0 10) 467 52 78 – www.paxhotel.nl *Plan I* **C2**

124 rm – 75/145 € 85/185 €

♦ Business ♦ Functional ♦

Hotel lining a major road. It is just as convenient for train travellers as for motorists. Bedrooms of various sizes, with standard furniture.

Tulip Inn rest 60 VISA

Willemsplein 1 ✉ 3016 DN – ✆ (0 10) 413 47 90 – reservations@ tulipinnrotterdam.nl – Fax (0 10) 412 78 90 – www.tulipinnrotterdam.nl **F3**

92 rm – 139/199 € 149/220 €, 14 €

Rest – Menu 23 € – Carte 43/52 €

♦ Chain hotel ♦ Business ♦ Functional ♦

This building, lining a Nieuwe Maas quay, offers good, functional and rather comfortable little bedrooms. The Erasmusbrug is spread out before your eyes.

Van Walsum VISA

Mathenesserlaan 199 ✉ 3014 HC – ✆ (0 10) 436 32 75 – info@ hotelvanwalsum.nl – Fax (0 10) 436 44 10 – www.hotelvanwalsum.nl closed 24 December-2 January *Plan I* **B2**

29 rm – 80/95 € 100/150 €

Rest – *(residents only)*

♦ Family ♦ Business ♦ Functional ♦

Imposing middle-class residence, with identically-furnished and double-glazed bedrooms of various sizes. The breakfast room opens on to the terrace.

Parkheuvel (van Loo) 8/40 VISA

Heuvellaan 21 ✉ 3016 GL – ✆ (0 10) 436 07 66 – info@parkheuvel.com – Fax (0 10) 436 71 40 – www.parkheuvel.com closed 15 July-5 August, 27 December-7 January and Sunday **E3**

Rest – Menu 48 € (weekday lunch), 85/140 € bi – Carte 68/103 €

Spec. In wijn gemarineerde ganzenlever met zoetzure blet. Ravioli van kip met langoustines. Met witte chocolademousse gevulde frambozen, balsamico azijn en basilicum.

♦ Contemporary ♦ Formal ♦

On the banks of the Maas and next to a park near the Euromast tower, a modern, round-shaped pavilion offering great harbour views from the large bay windows and terrace. Elaborate menu.

XXX **Old Dutch** ⛱ ⇔10/55 P VISA MC AE ①

Rochussenstraat 20 ✉ 3015 EK – ☎ (0 10) 436 03 44 – info@olddutch.net – Fax (0 10) 436 78 26 – www.olddutch.net

closed Saturday dinner in July and August, Saturday lunch and Sunday **E2**

Rest – Menu 35 € (weekday lunch), 50/85 € bi – Carte 51/70 €

♦ Traditional ♦ Formal ♦

The "Old Dutchman" is a pleasant restaurant, adorned with conventional furniture, occupying an inn built in 1932. Several standard menus. Wines from around the world.

XXX ✿ **La Vilette** (Mustert) A/C VISA MC AE ①

Westblaak 160 ✉ 3012 KM – ☎ (0 10) 414 86 92 – Fax (0 10) 414 33 91 – www.lavilette.nl

closed 16 July-5 August, 24 December-3 January, Saturday lunch and Sunday **E2**

Rest – Menu 34 € (weekday lunch), 43/56 € bi – Carte 52/63 €

Spec. Jakobsschelp en eendenlever met truffel en appelstroop. Gebakken langoustines met watermeloen, creme van Jamaicapeper. Bereldingen van chocolade en noga.

♦ Contemporary ♦ Formal ♦

Comfortable restaurant with a "select brasserie" décor and refined atmosphere in the evenings. Quality welcome and service and appetising modern menu.

XX **De Harmonie** ⛱ ⇔6/70 VISA MC AE ①

Westersingel 95 ✉ 3015 LC – ☎ (0 10) 436 36 10 – deharmonie@deharmonie.demon.nl – Fax (0 10) 436 36 08 – www.restaurantdeharmonie.nl

closed 26 December-2 January, Saturday lunch and Sunday **E2**

Rest – Menu 38 € (weekday lunch), 40/78 € bi – Carte 48/69 €

♦ Contemporary ♦ Fashionable ♦

A modern restaurant opposite the Museumpark in a chic avenue of fine houses. A modern, refined dining area opening onto the charming garden terrace.

XX **Zeezout** ⛱ A/C VISA MC AE ①

Westerkade 11b ✉ 3016 CL – ☎ (0 10) 436 50 49 – zeezout1@hetnet.nl – Fax (0 10) 225 18 47 – www.engelgroep.com

closed Saturday lunch, Sunday and Monday **E3**

Rest – *(booking essential)* Menu 32 € (weekday lunch), 42/70 € bi – Carte 42/83 €

♦ Seafood ♦ Cosy ♦

The chic and trendy atmosphere, fish and seafood menu and waterside terrace are this modern brasserie's assets, whose name – "Sea Salt" – gives the game away.

XX **Brancatelli** A/C ⇔60 VISA MC AE

Boompjes 264 ✉ 3011 XZ – ☎ (0 10) 411 41 51 – restaurant@brancatelli.nl – Fax (0 10) 404 57 34 – www.brancatelli.com **F2**

Rest – *(open until 11 p.m.)* Menu 30 € (weekday lunch), 50/80 € – Carte 36/51 €

♦ Italian ♦ Friendly ♦

Italian restaurant, with a modern setting, lining a lively quay. Rather authentic menu, accompanied by a selection of wines received directly from Italy.

X **De Engel** A/C ⇔15/50 VISA MC AE ①

Eendrachtsweg 19 ✉ 3012 LB – ☎ (0 10) 413 82 56 – restaurant@engel.nl – Fax (0 10) 414 51 96 – www.engelgroep.com

closed 25-26 December, 31 January, Saturday lunch and Sunday **E2**

Rest – Menu 37 € (weekday lunch), 40/104 € bi – Carte 48/67 €

♦ Traditional ♦ Trendy ♦

One of Rotterdam's fashionable establishments. Relaxed atmosphere and a modern interior, adorned with furniture of varying styles and well-prepared market cooking.

Oliva
8/13 VISA

Witte de Withstraat 15a ✉ 3012 BK – ✆ (0 10) 412 14 13 – info@restaurantoliva.nl – Fax (0 10) 412 70 69 – www.restaurantoliva.nl **E2**

Rest – Menu 32/42 € – Carte approx. 40 €

◆ Italian ◆ Trendy ◆

A trendy Italian restaurant in an old industrial building. Loft style décor, lively atmosphere, a simple menu and daily specials board.

Rosso
A/C

Van Vollenhovenstraat 15 (access by Westerlijk Handelsterrein) ✉ 3016 BE – ✆ (0 10) 225 07 05

closed last week July and Sunday **E3**

Rest – *(dinner only)* Menu 35/78 € bi – Carte approx. 50 €

◆ Contemporary ◆ Wine bar ◆

Bar-restaurant in a renovated 19th century warehouse, with dining area in vibrant red tones. Chic clientele and ambiance. Très à la mode!

AT THE AIRPORT

Plan I

Airport
rm A/C 425 P VISA AE

Vliegveldweg 59 ✉ 3043 NT – ✆ (0 10) 462 55 66 – info@airporthotel.nl – Fax (0 10) 462 22 66 – www.airporthotel.nl **B1**

96 rm – †69/195 € ††69/195 €, 17 € – 2 suites

Rest – *(closed Friday dinner, Saturday and Sunday)* Menu 32 €

◆ Business ◆ Functional ◆

Hotel located opposite the airport (shuttle always available), with functional, well-soundproofed rooms. Lounge and bar popular with business clientele. Comfortable and modern dining room. Traditional dishes.

Novotel
rm A/C 200 P VISA AE

Hargalaan 2 (near A 20) ✉ 3118 JA Schiedam – ✆ (0 10) 471 33 22 – h0517@accor.com – Fax (0 10) 470 06 56 – www.accorhotels.com **A2**

134 rm – †79/135 € ††79/135 €, 16 €

Rest – Carte 28/46 €

◆ Chain hotel ◆ Business ◆ Functional ◆

Chain hotel in the verdant outskirts of the town on a crossroads, near the ring road. Functional bedrooms, summer terrace and garden with children's playground by the swimming pool. A modern style brasserie.

De Zwethheul
A/C 8/80 P VISA AE

Rotterdamseweg 480 (at Zweth, canalside) ✉ 2636 KB Schipluiden – ✆ (0 10) 470 41 66 – info@zwethheul.nl – Fax (0 10) 470 65 22 – www.zwethheul.nl

closed 24 December-7 January, Saturday lunch, Sunday lunch and Monday

Rest – Menu 45 € (weekday lunch), 65/145 € bi – Carte 74/107 € **A1**

Spec. "Rosbief" van tonijn met zwarte peper, chaud-froid van krab. Het beste van het lam met asperges (May-June). Reerug met sinaasappel, jus van kruldkoek en stoofpeertjes (October-December).

◆ Contemporary ◆ Formal ◆

This remodelled former inn is now a restaurant serving fine meals, with a magnificent view of the boats sailing past. Attractive terrace under the trees by the water's edge.

Lepels
A/C 6/20 VISA

Korte Haven 5 ✉ 3111 BH Schiedam – ✆ (0 10) 246 73 58 – info@marcsmeeds.nl – Fax (0 10) 246 73 59 – www.marcsmeeds.nl

closed 23 July-7 August, 27 December-12 January, Saturday lunch, Sunday and Monday **A2**

Rest – Menu 30 € (weekday lunch), 43/76 € bi – Carte 43/60 €

◆ Contemporary ◆ Brasserie ◆

Trendy restaurant located between the covered market and the windmill, near a bascule bridge. Central open kitchen, black and white designer décor, soft lighting and lounge music.

NETHERLANDS

Bistrot Hosman Frères

AC ⇔10/40 VISA MC AE

Korte Dam 10 ✉ 3111 BG Schiedam – ✆ (0 10) 426 40 96 – Fax (0 10) 426 90 41 – www.hosman-freres.nl
closed late December-1 January, Saturday lunch, Sunday lunch and Monday **A2**
Rest – Menu 28/40 € – Carte 34/47 €
♦ Traditional ♦ Bistro ♦
Pleasant inn, located on a picturesque Old Town site, near four old windmills. "Bistrot"-type food enthusiasts will be happy there.

NORWAY
NORGE

PROFILE

◆ **Area:**
323 878 km²
(125 049 sq mi).

◆ **Population:**
4 640 000 inhabitants (est. 2006), density = 14 per km².

◆ **Capital:**
Oslo (conurbation 731 600 inhabitants).

◆ **Currency:**
Krone (kr or NOK) divided into 100 øre; rate of exchange: NOK 1 = € 0.12 = US$ 0.15 (Nov 2006).

◆ **Government:**
Constitutional parliamentary monarchy with single-chamber Parliament (since 1945).

◆ **Languages:**
Norwegian has two written variants: Bokmål (influenced by Danish) spoken by 80% of the population and Nynorsk (New Norwegian). Sami is the language of the Sami people in the far north. English is widely spoken.

◆ **Specific public holidays:**
Maundy Thursday and Good Friday (Thursday and Friday before Easter); Constitution Day (17 May); Boxing Day (26 December and 27 December).

◆ **Local Time:**
GMT + 1 hour in winter and GMT + 2 hours in summer.

◆ **Climate:**
Temperate northern maritime, with cold winters and mild summers (Oslo: January: -4°C,

July: 16°C). Colder interior, fairly high precipitation in the coastal regions.

◆ **International dialling Code:**
00 47 followed by full local number.

◆ **Emergency:**
Police: ✆ **112**; Ambulance service: ✆ **113**; Fire Brigade: ✆ **110**.

◆ **Electricity:**
220 volts AC, 50Hz; 2-pin round-shaped continental plugs.

FORMALITIES

Travellers from the European Union (EU), Switzerland, Iceland and the main countries of North and South America need a national identity card or passport (America: passport required) to visit Norway for less than three months (tourism or business purpose). For visitors from other countries a visa may be required, in addition to a passport, especially for those wishing to stay for longer than three months. We advise you to check with your embassy before travelling.

Drivers must have a valid national driving licence, together with the vehicle's current registration document or a vehicle on hire certificate. Third party insurance is compulsory but Green Cards are highly recommended. The minimum age for drivers in Norway is 18 or 20 depending on the type of vehicle.

MAJOR NEWSPAPERS

The main national newspapers are: *Aftenposten, Verdens Gang, Vårt Land, Dagbladet and Dagsavinsen.*

SMOKING-NO SMOKING

The laws in Norway prohibit smoking in all restaurants, bars and in the public areas of hotels. Some hotel bedrooms are still available for smokers.

USEFUL PHRASES

ENGLISH	NORWEGIAN
Yes	**Ja**
No	**Nei**
Good morning	**God morgen**
Goodbye	**Ha det bra**
Thank you	**Takk**
Please	**Vær så god**
Excuse me	**Unnskyld**
I don't understand	**Jeg forstår ikke**

HOTELS

→ CATEGORIES

The standard of accommodation is very high and ranges from luxury international hotels and comfortable chain hotels to mountain hotels, chalets, cabins and guesthouses. Bed and breakfast accommodation is developing in Norway.

→ PRICE RANGE

The price is per room. There is little difference between the price of a single and a double room. In the high season, between mid-June and mid-August, it is advisable to book in advance in tourist areas. There are several hotel passes, discount schemes and cheque systems in operation which offer reduced hotel rates. Hotels in Oslo and the main towns offer substantial discounted rates at weekends and in summer, which are quieter periods for business travel.

→ TAX

Included in the room price. A service charge (10-12%) is included in hotel bills.

→ CHECKOUT TIME

Usually between 11am and noon.

→ RESERVATIONS

By telephone or by the Internet. A credit card is usually required. Tourist Information Offices in Norway often have a reservation service.

→ TIPS FOR LUGGAGE HANDLING

At the discretion of the client. A small tip (15-20NOK) is usually appreciated.

→ BREAKFAST

Breakfast is usually included in the room price. Most hotels offer a substantial self-service buffet of cold meats, pickled herring, eggs, cheese, cereals, fruit, jam and a variety of breads and rolls between 7-8am and 11am.

Reception	**Resepsjon**
Single room	**Enkeltrom**
Double room	**Dobbeltrom**

Bed	**Seng**
Bathroom	**Bad**
Shower	**Dusj**

RESTAURANTS

There are various types of places to eat in Norway besides the traditional restaurants: brasseries, cafés, cafeterias, self-service eateries, pizzerias, bistros, snack bars and sandwich shops. Those who want variety will also find places serving food from all over the world. Norwegians often have a snack at any time of the day.

→ MEALS

Breakfast	**Frokost**	7/8am-10am
Lunch	**Lunsj**	11am-3pm
Dinner	**Middag**	6pm-10pm

***NB**: Breakfast tends to be a copious meal while lunch is usually a snack (open sandwiches). Dinner is a hot meal which is eaten fairly early. A smørbrød supper (Kueldsmat) is taken in the late evening.*

Restaurants serving modern international cuisine and fusion food are to be found throughout Norway, particularly in the cities. They offer a comprehensive à la carte menu as well as a fixed price menu. At lunch you may choose to have a light snack or open sandwich or the dish of the day *(dangens rett)*.

→ RESERVATIONS

Reservations can be made by telephone, Internet or fax. It is not always necessary to book a table except if you want to visit a gourmet restaurant or a popular establishment.

→ THE BILL

The bill (check) includes service charge, VAT and tip. No additional gratuity is expected but you may wish to reward exceptional service (5 -10%).

Appetizer	**Appetittvekker**
Meal	**Måltid**
Starter	**Forett**
Main dish	**Hovedrett**
Main dish of the day	**Dagens rett**
Dessert	**Dessert**
Water/ mineral water (still, sparkling)	**Vann/ mineralvann (uten kullsyre, med kullsyre)**
Wine (red, white, rosé)	**Vin (rødvin, hvitvin, rosévin)**
Beer	**Øl**
Bread	**Brød**
Meat	**Kjøtt**
Fish	**Fisk**
Salt/pepper	**Salt/pepper**
Cheese	**Ost**
Vegetables	**Grønnsaker**
Hot/cold	**Varm/kald**
The bill (check) please	**Regningen, takk**

LOCAL CUISINE

Norway has an abundance of fresh products: fish and seafood from its long coastline, freshwater fish from its lakes and waterways, lamb and mutton from its verdant pastures and venison from its forests and mountains. The Norwegians have perfected the ways of preserving fish and meat by smoking, drying, pickling and salting. The forest and mountain plateaux provide a profusion of berries, and chanterelles and other wild mushrooms are picked in the forests in the autumn.

Fresh prawns direct from the boat are delicious. Fish – cod, catfish, halibut, haddock, mackerel, ling, ocean perch, coalfish, blenny, Arctic char, grayling, bream, tench – is always well cooked. Poached cod served with boiled potatoes is a delicacy as is poached salmon **(kokt laks)**. Crayfish **(kreps)**, mountain trout **(øret)** preferably broiled and served with fresh lemon are great treats, not to mention smoked salmon, trout and **gravlax**. Fish soufflé **(fiske-grateng)** and a creamy fish soup with shrimps are recommended. The national speciality is **lutefisk**, dried cod treated with lye and salted, which is either boiled or baked; it is very much an acquired taste.

Meat lovers will want to try reindeer, elk, venison or grouse either roasted **(reinsdyrstex, reinodyrstek)** or served with a creamy game sauce. Reindeer steak with gravy and tart lingonberries, roast lamb, cured leg of mutton **(fenalår)**, salted lamb ribs **(pinnekjøtt)** are specialities. The national dish is a lamb and cabbage stew **(Fårikål)**. Other typical dishes include meat patties with onions and gravy **(kjøttpudding)** and meatballs. **Postei** is a meat pie and **lapskaus,** a kind of hash made with leftovers. **Spekemat**, cured meat, is served with flat bread **(flatbrød)**, soured cream and scrambled eggs. **Kjøttpålegg** is cold meat cuts and **spekepølse** air-dried sausage. Boiled, roasted or fried potatoes accompany nearly all dishes.

The secret of the open sandwich **(smørbrød)** is choosing the right mixture of ingredients: a thin slice of rye bread topped with almost anything savoury, cold meats, smoked salmon, smoked eel, pickled herrings, eggs, sausages, cheese and garnished with various salads. You can also have a hot dog **(pølse i brød)** or a waffle as a snack. The evening meal is the main meal of the day. A **koldtbord** is an extensive choice of cold meats, seafood, salads – and one or two hot dishes and is traditionally served at holiday periods. For dessert try the pale-coloured cloudberries **(multer)**, raspberries and strawberries which are full of flavour, or a pancake with syltetøy (fruit jam). The soft **Jarlsberg** is the best known Norwegian cheese. A great favourite is **gietost**, a sweet, brown goat's cheese. Other varieties are **mysost**, a brown whey cheese, and **pultost**, a soft fermented cheese with caraway seeds.

DRINK

Beer is the national drink. Norway produces the famous Pils lager: Ringnes (south) and Mack (north). **Aquavit** is a very strong drink made from potatoes and caraway seeds. The locals usually drink it with a beer chaser. **Linie Akvavit** is reputedly one of the best. It is shipped in casks all the way to Australia because crossing the Equator is deemed to improve the flavour considerably! The fruit juices are particularly delicious. Vinmonopolet stores have the monopoly for selling wines and spirits and are usually to be found in the larger towns.

OSLO
OSLO

Population (est. 2006): 538 411 (Conurbation 731 600) – Altitude: 96m

B. Pérousse/MICHELIN

Oslo is a pleasant, modern city situated at the head of Oslofjord, on low land surrounded by steep forested hills. Its green open spaces highlight the compact and busy town centre. Its temperate climate with good skiing in winter and long sunny periods during the warm spring and summer allows both locals and tourists to enjoy outdoor activities.

The carefree relaxed attitude of the people is evident as they stroll in the streets and along the harbour, enjoy a drink at pavement cafés and eat outside late into the night. Oslo is a university city with a strong cultural tradition. It boasts a wide choice of museums, a busy theatrical season and an International Jazz Festival in August.

The original Viking settlement was a thriving port by the time the city was founded in 1048 by Harald Handråde. Oslo became the capital of Norway in the late 13C but subsequently suffered various setbacks as the Hanseatic League gained control of the Baltic trade, the population was decimated by the plague and the country was annexed by Denmark. In 1624 after fire destroyed the town, Christian IV built a new Renaissance town and named it Christiana. After Norway's union with Sweden in 1814, the town grew rapidly. The country gained independence in 1905 and in 1925 the capital reverted to the original name of Oslo.

WHICH DISTRICT TO CHOOSE

Prestigious **hotels** with luxury amenities are mostly located along the main street, Karl Johans gate *Plan I* **C2** and near Oslo Central Station *Plan I* **D2** in the city centre. However, there are also less expensive hotels in Karl Johans gate and the neighbouring streets which are reasonably priced for their location. You will find moderately priced chain hotels in the fashionable suburbs of Frogner *Plan I* **A1** and Majorstuen *Plan I* **B1**.

Oslo **restaurants** have won many awards and there are establishments to suit every taste and price range. Karl Johans gate in the city centre has a good variety of places to eat and drink. Some of the more exclusive

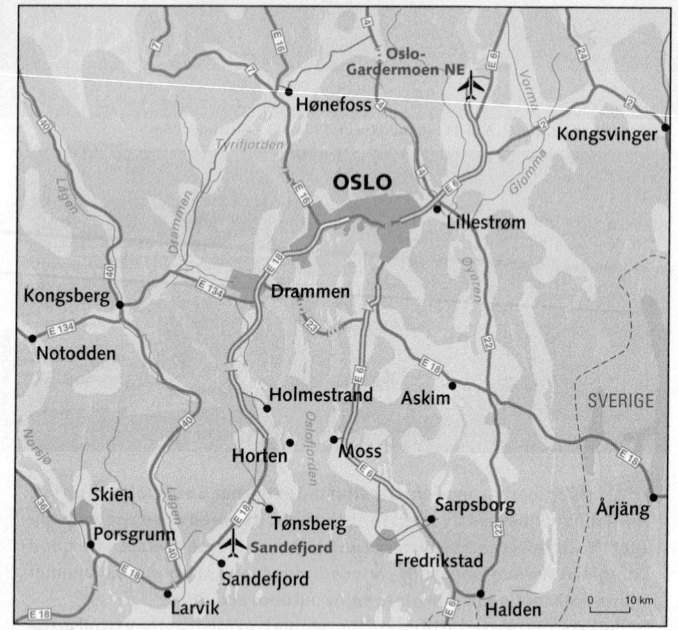

restaurants are to be found in Majorstuen and Frogner which also attract a young, trendy crowd. Grunerløkka *Plan I* **B1** is the area to visit for the more popular bars and restaurants with an informal and relaxed atmosphere and moderate prices. There are lively open-air bars and restaurants along the quaysides near Aker Brygge *Plan I* **B3**.

PRACTICAL INFORMATION

ARRIVAL – DEPARTURE

Oslo International Airport, Gardermoen – 47 km (30 mi) north of the city. ✆ 64 81 20 00; www.osl.no

Sandefjord Airport, Torp – 110 km (68 mi) southwest of the city. ✆ 33 42 70 00; www.torp.no

From Oslo International Airport to the city centre – By **taxi**: time 35min; taxis with Airport taxi logo on the side have special rates NOK600 (4 persons). ✆ 02 323; www.oslotaxi.no; by regular taxi about NOK600. By **express train** to Oslo S station, every 10min; time 19min; fare NOK160; tickets purchased at ticket counters and ticket machines (cash or credit cards). ✆ 47 815 00 77; www.flytoget.no. By **express bus** to Galleri bus terminal, every 20min; time 45min; fare NOK110 one way, NOK160 round trip. ✆ 22 80 49 71; www.flybussen.no/oslo

From Sandefjord Airport to the city centre – By **express bus** to Galleri Terminal: frequent service, time 2hr. *Trafikanten* ✆ 177 or 815 00 176. By **express train**: hourly service (bus or taxi to station 8km-5mi). ✆ 815 00 888; www.nsb.no

Railway Station – Oslo Central Station (Oslo S), Jernbanetorget *Plan I* **D2**. ✆ 177 or 815 00 176; www.trafikanten.no

TRANSPORT

→ BUS, TRAM, METRO

Oslo has an efficient integrated transport system. Single ticket NOK30; Day ticket NOK60. Oslo Pass (24, 48, 72hr) NOK195-395; family pass (2A+2C, 24hr) NOK395, gives unlimited transport, free entry to museums and various discounts. Oslo Pass must be validated by date and time from the start of travel. *Trafikanten*, Jernbanetorget 1 *Plan I* **D2**. Open Mon-Fri, 7am-8pm, Sat –Sun, 8am-6pm. ✆ 81 50 01 76; www.trafikanten.no

→ TAXIS

Taxis, which have a white Taxi sign on the roof, can be hailed in the streets at taxi stands near shopping centres, city squares or can be ordered by phone. *Oslo Taxi* ✆ 023 23; www.oslotaxi.no. *Norgestaxi* ✆ 08000; www.norgestaxi.no. *Taxi 2* ✆ 022 02.

USEFUL ADDRESSES

→ TOURIST INFORMATION

Norges Informasjonssenter – Fridtjof Nansens plass 5, N-0160 Oslo *Plan I* **C2**. Open Mon-Sun 9am-7pm; closed public holidays. ✆ 24 14 77 00; info@visitoslo.com; www.visitoslo.com

Tourist Information Centres also at Oslo Central Station (Oslo S) and at the airport.

→ POST OFFICES

Opening times Mon-Fri 8am-5pm; Sat 9am-3pm. Post boxes are pillar-box red. Main Post Offfice, Dronningensgate 15 *Plan I* **C2** has longer opening hours.

→ BANKS/CURRENCY EXCHANGE

Banks open mid-May to mid-September, Mon-Fri 9am-3pm; the rest of the year, Mon-Fri 9am-3.30pm (5pm Thu). Banks at Oslo Central Station Airport Express Train and at Oslo Airport Gardermoen open extended hours and have 24hr ATMs. ATMs are available all over the city. Credit cards are widely accepted. It is possible to exchange money and travellers' cheques at post offices.

→ PHARMACIES

Opening times 10am-5pm. *Jernbanetorget Apotek*, Jernbanetorget 4b *Plan I* **D2** is open 24hr. *Apoteket Sfinxen*, Bogstadveien 51and *Sagene Apotek*, Grimstadgata 21 are open Mon-Fri 8.30am-9pm, Sat 9am-8pm, Sun 5-8pm.

EXPLORING OSLO

VISITING

It is possible to visit the main sights and museums in Oslo in two days.

Museums and other sights are usually open 9-10am to 5-6pm; some close on Mondays.

Nasjonalgalleriet and **Munch Museum** *Plan I* **C2** – Important collection of Norwegian and international art (19C-20C French painting, Danish and Swedish art). 58 paintings by Edvard Munch including *Moonlight, The Dance of Life*.

Akershus Festning *Plan I* **C3** – Renaissance castle (17C) built on the site of a medieval fortress: large halls and dungeons. **Norges Hjemmefrontmuseum** (Resistance Museum): story of occupied Norway.

Bygdøy – *By car or by ferry from Rådhusbrygga 3*. The pleasant residential quarter is home to five important museums. **Norsk Folkemuseum**: open-air folk art museum displaying rural and urban architecture in wood. Viking Ship Museum **(Vikingskiphuset)**: outstanding display of three boats and their contents used for a funeral ceremony. **Fram Museum**: devoted to the polar vessel *Fram*, used by the Norwegian explorers Fridtjof Nansen and Roald Amundsen. The **Kon-Tiki Museum** illustrates the voyages of Thor Heyerdahl researching the routes followed by ancient civilisations. **Norsk Sjøfartsmuseum**: themed naval collections.

Ibsenmuseet *Plan I* **B2** – Museum dedicated to Norway's most famous dramatist housed in Ibsen's own apartment.

Vigelandsparken *Plan I* **A1** – The Vigeland Park displays monumental sculptures by Norway's most famous 20C sculptor, Gustav Vigeland.

Munchmuseet – Rotating exhibition of Edvard Munch's work.

Views – From the steeple of Domkirken *Plan I* **C2**.

Boat trips – Excursions to Drøbak, the islands and the fjord.

SHOPPING

Shops usually open Mon-Fri 10am-5pm (Thu 9am-6/8pm), Sat 10am-1/3pm. Shopping centres have extended opening hours.

The main shopping streets are **Karl Johans gate** *Plan I* **B2** and **Vikaterrassen** *Plan I* **B2**. There are many shopping centres: *Aker Brygge Plan I* **B3**; *Paleet*, Karl Johans gate 37-43; *Oslo City*, Stenersgate/Fred Olsens gate; *GlasMagasinet*, Stortorvet 9; *Steen & Strøm*, Nedre Slottsgate.

Explore *Basarhallene*, tiny boutiques around and near the main square, Stortorvet *Plan I* **C2** and *Kaare Berntsen Art and Antiques*, Universitetsgata 12 for handicrafts and antiques. For a wide choice of gifts, Norwegian arts and crafts, woollen garments, visit the *Tourist Office shop*; *Husfliden*, Møllergata 4; *Design Forum*, Øvre Slottsgate 29; *Unique design*, Rosenkrantz gate 13. *Sprell*, Thorvald Meyersgate 27 specialises in wooden toys and Scandinavian designs and *Juhls'*, Roald Amundsensgate 6; *Norway Designs*, Stortingsgaten 28 in designer silver jewellery.

WHAT TO BUY – Jewellery, pewter and enamelware, knitwear, trolls, reindeer leather goods, wooden toys and objects in painted wood (rosemaling); smoked meats and other specialities.

ENTERTAINMENT

Consult the monthly publication *What's On* for an updated calendar of events in Oslo available free from hotels and Tourist Information Offices.

Den Norske Opera *Plan I* **D2** – Opera, ballet.

National Theatret *Plan I* **C2** – Plays by Ibsen and other Norwegian playwrights in the original language.

Oslo Konserthuset *Plan I* **B2** – Home of the Norway Philarmonic Orchestra. Classical music; also pop and rock concerts.

Bryggeteater *Plan I* **B3** – Musical and dance performances.

Black Box Teater *Plan I* **B3**, **Oslo Nye Teater** *Plan I* **C2**, **Nordic Black Theatre**: Plays in English.

Valle Hovin Arena – Outdoor concerts.

Oslo Spektrum *Plan I* **D2** – Pop concerts and sporting events.

NIGHTLIFE

The most popular bars and clubs are to be found along **Karl Johans**

gate. **Grønland** is a multicultural area with lively venues: *Dattera til Hagen*, Grønland 10 and *Gloria Flames* no 18. You should also visit *Frognerveien 6*, Frognerveien and check out the streets around **Møllergata** *Plan I* **C2** and **Torgatta** *Plan I* **D2** lined with a wide range of bars and clubs. For trendy bars and pubs go to **Bogstadveien** *Plan I* **B1** and **Hegdehaugsveien**. The elegant *Kristiania Bar and Café* is situated in **Jernbanetorget**.

For live music visit *Stortorvets Gjæstgiveri*, Grensen 1; *Blå*, Brenneriveien 9c; *The Place*, Holmens gate 3; *Sør*, Torggata 11; *Mir*, Toftes gate 69; *Liv*, Olav gate 2; *Sam's Bar*, Markveien 32; *Barock*, Universitetsgate 26; *Galleria*, Kristian IV gate 12; *Bar Boca* and *Café Kaos*, Thorvald Meyers gate 30/56. The places for dancing are *Vice*, Pilestredet 9; *Macondo*, Badstugata 1. If you are a jazz fan you will enjoy *Oslo Jazzhus*, Toftesgate 69; *Smuget*, Rosencrantz gate 22. The popular Oslo Jazz Festival is held every summer.

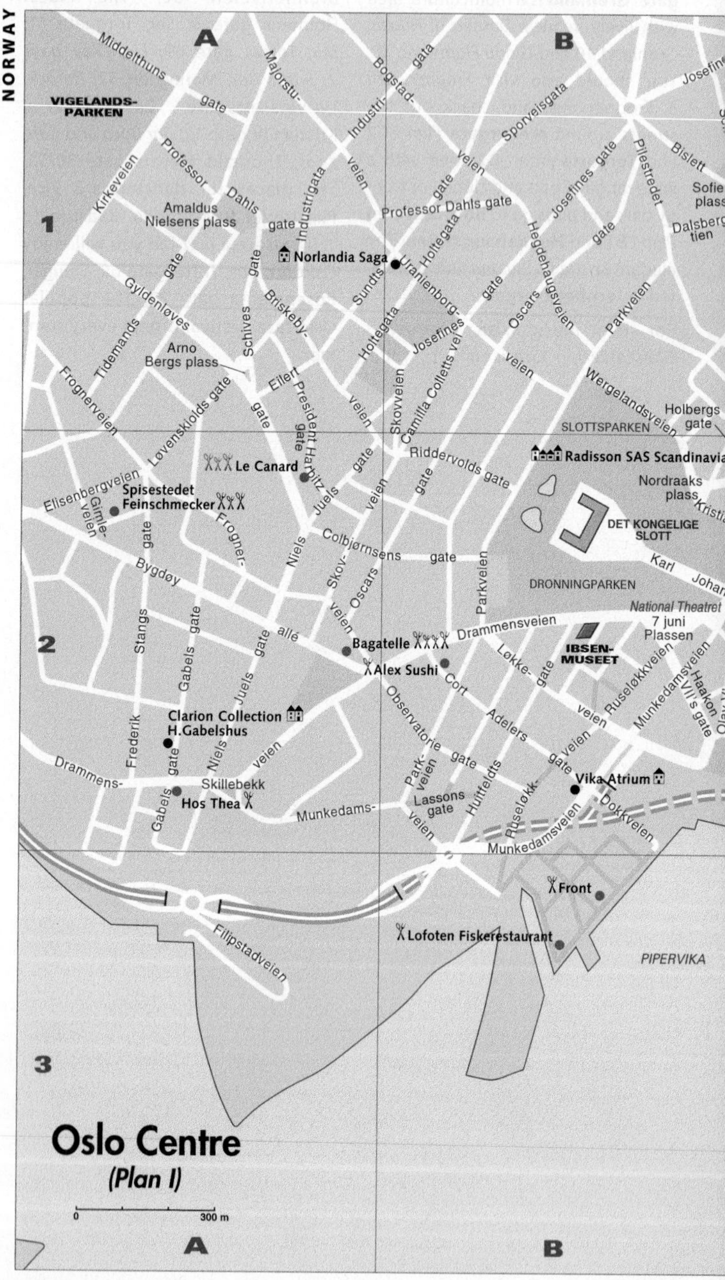
A
B
1
2
3
VIGELANDS-PARKEN
Amaldus Nielsens plass
Arno Bergs plass
Norlandia Saga
Le Canard
Spisestedet Feinschmecker
Radisson SAS Scandinavia
SLOTTSPARKEN
Holbergs gate
Nordraaks plass
DET KONGELIGE SLOTT
DRONNINGPARKEN
National Theatret
7 juni Plassen
IBSEN-MUSEET
Bagatelle
Alex Sushi
Clarion Collection H.Gabelshus
Hos Thea
Vika Atrium
Front
Lofoten Fiskerestaurant
PIPERVIKA
Sofie plass
Dalsbergstien
Bislett
Middelthuns gate
Majorstuveien
Bogstadveien
Industrigata
Professor Dahls gate
Kirkeveien
Sporveisgata
Josefines gate
Pilestredet
Hegdehaugsveien
Oscars gate
Parkveien
Wergelandsveien
Uranienborgveien
Holtegata
Sundts gate
Briskebyveien
Schives gate
Gyldenløves gate
Tidemands gate
Frognerveien
Løvenskiolds gate
Eilert Sundts gate
President Harbitz gate
Skovveien
Camilla Colletts vei
Riddervolds gate
Elisenbergveien
Gimleveien
Frognerveien
Niels Juels gate
Colbjørnsens gate
Bygdøy allé
Drammensveien
Karl Johans gate
Løkkeveien
Ruseløkkveien
Munkedamsveien
Haakon VII's gate
Stangs gate
Gabels gate
Frederik Stangs gate
Observatorie gate
Cort Adelers gate
Parkveien
Lassons gate
Huitfeldts gate
Dokkveien
Skillebekk
Filipstadveien
Oslo Centre
(Plan I)
0
300 m

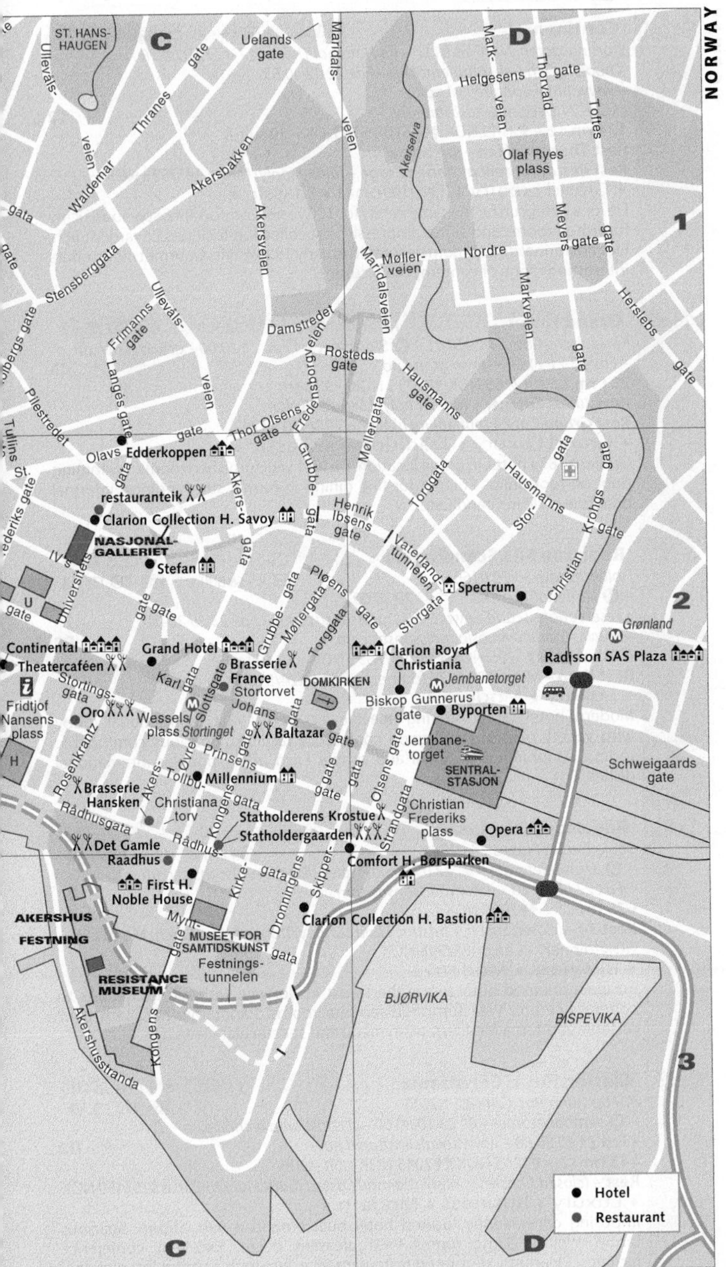

C
D
1
2
3
Hotel
Restaurant
Edderkoppen
restauranteik
Clarion Collection H. Savoy
NASJONAL-GALLERIET
Stefan
Spectrum
Continental
Theatercaféen
Grand Hotel
Brasserie France
DOMKIRKEN
Clarion Royal Christiania
Radisson SAS Plaza
Oro
Baltazar
Byporten
SENTRAL-STASJON
Millennium
Brasserie Hansken
Statholderens Krostue
Statholdergaarden
Opera
Det Gamle Raadhus
Comfort H. Børsparken
First H. Noble House
Clarion Collection H. Bastion
AKERSHUS FESTNING
MUSEET FOR SAMTIDSKUNST
RESISTANCE MUSEUM
BJØRVIKA
BISPEVIKA
ST. HANS-HAUGEN
Olaf Ryes plass
Grønland
Jernbanetorget
Stortinget
Stortorvet
Fridtjof Nansens plass
Christiania torv
Christian Frederiks plass
Festnings-tunnelen
Akerselva

Continental

Stortingsgaten 24-26 ✉ 0117 – Ⓜ National Theatret – ✆ 22 82 40 00 – booking@hotel-continental.no – Fax 22 42 40 65 – www.hotel-continental.no
closed 21 December to 2 January — C2
134 rm – 2145 NOK 1670/2575 NOK – 20 suites
Rest *Theatercaféen* – see below
Rest *Restauranteik at Annen Etage* – *(dinner only)* Menu 395/525 NOK
◆ Grand Luxury ◆ Traditional ◆ Classic ◆
De luxe hotel, run by the same family for 100 years. Comfortable, spacious, richly furnished rooms and suites. Impressive art collection includes Edvard Munch. Elegant formal dining room decorated in early 1920s style. Gourmet menu offers interesting range of contemporary cuisine.

Grand Hotel

Karl Johans Gate 31 ✉ 0101 – Ⓜ Stortinget – ✆ 23 21 20 00 – grand@rica.no – Fax 23 21 21 00 – www.grand.no — C2
281 rm – 2465 NOK 2715 NOK – 9 suites
Rest *Julius Fritzner* – *(dinner only)* Menu 595 NOK
Rest *Grand Café* – *(buffet lunch)* Menu 295/510 NOK
◆ Grand Luxury ◆ Traditional ◆ Classic ◆
Opulent 1874 hotel, in prime location. De luxe well furnished rooms. Swimming pool on roof. Julius Fritzner for fine dining in formal surroundings. Informal brasserie-style in Grand Café.

Radisson SAS Scandinavia

< Oslo and Fjord,
Holbergsgate 30 ✉ 0166 – Ⓜ National Theatret – ✆ 23 29 30 00 – reservations.scandinavia.oslo@radissonsas.com – Fax 23 29 30 01 – www.scandinavia.oslo.radissonsas.com — B2
476 rm – 1795 NOK 1595/2095 NOK – 12 suites
Rest *Enzo* – Menu 500 NOK (dinner) – Carte 424/515 NOK
◆ Luxury ◆ Modern ◆
Modern hotel block offering spectacular views. Vast international lobby with variety of shops and good conference facilities. Spacious comfortable rooms. Panoramic bar. Small and simple Enzo offers popular international dishes.

Radisson SAS Plaza

< Oslo and Fjord,
Sonja Henies Plass 3 ✉ 0134 – Ⓜ Jernbanetorget – ✆ 22 05 80 00 – sales.plaza@radissonsas.com – Fax 22 05 80 30 – www.radissonsas.com — D2
673 rm – 2095 NOK
Rest *34* – *(closed Easter, Christmas and Sunday) (tapas buffet lunch)* Menu 465 NOK (dinner) – Carte 485/595 NOK
◆ Business ◆ Modern ◆
Business-oriented hotel block, the tallest in Norway, with footbridge link to congress centre. Well furnished modern rooms. Panoramic bar. 34th floor restaurant offers a Mediterranean menu and spectacular views.

Clarion Royal Christiania

Biskop Gunnerus' Gate 3 ✉ 0106 – Ⓜ Jernbanetorget – ✆ 23 10 80 00 – cl.christiania@choice.no – Fax 23 10 80 80 – www.royalchristiania.no — D2
443 rm – 1845 NOK 2045 NOK – 60 suites
Rest – *(closed Christmas, New Year and Easter) (buffet lunch)* Carte 375/459 NOK
◆ Luxury ◆ Business ◆ Modern ◆
Imposing conveniently located hotel built around a vast atrium. Spacious lobby. Well lit large rooms with pleasant décor. Excellent conference facilities. Pleasantly decorated restaurant in atrium with a varied international menu.

Opera 240 VISA

Christian Frederiks plass 5 ✉ 0103 – Ⓜ Jernbanetorget – ✆ 24 10 30 00 – opera@thonhotels.no – Fax 24 10 30 10 – www.thonhotels.no/opera

closed 1 week Christmas **D2**

432 rm – 1595 NOK 1795 NOK – 2 suites

Rest – *(closed lunch Saturday and Sunday) (buffet lunch)* Menu 445 NOK (dinner) – Carte 465/615 NOK

◆ Business ◆ Modern ◆

A recent arrival in town, located next to the railway station and overlooking the harbour. Large modern building with functional yet contemporary furnishings and décor. Restaurant with huge windows affording panoramic views. Elaborate traditional cooking.

Clarion Collection H. Bastion without rest 50 VISA

Skippergaten 7 ✉ 0152 – ✆ 22 47 77 00 – cc.bastion@choice.no – Fax 22 33 11 80 – www.hotelbastion.no

closed 4-10 April **C3**

93 rm – 2195 NOK 1595/2395 NOK – 6 suites

◆ Business ◆ Modern ◆

Comfortable modern hotel handily placed for motorway. Welcoming rooms with good comforts and facilities. Furniture and paintings in part reminiscent of English style.

Edderkoppen 100 VISA

St Olavs Plass 1 ✉ 0165 – Ⓜ National Theatret – ✆ 23 15 56 00 – edderkoppen@scandic-hotels.com – Fax 23 15 56 11 – www.scandic-hotels.com

closed 23 December-2 January **C2**

235 rm – 1850 NOK 1150/2050 NOK – 6 suites

Rest – *(closed Sunday) (buffet lunch)* Menu 165/395 NOK – Carte 295/355 NOK

◆ Business ◆ Modern ◆

550 photographs of Norway's famous actors adorn the walls of this renovated building, incorporating a theatre. Modern functional well-equipped bedrooms. Modern and traditional fresh Norwegian and international dishes in Jesters and in the open-plan bar.

First H. Noble House without rest VISA

Kongens Gate 5 ✉ 0153 – ✆ 23 10 72 00 – noble.house@firsthotels.no – Fax 23 10 72 10 – www.firsthotels.no **C3**

55 rm – 1950 NOK 1950 NOK – 12 suites

◆ Business ◆ Classic ◆

Charming hotel in good location. Spacious rooms with parquet floors, top quality furniture and modern facilities. All rooms equipped with kitchenette. Hotel changing name and style in 2007.

Clarion Collection H. Gabelshus without rest 50 VISA

Gabelsgate 16 ✉ 0272 – ✆ 23 27 65 00 – cc.gabelshus@choice.no – Fax 23 27 65 60 – www.choicehotels.no

closed Easter and 22 December-2 January **A2**

113 rm – 2000 NOK – 1 suite

◆ Traditional ◆ Classic ◆

Attractive early 20C vine-clad hotel with extension in quiet district. Modern public rooms. Large well-fitted bedrooms; some on front with balconies, quieter at the rear.

Millennium

Tollbugaten 25 ✉ 0157 – ✆ 21 02 28 00 – millennium@firsthotels.no – Fax 21 02 28 30 – www.firsthotels.com **C2**

102 rm – 1550 NOK 1455/1750 NOK – 10 suites

Rest – *(closed Sunday and Bank Holidays) (dinner only)* Menu 399 NOK – Carte approx. 380 NOK

♦ Business ♦ Functional ♦

Functional modern hotel near harbour and restaurants. Internet access. Spacious well-equipped rooms; top floor with balconies; quietest on inside although overlooked. Simple restaurant on different levels serving global cuisine.

Stefan

Rosenkrantzgate 1 ✉ 0159 – ✆ 23 31 55 00 – stefan@thonhotels.no – Fax 23 31 55 55 – www.thonhotels.no/stefan

closed 1-9 April and 21 December-1 January **C2**

150 rm – 1525 NOK 1325/1525 NOK

Rest – *(closed Sunday)* Carte 199/234 NOK

♦ Business ♦ Functional ♦

Modern hotel on convenient corner site. Rooms are well equipped with functional furniture and good facilities. Good variety of room types. Families and groups catered for. Eighth floor restaurant with small terrace. Popular buffets.

Clarion Collection H. Savoy

Universitetsgata 11 ✉ 0164 – Ⓜ National Theatre – ✆ 23 35 42 00 – cc.savoy@choice.no – Fax 23 35 42 01 – www.choice.no

closed 21 December-2 January **C2**

93 rm – 1945 NOK

Rest *restauranteik* – see below

♦ Business ♦ Classic ♦

Classic early 20C hotel in the city centre behind the museum. Stylish public areas. Spacious well-kept bedrooms with good facilities.

Byporten without rest

Jernbanetorget 6 ✉ 0154 – Ⓜ Jernbanetorget – ✆ 23 15 55 00 – byporten@scandic-hotels.com – Fax 23 15 55 11 – www.scandic-hotels.com/byporten **D2**

235 rm – 1690 NOK 1490/1690 NOK – 4 suites

♦ Business ♦ Modern ♦

Modern hotel in vast office/commercial centre block by station. Functional soundproofed rooms with environmentally friendly decor. Breakfast in nearby public restaurant.

Comfort H. Børsparken without rest

Tollbugaten 4 ✉ 0152 – Ⓜ Jernbanetorget – ✆ 22 47 17 17 – co.borsparken@choice.no – Fax 22 47 17 18 – www.choicehotels.no 75 **C-D2**

198 rm – 1915 NOK 1680/1915 NOK

♦ Business ♦ Functional ♦

Modern functional chain hotel on corner site in city centre. Pleasant lobby opening onto tree-lined square. Compact practical rooms, well equipped for business clientele.

Norlandia Saga without rest 25

Eilert Sundtsgt. 39 ✉ 0259 – ✆ 22 43 04 85 – service@saga.norlandia.no – Fax 22 44 08 63 – www.norlandia.no/saga

closed Christmas-New Year **A-B1**

37 rm – 1225 NOK

♦ Family ♦ Classic ♦

Family-run hotel in quiet area. Cosy winter lounge with fire. Well-lit rooms with classic furnishings and facilities; rear rooms are quietest. Complimentary mid-week supper.

Vika Atrium without rest — 240 VISA MC AE
Munkedamsveien 45 ✉ 0121 – Ⓜ National Theatret – ☎ 22 83 33 00 – vika.atrium@thonhotels.no – Fax 22 83 09 57 – www.thonhotels.no/vikaatrium **B2**
79 rm ☕ – †1545 NOK ††1445/1745 NOK
◆ Business ◆ Functional ◆
Located in large office block built around an atrium. Comfortable lobby lounge. Well-serviced rooms with functional modern fittings. Good conference facilities.

Spectrum without rest — 30 VISA MC AE
Brugata 7 ✉ 0133 – Ⓜ Grønland – ☎ 23 36 27 00 – spectrum@thonhotels.no – Fax 23 36 27 50 – www.thonhotel.no/spectrum
closed 21 December-2 January **D2**
151 rm ☕ – †895 NOK ††895 NOK
◆ Business ◆ Functional ◆
Conveniently located hotel in pedestrian street not far from station. Two styles of room: "old" are fairly functional; "new" have more interesting décor and furniture.

Bagatelle (Hellstrøm) — VISA MC AE
Bygdøy Allé 3 ✉ 0257 – Ⓜ National Theatret – ☎ 22 12 14 40 – bagatelle@bagatelle.no – Fax 22 43 64 20 – www.bagatelle.no
closed Easter, 4 weeks July-August, Christmas and Sunday **A2**
Rest – *(booking essential) (dinner only)* Menu 800/1400 NOK – Carte 800/1000 NOK
Spec. Norwegian red King crab salad. Carpaccio of scallops and sea urchins. Game in season.
◆ Contemporary ◆ Design ◆
Highly reputed classic restaurant with colourful contemporary décor and numerous paintings on walls. Excellent innovative cuisine. Wine cellar may be viewed by diners.

Le Canard — 20 P VISA MC AE
President Harbitz Gate 4 ✉ 0259 – ☎ 22 54 34 00 – lecanard@lecanard.no – Fax 22 54 34 10 – www.lecanard.no
closed Easter, Christmas-New Year, 8 July-1 August, Sunday and Bank Holidays **A2**
Rest – *(dinner only)* Menu 650 NOK – Carte 495/625 NOK
Spec. Grilled scallops with foie gras, Jerusalem artichoke, red onion confit, orange syrup and Port glaze. Whole roasted duckling with lavender honey. Game and fowl in season.
◆ Inventive ◆ Formal ◆
1900 villa in residential district, fully refurbished in 2006. Stylish and modern interior with original wall fresco. Skilled and refined cooking. Knowledgeable service.

Statholdergaarden (Stiansen) — VISA MC AE
Rådhusgate 11, (entrance by Kirkegate) ✉ 0151 – Ⓜ Stortinget – ☎ 22 41 88 00 – post@statholdergaarden.no – Fax 22 41 22 24 – www.statholdergaarden.no
closed 1-10 April, 1, 17 and 27-28 May, 15 July-7 August, 23 December-3 January and Sunday **C2**
Rest – *(booking essential) (dinner only)* Menu 825 NOK – Carte 695/825 NOK
Spec. Langoustine and crisp filo filled with chanterelles, bell pepper cream, artichoke and shellfish vinaigrette. Pepper-glazed fillet of reindeer with cep foam and blackcurrant sauce. Calvados mousse with hazelnut brittle.
◆ Contemporary ◆ Formal ◆
Fine 17C house offers elegant dining room with original décor beneath beautiful period stucco ceilings, whose motifs reappear on the china. High quality cuisine.

NORWAY

XXX ✿

Spisestedet Feinschmecker

AC ⊙18 VISA MC AE D

Balchensgate 5 ✉ 0265 – ✆ 22 12 93 80 – kontakt@feinschmecker.no – Fax 22 12 93 88 – www.feinschmecker.no

closed Easter, 3 weeks in summer and Sunday **A2**

Rest – *(dinner only)* Menu 625/725 NOK – Carte 640/780 NOK

Spec. Poached turbot with saffron risotto, shrimp and clams. Grilled halibut with spinach, raisins and truffle vinaigrette. Parsley crusted rack of lamb with cassoulet of beans and celeriac.

♦ Contemporary ♦ Formal ♦

Busy restaurant in residential building. Spacious dining room has traditional feel and cosy atmosphere. Expect contemporary fare from the partially on-view kitchen.

XXX

Oro

AC ⊙20 VISA MC AE D

Tordenskioldsgate 6A ✉ 0160 – Ⓜ Stortinget – ✆ 23 01 02 40 – kontakt@ororestaurant.no – Fax 23 01 02 48 – www.ororestaurant.no

closed Easter, Christmas, July and Sunday **C2**

Rest – *(booking essential) (dinner only)* Menu 575 NOK – Carte 635/725 NOK

Rest *Del i Oro* – Menu 200/300 NOK – Carte 100/150 NOK

♦ Mediterranean ♦ Trendy ♦

Elegant, modern designer décor in muted tones with an informal atmosphere. Open-plan kitchen offers inventive cuisine with a Mediterranean influence. Booking a must. Del i Oro, the adjoining tapas bar with a large counter displaying cold and some warm dishes.

XX

Det Gamle Raadhus

VISA MC AE D

Nedre Slottsgate 1 ✉ 0157 – Ⓜ Stortinget – ✆ 22 42 01 07 – gamle.raadhus@gamle-raadhus.no – Fax 22 42 04 90 – www.gamle-raadhus.no

closed 1 week Easter, 3 weeks July, 1 week Christmas and Sunday **C3**

Rest – *(dinner only)* Menu 498 NOK – Carte 413/649 NOK

♦ Traditional ♦ Rustic ♦

Well-run restaurant operating for over a century located in Oslo's original City Hall, dating from 1641. Elegant rustic interior décor and English-style atmosphere in bar.

XX

Theatercaféen – at Continental H.

VISA MC AE D

Stortingsgaten 24-26 ✉ 0117 – Ⓜ National Theatret – ✆ 22 82 40 50 – theatercafeen@hotel-continental.no – Fax 22 41 20 94 – www.hotel-continental.no

closed Sunday lunch **C2**

Rest – *(light lunch)* Menu 305/557 NOK – Carte 457/719 NOK

♦ Traditional ♦ Brasserie ♦

An institution in the city and the place to see and be seen. Elaborate lunchtime sandwiches make way for afternoon/evening brasserie specials.

XX

restauranteik

AC VISA MC AE D

Universitetsgata 11 ✉ 0164 – Ⓜ Stortinget – ✆ 22 36 07 10 – eikefjord@restauranteik.no – Fax 22 36 07 11 – www.restauranteik.no

closed 4 weeks summer, 1 week Easter, 1 week Christmas, Sunday and Monday **C2**

Rest – *(dinner only) (set menu only)* Menu 355 NOK

♦ Contemporary ♦ Fashionable ♦

Restaurant in striking minimalist style; open-plan kitchen with chef's table. Good value set menu of 3 or 5 courses of interesting dishes.

XX

Baltazar

AC VISA MC AE D

Dronningensgt 2-7 ✉ 0154 – Ⓜ Jernbanetorget – ✆ 23 35 70 60 – baltazar@baltazar.no – Fax 23 35 70 61 – www.baltazar.no

closed Easter, 1 and 17 May, July, Christmas and Sunday **C2**

Rest – *(dinner only)* Menu 395/720 NOK – Carte 395/510 NOK

Rest *Enoteca* – Carte 280/350 NOK

♦ Italian ♦ Friendly ♦

In courtyard off Karl Johans gate beside cathedral. Serious Italian wine list; small a la carte or concise chef's menu: home-made pasta, fine Italian produce and local fish. The rustic décor of the wine bar is just right for an informal lunch.

Brasserie Hansken

Akersgata 2 ✉ 0158 – Ⓜ Stortinget – ✆ 22 42 60 88 – kontor@brasseriehansken.no – Fax 22 42 24 03 – www.brasseriehansken.no
closed 1 week Easter, 1 week Christmas and Sunday **C2**
Rest – *(booking essential)* Menu 325/625 NOK – Carte 385/698 NOK
♦ Modern ♦ Brasserie ♦
Busy restaurant in lively district with strictly contemporary bistro-style décor and dark wood fittings. Good quality brasserie fare. Terrace bar on the square in summer.

Brasserie France

Øvre Slottsgate 16 ✉ 0157 – Ⓜ Stortinget – ✆ 23 10 01 65 – bord@brasseriefrance.no – Fax 23 10 01 61 – www.brasseriefrance.no
closed Easter, 23 December-2 January and Sunday **C2**
Rest – *(dinner only except Saturday)* Menu 299/425 NOK – Carte 340/485 NOK
♦ French ♦ Brasserie ♦
French brasserie-style dining room at D'Artagnan; entrance from pedestrian street. Wall benches, bistro chairs and open kitchen at end of room. Interesting French dishes.

Hos Thea

Gabelsgate 11 ✉ 0272 – ✆ 22 44 68 74 – post@hosthea.no – www.hosthea.no
closed 5-30 July **A2**
Rest – *(dinner only)* Menu 395/450 NOK – Carte 405/510 NOK
♦ Traditional ♦ Family ♦
Discreet black façade in residential area conceals this typical little restaurant fitted out with simple Scandinavian-style décor. Family atmosphere. Appealing menu.

Statholderens Krostue – at Statholdergaarden

Rådhusgate 11, (entrance by Kirkegate) 1st floor ✉ 0151 – Ⓜ Stortinget – ✆ 22 41 88 00 – post@statholdergaarden.no – Fax 22 41 22 24 – www.statholdergaarden.no – closed 1-10 April, 1, 17 and 27-28 May, 8 July-8 August, 23 December-3 January, Sunday and Monday **C2**
Rest – Menu 495 NOK (dinner) – Carte 455/540 NOK
♦ Traditional ♦ Rustic ♦
Three vaulted basement rooms with bistro-style décor and warm candle-lit ambience. Changing themed menus for dinner and a la carte for light lunch; friendly service.

Lofoten Fiskerestaurant

Stranden 75 ✉ 0250 – ✆ 22 83 08 08 – lofoten@fiskerestaurant.no – Fax 22 83 68 66 – www.lofoten-fiskerestaurant.no
closed 24-31 December **B3**
Rest – Menu 250/550 NOK – Carte 490/550 NOK
♦ Seafood ♦ Brasserie ♦
A firm favourite with locals; attractive, modern fjord-side restaurant at Aker Brygge. Chef patron offers a tempting array of seafood and shellfish.

Alex Sushi

Cort Adelers Gate 2 ✉ 0254 – Ⓜ National Theatret – ✆ 22 43 99 99 – alex@alexsushi.no – Fax 22 43 99 98 – www.alexsushi.no
closed Christmas and New Year **B2**
Rest – *(dinner only)* Menu 375/925 NOK
♦ Japanese ♦ Design ♦
Swish Japanese restaurant features central oval sushi bar shaped like small boat with metallic roof. Dining room enlivened by modern art. Appealing tempura and miso dishes.

Front

Stranden 7 ✉ 0250 – ✆ 22 83 64 00 – post@restaurant-front.no – Fax 22 83 64 01 – www.restaurant-front.no **B3**
Rest – Menu 495 NOK – Carte 445/589 NOK
♦ Contemporary ♦ Brasserie ♦
A very popular newcomer on Aker Brygge quay, this contemporary brasserie/restaurant is flooded with light from big windows and has a smart front terrace. Tasty local dishes.

ENVIRONS OF OSLO

at Lillestrøm Northeast : 18 km by E 6

Arena

Nesgata 1 ✉ 2004 – ℘ 66 93 60 00
– arena@thonhotels.no – Fax 66 93 63 00
– www.thonhotels.no/arena
closed Christmas and Easter
262 rm – 1895 NOK – 16 suites
Rest *Madame Thrane* – *(dinner only)* Menu 295/395 NOK
Rest *Amfi* – *(buffet lunch)* Menu 285/515 NOK
♦ Business ♦ Functional ♦
Large modern hotel in trade fair centre with direct train access to airport and city centre. Spacious, contemporary rooms with every possible facility; a few singles. Madame Thrane for interesting contemporary dishes. Buffet-style service at the informal Amfi.

at Holmenkollen Northwest : 10 km by Bogstadveien, Sørkedalsveien and Holmenkollveien

Holmenkollen Park

Oslo and Fjord,
Kongeveien 26 ✉ 0787
– ℘ 22 92 20 00 – holmenkollen.park.hotel.rica@rica.no – Fax 22 14 61 92
– www.holmenkollenparkhotel.no
closed 22 December-3 January
210 rm – 1680 NOK 900/1930 NOK – 11 suites
Rest *De Fem Stuer* – *(buffet lunch)* Menu 345/635 NOK – Carte dinner 505/765 NOK
Rest *Galleriet* – *(closed Sunday) (buffet lunch)* Menu 225/535 NOK – Carte dinner 255/415 NOK
♦ Traditional ♦ Personalised ♦
Smart hotel near Olympic ski jump; superb views. Part built (1894) in old Norwegian "dragon style" decorated wood. Chalet-style rooms, some with balconies or views or saunas. International cuisine in De Fem Stuer. Informal Galleriet for a more popular menu.

at Oslo Airport Northeast : 45 km by E 6 at Gardermoen

Radisson SAS Airport

✉ 2061 – ℘ 63 93 30 00
– sales.airport.oslo@radissonsas.com – Fax 63 93 30 30
– www.gardermoen.radissonsas.com
346 rm – 2045 NOK 2295/2345 NOK – 4 suites
Rest – Menu 240/365 NOK – Carte 385/540 NOK
♦ Business ♦ Modern ♦
Ultra-contemporary business hotel on a semi-circular plan overlooking runway but well soundproofed. Rooms are a good size, well equipped and have varied décor. Modern restaurant offering a variety of international dishes to appeal to all comers.

Clarion Oslo Airport

(West : 6 km) ✉ 2060 – ℘ 63 94 94 94 – cl.oslo.airport@choice.no
– Fax 63 94 94 95 – www.choicehotels.no
357 rm – 1995 NOK – 1 suite
Rest – *(buffet lunch)* Menu 265/315 NOK – Carte approx. 463 NOK
♦ Business ♦ Functional ♦
Modern Norwegian design hotel in wood and red tiles on star plan. Compact functional rooms with good modern facilities. Well equipped for conferences. Families at weekend. Vast restaurant offers a standard range of international dishes to cater for all tastes.

POLAND

POLSKA

PROFILE

◆ **Area:**
312 677 km^2
(120 725 sq mi).

◆ **Population:**
38 635 000 inhabitants (est. 2005), density = 124 per km^2.

◆ **Capital:**
Warsaw (conurbation 2 135 000 inhabitants).

◆ **Currency:**
Złoty (zl or PLN); rate of exchange: PLN 1 = € 0.25 = US$ 0.32 (Nov 2006).

◆ **Government:**
Parliamentary republic (since 1990). Member of European Union since 2004.

◆ **Language:**
Polish.

◆ **Specific public holidays:**
National 3rd of May Holiday, Corpus Christi (9th Thursday after Easter), Independence Day (11 November).

◆ **Local Time:**
GMT + 1 hour in winter and GMT + 2 hours in summer.

◆ **Climate:**
Temperate continental with cold winters and warm summers (Warsaw: January: -2°C; July: 20°C).

◆ **International dialling Code:**
00 48 followed by the area code and then the local number. Directory enquiries: ✆ **118 912**.

◆ **Emergency:**
Ambulance: ✆ **999**; Fire Brigade: ✆ **998**; Police: ✆ **997**; Police from mobile: ✆ **112**.

◆ **Electricity:**
230V AC, 50Hz; 2 pin round-shaped continental plugs.

FORMALITIES

Travellers from the European Union (EU), Switzerland, Iceland and the main countries of North and South America need a national identity card or passport (America: passport required) to visit Poland for less than three months (tourism or business purpose). For visitors from other countries a visa may be required, in addition to a passport, especially for those wishing to stay for longer than three months. We advise you to check with your embassy before travelling.

The international car hire companies have branches in Warsaw. Nationals of EU countries require a valid national driving licence; nationals of non-EU countries require an International Driving Licence. Seat belts are compulsory for drivers and all passengers.

MAJOR NEWSPAPERS

The main daily newspapers are *Gazeta Wyborcza, Super Express, Rzeczpospolita* and *Nasz Dziennik* (Catholic newspaper). The major weeklies are *Przekroj, Polityka* and *Wprost*. Poland also has many regional papers, as *Gazeta Krakowska and Dziennik Polski* (Cracow) or *Gazeta Poznanska* (Poznan).

USEFUL PHRASES

ENGLISH	**POLISH**
Yes	**Tak**
No	**Nie**
Good morning	**Dzień dobry**
Goodbye	**Do widzenia**
Thank you	**Dziękuję**
Please	**Proszę**
Excuse me	**Przepraszam**
I don't understand	**Nie rozumiem**

HOTELS

→ CATEGORIES

Accommodation ranges from luxurious international hotels to smaller less expensive hotels; all are classified (1-5 stars). Economy inns and motels are located beside major roads. There are rooms to let *(wolne pokoje)* in tourist resorts. There is also rural and B&B accommodation ✆ 52 398 1434 (www.agritourism.pl). Many old and historic buildings have been converted into tourist accommodation – ✆ 22 433 60 30 (www.leisure-heritage.com).

→ PRICE RANGE

The price (quoted in Zloty and sometimes in euros also) is per room. Between April and October it is advisable to book in advance, particularly in Cracow. From November to March prices may be lower, some hotels offer special cheap rates.

→ TAX

7% but not included in the room price.

→ CHECKOUT TIME

Usually noon.

→ RESERVATIONS

By telephone or by Internet. A credit card number may be required.

→ TIP FOR LUGGAGE HANDLING

At the discretion of the customer.

→ BREAKFAST

It is not usually included in the price of the room and is generally served between 7am and 9.30/10am. Most hotels offer a hot and cold buffet but usually it is also possible to have breakfast served in the room.

Reception	**Recepcja**
Single room	**Pokój 1-Osobowy**
Double room	**Pokój 2-Osobowy**
Bed	**Łóżko**
Bathroom	**Łazienka**
Shower	**Prysznic**

RESTAURANTS

Traditional Polish cuisine, hearty and rustic, is served in the many **regional restaurants** and in most hotels but there is also modern Polish cooking by inventive chefs who re-interpret old recipes and create unique dishes using unusual combinations of ingredients. There is also the full range of international cuisine from Mediterranean to Asian. **Cafeteria (bar mleczny)** offer cheap, basic dishes; there are other fast food outlets.

→ MEALS

Breakfast	**Śniadanie**	7am – 9.30am
Lunch	**Obiad**	12 noon – 2pm
Dinner	**Kolacja**	8pm – midnight

Most restaurants in Poland offer à la carte menus. Menus are usually printed in Polish; they may also be printed in English or explained in English.

→ RESERVATIONS

Reservations are usually made by phone. For famous restaurants, it is advisable to book in advance.

→ THE BILL

The bill (check) does include VAT but not a service charge; in these circumstances tipping (10%) is at the discretion of the diners.

Drink or aperitif	**Drink**
Appetizer	**Przystawka**
Meal	**Posiłek**
Starter	**Przystawka**
Main dish	**Danie główne**
Main dish of the day	**Danie dnia**
Dessert	**Deser**
Water	**Woda**
Wine (red, white, rosé)	**Wino (czerwone, białe, różowe)**
Beer	**Piwo**
Bread	**Chleb**
Meat	**Mięso**
Fish	**Ryba**
Salt/pepper	**Sól/pieprz**
Cheese	**Ser**
Vegetables	**Warzywa**
Hot/cold	**Gorące/zimne**
The bill (check) please	**Rachunek proszę**

LOCAL CUISINE

The cuisine of Poland has been influenced by the Jewish population and by its eastern neighbours, and also by French and Italian royalty. Each region has developed its own particular dishes and culinary customs. Old recipes are passed on from generation to generation, because they preserve the unique flavour of Polish cooking.

On the Baltic coast herring is the most popular fish; in Pomerania and the lake districts there are fish and crayfish dishes; Podlasie offers a variety of cold meats and potato dishes; from the Polish highlands comes a unique **smoked sheep's milk cheese (oscypek)**, served in slices with a glass of spirits. There are dishes typical of just one region: Mazuria's **dzyndzałki** (small meat dumplings served with melted butter and cream), **małdrzyki** from Crakow, or **pork with prunes** in Wielkopolska. General Polish specialities include **sour soup (żurek)**, **cold soups**, **fruit soups**, **potato pancakes** and **black pudding**. **Pork** is ubiquitous and served in many different ways: as sausages with pickled cabbage, mushrooms and **prunes (bigos)**. **Goose** is popular, roasted, in the Jewish style **(gęsie pipki)**, or as pickled and smoked goose breast **(półgęsek)**. **Game** may be served marinated, as pâté or in sausages **(kiełbasa)**. There are numerous varieties of **dumplings** and **pancakes** unknown in other countries; every region produces **pierogi**, turnovers with various fillings: buckwheat and mushroom, cabbage and mushroom, buckwheat and cheese, minced offal and pickled cabbage, cottage cheese, potato and onion, berries of all kinds.

For dessert there is a variety of cream cakes and cheesecake **(sernik)**: two squares of puff pastry filled with a thick layer of cream and custard **(kremówka)**, **Toruń gingerbread**.

DRINK

There is a broad range of Polish beers which are of the lager type. Poland also produces many fruit juices and several mineral waters. **Juniper Beer** is the pride of Kurpie, in northeast of the country. **Pepper water** is made from onion juice, salt, pepper and vinegar. Imported wines and spirits tend to be expensive.

Polish **vodka** comes in many varieties. **White vodka** made from distilled spirit and water. **Flavoured vodka** is produced by adding various ingredients to give flavour, colour and aroma: fresh and dried fruit, spices, grass, flowers, seeds, aromatic oils, honey and sugar. It is worth mentioning by name **Żubrówka**, a light-yellow herbal vodka named bison vodka after the vanilla grass (called bison grass in Polish) which grows in the Bialowieska Forest, a refuge of European bison and the oldest primeval forest in Europe; **Jarzębiak**, made from rowanberries; **Żołądkowa Gorzka**, a spicy vodka made with unripe oranges and cloves; the famous **śliwowica from Łąck**, made from ripe plums and very potent (70%) owing to double distillation.

Poland is famous for its **mead (trójniak)**, an alcoholic drink (9-18%) made by fermenting diluted natural honey; the flavour may be enhanced by the addition of spices or herbs, as well as hops, also cinnamon, cloves, ginger, juniper berries, vanilla, mint, rose petals. Fruit mead is made by adding fruit juice instead of water. Mead may be drunk like wine, cold or hot; mulled mead is good for cold winter weather, served in ceramic cups rather than glasses. Other liqueurs sweetened with local honey are also famous: **krupnik kurpiowski** and **mioduszka**.

WARSAW
WARSZAWA

Population (est. 2005): 1 593 000 (conurbation 2 135 000) – Altitude: 106m

SIME / PHOTONONSTOP

The capital of Poland lies on the banks of the Vistula at the heart of the Mazovian lowlands. According to legend, a mermaid asked two young lovers, Wars and Sawa, to found a city and call it Warszawa, hence the city emblem of a mermaid in the Old Town Square. In fact the town was founded in the 10C and 11C when large villages spread along each side of the Vistula. It became the capital during the reign of Sigismund III in 1596, when the royal castle in Cracow was destroyed in a terrible fire. Over the centuries the city has expanded from its medieval core, which was laid waste during the Second World War and afterwards rebuilt as an almost exact copy of its former self from old documents and plans; it is now on the UNESCO World Heritage List.

Today Warsaw is a lively, bustling and modern metropolis, the most cosmopolitan, dynamic and progressive of Poland's cities, with good shops and restaurants. It is not only the seat of the government and administration but also a scientific, cultural and arts centre, with many theatres and concert halls, art galleries and museums, a university and institutes of higher education.

From 1826 to 1829 the Central Academy of Music numbered among its pupils F. Chopin who was born in 1810 in Żelazowa Wola (53 km west). Although he left Poland at 20, his work has a strong Polish accent.

WHICH DISTRICT TO CHOOSE

Most of the **hotels** are in the commercial district west of the Royal Way. There are **restaurants** in the commercial district and also in the Old Town *Plan I* **A2**. Both districts offer places where you can have a drink in the evening.

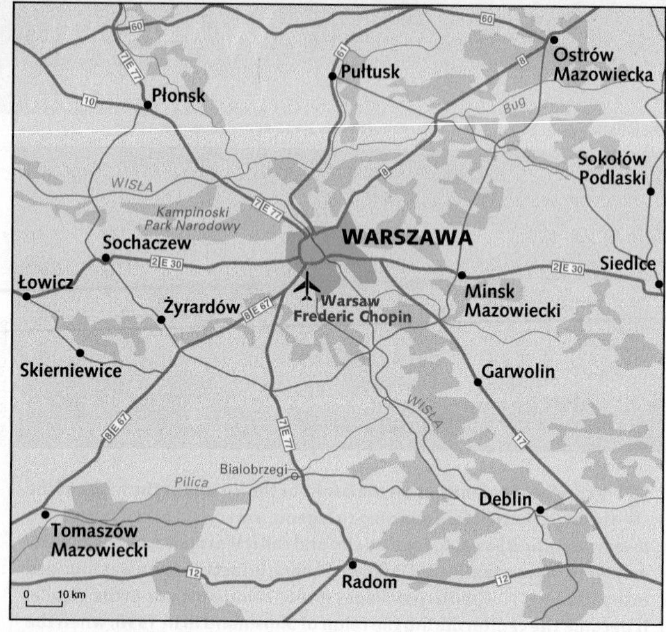

PRACTICAL INFORMATION

ARRIVAL – DEPARTURE

Warsaw F. Chopin (Okęcie) International Airport – About 10 km (6 mi) south of the city centre. ✆ 226 50 11 11 (info desk), 650 39 43 (flight information).

From the airport to the city centre – By **bus** 175 (611 at night) to the city centre. By **taxi**: it is advisable to order a taxi from one of the licensed firms: *Merc, MPT, Sawa-Taxi*; taxis touting for custom at the airport tend to be expensive. Initial charge 5-6zł.

Railway Stations – Dworzec Warszawa Centralna (Central), 54 Jerozolimskie Ave; **Dworzec Wschodni (West)**, 1 Lubelska St; for trains to the west; **Dworzec Zachodni (East)**, 144 Jerozolimskie Ave; for trains to the north and east.

TRANSPORT

→ TRAM, BUS AND METRO

Operate 5am-11pm. Single zł2.40; 1 day travelcard zł7.20; 3-day travelcard zł12; 30-day travelcard zł66; 90-day travelcard zł166; double fare for journeys outside the city limits; discounted fares for foreigners under 26 with valid ISIC card. All tickets can be bought at RUCH kiosks, from automatic ticket machines at stops, at newsagents and (for trams and buses) from the driver (additional fee) as rechargeable magnetic cards which must be validated (www.ztm.waw.pl).

→ TAXIS

Taxis are distinguished by a horizontal red and yellow line. It is advisable to take a taxi from a taxi rank, indicated by a blue sign, or book with one of the licensed firms: *MPT* ✆ 919, *Euro Taxi* ✆ 9662, *Halo Taxi* ✆ 9623, *Super-Taxi* ✆ 9622, *Volfra-Taxi* ✆ 9625. Initial charge 5-6zł; minimal day rate zł2 pkm (check the sticker on the window); official night (10pm-6am) and week-end rate zł4 pkm.

→ WARSAW TOURIST CARD

For free travel on public transport in Warsaw, free admission to 21 museums, discounts in some shops, restaurants and leisure centres.

USEFUL ADDRESSES

→ TOURIST INFORMATION

Tourist Help Line ✆ 48 22 94 31, May-Sep daily 8am-8pm, Oct-Apr daily 8am-6pm. **Tourist Information Centre**, 39 Krakowskie Przedmieście *Plan II* **D1**, May-Sep daily 9am-9pm, Oct-Apr daily 9am-6pm. **Dworzec Centralny (Central Railway Station)**, Jerozolimskie 54; May-Sep daily 8am-8pm, Oct-Apr daily 8am-6pm. **Dworzec Zachodni (Zachodni Coach Station)**, Jerozolimskie 144, May-Sep daily 10am-6pm, Oct-Apr daily 9am-5pm. **F. Chopin International Airport**, Arrival Hall, May-Sep daily 8am-8pm, Oct-Apr daily 8am-6pm. **Warsaw Tourist and Cultural Information**, Palace of Culture and Science (entrance Marszałkowska), daily 9am-6pm, ✆ 656 68 54, 656 71 36. **MUFA Warsaw Tourist Information Centre**, Zamkowy Square 1/13 *Plan II* **C1**; Mon-Fri 9am-6pm, Sat 10am-6pm, Sun 11am-6pm, ✆ 635 18 81; info@warsawtour.pl; www.warsawtour.pl

→ POST OFFICES

Mon-Fri 8am-8pm, Sat 8am-1pm. Main Post Office, **Świętokrzyska** 31/33 *Plan II* **C2**; open daily, 24-hr.

→ BANKS/CURRENCY EXCHANGE

Mon-Fri, 8am-6pm, Sat 8am-2pm. There are cash machines (24hr); most credit cards can be used in those connected to the Euronet system.

→ EMERGENCY

Ambulance: ✆ **999**; Fire Brigade: ✆ **998**; Police: ✆ **997**; Police from mobile: ✆ **112**.

BUSY PERIODS

It may be difficult to find a room at a reasonable price when special events are held in the city:

International Poster Biennial: March (even years) – Welcomes many artists of international reputation from all fields of culture and art; organised by the Poster Museum in Wilanów.

Mozart Festival: June-July – Mozart operas, symphonic and chamber music and masses performed in Warsaw Chamber Opera and churches.

International Festival of Organ Music: summer – in the cathedral.

Warsaw Autumn: September – International Festival of Contemporary Music.

Chopin Piano Competition: October, every fifth year (next in 2010) – International competition for young pianists playing music by Chopin, which attracts about 150 participants.

Jazz Jamboree: October – International Jazz Festival.

Old Music Festival: October-November – At the Royal Castle.

DIFFERENT FACETS OF THE CITY

It is possible to visit the main sights and museums in two to three days.

Most museums and sights are usually open Tues-Sat 10am-4pm. Some are closed on Mon; most are closed on Sun or vary their hours. To Wilanów Palace (8 km/5 mi south): bus 180 from Powązki Cemetery, daily 4.30am-10pm, every 15min.

VIEW OF WARSAW – **Pałac Kultury i Nauki** *Plan II* **C2**: panoramic view of the city and multimedia tourist information centre on 30th floor of the Palace of Culture and Science, a skyscraper (234m) in the Stalinist style of architecture, a 'gift' from the former USSR.

OLD TOWN *Plan II* **C1** – **Plac Zamkowy**: Castle Square marked by the Sigismund Column (1644). **Zamek Królewski**: the Royal Palace, reconstructed to create the luxury of the 17C and 18C. **Katedra Św Jana**: St John's Cathedral, a Gothic church with stained-glass windows depicting major figures from Polish history. **Rynek Starego Miasta**: Old Town Market Square, bordered by narrow-fronted houses and alive with cafés, restaurants, artists, souvenir stalls and horse-drawn carriages for hire.

MUSEUMS AND GALLERIES – **Muzeum Historyczne Warszawy** *Plan II* **C1**: the Warsaw History Museum; short film in English on the destruction and reconstruction of Warsaw. **Muzeum Narodowe** *Plan II* **D2**: National Museum devoted to medieval Polish art and other European artists; frescoes from Farras in Sudan. **Muzeum Kolekcji im. Jana Pawła II** *Plan II* **C1**: the John Paul II Collection of six centuries of outstanding European art; religious subjects, landscapes, mythology, portraits and works by the Impressionists. **Jewish History Museum**: the history of the Warsaw ghetto.

ROYAL ROAD – **Trakt Królewski**. The Royal Way (4 km/2.5 mi) linking the castle to the summer residence, is divided into several streets lined with historic buildings reflecting several centuries of history: St Anne's Church (**view** from the tower – *summer only*), Radziwiłł Palace, now the Residence of the President of Poland, Hotel Bristol, Warsaw University, Chopin's residence, Holy Cross Church (urn containing Chopin's heart), **Piłsudski** Square *(side street west)* with the changing of the guard every 1hr before the Tomb of the Unknown Soldier, Staszic Palace, St Aleksander's Church, Paderewski Monument in Ujazdowski Park.

ROYAL PALACES – **Park Łazienkowski** *Plan I* **B2**. 18C park (lakes, trees, lawns, flower beds; Botanic Gardens) containing Chopin Memorial; 18C orangery housing the royal theatre; Biały Dom, royal summer residence known as the White House; Pałac na Wodzie, royal residence designed by Merlini, standing on a tiny island: superbly furnished and decorated rooms; **Pałac Myśliwski**, second summer residence by Merlini; Teatr na Wyspie, amphitheatre on the edge of the lake; Belweder, 18C building now the official residence of the President of the Republic. **Wilanów** Residence of King John III Sobieski, a Baroque palace with lavishly furnished rooms, surrounded by a park and gardens: Baroque, English-style and Anglo-Chinese on the edge of the lake.

GOURMET TREATS

Warsaw is good for coffee and cakes (kawiarnia): for a range of patisserie; *Blikle*, Nowy Świat 33, famous for its traditional interior, doughnuts and cream cakes; *Antykwariat*, Żurawia 45; *Cafe Brama*, Krucza 16/22; *Coffeeheaven*, Nowy Świat 40. For a traditional Polish eating house: *U Fukiera*, Rynek Starego Miasta 27; *Dom Polski*, Francuska 11, with pleasant terrace garden; *Restauracja Polska 'Tradycja'*, Belwederska 18A; *Restauracja Polska*, Nowy Świat 21; *Restauracja Polska*, Chocimska 7.

SHOPPING

Shops are generally open from Mon-Fri 10am-7pm, Sat 9am-3pm. Food shops open earlier and close at 8pm or 10pm. Large shopping centres and tourist shops tend to open on Sundays.

There are some shops in the Old Town but the main shopping streets are: **Chmielna** *Plan II* **D2**, **Marszałkowska** *(Galeria Centrum)*, **Krakowskie Przedmieście** *Plan II* **D1**, **Nowy Świat** *Plan II* **D2**, **Świętojańska**, **Jerozolimskie** *(Smyk)*.

MARKETS – The street markets offer the lowest prices; the most famous **food market** is Polna St *Plan I* **B2**.

WHAT TO BUY – Woodcarvings, pottery, paintings on glass, embroidery, tapestries, striped woollen fabrics known as *pasiak* used to make skirts and aprons (all available in Cepelia shops). Amber, the gold of the north, is found in yellow, russet and brown, and used to make necklaces and earrings; sometimes it is mounted in silver as jewellery. Works of art and antiques (large selection in the *DESA* stores).

ENTERTAINMENT

What When Where, published in English, gives a calendar of current events in Warsaw and other towns. *What's up in Warsaw*, published monthly in English (no charge) also provides current information. Details about cultural events in Warsaw – theatre shows, concerts – can be obtained from the telephone Cultural Information Centre, ✆ 629 84 89 (Mon-Fri 10am-9pm, Sat-Sun 10am-6pm).

Tickets can be obtained at *ZASP Theatre Booking Office*, Jerozolimskie 25 *Plan II* **D2**, ✆ 621 94 54 or 621 93 83; *Empik*, Nowy Świat 15/17, ✆ 625 12 19; Marszałkowska 104/122, ✆ 551 4 37.

Grand Theatre-National Opera *Plan II* **D1** – National opera and ballet.

Warsaw Chamber Opera *Plan II* **C1** – Baroque opera.

National Philharmonic Hall *Plan II* **C2** – Two auditoria for orchestral concerts; venue for the Chopin Piano Competition.

Roma Music Theatre *Plan II* **D2** – Classical operettas and musicals.

National Theatre *Plan II* **D1** – Foremost Polish drama.

NIGHTLIFE

Warsaw has a lively clubbing scene, including *Piekarnia*, Młocińska 11; *Vanilla*, Sienkiewicza 6; *Techno*, Instytut Energetyki, Mory 8; *Lucid*, Jerozolimskie 179; *Organza*, Sienkiewicza 4; *Klubo Kawiarnia*, Czackiego; NoBo, Wilcza 58a.

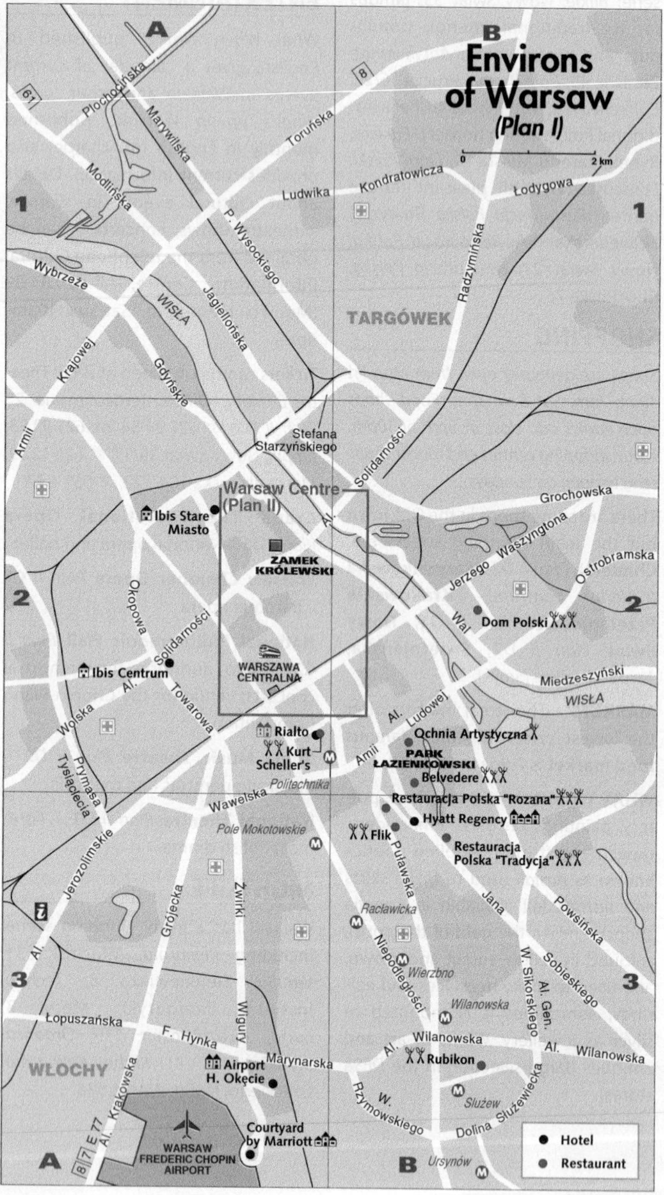

Environs of Warsaw
(Plan I)

0 2 km

A B
1 2 3

Płochocińska
Marywilska
Toruńska
Modlińska
Ludwika
Kondratowicza
Łodygowa
Radzymińska
P. Wysockiego
Wybrzeże
WISŁA
Jagiellońska
TARGÓWEK
Krajowej
Gdyńskie
Stefana Starzyńskiego
Armii
Al. Solidarności
Warsaw Centre (Plan II)
Ibis Stare Miasto
ZAMEK KRÓLEWSKI
Grochowska
Jerzego Waszyngtona
Ostrobramska
Okopowa
Wał
Dom Polski
Solidarności
Ibis Centrum
WARSZAWA CENTRALNA
Miedzeszyński
Al.
Towarowa
Wolska
Al. Ludowej
Ochnia Artystyczna
Rialto
Kurt Scheller's
Armii
PARK ŁAZIENKOWSKI
Belvedere
Prymasa Tysiąclecia
Politechnika
Wawelska
Restauracja Polska "Rozana"
Hyatt Regency
Pole Mokotowskie
Flik
Restauracja Polska "Tradycja"
Jerozolimskie
Grójecka
Żwirki
Puławska
Jana
Powsińska
Racławicka
Al.
Niepodległości
Wierzbno
W. Sikorskiego
Sobieskiego
Al. Gen.
Wilanowska
Łopuszańska
F. Hynka
Wigury
Wilanowska
Al. Wilanowska
Marynarska
Rubikon
WŁOCHY
Airport H. Okęcie
Krakowska
Al.
W. Rzymowskiego
Służew
Dolina Służewiecka
E 77
Courtyard by Marriott
WARSAW FREDERIC CHOPIN AIRPORT
Ursynów

- Hotel
- Restaurant

Le Royal Meridien Bristol

Krakowskie Przedmieście 42-44 ✉ 00 325 – Ⓜ Świętokrzyska – ✆ (022) 551 10 00 – bristol@lemeridien.com – Fax (022) 625 25 77 – www.lemeridien.com/warsaw 180 VISA MC AE **D1**

173 rm – ††1116 PLN, 100 PLN – 31 suites

Rest *Marconi* – *(dinner only)* Menu 59/69 PLN (lunch) – Carte 124/192 PLN

Rest *Malinowa* – *✆ (022) 55 11 832 (closed January, Sunday and Monday) (booking essential)* Menu 180 PLN – Carte 121/225 PLN

♦ Grand Luxury ♦ Classic ♦

Imposing late 19C façade, partly decorated in Art Nouveau style fronts classic hotel, a byword for luxury and meeting place for Warsaw high society. Spacious elegant rooms. Formal dining room with Art Nouveau décor and chandeliers adding opulence. Elaborate gourmet menu offers international cuisine with a strong French influence. Fairly informal restaurant with terrace offers a varied menu of Mediterranean fare.

Intercontinental

City, rm 500

Ul. Emilii Plater 49 ✉ 00 125 – Ⓜ Centrum – ✆ (022) 328 88 88 – wrs_reservation@interconti.com – Fax (022) 328 88 89 – www.warsaw.intercontinental.com VISA MC AE **C2**

306 rm – †684 PLN ††532/684 PLN – 21 suites

Rest *Frida* – *(closed lunch Sunday and Saturday)* Carte 130/186 PLN

Rest *Downtown* – Menu 89 PLN – Carte 52/69 PLN

Rest *Hemisphere* – *(closed Saturday-Sunday)* Carte 124/178 PLN

♦ Grand Luxury ♦ Business ♦ Modern ♦

Architecturally striking high-rise hotel. Richly furnished, contemporary bedrooms. Stunning 44th floor wellness centre. Frida for Mexican dishes from open-plan kitchen. Cosmopolitan New York-style in Downtown. Hemisphere with Hemingway theme and live music.

Hyatt Regency

rm 350 P VISA MC AE

Belwederska Ave 23 ✉ 00 761 – ✆ (022) 558 12 34 – info@hyattwarsaw.pl – Fax (022) 558 12 35 – www.warsaw.regency.hyatt.com *Plan I* **B3**

231 rm – †740 PLN ††490/780 PLN, 85 PLN – 19 suites

Rest *Venti Tre* – *✆ (022) 558 1094* – Menu 95 PLN (lunch) – Carte 106/128 PLN

Rest *Q Club* – *(closed Saturday, Sunday and Bank Holidays) (dinner only)* Carte 84/140 PLN

♦ Luxury ♦ Business ♦ Modern ♦

Striking glass-fronted and ultramodern corporate hotel beside Lazienki Park. Spacious bedrooms with every facility and comfort. Contemporary Italian fare in relaxed Venti Tre. Open kitchen with wood fired specialities. Q Club for contemporary Asian menu.

The Westin

rm 560 VISA MC AE

Al. Jana Pawła II 21 ✉ 00 854 – Ⓜ Świętokrzyska – ✆ (022) 450 80 00 – warsaw@westin.com – Fax (022) 450 81 11 – www.westin.com/warsaw **C2**

346 rm – †772 PLN ††539/772 PLN – 15 suites

Rest *Fusion* – Menu 90/130 PLN – Carte 80/140 PLN

♦ Luxury ♦ Business ♦ Modern ♦

Impressive modern façade, splendid glass atrium with glass lifts and spacious public areas. 'Heavenly beds' and modern facilities in comfortable bedrooms. Contemporary Fusion offers culinary delights as East meets West.

Sheraton

rm 700 VISA MC AE

Ul. B. Prusa 2 ✉ 00493 – Ⓜ Centrum – ✆ (022) 450 61 00 – warsaw@sheraton.com – Fax (022) 450 62 00 – www.sheraton.com/warsaw **D2**

331 rm – †772 PLN ††539/772 PLN, 90 PLN – 19 suites

Rest *The Oriental* – *(closed Saturday lunch and Sunday dinner)* Carte 154/192 PLN

Rest *Lalka* – Menu 90 PLN – Carte 96/171 PLN

♦ Luxury ♦ Business ♦ Modern ♦

Business hotel in well-located, imposing building. Comfortable, spacious rooms; extra amenities in business class. Authentic Asian fare in ornately decorated Oriental. All day bistro; Old City mural; Mediterranean/traditional Polish dishes in Lalka.

Marriott

City, rm 700

Al. Jerozolimskie 65-79 ✉ *00 697* – Ⓜ *Centrum* – 𝒞 *(022) 630 63 06 – warsaw-reservation@marriotthotels.com – Fax (022) 830 03 11 – www.marriott.com/wawpl*

VISA AE

C2

486 rm – †530 PLN ††360/530 PLN, ☕ 84 PLN – 32 suites

Rest *Parmizzano's* – Carte 115/269 PLN

Rest *Lila Weneda* – Menu 86 PLN (lunch) – Carte 69/134 PLN

♦ Business ♦ Modern ♦

Modern high-rise business hotel opposite station. Well-equipped up-to-date bedrooms with city views; good facilities for business travellers. Formal Parmizzano's offers Italian fare. Classic Polish cooking in Lila Weneda.

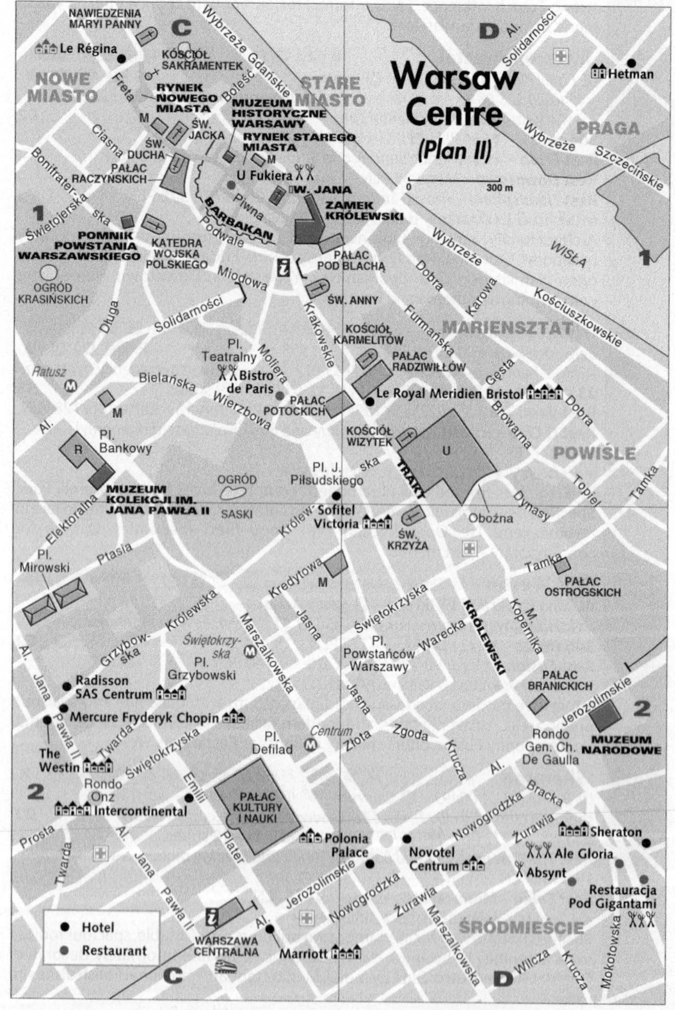

Sofitel Victoria

Ul. Królewska 11 ✉ 00 065 – Ⓜ Świętokrzyska – ✆ (022) 657 80 11 – sof.victoria@orbis.pl – Fax (022) 657 80 57 – www.sofitel.com **C1-2**

329 rm – 875 PLN – 12 suites

Rest *Canaletto* – Carte 120/165 PLN

♦ Business ♦ Classic ♦

Large hotel overlooking Pilsudski Square and Saxon Gardens. Rooms are well equipped and comfortable with muted classic décor. Good business facilities available. Formal restaurant with Italian influence.

Radisson SAS Centrum

Grzybowska 24 ✉ 00 132 – Ⓜ Świętokrzyska – ✆ (022) 321 88 88 – reservation.warsaw@radissonsas.com – Fax (022) 321 88 98 – www.radissonsas.com **C2**

292 rm – 720 PLN 420/720 PLN, 80 PLN – 19 suites

Rest *Latino Brasserie at Ferdy's* – Menu 69 PLN – Carte 80/150 PLN

♦ Business ♦ Modern ♦

Popular corporate hotel in business district with state of the art meeting facilities. Modern bedrooms in maritime, Scandinavian or Italian style. Informal bar-restaurant with Latin American influences.

Le Régina

U. Kościelna 12 ✉ 00 218 – Ⓜ Ratusz – ✆ (022) 531 60 00 – info@leregina.com – Fax (022) 531 60 01 – www.leregina.com **C1**

59 rm – 1400 PLN 1200/1400 PLN, 92 PLN – 2 suites

Rest *La Rotisserie* – Menu 95 PLN (weekday lunch) – Carte 150/248 PLN

♦ Luxury ♦ Design ♦

Boutique hotel close to the Old Town; neo-18C exterior but stylish, contemporary interior. Pleasant courtyard. Individually decorated, spacious high-tech bedrooms. Small, intimate restaurant offering original modern cuisine.

Polonia Palace

Al. Jerozolimskie 45 ✉ 00 692 – Ⓜ Centrum – ✆ (022) 318 2888 – centralreservation@syrena.com.pl – Fax (022) 318 28 89 – www.poloniapalace.com **D2**

197 rm – 880 PLN – 9 suites

Rest *Ludwikowska* – *(dinner only)* Carte 105/170 PLN

♦ Business ♦ Classic ♦

Architecturally striking hotel and celebrated landmark, dating from 1913. Sympathetically remodelled throughout, with bedrooms sleek and contemporary in style. Great detail in the ornate, gilded fine dining room with a menu of Polish and Mediterranean influences.

Mercure Fryderyk Chopin

Al. Jana Pawła II 22 ✉ 00 133 – Ⓜ Świętokrzyska – ✆ (022) 528 03 00 – h1597@accor.com – Fax (022) 528 03 03 – www.mercure.com **C2**

242 rm – 540 PLN, 60 PLN – 7 suites

Rest *Stanislas Brasserie* – ✆ (022) 528 03 60 – Carte 78/139 PLN

♦ Business ♦ Functional ♦

Located in business district, catering for business clientele. Practically appointed rooms. Comfortable brasserie-style restaurant for international dishes. Pleasant place for coffee.

Novotel Centrum

Ul. Marszalkowska 94/98 ✉ 00 510 – Ⓜ Centrum – ✆ (022) 621 02 71 – rez.nov.warszawa@orbis.pl – Fax (022) 625 04 76 **D2**

723 rm – 580 PLN, 30 PLN – 10 suites

Rest *Essencia* – Carte 85/117 PLN

♦ Business ♦ Functional ♦

1970s-style high-rise hotel in central location on main shopping street. Contemporary style, well-serviced bedrooms, all with city views. International cuisine and vibrant bar and lounge.

Rialto

Ul. Wilcza 73 ✉ 00 670 – Ⓜ Politechnika – ☎ (022) 584 87 00 – reservation@hotelrialto.com.pl – Fax (022) 584 87 01 – www.hotelrialto.com.pl *Plan I* **A2**

33 rm – †865 PLN ††865 PLN, ☕ 65 PLN – 11 suites

Rest *Kurt Scheller's* – see below

♦ Business ♦ Art Deco ♦

Boutique hotel with superb Art Deco features in converted 1906 building in discreet location. Individually decorated bedrooms with the latest in comfort and facilities.

Hetman

Klopotowskiego 36 ✉ 03 717 – ☎ (022) 511 98 00 – rez@hotelhetman.pl – Fax (022) 618 51 39 – www.hotelhetman.pl **D1**

68 rm ☕ – †350 PLN ††330/410 PLN

Rest – Carte 65/76 PLN

♦ Business ♦ Functional ♦

Modern hotel in a 19C converted apartment block, a short walk over the river from the Old Town and city centre. Large, uniform and immaculate bedrooms. International cuisine in restaurant.

Ibis Stare Miasto

Ul. Muranowska 2 ✉ 00 209 – ☎ (022) 310 10 00 – h3714@accor.com – Fax (022) 310 10 10 – www.ibishotel.com *Plan I* **A2**

333 rm – ††269 PLN, ☕ 28 PLN

Rest *L'Estaminet* – Carte 53/138 PLN

♦ Chain hotel ♦ Functional ♦

Modern hotel close to the Old Town with 24-hour bar and business centre. Larger rooms on 6th floor with balconies. Bistro-style restaurant providing simple traditional European dishes. Flexible breakfast times.

Ibis Centrum

Al. Solidarności 165 ✉ 00 876 – ☎ (022) 520 30 00 – h2894@accor.com – Fax (022) 520 30 30 – www.ibishotel.com *Plan I* **A2**

189 rm – †259 PLN ††199/259 PLN, ☕ 28 PLN

Rest *L'Estaminet* – Carte 53/138 PLN

♦ Chain hotel ♦ Functional ♦

Located at intersection of two main roads by Warsaw Trade Tower. Good size rooms are light and airy, well soundproofed with modern functional fittings. Bistro-style restaurant providing simple traditional European dishes.

Restauracja Polska "Tradycja"

Belwederska Ave 18A ✉ 00 762 – ☎ (022) 840 09 01 – Fax (022) 840 09 50 – www.restauracjatradycja.pl *Plan I* **B3**

Rest – *(booking essential)* Carte 62/122 PLN

♦ Traditional ♦ Family ♦

Several homely dining rooms offer traditional Polish atmosphere; live piano, candles and lace tablecloths. Professional service. Well-prepared traditional Polish cooking.

Restauracja Pod Gigantami

Al. Ujazdowskie 24 ✉ 00 478 – Ⓜ Centrum – ☎ (022) 629 23 12 – podgigantami@zapart.pl – Fax (022) 621 30 59 – www.podgigantami.pl closed Easter Sunday, 25 December and 1 January **D2**

Rest – Carte 102/117 PLN

♦ International ♦ Formal ♦

This early 20C house plays host to an elegant and charming restaurant, favoured by diplomats from nearby embassies. Attentive formal service and a carefully prepared European menu.

Restauracja Polska "Rozana"

Chocimska 7 ✉ 00 791 – Ⓜ Pole Mokotowskie – ☎ (022) 848 12 25 – Fax (022) 848 15 90 – www.restauracjapolska.com.pl closed 31 December *Plan I* **B3**

Rest – Carte 60.50/139 PLN

♦ Traditional ♦ Friendly ♦

Typical of the Restauracja Polska style: traditional homely ambience; professional service; classic Polish cuisine. Home-made dessert trolley and nightly pianist.

XXX

Ale Gloria

16

Pl. Trzech Krzyzy 3 ✉ 00 535 – Ⓜ Centrum – ✆ (022) 584 70 80 – alegloria@alegloria.pl – Fax (022) 584 70 81 – www.alegloria.pl **D2**

Rest – Carte 93/200 PLN

♦ Modern ♦ Design ♦

Prepare yourself for some subterranean enchantment. This fashionable restaurant, in what was once stables, has a magical, original feel. The menu is equally bold and individual.

XXX

Dom Polski

24

Ul. Francuska 11 ✉ 03 906 – ✆ (022) 616 24 32 – restauracjadompolski@wp.pl – Fax (022) 616 24 88 – www.restauracjadompolski.pl *Plan I* **B2**

Rest – Carte 55/164 PLN

♦ Traditional ♦ Friendly ♦

Elegant house in city suburb with pleasant terrace-garden. Comfortable dining rooms on two floors with welcoming ambience. Interesting well-presented traditional cuisine.

XXX

Belvedere

25

Ul. Agrykoli 1 (entry from Parkowa St) ✉ 00 460 – ✆ (022) 841 22 50 – restauracja@belvedere.com.pl – Fax (022) 841 71 35 – www.belvedere.com.pl

closed 23 December-6 January *Plan I* **B2**

Rest – *(booking essential)* Carte 86/207 PLN

♦ International ♦ Formal ♦

Elegant restaurant occupying late 19C orangery in Lazienki park. Dining room filled with statuesque plants. French-influenced international and Polish cuisine.

XX

Bistro de Paris

20

Pl. Piłsudskiego 9 ✉ 00 073 – Ⓜ Ratusz – ✆ (022) 826 01 07 – michelmoran@02.pl – Fax (022) 827 08 08 – www.restaurantbistrodeparis.com

closed Sunday **C1**

Rest – Carte 107/162 PLN

♦ French ♦ Family ♦

Expect French cooking with some eclectic touches but underscored by a traditional base. The smart façade is matched by the comfortable interior; service is taken seriously.

XX

Kurt Scheller's – at Rialto H.

Ul. Wilcza 73 ✉ 00 670 – Ⓜ Politechnika – ✆ (022) 584 87 00 – restaurant@hotelrialto.com.pl – Fax (022) 584 87 01 *Plan I* **A2**

Rest – Menu 50/70 PLN (lunch) – Carte 130/420 PLN

♦ Modern ♦ Fashionable ♦

Superb Art Deco style with reproduction 1930s furniture and posters. Modern slant on traditional Polish cooking by Kurt Scheller, renowned chef and teacher.

XX

Rubikon

12

Ul. Wróbla 3/5 ✉ 02 736 – Ⓜ Słuzew – ✆ (022) 847 66 55 – info@rubikon.waw.pl – www.rubikon.waw.pl *Plan I* **B3**

Rest – *(brunch at weekends)* Carte 75/100 PLN

♦ Italian ♦ Neighbourhood ♦

In a restored villa south of the city. Divided into various rooms over two floors, the style is modern with some Art Deco. Prime sourced produce, flavoursome cooking.

XX

U Fukiera

15

Rynek Starego Miasta 27 ✉ 00 272 – Ⓜ Ratusz – ✆ (022) 831 10 13 – fukier@tlen.pl – Fax (022) 831 58 08 – www.ufukiera.pl **C1**

Rest – Carte 90/325 PLN

♦ Traditional ♦ Rustic ♦

On historic central city square, well-known restaurant with character; 17C vaulted cellar and pleasant rear courtyard. Traditional Polish cuisine.

POLAND

Flik

Ul. Puławska 43 ✉ 02 508 – Ⓜ Pole Mokotowskie – ✆ (022) 849 44 34 – restauracja@flik.com.pl – Fax (022) 849 44 06 – www.flik.com.pl

closed 24 December

Plan I **B3**

Rest – Menu 59 PLN (lunch) – Carte 51/111 PLN

◆ Traditional ◆ Neighbourhood ◆

Welcoming neighbourhood restaurant with Polish art collection, overlooking park. Friendly service, well-prepared traditional fare. Famed for lunch buffet and business clientele.

Qchnia Artystyczna

Al. Ujazdowskie 6 (Ujazdowski Castle) ✉ 00 461 – Ⓜ Politechnika – ✆ (022) 625 76 27 – qchnia@qchnia.pl – Fax (022) 625 76 27 – www.qchnia.pl

closed Easter and Christmas

Plan I **B2**

Rest – Carte 60/95 PLN

◆ Modern ◆ Fashionable ◆

Translates as "artistic kitchen"; expect bold flavours using seasonal ingredients, from bizarrely laid out menu. Original and fresh decor; well regarded by fashionable locals.

Absynt

Ul. Wspólna 35 ✉ 00 519 – Ⓜ Centrum – ✆ (022) 621 18 81 – absynt@siesta.com.pl – Fax (022) 622 11 01 – www.kregliccy.com.pl

D2

Rest – Carte 80/106 PLN

◆ French ◆ Bistro ◆

Informal restaurant with a strong 'French' accent; more intimate basement. Good value, seasonally changing, classic French repertoire with a hint of modernity.

at Warsaw Frederick Chopin Airport Southwest : 10 km by Zwirki i Wigury

Plan I

Courtyard by Marriott

rm 420

Ul. Zwirki i Wigury 1 ✉ 00 906 – ✆ *(022) 650 01 00 – wcy@courtyard.com – Fax (022) 650 01 01 – www.courtyard.com/wawcy*

A3

219 rm – 540 PLN, 60 PLN – 7 suites

Rest *Brasserie* – Carte 86/160 PLN

◆ Business ◆ Modern ◆

Modern hotel opposite the airport entrance. Bar and cyber café with Internet access; conference facilities. Well-equipped modern bedrooms with effective soundproofing. Mezzanine brasserie offering an eclectic range of international dishes.

Airport H. Okęcie

rm 200

Ul. 17 Stycznia 24 ✉ 02 146 – ✆ *(022) 456 80 00 – reservation@airporthotel.pl – Fax (022) 456 80 29 – www.airporthotel.pl*

A3

165 rm – 460 PLN 520/560 PLN – 7 suites

Rest *Mirage* – Carte 72/94 PLN

◆ Business ◆ Classic ◆

Classic corporate hotel 800 metres from the airport. Large meeting rooms and bedrooms have the international traveller and conference delegate in mind. Sky Bar for drinks. Lively and popular 'Mirage' with open-plan kitchen and buffet.

PORTUGAL

PORTUGAL

PROFILE

- **Area:** 88 944 km² (34 341 sq mi).
- **Population:** 10 605 870 (est. 2006), density = 116 per km².
- **Capital:** Lisbon (conurbation 2 700 000 inhabitants).
- **Currency:** Euro (€); rate of exchange: € 1 = US$1.32 (Nov 2006).
- **Government:** Parliamentary republic (since 1976). Member of European Union since 1986.
- **Language:** Portuguese.
- **Specific public holidays:** Shrove Tuesday (February); Good Friday (Friday before Easter); Freedom Day (25 April), Corpus Christi (May or June); Portugal Day (10 June); Republic Day (5 October); Restoration of Independence Day (1 December); Immaculate Conception (8 December).
- **Local Time:** GMT in winter and GMT + 1 hour in summer.
- **Climate:** Temperate Mediterranean with warm winters and hot summers (Lisbon: January 15°C, July 26°C).

- **International dialling Code:** **00 351** followed by a nine-digit number. International directory enquiries : ✆ **098**.
- **Emergency:** Dial ✆ **112**.
- **Electricity:** 230-240 volts AC, 50 Hz; 2-pin round-shaped continental plugs.

FORMALITIES

Travellers from the European Union (EU), Switzerland, Iceland and the main countries of North and South America need a national identity card or passport (America: passport required) to visit Portugal for less than three months (tourism or business purpose). For visitors from other countries a visa may be required, in addition to a passport, especially for those wishing to stay for longer than three months. We advise you to check with your embassy before travelling.

A valid national driving licence is required by nationals of EU countries; an international driving licence is required by nationals of non-EU countries. Valid insurance cover is compulsory. Drivers must be at least 21 or 25 to hire a car and to have held a driving licence for more than 1 year.

MAJOR NEWSPAPERS

The main dailies are : *O Diário de Notícias*, *O Correio da Manhã* and *O Público* (from Lisbon) and *O Jornal de Notícias* (from Porto).

USEFUL PHRASES

ENGLISH	PORTUGUESE
Yes	**Sim**
No	**Não**
Good morning	**Bom dia**
Goodbye	**Adeus**
Thank you	**Obrigado (a)**
Please	**(se) faz favor**
Excuse me	**Desculpe**
I don't understand	**Não percebo**

HOTELS

→ CATEGORIES

Accommodation is classified in several different categories: **hotels** (1-5 stars); **inns** *(estalagens)*; smaller, **family-run guesthouses** (*residenciais* which do not serve meals); **more modest guesthouses** *(pensöes)*; **bed and breakfast in manor houses** *(turismo de habitação)*; **country houses** *(casas de campo)*; **farmhouses** *(agro-turismo)*. The **pousadas**, hotels in restored historic buildings (castles, palaces and convents) in beautiful sites or excursion centres, are state-owned; there are similar privately-owned hotels. As **pousadas** are very popular, it is wise to book in advance – www.pousadas.pt

→ PRICE RANGE

The price is per room. There is little difference between the price of a single and a double room.

Between April and October it is advisable to book in advance. From November to March prices may be slightly lower, some hotels offer special cheap rates and some may be closed.

→ TAX

Included in the room price (5% or 16%).

→ CHECK OUT TIME

Usually between 11am and noon.

→ RESERVATIONS

By telephone or by Internet; a credit card number may be required.

→ TIP FOR LUGGAGE HANDLING

At the discretion of the customer (about €1 per bag).

→ BREAKFAST

Breakfast is usually included in the price of the room and is generally served between 7am and 10am. Most hotels offer a buffet but usually it is possible to have continental breakfast served in the room.

Reception	**Recepção**
Single room	**Quarto indivudual**
Double room	**Quarto duplo**
Bed	**Cama**
Bathroom	**Casa de banho**
Shower	**Duche**

RESTAURANTS

Restaurants serve lunch from noon to 3pm and dinner from 7pm to 10pm, although some restaurants continue to serve after 10pm. Besides the traditional restaurants there are cafés and bars, which serve simpler fare.

Breakfast	**Pequeno-almoço**	7am – 10am
Lunch	**Almoço**	12.30pm – 2-3pm
Dinner	**Jantar**	6.30pm – 10-11pm sometimes later

Restaurants offer fixed price menus (starter, main course and dessert) or à la carte. Menus are usually printed in Portuguese and often in English. A fixed price menu is usually less expensive than the same dishes chosen from the à la carte. Hors-d'œuvre are often served prior to the meal and the cost is added to the bill if they are eaten.

In some of the more popular restaurants, particularly in the north, there are two prices against an item on the menu; the first is for a full portion *(dose)* and the second for a half-portion *(meia dose)*.

Reservations are usually made by phone, fax or Internet. For famous restaurants (including Michelin starred restaurants), it is advisable to book several days – in some instances weeks – in advance. A credit card number or a phone number may be required to guarantee the booking.

The bill (check) includes service charge and VAT. It is customary to leave a tip of about 10% of the total bill.

Drink or aperitif	**Bebida**	Wine (red, white, rosé)	**Vinho (tinto, branco, rosé)**
Aperitif	**Aperitivo**	Beer	**Cerveja**
Meal	**Comida, refeição**	Bread	**Pão**
Starter	**Entrada**	Meat	**Carne**
Main dish	**Prato principal**	Fish	**Peixe**
Main dish of the day	**Prato do dia**	Salt/pepper	**Sal/pimenta**
		Cheese	**Queijo**
Dessert	**Sobremesa**	Vegetables	**Hortaliças, vegetais**
Water, still, sparkling	**Água, sem gás, com gás**	Hot/cold	**Quente/frio**
		The bill (check) please	**A conta por favor**

LOCAL CUISINE

Portuguese meals are usually copious and prepared with olive oil and aromatic herbs.

Soup is served at most meals. **Caldo verde**, the most famous, consists of mashed potato mixed with finely shredded green cabbage, olive oil and slices of black pudding *(tora)*. Bread soup *(açorda)* is common to all regions but **gaspacho** – made of tomatoes, onions, cucumbers and chillies seasoned with garlic and vinegar, which is served cold with croutons – is mostly found in the south.

Fish is a basic element in Portuguese cooking. The commonest is **cod** *(bacalhau)* for which there are 365 different recipes; **caldeirada** is a stew of many types of fish. Seafood *(mariscos)* including octopus is plentiful. Shellfish are delicious and very varied, especially in the Algarve where **cataplana**, a special copper vessel, gives its name to a dish of clams and sausages spiced with herbs.

Pork is cooked and served in a variety of ways: **carne de porco à Alentejana**, pork marinated in wine and garnished with clams, **leitão assado**, roast suckling-pig and **presunto**, smoked ham. Other meat is usually minced and served as meatballs, although lamb and kid are sometimes roasted or served on skewers.

There are various types of cheese *(queijo)* made from ewe's milk (October to May) and goat's milk.

Nearly all cake and pastry recipes include eggs and come from old specialities prepared in convents: **Queijadas de Sintra**, with almonds and fresh ewe's milk, **Toucinho-do-Céu** and **Barriga-de-Freira.** The commonest dessert is the **pudim flan**, a sort of crème caramel; **leite-creme** is a creamier version. Particularly delicious is **pasteis de nata**, a small custard tart sprinkled with cinnamon. On festive occasions **Arroz doce** (rice pudding) sprinkled with cinnamon is served. In the Algarve the local figs *(figos)* and almonds *(amêndoas)* are made into appetising sweetmeats.

DRINK

Portugal has a rich variety of wines. **Vinho Verde** can be white or deep red; it is best enjoyed young and chilled; as an aperitif or with fish and seafood; its name which means green wine, comes from its early harvest and short fermentation period, which make it light and sparkling with a distinctive bouquet and a low alcohol content. **Bucelas** is a dry, somewhat acidic white wine. **Dão** wine may be a fresh white wine or a sweet red wine with a velvety texture and a heady bouquet. **Bairrada** is a robust, fragrant red with a natural sparkle. **Colares** is a velvety, dark red wine, famous since the 13C.

Portugal is best known for the world famous **Port**, named after Oporto. After fermentation brandy is added and the wine is matured in huge vats and then aged in wooden barrels (*pipes*). Port is red or white according to the colour of the grapes, and can be dry, medium or sweet. Port aged in casks matures through oxidation and turns an amber colour; port aged in the bottle matures by reduction and is a dark red colour. Red ports are blended: **Tinto** is young, distinctly coloured and fruity; **Tinto-alourado** or **Ruby** is older, rich in colour, fruity and sweet; **Alourado** or **Tawny** turns to a brownish gold as it ages; **Alourado-Claro** or **Light Tawny** is the culmination of the former.

Maderia wine, famous in England as Malmsey, comes in four principal types – **Sercial**, a dry wine with a good bouquet, amber in colour and served chilled as an aperitif; **Verdelho**, slightly sweeter but also drinkable as an aperitif; **Bual**, with a rich, full bodied flavour, primarily a dessert wine; **Malmsey**, now rare, is also a dessert wine with a honeyed flavour and a deep-red colour.

Dessert wines include **Setúbal** moscatel, a generous fruity wine, and fruity amber-coloured **Carcavelos**, which is also drunk as an aperitif.

The wide variety of Portuguese brandies includes cherry brandy from Alcobaça *(ginginha)*, arbutus berry brandy *(medronho)* and honey brandy *(brandimel)* from the Algarve. The most popular spirit is a grape marc *(bagaço* or *bagaceira)* which is served chilled.

The commonest beer is light and similar to lager. Fruit juices, still or sparkling, are also excellent and refreshing.

LISBON
LISBOA

Population (est. 2006): 570 000 (conurbation 2 700 000) – Altitude: at sea level

B. Morandi/MICHELIN

The capital of Portugal stands midway on the Atlantic coast on the Tagus estuary. At the time of the Great Discoveries (15C-16C), Lisbon became the cosmopolitan centre of a huge overseas empire.

The old town was built on 7 hills on the northern shore of the 'Straw Sea', as the bulge in the Tagus is called because of the golden reflections of the sun on the water. The attraction of the city lies in its light, its pastel ochres, pinks, blues and greens, its streets and squares with mosaic paving (small black and white stones named *empedrados*). With its narrow old streets, its magnificent vistas along wide avenues, its lively harbour, old trams, exotic gardens and *Fado* lyrical chants which celebrate nostalgia *(saudade)*, Lisbon is a delightful patchwork.

While Lisbon bears the stamp of its past, it has set its sights firmly on the future ever since Portugal became a member of the EEC (1986). New Business districts are growing, particularly around Campo Pequeno and Campo Grande, while the Centro Cultural de Belém (1992) was built to enhance the historical and cultural importance of this part of the city. The famous post-modern towers of Amoreiras, by the architect T. Taveira, caused a sensation when they first went up, while other towers have sprung up around Campo Grande to become landmarks within the city.

WHICH DISTRICT TO CHOOSE

For **hotels** there is a choice between the borders of the Parque Eduardo VII *Plan III* **G3** where most of the luxury hotels are to be found, and the residential districts such as Lapa *Plan I* **B3** near the embassies, which offers a number of charming hotels in old private houses, or Belém, which is further from the centre.

For **restaurants** it is best to go to the more central and lively districts such as Rossio *Plan I* **H1** and Baixa *Plan II* **F2** or climb up to Bairro Alto *Plan II* **E2** which has become the in-district in Lisbon.

If you are going out for a **drink**, take a stroll along the banks of the Tagus in Alcantara *Plan I* **B3** where the old docks *(Docas)* are now lined with bars and nightclubs.

PRACTICAL INFORMATION

ARRIVAL – DEPARTURE

Portela Airport – About 8 km (5 mi) north of the city centre. ✆ 218 413 700, 218 413 500; lisbon.airport@ana.pt; www.ana.pt

From the airport to the city centre – By **taxi**: 10 mins, €12.15 (+ €1.50 for luggage). By **shuttle bus** to Praça do Comércio *Plan II* **E2** and Cais do Sodré 15mins (7.45am-8.45pm, every 20min). Fare €3.00.

Railway Stations – **Estação de Santa Apolónia** *Plan I* **C3** for international routes and trains to the north of the country. ✆ 213 185 990; www.cp.pt – **Estação do Cais do Socré** for trains to Estoril and Cascais; departures approximately every 20min until 2.30am; journey time about 30min – **Estação do Rossio** for trains to the NW suburbs including Sintra and Leiria; departures to Sintra approximately every 20min until 2.30am; journey time about 30min – **Estação Sul e Sueste** for trains to Alentejo and Algarve via the ferry which crosses the river to Barreiro railway station – **Estação do Oriente** intermodal transport terminal (bus, metro and train) serving the north: the station is linked to Santa Apolónia and Sintra railway stations.

TRANSPORT

→ METRO

4 lines (Gaivota, Girassol, Caravela and Oriente) operate from 6.30am to 1am; the stations are works of art. Single ticket €0.70; 10 tickets €6.65; 1-day ticket €1.40 ✆ 213 500 115 – www.metrolisboa.pt

→ BUSES, TRAMS AND FUNICULAR

There are 6 main bus routes and 3 funiculars. The buses and trams *(eléctricos)* operate from 7am to 1am, every 11-15min until 9.30pm; the last no 45 bus (Cais do Sodré, Baixa, Av. da Liberdade) is at 1.55am. Tram routes no 15 and 28 serve the main sights. Funiculars operate from 7am to 11pm. Tickets can be bought individually on both buses and trams; single fare €1.20, 1-day ticket €3.40, 5-day ticket €13.20 on sale in metro stations and in kiosks *(Venda de Passe)*. The '7 Colinas' card is a contact-free card on which multimodal tickets can be credited. The journeys cover the Carris (bus, trams and funiculars) and metro. 1-day ticket €3.30, 5-day ticket €13.20. Bus and tram route maps (€5) available at the kiosks, ✆ 213 613 000, www.carris.pt

→ LISBOA CARD

Valid for unlimited travel on public transport (metro, buses, trams except trams no 15 and 28) and for free or reduced admission to most museums and cultural sites; on sale at certain venues and museums; €13.25 (24hr); €23 (48hr); €28 (72hr); ✆ 213 610 250 or 210 312 810. www.askmelisboa.com

→ TAXIS

Taxis are usually beige or cream but older ones are still black with green roofs; they are occupied if the illuminated sign on the roof is lit. They are numerous and relatively cheap. Initial charge €2 (daytime rate), €2.35 (night rate); €1.50 fixed rate for luggage; €0.75 surcharge if called by phone; 20% surcharge between 10pm and 6am. Journeys within the city are metered; outside the tariff is per km, including the return trip to the pick-up point and any road tolls, price to be agreed in advance. Tipping at 10% or by rounding up. ✆ 218 119 000 *(Rádio Táxis de Lisboa)*, ✆ 214 186 206 or 217 996 460 *(Autocoop)*, ✆ 213 649 538 *(Auto Táxis Progresso do Príncipe Real)*, ✆ 218 155 061 or 218 111 100 *(Teletáxis)*.

→ RIVER BOAT AND FERRY STATIONS

Five ferries *(cacilheiros)* link Lisbon with the opposite bank of the Tagus; departures every 15min; tickets available at the ferry stations; also boat rides on the Tagus (2hr) 11am-5pm daily; €15 (€7.50 child 6-12 yrs), ✆ 808 20 30 50; www.transtejo.pt

USEFUL ADDRESSES

→ TOURIST INFORMATION

Tourist Office, Palácio Foz, Praça dos Restauradores *Plan II* **H1**; open 9am-8pm, ✆ 213 463 314/213 463 658. **Airport Tourist Office**; open 7am-midnight, ✆ 218 494 323. **Lisboa Welcome Center Plan**, Praça do Comércio; ✆ 210 312 810; open 9am-8pm; café, restaurant, food shop, designer and fashion shop, art gallery. **Tourist Help Line** ✆ 800 296 296; www.atl-turismolisboa.pt; www.visitlisboa.com

→ POST OFFICES

Opening times Mon-Fri 8.30am-6pm, Sat 9am-6pm, Sun and public holidays 9am-1pm and 2-5pm; Airport 24 hrs.

→ BANKS/CURRENCY EXCHANGE

Opening times Mon-Fri, 8.30am-3pm. National network (24hrs) of ATMs (MB-*multibanco*) for withdrawing money using all major bank cards.

→ EMERGENCY

✆ **112**; Police: ✆ **213 466 141**.

BUSY PERIODS

It may be difficult to find a room at a reasonable price (except at weekends) during special events:

Meia Martona Internacional de Lisboa: March – Lisbon International Half Marathon.

Holy Week: Easter.

Summer Festivals: 12-29 June – Popular saints' festivals with processions of young people in traditional costume *(marchas populares)*.

Meia Martona de Portugal: September – Portugal Half Marathon.

EXPLORING LISBON

DIFFERENT FACETS OF THE CITY

It is possible to visit the main sights and museums in three days.

Museums and sights are usually open from 10am to 5pm. Most are closed on Mondays and on Tuesday mornings and public holidays (national palaces are closed on Wednesdays).

HISTORIC CITY – Mosteiro dos Jerónimos *Plan I* **A3** – 16C Manueline Gothic monastery: church and cloisters. **Torre de Belém** – 16C Manueline defensive tower. **Baixa** *Plan II* **F2** – District re-built to the plans of the Marquis of Pombal in 1755 after the earthquake. **Alfama** – Cobbled maze of narrow twisting streets and steps. **Cathedral** *Plan II* **F2** – Romanesque cathedral, built as a 12C fortress but remodelled in 17C and 18C; Treasury. **Castelo de São Jorge** *Plan II* **F2** – 5C Visigoth castle, with 9C Moorish extensions and 12C modifications, converted into a shaded flower garden with magnificent **views**. **Palácio dos Marqueses de Fronteira** *Plan I* **B2** – 17C hunting lodge set in formal gardens: outstanding decorative tiles.

ARTISTIC LISBON – Museu Nacional de Arte Antiga *Plan I* **B3** – 17C palace: 12C to early 19C paintings, sculptures and decorative art. **Museu de Artes Decorativas** *Plan II* **F2** – 17C and 18C interiors with silver, porcelain, tapestries and furniture. **Museu Nacional do Azulejo** *Plan I* **D3** – Former convent displaying decorative tiles: 15C Hispano-Moorish to the present day. **Museu da Marinha** *Plan I* **A3** – Portuguese ships and maritime history. **Museu Calouste Gulbenkian** *Plan III* **G2** – Oriental and European art beautifully presented. **Casa do Fado e da Guitarra Portuguesa** *Plan II* **F2** – History of **Fado**.

OUTDOOR LISBON – Parque das Naçoes *Plan I* **D1** – Site of Expo'98: contemporary works of art, gardens and pedestrianised areas, bars, restaurants, entertainment venues and shopping centre; **Torre Vasco da Gama**, belvedere with **views** of the Tagus. **Parque Eduardo VII** *Plan III* **G3** – Elegant landscaped park with a magnificent **view** over the Baixa and the Tagus. **Jardim Zoológico** *Plan I* **B2** – Magnificent palm trees in one of the finest gardens for subtropical plants in Europe.

GOURMET TREATS

A favourite pastime in Lisbon is to go to a bar or café for an after-lunch or after-dinner coffee *(bica)*; excellent cafés and pastry shops can be found all over the city. *Confeitaria Nacional*, Pç Figueira 18B – one of the best old cafés in Lisbon, has a huge choice of pastries and traditional sweets; *Pastelaria Suiça*, Praça. D. Pedro IV/ Rossio – for an outdoor terrace where you can consume snacks, excellent cakes and fruit juices with views of the Castelo de São Jorge; *Pastéis de Belém Café*, Rua Belém 84/8 – serving the famous cakes of this name; *Pastelaria Benard*, Rua Garrett 104 – for delicious pastries or a meal served in its quiet, dignified atmosphere.

For traditional family cuisine at reasonable prices it is worth trying one of the museum cafeterias or restaurants, which are often set in attractive surroundings: patios, gardens, modern décor.

SHOPPING

Shops are usually open from 9am to 1pm and 3-7pm. On Saturdays they close at 1pm. Shopping centres are usually open 10am-11pm.

The traditional shopping district is **Baixa** *Plan II* **F2**. **Chiado** *Plan II* **E2**, in particular Rua do Carmo and Rua do Garret, has shops selling international brand names, also bookshops and some old boutiques. For fashion try Av. Da Liberdade, Pç. D. Pedro IV, Rua do Carmo and the Bairro Alto district.

Shopping centres outside the city centre but worth visiting: **Amoreiras Shopping Centre**, Av. Eng. Duarte Pacheco *Plan I* **B2**; **Colombo**, Avenida do Colégio Militar *Plan I* **B1**; **Vasco da Gama**, Parque das Naçoes *Plan I* **B1**.

MARKETS – **Feira da Ladra**, Campo Sta Clara *Plan I* **C3** is a good flea market for second-hand silverware, furniture, old books, clothes, etc. (Tues, 7am-1pm and Sat, 7am-6pm).

WHAT TO BUY – Wines, port, cheeses, footwear, handbags, embroidery, lace, household textiles, clothing, Vista Alegre porcelain, crystal from the Alcobaça and Marinha Grande regions, decorative tiles *(azulejos)*, regional pottery, copper utensils, wicker baskets.

ENTERTAINMENT

Agenda Cultural, a monthly publication, provides information on cultural events, available free of charge at the main tourist offices, hotels and kiosks (www.agendacultural.pt). *Lisboa em*, another monthly publication (in Portuguese and English) publishes details of cultural events as well as practical information, available free of charge at tourist sights and in some bars. *What's on in Lisbon* (in English) lists concerts and other events (publituris@mail.telepac.pt)

Tickets can be obtained at the following kiosks: *ABEP*, Praça dos Restauradores, ✆ 213 425 360; *Quiosque Cultural de São Mamede*, R. de São Mamede.

Coliseu dos Recreios *Plan II* **E2** – Opera, concerts and a wide range of other events.

Teatro Nacional de São Carlos *Plan II* **E2** – Opera, ballet and concerts of classical music.

Grande Auditório Gulbenkian *Plan III* **G2** – Musical concerts.

Centro Cultural de Belém *Plan I* **A3** – Concerts and temporary exhibitions.

Comuna *Plan III* **G2** – Traditional programme of theatre with a bistro-style café-theatre for contemporary music concerts (rock, jazz) (Sat at 10pm).

Culturgest – Caixa Geral de Depósitos *Plan II* **E2** – Cultural centre with two auditoria and two exhibition galleries and a programme of musical events of high quality.

Escola Portuguesa de Arte Equestre (Palácio Nacional de Queluz, 2475 Queluz) – School maintaining Portuguese equestrian art, particularly with Lusitanian thoroughbreds.

Praça de Touros do Campo Pequeno *Plan III* **H1** – Neo-Moorish red-brick arena for bullfights *(touradas)* (May-Sep, Thur at 10pm – the bulls are not killed).

NIGHTLIFE

Nightclubs rarely get going until after midnight. The best-known districts are **Chiado** and **Bairro Alto** *Plan II* **E2** ; there is also a string of restaurants, bars and nightclubs along the docks in **Alcântara** and **Santo Amaro** *Plan I* **B3**. Another address is **Avenida 24 de Julho**. **Principe Real**, a small elegant district, is the centre of gay nightlife.

For **fado** restaurants go to the historic **Alfama district** *Plan II* **F2** or **Chiado** and **Bairro Alto**: *Sr. Vinho*, Rua do Meio-à-Lapa 18; *A Severa*, Rua das Gàveas 51; *Adega Machado*, Rua do Norte 91.

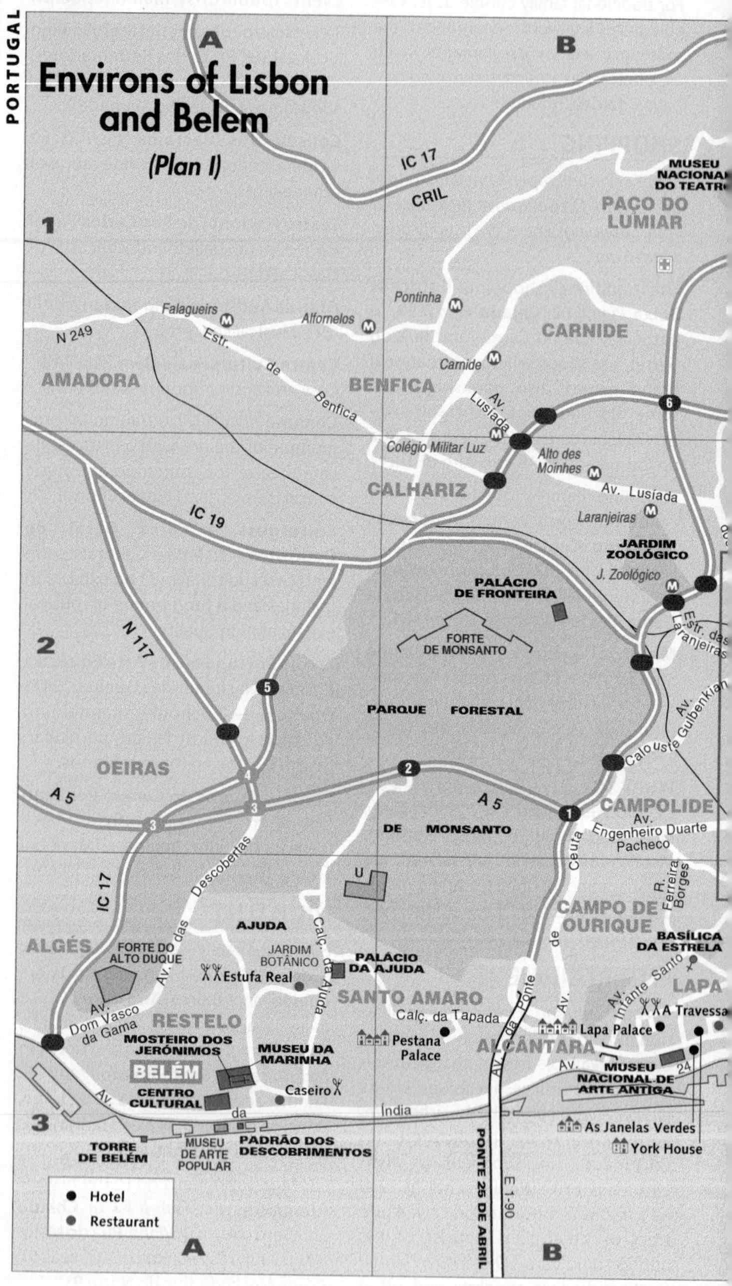
Environs of Lisbon and Belem
(Plan I)
A
B
1
2
3
IC 17
CRIL
MUSEU NACIONAL DO TEATRO
PAÇO DO LUMIAR
Pontinha
Falagueirs
Alfornelos
N 249
Estr. de Benfica
CARNIDE
Carnide
AMADORA
BENFICA
Av. Lusíada
Colégio Militar Luz
Alto des Moinhes
CALHARIZ
Av. Lusíada
Laranjeiras
IC 19
JARDIM ZOOLÓGICO
J. Zoológico
PALÁCIO DE FRONTEIRA
FORTE DE MONSANTO
Estr. das Laranjeiras
N 117
PARQUE FORESTAL DE MONSANTO
Av. Calouste Gulbenkian
OEIRAS
A 5
A 5
CAMPOLIDE
Av. Engenheiro Duarte Pacheco
Av. Ceuta
R. Ferreira Borges
IC 17
Av. das Descobertas
CAMPO DE OURIQUE
AJUDA
Calç. da Ajuda
BASÍLICA DA ESTRELA
ALGÉS
FORTE DO ALTO DUQUE
JARDIM BOTÂNICO
PALÁCIO DA AJUDA
Estufa Real
SANTO AMARO
LAPA
Av. Infante Santo
A Travessa
Av. Dom Vasco da Gama
RESTELO
Calç. da Tapada
Av. da Ponte
Lapa Palace
Pestana Palace
MOSTEIRO DOS JERÓNIMOS
MUSEU DA MARINHA
ALCÂNTARA
BELÉM
Av. 24
MUSEU NACIONAL DE ARTE ANTIGA
CENTRO CULTURAL
Caseiro
Av. da Índia
TORRE DE BELÉM
MUSEU DE ARTE POPULAR
PADRÃO DOS DESCOBRIMENTOS
PONTE 25 DE ABRIL
E 1-90
As Janelas Verdes
York House
Hotel
Restaurant

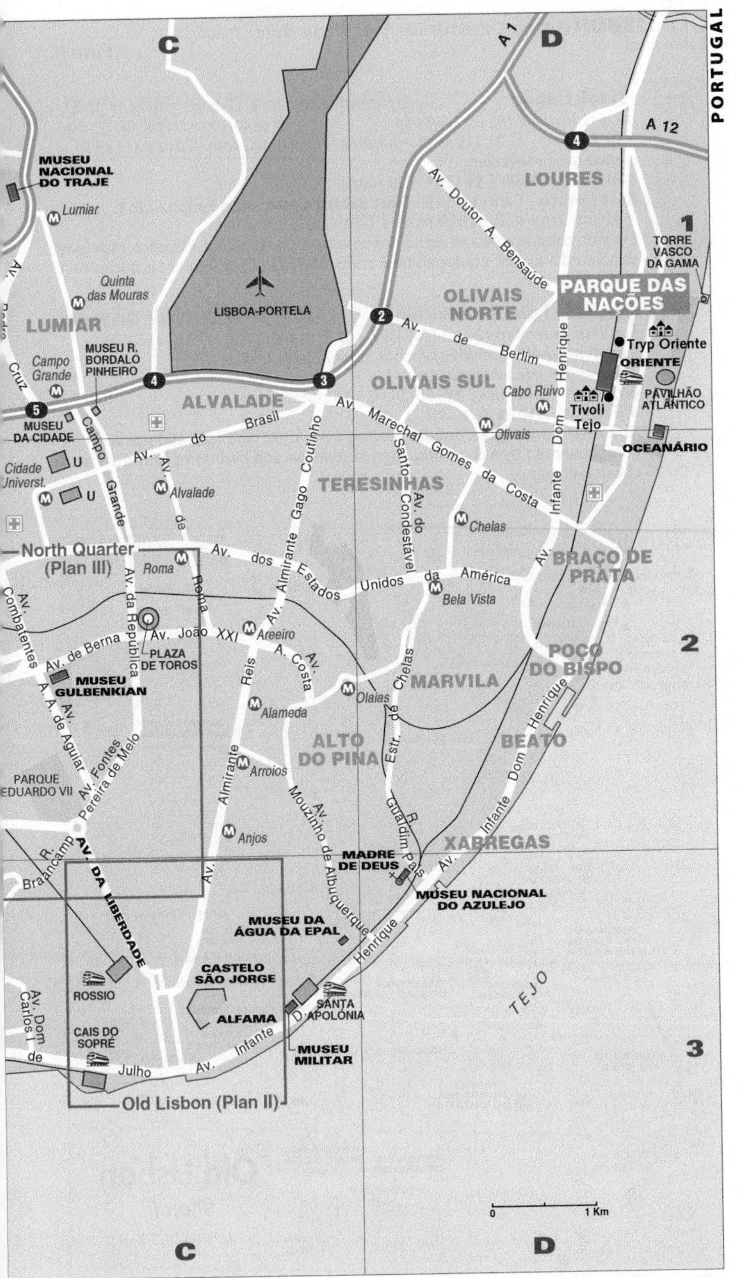
C
D
A 1
A 12
MUSEU NACIONAL DO TRAJE
Lumiar
Quinta das Mouras
LUMIAR
LISBOA-PORTELA
LOURES
Av. Doutor A. Bensaúde
TORRE VASCO DA GAMA
PARQUE DAS NAÇÕES
OLIVAIS NORTE
Av. de Berlim
Tryp Oriente
ORIENTE
MUSEU R. BORDALO PINHEIRO
Campo Grande
ALVALADE
OLIVAIS SUL
Cabo Ruivo
Tivoli Tejo
PAVILHÃO ATLÂNTICO
MUSEU DA CIDADE
OCEANÁRIO
Olivais
Av. do Brasil
Av. Marechal Gomes da Costa
Cidade Universt.
Campo Grande
Av. de Alvalade
Alvalade
Av. Almirante Gago Coutinho
TERESINHAS
Av. do Condestável
Santo Condestável
Av. Infante Dom Henrique
Chelas
North Quarter (Plan III)
Roma
Av. dos Estados Unidos da América
Bela Vista
BRAÇO DE PRATA
Av. Roma
Av. Combatentes
Av. da República
Av. João XXI
Areeiro
Av. de Berna
PLAZA DE TOROS
A. Costa
Av. Almirante Reis
Olaias
Estr. de Chelas
MARVILA
POÇO DO BISPO
MUSEU GULBENKIAN
Av. A. A. de Aguiar
Alameda
ALTO DO PINA
BEATO
Av. Infante Dom Henrique
PARQUE EDUARDO VII
Av. Fontes Pereira de Melo
Arroios
Av. Mouzinho de Albuquerque
R. Guardim Pais
Anjos
XABREGAS
MADRE DE DEUS
R. Braamcamp
AV. DA LIBERDADE
MUSEU NACIONAL DO AZULEJO
MUSEU DA ÁGUA DA EPAL
CASTELO SÃO JORGE
TEJO
ROSSIO
ALFAMA
SANTA APOLÓNIA
Av. Dom Carlos I
CAIS DO SOPRÉ
Av. 24 de Julho
Av. Infante D. Henrique
MUSEU MILITAR
Old Lisbon (Plan II)
0
1 Km
1
2
3

OLD LISBON *(Alfama, Castelo de São Jorge, Rossio, Baixa, Chiado, Bairro Alto)*

Plan II

Tivoli Lisboa ⋞ city from the terrace, ⅀ (heated) ♿ AC ⇸rm SAT 📶 40/200 VISA MC AE ⓓ

av. da Liberdade 185 ✉ 1269-050 – Ⓜ Avenida – ✆ 21 319 89 00 – htlisboa@tivolihotels.com – Fax 21 319 89 50 – www.tivolihotels.com **E1**

300 rm ☕ – †400 € ††420 € – 29 suites

Rest *Terraço* – Carte 36/60 € – **Rest *Beatriz Costa*** – Carte approx. 36 €

♦ Business ♦ Traditional ♦ Classic ♦

Elegant, comfortable and with fine views from the top floor. Pleasant, tastefully decorated and well-equipped bedrooms. The Terraço restaurant is both smart and traditional.

Avenida Palace without rest AC SAT 📶 25/100 VISA MC AE ⓓ

Rua 1º de Dezembro 123 ✉ 1200-359 – Ⓜ Restauradores – ✆ 21 321 81 00 – reservas@hotel-avenida-palace.pt – Fax 21 342 28 84 – www.hotel-avenida-palace.pt **E1**

64 rm ☕ – †140/180 € ††170/205 € – 18 suites

♦ Traditional ♦ Classic ♦

An elegant, prestigious building dating from 1892, with splendid public areas, complemented by a charming English-style bar and bedrooms furnished with classical elegance.

Old Lisbon (Plan II)

Sofitel Lisboa 25/250 VISA

Av. da Liberdade 127 ✉ 1269-038 – Ⓜ Avenida – ☎ 21 322 83 00 – h1319@accor.com – Fax 21 322 83 60 – www.sofitel.com E1

167 rm – 265/315 € 335/365 €, ☕ 17 € – 4 suites

Rest Ad Lib – see below

◆ Business ◆ Design ◆

A friendly welcome, comfortable and with a contemporary classic feel. Enjoy a pleasant stay in agreeable surroundings.

Lisboa Plaza 25/140 P VISA

Travessa do Salitre 7 ✉ 1269-066 – Ⓜ Avenida – ☎ 21 321 82 18 – plaza.hotels@heritage.pt – Fax 21 347 16 30 – www.heritage.pt E1

94 rm – 146/215 € 156/235 €, ☕ 14 € – 12 suites

Rest – Menu 35 €

◆ Business ◆ Traditional ◆ Classic ◆

Near the famous Avenida da Liberdade. Very traditional with distinguished and tasteful atmosphere and classic décor. A large buffet is available in the dining room.

Lisboa Regency Chiado without rest VISA

Rua Nova do Almada 114 ✉ 1200-290 – Ⓜ Baixa-Chiado – ☎ 21 325 61 00 – reservations.chiado@madeiraregency.pt – Fax 21 325 61 61 – www.regency-hotels-resorts.com E2

40 rm ☕ – 153/388 € 173/388 €

◆ Business ◆ Personalised ◆

Pleasantly situated in a building in the old part of the city. Friendly, professional service with bedrooms decorated in oriental style.

NH Liberdade 25/50 VISA

Av. da Liberdade 180-B ✉ 1250-146 – Ⓜ Avenida – ☎ 21 351 40 60 – nhliberdade@nh-hotels.com – Fax 21 314 36 74 – www.nh-hotels.com E1

58 rm ☕ – 106/227 € 118/250 € – 25 suites

Rest – *(closed Saturday, Sunday and Bank Holidays)* Menu 27 €

◆ Business ◆ Chain hotel ◆ Modern ◆

Situated in Lisbon's most important business district. A comfortable and functional hotel with all the quality and characteristic style of this hotel chain.

Tivoli Jardim (heated) rm 25 P VISA

Rua Julio Cesar Machado 7 ✉ 1250-135 – Ⓜ Avenida – ☎ 21 359 10 00 – htjardim@mail.telepac.pt – Fax 21 359 12 45 – www.tivolihotels.com E1

119 rm ☕ – 310 € 320 €

Rest – Menu 26 €

◆ Business ◆ Functional ◆

Modern efficiency for the business traveller. A large foyer, conference rooms and pleasantly decorated bedrooms. The brightly-lit dining room offers traditional dishes.

Britania without rest VISA

Rua Rodrigues Sampaio 17 ✉ 1150-278 – Ⓜ Avenida – ☎ 21 315 50 16 – britania.hotel@heritage.pt – Fax 21 315 50 21 – www.heritage.pt E1

33 rm – 157/225 € 167/245 €, ☕ 14 €

◆ Business ◆ Traditional ◆ Art Deco ◆

The lounge area consists of a bar which boasts a beautiful wooden floor and paintings of Portugal's former colonies. Spacious Art Deco-style rooms.

Veneza without rest P VISA

av. da Liberdade 189 ✉ 1250-141 – Ⓜ Avenida – ☎ 21 352 26 18 – veneza@3khoteis.com.pt – Fax 21 352 66 78 – www.3khoteis.com.pt E1

37 rm – 79/89 €, ☕ 8 €

◆ Traditional ◆ Business ◆ Cosy ◆

In a small former palace with a lovely façade. A perfect balance of old grandeur and modern day functionality.

Olissippo Castelo without rest

Rua Costa do Castelo 126 ✉ 1100-179 – Ⓜ Rossio – ☎ 218 82 01 90 – info.oc@olissippohotels.com – Fax 218 82 01 94 – www.olissippohotels.com **F2**

24 rm – †128/175 € ††144/185 €

♦ Traditional ♦ Classic ♦

A hotel located next to the Castelo São Jorge, with one of its walls built into the castle's defensive surround. Luxurious bedrooms (a dozen with their own garden terrace) and magnificent views.

Solar do Castelo without rest

Rua das Cozinhas 2 ✉ 1100-181 – ☎ 21 880 60 50 – solar.castelo@heritage.pt – Fax 21 887 09 07 – www.heritage.pt **F2**

14 rm – †196/282 € ††210/310 €, 14 €

♦ Family ♦ Cosy ♦

A small 18C palace in an area with lots of historic monuments. A comfortable and completely renovated interior. Modern bedrooms with attractive design details.

Metropole without rest

Praça Dom Pedro IV-30 (Rossio) ✉ 1100-200 – Ⓜ Rossio – ☎ 21 321 90 30 – metropole@almeidahotels.com – Fax 21 346 91 66 – www.almeidahotels.com **E2**

36 rm – †120/160 € ††130/170 €

♦ Traditional ♦ Classic ♦

An early-20C building in the heart of old Lisbon. High-quality traditional bedrooms, particularly those with a balcony looking towards Rossio square.

Solar dos Mouros without rest

Rua do Milagre de Santo António 6 ✉ 1100-351 – Ⓜ Baixa-Chiado – ☎ 218 85 49 40 – reservation@solardosmouros.pt – Fax 218 85 49 45 – www.solardosmouros.com **F2**

11 rm – †88/186 € ††106/216 €, 14 €

♦ Family ♦ Personalised ♦

A typical house which has been modernised and furnished with personal touches, including four paintings by the owner himself. Colourful bedrooms, some with excellent views.

Lisboa Tejo without rest

Rua dos Condes de Monsanto 2 ✉ 1100-159 – Ⓜ Rossio – ☎ 21 886 61 82 – hotellisboatejo.reservas@evidenciagrupo.com – Fax 21 886 51 63 – www.evidenciahoteis.com **F2**

51 rm – †80/105 € ††85/120 € – 7 suites

♦ Business ♦ Traditional ♦ Personalised ♦

Moderate prices and pleasant, well-appointed bedrooms in the Baixa Pombalina district. A modern, refurbished and central hotel with a traditional atmosphere and elegant décor.

Tavares

Rua da Misericórdia 37 ✉ 1200-270 – Ⓜ Baixa-Chiado – ☎ 21 342 11 12 – reservas@tavaresrico.pt – Fax 21 347 81 25 – www.tavaresrico.pt closed Saturday lunch and Sunday lunch **E2**

Rest – Carte 68/85 €

♦ Inventive ♦ Formal ♦

Founded in 1784, Lisbon's oldest restaurant has retained all its aristocratic elegance and ambience. A sumptuous decor of gilded work, mirrors and chandeliers.

Gambrinus

18/30

Rua das Portas de Santo Antão 25 ✉ 1150-264 – Ⓜ Restauradores – ☎ 21 342 14 66 – Fax 21 346 50 32 **E1**

Rest – Carte 40/66 €

♦ Traditional ♦ Formal ♦

In the historic centre of the city near the Rossio district. A restaurant with a well-established reputation backed up by fine cuisine and an excellent wine list.

XXX **Casa do Leão**

Castelo de São Jorge ✉ 1100-129 – Ⓜ Rossio – ☎ 21 887 59 62 – guest@pousadas.pt – Fax 21 887 63 29 – www.pousadas.pt F2

Rest – Carte approx. 37 €

◆ Traditional ◆ Formal ◆

Situated in the walls of the castle of São Jorge. An elegant restaurant in traditional Portuguese-style with an exclusive ambience.

XX **Solar dos Presuntos**

Rua das Portas de Santo Antão 150 ✉ 1150-269 – Ⓜ Restauradores – ☎ 21 342 42 53 – restaurante@solardospresuntos.com – Fax 21 346 84 68

closed August, Sunday and Bank Holidays E1

Rest – Carte 27/42 €

◆ Minho cuisine ◆ Family ◆

A locally-run, comfortable restaurant with a wide selection of well-prepared traditional dishes and some specialities from Minho.

XX **Ad Lib** – Hotel Sofitel Lisboa

Av. da Liberdade 127 ✉ 1269-038 – Ⓜ Avenida – ☎ 21 322 83 50 – h1319@accor.com – Fax 21 322 83 60

closed Saturday lunch and Sunday lunch E1

Rest – Carte 34/45 €

◆ Contemporary ◆ Bistro ◆

A friendly welcome, comfortable and with a contemporary classic feel. Enjoy a pleasant stay in agreeable surroundings.

FADO RESTAURANTS *You can hear the typical Portuguese fado songs while dining in these restaurants.* *Plan II*

XX **Clube de Fado**

São João da Praça 94 ✉ 1100-521 – ☎ 21 885 27 04 – info@clube-de-fado.com – Fax 21 888 26 94 – www.clube-de-fado.com F2

Rest – *(dinner only)* Carte 30/49 €

◆ Traditional ◆ Musical ◆

A restaurant with a well cared-for appearance, a pleasant ambience and a bar with a friendly atmosphere. Simple décor.

XX **A Severa**

Rua Das Gáveas 51 ✉ 1200-206 – Ⓜ Baixa-Chiado – ☎ 21 342 83 14 – Fax 21 346 40 06 – www.asevera.com E2

Rest – Carte approx. 56 €

◆ Traditional ◆ Musical ◆

A traditional fado restaurant run by a large family who base their success on good cuisine. Comfortable and with classic Portuguese décor.

NORTH QUARTER *(Av. da Liberdade, Parque Eduardo VII, Museu Gulbenkian)* *Plan III*

Four Seasons H. Ritz Lisbon

25/500

Rua Rodrigo da Fonseca 88 ✉ 1099-039 – Ⓜ Marquês de Pombal – ☎ 21 381 14 00 – fsh.lisbon@fourseasons.com – Fax 21 383 17 83 – www.fourseasons.com G3

262 rm – †320/420 € ††345/445 €, ☐ 26 € – 20 suites

Rest *Varanda* – Carte 58/70 €

◆ Luxury ◆ Business ◆ Classic ◆

Luxury is the keynote in these exquisite bedrooms, more than matched by the superb public rooms. The exclusive restaurant in classic style serves sophisticated, immaculately presented cuisine.

Le Meridien Park Atlantic Lisboa 25/550

Rua Castilho 149 ✉ 1099-034 – Ⓜ Marquês de Pombal – ✆ 21 381 87 00 – reservas.lisboa@lemeridien.pt – Fax 21 389 05 05 VISA MC AE

G3

314 rm – ††305/395 €, ☕ 21.50 € – 17 suites

Rest *L'Appart* – Carte 32/48 €

♦ Business ♦ Chain hotel ♦ Modern ♦

A full range of facilities and professional service in the comfort of modern bedrooms and suites. Bathrooms fitted with marble and high quality furnishings. A pleasantly decorated restaurant offering à la carte, buffet or dish of the day.

Real Palacio ⇷rm 25/230 VISA MC AE

Rua Tomás Ribeiro 115 ✉ 1050-228 – Ⓜ São Sebastião – ✆ 213 19 95 00 – realpalacio@hoteisreal.com – Fax 213 19 95 01 – www.hoteisreal.com

G2

143 rm ☕ – †100/254 € ††120/275 € – 4 suites

Rest *Guarda Real* – Carte 30/43 €

♦ Business ♦ Classic ♦

The Real Palacio is a mix of the modern and traditional with its stylish marble and elegant woodwork. Panelled meeting rooms and fully-equipped bedrooms. Options in the restaurant include the à la carte menu and an extensive buffet.

Holiday Inn Lisbon Continental ⇷rm 25/180

Rua Laura Alves 9 ✉ 1069-169 – Ⓜ Campo Pequeno – ✆ 21 004 60 00 – hic@grupo-continental.com – Fax 21 797 36 69 – www.holiday-inn.com VISA MC AE

H1

210 rm – †85/180 € ††95/205 €, ☕ 11.50 € – 10 suites

Rest – Menu 18 €

♦ Business ♦ Chain hotel ♦ Functional ♦

A hotel with a modern exterior that is very popular for business meetings. Pleasant, well-appointed bedrooms and adequate public areas. The dining room is not up to the standards of the rest of the hotel.

Real Parque ⇷rm 25/100 VISA MC AE

Av. Luís Bívar 67 ✉ 1069-146 – Ⓜ São Sebastião – ✆ 21 319 90 00 – realparque@hoteisreal.com – Fax 21 357 07 50 – www.hoteisreal.com

G2

147 rm ☕ – †80/175 € ††90/200 € – 6 suites

Rest *Cozinha do Real* – Carte 24/36 €

♦ Business ♦ Classic ♦

Ideal for meetings, business and leisure travel. Elegant furnishings, quality and good taste everywhere. A modern exterior, classic contemporary décor and a charming lounge area. Good food served in a pleasant dining room.

Aviz 25 VISA MC AE

Rua Duque de Palmela 32 ✉ 1250-098 – Ⓜ Marquês de Pombal – ✆ 21 040 20 00 – geral@hotelaviz.com – Fax 21 040 21 98 – www.hotelaviz.com

G3

56 rm ☕ – †120/160 € ††140/320 € – 14 suites

Rest – Carte 27/47 €

♦ Traditional ♦ Classic ♦

The name pays homage to a famous luxury hotel that has now disappeared. Elegant lobby, plus well-appointed rooms with marble bathrooms. Traditional decor in the restaurant, adorned with objects from the former "Aviz".

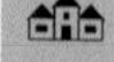

AC Lisboa 25/60 VISA MC AE

Rua Largo Andaluz 13 ✉ 1050-121 – Ⓜ Marquês de Pombal – ✆ 210 05 09 30 – aclisboa@ac-hotels.com – Fax 210 05 09 31 – www.ac-hotels.com H3

81 rm ☕ – ††180 € – 2 suites

Rest – Menu 22 €

♦ Business ♦ Chain hotel ♦ Modern ♦

Located in the rear part of the palace, this hotel has a modern façade and a reception area that is typical of the AC chain. Pleasant lounge and meeting areas, plus modern, well-appointed bedrooms. An attractive, albeit soberly decorated restaurant.

Suites do Marquês 25/50 VISA

Av. Duque de Loulé 45 ✉ 1050-086 – Ⓜ Picoas – ☎ 21 351 04 80 – suitesdomarques@viphotels.com – Fax 21 353 18 65 – www.viphotels.com

80 rm – 98/109 €, 8.50 € – 4 suites – **Rest** – Carte approx. 30 € **H3**

♦ Business ♦ Functional ♦

Central location near the famous Praça Marquês de Pombal square. All the comfort and characteristic style of the Meliá chain in large, quiet and functional bedrooms.

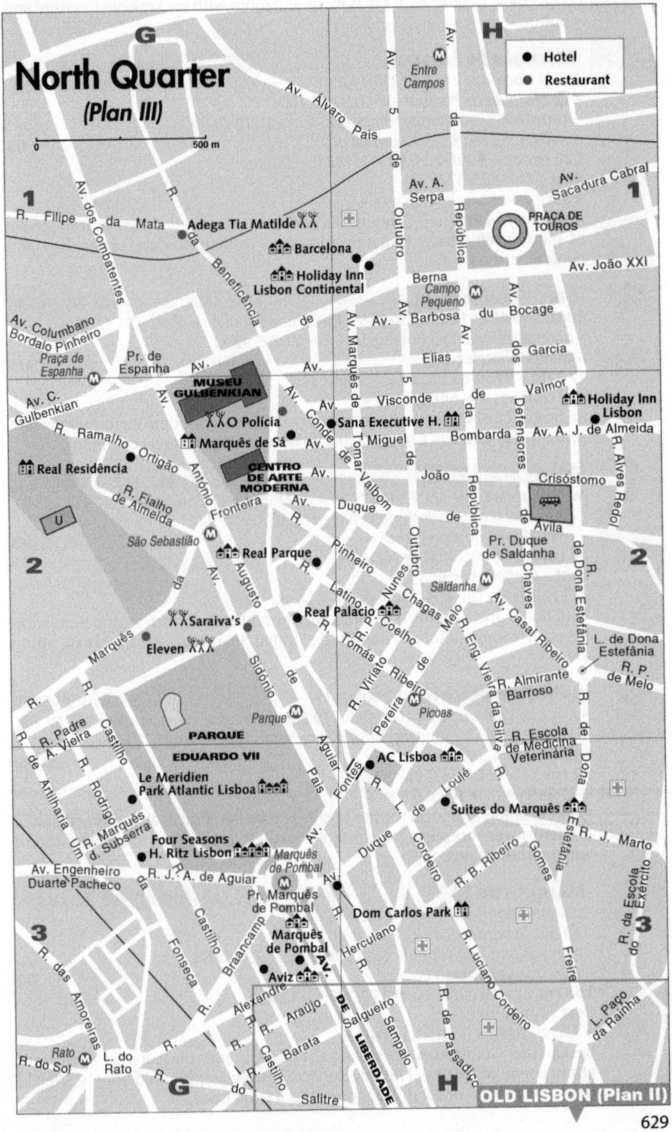

North Quarter

(Plan III)

0 — 500 m

● Hotel
● Restaurant

OLD LISBON (Plan II)

PORTUGAL

Holiday Inn Lisbon

25/300

Av. António José de Almeida 28-A ✉ 1000-044 – Ⓜ Alameda – ✆ 21 004 40 00 – hil@grupo-continental.com – Fax 21 793 66 72

VISA MC AE

H2

161 rm – †80/110 € ††95/140 €, ☕ 11.50 € – 8 suites

Rest – Menu 19 €

◆ Business ◆ Chain hotel ◆ Modern ◆

Centrally located; ideal for the business or leisure traveller. Few public rooms but comfortable bedrooms. A pleasant dining room with wickerwork furniture and a buffet.

Marquês de Pombal

25/110

Av. da Liberdade 243 ✉ 1250-143 – Ⓜ Marquês de Pombal – ✆ 21 319 79 00 – info@hotel-marquesdepombal.pt – Fax 21 319 79 90 – www.hotel-marquesdepombal.pt

VISA MC AE

G3

120 rm ☕ – †99/170 € ††111/182 € – 3 suites

Rest – Carte 25/37 €

◆ Business ◆ Modern ◆

A recently-built hotel. Conferences and business meetings in an atmosphere of modern efficiency. Elegantly furnished with up-to-date technology and conference hall.

Barcelona without rest

25/230 VISA MC AE

Rua Laura Alves 10 ✉ 1050-138 – Ⓜ Campo Pequeno – ✆ 21 795 42 73 – hotelbarcelona@viphotels.com – Fax 21 795 42 81 – www.viphotels.com

H1

120 rm – ††69/89 €, ☕ 6 € – 5 suites

◆ Business ◆ Modern ◆

An up-to-date hotel in the financial district of the city. Modern surroundings with avant-garde touches. Cheery colourful décor and good level of comfort.

Dom Carlos Park

25/40 VISA MC AE

Av. Duque de Loulé 121 ✉ 1050-089 – Ⓜ Marquês de Pombal – ✆ 21 351 25 90 – comercial@domcarloshoteis.com – Fax 21 352 07 28 – www.domcarloshoteis.com

G-H3

76 rm ☕ – †79/130 € ††94/160 €

Rest – *(Coffee shop only)*

◆ Traditional ◆ Business ◆ Classic ◆

Traditional and elegant hotel in a very good location with restful ambience. Pleasant rooms with bathrooms decorated in marble and a small sitting area.

Sana Executive H. without rest

25/55

Av. Conde Valbom 56 ✉ 1050-069 – Ⓜ São Sebastião – ✆ 21 795 11 57 – sanaexecutive@sanahotels.com – Fax 21 795 11 66 – www.sanahotels.com

VISA MC AE

G-H2

72 rm ☕ – †60/155 € ††70/165 €

◆ Business ◆ Modern ◆

Good location and ideal for the business traveller. Practical and functional. A modern foyer-reception, comfortable, well-equipped rooms and bathrooms with marble fittings.

Marquês de Sá

25/300 VISA MC AE

Av. Miguel Bombarda 130 ✉ 1050-167 – Ⓜ São Sebastião – ✆ 21 791 10 14 – reservas.oms@olissippohotels.com – Fax 21 793 69 83 – www.olissippohotels.com

G2

163 rm ☕ – †100/135 € ††110/165 € – 1 suite

Rest – Menu 14 €

◆ Business ◆ Functional ◆

Beside the Gulbenkian Foundation. Business and pleasure in a pleasant atmosphere of quality. Friendly service and well-appointed rooms. Well-lit dining room with décor in blue tones and a large foyer.

Real Residência

rm 25/70 VISA AE

Rua Ramalho Ortigão 41 ✉ 1070-228 – Ⓜ São Sebastião – ✆ 21 382 29 00 – realresidencia@hoteisreal.com – Fax 21 382 29 30 – www.hoteisreal.com **G2**

24 suites – 80/120 € 100/130 €

Rest – Carte 19/24 €

♦ Traditional ♦ Classic ♦

Quality, comfort and elegance. Large, well-equipped apartments: bathrooms fitted with marble, traditional décor of good quality furnishings and fittings. The smallish dining room is pleasant and combines modern elements with attractive rustic details.

Eleven

park, city and river Tejo, 20/40 VISA AE

Rua Marquês de Fronteira ✉ 1070 – Ⓜ São Sebastião – ✆ 21 386 22 11 – 11@restauranteleven.com – Fax 21 386 22 14 – www.restauranteleven.com **G2**

closed Sunday and Monday

Rest – Menu 85 € – Carte 48/73 €

Spec. Crocante de camarão sobre risotto de coco, molho caril de Madras e erva limão. Jarrette de vitela com puré de batata ratte, cúrcuma e legumes glaceados. Soufflé de maracujá.

♦ Inventive ♦ Design ♦

This establishment has already gained wide acceptance in a short time. Excellent, modern facilities, a private lobby bar and a dining room with magnificent views. Enticing creative cooking.

Saraiva's

VISA AE

Rua Engenheiro Canto Resende 3 ✉ 1050-104 – Ⓜ Parque – ✆ 21 354 06 09 – Fax 21 353 19 87 **G2**

closed Friday dinner, Saturday and Bank Holidays

Rest – Carte 20/33 €

♦ Traditional ♦ Design ♦

Carpeted floors and elegant modern-style furnishings. Very professional service, a well-heeled clientele and a lively ambience.

Adega Tia Matilde

40 VISA AE

Rua da Beneficência 77 ✉ 1600-017 – Ⓜ Praça de Espanha – ✆ 21 797 21 72 – adegatiamatilde@netcabo.pt – Fax 21 797 21 72 **G1**

closed Saturday dinner and Sunday

Rest – Carte 25/39 €

♦ Traditional ♦ Family ♦

A popular establishment, friendly and professional. Portuguese specialities. Classic-modern style with plants and fresh flowers on the tables.

Varanda da União

VISA AE

Rua Castilho 14 C-7º ✉ 1250-069 – Ⓜ Marquês de Pombal – ✆ 21 314 10 45 – Fax 21 314 10 46 – www.varandadauniao.restaunet.pt *Plan II* **E1**

closed Saturday lunch and Sunday

Rest – Carte 26/40 €

♦ Traditional ♦ Formal ♦

A fine panorama of Lisbon rooftops from the 7th floor of a residential building. A large number of waiting staff and success based on the quality of the cuisine.

O Polícia

10/40 VISA AE

Rua Marquês Sá da Bandeira 112 ✉ 1050-150 – Ⓜ São Sebastião – ✆ 21 796 35 05 – Fax 21 796 97 91 – www.opolicia.restaunet.pt **G2**

closed Saturday dinner, Sunday and Bank Holidays

Rest – Carte 26/37 €

♦ Traditional ♦ Brasserie ♦

Renowned for fish. Well-decorated establishment with large dining room, friendly service and a busy atmosphere. Reservation recommended.

PORTUGAL

PARQUE DAS NAÇÕES

Plan I

Tivoli Tejo

rm 25/250 VISA

Av. D. João II (Parque das Nações) ✉ 1990-083 – Ⓜ Oriente – ✆ 21 891 51 00 – httejo@tivolihotels.com – Fax 21 891 53 45 – www.tivolihotels.com **D1**

262 rm – 🛉120/170 € 🛉🛉130/190 € – 17 suites

Rest – Menu 20 €

Rest *VIII Colina* – Carte 28/37 €

♦ Chain hotel ♦ Business ♦ Classic ♦

An attractive building next to the Oriente railway station, with contemporary bedrooms and compact bathrooms. Although on the small side, the hotel's public areas are comfortable and well-appointed. The VIII Colina restaurant enjoys wonderful panoramic views of the city.

Tryp Oriente

rm 25/100 VISA

Av. D. João II (Parque das Nações) ✉ 1990-083 – Ⓜ Oriente – ✆ 21 893 00 00 – tryp.oriente@solmeliaportugal.com – Fax 21 893 00 99 – www.tryporiente.solmelia.com **D1**

205 rm – 🛉75/119 € 🛉🛉87/136 € – 1 suite

Rest – Menu 17 €

♦ Chain hotel ♦ Business ♦ Functional ♦

Within the confines of the Expo site, this functional hotel has a lobby-bar and lounge, spacious guestrooms, and great views from the upper floors. The bright restaurant, with separate access, offers a limited menu.

AT WEST

Plan I

Lapa Palace

25/250 VISA

Rua do Pau de Bandeira 4 ✉ 1249-021 – ✆ 21 394 94 94 – info@lapa-palace.com – Fax 21 395 06 65 – www.lapa-palace.com **B3**

92 rm – 🛉🛉340/445 € – 9 suites

Rest *Hotel Cipriani* – Carte 54/62 €

♦ Grand Luxury ♦ Classic ♦

Lavish, traditional elegance on a hill with the Tagus as a backdrop. A 19C palace with intimate corners and evocative gardens with a small waterfall tumbling through the trees. The restaurant is renowned for its refined cuisine focusing on Portuguese and Italian specialities.

Pestana Palace

rm 25/520 VISA

Rua Jau 54 ✉ 1300-314 – ✆ 21 361 56 00 – sales.cph@pestana.com – Fax 21 361 56 01 – www.pestana.com **B3**

173 rm – 🛉370 € 🛉🛉390 € – 17 suites

Rest *Valle Flor* – Carte 54/70 €

♦ Luxury ♦ Classic ♦

An attractive restored 19C palace decorated in keeping with its period of construction, including sumptuous lounges and meticulously appointed bedrooms. The elegant exterior is a veritable botanical paradise. A magnificent restaurant, both for its cuisine and the beauty of its luxurious dining rooms.

As Janelas Verdes without rest

VISA

Rua das Janelas Verdes 47 ✉ 1200-690 – ✆ 21 396 81 43 – jverdes@heritage.pt – Fax 21 396 81 44 – www.heritage.pt **B3**

29 rm – 🛉177/270 € 🛉🛉190/295 €, 14 €

♦ Traditional ♦ Cosy ♦

Partly occupying a seigneurial 18C mansion, with a delightful lounge-library and good views. The overall sensation here is warm, romantic and charmingly traditional.

York House

AC 25/30 VISA MC AE

Rua das Janelas Verdes 32 ✉ 1200-691 – Ⓜ Cais do Sodré – ✆ 21 396 24 35 – reservations@yorkhouselisboa.com – Fax 21 397 27 93 – www.yorkhouselisboa.com **B3**

32 rm – 100/130 € 120/200 €, 14 €

Rest – *(closed Sunday and Monday)* Carte approx. 38 €

♦ Traditional ♦ Cosy ♦

Housed in a 17C convent, but with an interior that has been completely modernised, with furniture that combines the traditional and the contemporary. Traditionally decorated restaurant, including a striking panel of old azulejos.

A Travessa

VISA MC AE

Travessa do Convento das Bernardas 12 ✉ 1200-638 – Ⓜ Cais do Sodré – ✆ 21 390 20 34 – info@atravessa.com – Fax 21 394 08 39 – www.atravessa.com

closed Sunday **B3**

Rest – Carte 27/40 €

♦ French ♦ Cosy ♦

Part of a 17C convent, in which the dining room, located in what was once the refectory, is crowned by a delightful vaulted ceiling. The terrace, occupying the cloisters, adds further charm to the setting.

BELÉM

Plan I

Estufa Real

AC 19 P VISA MC AE

Jardim Botânico da Ajuda-Calçada do Gãlvao ✉ 1400 – ✆ 21 361 94 00 – estufa.real@mail.telepac.pt – Fax 21 361 90 18

closed Saturday **A3**

Rest – *(lunch only)* Carte 25/41 €

♦ Traditional ♦ Fashionable ♦

A relaxing location in the Jardim Botânico da Ajuda. A lovely glassed-in conservatory with attractive modern design details.

Caseiro

AC VISA MC AE

Rua de Belém 35 ✉ 1300-354 – Ⓜ Cais do Sodré – ✆ 21 363 88 03 – Fax 21 364 23 39

closed August and Sunday **A3**

Rest – Carte 24/32 €

♦ Traditional ♦ Rustic ♦

Traditional establishment serving delicious, simply prepared dishes which have made this restaurant well known in the locality.

SPAIN
ESPAÑA

PROFILE

◆ **Area:**
504 782 km^2 (194 897 sq mi).

◆ **Population:**
40 397 842 inhabitants (est. 2006), density = 81 per km^2.

◆ **Capital:**
Madrid (conurbation 4 858 000 inhabitants).

◆ **Currency:**
Euro (€); rate of exchange: € 1 = US$ 1.32 (Nov 2006).

◆ **Government:**
Constitutional parliamentary monarchy (since 1978). Member of European Union since 1986.

◆ **Languages:**
Spanish (Castilian) but also Catalan in Catalonia, Gallego in Galicia, Euskera in the Basque Country, Valencian in the Valencian Region and Mallorquin in the Balearic Isles.

◆ **Specific public holidays:**
Epiphany (6 January); San Jose (19 March); Maundy Thursday (the day before Good Friday); Good Friday (Friday before Easter); National Day (12 October); Constitution Day (6 December); Immaculate Conception (8 December). Some public holidays may be replaced by the autonomous communities with another date.

◆ **Local Time:**
GMT + 1 hour in winter and GMT + 2 hours in summer.

◆ **Climate:**
Temperate Mediterranean with mild winters (colder in interior) and sunny, hot summers (Madrid: January: 6°C, July: 25°C).

◆ **International dialling Code:**
00 34 followed by full 9-digit number. Directory enquiries: ✆ **1003**. International directory enquiries: ✆ **025**. On-line telephone directory: www.paginas-blancas.es

◆ **Emergency:**
Dial ✆ **112**; Medical Assistance: ✆ **061**; National Police: ✆ **091**.

◆ **Electricity:**
220 or 225 volts AC (previously 110 V), 50 Hz; 2-pin round-shaped continental plugs.

FORMALITIES

Travellers from the European Union (EU), Switzerland, Iceland and the main countries of North and South America need a national identity card or passport (America: passport required) to visit Spain for less than three months (tourism or business purpose). For visitors from other countries a visa may be required, in addition to a passport, especially for those wishing to stay for longer than three months. We advise you to check with your embassy before travelling.

An International Driving Licence or an EU driving licence is required. Third party insurance is compulsory in Spain. For traffic offences on-the-spot payment of fines (reduced by 30%) is compulsory for non-residents. The minimum age for driving is 18 and for car hire is 21. For information in English on regulations and road conditions contact the National Traffic Agency ✆ 900 12 35 05; www.dgt.es

MAJOR NEWSPAPERS

The main dailies distributed nationally are *El País*, *ABC* and *El Mundo* (from Madrid), *La Vangardia* and *El Periódico* (from Barcelona). Major regional newspapers: *El Correo* (Bilbao), *La Voz de Galicia* (A Coruña), *Levante* (Valencia) and *El Correo de Andalucia* (Sevilla).

SMOKING-NO SMOKING

In Spain, hotels must provide bedrooms for non-smokers. Restaurants and bars can have areas for smokers and non-smokers.
However, some establishments have made the choice to accept only non smokers and others only smokers.
We indicate these options in the following way:
Rest. no smoking – It is forbidden to smoke in these premises.
Rest. smoking – Smoking is permitted in these premises.

USEFUL PHRASES

ENGLISH	**SPANISH**
Yes	**Si**
No	**No**
Good morning	**Buenos diasl**
Goodbye	**Hasta luego, adios**
Thank you	**Gracias**
Please	**Por favor**
Excuse me	**Perdone**
I don't understand	**No entiendo**

HOTELS

→ CATEGORIES

Accommodation ranges from luxurious international hotels, classified from 1-5 stars, via smaller hotels *(hostales)* and family-run guesthouses *(pensiones)*, classified from 1-3 stars to rural accommodation, sometimes in private houses. Most hotels have a restaurant except *hoteles-residencias*, which usually serve only breakfast. Ratings are granted by the regional governments and standards may vary from region to region. The state-run network of luxury hotels *(paradores)*, classified from 3-5 stars and located in restored historic buildings (castles, palaces, monasteries etc), often has special weekend offers in addition to a 5-night 'go as you please' accommodation card – www.parador.es

→ PRICE RANGE

The price is per room. There is little difference between the price of a single and a double room.

Between April and October it is advisable to book in advance, particularly on the coast. From November to March prices may be slightly lower, some hotels offer special cheap rates and some may be closed. At the weekend out of season chain hotels in the capital usually offer lower rates.

→ TAX

On the mainland 7%, which is not always included in the room price.

→ CHECK OUT TIME

Usually at noon.

→ RESERVATIONS

By telephone or by Internet. A credit card number may be required.

➜ TIP FOR LUGGAGE HANDLING

At the discretion of the customer (about €1).

➜ BREAKFAST

It is not always included in the price of the room and is generally served from 8am to 11am. Most hotels offer a buffet but usually it is possible to have continental breakfast served in the room.

Reception	**Recepción**	Bed	**Cama**
Single room	**Habitación individual**	Bathroom	**Baño**
		Shower	**Ducha**
Double room	**Habitación doble**		

RESTAURANTS

Spaniards usually eat lunch between 1pm and 3.30pm and dinner from 8.30 to 11pm. Besides the traditional **restaurants** there are the ubiquitous **tapas bars**, serving the traditional appetizers, which come in two different sizes: small saucer-size portions *(tapas)* or more substantial portions *(raciones)*; two or three *tapas* or one or two *raciones*, together with a draught beer *(una caña)* or a glass of sherry *(una copa de fino)*, make a good light lunch. In the smallest village as in the large towns, the many **bars** are a local focal point where people look in for refreshment at any time of day. In summer **terraces** spring up on the pavements and in shady alleys where you can sit down for a drink or a whole meal. The **beach bars** *(chiringuitos)* are particularly popular as you can enjoy a drink or a meal without changing out of swimming garb.

Breakfast	**Desayuno**	7am – 10am
Lunch	**Almuerzo**	1.30pm – 3.30pm
Dinner	**Cena**	9pm – 11pm

Spanish restaurants offer fixed price menus *(menú del día)*, comprising starter, main course, dessert and drink, or à la carte. Menus are usually printed in Spanish and English, and sometimes also in French and German, depending on the location. A fixed-price menu is usually less expensive than the same number of dishes chosen à la carte.

Reservations are usually made by phone, fax or Internet. For famous restaurants (including Michelin starred restaurants), it is advisable to book several days – or weeks in some instances – in advance. A credit card number or a phone number may be required to guarantee the booking.

The **bill** (check) includes service charge and VAT. Tipping is optional but, if you are particularly pleased with the service, it is customary to add between 5% and 10% of the total bill.

Drink or aperitif	**Bebida**	Meat (medium, rare, blue)	**Carne (muy hecha, medio hecha, poco hecha)**
Appetizers	**Tapas/Aperitivo**	Fish	**Pescados**
Meal	**Comida**	Salt/pepper	**Sal/pimienta**
Starter	**Entrante**	Cheese	**Queso**
Main dish	**Plato principal**	Vegetables	**Legumbres**
Main dish of the day	**Plato de día**	Hot/cold	**Caliente/frío**
Dessert	**Postre**	The bill (check) please	**La nota, por favor**
Water	**Agua**		
Wine (red, white, rosé)	**Vino (tinto, blanco, rosado)**		
Beer	**Cerveza**		
Bread	**Pan**		

LOCAL CUISINE

Spanish food is distinctively Mediterranean – cooked with olive oil, seasoned with aromatic herbs and spiced with garlic and peppers – but it also varies enormously from region to region.

The commonest dish is stew *(cocido*; also known as *olla, pote, escudella...)* made with pulses (beans or chick-peas), vegetables and meat, cooked together slowly but served as two or three separate courses. Other dishes served throughout the country include garlic soup (made of bread, garlic, oil and paprika with additional regional ingredients), spicy pork sausages (**chorizo**), delicious lean Serrano hams and omelette (**tortilla**) such as the famous **Spanish omelette** which contains potatoes. Fish and seafood are also used in a great many dishes, particularly along the coasts. There are also many savoury rice dishes, particularly in the eastern region, including the well-known **paella** which was first produced in the mid-19C in Valencia and consist of saffron rice with a variety of fish, meat and vegetables. Meat plays a leading role in Spanish cooking; beef and veal, pork, both cooked and cured, lamb and goat, and game of all kinds. Some of the more unusual specialities include **perdices con chocolate** (partridge with chocolate) from Aragon, **mar y muntanya** in Girona (fish and meat in the same dish, usually lobster and chicken); **gazpacho**, a cold soup made of cucumber, tomato, oil, garlic and bread; **habas a la granadina** (broad beans Granada style); **roast suckling pig** in Segovia; **bacalao al ajoarriero** (salt cod) from Castile, and **migas**, a dish of breadcrumbs softened in water and then gently fried, which must be ordered in advance.

The ubiquitous **tapas**, invented in Seville but now found throughout Spain, appear on the counters of most bars and cafés just before lunch and dinner. This often vast array of colourful appetisers may include cheese, ham, sausage or a selection of vegetarian, fish, seafood or meat dishes.

Every region of Spain has its own cheeses; hard cheeses such as Roncal from Navarra and Manchego from La Mancha; soft creamy curd cheeses from Burgos and Valladolid.

Spain has a wide range of sweets, many of Arab origin: **quesada**, a mixture of cream cheese, honey and milk, from Santander; nougat (**turrón**) in Valencia; **pan de Alá**, **tocino de cielo** and **roscos de vino** in Murcia; **tortas de aceite** (olive oil cakes), once an essential part of breakfast in Seville but now found throughout Spain; **yemas de Santa Teresa**, a sweet made of sugar and egg yolk in Avila; **mazapán** (marzipan made with sugar and almonds) from Toledo.

DRINK

Wine is produced in most of the regions of Spain, which has 50 wine producing areas recognised by the Instituto Nacional de Denominaciones de Origen (INDO). The red table wines of **La Rioja** have an international reputation. Castile produces some reds and rosés of international renown – Cigales, Rueda, Ribera de Duero, Toro, Bierzo. The art of viniculture goes back centuries in Catalonia, which produces excellent light wines: reds in Priorato, fruity white in Penedès and Tarragona as an appetiser or with fish. The main source of Spanish wine is La Mancha; the best known are the light reds and white from Valdepeñas. The full-flavoured reds of Aragon are ideal with meat dishes. From Levante come crisp, dry white Valencias and red Jumillas. The light whites of Galicia go well with the local cuisine.

Andalusia is famous for its **dessert wines** and sherries (Jerez), Manzanilla, Montilla-Moriles and Málaga. The sparkling wines known as **cavas** are produced in the region of Barcelona. In the northern provinces of Asturias and Cantabria **cider** *(sidra)*, made from locally-grown apples, is often drunk at meals. Orgeat **(horchata)**, a sweet, light, refreshing drink made from chufa (tiger nut), is enjoyed in summer all over Spain.

Population (est. 2006): 3 155 359 (conurbation 6 000 000) – Altitude: 646m

J. Malburet/MICHELIN

Madrid is one of Europe's most hospitable, cosmopolitan and lively cities, with wide avenues, attractive parks and a great sense of joie de vivre. In 1561 Charles V moved his capital from Toledo to Madrid; at this time Spain ruled over a vast empire. Madrid was chosen because it was more or less in the geographic centre of Spain and has attracted people from every corner of the country.

As the capital of Spain, Madrid is the leading city for banks and insurance, administrative and political institutions. It is an important industrial and technological centre with most of these activities developing on the outskirts of the city.

When Charles V made it the capital of Spain in 1561 it began to grow and it was further transformed in the 18C under the Bourbons. The City's main monuments, Classical and Baroque in style, were built during the 17C, 18C and 19C. As a result of the artistic legacies of the Habsburgs and Bourbons, Madrid is home to an exceptional wealth of paintings, enhanced considerably in recent years by the superb collections on display in the Museo Thyssen-Bornemisza and the Centro de Arte Reina Sofía.

WHICH DISTRICT TO CHOOSE

The central districts of Madrid are well provided with **places to stay**, **restaurants**, sights and attractions. The Centro district, especially round Sol, Callao *Plan I* **B2** is good for dinner or a drink in one of the many local cafés and restaurants. Barrio de los Austrias *Plan II* **E3** is also excellent for **tapas**, dinner or a drink. Home of the 17C literary community, Huertas *Plan II* **G3** is now packed with bars and restaurants and attracts an interesting mixture of late-night revellers. Malasaña *Plan II* **F1** is transformed at night by the crowds of young people heading for the many bars, although there are some quieter cafés. The rich and famous congregate in the upmarket bars and restaurants in Alonso Martínez *Plan II* **G2**. Chueca is now Madrid's gay area with a multitude of small and sophisticated boutiques.

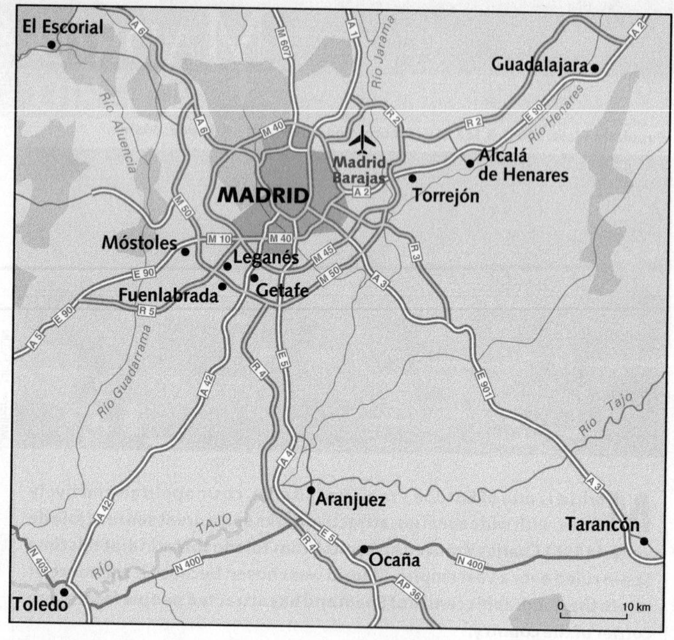

PRACTICAL INFORMATION

ARRIVAL – DEPARTURE

Madrid-Barajas Airport – About 13 km (8 mi) east of the city centre. ✆ 913 936 000. Airport Information ✆ 902 353 570, 913 058 345; AENA ✆ 902 404 704; www.aena.es

From the airport to the city centre – By **taxi**: Fare €18-€20 + charge for luggage; journey time 25 min. By **Metro Line 8** €1; (Terminals 1&2) 6am-2.00am, every 4-7min; journey time 50min; terminus Nuevos Ministerios. (Terminal 4, Inauguration Metro Spring 2007); ✆ 902 444 403; www.metromadrid.es By **bus** (red buses): Terminals 1, 2 & 3 (lines **101** and **200**, approx 15 min) and terminal 4 (line **204**, terminus Intercambiador de Avenida América and **'Shuttle Bus'**, free passenger transport between terminals, every 3 min); journey time 30min; €3; terminus Intercambiador de Avenida América.

Railway Stations – **Chamartín Station** *Plan V* **M1** for services to the north of Spain and to France. **Atocha Station** *Plan II* **H3** for services to the south of Spain. ✆ 902 240 202 (24hr information line; bookings 5.30am-11.50pm); www.renfe.es

TRANSPORT

→ METRO AND BUS

Single journey €1; **Metrobus** 10-trip ticket *(un bono de 10 viajes)* €6.15; these tickets are valid on both bus and metro networks and are available from underground stations, bus ticket offices, newsstands and tobacconists *(estancos)*. The **Tourist Travel Card** *(abono turístico de transportes)*, valid for from 1 to 7 days for unlimited travel on all public transport in Zone A or Zone T in the Madrid region and available at Metro ticket offices, at Chamartín and Atocha Stations, and at the Travel Information Point at the Airport station. Metro trains operate on 12 lines from 6am-1.30am. ✆ 902 444 403; www.metromadrid.es. Bus services operate on 189 routes generally from 6am-11.30pm. ✆ 902 507 850; www.emtmadrid.es

→ TAXIS

Taxis are distinguished by their white paintwork with a red diagonal stripe on the rear doors; they show a green light *(Libre)* on the windscreen when not engaged and can be hailed in the street. Minimum pick up charge is €1.75; supplementary charge between 10pm and 6am. It is customary to round up taxi fares. *Radio-Taxi* ✆ 914 475 180; *Tele-Taxi* ✆ 914 459 008; *Radio-Teléfono Taxi* ✆ 902 (or 915) 478 200.

→ MADRID CARD

1-day ticket €38; 2-day ticket €48, 3-day ticket €58; available from Madrid Tourist Office, Madrid Municipal Tourism, tobacco shops *(estancos)*, Barajas Airport, Atocha Station, at news-stands (64 Gran Vía, 11 Puerta del Sol, Madrid Visión, beside the Prado Museum); valid for travel by all public transport plus admission to more than 40 museums; also valid for discounts in some night clubs, shops and restaurants. To buy the card by phone: 902 088 908; information: ✆ 915 241 370 (Mon-Fri, 10-14/15-19, Saturday 10-14); www.madridcard.com

→ MADRID VISION SIGHTSEEING TOURS

1-day ticket €14.50 and 2-days ticket €19, no charge for holders of Madrid Card. Service operates all year, 9.30/10am-7pm/midnight – Route 1 (thema: Historical Madrid) from the Teatro Real; Route 2 (thema: Modern Madrid) from the Prado Museum. ✆ 917 791 888; www.madridvision.es

USEFUL ADDRESSES

→ TOURIST INFORMATION

Municipal Tourist Office *Plan II* **F2** 27 Plaza Mayor, ✆ 915 881 636; Mercado Puerta de Toledo; 2 Duque de Medinaceli; **Barajas Airport Tourist Office**, (Terminal 1 – arrivals); **Chamartín Railway Station** *Plan V* **M1**, Gate 15; **Atocha Station** *Plan II* **H3**; ✆ 902 100 007; info@turmadrid.com; turismo@madrid.org; turismo@comadrid.es; www.madrid.org

→ POST OFFICES

Opening times Mon-Sat, 8.30am-2.30pm (1pm Sat). Main Office, Plaza de Cibeles (Mon-Fri 8.30am-9.30pm and Sat 8.30am-2pm). ✆ 902 197 197. Stamps can be bought in tobacconists *(estancos)*.

→ BANKS / CURRENCY EXCHANGE

Opening times Mon-Fri, 8.30am-2pm, Sat 9am-1pm but closed Saturdays in summer.

→ EMERGENCY

Dial ✆ **112**; for National Police ✆ **091**; for Medical assistance and Ambulance ✆ **061**.

BUSY PERIODS

It may be difficult to find a room at a reasonable price when special events are held in the city:

Madrid Regional Festival: 1-4 May.

Feria de San Isidro: from 15 May for a month – Concerts, open-air dancing, outdoor picnics and a famous bullfighting festival, lasting six weeks.

Veranos de la Villa: Summer – Variety of cultural performances.

Autumn Festival: mid-October to mid-November – Theatre, dance, music.

Festival Internacional de Jazz: November.

DIFFERENT FACETS OF THE CITY

It is possible to visit the main sights and museums in two to three days.

Museums and sights are usually open from 9/10am to 5pm. Some close on Mondays.

Museum Card (Paseo del Arte): €12; special ticket valid for and available at the 3 main museums; www.munimadrid.es

ARTISTIC CITY – **Museo del Prado** *Plan III* **I3**: one of the greatest galleries of Classical paintings in the world, housing the collections of Spanish painting made by the Habsburg and Bourbon kings; also works by Flemish painters and many paintings from the Italian School favoured by Emperor Charles V and Philip II. **Museo Thyssen-Bornemisza** *Plan II* **G2**: the museum contains approximately 800 works (mainly paintings) from the late 13C to the present day – one of the largest private collections, assembled by Baron Heinrich Thyssen-Bornemisza. **Museo Nacional Centro de Arte Reina Sofía** *Plan II* **G3**: an outstanding collection of contemporary art housed in a former hospital. **Monasterio de las Descalzas Reales** *Plan II* **F2**: the convent of the Poor Clares, founded by Joanna of Austria in the palace where she was born, served for two centuries as a retreat for nobles, who heaped gifts upon the order. **Museo Arqueológico Nacional** *Plan III* **I2**: this museum, founded in 1867 by Queen Isabel II, traces the development of artistic creativity; Prehistoric Art and Archaeology, Iberian and Classical Antiquities, Medieval and Renaissance Decorative Art, 16-19C Art.

HABSBURG AND BOURBON MADRID *Plan II* **E2-F2** – **Plaza Mayor**: the architectural centre of Habsburg Madrid, built in the 17C, and surrounded by historic houses. **Palacio Real** : the official residence of the royal family until 1931 was built by the Bourbons to replace the old Habsburg Alcázar which was destroyed in a fire. The north front faces the **Jardines de Sabatini**; the west is flanked by the **Campo del Moro** *Plan II* **E2** and the Manzanares River. On the east side is the Plaza de Oriente, where you can stroll up to the magnificent equestrian statue of Philip IV by Pietro Tacca (17C), and the **Teatro Real** *Plan II* **E2**, a hexagonal neo-Classical building by López de Aguacio, inaugurated as an opera house in 1850 for Isabel II.

OUTDOOR MADRID *Plan III* **I2-I3**– **Parque del Buen Retiro**: 32 acres in the middle of the city, created in the 17C, with dense clumps of trees, formal flower-beds, fountains, temples, colonnades and statues, lake with boats for hire, music, puppets, exhibitions in the **Palacio de Cristal**. Flanking the park is **Calle de Alfonxo XII** running north to **Puerta de Alcalá**, built (1769-78) by Sabatini to celebrate the triumphant entrance of Charles III into Madrid: impressive perspective at night. **Casa de Campo** *Plan I* **A2**: 4,000 acres on the right bank of the Manzanares River, once part of the royal estate, with the Zoo, an amusement park, rowing boats on the lake, swimming and tennis.

GOURMET TREATS

In Madrid going out for **tapas** *(ir de tapeo)* is a tradition; the most popular district is in and around Plaza Mayor but there are hundreds of bars throughout the city which serve tapas – small portions of a variety of savoury dishes served as appetizers – accompanied by a draught beer *(una caña)* or a small glass of wine or sherry *(una copa de fino)*. Wine from La Mancha is usually served in Madrid during the *chateo*, when people go from bar to bar having a glass of wine in each.

Gourmets may argue whether Madrid has its own cuisine but several dishes can be considered typical. **Cocido madrileño** is a huge succulent stew combining chickpeas with vegetables (cabbage, celery, carrots, turnips and potatoes) and chicken, beef and pork. **Callos** (tripe) is found in some of the well-known restaurants. Other typical dishes include **sopa de ajo** (garlic soup), **caracoles** (snails), **tortilla de patatas** (potato omelette), **besugo al horno** (baked bream) and **bacalao** (cod).

The year is marked by seasonal sweets – **torrijas** in the spring and Holy Week, **barquillos** (rolled wafers), **bartolillos con crema** (a type of small pie with custard), **buñuelos** (a type of fritter filled with custard and whipped cream); **mazapán** (marzipan) in November, **turrón** (nougat) at Christmas and **rosquillas de anís** (aniseed-flavoured doughnuts) during the festival of San Isidro.

SHOPPING

Department stores are usually open 10am-8.30pm. Smaller shops and boutiques open 10am-2pm and 5-8pm. The majority of shops close on Sundays.

The shopping district par excellence is **Sol-Callao** *Plan II* **F2** including **Preciados**, the pedestrianised precinct north of Puerta de Sol. Other streets with large department stores are **Princesa** *Plan IV* **K3**, **Goya** and **Castellana** *Plan I* **C2**. For designer boutiques and an impressive collection of stores selling luxury goods visit **Almirante** *Plan II* **G2**, **Conde Xiquena** and **Salamanca** *Plan IV* **L2**: Serrano and Ortega y Gasset. The shops in and around Plaza Mayor sell traditional articles such as espadrilles, fabrics, ropes, hats and religious articles.

MARKETS – The best known flea market is **El Rastro** *Plan I* **C2**; there are other markets in **Las Cortes** *Plan II* **G2** and **Serrano** *Plan III* **J1**.

WHAT TO BUY – Leather goods, shoes, jewellery, pottery and wrought-iron.

ENTERTAINMENT

The *Guia del Ocio*, a weekly publication, contains information on shows, entertainment, night life and restaurants – www.guiadelocio.es; www.cajamadrid.es (for theatre tickets)

Teatro Real *Plan II* **E2** – Offers a season of opera.

Auditorio Nacional *Plan V* **M3** – Varied programme of classical music

Zarzuela Theatre *Plan II* **G2** – Wide range of shows including ballets and Spanish operettas (*zarzuelas*).

Plaza de la Ventas *Plan I* **C2** – Bull fights on Sunday afternoons; ✆ 913 562 200; reservations ✆ 902 150 025; www.las-ventas.com; reservations www.mundotoro.com; www.ticketstoro.com; www.tauroentrada.com

Warner Brothers Movie World Park – Entertainment for young and old with Hollywood characters, thrilling rides and live performances; www.warnerbrospark.com

NIGHTLIFE

Madrid is a great city for a night out any evening of the week; as people tend to eat late some places stay open until the early hours. **Malasaña** *Plan II* **E1** has many cafés and bars with live music, as well as moderately-priced restaurants. Young people generally frequent **Argüelles** *Plan I* **B1** and **Moncloa** *Plan I* **A2**. Other districts with a lively nightlife – popular bars, pubs, fast-food outlets and ice cream parlours – are **Huertas** *Plan II* **G3** and **Alonso Martínez** *Plan II* **G2**. **Paseo de la Castellana, Paseo de Recoletos** and **Paseo del Prado** *Plan II* **H3** cater to more expensive tastes. For open-air terraces in the summer months and especially at night, try the district of **Paseo de la Castellana** and **Parque del Oeste** *Plan I* **A2**.

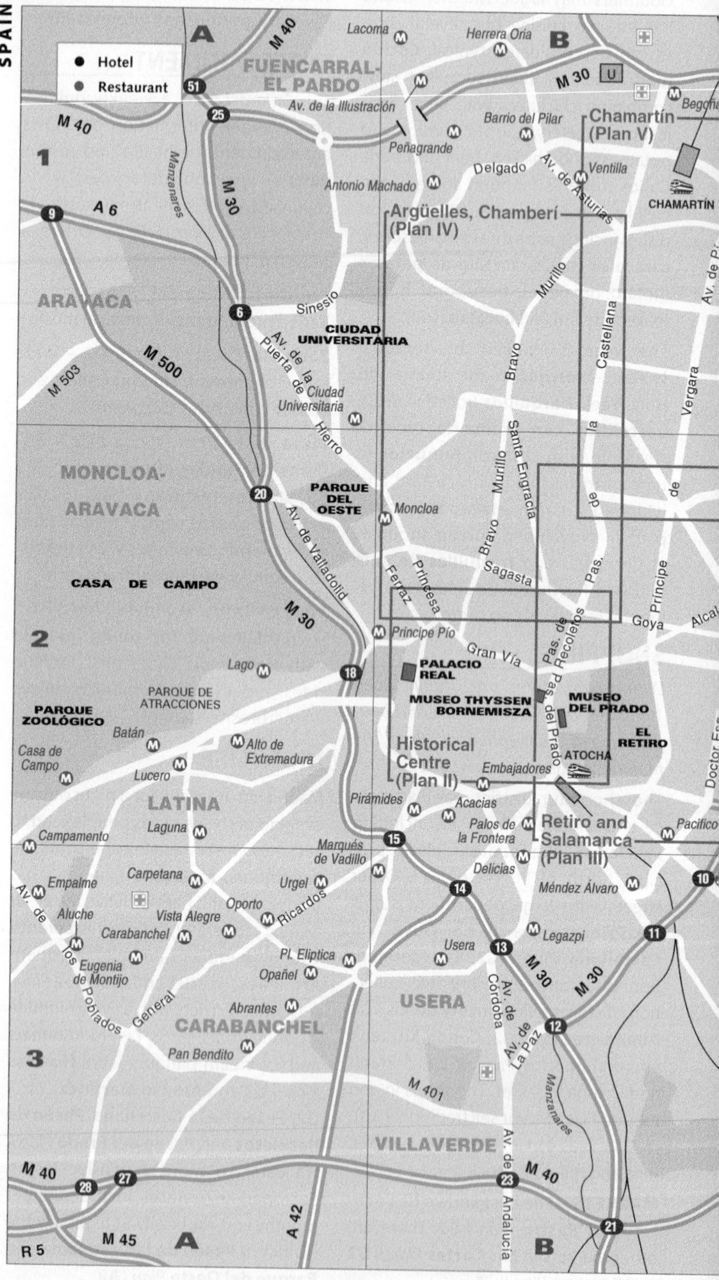
Hotel
Restaurant
A
B
1
2
3
FUENCARRAL-EL PARDO
Lacoma
Herrera Oria
M 40
M 30
Av. de la Illustración
Peñagrande
Barrio del Pilar
Begoña
Chamartín (Plan V)
Delgado
Av. de Asturias
Ventilla
CHAMARTÍN
Antonio Machado
Manzanares
M 30
A 6
Argüelles, Chamberí (Plan IV)
Murillo
Castellana
Av. de P
ARAVACA
Sinesio
CIUDAD UNIVERSITARIA
Av. de la Puerta de Hierro
Ciudad Universitaria
M 500
M 503
Bravo
Vergara
la
MONCLOA-ARAVACA
PARQUE DEL OESTE
Moncloa
Av. de Valladolid
Santa Engracia
Murillo
Bravo
de
de
Sagasta
Pas.
Príncipe
CASA DE CAMPO
Ferraz
Princesa
M 30
Príncipe Pío
Goya
Alcal
Gran Vía
Pas. de Recoletos
Lago
PALACIO REAL
MUSEO THYSSEN BORNEMISZA
Pas. del Prado
MUSEO DEL PRADO
PARQUE DE ATRACCIONES
PARQUE ZOOLÓGICO
Batán
Alto de Extremadura
Historical Centre (Plan II)
EL RETIRO
Casa de Campo
Lucero
Embajadores
ATOCHA
Doctor Es
LATINA
Pirámides
Acacias
Laguna
Palos de la Frontera
Retiro and Salamanca (Plan III)
Pacífico
Campamento
Marqués de Vadillo
Delicias
Empalme
Carpetana
Urgel
Méndez Álvaro
Oporto
Ricardos
Av. de los Poblados
Aluche
Vista Alegre
Carabanchel
Legazpi
Pl. Elíptica
Usera
Eugenia de Montijo
Opañel
M 30
M 30
Av. de Córdoba
General
Abrantes
USERA
Av. de La Paz
CARABANCHEL
Pan Bendito
Manzanares
M 401
VILLAVERDE
Av. de Andalucía
M 40
M 40
A 42
M 45
R 5
51
25
9
6
20
18
15
14
13
12
11
10
28
27
23
21

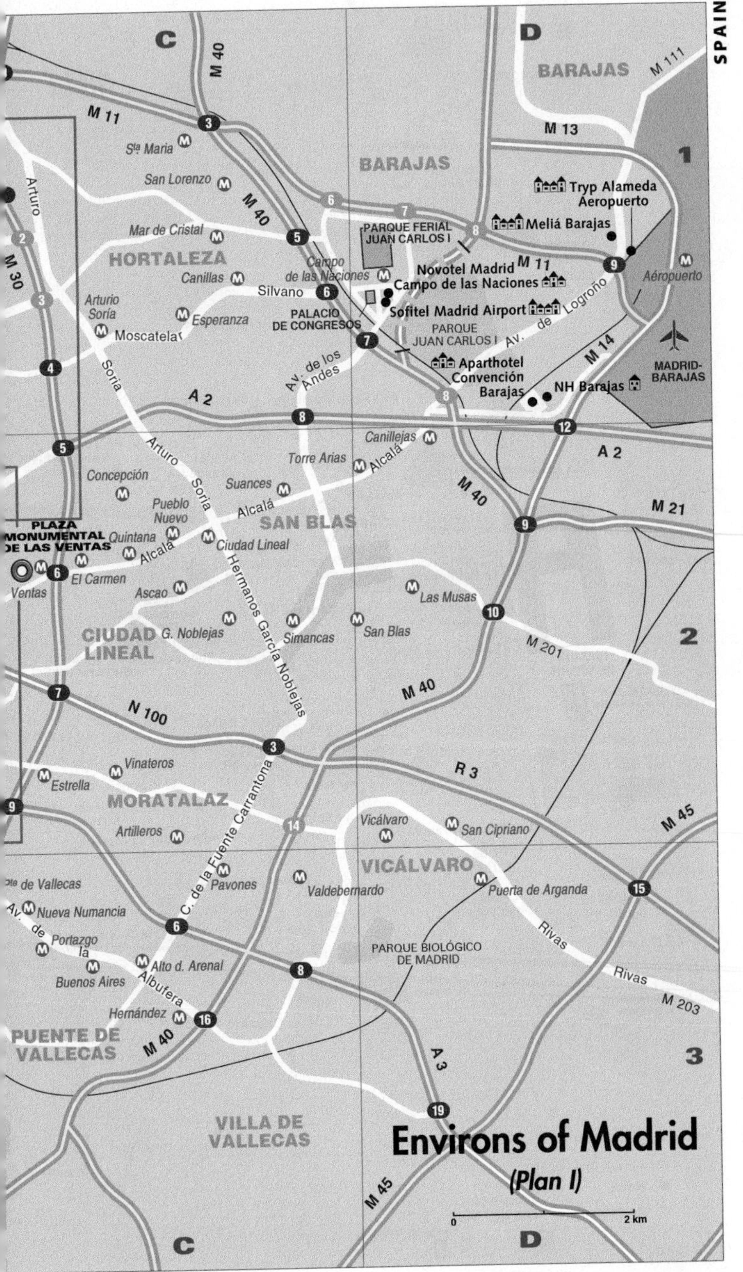
Environs of Madrid
(Plan I)
C
D
1
2
3
BARAJAS
HORTALEZA
SAN BLAS
CIUDAD LINEAL
MORATALAZ
VICÁLVARO
PUENTE DE VALLECAS
VILLA DE VALLECAS
Tryp Alameda Aeropuerto
Meliá Barajas
Novotel Madrid Campo de las Naciones
Sofitel Madrid Airport
Aparthotel Convención Barajas
NH Barajas
PARQUE FERIAL JUAN CARLOS I
PALACIO DE CONGRESOS
PARQUE JUAN CARLOS I
MADRID-BARAJAS
PLAZA MONUMENTAL DE LAS VENTAS
PARQUE BIOLÓGICO DE MADRID
Aeropuerto
Sta Maria
San Lorenzo
Mar de Cristal
Canillas
Campo de las Naciones
Silvano
Arturio Soria
Esperanza
Moscatelar
Canillejas
Torre Arias
Suances
Concepción
Pueblo Nuevo
Quintana
Ciudad Lineal
El Carmen
Ventas
Ascao
G. Noblejas
Simancas
San Blas
Las Musas
Vinateros
Estrella
Artilleros
Vicálvaro
San Cipriano
Pavones
Valdebernardo
Puerta de Arganda
Nueva Numancia
Portazgo
Buenos Aires
Alto d. Arenal
Hernández
Av. de los Andes
Av. de Logroño
Arturo Soria
Alcalá
Hermanos García Noblejas
C. de la Fuente Carrantona
Av. de la Albufera
Rivas
M 11
M 13
M 14
M 21
M 30
M 40
M 45
M 111
M 201
M 203
A 2
A 3
N 100
R 3
0
2 km

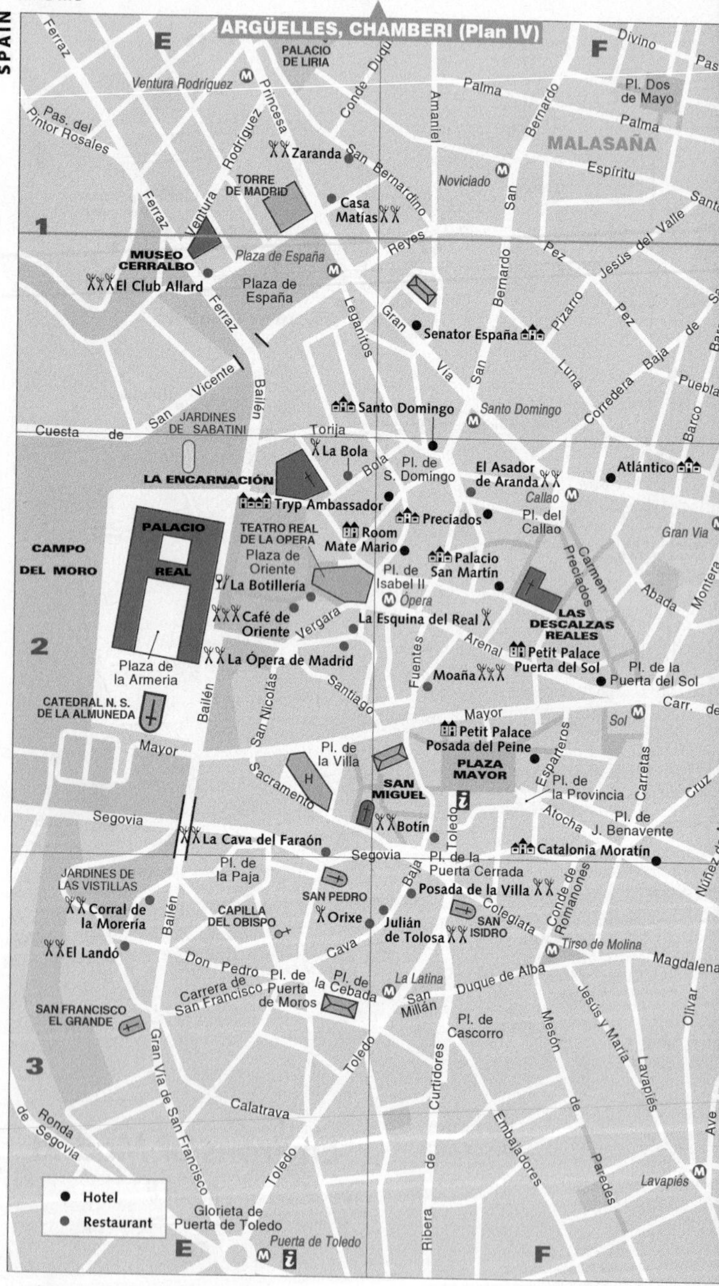
ARGÜELLES, CHAMBERI (Plan IV)
PALACIO DE LIRIA
MALASAÑA
TORRE DE MADRID
MUSEO CERRALBO
Zaranda
Casa Matías
El Club Allard
Plaza de España
Senator España
JARDINES DE SABATINI
Santo Domingo
La Bola
LA ENCARNACIÓN
Tryp Ambassador
Pl. de S. Domingo
El Asador de Aranda
Atlántico
Preciados
Pl. del Callao
PALACIO REAL
CAMPO DEL MORO
TEATRO REAL DE LA OPERA
Plaza de Oriente
Room Mate Mario
Palacio San Martín
LAS DESCALZAS REALES
La Botillería
Café de Oriente
La Esquina del Real
Pl. de Isabel II
Petit Palace Puerta del Sol
Pl. de la Puerta del Sol
La Ópera de Madrid
Moaña
Plaza de la Armeria
CATEDRAL N. S. DE LA ALMUNEDA
Petit Palace Posada del Peine
PLAZA MAYOR
Pl. de la Villa
SAN MIGUEL
Pl. de la Provincia
Botín
La Cava del Faraón
Pl. de J. Benavente
Catalonia Moratín
Pl. de la Puerta Cerrada
Pl. de la Paja
JARDINES DE LAS VISTILLAS
SAN PEDRO
Posada de la Villa
Corral de la Morería
CAPILLA DEL OBISPO
Orixe
Julián de Tolosa
SAN ISIDRO
El Landó
Pl. de Puerta de Moros
Pl. de la Cebada
SAN FRANCISCO EL GRANDE
Pl. de Cascorro
Glorieta de Puerta de Toledo
Hotel
Restaurant

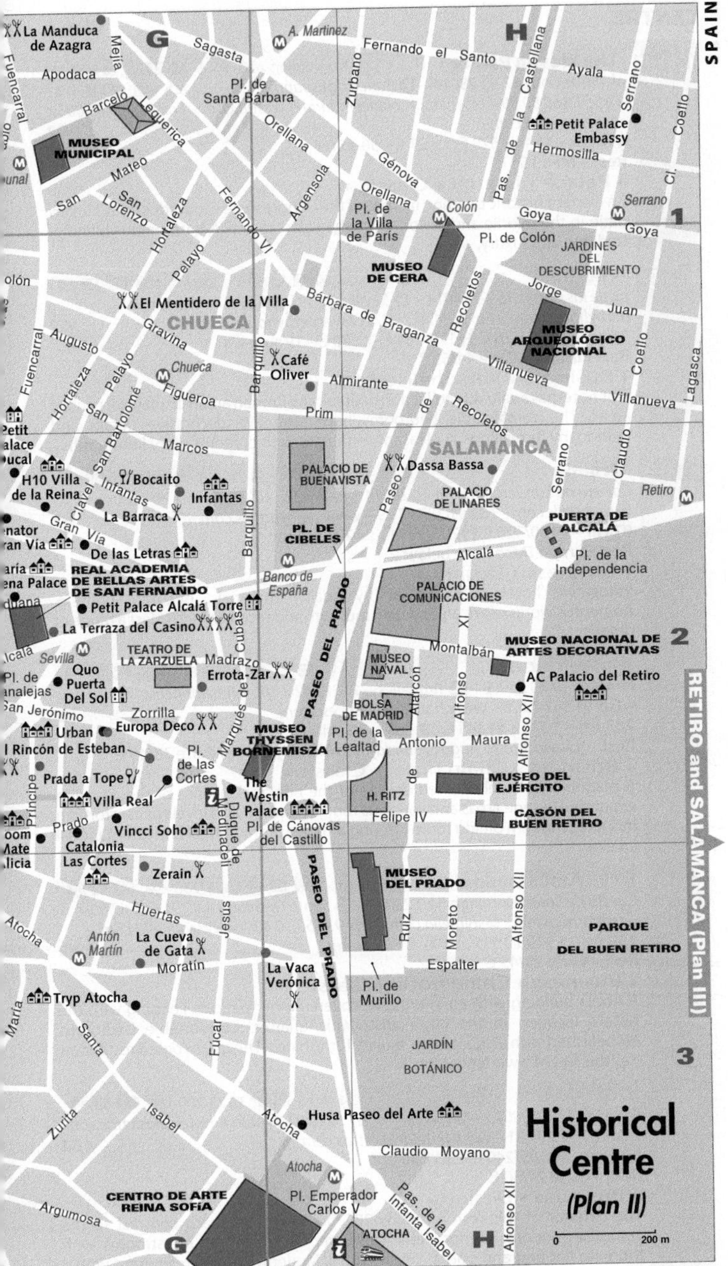
Historical Centre
(Plan II)
RETIRO and SALAMANCA (Plan III)
CHUECA
SALAMANCA
MUSEO MUNICIPAL
MUSEO DE CERA
MUSEO ARQUEOLÓGICO NACIONAL
PALACIO DE BUENAVISTA
PALACIO DE LINARES
PUERTA DE ALCALÁ
PL. DE CIBELES
PALACIO DE COMUNICACIONES
MUSEO NACIONAL DE ARTES DECORATIVAS
MUSEO NAVAL
BOLSA DE MADRID
MUSEO THYSSEN BORNEMISZA
MUSEO DEL EJÉRCITO
CASÓN DEL BUEN RETIRO
MUSEO DEL PRADO
PARQUE DEL BUEN RETIRO
JARDÍN BOTÁNICO
CENTRO DE ARTE REINA SOFíA
REAL ACADEMIA DE BELLAS ARTES DE SAN FERNANDO
TEATRO DE LA ZARZUELA
JARDINES DEL DESCUBRIMIENTO
H. RITZ
ATOCHA
PASEO DEL PRADO
La Manduca de Azagra
El Mentidero de la Villa
Café Oliver
Dassa Bassa
Bocaito
Infantas
La Barraca
H10 Villa de la Reina
De las Letras
Petit Palace Alcalá Torre
La Terraza del Casino
Quo Puerta del Sol
Errota-Zar
Europa Deco
Urban
Rincón de Esteban
Prada a Tope
Villa Real
The Westin Palace
Vincci Soho
Catalonia Las Cortes
Zerain
La Cueva de Gata
La Vaca Verónica
Tryp Atocha
Husa Paseo del Arte
Petit Palace Embassy
AC Palacio del Retiro
Sagasta
Fernando el Santo
Ayala
Serrano
Coello
Hermosilla
Goya
Colón
Pl. de Colón
Pl. de Santa Bárbara
Orellana
Génova
Zurbano
Pl. de la Villa de París
Bárbara de Braganza
Recoletos
Villanueva
Jorge Juan
Almirante
Prim
Claudio Coello
Lagasca
Retiro
Alcalá
Pl. de la Independencia
Montalbán
Alfonso XII
Antonio Maura
Felipe IV
Pl. de Cánovas del Castillo
Pl. de la Lealtad
Banco de España
Gran Vía
Fuencarral
Apodaca
Barceló
Lequerica
Mejía
San Mateo
San Lorenzo
Hortaleza
Pelayo
Fernando VI
Argensola
Augusto Figueroa
Gravina
Chueca
San Bartolomé
Marcos
Clavel
Infantas
Barquillo
Cubas
Madrazo
Marqués de Cubas
Zorrilla
Sevilla
San Jerónimo
Pl. de las Cortes
Duque de Medinaceli
Príncipe
Prado
Huertas
Antón Martín
Moratín
Jesús
Atocha
Fúcar
Santa Isabel
María
Zurita
Argumosa
Ruiz de Alarcón
Moreto
Espalter
Pl. de Murillo
Claudio Moyano
Pl. Emperador Carlos V
Pas. de la Infanta Isabel
Pas. de la Castellana
A. Martínez
Serrano
G
H
1
2
3
0
200 m

CENTRE

Plan II

The Westin Palace

No smokers rest. – 25/500

pl. de las Cortes 7 ✉ 28014 – Ⓜ Banco de España – ✆ 91 360 80 00 – reservation.palacemadrid@westin.com – Fax 91 360 81 00 – www.westin.com — VISA MC AE

G2

418 rm – ††495/625 €, ☕ 27 € – 50 suites

Rest – Menu 56 €

◆ Palace ◆ Luxury ◆ Classic ◆

An elegant historic building in front of the Congreso de Diputados with a lovely patio in the middle and a Modernist-style glass dome. A harmonious blend of tradition and luxury.

Villa Real

35/200 VISA MC AE

pl. de las Cortes 10 ✉ 28014 – Ⓜ Sevilla – ✆ 91 420 37 67 – villareal@derbyhotels.com – Fax 91 420 25 47 – www.derbyhotels.com

G2

96 rm – †160/326 € ††170/364 €, ☕ 20 € – 19 suites

Rest *Europa* – Carte 44/55 €

◆ Business ◆ Personalised ◆

This hotel has a valuable collection of Greek and Roman art on display in its public areas. The comfortable bedrooms have attractive decorative details and mahogany furnishings. A pleasant restaurant with contemporary lithographs.

Urban

25/120 VISA MC AE

Carrera de San Jerónimo 34 ✉ 28014 – Ⓜ Sevilla – ✆ 91 787 77 70 – urban@derbyhotels.com – Fax 91 787 77 79 – www.derbyhotels.com

G2

87 rm – †180/326 € ††200/364 €, ☕ 20 € – 9 suites

Rest *Europa Deco* – see below

◆ Business ◆ Design ◆

Innovative hotel, characterized by quality materials, beautiful lighting, numerous works of art, an Egyptian museum and rooms which boast a range of details.

Husa Princesa

25/500 VISA MC AE

Princesa 40 ✉ 28008 – Ⓜ Argüelles – ✆ 91 542 21 00 – husaprincesa@husa.es – Fax 91 542 73 28 – www.hotelhusaprincesa.com

Plan IV **K3**

263 rm – †275 € ††345 €, ☕ 23 € – 12 suites

Rest – *(closed 1 to 15 August, Sunday and Monday dinner)* Carte 38/49 €

◆ Business ◆ Chain hotel ◆ Classic ◆

A magnificent hotel situated on one of the principal arteries of the city with expansive lounge areas and spacious rooms offering high levels of comfort. An intimate, modern dining room offering a choice of traditional and international cuisine.

Tryp Ambassador

25/280 VISA MC AE

Cuesta de Santo Domingo 5 ✉ 28013 – Ⓜ Santo Domingo – ✆ 91 541 67 00 – tryp.ambassador@solmelia.com – Fax 91 559 10 40 – www.solmelia.com

E-F2

159 rm – ††108/199 €, ☕ 17 € – 24 suites

Rest – Carte 28/45 €

◆ Business ◆ Chain hotel ◆ Classic ◆

A noble building with an impressive covered inner patio in keeping with the hotel's location in the city's aristocratic quarter. Comfortable bedrooms embellished with elegant, high-quality furnishings. The glass-roofed restaurant has the feel of a winter garden.

De las Letras

25/200 VISA MC AE

Gran Vía 11 ✉ 28013 – Ⓜ Sevilla – ✆ 91 523 79 80 – info@hoteldelasletras.com – Fax 91 523 79 81 – www.hoteldelasletras.com

G2

103 rm – ††105/240 €, ☕ 12.50 €

Rest – Carte 24/30 €

◆ Business ◆ Design ◆

The exterior of this restored early-20C building is in sharp contrast to the colourful modern interior. New York-style design in the guestrooms with intimate lighting and poems on the walls. Modern, original restaurant with a menu that allows you to create your own dishes.

Vincci Soho No smokers rest. 25/300 VISA MC AE

Prado 18 ✉ 28014 – Ⓜ Antón Martín – ☎ 91 141 41 00 – reservas.soho@vinccihoteles.com – Fax 91 141 41 01 – www.vinccihoteles.com **G2**

167 rm – †74/196 € ††74/241 €, ☕ 15 € – 2 suites

Rest – Carte 23/39 €

♦ Business ♦ Personalised ♦

The completety renovated interior comes as something of a surprise, with its chilled-out ambience and minimalist and avant-garde features. Pleasantly comfortable and well-appointed. Both the restaurant and cafeteria are attractively designed, creating an impressive overall effect.

María Elena Palace VISA MC AE

Aduana 19 ✉ 28013 – Ⓜ Sol – ☎ 91 360 49 30 – mariaelenapalace@chh.es – Fax 91 360 47 89 – www.chh.es **G2**

64 rm ☕ – †100/180 € ††115/225 €

Rest – Menu 23 €

♦ Business ♦ Traditional ♦ Classic ♦

The hotel's main features are its open lobby area and a magnificent patio crowned with glass vaulting. Classic bedrooms with good quality furnishings, carpets and marble bathrooms.

Catalonia Las Cortes No smokers rest. 25/60 VISA MC AE

Prado 6 ✉ 28014 – Ⓜ Antón Martín – ☎ 91 389 60 51 – lascortes@hoteles-catalonia.es – Fax 91 389 60 52 – www.hoteles-catalonia.com **G2**

65 rm – †143/197 € ††189/232 €, ☕ 13 €

Rest – *(dinner only)* Carte 25/45 €

♦ Traditional ♦ Classic ♦

An 18C palace which once belonged to the Dukes of Noblejas. A traditional yet contemporary interior that is striking for its brightness. Well-appointed guestrooms.

Senator España 25/200 VISA MC AE

Gran Vía 70 ✉ 28013 – Ⓜ Plaza de España – ☎ 91 522 82 65 – senator.espana@playasenator.com – Fax 91 522 82 64 – www.playasenator.com **F1**

171 rm – †95/230 € ††115/280 €, ☕ 13 €

Rest – Menu 16 €

♦ Business ♦ Chain hotel ♦ Functional ♦

Excellent leisure facilities, including a beauty centre and hydromassage pools. The hotel's bedrooms are fully sound-proofed and well-appointed. The restaurant offers diners the combination of a salad buffet and a reasonably creative menu.

H10 Villa de la Reina 25/40 VISA MC AE

Gran Vía 22 ✉ 28013 – Ⓜ Gran Vía – ☎ 91 523 91 01 – h10.villa.delareina@h10.es – Fax 91 521 75 22 – www.h10hotels.com **G2**

73 rm ☕ – †120/190 € ††140/205 € – 1 suite

Rest – *(dinner only)* Carte 23/28 €

♦ Business ♦ Chain hotel ♦ Stylish ♦

An attractive building from the early part of the last century, with an entrance-reception area adorned with attractive marble and wood. The charm of yesteryear has been retained in the hotel, which offers guests high levels of comfort in every room.

Infantas Smokers rest. 30 VISA MC AE

Infantas 29 ✉ 28004 – Ⓜ Chueca – ☎ 91 521 28 28 – hotelinfantas@lussohoteles.com – Fax 91 521 66 88 – www.lussohoteles.com **G2**

40 rm – †85/165 €, ☕ 13 €

Rest *Ex Libris* – Carte 34/44 €

♦ Business ♦ Modern ♦

The Infantas occupies an old building that has been completely remodelled with a more contemporary feel. Well-equipped bedrooms and bathrooms, plus a minimalist-style restaurant serving creative cuisine.

Palacio San Martín No smokers rest.

pl. San Martín 5 ✉ 28013 – Ⓜ Sol – ✆ 91 701 50 00 – sanmartin@intur.com – Fax 91 701 50 10 – www.intur.com 25 VISA MC AE **F2**

93 rm – †111/173 € ††111/214 €, ☕ 16 € – 1 suite

Rest – *(closed August, Sunday and Bank Holidays)* Carte 36/41 €

◆ Business ◆ Stylish ◆

A historic building which in the 1950s was the United States Embassy. A patio with a glass roof serves as a lounge area. Traditional-style bedrooms, plus a panoramic restaurant on the top floor.

Husa Paseo del Arte 25/180 VISA MC AE

Atocha 123 ✉ 28012 – Ⓜ Atocha – ✆ 91 298 48 00 – paseodelarte@husa.es – Fax 91 298 48 50 – www.husa.es **G3**

260 rm – †56/200 € ††56/250 €, ☕ 17 €

Rest – Menu 20 €

◆ Business ◆ Modern ◆

As its name indicates, the hotel is an excellent base from which to explore Madrid's most famous museums. Bright, open public areas, along with functional bedrooms of a high standard. The restaurant occupies the inner patio, with its glass roof and small garden.

Room Mate Alicia without rest VISA MC AE

Prado 2 ✉ 28014 – Ⓜ Sevilla – ✆ 91 389 60 95 – alicia@room-matehoteles.com – Fax 91 369 47 95 – www.room-matehoteles.com **G2**

34 rm ☕ – †80/130 € ††100/140 €

◆ Business ◆ Modern ◆

The façade of this sensitively restored old building provides an interesting contrast with the modern interior. Spacious bedrooms with impeccable decor and designer furniture.

Senator Gran Vía 25 VISA MC AE

Gran Vía 21 ✉ 28013 – Ⓜ Gran Vía – ✆ 91 531 4151 – senator.granvia@playasenator.com – Fax 91 524 07 99 – www.playasenator.com **G2**

136 rm – †75/200 € ††85/250 €, ☕ 13 €

Rest – Menu 16 €

◆ Business ◆ Chain hotel ◆ Functional ◆

Behind the Senator's distinctive classical façade is an interior with the latest in modern comforts, including avant-garde bedrooms. Dining options include a simply-styled restaurant offering à la carte and buffet dining and a spacious cafeteria.

Santo Domingo No smokers rest. 25/200 VISA MC AE

pl. de Santo Domingo 13 ✉ 28013 – Ⓜ Santo Domingo – ✆ 91 547 98 00 – reserva@hotelsantodomingo.com – Fax 91 547 59 95 – www.hotelsantodomingo.net

120 rm – ††149/191 €, ☕ 12.50 € **F2**

Rest – Menu 34 €

◆ Business ◆ Traditional ◆ Personalised ◆

Numerous works of art decorate the walls of this hotel. Comfortable rooms with modern bathrooms, some with hydro-massage baths.

Preciados 25/120 VISA MC AE

Preciados 37 ✉ 28013 – Ⓜ Callao – ✆ 91 454 44 00 – preciadoshotel@preciadoshotel.com – Fax 91 454 44 01 – www.preciadoshotel.com **F2**

68 rm – †100/400 € ††110/450 €, ☕ 16.05 € – 5 suites

Rest – Carte 32/41 €

◆ Business ◆ Modern ◆

The severe 19C Classicism of this hotel's architecture is in complete contrast to its modern and well-appointed facilities. A small but pleasant lounge.

Tryp Atocha without rest 25/210 VISA MC AE

Atocha 83 ✉ 28012 – Ⓜ Antón Martín – ✆ 91 330 05 00 – tryp.atocha@solmelia.com – Fax 91 420 15 60 – www.solmelia.com **G3**

150 rm – †112/130 € ††145/159 €, ☕ 15 €

◆ Business ◆ Chain hotel ◆ Functional ◆

This small palace dating from 1913 offers guests modern, functional facilities. The spacious lounge areas include the glass-adorned "salón de actos" and a superb staircase.

Catalonia Moratín without rest

Atocha 23 ✉ 28012 – Ⓜ Sol – ✆ 91 369 71 71 – moratin@hoteles-catalonia.es – Fax 91 360 12 31 – www.hoteles-catalonia.es 25/30 VISA MC AE

F2-3

59 rm – †70/200 € ††80/250 €, ☕ 14 € – 4 suites

◆ Business ◆ Chain hotel ◆ Functional ◆

An 18C building combining original features, such as the staircase, and other more practical designs. Inner patio with a glass roof, plus modern bedrooms.

Atlántico without rest

Gran Vía 38 ✉ 28013 – Ⓜ Callao – ✆ 91 522 64 80 – informacion@hotelatlantico.es – Fax 91 531 02 10 – www.hotelatlantico.es

F2

116 rm – †90/125 € ††120/180 €, ☕ 10 €

◆ Business ◆ Family ◆ Classic ◆

The comfort in this centrally located mansion has increased following a recent expansion. Harmonious decor in the bedrooms with matching wallpaper and curtains.

Husa Moncloa

Serrano Jover 1 ✉ 28015 – Ⓜ Argüelles – ✆ 91 542 45 85 – husamoncloa@husa.es – Fax 91 542 71 69 – www.hotelhusamoncloa.com

Plan IV **K3**

116 rm – †169 € ††199 €, ☕ 15 € – 12 suites

Rest – *(in Hotel Husa Princesa)*

◆ Business ◆ Chain hotel ◆ Classic ◆

This hotel acts as an annexe to the Husa Princesa hotel. Breakfast only is served here, so guests can use the facilities of its neighbour. Large, well-appointed bedrooms.

Petit Palace Alcalá Torre without rest

Virgen de los Peligros 2 ✉ 28013 – Ⓜ Sevilla – ✆ 91 532 19 01 – alcala@hthoteles.com – Fax 91 522 91 30 – www.hthoteles.com

G2

66 rm – ††115/360 €, ☕ 15 €

◆ Chain hotel ◆ Minimalist ◆

An historic building with an unusual layout. Typical modern and functional furniture associated with this hotel chain, hydromassage showers and impressive views from the tower's rooms.

Petit Palace Puerta del Sol without rest

Arenal 4 ✉ 28013 – Ⓜ Sol – ✆ 91 521 05 42 – sol@hthoteles.com – Fax 91 521 05 61 – www.hthoteles.com VISA MC AE

F2

64 rm – ††89/200 €, ☕ 12 €

◆ Chain hotel ◆ Functional ◆

A modern hotel with a spacious reception area, lounge and free-Internet access zone. Functional bedrooms with hydromassage showers.

Petit Palace Ducal without rest 25/50 VISA MC AE

Hortaleza 3 ✉ 28004 – Ⓜ Gran Vía – ✆ 91 521 10 43 – duc@hthoteles.com – Fax 91 521 50 64 – www.hthoteles.com

G2

58 rm – †75/145 € ††75/175 €, ☕ 11 €

◆ Chain hotel ◆ Functional ◆

Hidden behind the 19C façade is a hotel with a contemporary feel and contrasting black and white colour scheme. Comfortable bedrooms with hydromassage showers.

Quo Puerta Del Sol without rest VISA MC AE

Sevilla 4 ✉ 28014 – Ⓜ Sevilla – ✆ 91 532 90 49 – puertadelsol@hotelesquo.com – Fax 91 531 28 34 – www.hotelesquo.com

G2

61 rm – †125/205 € ††138/257 €, ☕ 17 € – 1 suite

◆ Business ◆ Design ◆

The hotel's excellent facilities and refined minimalist decor more than compensate for the lack of public areas and bedrooms that are on the small side.

SPAIN

Petit Palace Posada del Peine without rest

Postas 17 ✉ 28012 – Ⓜ Sol – ✆ 91 523 81 51 – pos@hthoteles.com – Fax 91 523 29 93 – www.hthoteles.com **F2**

69 rm – ††90/200 €, ☕ 12 €

◆ Chain hotel ◆ Functional ◆

An historic Madrid hotel dating from 1610. Completely refurbished, guests can now look forward to comfortable rooms, attractive decor and the latest technology.

Room Mate Mario without rest

Campomanes 4 ✉ 28013 – ✆ 91 548 85 48 – mario@room-matehoteles.com – Fax 91 559 12 88 – www.room-matehoteles.com **F2**

54 rm ☕ – †80/140 € ††90/150 €

◆ Chain hotel ◆ Modern ◆

A small hotel with a decorative avant-garde design combining different colours, styles and furniture, and bedrooms with excellent facilities.

La Terraza del Casino

Alcalá 15-3º ✉ 28014 – Ⓜ Sevilla – ✆ 91 521 87 00 – laterraza@casinodemadrid.es – Fax 91 523 44 36 – www.casinodemadrid.es

closed August, Saturday lunch, Sunday and Bank Holidays **G2**

Rest – Menu 110 € – Carte 60/85 €

Spec. Esféricos de mozzarella. Pez de San Pedro con texturas de limón. Jarrete de ternera con papillote de verduras.

◆ Inventive ◆ Formal ◆

In the 19C Madrid Casino building. The lounges have a classy feel and the very attractive terrace is a delightful setting in which to eat.

El Club Allard

Ferraz 2 ✉ 28008 – Ⓜ Plaza España – ✆ 91 559 09 39 – rverdes@antuvi.es – Fax 91 559 12 29

closed August, Sunday and Bank Holidays **E1**

Rest – Carte 43/59 €

◆ Inventive ◆ Formal ◆

Occupying the ground floor of an early-20C Modernist building with an impressive high-ceilinged dining room. Imaginative, meticulously prepared cuisine based on in-season ingredients fresh from the market.

Café de Oriente

pl. de Oriente 2 ✉ 28013 – Ⓜ Ópera – ✆ 91 547 15 64 – cafeoriente@grupolezama.com – Fax 91 547 77 07 – www.grupolezama.es **E2**

Rest – Carte 45/57 €

◆ International ◆ Formal ◆

In front of the Palacio Real with a luxury café and an attractive wine cellar-style dining room. International menu with a modern twist.

La Manduca de Azagra

Sagasta 14 ✉ 28004 – Ⓜ Alonso Martínez – ✆ 91 591 01 12 – Fax 91 591 01 13

closed August, Sunday and Bank Holidays **G1**

Rest – Carte 37/46 €

◆ Navarrese specialities ◆ Minimalist ◆

A privileged central location for this spacious restaurant with a minimalist feel in both its design and lighting. The cuisine here is based on quality products.

Moaña

Hileras 4 ✉ 28013 – Ⓜ Ópera – ✆ 91 548 29 14 – Fax 91 541 65 98

closed Sunday dinner **F2**

Rest – Carte 39/59 €

◆ Galician specialities ◆ Formal ◆

A hotel with an elegant and comfortable feel in the heart of the old quarter. Bar, a number of private rooms and a live fish and seafood tank.

XX **El Mentidero de la Villa** Smokers rest. 8/45

Santo Tomé 6 ✉ 28004 – Ⓜ Colón – ✆ 91 308 12 85 – info@mentiderodelavilla.com – Fax 91 651 34 88 – www.elmentiderodelavilla.es

closed Holy Week, August, Saturday lunch, Sunday and Bank Holidays **G1**

Rest – Carte 38/50 €

◆ International ◆ Cosy ◆

A welcoming, intimate restaurant with a well-conceived layout and original decor. Exquisite culinary preparation of daring international cuisine.

XX **Errota-Zar** 4/20

Jovellanos 3-1° ✉ 28014 – Ⓜ Banco de España – ✆ 91 531 97 90 – errota@errota-zar.com – Fax 91 531 25 64 – www.errota-zar.com

closed Holy Week, August, Sunday and Bank Holidays **G2**

Rest – Carte 42/51 €

◆ Basque ◆ Family ◆

In front of the Zarzuela theatre. The sober but elegant dining room serves Basque cuisine accompanied by an extensive wine and cigar list. One private room is also available.

XX **Casa Matías**

San Leonardo 12 ✉ 28015 – Ⓜ Plaza de España – ✆ 91 541 76 83 – Fax 91 541 93 70

closed Sunday dinner **E1**

Rest – Carte 40/47 €

◆ Grills ◆ Rustic ◆

This Basque-style cider house, adorned with large casks of its trademark brew for customers to taste, has two spacious rustic-modern rooms, one with an open grill.

XX **Julián de Tolosa** Smokers rest.

Cava Baja 18 ✉ 28005 – Ⓜ La Latina – ✆ 91 365 82 10 – Fax 91 366 33 08

closed Sunday dinner **F3**

Rest – Carte 39/50 €

◆ Grills ◆ Rustic ◆

A pleasant restaurant in neo-rustic style offering the best T-bone steaks in the city. The limited menu is more than compensated for by the quality of the food.

XX **Posada de la Villa**

Cava Baja 9 ✉ 28005 – Ⓜ La Latina – ✆ 91 366 18 60 – povisa@posadadelavilla.com – Fax 91 366 70 90 – www.posadadelavilla.com

closed August and Sunday dinner except May **F3**

Rest – Carte 25/40 €

◆ Spanish ◆ Rustic ◆

An old inn with a friendly ambience and Castilian décor. Regional menu and traditional roasts cooked in a wood-fired oven. Madrid-style chickpea stew a speciality.

XX **Europa Deco** – Hotel Urban

Carrera de San Jerónimo 34 ✉ 28014 – Ⓜ Sevilla – ✆ 91 787 77 80 – europadeco@derbyhotels.com – Fax 91 787 77 70 – www.derbyhotels.com

Rest – Carte 48/59 € **G2**

◆ Inventive ◆ Trendy ◆

The name on everyone's lips, with its innovative design and excellent restaurant, serving Mediterranean and international fusion cuisine, produced using both fresh local produce and more exotic ingredients.

XX ✿ **Zaranda** Smokers rest.

San Bernardino 13 ✉ 28015 – Ⓜ Plaza España – ✆ 91 541 20 26 – zaranda@zaranda.es – www.zaranda.es

closed August, Saturday lunch, Sunday and Bank Holidays **E1**

Rest – Menu 45 € – Carte 43/69 €

Spec. Risotto de espárragos verdes y colmenillas. Lomo rosa de cordero recental con caviar de berenjena y pimientos. Ópera de pistacho y mandarina.

◆ Inventive ◆ Friendly ◆

Contemporary design dominated by blue tones, with one attractively arranged public dining room and one private, cave-like room in the basement. Reliable yet imaginative menu.

SPAIN

XX **El Asador de Aranda** No smokers rest. AC VISA MC AE

Preciados 44 ✉ 28013 – Ⓜ Cuzco – ☎ 91 547 21 56 – Fax 91 556 62 02 – www.asadordearanda.com

closed 24 July-13 August and Monday dinner **F2**

Rest – Carte approx. 31 €

♦ Roast lamb ♦ Rustic ♦

An attractive Castilian restaurant with beautiful wood ceilings. Traditional dishes and roast meats cooked in a wood fired oven a speciality.

XX **La Ópera de Madrid** AC VISA MC AE

Amnistía 5 ✉ 28013 – Ⓜ Ópera – ☎ 91 559 50 92 – Fax 91 559 50 92 – www.laoperarestaurante.com

closed August, Sunday and Monday dinner **E2**

Rest – Carte 28/43 €

♦ International ♦ Cosy ♦

A good place to start an evening out or to discuss a play seen in the nearby theatre while enjoying something delicious. Elegant décor and a well-balanced menu.

XX **El Landó** Smokers rest. AC ⇔4/15 VISA MC AE

pl. Gabriel Miró 8 ✉ 28005 – Ⓜ La Latina – ☎ 91 366 76 81 – blake.gonzalez@telefonica.net – Fax 91 366 25 56

closed Holy Week, August and Sunday **E3**

Rest – Carte approx. 44 €

♦ Spanish ♦ Formal ♦

Near to the Basílica de San Francisco el Grande, this restaurant has a bar, dining room in the basement and private room, all classically furnished with a profusion of wood.

XX **Corral de la Morería** No smokers rest. AC VISA MC AE

Morería 17 ✉ 28005 – Ⓜ Ópera – ☎ 91 365 84 46 – info@corraldelamoreria.com – Fax 91 364 12 19 – www.corraldelamoreria.com **E3**

Rest – Espectáculo flamenco – *(dinner only)* Carte 40/79 €

♦ Spanish ♦ Musical ♦

A restaurant with a highly respected flamenco show, with tables set close together around the stage. A la carte and gastronomic fixed menu options.

XX **Botín** No smokers rest. AC VISA MC AE

Cuchilleros 17 ✉ 28005 – Ⓜ Puerta del Sol – ☎ 91 366 42 17 – Fax 91 366 84 94 – www.botin.es **F2**

Rest – Carte 36/49 €

♦ Spanish ♦ Rustic ♦

Founded in 1725 and said to be the oldest restaurant in the world. The old-style décor, traditional wine-cellar and wood-fired oven all convey a strong feeling of the past.

XX **El Rincón de Esteban** Smokers rest. AC VISA MC AE

Santa Catalina 3 ✉ 28014 – Ⓜ Sevilla – ☎ 91 429 92 89 – Fax 91 365 87 70

closed August and Sunday **G2**

Rest – Carte 49/64 €

♦ Spanish ♦ Family ♦

Frequented by politicians because of its proximity to the Palacio de Congresos. Intimate and elegant and offering traditional-style dishes.

XX **La Cava del Faraón** AC VISA MC AE

Segovia 8 ✉ 28005 – Ⓜ Tirso de Molina – ☎ 91 542 52 54 – f@defuny.com – Fax 91 457 45 30

closed Monday **E2**

Rest – *(dinner only)* Carte 30/45 €

♦ Egyptian ♦ Exotic ♦

A typical Egyptian setting with a tea-room, domed ceilings and a dining room where you can sample the cuisine of the country and enjoy a belly-dancing performance.

La Esquina del Real
Smokers rest. AC VISA MC AE ①

Amnistía 2 ✉ 28013 – Ⓜ Ópera – ☏ 91 559 43 09
closed 15 August-15 September, Saturday lunch and Sunday **E-F2**
Rest – Carte 37/51 €
♦ International ♦ Friendly ♦
An intimate and pleasant rustic-style restaurant with stone and brick walls. Friendly service and French dishes.

Orixe
AC VISA MC AE ①

Cava Baja 17 ✉ 28005 – ☏ 91 354 04 11 – info@orixerestaurante.com – Fax 91 458 39 01 – www.orixerestaurante.com
closed 16 to 31 July, Sunday dinner and Monday **E3**
Rest – Carte approx. 40 €
♦ Galician specialities ♦ Friendly ♦
A good address in which to enjoy the flavour of traditional Galician cuisine. Bar at the entrance, in addition to several dining rooms, all with a contemporary feel and decor.

Zerain
AC ⇔8/23 VISA MC AE ①

Quevedo 3 ✉ 28014 – Ⓜ Antón Martín – ☏ 91 429 79 09 – Fax 91 429 17 20
closed August and Sunday **G3**
Rest – Carte 29/35 €
♦ Basque ♦ Rustic ♦
A Basque cider house with huge barrels. Friendly atmosphere and attractive décor with pictures of the Basque country. Traditional cider house menu at reasonable prices.

La Barraca
AC ⇔6/30 VISA MC AE ①

Reina 29 ✉ 28004 – Ⓜ Banco de España – ☏ 91 532 71 54 – info@labarraca.es – Fax 91 523 82 74 – www.labarraca.es **G2**
Rest – Carte 26/36 €
♦ Rice specialities ♦ Rustic ♦
Popular with tourists because of its renown and its location. Traditional Valencian décor with lots of ceramic tiles. Rice dishes a speciality.

Café Oliver
AC VISA MC AE

Almirante 12 ✉ 28004 – Ⓜ Chueca – ☏ 91 521 73 79 – info@cafeoliver.com – www.cafeoliver.com **G1**
Rest – Carte 34/40 €
♦ International ♦ Bistro ♦
Despite its size, the Café Oliver retains its intimacy thanks to its stone walls and individual table lighting. An interesting mix of traditional, international and Arab-influenced cuisine.

La Cueva de Gata
Smokers rest. AC ⇔4/30

Moratín 19 ✉ 28014 – Ⓜ Antón Martín – ☏ 91 360 09 43 – www.cuevadegata.com
closed 1 to 20 August and Sunday **G3**
Rest – Carte 30/35 €
♦ Spanish ♦ Formal ♦
Run by two brothers, this restaurant has a small bar and tapas section at the entrance, leading onto a traditional dining room. Cave-like private room on the lower floor.

La Bola
No smokers rest. AC

Bola 5 ✉ 28013 – Ⓜ Santo Domingo – ☏ 91 547 69 30 – labola1870@hotmail.com – Fax 91 541 71 64 – www.labola.es
closed Sunday dinner **E2**
Rest – Carte approx. 30 €
♦ Spanish ♦ Friendly ♦
A long-established Madrid tavern with the flavour of old Madrid. Traditional stewed dishes a speciality. Try the meat and chickpea stew.

SPAIN

La Vaca Verónica
Smokers rest. AC VISA MC AE DC

Moratín 38 ✉ 28014 – Ⓜ Antón Martín – ☎ 91 429 78 27
closed Saturday lunch **G3**
Rest – Carte approx. 30 €
◆ International ◆ Friendly ◆
This delightfully intimate and friendly restaurant is decorated in original style with colourful paintings, mirrored ceilings and candles on every table.

La Botillería del Café de Oriente
AC VISA MC AE DC

pl. de Oriente 4 ✉ 28013 – Ⓜ Ópera – ☎ 91 548 46 20 – cafeoriente@grupolezama.com – Fax 91 547 77 07 – www.grupolezama.es **E2**
Tapa 2 € **Ración** approx. 12 €
◆ Spanish ◆ Tapas bar ◆
In an area that is very lively at night. Traditional Viennese café-style décor and a wide variety of canapes accompanied by good wines served by the glass.

Prada a Tope
Smokers rest. AC VISA AE

Principe 11 ✉ 28012 – Ⓜ Sevilla – ☎ 91 429 59 21 – www.pradaatope.es
closed August, Sunday dinner and Monday **G2**
Tapa 6 € **Ración** approx. 12 €
◆ Spanish ◆ Tapas bar ◆
A traditional establishment with a bar and rustic-style tables. Wood décor, photos on the walls and the opportunity to buy various products.

Bocaito
Smokers rest. AC VISA MC AE DC

Libertad 6 ✉ 28004 – Ⓜ Chueca – ☎ 91 532 12 19 – bocaito@bocaito.com – Fax 91 522 56 29 – www.bocaito.com
closed August, Saturday lunch and Sunday **G2**
Tapa 3 € **Ración** approx. 11 €
◆ Spanish ◆ Tapas bar ◆
A taurine atmosphere and décor. Ideal for sampling tapas either at the splendid bar or at a table. Deep-fried and egg-based tapas are specialities.

Taberna de San Bernardo
Smokers rest. AC VISA MC

San Bernardo 85 ✉ 28015 – Ⓜ San Bernardo – ☎ 91 445 41 70 *Plan IV* **K3**
Tapa 1.80 € **Ración** approx. 6.50 €
◆ Spanish ◆ Tapas bar ◆
An informal, rustic tavern with three separate sections. Popular house specialities include two vegetarian dishes - papas con huevo and fritura de verduras.

RETIRO and SALAMANCA *Plan III*

Ritz
No smokers rest. AC 25/250 VISA MC AE DC

pl. de la Lealtad 5 ✉ 28014 – Ⓜ Banco de España – ☎ 91 701 67 67 – reservations@ritz.es – Fax 91 701 67 76 – www.ritzmadrid.com **I2**
137 rm – †510 € ††610 €, ☕ 30 € – 30 suites
Rest – Carte approx. 90 €
◆ Grand Luxury ◆ Traditional ◆ Classic ◆
An internationally prestigious hotel occupying a former palace dating from the early 20C, with long-standing associations with the diplomatic world. Extraordinarily beautiful public areas and sumptuously decorated guestrooms. The Ritz's restaurant has an elegant dining room and pleasant summer terrace.

Villa Magna
No smokers rest. AC 25/400 VISA MC AE DC

Paseo de la Castellana 22 ✉ 28046 – Ⓜ Rubén Darío – ☎ 91 587 12 34 – villamagna@hyattintl.com – Fax 91 431 22 86 – www.madrid.park.hyatt.com **I1**
164 rm – †255/465 € ††255/520 €, ☕ 27 € – 18 suites
Rest – *(closed August, Sunday and Bank Holidays)* Menu 39 €
Rest *Tsé Yang* – Carte approx. 50 €
◆ Luxury ◆ Classic ◆
Luxury and elegance from the period of Charles IV are to the fore in the detail, decor and furnishings of the Villa Magna. Spacious public areas and lounges with contrasting designs and furnishings. Refined restaurant with attractive wood panelling.

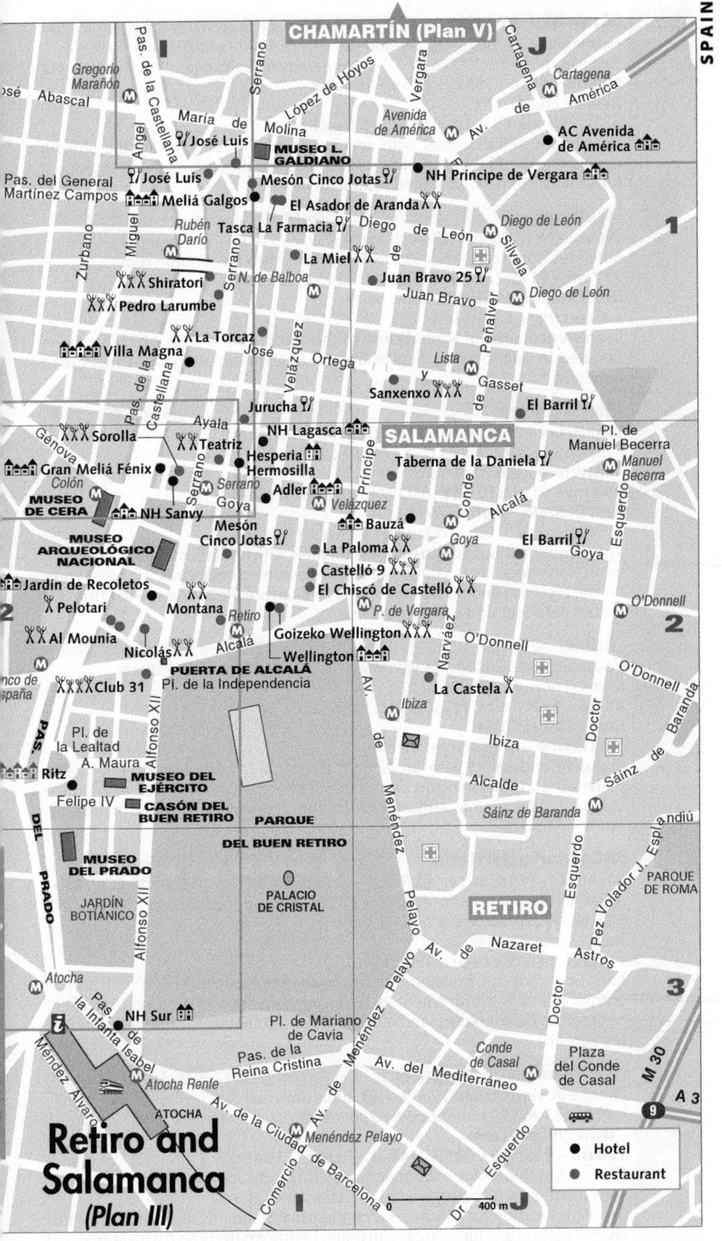
CHAMARTÍN (Plan V)
Retiro and Salamanca
(Plan III)
SALAMANCA
RETIRO
MUSEO L. GALDIANO
MUSEO DE CERA
MUSEO ARQUEOLÓGICO NACIONAL
PUERTA DE ALCALÁ
MUSEO DEL EJÉRCITO
CASÓN DEL BUEN RETIRO
PARQUE DEL BUEN RETIRO
PALACIO DE CRISTAL
MUSEO DEL PRADO
JARDÍN BOTÁNICO
PARQUE DE ROMA
ATOCHA
AC Avenida de América
NH Príncipe de Vergara
José Luis
Mesón Cinco Jotas
Meliá Galgos
El Asador de Aranda
Tasca La Farmacia
La Miel
Juan Bravo 25
Shiratori
Pedro Larumbe
La Torcaz
Villa Magna
Sanxenxo
El Barril
Jurucha
NH Lagasca
Sorolla
Teatriz
Hesperia Hermosilla
Taberna de la Daniela
Gran Meliá Fénix
Adler
NH Sanvy
Bauzá
La Paloma
Castelló 9
El Chiscó de Castelló
Jardín de Recoletos
Pelotari
Montana
Goizeko Wellington
Wellington
Al Mounia
Nicolás
Club 31
La Castela
Ritz
NH Sur
Hotel
Restaurant
0 400 m
M 30
A 3

SPAIN

Gran Meliá Fénix

25/100 VISA AE

Hermosilla 2 ✉ 28001 – Ⓜ Serrano – ✆ 91 431 67 00 – gran.melia.fenix@solmelia.com – Fax 91 576 06 61 – www.granmeliafenix.com **I2**

199 rm – ††180/365 €, ☕ 25 € – 16 suites

Rest – Carte 41/55 €

♦ Luxury ♦ Chain hotel ♦ Classic ♦

An elegant, refined hotel with spacious public areas, such as the striking cupola-crowned lobby, and impressive, traditional bedrooms with top-notch furnishings. Somewhat limited restaurant facilities.

Wellington

25/200 VISA AE

Velázquez 8 ✉ 28001 – Ⓜ Velázquez – ✆ 91 575 44 00 – wellington@hotel-wellington.com – Fax 91 576 41 64 – www.hotel-wellington.com

237 rm – †175/275 € ††210/350 €, ☕ 25 € – 25 suites **I2**

Rest *Goizeko Wellington* – see below

♦ Luxury ♦ Classic ♦

In an elegant area of Madrid close to the Retiro. Classic style which has been updated in public rooms and bedrooms. Bullfighting aficionados meet here regularly.

Meliá Galgos

25/300 VISA AE

Claudio Coello 139 ✉ 28006 – Ⓜ Gregorio Marañón – ✆ 91 562 66 00 – melia.galgos@solmelia.com – Fax 91 561 76 62 – www.meliagalgos.solmelia.com **I1**

350 rm – †103/310 € ††103/392 €, ☕ 17 € – 6 suites

Rest *Diábolo* – Carte 40/60 €

♦ Business ♦ Chain hotel ♦ Functional ♦

The Galgos mainly caters to business clientele with facilities to match, including attractive lounge areas, comfortable, well-appointed bedrooms, a fitness centre on the top floor and a solarium on the roof terrace. Restaurant with attractive traditional decor and excellent service.

Adler

Smokers rest. VISA AE

Velázquez 33 ✉ 28001 – Ⓜ Velázquez – ✆ 91 426 32 20 – hoteladler@iova-sa.com – Fax 91 426 32 21 **I2**

45 rm – †220/350 € ††250/430 €, ☕ 22 €

Rest – Carte 52/64 €

♦ Luxury ♦ Personalised ♦

Exclusive and select with an elegant interior refurbished with high-quality materials and furnishings. Comfortable bedrooms with facilities of a similar standard. Welcoming atmosphere in the restaurant, with its meticulous attention to detail.

AC Palacio del Retiro

No smokers rest. 25/40 VISA AE

Alfonso XII - 14 ✉ 28014 – Ⓜ Retiro – ✆ 91 523 74 60 – pretiro@ac-hotels.com – Fax 91 523 74 61 – www.ac-hotels.com *Plan II* **H2**

50 rm – ††220/340 €, ☕ 27 € – 1 suite

Rest – Carte 41/48 €

♦ Luxury ♦ Personalised ♦

Imposing, early 20C building. The reception area occupies the former carriage entrance and is complemented by an elegant lounge area and excellent bedrooms. Dark colours and design details combine to create a modern restaurant.

NH Príncipe de Vergara

Smokers rest. 25/250 VISA AE

Príncipe de Vergara 92 ✉ 28006 – Ⓜ Av. de América – ✆ 91 563 26 95 – nhprincipedevergara@nh-hotels.com – Fax 91 563 72 53 – www.nh-hotels.com **J1**

170 rm – †95/180 € ††95/214 €, ☕ 18.50 € – 3 suites

Rest – *(closed Saturday and Sunday in August)* Carte approx. 38 €

♦ Business ♦ Chain hotel ♦ Functional ♦

Excellent location for this hotel with the usual standards associated with this chain. Practical and functional, with bright bedrooms decorated with light wood panelling. Cosy basement restaurant offering a traditional menu with a modern twist.

NH Sanvy 25/160 VISA

Goya 3 ✉ 28001 – Ⓜ Serrano – ✆ 91 576 08 00 – nhsanvy@nh-hotels.com – Fax 91 575 24 43 – www.nh-hotels.com **I2**

139 rm – †107/195 € ††107/225 €, ☕ 18 € – 10 suites

Rest *Sorolla* – see below

♦ Business ♦ Chain hotel ♦ Functional ♦

A functional hotel with a good level of comfort throughout. Impeccable contemporary decor, plus a large terrace on the fourth floor, with a swimming pool and solarium.

Bauzá 25/350 VISA

Goya 79 ✉ 28001 – Ⓜ Goya – ✆ 91 435 75 45 – info@hotelbauza.com – Fax 91 431 09 43 – www.hotelbauza.com **J2**

169 rm – †101/135 € ††140/240 €, ☕ 14 € – 8 suites

Rest – Carte 36/45 €

♦ Business ♦ Design ♦

An upbeat design, including a cosy lounge-library with a fireplace, and bedrooms with every creature comfort, some with a terrace. Bright, modern restaurant with decor in varying shades of white and an innovative menu.

Petit Palace Embassy No smokers rest.

Serrano 46 ✉ 28001 – Ⓜ Serrano – ✆ 91 431 30 60 – emb@hthoteles.com – Fax 91 431 30 62 – www.hthoteles.com 25/50 VISA **H1**

75 rm – †135/300 € ††145/350 €, ☕ 15 €

Rest – *(closed August, Saturday, Sunday and Bank Holidays)* Carte 41/55 €

♦ Chain hotel ♦ Design ♦

The combination of a 19C building and a contemporary designer interior has created a hotel that is bold yet welcoming. Well-appointed bedrooms, each with their own computer. Modern feel to the restaurant with a predominance of grey and metallic tones.

AC Avenida de América 25/50 VISA

Cartagena 83 ✉ 28028 – Ⓜ Av. de América – ✆ 91 724 42 40 – acamerica@ac-hotels.com – Fax 91 724 42 41 – www.ac-hotels.com **J1**

145 rm – ††110/130 €, ☕ 12 €

Rest – *(coffee shop) (dinner only)*

♦ Business ♦ Chain hotel ♦ Functional ♦

Ideal for business executives and with good communications. Modern and functional with a coffee shop that is also a bar depending on the time of day.

Jardín de Recoletos VISA

Gil de Santivañes 4 ✉ 28001 – Ⓜ Serrano – ✆ 91 784 16 40 – rc@vphoteles.com – Fax 91 781 16 41 – www.vphoteles.com **I2**

43 rm ☕ – †130.51/197.66 € ††138.25/204.80 €

Rest – Menu 23 €

♦ Business ♦ Classic ♦

Attractive façade with balustraded balconies. Elegant lobby-reception area with a glazed ceiling, spacious, study-like bedrooms and a pleasant patio-terrace. Small dining room decorated with landscape-inspired murals.

NH Lagasca No smokers rest. 25/60 VISA

Lagasca 64 ✉ 28001 – Ⓜ Serrano – ✆ 91 575 46 06 – nhlagasca@nh-hotels.com – Fax 91 575 16 94 – www.nh-hotels.com **I2**

100 rm – ††128/215 €, ☕ 16 €

Rest – *(closed 24 to 30 December, 30 July-26 August, Saturday and Sunday)* Menu 18 €

♦ Business ♦ Chain hotel ♦ Functional ♦

Good and comfortable rooms in a functional hotel where great thought is given to the needs and comfort of guests. Professional management.

SPAIN

Hesperia Hermosilla without rest VISA AE
Hermosilla 23 ✉ 28001 – Ⓜ Serrano – ✆ 91 246 88 00 – hotel@hesperia-hermosilla.com – Fax 91 246 88 01 – www.hesperia-hermosilla.es
67 rm – ††80/195 €, ☕ 15 € I2
♦ Business ♦ Chain hotel ♦ Functional ♦
The interior of this early-20C building has been transformed into a hotel with a thoroughly modern ambience. Attractive glazed patio, a delightful staircase and comfortable rooms covered with wall hangings.

NH Sur without rest 25/30 VISA AE
Paseo Infanta Isabel 9 ✉ 28014 – Ⓜ Atocha – ✆ 91 539 94 00 – nhsur@nh-hotels.com – Fax 91 467 09 96 I3
68 rm – †58/136 € ††58/165 €, ☕ 13 €
♦ Business ♦ Chain hotel ♦ Functional ♦
Decor in keeping with the contemporary ethos of the NH chain. Public areas limited to a breakfast room with TV. Comfortable rooms, although the single rooms are on the small side.

Club 31 Smokers rest. 6/16 VISA AE
Alcalá 58 ✉ 28014 – Ⓜ Retiro – ✆ 91 531 00 92 – club31@club31.net – Fax 91 531 00 92 – www.club31.net I2
Rest – Carte approx. 64 €
♦ International ♦ Formal ♦
This highly respected and well-established restaurant offers a mix of traditional and modern decor, and a menu featuring a range of international cuisine. Impressive cellar.

Sanxenxo 10/12 VISA AE
José Ortega y Gasset 40 ✉ 28006 – Ⓜ Núñez de Balboa – ✆ 91 577 82 72 – combarro@combarro.com – Fax 91 435 95 12 – www.combarro.com
closed Holy Week, August and Sunday dinner J1
Rest – Carte 57/70 €
♦ Galician specialities ♦ Formal ♦
Superb setting with dining rooms laid out on two floors with a decorative emphasis on granite and wood. Traditional Galician cuisine focusing on high-quality fish and seafood.

Pedro Larumbe VISA AE
Serrano 61 (2nd floor) ✉ 28006 – Ⓜ Rubén Darío – ✆ 91 575 11 12 – info@larumbe.com – Fax 91 576 60 19 – www.larumbe.com
closed Holy Week, 15 days in August, Saturday lunch, Sunday and Bank Holidays
Rest – Carte 43/60 € I1
♦ International ♦ Retro ♦
On the top floor of a small palace, with three majestic dining rooms with personalised decor and exquisitely tasteful detail. International cuisine with a creative touch.

Goizeko Wellington – Hotel Wellington VISA AE
Villanueva 34 ✉ 28001 – Ⓜ Retiro – ✆ 91 577 01 38 – goizeko@goizekowellington.com – Fax 91 555 60 26 – www.goizekogaztelupe.com
closed Sunday and Saturday lunch in July-August I2
Rest – Carte 60/90 €
♦ Spanish ♦ Minimalist ♦
A combination of classic and modern decor and an elegant setting form the backdrop to this restaurant where the menu is a fusion of traditional and international cuisine with a creative flourish. Extensive cellar.

Sorolla – Hotel NH Sanvy P VISA AE
Hermosilla 4 ✉ 28001 – Ⓜ Serrano – ✆ 91 576 08 00 – Fax 91 575 24 43
closed August and Sunday I2
Rest – Carte 35/43 €
♦ Spanish ♦ Formal ♦
Impressive, classically furnished dining room, as well as four private rooms. Traditional cuisine complemented by grilled dishes and a fine selection of coffees and herbal teas.

XXX **Shiratori** AC P VISA MC AE ⓓ

Paseo de la Castellana 36 ✉ 28046 – Ⓜ Rubén Darío – ☎ 91 577 37 34 – jarmas@r-shiratori.com – Fax 91 577 44 55

closed Holy Week, 6 to 26 August, Sunday and Bank Holidays **I1**

Rest – Carte 42/63 €

♦ Japanese ♦ Exotic ♦

A spacious restaurant serving a selective range of Japanese specialities in a relaxed atmosphere typical of the country. A choice of menus, with dishes created in front of diners.

XXX **Castelló 9** AC ⇔10/20 VISA MC AE ⓓ

Castelló 9 ✉ 28001 – Ⓜ Príncipe de Vergara – ☎ 91 435 00 67 – Fax 91 435 91 34 – www.castello9.es

closed 3 to 10 December, Holy Week, August, Sunday and Bank Holidays

Rest – Carte 35/46 € **I2**

♦ International ♦ Formal ♦

Classic elegance in the Salamanca district. Intimate dining rooms offering an international à la carte choice plus a tasting menu featuring a variety of shared dishes.

XX **La Paloma** Smokers rest. AC ⇔8/13 VISA MC AE ⓓ

Jorge Juan 39 ✉ 28001 – Ⓜ Príncipe de Vergara – ☎ 91 576 86 92 – Fax 91 575 51 41

closed Holy Week, August, Sunday and Bank Holidays **I2**

Rest – Carte 47/53 €

♦ International ♦ Trendy ♦

A highly professional feel and superb service are the hallmarks of this restaurant attracting an elegant clientele. A dining room on two floors, where the cuisine is based around international and traditional dishes.

XX **La Torcaz** Smokers rest. AC ⇔8/12 VISA MC AE ⓓ

Lagasca 81 ✉ 28006 – Ⓜ Núñez de Balboa – ☎ 91 575 41 30 – Fax 91 431 83 88 – www.latorcaz.com

closed Holy Week, August, Sunday and Bank Holidays **I1**

Rest – Carte 38/47 €

♦ International ♦ Formal ♦

A cosy restaurant with an attractive wine display case. Fusion of modern and traditional furnishings, excellent service and an impressive wine list.

XX **Dassa Bassa** AC VISA AE ⓓ

Villalar 7 ✉ 28001 – Ⓜ Retiro – ☎ 91 576 73 97 – dassabassa@dassabassa.com – www.dassabassa.com

closed Holy Week, 14 days in August, Sunday, Monday and Bank Holidays

Rest – Carte 41/56 € *Plan II* **H2**

♦ Inventive ♦ Design ♦

Occupying what was once a charcoal factory, the Dassa Barra has a large entrance and four modern dining rooms decorated with designer features. Creative cuisine with an accent on distinctive flavours.

XX **La Miel** Smokers rest. AC VISA MC AE ⓓ

Maldonado 14 ✉ 28006 – Ⓜ Núñez de Balboa – ☎ 91 435 50 45 – manuelcoto@restaurantelamiel.com – www.restaurantelamiel.com

closed Holy Week, 21 days in August and Sunday **I1**

Rest – Carte 35/45 €

♦ International ♦ Family ♦

A traditional, comfortable restaurant run by the proprietors. Attentive service, a good menu of international dishes and an impressive wine cellar.

XX **Montana** Smokers rest. AC VISA MC AE ⓓ

Lagasca 5 ✉ 28001 – Ⓜ Retiro – ☎ 91 435 99 01 – restaurantemontana@hotmail.com – Fax 91 297 47 40 – www.restaurantemontana.es

closed Holy Week, 15 days in August and Sunday **I2**

Rest – Carte 28/45 €

♦ Spanish ♦ Minimalist ♦

This small restaurant is run by a young team with great enthusiasm. A modern feel, attentive service, and traditional cuisine enlivened with creative panache.

SPAIN

XX **Al Mounia** AC VISA MC AE

Recoletos 5 ✉ 28001 – Ⓜ Banco de España – ✆ 91 435 08 28 – almounia@terra.es – Fax 91 575 01 73

closed Holy Week, August, Sunday and Monday **I2**

Rest – Carte 21/33 €

♦ North African ♦ Exotic ♦

An exotic restaurant near the National Archaeological Museum. Moroccan decor featuring sculpted wood, moulded plasterwork, attractive rugs and typical low tables. Traditional dishes from North Africa.

XX **Teatriz** AC ⇔10/40 VISA MC AE ⓓ

Hermosilla 15 ✉ 28001 – Ⓜ Serrano – ✆ 91 577 53 79 – Fax 91 431 69 10 – www.grupovips.com **I2**

Rest – Carte 33/46 €

♦ International ♦ Design ♦

In the stalls of the former Teatro Beatriz. A tapas bar near the entrance and a dining area and a bar on the stage, all with attractive Modernist décor.

XX **Nicolás** Smokers rest. AC ⇔4/14 VISA MC AE ⓓ

Villalar 4 ✉ 28001 – Ⓜ Retiro – ✆ 91 431 77 37 – resnicolas@hotmail.com – Fax 91 577 86 65

closed Holy Week, August, Sunday and Monday **I2**

Rest – Carte 23/40 €

♦ Spanish ♦ Minimalist ♦

Modern decor provides the backdrop for this restaurant with a minimalist air. The traditional menu is a little limited, although compensated by the good choice of home cooking. Select wine list.

XX **El Chiscón de Castelló** Smokers rest. AC ⇔6/20 VISA MC AE

Castelló 3 ✉ 28001 – Ⓜ Príncipe de Vergara – ✆ 91 575 56 62 – Fax 91 575 56 05 – www.elchiscon.com

closed August, Sunday and Bank Holidays **I2**

Rest – Carte 27/44 €

♦ Spanish ♦ Friendly ♦

Hidden behind the typical façade is a warmly decorated interior that gives it the feel of a private house, particularly on the first floor. Well-priced traditional cuisine.

XX **El Asador de Aranda** No smokers rest. AC ⇔8/12 VISA MC AE ⓓ

Diego de León 9 ✉ 28006 – Ⓜ Núñez de Balboa – ✆ 91 563 02 46 – Fax 91 556 62 02 – www.asadordearanda.com

closed 7 August to 3 September and Sunday dinner **I1**

Rest – Carte 28/36 €

♦ Roast lamb ♦ Rustic ♦

Classic Castilian décor and a wood-fired oven for roasting meat. The main dining room with stained-glass windows is on the 1st floor.

X **Pelotari** AC ⇔15/20 VISA MC AE ⓓ

Recoletos 3 ✉ 28001 – Ⓜ Colón – ✆ 91 578 24 97 – informacion@asador-pelotari.com – Fax 91 431 60 04 – www.asador-pelotari.com

closed Sunday **I2**

Rest – Carte 33/44 €

♦ Basque ♦ Rustic ♦

A typical Basque rotisserie run by two owners, one in the kitchen, the other front of house. Four dining rooms (two convertible into private dining areas), where the traditional decor is typical of this region in the north of the country.

X **La Castela** Smokers rest. AC ⇔12 VISA MC AE ⓓ

Doctor Castelo 22 ✉ 28009 – Ⓜ Ibiza – ✆ 91 574 00 15 – info@lacasela.com – www.lacastela.com

closed Holy Week, August and Sunday **J2**

Rest – Carte approx. 39 €

♦ Spanish ♦ Formal ♦

La Castela perpetuates the tradition of historic Madrid taverns, with its tapas bar at the entrance. Simple but attractive traditional dining room with a similarly conservative menu.

Juan Bravo 25
Smokers rest.

Juan Bravo 25 ✉ 28006 – Ⓜ Núñez de Balboa – ✆ 91 411 60 25 – jmb@juanbravo25.com – Fax 91 411 82 31 – www.juanbravo25.com
closed 15 to 30 August and Sunday **J1**

Tapa 2.95 € **Ración** approx. 12.50 €

♦ Spanish ♦ Tapas bar ♦

A large cervecería located on a mezzanine with a central bar overflowing with pinchos and tapas in true Basque style. The adjoining dining room offers traditional menu choices.

José Luis
Smokers rest.

General Oráa 5 ✉ 28006 – Ⓜ Gregorio Marañón – ✆ 91 561 64 13 – joseluis@nexo.es **I1**

Tapa 2 € **Ración** approx. 12 €

♦ Spanish ♦ Tapas bar ♦

A well-known establishment with a wide range of canapés, Basque-style tapas and servings of different dishes in elegant surroundings with traditional décor.

Mesón Cinco Jotas

Puigcerdá ✉ 28001 – Ⓜ Serrano – ✆ 91 575 41 25 – m5jjorgejuan@osborne.es – Fax 91 575 56 35 – www.mesoncincojotas.com **I2**

Tapa 3.50 € **Ración** approx. 9 €

♦ Spanish ♦ Tapas bar ♦

Renowned for the high quality of its Iberian products, including tapas and raciones, this typical eatery has a splendid terrace and three cosy dining rooms arranged on three floors.

Tasca La Farmacia
No smokers rest.

Diego de León 9 ✉ 28006 – Ⓜ Núñez de Balboa – ✆ 91 564 86 52 – Fax 91 556 62 02
closed 17 July-13 August and Sunday **I1**

Tapa 2.25 € **Ración** approx. 4.60 €

♦ Codfish specialities ♦ Tapas bar ♦

A traditional establishment with a beautiful tiled bar. Don't miss the opportunity to try the tapas or larger servings of salt-cod dishes.

Mesón Cinco Jotas

Serrano 118 ✉ 28006 – Ⓜ Núñez de Balboa – ✆ 91 563 27 10 – m5jserrano@osborne.es – Fax 91 561 32 84 – www.mesoncincojotas.com **I1**

Tapa 3.50 € **Ración** approx. 9 €

♦ Spanish ♦ Tapas bar ♦

Contemporary in feel, with a good selection of tapas, toasts and raciones, with the emphasis on Iberian pork products. Pleasant dining room.

El Barril

Goya 86 ✉ 28009 – Ⓜ Goya – ✆ 91 578 39 98 – www.elbarrildegoya.com
closed Sunday dinner **J2**

Ración approx. 24 €

♦ Seafood ♦ Tapas bar ♦

A seafood restaurant with an impressive bar displaying an extensive selection of high-quality products. Good menu choices in the dining room to the rear.

José Luis
Smokers rest.

Serrano 89 ✉ 28006 – Ⓜ Gregorio Marañón – ✆ 91 563 09 58 – joseluis@nexo.es – Fax 91 563 31 02 **I1**

Tapa 2 € **Ración** approx. 12 €

♦ Spanish ♦ Tapas bar ♦

Two restaurants in one with two entrances, two bars and two dining rooms. Pleasant summer terrace. Basque tapas and raciones, plus a small menu.

Taberna de la Daniela
Smokers rest.

General Pardiñas 21 ✉ 28001 – Ⓜ Goya – ✆ 91 575 23 29 – Fax 91 435 24 22 **J2**

Tapa 2.35 € **Ración** approx. 9.80 €

♦ Spanish ♦ Tapas bar ♦

A typical tavern in the Salamanca district, with an azulejo-adorned façade and several dining rooms in which to enjoy a range of tapas and raciones. An address famous for its cocido madrileño, the city's typical stew.

SPAIN

El Barril AE VISA MC AE

Don Ramón de la Cruz 91 ✉ 28006 – Ⓜ Manuel Becerra – ✆ 91 401 33 05 – www.elbarrilalcantara.com **J1**

Ración approx. 22 €

◆ Seafood ◆ Tapas bar ◆

A seafood restaurant renowned for its high-quality cuisine and excellent service. Eat in the bar-cervecería or in one of the two dining rooms.

Jurucha Smokers rest.

Ayala 19 ✉ 28001 – Ⓜ Serrano – ✆ 91 575 00 98 – jurucha@telefonica.net closed August, Sunday and Bank Holidays **I1**

Tapa 1.60 € **Ración** approx. 4 €

◆ Spanish ◆ Tapas bar ◆

A must on any tapas tour of Madrid. Delicious Basque-style tapas and pinchos, including omelettes and croquettes.

ARGÜELLES *Plan IV*

Sofitel Madrid Plaza de España without rest

Tutor 1 ✉ 28008 – Ⓜ Ventura Rodríguez – ✆ 91 541 98 80 – h1320@accor.com – Fax 91 542 57 36 – www.sofitel.com VISA MC AE **K3**

96 rm – 🚹276 € 🚹🚹281 €, ☕ 23 € – 1 suite

◆ Business ◆ Chain hotel ◆ Cosy ◆

Well refurbished with high-quality furnishings in the bedrooms and marble fittings in the bathrooms. A perfect balance of elegance and comfort.

El Molino de los Porches VISA MC AE

Paseo Pintor Rosales 1 ✉ 28008 – Ⓜ Ventura Rodríguez – ✆ 91 548 13 36 – Fax 91 547 97 61 – www.asadorelmolino.com closed Sunday dinner and Monday **K3**

Rest – Carte approx. 40 €

◆ Grills ◆ Rustic ◆

A hotel located in the Parque del Oeste with several lounges and a pleasant glazed-in terrace. The meat produced from the wood-fired oven and charcoal grill is delicious.

CHAMBERÍ *Plan IV*

AC Santo Mauro No smokers rest. 25/50

Zurbano 36 ✉ 28010 – Ⓜ Alonso Martínez – ✆ 91 319 69 00 – santo-mauro@ac-hotels.com – Fax 91 308 54 77 VISA MC AE **L3**

43 rm – 🚹261/366 € 🚹🚹315/441 €, ☕ 27 € – 8 suites

Rest *Santo Mauro* – Carte approx. 73 €

◆ Palace ◆ Grand Luxury ◆ Classic ◆

A hotel in a beautiful French-style palace with garden situated in a classy district of Madrid. Elegant with touches of luxury in the rooms. The restaurant is in a beautiful library-room which lends distinction to the food.

Intercontinental Madrid 25/450

Paseo de la Castellana 49 ✉ 28046 – Ⓜ Gregorio Marañón – ✆ 91 700 73 00 – madrid@ichotelsgroup.com – Fax 91 319 58 53 – www.madrid.intercontinental.com VISA MC AE **L3**

279 rm – 🚹🚹199/259 €, ☕ 28 € – 28 suites

Rest – Carte 52/69 €

◆ Luxury ◆ Classic ◆

Superb facilities, including an elegant domed lobby with a profusion of marble, a pleasant interior patio-terrace, and bedrooms with the Intercontinental's usual high levels of comfort. A refined menu of international cuisine is the order of the day in the restaurant adjoining the lobby-bar.

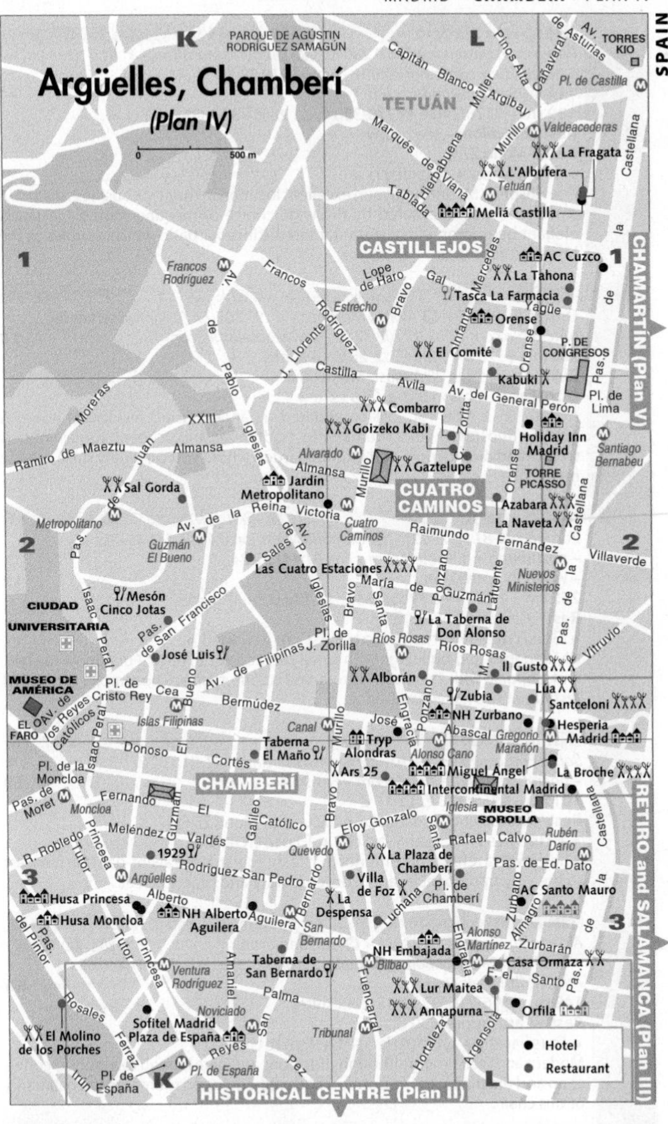

Miguel Ángel

25/200 VISA

Miguel Ángel 31 ✉ 28010 – Ⓜ Gregorio Marañón – ☎ 91 442 00 22 – comercial.hma@oh-es.com – Fax 91 442 53 20 – www.miguelangelhotel.com

243 rm – 350 €, ☕ 24 € – 20 suites – **Rest *Arco*** – Carte 44/52 € **L3**

◆ Luxury ◆ Classic ◆

A prestigious and up-to-date hotel located in the Castellana district of Madrid. Well-appointed rooms and large public areas with classically elegant decor. Superb restaurant with a terrace for the summer months.

SPAIN

Hesperia Madrid

Paseo de la Castellana 57 ✉ 28046 – Ⓜ Gregorio Marañón – ☎ 91 210 88 00 – hotel@hesperia-madrid.com – Fax 91 210 88 99 – www.hesperia-madrid.com **L2**

139 rm – 170/340 € 170/390 €, 28 € – 32 suites

Rest *Santceloni* – see below

Rest – Menu 27 €

♦ Business ♦ Modern ♦

The Hespería Madrid enjoys an excellent location in the city's business district. A small lobby, compensated by the wide choice of meeting rooms. Classically elegant bedrooms, plus a restaurant in the interior patio which doubles as the breakfast room.

Orfila

No smokers rest. 25/80

Orfila 6 ✉ 28010 – Ⓜ Alonso Martínez – ☎ 91 702 77 70 – inforeservas@hotelorfila.com – Fax 91 702 77 72 – www.hotelorfila.com **L3**

28 rm – 320 € 390 €, 25 € – 4 suites

Rest – *(closed 4 to 28 August)* Menu 80 €

♦ Palace ♦ Luxury ♦ Classic ♦

A hotel in a late 19C palace situated in an exclusive residential zone. A grand atmosphere and rooms with traditional and elegant furnishings. A welcoming dining room and interior garden where you can enjoy the à la carte menu.

NH Zurbano

25/180

Zurbano 79-81 ✉ 28003 – Ⓜ Gregorio Marañón – ☎ 91 441 45 00 – nhzurbano@nh-hotels.com – Fax 91 441 32 24 – www.nh-hotels.com **L2**

255 rm – 65/149 € 65/164 €, 14.50 € – 11 suites

Rest – Carte approx. 35 €

♦ Business ♦ Chain hotel ♦ Functional ♦

Divided into two buildings with separate facilities in each. Functional in style, and popular with business visitors and sports teams. The simple, functional restaurant has its own entrance.

NH Embajada

25/60

Santa Engracia 5 ✉ 28010 – Ⓜ Alonso Martínez – ☎ 91 594 02 13 – nhembajada@nh-hotels.com – Fax 91 447 33 12 **L3**

101 rm – 59/178 €, 14 €

Rest – *(closed August, Saturday and Sunday)* Menu 25 €

♦ Business ♦ Chain hotel ♦ Functional ♦

A hotel with a refurbished interior that leans towards the avant-garde in contrast to the very traditional façade. Contemporary and practical feel.

NH Alberto Aguilera

Smokers rest. 25/100

Alberto Aguilera 18 ✉ 28015 – Ⓜ San Bernardo – ☎ 91 446 09 00 – nhalbertoaguilera@nh-hotels.com – Fax 91 446 09 04 – www.nh-hotels.com **K3**

148 rm – 63/166 €, 15 € – 5 suites

Rest – Carte approx. 30 €

♦ Business ♦ Chain hotel ♦ Functional ♦

Modern and welcoming although the public areas are limited to a lounge-coffee shop and the dining room. Comfort and well-equipped rooms are the hallmarks of this chain.

Tryp Alondras

José Abascal 8 ✉ 28003 – Ⓜ Alonso Cano – ☎ 91 447 40 00 – tryp.alondras@solmelia.com – Fax 91 593 88 00 – www.solmelia.com **L2**

72 rm – 85/130 €, 9.50 €

Rest – *(coffee shop) (dinner only)*

♦ Business ♦ Chain hotel ♦ Classic ♦

A friendly hotel with a small lobby-reception and a minimalist modern cafeteria which is in contrast to the old-style, traditional feel of the bedrooms.

XXXX ✿✿ **Santceloni** – Hotel Hesperia Madrid A/C ⇔7/20 VISA MC AE D

Paseo de la Castellana 57 ✉ 28046 – Ⓜ Gregorio Marañón – ✆ 91 210 88 40 – santceloni@hesperia-madrid.com – Fax 91 210 88 92 – www.restaurantesantceloni.com

closed Holy Week, August, Saturday lunch, Sunday and Bank Holidays

Rest – Carte 95/130 € **L2**

Spec. San Pedro con puré de coliflor y escabeche de piña y menta. Jarrete de ternera blanca con puré de patata. Sorpresas de fruta de la pasión.

♦ Inventive ♦ Minimalist ♦

An extraordinary culinary experience. An elegant modern dining room on two levels where the service is understandably impeccable. The kitchen is visible from the hotel's lounges.

XXXX ✿✿ **La Broche** No smokers rest. A/C VISA MC AE D

Miguel Ángel 29 ✉ 28010 – Ⓜ Gregorio Marañón – ✆ 91 399 34 37 – info@labroche.com – Fax 91 399 37 78 – www.labroche.com

closed Holy Week, August, Saturday and Sunday **L3**

Rest – Menu 85 € – Carte 66/84 €

Spec. Puntas de espárragos verdes y blancos con perrechicos, jugo de pimiento y emulsión de tortilla (Spring). Tacos de merluza asados en picada tradicional de frutos secos y patatas guisadas (March-June). Lascas de roast beef y morcilla, ensalada de anisados y helado de foie-gras (Spring).

♦ Inventive ♦ Minimalist ♦

A spacious restaurant with bare white walls which allow all attention to be focused on the very innovative cuisine.

XXXX **Las Cuatro Estaciones** A/C VISA MC AE D

General Ibáñez de Íbero 5 ✉ 28003 – Ⓜ Guzmán El Bueno – ✆ 91 553 63 05 – Fax 91 535 05 23

closed Holy Week, August, Saturday lunch and Sunday **K2**

Rest – Carte 50/71 €

♦ International ♦ Formal ♦

This original restaurant recalls the decorative trends of the 1980s. The carpeted dining room is laid out on several levels. Private bar and well-balanced cellar.

XXX **Il Gusto** A/C VISA MC AE D

Espronceda 27 ✉ 28003 – Ⓜ Alonso Cano – ✆ 91 535 39 02 – Fax 91 535 08 61 – www.restauranteilgusto.com **L2**

Rest – Carte 32/46 €

♦ Italian ♦ Design ♦

Discover the delicious nuances of Italian cuisine in this modern restaurant with an entrance hall and elegant restaurant, where the decor is a combination of wood and marble.

XXX **Annapurna** A/C VISA MC AE D

Zurbano 5 ✉ 28010 – Ⓜ Alonso Martínez – ✆ 91 319 87 16 – info@annapurnarestaurante.com – Fax 91 308 32 49 – www.annapurnarestaurante.com

closed Saturday lunch, Sunday and Bank Holidays **L3**

Rest – Carte 26/36 €

♦ Indian ♦ Exotic ♦

A restaurant with a bar for a pre-dinner drink, and a spacious dining room with views of one private and one inner garden. Colourful and exotic dishes including tasting menus, all evoking the diversity of Indian cuisine.

XXX **Lur Maitea** A/C VISA MC AE D

Fernando el Santo 4 ✉ 28010 – Ⓜ Alonso Martínez – ✆ 91 308 03 05 – alex@lurmaitearestaurante.com – Fax 91 391 38 21 – www.lurmaitearestaurante.com

closed Holy Week, August and Sunday **L3**

Rest – Carte 43/56 €

♦ Basque ♦ Formal ♦

Lur Maitea has become one of Madrid's most respected addresses. Elegant dining room with a parquet floor and decor influenced by varying shades of blue. Contemporary Basque cuisine.

SPAIN

XX **Alborán** AC 10/30 VISA MC AE

Ponzano 39-41 ✉ 28003 – Ⓜ Alonso Cano – ✆ 91 399 21 50 – alboran@alboran-rest.com – Fax 91 399 21 50 – www.alboran-rest.com
closed Sunday dinner L2
Rest – Carte 28/40 €
♦ Spanish ♦ Rustic ♦
A coffee shop with tapas near the entrance and two dining areas with high-quality furnishings. Decor of a maritime theme with wooden floors and walls.

XX **Casa Ormaza** Smokers rest. AC VISA MC AE

Zurbano 13 ✉ 28010 – Ⓜ Alonso Martínez – ✆ 91 319 88 48 – casaormaza@hotmail.com L3
Rest – Carte 33/44 €
♦ Spanish ♦ Formal ♦
A private bar at the entrance in addition to the pleasant dining room with various sections, traditional furniture, a slate floor and ochre-coloured decor.

XX **La Plaza de Chamberí** AC VISA MC AE

pl. de Chamberí 10 ✉ 28010 – Ⓜ Iglesia – ✆ 91 446 06 97 – Fax 91 594 21 20 – www.restaurantelaplazadechamberi.com
closed Sunday L3
Rest – Carte 33/37 €
♦ Spanish ♦ Formal ♦
A well-established, colourful local restaurant, with an old-style dining room laid out on two levels. The menu here is dominated by traditional recipes.

XX **Lúa** Smokers rest. AC VISA MC AE

Zurbano 85 ✉ 28003 – Ⓜ Gregorio Marañón – ✆ 91 395 28 53
closed 15 to 30 August and Sunday L2
Rest – *(set menu only)* Menu 35 €
♦ Inventive ♦ Cosy ♦
A small restaurant with a young and lively atmosphere and a dining room split into three sections. The cuisine here is based around a daily tasting-style menu with a creative, contemporary slant.

X **Villa de Foz** Smokers rest. AC 15 VISA MC AE

Gonzalo de Córdoba 10 ✉ 28010 – Ⓜ Bilbao – ✆ 91 446 89 93 – www.villadefoz.es
closed August and Sunday L3
Rest – Carte 30/38 €
♦ Galician specialities ♦ Trendy ♦
Good traditional Galician cuisine in a modern dining room. The menu is limited but the food is of very high quality.

X **Ars 25** AC VISA MC AE

Viriato 25 ✉ 28010 – Ⓜ Iglesia – ✆ 91 593 80 44 – restars25@yahoo.es
closed Holy Week, August, Sunday and Monday L3
Rest – Carte 44/50 €
♦ Inventive ♦ Trendy ♦
Enthusiastically run by its two young owners, Ars 25 occupies a former print works, which gives it its somewhat impersonal atmosphere. Creative cuisine.

Mesón Cinco Jotas AC VISA MC AE

Paseo de San Francisco de Sales 27 ✉ 28003 – Ⓜ Guzmán El Bueno – ✆ 91 544 01 89 – m5jsfsales@osborne.es – Fax 91 549 06 51 – www.mesoncincojotas.com K2
Tapa 3.50 € **Ración** approx. 9 €
♦ Spanish ♦ Tapas bar ♦
In the style of this chain with two areas where you can have a single dish or eat à la carte. Also a variety of tapas, fine hams and pork products.

Zubia Smokers rest. AC

Espronceda 28 ✉ 28003 – Ⓜ Ríos Rosas – ✆ 91 441 04 32 – info@restaurantezubia.com – Fax 91 441 10 43 – www.restaurantezubia.com
closed Holy Week, 15 days in August, Saturday lunch and Sunday L2
Tapa 1.50 € **Ración** approx. 10 €
♦ Spanish ♦ Tapas bar ♦
Enjoy a good choice of tapas and raciones standing at the Zubia's bar, or seated at the small number of adjoining tables or in the small interior dining room.

José Luis Smokers rest.

Paseo de San Francisco de Sales 14 ✉ 28003 – Ⓜ Islas Filipinas – ✆ 91 441 20 43 – joseluis@nexo.es **K2**

Tapa 2.40 € **Ración** approx. 10 €

◆ Spanish ◆ Tapas bar ◆

One of the more simple establishments in this well-known chain. A variety of Basque-style tapas and larger portions of dishes. Also a terrace.

La Taberna de Don Alonso Smokers rest.

Alonso Cano 64 ✉ 28003 – Ⓜ Ríos Rosas – ✆ 91 533 52 49

closed 23 July-21 August, Sunday dinner and Monday **L2**

Tapa 2 € **Ración** approx. 11 €

◆ Spanish ◆ Tapas bar ◆

A tavern with a selection of Basque-style tapas and a blackboard listing tapas prepared to order and larger servings of dishes available. Wine by the glass.

Taberna El Maño Smokers rest.

Vallehermoso 59 ✉ 28015 – Ⓜ Canal – ✆ 91 448 40 35

closed 1 to 7 January, Holy Week, 6 August-6 September, Sunday dinner and Monday **K3**

Tapa 3 € **Ración** approx. 12 €

◆ Spanish ◆ Tapas bar ◆

An old-fashioned, typical eatery with a bullfighting-inspired decor. A wide choice of pinchos, tapas and raciones created from high-quality ingredients.

1929 Smokers rest.

Rodríguez San Pedro 66 ✉ 28015 – Ⓜ Argüelles – ✆ 91 549 91 16 – www.taberna1929madrid.com

closed Sunday and August **K3**

Tapa 2.75 € **Ración** approx. 7.50 €

◆ Spanish ◆ Tapas bar ◆

A rustic ambience pervades this bar-restaurant run by its owner. Busy bar, a few barrels doubling as tables and two dining rooms in which to enjoy the chef's specialities.

CASTILLEJOS and CUATRO CAMINOS *Plan IV*

Meliá Castilla 25/800

Capitán Haya 43 ✉ 28020 – Ⓜ Cuzco – ✆ 91 567 50 00 – melia.castilla@solmelia.com – Fax 91 567 50 51 – www.meliacastilla.solmelia.com **L1**

904 rm – ††140/350 €, ☕ 21 € – 12 suites

Rest *L'Albufera* and ***La Fragata*** – see below

◆ Business ◆ Chain hotel ◆ Modern ◆

The main selling-points of this macro-hotel are its extensive public areas, large auditorium, numerous function rooms for banquets and conferences, and elegant, classically designed bedrooms.

AC Cuzco No smokers rest. 25/130

Paseo de la Castellana 133 ✉ 28046 – Ⓜ Cuzco – ✆ 91 556 06 00 – reservas.accuzco@ac-hotels.com – Fax 91 556 03 72 – www.ac-hotels.com **L1**

315 rm – ††93.46/225 €, ☕ 19 € – 4 suites

Rest – Carte approx. 45 €

◆ Business ◆ Functional ◆

Completely renovated in line with the comfort, design and contemporary feel of the AC chain. Well-appointed bedrooms.

Holiday Inn Madrid 25/400

pl. Carlos Trías Beltrán 4 (entrance by Orense 22-24) ✉ 28020 – Ⓜ Santiago Bernabeu – ✆ 91 456 80 00 – tojsp.reservations@ichotelsgroup.com – Fax 91 456 80 01 – www.holiday-inn.com **L2**

280 rm – †160/200 € ††190/230 €, ☕ 20 € – 33 suites

Rest *Big Blue* – Carte 32/45 €

◆ Business ◆ Chain hotel ◆ Functional ◆

Well-located next to the Azca business district with its numerous offices and leisure facilities. Modern rooms and an extensive range of guest services. Cheerful, modernist decor in the Big Blue restaurant.

SPAIN

Orense 25/50 VISA AE

Pedro Teixeira 5 ✉ 28020 – Ⓜ Santiago Bernabeu – ✆ 91 597 15 68 – reservas@hotelorense.com – Fax 91 597 12 95 – www.hotelorense.com L1

140 rm – †190 € ††225 €, ☕ 14 €

Rest – Menu 17 €

♦ Traditional ♦ Cosy ♦

A modern hotel featuring comfortable well-appointed rooms with attractive decor. Small lounge area but a good range of meeting rooms. .

Jardín Metropolitano 25/250 VISA AE

Av. Reina Victoria 12 ✉ 28003 – Ⓜ Cuatro Caminos – ✆ 91 183 18 10 – metropolitano@vphoteles.com – Fax 91 183 18 11 – www.vphoteles.com K-L2

96 rm ☕ – †88.40/158.08 € ††102.92/197.60 € – 6 suites

Rest – Carte 32/45 €

♦ Business ♦ Classic ♦

A modern hotel occupying a building arranged around a central patio crowned by a large skylight. Classic, spacious and well-appointed bedrooms.

XXX **L'Albufera** – Hotel Meliá Castilla P VISA AE

Capitán Haya 45 ✉ 28020 – Ⓜ Cuzco – ✆ 91 567 51 97 – Fax 91 567 50 51 L1

Rest – Carte approx. 50 €

♦ Rice specialities ♦ Formal ♦

A restaurant with three attractive dining rooms and another in a conservatory in a central patio with numerous plants.

XXX **Azabara** 5/14 VISA AE

Hernani 75 ✉ 28020 – Ⓜ Nuevos Ministerios – ✆ 91 417 59 79 – gonzalezyugarte@gyu.e.telefonica.net – Fax 91 417 57 14 L2

Rest – Carte 56/67 €

♦ Spanish ♦ Retro ♦

An impeccable, elegant restaurant with traditional decor in the style of the 1920s, with a predominance of black and individual lighting on each table.

XXX **Combarro** 6/30 VISA AE

Reina Mercedes 12 ✉ 28020 – Ⓜ Alvarado – ✆ 91 554 77 84 – combarro@combarro.com – Fax 91 534 25 01 – www.combarro.com

closed Holy Week, August and Sunday dinner L2

Rest – Carte 57/70 €

♦ Galician specialities ♦ Formal ♦

Galician cooking based on quality products which are on view in the live fish and seafood display tanks. Public bar, dining room on the first floor and various rooms in the basement, all decorated and furnished with classical elegance.

XXX **La Fragata** – Hotel Meliá Castilla P VISA AE

Capitán Haya 45 ✉ 28020 – Ⓜ Cuzco – ✆ 91 567 51 96 – Fax 91 567 50 51

closed August and Bank Holidays L1

Rest – Carte 45/59 €

♦ Spanish ♦ Formal ♦

Enjoy a pre-dinner drink at La Fragata's charming bar before heading to the dining room overlooking a plant-filled patio. Traditional à la carte menu specialising in grilled fish and meat.

XXX **Goizeko Kabi** Smokers rest. VISA AE

Comandante Zorita 37 ✉ 28020 – Ⓜ Alvarado – ✆ 91 533 01 85 – Fax 91 533 02 14 – www.goizeko-gaztelupe.com

closed Sunday L2

Rest – Carte 45/58 €

♦ Basque ♦ Formal ♦

A Basque restaurant with prestige in the city. Elegant and comfortable although the tables are a little close together.

SPAIN

La Tahona No smokers rest. 20/40

Capitán Haya 21 (side) 28020 – Cuzco – 91 555 04 41 – Fax 91 556 62 02 – www.asadordearanda.com

closed 7 August to 3 September and Sunday dinner L1

Rest – Carte approx. 30 €

◆ Roast lamb ◆ Rustic ◆

The entrance bar, with its wood oven and wood-inspired craftwork, leads to various rooms with a medieval Castillian ambience. Traditionally roasted dishes, plus a good house red.

La Naveta

Hernani 75 28020 – Nuevos Ministerios – 91 417 59 79 – gonzalezyugarte@gyu.e.telefonica.net – Fax 91 417 57 14 L2

Rest – Carte 54/89 €

◆ Traditional ◆ Trendy ◆

La Naveta has a wide, elegantly laid-out tapas bar and an air-conditioned terrace-style dining room with tables on different levels and designer chairs.

Gaztelupe 4/30

Comandante Zorita 32 28020 – Alvarado – 91 534 90 28 – Fax 91 554 65 66 – www.goizeko-gaztelupe.com

closed Sunday dinner L2

Rest – Carte 33/50 €

◆ Basque ◆ Friendly ◆

A bar at the entrance, refurbished dining areas with decor in regional style, and two private rooms in the basement. An extensive menu of traditional Basque dishes.

El Comité Smokers rest.

pl. de San Amaro 8 28020 – Santiago Bernabeu – 91 571 87 11 – Fax 91 435 43 27

closed Saturday lunch and Sunday L1

Rest – Carte 40/50 €

◆ French ◆ Bistro ◆

Restaurant in a welcoming bistro-style with café-type furniture and lots of old photos on the walls. French cuisine.

Sal Gorda Smokers rest.

Beatríz de Bobadilla 9 28040 – Guzmán El Bueno – 91 553 95 06

closed August and Sunday K2

Rest – Carte approx. 32 €

◆ Spanish ◆ Formal ◆

A warm, inviting and professionally run restaurant with a regular and loyal clientele. Traditional decor with a slightly outdated feel.

Kabuki

av. Presidente Carmona 2 28020 – Santiago Bernabeu – 91 417 64 15 – Fax 91 556 02 32

closed Holy Week, 7 to 27 August, Saturday lunch, Sunday and Bank Holidays L1-2

Rest – Carte 48/61 €

◆ Japanese ◆ Minimalist ◆

An intimate Japanese restaurant with tasteful, minimalist decor. A modern terrace, in addition to a bar/kitchen serving popular dishes such as sushi.

Tasca La Farmacia No smokers rest.

Capitán Haya 19 28020 – Cuzco – 91 555 81 46 – Fax 91 556 62 02

closed 14 August-10 September and Sunday L1

Tapa 2.25 € **Ración** approx. 6 €

◆ Codfish specialities ◆ Tapas bar ◆

This charming restaurant is adorned with azulejos, stone arches, exposed brickwork, wrought-iron latticework and attractive glass in the ceiling of the dining room. Famous for its cod dishes.

CHAMARTÍN

Plan V

Puerta América
25/750 VISA

av. de América 41 ✉ 28002 – Ⓜ Cartagena – ☎ 91 744 54 00 – hotel.puertamerica@hoteles-silken.com – Fax 91 744 54 01 – www.hotelpuertamerica.com **N3**

330 rm – ††170/360 €, ☕ 25 € – 12 suites

Rest *Lágrimas Negras* – Carte 60/74 €

◆ Business ◆ Design ◆

A colourful designer hotel with the creative work of a prestigious artist displayed on each of its floors. Highly original bedrooms, plus a modern restaurant with a bar area, high ceilings and something of a New York ambience.

NH Eurobuilding
25/900 VISA

Padre Damián 23 ✉ 28036 – Ⓜ Cuzco – ☎ 91 353 73 00 – nheurobuilding@nh-hotels.com – Fax 91 345 45 76 – www.nh-hotels.com **M2**

455 rm – ††102.80/230 €, ☕ 20 € – 4 suites

Rest *Magerit* – *(closed August and Sunday)* Carte approx. 40 €

◆ Business ◆ Chain hotel ◆ Functional ◆

In keeping with the NH chain's philosophy, the rooms here are well-appointed, modern and spacious. Numerous meeting rooms and a spa complex. High-quality restaurant with a warm, traditional atmopshere.

AC Aitana
No smokers rest. VISA

Paseo de la Castellana 152 ✉ 28046 – Ⓜ Cuzco – ☎ 91 458 49 70 – aitana@ac-hotels.com – Fax 91 458 49 71 – www.ac-hotels.com **M2**

109 rm – †99/225 € ††99/246 €, ☕ 19 € – 2 suites

Rest – Carte approx. 35 €

◆ Business ◆ Chain hotel ◆ Functional ◆

The interior design and furniture here have an avant-garde feel, with a predominance of wood. Contemporary bedrooms with parquet flooring. The restaurant is used for breakfast, lunch and dinner.

Confortel Pío XII
No smokers rest. 25/350 VISA

av. Pío XII-77 ✉ 28016 – Ⓜ Pio XII – ☎ 91 387 62 00 – infopioxii@confortel.com – Fax 91 302 65 22 – www.confortelhoteles.com **N1**

214 rm – †140 € ††250 €, ☕ 14 €

Rest – Menu 22 €

◆ Business ◆ Chain hotel ◆ Modern ◆

Comfortable rooms decorated in soft tones, and with modern furnishings and wooden floors. Large, panelled meeting rooms and good facilities for disabled guests. Good restaurant, albeit lacking decoration on the walls.

NH La Habana
25/250 VISA

Paseo de la Habana 73 ✉ 28036 – Ⓜ Colombia – ☎ 91 443 07 20 – nhhabana@nh-hotels.com – Fax 91 457 75 79 – www.nh-hotels.com **M2**

155 rm – †59/158 € ††60/175 €, ☕ 15 € – 1 suite

Rest – *(closed August)* Carte 23/34 €

◆ Business ◆ Chain hotel ◆ Functional ◆

A modern hotel gearing mainly to business visitors. Comfortable guestrooms, albeit on the small side, with modern furnishings and wooden flooring.

Confortel Suites Madrid
No smokers rest. 25/350 VISA

López de Hoyos 143 ✉ 28002 – Ⓜ Alfonso XIII – ☎ 91 744 50 00 – info@confortelsuitesmadrid.com – Fax 91 415 30 73 – www.confortelhoteles.com **N3**

120 rm – ††135/350 €, ☕ 16 €

Rest – *(closed August, Saturday and Sunday)* Menu 16 €

◆ Business ◆ Chain hotel ◆ Modern ◆

A large, business-orientated hotel with reasonably spacious guestrooms, almost all with their own lounge, which are gradually being refurbished in a more contemporary style.

Chamartín
(Plan V)

● Hotel
● Restaurant

Don Pío without rest — 25/80 VISA

av. Pío XII-25 ✉ 28016 – Ⓜ Pio XII – ☎ 91 353 07 80 – hoteldonpio@ hoteldonpio.com – Fax 91 353 07 81 – www.hoteldonpio.com **N2**

41 rm – †78/145 € ††103/160 €, ☕ 13 €

◆ Business ◆ Traditional ◆ Cosy ◆

An attractive patio foyer with a classic-modern skylight which runs through the building. The bedrooms are quite large and have facilities such as hydro-massage.

SPAIN

Castilla Plaza

Paseo de la Castellana 220 ✉ 28046 – Ⓜ Plaza Castilla – ✆ 91 567 43 00 – castilla-plaza@abbahoteles.com – Fax 91 315 54 06 – www.abbacastillaplazahotel.com **M1**

181 rm – 90/250 € 125/300 €, ☕ 15 € – **Rest** – Menu 25 €

◆ Business ◆ Modern ◆

An impressive, glass-fronted building which, along with the Kio Torres, forms part of the architectural complex known as the Puerta de Europa. Comfortable, modern and with a wealth of detail. The menu in the attractively laid-out restaurant focuses on traditional cuisine.

Aristos

av. Pío XII-34 ✉ 28016 – Ⓜ Pio XII – ✆ 91 345 04 50 – hotelaristos@elchaflan.com – Fax 91 345 10 23 – www.hotelaristos.com **N1**

22 rm – 102.15 € 138.85 €, ☕ 8.75 € – 1 suite

Rest ***El Chaflán*** – see below

◆ Traditional ◆ Functional ◆

An attractive red-brick façade, functional facilities and well-appointed rooms with white wooden flooring and contemporary furnishings.

Zalacain

4/20

Álvarez de Baena 4 ✉ 28006 – Ⓜ Gregorio Marañón – ✆ 91 561 48 40 – Fax 91 561 47 32 – www.restaurantezalacain.com

closed Holy Week, August, Saturday lunch, Sunday and Bank Holidays

Rest – Menu 93 € – Carte 57/78 € **M3**

Spec. Ensalada de langostinos al estilo clásico de Zalacain. Urta a la plancha con aceite de hoja de limonero y trío de pimientos. Pichón al chocolate con especias y frutos secos.

◆ International ◆ Formal ◆

A warm and intimate setting with a keen sense of aesthetic detail. An elegant atmosphere in which to enjoy a mix of traditional and international cuisine.

Príncipe de Viana

Manuel de Falla 5 ✉ 28036 – Ⓜ Cuzco – ✆ 91 457 15 49 – principeviana@ya.com – Fax 91 457 52 83

closed August, Saturday lunch, Sunday and Bank Holidays **M2**

Rest – Carte approx. 65 €

◆ Basque ◆ Formal ◆

Well-known restaurant serving Basque-Navarrese inspired cooking. Traditional dining areas and excellent service.

El Bodegón

12/30

Pinar 15 ✉ 28006 – Ⓜ Gregorio Marañón – ✆ 91 562 88 44 – Fax 91 562 97 25

Rest – Carte 55/62 € **M3**

◆ Spanish ◆ Formal ◆

Classical design and elegance are to the fore in this restaurant set out on several levels, where the culinary emphasis is on traditional cuisine. Private bar for a pre-dinner aperitif.

El Chaflán – Hotel Aristos

av. Pío XII-34 ✉ 28016 – Ⓜ Pio XII – ✆ 91 350 61 93 – restaurante@elchaflan.com – Fax 91 345 10 23 – www.elchaflan.com

closed 15 days in August, Saturday lunch and Sunday **N1**

Rest – Menu 66 € – Carte 53/73 €

Spec. Alcachofas con castañuelas y naranja al oloroso. Atún rojo al pil-pil de tomate, cous-cous de arroz. Rissotto de hongos.

◆ Inventive ◆ Minimalist ◆

A restaurant in minimalist style which prides itself on its service. An olive tree has pride of place in the centre of the room. Interesting and innovative cuisine.

Aldaba

4/10

av. de Alberto Alcocer 5 ✉ 28036 – Ⓜ Cuzco – ✆ 91 359 73 86 – Fax 91 345 21 93

closed Holy Week, August, Saturday lunch, Sunday and Bank Holidays

Rest – Carte 40/62 € **M2**

◆ Spanish ◆ Friendly ◆

A bar near the entrance from which follows a pleasant dining room in classic-modern style. There are also private rooms. Excellent wine list.

XXX

El Olivo

General Gallegos 1 ✉ 28036 – Ⓜ Cuzco – ☎ 91 359 15 35 – bistrotelolivosl@retemail.es – Fax 91 345 91 83 – www.elolivorestaurante.com

closed 15 to 31 August, Sunday and Monday **M2**

Rest – Carte 37/63 €

♦ International ♦ Friendly ♦

Note the attractive bar, full of fino and other sherry bottles, the dining room embellished in varying shades of green, and the decorative details alluding to olive oil. Cosmopolitan, Mediterranean cuisine.

XXX

El Foque

Smokers rest.

Suero de Quiñones 22 ✉ 28002 – Ⓜ Cruz del Rayo – ☎ 91 519 25 72 – restaurante@elfoque.com – Fax 91 561 07 99 – www.elfoque.com

closed Sunday **M3**

Rest – Carte 39/42 €

♦ Codfish specialities ♦ Friendly ♦

A good location next to the National Music Auditorium. Refined dining room on two levels with maritime decor including a mast and sails. Cod specialities.

XX

Carta Marina

4/12

Padre Damián 40 ✉ 28036 – Ⓜ Cuzco – ☎ 91 458 68 26 – Fax 91 457 08 21

closed Holy Week, August and Sunday **M2**

Rest – Carte 41/55 €

♦ Galician specialities ♦ Formal ♦

A restaurant with wood decor and an attractive private bar. Pleasant dining rooms with terrace. Traditional Galician cooking.

X

Casa d'a Troya

24

Emiliano Barral 14 ✉ 28043 – Ⓜ Avenida de la Paz – ☎ 91 416 44 55 – Fax 91 416 42 80

closed 24 December-2 January, Holy Week, 15 July-August, dinner Monday to Thursday, Sunday and Bank Holidays **N3**

Rest – Carte 45/60 €

Spec. Pulpo a la gallega. Merluza a la gallega. Tarta de Santiago.

♦ Galician specialities ♦ Family ♦

A family-run restaurant offering excellent Galician food prepared in a traditionally simple way. A bar-entrance area and traditional furnishings in the dining room.

Mesón Cinco Jotas

Padre Damián 42 ✉ 28036 – Ⓜ Cuzco – ☎ 91 350 31 73 – m5jpdamian@osborne.es – Fax 91 345 79 51 – www.mesoncincojotas.com **M2**

Tapa 3.50 € **Ración** approx. 9 €

♦ Spanish ♦ Tapas bar ♦

This establishment belongs to a chain specialising in ham and other pork products. Two attractive eating areas plus a limited choice of set menus.

PARQUE FERIAL

Plan I

Sofitel Madrid Campo de las Naciones

av. de la Capital de España Madrid 10 — 50/120

✉ 28042 – Ⓜ Campo de las Naciones – ☎ 91 721 00 70 – h1606@accor.com – Fax 91 721 05 15 – www.sofitel.com **D1**

176 rm – †100/350 € ††110/350 €, ☕ 25 € – 3 suites

Rest *Mare Nostrum* – *(closed 20 to 30 December, August, Saturday and Sunday)* Carte 54/63 €

♦ Business ♦ Chain hotel ♦ Classic ♦

Close to Madrid's exhibition site. Impressive entrance area and attractive dining room in the style of an Andalucian patio. Well-appointed, comfortable guestrooms. Distinguished ambience in the Mare Nostrum restaurant, with its interesting menu.

SPAIN

Novotel Madrid Campo de las Naciones No smokers rest.
Amsterdam 3 25/200 VISA
✉ 28042 – Ⓜ Campo de las Naciones – ☎ 91 721 18 18 – h1636@accor.com – Fax 91 721 11 22 – www.novotel.com D1
240 rm – 59/224 € 59/234 €, 16 € – 6 suites
Rest ***Claravía*** – Carte approx. 40 €
♦ Business ♦ Chain hotel ♦ Functional ♦
A contemporary chain hotel near the city's exhibition area. Reasonably spacious public areas, and bedrooms with functional facilities and furnishings. Bright dining room with a terrace for the summer months.

AT BARAJAS AIRPORT

Plan I

Meliá Barajas 25/675 VISA
av. de Logroño 305 (A2 and detour to Barajas city: 15km) ✉ 28042 – Ⓜ Barajas – ☎ 91 747 77 00 – reservas.tryp.barajas@solmelia.com – Fax 91 747 87 17 – www.meliabarajas.solmelia.com D1
220 rm – 210 €, 18 € – 9 suites
Rest – Menu 27.50 €
♦ Business ♦ Chain hotel ♦ Classic ♦
Comfortable and traditional with extremely well-equipped rooms and refurbished bathrooms. A number of conference/meeting rooms around the swimming pool and garden. One dining room serves à la carte cuisine, the other food prepared on a charcoal grill.

Tryp Alameda Aeropuerto 25/280 VISA
av. de Logroño 100 (A2 and detour to Barajas city: 15km) ✉ 28042 – Ⓜ Barajas – ☎ 91 747 48 00 – tryp.alameda.aeropuerto@solmelia.com – Fax 91 747 89 28 – www.trypalamedaaeropuerto.solmelia.com D1
145 rm – 79/180 € 85/200 €, 16 € – 3 suites
Rest – Menu 24 €
♦ Business ♦ Chain hotel ♦ Modern ♦
Bright and comfortable guest rooms furnished in modern style with cherry tones and well-equipped bathrooms. The hotel's lounges and meeting areas are in the process of being refurbished.

Aparthotel Convención Barajas without rest 25
Noray 10 (A2 detour to Barajas city and industrial zone :10km) ✉ 28042 – Ⓜ Canillejas – ☎ 91 371 74 10 – aparthotel@hotel-convencion.com – Fax 91 371 79 01 – www.hotel-convencion.com VISA
95 suites – 68/144 € 68/180 €, 11.68 € D1
♦ Business ♦ Functional ♦
Two towers with few areas in common although they have spacious apartment-type bedrooms with a small sitting room and kitchen.

NH Barajas without rest VISA
Catamarán 1 (A2 detour to Barajas city and industrial zone: 10km) ✉ 28042 – ☎ 91 742 02 00 – exbarajas@nh-hoteles.es – Fax 91 741 11 00 – www.nh-hotels.com D1
173 rm – 60/128 €, 9 €
♦ Business ♦ Chain hotel ♦ Functional ♦
This budget hotel, part of the NH chain, offers reasonable comfort and value for money, although its lounges and public areas are somewhat on the small side.

Barcelona

BARCELONA

Population (est. 2006): 1 593 075 (conurbation 5 226 354) – Altitude: at sea level

R. Mattès / MICHELIN

Barcelona is perhaps the most cosmopolitan of all Spanish cities, combining the traditional and the avant-garde to create an identity which is open and welcoming. Barcelona is not only the capital of an autonomous community but a major Mediterranean port and industrial centre. It is also a Catalan town where Catalan is considered the official language along with Castilian Spanish. Barcelona is a university town and an important cultural centre with an opera house and many museums, theatres and concert halls. It has been the place of residence for many artists – Picasso, Miró, Dalí, Tàpies, the sculptor Subirachs and the architects Gaudí, Josep Lluís Sert, Bofill and Bohigas – and is now a centre for modern art, with cultural and nocturnal attractions which regularly attract millions of visitors.

The city was founded by the Phocaeans, prospered under the Romans and in the 12C became the capital of Catalonia. In the mid 19C, when the ban on building outside its fortifications was lifted, the ramparts were demolished and the city spread in an elegant town-planning grid divided by great diagonal avenues. There was a flurry of building on Montjuïc for the International Exhibition in 1929 and another surge of development took place when the Olympic Games were held in Barcelona in 1992.

WHICH DISTRICT TO CHOOSE

For **hotels** the selection is wide and varied. The most charming buildings are situated in the narrow streets of the Old Town, formerly enclosed within the city walls, an attractive location close to the harbour and the lively Barceloneta *Plan II* **H2** and Ribera *Plan II* **G1** districts. The most modern buildings are to be found in the Vila Olimpica *Plan I* **C2**. Many more hotels are located in the streets near the Passeig de Gràcia *Plan II* **E1** and the large avenues of Eixample, the districts with a formal grid plan of wide streets south and north of the Diagonal in the extended city.

As for **restaurants**, the cuisine of Catalonia in general and of Barcelona in particular is improving constantly;

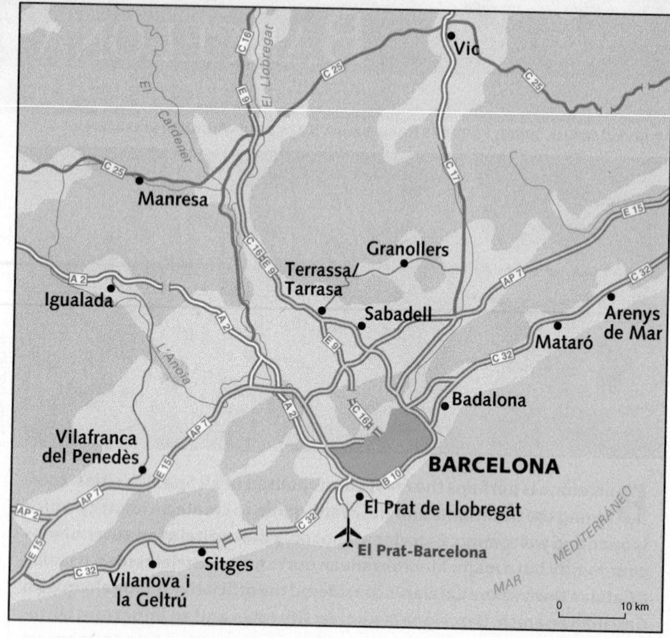

magnificent inventive dishes are often created in restaurants of rare beauty: early 20C modernist houses and more futuristic architecture.

PRACTICAL INFORMATION

ARRIVAL – DEPARTURE

Barcelona Airport – In El Prat de Llobregat, about 13 km (8 mi) southwest of the city centre. AENA ✆ 902 404 704, www.aena.es

From the airport to the city centre – By **taxi**: €15-€20 + charge for luggage. By **train**: Rodalíes/Cercanías (marked C beside Terminal A) €2.40 every 30min from 5.12am to 11.44pm. Journey time: 30min. By **Aerobús (A1)**: €3.75; every 10mins from 5.30am to 01.00am, via Sants Station, Avenida Roma/Comte d'Urgell, Passeig de Gràcia/Conseil de Cent, Plaça Catalunya. Other bus: line **46**, €1.20 (last stop Pl. España, every 30 min); line **N17**, €1.20 (last stop Pl. Catalunya, every 30 min).

Railway Station – Estació de França *Plan II* **H1** regional and long-distance services to Paris, Geneva, Zurich and Milan; trains to El Prat Airport. Estació de Sants *Plan III* **I3** Domestic and international services; trains to El Prat Airport. ✆ 902 24 02 02 (information and booking for domestic services) and ✆ 902 24 34 02 (international services); www.renfe.es

TRANSPORT

→ BUSES AND METRO

The majority of bus services operate 4.30am-11pm. The 6 metro lines operate Mon-Thu and Sun 5am-midnight (2am Fri, Sat and preceding public holidays). Single ticket €1.20; T-Día (1 day) ticket €5 to €14.20 (according to the zone), T-10

(10 trips) €6.65 to €28.80 (according to the zone), T-50/30 (50 trips in 30 days) €27.55 to €106 (according to the zone), valid for underground, bus and local trains and available from underground ticket offices, tobacco shops (*estancos*), regional train offices (FGC), Barcelona Metropolitan Transport (TMB) office and in Savings Banks (Caixas). 2-day ticket €9.20; 3-day ticket €13.20, 4-day ticket €16.80, 5-day ticket €20, monthly ticket €42.75 to €121 (according to the zone), valid for underground, bus and regional trains, available from underground ticket offices and Tourist Offices. Information ✆ 93 318 70 74; www.tmb.net

→ BARCELONA CARD

2-day €23, 3-day €28, 4-day €31, 5-day €34, valid for travelling on all Barcelona public transport plus discounts (30%-50%) on some museums, art galleries, shops, nightclubs and restaurants, available from Tourist Offices, and El Corte Inglés.

→ TAXIS

The city's black and yellow taxis are not expensive and can be hailed in the street. Minimum pick up charge is €1.95; supplementary charge between 10pm and 6am. It is customary to round up taxi fares. *Radio-Taxi* ✆ 932 250 000; *Servi-Taxi* ✆ 933 300 300; *Taxi-Radio-Móvil* ✆ 933 581 111, www.bcntaxi.com

→ TOURIST BUS

€18 official sightseeing tour (2hrs) with 3 routes (north and south of the city and Forum route) and 42 stops from 9am or 9.30am every 6 to 20min, until 7pm or 8pm according to season Ticket available from the bus and Tourist Offices.

USEFUL ADDRESSES

→ TOURIST INFORMATION

Barcelona Tourist Information, 17-S Plaza Catalunya *Plan II* **E1** ✆ 932 853 832/3/4; **Catalonia Tourist Information**, Palau Robert 107 Passeig de Gràcia *Plan III* **K2** ✆ 932 388 091/2/3; **Barcelona Airport Tourist Office** Terminal A: 934 784 704; Terminal B: 934 780 565; **Sants Station** (Hall) ✆ 932 853 832; turisme.bcn@bcn.servicom.es, www.gencat.es, www.barcelonaturisme.com, www.catalunyaturisme.com, www.tourspain.es

→ POST OFFICES

G.P.O., Plaça de Antoni López (at the end of Via Laietana) *Plan II* **G2** Mon-Sat, 8.30am-10pm; branch post offices at 282 C. Aragó *Plan III* **K1** and 54 Via Laietana *Plan II* **F2** close at 8.30pm. Opening times 9am to 4-5pm. Stamps can be bought in tobacconists *(estancos)*.

→ BANKS / CURRENCY EXCHANGE

Opening times Mon-Fri 8.30am to 2pm; Sat (Oct to May) 8.30am-12.30pm.

→ EMERGENCY

Dial ✆ **112**; for National Police: ✆ **091**; for Medical assistance and Ambulance: ✆ **061**.

BUSY PERIODS

It may be difficult to find a room at a reasonable price when special events are held in the city:

Carnival: February – Parades and fireworks.

Sant Medir: 3 March – Festival and procession in Gràcia district.

Sant Jordi: 23 April – St George's Day with bookstalls throughout the city.

Corpus Christi: June – Parades of giants and carnival figures.

Sant Joan: 23 June – St John's Day with bonfires and fireworks at night.

Assumption: 15 August – Gràcia district.

Cardona: 9-13 September – Celebration with bull-centred events.

La Mercè: 24 September – 4-day Patronal festival of Barcelona.

DIFFERENT FACETS OF THE CITY

It is possible to visit the main sights and museums in two to three days.

Barcelona Art ticket: €20. Voucher for 7 museums and art galleries, available from museums, Tourist Offices, Savings Banks.

Museums and sights are usually open from 10am to 6pm or later according to season. Some close on Mondays; others on Tuesdays.

ARTISTIC CITY – **Museu Nacional d'Art de Catalunya** *Plan I* **B3**: remarkable Romanesque and Gothic collections from many churches in Catalunya and Aragón. **Fundació Joan Miró**: over 10 000 exhibits (paintings, sculptures, drawings, collages and other graphic works) housed in a modern building in the artist's native city. **Fundació Antoni Tàpies** *Plan II* **E1**: 300 paintings and sculptures tracing the development of this local artist since 1948, housed in a Modernist building. **Museu d'Art Contemporàni de Barcelona** (MACBA) *Plan II* **E1**: works influenced by Constructivism and Abstract art, creations by experimental artists and names associated with the 1980s. **Drossanes and Museu Maritim** *Plan II* **F3**: Catalan naval history presented in an historic former shipyard building. **Museu Picasso** *Plan II* **G1**: works by Picasso presented in two Gothic palaces.

MODERNIST ARCHITECTURE – **La Sagrada Familia** *Plan III* **L1**: the unfinished church planned by Gaudí in 1883 and continued (1940-81) after his death. **Palau Güell** *Plan II* **F3**: family residence designed by Gaudí in 1889 for his patron and admirer the banker, Eusebi Güell. **Palau de la Música Catalana** *Plan II* **F1**: Barcelona's most important concert hall and the most famous work by Domenech I Montaner with lavish external mosaic decoration and an inverted internal cupola. **Passeig de Gràcia** *Plan II* **E1**: elegant street adorned with wrought-iron street lamps by Pere Falqués (1900) and the finest examples of Modernist architecture in Barcelona. **Park Güell** *Plan I* **B1**: the most famous of Gaudí's undertakings commissioned by Güell. Information telephone number of the Modernisme Route, from city of Barcelona ✆ 902 076 621 and from outside of the city ✆ +34 933 177 652; www.rutadelmodernisme.com

OLD TOWN – **Gothic City** *Plan II* **F2**: a network of streets, square and hidden corners, incorporating the **Cathedral**, many **medieval monuments** and **Roman walls**, on the site of an ancient fortified Roman village. **Santa Maria del Mar** *Plan II* **G2**: fine example of Catalan Gothic, built in the 14C by local sailors.

LOCAL COLOUR – **La Rambla** *Plan II* **F2**: the most famous street in Barcelona, in five different sections, where a colourful crowd of locals, tourists and down-and-outs strolls along beneath the plane trees at all hours of the day, passing the bird- and flower-sellers and the news-stands which sell papers and magazines in every language. **Plaça Reial** *Plan II* **F2**: vast pedestrian-only square shaded by palm trees and lined with cafés and neo-Classical buildings (19C); central fountain flanked by lamp-posts designed by Gaudí.

GOURMET TREATS

In Barcelona going out for **tapas** *(ir de tapeo)* is as popular as elsewhere in Spain; hundreds of bars throughout the city serve a **tapa** – small portions of a variety of savoury dishes served as appetizers – accompanied by a draught beer *(una caña)* or a small glass of wine or sherry *(una copa de fino)*. Barcelona has a long gastronomic tradition, more influenced by France and Italy than other regions. The typical dish is **escudella i carn d'olla**, once eaten on a daily basis but now not so frequent; it consists of two courses *(vuelcos)*: a thin noodle and rice soup and then the vegetables and meat, inlcuding the famous *pilota*, a ball made from minced meat, parsley, breadcrumbs and egg. Other specialities of Barcelona are **fideos a la cazuela** (noodles cooked in an earthenware dish), **habas a la catalana** (broad beans Catalonia style) in which the beans are prepared with herbs and spices and **butifarra** (sausages).

For dessert there is **crema catalana**, similar to **natillas** (a custard covered with a layer of caramel). The most traditional sweets are cakes prepared for various feast days: **pa de pessic** and **coques** for St John's Eve, **panellets**, made from almonds and pine nuts in November and **mel i mató** with cottage cheese.

SHOPPING

Department stores are usually open 10am-8.30pm. Smaller shops and boutiques open 10am-2pm and 5-8pm. The majority of shops close on Sundays.

Between **Plaça Catalunya** *Plan II* **E1** and **C. Portaferrisso** *Plan II* **F2** and along **Av. Portal de l'Angel** *Plan II* **F3**: two department stores and many shops selling fashion, accessories and other articles. **Eixample** *Plan III* **K1**: select fashion and jewellery shops. **Passeig de Gràcia** *Plan II* **E1**: shopping arcades. **Diagonal** *Plan II* **K1**: two department stores and the most famous **designer boutiques** in the city.

MARKETS – Boquería Market *Plan II* **F2**: a succession of stalls selling fresh vegetables, meat and fish, as well as bars for a bite to eat or a drink. **Mercat de les Encants** *Plan I* **C2**: a flea market selling all kinds of new, old and even antique articles (Mon, Wed, Fri-Sat, 8am-7pm). **Mercat de Sant Antoni** *Plan III* **J2**: another flea market (Mon, Wed, Fri-Sat, 8am-7pm); on Sunday mornings: old books, collector cards, movie posters and records.

ENTERTAINMENT

The *Guía del Ocio*, a weekly publication containing a list of every cultural event in the city, is on sale at newspaper stands. The city airport and tourist offices supply a full range of booklets and leaflets produced by the Generalitat de Catalunya's Department of Industry, Commerce and Tourism.

Gran Teatre de Liceu *Plan II* **F2** – The opera house, rebuilt in 1994 following a fire.

Palau de la Música Catalana *Plan II* **F1**; **Auditorio** *Plan I* **C2** – Barcelona's biggest concert halls.

Palau Sant Jordi *Plan I* **B3**; **Velódromo de Horta** *Plan I* **C2**; **Plaza de Toros Monumental** *Plan III* **L1**; **Sot del Migdia** *Plan I* **B3** – Venues for major pop and rock concerts.

Plaza de Toros Monumental *Plan III* **L1** – Bullfights on Sunday afternoons; reservations ✆ 934 533 821; Fax 934 516 998 (11am-2pm and 4-8pm); www.torosbarcelona.com; www.mundotoro.com; www.ticketstoro.com; www.tauroentrada.com

NIGHTLIFE

The district south of **Av. Diagonal** between **C. Pau Claris** and **C. Aribau** *Plan III* **K2** abounds in bars, cafés, clubs and discotheques, which cater to all tastes with a variety of styles of music. There are more nightspots north of **Av. Diagoal**, in **C. Santaló** and around **Plaça Francesc Macià** *Plan III* **J2**. The streets of **C. Aribau** and **C. Muntaner** *Plan III* **J1** are also very lively at night. The district of **Av. de Tibidabo** *Plan I* **B1** *(terminus of the Tramvia blau)* provides a more relaxed environment which is popular in summer. There are several small nightclubs and outdoor cafés in the squares in the **Gràcia** district *Plan III* **K1**. The **Spanish Village** *(Poble Espanyol)* on Montjuïc is a striking and unique location and there is a good selection of bars with music and discotheques in the Olympic Village in **Poble Nou** *Plan I* **D2**.

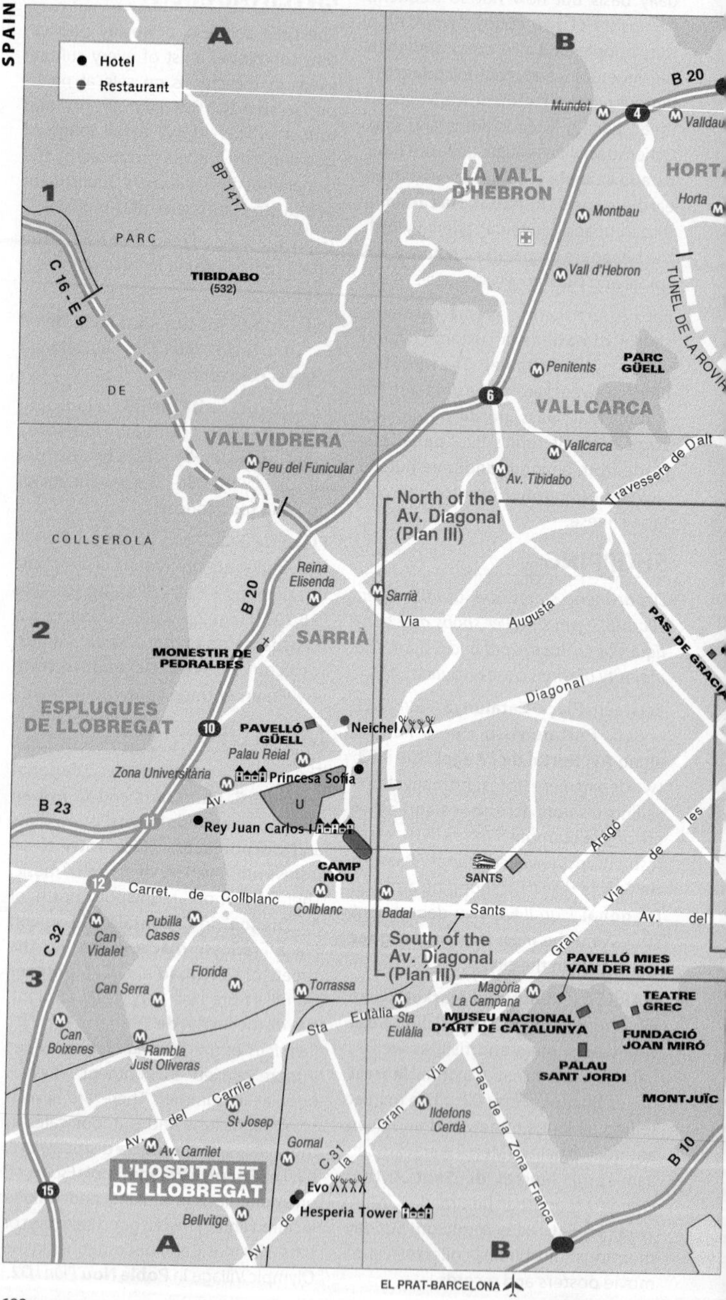

● Hotel
● Restaurant

A
B
1
2
3

B 20
Mundet
4
Valldaura
HORTA
Horta
LA VALL D'HEBRON
Montbau
Vall d'Hebron
TÚNEL DE LA ROVIRA
Penitents
PARC GÜELL
VALLCARCA
6
Vallcarca
Av. Tibidabo
Travessera de Dalt

BP 1417
PARC
TIBIDABO
(532)
C 16 - E 9
DE
VALLVIDRERA
Peu del Funicular
COLLSEROLA

North of the Av. Diagonal (Plan III)

Reina Elisenda
Sarrià
Via Augusta
B 20
SARRIÀ
PAS. DE GRACIA
MONESTIR DE PEDRALBES
Diagonal
ESPLUGUES DE LLOBREGAT
10
PAVELLÓ GÜELL
Neichel
Palau Reial
Zona Universitària
Princesa Sofía
Av.
U
B 23
11
Rey Juan Carlos I

CAMP NOU
SANTS
Aragó
Gran Via de les
12
Carret. de Collblanc
Collblanc
Badal
Sants
Av. del
C 32
Can Vidalet
Pubilla Cases
South of the Av. Diagonal (Plan III)
PAVELLÓ MIES VAN DER ROHE
Florida
Torrassa
Magòria La Campana
TEATRE GREC
Can Serra
Sta Eulàlia
Sta Eulàlia
MUSEU NACIONAL D'ART DE CATALUNYA
Can Boixeres
Rambla Just Oliveras
FUNDACIÓ JOAN MIRÓ
PALAU SANT JORDI
Gran Via
Pas. de la Zona Franca
MONTJUÏC
Av. del Carrilet
St Josep
Ildefons Cerdà
Av. Carrilet
Gornal
C 31
B 10
L'HOSPITALET DE LLOBREGAT
Evo
15
Hesperia Tower
Bellvitge
Av. de la Gran Via
A
B
EL PRAT-BARCELONA

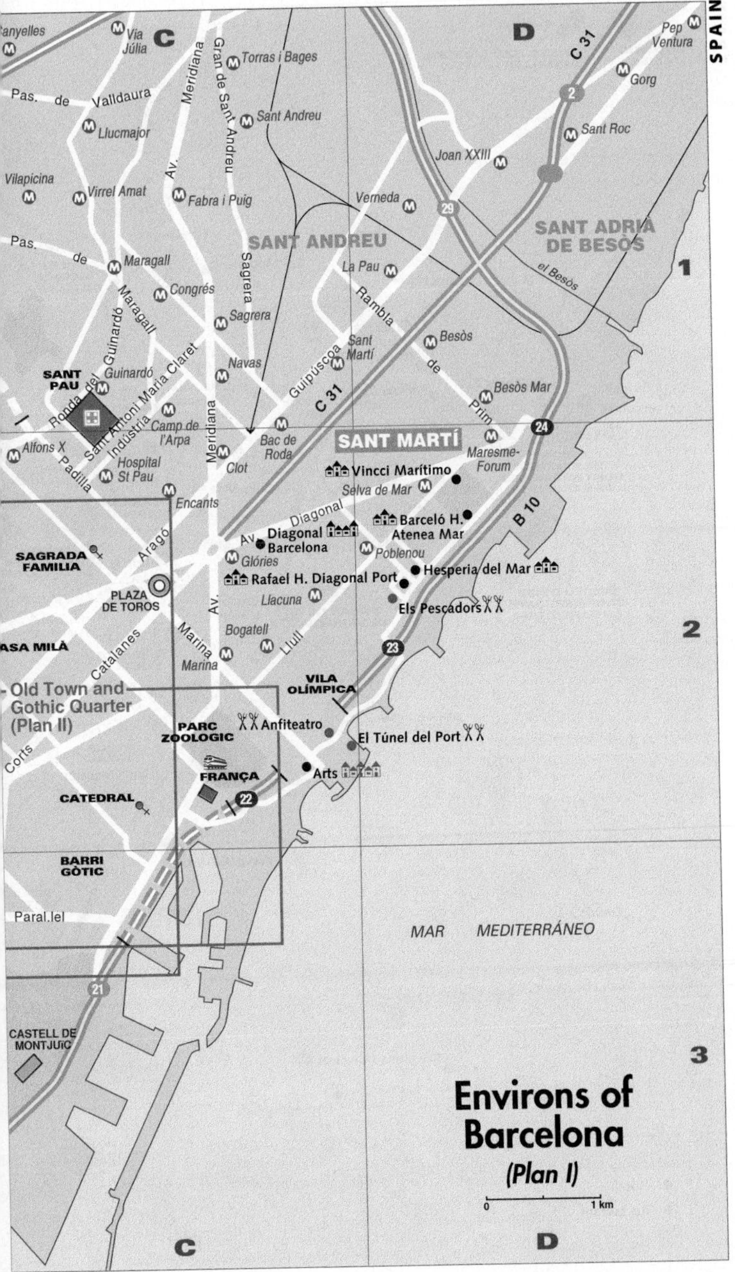
C
D
Via Júlia
Torras i Bages
Pep Ventura
Gorg
Pas. de Valldaura
Meridiana
Gran de Sant Andreu
Sant Andreu
Llucmajor
Sant Roc
Joan XXIII
Vilapicina
Virrel Amat
Av.
Fabra i Puig
Verneda
SANT ANDREU
SANT ADRIÀ DE BESÒS
el Besòs
Pas. de Maragall
Maragall
Congrés
Sagrera
La Pau
Rambla de Prim
Sagrera
Sant Martí
Besòs
Navas
Guipúscoa
SANT PAU
Guinardó
Ronda del Guinardó
Sant Antoni Maria Claret
Camp de l'Arpa
Indústria
C 31
Besòs Mar
Meridiana
Bac de Roda
SANT MARTÍ
Maresme-Forum
Alfons X
Padilla
Hospital St Pau
Clot
Vincci Marítimo
Selva de Mar
Encants
Av. Diagonal
Diagonal Barcelona
Barceló H. Atenea Mar
B 10
SAGRADA FAMILIA
Aragó
Glòries
Poblenou
Hesperia del Mar
Rafael H. Diagonal Port
PLAZA DE TOROS
Llacuna
Els Pescadors
Marina
Bogatell
Llull
ASA MILÀ
Catalanes
Marina
VILA OLÍMPICA
Old Town and Gothic Quarter (Plan II)
PARC ZOOLOGIC
Anfiteatro
El Túnel del Port
Corts
FRANÇA
Arts
CATEDRAL
BARRI GÒTIC
Paral.lel
MAR MEDITERRÁNEO
CASTELL DE MONTJUÏC
1
2
3
2
24
23
22
21
29
Environs of Barcelona (Plan I)
0
1 km
C
D

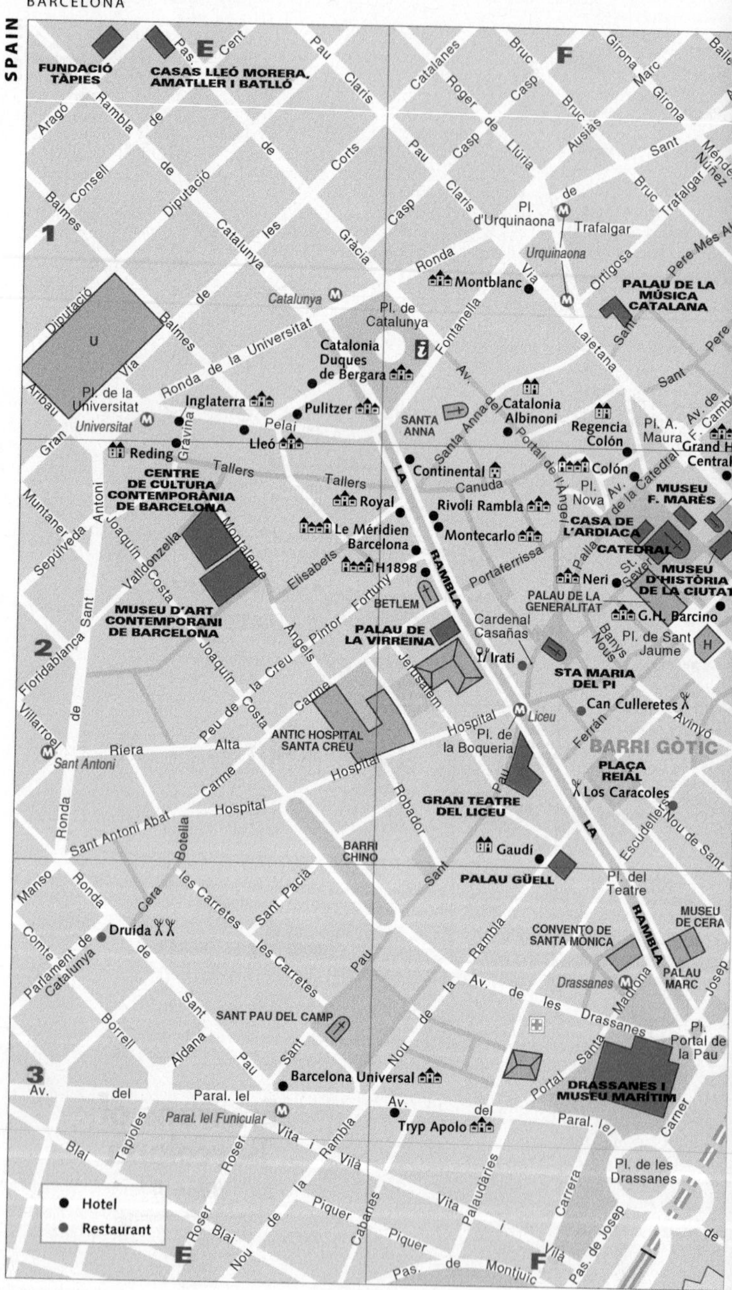
FUNDACIÓ TÀPIES
CASAS LLEÓ MORERA, AMATLLER I BATLLÓ
PALAU DE LA MÚSICA CATALANA
Pl. d'Urquinaona
Urquinaona
Montblanc
Catalunya
Pl. de Catalunya
Catalonia Duques de Bergara
Inglaterra
Pulitzer
Pl. de la Universitat
Universitat
Lleó
Reding
SANTA ANNA
Catalonia Albinoni
Regencia Colón
Pl. A. Maura
Grand H Central
Continental
Colón
Pl. Nova
MUSEU F. MARÈS
CENTRE DE CULTURA CONTEMPORÀNIA DE BARCELONA
Royal
Rivoli Rambla
Le Méridien Barcelona
Montecarlo
CASA DE L'ARDIACA
CATEDRAL
H1898
Neri
MUSEU D'HISTÒRIA DE LA CIUTAT
PALAU DE LA GENERALITAT
G.H. Barcino
BETLEM
MUSEU D'ART CONTEMPORANI DE BARCELONA
PALAU DE LA VIRREINA
Irati
Pl. de Sant Jaume
STA MARIA DEL PI
Can Culleretes
Liceu
ANTIC HOSPITAL SANTA CREU
Pl. de la Boqueria
BARRI GÒTIC
PLAÇA REIAL
Sant Antoni
Los Caracoles
GRAN TEATRE DEL LICEU
BARRI CHINO
Gaudí
PALAU GÜELL
Pl. del Teatre
Druída
CONVENTO DE SANTA MÒNICA
MUSEU DE CERA
Drassanes
PALAU MARC
SANT PAU DEL CAMP
Pl. Portal de la Pau
Barcelona Universal
DRASSANES I MUSEU MARÍTIM
Paral. lel Funicular
Tryp Apolo
Pl. de les Drassanes
LA RAMBLA
Hotel
Restaurant

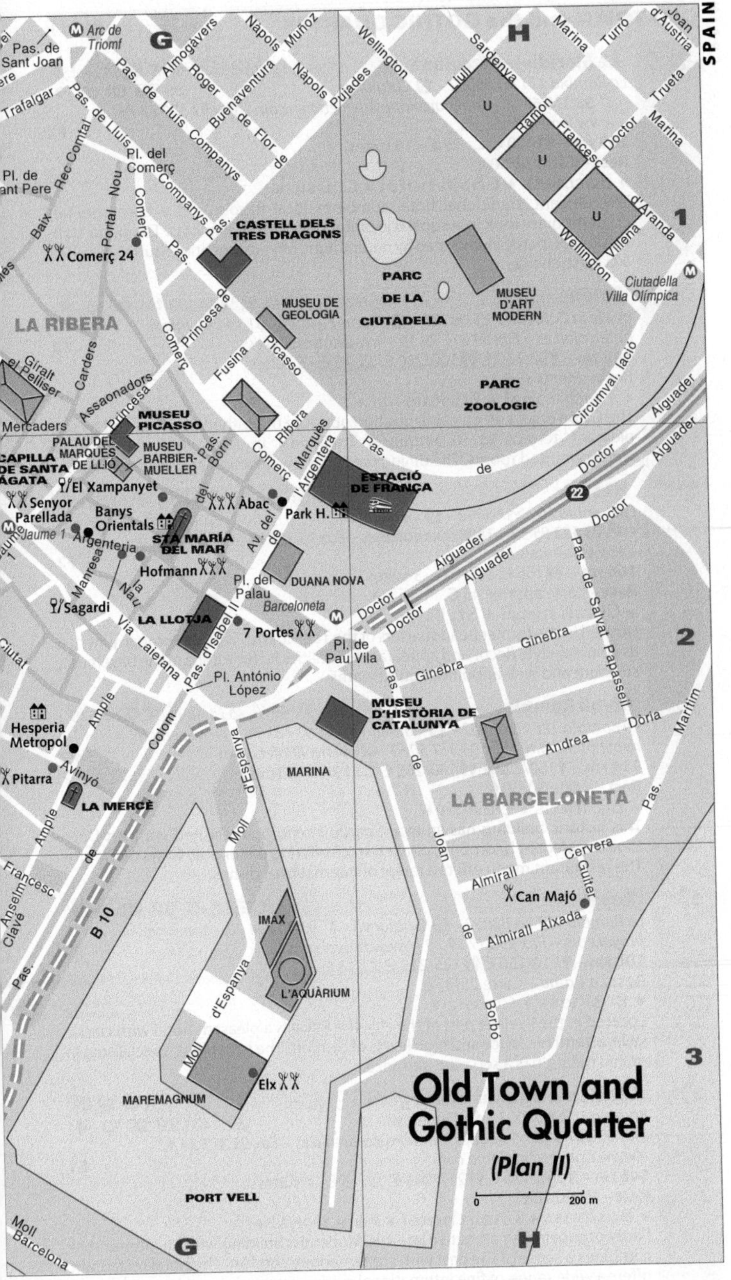
Old Town and Gothic Quarter
(Plan II)
PARC DE LA CIUTADELLA
PARC ZOOLOGIC
MUSEU D'ART MODERN
MUSEU DE GEOLOGIA
CASTELL DELS TRES DRAGONS
LA RIBERA
MUSEU PICASSO
PALAU DEL MARQUES DE LLIÓ
MUSEU BARBIER-MUELLER
CAPILLA DE SANTA ÀGATA
STA MARÍA DEL MAR
ESTACIÓ DE FRANÇA
DUANA NOVA
LA LLOTJA
MUSEU D'HISTÒRIA DE CATALUNYA
LA BARCELONETA
MARINA
IMAX
L'AQUÀRIUM
MAREMAGNUM
PORT VELL
LA MERCÈ
Comerç 24
El Xampanyet
Senyor Parellada
Banys Orientals
Àbac
Park H.
Hofmann
Sagardi
7 Portes
Hesperia Metropol
Pitarra
Can Majó
Elx
Arc de Triomf
Ciutadella Villa Olímpica
Jaume 1
Barceloneta
Pl. de Pau Vila
Pl. del Palau
Pl. António López
Pl. del Comerç
B 10
0
200 m

OLD TOWN and the GOTHIC QUARTER

Plan II

Le Méridien Barcelona

No smokers rest. 25/150

La Rambla 111 ✉ 08002 – Ⓜ Catalunya – ✆ 93 318 62 00 – info.barcelona@lemeridien.com – Fax 93 301 77 76 – www.lemeridien.com

VISA MC AE

F2

202 rm – 400 €, 25 € – 10 suites

Rest – Carte 38/50 €

♦ Business ♦ Chain hotel ♦ Classic ♦

This elegant, traditional hotel combines local flavour and a cosmopolitan contemporary look in a superb location right on the Ramblas. The patio-style restaurant, partly illuminated by natural light, offers a lunchtime buffet as well as à la carte choices.

Colón

No smokers rest. 25/150 VISA MC AE

av. de la Catedral 7 ✉ 08002 – Ⓜ Jaume I – ✆ 93 301 14 04 – info@hotelcolon.es – Fax 93 317 29 15 – www.hotelcolon.es

F2

140 rm – 90/160 € 100/230 €, 15 € – 5 suites

Rest – Menu 35 €

♦ Traditional ♦ Functional ♦

The Colón enjoys an enviable position opposite the cathedral, enhanced by the pleasant terrace at its entrance. Traditional in style with comfortable, well-appointed rooms. The dining room has a welcoming and intimate feel.

H1898

No smokers rest. 25/200

La Rambla 109 ✉ 08002 – Ⓜ Catalunya – ✆ 93 552 95 52 – 1898@nnhotels.es – Fax 93 552 95 50 – www.nnhotels.es

VISA MC AE

F2

166 rm – 165 €, 19 € – 3 suites

Rest – Carte approx. 45 €

♦ Chain hotel ♦ Stylish ♦

Housed in the former headquarters of the Tabacos de Filipinas company, hence its colonial-style decor and appearance. Facilities include a spa in the basement, solarium and well-appointed guestrooms.

Rivoli Rambla

25/100 VISA MC AE

La Rambla 128 ✉ 08002 – Ⓜ Catalunya – ✆ 93 481 76 76 – reservas@rivolihotels.com – Fax 93 317 50 53 – www.rivolihotels.com

F2

114 rm – 160/222 € 180/265 €, 19 € – 15 suites

Rest – Carte 30/39 €

♦ Business ♦ Design ♦

This historic building has an avant-garde interior embellished with Art Deco touches, elegant bedrooms, plus a terrace offering panoramic views of the city. The restaurant menu offers a range of international dishes.

Royal

VISA MC AE

La Rambla 117 ✉ 08002 – Ⓜ Catalunya – ✆ 93 301 94 00 – hotelroyal@hroyal.com – Fax 93 317 31 79 – www.hroyal.com

F2

108 rm – 110/150 € 125/215 €, 13 €

Rest ***La Poma*** – Carte 25/37 €

♦ Business ♦ Classic ♦

Located in the liveliest part of the city, the Royal is a pleasant hotel with classic style, attentive service and high levels of comfort. The restaurant, specialising in grilled meats, has a separate entrance.

Catalonia Duques de Bergara

Bergara 11 ✉ 08002 – Ⓜ Catalunya – ✆ 93 301 51 51 – duques@hoteles-catalonia.es – Fax 93 317 34 42 – www.hoteles-catalonia.com

25/400 VISA MC AE

E1

146 rm – 147/175 € 217/249 €, 13 € – 2 suites

Rest – Menu 18 €

♦ Business ♦ Chain hotel ♦ Functional ♦

Partly occupying an attractive late 19C Modernist building with an interior that combines a sense of the past with contemporary comfort. The hotel restaurant offers a wide range of fine international cuisine. Swimming pool-solarium.

Montecarlo without rest AC SAT VISA MC AE

La Rambla 124 ✉ *08002* – Ⓜ *Liceu* – ✆ *93 412 04 04 – hotel@montecarlobcn.com – Fax 93 318 73 23 – www.montecarlobcn.com* **F2**

54 rm – 135 € 198/347 €, ☕ 9 € – 1 suite

◆ Traditional ◆ Design ◆

This magnificent hotel, housed in a 19C palace, harmoniously combines the classicism of the past with the modern design features of its exquisitely furnished guestrooms.

Neri AC SAT VISA MC AE

Sant Sever 5 ✉ *08002* – Ⓜ *Liceu* – ✆ *93 304 06 55 – info@hotelneri.com – Fax 93 304 03 37 – www.hotelneri.com* **F2**

21 rm – 200/325 €, ☕ 20 € – 1 suite

Rest – Menu 64 €

◆ Business ◆ Design ◆

A large 18C mansion with a unique and bold avant-garde look just a few yards from the cathedral. Small library-lounge, superb bedrooms and an intimate restaurant dominated by two stone arches in which the cuisine is equally innovative.

Montblanc AC SAT 25/450 VISA MC AE

Via Laietana 61 ✉ *08003* – Ⓜ *Urquinaona – ✆ 93 343 55 55 – montblanc@hcchotels.es – Fax 93 343 55 58 – www.hcchotels.es* **F1**

157 rm – 112/175 € 128/215 €, ☕ 16 €

Rest – Menu 20 €

◆ Traditional ◆ Functional ◆

A hotel in classic yet contemporary style with spacious lounges and an elegant piano bar. The comfortable bedrooms are modern in style with carpeted floors and marble bathrooms. The circular dining room offers a choice of Catalan and international dishes.

Tryp Apolo No smokers rest. AC SAT 25/500 VISA MC AE

av. del Paral.lel 57-59 ✉ *08004* – Ⓜ *Paral.lel – ✆ 93 343 30 00 – tryp.apolo@solmelia.com – Fax 93 443 00 59 – www.solmelia.com* **F3**

290 rm – 90/220 €, ☕ 15 € – 24 suites

Rest – *(closed July and August)* Carte 20/36 €

◆ Business ◆ Chain hotel ◆ Functional ◆

Friendly, functional and ideal for the business traveller. Lounges fitted with marble and bedrooms that have recently been refurbished. The bright restaurant overlooks a garden terrace.

Barcelona Universal No smokers rest. AC SAT 25/100 VISA MC AE

av. del Paral.lel 80 ✉ *08001* – Ⓜ *Paral.lel – ✆ 93 567 74 47 – bcnuniversal@nnhotels.com – Fax 93 567 74 40 – www.nnhotels.com* **E3**

164 rm – 112/180 € 112/200 €, ☕ 13.50 € – 3 suites

Rest – *(dinner only)* Carte approx. 36 €

◆ Business ◆ Functional ◆

A new hotel built in modern style with large, well-appointed bedrooms embellished with wooden floors and well-equipped bathrooms. The panoramic swimming pool on the roof is an added bonus. Contemporary-style restaurant adorned with a profusion of wood.

G.H. Barcino without rest AC VISA MC AE

Jaume I-6 ✉ *08002* – Ⓜ *Jaume I* – ✆ *93 302 20 12 – reserve@gargallo-hotels.com – Fax 93 301 42 42 – www.gargallohotels.es* **F2**

53 rm – 122/195 € 142/240 €, ☕ 15 €

◆ Traditional ◆ Classic ◆

Right in the heart of the Gothic Quarter. The hotel's main selling points are the elegant entrance hall and attractively designed bedrooms, all equipped with modern bathrooms. Some rooms on the top floor enjoy views of the cathedral from their terrace.

SPAIN

Inglaterra

25 VISA

Pelai 14 ✉ 08001 – Ⓜ Universitat – ☎ 93 505 11 00 – recepcion@hotel-inglaterra.com – Fax 93 505 11 09 – www.hotel-inglaterra.com **E1**

55 rm – 99/230 € 119/260 €, 13 €

Rest – *(coffee shop only)*

♦ Traditional ♦ Functional ♦

A smart, modern hotel with a classical façade and welcoming feel. Multi-purpose function areas, plus bedrooms with large wooden headboards. Pleasant terrace-solarium.

Pulitzer

No smokers rest. VISA

Bergara 8 ✉ 08002 – Ⓜ Catalunya – ☎ 93 481 67 67 – info@hotelpulitzer.es – Fax 93 481 64 64 – www.hotelpulitzer.es **E1**

91 rm – 150/220 € 180/240 €, 15 €

Rest – *(closed August and Sunday) (lunch only except Thursday, Friday and Saturday)* Carte 24/34 €

♦ Business ♦ Functional ♦

Modern facilities with a spacious lounge area and café. Functional, comfortable rooms with wood floors. The restaurant has a contemporary design and looks out onto a terrace.

Grand H. Central

No smokers rest. 25/40 VISA

Via Laietana 30 ✉ 08003 – Ⓜ Jaume I – ☎ 93 295 79 00 – info@grandhotelcentral.com – Fax 93 268 12 15 – www.grandhotelcentral.com **F2**

147 rm – 145/216 €, 16 € – **Rest *Actual*** – Carte 18/35 €

♦ Business ♦ Design ♦

A new-generation hotel combining functionality, modernity and a keen eye on contemporary design. Terrace with panoramic views, and comfortable bedrooms. A dynamic, informal restaurant with a focus on creative cuisine.

Lleó

25/150 VISA

Pelai 22 ✉ 08001 – Ⓜ Universitat – ☎ 93 318 13 12 – reservas@hotel-lleo.es – Fax 93 412 26 57 – www.hotel-lleo.es **E1**

89 rm – 115/125 € 135/160 €, 10 € – **Rest** – *(coffee shop only)*

♦ Family ♦ Personalised ♦

A well-run family hotel with an elegant façade, bedrooms offering adequate levels of comfort and a large lounge area.

Catalonia Albinoni without rest

VISA

av. Portal de l'Ángel 17 ✉ 08002 – Ⓜ Catalunya – ☎ 93 318 41 41 – albinoni@hoteles-catalonia.es – Fax 93 301 26 31 – www.hoteles-catalonia.es **F1**

74 rm – 125/165 € 157/177 €, 13 €

♦ Business ♦ Chain hotel ♦ Functional ♦

In the former Rocamora Palace and near the Gothic Quarter. The foyer area has original decorative details and bedrooms in the style of the period.

Reding

VISA

Gravina 5-7 ✉ 08001 – Ⓜ Universitat – ☎ 93 412 10 97 – reding@occidental-hoteles.com – Fax 93 268 34 82 – www.hotelreding.com **E1-2**

44 rm – 134/200 € 144/225 €, 12 €

Rest – *(closed Sunday and Bank Holidays)* Menu 11 €

♦ Traditional ♦ Functional ♦

Located close to Plaça de Catalunya. Despite being on the small side, the lounge areas and bedrooms are comfortable and well equipped. The hotel's dining room offers a menu featuring traditional and Catalan dishes.

Banys Orientals

VISA

L'Argenteria 37 ✉ 08003 – Ⓜ Jaume I – ☎ 93 268 84 60 – reservas@hotelbanysorientals.com – Fax 93 268 84 61 – www.hotelbanysorientals.com **G2**

43 rm – 82 € 98 €, 10 €

Rest *Senyor Parellada* – see below

♦ Business ♦ Design ♦

Comfortable minimalist rooms with design features galore, wooden floors and four-poster-style beds. No lounge area.

Park H. without rest
av. Marquès de l'Argentera 11 ✉ 08003 – Ⓜ Barceloneta – ☎ 93 319 60 00 – parkhotel@parkhotelbarcelona.com – Fax 93 319 45 19 – www.parkhotelbarcelona.com – **91 rm** ☕ – 🚹110/142 € 🚹🚹135/185 € G2

◆ Traditional ◆ Modern ◆

A modern, avant-garde feel permeates this well-maintained hotel with a friendly atmosphere and large breakfast room. Pleasant entrance-cum-reception area with adjoining bar.

Gaudí
Nou de la Rambla 12 ✉ 08001 – Ⓜ Liceu – ☎ 93 317 90 32 – gaudi@hotelgaudi.es – Fax 93 412 26 36 – www.hotelgaudi.es F2
73 rm – 🚹80/130 € 🚹🚹100/160 €, ☕ 10 € – **Rest** – *(coffee shop only)*

◆ Family ◆ Functional ◆

The Gaudí's main features are its Modernist fountain in the foyer and an attractive cafeteria. The hotel's bedrooms, some with balcony, are gradually being refurbished.

Regencia Colón without rest
Sagristans 13 ✉ 08002 – Ⓜ Jaume I – ☎ 93 318 98 58 – info@hotelregenciacolon.com – Fax 93 317 28 22 – www.hotelregenciacolon.com F1-2
50 rm – 🚹50/115 € 🚹🚹50/160 €, ☕ 10 €

◆ Traditional ◆ Functional ◆

A great base from which to explore one of the city's most distinctive districts. Functional bedrooms with modern bathrooms and wood flooring.

Hesperia Metropol without rest
Ample 31 ✉ 08002 – Ⓜ Drassanes – ☎ 93 310 51 00 – hotel@hesperia-metropol.com – Fax 93 319 12 76 – www.hoteles-hesperia.es G2
68 rm – 🚹60/165 € 🚹🚹60/180 €, ☕ 10.50 €

◆ Business ◆ Chain hotel ◆ Functional ◆

Situated in the Old Town with comfortable and well-decorated rooms. Friendly atmosphere and pleasant staff.

Continental without rest
Rambles 138-2º ✉ 08002 – Ⓜ Catalunya – ☎ 93 301 25 70 – barcelona@hotelcontinental.com – Fax 93 302 73 60 – www.hotelcontinental.com F2
35 rm ☕ – 🚹75 € 🚹🚹105 €

◆ Family ◆ Personalised ◆

Friendly hotel located close to the Plaza Catalunya square which gets much of its character from the bedrooms which are furnished in an English style.

Àbac 10/14
(possible transfer to av. del Tibidabo 7), Rec 79-89 ✉ 08003 – Ⓜ Barceloneta – ☎ 93 319 66 00 – info@restaurantabac.com – Fax 93 319 45 19 – www.restaurantabac.com
closed 6 to 13 January, 3 weeks in August, Sunday and Monday lunch
Rest – Menu 84.14 € – Carte 60/94 € G2

Spec. Prensado de acelgas y setas, ensalada de germinados. Rémol con mantequilla de almendras tostadas. Cordero lechal a la vainilla.

◆ Inventive ◆ Minimalist ◆

Modern restaurant with minimalist design details. Excellent service and creative Mediterranean cuisine. Popular with a young clientele.

Hofmann 6/20
L'Argenteria 74-78 (1º) ✉ 08003 – Ⓜ Jaume I – ☎ 93 319 58 89 – restaurante@hofmann-bcn.com – Fax 93 319 58 82 – www.hofmann-bcn.com G2
closed Christmas, Holy Week, August, Saturday and Sunday
Rest – Carte 52/69 €

Spec. Nuestra tradicional tarta de sardinas con tomate y cebollitas nuevas. Foie de pato con salsa Oporto y manzana en tres texturas. Crujientes templados de vainilla con uvas pasas.

◆ Inventive ◆ Design ◆

Housed in an old building which doubles as a catering school, the Hofmann is known for its classical design and innovative, imaginatively presented cuisine.

XX **Druída** AC 16 VISA MC AE D

Parlament 54 ✉ 08015 – Ⓜ Sant Antoni – ✆ 93 441 10 45 – druida@restaurantedruida.com – Fax 93 324 84 67 – www.restaurantedruida.com
closed 16 to 31 August, Sunday dinner and Monday **E3**
Rest – Carte 30/48 €
♦ Inventive ♦ Formal ♦
A cosy restaurant adorned with Louis XV-style furniture and chairs, and designer crockery. A creative menu, plus a dining room with views of the kitchen.

XX **Senyor Parellada** – Hotel Banys Orientals AC VISA MC AE D

L'Argenteria 37 ✉ 08003 – Ⓜ Jaume I – ✆ 93 310 50 94 – fondaparellada@hotmail.com – Fax 93 268 31 57 **G2**
Rest – Carte 23/28 €
♦ Catalan cuisine ♦ Cosy ♦
A pleasant restaurant with classic-contemporary decor, bar and several attractive dining rooms. The small central patio, crowned by a glass roof, is worthy of particular note.

XX **7 Portes** AC VISA MC AE D

Passeig d'Isabel II-14 ✉ 08003 – Ⓜ Barceloneta – ✆ 93 319 30 33 – reservas@7portes.com – Fax 93 319 30 46 – www.7portes.com **G2**
Rest – Carte approx. 40 €
♦ Catalan cuisine ♦ Retro ♦
A venerable Barcelona institution dating back to 1836, whose dining areas retain their old-fashioned feel. The traditional menu is strong on fish, seafood and rice dishes.

XX **Comerç 24** VISA MC

Comerç 24 ✉ 08003 – Ⓜ Arc de Triomf – ✆ 93 319 21 02 – info@comerc24.com – Fax 93 319 10 74 – www.carlesabellan.com
closed 21 days in August, Sunday and Monday **G1**
Rest – Carte 27/46 €
♦ Inventive ♦ Design ♦
A modern restaurant with avant-garde décor offering different menus of creative cuisine. Popular with a younger clientele.

XX **Elx** AC VISA MC AE

Moll d'Espanya-Maremagnum (Local 9) ✉ 08039 – Ⓜ Drassanes – ✆ 93 225 81 17 – Fax 93 225 81 20 – www.restauratelx.com **G3**
Rest – Carte 19/32 €
♦ Rice specialities ♦ Formal ♦
A restaurant with impressive views of the marina, a modern-rustic dining room and pleasant covered terrace. Popular for its fish, seafood and good choice of rice-based dishes.

X **Pitarra** AC 12/30 VISA MC AE D

Avinyó 56 ✉ 08002 – Ⓜ Liceu – ✆ 93 301 16 47 – Fax 93 301 85 62 – www.pitarra.com
closed August, Sunday and dinner Bank Holidays **G2**
Rest – Carte 22/39 €
♦ Catalan cuisine ♦ Cosy ♦
A pleasant and welcoming interior adorned with old clocks and mementoes of the poet Pitarra. The comprehensive, moderately priced menu is strong on traditional cuisine.

X **Can Majó** AC VISA MC AE D

Almirall Aixada 23 ✉ 08003 – Ⓜ Barceloneta – ✆ 93 221 54 55 – majocan@terra.es – Fax 93 221 54 55
closed Sunday dinner and Monday **H3**
Rest – Carte 33/43 €
♦ Seafood ♦ Family ♦
This popular, family-run restaurant is renowned for its impressive fish and seafood menu. Attractive seafood counter plus a panoramic terrace.

SPAIN

Can Culleretes

Quintana 5 ✉ 08002 – Ⓜ Liceu – ✆ 93 317 64 85 – culleretes@hotmail.com – Fax 93 412 59 92 – www.culleretes.com
closed July, Sunday dinner and Monday – **Rest** – Carte 21/30 € **F2**

♦ Catalan cuisine ♦ Friendly ♦

A family-run restaurant dating back to 1786. Traditional décor with beams and lots of paintings, creating a welcoming atmosphere.

Los Caracoles

No smokers rest. ⇔10/20

Escudellers 14 ✉ 08002 – Ⓜ Liceu – ✆ 93 302 31 85 – caracoles@versin.com – Fax 93 302 07 43 – **Rest** – Carte 30/45 € **F2**

♦ Catalan cuisine ♦ Retro ♦

Established in 1835, this typically rustic restaurant in the city's old quarter has retained all its old charm. Interesting menu and as popular as ever.

Sagardi

L'Argenteria 62 ✉ 08003 – Ⓜ Jaume I – ✆ 93 319 99 93 – sagardi@sagardi.es – Fax 93 268 48 86 – www.sagardi.com **G2**
Tapa 1.50 € **Ración** approx. 14 €

♦ Basque ♦ Tapas bar ♦

A Basque cider house situated near the historic church of Santa María del Mar. A very wide range of Basque-style tapas and dining room with cider barrels and charcoal grill.

Irati

Cardenal Casanyes 17 ✉ 08002 – Ⓜ Liceu – ✆ 93 302 30 84 – sagardi@sagardi.com – Fax 93 412 73 76 – www.sagardi.com **F2**
Tapa 1.50 € **Ración** approx. 14 €

♦ Basque ♦ Tapas bar ♦

This traditional-style Basque tavern close to the Liceo theatre offers a good choice of typical Basque dishes with an innovative touch.

El Xampanyet

No smokers rest.

Montcada 22 ✉ 08003 – Ⓜ Jaume I – ✆ 93 319 70 03
closed Holy Week, August, Sunday and Monday **G2**
Tapa 2.50 € **Ración** approx. 6 €

♦ Spanish ♦ Tapas bar ♦

This well-established family-run tavern is attractively adorned with typical azulejo panelling. A varied selection of tapas with the emphasis on fish and meat.

SOUTH of AV. DIAGONAL *Plan III*

Rey Juan Carlos I

No smokers rest. (heated) 25/1000

av. Diagonal 661 ✉ 08028 – Ⓜ Zona Universitaria – ✆ 93 364 40 40 – hotel@hrjuancarlos.com – Fax 93 364 42 64 – www.hrjuancarlos.com *Plan I* **A2**
375 rm – †250/315 € ††300/420 €, ☕ 22 € – 37 suites
Rest *The Garden* – *(closed August, Sunday and Monday)* Carte approx. 75 €
Rest *Café Polo* – *(buffet)* Menu 34 €

♦ Luxury ♦ Business ♦ Modern ♦

A hotel with impressive modern facilities surrounded by an area of parkland with a small lake and swimming pool. An exclusive atmosphere pervades this hotel, which is tastefully decorated throughout. The Garden restaurant has a pleasant terrace.

Palace

Smokers rest. 25/330

Gran Via de les Corts Catalanes 668 ✉ 08010 – Ⓜ Urquinaona – ✆ 93 510 11 30 – palace@hotelpalacebarcelona.com – Fax 93 318 01 48 – www.hotelpalacebarcelona.com **L2**
114 rm – †190/355 € ††190/380 €, ☕ 21 € – 6 suites
Rest Caelis – see below

♦ Grand Luxury ♦ Classic ♦

An emblematic name, both in terms of its opulence and tradition. The Palace occupies an elegant building dating from 1919, with an impressively attractive cupola-crowned lounge and splendid guestrooms.

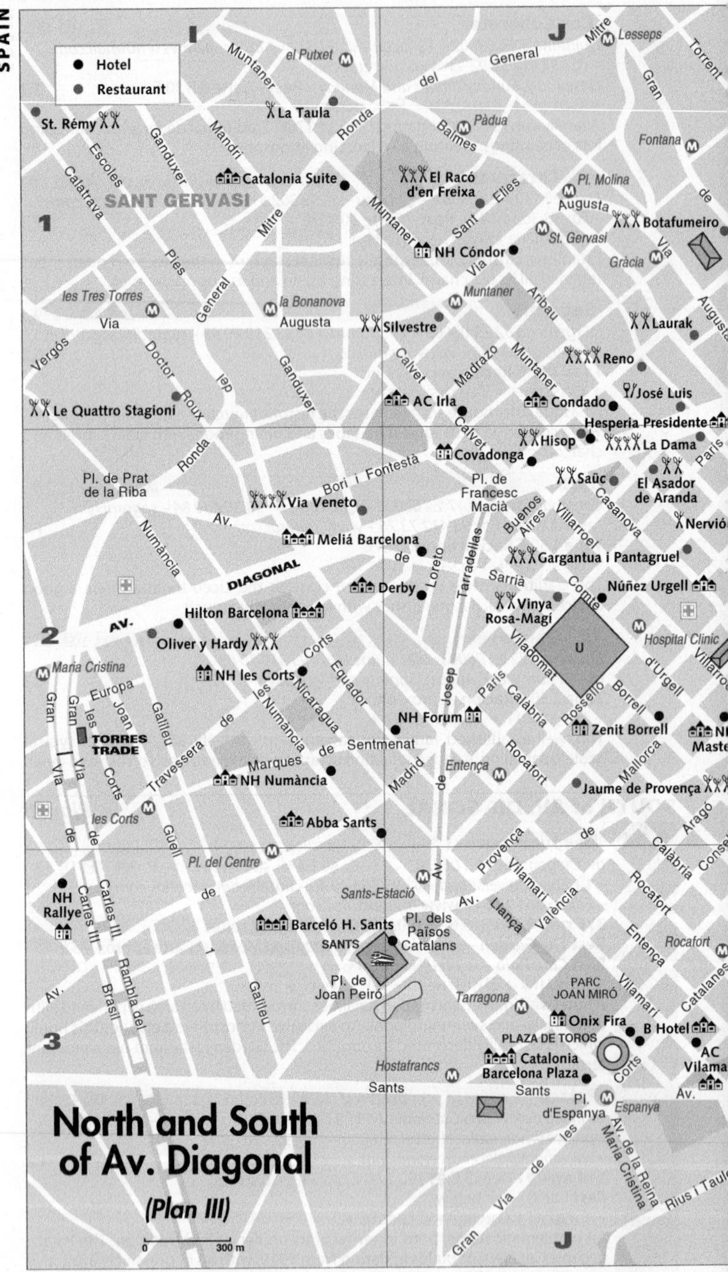
Hotel
Restaurant
St. Rémy
La Taula
Catalonia Suite
El Racó d'en Freixa
Botafumeiro
NH Cóndor
Silvestre
Laurak
Reno
José Luis
Le Quattro Stagioni
AC Irla
Condado
Hesperia Presidente
Hisop
La Dama
Covadonga
Saüc
El Asador de Aranda
Via Veneto
Nervió
Meliá Barcelona
Gargantua i Pantagruel
Derby
Núñez Urgell
Vinya Rosa-Magí
Hilton Barcelona
Oliver y Hardy
NH les Corts
NH Forum
Zenit Borrell
NH Master
NH Numància
Jaume de Provença
Abba Sants
NH Rallye
Barceló H. Sants
Onix Fira
B Hotel
AC Vilamarí
Catalonia Barcelona Plaza
SANT GERVASI
TORRES TRADE
SANTS
PARC JOAN MIRÓ
PLAZA DE TOROS
DIAGONAL
Av.
Pl. de Prat de la Riba
Pl. de Francesc Macià
Pl. del Centre
Pl. dels Països Catalans
Pl. de Joan Peiró
Pl. d'Espanya
el Putxet
Lesseps
Pàdua
Fontana
Pl. Molina
St. Gervasi
Gràcia
les Tres Torres
la Bonanova
Muntaner
Maria Cristina
Hospital Clinic
Entença
les Corts
Sants-Estació
Tarragona
Rocafort
Hostafrancs
Espanya
Muntaner
Mandri
Ganduxer
Escoles
Calatrava
Pies
General Mitre
Ronda
Balmes
Sant Elies
Augusta
Via Augusta
Vergós
Doctor Roux
Calvet
Madrazo
Aribau
Bori i Fontestà
Numància
Buenos Aires
Villarroel
Casanova
Sarrià
Tarradellas
Loreto
Comte d'Urgell
Viladomat
París
Calàbria
Rosselló
Borrell
Corts
Equador
Nicaragua
Travessera de les Corts
Marques de Sentmenat
Galileu
Josep
Europa
Joan
Gran Via de Carles III
Madrid
Mallorca
Aragó
Provença
Vilamarí
Llança
València
Consell de Cent
Catalanes
Güell
Rambla del Brasil
Gran Via de les Corts Catalanes
Av. de la Reina Maria Cristina
Rius i Taulet
I
J
1
2
3
North and South of Av. Diagonal
(Plan III)
0
300 m

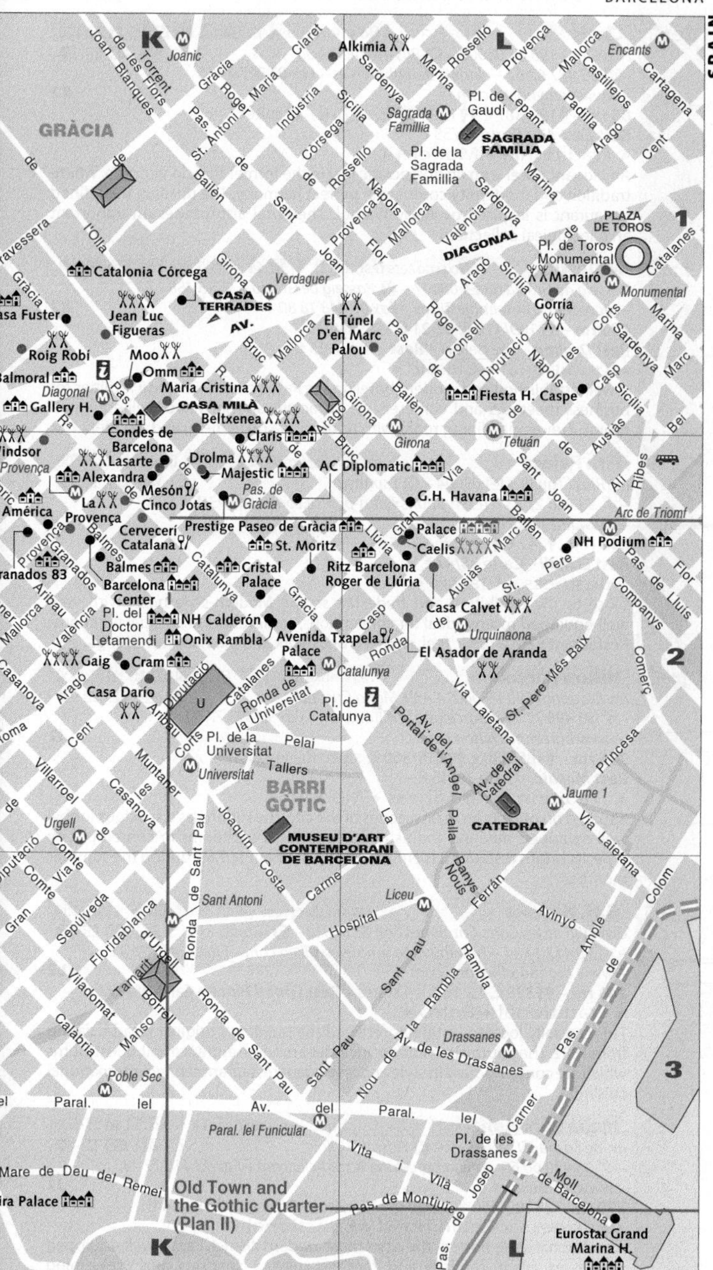

GRÀCIA
SAGRADA FAMILIA
PLAZA DE TOROS
CASA TERRADES
CASA MILÀ
BARRI GÒTIC
MUSEU D'ART CONTEMPORANI DE BARCELONA
CATEDRAL
DIAGONAL
Catalonia Córcega
Jean Luc Figueras
Casa Fuster
Roig Robí
Moo
Omm
Maria Cristina
Balmoral
Gallery H.
Condes de Barcelona
Beltxenea
Claris
Windsor
Lasarte
Drolma
Majestic
AC Diplomatic
Alexandra
Mesón Cinco Jotas
La Provença
América
Cervecerí Catalana
Prestige Paseo de Gràcia
St. Moritz
Granados 83
Balmes
Barcelona Center
Cristal Palace
Ritz Barcelona
Roger de Llúria
NH Calderón
Onix Rambla
Avenida Palace
Txapela
Gaig
Cram
Casa Darío
Alkimia
Manairó
Gorría
El Túnel D'en Marc Palou
Fiesta H. Caspe
G.H. Havana
Palace
Caelis
NH Podium
Casa Calvet
El Asador de Aranda
Eurostar Grand Marina H.
Ira Palace
Old Town and the Gothic Quarter (Plan II)
Pl. de Gaudí
Pl. de la Sagrada Família
Pl. de Toros Monumental
Pl. del Doctor Letamendi
Pl. de Catalunya
Pl. de la Universitat
Pl. de les Drassanes
Joanic
Encants
Sagrada Família
Verdaguer
Monumental
Diagonal
Provença
Girona
Tetuán
Pas. de Gràcia
Arc de Triomf
Urquinaona
Catalunya
Universitat
Jaume 1
Urgell
Sant Antoni
Liceu
Drassanes
Poble Sec
Paral. lel Funicular
K
L
1
2
3

SPAIN

Claris No smokers rest. 25/120
Pau Claris 150 ✉ 08009 – Ⓜ Passeig de Gràcia
– ☎ 93 487 62 62 – claris@derbyhotels.es – Fax 93 215 79 70
– www.derbyhotels.com **K2**
80 rm – 199/387 € 199/430 €, 20 € – 40 suites
Rest *East 47* – Carte 45/55 €
◆ Traditional ◆ Modern ◆
An elegant hotel with an aristocratic feel in the former Palacio Vedruna, where tradition and modernity combine in perfect harmony. The decor in the refined restaurant is inspired by Andy Warhol. The hotel also houses an important archaeological collection.

Majestic No smokers rest. 25/400
Passeig de Gràcia 68 ✉ 08007 – Ⓜ Passeig de Gràcia – ☎ 93 488 17 17
– recepcion@hotelmajestic.es – Fax 93 448 18 80 **K2**
273 rm – 169/410 €, 21 € – 31 suites
Rest *Drolma* – see below – **Rest** – Menu 35 €
◆ Traditional ◆ Classic ◆
A well-established and modern hotel on the Paseo de Gràcia. Good facilities for business meetings and conferences. Attractive, spacious and well-equipped rooms. Functional dining room with both an à la carte menu and a buffet.

Fira Palace No smokers rest. 25/1300
av. Rius i Taulet 1 ✉ 08004 – Ⓜ Espanya
– ☎ 93 426 22 23 – reservations@fira-palace.com – Fax 93 425 50 47
– www.fira-palace.com **J-K3**
258 rm – 242 € 282 €, 15 € – 18 suites
Rest *El Mall* – Carte 35/47 €
◆ Business ◆ Classic ◆
Close to the exhibition and trade fair sector. Modern-style hotel with very well-equipped rooms. Ideal for conventions, conferences and social functions. Restaurant with a rustic feel, exposed brickwork and pleasant furnishings.

Hilton Barcelona No smokers rest. 25/600
av. Diagonal 589 ✉ 08014 – Ⓜ Maria Cristina
– ☎ 93 495 77 77 – barcelona@hilton.com – Fax 93 495 77 00
– www.barcelona.hilton.com **I2**
275 rm – 185/330 € 215/360 €, 20 € – 11 suites
Rest *Mosaic* – Carte 36/45 €
◆ Traditional ◆ Business ◆ Modern ◆
Situated on one of the main arteries of the city, the Hilton has a spacious lobby, well-equipped meeting rooms and comfortable bedrooms in contemporary style. Its bright restaurant is enhanced by a pleasant terrace during the summer months.

G.H. Havana No smokers rest. 25/150
Gran Via de les Corts Catalanes 647 ✉ 08010 – Ⓜ Girona
– ☎ 93 412 11 15 – hotelhavana@hoteles-silken.com – Fax 93 412 26 11
– www.granhotelhavana.com **L2**
141 rm – 325 €, 16 € – 4 suites – **Rest *Grand Place*** – Carte 28/43 €
◆ Traditional ◆ Retro ◆
This centrally located hotel has retained the building's original façade, dating from 1882. The refurbished interior includes a modern entrance hall, guestrooms which are contemporary in style and an elegant restaurant serving international cuisine.

Meliá Barcelona No smokers rest. 25/500
av. de Sarrià 50 ✉ 08029 – Ⓜ Hospital Clinic
– ☎ 93 410 60 60 – melia.barcelona@solmelia.com – Fax 93 410 77 44
– www.solmelia.es **J2**
299 rm – 100/360 €, 20 € – 15 suites – **Rest** – Carte 30/53 €
◆ Business ◆ Chain hotel ◆ Functional ◆
A traditional-style hotel in the city's most modern district. Large, well-equipped rooms, excellent services and facilities, plus a spacious and welcoming restaurant.

SPAIN

Princesa Sofía

25/1000

pl. Pius XII-4 ✉ 08028 – Ⓜ Maria Cristina – ✆ 93 508 10 00 – psofia@expogrupo.com – Fax 93 508 10 01 – www.princesasofia.com

VISA MO AE ①

Plan I **A2**

475 rm – ††190/380 €, ☕ 20 € – 25 suites

Rest – Carte approx. 60 €

♦ Business ♦ Classic ♦

In the city's main business and commercial district. The hotel's excellent facilities, luxurious lounges and comfortable rooms make it an ideal location for business trips and conventions. The modern-style restaurant offers à la carte and buffet options.

AC Diplomatic

25/70 VISA MO AE ①

Pau Claris 122 ✉ 08009 – Ⓜ Passeig de Gràcia – ✆ 93 272 38 10 – diplomatic@ac-hotels.com – Fax 93 272 38 11 – www.ac-hotels.com

K2

209 rm – ††160/255 €, ☕ 19 € – 2 suites

Rest – Carte 30/39 €

♦ Business ♦ Chain hotel ♦ Functional ♦

Located at the heart of the Ensanche district, this functional hotel offers guests comfortable, contemporary bedrooms with modern bathrooms and good soundproofing.

NH Calderón

25/200 VISA MO AE ①

Rambla de Catalunya 26 ✉ 08007 – Ⓜ Passeig de Gràcia – ✆ 93 301 00 00 – nhcalderon@nh-hotels.com – Fax 93 412 41 93 – www.nh-hotels.com

K2

224 rm – ††100/240 €, ☕ 17.50 € – 29 suites

Rest – Carte approx. 32 €

♦ Business ♦ Chain hotel ♦ Functional ♦

This hotel's location in the city's main financial district makes it an ideal base for business travellers. Excellent facilities and high levels of comfort.

Fiesta H. Caspe

No smokers rest. 25/200

Casp 103 ✉ 08013 – Ⓜ Arc de Triomf – ✆ 93 246 70 00 – caspe@fiesta-hotels.com – Fax 93 246 70 01 – www.fiestahotelgroup.com

VISA MO AE ①

L1

141 rm – †60/230 € ††60/260 €, ☕ 14 €

Rest *3 Plats* – Carte 21/26 €

♦ Business ♦ Chain hotel ♦ Functional ♦

The hotel's lounge area and modern foyer are both embellished with design furniture. Wide choice of meeting rooms and guest bedrooms with a shower and bathtub as standard. A combination of Mediterranean and international cuisine is on offer in the restaurant.

Barcelona Center

25/200 VISA MO AE ①

Balmes 103 ✉ 08008 – Ⓜ Diagonal – ✆ 93 273 00 00 – barcelona@hotelescenter.com – Fax 93 273 00 02 – www.hotelescenter.com

K2

129 rm – †120/220 € ††120/275 €, ☕ 17 € – 3 suites

Rest – *(coffee shop only)*

♦ Chain hotel ♦ Cosy ♦

This hotel shelters behind a striking, well-preserved façade. Distinctive public areas, superbly appointed modern bedrooms and an enormous terrace-solarium.

Catalonia Barcelona Plaza

(heated) 25/600

pl. d'Espanya 6 ✉ 08014 – Ⓜ Espanya – ✆ 93 426 26 00 – plaza@hoteles-catalonia.es – Fax 93 426 04 00 – www.hoteles-catalonia.com

VISA MO AE ①

J3

338 rm – †140/175 € ††217/249 €, ☕ 13 € – 9 suites

Rest *Gourmet Plaza* – Carte 30/40 €

♦ Business ♦ Chain hotel ♦ Functional ♦

A modern hotel facing Barcelona's main exhibition centre with excellent facilities aimed mainly at business clientele, as well as a functional restaurant decorated in minimalist style.

SPAIN

Barceló H. Sants
No smokers rest. 25/1500

pl. dels Països Catalans ✉ 08014 – Ⓜ Sants-Estació – ✆ 93 503 53 00 – sants@bchoteles.com – Fax 93 490 60 45 – www.bchoteles.com **J3**

364 rm – ††90/180 €, ☕ 12 € – 13 suites

Rest – *(closed August and Sunday)* Carte 33/56 €

♦ Business ♦ Chain hotel ♦ Functional ♦

Located within the confines of the Sants railway station with views of the city. Functional in style with good facilities and a spacious lobby. The well-lit dining room offers two contrasting sections, one for à la carte, the other a more relaxed buffet.

Condes de Barcelona
25/200

passeig de Gràcia 73-75 ✉ 08008 – Ⓜ Passeig de Gràcia – ✆ 93 445 00 00 – reservas@condesdebarcelona.com – Fax 93 445 32 32 – www.condesdebarcelona.com **K2**

232 rm – ††105/315 €, ☕ 16 € – 3 suites – **Rest *Lasarte*** – see below

♦ Traditional ♦ Modern ♦

A hotel-monument occupying two emblematic buildings (Casa Batlló and Casa Daurella) combining modern comforts with period detail. Attractive terrace-solarium.

Avenida Palace
No smokers rest. 25/300

Gran Via de les Corts Catalanes 605 ✉ 08007 – Ⓜ Passeig de Gràcia – ✆ 93 301 96 00 – avpalace@husa.es – Fax 93 318 12 34 – www.avenidapalace.com **K2**

136 rm – ††110/275 €, ☕ 20 € – 14 suites

Rest – Menu 21 €

♦ Traditional ♦ Classic ♦

An elegant, traditional-style hotel in which the attention to detail is evident throughout and the recently refurbished rooms offer high levels of comfort. The restaurant has a distinguished atmosphere, pleasant furnishings and impeccable service.

Ritz Barcelona Roger de Llúria
25/60

Roger de Llúria 28 ✉ 08010 – Ⓜ Urquinaona – ✆ 93 343 60 80 – ritzbcn@rogerdelluria.com – Fax 93 343 60 81 – www.rogerdelluria.com **L2**

46 rm – †105/205 € ††116/315 €, ☕ 17.50 € – 2 suites

Rest – *(closed August and Sunday)* Carte 28/39 €

♦ Traditional ♦ Classic ♦

A hotel with a welcoming and intimate feel, a small foyer and large, extremely comfortable and well-appointed bedrooms. The spacious restaurant is traditionally furnished in elegant style.

Omm
25/30

Rosselló 265 ✉ 08008 – Ⓜ Diagonal – ✆ 93 445 40 00 – reservas@hotelomm.es – Fax 93 445 40 04 – www.hotelomm.es **K1**

91 rm – ††200/400 €, ☕ 21 €

Rest *Moo* – see below

♦ Business ♦ Design ♦

Hiding behind the original façade is a boutique hotel with a bright, spacious lounge area with a designer feel laid out in three parts. Contemporary rooms with restrained decor, plus a restaurant serving varied and inventive cuisine.

Abba Sants
No smokers rest. 25/200

Numància 32 ✉ 08029 – Ⓜ Sants-Estació – ✆ 93 600 31 00 – abba-sants@abbahoteles.com – Fax 93 600 31 01 **I2**

140 rm – ††80/280 €, ☕ 15.50 €

Rest – Menu 26 €

Rest *Amalur* – *(closed August)* Carte 40/45 €

♦ Business ♦ Chain hotel ♦ Modern ♦

A newly constructed hotel of modern design. Adequate public areas and bedrooms, which are smallish but comfortable. Functional dining room where the menu is a mix of traditional and Basque cuisine.

Gallery H. No smokers rest.

Rosselló 249 ✉ 08008 – Ⓜ Diagonal – ✆ 93 415 99 11 – email@galleryhotel.com – Fax 93 415 91 84 – www.galleryhotel.com 25/200 VISA

108 rm – 110/255 € 115/285 €, 17 € – 5 suites **K1**

Rest – Menu 22 €

◆ Business ◆ Modern ◆

This spacious, modern hotel has a roomy foyer, a number of meeting rooms and comfortable bedrooms with attractive, fully equipped bathrooms. The pleasant atmosphere in the restaurant is enhanced by the large windows, interior patio and welcoming terrace.

St. Moritz 25/200 VISA

Diputació 264 ✉ 08007 – Ⓜ Passeig de Gràcia – ✆ 93 412 15 00 – stmoritz@hcchotels.es – Fax 93 412 12 36 – www.hcchotels.es **K2**

91 rm – 139/220 € 157/265 €, 18 €

Rest – Menu 25 €

◆ Business ◆ Functional ◆

A well-run hotel with a traditional façade, well-appointed rooms and a number of private rooms suitable for any social function.

Prestige Paseo de Gràcia without rest

Passeig de Gràcia 62 ✉ 08007 – Ⓜ Passeig de Gràcia – ✆ 93 272 41 80 – reservas@prestigehotels.com – Fax 93 272 41 81 – www.prestigepaseodegracia.com VISA **K2**

45 rm – 190/300 € 220/420 €, 17.50 €

◆ Traditional ◆ Minimalist ◆

The design concept figures strongly here, with aesthetically pleasing pure lines and minimalist decor which is most evident in the hotel's bedrooms.

Cram VISA

Aribau 54 ✉ 08011 – Ⓜ Universitat – ✆ 93 216 77 00 – info@hotelcram.com – Fax 93 216 77 07 – www.hotelcram.com **K2**

67 rm – 155/400 €, 20 € – **Rest *Gaig*** – see below

◆ Business ◆ Design ◆

Bedrooms on the small side are more than compensated for by the use of innovative technology and cutting-edge work by leading interior designers.

Granados 83 No smokers rest. 25 VISA

Enric Granados 83 ✉ 08008 – Ⓜ Passeig de Gràcia – ✆ 93 492 96 70 – granados83@derbyhotels.com – Fax 93 492 96 90 – www.derbyhotels.com

77 rm – 160/349 € 160/389 €, 16 € **K2**

Rest – Carte 42/57 €

◆ Chain hotel ◆ Design ◆

A unique avant-garde hotel with a profusion of glass, steel and brick. Splendid bedrooms with excellent facilities, decorated with 10C Asiatic art. Pleasant restaurant terrace.

NH Podium No smokers rest. 25/240

Bailén 4 ✉ 08010 – Ⓜ Arc de Triomf – ✆ 93 265 02 02 – nhpodium@nh-hotels.com – Fax 93 265 05 06 VISA **L2**

140 rm – 118/158 € 124/204 €, 19 € – 5 suites

Rest *Corella* – Carte 31/36 €

◆ Business ◆ Chain hotel ◆ Functional ◆

In the Modernist part of the Ensanche area. A traditional façade and a modern interior with avant-garde design details. Welcoming and well-lit rooms. Intimate restaurant with pleasant décor and contemporary paintings.

Balmes No smokers rest. 25/30 VISA

Mallorca 216 ✉ 08008 – Ⓜ Diagonal – ✆ 93 451 19 14 – balmes@derbyhotels.es – Fax 93 451 00 49 – www.derbyhotels.com **K2**

93 rm – 90/192 € 90/210 €, 13 € – 8 suites

Rest – *(closed Saturday and Sunday) (lunch only)* Menu 10.90 €

◆ Traditional ◆ Functional ◆

A modern-style hotel with pleasantly furnished rooms, wooden floors and exposed brick walls. One of the hotel's main features is its pleasant pool and terrace.

SPAIN

Derby
AC SAT ✆ 25/60 VISA MC AE

Loreto 21 ✉ 08029 – Ⓜ Entença – ✆ 93 322 32 15 – derby@derbyhotels.com – Fax 93 410 08 62 – www.derbyhotels.com J2

111 rm – †85/210 € ††85/234 €, ☕ 14 € – 4 suites

Rest – *(coffee shop only)*

♦ Traditional ♦ Functional ♦

A classic hotel in the business district of the city. Spacious public areas and a coffee shop with a separate entrance, an English-style bar and comfortable rooms.

AC Vilamarí
Fitness ♿ AC SAT ✆ 25/35 VISA MC AE

Vilamarí 34-36 ✉ 08015 – Ⓜ Espanya – ✆ 93 289 09 09 – acvilamari@ac-hotels.com – Fax 93 289 05 01 – www.ac-hotels.com J3

90 rm – ††75/210 €, ☕ 13 €

Rest – *(closed August)* Menu 22 €

♦ Business ♦ Chain hotel ♦ Functional ♦

Meticulous in style, this hotel successfully combines functionality with the world of design. Comfortable bedrooms, half of which have bathtubs, the remainder showers. The subtly-lit restaurant is modern yet intimate.

Alexandra
♿ AC SAT ✆ 25/100 VISA MC AE

Mallorca 251 ✉ 08008 – Ⓜ Passeig de Gràcia – ✆ 93 467 71 66 – informacion@hotel-alexandra.com – Fax 93 488 02 58 – www.hotel-alexandra.com K2

106 rm – †165/280 € ††195/330 €, ☕ 17 € – 3 suites

Rest – *(set menu only)* Menu 22 €

♦ Business ♦ Functional ♦

A modern and welcoming hotel with spacious, well-equipped rooms, pleasant furnishings, carpeted floors and bathrooms with marble fittings. Pleasant public areas.

NH Master
AC 25/100 VISA MC AE

València 105 ✉ 08011 – Ⓜ Hospital Clinic – ✆ 93 323 62 15 – nhmaster@nh-hotels.com – Fax 93 323 43 89 – www.nh-hotels.com J2

80 rm – †70.09/130 € ††70.09/174 €, ☕ 13 € – 1 suite

Rest – Menu 12.50 €

♦ Business ♦ Chain hotel ♦ Functional ♦

Both central and modern with the characteristic style of this hotel chain. Pleasantly decorated and functional bedrooms which are ideal for business travellers.

Cristal Palace
AC SAT ✆ 25/100 VISA MC AE

Diputació 257 ✉ 08007 – Ⓜ Passeig de Gràcia – ✆ 93 487 87 78 – reservas@eurostarscristalpalace.com – Fax 93 487 90 30 – www.eurostarscristalpalace.com K2

147 rm – †79/250 € ††99/275 €, ☕ 12.88 € – 1 suite

Rest – Menu 18.69 €

♦ Business ♦ Modern ♦

Modern in design with a glass façade and well-equipped rooms offering high levels of comfort. Efficiently managed by friendly staff.

NH Numància
AC SAT ✆ 25/65 VISA MC AE

Numància 74 ✉ 08029 – Ⓜ Sants-Estació – ✆ 93 322 44 51 – nhnumancia@nh-hotels.com – Fax 93 410 76 42 – www.nh-hotels.com I2

140 rm – †70.09/130 € ††70.09/174 €, ☕ 13 €

Rest – Menu 22 €

♦ Business ♦ Chain hotel ♦ Functional ♦

Close to Sants train station. Pleasant public areas and comfortable bedrooms with modern décor and furnishings.

América without rest
Fitness ♿ AC SAT ✆ 25/50 VISA MC AE

Provença 195 ✉ 08008 – Ⓜ Provença – ✆ 93 487 62 92 – america@hotel-america-barcelona.com – Fax 93 487 25 18 – www.hotelamericabarcelona.com K2

60 rm – †100/196 € ††100/230 €, ☕ 14.50 €

♦ Traditional ♦ Cosy ♦

A modern and spacious hotel with a combined reception and public areas. Comfortable bedrooms with minimalist décor and personalised service.

B Hotel without rest 25/130 VISA AE
Gran Via de les Corts Catalanes 389 ✉ 08015 – Ⓜ Espanya – ✆ 93 552 95 00 – b-hotel@nnhotels.es – Fax 93 552 95 01 – www.b-hotel.es **J3**
84 rm – 100/240 € 100/295 €, 12 €
♦ Chain hotel ♦ Modern ♦
A thoroughly contemporary feel, plus a good location in the city. Bright public areas, modern bedrooms, rooftop terrace-solarium with excellent views, and a swimming pool.

Núñez Urgell without rest 25/150 VISA AE
Comte d'Urgell 232 ✉ 08036 – Ⓜ Hospital Clinic – ✆ 93 322 41 53 – nunezurgell@nnhotels.es – Fax 93 419 01 06 – www.nnhotels.com **J2**
106 rm – 90/240 € 100/295 €, 12.50 € – 2 suites
♦ Business ♦ Functional ♦
A hotel with a welcoming foyer, coffee shop and comfortable bedrooms, most of which are pleasantly furnished and have a terrace-balcony.

Onix Rambla 25/80 VISA AE
Rambla de Catalunya 24 ✉ 08007 – Ⓜ Catalunya – ✆ 93 342 79 80 – reservas.hotelsonix@icyesa.es – Fax 93 342 51 52 – www.horelsonix.es **K2**
40 rm – 80/127 € 90/157 €, 10 €
Rest – *(coffee shop only)*
♦ Business ♦ Functional ♦
The Onix Rambla's seigneurial exterior contrasts with its welcoming, contemporary interior; reasonably spacious and functionally furnished rooms with wood flooring.

Zenit Borrell 25/60 VISA AE
Comte Borrell 208 ✉ 08029 – Ⓜ Hospital Clinic – ✆ 93 452 55 66 – borrell@zenithoteles.com – Fax 93 452 55 60 – www.zenithoteles.com **J2**
73 rm – 50/250 €, 11 € – 1 suite
Rest – Menu 12 €
♦ Traditional ♦ Modern ♦
The emphasis here is on impeccable taste with bedrooms that have contemporary furnishings, wood floors and top-notch bathrooms. Small, Modernist-style lounge area.

NH Forum No smokers rest. 25/50 VISA AE
Ecuador 20 ✉ 08029 – Ⓜ Sants-Estació – ✆ 93 419 36 36 – nhforum@nh-hotels.com – Fax 93 419 89 10 – www.nh-hotels.com **J2**
47 rm – 95/151 €, 13 € – 1 suite
Rest – *(closed August, Saturday, Sunday and Bank Holidays)* Carte 27/35 €
♦ Business ♦ Chain hotel ♦ Functional ♦
A modern hotel with the characteristic style of the NH chain. Pleasant and well-equipped rooms.

NH Rallye No smokers rest.
Travessera de les Corts 150 ✉ 08028 25/250 VISA AE
– Ⓜ Les Corts – ✆ 93 339 90 50 – nhrallye@nh-hotels.com – Fax 93 411 07 90 – www.nh-hotels.com **I3**
105 rm – 67/139 € 77/186 €, 13.50 € – 1 suite
Rest – *(closed August)* Carte 24/35 €
♦ Business ♦ Chain hotel ♦ Functional ♦
A modern, functional hotel with the characteristic style of the NH chain. Comfortable, well-equipped rooms, plus an attractive terrace-bar on the top floor.

NH les Corts 25/80 VISA AE
Travessera de les Corts 292 ✉ 08029 – Ⓜ Les Corts – ✆ 93 322 08 11 – nhlescorts@nh-hotels.com – Fax 93 322 09 08 – www.nh-hotels.com
80 rm – 88/131 € 99/168 €, 13.50 € – 1 suite **I2**
Rest – *(coffee shop) (dinner only)*
♦ Business ♦ Chain hotel ♦ Functional ♦
Pleasant rooms, each with a terrace, furnished in brightly coloured modern decor. Multi-functional meeting rooms are also available. Efficiently managed by friendly staff.

Onix Fira without rest 25/80 VISA

Llançà 30 ✉ 08015 – Ⓜ Espanya – ☎ 93 426 00 87 – reservas.hotelsonix@icyesa.es – Fax 93 426 19 81 – www.hotelsonix.com **J3**

80 rm – 88/132 € 99/163 €, 9 €

◆ Business ◆ Functional ◆

Close to the old bullring. An intimate and comfortable hotel with a large coffee shop and functional rooms. Décor with an attractive use of marble.

XXXX ✿ **Caelis** – Hotel Palace VISA

Gran Via de les Corts Catalanes 668 ✉ 08010 – Ⓜ Urquinaona – ☎ 93 510 12 05 – restaurante@caelis.com – Fax 93 510 12 05

closed 7 days in July, August, 7 days in September, Saturday lunch, Sunday, Monday and Bank Holidays **L2**

Rest – Menu 70 € – Carte 69/100 €

Spec. Macarrones gratinados, tipo mar y montaña, rellenos con bogavante, apio y trufa negra. Cochinillo crujiente con frutos secos y sorbete de manzana verde. Trufa negra (January-March).

◆ Inventive ◆ Design ◆

An amazing décor with a classical entrance contrasting with a modern designed dining room. Excellent setting for the inventive cuisine.

XXXX **La Dama** VISA

av. Diagonal 423 ✉ 08036 – Ⓜ Diagonal – ☎ 93 202 06 86 – reservas@ladama-restaurant.com – Fax 93 200 72 99 – www.ladama-restaurant.com

closed 3 weeks in August **J2**

Rest – Carte 49/67 €

◆ International ◆ Retro ◆

An elegant restaurant with Modernist decorative details both inside and on the façade. Professional staff.

XXXX ✿ **Drolma** – Hotel Majestic Smokers rest. 12/16 VISA

Passeig de Gràcia 68 ✉ 08007 – Ⓜ Passeig de Gràcia – ☎ 93 496 77 10 – drolma@hotelmajestic.es – Fax 93 445 38 93

closed Sunday **K2**

Rest – Menu 135 € – Carte 100/138 €

Spec. Puré de patatas, zabaione y trufas negras (December-March). Cabrito embarrado a la cuchara. Grouse con cap i pota y col (October-November).

◆ International ◆ Formal ◆

Traditional-style, predominantly wood, décor creating an elegant and refined atmosphere. Professional staff.

XXXX ✿ **Gaig** – Hotel Cram 4/40 VISA

Aragó 214 ✉ 08011 – Ⓜ Passeig de Gràcia – ☎ 93 429 10 17 – info@restaurantgaig.com – Fax 93 429 70 02 – www.restaurantgaig.com

closed Holy Week, 21 days in August, Sunday, Monday lunch and Bank Holidays dinner **K2**

Rest – Menu 74.20 € – Carte 58/79 €

Spec. Atún marinado y ensalada de contrastes. Arroz bomba del delta con pichón. Serrín dulce y cinco tipos de chocolate.

◆ Inventive ◆ Design ◆

A refined setting with professional service of the highest order. Creative cuisine which takes its inspiration from the Mediterranean and Catalunya.

XXXX **Beltxenea** VISA

Mallorca 275 entlo ✉ 08008 – Ⓜ Diagonal – ☎ 93 215 30 24 – Fax 93 487 00 81

closed Christmas, Holy Week, August, Saturday lunch and Sunday **K1**

Rest – Carte 41/51 €

◆ Basque ◆ Formal ◆

An elegant restaurant in a historic building with an atmosphere of the past. A dining room with views of the garden and an attractive, carved wooden fireplace.

XXX **Casa Calvet** No smokers rest. AC ⇔5/12 VISA MC AE

Casp 48 ✉ 08010 – Ⓜ Urquinaona – ✆ 93 412 40 12 – restaurant@casacalvet.es – Fax 93 412 43 36 – www.casacalvet.es
closed Holy Week, 15 days in August, Sunday and Bank Holidays **L2**
Rest – Carte 49/63 €
◆ Inventive ◆ Formal ◆
A restaurant in an attractive building designed by Gaudí. The dining room is welcoming and there is an excellent à la carte menu.

XXX ✿ **Lasarte** – Hotel Condes de Barcelona Smokers rest. AC VISA MC AE

Mallorca 259 ✉ 08008 – Ⓜ Passeig de Gràcia – ✆ 93 445 32 42 – info@restaurantlasarte.com – Fax 93 445 32 32 – www.restaurantlasarte.com
closed August, Saturday, Sunday and Bank Holidays **K2**
Rest – Menu 85 € – Carte 69/78 €
Spec. Mosaico de frutos del mar con crema de limón al caviar. Costillar de cordero asado con gnocchis al aceite de olivas negras y tiras de espárragos. Canelón de manzana verde con jugo helado de coco y granizado de ron.
◆ Inventive ◆ Formal ◆
A restaurant supervised by the famous chef Martin Barasategui from Lasarte in the Basque country. Two comfortable dining rooms in a modern style offering a creative menu with some traditional Basque dishes.

XXX **Jaume de Provença** AC VISA MC AE

Provença 88 ✉ 08029 – Ⓜ Entença – ✆ 93 430 00 29 – restaurant@jaumeprovenza.com – Fax 93 439 29 50 – www.jaumeprovenza.com
closed Holy Week, August, Sunday dinner and Monday **J2**
Rest – Carte 36/53 €
◆ International ◆ Formal ◆
A traditional-style restaurant with a small bar, which leads to a spacious dining room with an intimate atmosphere and attentive service.

XXX **Windsor** AC VISA MC AE

Còrsega 286 ✉ 08008 – Ⓜ Diagonal – ✆ 93 415 84 83 – info@restaurantwindsor.com – Fax 93 238 66 08 – www.restaurantwindsor.com
closed 1 to 7 January, Holy Week, August, Saturday lunch and Sunday
Rest – Carte 35/55 € ✿ **K2**
◆ Catalan cuisine ◆ Formal ◆
An elegant restaurant with a beautiful interior patio, several dining areas and a private bar. An interesting menu and a good wine list.

XXX **Gargantua i Pantagruel** AC ⇔6/28 VISA MC AE

Còrsega 200 ✉ 08036 – Ⓜ Hospital Clinic – ✆ 93 453 20 20 – gip@gargantuaipantagruel.com – Fax 93 419 29 22 – www.gargantuaipantagruel.com
closed August and Sunday dinner – **Rest** – Carte 35/54 € **J2**
◆ Catalan cuisine ◆ Trendy ◆
The main restaurant and private rooms are classic in style, enhanced by contemporary design features. Traditional cuisine with a modern twist, including dishes from Lérida.

XXX **Oliver y Hardy** AC VISA MC AE

av. Diagonal 593 ✉ 08014 – Ⓜ Maria Cristina – ✆ 93 419 31 81 – oliveryhardy@husa.es – Fax 93 419 18 99 – www.husarestauracion.com
closed Holy Week, Saturday lunch and Sunday – **Rest** – Carte 28/51 € **I2**
◆ International ◆ Formal ◆
A renowned dinner venue divided between a nightclub and restaurant. Refined dining room with a terrace used for private functions.

XXX **Maria Cristina** AC VISA MC AE

Provença 271 ✉ 08008 – Ⓜ Provença – ✆ 93 215 32 37 – Fax 93 215 83 23
closed 15 to 25 August, Saturday lunch and Sunday **K1**
Rest – Carte 40/51 €
◆ Catalan cuisine ◆ Formal ◆
The attractive opaque glass frontage leads to a small foyer and several dining rooms with a mixed classic-modern ambience. Traditional cuisine based on high-quality products.

Moo - Hotel Omm
No smokers rest. AC VISA MC AE DC

Rosselló 265 ✉ 08008 – Ⓜ Diagonal – ✆ 93 445 40 00 – restaurante.moo@hotelomm.es – Fax 93 445 40 04 – www.hotelomm.es
closed 21 days in August and Sunday K1
Rest – Menu 70 € – Carte 45/65 €
Spec. Tartar de salmón salvaje con helado de humo. Lubina con guisantes y cilantro. Viaje a La Habana.
♦ Inventive ♦ Design ♦
Cosmopolitan in feel with a cafeteria and an open contemporary dining room featuring skylights and decorative designer details. Innovative cuisine and an original wine list.

El Asador de Aranda
AC VISA MC AE DC

Londres 94 ✉ 08036 – Ⓜ Tibidabo – ✆ 93 414 67 90 – Fax 93 414 67 90 – www.asadoraranda.com
closed Holy Week and Sunday dinner L2
Rest – Carte 30/36 €
♦ Roast lamb ♦ Rustic ♦
In a street off the Avenida Diagonal. A spacious restaurant with traditional Castilian-style décor, bar and a wood-fired oven for roasting suckling pig and lamb.

La Provença
AC VISA MC AE DC

Provença 242 ✉ 08008 – Ⓜ Diagonal – ✆ 93 323 23 67 – restofi@laprovenza.com – Fax 93 451 23 89 – www.laprovenza.com K2
Rest – Carte 22/27 €
♦ Catalan cuisine ♦ Trendy ♦
A fusion of the traditional and modern restaurant close to the Paseo de Gràcia in a comfortable, cheerful setting. The well-priced menu is based on fresh market produce.

El Asador de Aranda
AC VISA MC AE DC

Pau Claris 70 ✉ 08010 – Ⓜ Urquinaona – ✆ 93 342 55 77 – asador@asadoraranda.com – Fax 93 342 55 78 – www.asadoraranda.com
closed Holy Week and Sunday dinner J2
Rest – Carte 30/36 €
♦ Roast lamb ♦ Rustic ♦
The standard features of this chain are evident here with a bar at the entrance, a roasting oven in open view and two inviting dining rooms with elegant Castilian decor.

El Túnel D'en Marc Palou
Smokers rest. AC VISA MC AE DC

Bailén 91 ✉ 08009 – Ⓜ Girona – ✆ 93 265 86 58 – Fax 93 246 01 14
closed August, Sunday and Monday dinner L1
Rest – Carte 32/41 €
♦ Inventive ♦ Trendy ♦
In a glass-fronted corner building with three small and contemporary dining rooms on various levels. A refined setting for cuisine that is interestingly inventive.

Vinya Rosa-Magí
Smokers rest. AC ⇔6/20 VISA MC AE DC

av. de Sarrià 17 ✉ 08029 – Ⓜ Hospital Clinic – ✆ 93 430 00 03 – info@vinyarosamagi.com – Fax 93 430 00 41 – www.vinyarosamagi.com
closed Saturday lunch and Sunday J2
Rest – Carte 37/57 €
♦ International ♦ Friendly ♦
This small restaurant has an intimate and welcoming atmosphere and attractive décor details. Cosmopolitan cuisine.

Gorría
AC VISA MC AE DC

Diputació 421 ✉ 08013 – Ⓜ Sagrada Familia – ✆ 93 245 11 64 – info@restaurantegorria.com – Fax 93 232 78 57 – www.restaurantegorria.com
closed Holy Week, August, Sunday, Monday dinner and Bank Holidays dinner L1
Rest – Carte 35/46 €
♦ Basque ♦ Rustic ♦
A well-established and pleasant restaurant with good service. Very good menu and cuisine.

XX

Casa Darío

4/40 VISA

Consell de Cent 256 ✉ 08011 – Ⓜ Universitat – ✆ 93 453 31 35 – casadario@casadario.com – Fax 93 451 33 95 – www.casadario.com

closed August and Sunday **K2**

Rest – Carte 32/51 €

◆ Seafood ◆ Formal ◆

A long-standing, popular restaurant known for its high-quality cuisine. Private bar, three dining rooms and three private rooms. Galician and seafood specialities.

XX ✿

Saüc

Smokers rest. VISA

Passatge Lluís Pellicer 12 ✉ 08036 – Ⓜ Hospital Clinic – ✆ 93 321 01 89 – sauc@saucrestaurant.com – www.saucrestaurant.com

closed 1 to 7 January, 21 days in August, Sunday, Monday and Bank Holidays

Rest – Menu 54 € – Carte 51/60 € **J2**

Spec. Papada crujiente, calamares y alcachofas, jugo de asado. Cabrito confitado, peras, perfume de ajo y cítricos. Sablé especiado de piña, crema de azafrán y sorbete de mandarina.

◆ Inventive ◆ Family ◆

The couple who run this restaurant, functional in style but with the occasional avant-garde touch, offer a personal slant on regional cuisine based on high-quality products.

XX

Manairó

Smokers rest. VISA

Diputació 424 ✉ 08013 – Ⓜ Monumental – ✆ 93 231 00 57 – info@manairo.com – Fax 93 265 23 81 – www.manairo.com

closed 1 to 7 January, 7 to 31 August, Sunday and Monday **L1**

Rest – Carte 33/52 €

◆ Inventive ◆ Cosy ◆

This establishment has already built up a strong reputation locally. The small lounge is decorated with works by a range of artists and the restaurant serves food produced by the marriage of innovative techniques with culinary tradition.

X

Nervión

Smokers rest. VISA

Còrsega 232 ✉ 08036 – Ⓜ Diagonal – ✆ 93 218 06 27

closed Holy Week, August, Sunday and Bank Holidays **J2**

Rest – Carte 28/44 €

◆ Basque ◆ Cosy ◆

A small and well-managed restaurant. Delicious traditional Basque dishes and friendly service.

Mesón Cinco Jotas

VISA

Rambla de Catalunya 91-93 ✉ 08008 – Ⓜ Diagonal – ✆ 93 487 89 42 – m5jrambla@osborne.es – Fax 93 487 91 21 – www.mesoncincojotas.com

Tapa 3.50 € **Ración** approx. 12 € **K2**

◆ Spanish ◆ Tapas bar ◆

A spacious bar with traditional wood décor where customers can sample a good selection of fine hams and other pork products. Beyond the bar there is a dining room.

Txapela

VISA

Passeig de Gràcia 8-10 ✉ 08007 – Ⓜ Passeig de Gràcia – ✆ 93 412 02 89 – txapela@angrup.com – Fax 93 412 24 78 **K2**

Tapa 2 €

◆ Basque ◆ Tapas bar ◆

A Basque-style bar and restaurant situated on the Paseo de Gràcia. Spacious and with a pleasant terrace.

Cervecería Catalana

VISA

Mallorca 236 ✉ 08008 – Ⓜ Diagonal – ✆ 93 216 03 68 – jahumada@62online.com – Fax 93 488 17 97 **K2**

Tapa 5 € **Ración** approx. 9 €

◆ Spanish ◆ Brasserie ◆

A bar specialising in different beers with wood décor and a wide range of well-presented tapas made from carefully selected ingredients.

SPAIN

SANT MARTÍ

Plan I

Arts

Marina 19 ✉ 08005 – Ⓜ Ciutadella-Vila Olímpica – ☎ 93 221 10 00 – rc.barcelonareservations@ritzcarlton.com – Fax 93 221 10 70 – www.hotelartsbarcelona.com **C2**

25/900 VISA MC AE

397 rm – 370/500 €, ☕ 26 € – 86 suites – **Rest** – Menu 65 €
Rest *Arola* – *(closed January, Monday and Tuesday)* Carte 43/62 €

◆ Grand Luxury ◆ Design ◆

Housed in one of the two towers overlooking the Olympic port, this superb hotel is justifiably renowned for the luxurious design of its guestrooms and lounges. The Arts has several restaurants, most notably the Arola, renowned for its creative cuisine.

Eurostar Grand Marina H.

25/500 VISA MC AE

Moll de Barcelona (World Trade Center) ✉ 08039 – ☎ 93 603 90 00 – info@grandmarinahotel.com – Fax 93 603 90 90 – www.grandmarinahotel.com Plan III **L3**

258 rm – 160/900 €, ☕ 22 € – 15 suites
Rest – Carte approx. 65 €

◆ Grand Luxury ◆ Modern ◆

A circular building in a very modern style with a patio in the middle. Rooms with a high level of comfort, attractive design details and original works of art. A well-lit restaurant with good service.

Diagonal Barcelona

No smokers rest. 25/250 VISA MC AE

av. Diagonal 205 ✉ 08018 – Ⓜ Glòries – ☎ 93 489 53 00 – reservas.diagonal@hoteles-silken.com – Fax 93 489 53 09 – www.hoteldiagonalbarcelona.com **C2**

228 rm – 100/310 € 100/340 €, ☕ 17 € – 12 suites
Rest – *(closed Sunday)* Carte 33/45 €

◆ Business ◆ Design ◆

Pure design is what you get when you ask several well-known artists to give free rein to their creativity. Ultra-modern bedrooms with baths on view and a sun terrace on the roof.

Barceló H. Atenea Mar

No smokers rest. 25/400 VISA MC AE

Passeig Garcia Faria 47 ✉ 08019 – Ⓜ Selva de Mar – ☎ 93 531 60 40 – ateneamar@bchoteles.com – Fax 93 531 60 90 – www.bchoteles.com **D2**

191 rm – 90/150 € 100/175 €, ☕ 13 € – **Rest *El Comedor*** – Carte 30/37 €

◆ Business ◆ Chain hotel ◆ Functional ◆

On an avenue facing out to sea, the Atenea Mar offers a number of modular meeting rooms, reasonable fitness area and functional bedrooms, the majority with Mediterranean views. Restaurant with a separate entrance and menu based on traditional seasonal cuisine.

Rafael H. Diagonal Port

25/175 VISA MC AE

Lope de Vega 4 ✉ 08005 – Ⓜ Poblenou – ☎ 93 230 20 00 – diagonalport@rafaelhoteles.com – Fax 93 230 20 10 – www.rafaelhoteles.com **D2**

115 rm – 90/210 € 90/240 €, ☕ 14 € – **Rest** – Menu 20 €

◆ Business ◆ Functional ◆

A modern, functional hotel with spacious public areas, comfortable, carpeted bedrooms, bathrooms fitted with marble and good soundproofing.

Hesperia del Mar

No smokers rest. 25/175 VISA MC AE

Espronceda 6 ✉ 08005 – Ⓜ Poblenou – ☎ 93 502 97 00 – hotel@hesperia-delmar.com – Fax 93 502 97 01 – www.hesperia-delmar.com **D2**

78 rm – 95/180 € 110/190 €, ☕ 15 € – 6 suites
Rest – Carte approx. 35 €

◆ Business ◆ Chain hotel ◆ Functional ◆

This hotel is located close to the sea in an area in the process of redevelopment. Facilities here include spacious lounge areas, well-equipped guest rooms with modern, practical furnishings and a bright, airy restaurant.

Vincci Marítimo No smokers rest. 25/250

Llull 340 ✉ 08019 – Ⓜ Selva de Mar – ✆ 93 356 26 00 – maritimo@vinccihoteles.com – Fax 93 356 06 69 – www.vinccihoteles.com VISA MC AE **D2**

144 rm – 78/196 € 78/241 €, ☕ 14 €

Rest – Menu 16 €

♦ Business ♦ Chain hotel ♦ Design ♦

A good level of general comfort, although the hotel's outstanding feature is its designer decor with original avant-garde features in the bathrooms and on the bed headboards. The restaurant is bright and simply designed.

Els Pescadors 5/30 VISA MC AE

pl. Prim 1 ✉ 08005 – Ⓜ Poblenou – ✆ 93 225 20 18 – contacte@elspescadors.com – Fax 93 224 00 04 – www.elspescadors.com

closed Holy Week **D2**

Rest – Carte 32/46 €

♦ Rice specialities ♦ Formal ♦

This restaurant has one dining room in the style of an early 20C café-bar and two with more modern decor. A varied menu of fish and seafood, including cod and rice dishes.

Anfiteatro VISA MC AE

av. Litoral (Parc del Port Olímpic) ✉ 08005 – Ⓜ Ciutadella-Vila Olímpica – ✆ 659 69 53 45 – anfiteatrobcn@telefonica.net – Fax 93 457 14 19

closed 8 January-4 February, 6 to 19 August, Sunday dinner and Monday **C2**

Rest – *(only set meal)* Menu 45 €

♦ Inventive ♦ Trendy ♦

This modern restaurant has a friendly atmosphere, an abundance of natural light and careful attention to detail. A large fountain adds to the overall charm.

El Túnel del Port 20/40 VISA MC AE

Moll de Gregal 12 (Port Olímpic) ✉ 08005 – Ⓜ Ciutadella-Vila Olímpica – ✆ 93 221 03 21 – eltunel@eltuneldelport.com – Fax 93 221 35 86 – www.eltuneldelport.com

closed Sunday dinner and Monday **C2**

Rest – Carte 34/52 €

♦ Catalan cuisine ♦ Formal ♦

A traditional restaurant in an elegant setting with service in keeping with its reputation. Two dining rooms, one private section and two large-capacity terraces.

NORTH of AV. DIAGONAL *Plan III*

Casa Fuster Smokers rest. 25/110 VISA MC AE

passeig de Gràcia 132 ✉ 08008 – Ⓜ Diagonal – ✆ 93 255 30 00 – casafuster@hotelescenter.es – Fax 93 255 30 02 – www.hotelcasafuster.com **K1**

76 rm – 180/501 €, ☕ 25 € – 20 suites

Rest ***Galaxó*** – Carte 45/65 €

♦ Luxury ♦ Modern ♦

Magnificent hotel housed in a beautiful Modernist building dating back to 1908. It has an attractive café-lounge and the bedrooms are equipped to the highest level with well-appointed bathrooms. You can enjoy sophisticated, innovative cooking in the hotel's elegant restaurant.

Balmoral 25/150 VISA MC AE

Via Augusta 5 ✉ 08006 – Ⓜ Diagonal – ✆ 93 217 87 00 – info@hotelbalmoral.com – Fax 93 415 14 21 – www.hotelbalmoral.com **K1**

106 rm – 100/194 € 120/240 €, ☕ 12 €

Rest – *(coffee shop only)*

♦ Traditional ♦ Classic ♦

A comfortable, traditional-style hotel offering professional service. Bright, well-appointed bedrooms and a choice of panelled-off function rooms.

Hesperia Presidente 25/130 VISA

av. Diagonal 570 ✉ 08021 – Ⓜ Hospital Clinic – ✆ 93 200 21 11 – hotel@hesperia-presidente.com – Fax 93 209 51 06 – www.hesperia-presidente.com **J2**

139 rm – 🚹120/230 € 🚹🚹120/270 €, ☕ 15 € – 12 suites

Rest – Carte 30/41 €

◆ Business ◆ Chain hotel ◆ Functional ◆

This completely restored building has been refurbished in light tones. Well-equipped bedrooms and spacious public areas with views of the Diagonal. The restaurant menu is based on Catalan and Mediterranean dishes.

AC Irla without rest 25/30 VISA

Calvet 40-42 ✉ 08021 – Ⓜ Muntaner – ✆ 93 241 62 10 – acirla@ac-hotels.com – Fax 93 241 62 11 **J1**

36 rm – 🚹🚹90/245 €, ☕ 13 €

◆ Business ◆ Chain hotel ◆ Functional ◆

A welcoming ambience created from a combination of quality materials, functionality and design concepts. Spacious bathrooms with showers.

Catalonia Suite No smokers rest. 25/90 VISA

Muntaner 505 ✉ 08022 – Ⓜ El Putxet – ✆ 93 212 80 12 – suite@hoteles-catalonia.es – Fax 93 211 23 17 – www.hoteles-catalonia.com **I1**

117 rm – 🚹108/139 € 🚹🚹165/177 €, ☕ 13 €

Rest – Menu 18 €

◆ Business ◆ Chain hotel ◆ Functional ◆

Located in an exclusive residential and business district, the Catalonia Suite offers guests functional, elegantly decorated rooms in a welcoming, restful atmosphere.

Catalonia Córcega VISA

Còrsega 368 ✉ 08037 – Ⓜ Verdaguer – ✆ 93 208 19 19 – corcega@hoteles-catalonia.es – Fax 93 208 08 57 – www.hoteles-catalonia.com **K1**

77 rm – 🚹122/153 € 🚹🚹165/177 €, ☕ 13 € – 2 suites

Rest – Menu 13 €

◆ Business ◆ Chain hotel ◆ Functional ◆

A modern hotel with attractive, spacious rooms, a mix of contemporary and traditional furniture and facilities in keeping with its rating, although the hotel lounge is on the small side. Fixed menu in the restaurant with a small à la carte choice.

Condado without rest VISA

Aribau 201 ✉ 08021 – Ⓜ Diagonal – ✆ 93 200 23 11 – administracion@condadohotel.com – Fax 93 200 25 86 – www.condadohotel.com **J1**

75 rm – 🚹🚹90/180 €, ☕ 11 € – 1 suite

◆ Traditional ◆ Classic ◆

The result of the building's complete refurbishment is a mix of the traditional and contemporary, with quality furnishings in light tones. Large, bright bedrooms with wood floors.

NH Cóndor Smokers rest. 25/50 VISA

Via Augusta 127 ✉ 08006 – Ⓜ Muntaner – ✆ 93 209 45 11 – nhcondor@nh-hotels.es – Fax 93 202 27 13 – www.nh-hotels.com **J1**

66 rm – 🚹80/130 € 🚹🚹80/158 €, ☕ 13 € – 12 suites

Rest – *(closed August, Saturday and Sunday)* Menu 20 €

◆ Business ◆ Chain hotel ◆ Functional ◆

A functional and comfortable hotel with all the characteristic style of this hotel chain. Modern furnishings and wood décor creating an intimate atmosphere.

Covadonga without rest 25/50 VISA

av. Diagonal 596 ✉ 08021 – Ⓜ Hospital Clinic – ✆ 93 209 55 11 – covadonga@hcchotels.com – Fax 93 209 58 33 – www.hcchotels.es **J2**

101 rm – 🚹108/169 € 🚹🚹125/210 €, ☕ 15 €

◆ Traditional ◆ Functional ◆

A good location in a lively shopping area. A classical façade, intimate ambience, and bright rooms with all creature comforts. Popular with groups.

XXXX ✿ **Neichel**

Beltran í Rózpide 1 ✉ 08034 – Ⓜ Maria Cristina – ✆ 93 203 84 08 – neichel@relaischateaux.com – Fax 93 205 63 69 – www.neichel.es
closed 1 to 7 January, 1 to 19 August, Sunday, Monday and Bank Holidays
Rest – Menu 80 € – Carte 59/79 € *Plan I* **A2**

Spec. Tartar de centollo y bogavante, carpaccio de vieiras ahumadas, rúcula a la vinagreta de naranja y piñones. Gambas de Palamós y espardenyes con alcachofas, emulsión de erizos de mar y salicornio. Tarta fina de albaricoque caliente y caramelizado, helado de mató, ratafía y almendras amargas.

♦ Inventive ♦ Design ♦

Creative and innovative cuisine to satisfy even the most demanding palate. An elegant and pleasant restaurant with a garden.

XXXX ✿ **Via Veneto**

Ganduxer 10 ✉ 08021 – Ⓜ Hospital Clinic – ✆ 93 200 72 44 – pmonje@adam.es – Fax 93 201 60 95 – www.viavenetorestaurant.com
closed 1 to 20 August, Saturday lunch and Sunday **I2**
Rest – Menu 70 € – Carte 58/73 €

Spec. Espardenyes salteadas con patatas y panceta del coll. Costillar de cordero lechal asado con costra de finas hierbas y flores de calabacín rellenas de sanfaina. Tres en uno de chocolate.

♦ International ♦ Retro ♦

A restaurant with elegant Belle Époque décor and impeccable service with an interesting menu. A highly professional staff.

XXXX ✿ **Jean Luc Figueras**

Santa Teresa 10 ✉ 08012 – Ⓜ Passeig de Gràcia – ✆ 93 415 28 77 – jlf@jeanlucfigueras.com – Fax 93 218 92 62 – www.jeanlucfigueras.com
closed Sunday – **Rest** – Carte 67/92 € **K1**

Spec. Steak tartar con caviar iraní, mascarpone de mostaza y patatas pont-neuf. Pato Colvert relleno de sémola y con su jugo de asado. Lubina de costa con hinojo y borracho de coco (January-September).

♦ Inventive ♦ Cosy ♦

A very pleasant setting in which to enjoy creative and innovative dishes. Several elegant dining areas and décor with exquisitely tasteful design details.

XXXX **Reno**

Tuset 27 ✉ 08006 – Ⓜ Passeig de Gràcia – ✆ 93 200 91 29 – reno@restaurantreno.com – Fax 93 414 41 14 – www.restaurantreno.com
closed August – **Rest** – Carte approx. 66 € **J1**

♦ Catalan cuisine ♦ Formal ♦

A traditional-style restaurant with a welcoming atmosphere and a menu firmly rooted in the gastronomic culture of the region but with a modern twist. A very good wine list.

XXX ✿ **El Racó d'en Freixa** Smokers rest. ⇔4/14

Sant Elies 22 ✉ 08006 – Ⓜ Plaça Molina – ✆ 93 209 75 59 – info@elracodenfreixa.com – Fax 93 209 79 18 – www.elracodenfreixa.com
closed Holy Week, 21 days in August, Sunday and Monday **J1**
Rest – Carte 71/76 €

Spec. Bocadillo de habas y gambas a la menta con ensalada extraña (December-May). Liebre a la royal con berenjenas fundentes. Chocolate 2007, leche, cacao, avellanas y azúcar.

♦ Inventive ♦ Family ♦

Recently redecorated in a more contemporary style with pure, minimalist lines and designer touches to mirror the excellent service and interestingly creative cuisine.

XXX **Botafumeiro**

Gran de Gràcia 81 ✉ 08012 – Ⓜ Fontana – ✆ 93 218 42 30 – info@botafumeiro.es – Fax 93 217 13 05 – www.botafumeiro.es **J1**
Rest – Carte 50/70 €

♦ Seafood ♦ Formal ♦

A well-known restaurant in the Gràcia district of the city with a maritime feel to it and a menu to match.

SPAIN

XX **Roig Robí**

Sèneca 20 ✉ 08006 – Ⓜ Diagonal – ✆ 93 218 92 22 – roigrobi@roigrobi.com – Fax 93 415 78 42 – www.roigrobi.com

closed 3 weeks in August, Saturday lunch and Sunday **K1**

Rest – Carte 53/67 €

◆ Catalan cuisine ◆ Family ◆

A modern restaurant in a splendid setting with a pleasant garden-terrace. A very varied and original menu.

XX **Alkimia** Smokers rest.

Indústria 79 ✉ 08025 – Ⓜ Sagrada Familia – ✆ 93 207 61 15 – alkimia@telefonica.net

closed 7 days in Holy Week, 7 to 27 August, Saturday, Sunday and Bank Holidays **K1**

Rest – Menu 60 € – Carte 47/70 €

Spec. Canelón de pollo de payés con bechamel de almendra y ensalada fresca. Rodaballo con crema espumosa de mantequilla, calabaza y sus pipas. Pies de cerdo con endivias glaseadas y picada de nueces.

◆ Inventive ◆ Minimalist ◆

Dining room with soothing, minimalist decor, very good service and individual lighting. Modern cuisine based on Catalonian traditions and a "sampler" menu for tasting a variety of dishes.

XX **Laurak** No smokers rest. 6/16

La Granada del Penedès 14-16 ✉ 08006 – Ⓜ Passeig de Gràcia – ✆ 93 218 71 65 – Fax 93 218 98 67 – www.laurak.net

closed 23 December-2 January, 6 to 28 August, Sunday and Monday dinner

Rest – Carte approx. 61 € **J1**

◆ Basque ◆ Design ◆

A modern restaurant which is efficiently run by the owner-chef. Airy dining room with a wooden floor, design features and two private sections.

XX **Hisop** Smokers rest.

Passatge de Marimon 9 ✉ 08021 – Ⓜ Hospital Clinic – ✆ 93 241 32 33 – hisop@hisop.com – www.hisop.com

closed 1 to 7 January, 8 to 24 August, Saturday lunch and Sunday **J2**

Rest – Carte 44/57 €

◆ Inventive ◆ Minimalist ◆

Hisop enjoys an excellent local reputation based upon its highly creative cuisine and good service. A minimalist look with floral decoration on the walls.

XX **St. Rémy**

Iradier 12 ✉ 08017 – ✆ 93 418 75 04 – Fax 93 434 04 34 – www.stremyrestaurant.com

closed Sunday dinner **I1**

Rest – Carte 26/35 €

◆ Catalan cuisine ◆ Formal ◆

A restaurant laid out on two levels, with spacious dining rooms embellished with contemporary designer furniture and pleasant lighting effects. Moderately priced Catalan cuisine.

XX **Le Quattro Stagioni** 8/16

Dr. Roux 37 ✉ 08017 – Ⓜ Les Tres Torres – ✆ 93 205 22 79 – restaurante@4stagioni.com – Fax 93 205 78 65 – www.4stagioni.com

closed Holy Week, Sunday and Monday lunch (July-August), Sunday dinner and Monday for rest of the year **I1**

Rest – Carte 24/33 €

◆ Italian ◆ Cosy ◆

A well-run restaurant with comfortable dining areas with modern décor and a pleasant patio-terrace. Cuisine in the Italian tradition.

XX

Silvestre

Santaló 101 ✉ 08021 – Ⓜ Muntaner – ☎ 93 241 40 31 – Fax 93 241 40 31
closed Holy Week, 21 days in August, Saturday lunch, Sunday and Bank Holidays **J1**
Rest – Carte 29/35 €
◆ Catalan cuisine ◆ Cosy ◆
The couple who own this restaurant have created a popular eatery with several sections which add intimacy to this classic setting. Good value for money and seasonal produce.

X

La Taula

No smokers rest.

Sant Màrius 8-12 ✉ 08022 – Ⓜ El Putxet – ☎ 93 417 28 48 – Fax 93 434 01 27 – www.lataula.com
closed August, Saturday lunch, Sunday and Bank Holidays **I1**
Rest – Carte 18/35 €
◆ International ◆ Cosy ◆
Small, cosy and with good attention to detail. A busy, lively atmosphere pervades this restaurant where the cuisine is centred around two types of menu and a list of chef's recommendations.

José Luis

Smokers rest.

av. Diagonal 520 ✉ 08006 – Ⓜ Diagonal – ☎ 93 200 83 12 – barcelona@joseluis.es – Fax 93 200 83 12 – www.joseluis.es **J2**
Tapa 7 € **Ración** approx. 14 €
◆ Spanish ◆ Tapas bar ◆
On the city's main artery. A tapas bar with tables and on the first floor two pleasant dining areas.

AT L'HOSPITALET de LLOBREGAT *Plan I*

Hesperia Tower

25/1400

Gran Via 144 ✉ 08907 – Ⓜ Bellvitge – ☎ 93 413 50 00 – hotel@hesperia-tower.com – Fax 93 413 50 10 – www.hesperia-tower.com **A3**
258 rm – 175/340 €, 22 € – 22 suites
Rest Evo – see below – **Rest *Bouquet*** – Carte approx. 60 €
◆ Business ◆ Chain hotel ◆ Modern ◆
An innovative "high tech" architectural design is behind this hotel, with its spacious public areas and lounges, conference centre and welll-equipped guestrooms. Creative dishes are to the fore in the restaurant on the second floor.

XXXX

Evo – Hotel Hesperia Tower

Smokers rest. city and mountain with the sea far off,

Gran Via 144 ✉ 08079 – Ⓜ Bellvitge – ☎ 93 413 50 30 – evo@hesperia-tower.com – www.evorestaurante.com
closed August, Saturday and Bank Holidays **A3**
Rest – Menu 135 €
Spec. Espardenyes salteadas con cebolla y tomate. Merluza pochada con pimientos del piquillo. Babá con frutos rojos y pistachos.
◆ Inventive ◆ Design ◆
A highly original design based on a panoramic dining room built beneath a glass dome. Innovative cuisine with its roots in traditional dishes and fresh market produce.

AT EL PRAT AIRPORT

Ciutat del Prat

No smokers rest. 25/100

av. Remolar 46 ✉ 08820 – ☎ 93 378 83 33 – ciutatdelprat@euro-mar.com – Fax 93 478 60 63 – www.euro-mar.com
130 rm – 74/150 €, 10 €
Rest – Menu 25 €
◆ Business ◆ Cosy ◆
Modern building with brightly coloured, fully furnished rooms and marble bathrooms. The lounge areas are cheerful and comfortable; the restaurant is elegantly furnished and decorated.

Tryp Barcelona Aeropuerto No smokers rest. 25/300

pl. del Pla de L'Estany 1-2 ✉ 08820 – ✆ 93 378 10 00 VISA MO AE

– tryp.barcelona.aeropuerto@solmelia.com – Fax 93 378 10 01

– www.tripbarcelonaaeropuerto.solmelia.com

205 rm – 60/225 €, 13 €

Rest – Menu 19.72 €

♦ Business ♦ Chain hotel ♦ Functional ♦

Functional establishment located in a business park close to the airport. The interesting lobby layout means that it opens directly onto all the corridors leading to the hotel's comfortable, practical bedrooms.

VALENCIA
VALENCIA

Population (est. 2006): 746 612 (conurbation 2 172 840) – Altitude: 13m

TURISMO VALENCIA Convention Bureau

Valencia is internationally renowned for its *Fallas* festival and, thanks to its enviable location on the Mediterranean, its delightful climate and magnificent beaches. However, the city offers much more to its increasing number of visitors who come here to admire the charming historical centre and avant-garde buildings such as the Ciudad de las Artes y las Ciencias, a work by the visionary architect Santiago Calatrava, and the Palacio de Congresos, designed by Norman Foster, both of which have become Valencia's new architectural emblems. The city has been transformed by these cutting-edge urban projects, with a reputation that has been enhanced further by the choice of Valencia as the venue for the 2007 America's Cup.

WHICH DISTRICT TO CHOOSE

Most of Valencia's **hotels** are situated in the historic centre and the area around the Ciudad de las Artes y las Ciencias. Among the city's wide choice of **restaurants** it is particularly worth mentioning those located in Playa de Levante (Les Arenes), which serve a good selection of seafood, paella and delicious rice dishes

PRACTICAL INFORMATION

ARRIVAL – DEPARTURE

Valencia-Manises airport – 8km/5mi W of the city. ✆ 961 530 229 (Arrivals), 902 404 704 (AENA (Spanish Airport Authority) information), www.aena.es; IBERIA, ✆ 902 400 500 (Reservations), www.iberia.com

From the airport to the city centre – By **bus: Aero-Bus** to Avenida del Cid, departures every 20min, cost: €2.50; bus n° **150** to the main bus station (Estación Central de Autobuses), cost: €1.05, ✆ 963 160 707 (bus information), www.etmvalencia.com/metrobus. By **taxi**: approximately €14 + €2.75 (airport supplement), ✆ 963 703 333 (Radio-taxi). By **Metro**: a metro line from the city to the airport is scheduled to open in 2007. ✆ 900 46 10 46, www.metrovalencia.com

Ferries to the Balearic Islands – Transmediterránea, Muelle de Poniente, ✆ 963 164 855, www.trasmediterranea.es

Train stations – Estación del Norte and Estación del Cabañal; RENFE (Spanish State Railways) information, ✆ 902 24 02 02 (Reservations), ✆ 902 24 34 02 (information on international services), www.renfe.es

TRANSPORT

→ METRO AND BUS

Valencia's metro system currently consists of 4 lines (three metro and one tram). The extension of line 5, scheduled for completion in 2007, will provide a link between the beach, city and the airport. The metro network is divided into different zones and the ticket price varies depending on the destination. The city centre is situated in Zone A, where a ticket costs €1.20 (a **Bonometro** card covering 10 trips costs €5.60). Combined bus and metro tickets *(billetes integrados)* are also available; for Zone A buy a **B10** ticket (€6.50). Open 5am-11.30pm; www.metrovalencia.com

Valencia also has an excellent bus network. Tickets cost €1.10, or €5.20 for the **Bonobús**, valid for 10 journeys that do not require a transfer (transfers are permitted on night buses). A good option for visitors are tickets **T1**, **T2** and **T3**, valid for an unlimited number of journeys by bus for a one-, two- or three-day period (€3.10/€5.50/€8 respectively). ✆ 963 15 85 15, www.emtvalencia.es

→ TAXI

Taxis can be hailed in the street or are available at taxi ranks. ✆ 963 703 333 (Radio-taxi), ✆ 963 959 560 (Autotaxis), ✆ 963 571 313 (Tele Taxi).

→ VALENCIA TOURIST CARD

The Valencia Tourist Card, available online and on sale in the city's tourist offices, hotels, tobacconists and newspaper stalls, offers unlimited public transport (bus, metro and tram in the city or Zone A), as well as discounts on museum entry and in participating shops and restaurants. Valid for 1, 2 or 3 days (€6, €10 and €15 respectively). ✆ 900 70 18 18, www.etmvalencia.es/valcard

→ TOURIST BUS

This 1hr30min tour covers the city's old quarter, the banks of the former bed of the River Turia and the Ciudad de las Artes y las Ciencias. Departures from plaza de la Reina, hourly from 10.30am; €12, no charge for children aged 6 and under, 6€ for children aged 7-11.

Excursion to the Albufera (tourist bus + boat trip). This 2-hr excursion operates from March to November (not every day), with departures from plaza de la Reina. ✆ 96 341 44 00, www.valenciabusturistic.com

→ TOURIST TRAIN

This 30-min tour passes through the Turia gardens, then continues to the Ciudad de las Artes y las Ciencia. ✆ 619 763 010, www.turisvalencia.es

USEFUL ADDRESSES

→ TOURIST INFORMATION

Reina: plaza la Reina, 19; ✆ 963 153 931; open Mon-Sat, 9am-7pm (Sun and public hols, 10am-2pm). **Airport**: Planta de Llegadas; ✆ 961 530 229; open Mon-Fri, 8.30am-8.30pm (Sat-Sun and public hols, 9.30am-5.30pm). **Beach**: paseo de Neptuno, 2; ✆ 963 557 108/963 525 478 – ext. 3987; open Mon-Fri, 10am-7pm (Sat-Sun and public hols, 10am-6pm). **Railway station**: Játiva, 24 (Estación del Norte); ✆ 963 528 573; open Mon-Sat, 9am-7pm (Sun and public hols, 10am-2pm). **Diputación**: Poeta Querol (Teatro Principal building); ✆ 963 514 907; open Mon-Fri, 9.30am-7pm; Sat, 10am-2pm; Sun, 11am-2pm. **Paz**: Paz, 48; ✆ 963 986 422; open Mon-Fri, 9am-2.30pm and 4.30-8pm. www.turisvalencia.es

→ POST OFFICES

Plaza del Ayuntamiento, 24; ✆ 963 944 711; open Mon-Fri, 8.30am-8.30pm; Sat, 9.30am-2pm. www.correos.es. Stamps can also be bought at tobacconist shops.

→ BANKS / CURRENCY EXCHANGE

Open Mon-Fri, 8.30am-2pm; Sat, 9am-1pm (closed Sat in summer). Cash dispensing machines available (24hr).

→ EMERGENCY

General emergencies ✆ **112**; Police ✆ **091**; Medical emergencies and ambulance ✆ **061**.

BUSY PERIODS

Fallas: 15-19 Mar – A renowned festival which has been officially designated of "international tourist interest".

Corpus Christi: 7 Jun – A colourful and spectacular procession, the origins of which date back to 1355.

Semana Santa (Holy Week): 1-8 Apr – The brotherhoods of the fishermen's districts are of particular interest during Valencia's Holy Week.

La Virgen de los Desamparados (Virgen of the Abandoned): 2nd Sun in May – Festival celebrating the city's patron saint.

Feria de Julio (July Fair): A varied programme of theatre, pop, rock, flamenco, jazz etc. Star attractions include the "Certamen Internacional de Bandas de Música" (first half of July), the bullfighting festival (second half of the month) and the colourful "battle of the flowers" (last Sun in July).

Mostra de Valencia Cinema del Mediterrani: This Mediterranean film festival is held in early Oct.

Día de la Comunidad: 9 Oct – The day of the Comunidad Valenciana, the Day of Lovers (Día de los Enamorados) and the International Fireworks Festival are all held on the same day.

DIFFERENT FACETS OF THE CITY

The majority of museums and cultural centres are open from 10am-6pm, excluding Mondays, when most are closed.

OLD CITY (CIUDAD VIEJA) – The city's historical quarter is home to numerous medieval buildings, including the **cathedral**, most of which dates from the 14C and 15C. The highlight of the building is **El Miguelete** (1418), the name affectionately given by the city's residents to the main bell of the bell tower. Other features of interest include the towers flanking the gateways in the old walls: on one side the **Torres de Serranos** (late 14C), and on the other, the **Torres de Quart** (15C). Also worthy of note are the **Palau de la Generalitat**, an attractive 15C Gothic palace, and **La Lonja**, a late-15C Flamboyant Gothic building, whose main feature is its magnificent trading hall, adorned with elegant spiral columns.

LA CIUDAD DE LAS ARTES Y LAS CIENCIAS – This cultural and leisure complex covering 350 000m²/418 600sq yd is made up of a series of spectacular avant-garde buildings, with facilities based around three distinct themes: art, science and nature. The main attractions are as follows: **L'Oceanogràfic**, a magnificent maritime park built by the architect Félix Candela; **L'Umbracle**, which functions as an open-air gallery-garden; and three impressive buildings designed by the architect Santiago Calatrava: the **Museo de les Ciències Príncipe Felipe**, considered the largest interactive museum in Europe; **L'Hemisfèric**, in the shape of a human eye; and the **Palau de les Arts**.

MAIN MUSEUMS – **Museo Nacional de Cerámica y de las Artes Suntuarias González Martí**: the sumptuous Baroque-style Palacio del Marqués de Dos Aguas is home to the superb collection of the National Ceramics Museum. **IVAM (Instituto Valenciano de Arte Moderno)** is dedicated to contemporary art with over 7 000 objects on display. The **Museo de Bellas Artes San Pío V**, which is devoted to fine arts, includes a superb collection of Gothic altarpieces, European Baroque paintings, as well as canvases from the Golden Age of Spanish art. One of the city's most visited museums is the **Museo Fallero**, which showcases the origins and evolution of the city's famous Fallas festival.

MARITIME VALENCIA – The city's port has been an important feature of Valencian commercial life since the 15C, when silk and ceramics were exported across Europe. The **Atarazanas**, medieval shipyards located close to the port, bear witness to the importance of shipbuilding in centuries past. In addition, locals and visitors alike flock to the city's beaches, such as the **Playa de Las Arenas (Levante)**, teeming with restaurants, and the **Playa de la Malvarrosa**, home to the **Casa-Museo de Blasco Ibáñez**, a chalet which once belonged to this famous writer. Two other museums worth visiting in industrial buildings close to the port are the **Museo de la Semana Santa Marinera**, devoted to local Holy Week celebrations, and the **Museo del Arroz**, providing an insight into the city's rice industry during the 20C.

GOURMET TREATS

Valencia's gastronomy, spearheaded by its famous paella and other rice-based dishes, enjoys an excellent reputation. The city's signature dish, **paella**, is traditionally cooked on a wood fire in a wide, flat-bottomed dish (also known as a "paella") similar to a frying pan with handles on each side. The dish takes a variety of forms, including vegetarian, seafood, meat and chicken, mixed (meat and fish), rabbit etc. Valencia's other rice-based dishes are well worth tasting, such as the typical **arroz a banda**, accompanied by *alioli* (an olive oil and garlic-based sauce), and **arroz negro** or black rice, prepared in a traditional paella dish and cooked with squid in its own ink, hence the dark colour. Another famous dish similar to paella is **fideuà**, prepared in the same way as *arroz a banda*, but with thick noodles instead of rice. Renowned local fish dishes include **all i pebre d'anguiles**, a stew with eel, garlic and peppers. Local desserts include sweet **cocas**, **arnadí** (a cake made from pumpkin or sweet potato), **pan quemado** (a large roll), **arrop i talladotes** (a type of fruit slice served with brown syrup) and **monas**, round rolls which are a delicacy traditionally eaten at Easter. Special mention should also be made of **horchata**, a delicious cold drink made from tiger nuts and served chilled or with crushed ice, and often accompanied by *fartons* (long, sweet pastries which are dunked in the drink).

SHOPPING

Shopping centres are generally open from 10am-8.30pm, with smaller shops opening from 10am-2pm and 5-8pm. Most shops are closed on Sundays.

Valencia's old quarter is teeming with shops selling souvenirs, with the busiest area along streets branching out from plaza de la Virgen, plaza del Ayuntamiento and plaza del Patriarca. Arts and crafts shops are predominantly centred around the cathedral, while the majority of the city's luxury boutiques (clothing, jewellery, porcelain) are located in the streets to the south of the old quarter (Poeta Querol, Colón, Cirilo and Amorós etc).

MARKETS – Valencia's *mercados* are generally held on Sundays, with the best-known taking place around the **Mestalla** football stadium, where the focus is on second-hand goods; in **plaza Redonda**, selling plants, animals, books, paintings and music; and in **La Lonja**, a wonderful setting in which to buy and sell stamps and coins.

WHAT TO BUY – **Ceramics** take pride of place in Valencia, with the most famous pieces produced by the internationally renowned *Lladró* company (Poeta Querol, 9). The best **fans** *(abanicos)*, another traditional item, are either hand-painted or made with ribs of marble or wood.

ENTERTAINMENT

The *Guía del Ocio* is a weekly publication providing a full listing of the city's cultural and leisure activities. Valencia's tourist offices are also able to provide up-to-date information on the latest events taking place in the city. For further information, log onto www.guiadelocio.com and www.lanetro.com.

Palau de la Música – A venue dedicated to classical music. www.palaudevalencia.com

Palau de les Arts – Renowned for its avant-garde design, the Palau de les Arts hosts a varied season of opera. www.lesarts.com

Teatro Principal – This theatre is a member of the "Teatres de la Generalitat Valenciana" network. www.cult.gva.es/tgv

Plaza de Toros de Valencia (Bullring) – www.tauroentrada.com; www.mundotoro.com and www.ticketstoros.com

NIGHTLIFE

Valencia is particularly lively in the evening, with numerous cafés, bars, pubs and nightclubs to suit every taste. The **El Carmen** district is at the heart of the city's nightlife with its array of pleasant outdoor terraces in plaza de La Virgen and in busy streets such as Caballeros and Quart (café *Bolsería*; Bolsería, 41). Another popular district in the evening is the area around **plaza Cánovas del Castillo** (*Boss nightclub*) and the **Gran Vía del Marqués del Turia** (*Gran Café*; *La Dama*; *Plaza* and *Las Ánimas*, the latter located at Pizarro, 31).

32nd America's CUP

VALENCIA

The America's Cup is much more than just an historic regatta – it is a friendly competition between nations and a quest for technical supremacy in the world of sailing.

History

The origins of this unique competition date back to 1851 with a regatta organised as part of the Great Exhibition held in London. This race through the English Channel involved a circuit around the Isle of Wight, with the winning team receiving a silver jug with a value of one hundred guineas. With the passing of time, this trophy became known as the ***"100 Guinea Cup"***. The schooner ***"America"*** won the race with overwhelming ease, ending the British Empire's long-standing supremacy of the seas, and demonstrating to the world the boat's technological supremacy. It is said that while watching the race, Queen Victoria asked one of her attendants which boat was in first place, and received the reply: ***"the America, Your Majesty"***; upon asking who was second, the response was clear; ***"there is no second, Your Majesty"***.

Six years later, the boat's owner, John Stevens, donated the cup to his club, the New York Yacht Club (NYYC), on the condition that the club accepted any challenge from any other club which wanted to compete for it. It was at this very moment that this unique competition was born, and which would henceforth be known as the ***"America's Cup"*** in honour of the very first boat to defeat its British adversaries in the latters' own waters.

In 1887, following a number of ***"challenges"***, George Schuyler, the last survivor of the crew of the schooner ***"America"***, passed the Cup into the permanent possession of the NYYC, a donation which was accompanied by a ***"Deed of Gift"*** laying down the terms in which challenges could be made and which stated that this was to be a ***"friendly competition between nations"***. From that moment on,

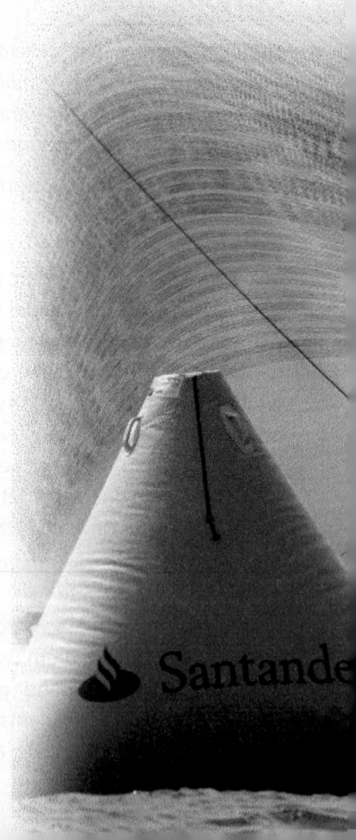

regattas would be subject to ***"mutual agreement"*** established between boats and in the event of failing to reach such an agreement, the competition would abide by the conditions stated in the aforementioned deed.

Today, the competition is divided into two parts, starting with the Louis Vuitton Cup - a series of challenger races in which competitors hoping to challenge the reigning champion fight it out in a series of head-to-head and fleet races. The winner of this cup will go on to challenge the current holder of the America's Cup, namely the Swiss Alinghi boat, which won the trophy in 2003 representing the Société Nautique de Genève, in so doing becoming the fourth country in the history of the competition to triumph in this famed race.

Valencia venue for the 2007 - America's Cup

The choice of Valencia as the venue for the 2007 competition resulted from Switzerland earning the right to organise the series of races in its role as reigning champion. As it is compulsory for the regattas to take place at sea, the Swiss were forced to find a venue outside their own country, and following an assessment of various proposals from a number of candidates, finally chose Valencia. Determining factors in this decision were the city's excellent meteorological and sailing conditions, its great maritime tradition, its obvious attractions for visitors, and the superb project of regeneration which will see the conversion of the inner basin of the city's commercial port into the America's Cup venue, with team bases and other related buildings and offices set up around its rim.

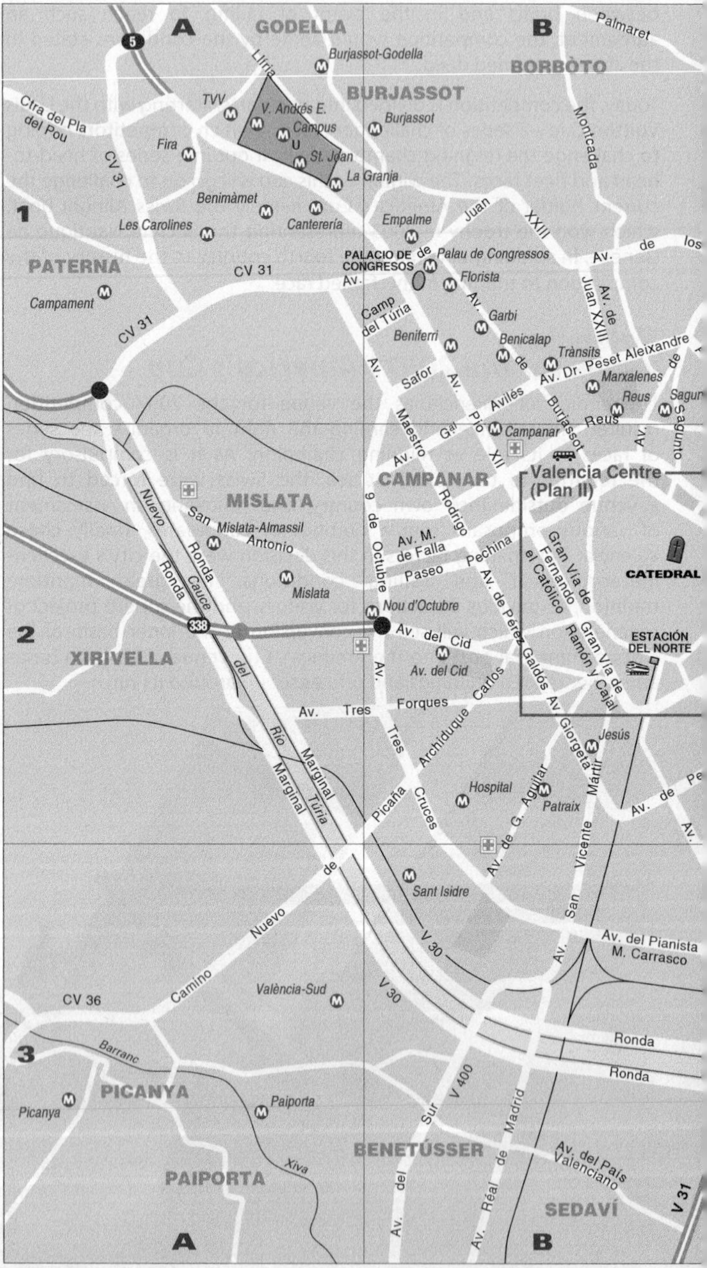

GODELLA
BURJASSOT
BORBÒTO
PATERNA
MISLATA
CAMPANAR
XIRIVELLA
PICANYA
PAIPORTA
BENETÚSSER
SEDAVÍ

Valencia Centre (Plan II)
CATEDRAL
ESTACIÓN DEL NORTE
PALACIO DE CONGRESOS

Burjassot-Godella
TVV
V. Andrés E.
Campus
St. Joan
La Granja
Burjassot
Fira
Benimàmet
Cantereria
Les Carolines
Campament
Empalme
Palau de Congressos
Florista
Garbi
Benicalap
Beniferri
Tránsits
Marxalenes
Reus
Sagunt
Campanar
Mislata-Almassil
Mislata
Nou d'Octubre
Av. del Cid
Jesús
Hospital
Patraix
Sant Isidre
València-Sud
Paiporta
Picanya

Palmaret
Llíria
Ctra del Pla del Pou
Montcada
CV 31
Av. de Juan XXIII
Av. de los
Camp del Túria
Av. Dr. Peset Aleixandre
Av. Pio XII
Av. Maestro Rodrigo
Av. Gal Avilés
Burjassot
Reus
Av. Saguntó
Safor
Nuevo Cauce
Ronda
San Antonio
Av. 9 de Octubre
Av. M. de Falla
Paseo Pechina
Av. de Pérez Galdós
Gran Vía de Fernando el Católico
Gran Vía de Ramón y Cajal
Av. Giorgeta
Av. del Cid
Av. Tres Forques
Archiduque Carlos
Av. Tres Cruces
Picaña
Ronda del Río
Marginal Túria
Av. de G. Aguilar
Av. San Vicente Mártir
Av. de Pe
V 30
Av. del Pianista M. Carrasco
Camino Nuevo de
CV 36
Barranc
Xiva
V 400
Av. del Sur
Av. Réal de Madrid
Av. del País Valenciano
V 31
Ronda
VALENCIA-MANISES
A
B
1
2
3

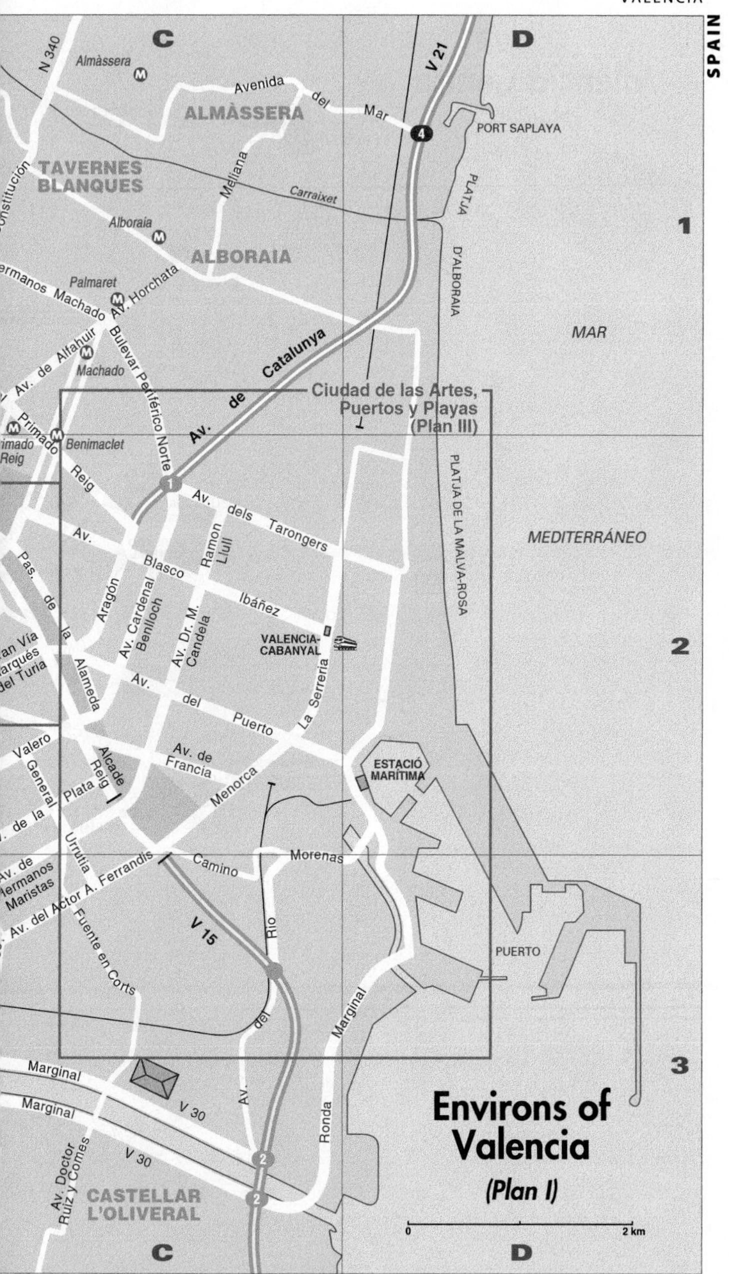

Environs of Valencia

(Plan I)

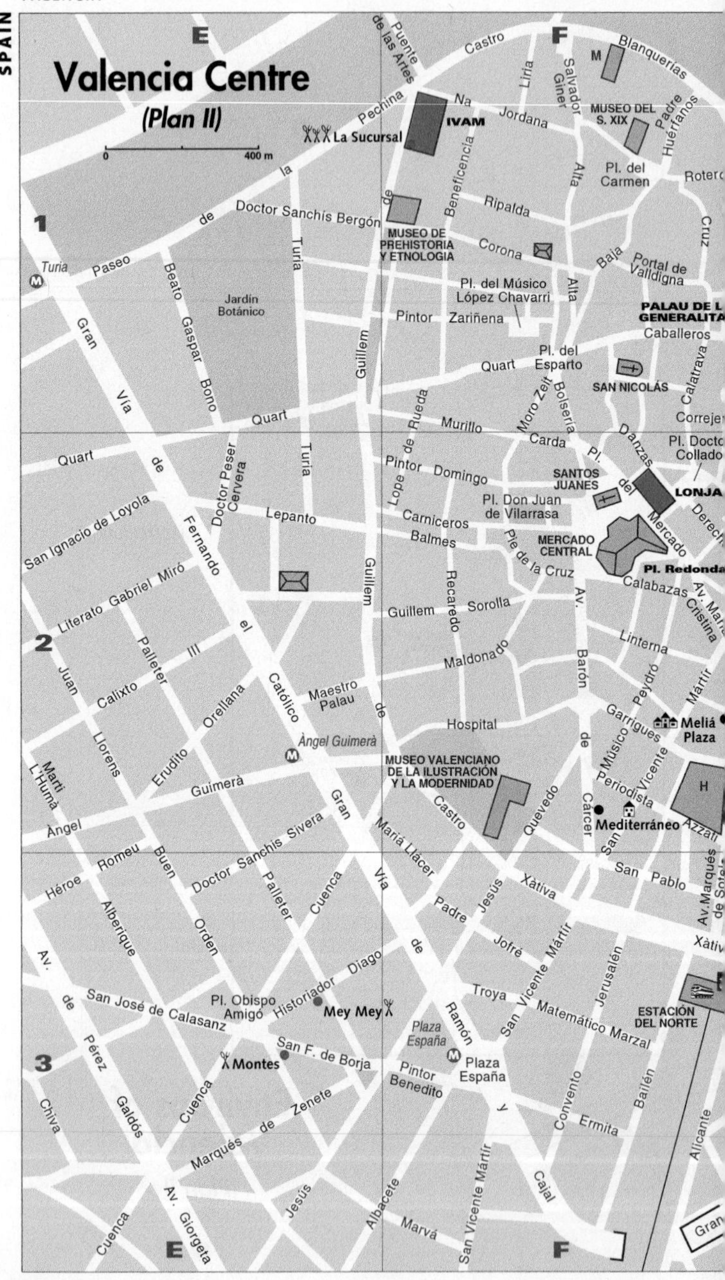
Valencia Centre
(Plan II)
0
400 m
E
F
1
2
3
IVAM
MUSEO DEL S. XIX
MUSEO DE PREHISTORIA Y ETNOLOGIA
La Sucursal
Jardín Botánico
PALAU DE L GENERALITA
SAN NICOLÁS
SANTOS JUANES
LONJA
MERCADO CENTRAL
Pl. Redonda
Meliá Plaza
MUSEO VALENCIANO DE LA ILUSTRACIÓN Y LA MODERNIDAD
Mediterráneo
ESTACIÓN DEL NORTE
Mey Mey
Montes
Turia
Àngel Guimerà
Plaza España
Pl. del Músico López Chavarri
Pl. del Carmen
Pl. del Esparto
Pl. Doctor Collado
Pl. Don Juan de Vilarrasa
Pl. Obispo Amigó
Paseo de la Pechina
Doctor Sanchis Bergón
Gran Vía de Fernando el Católico
Gran Vía de Ramón y Cajal
Quart
Lepanto
Guillem de Castro
Blanquerías
Calixto III
Xàtiva
San Vicente Mártir
Av. Barón de Cárcer
Av. de Pérez Galdós
Av. Giorgeta
San José de Calasanz
Marqués de Zenete
Matemático Marzal
Alicante
Puente de las Artes

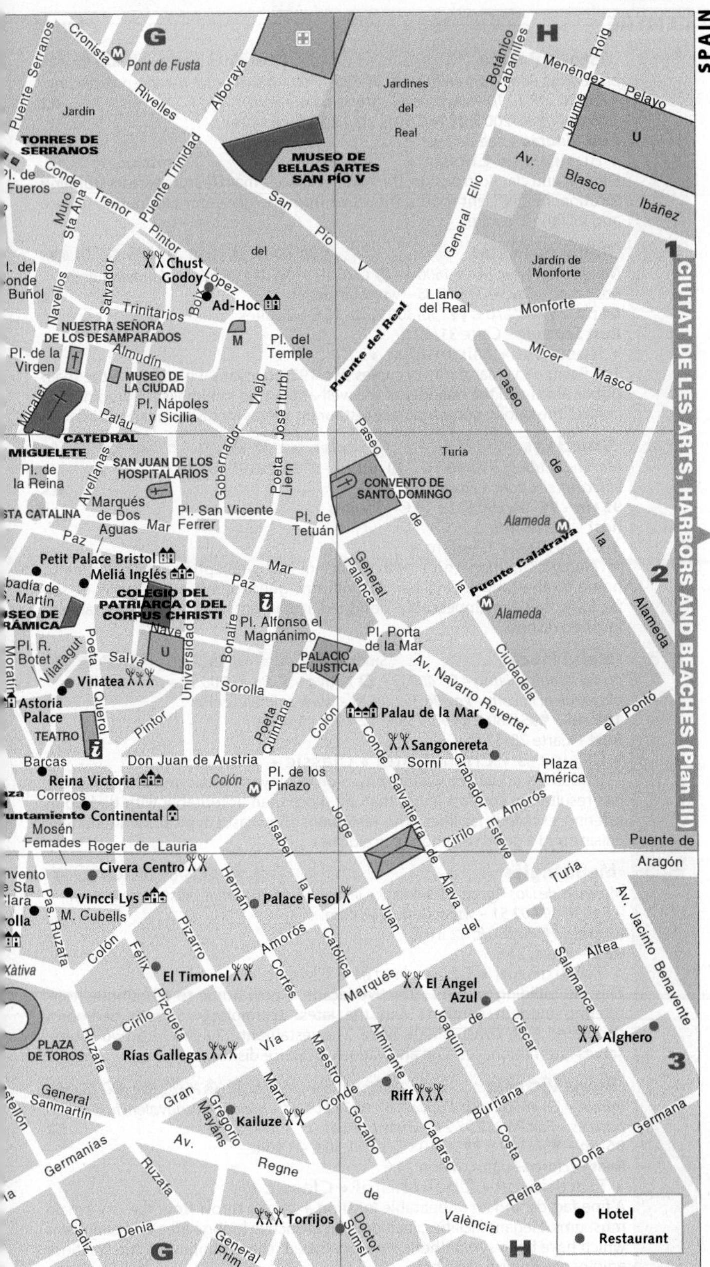
SPAIN
CIUTAT DE LES ARTS, HARBORS AND BEACHES (Plan III)
TORRES DE SERRANOS
MUSEO DE BELLAS ARTES SAN PÍO V
Jardines del Real
Jardín
Pont de Fusta
Chust Godoy
Ad-Hoc
NUESTRA SEÑORA DE LOS DESAMPARADOS
MUSEO DE LA CIUDAD
Pl. Nápoles y Sicilia
CATEDRAL
MIGUELETE
SAN JUAN DE LOS HOSPITALARIOS
Pl. de la Reina
Pl. de la Virgen
Pl. del Temple
Llano del Real
Jardín de Monforte
Puente del Real
CONVENTO DE SANTO DOMINGO
Pl. San Vicente Ferrer
Pl. de Tetuán
Alameda
Puente Calatrava
Turia
Petit Palace Bristol
Meliá Inglés
COLEGIO DEL PATRIARCA O DEL CORPUS CHRISTI
Pl. Alfonso el Magnánimo
PALACIO DE JUSTICIA
Pl. Porta de la Mar
Vinatea
Astoria Palace
TEATRO
Palau de la Mar
Sangonereta
Plaza América
Reina Victoria
Continental
Colón
Pl. de los Pinazo
Puente de Aragón
Civera Centro
Vincci Lys
Palace Fesol
El Timonel
El Ángel Azul
Alghero
PLAZA DE TOROS
Rías Gallegas
Riff
Kailuze
Torrijos
Hotel
Restaurant

SPAIN

CENTRE

Plan II

Astoria Palace

25/500

pl. Rodrigo Botet 5 ✉ 46002 – ✆ 96 398 10 00 – info@hotel-astoria-palace.com – Fax 96 398 10 10 – www.hotel-astoria-palace.com **G2**

196 rm – †96/200 € ††96/250 €, ☕ 12.50 € – 8 suites

Rest *Vinatea* – see below

◆ Business ◆ Classic ◆

Elegant and classic in design, the Astoria Palace's main features are its stunning location, magnificent rooms, the views from the glass-fronted lounge-terrace and its fitness centre.

Palau de la Mar

25/30

Navarro Reverter 14 ✉ 46004 – Ⓜ Colón – ✆ 96 316 28 84 – palaudelamar@hospes.es – Fax 96 316 28 85 – www.hospes.es **H2**

64 rm – †150/270 € ††150/300 €, ☕ 16 € – 2 suites

Rest *Senzone* – Carte 31/49 €

◆ Business ◆ Minimalist ◆

The Palau de la Mar partly occupies two 19C mansions which house the main public areas and the majority of the well-appointed minimalist bedrooms. Spa centre. The bright, contemporary restaurant serves Mediterranean cuisine.

Vincci Lys

No smokers rest. 25/70

Martínez Cubells 5 ✉ 46002 – Ⓜ Xàtiva – ✆ 96 350 95 50 – lys@vinccihoteles.com – Fax 96 350 95 52 **G3**

95 rm – ††104/290 €, ☕ 14 € – 5 suites

Rest – Menu 16 €

◆ Business ◆ Classic ◆

An elegant, traditional hotel with a spacious lobby-reception area which is also home to the lounge and bar. Magnificent guestrooms, a full range of spa facilities, and an impeccably designed restaurant offering Mediterranean-inspired dishes.

Meliá Plaza

Smokers rest. 80

pl. del Ayuntamiento 4 ✉ 46002 – Ⓜ Xàtiva – ✆ 96 352 06 12 – reservas@plazavalencia.com – Fax 96 352 04 26 – www.solmelia.com **F2**

100 rm – †95/180 € ††95/255 €, ☕ 12 € – 1 suite

Rest – Carte 28/37 €

◆ Business ◆ Chain hotel ◆ Classic ◆

The hotel's gradual renovation, based on quality materials and elegant decor, has resulted in comfort levels that are more than acceptable with bedrooms offering excellent facilities. The restaurant showcases typical Mediterranean cuisine and a good selection of rice dishes.

Meliá Inglés

25/60

Marqués de Dos Aguas 6 ✉ 46002 – ✆ 96 351 64 26 – ingles@sh-hoteles.com – Fax 96 394 02 51 – www.sh-hoteles.com **G2**

63 rm – ††95/200 €, ☕ 10 €

Rest – Menu 21 €

◆ Traditional ◆ Chain hotel ◆ Classic ◆

This old building with its attractive façade is now home to a boutique hotel offering modern comforts and the latest technology. Superb bedrooms decorated with consummate taste. The restaurant, divided into two rooms, serves international cuisine and various local rice dishes.

Reina Victoria

No smokers rest. 25/75

Barcas 4 ✉ 46002 – Ⓜ Xàtiva – ✆ 96 352 04 87 – hreinavictoriavalencia@husa.es – Fax 96 352 27 21 – www.husa.es **G2**

95 rm – †56/139 € ††56/198 €, ☕ 11.50 € – 1 suite

Rest – *(closed August)* Menu 24 €

◆ Traditional ◆ Chain hotel ◆ Classic ◆

A fine façade and an unbeatable location a stone's throw from the city's main museums. Elegant facilities, including an attractive lounge area and bedrooms which have been sympathetically modernised. The restaurant on the first floor adjoins the English-style bar.

Ad-Hoc Smokers rest.

Boix 4 ✉ 46003 – Ⓜ Colón – ✆ 96 391 91 40
– adhoc@adhochoteles.com
– Fax 96 391 36 67 – www.adhochoteles.com **G1**

28 rm – 86/162 € 86/199 €, 10 €

Rest – *(closed Friday lunch, Saturday lunch and Sunday)* Menu 25 €

◆ Traditional ◆ Rustic ◆

Occupying an attractive 19C building, this hotel has a welcoming lounge area and neo-rustic, simply decorated bedrooms with bare brick, exposed beams and clay tiles. A pleasant restaurant with an appetising choice of desserts.

Petit Palace Bristol without rest 25/75

Abadía de San Martín 3 ✉ 46002 – Ⓜ Colón
– ✆ 96 394 51 00 – bristol@hthoteles.com
– Fax 96 394 38 50 – www.hthoteles.com **G2**

43 rm – 65/180 € 65/190 €, 11 €

◆ Traditional ◆ Modern ◆

Housed in a building which has retained its original 19C façade, this hotel has a multi-function lobby and modern bedrooms, all with a hydromassage column in their bathroom.

Sorolla without rest 25/45

Convento Santa Clara 5 ✉ 46002 – Ⓜ Xàtiva
– ✆ 96 352 33 92 – reservas@hotelsorolla.com
– Fax 96 352 14 65 – www.hotelsorolla.com **G3**

58 rm – 77/195 €, 8 €

◆ Traditional ◆ Functional ◆

With its glass-fronted façade and attractively renovated reception, the Sorolla's overall feel is pleasantly contemporary. Comfortable, functional bedrooms with parquet flooring.

Mediterráneo without rest

Barón de Cárcer 45 ✉ 46001 – Ⓜ Xàtiva – ✆ 96 351 01 42
– riasmediter@terra.es – Fax 96 351 01 42
– www.mediterraneovalencia.com **F2**

34 rm – 56/95 € 56/140 €, 7 €

◆ Family ◆ Functional ◆

A centrally located hotel with an elegant and welcoming entrance hall-cum-reception area in wood and marble. Classic bedrooms and a breakfast room on the first floor.

Continental without rest

Correos 8 ✉ 46002 – Ⓜ Colón – ✆ 96 353 52 82 – continental@contitel.es
– Fax 96 353 11 13 – www.contitel.es **G2**

46 rm – 48/65 € 62/107 €

◆ Traditional ◆ Functional ◆

The Continental enjoys a good central location. Contemporary in style with functional furnishings and comfortable bedrooms, half of which look onto an inner patio. Limited public areas.

Rías Gallegas Smokers rest. 4/24

Cirilo Amorós 4 ✉ 46004 – Ⓜ Xàtiva – ✆ 96 352 51 11 – riasgallegas@riasgallegas.es – Fax 96 351 99 10 – www.riasgallegas.es
closed Holy Week, August, Sunday and Monday dinner **G3**

Rest – Carte 47/64 €

◆ Galician specialities ◆ Formal ◆

Specialising in traditional Galician cuisine, the menu here understandably focuses on fish and seafood. Exclusive dining room on two levels, professional service and delightful table settings.

XXX ✿ **Torrijos** 8/40 VISA

Dr. Sumsi 4 ✉ 46005 – Ⓜ Colón – ✆ 96 373 29 49 – info@restaurantetorrijos.com – Fax 96 373 29 49 – www.restaurantetorrijos.com

closed 10 days in January, 10 days in April, 1 to 15 September, Sunday and Monday **G-H3**

Rest – Menu 65 € – Carte 46/60 €

Spec. Percebes y mero en ensalada con manzana verde y apio. Ventresca de congrio con arroz meloso en su tinta. Arena de cacao, caramelo, granizado de Paradis y lima.

♦ Inventive ♦ Formal ♦

An elegant, modern ambience, excellent service and an attractive, innovative menu. Attractive, glass-fronted wine cellar and two private rooms, one with views of the kitchen.

XXX ✿ **La Sucursal** VISA

Guillén de Castro 118 ✉ 46003 – ✆ 96 374 66 65 – info@restaurantelasucursal.com – Fax 96 392 41 54

closed 15 to 31 August, Saturday lunch and Sunday **F1**

Rest – Menu 65 € – Carte approx. 52 €

Spec. Yema de huevo con carpaccio, trufa y polenta cremosa (November-February). Ventresca de atún con vinagreta de piñones (May-October). Arroz caldoso de bogavante.

♦ Inventive ♦ Minimalist ♦

Part of the Instituto Valenciano de Arte Moderno, with a cafeteria open to the public on the ground floor and a minimalist room on the first. A fusion of innovative and traditional cuisine.

XXX **Vinatea** – Hotel Astoria Palace Smokers rest. 25 VISA

Vilaragut 4 ✉ 46002 – ✆ 96 398 10 00 – info@hotel-astoria-palace.com – Fax 96 398 10 10 **G2**

Rest – Carte approx. 43 €

♦ International ♦ Formal ♦

Excellent levels of comfort, with a separate entrance, offering interesting gastronomic choice. Refined classical décor with elegant furniture.

XXX **Riff** Smokers rest. 40 VISA

Conde de Altea 18 ✉ 46005 – Ⓜ Colón – ✆ 96 333 53 53 – restaurante@restaurante-riff.com – Fax 96 335 31 78 – www.restaurante-riff.com

closed 15 to 31 August, Sunday and Monday **H3**

Rest – Carte 46/53 €

♦ Inventive ♦ Minimalist ♦

Hot on the heels of the latest trends in the restaurant world with its creative cuisine and minimalist design. The restaurant also has its own delicatessen next door.

XX **Kailuze** Smokers rest. 16 VISA

Gregorio Mayáns 5 ✉ 46005 – Ⓜ Xàtiva – ✆ 96 335 45 39 – kailuze@menjariviure.com – Fax 96 335 48 93 – www.kailuze.com

closed August, Saturday lunch and Sunday **G3**

Rest – Carte 43/57 €

♦ Basque ♦ Formal ♦

Warm decor, excellent service and reliable Basque-Navarran cuisine are the hallmarks of this restaurant with a reception area and cosy dining room.

XX **El Ángel Azul** Smokers rest. 12/15 VISA

Conde de Altea 33 ✉ 46005 – Ⓜ Colón – ✆ 96 374 56 56 – www.angelazul.com

closed 14 August-14 September, Sunday and Monday **H3**

Rest – Carte 38/50 €

♦ Inventive ♦ Formal ♦

A centrally located restaurant with an elegant main dining room and two rooms for private functions. Creative à la carte choices, in addition to several tasting menus.

SPAIN

XX

Civera Centro

Mosén Femades 10 ✉ 46002 – Ⓜ Xàtiva – ✆ 96 352 97 64 – civeracentro@marisqueriascivera.com – Fax 96 346 50 50 – www.marisqueriascivera.com
closed Holy Week and 15 days in July **G3**
Rest – Carte 29/48 €
◆ Seafood ◆ Formal ◆
A restaurant renowned for the high quality of its ingredients. Tapas bar, maritime-influenced decor in the dining room and various private rooms. The seafood platter is a house speciality.

XX

Chust Godoy

Smokers rest. ⟺10

Boix 6 ✉ 46003 – ✆ 96 391 38 15 – chustgodoy@chustgodoy.com – Fax 96 392 22 39 – www.chustgodoy.com
closed Holy Week, August, Saturday lunch and Sunday **G1**
Rest – Carte 37/47 €
◆ Traditional ◆ Family ◆
Professionally run by the owner-chef and his wife, the Chust Godoy has one neo-rustic dining room and one cellar-type private area. Menu based on seasonal market products, with a good choice of savoury rice dishes.

XX

Sangonereta

Sorni 31 ✉ 46004 – Ⓜ Colón – ✆ 96 373 81 70 – rtesangonereta@hotmail.com – Fax 96 373 81 70
closed Holy Week, 21 days in August, Saturday lunch and Sunday **H2**
Rest – Carte 33/44 €
◆ Inventive ◆ Formal ◆
A classic layout for this restaurant whose name refers to a character from a Spanish TV series. Creative cuisine, including a tasting menu.

XX

El Timonel

Félix Pizcueta 13 ✉ 46004 – Ⓜ Colón – ✆ 96 352 63 00 – restaurante@eltimonel.com – Fax 96 351 17 32 – www.eltimonel.com
closed Monday **G3**
Rest – Carte 25/37 €
◆ Traditional ◆ Family ◆
This family-run restaurant has the owner/father front of house and the son in the kitchen. Warm decor inspired by the sea provides the backdrop for gastronomic cuisine.

XX

Alghero

Smokers rest.

Burriana 52 ✉ 46005 – ✆ 96 333 35 79 – correo@restaurantealghero.com – www.restaurantealghero.com
closed 15 days around Holy Week, 15 to 31 August, Sunday and Monday **H3**
Rest – Carte 32/37 €
◆ Mediterranean ◆ Formal ◆
An attractive restaurant with elegant, traditional furnishings and a menu centred on creative Mediterranean cuisine, including Italian-influenced dishes.

X

Palace Fesol

Smokers rest. ⟺40

Hernán Cortés 7 ✉ 46004 – Ⓜ Colón – ✆ 96 352 93 23 – palacefesol@palacefesol.com – Fax 96 353 00 68 – www.palacefesol.com
closed Holy Week **G3**
Rest – Carte 25/39 €
◆ Regional ◆ Family ◆
A restaurant with a great family tradition. Bar for a pre-dinner drink, a neo-rustic dining room decorated with azulejos on the walls, plus an attractive private room on the first floor. Traditional menu including rice dishes.

X

Montes

Smokers rest.

pl. Obispo Amigó 5 ✉ 46007 – Ⓜ Pl. Espanya – ✆ 96 385 50 25
closed August, Sunday dinner and Monday **E3**
Rest – Carte 25/33 €
◆ Traditional ◆ Family ◆
Pleasantly decorated main dining room with excellent service. The entrance is via an attractive hall with bar which leads to an elongated dining room.

SPAIN

Mey Mey
Smokers rest.

Historiador Diago 19 ✉ 46007 – Ⓜ Pl. Espanya – ✆ 96 384 07 47 – Fax 96 185 71 76 – www.mey-mey.com
closed Holy Week and last 3 weeks August **E3**
Rest – Carte 20/28 €
◆ Chinese ◆ Exotic ◆
Attractive decor in keeping with that of a traditional Chinese restaurant – note the circular fountain full of colourful fish. Cantonese menu, including a selection of steamed dishes.

CIUDAD DE LAS ARTES, HARBOURS AND BEACHES *Plan III*

Meliá Valencia Palace
25/800

paseo de la Alameda 32 ✉ 46023 – ✆ 96 337 50 37 – melia.valencia.palace@solmelia.com – Fax 96 337 55 32 – www.sh-hoteles.com **J2**
243 rm – ††105/206 €, ☕ 14 € – 5 suites
Rest – Carte 33/41 €
◆ Business ◆ Chain hotel ◆ Classic ◆
The hotel offers its guests a high standard of comfort and facilities, including the spectacular entrance hall, reflecting the latest trends in interior design, and the bedrooms, furnished with impeccable taste. A mix of modern and traditional cuisine in the restaurant, decorated in functional minimalist style.

Las Arenas
No smokers rest. 25/500

Eugenia Viñes 22 ✉ 46011 – ✆ 96 312 06 00 – reservas@hotel-lasarenas.com – Fax 96 312 06 16 – www.hotel-lasarenas.com **K2**
243 rm – †140/350 € ††160/400 €, ☕ 18 € – 10 suites
Rest – Carte 41/51 €
◆ Business ◆ Chain hotel ◆ Classic ◆
A luxury hotel located on the beachfront. Split between three buildings with welcoming lounges, superb meeting rooms and well-appointed bedrooms. Mediterranean-inspired cuisine is to the fore in the hotel restaurant.

NH Las Artes I
No smokers rest. 25/250

av. Instituto Obrero 28 ✉ 46013 – ✆ 96 335 13 10 – nhlasartes@nh-hotels.com – Fax 96 374 86 22 – www.nh-hotels.com
172 rm – †65/150 € ††65/200 €, ☕ 14 € – 2 suites **J2**
Rest – Menu 20 €
◆ Business ◆ Chain hotel ◆ Functional ◆
A contemporary hotel offering excellent facilities and refined comfort. Great attention to detail in the bedrooms, plus an extensive range of guest services.

Holiday Inn Valencia
No smokers rest. 25/130

paseo de la Alameda 38 ✉ 46023 – ✆ 96 303 21 00 – reservas@holidayinnvalencia.com – Fax 96 303 21 26 – www.valencia.holiday-inn.com **J2**
200 rm – ††90/250 €, ☕ 15 € – **Rest** – Menu 10.50 €
◆ Business ◆ Chain hotel ◆ Functional ◆
A modern hotel geared towards business travellers with the standards and comforts associated with this international chain. Terrace-bar with fine views and a restaurant connected to the hall-cafeteria.

Neptuno

paseo de Neptuno 2 ✉ 46011 – Ⓜ Les Arenes – ✆ 96 356 77 77 – reservas@hotelneptunovalencia.com – Fax 96 356 04 30 – www.hotelneptunovalencia.com **K2**
48 rm ☕ – †115/200 € ††130/245 €
Rest *Tridente* – *(closed Sunday dinner and Monday)* Carte 43/54 €
◆ Business ◆ Modern ◆
The guestrooms in this contemporary beachfront hotel are minimalist in design and furnished with quality fabrics and furnishings, with bathrooms which include hydromassage bathtubs. A modern restaurant with a glass-fronted wine cellar and views of the kitchens.

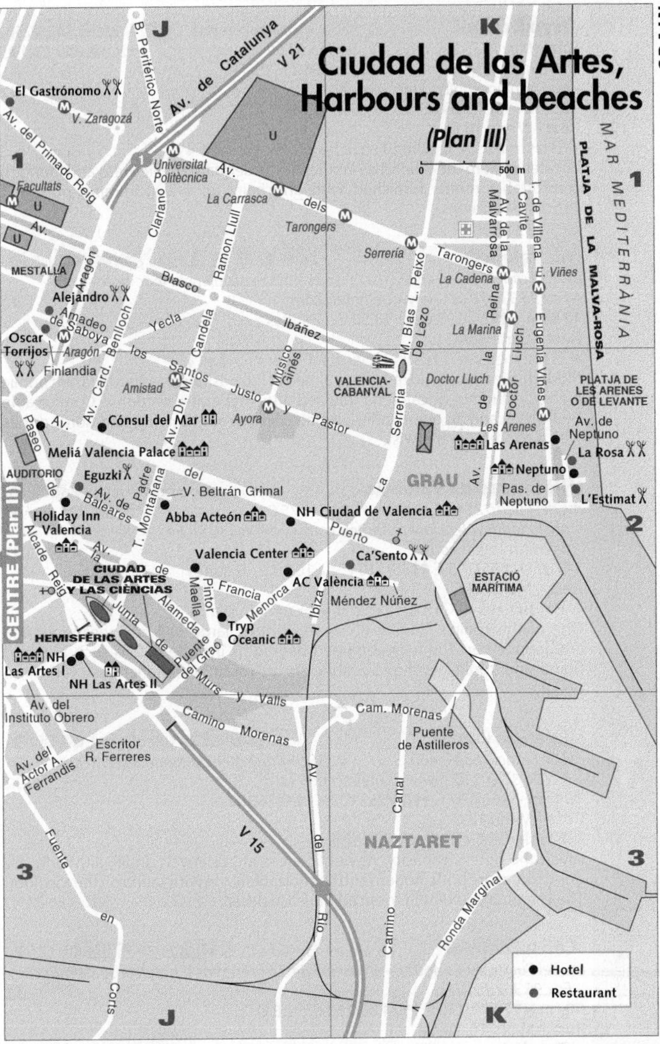

Ciudad de las Artes, Harbours and beaches (Plan III)

Abba Acteón No smokers rest. 25/400 VISA

Vicente Beltrán Grimal 2 ✉ 46023 – ☎ 96 331 07 07 – reservas-acteon@abbahoteles.com – Fax 96 330 22 30 – www.abba-acteonhotel.com **J2**

182 rm – †72/260 € ††72/278 €, ☐ 12.50 € – 5 suites

Rest *Amalur* – *(closed Sunday)* Carte 24/36 €

♦ Business ♦ Chain hotel ♦ Modern ♦

Quality and design are the buzzwords in this hotel, with its spacious bedrooms decorated with elegant materials, including marble in the bathrooms. Open, modern and attractively arranged restaurant.

SPAIN

Tryp Oceanic No smokers rest. 25/250 VISA AE

Pintor Maella 35 ✉ 46023 – ☎ 96 335 03 00 – tryp.oceanic@solmelia.com – Fax 96 335 03 11 – www.trypoceanic.solmelia.com **J2**

195 rm – 77/160 €, 12 € – 2 suites

Rest – Menu 18 €

♦ Business ♦ Chain hotel ♦ Functional ♦

Located next to the Ciudad de las Ciencias. Adequate public areas and lounges, comfortable rooms furnished with armchairs, plus a swimming pool and surrounding lawns.

AC València 25/80 VISA AE

av. de Francia 67 ✉ 46023 – ☎ 96 331 70 00 – acvalencia@ac-hotels.com – Fax 96 331 70 01 – www.ac-hotels.com **J2**

174 rm – 60/195 €, 13.50 € – 2 suites

Rest – Carte 36/41 €

♦ Business ♦ Chain hotel ♦ Functional ♦

Modern, functional and resolutely aimed at the business market. Pleasant public areas, including a cafeteria divided into separate sections. Comfortable bedrooms, and an open, multi-purpose dining room serving traditional dishes with a contemporary twist.

NH Ciudad de Valencia No smokers rest. 30/80 VISA AE

av. del Puerto 214 ✉ 46023 – ☎ 96 330 75 00 – nhciudaddevalencia@nh-hotels.com – Fax 96 330 98 64 – www.nh-hotels.com **J2**

147 rm – 55/185 € 55/210 €, 10.50 € – 2 suites

Rest – Menu 17 €

♦ Business ♦ Chain hotel ♦ Functional ♦

One of the chain's standard-bearers, with its large hall and reception area and lounge-bar. The fully-equipped bedrooms include details such as wood floors and triple glazing. Sizeable dining room with functional yet warm decor.

Valencia Center 25/100 VISA AE

av. de Francia 33 ✉ 46023 – ☎ 96 335 07 00 – valencia@hotelescenter.es – Fax 96 335 07 02 – www.hotelescenter.es **J2**

134 rm – 60/197 € 60/252 €, 14 € – 6 suites

Rest – Menu 18 €

♦ Business ♦ Functional ♦

Given the hotel's capacity, its public areas are relatively small, although the guestrooms are both modern and comfortable. Gym with sauna on the top floor. The cafeteria and dining room adjoin each other.

Cónsul del Mar Smokers rest. 25/50 P VISA AE

av. del Puerto 39 ✉ 46021 – ☎ 96 362 54 32 – reservas@hotelconsuldelmar.com – Fax 96 362 16 25 **J2**

60 rm – 70.40/150 € 74.80/160 €, 8 €

Rest – Menu 16 €

♦ Traditional ♦ Classic ♦

With its attractive period architecture, this hotel takes you back to the 1900s. Refined furnishings in the bedrooms with bathrooms full of personalised touches.

NH Las Artes II without rest 25 VISA AE

av. Instituto Obrero 26 ✉ 46013 – ☎ 96 335 60 62 – exlasartes@nh-hotels.com – Fax 96 333 46 83 – www.nh-hotels.com **J2**

121 rm – 55/110 € 55/150 €, 10 €

♦ Business ♦ Chain hotel ♦ Functional ♦

A functional chain hotel with the expected level of facilities but limited public areas. Simply furnished yet colourful guestrooms.

Oscar Torrijos Smokers rest.

Finlandia 7 ✉ 46010 – Ⓜ Aragón – ☏ 96 393 63 00 – oscartorrijos@telefonica.net – Fax 96 393 63 00

closed Holy Week, 15 August-15 September and Sunday **J1**

Rest – Carte 43/55 €

♦ Mediterranean ♦ Neighbourhood ♦

The bar at the entrance offers views of the kitchen. A modern dining room with a glass-fronted wine cellar, where the focus is on attentively prepared cuisine, including two tasting menus.

El Gastrónomo Smokers rest.

av. Primado Reig 149 ✉ 46020 – Ⓜ Benimaclet – ☏ 96 369 70 36 – www.elgastronomorestaurante.com

closed Holy Week, August, Sunday and Monday dinner **J1**

Rest – Carte 27/39 €

♦ International ♦ Formal ♦

A resolutely old-style restaurant both in terms of the way it's run and the nutritious cuisine on offer here.

Ca'Sento Smokers rest. 16

Méndez Núñez 17 ✉ 46024 – ☏ 96 330 17 75

closed Holy Week, August, Sunday and Monday **K2**

Rest – *(booking essential)* Menu 90 € – Carte 75/90 €

Spec. Ortigas de mar rebozadas con pan de agua y jugo de moluscos. Lubina asada con cebollitas escabechadas al aroma de canela y clavo. Bizcocho de mascarpone con calabaza caramelizada y canutillos de piñones.

♦ Inventive ♦ Family ♦

This long-standing family-run restaurant comes as a pleasant surprise in this part of the city. The cooking here is based solidly around fish, seafood and simple flavours, with a slight slant towards new culinary trends.

Alejandro Smokers rest. 4/10

Amadeo de Saboya 15 ✉ 46010 – Ⓜ Aragón – ☏ 96 393 40 46 – Fax 96 320 29 16 – www.restaurantealejandrodeltoro.com

closed Saturday lunch and Sunday **J1**

Rest – Menu 55 € – Carte approx. 56 €

Spec. Hervido valenciano con aire de zanahoria. Coca de boquerón de luz marinado con pimiento murciano escalivado con Módena. Sopa de melón de la Galia con kiwi, sorbete de limón y almendra marcona.

♦ Inventive ♦ Friendly ♦

The Alejandro's young owner-chef is developing a reputation for his creative contemporary cuisine. The traditional-style dining room is welcoming in feel, with the occasional minimalist detail and a glass-fronted wine cellar.

La Rosa Smokers rest.

av. de Neptuno 70 ✉ 46011 – Ⓜ Les Arenes – ☏ 96 371 20 76 – Fax 96 371 25 65

closed Holy Week and 14 August-5 September **K2**

Rest – *(only lunch in winter)* Carte 33/45 €

♦ Rice specialities ♦ Family ♦

La Rosa's dining rooms are embellished with a profusion of wood and decoration relating to the America's Cup. Pleasant glass-fronted terrace and a fish- and seafood-inspired menu including delicious rice dishes.

Eguzki Smokers rest.

av. Baleares 1 ✉ 46023 – ☏ 96 337 50 33 – Fax 96 337 50 33

closed August, Sunday and Bank Holidays **J2**

Rest – Carte 35/50 €

♦ Basque ♦ Family ♦

This Basque restaurant with an attractive stone façade is run with great enthusiasm by the family that owns it. A hall-bar on the ground floor and a pleasant dining room one floor up.

SPAIN

L'Estimat AC VISA

av. de Neptuno 16 ✉ 46011 – ✆ 96 371 10 18 – info@lestimat.com – Fax 96 372 73 85 – www.lestimat.com

closed 14 August-12 September, Sunday dinner, Monday dinner and Tuesday **K2**

Rest – Carte 30/46 €

♦ Traditional ♦ Family ♦

A house with an entrance hall adorned with two aquariums, a kitchen in full view of diners, and a spacious, maritime-inspired dining room with a menu featuring regional cuisine and a good selection of rice dishes.

SWEDEN
SVERIGE

PROFILE

◆ **AREA:**
449 964 km²
(173 731 sq mi).

◆ **POPULATION:**
9 003 000 inhabitants (est. 2006), density = 20 per km².

◆ **CAPITAL:**
Stockholm 781 000 (conurbation 1 912 000 inhabitants).

◆ **CURRENCY:**
Swedish Kronor (Skr or SEK); rate of exchange: SEK 1 = € 0.11 = US$ 0.14 (Nov 2006).

◆ **GOVERNMENT:**
Constitutional parliamentary monarchy (since 1950). Member of European Union since 1995.

◆ **LANGUAGE:**
Swedish; many Swedes also speak good English.

◆ **SPECIFIC PUBLIC HOLIDAYS:**
Epiphany (6 January), Good Friday (Friday before Easter), National Day, 6 June, Midsummer's Day (Saturday between June 20-26), Halloween (Saturday between Oct 31-Nov 6), Christmas Day (25 December), Boxing Day (26 December).

◆ **LOCAL TIME:**
GMT + 1 hour in winter and GMT + 2 hours in summer.

◆ **CLIMATE:**
Temperate continental with cold winters and mild summers (Stockholm: January: -3°C, July: 16°C).

◆ **INTERNATIONAL DIALLING CODE:**
00 46 followed by

area code without the initial **0** and then the local number. International Directory Enquiries: ✆ **079 77.**

◆ **EMERGENCY:**
Dial ✆ **112** for Police, Fire Brigade, Ambulance, Poison hot-line, on-call doctors and 24hr Roadside breakdown service.

◆ **ELECTRICITY:**
220 volts AC, 50 Hz; 2-pin round-shaped continental plugs.

FORMALITIES

Travellers from the European Union (EU), Switzerland, Iceland and the main countries of North and South America need a national identity card or passport (America: passport required) to visit Sweden for less than three months (tourism or business purpose). For visitors from other countries a visa may be required, in addition to a passport, especially for those wishing to stay for longer than three months. We advise you to check with your embassy before travelling.

The major international car hire companies have offices in Stockholm and Gothenburg and at Arlanda and Landvetter airports. Drivers must not drink any alcoholic beverages.

MAJOR NEWSPAPERS

The main daily newspapers are *Dagens Nyheter* (Stockholm), *Göteborgs-Posten* (Göteborg) and *Sydsvenska Dagbladet* (Malmö); also *Expressen* and *Aftonbladet*. Most of the dailies are sold by subscription, with early morning home delivery.

USEFUL PHRASES

ENGLISH	**SWEDISH**
Yes	**Ja**
No	**Nej**
Good morning	**God Morgon**
Goodbye	**Adjö, Hej då**
Please	**Varsågod, Tack**
Thank you	**Tack**
Excuse me	**Urśåkta**
I don't understand	**Jag förstår inte**
Hi, Hello	**Hej**

HOTELS

→ CATEGORIES

Accommodation ranges from luxurious 5-star international hotels, to smaller, family-run guesthouses and bed and breakfast establishments *(rum & frukost).*

→ PRICE RANGE

The price is per room. There is little difference between the price of a single and a double room. Between April and October it is advisable to book in advance. From November to March prices may be slightly lower, some hotels offer discounts throughout the year and during the summer. In Stockholm hotel chains frequently offer special discounts or hotel cheques.

→ TAX

Included in the room price, together with service charge and breakfast.

→ CHECK OUT TIME

Usually between 10am and noon.

→ RESERVATIONS

By telephone or by Internet. A credit card number or a deposit may be required.

→ BREAKFAST

It is usually included in the price of the room and is generally served between 7am and 10am. Most hotels offer a generous self-service buffet but usually it is possible to have continental breakfast served in the room.

Reception	**Reception**
Single room	**Enkelrum**
Double room	**Dubbelrum**
Bed	**Säng**
Bathroom	**Badrum**
Shower	**Dusch**

RESTAURANTS

Besides the traditional **restaurants** there are **brasseries** which serve simpler meals.

Breakfast	**Frukost**	7am – 10am
Lunch	**Lunch**	11am – 2pm
Dinner	**Middag**	6pm – 10pm

All restaurants display a menu in the window; the prices include VAT (Moms) and a service charge. Menus are usually printed in Swedish and English. Many formal restaurants are closed at lunchtime but the dish of the day *(dagens rätt)* is usually good value as it includes unlimited salad, a soft drink bread and coffee. An alternative is to try a café for one of the tempting open sandwiches which make a refreshing and sustaining snack. At any time of year, as soon as the sun shines, the locals sit out on the terraces and at pavement tables.

→ RESERVATIONS

Reservations are usually made by phone or Internet. For famous restaurants (including Michelin starred restaurants), it is advisable to book several days – or weeks in some instances – in advance. A phone number may be required as guarantee.

→ THE BILL

The bill (check) includes service charge (13-15%) and VAT. Tipping is optional but, if you are particularly pleased with the service, it is customary to round up the total – 10% in larger restaurants and the value of the small change elsewhere. In winter there is often a compulsory cloakroom charge of Skr 20.

Drink or aperitif	**Drycker**
Meal	**Måltid**
First course, starter	**Förrätt**
Main dish	**Huvudrätt / Varmrätt**
Main dish of the day	**Dagens rätt**
Dessert	**Efterrätt**
Water	**Vatten**
Wine (red, white, rosé)	**Vin (röd, vitt, rosé)**
Beer	**Öl**
Bread	**Bröd**
Meat (rare, medium, well done)	**Kött (blodig, medium, välstekt)**
Fish	**Fisk**
Salt/pepper	**Salt / peppar**
Cheese	**Ost**
Vegetables	**Grönsaker**
Hot/cold	**Varm / kall**
The bill (check) please	**Får jag be om notan, tack**

LOCAL CUISINE

Breakfast is a mouth-watering display of bread, rolls, pastries, crispbread, sliced sausage, cheese, boiled and scrambled eggs, meatballs, pickles, cereals, yoghurt and fruit, accompanied with thin yoghurt *(filmjölk)*, milk, fruit juices, tea and coffee.

The great Swedish buffet *(smörgåsbord)* is served as a celebratory meal and should be approached in a leisurely way. Start with herring in many delectable forms in a mustard or horseradish sauce accompanied by boiled potatoes, garnished with fresh herbs and juniper berries; this stage is usually accompanied with beer and acquavit. Next try the thin slices of salmon cured in dill and then cleanse the palate with a course of cheese or eggs stuffed with caviar and shrimps. After that comes the main course of cold meat or fish or a hot dish of meatballs.

Seafood is always popular: cod (torsk), haddock, Baltic herring and fermented herring *(surströmming)*, whitefish and whitefish caviar, prawns *(räkor)*, mussels *(blåmusslor)*, crab and lobster *(hummer)*, salmon *(lax)* and trout *(forell)*. **Eel** *(ål)* is a delicacy served in a wide variety of ways. August is the time for **crayfish** *(kräftor)* parties when these delicious freshwater shellfish, boiled with dill, salt and sugar, are served cold with hot buttered toast and caraway cheese accompanied by the odd schnapps and beer. **Lutfisk**, dried and boiled ling, is served on Christmas Eve. **Janssons frestelse** (Jansson's Temptation) is a gratin of anchovies, potatoes, onions and cream baked in the oven.

Menus feature pork *(fläsk)*, beef *(biff)*, veal *(kalvkött)*, lamb *(lammkött)*, chicken *(kyckling)* and sausage *(korv)*. A very popular meat dish is succulent **meatballs** *(köttbullar)*, mixed with herbs and served in a cream sauce with mashed potatoes. Goose makes a festive dinner on St Martin's Eve. Venison, reindeer *(ren)* and elk *(älg)* may appear on the menu in season: **smoked reindeer, roast** with boiled potatoes, cream sauce and blackcurrant or redcurrant jelly. Wild berries figure largely in many dishes: blueberries for soup and fruit pies, loganberries for juice and jam, lingonberries to accompany meatballs, elk and pancakes. Often served for lunch on Thursday is pea soup *(ärtsoppa)* and pancake.

Sweet cakes and pastries are popular: waffles *(våfflor)*, mini pancakes (plättar) served with cream and jam, cinnamon buns *(kanelbullar)*, gingerbread biscuits *(pepparkaka)*, saffron cakes *(lussekatt)* are usually available in December, a cake made of eggs and sugar *(spettekaka)*, a regional speciality from Skåne.

DRINK

Most Swedes prefer to drink **beer**, which is produced in 3 grades – light, ordinary and export. Wine is widely available in nearly all restaurants, most of which offer an interesting range from France and other countries, often by the glass. As alcohol is expensive and sold only in government-owned shops *(Systembolaget)* (Mon-Fri 9.30am-6pm, Sat 10am-3pm), soft drinks, mineral water, light beer and coffee are usually drunk at meal times. The coffee is fairly strong and tea is usually made with warm water. In December you can warm up with a glass of spicy mulled wine *(glögg)*. The most popular Swedish spirit is aquavit *(akvavit)* and the most popular brand is Skåne. Aquavit is distilled from barley or potatoes but each brand is flavoured with juniper or coriander or myrtle or some other herb. It is served in tiny glasses and quaffed ice cold usually at the beginning of a meal with the fish course.

STOCKHOLM

STOCKHOLM

Population: 782 000 (conurbation 1 912 000) – Altitude: sea level

R. Mattès/MICHELIN

Enthusiastic admirers say that Stockholm is the most beautiful city in the world. The Swedish capital is set in an archipelago so that the city, which is built on 14 islands linked by bridges, is surrounded on all sides by water. It is located where freshwater Lake Mälaren joins the Baltic Sea, amid a seascape of countless islands, each seemingly more beautiful than the last. Parks and gardens add to Stockholm's undeniable beauty and contrast with the high-rise buildings of the commercial centre. The residence of the royal household is not far from Stockholm at Drottningholm.

Stockholm is modern and efficient, with a rich historical and cultural heritage. During the summer Stockholmers live outdoors, like the citizens of Oslo and Copenhagen, making for the city's animated streets and parks, where there are staged entertainments. Stockholm is rich in cultural activities with a wide selection of museums, theatres, art galleries and music performances. Early in December brightly decorated stalls are set up in the Old Town square for the Christmas Fair.

WHICH DISTRICT TO CHOOSE

Many of the **hotels** are located in the Old Town (Gamla Stan) *Plan I* **C2** and in Norrmalm *Plan I* **B2** but there are a good number in the suburbs and at the airport.

Stockhom has a great diversity of **restaurants** and the highest concentrations are to be found in Norrmalm, Östermalm *Plan I* **C1**, Södermalm *Plan I* **C3** and Gamla Stan; the latter boasts many restaurants, some of them established in picturesque old houses; the triangle formed by Birger Jarlsgatan and Nybrogatan up to Östermalmstorg has a good selection of restaurants, brasseries, cafés and snack bars. There are also restaurants in the suburbs where there are hotels and at the airport.

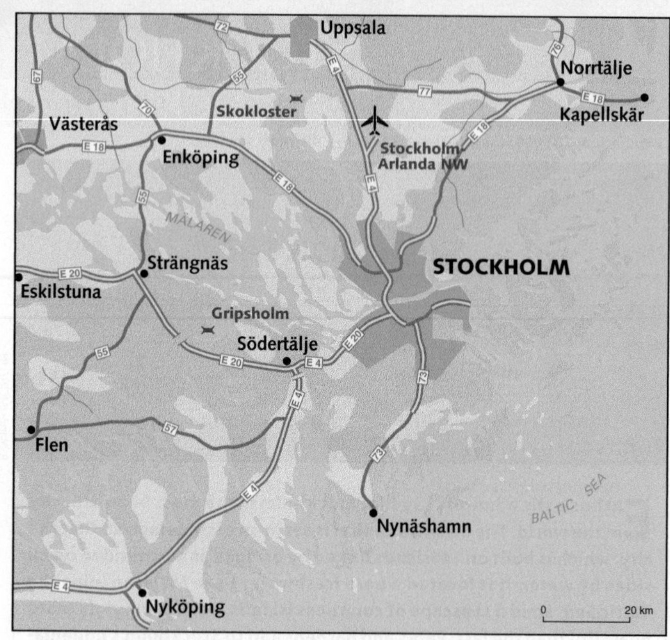

PRACTICAL INFORMATION

ARRIVAL – DEPARTURE

Stockholm Arlanda Airport – About 40 km (25 mi) northwest of city centre, ✆ 0(8) 797 60 00.

From the airport to the city centre – By **train**: Arlanda Express (20min) to Centralstation (5am-12.35am, every 15min), SEK 200. By **airport bus** *(Flygbuss)* (40min) to Cityterminalen, the central bus station (6.30am-11.45pm every 5-10min), SEK 95. By **taxi**: 35min, SEK 375.

Railway Station – **Centralstation** *Plan I* **B2** for services from the main towns of Sweden. www.sj.se

Ferry Terminal – Ferry services from Helsinki (Finland) – *Silja Line*, ✆ (0)8 22 21 40; www.silja.com; *Viking Line*, ✆ (0)8 452 40 00; www.vikingline.se. From Tallinn (Estonia) – *Tallink*, www.tallink.se

TRANSPORT

→ BUS, TRAM AND METRO

Buses (450 routes), trams, the underground railway *(Tunnelbanan)* and suburban trains. Timetables and maps from the buses or at Stockholm's Local Traffic Information Centre in Central Station. The metro is often quicker as it offers a more direct route. The tram No 7 (June-August daily 11am-6/7pm) takes in quite a few of the main attractions. **Travel passes** for unlimited travel by bus, metro and regional train and ferries to Djurgården: 1-day card SEK 95; 3-day card SEK 180, available from travel centres and newsagents *(pressbyrå)*. **Ticket coupons** *(rabattkuponger)* valid on buses and underground, a single ticket is 40 SEK and a 10 ticket booklet 180 SEK, available at any underground station. **Monthly**

card *(månadskort)* for unlimited travel on public transport for 30 days SEK 620.

→ TAXIS

Taxis can be hailed in the street or picked up at a taxi rank. A 10% tip is included in the amount shown on the meter. The basic charge is SEK 42 within the city area plus SEK 10 per km. Special fares operate after midnight, at weekends and on public holidays. *Taxi Stockholm* ✆ (0)8 15 00 00, *Taxi Kurir* ✆ (0)8 30 00 00, *Top Cab* ✆ (0)8 33 33 33.

→ BOATS

Ferry between **Skeppsbron** and **Djurgården**, daily (extra service in summer from Nybroplan stopping at Skeppsholmen and Vasamuseet).

Boat tours under the Bridges of Stockholm, discovering the network of waterways of this island city; daily from **Strömkajen** or **Nybroplan**. Combined sightseeing boat and bus tour. Information and bookings from Stockholm Sight-seeing, Skeppsbron 22. ✆ (0)8 587 140 20; www.stockholmsightseeing.com

Boat tours to different parts of the **National City Park**: round Djurgården April to mid-Dec daily; round Brunnsviken (north of city centre) late June to early August daily (last tour in English); Fjäderholmarna Islands (east of Djurgården) from May to mid-Sep daily. ✆ (0)8 587 140 40.

→ STOCKHOLM CARD

Valid for free public transport (city centre and suburbs but not airport buses), parking, a sightseeing tour by boat and free admission to 70 museums and other attractions. 24hr-card SEK 220 ; 48hr-card SEK 380; 72hr-card SEK 540.

USEFUL ADDRESSES

→ TOURIST OFFICES

Tourist Centre, Sweden House, Hamngatan 27 (entrance in Kungsträdgården) *Plan I* **C2**; open Mon-Fri 9am-6pm, Sat-Sun 9am-3pm; ✆ (0)8 508 28 508 (Mon-Fri), 789 24 90 (weekends; Excursion Shop and Tourist Centre only). **Kaknästornet**, Ladugårdsgärdet, ✆ (0)8 667 21 05 (9am-10pm); kaknas@stoinfo.se. **Stadshuset** (Town Hall), Hantverkargatan 1, ✆ (0)8 508 29 059; www.stockholmtown.com.

Accommodation Booking Office – Hotel Centralen *Plan I* **B2**, ✆ (0)8 508 28 508.

→ POST OFFICES

Opening times Mon-Sat 10am-6pm (Sat 1pm).

→ BANKS/CURRENCY EXCHANGE

Opening times Mon-Fri 9.30am-3pm; most banks in the city centre close at 3.30pm. Banking facilities at the Arlanda Airport daily 7am-10pm. Exchange facilities at the Tourist Centre and in most large hotels. There are cash dispensers all over the city. Credit cards are widely accepted and require a PIN.

♦ EMERGENCY

Dial ✆ **112** for Police, Fire Brigade, Ambulance, Poison hot-line, on-call doctors and 24hr Roadside breakdown service.

BUSY PERIODS

Restaurant Festival: early June – Kungsträdgården becomes a large outdoor restaurant.

Midsummer Eve: June (next to last Saturday) – Major Swedish festival celebrated at Skansen; maypole and ring dancing.

Music at the Palace: June-August – Summer concert season starts in the Royal Palace.

Drottningholms Slottsteater: June-August – Summer season of concerts, opera and dance in the 18C court theatre.

Stockholm International Jazz and Blues Festival: July.

Christmas Markets: early December – Christmas goods on sale at traditional markets at Skansen, Rosendals Slott, Stortorget in Gamla Stan and Drottningholms Slott.

DIFFERENT FACETS OF THE CITY

It is possible to visit the main sights and museums in two to three days.

Museums and sights are usually open from 10/11am to 4-6pm; some close on Mondays.

GAMLA STAN – Historic heart of the city, an architecturally harmonious maze of narrow 17C streets and several prestigious buildings erected on three islands – Stadsholmen, Riddarholmen and Helgeandsholmen. **Kungliga Slottet** *Plan II* **F**: Royal castle rebuilt in the baroque style after a fire; now houses several museums and is occasionally used for official receptions; Royal Armoury in the vaults; Royal Treasury; changing of the guard weekdays at noon and Sundays and holidays at 1.10pm. **Storkyrkan** *Plan II* **F**: Cathedral, consecrated in 1306 and later remodelled, with a magnificent wooden 15C sculpture depicting St George and the Dragon by Bernt Notke from Lübeck. **Stortorget** *Plan II* **F**: Old Town main square, fronted by a late 18C rococo-style building, the former **Börsen** (Stock Exchange), now the Royal Academy, where the winner of the Nobel Prize for literature is announced. **Riddarholmskyrkan** *Plan II* **E**: set on a small island, one of the oldest churches in Stockholm, containing the tombs of the Swedish monarchs, now houses a museum. **Medeltidsmuseet** *Plan II* **E**: situated on Helgeandsholmen, beneath the Parliament House, contains medieval ruins.

NORRMALM – Modern, functional district north of the old town consisting of wide straight streets with offices and shops clustered round Sergels Torg. **Kungsträdgården** *Plan I* **C2**: a popular meeting place offering a range of activities – large chessboards and boules alleys – on the site of the royal vegetable plot. **Nationalmuseum** *Plan I* **C2**: national museum of fine arts.

DJURGÅRDEN – Vast park containing three museums in former hunting ground: picnicking, rambling, horse-riding and other outdoor pursuits. **Skansen** *Plan I* **D2**: zoo and the world's first open-air museum, founded in 1891, containing 150 houses from different regions of Sweden; the interiors have all been reconstructed. **Vasamuseet** *Plan I* **D2**: *Vasa* warship which sank in 1628 in Stockholm harbour and was raised and restored in 1961. **Nordiska Museet** *Plan I* **D2**: cultural history of Sweden with a particularly interesting section on the Lapps.

OUTSKIRTS – **Drottningholm Slott** *(1hr by boat from Stadshusbron on Kungsholmen)*: late 17C royal castle in the Baroque style, the official residence of the monarch; monumental staircase, Court Theatre, formal gardens, French gardens, English park. **Millesgården**: Museum dedicated to the sculptor Carl Milles (1875-1955) in his former residence magnificently set on the island of Lidingö. **Archipelago**: take a mini-cruise to visit some of the 24 000 islands and reefs in the area around Stockholm, where many locals have island summer houses; swimming possible.

GOURMET TREATS

For a light lunch go into **Östermalms Saluhall** (covered market) *Plan I* **C1** where individual stalls sell an array of fish, meat, cheese and vegetables and offer a range of open sandwiches, salads and snacks, served directly at the counter or on tables set inside the market hall.

Many of Stockholm's cafés are distinctive places in pleasantly rural or lakeside settings with excellent views. They also provide a mouth-watering selection of open sandwiches and home-made delicacies: pastries, apple, walnut and fudge, raspberry and blueberry pies, cheesecakes or waffles with cloudberry jam. Quite a number offer light lunches. Coffee may be expensive but you are often entitled to a second cup. Museum cafés often offer good value for money.

SHOPPING

Stores are usually open on weekdays from 9/10am to 6/7pm. On Friday some department stores close at 8-9pm. In Central Stockholm department stores open on Sundays 12-4pm.

Stockholm has a great variety of shops from small boutiques to large stores. The largest department store is *Åhléns* (Klarabergsgatan 50) and the most exclusive is *NK* (Hamngatan 18-20). The main shopping streets in the centre of Stockholm are **Hamngatan** *Plan I* **C2**, **Biblioteksgatan**, **Drottninggatan** *Plan I* **B2**, **Sturegallerian**; also in the Old Town mainly **Västerlånggatan** *Plan I* **C2**, which has many speciality shops. Certain streets or districts in the city centre tend to specialise in one kind of shop: department stores in **Hamngatan**; expensive boutiques on **Biblioteksgatan**; design shops in **Strandvägen**; individual shops selling trendy clothes in pedestrianised **Drottninggatan**, the rendezvous for the young. When looking for bargains *Rea* means sale, *Extrapris* means discount and *Fynd* indicates a special offer.

WHAT TO BUY – Glassware (Orrefors, Kosta, Boda), ceramics and textiles; the museum shops are good for gifts.

ENTERTAINMENT

For information about times and venues consult *What's On*, a monthly publication from the Tourist Office, and the *På Stan* section of the Thursday edition of the daily newspaper *Dagens Nyheter*.

MUSIC – **Opera** *Plan I* **C2**. **Berwaldhallen** *Plan I* **D1**. **Konserthuset** *Plan I* **B2**. Many city churches. **Skeppsholmen** *Plan I* **D2**: for the Stockholm Jazz and Blues Festival in July. **Cirkus** (Djurgården) for rock and pop concerts. **Skansen** *Plan I* **D1** and **Gröna Lund**: for concerts in summer. **Stampen** (Stora Nygatan 5) *Plan II* **E1**: for jazz and swing. **Fasching Jazzclub** (Kungsgatan) *Plan I* **B2**.

THEATRE – **Kungliga Dramatiska Teatern** *Plan I* **C2**: the stamping ground of Strindberg and Bergman. **Stadsteatern** for contemporary theatre.

NIGHTLIFE

For information on nightclubs consult *What's On*, a monthly publication from the Tourist Office, and the *På Stan* section of the Thursday edition of the daily newspaper *Dagens Nyheter*. The area around **Kungsträdgården** *Plan I* **C2** and **Stureplan** *Plan I* **C1** has a thriving nightlife: *Café Opera* (Operahuset, Kungsträdgården), known for its celebrity clientele and long queues, has dancing every night; *Sturecompagniet* (Stureplan) a multi-storey complex of drinking and dancing spots.

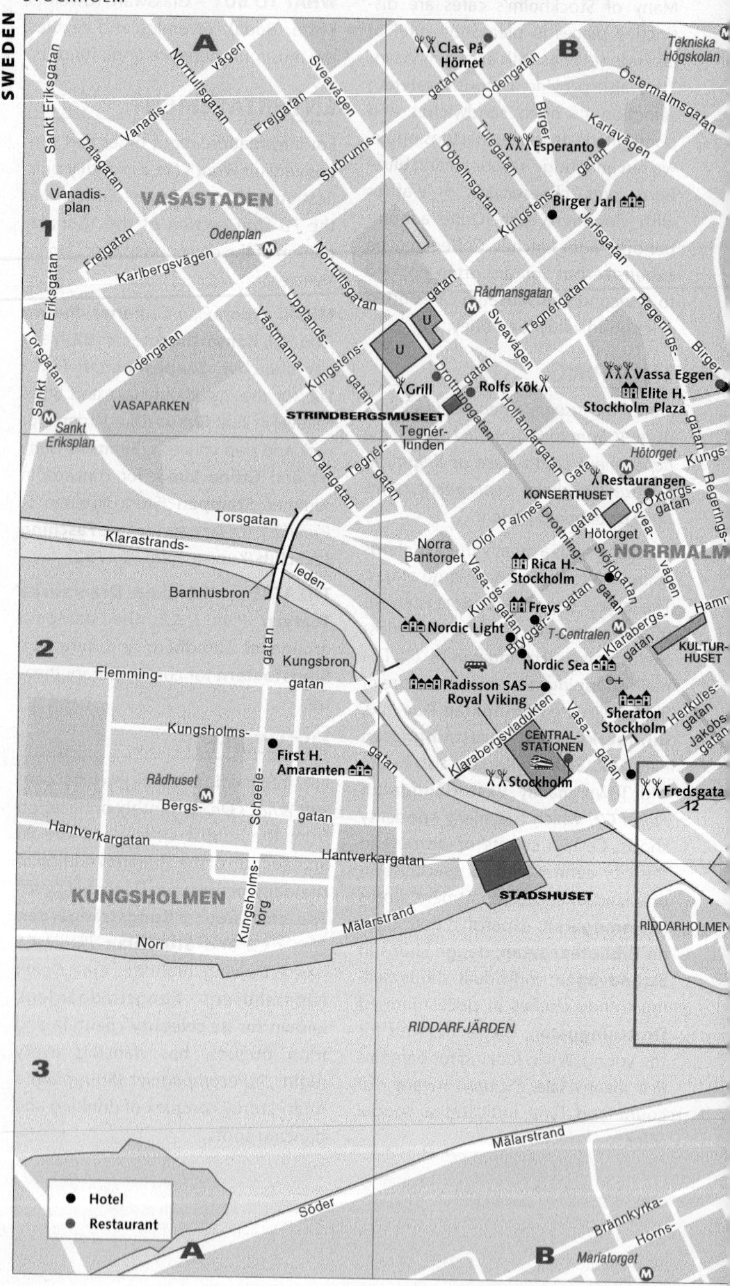
A
B
1
2
3
Clas På Hörnet
Tekniska Högskolan
Östermalmsgatan
Odengatan
Birger
Karlavägen
Tulegatan
Esperanto
gatan
Döbelnsgatan
Kungstens-
Birger Jarl
Jarlsgatan
Sankt Eriksgatan
Norrtullsgatan
vägen
Sveavägen
Dalagatan
Vanadis-
Frejgatan
Surbrunns-
Vanadis-
plan
VASASTADEN
Odenplan
Freigatan
Karlbergsvägen
Norrtullsgatan
Eriksgatan
Upplands-
Västmanna-
gatan
Rådmansgatan
Tegnérgatan
Regerings-
Torsgatan
Odengatan
Sveavägen
U
U
Kungstens-
Drottninggatan
gatan
Vassa Eggen
Elite H.
Stockholm Plaza
Sankt
VASAPARKEN
Grill
Rolfs Kök
Sankt
Eriksplan
STRINDBERGSMUSEET
Tegnér-
lunden
Holländargatan
gatan
Hötorget
Kungs-
Dalagatan
Tegnér-
gatan
Gata
Restaurangen
KONSERTHUSET
Oxtorgs-
gatan
Regerings-
Torsgatan
Olof Palmes
Drottning-
gatan
Svea-
vägen
Klarastrands-
Norra
Bantorget
Hötorget
NORRMALM
leden
Vasa-
Rica H.
Stockholm
Slöjdgatan
Barnhusbron
Kungs-
gatan
Freys
gatan
Nordic Light
Brygg-
T-Centralen
Klarabergs-
gatan
Hamn
KULTUR-
HUSET
gatan
Kungsbron
Flemming-
gatan
Nordic Sea
Radisson SAS
Royal Viking
Sheraton
Stockholm
Herkules-
gatan
Jakobs-
gatan
Kungsholms-
Klarabergsviadukten
Vasa-
gatan
CENTRAL-
STATIONEN
First H.
Amaranten
gatan
Rådhuset
Stockholm
Fredsgata
12
Bergs-
gatan
Scheele-
Hantverkargatan
Hantverkargatan
STADSHUSET
KUNGSHOLMEN
Kungsholms-
torg
Mälarstrand
Norr
RIDDARHOLMEN
RIDDARFJÄRDEN
Mälarstrand
Söder
Brännkyrka-
Horns-
Mariatorget
Hotel
Restaurant

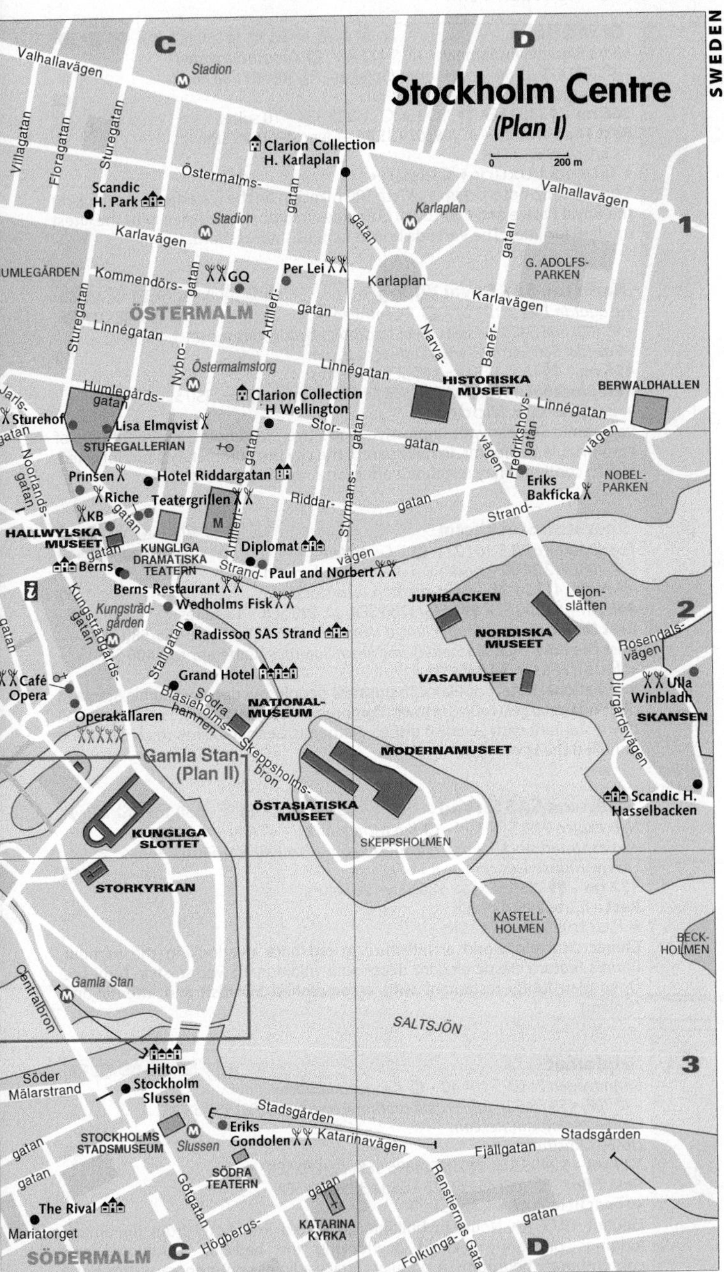

Stockholm Centre
(Plan I)
0
200 m
C
D
1
2
3
Valhallavägen
Stadion
Villagatan
Floragatan
Sturegatan
Clarion Collection H. Karlaplan
Östermalms-
gatan
Scandic H. Park
Stadion
Karlavägen
Karlaplan
HUMLEGÅRDEN
Kommendörs-
gatan
GQ
Per Lei
Karlaplan
G. ADOLFS-PARKEN
Karlavägen
ÖSTERMALM
Artilleri-
Linnégatan
Narva-
Banér-
Nybro-
Östermalmstorg
Linnégatan
HISTORISKA MUSEET
BERWALDHALLEN
Humlegårds-
gatan
Clarion Collection H Wellington
Jarls-
gatan
Sturehof
Lisa Elmqvist
Stor-
STUREGALLERIAN
gatan
Fredrikshovs-
gatan
vägen
Noorlands-
gatan
Prinsen
Hotel Riddargatan
Eriks Bakficka
NOBEL-PARKEN
Riche
Teatergrillen
Riddar-
gatan
Styrmans-
KB
Strand-
HALLWYLSKA MUSEET
KUNGLIGA DRAMATISKA TEATERN
Diplomat
vägen
Berns
Strand-
Paul and Norbert
Berns Restaurant
JUNIBACKEN
Lejon-slätten
Kungsträd-gården
Wedholms Fisk
Kungsträdgårds-gatan
Radisson SAS Strand
NORDISKA MUSEET
Rosendals-vägen
Stallgatan
Café Opera
Grand Hotel
VASAMUSEET
Ulla Winbladh
SKANSEN
Södra Blasieholms-hamnen
NATIONAL-MUSEUM
Djurgårdsvägen
Operakällaren
MODERNAMUSEET
Gamla Stan (Plan II)
Skeppsholms-bron
ÖSTASIATISKA MUSEET
Scandic H. Hasselbacken
KUNGLIGA SLOTTET
SKEPPSHOLMEN
STORKYRKAN
KASTELL-HOLMEN
BECK-HOLMEN
Centralbron
Gamla Stan
SALTSJÖN
Hilton Stockholm Slussen
Söder Mälarstrand
Stadsgården
STOCKHOLMS STADSMUSEUM
Slussen
Eriks Gondolen
Katarinavägen
Fjällgatan
Stadsgården
SÖDRA TEATERN
Renstiernas Gata
Götgatan
The Rival
Mariatorget
KATARINA KYRKA
SÖDERMALM
Högbergs-
gatan
Folkunga-

Grand Hôtel

350 VISA

Södra Blasieholmshamnen 8 ✉ *S-111 47* – Ⓜ *Kungsträdgården* – ✆ *(08) 679 35 00* – *info@grandhotel.se* – *Fax (08) 611 86 86* – *www.grandhotel.se* **C2**

366 rm – 🚹3400 SEK 🚹🚹3800 SEK, ☕ 235 SEK – 10 suites

Rest *The Veranda* – ✆ *(08) 679 35 86* – Menu 495/595 SEK – Carte 405/680 SEK

♦ Grand Luxury ♦ Classic ♦

Sweden's top hotel occupies a late 19C mansion on the waterfront overlooking the Royal Palace and Old Town. Combines traditional elegance with the latest modern facilities. The Veranda boasts famous smörgåsbord.

Radisson SAS Royal Viking

130 VISA

Vasagatan 1 ✉ *S-101 24* – Ⓜ *T-Centralen* – ✆ *(08) 506 540 00* – *sales.royal.stockholm@radissonsas.com* – *Fax (08) 506 540 02* – *www.radissonsas.com* **B2**

456 rm – 🚹🚹1895 SEK, ☕ 125 SEK – 3 suites

Rest *Stockholm Fisk* – ✆ *(08) 506 541 02* – Carte approx. 550 SEK

♦ Business ♦ Modern ♦

Panoramic Sky Bar with impressive views over Stockholm, above 9 floors of comfortable bedrooms. In busy part of the city but completely soundproofed. Stylish contemporary restaurant offers an array of seafood dishes.

Sheraton Stockholm

380 VISA

Tegelbacken 6 ✉ *S-101 23* – Ⓜ *T-Centralen* – ✆ *(08) 412 34 00* – *stockholm.sheraton@sheraton.com* – *Fax (08) 412 34 09* – *www.sheraton.com/stockholm* **B2**

445 rm – 🚹3200 SEK 🚹🚹1495/3200 SEK, ☕ 220 SEK – 17 suites

Rest *Dining Room* – *(buffet lunch)* Menu 135/245 SEK – Carte 455/580 SEK

Rest *Die Ecke* – *(closed Sunday and lunch Saturday)* Carte approx. 400 SEK

♦ Business ♦ Modern ♦

International hotel popular with business people, overlooking Gamla Stan and offering the largest rooms in town. Comprehensive guest facilities. Open-plan all day restaurant with Swedish dishes. Authentic German dishes in classic wood panelled Die Ecke.

Radisson SAS Strand

50 VISA

Nybrokajen 9 ✉ *S-103 27* – Ⓜ *Kungsträdgården* – ✆ *(08) 506 640 00* – *sales.strand.stockholm@radissonsas.com* – *Fax (08) 506 640 01* – *www.radissonsas.com* **C2**

132 rm – 🚹🚹2595 SEK, ☕ 180 SEK – 20 suites

Rest – Carte 295/425 SEK

♦ Business ♦ Classic ♦

Characterful old world architecture in red brick overlooking the harbour. Rooms feature classic elegant décor with traditional Swedish-style furniture. Open-plan lobby restaurant with accomplished Swedish and international cooking.

Diplomat

VISA

Strandvägen 7c ✉ *S-104 40* – Ⓜ *Kungsträdgården* – ✆ *(08) 459 68 00* – *info@diplomathotel.com* – *Fax (08) 459 68 20* – *www.diplomathotel.com*

closed Christmas **C2**

129 rm – 🚹2495 SEK 🚹🚹2995/4895 SEK, ☕ 170 SEK

Rest *T Bar* – ✆ *(08) 459 68 02* – Carte 325/508 SEK

♦ Traditional ♦ Classic ♦

Elegant 1911 Art Nouveau building converted into hotel from diplomatic lodgings pleasantly located overlooking the harbour. Traditional and contemporary bedrooms. A popular terrace adjoins contemporary-style hotel restaurant offering traditional Swedish cooking.

Berns 180 VISA

Näckströmsgatan 8, Berzelii Park ✉ S-111 47 – Ⓜ Kungsträdgården – ✆ (08) 566 322 00 – frontoffice@berns.se – Fax (08) 566 322 01 – www.berns.se **C2**

61 rm – 3500 SEK 4250 SEK – 4 suites

Rest *Berns Restaurant* – see below

♦ Business ♦ Stylish ♦

Boutique hotel with a modern minimalist interior décor verging on trendy; details in cherry wood and marble. Modern facilities in bedrooms, some have balconies.

Nordic Light 40 VISA

Vasaplan ✉ S-101 37 – Ⓜ T-Centralen – ✆ (08) 505 630 00 – info@nordichotels.se – Fax (08) 505 630 30 – www.nordiclighthotel.com **B2**

175 rm – 3030 SEK

Rest – Carte 360/465 SEK

♦ Business ♦ Design ♦

Sister hotel to Nordic Sea boasting most facilities. Modern harmonious black and white designer décor features symphony of lights on the Nordic Lights theme. Also, an ice bar! Modern restaurant in the main hall: modish cooking.

Nordic Sea without rest 100 VISA

Vasaplan ✉ S-101 37 – Ⓜ T-Centralen – ✆ (08) 505 630 00 – info@nordichotels.se – Fax (08) 505 630 90 – www.nordicseahotel.com **B2**

367 rm – 2140 SEK 1440/2570 SEK

♦ Business ♦ Design ♦

Stylish modern hotel with an appropriately nautical theme. Accordingly, the modish bedrooms all have a cool blue backdrop.

First H. Amaranten rest VISA

Kungsholmsgatan 31 ✉ S-104 20 – Ⓜ Rådhuset – ✆ (08) 692 52 00 – amaranten@firsthotels.se – Fax (08) 652 62 48 – www.firsthotels.com/amaranten **A2**

422 rm – 1998 SEK 1398/2398 SEK – 1 suite

Rest *Amaranten* – *(closed Sunday)* Menu 265/365 SEK

♦ Business ♦ Modern ♦

Modernised, commercial hotel conveniently located with easy access to subway. Stylish, quiet public areas with American Bar; compact but up-to-date bedrooms. Stylish modern eating area with a large menu of modern Swedish cooking.

Scandic H. Park 50 VISA

Karlavägen 43 ✉ S-102 46 – Ⓜ Stadion – ✆ (08) 517 348 00 – park@scandic-hotels.com – Fax (08) 517 348 11 – www.scandic-hotels.com/park **C1**

190 rm – 2700 SEK 1700/2500 SEK – 8 suites

Rest *Park Village* – Carte 310/440 SEK

♦ Business ♦ Modern ♦

Convenient location by one of the city's prettiest parks (view from suites). All rooms are a good size, modern and comfortable with good range of facilities and comforts. Modern restaurant with small summer terrace; traditional Swedish and international fare.

Birger Jarl 150 VISA

Tulegatan 8 ✉ S-104 32 – Ⓜ Rådmansgatan – ✆ (08) 674 18 00 – info@birgerjarl.se – Fax (08) 673 73 66 – www.birgerjarl.se **B1**

230 rm – 2520 SEK 2800 SEK – 5 suites

Rest – *(closed lunch Saturday and Sunday)* Carte 297/388 SEK

♦ Business ♦ Modern ♦

Modern hotel building in quieter part of city. Lobby features many art and sculpture displays. Some rooms decorated by local artists of international reputation. Simple and stylish restaurant with unfussy Swedish cooking.

Elite H. Stockholm Plaza

VISA AE

Birger Jarlsgatan 29 ✉ S-103 95 – Ⓜ Östermalmstorg – ✆ (08) 566 220 00 – info.stoplaza@elite.se – Fax (08) 566 220 20 – www.elite.se
closed 23-27 December **B1**

139 rm – 2095 SEK 1490/2495 SEK – 4 suites

Rest *Vassa Eggen* – see below

◆ Business ◆ Functional ◆

Well preserved 1884 building with up-to-date comforts. Compact well-run commercial hotel with conference rooms, basement sauna and high percentage of single rooms.

Freys

30 VISA AE

Bryggargatan 12 ✉ S-101 31 – Ⓜ T-Centralen – ✆ (08) 506 213 00 – freys@freyshotels.com – Fax (08) 506 213 13 – www.freyshotels.com
closed 22-27 December **B2**

123 rm – 1795 SEK 1895 SEK – 1 suite

Rest *Belgobaren* – Menu 295 SEK (dinner) – Carte 278/440 SEK

◆ Business ◆ Functional ◆

Completely renovated hotel near Central station. Local paintings for sale. First-floor terrace. Fairly compact rooms with informal furnishings; superior rooms with balconies. Belgian specialities, including more than 100 different beers, on exclusive menu.

Hotel Riddargatan without rest

VISA AE

Riddargatan 14 ✉ S-114 35 – Ⓜ Östermalmstorg – ✆ (08) 555 730 00 – hotelriddargatan@profilhotels.se – Fax (08) 555 730 11 – www.profilhotels.se
closed 22 December- 2 January **C2**

56 rm – 2350 SEK 1425/2350 SEK – 2 suites

◆ Business ◆ Design ◆

Modern-style hotel in quiet location behind the Royal Dramatik Theatre, near shops and restaurants. Swedish design bedrooms with good Internet facilities.

Rica H. Stockholm

60 VISA AE

Slöjdgatan 7 ✉ S-111 57 – Ⓜ T-Centralen – ✆ (08) 723 72 00 – info.stockholm@rica.se – Fax (08) 723 72 09 – www.rica.se
closed 22 December-2 January **B2**

292 rm – 2295 SEK 1180/2345 SEK

Rest *Oasen* – *(closed Saturday and Sunday) (lunch only) (snacks only)*
Carte approx. 90 SEK

◆ Business ◆ Functional ◆

Conveniently located at heart of shopping district so popular with tourists. Rooms distributed around atrium, beneath which is a winter garden. Functional modern bedrooms. Street-side restaurant offering narrow range of daily changing platters.

Clarion Collection H. Wellington without rest

VISA AE

Storgatan 6 ✉ S-114 51 – Ⓜ Östermalmstorg – ✆ (08) 667 09 10 – cc.wellington@choice.se – Fax (08) 667 12 54 – www.wellington.se
closed 21 December- 7 January **C1**

58 rm – 2395 SEK 1595/2695 SEK – 2 suites

◆ Business ◆ Functional ◆

Apartment block converted to hotel in 1960s, well placed for shopping and clubs. Compact, refurbished and well-equipped rooms; good city views from upper floor balconies.

Clarion Collection H. Karlaplan without rest

VISA AE

Skeppargatan 82 ✉ S-114 59 – ✆ (08) 31 32 20 – info.karlaplan@choicehotels.se – Fax (08) 31 32 21 – www.hotelkarlaplan.se **C-D1**

85 rm – 1399 SEK 2399 SEK

◆ Business ◆ Modern ◆

18C building on edge of city centre. Functionality is the key here, with both breakfast room and bedrooms being simple and unfussily adorned. Buffet included in room rate.

XXXXX ✿ **Operakällaren** (Catenacci) ⇸ ⊕20 VISA MC AE ⓓ

Operahuset, Karl XII's Torg ✉ S-111 86 – Ⓜ Kungsträdgården – ✆ (08) 676 58 01 – matsal@operakallaren.se – Fax (08) 676 58 72 – www.operakallaren.se

closed mid July-mid August, 25 December-8 January, Sunday and Monday **C2**

Rest – *(dinner only)* Carte 660/883 SEK

Spec. Half a Scottish lobster with vanilla dressing and sweet and sour mushrooms. Knuckle of veal poached in red wine and beer, tortellini and kidney. Cloudberry gazpacho with white chocolate panna cotta.

♦ Traditional ♦ Formal ♦

Magnificent dining room with original 19C carved wood décor and fresco paintings situated in the historic Opera House. Classically based menu of gourmet dishes.

XXX **Vassa Eggen** – at Elite H. Stockholm Plaza AC ⇸ VISA MC AE ⓓ

Birger Jarlsgatan 29 ✉ S-114 25 – Ⓜ Östermalmstorg – ✆ (08) 21 61 69 – info@vassaeggen.com – Fax (08) 20 34 46 – www.vassaeggen.com

closed 23-27 December **B1**

Rest – *(closed Sunday dinner)* Menu 385 SEK (lunch) – Carte 655/745 SEK

♦ Innovative ♦ Fashionable ♦

Refined restaurant popular with those in the know. Modern style reflected in both the décor and the cuisine, which is ambitious and innovative.

XXX ✿ **Esperanto** (Hoglander/ Isaksson) AC ⇸ VISA MC AE

Kungstensgatan 2 ✉ S-114 25 – Ⓜ Tekniska Högskolan – ✆ (08) 696 2323 – esperanto@sollevi.se – www.esperantorestaurant.se **B1**

closed 6 weeks summer, 2 weeks Christmas-New Year, Sunday and Monday

Rest – *(dinner only) (set menu only)* Menu 695/895 SEK

Spec. Monkfish with lentils and a melon and crustacean sorbet. Venison with autumn leaves, marrow, nuts, dried fruits and chestnut crème with foie gras. Rice wafer with mango, sticky rice and sorbet.

♦ Innovative ♦ Formal ♦

Found on the first floor of a converted theatre. Candlelight adds warmth to the understated décor of the dining room. Structured and well-organised service; original and precise cooking.

XX ✿ **Fredsgatan 12** (Couet) ⇸ ⊕50 VISA MC AE ⓓ

Fredsgatan 12 ✉ S-111 52 – Ⓜ T-Centralen – ✆ (08) 24 80 52 – info@fredsgatan12.com – Fax (08) 23 76 05 – www.fredsgatan12.com

closed 12 July-14 August, 22 December-2 January, Sunday and lunch Saturday **B2**

Rest – *(booking essential)* Menu 350 SEK (lunch) – Carte 490/840 SEK

Spec. Plums with foie gras and tonka beans. Roe deer with cocoa beans and berbere. Arctic bramble "pearls" with warm caramel.

♦ Innovative ♦ Fashionable ♦

A strikingly redesigned restaurant in a wing of the Academy of Arts. Divided into a number of areas, all with a modern and stylish feel. Creative and original modern cuisine.

XX **Paul and Norbert** ⇸ VISA MC AE ⓓ

Strandvägen 9 ✉ S-114 56 – Ⓜ Kungsträdgården – ✆ (08) 663 81 83 – restaurang.paul.norbert@telia.se – Fax (08) 661 72 36 – www.paulochnorbert.se

closed Christmas and New Year, Monday lunch and Sunday **C2**

Rest – *(booking essential)* Menu 350/850 SEK – Carte 585/715 SEK

♦ Traditional ♦ Formal ♦

Small sophisticated well-run restaurant on harbour with stylish modern décor and artwork. Some tables in booths. Numerous menus featuring seasonal produce.

SWEDEN

XX

GQ

Kommendörsgatan 23 ✉ S-114 48 – Ⓜ Stadion – ✆ (08) 545 674 30 – upplev@gqrestaurang.se – Fax (08) 662 25 06 – www.gqrestaurang.se
closed 2 July-15 August, 22 December-8 January and Sunday **C1**
Rest – *(set menu only)* Menu 295 SEK (lunch) – Carte 525/695 SEK
♦ Innovative ♦ Trendy ♦
"Gastronomic intelligence" in a trendy, eye-catching restaurant with its own cookery school. Specially chosen wines complement seriously considered and ambitious dishes.

XX

Berns Restaurant – at Berns H.

Näskströmsgatan 8, Berzelii Park ✉ S-111 47 – Ⓜ Kungsträdgården – ✆ (08) 566 322 22 – info@berns.se – Fax (08) 566 323 23 – www.berns.se **C2**
Rest – Carte 215/435 SEK
♦ Modern ♦ Fashionable ♦
A stunningly-restored 19C rococo ballroom with galleries overlooking the dining room. Modern international cuisine. Live music. The place to be seen in.

XX

Wedholms Fisk

Nybrokajen 17 ✉ S-111 48 – Ⓜ Kungsträdgården – ✆ (08) 611 78 74 – info@wedholmsfisk.se – Fax (08) 678 60 11 – www.wedholmsfisk.se
closed Sunday and Saturday lunch – **Rest** – Carte 400/980 SEK **C2**
♦ Seafood ♦ Formal ♦
Classic 19-20C building near harbour. Elegant restaurant serving a good choice of fish and shellfish, simply but accurately prepared; similar dishes in the bar.

XX

Per Lei

Artillerigatan 56 ✉ S-114 45 – Ⓜ Karlaplan – ✆ (08) 411 38 11 – info@perlei.se – Fax (08) 662 64 45 – www.perlei.se
closed 2 July- 6 August, 2 days Christmas, Sunday and Saturday lunch **C1**
Rest – *(booking essential) (light lunch)* Menu 225/445 SEK – Carte approx. 500 SEK
♦ Italian influences ♦ Cosy ♦
Popular neighbourhood restaurant in converted boutique; elegant décor with Murano chandelier. Modern Italian menu: two dinner menus of three or five courses. Refined cooking.

XX

Stockholm

Centralplan/Ingång från Vasagatan ✉ 101 35 – Ⓜ T-Centralen – ✆ (08) 20 20 49 – Fax (08) 613 62 55 – www.restaurangstockholm.se
closed July, 1 week Christmas, Sunday and Saturday lunch **B2**
Rest – Menu 265 SEK (lunch) – Carte dinner 420/560 SEK
♦ Modern ♦ Fashionable ♦
Restaurant within a glass cube in front of the central station. Stylish and retro-style decoration, with lounge bar. Friendly and organised service; classic Swedish cuisine with some modern touches.

XX

Teatergrillen

Nybrogatan 3 ✉ S-111 48 – Ⓜ Östermalmstorg – ✆ (08) 545 035 65 – riche@riche.se – Fax (08) 545 035 69 – www.teatergrillen.se
closed Sunday, Saturday lunch and Monday dinner **C2**
Rest – Menu 495 SEK (lunch) – Carte 485/705 SEK
♦ Traditional ♦ Brasserie ♦
Intimate, traditional city institution, most pleasant in the evening. Menus are more expensive than its sister Riche. Expect traditional cooking of Scandinavian classics.

XX

Café Opera

Operahuset, Karl XII's Torg ✉ S-111 86 – Ⓜ Kungsträdgården – ✆ (08) 676 58 09 – info@cafeopera.se – Fax (08) 676 58 71 – www.cafeopera.se – closed Midsummer Eve, 24 December and Monday except Summer and December
Rest – *(booking essential) (dinner only - music and dancing after 12pm)* Carte 365/605 SEK **C2**
♦ International ♦ Brasserie ♦
Characterful rotunda-style historic restaurant with ceiling painted in 1895, Corinthian pillars, fine mouldings and covered terrace. Swedish-influenced, international menu.

XX

Clas På Hörnet with rm

Surbrunnsgatan 20 ✉ S-113 48 – Ⓜ Tekniska Högskolan – ✆ (08) 16 51 30 – boka@claspahornet.se – Fax (08) 612 53 15 – www.claspahornet.se **B1**

10 rm – 2395 SEK

Rest – *(closed Saturday lunch and Sunday)* Carte 260/555 SEK

♦ Traditional ♦ Rustic ♦

Well-established and busy restaurant in part 18C inn with character. Simple traditional rustic cooking using good quality local produce. Cosy, well-equipped bedrooms.

X

Restaurangen

Oxtorgsgatan 14 ✉ S-111 57 – Ⓜ Hötorget – ✆ (08) 22 09 52 – reservation@restaurangentm.com – Fax (08) 22 09 54 – www.restaurangentm.com closed 1 month in summer, Christmas and New year's Eve, Saturday lunch and Sunday **B2**

Rest – *(booking essential) (light lunch)* Carte 300/500 SEK

♦ Inventive ♦ Trendy ♦

Contemporary interior with clean-cut minimalist décor and modern furnishings. Unusual menu concept based on a tasting of several small dishes.

X

Grill

Drottninggatan 89 ✉ S-113 60 – Ⓜ Rådmansgatan – ✆ (08) 31 45 30 – info@grill.se – Fax (08) 31 45 80 – www.grill.se closed mid July-early August and lunch Saturday and Sunday **B1**

Rest – *(light buffet lunch)* Carte 165/335 SEK

♦ Grills ♦ Minimalist ♦

Stylish city centre restaurant with spacious lounge area; modern minimalist décor. Open-plan kitchen. Menu based on different cooking methods - grilling, rotisserie, BBQ etc.

X

Rolfs Kök

Tegnérgatan 41 ✉ S-111 61 – Ⓜ Rådmansgatan – ✆ (08) 10 16 96 – info@rolfskok.se – Fax (08) 789 88 80 – www.rolfskok.se closed July, 1 week August, 24-26 December, 31 December-1 January and lunch Saturday and Sunday **B1**

Rest – *(booking essential) (light lunch)* Carte 315/545 SEK

♦ International ♦ Bistro ♦

Compact, trendy bar-restaurant; buzzy atmosphere guaranteed. Home-made fresh bread and ice cream. Modern international cooking. Up to 750 wines can be ordered by the glass!

X

Lisa Elmqvist

Östermalms Saluhall ✉ 114 39 – Ⓜ Östermalmstorg – ✆ (08) 553 40410 – info@lisaelmqvist.se – Fax (08) 553 4 04 24 – www.lisaelmqvist.se closed Sunday and Bank Holidays **C1**

Rest – *(booking essential) (bookings not accepted on Saturday) (lunch only) (communal dining)* Carte 311/463 SEK

♦ Seafood ♦ Friendly ♦

A fourth generation family affair where shared tables and fresh seafood combine to create a contented and lively atmosphere. Open kitchen with seasonal fish display and deli.

BRASSERIES AND BISTRO *Plan I*

X

Prinsen

Mäster Samuelsgatan 4 ✉ S-111 44 – Ⓜ Östermalmstorg – ✆ (08) 611 13 31 – kontoret@restaurangprinsen.se – Fax (08) 611 70 79 – www.restaurangprinsen.se closed 24-26 and 31 December and Sunday lunch **C2**

Rest – *(booking essential)* Carte 363/583 SEK

♦ Traditional ♦ Brasserie ♦

Long-standing, busy and well-run brasserie with literary associations. Spread over ground and lower floor with traditional décor and well-priced Swedish and French classics.

SWEDEN

KB

40

Smålandsgatan 7 ✉ S-111 46 – Ⓜ Östermalmstorg – ✆ (08) 679 60 32 – info@konstnarsbaren.se – Fax (08) 611 39 32 – www.konstnarsbaren.se **C2**

Rest – Menu 295 SEK (dinner) – Carte 232/625 SEK

♦ Traditional ♦ Brasserie ♦

19C building with impressive façade and original wall frescoes in bar - a home of Swedish artists with interesting modern art on the walls. Traditional Swedish cooking.

Eriks Bakficka

Fredrikshovsgatan 4 ✉ S-115 23 – ✆ (08) 660 15 99 – info.bakfickan@eriks.se – Fax (08) 663 25 67 – www.eriks.se

closed July, 23-25 and 31 December, 1 January and lunch Saturday and Sunday **D2**

Rest – Menu 535 SEK (dinner) – Carte 295/555 SEK

♦ Modern ♦ Bistro ♦

Quiet residential setting and well-run bistro and bar-counter with small terrace. Cosy dining rooms in the basement. Traditional Swedish dishes with modern global twists.

Sturehof

Stureplan 2-4 ✉ S-114 46 – Ⓜ Östermalmstorg – ✆ (08) 440 57 30 – info@sturehof.com – Fax (08) 678 11 01 – www.sturehof.com **C1**

Rest – Carte 335/705 SEK

♦ Traditional ♦ Brasserie ♦

Very popular classic café-brasserie with closely packed tables and a busy atmosphere due to the steady stream of local business clientele. Good choice of seafood dishes.

Riche

Birger Jarlsgatan 4 ✉ S-114 53 – Ⓜ Östermalmstorg – ✆ (08) 545 035 60 – riche@riche.se – Fax (08) 545 035 69 – www.riche.se

closed Sunday **C2**

Rest – Carte 360/605 SEK

♦ Traditional ♦ Brasserie ♦

Lively bar and bustling restaurant, very different from, but with same menu as, its sister Teatergrillen. Serves classic Scandinavian as well as international dishes.

at Gamla Stan (Old Stockholm) *Plan II*

First H. Reisen

20

Skeppsbron 12 ✉ S-111 30 – Ⓜ Gamla Stan – ✆ (08) 22 32 60 – reisen@firsthotels.se – Fax (08) 20 15 59 – www.firsthotels.com/reisen **F1**

137 rm – †2398 SEK ††1498/2798 SEK, ☕ 160 SEK – 7 suites

Rest *Reisen Bar and Dining Room* – *(light lunch)* Carte 125/220 SEK

♦ Business ♦ Modern ♦

19C hotel on waterfront with original maritime décor. Popular piano bar. Sauna in 17C vault. De luxe and superior rooms offer quayside view and small balconies. Maritime interior and a warm and welcoming atmosphere. Traditional Swedish and international menu.

Victory

55

Lilla Nygatan 5 ✉ S-111 28 – Ⓜ Gamla Stan – ✆ (08) 506 400 00 – info@victoryhotel.se – Fax (08) 506 400 10 – www.victoryhotel.se

closed 19 December- 6 January **E1**

45 rm – †2650 SEK ††1850/2650 SEK, ☕ 170 SEK – 3 suites

Rest *Leijontornet* – see below

♦ Historic ♦ Classic ♦

Pleasant 17C hotel with Swedish rural furnishings and maritime antiques. Rooms named after sea captains with individually-styled fittings, mixing modern and antique.

Rica H. Gamla Stan without rest

Lilla Nygatan 25 ✉ S-111 28 – Ⓜ Gamla Stan
– ✆ (08) 723 72 50 – info.gamlastan@rica.se – Fax (08) 723 72 59
– www.rica.se **F1**

50 rm – single 1895 SEK, double 1960 SEK – 1 suite

♦ Business ♦ Classic ♦

Conveniently located 17C house with welcoming style. Well-furnished rooms with traditional décor and antique-style furniture. Pleasant top-floor terrace with rooftop outlook.

Lady Hamilton without rest

Storkyrkobrinken 5 ✉ S-111 28 – Ⓜ Gamla Stan
– ✆ (08) 506 401 00 – info@ladyhamiltonhotel.se – Fax (08) 506 401 10
– www.ladyhamiltonhotel.se **E-F1**

34 rm – single 2450 SEK, double 1750/2450 SEK, breakfast 140 SEK

♦ Historic ♦ Classic ♦

15C houses of character full of fine Swedish rural furnishings. Rooms boast antique pieces and modern facilities. Sauna and 14C well plunge pool in basement.

Lord Nelson without rest

Västerlånggatan 22 ✉ S-111 29 – Ⓜ Gamla Stan
– ✆ (08) 506 401 20 – info@lordnelsonhotel.se – Fax (08) 506 401 30
– www.lordnelsonhotel.se **E1**
closed 16 December- 6 January

29 rm – single 2150 SEK, double 1490/2150 SEK, breakfast 90 SEK

♦ Historic ♦ Classic ♦

Charming late 17C house located in lively Old Town with ship-style interior and maritime antiques. Small cabin-style rooms with good level of comfort and compact bathrooms.

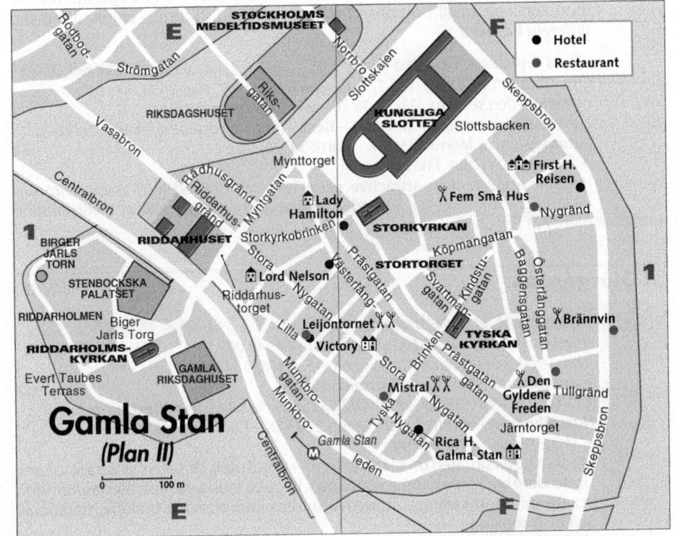

SWEDEN

XX **Leijontornet** – at Victory H.

Lilla Nygatan 5 ✉ S-111 28 – Ⓜ Gamla Stan – ✆ (08) 506 400 80 – info@leijontornet.se – Fax (08) 506 400 85 – www.leijontornet.se
closed 23 December-7 January, Saturday lunch and Sunday **E1**
Rest – *(booking essential) (light lunch)* Menu 325/895 SEK – Carte 270/650 SEK
◆ Traditional ◆ Formal ◆
Characterful restaurant with remains of a 14C fortified tower and a glass-fronted wine cellar sunk into floor. Light lunch in bistro; dinner in main basement dining room.

XX ✿ **Mistral** (Andersson)

Lilla Nygatan 21 ✉ S-111 28 – Ⓜ Gamla Stan – ✆ (08) 10 12 24 – rest.mistral@telia.com – Fax 10 12 17
closed Easter, July, Christmas, New Year and Sunday-Tuesday **F1**
Rest – *(booking essential) (dinner only) (set menu only)* Menu 995 SEK
Spec. Marinated carrot in saffron with raw prawns and fried turnip. Slow poached neck of lamb with coffee and thyme. Apple ice cream with walnut oil.
◆ Innovative ◆ Minimalist ◆
Very small personally-run restaurant with simple décor. Open-plan kitchen prepares original and creative dishes menus of 10 courses. Service is thoughtful and knowledgeable.

X **Fem Små Hus**

Nygränd 10 ✉ S-111 30 – Ⓜ Gamla Stan – ✆ (08) 10 87 75 – info@femsmahus.se – Fax (08) 14 96 95 – www.femsmahus.se – closed July
Rest – *(dinner only)* Menu 375/545 SEK – Carte 445/630 SEK **F1**
◆ Traditional ◆ Rustic ◆
Characterful restaurant located in 17C cellars of five adjacent houses and filled with antiques. Popular with tourists. Several menus available offering traditional cuisine.

X **Brännvin**

Skeppsbrokajen, Tullhus 2 ✉ S-111 30 – Ⓜ Gamla Stan – ✆ (08) 22 57 55 – info@brannvin-stockholm.se – www.brannvin-stockholm.se
closed 23 December- 1 May, Sunday and Monday **F1**
Rest – Carte 380/430 SEK
◆ Traditional ◆ Bistro ◆
Modern quayside bistro; its neat terrace runs to the water's edge. Interesting food concept: small portions of traditional Swedish dishes emphasising the different flavours.

X **Den Gyldene Freden**

Österlånggatan 51 ✉ S-103 17 – Ⓜ Gamla Stan – ✆ (08) 24 97 60 – info@gyldenefreden.se – Fax (08) 21 38 70 – www.gyldenefreden.se
closed Sunday and Bank Holidays – **Rest** – *(booking essential)(dinner only and Saturday lunch)* Menu 495 SEK – Carte 345/675 SEK **F1**
◆ Traditional ◆ Rustic ◆
Popular restaurant in attractive early 18C inn, divided into assorted rooms including vaulted cellar. Friendly service and robust cooking incorporating plenty of flavours.

at Djurgården

Plan I

Scandic H. Hasselbacken 250

Hazeliusbacken 20 ✉ S-100 55 – ✆ (08) 517 343 00 – hasselbacken@scandic-hotels.com – Fax (08) 517 343 11 – www.scandic-hotels.com/hasselbacken **D2**
111 rm – †2090 SEK ††1990/2390 SEK – 1 suite – **Rest *Restaurang Hasselbacken*** – *(buffet lunch)* Menu 220 SEK – Carte approx. 265 SEK
◆ Business ◆ Modern ◆
Modern hotel situated on island in former Royal park, close to the Vasa Museum. Up-to-date bedrooms, some with views. Regular musical events. Restaurant with ornate mirrored ceilings, attractive terrace and pleasant outlook; traditional Swedish cooking.

SWEDEN

Ulla Winbladh

Rosendalsvägen 8 ✉ S-115 21 – ✆ (08) 534 897 01 – info@ullawinbladh.se – Fax (08) 545 001 67 – www.ullawinbladh.se
closed 24 and 25 December D2
Rest – (booking essential) Carte 202/585 SEK
♦ Traditional ♦ Formal ♦
Pleasant late 19C pavilion in former Royal hunting ground houses several welcoming dining rooms and extensive terraces in summer. Traditional Swedish cuisine.

at Södermalm

Plan I

Hilton Stockholm Slussen

300 VISA
Guldgränd 8 ✉ S-104 65 – Ⓜ Slussen – ✆ (08) 517 353 00 – stockholm-slussen@hilton.com – Fax (08) 517 353 11 – www.stockholm-slussen.hilton.com C3
276 rm – 3290 SEK 1590/3290 SEK, 150 SEK – 13 suites
Rest *Eken* – (dinner only) Menu 520 SEK – Carte 250/525 SEK
♦ Business ♦ Modern ♦
Busy commercial hotel, overlooking Old Town and surrounding water, housed in three buildings with central lobby. Stylish rooms with elegant, coloured Scandinavian wood panels. Traditional and modern Swedish cuisine.

Clarion H. Stockholm

500 VISA
Ring Vägen 98 ✉ 104 60 – Ⓜ Skanstull – ✆ 462 1000 – cl.stockholm@choice.se – Fax 08462 10 99 – www.clarionstockholm.se
531 rm – 2490 SEK 2790 SEK – 1 suite
Rest *Greta's Kok* – (closed Sunday) (dinner only) Carte 300/515 SEK
♦ Business ♦ Modern ♦
Displaying more character than most purpose built hotels. Impressive collection of Nordic art throughout. Comfortable lounge space. Good bathrooms. Restaurant named after Greta Garbo who was born locally; international menu.

The Rival

50 VISA
Mariatorget 3 ✉ S-118 91 – Ⓜ Mariatorget – ✆ (08) 545 789 00 – rival@rival.se – Fax (08) 545 789 24 – www.rival.se C3
97 rm – 2290 SEK 2190/2890 SEK, 145 SEK – 2 suites
Rest *The Bistro* – (dinner only) Carte 295/600 SEK
♦ Business ♦ Stylish ♦
Modern boutique hotel and Art Deco cinema in 1930s building. Stylish bedrooooms with cinema theme décor and high-tech facilities. First floor open-plan bar and bistro/restaurant. Classic Swedish cooking in the bistro; more modern dishes in the restaurant.

Eriks Gondolen

< Stockholm and water, VISA
Stadsgården 6 (11th floor) ✉ S-104 56 – Ⓜ Slussen – ✆ (08) 641 70 90 – info@eriks.se – Fax (08) 641 11 40 – www.eriks.se – closed 17 April, 10 July-13 August, 24-26 December, 1 January, Saturday and Sunday C3
Rest – Menu 295/535 SEK – Carte 370/615 SEK
♦ Traditional ♦ Brasserie ♦
Glass-enclosed suspended passageway, renowned for stunning panoramic view of city and water. Open-air dining and barbecue terraces on 12th floor. Traditional Swedish fare.

at Arlanda Airport

Radisson SAS Sky City

VISA
at Terminals 4-5, 2nd floor above street level (Stockholm-Arlanda, Sky City) ✉ 190 45 – ✆ (08) 506 740 00 – reservations.skycity.stockholm@radissonsas.com – Fax (08) 506 740 01 – www.radissonsas.com – **229 rm** – 2195 SEK 1350/2195 SEK, 135 SEK – 1 suite – **Rest *Stockholm Fish*** – Carte approx. 350 SEK
♦ Business ♦ Modern ♦
The perfect place not to miss your plane: modern, corporate airport hotel. Varied décor to rooms: older Scandinavian or a choice of three modern styles. Balcony restaurant overlooking airport terminal offering fish-based menu.

Radisson SAS Arlandia

100

Benstocksvägen (Stockholm-Arlanda, Southeast : 1 km) ✉ *190 45 –* ☎ *(08) 506 840 00 – reservations.arlandia.stockholm@radissonsas.com – Fax (08) 506 840 01 – www.radissonsas.com*
closed 23 December-3 January
327 rm – 1800 SEK 1095/1800 SEK – 8 suites
Rest *Cayenne* – *(buffet lunch)* Menu 197 SEK – Carte approx. 250 SEK
♦ Business ♦ Functional ♦
A short shuttle ride from the terminal. Bright and modern corporate hotel and congress hall. Ecological, maritime and Scandinavian themed bedrooms. Contemporary-styled restaurant and adjacent bar for light snacks, pastas and traditional Scandinavian fare.

ENVIRONS OF STOCKHOLM

to the North 2 km by Sveavägen (at beginning of E 4)

Stallmästaregården

200

Nortull (North : 2 km by Sveavägen (at beginning of E 4)) ✉ *S-113 47 –* ☎ *(08) 610 13 00 – info@stallmastaregarden.se – Fax (08) 610 13 40 – www.stallmastaregarden.se*
closed 25-30 December
46 rm – 2095 SEK 1350/2395 SEK – 3 suites
Rest Stallmästaregården restaurant – see below
♦ Inn ♦ Classic ♦
Attractive 17C inn with central courtyard and modern bedroom wing. Quieter rooms overlook waterside and park. 18C-style rustic Swedish décor with modern comforts.

XX Stallmästaregården – at Stallmästaregården H.

Nortull (North : 2 km by Sveavägen (at beginning of E 4)) ✉ *S-113 47 –* ☎ *(08) 610 13 00 – info@stallmastaregarden.se – Fax (08) 610 13 40 – www.stallmastaregarden.se*
closed 25-30 December
Rest – Menu 425 SEK (dinner) – Carte 385/640 SEK
♦ Modern ♦ Inn ♦
Part 17C inn with elegant 18C Swedish décor. Beautiful waterside terrace in summer. Open kitchen. Modern Swedish cuisine.

at Ladugårdsgärdet

Villa Källhagen

55

Djurgårdsbrunnsvägen 10 (East: 3 km by Strandvägen) ✉ *S-115 27 –* ☎ *(08) 665 03 00 – villa@kallhagen.se – Fax (08) 665 03 99 – www.kallhagen.se*
closed 25-27 December
34 rm – 2400 SEK – 2 suites
Rest Villa Källhagen – see below
Rest *Bistro* – Carte approx. 380 SEK
♦ Inn ♦ Modern ♦
A relaxing hotel in a lovely waterside setting with extensive open-air terraces among the trees. Contemporary bedrooms, all with views. Simple bistro with international menu.

XX Villa Källhagen – at Villa Källhagen

Djurgårdsbrunnsvägen 10 (East: 3 km by Strandvägen) ✉ *S-115 27 –* ☎ *(08) 665 03 00 – villa@kallhagen.se – Fax (08) 665 03 99 – www.kallhagen.se*
closed 25-27 December
Rest – Carte 373/595 SEK
♦ International ♦ Brasserie ♦
Busy restaurant with terrace in great spot overlooking lake. Popular lunch with mostly traditional fare; more international influences at dinner. Raised area the best place to sit.

at Fjäderholmarna Island

Fjäderholmarnas Krog ← neighbouring islands and sea,
Stora Fjäderholmen ✉ *S-100 05* – ✆ *(08) 718 33 55* VISA MC AE
– fjaderholmarna@atv.se – Fax (08) 716 39 89
– www.fjaderholmarnaskrog.se
Easter to early October and 1-23 December
Rest – *(booking essential)* Carte 370/705 SEK
♦ Seafood ♦ Friendly ♦
Delightful waterside setting on archipelago island with fine view. Fresh produce, mainly fish, delivered daily by boat. Wide selection of traditional Swedish dishes.

at Nacka Strand Southeast : 10 km by Stadsgården or 20 mins by boat from Nybrokajen

Hotel J ← Sea, 30 P VISA MC AE
Ellensviksvägen 1 ✉ *S-131 28* – ✆ *(08) 601 30 00*
– nackastrand@hotelj.com
– Fax (08) 601 30 09 – www.hotelj.com
closed 23-30 December
41 rm – †1795 SEK ††1575/2195 SEK – 4 suites
Rest Restaurant J – see below
♦ Luxury ♦ Design ♦
Former politician's early 20C summer residence in quiet waterside setting. 'Boutique'- style hotel with maritime theme. Stylish spacious rooms, some with sea view.

Restaurant J ← Sea, VISA MC AE
Augustendalsvägen 52 ✉ *S-131 28* – ✆ *(08) 601 30 25 – info@restaurantj.com*
– Fax (08) 601 30 09 – www.restaurantj.com
Rest – Menu 450/550 SEK – Carte 390/630 SEK
♦ Traditional ♦ Brasserie ♦
Bright, informal restaurant with sleek maritime décor and attractive terrace beside marina. Selective menu of Swedish and international dishes.

at Lilla Essingen West : 5.5 km by Norr Mälarstrand

Lux Stockholm (Norström) ← VISA MC AE
Primusgatan 116 ✉ *S-112 67* – ✆ *(08) 619 01 90 – info@luxstockholm.com*
– Fax (08) 619 04 47 – www.luxstockholm.com
closed 22 December-7 January, Saturday lunch, Sunday and Monday
Rest – *(booking essential) (light lunch)* Menu 650/895 SEK
– Carte 590/695 SEK
Spec. "Taste of the sea" with crab, caviar and scallop cream. Mushroom grilled pike-perch with crispy potato, langoustine and blackened skate. Hazelnut and goat's milk sorbet, apple and salted caramel.
♦ Innovative ♦ Fashionable ♦
Former Electrolux factory overlooking waterways. Light and airy with green and white décor. Delightful terrace. Innovative Swedish cooking with distinctive twists.

at Bromma West : 5.5 km by Norr Mälarstrand and Drottningholmsvägen

Sjöpaviljongen ← VISA MC AE
Traneberg Strand 4, Alvik (East : 1.5 km) ✉ *167 40* – Ⓜ *Alvik* – ✆ *(08) 704 04 24*
– info@sjopaviljongen.se – Fax (08) 704 82 40 – www.sjopaviljongen.se
closed 23 December-7 January and Sunday dinner
Rest – *(booking essential) (light lunch)* Menu 375 SEK (dinner) – Carte 168/475 SEK
♦ Traditional ♦ Friendly ♦
Modern pavilion in attractive lakeside setting. Swedish-style décor with busy, bustling atmosphere. Good value classic Swedish cuisine. Mature service.

to the Northwest 8 km by Sveavägen and E 18 towards Norrtälje

XXX **Ulriksdals Wärdshus**

(take first junction for Ulriksdals Slott) ✉ 170 79 Solna – ✆ (08) 85 08 15 – info@ulriksdalswardshus.se – Fax (08) 85 08 58 – www.ulriksdalswardshus.se
closed 1 week Febuary, 1 week March, 13-27 July, 24-27 December, Monday September-April and Tuesday dinner except December
Rest – *(booking essential)* Menu 300 SEK (lunch) – Carte 350/615 SEK
♦ Traditional ♦ Inn ♦
19C former inn in Royal Park with classic winter garden-style décor. Wine cellar features in Guinness Book of Records. Extensive smörgåsbord at weekends.

at Sollentuna Northwest : 15 km by Sveavägen and E 4, (exit Sollentuna c)

XXXX ✿✿ **Edsbacka Krog** (Lingström)

Sollentunavägen 220 ✉ 191 35 – ✆ (08) 96 33 00 – info@edsbackakrog.se – Fax (08) 96 40 19 – www.edsbackakrog.se
closed Midsummer weekend, 8 July-2 August, 22 December-3 January, Sunday and Bank Holidays
Rest – *(dinner only and Saturday lunch)* Menu 750 SEK – Carte 735/935 SEK
Spec. "Palette" of Swedish specialities. Game in season. Chocolate composition.
♦ Innovative ♦ Inn ♦
Charming part 17C inn in small park with elegantly understated décor, divided into five rooms. Attention to detail in service and menus, with highly accomplished and original modern cooking.

X **Bistro Edsbacka**

Sollentunavägen 223 ✉ 191 35 – ✆ (08) 631 00 34 – bistro@edsbackakrog.se – Fax (08) 96 40 14 – www.edsbacka.se
closed Midsummer weekend, 22-25 December, 1 January and lunch in July
Rest – *(booking essential)* Menu 395/425 SEK – Carte 250/565 SEK
♦ Traditional ♦ Bistro ♦
Simple modern bistro, contrasting the restaurant opposite, with black and white décor. Smart rear terrace shielded from traffic. Good value menu of classic Swedish dishes.

GOTHENBURG
GÖTEBORG

Population (est. 2006): 489 500 (conurbation 872 200) – Altitude: sea level

Assner GÖRAN/VISITSWEDEN

Not without reason Gothenburg has been designated by Swedes themselves as Sweden's most friendly town. Sweden's second city and gateway to the west is favourably located on the west coast, equidistant from three Scandinavian capitals – Stockholm, Copenhagen and Oslo. With strong maritime traditions Gothenburg, at the mouth of the River Göta, is Scandinavia's number one seaport and a bustling commercial centre, including the head offices of some of Sweden's best known industrial companies – Volvo, SKF and Hasselblad. It is set among hills, bridges, water and islands and is known for its seafood restaurants. The coast to the south boasts miles of sandy beaches backed by dunes – the Swedish Riviera. The archipelago provides many places for cycling, fishing, surfing and bathing.

The city boasts excellent facilities for conferences, trade fairs, sporting events and rock concerts but its popularity is mostly due to its cosmopolitan, lively and friendly welcome. Shoppers may enjoy Nordstan, Northern Europe's largest indoor shopping centre. Ullevi, Scandinavia's largest stadium with 47 000 seats, and Scandinavium (12 500 seats) are stages for events ranging from rock concerts to sports events. The annual Gothia Cup is the world's greatest junior football tournament, with about 31 000 participants.

WHICH DISTRICT TO CHOOSE

Most **hotels** are to be found in and around the city centre *Plan I* **B1** and Götaplatsen *Plan I* **C3**. **Restaurants** follow much the same pattern; some are in the parks and some on the waterfront or accessible by boat. For lunch the best places are cafés, which offer good food at reasonable prices, or the traditional *konditori* (bakery with tearoom attached) in Haga and Linné. For a **drink only**, choose one of the places in Avenyn *Plan I* **B2** or Haga *Plan I* **A3**.

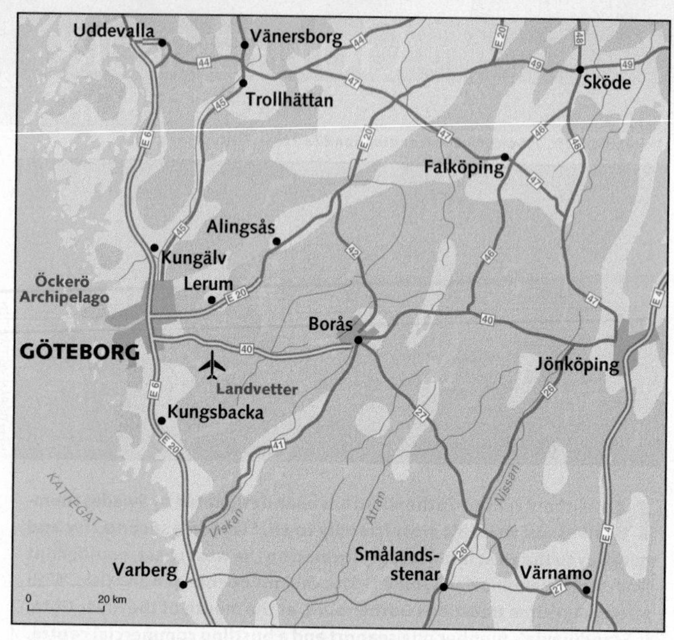

PRACTICAL INFORMATION

ARRIVAL – DEPARTURE

Landvetter Airport – About 25 km (16 mi) east of the city centre, ✆ 94 10 00. ✆ (0)31 94 10 00; www.landvetter.lfv.se

From the airport to the city centre – By **taxi** (30min) SEK 330. By **airport bus** *(Flygbuss)* (30min) every 15min, SEK 70; ✆ (0)31 80 12 35.

Railway Stations – There are regular train services to **Gothenburg Centralstationen** *Plan I* **B2** from the major towns in Sweden; www.sj.se

Ferry Terminal – There are regular ferry services from Kiel (Germany), Frederikshavn (Denmark) ✆ (0)31 704 00 00; www.stenaline.com; Harwich and Newcastle (England), Kristiansand (Norway) ✆ (0)31 650 650; www.dfdsseaways.com

TRANSPORT

→ BUS AND TRAM

The blue and white tram cars are named after personalities with Gothenburg connections. Tickets, timetables, routes and fares for buses and trams are available at Travel Information Centres *(tidpunkten)* at Brunnsparken, Drottningtorget, Nils Ericssons-platsen or Folkungabron. Tickets also sold by bus/tram drivers: Single ticket SEK 20. ✆ (0)771 414 300 (enquiries).

Vintage trams (Lisebergslinjen) operate in summer (12 noon to 6pm) between Central Station and Liseberg.

Punts *(paddan)* are a fascinating way to explore this maritime city, gliding along the canals past stately canalside buildings and under 20 bridges *(depart from the bridge at Kungsportsplatsen)*, SEK 80.

→ TAXIS

Taxis can be hired at a taxi stand – Central Station, Kungsportsplatsen, Kungsportsavenyn. When the *Ledig* sign is lit up, the taxi is free. The basic charge is SEK 29 plus SEK 9 per km within the city area. *Taxi Göteborg*, ✆ (0)31 65 00 00.

→ GOTHENBURG CARD

This card *(Göteborgskortet)* is valid for free boat and tram rides, parking in municipal car parks, a sightseeing tour, admission to the Liseberg amusement park and museums and discounts in certain shops and restaurants. 1-day card SEK 210, 2-day card SEK 295 on sale at Tourist Information Offices, the amusement park, newspaper kiosks *(pressbyrån)*, hotels and campsites.

USEFUL ADDRESSES

→ TOURIST OFFICE

Göteborgs Turistbyrå, Kungsportsplatsen 2 *Plan I* **B2**; ✆ (0)31 61 25 00; www.goteborg.com. Nordstan Shopping Centre, Nordstadstorget; ✆ (0)31 15 07 05; www.goteborg.com; www.scandinavium.se. For information and tickets to concerts, theatres and sports events: *Scandinavium*, Ullevi, Skånegatan, ✆ (0)31 811 020.

→ POST OFFICES

Opening times are Mon-Fri 9am-6pm, Sat 10am-1pm.

→ BANKS/CURRENCY EXCHANGE

Opening times 9.30am-3pm; some stay open until 5.30pm. At Landvetter Airport, Mon-Fri 8am-6pm, Sat until 5pm, Sun 12.30-8pm. Bank cash machines (ATMs) are open 24hrs (pin number required).

→ EMERGENCY

✆ **112** for Police, Fire Brigade, Ambulance, Poison hot-line, on-call doctors and 24hr Roadside breakdown service.

BUSY PERIODS

It may be difficult to find a room at a reasonable price (except at weekends) during special events:

International Film Festival: late January.

International Travel and Tourism Fair: Spring – In the exhibition centre Svenska Mässan.

Göteborgsvarvet: mid May-Half marathon.

Gothia Cup: mid July-Football cup.

Book Fair: Autumn – In the exhibition centre Svenska Mässan.

EXPLORING GOTHENBURG

In two days there is time to visit the main sights and museums.

Opening times are usually from 10/11am-4/6pm but closed on Mondays and public holidays.

VISITING

Waterfront: **Göteborgs-Utkiken** *Plan I* **B1** – Distinctive red and white office skyscraper (late 1980s) with **panoramic view** of the town from the café *(lift)*. **Lilla Bommens Hamn** *Plan I* **B1** – Departure point for local excursions by boat; 4-masted barque *Viking* (1906) converted to a restaurant. **Göteborgsoperan** *Plan I* **B1** – Modern opera house resembling a ship. **Göteborgs Maritima Centrum** *Plan I* **A1** – Floating museum of 11 historic vessels and boats. **Masthuggskyrkan** *Plan I* **B2** – Church built in the Swedish National Romantic style with an interesting wooden interior and a good view of the city.

Göteborgs Stadsmuseum *Plan I* **B2** – Historical and industrial museums housed in the Swedish East India House (1750-62), which served as HQ, warehouse and auction room. **Sjöfartsmuseet** – History of the Gothenburg East India trade: merchant ship *Finland*.

Town Centre: **Gustaf Adolfs Torg** is bordered by the stock exchange, **Börsen** (1849), **Wenngren's House** (1759), **Stadshuset** (1758) and **Rådhuset** (1672). **Avenyn** *Plan I* **B2** – The main artery of Gothenburg, properly called Kungsportsavenyn, a tree-lined boulevard, lined with cafés and restaurants, running south from Kungsportsplatsen over the canal and through the park to the Götaplatsen.

Göteborgs Konstmuseum *Plan I* **C3** – Collection of 19C and 20C Scandinavian art, 17C Dutch and Flemish art, 16C-18C Italian and Spanish art, 19C and 20C French art as well as contemporary international art: Göteborg Colourists, humerous pictures by Ivar Arosenius.

Röhsska Konstslöjdmuseet *Plan I* **C3** – Arts and crafts museum: latest in Nordic and international design.

Trädgårdsföreningen *Plan I* **C2** – Laid out by the horticultural society in 1842 with a Butterfly house, Palm House and rose garden beside the canal.

Liseberg *Plan I* **D3** – Fantastic amusement park with many rides, bandstands, theatres, dancing, cafés and restaurants in a pleasant green setting.

Botaniska Trädgården – Botanical gardens with Rock Garden, Bamboo Grove, Japanese Dale, Rhododendron Valley, wide expanses of lawn, winding paths and woodland.

SHOPPING

The main shopping streets are **Nordstan Mall**, **Avenyn**, **Linnégatan** and **Haga**. *NK* (Östra Hamngatan 42) and *Åhléns* (Nordstan) are two leading department stores. *Kronhusbodarna* (Kronhusgtan) is good for buying glassware and handicrafts; *Bohusslöjden* (Kungsportsavenyn 25) for local handicrafts.

MARKETS – The **fish and seafood** market (closed Monday) is held in the fish church *(Feskekörke)*, so called because of its architecture.

WHAT TO BUY – Glassware (Orrefors, Kosta, Boda), textiles, craft work, wood carvings; the museum shops are good for gifts.

ENTERTAINMENT

Theatre, cinema, bars and restaurants, clubs and other listings are printed in the Friday edition of *Göteborg Posten* and its weekly supplement *Aveny*.

Göteborgsoperan *Plan I* **B1** – Opera, ballet, light opera, musicals.

Konserthuset *Plan I* **C3** – Home of the Gothenburg Symphony Orchestra; also Stenhammar Room for chamber music recitals.

City Theatre and Folkteatern *Plan I* **C3**.

NIGHTLIFE

Gothenburg has a lively nightlife: *Dojan* (Vallgatan) the oldest and biggest music pub in the city with dance floor and rock bar and live performances on Thursdays and Sundays; *Henriksberg* (Stigbergsliden) old premises with nightclub, pub and restaurant. There is also the *Casino Cosmopol* (Packhusplatsen).

Radisson SAS Scandinavia 450

Södra Hamngatan 59-65 ✉ *S-401 24 – (031) 758 50 00 – info.gothenburg@radissonsas.com – Fax (031) 758 50 01 – www.gothenburg.radissonsas.com* VISA MC AE **B2**

332 rm – 2070 SEK – 17 suites

Rest *Atrium Bar & Restaurant* – *(buffet lunch)* Carte 400/550 SEK

◆ Business ◆ Modern ◆

Grand commercial hotel with impressive atrium courtyard complete with water features and glass elevators. Renovated, airy rooms boast choice of décor and impressive mod cons. A range of international dishes offered in restaurant housed within the atrium.

Elite Park Avenue 550

Kungsportsavenyn 36-38 ✉ *S-400 15 – (031) 727 1000 – Fax (031) 727 10 10 – www.elite.se* VISA MC AE **C3**

301 rm – 1850 SEK 1535/2600 SEK

Rest *Park Aveny Cafe* – Carte 385/525 SEK

◆ Business ◆ Modern ◆

Fully refurbished purpose-built hotel built in the 1950's on busy main street. Offers high levels of comfort with well proportioned bedrooms in creams and chocolates. Professional service. Informal café restaurant with large bar and opening onto pavement terrace; French classics on the menu.

Gothia Towers 1500 VISA MC AE

Mässans Gata 24 ✉ *S-402 26 – (031) 750 88 00 – hotelreservations@gothiatowers.com – Fax (031) 750 88 82 – www.gothiatowers.com* **D3**

695 rm – 1845 SEK 1145/2095 SEK – 9 suites

Rest *Heaven 23* – *(buffet lunch)* Menu 215/515 SEK – Carte 475/560 SEK

Rest *Incontro* – *(closed Sunday dinner) (buffet lunch)* Menu 125/495 SEK – Carte 310/450 SEK

◆ Business ◆ Modern ◆

Large twin tower hotel owned by Gothenburg Exhibition Centre, popular with conference delegates and business people. Elegant modern Scandinavian décor. Top floor Heaven 23, for spectacular city views and modern cuisine. Modern Italian dishes in Incontro.

Elite Plaza 50 VISA MC AE

Västra Hamngatan 3 ✉ *S-402 22 – (031) 720 40 40 – info.gbgplaza@elite.se – Fax (031) 720 40 10 – www.elite.se*

closed 23-25 December **B2**

143 rm – 2925 SEK

Rest *Swea Hof* – see below

◆ Luxury ◆ Modern ◆

Discreet and stylishly converted late 19C building. Rooms embody understated luxury with those overlooking the atrium sharing its lively atmosphere. Smart cocktail bar.

Clarion Collection H. Odin without rest 30

Odinsgatan 6 ✉ *S-411 03 – (031) 745 22 00 – info.cc.odin@choicehotels.se – Fax (031) 711 24 60 – www.hotelodin.se* P VISA MC AE **C2**

112 rm – 2055 SEK – 24 suites

◆ Business ◆ Modern ◆

Central location near railway station. Smart, Scandic-style, well-equipped, serviced apartments with mini-kitchen; also spacious and appealing suites.

Scandic H. Rubinen 40 VISA MC AE

Kungsportsavenyn 24 ✉ *S-400 14 – (031) 751 54 00 – rubinen@scandic-hotels.com – Fax (031) 751 54 11 – www.scandic-hotels.com/rubinen* **C3**

190 rm – 2190 SEK – 1 suite

Rest – *(closed Sunday lunch)* Carte 336/458 SEK

◆ Business ◆ Modern ◆

Well-located central hotel with smart, modern style. Comfy rooms exude a rich "red" theme, including a painting in that style. Junior suites boast delightful roof terraces. Modish restaurant with dominant bar; trendy "New Latino" style cuisine.

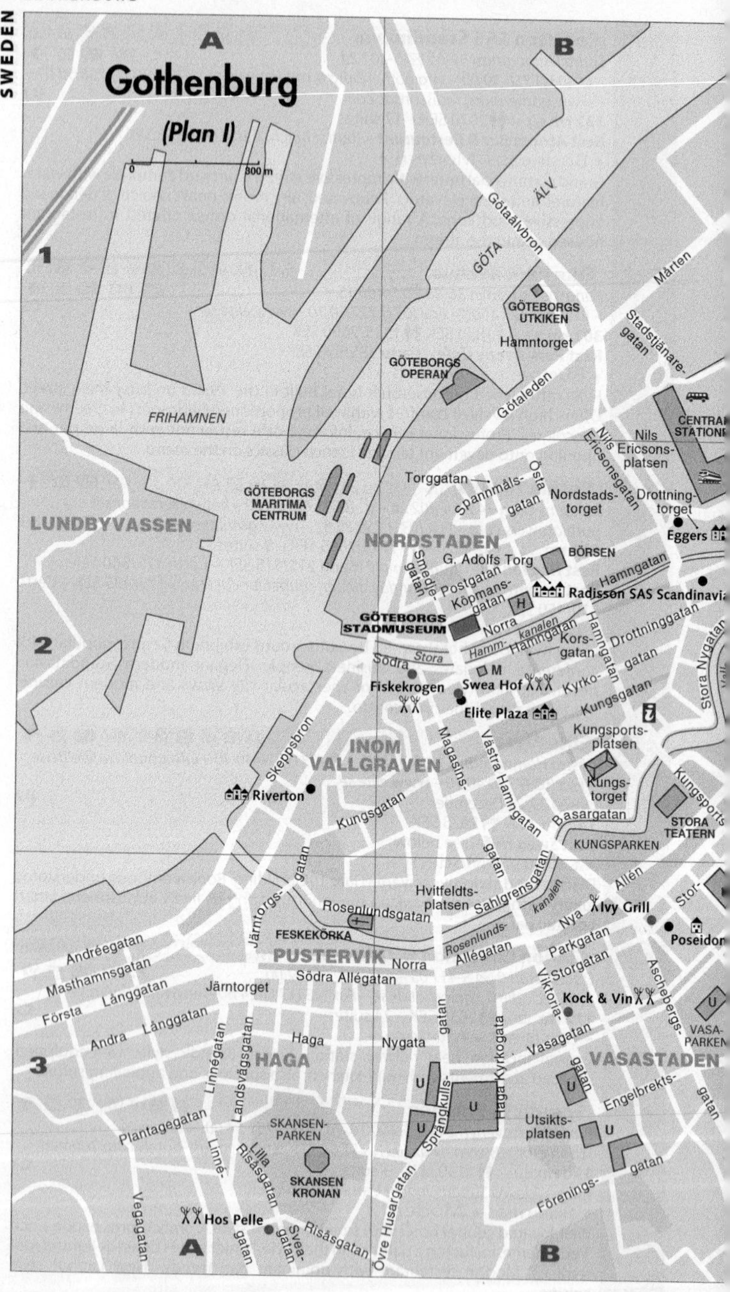

Gothenburg
(Plan I)
0
300 m
A
B
1
2
3
FRIHAMNEN
LUNDBYVASSEN
GÖTA
ÄLV
Götaälvbron
GÖTEBORGS UTKIKEN
Hamntorget
GÖTEBORGS OPERAN
Götaleden
Mårten
Stadstjänare-gatan
CENTRAL STATION
Nils Ericsons-platsen
Nils Ericsonsgatan
Drottning-torget
Eggers
GÖTEBORGS MARITIMA CENTRUM
Torggatan
Spannmåls-gatan
Östra
Nordstads-torget
NORDSTADEN
Smedje-gatan
G. Adolfs Torg
BÖRSEN
Postgatan
Köpmans-gatan
Hamngatan
Radisson SAS Scandinavia
GÖTEBORGS STADMUSEUM
Norra Hamngatan
Stora Hamm-kanalen
Södra
Kors-gatan
Drottninggatan
Hamngatan
M
Fiskekrogen
Swea Hof
Kyrko-gatan
Kungsgatan
Elite Plaza
Stora Nygatan
Kungsports-platsen
Skeppsbron
INOM VALLGRAVEN
Magasins-gatan
Västra Hamngatan
Kungs-torget
Riverton
Kungsgatan
Basargatan
Kungsports
STORA TEATERN
KUNGSPARKEN
Järntorgs-gatan
Hvitfeldts-platsen
Sahlgrensgatan
Rosenlundsgatan
kanalen
Nya Allén
Ivy Grill
Stor-
Poseidon
FESKEKÖRKA
Andréegatan
Masthamnsgatan
PUSTERVIK
Norra Allégatan
Rosenlunds-kanalen
Parkgatan
Storgatan
Aschebergs-gatan
Södra Allégatan
Järntorget
Första Långgatan
Andra Långgatan
Viktoria-gatan
Kock & Vin
Linnégatan
Landsvägsgatan
Haga
Nygata
gatan
Vasagatan
VASA-PARKEN
HAGA
VASASTADEN
U
Haga Kyrkogata
Sprängkulls-gatan
Engelbrekts-gatan
Plantagegatan
SKANSEN-PARKEN
Utsikts-platsen
Linné-gatan
Lilla Risåsgatan
SKANSEN KRONAN
Förenings-gatan
Vegagatan
Hos Pelle
Svea-gatan
Risåsgatan
Övre Husargatan

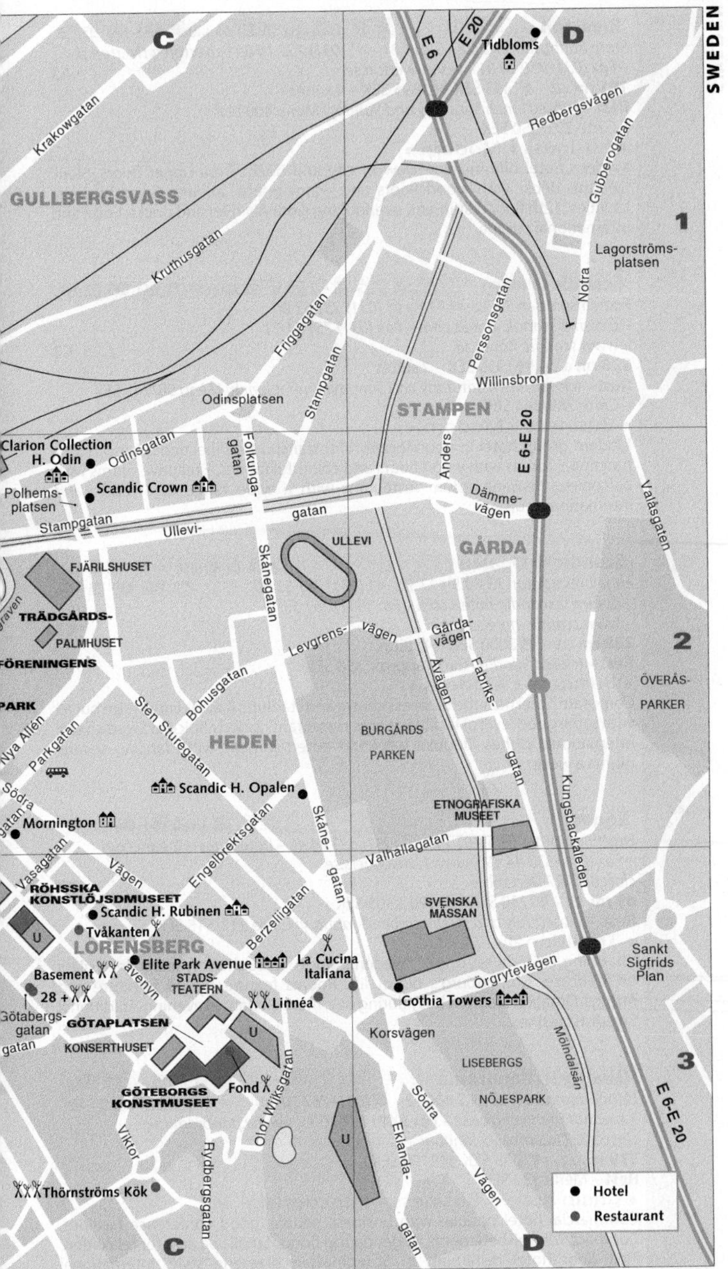
C
D
E 6
E 20
Tidbloms
Redbergsvägen
Krakowgatan
Gubberogatan
GULLBERGSVASS
1
Lagorströms-
platsen
Kruthusgatan
Notra
Perssonsgatan
Friggagatan
Stampgatan
Willinsbron
Odinsplatsen
STAMPEN
E 6-E 20
Clarion Collection
H. Odin
Odinsgatan
Folkunga-
gatan
Anders
Scandic Crown
Polhems-
platsen
Dämme-
vägen
Valåsgaten
Stampgatan
Ullevi-
gatan
ULLEVI
GÅRDA
FJÄRILSHUSET
Skånegatan
TRÄDGÅRDS-
PALMHUSET
FÖRENINGENS
PARK
Levgrens-
vägen
Gårda-
vägen
2
Avägen
Fabriks-
gatan
ÖVERÅS-
PARKER
Bohusgatan
Sten Sturegatan
Nya Allén
Parkgatan
HEDEN
BURGÅRDS
PARKEN
Södra
Scandic H. Opalen
Kungsbackaleden
Mornington
ETNOGRAFISKA
MUSEET
Engelbrektsgatan
Skåne-
gatan
Valhallagatan
Vasagatan
Vägen
RÖHSSKA
KONSTLÖJSDMUSEET
Scandic H. Rubinen
SVENSKA
MÄSSAN
Berzeliigatan
Tvåkanten
LORENSBERG
U
Elite Park Avenue
La Cucina
Italiana
Basement
avenyn
STADS-
TEATERN
Sankt
Sigfrids
Plan
Örgrytevägen
28 +
Linnéa
Gothia Towers
Götabergs-
gatan
GÖTAPLATSEN
Korsvägen
Mölndalsån
KONSERTHUSET
LISEBERGS
NÖJESPARK
3
Olof Wijksgatan
Fond
GÖTEBORGS
KONSTMUSEET
Södra
Vägen
E 6-E 20
Viktor
Eklanda-
gatan
Rydbergsgatan
Thörnströms Kök
Hotel
Restaurant

SWEDEN

Riverton
Stora Badhusgatan 26 ✉ *S-411 21* – ✆ *(031) 750 10 00 – riverton@riverton.se – Fax (031) 750 10 01 – www.riverton.se* **A2**
191 rm – 1495 SEK 1895 SEK – 4 suites
Rest – *(closed lunch Saturday and Sunday)* Menu 406 SEK – Carte 295/550 SEK
♦ Business ♦ Modern ♦
Modern hotel offering fine view of city and docks from upper floors. Sleek Swedish décor with wood floors and warm bright colours. Good business facilities. 12th floor restaurant, overlooking Göta Älv river and docks. Local and international cuisine.

Scandic Crown
Polhemsplatsen 3 ✉ *S-411 11* – ✆ *(031) 751 51 00 – crown@scandic-hotels.com – Fax (031) 751 51 11 – www.scandic-hotels.se* **C2**
336 rm – 1950 SEK – 2 suites
Rest – *(closed lunch Saturday and Sunday) (buffet lunch)* Menu 98/245 SEK – Carte 289/364 SEK
♦ Business ♦ Modern ♦
Modern group hotel in good location for transport connections. Fresh bright functional rooms with wood floors and colourful fabrics. Executive rooms with balconies. Pleasant atrium restaurant with a wide range of Swedish and international cuisine.

Scandic H. Opalen
Engelbrektsgatan 73 ✉ *S-412 52* – ✆ *(031) 751 53 00 – opalen@scandic-hotels.com – Fax (031) 751 53 11 – www.scandic-hotels.com* **C2**
238 rm – 2000 SEK – 4 suites
Rest – *(closed Sunday)* Carte approx. 350 SEK
♦ Business ♦ Modern ♦
Corporate hotel near the business centre and stadium. Rooms vary in size but all with same good level of facilities. Large restaurant, varied choice of Swedish and international dishes. Popular weekend entertainment with dancing several nights a week.

Eggers
Drottningtorget ✉ *S-401 25* – ✆ *(031) 333 44 40 – hotel.eggers@telia.com – Fax (031) 333 44 49 – www.hoteleggers.se*
closed 23-27 December **B2**
69 rm – 1780 SEK 1190/2305 SEK
Rest – *(closed July and 20 December-8 January)* Carte 212/515 SEK
♦ Traditional ♦ Classic ♦
Charming 1850s hotel, one of Sweden's oldest: wrought iron and stained glass on staircase, Gothenburg's oldest lift. Rooms feature period furniture and fittings. Ornate restaurant busy during day, more elegant in evening. Traditional Swedish cuisine.

Quality H. Panorama
Eklandagatan 51-53 ✉ *S-400 22* – ✆ *(031) 767 70 00 – q.panorama@choice.se – Fax (031) 767 70 75 – www.panorama.se*
closed 22 December-5 January
339 rm – 1895 SEK 2195 SEK
Rest – Menu 330 SEK
♦ Chain hotel ♦ Business ♦ Functional ♦
Commercial hotel popular with business people; good conference facilities. Compact, refurbished rooms, larger on top floors. Small spa area for relaxation. First floor hotel restaurant in Scandinavian brasserie style. International menu.

Novotel Göteborg
Klippan 1 (Southwest : 3.5 km by Andréeg taking Kiel-Klippan Ö exit, or boat from Rosenlund) ✉ *S-414 51 – ✆ (031) 720 22 00 – info@novotel.se – Fax (031) 720 22 99 – www.novotel.se*
144 rm – 1530 SEK 1260/1630 SEK – 5 suites
Rest *Carnegie Kaj* – *(buffet lunch)* Carte 298/423 SEK
♦ Chain hotel ♦ Business ♦ Functional ♦
Converted brewery on waterfront with view of Göta Älv. Central atrium-style lobby. Spacious rooms with international-style décor and sofabeds. Restaurant overlooking the harbour. International cooking to appeal to all tastes.

Mornington
Kungsportsavenyn 6 ✉ *S-411 36 – ✆ (031) 767 34 00 – goteborg@mornington.se – Fax (031) 711 34 39 – www.mornington.se* C2
91 rm – 1990 SEK 1275/1990 SEK
Rest *Brasserie Lipp* – Carte 364/435 SEK
♦ Business ♦ Modern ♦
Modern office block-style façade conceals hotel on famous shopping street. Compact rooms of dark brown, comfortable functional furniture with slightly English "feel" to them. Pleasant brasserie-style restaurant, hearty home cooking and international fare.

Tidbloms
Olskroksgatan 23 ✉ *S-416 66 – ✆ (031) 707 50 00 – info@tidbloms.se – Fax (031) 707 50 99 – www.tidbloms.se* D1
42 rm – 1195 SEK 945/1495 SEK
Rest – *(closed Sunday)* Menu 155 SEK
♦ Business ♦ Functional ♦
Old red brick hotel in quiet residential area. Quaint turret and semi-circular veranda-cum-conservatory. Sunny rooms with standard comforts. Rustic restaurant in the round, serving modern international cuisine.

Poseidon without rest
Storgatan 33 ✉ *S-411 38 – ✆ (031) 10 05 50 – info@hotelposeidon.com – Fax (031) 13 83 91 – www.hotelposeidon.com* B3
49 rm – 1050 SEK 895/1450 SEK
♦ Family ♦ Functional ♦
Informal hotel in residential area not far from main shopping street. Comfortable neutral décor and functional furnishings in rooms. Accommodation for families available.

Sjömagasinet (Mannerström)
Klippans Kulturreservat 5 (Southwest : 3.5 km by Andréeg taking Kiel-Klippan Ö exit, or boat from Rosenlund. Also evenings and weekends in summer from Lilla Bommens Hamn) ✉ *S-414 51 – ✆ (031) 775 59 20 – info@sjomagasinet.se – Fax (031) 24 55 39 – www.sjomagasinet.se*
closed 9 April, 22 June, 23-26 and 31 December-2 January and Sunday January-March
Rest – *(booking essential) (buffet lunch in summer)* Menu 395/695 SEK (lunch) – Carte 675/920 SEK
Spec. Mannerström's herring platter with matured cheese and crispbread. Pan-fried angler fish with brisket of beef, sweetbread and potato purée with duck liver. Chocolate cream with olive oil and pear.
♦ Seafood ♦ Rustic ♦
Delightful 18C former East India Company waterfront warehouse. Forever busy restaurant on two floors with ship's mast and charming terrace. Accomplished seafood cooking.

SWEDEN

XXX **Thörnströms Kök** AC ⅟ ⇔6 VISA MC AE ⓓ

Teknologgatan 3 ✉ S-411 32 – ✆ (031) 16 20 66 – info@thornstromskok.com – Fax (031) 16 40 17 – www.thornstromskok.com

closed 20 June-10 August, 22 December-3 January, Sunday, Monday and Bank Holidays **C3**

Rest – *(booking essential) (dinner only)* Menu 465/650 SEK – Carte 395/605 SEK

♦ Traditional ♦ Neighbourhood ♦

Eternally popular and stylishly elegant restaurant, set in a quiet area near university. Accomplished, well-priced international gourmet dishes; expect very good service.

XXX **Swea Hof** – at Elite Plaza H. AC VISA MC AE ⓓ

Västra Hamngatan 3 ✉ S-404 22 – ✆ (031) 720 40 40 – Fax (031) 720 40 10

closed 23-25 December **B2**

Rest – Menu 600 SEK (dinner) – Carte 475/715 SEK

♦ Modern ♦ Formal ♦

Striking atrium-style restaurant in heart of hotel with glass roof on metal framework and open-plan kitchen. Dinner menu offers elaborate and accomplished modern cuisine.

XX ✿ **Basement** (Wagner) AC ⅟ VISA MC AE ⓓ

Götabergsgatan 28 ✉ S-411 34 – ✆ (031) 28 27 29 – bokning@restbasement.com – Fax (031) 28 27 37 – www.restbasement.com

closed July, Christmas, New Year and Sunday **C3**

Rest – *(dinner only)* Menu 660/1050 SEK

Spec. Local seafood in maple syrup and vanilla sauce. Saddle of venison with mocha sauce and truffle risotto. Baked chocolate fondant.

♦ Modern ♦ Fashionable ♦

Restaurant below street level with white walls enlivened by contemporary paintings and lithographs. Imaginative and precise cuisine using top quality Swedish produce.

XX ✿ **28 +** (Lyxell) AC ⅟ ⇔20 VISA MC AE ⓓ

Götabergsgatan 28 ✉ S-411 34 – ✆ (031) 20 21 61 – 28plus@telia.com – Fax (031) 81 97 57 – www.28plus.se

closed Easter, July-21 August, 23-26 December, 31 December-2 January and Sunday **C3**

Rest – *(dinner only)* Carte 545/775 SEK

Spec. Veal carpaccio with oysters and parsley oil. Steamed fillet of turbot with horseradish jelly and cucumber linguini. Valrhona chocolate mousse with cocoa jelly and arctic raspberries.

♦ Modern ♦ Cosy ♦

Descend to dining room divided into three, with bright white décor and accessible wine cellar. Skilled and unfussy cooking with classical base. A chef describes the cheeses.

XX **Linnéa** AC ⅟ VISA MC AE ⓓ

Södra Vägen 32 ✉ S-412 52 – ✆ (031) 16 11 83 – info@restauranglinnea.com – Fax (031) 18 12 92 – www.restauranglinnea.com

closed Easter, 30 June-13 August 25 December-9 January, Sunday, Saturday lunch and Bank Holidays **C3**

Rest – Menu 325/425 SEK – Carte 361/588 SEK

♦ Modern ♦ Neighbourhood ♦

Well-run restaurant; changing summer and winter décor. Simple lunch venue; more formal and elaborate for dinner - stylish place settings. Well-prepared modern Swedish cuisine.

Fiskekrogen

Lilla Torget 1 ✉ S-411 18 – ✆ (031) 10 10 05 – info@fiskekrogen.com – Fax (031) 10 10 06 – www.fiskekrogen.com

closed July, 2 weeks Christmas and Sunday **B2**

Rest – *(buffet lunch)* Menu 225/625 SEK – Carte 470/745 SEK

♦ Seafood ♦ Brasserie ♦

Busy 1920s restaurant with reputation for its seafood. Striking room with high ceiling, wood panelling, columns and modern Scandinavian art. Good choice seafood buffet lunch.

Hos Pelle

Djupedalsgatan 2 ✉ S-413 07 – ✆ (031) 12 10 31 – info@hospelle.com – Fax (031) 775 38 32 – www.hospelle.com

closed 5 weeks summer, 24-26 December, 1 January and Sunday **A3**

Rest – *(dinner only)* Menu 300 SEK

♦ Traditional ♦ Neighbourhood ♦

Popular local restaurant with comfortable atmosphere, displaying Swedish art. Serves classic and modern Swedish cuisine prepared to high standard. Ground floor bistro.

Kock & Vin

Viktoriagatan 12 ✉ S-411 25 – ✆ (031) 701 79 79 – info@kockvin.se – www.kockvin.se

closed 22-23 June, 9 July-5 August, Christmas, New Year and Sunday **B3**

Rest – *(dinner only)* Menu 545/755 SEK – Carte 485/575 SEK

♦ Modern ♦ Romantic ♦

Attractive candlelit neighbourhood restaurant. Modern paintings but 19C painted ceiling. A la carte or set menu with complementary wines; best of Swedish ingredients.

Fond

Götaplatsen ✉ S-412 56 – ✆ (031) 81 25 80 – fond@fondrestaurang.com – Fax (031) 18 37 90 – www.fondrestaurang.com

closed 4 weeks summer, 2 weeks Christmas, Sunday, Saturday lunch and Bank Holidays **C3**

Rest – Carte 530/745 SEK

Spec. Deep-fried langoustine with glazed carrots and orange flavoured butter cream sauce. Fried brill with Jerusalem artichoke, baby potatoes with crab and dill. Kalvdans with blackberry sorbet and candied nuts.

♦ Modern ♦ Trendy ♦

Bright semi-circular glass structure outside Art Museum houses contemporary restaurant. Traditional Swedish lunch as lighter option and modern elaborate dinner menus.

La Cucina Italiana

Skånegatan 33 ✉ S-412 52 – ✆ (031) 16 63 07 – pietro@swipnet.ie – Fax (031) 16 63 07 – www.lacucinaitaliana.nu

closed Easter, Midsummer, Christmas, New Year and Sunday **C3**

Rest – *(booking essential) (dinner only)* Carte 409/554 SEK

♦ Italian ♦ Bistro ♦

Snugly intimate and authentic Italian restaurant, away from the city centre, with a smart line in modern furnishings. Good value modish menus which change daily.

Tvåkanten

28

Kungsportsavenyn 27 ✉ S-411 36 – ✆ (031) 18 21 15 – info@tvakanten.se – Fax (031) 81 11 98 – www.tvakanten.se

closed 22-23 June, 23-24 December and Sunday lunch **C3**

Rest – Menu 260/845 SEK – Carte 380/700 SEK

♦ Traditional ♦ Brasserie ♦

Busy characterful restaurant with simpler lunch and more extensive dinner menus. Dining rooms with brick walls, plus elegant first-floor private dining room. Rustic fare.

Ivy Grill

Vasaplatsen 2 ✉ *S-411 28 – ✆ (031) 711 44 04 – info@ivygrill.com – Fax (031) 711 29 55 – www.ivygrill.com* **B3**

Rest – *(dinner only)* Carte 250/350 SEK

♦ Grills ♦ Brasserie ♦

Step down from the lively bar to this trendy restaurant with its unusual décor. Menu specialises in grills; simple lunch on the terrace in summer only.

at Eriksberg West : 6 km by Götaälvbron and Lundbyleden, or boat from Rosenlund

Quality Hotel 11

Maskingatan 11 ✉ *S-417 64 – ✆ (031) 779 11 11 – q.hotel11@choice.se – Fax (031) 779 11 10 – www.hotel11.se*

260 rm – †2007 SEK ††1035/2007 SEK

Rest ***Kök & Bar 67*** – Menu 150/225 SEK – Carte 283/429 SEK

♦ Business ♦ Functional ♦

Striking former shipbuilding warehouse, part see-through there is so much glass! Rooms feature stylish modern Scandinavian interior design with pale wood and bright fabrics. Upper floor restaurant with bar area, waterway views and international cooking.

River Café

Göta Älv river and harbour,

Dockepiren ✉ *S-417 64 – ✆ (031) 51 00 00 – info@rivercafe.se – Fax (31) 51 00 01 – www.rivercafe.se*

closed Sunday

Rest – Menu 250/650 SEK

♦ Modern ♦ Friendly ♦

Delightfully set on the pier in Eriksburg with fine view to harbour. Agreeable bar; elegant first-floor restaurant with panoramic glass frontage. Modish worldwide menus.

at Landvetter Airport East : 30 km by Rd 40

Landvetter Airport H.

✉ *S-438 13 – ✆ (031) 97 75 50 – info@landvetterairporthotel.se – Fax (031) 94 64 70 – www.landvetterairporthotel.se*

103 rm – †1595 SEK ††1595 SEK – 1 suite

Rest – *(buffet lunch)* Menu 198 SEK (lunch) – Carte 214/454 SEK

♦ Business ♦ Modern ♦

Hotel benefitting from immediate proximity to airport. Rooms are bright and welcoming and feature typical Swedish décor in bright colours. Full modern and business facilities. Relaxed restaurant and terrace off the main lobby. Offers Swedish and global fare.

SWITZERLAND

SUISSE, SCHWEIZ, SVIZZERA

PROFILE

◆ **Area:**
41 284 km^2
(15 940 sq mi).

◆ **Population:**
7 460 000 (est. 2006), density = 181 per km^2.

◆ **Capital:**
Bern (Berne) (conurbation 349 100 inhabitants).

◆ **Currency:**
Swiss Franc (CHF); rate of exchange CHF 1 = € 0.60 = US$ 0.75 (Nov 2006).

◆ **Government:**
Federation of 26 cantons with 2 assemblies (National Council and Council of State) forming the Federal Assembly.

◆ **Languages:**
German (64% of population), French (20%), Italian (7%) are spoken in all administrative departments, shops, hotels and restaurants. Romansh (1%) in the Grisons canton.

◆ **Sepcific public holidays:**
Berchtold's Day (2 January); Good Friday (Friday before Easter); Swiss National Holiday (1 August); St. Stephen's Day (26 December). Thanksgiving (Jeûne Fédéral in French; Bettag in German) is observed in all cantons, except Geneva, on the third Sunday in September; the Geneva canton holds Thanksgiving on the second Thursday in September.

◆ **Local Time:**
GMT + 1 hour in winter, GMT+ 2 hours in summer.

◆ **Climate**
Temperate continental, varies with altitude – most of the country has

cold winters and warm summers (Bern: January: 0°C, July: 19°C).

◆ **International dialling Code**
00 41 followed by the area or city code (Geneva: **22**, Bern: **31**, Zurich: **44** or **43**) and then the local number.

◆ **Emergency**
Police: ✆ **117**; Medical emergencies: ✆ **144**; Fire Brigade: ✆ **118**. Anglo-Phone (24 hr information and helpline in English): ✆ **0900 576 444**.

◆ **Electricity:**
220 volts AC, 50 Hz; 2-pin round-shaped continental plugs.

FORMALITIES

Travellers from the European Union (EU), Iceland and the main countries of North and South America need a national identity card or passport (America: passport required) to visit Switzerland for less than three months (tourism or business purpose). For visitors from other countries a visa may be required, in addition to a passport, especially for those wishing to stay for longer than three months. We advise you to check with your embassy before travelling.

A valid driving licence or international driving permit, car registration papers and a nationality plate of the approved size are required. An international Insurance Certificate (Green Card) is advisable. Roads are toll-free but all vehicles must display a road tax disc (vignette) which is available at border posts. It can be purchased in advance from the Swiss National Tourist Office.

MAJOR NEWSPAPERS

Le Matin, La Tribune de Genève, 24 Heures are the main French-language papers; *Neue Zürcher Zeitung, Basler Zeitung, Tages-Anzeiger, Berner Zeitung* are published in German.

USEFUL PHRASES

ENGLISH	FRENCH	GERMAN	ITALIAN
Yes	**Oui**	**Ja**	**Si**
No	**Non**	**Nein**	**No**
Good morning	**Bonjour**	**Guten Morgen**	**Buongiorno**
Goodbye	**Au revoir**	**Auf Wiedersehen**	**Arrivederci**
Thank you	**Merci**	**Danke**	**Grazie**
Please	**S'il vous plaît**	**Bitte**	**Per favore**
Excuse me	**Excusez-moi**	**Verzeihung**	**Mi scusi**
I don't understand	**Je ne comprends pas**	**Ich verstehe nicht**	**Non capisco**

HOTELS

→ CATEGORIES

Prestigious international hotels offer high standards of accommodation and service. Motels, resorts, moderately priced hotels, garni (hotel with no restaurant) provide a very good standard of comfort. Inns (Gasthaus), B&Bs and guesthouses (pension) have clean, simple accommodation. The Swiss Hotel Association has a star-rating classification but this is on a voluntary basis.

→ PRICE RANGE

Prices may be quoted per person or per room. Make sure to check when you contact the hotel directly. Hotel prices usually include breakfast in summer but tend to quoted for half-board in winter.

→ TAX

Prices are inclusive of VAT (7.6%) and service charge but an additional tax may be payable depending on the canton.

→ CHECK OUT TIME

Between 11am and noon.

→ RESERVATIONS

Bookings can be made by phone or on the Internet. Discounts apply for booking on line.

→ TIPS FOR LUGGAGE HANDLING

No gratuities are expected but it is at the discretion of the customer (2CHF per item) whether to tip the porter.

→ BREAKFAST

Breakfast is usually included in the price of the room and consists of a self-service buffet. You may be able to order continental breakfast to be served in the room.

Reception	**Réception**	**Empfang**	**Ufficio ricevimento**
Single room	**Chambre simple**	**Einzelzimmer**	**Camera singola**
Double room	**Chambre double**	**Doppelzimmer**	**Camera doppia**
Bed	**Lit**	**Bett**	**Letto**
Bathroom	**Salle de bains**	**Bad**	**Bagno**
Shower	**Douche**	**Dusche**	**Doccia**

RESTAURANTS

Set menus usually include an entrée, a meat dish with vegetables and dessert. A la carte dishes are very generous. Inns serve simple local cuisine, 'cuisine du terroir'.

Wirtschaft is a modest local inn or pub. **Grotto** means, in the Ticino area, a typical restaurant serving local wines and a selection of dishes of the region. In Switzerland **Café** is a tea-room.

→ MEALS

Breakfast	**Petit-déjeuner**	**Frühstück**	**La collazione**	6am – 10am
Lunch	**Déjeuner**	**Mittagessen**	**Il pranzo**	noon –2-3pm
Dinner	**Dîner**	**Abendessen**	**La cena**	8pm – 11.30pm

NB: The Swiss often call the midday meal 'dinner'.

→ RESERVATIONS

Booking should be made by phone or by email. It is advisable to book, especially if you want to visit a popular restaurant or a restaurant which has won special commendation.

→ THE BILL

The bill (check) includes service charge and VAT. No extra tip required unless you wish to reward exceptional service.

Drink or aperitif	**Apéritif**	**Aperitif**	**Aperitivo**
Appetizer	**Amuse-bouche**	**Appetitanreger**	**Antipasto**
Meal	**Repas**	**Essen**	**Pasto**
First course, starter	**Entrée**	**Vorspeise**	**Primo piatto**
Main dish	**Plat principal**	**Hauptgericht**	**Piatto principale**
Main dish of the day	**Plat du jour**	**Tagesteller**	**Piatto del giorno**
Dessert	**Dessert**	**Nachtisch**	**Dolce**
Water/mineral water (still, sparkling)	**Eau/eau minérale (plate, gazeuse)**	**Wasser/ Mineralwasser (ohne/mit Kohlensäure)**	**Acqua/acqua minerale (naturale, gasata)**
Wine (red, white, rosé)	**Vin (rouge, blanc, rosé)**	**Wein (rot, weiss, rosé)**	**Vino (rosso, bianco, rosatello)**
Beer	**Bière**	**Bier**	**Birra**
Bread	**Pain**	**Brot**	**Pane**
Meat (rare, medium, well done)	**Viande (saignant, à point, bien cuit)**	**Fleisch (blutig, mittel, gut durchgebraten)**	**Carne (al sangue, a puntino, ben cotto)**
Fish	**Poisson**	**Fisch**	**Pesce**
Salt/pepper	**Sel/poivre**	**Salz/Pfeffer**	**Sale/pepe**
Cheese	**Fromage**	**Käse**	**Formaggio**
Vegetables	**Légumes**	**Gemüse**	**Verdure**
Hot/cold	**Chaud/froid**	**Heiss/Kalt**	**Caldo/freddo**
The bill (check) please	**L'addition s'il vous plaît**	**Die Rechnung bitte**	**Il conto per favore**

LOCAL CUISINE

Switzerland combines the gastronomic traditions of France, Germany and Italy and is rich in culinary specialities, often simple but wholesome and tasty.

The national dish of German Swiss is the golden **Rösti**, often topped with cheese, ham or fried egg. The **fondue** made from the hard cheeses, Vacherin and Gruyère, melted with spices, kirsch and wine, is a national institution among the French Swiss. The fondue is eaten by dipping little cubes of bread, held on a long fork, into the pot. **Raclette** is a Valais speciality – melted Valais cheese is eaten with gherkins and potatoes. Other tasty cheeses are Emmental, Vacherin Mont d'Or, Tête de moine, L'Etivaz, Formaggio d'alpe ticinese. **Bündnerfleisch**, thin slices of smoked, dried beef is a Grisons delicacy. Varieties of sausages (Wurst, saucisse, salsiccia) are numerous: Cervelat, Schüblig (long beef and pork sausage), Longeole (raw sausage with spices and white wine), boutefas, saucisson neuchâtelois, saucisse d'Ajoie, saucisson vaudois, dried house sausages from the Valais, salami, mortadella ticinese, cicitt (goat sausages), salsiz (small sausages), veal and venison sausages. The monumental **Berner Platte** brings together bacon, sausages, ham, boiled beef, pickled cabbage (Sauerkraut), potatoes or green beans.

Among regional specialities are: air-dried Graubünden meat, **Capuns** (stuffed mangel leaves), **Beinwurst** (pork ragout in wine sauce), Schaffhauser **Bölletüne** (onion pie), **busecca** (entrails and vegetable soup), **Papet vaudois** (cream-leek casserole), **geschnetzeltes Kalbsfleisch** (minced veal or calf's liver with cream), **Leberspiessli** (calf's liver on a spit with bacon), **Pastetli** (puff pastry with creamy diced veal), **cardoons au gratin**. The rivers and lakes provide a wide variety of fish (pike, trout, carp, tench, perch, which are prepared to traditional recipes: baked, in white wine sauce, in pastry, pickled.

Desserts and sweets should not be missed: tarte au vin (wine cake), torta di pane (bread cake), kirsch cake, meringues, Schaffhauserzungen (baked biscuits), Leckerli (spiced honey and almond bread). Swiss chocolate, of time-honoured renown, is used to make delicious cakes and sweets.

DRINK

The wine growing tradition of Switzerland goes back to the Roman era. The diversity of vines, soil and climate accounts for the quality and originality of its wines. The Vaud produces excellent vintages in the regions La Côte, Lavaux and Chablais: Chasselas, Salvagnin and fruity, light Pinot Noir. The best known wines from the Valais, the largest wine canton, include **Fendant**, Johannisberg (white) and the fragrant red **Dôle**. The Geneva canton produces interesting dry whites: Chasselas, Pinot Gris and full-bodied Aligoté as well as the mellow, aromatic **Gewürztraminer**. The fruity red Gamay and dry Pinot Noir and the lively fresh rosé, **Oeil-de-Perdrix**, are also noteworthy. The principal wines from Neuchâtel are Chasselas, Pinot Noir and the delicately fruity **Oeil-de-Perdrix**. The warm climate of the south yields outstanding wines: tannic Merlot del Ticino and Merlot Bianco. The red, white, rosé wines from the eastern area of the country and the Alpine Valley of the Rhine are most appreciated for their light and subtle quality. There are also some excellent dessert wines (Malvoisie, Johannisberg).

Kirsch from Zug, Marc (grape schnapps), Grappa from Ticino, Williams (pear schnapps) from the Valais, Zwetschgenwasser (plum eau-de-vie), Damassine (wild plum schnapps), pleasantly round off a meal. Strong absinthe is a speciality of the Watch Valley (Val-de-Travers). Beer, in particular Feldschlösschen from Basle and Cardinal from Fribourg, and strong alcoholic cider are also popular.

BERN
BERNE

Population: 122 200 (conurbation 349 100) – Altitude: 548m

The attraction of Bern is enhanced by its situation on a spur overlooking a verdant loop of the Aare, facing the Alps. The old town, a World Heritage Site, is characterised by its long stretch of arcades, home to a wide range of shops, its attractive towers and flower-decked fountains; it is best explored on foot.

The foundation of Bern on a former hunting ground by Duke Berchtold V of Zähringen dates back to the 12C. It was named after the first animal killed by the duke and his followers while hunting during the construction of the city. This was a bear (Bär); it appears on its coat of arms and is the town's mascot. From the 14C to the 16C, the town followed a clever policy of expansion and played a dominant part in the Confederation. When the Constitution was drafted in 1848, Bern was chosen as the seat of the federal authority. It holds a privileged position at the dividing line between the Latin and German cultures. It is the seat of the Swiss federal authorities, 70 embassies and the headquarters of several international organisations. Its famous sons include the artists Ferdinand Hodler and Paul Klee and it was home to the Nobel prize-winning physicist, Albert Einstein, who worked out his theory of relativity while employed as a clerk at the Bern patent office.

WHICH DISTRICT TO CHOOSE

The attractive old town is where you will find luxury **accommodation** in tastefully converted old town houses and with stunning views. It is also relatively easy to find moderately priced hotels in the quiet cobbled streets. There are business hotels near the station and the Bern Expo complex.

There is a great variety of **restaurants** where you can treat yourself in the old town from establishments offering refined international cuisine and brasseries with a congenial ambience to charming inns serving traditional and seasonal dishes.

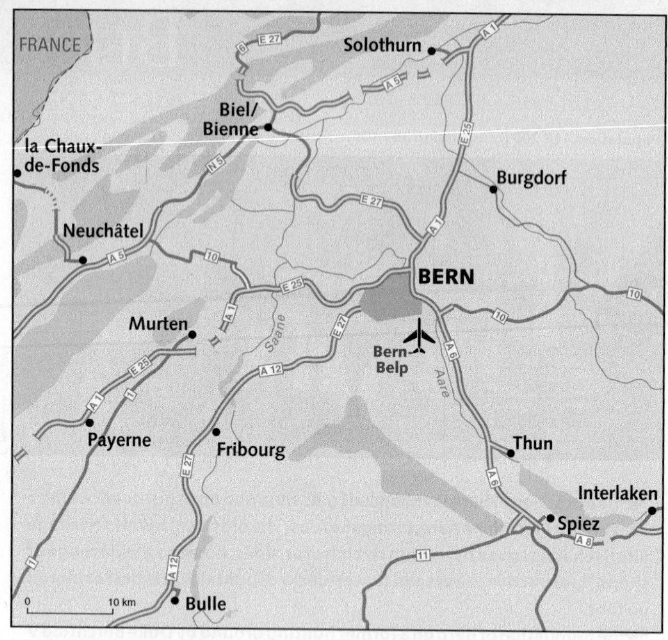

PRACTICAL INFORMATION

ARRIVAL – DEPARTURE

Bern-Belp International Airport – 9 km (5.5 mi) southeast of the city. ✆ 031 960 21 11, www.alpar.ch

From the airport to the city centre – By **taxi**: 45-50CHF, time 20-30min. By **shuttle bus**: 15CHF, every 30min, time: 20min. By **Airliner** Regional bus: 3CHF, 1-2 buses an hour.

Railway Station – Bahnhof, Bahnhofplatz *Plan II* **C2**: inter-city and intercontinental services. Fast trains to Zurich and Geneva airports. ✆ 0900 300 300; www.sbb.ch

TRANSPORT

→ BUSES AND TRAMS

The bus and tram network is very efficient. A short cable-railway links the Marzili quarter to the Bundeshaus. Single ticket 1.90CHF (1-6 stops, valid 30min), 3.20CHF (7 or more stops, valid 1hr). Buy your ticket from the ticket machine at the bus or tram stop. The BernCard – 19CHF (€12, 24hr), 29CHF (€18, 48hr), 35CHF (€22, 72hr) – which gives unlimited travel, free admission to museums and gardens and various reductions, is available from the Tourist Office, museums and hotels. *BernMobil*, ✆ 031 321 88 88; www.bernmobil.ch

→ TAXIS

There are taxi ranks in **Casinoplatz** *Plan II* **D2** and at the railway station or taxis can also be ordered by phone. An average ride in town costs 12-15CHF. Supplements are charged for evenings and luggage. *Bären Taxi* ✆ 031 371 11 11; *Nova-Taxi* ✆ 031 331 33 13.

USEFUL ADDRESSES

→ TOURIST OFFICES

Bern Tourismus – In **Bahnhof** *Plan II* **C2**: open Jun-Sep, daily 9am-8.30pm; Oct-May, Mon-Sat 9am-6.30pm, Sun 10am-5pm. **Bärengraben**: open Jun-Sep, daily 9am-6pm; Oct, Mar-May, daily 10am-4pm; Nov-Feb, Fri-Sun 11am-4pm. ✆ 031 328 12 12; www.bernetourism.ch

→ POST OFFICES

Main Post Office (Schanzenpost), Schanzenstrasse *Plan II* **C2**; open Mon-Fri 7.30am-9pm, Sat 8am-4pm, Sun 4pm-9pm.

→ BANKS/CURRENCY EXCHANGE

Banks open Mon-Fri 8.30am-4.30pm (6pm Thu). Exchange offices at the railway station open extended hours.

There are cash dispensers all over the city. Credit cards are widely accepted and require a PIN.

→ PHARMACIES

Bahnhof Apotheke, Bahnhof (upper level) *Plan II* **C2** is open daily, 6.30am-10pm.

→ EMERGENCY

Police ✆ **117**. Fire Brigade ✆ **118**. Medical Emergency service ✆ **144**.

BUSY PERIODS

It may be difficult to find a room at a reasonable price during special events:

International Jazz Festival Gala: one weekend in May – In the Kursaal.

Zibelemärit: Fourth Monday in November – Traditional onion market to mark the beginning of winter.

EXPLORING BERN

It is possible to visit the main sights and museums in two days.

Museums and other sights are usually open from 9-10am to 5pm. Some close on Mondays.

VISITING

Old Town – Marktgasse *Plan II* **D2**: fine 17-18C houses and arcades, fountains, clock tower **(Zeitglockenturm)** with painted figurines. **Kramgasse** *Plan II* **E1**: old houses with oriel windows and corner turrets, Samson fountain, **Einsteinhaus** (home of Nobel physicist). 15C **Rathaus** with double staircase and covered porch. **Nydeggbrücke** *Plan II* **F1**: view of the town, river and wooded setting. **Bärengraben**: city mascots, Bern Show (history of the town). **Junkerngasse** lined with old houses (Baroque **Erlacher Hof**). Gothic **Münster Sankt Vincenz** *Plan II* **H2** (panorama from belltower, painted tympanum of main portal, stained glass in chancel, 16C stalls). **Bundeshaus** *Plan II* **D2**, home of the Federal Council and Swiss Parliament; view from the terrace.

Kunstmuseum *Plan II* **C1** – Splendid collection of 13C-20C paintings: Swiss Primitives, Hodler, French schools and contemporary Swiss art.

Zentrum Paul Klee *Plan I* **B2** – Three spectacular buildings are devoted to the life and works of the artist Paul Klee.

Bernisches Historisches Museum *Plan I* **A2** – Collection of historical, archaeological and ethnographic exhibits.

Schweizerisches Alpines Museum *Plan II* **D2** – A good introduction to the Alps: Alpine life, traditional customs and folklore.

Naturhistorisches Museum *Plan I* **A2** – One of the largest natural history museums in the country: remarkable

Wattenwyl Hall, dioramas and fine collections.

Museum für Kommunikation *Plan I* **A2** – It traces the history of communication from smoke signals to digital systems.

Excursions – The **Gurten** *(2.5 km-1.5 mi S by road and funicular)*: views. **Murten** (*18km-11mi W*): picturesque fortified town. **Fribourg** *(27 km-18 mi SW)*: in a remarkable site, it marks the boundary between Switzerland's French- and German-speaking areas.

SHOPPING

Shops open Mon 2pm (department stores 9am)-6.30pm; Tue-Fri 9am-6.30pm (9pm Thu); Sat 8am-4pm; closed Sun except shops at the railway station.

The main shopping streets are **Spitalgasse** *Plan II* **C2** (*Globus* No 37, *Loeb* No 47-57), **Marktgasse** *Plan II* **D2**, **Kramgasse** and **Gerechtigkeitsgasse** *Plan II* **E1**. Smaller specialist boutiques (antiques, wooden toys, arts and crafts) are located in the side streets near the river bank. Visit *Grieder*, Waisenhausplatz 3; *Bürki*, Münzgraben 2; *Gygax* and *Bally*, Spitalgasse 4/9 for leather goods. *Indigo Moda Donna*, Spitalgasse 27; *Jutta van D* and *Stoff-Ciolina*, Kramgasse 8/52; *Bayard Wartmann*, Marktgasse 45 specialise in ladies fashion.

MARKETS – In **Bundesplatz** and **Bärenplatz** *Plan II* **D2**, **Waisenhausplatz** *Plan II* **D1** on Tue, Sat mornings. **Craft market**: Mar-Dec, every first Sun on the Münster platform *Plan II* **E2**. Traditional **onion market** *(Zwiebelmarkt)* on the fourth Mon in Nov at various locations in the city. **Christmas market** on Münsterplatz *Plan II* **E2**.

WHAT TO BUY – Designer items, watches, jewellery, chocolates (Toblerone), handicrafts, toys.

ENTERTAINMENT

Stadttheater *Plan II* **D1** – Drama, music.

Theater am Käfigturm *Plan II* **C2** and **Schlachthaus Theater** *Plan II* **E1** – Cultural events.

Kursaal *Plan II* **D1** – Nightclub, cabaret; international variety shows, Jazz Festival.

Puppentheater *Plan II* **E1** – Puppet theatre, shadow play, masques.

Narrenpack Theater *Plan II* **E1** – Lively folk theatre.

Zytglogge Theater *Plan II* **D1** – Plays in dialect.

Gaskessel *Plan I* **A2**, **Reitschule Bern** *Plan II* **C1**, **Dampfzentrale** *Plan I* **A2** – Cultural centres.

NIGHTLIFE

There is a multitude of bars, cafés, restaurants in **Spitalgasse** *Plan II* **C2**, **Marktgasse** *Plan II* **D2**. Enjoy the evening at the elegant *Belle Epoque* and *Klötzkeller*, the oldest tavern in town, Gerechtigkeitsgasse 18/62; *Kreissaal*, Brunngasshalde 63; *Kornhaus*, Kornhausplatz 18; *Arcady* piano bar, Bahnhofplatz 11; *Bierhübeli*, Neubrückstrasse 43; *Schwellenmätteli*, Dalmaziquai 11. Listen to music at *Markthalle Bern*, Bubenbergplatz 9; *Nordsüd* and *Propeller*, Aabergergasse 10/30; *Lirum Larum*, Kramgasse 19A. Trendy places to visit are *Lorenzini*, Hotelgasse 10; *Pery Bar*, Zeughausgasse 3. Dance the night away at *Via Felsenau*, Spinnereiweg 17; *Guayas*, Parkterrasse 16; *Le Club*, Kornhausstrasse 3; *Silo*, Mühlenplatz 11. *Marian's Jazzroom* (Hotel Innere Enge), Engestrasse 54 and *Mahogany Hall*, Klösterlistutz 18 are popular with jazz connoisseurs. Lady luck beckons at the *Grand Casino*, Herrengasse 25.

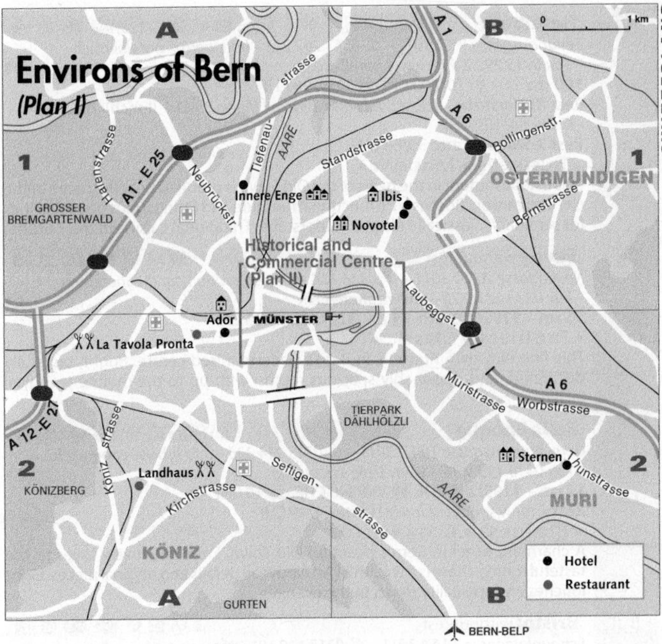

Environs of Bern
(Plan I)

A
B
1
2
A1 - E 25
A 1
A 6
A 12 - E 27
Halenstrasse
Neubrückstr.
Tiefenau-strasse
AARE
Standstrasse
Bollingenstr.
Bernstrasse
OSTERMUNDIGEN
GROSSER BREMGARTENWALD
Innere Enge
Ibis
Novotel
Historical and Commercial Centre (Plan II)
MÜNSTER
Ador
La Tavola Pronta
Laubeggst.
Muristrasse
Worbstrasse
TIERPARK DÄHLHÖLZLI
Sternen
Thunstrasse
MURI
Landhaus
Könizstrasse
KÖNIZBERG
Kirchstrasse
Seftigen-strasse
KÖNIZ
GURTEN
BERN-BELP
0 — 1 km
● Hotel
● Restaurant

HISTORICAL AND COMMERCIAL CENTRE *Plan II*

Bellevue Palace rm 15/350 VISA AE

Kochergasse 3 ✉ 3001 – ✆ 0313 204 545 – info@bellevue-palace.ch
– Fax 0313 114 7 43 – www.bellevue-palace.ch **D2**
115 rm – 350/430 CHF 460/540 CHF – 15 suites
Rest *Bellevue Grill / Bellevue Terrasse* – *(Grill: closed May - October and lunch in winter; Terrasse: closed dinner in winter)* Menu 68 CHF (lunch)/125 CHF – Carte 76/150 CHF

♦ Palace ♦ Classic ♦

This recently renovated luxury hotel breathes an air of aristocratic refinement, effortlessly combining tradition and modernity. Beautiful views of the river from the terrace.

Allegro rm rm 15/350 VISA AE

Kornhausstr. 3 ✉ 3013 – ✆ 0313 395 500 – info@kursaal-bern.ch
– Fax 0313 395 5 10 – www.kursaal-bern.ch **D1**
171 rm – 220/255 CHF 300/450 CHF, 25 CHF
Rest *Meridiano* – see below
Rest *Yù* – *(closed Saturday lunch)* Menu 28 CHF (lunch)/128 CHF – Carte 61/137 CHF
Rest *Allegretto* – Menu 40 CHF (lunch)/75 CHF – Carte 55/114 CHF

♦ Business ♦ Modern ♦

A trend-setting hotel especially tailored to business guests, with its modern and functional furnishings. There is also a casino in the hotel. Friendly atmosphere and contemporary cuisine in Allegretto.

Hotelbern 15/120 VISA

Zeughausgasse 9 ✉ 3011 – ✆ 0313 292 222 – hotelbern@hotelbern.ch – Fax 0313 292 2 99 – www.hotelbern.ch **D1**

100 rm – 170/260 CHF 225/290 CHF

Rest *Kurierstube* – *(closed July and Sunday)* Menu 35 CHF (lunch)/78 CHF – Carte 54/109 CHF

Rest *7 Stube* – Carte 39/88 CHF

♦ Business ♦ Modern ♦

This establishment in the heart of the Old Town is proud to bear the name of the city and canton. Rooms with functional furniture and fittings, plus good facilities for seminars. Classically elegant Kurierstube. Traditional cuisine in the 7 Stube.

Savoy without rest VISA

Neuengasse 26 ✉ 3011 – ✆ 0313 114 405 – reservation-sar@zghotels.ch – Fax 0313 121 9 78 – www.zghotels.ch **C1**

56 rm – 180/205 CHF 250/320 CHF, 25 CHF

♦ Business ♦ Classic ♦

This fine old town house is in Bern's pedestrianised centre. Bright, tastefully decorated, and reasonably spacious rooms, with up-to-the-minute technical facilities.

Belle Epoque rm rm VISA

Gerechtigkeitsgasse 18 ✉ 3011 – ✆ 0313 114 336 – info@belle-epoque.ch – Fax 0313 113 9 36 – www.belle-epoque.ch **E1**

17 rm – 195/285 CHF 280/340 CHF, 19 CHF

Rest – *(only snacks at lunch)* Carte 54/99 CHF

♦ Business ♦ Cosy ♦

A charming hotel in Bern's beautiful Old Town. From the lovely foyer to the tasteful rooms, there is a wealth of Art Nouveau details and original pieces. Light lunches and speciality roasts in the evening.

Bristol without rest VISA

Schauplatzgasse 10 ✉ 3011 – ✆ 0313 110 101 – reception@bristolbern.ch – Fax 0313 119 4 79 – www.bristolbern.ch **C2**

92 rm – 200/220 CHF 260/310 CHF

♦ Business ♦ Modern ♦

This old town house has been completely refurbished and accommodates its guests in modern rooms with massive wooden furniture. Small sauna shared with the Hotel Bern.

Bären without rest VISA

Schauplatzgasse 4 ✉ 3011 – ✆ 0313 113 367 – reception@baerenbern.ch – Fax 0313 116 9 83 – www.baerenbern.ch **C2**

57 rm – 200/220 CHF 260/310 CHF

♦ Business ♦ Modern ♦

Just a stone's throw from the Bundesplatz, a hotel with rooms furnished in contemporary style with a good range of technical facilities for business travellers.

Kreuz rest rm 15/120 VISA

Zeughausgasse 41 ✉ 3011 – ✆ 0313 299 595 – info@hotelkreuz-bern.ch – Fax 0313 299 5 96 – www.hotelkreuz-bern.ch **D1**

100 rm – 125/150 CHF 180/210 CHF

Rest – *(1st floor) (closed 30 June - 6 August, Saturday and Sunday)* Carte 31/63 CHF

♦ Business ♦ Modern ♦

This hotel specialises in meetings and conferences. Rooms are in functional style with grey, fitted furniture. Seminar rooms of various types are available.

City am Bahnhof without rest VISA

Bubenbergplatz 7 ✉ 3011 – ✆ 0313 115 377 – cityab@fhotels.ch – Fax 0313 110 6 36 – www.fhotels.ch **C2**

58 rm – 112/210 CHF 144/240 CHF, 18 CHF

♦ Business ♦ Functional ♦

The hotel is in the immediate vicinity of the train station. The guest rooms are furnished in a modern style and feature parquet floors throughout.

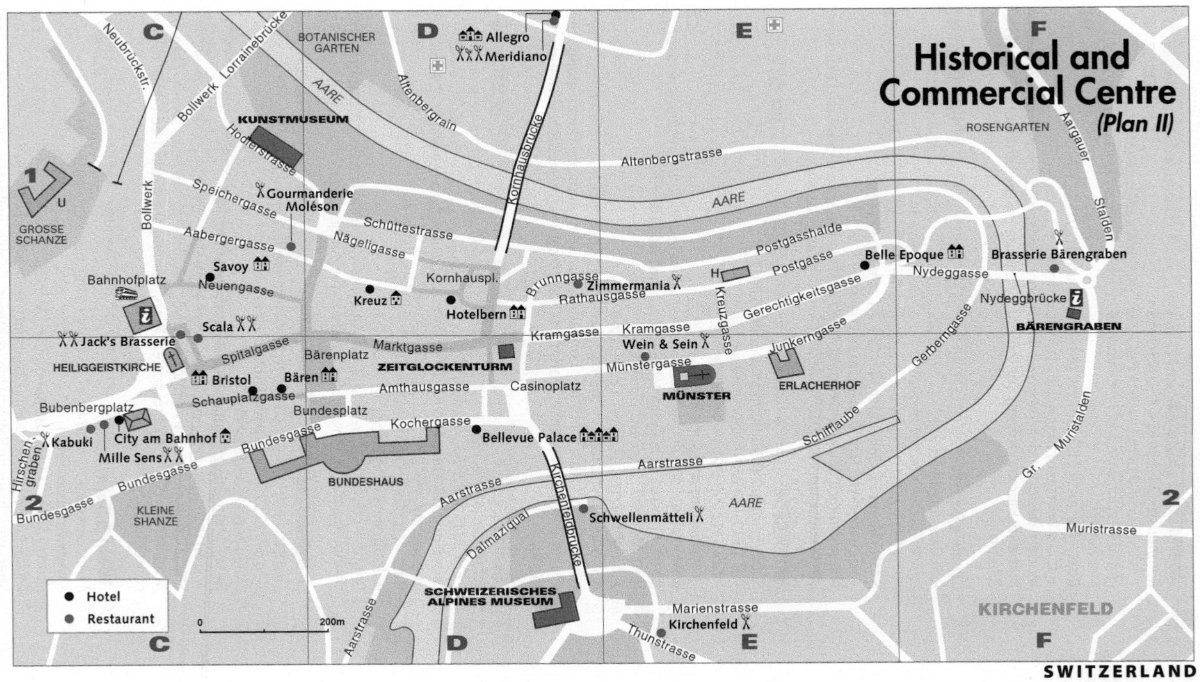

SWITZERLAND

XXX **Meridiano** – Hotel Allegro ⋖ Bern and Mountains, AC P VISA MC AE
Kornhausstr. 3 ✉ 3013 – ✆ 0313 395 245 – info@kursaal-bern.ch – Fax 0313 395 5 10 – www.allegro-hotel.ch
closed 1 - 7 January, 5 - 11 February, 16 - 29 July, Saturday lunch, Sunday and Monday **D1**
Rest – Menu 55 CHF (lunch)/168 CHF – Carte 102/155 CHF
♦ Contemporary ♦ Fashionable ♦
Modern design and the one-of-a-kind panoramic terrace create a special appeal in the restaurant, serving contemporary cuisine on the 6th floor of the Hotel Allegro.

XX **Jack's Brasserie** AC VISA MC AE
Bahnhofplatz 11 ✉ 3011 – ✆ 0313 268 080 – jacks@schweizerhof-bern.ch – Fax 0313 268 0 84 – www.schweizerhof-bern.ch **C2**
Rest – Menu 55 CHF (lunch)/85 CHF – Carte 62/115 CHF
♦ Contemporary ♦ Brasserie ♦
The restaurant, filled with upholstered seats in the style of a refined brasserie, offers contemporary cuisine as well as traditional classics.

XX **Mille Sens** VISA MC AE
Bubenbergplatz 9, (in the market hall) ✉ 3011 – ✆ 0313 292 929 – info@millesens.ch – Fax 0313 292 9 91 – www.millesens.ch
closed Sunday and Bank Holidays **C2**
Rest – *(closed also dinner from June-August except on Saturday) (only menu at lunch)* Menu 65 CHF (lunch)/138 CHF – Carte 78/110 CHF
Rest *Marktplatz* – Carte 53/98 CHF
♦ Contemporary ♦ Trendy ♦
A modern restaurant in the midst of busy shops: black leather chairs, smart white tablecloths, parquet beneath your feet and air ducts along the ceiling. The no-nonsense 'Marktplatz' bistro serves a concise and well-priced menu.

XX **Scala** VISA MC AE
Schweizerhofpassage 7 ✉ 3011 – ✆ 0313 264 545 – info@ristorante-scala.ch – Fax 0313 264 5 46 – www.ristorante-scala.ch
closed mid July - mid August, Saturday except dinner from November - December and Sunday **C1**
Rest – *(1st floor)* Carte 56/100 CHF
♦ Italian ♦ Fashionable ♦
Bright, modern restaurant in elegant Italian style on the first floor of one of Bern's shopping arcades. Parquet floors add to the congenial ambience.

X **Kirchenfeld** ⇔30 VISA MC AE
Thunstr. 5 ✉ 3005 – ✆ 0313 510 278 – restaurant@kirchenfeld.ch – Fax 0313 518 4 16 – www.kirchenfeld.ch
closed Sunday and Monday **E2**
Rest – Menu 56 CHF (lunch)/62 CHF – Carte 50/90 CHF
♦ Contemporary ♦ Brasserie ♦
Stucco decoration and antiques give this establishment a stylish note. A tasty range of meals are served here, ranging from the traditional to the contemporary.

X **Wein & Sein** (Blum) VISA MC
Münstergasse 50 ✉ 3011 – ✆ 0313 119 844 – blum@weinundsein.ch – www.weinundsein.ch
closed 15 July - 13 August, Sunday and Monday **E2**
Rest – *(dinner only) (booking essential) (set menu only)* Menu 88 CHF
Spec. Verschiedene Kaltschalen (summer). Sommerwild (May - July). Gebackene Desserts (winter)
♦ Contemporary ♦ Trendy ♦
This is an attractive, typical Bern cellar restaurant, with a wine bar. It presents a contemporary menu, changed daily – the fare is written on a board.

Schwellenmätteli - Rest Terrasse

Dalmaziquai 11 ✉ 3005 – ✆ 0313 505 007
– www.schwellenmaetteli.ch **D2**
Rest – *(booking essential)* Carte 48/93 CHF
Rest *Casa* – *(closed Monday)* Carte 47/90 CHF
♦ Contemporary ♦ Trendy ♦
This modern restaurant serving modern cuisine has a beautiful setting on the Aare river. The unique terrace overlooking the river offers breathtaking views. Contemporary Italian cuisine is served in the Casa.

Zimmermania

Brunngasse 19 ✉ 3011 – ✆ 0313 111 542 – Fax 0313 122 8 22
closed 7 July - 5 August, Monday, Sunday and Bank Holidays **D1**
Rest – Menu 33 CHF (lunch)/68 CHF – Carte 44/101 CHF
♦ Traditional ♦ Bistro ♦
This Bern bistro, a tradition for over 150 years, is located in a side street in the old town. Traditional cuisine is enjoyed in a cosy atmosphere.

Gourmanderie Moléson

Aarbergergasse 24 ✉ 3011 – ✆ 0313 114 463 – info@moleson-bern.ch
– www.moleson-bern.ch **C1**
Rest – *(closed Saturday lunch, Sunday and Bank Holidays)* Menu 66 CHF – Carte 62/101 CHF
♦ Brasserie ♦ Brasserie ♦
Cooking like in grandmother's time is the motto of this cosy restaurant in the Old Town. Specialities are traditional Bernese dishes and Alsatian Flammkuchen.

Brasserie Bärengraben

Grosser Muristalden 1 ✉ 3006 – ✆ 0313 314 218
– edy_juillerat@hotmail.com – Fax 0313 312 5 60
– www.brasseriebaerengraben.ch **F1**
Rest – *(booking essential)* Menu 66 CHF – Carte 38/85 CHF
♦ Brasserie ♦ Brasserie ♦
One of the most popular and traditional Brasseries in the city is accommodated in the historic little customs house on the Nydeggbrücke near the Bärengraben.

Kabuki

Bubenbergplatz 9, (in the market hall) ✉ 3011
– ✆ 0313 292 919 – kabuki@kabuki.ch
– Fax 0313 292 9 17 – www.kabuki.ch
closed 30 July - 5 August, Sunday and Bank Holidays **C2**
Rest – Menu 92 CHF (dinner) – Carte 41/99 CHF
♦ Japanese ♦ Exotic ♦
An understated, modern style and a long sushi bar define the ambience of this restaurant in the basement of the market hall.

ENVIRONS OF BERN *Plan I*

Innere Enge

Engestr. 54 ✉ 3012 – ✆ 0313 096 111
– reservation-ieb@zghotels.ch
– Fax 0313 096 1 12 – www.zghotels.ch **A1**
27 rm – †195/300 CHF ††230/400 CHF, ☕ 25 CHF
Rest – Menu 50 CHF (lunch)/78 CHF – Carte 44/102 CHF
♦ Business ♦ Classic ♦
Quiet establishment almost in the countryside. The rooms are fitted with elegant furniture and feature Provençal colour schemes. Breakfast is served in the historic Pavillon. The Jazz Cellar is a city institution. Welcoming bistro-style café and restaurant.

SWITZERLAND

Novotel

Guisanplatz 2 ✉ 3014 – ✆ 0313 390 909 – H5009@accor.com – Fax 0313 390 9 10 – www.novotel.com **B1**

112 rm – 150/225 CHF 150/246 CHF, 25 CHF

Rest – Menu 36 CHF – Carte 47/97 CHF

♦ Chain hotel ♦ Modern ♦

Modern rooms with good technical mod cons, plus a light, contemporary restaurant, right next to the Bern Expo complex. The bar pays tribute to Germany's 1954 World Cup win - "The Miracle of Bern" - at the now rebuilt Wankdorf Stadium nearby.

Sternen

Thunstr. 80 ✉ 3074 Muri – ✆ 0319 507 111 – info@sternenmuri.ch – Fax 0319 507 1 00 – www.sternenmuri.ch **B2**

44 rm – 140/180 CHF 190/245 CHF

Rest – Menu 37 CHF (lunch) – Carte 45/97 CHF

♦ Traditional ♦ Functional ♦

Village centre hotel in typical Bernese country style. Bright, functional rooms in the original house and annex. The "Läubli" serves contemporary dishes.

Ador

Laupenstr. 15 ✉ 3008 – ✆ 0313 880 111 – info@hotelador.ch – Fax 0313 880 1 10 – www.hotelador.ch

closed 22 December - 2 January, Sunday and Bank Holidays **A2**

52 rm – 120/170 CHF 160/240 CHF

Rest – Carte 37/69 CHF

♦ Business ♦ Modern ♦

A hotel near the train station, particularly tailored to business guests, with rooms furnished in a functional, modern style that offer the latest technology.

Ibis without rest

Guisanplatz 4 ✉ 3014 – ✆ 0313 351 200 – H5007@accor.com – Fax 0313 351 2 10 – www.ibishotel.com **B1**

96 rm – 99/119 CHF 99/119 CHF, 14 CHF

♦ Chain hotel ♦ Minimalist ♦

Simple, practical and affordable, the bedrooms here are clean and bright. A snack menu is available around the clock at the bar.

Landhaus - Rest Rôtisserie with rm

Schwarzenburgstr. 134 ✉ 3097 Liebefeld – ✆ 0319 710 758 – info@landhaus-liebefeld.ch – Fax 0319 720 2 49 – www.landhaus-liebefeld.ch

closed Sunday **A2**

6 rm – 160 CHF 240/260 CHF

Rest – *(booking essential)* Menu 83/115 CHF – Carte 56/111 CHF

Rest *Gaststube* – Carte 53/92 CHF

♦ Contemporary ♦ Formal ♦

The charming Rotisserie is located in the former regional court building. Contemporary cuisine is served, and guests will enjoy the cosy garden terrace. Favourite classic dishes as well as seasonal specialities are served in the Gaststube restaurant. Elegant, bright and modern guest rooms.

La Tavola Pronta

Laupenstr. 57 ✉ 3008 – ✆ 0313 826 633 – Fax 0313 815 6 93 – www.latavolapronta.ch

closed 3 weeks in July - August, Saturday lunch and Sunday **A2**

Rest – *(booking essential)* Menu 57 CHF (lunch)/96 CHF – Carte 66/103 CHF

♦ Italian ♦ Cosy ♦

This small cellar restaurant, a comfortable lounge with a fireplace, has a very welcoming atmosphere. The classic Piedmont fare is written on a mirror.

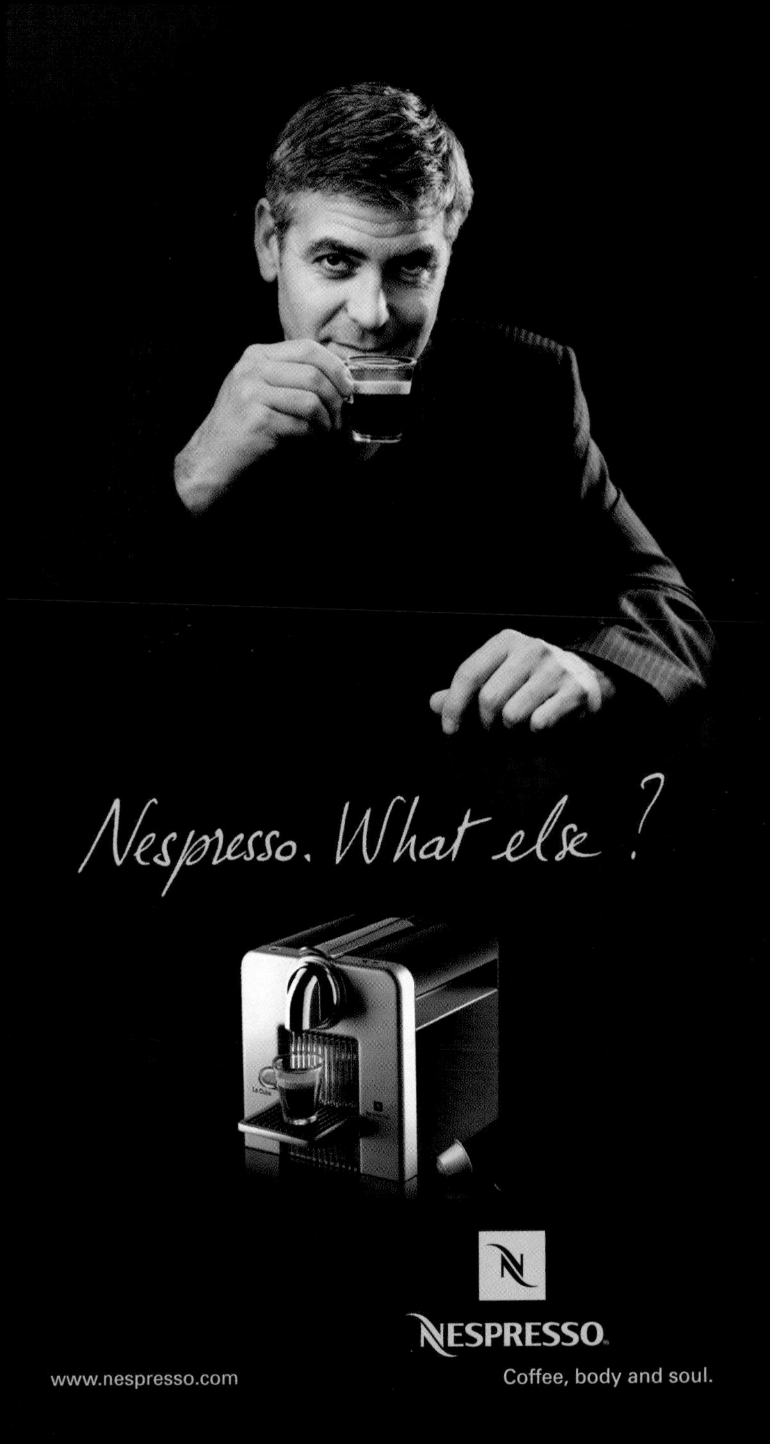
Nespresso. What else?
Le Cube
NESPRESSO
www.nespresso.com
Coffee, body and soul.

GENEVA
GENÈVE

Population (est. 2005): 178 700 (conurbation 698 000) – Altitude: 375m

AGE Moya / HOA QUI

An exceptional location on the shimmering shores of Lake Geneva, set against a backdrop of lush vegetation and wooded mountains, makes Geneva one of Switzerland's most privileged cities. It enjoys a pristine natural environment and the best possible living conditions. Visitors will be charmed by the opulent mansions, the harbour and its Jet d'Eau, the green spaces, its busy streets and elegant shopping centres.

Geneva is home to the second seat of the United Nations after New York and it houses the headquarters of several UN agencies as well as many international bodies. But Geneva, clustering around its cathedral, also remains the town of Calvin and the stronghold of the Reformation. The city was occupied by French troops in 1798 and for 16 years it was the capital of the French department of Léman. After the collapse of the Napoleonic Empire, it joined the Swiss Confederation on 19 May 1815 when the unification treaty was signed. The metropolis of French-speaking Switzerland, Geneva is an intellectual city which has welcomed many luminaries such as Jean-Jacques Rousseau and Voltaire as well as many eminent writers and men of science. These diverse influences are bound together by a very Helvetian atmosphere of order and discipline.

WHICH DISTRICT TO CHOOSE

The city offers exceptionally high standards of **accommodation** to suit the most demanding visitors. Opulent hotels with splendid views are located along the quays on both sides of the lake and there are charming, quiet hotels at moderate prices near the station, in the little streets by the Rhône. You will find business hotels by the station *Plan II* **E3**, near the airport *Plan I* **A1** and the Palais des Expositions *Plan I* **B1** and modern chain hotels on the outskirts.

The quality and number of **restaurants** in Geneva rank very high with many award-winning establishments. Elegant restaurants overlook the lake or are to be found

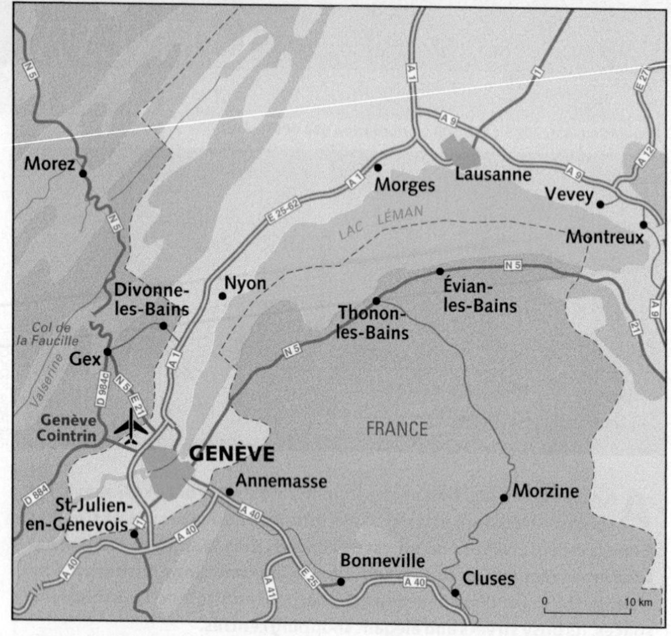

in the surrounding countryside *(see listing)*. Delightful small restaurants and modern brasseries in the town centre and country inns in the environs serve regional and seasonal specialities.

PRACTICAL INFORMATION

ARRIVAL – DEPARTURE

Geneva International Airport – Cointrin *Plan I* **A1**. ✆ 022 717 71 11; www.gva.ch

From the airport to the city centre – By **taxi**: 30-35CHF; time 15min. By **train**: 3CHF; every 10min; time 8min. By **bus**: 3CHF; No 10 to Geneva city (every 10min), No 20 to Meyrin, UN complex and the lake (every 20min), No 18 to UN (every 30min); time 20min.

Railway Stations – Cornavin Station, place Cornavin *Plan II* **E3** and **Geneva Airport Station**: international and inter-city services. ✆ 0900 300 300; www.cff.ch. **Eaux Vives Station**: services to Évian, Annecy and Annemasse over the border in France.

TRANSPORT

→ BUSES, TRAMS, TRAINS, BOATS

The city is served by an efficient public transport network. A single All Geneva ticket costs 3-5CHF and is valid 1hr. A day card is 10-12CHF and a 9am-midnight card 7-11.60CHF (city), 12-20CHF (Regional). Also Tourist Cards: 20CHF (valid 48hr), 30CHF (72hr). A short hop ticket 2CHF is valid for 3 stops or 1 ferry crossing. ✆ 0900 022 021; www.unireso.com, www.tpg.ch

→ TAXIS

Metered taxis can be hailed at taxi ranks, near the stations and at the airport or can be ordered by phone. Fares are based on a standard charge of 6.30CHF and 3.20CHF/km. There are supplements for travel at night, Sundays and public holidays (3.80CHF) and luggage (1.50CHF). Tips and VAT are included but it is usual to round up the fare. *Taxiphone* ✆ 022 331 41 33. *Ambassador* ✆ 022 731 41 41. *Europa* ✆ 022 906 79 79, 0800 141 141.

USEFUL ADDRESSES

→ TOURIST OFFICE

Geneva Tourism – Rue du Mont-Blanc 18 *Plan II* **E3**, P.O.Box 1602, CH – 1211 Geneva 1. Open 9am (10am Mon) to 6pm; closed Sun, Sep to mid-Jun. ✆ 022 909 70 00; www.geneva-tourism.ch

→ POST OFFICES

Main Post Office, Rue du Mont-Blanc 18 *Plan II* **E3** is open Mon-Fri 7.30am-6pm; Sat 9am-4pm. The post office Cornavin Station at 16 Rue des Gares *Plan II* **E3** is open Mon-Fri, 8am-8pm; Sat 8am-noon, Sun 4-7pm.

→ BANKS/CURRENCY EXCHANGE

Banks open Mon-Fri 8am-4.30pm (5.30pm). Exchange offices at Cornavin Station and at the airport open longer hours. There are cash dispensers, which require a PIN, all over the city. Credit cards are widely accepted for all transactions.

→ EMERGENCY

Police ✆ **117**; Fire Brigade: ✆ **118**; Medical Emergency Service: ✆ **144**.

BUSY PERIODS

It may be difficult to find a room at a reasonable price during special events:

International Motor Show: early March.

Geneva Festival: first two weeks in August – Various shows and attractions (floral floats, fireworks).

Feast of the Escalade: December – Commemorates the successful defence of the town against the Savoyards in 1602: torchlight procession, chocolate cauldrons.

EXPLORING GENEVA

It is possible to visit the main sights and museums in two days.

Museums and other sights are usually open from 10-11am to 5pm. Some close on Mondays.

VISITING

Boat trips on the lake and on the Rhône from Quai du Mont-Blanc *Plan II* **F3**, Quai des Moulins en l'Île *Plan III* **G1** and Quai Gustave-Ador, Jardin Anglais *Plan III* **H1**.

HARBOUR AND LAKESHORES – Splendid views of the majestic **Jet d'Eau** *Plan III* **H1** and bustling harbour. **North Bank** – Parks **(Villa Barton, La Perle du Lac, Mon Repos)** *Plan II* **F1**: the finest landscaped area lined with 19C mansions (Musée d'Histoire des Sciences in Villa Bartoloni, Parc de la Perle du Lac); views of Little Lake. **Conservatoire** and **Jardin Botanique** *Plan II* **E1**: living plant museum and rock garden. **South Bank** – **Jardin Anglais** *Plan III* **H1**: floral clock, panorama of harbour and the Jura mountain range, marina; **Parc de la Grange** (wonderful rose garden) *Plan I* **C2** and **Parc des Eaux-Vives** *Plan I* **D2**.

INTERNATIONAL DISTRICT – Place des Nations leads to the imposing

Palais des Nations (Armillary Sphere) *Plan II* **E1** in Ariana Park: tour including the Salle des Pas Perdus, the impressive Assembly Room and the Council Chamber. **Musée Ariana** *Plan II* **E1**: Overview of ten centuries of ceramic-making in Europe. **Musée International de la Croix Rouge et du Croissant Rouge** *Plan I* **B2** the museum traces events which have left their mark on history. **Domaine de Penthes – Musée des Suisses à l'Étranger** *Plan I* **B1**: focus on the Papal Guard, Swiss mercenaries and celebrities.

OLD TOWN *Plan III* **H2** – Narrow streets and squares lined with old houses and aristocratic residences: **Grand-Rue**, **Rue des Granges**, **Place du Bourg-de-Four** with flower-decked fountain. Impressive **Cathédrale St-Pierre**: superb view from the tower; archaeological site. **Hôtel de Ville** (16C-17C): Tour Baudet, Alabama Room where the Geneva Convention was signed. Elegant **Maison Tavel**, the oldest house in the city: museum devoted to the history of Geneva.

Musée d'Art et d'Histoire *Plan III* **H2** – An outline of the history of civilisation from prehistoric times to the 21C: archaeology, applied art, coins, paintings.

Petit Palais *Plan III* **H2** – 19C mansion housing the **Musée d'Art Moderne**: French and European avant-garde painting (Impressionism, Surrealism, Abstract art).

Musée d'Histoire Naturelle *Plan I* **C3** – Dioramas of regional fauna; displays devoted to paleontology, mineralogy and the geology of the country.

Patek Philippe Museum *Plan III* **G2** – Housed in a beautifully restored factory, it displays a collection of magnificent timepieces.

Musée de l'Horlogerie et de l'Émaillerie *Plan I* **C3** – An illuminating history of the science of horology from its origins to the present day and the art of enamelling.

Musée International de l'Automobile *Plan I* **B1** – A fabulous array of vintage vehicles, some owned by famous people.

SHOPPING

Shops are usually open Mon-Wed 9am-7pm (9pm Thu, 7.30pm Fri, 6pm Sat).

The main shopping areas are located on the North bank: **Quai des Bergues** *Plan III* **G1**, **Quai du Mont-Blanc** *Plan II* **F3** and **Rue du Mont-Blanc** *Plan II* **E3**. South bank: around the chic **Rue du Rhône**, in the **Rues du Molard** *Plan III* **H2**, **de la Confédération du Marché** *Plan III* **G1** and **de la Croix-d'Or de Rive** *Plan III* **H2** and **de la Corraterie** *Plan III* **H1**, **cours de Rive** *Plan III* **H2** and **galerie Malbuisson**. The more popular **Saint-Gervais** and **Pâquis** *Plan II* **F3** areas are also worth a visit. Department stores: *Globus*, 48 Rue du Rhône and Rue de la Confédération; *Manor*, Rue Cornavin 6. Browse in **Grand-Rue** *Plan III* **G2** for bookstores, art galleries, antique shops. Visit *Aux Arts du Feu*, 18 Quai du Général Guisan (antiques); *Linen Langenthal*, 13 Rue du Rhône (fine linen, lace); *Les Galeries du Lac*, 16 Chemin de la Voie-Creuse and *Molard Souvenirs*, Rue de la Croix-d'Or (gifts); *Buzzano*, 15 Rue de Rive and 1 Rue de la Croix-d'Or and *Bally*, 18 Rue du Marché (leather goods); *Pinocchio*, 10 Rue Etienne-Dumont (wooden toys); *Chocolaterie du Rhône*, 3 Rue de la Confédération; *Arn Chocolatier*, 12 Rue Bourg-de-Four; *La Bonbonnière*, 11 Rue de Rive and *Teuscher Confiserie*, 2 Rue du Rhône (chocolates).

MARKETS – Plaine de Plainpalais *Plan III* **G2**: **produce market** open Tue, Fri 8am-1pm, Sun 8am-6pm; **flea market** (antiques and other goods) Wed, Sat 8am-5pm. Place de la Fusterie *Plan III* **G1**: **produce market** open Wed, Sat 8am-6.45pm; **handicrafts** Thu 8am-7pm; books Fri 8am-6.45pm. **Produce market** in Place de la Navigation *Plan II* **F3**: Tue, Fri 8am-1pm; Place de Grenus *Plan II* **E3**: Sat 8am-1.30pm; Boulevard Helvétique *Plan III* **H2**: Wed 8am-1pm, Sat 8am-1.30pm. **Flower market**: Place du Molard *Plan III* **H2** daily.

WHAT TO BUY – Jewellery, watches, linen, lace, cuckoo clocks, music boxes, toys, chocolates (Pavés de Genève).

ENTERTAINMENT

Consult Genève-Agenda, a monthly publication listing events and entertainment in the city. It is available free from the Tourist Office, hotels, stations and many public places.

Grand Théâtre *Plan III* **G2** – Opera, ballet and music.

Bâtiment des Forces Motrices *Plan I* **B3** – Plays, opera and conferences.

Conservatoire de Musique and **Victoria Hall** *Plan III* **G2** – Classical music concerts.

Comédie d e Genève *Plan III* **G2** – Contemporary and classical drama.

Les Salons *Plan III* **G2** – Musical performances and plays by modern authors.

Casino-Théâtre *Plan III* **G3** – Satirical reviews, operetta and variety shows.

Les Marionettes de Genève *Plan III* **G3** and **Am Stram Gram** *Plan I* **C3** – Puppet theatre and shows for children.

Forum Meyrin *Plan I* **A1** – Drama, dance, classical and modern music performances.

NIGHTLIFE

The bustling area between **Cornavin Station** and **Les Pâquis** abounds in cinemas, bars, pubs and restaurants. You may also visit **Carouge** *Plan I* **C3** to the south of the city for its lively cafés and restaurants. Enjoy a drink at the microbrewery *Les Brasseurs*, Place Cornavin ; *Mortimer* and *Clémence* around Place du Bourg-de-Four; *Bohême* piano bar, *Griffin's*, Boulevard Helvétique 56/36. A fashionable crowd flocks to *Demi-Lune* café, 3 Rue Etienne-Dumont; *Brasserie Lipp*, 8 Rue de la Confédération; *La Coupole*, 116 Rue du Rhône; *Club 58*, 15 Rue des Glacis-de-Rive; the stylish cafés in the **Eaux-Vives quartier** *Plan I* **D2**. For live music and dancing, visit *Au Chat Noir*, 13 Rue Vautier; *L'Usine*, 4 Place des Volontaires; *Le Baroque*, 12 Place de la Fusterie; *CREM*, Boulevard Helvétique 10; *Arthur's Club*, 20 Rue du Pré-Bois and *Macumba*, 403 Route d'Annecy (France). Go to *Grand Casino du Lac*, 20 Route de Pré-Bois, for a sophisticated evening.

Around Geneva
(Plan I)

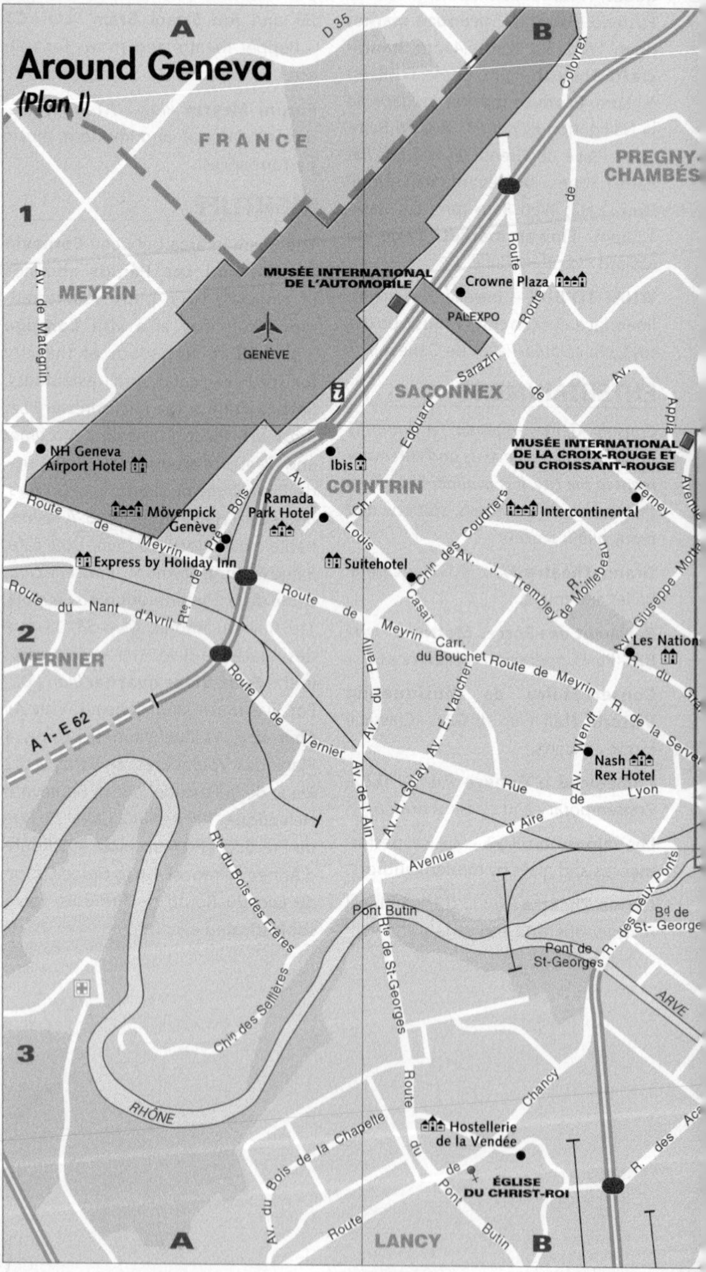

A
B
1
2
3
D 35
Colovrex
FRANCE
PREGNY-
CHAMBÉS
MEYRIN
Av. de Mategnin
MUSÉE INTERNATIONAL
DE L'AUTOMOBILE
GENÈVE
PALEXPO
Crowne Plaza
Route de Colovrex
Route Edouard Sarazin
SACONNEX
Av. Appia
NH Geneva
Airport Hotel
MUSÉE INTERNATIONAL
DE LA CROIX-ROUGE ET
DU CROISSANT-ROUGE
Ibis
COINTRIN
Ramada
Park Hotel
Av. Louis Casaï
Ch. des Coudriers
Intercontinental
Ferney
Mövenpick
Genève
Route de Meyrin
Rte de Pré Bois
Express by Holiday Inn
Suitehotel
Av. J. Trembley
R. de Moillebeau
Av. Giuseppe Motta
Route du Nant d'Avril
VERNIER
Carr.
du Bouchet
Route de Meyrin
Les Nations
R. du Grand-Pré
Av. du Pailly
Av. E. Vaucher
R. Wendt
R. de la Servette
A 1- E 62
Route de Vernier
Av. de l'Ain
Av. H. Golay
Nash
Rex Hotel
Rue de Lyon
Av. Wendt
Avenue d'Aire
Rte du Bois des Frères
Pont Butin
Rte de St-Georges
R. des Deux Ponts
Bd de St- Georges
Pont de
St-Georges
ARVE
Chin des Sellières
RHÔNE
Route de Chancy
Hostellerie
de la Vendée
Av. du Bois de la Chapelle
Route du Pont Butin
ÉGLISE
DU CHRIST-ROI
R. des Acacias
Route
LANCY

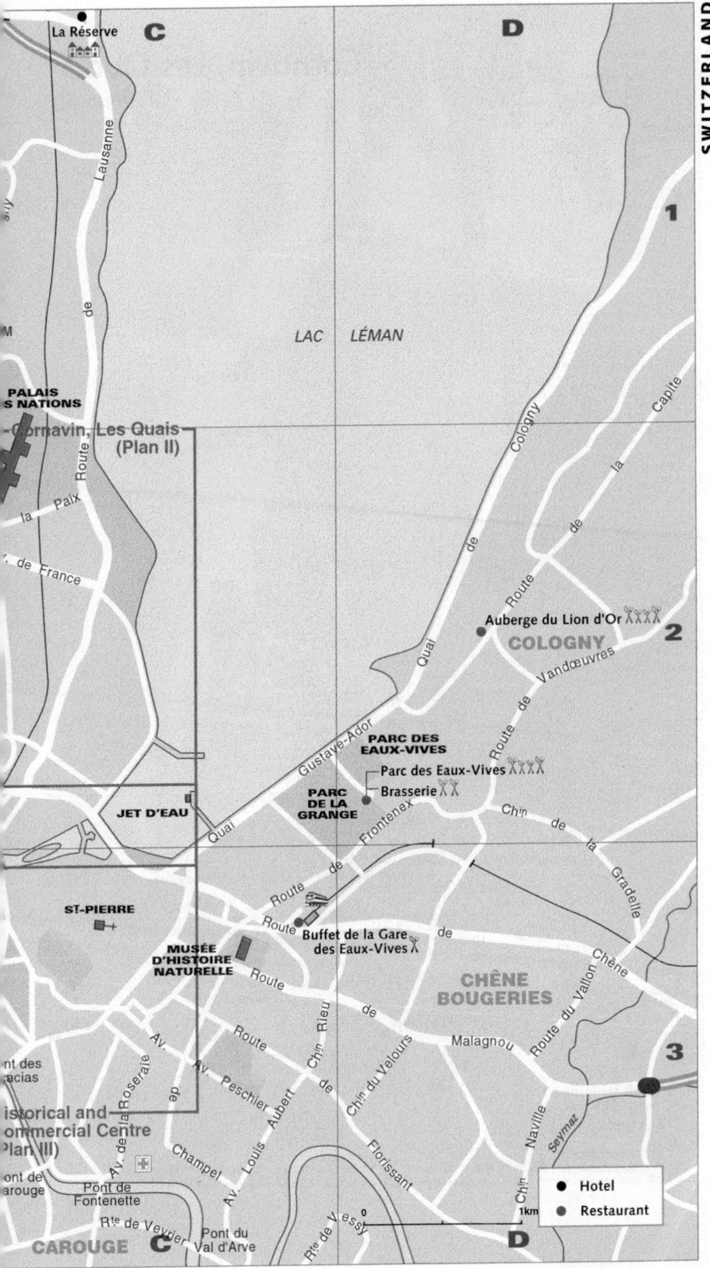
La Réserve
C
D
Route de Lausanne
LAC LÉMAN
PALAIS
S NATIONS
Cornavin, Les Quais
(Plan II)
la Paix
de France
Route de Cologny
Quai
Route de la Capite
Auberge du Lion d'Or
COLOGNY
Route de Vandœuvres
Quai Gustave-Ador
PARC DES EAUX-VIVES
Parc des Eaux-Vives
Brasserie
PARC DE LA GRANGE
JET D'EAU
Route de Frontenex
Chin de la Gradelle
ST-PIERRE
Buffet de la Gare des Eaux-Vives
MUSÉE D'HISTOIRE NATURELLE
Route de Chêne
CHÊNE BOUGERIES
Route de Malagnou
Route du Vallon
Chin Rieu
Chin du Velours
Route de Florissant
Av. Peschier
Av. Louis Aubert
Av. de Champel
Av. de la Roseraie
Historical and
Commercial Centre
(Plan III)
Pont de Fontenette
Rte de Veyrier
Pont du Val d'Arve
Rte de Vessy
Chin Naville
Seymaz
CAROUGE
0
1km
Hotel
Restaurant
1
2
3

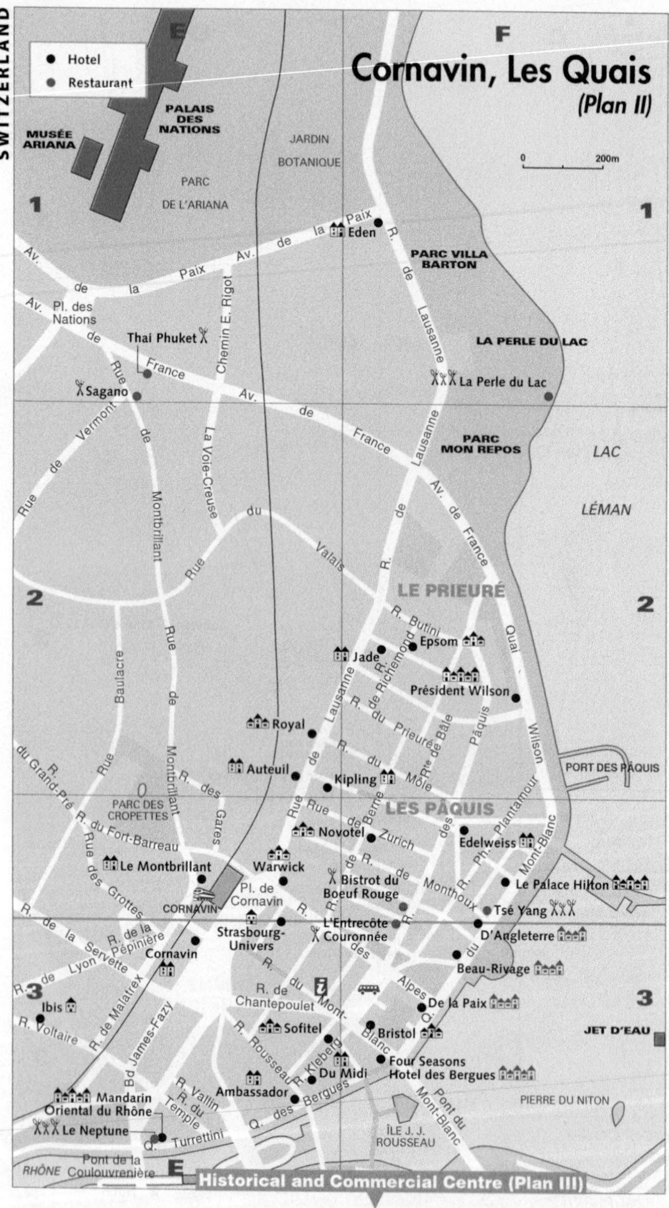
Cornavin, Les Quais
(Plan II)
Hotel
Restaurant
PALAIS DES NATIONS
MUSÉE ARIANA
JARDIN BOTANIQUE
PARC DE L'ARIANA
PARC VILLA BARTON
LA PERLE DU LAC
PARC MON REPOS
LAC LÉMAN
LE PRIEURÉ
LES PÂQUIS
PORT DES PÂQUIS
PARC DES CROPETTES
CORNAVIN
JET D'EAU
PIERRE DU NITON
ÎLE J. J. ROUSSEAU
RHÔNE
Eden
Thai Phuket
Sagano
La Perle du Lac
Epsom
Jade
Président Wilson
Royal
Auteuil
Kipling
Novotel
Edelweiss
Le Montbrillant
Warwick
Bistrot du Boeuf Rouge
Le Palace Hilton
Tsé Yang
L'Entrecôte Couronnée
D'Angleterre
Cornavin
Strasbourg-Univers
Beau-Rivage
Ibis
De la Paix
Sofitel
Bristol
Du Midi
Four Seasons Hotel des Bergues
Ambassador
Mandarin Oriental du Rhône
Le Neptune
Pont de la Coulouvrenière
Pont du Mont-Blanc
Historical and Commercial Centre (Plan III)

RIGHT BANK

Plan II

Four Seasons Hotel des Bergues

33 quai des Bergues ✉ 1201
– ✆ 0229 087 000 – info.gen@fourseasons.com – Fax 0229 087 4 00
– www.fourseasons.com
82 rm – 525/1550 CHF 740/1600 CHF, 50 CHF – 21 suites
Rest *Il Lago* – Menu 77 CHF (lunch)/180 CHF – Carte 110/172 CHF
25/150 VISA MC AE — **F3**

◆ Palace ◆ Stylish ◆

Recently renovated, the oldest and most luxurious hotel in Geneva (1834) offers lounges adorned with gleaming marble, an elegant bar, guestrooms and suites decorated in Empire style. Italian restaurant with opulent, classical decor and delightful hand-painted wallpaper in one of the dining rooms.

Mandarin Oriental du Rhône

1 quai Turrettini ✉ 1201 – ✆ 0229 090 000
– mogva-enquiry@mohg.com – Fax 0229 090 0 10
– www.mandarinoriental.com
180 rm – 570/990 CHF 750/1150 CHF, 40 CHF – 10 suites
Rest *Le Neptune* – see below
Rest *Café Rafael* – *✆ 0229 090 005* – Menu 61 CHF – Carte 81/120 CHF
15/150 VISA MC AE — **E3**

◆ Grand Luxury ◆ Art Deco ◆

Central location on the right bank of the Rhône. Sumptuous rooms with Art Deco furnishings and sparkling marble bathrooms. The Café Rafael offers a choice of traditional recipes showing occasional local influence.

Président Wilson

47 quai Wilson ✉ 1201 – ✆ 0229 066 666
– sales@hotelpwilson.com – Fax 0229 066 6 67 – www.hotelpwilson.com
219 rm – 690/790 CHF 790/890 CHF, 40 CHF – 11 suites
Rest *Spice's* – *(closed 3 weeks in July - August, Saturday lunch and Sunday)*
Menu 59 CHF (lunch)/135 CHF – Carte 108/172 CHF – **Rest *L'Arabesque*** –
Menu 55 CHF (lunch)/98 CHF – Carte 57/104 CHF – **Rest *Pool Garden*** –
(opened May - September) Menu 49 CHF (lunch)/75 CHF – Carte 83/156 CHF
15/600 VISA MC AE — **F2**

◆ Grand Luxury ◆ Stylish ◆

Wood and marble abound in this hotel whose finest rooms look onto the lake. Spice's Café has "World Cuisine" in a modern setting, while the Arabesque offers mouthwatering Lebanese delights. Try eating al fresco in the Pool Garden in summer.

Le Palace Hilton

19 quai du Mont-Blanc ✉ 1201
– ✆ 0229 089 081 – info@hiltongeneve.com – Fax 0229 089 0 90
– www.hiltongeneve.com
409 rm – 330/690 CHF 330/790 CHF, 41 CHF – 14 suites
Rest – *(new concept of restoration from mid 2007)*
15/800 VISA MC AE — **F3**

◆ Grand Luxury ◆ Classic ◆

This imposing, well-appointed hotel is situated on the lakeside. The public areas, guestrooms and suites are all being refurbished in contemporary style, using the finest materials.

Beau-Rivage

13 quai du Mont-Blanc ✉ 1201 – ✆ 0227 166 666 – info@beau-rivage.ch
– Fax 0227 166 0 60 – www.beau-rivage.ch
81 rm – 650/1100 CHF 750/1200 CHF, 42 CHF – 12 suites
Rest *Le Chat Botté* – Menu 65 CHF (lunch)/180 CHF – Carte 111/180 CHF
Rest *Le Patara* – *✆ 0227 315 566 (closed 6 - 9 April, 26 - 28 May, 23 December - 7 January, Saturday lunch and Sunday lunch)* Menu 37 CHF (lunch)/115 CHF – Carte 76/103 CHF
15/120 VISA MC AE — **F3**

◆ Grand Luxury ◆ Stylish ◆

Run by the same family since 1865, this typical hotel facing the lake has elegant, traditionally furnished guestrooms, as well as an attractive atrium decorated with columns and a fountain. Contemporary cuisine and stylish atmosphere in the Le Chat Botté restaurant; Thai specialities in the Patara.

SWITZERLAND

D'Angleterre rm 15/35

17 quai du Mont-Blanc ✉ 1201 – ✆ 0229 065 555 – angleterre@rchmail.com – Fax 0229 065 5 56 – www.hotelangleterre.ch **F3**

45 rm – †530/950 CHF ††530/950 CHF, ☐ 42 CHF

Rest *Windows* – Menu 42 CHF (lunch)/169 CHF – Carte 103/153 CHF

♦ Grand Luxury ♦ Stylish ♦

An elegant neo-Classical building (1872) facing Lake Léman. Attention to detail, tasteful guestrooms with individual touches, and colonial decor in the cosy Leopard Lounge. The veranda restaurant with its exclusive atmosphere and lake views serves contemporary cuisine.

De la Paix rm 24/110

11 quai du Mont-Blanc ✉ 1201 – ✆ 0229 096 000 – reservation@hoteldelapaix.ch – Fax 0229 096 0 01 – www.hoteldelapaix.ch **F3**

84 rm – †360/750 CHF ††550/920 CHF, ☐ 40 CHF – **Rest *Vertig'O*** – *(closed 13 July - 6 August and Sunday)* Menu 49 CHF (lunch)/115 CHF – Carte 90/126 CHF

♦ Luxury ♦ Classic ♦

Built in 1865 and renovated in 2005, this hotel boasts exuberant public rooms, including a stunning gold-adorned patio. The guestrooms are decorated along two themes: "water droplets" and "floating rose petals". Contemporary cuisine is served in the modern bistro.

Intercontinental rm 15/450

7-9 ch. du Petit-Saconnex ✉ 1209 – ✆ 0229 193 939 – geneva@interconti.com – Fax 0229 193 8 38 – www.intercontinental.com/geneva *Plan I* **B2**

304 rm – †280/655 CHF ††280/655 CHF, ☐ 40 CHF – 24 suites

Rest *Woods* – Menu 59 CHF (lunch)/107 CHF – Carte 75/120 CHF

♦ Chain hotel ♦ Classic ♦

Next door to the Palais des Nations and ideal for conferences, this 1960s-built hotel has given its public areas a facelift, while the rooms await a similar overhaul. Extensive conference facilities. Spacious and comfortable restaurant serving contemporary cuisine in a modern setting.

Bristol rm 15/100

10 r. du Mont-Blanc ✉ 1201 – ✆ 0227 165 700 – reservations@bristol.ch – Fax 0227 389 0 39 – www.bristol.ch **F3**

95 rm – †335/600 CHF ††460/640 CHF, ☐ 34 CHF – 5 suites

Rest *Relais Bristol* – Menu 50 CHF (lunch)/94 CHF – Carte 66/108 CHF

♦ Business ♦ Classic ♦

An opulent entrance hall leads to the reception area of this hotel near the lake. Spacious, refurbished rooms, fitness centre, sauna, steam room and collection of old canvasses. Cuisine with a modern twist is served in a spruce, classic dining room. Piano bar.

Epsom rm rm 15/60

18 r. Richemont ✉ 1202 – ✆ 0225 446 666 – epsom@manotel.com – Fax 0225 446 6 99 – www.manotel.com **F2**

153 rm – †320/550 CHF ††320/550 CHF, ☐ 30 CHF

Rest *Portobello* – Menu 40 CHF (lunch)/59 CHF – Carte 60/111 CHF

♦ Business ♦ Classic ♦

Very contemporary hotel on a quiet city-centre street. Relaxing atmosphere, homely rooms and high-tech conference facilities. Modern rôtisserie with a glass roof.

Royal rm rm 30/250

41 r. de Lausanne ✉ 1201 – ✆ 0229 061 414 – royal@manotel.com – Fax 0229 061 4 99 – www.manotel.com/royal **E2**

197 rm – †320/550 CHF ††320/550 CHF, ☐ 30 CHF – 5 suites

Rest *Rive Droite* – Menu 65 CHF – Carte 66/94 CHF

♦ Business ♦ Classic ♦

Located on a busy boulevard between the lake and the railway station, this elegant, comfortable hotel has been renovated in stages, providing a good choice of rooms. Contemporary cuisine, stylish ambience and an arcaded terrace in the hotel's Rive Droite restaurant.

Warwick AC rm 15/150 VISA MC AE

14 r. de Lausanne ✉ 1201 – ✆ 0227 168 000 – res.geneva@warwickhotels.com – Fax 0227 168 0 01 – www.warwickgeneva.com **E3**

167 rm – 199/330 CHF 199/330 CHF, 27 CHF

Rest *La Brasserie* – *(closed Sunday lunch)* Menu 25 CHF (lunch) – Carte 62/102 CHF

♦ Business ♦ Functional ♦

Located in front of the station, the Warwick is ideal for tourists and conference guests travelling by train. Contemporary, functional rooms. The restaurant cultivates a Parisian bistro atmosphere.

Sofitel AC rm VISA MC AE

18-20 r. du Cendrier ✉ 1201 – ✆ 0229 088 080 – h1322@accor.com – Fax 0229 088 0 81 – www.sofitel.com **E3**

95 rm – 370/510 CHF 370/550 CHF, 35 CHF

Rest – Menu 45 CHF (lunch)/85 CHF – Carte 65/108 CHF

♦ Chain hotel ♦ Stylish ♦

This chain hotel, centrally located between the lake and the railway station, has recently renovated public areas and guestrooms. Classical lobby and piano-bar. The restaurant features traditional cuisine served in the retro-style dining room or on the terrace.

Novotel AC rm 25 VISA MC AE

19 r. de Zurich ✉ 1201 – ✆ 0229 099 000 – h3133@accor.com – Fax 0229 099 0 02 – www.novotel.com **F3**

196 rm – 230/450 CHF 230/450 CHF, 27 CHF – 10 suites

Rest – *(closed Saturday and Sunday)* Menu 29 CHF (lunch)/39 CHF – Carte 58/91 CHF

♦ Chain hotel ♦ Functional ♦

A chain hotel recognisable by its glass façade, ideally located close to both the train station and lake. Good-sized, well-appointed bedrooms, in the process of being renovated. Contemporary-style "spice"-themed decor in the restaurant. Traditional cuisine.

Nash Rex Hotel without rest VISA MC AE

42 av. Wendt ✉ 1203 – ✆ 0225 447 474 – hotel.rex@nash-holding.com – Fax 0225 447 4 99 – www.nashrex.com *Plan I* **B2**

70 rm – 195/500 CHF 195/500 CHF, 18 CHF

♦ Business ♦ Classic ♦

Opened in 2004 in a residential area, this hotel offers opulent-looking reception areas and rooms of various sizes: at its best, the accommodation is bright, spacious and furnished with period pieces.

Le Montbrillant rm 15/40 P VISA MC AE

2 r. de Montbrillant ✉ 1201 – ✆ 0227 337 784 – contact@montbrillant.ch – Fax 0227 332 5 11 – www.montbrillant.ch **E3**

82 rm – 159/190 CHF 238/360 CHF

Rest – Menu 38 CHF (lunch)/78 CHF – Carte 45/92 CHF

♦ Family ♦ Personalised ♦

Good accommodation for visitors who wish to be near the railway station. Typical Swiss decor, rooms of varying sizes and studios with a small kitchen. The Parisian brasserie has a friendly atmosphere and serves a mix of traditional and Italian cuisine (pizza baked in a wood oven).

Les Nations without rest VISA MC AE

62 r. du Grand-Pré ✉ 1202 – ✆ 0227 480 808 – info@hotel-les-nations.com – Fax 0227 343 8 84 – www.hotel-les-nations.com *Plan I* **B2**

71 rm – 175/280 CHF 220/350 CHF

♦ Business ♦ Classic ♦

Popular with UN staff, this renovated hotel is located on a busy road. The hotel corridors are adorned with antiques grouped by theme, while the guestrooms all feature individual touches.

SWITZERLAND

Auteuil without rest
33 r. de Lausanne ✉ 1201 – ☎ 0225 442 222 – auteuil@manotel.com – Fax 0225 442 2 99 – www.manotel.com **E2**
104 rm – †290/450 CHF ††290/450 CHF, ☕ 28 CHF
◆ Business ◆ Classic ◆
A contemporary reception hall with Warhol-style portraits of the stars leads on to modern rooms in dark wood, designer bathrooms and a very trendy breakfast room.

Cornavin without rest
Cornavin Station ✉ 1201 – ☎ 0227 161 212 – cornavin@fhotels.ch – Fax 0227 161 2 00 – www.fassbindhotels.com **E3**
164 rm – †251/387 CHF ††301/437 CHF, ☕ 18 CHF
◆ Business ◆ Modern ◆
Patronised by Tintin in "The Calculus Affair", this hotel is home to the world's biggest clock. Modern guest rooms with Le Corbusier armchairs, and a panoramic breakfast room.

Kipling without rest
27 r. de la Navigation ✉ 1201 – ☎ 0225 444 040 – kipling@manotel.com – Fax 0225 444 0 99 – www.manotel.com **E-F2**
62 rm – †260/350 CHF ††260/350 CHF, ☕ 18 CHF
◆ Business ◆ Modern ◆
A delicate waft of incense greets you as you enter this colonial-styled hotel dedicated to the author of "The Jungle Book".

Jade without rest
55 r. Rothschild ✉ 1201 – ☎ 0225 443 838 – jade@manotel.com – Fax 0225 443 8 99 – www.manotel.com **F2**
47 rm – †260/350 CHF ††260/350 CHF, ☕ 18 CHF
◆ Business ◆ Modern ◆
The interior of this hotel has been designed according to the principles of the fashionable Chinese philosophy of Feng Shui. The result is a refined, modern setting aiming to promote harmony and serenity.

Du Midi
4 pl. Chevelu ✉ 1201 – ☎ 0225 441 500 – info@hotel-du-midi.ch – Fax 0225 441 5 20 – www.hotel-du-midi.ch **E-F3**
78 rm – †250/350 CHF ††300/450 CHF, ☕ 26 CHF – **Rest** – *(closed Saturday and Sunday)* Menu 35 CHF (lunch)/100 CHF – Carte 54/88 CHF
◆ Business ◆ Functional ◆
This comfortable, family-run hotel stands on a small square overlooking the River Rhône. Large lobby decorated with columns, a cosy lounge and classical-contemporary guestrooms. Warm, modern dining room with a summer terrace.

Edelweiss
2 pl. de la Navigation ✉ 1201 – ☎ 0225 445 151 – edelweiss@manotel.com – Fax 0225 445 1 99 – www.manotel.com **F3**
42 rm – †260/350 CHF ††260/350 CHF, ☕ 18 CHF
Rest – *(dinner only)* Menu 55 CHF – Carte 50/97 CHF
◆ Business ◆ Cosy ◆
The outside of this establishment gives a good idea of the pleasures within. It's a real Swiss chalet, with cosy bedrooms and a congenial galleried dining room where you can enjoy traditional fare and typical cheese dishes to the accompaniment of music.

Ambassador
21 quai des Bergues ✉ 1201 – ☎ 0229 080 530 – info@hotel-ambassador.ch – Fax 0227 389 0 80 – www.hotel-ambassador.ch **E3**
80 rm – †210/400 CHF ††280/400 CHF, ☕ 24 CHF – **Rest** – *(closed Sunday lunch, Saturday and Bank Holidays)* Menu 39 CHF (lunch)/67 CHF – Carte 53/98 CHF
◆ Business ◆ Classic ◆
Traffic hurries by outside, following the river Rhône, but excellent soundproofing in the bedrooms keeps out all but a murmur. Traditional meals served in wood-fitted dining room or on the terrace in summer.

Eden 20

135 r. de Lausanne ✉ 1202 – ☎ 0227 163 700 – eden@eden.ch
– Fax 0227 315 2 60 – www.eden.ch **F1**

54 rm – 175/265 CHF 235/320 CHF

Rest – *(closed 21 July - 12 August, 22 December - 7 January, Saturday and Sunday)* Menu 33/45 CHF – Carte 45/70 CHF

♦ Business ♦ Classic ♦

This establishment facing the Palais des Nations is regularly refurbished. Bright and functional classically furnished rooms. Traditional restaurant where local people rub shoulders with guests and passers-by.

Strasbourg-Univers without rest

10 r. Pradier ✉ 1201 – ☎ 0229 065 800
– info@hotel-strasbourg-geneva.ch
– Fax 0227 384 2 08 – www.strasbourg-geneva.ch **E3**

51 rm – 170/210 CHF 220/270 CHF

♦ Business ♦ Functional ♦

Close to the station and the Cornavin car park, this refurbished establishment has small, functional rooms with cosy public areas.

Ibis without rest

10 r. Voltaire ✉ 1201 – ☎ 0223 382 020 – h2154@accor.com
– Fax 0223 382 0 30 – www.ibishotel.com **E3**

65 rm – 136 CHF 136 CHF, 14 CHF

♦ Chain hotel ♦ Minimalist ♦

This completely refurbished establishment is typical of the new generation of Ibis hotels. Contemporary comfort in rooms with modern, no-nonsense furnishings.

Le Neptune – Hotel Mandarin Oriental du Rhône

1 quai Turrettini ✉ 1201 – ☎ 0229 090 006
– mogva-enquiry@mohg.com – Fax 0229 090 0 10
– www.mandarinoriental.com
closed August, Saturday and Sunday **E3**

Rest – Menu 98 CHF (lunch)/175 CHF – Carte 160/220 CHF

Spec. Tuilé d'aubergine et confit de poivron doux, tartine de jambon Jabugo et vinaigrette de tomate au Xérès. Ravioli de homard à la fondue de tomate et basilic, jus de crustacé. Tournedos de thon rouge sur le grill, fritots de pomme de terre, mousseline béarnaise.

♦ Contemporary ♦ Formal ♦

Culinary artistry and modern cuisine from the Mandarin Oriental du Rhône's Le Neptune restaurant – the god himself appears in the wall-paintings.

Tsé Yang 20

19 quai du Mont-Blanc ✉ 1201 – ☎ 0227 325 081
– Fax 0227 310 5 82 **F3**

Rest – *(1st floor)* Menu 45 CHF (lunch)/139 CHF – Carte 63/165 CHF

♦ Chinese ♦ Exotic ♦

Elegant restaurant with oriental décor and carved wooden partitions. Savour Chinese specialities while admiring the view over Lake Léman.

La Perle du Lac Lake, 8/60

126 r. de Lausanne ✉ 1202 – ☎ 0229 091 020 – info@laperledulac.ch
– Fax 0229 091 0 30 – www.laperledulac.ch
closed 24 December - 24 January and Monday **F1**

Rest – Menu 62 CHF (lunch)/120 CHF – Carte 105/140 CHF

♦ Contemporary ♦ Formal ♦

Established over a century ago, this chalet with a spacious panoramic terrace is located in a park facing the lake. Bold colours enliven the more modern of the two dining rooms.

Thai Phuket

33 av. de France ✉ 1202 – ✆ 0227 344 100 – Fax 0227 344 2 40 **E1**

Rest – *(closed Saturday lunch)* Menu 35 CHF (lunch)/90 CHF – Carte 48/80 CHF

◆ Thai ◆ Exotic ◆

A respected address with attentive service from waitresses dressed in traditional costume. Vintage wines, including top clarets, and a superb aquarium of exotic fish.

Bistrot du Bœuf Rouge

17 r. Alfred-Vincent ✉ 1201 – ✆ 0227 327 537 – Fax 0227 314 6 84 – www.boeufrouge.ch

closed 3 weeks in July, 23 December - 3 January, Saturday, Sunday and Bank Holidays **F3**

Rest – Menu 37 CHF (lunch)/54 CHF – Carte 51/88 CHF

◆ Lyonnais cuisine ◆ Brasserie ◆

A typically French brasserie ornamented with mirrors, a bar and comfortable benches. The menu features specialities from the city of Lyon, local dishes and daily specials.

Sagano

80

86 r. de Montbrillant ✉ 1202 – ✆ 0227 331 150 – Fax 0227 332 7 55 **E1**

Rest – *(closed Saturday lunch and Sunday)* Menu 40 CHF (lunch)/90 CHF – Carte 46/90 CHF

◆ Japanese ◆ Exotic ◆

Hungry for a taste of the exotic with a little zen? Head for this Japanese restaurant with its tatami mats and low tables. A culinary voyage from the Land of the Rising Sun.

L'Entrecôte Couronnée

5 r. des Pâquis ✉ 1201 – ✆ 0227 328 445 – Fax 0227 328 4 46

closed Christmas - New Year, Saturday lunch and Sunday **F3**

Rest – Menu 58 CHF – Carte 60/82 CHF

◆ Contemporary ◆ Bistro ◆

This is the place to experience the real Geneva. Bistro-style ambience with contemporary food. Plenty of prints and paintings evoke the spirit of this old city.

LEFT BANK *Plan III*

Swissôtel Métropole Geneva

rm 15/90

34 quai Général-Guisan ✉ 1204 – ✆ 0223 183 200 – geneva@swissotel.com – Fax 0223 183 3 00 – www.swissotel-geneva.com **H1**

118 rm – 320/810 CHF 350/880 CHF, 37 CHF – 9 suites

Rest ***Le Grand Quai*** – Carte 69/124 CHF

◆ Luxury ◆ Classic ◆

Built in 1854 overlooking the landmark Jet d'Eau. Attractive, traditional guest rooms, many with lake views, plus new king-size suites and a panoramic roof terrace and fitness centre. Le Grand Quai, with its trompe l'œil frescoes, serves traditional French fare.

Les Armures

1 r. du Puits-Saint-Pierre ✉ 1204 – ✆ 0223 109 172 – armures@span.ch – Fax 0223 109 8 46 – www.hotel-les-armures.ch **H2**

32 rm – 370/470 CHF 465/595 CHF

Rest – *(closed Easter, Christmas and New Year)* Menu 55 CHF – Carte 49/91 CHF

◆ Traditional ◆ Historic ◆

An elegant 17C town house tucked away in the heart of the old town. Attractive bedroom decor with antique furniture and exposed beams. A choice of traditional dishes in the newly renovated restaurant, including fondue served in the "carnotset" (drinking den).

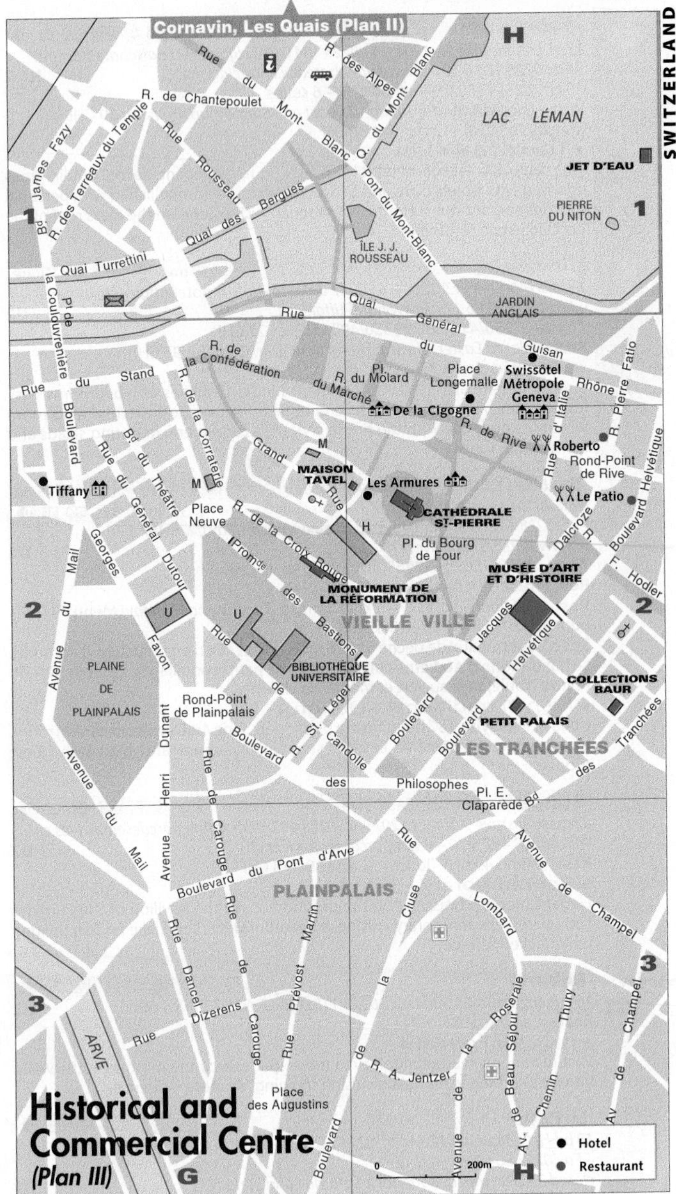

Historical and Commercial Centre
(Plan III)

De la Cigogne

17 pl. Longemalle ✉ 1204 – ✆ 0228 184 040 – cigogne@relaischateaux.com – Fax 0228 184 0 50 – www.relaischateaux.com/cigogne **H1-2**
46 rm – 380 CHF 480 CHF – 6 suites
Rest – *(closed Saturday in July - August and Sunday lunch)* Menu 59 CHF (lunch)/105 CHF – Carte 72/121 CHF
♦ Traditional ♦ Historic ♦
The early-20C façade overlooks a busy square. Elegant decor, public areas adorned with objets d'art, and bedrooms and suites embellished with personal touches and antique furniture. Traditional cuisine beneath the glass roof of the Art Deco-style restaurant.

Tiffany

rm

1 r. des Marbriers ✉ 1204 – ✆ 0227 081 616 – info@hotel-tiffany.ch – Fax 0227 081 6 17 – www.hotel-tiffany.ch **G2**
46 rm – 250/410 CHF 350/490 CHF, 21 CHF
Rest – *(closed Easter, Christmas and New Year)* Carte 57/97 CHF
♦ Traditional ♦ Classic ♦
Built on the site of a late-19C monument. Modern facilities with bedrooms, cosy lounge and bar all showing Belle Époque influence. Retro-style dining room which fits perfectly with the house style. A la carte menu featuring salads and low-calorie dishes.

Parc des Eaux-Vives with rm

rest rm 15/80 30/40

82 quai Gustave-Ador ✉ 1207 – ✆ 0228 497 575 – info@parcdeseauxvives.ch – Fax 0228 497 5 70 – www.parcdeseauxvives.ch *Plan I* **D2**
7 rm – 550/750 CHF 650/850 CHF, 29 CHF
Rest *Brasserie* – see below
Rest – *(1st floor) (closed 3 weeks in January, Sunday and Monday)* Menu 79 CHF (lunch)/220 CHF – Carte 157/226 CHF
Spec. Les ormeaux de pêche à pied, radis noir et céleri en réduction d'agrumes. Le bar de ligne d'Audierne cuit en étuvée de petits coquillages. Le lapin "Rex du Poitou" roulé, saisi au vert et moutarde violette.
♦ French traditional ♦ Design ♦
Housed in a lavish 18C building in a public park. Fine Art Deco-style dining room, mouth-watering, creative cuisine, summer restaurant and high-tech guest rooms.

Brasserie – Parc des Eaux-Vives

82 quai Gustave-Ador ✉ 1207 – ✆ 0228 497 575 – info@parcdeseauxvives.ch – Fax 0228 497 5 70 – www.parcdeseauxvives.ch *Plan I* **D2**
Rest – Menu 49 CHF (lunch) – Carte 59/113 CHF
♦ Contemporary ♦ Trendy ♦
Elegant modern brasserie on the ground floor of the pavilion of the Parc des Eaux-Vives. Contemporary cuisine, a beautiful view of the lake and an inviting teak-decked terrace.

Roberto

15

10 r. Pierre Fatio ✉ 1204 – ✆ 0223 118 033 – Fax 0223 118 4 66 **H2**
Rest – Carte 80/120 CHF
♦ Italian ♦ Formal ♦
Vast restaurant made to look even more spacious by the mirrors on the walls. Intimate ambience for Italian cuisine showing Milanese influence.

Le Patio

19 bd Helvétique ✉ 1207 – ✆ 0227 366 675 – lepatio.ch@freesurf.ch – Fax 0227 864 0 74
closed 25 December - 3 January, Saturday and Sunday **H2**
Rest – Carte 68/107 CHF
♦ Contemporary ♦ Fashionable ♦
This establishment has two modern dining rooms, one of them designed as a winter garden. A selection of seasonal recipes and Provençal specialities make easy bedfellows.

Buffet de la Gare des Eaux-Vives (Labrosse)

7 av. de la Gare des Eaux-Vives ✉ 1207 – ✆ 0228 404 430 – Fax 0228 404 4 31
closed 21 July - 5 August, 25 December - 7 January, Saturday and Sunday

Plan I **C-D3**

Rest – Menu 56 CHF (lunch)/155 CHF – Carte 94/131 CHF

Spec. Langoustine rôtie et carpaccio de Saint Jacques en robe de San Daniele (spring - summer). Loup de ligne doré à la peau, tartine de tomates et olives, pesto de roquette sauvage et fenouil confit (spring). Côte de veau dorée, ravioles de jarret confit et pommes de terre écrasées aux morilles, jus au savagnin (spring).

♦ Contemporary ♦ Formal ♦

Not your ordinary station buffet, here is a boldly contemporary yet sober interior with a railway fresco, a waterside summer terrace and an inventive up-to-the-minute menu.

ENVIRONS AND COINTRIN AIRPORT

Plan I

La Réserve

301 rte de Lausanne ✉ 1293 Bellevue – ✆ 0229 595 959 – info@lareserve.ch – Fax 0229 595 9 60 – www.lareserve.ch

C1

87 rm – †430/990 CHF ††540/990 CHF, ☕ 45 CHF – 15 suites

Rest *Le Loti* – Carte 69/162 CHF

Rest *Tsé-Fung* – Menu 70/150 CHF – Carte 65/245 CHF

♦ Grand Luxury ♦ Design ♦

Most of the modern guestrooms and suites of this hotel have terraces overlooking the hotel gardens and swimming pool. The splendid decor of the hotel is the work of the designer Garcia. Superb hotel spa. Choose between Chinese cuisine and glossy décor in the Le Tsé Fung restaurant and contemporary dishes in the Loti.

Crowne Plaza

15/600

34 r. François-Peyrot ✉ 1218 Grand-Saconnex – ✆ 0227 470 202 – reservations@cpgeneva.ch – Fax 0227 470 3 03 – www.crowneplaza.com

B1

496 rm – †230/500 CHF ††270/570 CHF, ☕ 34 CHF

Rest *Carlights* – Carte 50/99 CHF

Rest *L'Olivo* – *(closed 21 December - 8 January, Saturday and Sunday)* Carte 63/110 CHF

♦ Business ♦ Classic ♦

This business hotel near the airport specialises in conferences and congresses. Contemporary-style guestrooms, modern public areas and a fully-equipped wellness centre. Fusion cuisine and designer decor in the Carlights restaurant; daily dishes and a Mediterranean atmosphere in the Olivo.

Mövenpick Genève

rest rm 15/800

20 rte de Pré-Bois ✉ 1216 Cointrin – ✆ 0227 171 111 – hotel.geneva.airport@moevenpick.com – Fax 0227 171 1 22 – www.moevenpick-geneva-airport.com

A2

344 rm – †185/430 CHF ††199/530 CHF, ☕ 34 CHF – 6 suites

Rest *Latitude* – Carte 55/100 CHF

Rest *Kamome* – *(closed Saturday lunch, Monday lunch and Sunday)* Menu 42 CHF (lunch)/110 CHF – Carte 62/105 CHF

♦ Chain hotel ♦ Modern ♦

Business hotel near the airport. Facilities include a lounge, bars, casino and guestrooms of different categories (the executive rooms are the most recent). The Le Latitude restaurant serves "fusion" cuisine in a modern setting, while Le Kamome specialises in Japanese food, with a sushi bar and teppanyaki grill.

SWITZERLAND

Ramada Park Hotel

75 av. Louis-Casaï ✉ 1216 Cointrin – ✆ 0227 103 000 – resa@ramadaparkhotel.ch – Fax 0227 103 1 00 – www.ramadaparkhotel.ch

15/550 VISA AE

A2

302 rm – 195/480 CHF 195/480 CHF, 36 CHF – 6 suites

Rest *La Récolte* – Menu 34 CHF – Carte 51/95 CHF

◆ Chain hotel ◆ Classic ◆

Next door to the airport, a hotel with a wide range of amenities including a newspaper kiosk, a hairdresser's, a sauna and fitness centre, and meeting rooms. The bedrooms are modern. Some weeks the contemporary restaurant stages a themed menu.

Hostellerie de la Vendée

28 ch. de la Vendée ✉ 1213 Petit-Lancy – ✆ 0227 920 411 – info@vendee.ch – Fax 0227 920 5 46 – www.vendee.ch closed 6 - 9 April and 23 December - 7 January

15/60 VISA AE

B3

34 rm – 150/360 CHF 190/390 CHF

Rest – *(closed Saturday lunch, Sunday and Bank Holidays)* Menu 59 CHF (lunch)/150 CHF – Carte 85/148 CHF – **Rest *Bistro*** – *(closed Saturday lunch, Sunday and Bank Holidays)* Menu 41/62 CHF – Carte 63/100 CHF

◆ Business ◆ Classic ◆

This 1960s building stands in a residential part of town. Visitors are advised to opt for one of the contemporary-style renovated rooms. Enjoy traditional dishes with a modern twist in the light, comfortable dining room and the adjoining orangery, or sample simpler fare in the bistro.

NH Geneva Airport Hotel

21 av. de Mategnin ✉ 1217 Meyrin – ✆ 0229 899 000 – nhgenevaairport@nh-hotels.ch – Fax 0229 899 9 99 – www.nh-hotels.com

15/60 VISA AE

A2

190 rm – 130/450 CHF 150/450 CHF, 27 CHF

Rest *Le Pavillon* – *(closed Saturday lunch and Sunday lunch)* Carte 51/89 CHF

◆ Chain hotel ◆ Design ◆

A circular red-brick construction whose outer appearance provides a foretaste of the contemporary interior. Designer hall and lobby, friendly bar and well-kept rooms. Modern cuisine is served in the contemporary setting beneath the Pavillon's cupola.

Suitehotel

28 av. Louis-Casaï ✉ 1216 Cointrin – ✆ 0227 104 646 – H5654@accor.com – Fax 0227 104 6 00 – www.suite-hotel.com

VISA AE

B2

86 rm – 172/230 CHF 172/230 CHF, 10 CHF

Rest *Swiss Bistro* – *(closed Sunday lunch and Saturday)* Carte 33/77 CHF

◆ Chain hotel ◆ Modern ◆

This hotel located between the airport and the town centre offers up-to-the-minute rooms, each with an office which can be separated off by a sliding door. The public areas are bright and modern. Contemporary-style brasserie serving bistro-type meals with a Swiss twist.

Express by Holiday Inn without rest

16 rte de Pré-Bois ✉ 1216 Cointrin – ✆ 0229 393 939 – info@expressgeneva.com – Fax 0229 393 9 30 – www.expressgeneva.com

15/25 VISA AE

A2

154 rm – 139/230 CHF 139/230 CHF

◆ Chain hotel ◆ Modern ◆

This modern, mid-range chain hotel near the airport is designed with business travellers in mind. Functional guestrooms.

Ibis

10 ch. de la Violette ✉ 1216 Cointrin – ✆ 0227 109 500 – H3535@accor.com – Fax 0227 109 5 95 – www.ibishotel.com

VISA AE

A2

109 rm – 99/162 CHF 99/162 CHF, 14 CHF

Rest – *(dinner only)* Carte approx. 40 CHF

◆ Chain hotel ◆ Minimalist ◆

Situated near the motorway and Geneva airport, this hotel has all the facilities you would expect of the Ibis chain. Functional rooms with bathrooms. Tavern atmosphere and contemporary cuisine in the restaurant.

Auberge du Lion d'Or (Byrne/Dupont) Lake, AC, P, VISA

5 pl. Pierre-Gautier ⊠ 1223 Cologny – ✆ 0227 364 432 – info@liondor.ch – Fax 0227 867 4 62 – www.liondor.ch

closed 22 December - 7 January, Saturday and Sunday **D2**

Rest – Menu 70 CHF (lunch)/170 CHF – Carte 134/173 CHF

Rest *Le Bistro de Cologny* – Carte 71/118 CHF

Spec. Nem croustillant de ris de veau au gomasio, émulsion de carotte confite au gingembre et à la citronelle. Pavé de loup de mer, marmelade de citron, compression d'artichaut et épinard cremolata. Filet de bœuf du pays, ficelé et rôti, inspiration béarnaise, poêlée de chanterelles au persil plat.

♦ Contemporary ♦ Luxury ♦

Enjoy fine views of the lake and mountains through the large bay windows in the Wilmotte-designed dining room, from the modern bar, or the outdoor terrace. Modern cuisine served in the bistro or outdoors in a flower-filled garden in summer.

Domaine de Châteauvieux (Chevrier) with rm AC rm

16 ch. de Châteauvieux ⊠ 1242 Satigny 15 P VISA

– ✆ 0227 531 511 – info@chateauvieux.ch – Fax 0227 531 9 24 – www.chateauvieux.ch

closed 22 July - 8 August and 24 December - 8 January

13 rm – †220/360 CHF ††270/410 CHF

Rest – *(closed Sunday and Monday)* Menu 88 CHF (lunch)/240 CHF – Carte 180/252 CHF

Spec. Menu truffe noire (January - February). Menu truffe blanche (September - December). Menu gibier à plume (October - December).

♦ Innovative ♦ Luxury ♦

This restaurant occupies an old farmhouse surrounded by vineyards. Fine cuisine, prestigious crus and all the little touches you would expect from a high-class restaurant.

ZURICH

ZÜRICH

Population (est. 2006): 347 500 (conurbation 1 081 700) – Altitude: 409m

AGE RAGA/HOA QUI

The site of Zurich, framed by the wooded slopes of the Uetliberg and the Zürichberg at the point where the Limmat, flowing out of Lake Zürich, meets the Sihl river, is particularly charming. It is Switzerland's largest city and an important financial, industrial and commercial centre. It has a reputation for good living with a rich cultural life, outdoor cafés and gourmet restaurants; it is also a busy university city.

Zurich became a stronghold of the Reformation movement in the 16C. The pastor Ulrich Zwingli denounced social institutions and corruption and instituted controversial religious reforms. Several cantons formed an alliance against Zurich; the city was excluded from the direction of federal affairs and war broke out in 1531. However, his religious theories spread throughout German Switzerland. In the early 20C, the city was the cradle of the avant-garde Dada Movement as a reaction to established art. Its members included friends and artists from a variety of backgrounds, among them Tristan Tzara, Maurice Janco, Jean Arp and Sophie Taeuber.

WHICH DISTRICT TO CHOOSE

For the finest **accommodation** and boutique hotels look in the old city, around Niederdorfstrasse *Plan II* ***D2*** and Bahnhofstrasse *Plan II* **C2**. Business travellers will find first-class hotels with all facilities near the airport, in the city centre and in the downtown area. Hotels in the lake-side area and on the outskirts will suit visitors who appreciate peace and tranquillity. There are also delightful smaller hotels with an intimate atmosphere in the city.

The city boasts a variety of **eating places** in the old town, in a pleasant location along the quays and in the up and coming area to the west near the Schiffbau complex *Plan I* ***A3***. For a gourmet experience, visit also the starred restaurants at Küsnacht, Uetikon am See (SE) and Gattikon (S) on the outskirts of the city.

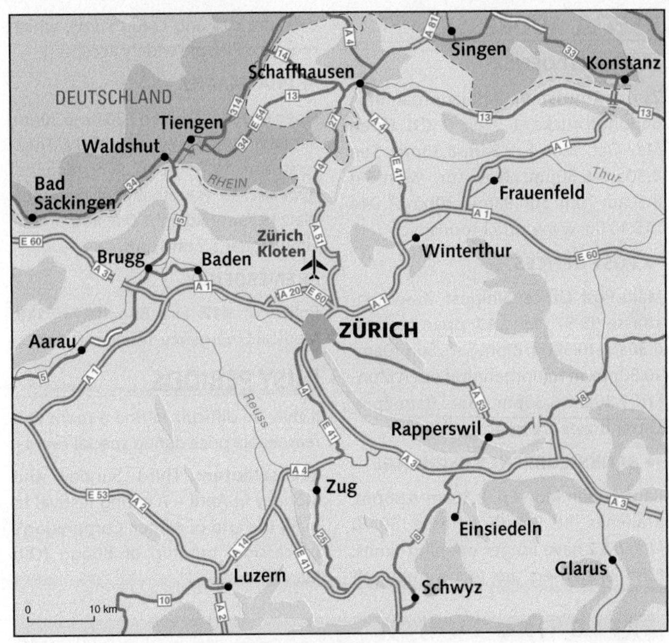

PRACTICAL INFORMATION

ARRIVAL – DEPARTURE

Zurich International Airport (Kloten) – 10 km (6 mi) north of the city. ✆ 0438 162 211; www.zurichairport.com

From the airport to the city centre – By **taxi**: about 50CHF, time 20-40min. By **train**: 5.80CHF, every 10-15min, time 10min. By **shuttle minibus** to hotels: about 20CHF, every 45min. By **bus**: several buses go to the city centre, 3.80CHF, time 20-30min.

Railway Station – Zürich Hauptbahnhof *Plan II* **C1**; main station for international and intercity trains. ✆ 0900 300 300; www.sbb.ch

TRANSPORT

→ BUS, METRO, TRAM, TRAIN, BOAT

The city operates an efficient public transport network in the city centre and suburbs. Single ticket 3.80CHF; day ticket 7.60CHF (€5.15); 9 o'clock Pass 22CHF (€14.85). Tickets are available from ticket machines and offices. Make sure you validate the ticket before boarding at the ticket machine or the special orange-coloured machine. Zurich Card gives unlimited travel, free entry to several museums and various discounts: 15CHF (€10.15, 24hr); 30CHF (€20.25, 72hr). It is available from the Tourist Office, hotels, museums and stations. ✆ 0848 988 988; www.vbz.ch

→ TAXIS

Metered taxis can be hailed at taxi stands, near the stations, at the airport or ordered by phone. Tips are included in the fare. Average ride in town: 25CHF. *Alpha Taxi AG* ✆ 044 777 77 77; www.alphataxi.ch; *Taxi 444 AG* ✆ 044 444 44 44; www.taxi444.ch

USEFUL ADDRESSES

→ TOURIST OFFICE

Zürich Tourismus – In Hauptbahnhof, Bahnhofbrücke 1 *Plan II* ***C1***. Open May-Oct, Mon-Sat 8am-8.30pm; Sun 8.30am-6.30pm; Nov-Apr, Mon-Sat 8.30am-7pm; Sun 9am-6.30pm. ✆ 044 215 40 00; www.zurichtourism.ch

→ POST OFFICES

Main Post Office: Sihlpost, Kasernenstrasse 95-97 *Plan I* ***A3***: open Mon-Fri 6.30am-10.30pm (8pm Sat), Sun 10am-10.30pm. In Hauptbahnhof open Mon-Fri 7.30am-6.30pm, Sat 8am-7pm. Letter boxes are bright yellow.

→ BANKS/CURRENCY EXCHANGE

Banks open Mon-Fri, 8.30am-4.30pm. Branches at Bahnhofstrasse 39/70 *Plan II* **C2** have longer opening times. Cash dispensers are to be found all over the city and credit cards, which require a PIN, are widely accepted.

→ PHARMACIES

Opening times Mon-Fri 7.30am-6.30pm, Sat 8am-4pm. *Bellevue Apotheke*, Theaterstrasse 14, is open 24hr. *Bahnhof Apotheke*, in Hauptbahnhof, Bahnhofplatz 15, 7am-midnight. *Odeon Apotheke*, Limmatquai 2, 7am-11pm.

→ EMERGENCY

Police: ✆ **117**. Fire Brigade: ✆ **118**. Medical Emergency Service: ✆ **144**.

BUSY PERIODS

It may be difficult to find a room at a reasonable price during special events:

Sechseläuten: Third Sunday and Monday in April – A spring festival to mark the end of winter. Corporation's procession; burning of Böögg (Old Man Winter).

EXPLORING ZURICH

It is possible to visit the main sights and museums in two days.

Museums and other sights are usually open from 9-10am to 5-6pm. Some close on Mondays.

VISITING

Grossmünster *Plan II* **D2** – Imposing 11C-13C cathedral with domed towers (statue of Charlemagne) and Romanesque cloisters.

Old Town *Plan II* **C2** – Follow the tree-lined **Bahnhofstrasse** to Paradeplatz – take Bleicherweg *Plan II* **C3** to view the old moat, **Schanzengraben**; Post-strasse leads to **Münsterhof** and 13C **Fraumünster** – Romanesque chancel, stained-glass windows, cloisters. Proceed to **St Peterkirche** (7C): 16C clock; and pretty **Weinplatz** (view of the east bank). **Schipfe**, the heart of the old town, boasts narrow, medieval streets lined with old houses (Augustinerstrasser). The shady **Lindenhof** (views of old quarter on opposite bank) marks the site of Celtic and Roman encampments.

Schweizerisches Landesmuseum *Plan II* **C1** – Magnificent collections of the Swiss National Museum tracing Switzerland's artistic and cultural heritage.

Kunsthaus *Plan II* **D2** – The Fine Arts Museum displays medieval sculpture, Swiss and German 15C Primitives and paintings by major European artists (Hodler, Cézanne, Renoir, Matisse, Braque, Picasso); also works by E. Munch, Man Ray, Arp and Giacometti.

Museum Rietberg *Plan I* **A3** – The eclectic collection of a private art patron: art from Asia, Africa, the South Sea Islands, South America and the Near East.

Sammlung Bührle – Splendid collection of paintings and sculpture assembled by a private collector: the exhibits illustrate all major European trends from the Dutch schools, the Impressionist movement to Cubism and Fauvism.

Boat trips – Cruises on Lake Zurich and the River Limmat from Bürkliplatz landing-stage *Plan II* **C3**.

Views – From Jules Verne Bar Panorama *Plan II* **C2**. Top of Uetliberg Tower. Bürkliplatz *Plan II* **C3**.

Excursions – **Uetliberg** and **Felsenegg** *(2hr round trip by train)*. **Albis Pass Road**, former Abbey of Kappel and plunging views of the lake beyond Hütten *(53 km-33 mi SW)*. **Eglisau** *(27 km-17 mi N)*.

SHOPPING

Department stores are usually open Mon-Fri 9am-8pm, Sat 8am-4pm. Smaller shops open later and close on Mon.

Bahnhofstrasse *Plan II* **C2**, the most famous shopping boulevard, is lined by smart boutiques and department stores *(Globus, Vilan, Jelmoli)*. You will also find boutiques, antique stores, trendy shops (*Trois Pommes* No 18) in the narrow streets around **Weinplatz**, **Münsterhof** and in the district around **Nieder-dorfstrasse** *Plan II* **D2** in the picturesque Old Town. There are also some fine shops in **Rennweg** *Plan II* **C2**, **Limmatquai** and **Langstrasse** *Plan I* **A3**. Visit *Fabric Frontline*, Ankerstrasse 118 (fine silks). For designer collectibles browse in *Time Tunnel*, Stüssihof-statt 7. For mouthwatering chocolates and specialities, do not miss *Sprüngli* and *Merkur*, Bahnhofstrasse 21/106; *Teuscher*, Storchengasse 9 and *Globus* Delikatessen. *Pastorini*, Weinplatz 3, specialises in wooden toys, and *Schweizer Heimatwerk*, Rudolf Brun-Brücke, in gifts and handicrafts. *Christie's*, Steinwiesstrasse 26, and *Sotheby's*, Gessnerallee 1, hold international auctions of art and antiques.

MARKETS – **Flea market** on Bürkliplatz *Plan II* **C3** (May-Oct, Sat 6am-3.30pm).

WHAT TO BUY – Designer items, jewellery, watches, toys, children's clothes, lace, linen, dolls, wall hangings, confectionery (truffles, chocolates, Luxemburgerli), cheese and other delicacies.

ENTERTAINMENT

Consult ZüriTipp (in German), the Friday supplement of Tages-Anzeiger, for listings of cultural events. English language web site www.zürtipp.ch/essentials

Opernhaus *Plan II* **D3** – Opera.

Tonhalle *Plan II* **C3** – Large hall inaugurated by Johannes Brahms in 1895.

Schauspielhaus *Plan II* **D2** – Plays.

Theatre Neumarkt and **Theater Stock** *Plan II* **D2** – Contemporary theatre.

Bernhard-Theater *Plan II* **D3** – Comedy, cabaret.

Theatersaal Rigiblick *Plan I* **B2** – Plays, dance, music.

Theatre Stadelhofen *Plan II* **D3** – Puppet plays, object and figure theatre.

Herzbaracke (Bellevuesteg) *Plan II* **D3** – Floating theatre for variety entertainment.

NIGHTLIFE

The Old Town (**Bahnhofstrasse**, **Niederdorfstrasse** and **the quays**) boasts a multitude of eating, drinking and entertainment venues. To the west, the area around **Escher-Wyss Platz/Pfingstweidstrasse** is lively with cafés, restaurants, nightclubs. Trendy venues include *4.Akt*, Heinrichstrasse 262; *Toni Molkerei*, Förrlibuckstrasse 109; *Rohstofflager*, Duttweilerstrasse; *Labor Bar*, Schiffbaustrasse 3; *Supermarket*, Geroldstrasse 17; *X-Tra* and *Indochine*, Limmatstrasse 118/275; *Kunsthaus*, Heimplatz 1. Relax at the famous *Café Odéon* and *Café Select*, Limmatquai 2/16; at the *Splendid* piano bar, Rosengasse 5 and the sophisticated *Kronenhalle*, Rämistrasse 4. Listen to cool jazz at *Blue Note*, Stockerstrasse 45; *Casa Bar*, Münstergasse30;*Moods*,Schiffbaustrasse 6. Visit *Grand Casino Baden*, Haselstrasse 2, Baden, for an elegant evening out.

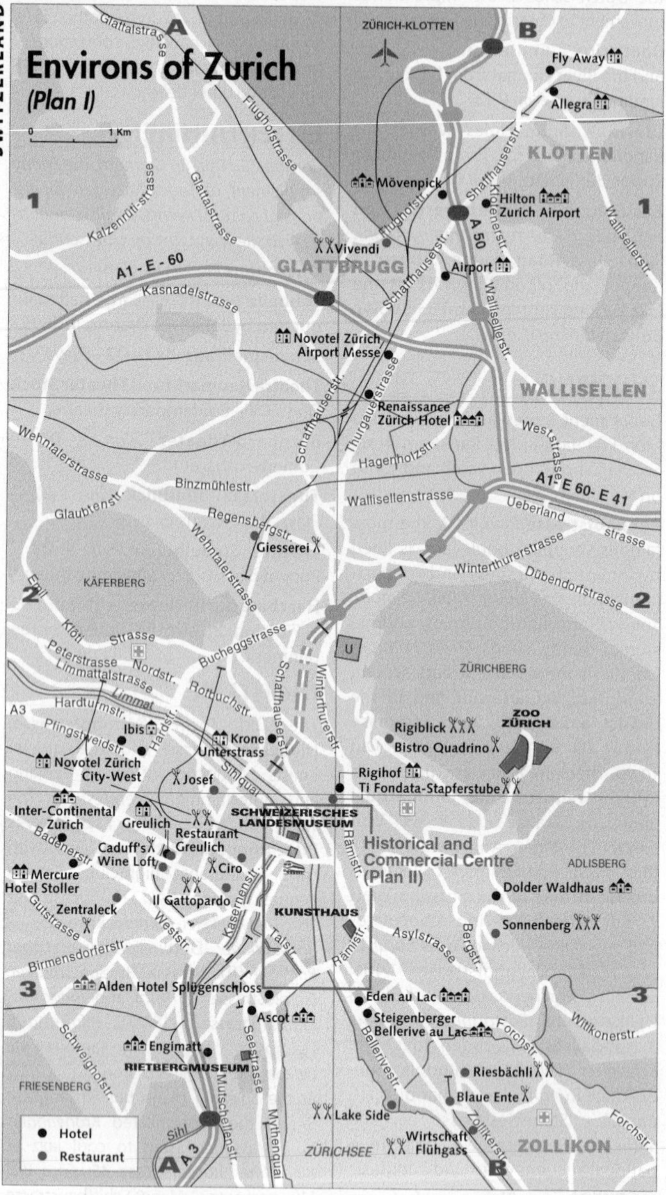

Environs of Zurich
(Plan I)

0 1 Km

A B
1 2 3

Glattalstrasse
Flughofstrasse
ZÜRICH-KLOTTEN
Fly Away
Allegra
KLOTTEN
Shaffhauserstr.
Katzenrüti-strasse
Glattalstrasse
Mövenpick
Hilton
Zurich Airport
Klotenerstr.
Wallisellerstr.
A 50
Flughofstr.
Vivendi
GLATTBRUGG
Airport
A1 - E - 60
Kasnadelstrasse
Schaffhauserstr.
Wallisellerstr.
Novotel Zürich
Airport Messe
Thurgauerstrasse
Schaffhauserstr.
Renaissance
Zürich Hotel
WALLISELLEN
Weststrasse
Wehntalerstrasse
Hagenholzstr.
Binzmühlestr.
A1- E 60- E 41
Glaubtenstr.
Wallisellenstrasse
Ueberland
strasse
Regensbergstr.
Giesserei
Wehntalerstrasse
Winterthurerstrasse
Dübendorfstrasse
KÄFERBERG
Emil
Klöti
Strasse
Bucheggstrasse
U
Peterstrasse
Nordstr.
Limmattalstrasse
Schaffhauserstr.
Winterthurerstr.
ZÜRICHBERG
Rotbuchstr.
Limmat
A3
Hardturmstr.
Pfingstweidstr.
Ibis
Hardstr.
Krone
Unterstrass
Rigiblick
Bistro Quadrino
ZOO ZÜRICH
Novotel Zürich
City-West
Sihlquai
Josef
Rigihof
Ti Fondata-Stapferstube
Inter-Continental
Zurich
Greulich
SCHWEIZERISCHES
LANDESMUSEUM
Restaurant
Greulich
Rämistr.
Historical and
Commercial Centre
(Plan II)
ADLISBERG
Badenerstr.
Caduff's
Wine Loft
Ciro
Mercure
Hotel Stoller
Dolder Waldhaus
Gutstrasse
Zentraleck
Il Gattopardo
Kasernenstr.
KUNSTHAUS
Sonnenberg
Weststr.
Talstr.
Rämistr.
Asylstrasse
Bergstr.
Birmensdorferstr.
Alden Hotel Splügenschloss
Eden au Lac
Ascot
Steigenberger
Bellerive au Lac
Witikonerstr.
Forchstr.
Schweighofstr.
Engimatt
RIETBERGMUSEUM
Seestrasse
Bellerivestr.
Riesbächli
FRIESENBERG
Blaue Ente
Mutschellenstr.
Mythenquai
Lake Side
Zollikerstr.
Forchstr.
Sihl
A3
Wirtschaft
Flühgass
ZÜRICHSEE
ZOLLIKON

● Hotel
● Restaurant

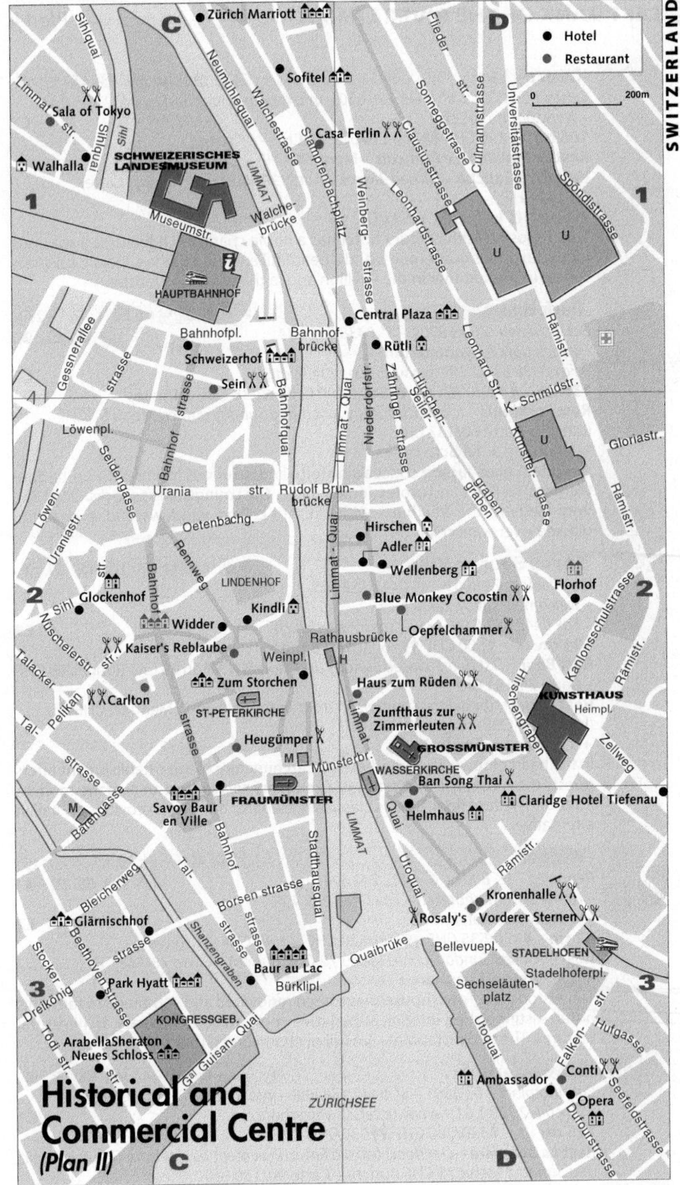
Historical and Commercial Centre (Plan II)
Hotel
Restaurant
Zürich Marriott
Sofitel
Sala of Tokyo
Walhalla
Casa Ferlin
SCHWEIZERISCHES LANDESMUSEUM
HAUPTBAHNHOF
Central Plaza
Schweizerhof
Rütli
Sein
Hirschen
Adler
Wellenberg
Blue Monkey Cocostin
Florhof
Glockenhof
Kindli
Widder
Oepfelchammer
Kaiser's Reblaube
Zum Storchen
Haus zum Rüden
Carlton
ST-PETERKIRCHE
Zunfthaus zur Zimmerleuten
KUNSTHAUS
Heugümper
GROSSMÜNSTER
WASSERKIRCHE
Ban Song Thai
FRAUMÜNSTER
Savoy Baur en Ville
Claridge Hotel Tiefenau
Helmhaus
Kronenhalle
Rosaly's
Vorderer Sternen
Glärnischhof
Baur au Lac
STADELHOFEN
Park Hyatt
KONGRESSGEB.
ArabellaSheraton Neues Schloss
Conti
Ambassador
Opera
ZÜRICHSEE
LIMMAT

LEFT BANK OF THE RIVER LIMMAT *Plan II*

Baur au Lac
rm rm 15/60 VISA
Talstr. 1 ✉ 8001 – ✆ 0442 205 020 – info@bauraulac.ch – Fax 0442 205 0 44 – www.bauraulac.ch **C3**
106 rm – †490 CHF ††740 CHF, ☕ 42 CHF – 17 suites
Rest *Le Pavillon/Le Français* – Menu 90 CHF – Carte 82/184 CHF
Rest *Rive Gauche* – *(closed 3 weeks in July - August and Sunday)* Carte 66/152 CHF
♦ Grand Luxury ♦ Stylish ♦
This imposing 19th century hotel has a noble character. It features a spacious lobby, luxurious guest rooms and a beautiful enclosed garden. Classic cuisine is served in the summer in the Pavillon and in the winter in Français.

Park Hyatt
rm 15/280 VISA
Beethovenstr. 21 ✉ 8002 – ✆ 0438 831 234 – zurich.park@hyattintl.com – Fax 0438 831 2 35 – www.zurich.park.hyatt.ch **C3**
138 rm – †440/990 CHF ††560/1140 CHF, ☕ 38 CHF – 4 suites
Rest *Parkhuus* – *(closed Saturday lunch and Sunday dinner)* Menu 57 CHF (lunch) – Carte 60/137 CHF
♦ Luxury ♦ Modern ♦
A modern glass façade conceals tasteful and luxurious rooms with up-to-date technical facilities and professional service. The Lounge offers snacks. Onyx Bar. Very elegant: the Parkhuus with floor-to-ceiling windows and a beautiful glassed-over wine cellar on 2 floors.

Savoy Baur en Ville
15/70 VISA
Paradeplatz ✉ 8001 – ✆ 0442 152 525 – welcome@savoy-zuerich.ch – Fax 0442 152 5 00 – www.savoy-zuerich.ch **C3**
104 rm ☕ – †500 CHF ††760 CHF – 8 suites
Rest *Baur* – *(1st floor) (closed Sunday and Monday)* Menu 68 CHF (lunch)/98 CHF – Carte 74/151 CHF
Rest *Orsini* – *(booking essential) (in front of the cathedral)* Menu 66 CHF (lunch)/89 CHF – Carte 72/153 CHF
♦ Luxury ♦ Stylish ♦
In the heart of town, the grandiose 19C architecture of this establishment offers guests the most stylish of settings. Exemplary service and an elegant, modern interior. The first-floor Baur is classically elegant; the Orsini provides an Italian alternative.

Widder
rest 15/120 VISA
Rennweg 7 ✉ 8001 – ✆ 0442 242 526 – home@widderhotel.ch – Fax 0442 242 4 24 – www.widderhotel.ch **C2**
42 rm – †450/535 CHF ††690/820 CHF, ☕ 48 CHF – 7 suites
Rest – *(closed Sunday lunch)* Menu 72 CHF (lunch) – Carte 78/142 CHF
♦ Luxury ♦ Design ♦
Ten historic Old Town houses have been renovated and combined to form this hotel. Distinguished interior, superlative comfort, contemporary architectural features. The two restaurants are full of charm and character.

Schweizerhof
rm 15/40 VISA
Bahnhofplatz 7 ✉ 8001 – ✆ 0442 188 888 – info@hotelschweizerhof.com – Fax 0442 188 1 81 – www.hotelschweizerhof.com **C1**
115 rm ☕ – †320/500 CHF ††530/715 CHF
Rest *La Soupière* – *(1st floor) (closed Saturday except dinner from October - June and Sunday)* Menu 75 CHF (lunch) – Carte 90/130 CHF
♦ Luxury ♦ Stylish ♦
This historic establishment stands in the very heart of town directly opposite the main station. Beyond the imposing façade is an interior of contemporary elegance and great comfort. La Soupière restaurant has a classically tasteful ambience.

Zum Storchen rm rm 15/20 VISA

Weinplatz 2 ✉ 8001 – ✆ 0442 272 727 – info@storchen.ch – Fax 0442 272 7 00 – www.storchen.ch **C2**

70 rm – 340/450 CHF 540/720 CHF

Rest *Rôtisserie* – *(1st floor)* Carte 69/118 CHF

♦ Traditional ♦ Functional ♦

This traditional hotel - one of the city's oldest - stands right on the Limmat. Elegant, comfortable rooms, with tasteful toile de Jouy fabrics, ensure a relaxing stay. The restaurant's lovely riverside terrace offers a fine view of the Old Town.

ArabellaSheraton Neues Schloss rm 20 VISA

Stockerstr. 17 ✉ 8002 – ✆ 0442 869 400 – neuesschloss@arabellasheraton.com – Fax 0442 869 4 45 – www.arabellasheraton.com **C3**

60 rm – 225/485 CHF 225/485 CHF, 35 CHF

Rest *Le Jardin* – *(closed Sunday and Bank Holidays)* Carte 59/102 CHF

♦ Traditional ♦ Modern ♦

Not far from the lakeside, this establishment makes an excellent base for your stay in Zurich. The recently renovated rooms have elegant wooden furnishings in contemporary style. The ground floor restaurant is lavishly decorated with indoor plants.

Glärnischhof rm 25 VISA

Claridenstr. 30 ✉ 8002 – ✆ 0442 862 222 – info@hotelglaernischhof.ch – Fax 0442 862 2 86 – www.hotelglaernischhof.ch **C3**

62 rm – 240/370 CHF 290/490 CHF

Rest *Le Poisson* – *(closed Saturday and Sunday)* Menu 58 CHF (lunch)/98 CHF – Carte 70/118 CHF

Rest *Vivace* – Carte 45/104 CHF

♦ Business ♦ Modern ♦

This building on the edge of the city centre has functional rooms with fine wood furnishings and fresh and bright colour schemes. The restaurants' names spell out their wares: fish dishes in Le Poisson, Italian cuisine in Vivace.

Glockenhof rm rest rm 15/40 VISA

Sihlstr. 31 ✉ 8001 – ✆ 0442 259 191 – info@glockenhof.ch – Fax 0442 259 2 92 – www.glockenhof.ch **C2**

95 rm – 200/350 CHF 300/480 CHF

Rest – Menu 45 CHF (lunch) – Carte 45/74 CHF

♦ Business ♦ Modern ♦

Its city centre location is only one of the advantages of this well-run hotel. Choose from traditionally decorated rooms or tasteful modern ones. Enjoy the pleasantly relaxed terrace of the traditional Glogge-Stube restaurant or Bistro Glogge-Egge.

Kindli VISA

Pfalzgasse 1 ✉ 8001 – ✆ 0438 887 676 – reservations@kindli.ch – Fax 0438 887 6 77 – www.kindli.ch **C2**

21 rm – 200/360 CHF 300/420 CHF

Rest *Zum Kindli* – *(closed Sunday and Bank Holidays)* Carte 66/112 CHF

♦ Traditional ♦ Cosy ♦

This historic town house with a friendly, informal ambience is decorated in English country-house style; Laura Ashley design sets the tone in its individually styled rooms. Family atmosphere. Discreetly elegant restaurant offers contemporary cooking.

Walhalla without rest 15/20 VISA

Limmatstr. 5 ✉ 8005 – ✆ 0444 465 400 – walhalla-hotel@bluewin.ch – Fax 0444 465 4 54 – www.walhalla-hotel.ch **C1**

48 rm – 135/160 CHF 180/220 CHF, 16 CHF

♦ Business ♦ Functional ♦

Good public transport access, by a tram stop behind the main station. Rooms with dark wood furniture and paintings of gods disporting themselves.

SWITZERLAND

XX **Kaiser's Reblaube** VISA

Glockengasse 7 ✉ 8001 – ☎ 0442 212 120 – rest.reblaube@bluewin.ch – Fax 0442 212 1 55 – closed 24 July - 13 August, Monday dinner except from October - March, Saturday lunch and Sunday **C2**

Rest – *(booking essential)* Menu 58 CHF (lunch)/145 CHF – Carte 75/121 CHF

♦ Contemporary ♦ Rustic ♦

Historic townhouse hidden in a maze of streets. Modern cooking in the first floor Goethe-Stübli; modern cuisine in the lively wine bar, which has a garden.

XX **Sein** ⇔18 VISA

Schützengasse 5 ✉ 8001 – ☎ 0442 211 065 – restaurantsein@bluewin.ch – Fax 0442 126 5 80 – www.zürichsein.ch – closed 14 July - 5 August, 24 - 28 December, Saturday, Sunday and Bank Holidays **C1**

Rest – Menu 65 CHF (lunch) – Carte 68/122 CHF

Rest *Tapas Bar* – Carte approx. 60 CHF

♦ Contemporary ♦

The Sein, located near the train station, is a restaurant with a modern design. In the evening, a gourmet menu is featured; simpler fare is offered midday. Contemporary cuisine.

XX **Carlton** ⇔30/60 VISA

Bahnhofstr. 41 ✉ 8001 – ☎ 0442 271 919 – info@carlton.ch – Fax 0442 271 9 27 – www.carlton.ch **C2**

Rest – *(closed Sunday and Bank Holidays)* Menu 49 CHF (lunch) – Carte 65/115 CHF

♦ Contemporary ♦ Trendy ♦

A spacious restaurant, elegantly decorated in Art Deco style. The kitchen produces modern dishes, the wine cellar is open to diners and they also serve afternoon tea.

XX **Sala of Tokyo** VISA

Limmatstr. 29 ✉ 8005 – ☎ 0442 715 290 – sala@active.ch – Fax 0442 717 8 07 – www.sala-of-tokyo.ch – closed 3 weeks in July - August, 24 December - 9 January, Saturday lunch, Sunday and Monday **C1**

Rest – Menu 125 CHF – Carte 49/120 CHF

♦ Japanese ♦ Exotic ♦

Wood-panelled interior with sushi-bar and restaurant, to the rear a section in contemporary style with yakitori grills. The kitchen is sure to bring a smile to your lips.

X **Heugümper** ⇔35 VISA

Waaggasse 4 ✉ 8001 – ☎ 0442 111 660 – info@restaurantheuguemper.ch – Fax 0442 111 6 61 – www.restaurantheuguemper.ch closed 14 July - 19 August, 23 December - 3 January, Saturday except dinner from October - December, Sunday and Bank Holidays **C2**

Rest – Menu 138 CHF – Carte 63/131 CHF

♦ Contemporary ♦ Bistro ♦

In the part of the Old Town around the Fraumünster this restaurant consists of a smart bistro and an elegant dining room, both serving dishes with a modern twist.

RIGHT BANK OF THE RIVER LIMMAT *Plan II*

Zürich Marriott rm rm 15/250

Neumühlequai 42 ✉ 8001 – ☎ 0443 607 070 – marriott.zurich@marriotthotels.com – Fax 0443 607 7 77 VISA **C1**

252 rm – †325/455 CHF ††325/455 CHF, ☕ 35 CHF – 9 suites

Rest *White Elephant* – *(closed Saturday lunch and Sunday lunch)* Menu 38 CHF (lunch)/69 CHF (Buffet) – Carte 51/96 CHF

Rest *Parkview* – *(dinner only)* Carte 55/103 CHF

♦ Chain hotel ♦ Classic ♦

This multistory hotel has its own underground garage and is located right on the river. The guest rooms are of different sizes and designs and feature contemporary comfort. The White Elephant features modern, clean lines. Parkview serves contemporary cuisine.

Sofitel

rm 15/40 VISA AE

Stampfenbachstr. 60 ✉ 8006 – ✆ 0443 606 060 – h1196@accor.com – Fax 0443 606 0 61 – www.sofitel.com **C1**

134 rm – 180/535 CHF 220/535 CHF, 32 CHF – 4 suites

Rest *Bel Etage* – Carte 55/106 CHF

♦ Chain hotel ♦ Stylish ♦

Attractive décor throughout, based on the use of wood and warm colours, from the foyer in the style of an elegant Swiss chalet to the soundproofed rooms. A wide-ranging menu is served in the Bel Etage restaurant.

Central Plaza

rm rm 30 VISA AE

Central 1 ✉ 8001 – ✆ 0442 565 656 – info@central.ch – Fax 0442 565 6 57 – www.central.ch **D1**

97 rm – 232/395 CHF 232/395 CHF, 18 CHF – 4 suites

Rest *King's Cave* – *(closed Saturday lunch and Sunday lunch)* Carte 41/96 CHF

♦ Business ♦ Modern ♦

This establishment is right on the River Limmat directly opposite the main station. Rooms are all in the same modern and comfortable style, calculated to meet guests' every need. The vaulted cellars house the King's Cave grill.

Florhof

rm VISA AE

Florhofgasse 4 ✉ 8001 – ✆ 0442 502 626 – info@florhof.ch – Fax 0442 502 6 27 – www.florhof.ch **D2**

34 rm – 220/275 CHF 330/380 CHF

Rest – *(closed 14 - 29 April, 22 December - 6 January, Monday except dinner in summer, Saturday lunch, Sunday and Bank Holidays)* Menu 44 CHF (lunch)/ 88 CHF – Carte 82/121 CHF

♦ Family ♦ Personalised ♦

Tasteful décor characterises the rooms in this lovely old patrician mansion from the 16C. Careful attention to detail and excellent technical facilities throughout. Tempting dishes await diners in the elegant restaurant.

Ambassador

rm VISA AE

Falkenstr. 6 ✉ 8008 – ✆ 0442 589 898 – welcome@ambassadorhotel.ch – Fax 0442 589 8 00 – www.ambassadorhotel.ch **D3**

45 rm – 210/360 CHF 330/460 CHF, 24 CHF

Rest – Menu 48 CHF (dinner) – Carte 54/110 CHF

♦ Business ♦ Functional ♦

This stately hotel is located right by the opera house on the edge of the city centre. Rooms and suites furnished in contemporary style and provided with excellent technical facilities. Restaurant with fantastical murals depicting scenes from the opera.

Wellenberg without rest

VISA AE

Niederdorfstr. 10 ✉ 8001 – ✆ 0438 884 444 – reservation@hotel-wellenberg.ch – Fax 0438 884 4 45 – www.hotel-wellenberg.ch **D2**

45 rm – 195/360 CHF 310/450 CHF

♦ Business ♦ Functional ♦

This establishment is located right in the middle of the Old Town. Modern bedrooms, some in Art Deco style. Elegant breakfast room with a sun terrace and pergola.

Claridge Hotel Tiefenau

rm P VISA AE

Steinwiesstr. 8 ✉ 8032 – ✆ 0442 678 787 – info@claridge.ch – Fax 0442 512 4 76 – www.claridge.ch

closed 22 December - 1 January **D3**

31 rm – 179/290 CHF 199/420 CHF

Rest *Orson's* – *(closed Sunday)* Carte 55/106 CHF

♦ Traditional ♦ Stylish ♦

This hotel is housed in a building dating from 1835 and is near the city centre. The guest rooms, each with a different design, are partly outfitted with attractive Louis XV-style furnishings. In Orson's, modern, Asian-inspired cuisine is served.

Opera without rest
Dufourstr. 5 ✉ 8008 – ✆ 0442 589 999 – welcome@operahotel.ch – Fax 0442 589 9 00 – www.operahotel.ch **D3**
62 rm – †195/330 CHF ††300/450 CHF, ☕ 24 CHF
♦ Business ♦ Functional ♦
Directly opposite the opera house to which this business hotel owes its name. Well-maintained rooms with contemporary comforts.

Adler
Rosengasse 10, Hirschenplatz ✉ 8001 – ✆ 0442 669 696 – info@hotel-adler.ch – Fax 0442 669 6 69 – www.hotel-adler.ch **D2**
52 rm ☕ – †140/270 CHF ††210/270 CHF
Rest *Swiss Chuchi* – Carte 40/98 CHF
♦ Business ♦ Functional ♦
Rooms with bright, functional wooden furniture and up-to-the-minute technical facilities are also hung with pictures of the old city by Hans Blum. Country-style ambience in the rustic Swiss-Chuchi restaurant facing the street.

Helmhaus without rest
Schifflände 30 ✉ 8001 – ✆ 0442 669 595 – hotel@helmhaus.ch – Fax 0442 669 5 66 – www.helmhaus.ch **D3**
24 rm ☕ – †175/260 CHF ††240/380 CHF
♦ Business ♦ Functional ♦
In the very heart of the city, this hotel offers rooms most of which have bright and functional décor featuring white built-in furniture. Breakfast on the first floor.

Hirschen without rest
Niederdorfstr. 13 ✉ 8001 – ✆ 0432 683 333 – info@hirschen-zuerich.ch – Fax 0432 683 3 34 – www.hirschen-zuerich.ch **D2**
27 rm ☕ – †135/160 CHF ††175/220 CHF
♦ Family ♦ Functional ♦
The 300 year-old Hirschen offers practical, modern rooms and a wine bar in the vaulted cellars, which date back to the 16C.

Rütli without rest
Zähringerstr. 43 ✉ 8001 – ✆ 0442 545 800 – info@rutli.ch – Fax 0442 545 8 01 – www.rutli.ch – closed 22 December - 3 January **D1**
62 rm ☕ – †145/195 CHF ††220/290 CHF
♦ Business ♦ Functional ♦
This hotel is near the train station and features an attractive reception area, guest rooms furnished in a clean, modern style and a generous breakfast buffet.

Conti
Dufourstr. 1 ✉ 8008 – ✆ 0442 510 666 – ristorante.conti@bindella.ch – Fax 0442 510 6 86 – www.bindella.ch – closed Christmas **D3**
Rest – Carte 64/136 CHF
♦ Italian ♦ Formal ♦
This restaurant, in the immediate vicinity of the Opera House, offers a classic and refined interior with a beautiful high stucco ceiling and a display of artwork.

Kronenhalle
Rämistr. 4 – ✆ 0442 629 900 – kronenhalle@bluewin.ch – Fax 0442 629 9 19 – www.kronenhalle.com –closed 6 - 12 August **D3**
Rest – *(booking essential)* Carte 75/145 CHF
♦ Traditional ♦ Formal ♦
Located in Bellevueplatz, this Zurich institution has visibly maintained its long tradition. The art collection is not to be missed!

Haus Zum Rüden
Limmatquai 42 (1st floor) ✉ 8001 – ✆ 0442 619 566 – info@hauszumrueden.ch – Fax 0442 611 8 04 – www.hauszumrueden.ch closed Christmas, Saturday and Sunday **D2**
Rest – Menu 58 CHF (lunch)/138 CHF – Carte 72/147 CHF
♦ French traditional ♦ Rustic ♦
This restaurant, with an amazing wooden ceiling, is in a 13C guild house. The elegant, historical atmosphere is in keeping with a classic menu.

Zunfthaus zur Zimmerleuten
25/120 VISA MC AE
Limmatquai 40 ✉ 8001 – ✆ 0442 505 363 – zimmerleuten@kramergastronomie.ch – Fax 0442 505 3 64 – www.kramergastronomie.ch
closed Christmas **D2**
Rest – *(1st floor)* Menu 30 CHF (lunch) – Carte 59/120 CHF
Rest *Küferstube* – Menu 38/85 CHF – Carte 36/93 CHF
♦ Traditional ♦ Rustic ♦
The restaurant is located on the 1st floor of the trade guild house, built in 1708. Carved wooden benches lend ambiance to the space. Beautiful terrace. Old taps and dark wood characterize the atmosphere of the küferstube.

Ti Fondata-Stapferstube
30 VISA MC AE
Culmannstr. 45 ✉ 8006 – ✆ 0443 501 100 – massimiliano@restauranti.ch – Fax 0443 501 1 01 – www.restauranti.ch
closed 23 July - 6 August, 24 December - 2 January, Monday from June - September, Saturday lunch, Sunday and Bank Holidays *Plan I* **A3**
Rest – Carte 63/118 CHF
♦ Italian ♦ Friendly ♦
This traditional restaurant, under new management, offers an experience typical of the Ticino region: fresh, traditional cuisine and a large selection of Ticino wines and grappas.

Casa Ferlin
A/C VISA MC AE
Stampfenbachstr. 38 ✉ 8006 – ✆ 0443 623 509 – casaferlin@bluewin.ch – Fax 0443 623 5 34 – www.casaferlin.ch **C-D1**
closed mid July - mid August, 23 December - 2 January, Saturday and Sunday
Rest – *(booking essential)* Menu 52 CHF (lunch)/105 CHF – Carte 63/138 CHF
♦ Italian ♦ Rustic ♦
This classically styled restaurant, with its open fireplace and rustic furnishings, has been family run since 1907: it's one of the oldest Italian restaurants in the city.

Vorderer Sternen
VISA MC AE
Theaterstr. 22 ✉ 8001 – ✆ 0442 514 949 – info@vorderer-sternen.ch – Fax 0442 529 0 63 – www.vorderer-sternen.ch **D3**
Rest – *(1st floor)* Carte 46/85 CHF
♦ Traditional ♦ Rustic ♦
Straightforward café on the ground floor, above it a homely restaurant with dark wood décor. A traditional menu is offered.

Blue Monkey Cocostin
20 VISA MC AE
Stüssihofstatt 3 ✉ 8001 – ✆ 0442 617 618 – kontakt@bluemonkey.ch – Fax 0442 627 1 23 – www.bluemonkey.ch
closed Saturday lunch and Sunday lunch **D2**
Rest – *(1st floor)* Menu 39 CHF (lunch)/56 CHF – Carte 55/98 CHF
♦ Thai ♦ Exotic ♦
A Thai restaurant has been established on two floors of the historic guildhall called the Zunfthaus zur Schneidern. Ground floor bar-bistro, fine dining above.

Oepfelchammer
30 VISA MC AE
Rindermarkt 12 ✉ 8001 – ✆ 0442 512 336 – Fax 0442 627 5 33 – www.oepfelchammer.ch
closed 18 July - 16 August, 24 December - 8 January, Monday, Sunday and Bank Holidays **D2**
Rest – *(1st floor)* Carte 56/95 CHF
♦ Traditional ♦ Rustic ♦
The famous 19C Swiss writer Gottfried Keller was a regular in the wine bar in this 14C establishment. Good solid fare in the restaurant including local specialities.

Rosaly's
VISA MC AE
Freieckgasse 7 ✉ 8001 – ✆ 0442 614 430 – info@rosalys.ch – Fax 0442 614 4 13 – www.rosalys.ch **D3**
Rest – *(closed Saturday lunch and Sunday lunch)* Carte 43/89 CHF
♦ Contemporary ♦ Trendy ♦
Contemporary, simply furnished restaurant with relaxed atmosphere, offering interesting international dishes prepared in a refined traditional style.

SWITZERLAND

Ban Song Thai

VISA MC AE

Kirchgasse 6 ✉ 8001 – ✆ 0442 523 331 – bansong@bluewin.ch – Fax 0442 523 3 15 – www.bansongthai.ch
closed 23 July - 13 August, 24 December - 2 January, Monday from mid May - mid September, Saturday lunch and Sunday **D2**
Rest – *(booking essential)* Menu 62 CHF – Carte 44/97 CHF
♦ Thai ♦ Exotic ♦
This restaurant is very close to the Kunsthaus and Cathedral. Its name evokes its offerings - you are cordially invited by your hosts to take a gastronomic trip to Thailand.

NEAR THE AIRPORT *Plan I*

Renaissance Zürich Hotel

rm 15/300 VISA MC AE

Talackerstr. 1 ✉ 8152 Glattbrugg – ✆ 0448 745 000 – renaissance.zurich@renaissancehotels.com – Fax 0448 745 0 01 – www.renaissancehotels.com/zrhrn **B2**
196 rm – 195/390 CHF 195/580 CHF, 32 CHF – 8 suites
Rest *Asian Place* – *(closed 14 July - 19 August, 24 December - 2 January, Saturday lunch and Sunday)* Carte 54/129 CHF
Rest *Brasserie* – Menu 39 CHF (lunch) – Carte 55/107 CHF
♦ Business ♦ Functional ♦
The hotel features a large, public recreation area in the underground level and spacious rooms with dark-toned solid wood furnishings. Cuisine options in the Asian Place range from Chinese to Thai, Japanese to Indonesian. The Brasserie serves traditional fare.

Hilton Zurich Airport

rm rm 15/150 VISA MC AE

Hohenbühlstr. 10 ✉ 8152 Glattbrugg – ✆ 0448 285 050 – zurich@hilton.ch – Fax 0448 285 1 51 – www.hilton.de/zuerich **B1**
310 rm – 179/369 CHF 179/369 CHF, 35 CHF – 13 suites
Rest *Market Place* – Menu 49 CHF – Carte 58/113 CHF
♦ Chain hotel ♦ Functional ♦
The hotel, near the airport, offers newly renovated rooms filled with light-toned maple furnishings. New executive rooms.

Mövenpick

rm rm 15/220 VISA MC AE

Walter Mittelholzerstr. 8 ✉ 8152 Glattbrugg – ✆ 0448 088 888 – hotel.zurich.airport@moevenpick.com – Fax 0448 088 8 77 – www.moevenpick-zurich.com **B1**
333 rm – 195/345 CHF 195/345 CHF, 31 CHF
Rest *Appenzeller Stube* – *(closed 4 weeks in July - August and Saturday lunch)* Menu 45 CHF (lunch)/85 CHF – Carte 54/121 CHF
Rest *Mövenpick Rest.* – Carte 41/112 CHF – **Rest *Dim Sum*** – *(closed 4 weeks in July - August, Saturday lunch and Sunday)* Carte 42/112 CHF
♦ Chain hotel ♦ Modern ♦
Close to the Autobahn, the hotel offers modern, comfortable, spacious rooms, both superior and standard class, some with private gym equipment. The Appenzeller Stube features a characteristically Swiss atmosphere. International cuisine in the Mövenpick restaurant.

Novotel Zürich Airport Messe

rm rm 15/150 VISA MC AE

Talackerstr. 21 ✉ 8152 Glattbrugg – ✆ 0448 299 000 – h0884@accor.com – Fax 0448 299 9 99 – www.novotel.com **A-B1**
255 rm – 159/205 CHF 159/205 CHF, 25 CHF
Rest – Carte 40/82 CHF
♦ Chain hotel ♦ Modern ♦
On the edge of the city centre, just a few minutes from the new trade show centre, this business hotel offers spacious, modern rooms with light-coloured, solid wood furnishings. Colourful artwork adorns the walls of the modern restaurant where international cuisine is served.

Airport rm 15 VISA

Oberhauserstr. 30 ✉ 8152 Glattbrugg – 0448 094 747 – reservation@hotel-airport.ch – Fax 0448 094 7 74 – www.hotel-airport.ch **B1**

44 rm – 120/190 CHF 150/220 CHF, 20 CHF

Rest *Edo Garden* – Carte 49/112 CHF

Rest *Fujiya of Japan* – Carte 54/113 CHF

♦ Business ♦ Functional ♦

This hotel, with its functional and contemporary furnishings as well as its location – only a few minutes from the airport – particularly meets the needs of business travellers. Edo Garden offers Japanese cuisine and teppanyaki specialities are served in Fujiya of Japan.

Allegra rm 15/30 VISA

Hamelirainstr. 3 ✉ 8302 Kloten – 0448 044 444 – reservation@hotel-allegra.ch – Fax 0448 044 1 41 – www.hotel-allegra.ch **B1**

132 rm – 133/173 CHF 156/226 CHF, 15 CHF

Rest – Carte 39/77 CHF

♦ Business ♦ Modern ♦

The modern business hotel features spacious rooms with functional, colourful furnishings. The hotel has a free bus service to and from the airport.

Fly Away rm VISA

Marktgasse 19 ✉ 8302 Kloten – 0448 044 455 – reservation@hotel-flyaway.ch – Fax 0448 044 4 50 – www.hotel-flyaway.ch

closed 24 December - 2 January (Hotel only) **B1**

42 rm – 120/175 CHF 140/197 CHF, 15 CHF

Rest – Carte 45/92 CHF

♦ Business ♦ Functional ♦

This hotel is near the train station and offers spacious rooms, similar in design layout, furnished in a timeless and functional style.

Vivendi VISA

Europastr. 2 ✉ 8152 Glattbrugg – 0432 113 242 – info@restaurant-vivendi.ch – Fax 0432 113 2 41 – www.restaurant-vivendi.ch

closed 23 December - 2 January, Saturday, Sunday and Bank Holidays

Rest – Carte 48/99 CHF **B1**

♦ Traditional ♦ Friendly ♦

Clean lines and a pleasantly muted colour scheme set the tone in this modern restaurant, which serves traditionally presented cuisine with modern touches.

ENVIRONS OF ZURICH *Plan I*

Eden au Lac 20 VISA

Utoquai 45 ✉ 8008 – 0442 662 525 – info@edenaulac.ch – Fax 0442 662 5 00 – www.edenaulac.ch **B3**

45 rm – 420/490 CHF 640/710 CHF, 40 CHF – 5 suites

Rest – Menu 65 CHF (lunch)/120 CHF – Carte 72/144 CHF

♦ Luxury ♦ Classic ♦

Having set the architectural tone for Zurich's lakeside since 1909, this neo-Baroque hotel is now a listed cultural monument. Inside you will find everything you expect from a luxury hotel. The restaurant offers contemporary cuisine.

Steigenberger Bellerive au Lac rm rm 15/25 VISA

Utoquai 47 ✉ 8008 – 0442 544 000 – bellerive@steigenberger.ch – Fax 0442 544 0 01 – www.zuerich.steigenberger.ch **B3**

51 rm – 230/410 CHF 270/560 CHF

Rest – *(new concept of restoration planned)*

♦ Traditional ♦ Stylish ♦

This hotel, located on the riverbank, offers a modern and elegant 1920s-style décor. The rooms offer the very latest in terms of design, technology and comfort.

SWITZERLAND

Alden Hotel Splügenschloss - (Suitenhotel)

Splügenstr. 2 ✉ 8002 – ☏ 0442 899 999 – welcome@alden.ch – Fax 0442 899 9 98 – www.alden.ch **A3**

10 rm – 700/1500 CHF 700/1500 CHF – 12 suites

Rest *Gourmet* – *(closed Saturday and Sunday)* Menu 65 CHF (lunch) – Carte 88/143 CHF – **Rest *Bar / Bistro*** – Carte 50/95 CHF

♦ Grand Luxury ♦ Design ♦

Behind luxurious facade of this building, dating from 1895, are the most modern suites with elegant designer furnishings. Contemporary cuisine is served in the refined Gourmet.

Ascot

Tessinerplatz 9 ✉ 8002 – ☏ 0442 081 414 – info@ascot.ch – Fax 0442 081 4 20 – www.ascot.ch **A3**

74 rm – 220/440 CHF 220/550 CHF

Rest *Lawrence* – *(closed Saturday and Sunday)* Menu 62 CHF (lunch) – Carte 62/126 CHF

♦ Traditional ♦ Classic ♦

This stylishly decorated establishment offers rooms with furniture in either mahogany or limewashed oak. The Lawrence is decorated in Tudor style.

Inter-Continental Zurich

Badenerstr. 420 ✉ 8040 – ☏ 0444 044 444 – zurich@interconti.com – Fax 0444 044 4 40 – www.intercontinental.com/zurich **A3**

364 rm – 180/370 CHF 180/370 CHF, 30 CHF

Rest *Relais des Arts* – *(closed Saturday and Sunday)* Menu 49 CHF (lunch) – Carte 60/96 CHF

♦ Business ♦ Functional ♦

Among the amenities of this hotel - as well as its comfortable and functional contemporary style rooms - is its accessibility to the airport and the motorway. Guests are invited to dine in the bright and elegant surroundings of the Relais des Arts.

Dolder Waldhaus

Zurich and lake,

Kurhausstr. 20 ✉ 8032 – ☏ 0442 691 000 – reservations@dolderwaldhaus.ch – Fax 0442 691 0 01 – www.dolderwaldhaus.ch **B3**

70 rm – 240/310 CHF 370/460 CHF, 20 CHF

Rest – Carte 57/106 CHF

♦ Business ♦ Classic ♦

This hotel offers a quiet setting and modern guest rooms with a balcony and a view of the city and lake. Modern apartments are available for families and longer-term guests. Restaurant with a refined ambiance and attractive terrace.

Engimatt

Engimattstr. 14 ✉ 8002 – ☏ 0442 841 616 – info@engimatt.ch – Fax 0442 012 5 16 – www.engimatt.ch **A3**

73 rm – 195/280 CHF 235/430 CHF

Rest – Menu 43 CHF (lunch)/79 CHF – Carte 45/84 CHF

♦ Business ♦ Modern ♦

The hotel is near the city centre and is yet surrounded by greenery. All guest rooms feature individual and modern furnishings and a balcony. The Orangerie restaurant is in the style of a modern glass conservatory with a beautiful garden terrace.

Mercure Hotel Stoller

Badenerstr. 357 ✉ 8003 – ☏ 0444 054 747 – h5488@accor.com – Fax 0444 054 8 48 – www.mercure.com **A3**

78 rm – 142/199 CHF 169/210 CHF, 20 CHF

Rest *Ratatouille* – Carte 49/102 CHF

♦ Chain hotel ♦ Functional ♦

On the edge of the city centre close to a tram stop. Rooms in similar style with furnishings in grey veneer. Quieter rooms with balcony to the rear. The two-room Ratatouille is furnished in dark wood: it opens up its street café in summer.

Greulich

Herman Greulich-Str. 56 ✉ 8004 – ✆ 0432 434 243 – mail@greulich.ch – Fax 0432 434 2 00 – www.greulich.ch

closed Christmas **A3**

18 rm – 180/195 CHF 255/275 CHF, 22 CHF

Rest *Restaurant Greulich* – see below

◆ Business ◆ Modern ◆

Garden rooms as well as junior suites in an inner courtyard with a birch grove are highlighted by the clean, modern design of their furnishings.

Krone Unterstrass

Schaffhauserstr. 1 ✉ 8006 – ✆ 0443 605 656 – info@hotel-krone.ch – Fax 0443 605 6 00 – www.hotel-krone.ch **A2**

57 rm – 170/210 CHF 230/250 CHF, 18 CHF

Rest – Carte 49/97 CHF

◆ Business ◆ Modern ◆

Just above the city centre, this establishment offers classically comfortable, newly refitted rooms in a tasteful, modern style. One of the restaurants boasts a splendid open fireplace.

Novotel Zürich City-West

Schiffbaustr. 13 ✉ 8005 – ✆ 0442 762 222 – H2731@accor.com – Fax 0442 762 3 23 – www.novotel.com **A2**

142 rm – 150/299 CHF 150/299 CHF, 25 CHF

Rest – Carte 39/105 CHF

◆ Chain hotel ◆ Modern ◆

The black glass facade of this hotel and the white built-in furnishings of the modern guest rooms offer ample space.

Rigihof

Universitätstr. 101 ✉ 8006 – ✆ 0443 601 200 – info@hotel-rigihof.ch – Fax 0443 601 2 07 – www.hotel-rigihof.ch **B2**

66 rm – 190/275 CHF 250/360 CHF

Rest *Bauhaus* – Menu 42 CHF (dinner) – Carte 50/91 CHF

◆ Business ◆ Design ◆

Designed in timeless Bauhaus style, the hotel offers rooms that are linked in an artistic way to personalities associated with Zurich and are named after them. Bold lines and colours distinguish the Bauhaus restaurant.

Ibis

Schiffbaustr. 11 ✉ 8005 – ✆ 0442 762 100 – h2942@accor.com – Fax 0442 762 1 01 – www.ibishotel.com **A2**

155 rm – 99/134 CHF 99/134 CHF, 14 CHF

Rest – *(closed Saturday lunch and Sunday lunch)* Carte 36/57 CHF

◆ Chain hotel ◆ Minimalist ◆

This hotel is on the site of the old shipbuilding sheds: practical rooms provide all the essentials for what is a very reasonable price.

Rigiblick - Rest Spice (Eppisser) with rm

< Zurich,

Germaniastr. 99 ✉ 8006 – ✆ 0432 551 570 – eppisser@restaurantrigiblick.ch – Fax 0432 551 5 80 – www.restaurantrigiblick.ch

closed Sunday and Monday **B2**

7 rm – 380/750 CHF 380/750 CHF

Rest *Bistro Quadrino* – see below

Rest – *(booking essential)* Menu 54 CHF (lunch)/145 CHF – Carte 105/130 CHF

Spec. Gebratenes Entenlebermedaillon auf glasierten Baby-Bananen mit Sumatra-Kaffeereduktion. Bio Rindsfiletmedaillon aus Ennetbürgen mit Sweet & Sour - Chili Dressing. Knusprige Ananasravioli auf exotischem Früchte Relish.

◆ Euro-asiatic ◆ Fashionable ◆

A clean, pure, elegant style defines the ambiance in the Spice restaurant. Eurasian cuisine is served, as is a spectacular view. Modern junior suites.

SWITZERLAND

XXX **Sonnenberg** < Zurich and lake, VISA

Hitziweg 15 ✉ 8032 – ✆ 0442 669 797 – restaurant@sonnenberg-zh.ch – Fax 0442 669 7 98 – www.sonnenberg-zh.ch **B3**

Rest – *(booking essential)* Carte 69/151 CHF

♦ French traditional ♦ Fashionable ♦

Located high up in the FIFA building with a spectacular view of the city, lake and mountains. The crescent-shaped panoramic restaurant serves classical French cuisine.

XX **Wirtschaft Flühgass** 20 VISA

Zollikerstr. 214 ✉ 8008 – ✆ 0443 811 215 – info@fluehgass.ch – Fax 0444 227 5 32 – www.fluehgass.ch

closed 14 July - 12 August, 23 December - 2 January, Saturday except dinner from November - December and Sunday **B3**

Rest – *(booking essential)* Menu 95/135 CHF – Carte 54/125 CHF

♦ French traditional ♦ Family ♦

The old 16C wine bar is now a congenial restaurant serving cuisine with a traditional French flavour.

XX **Riesbächli** VISA

Zollikerstr. 157 ✉ 8008 – ✆ 0444 222 324 – Fax 0444 222 9 41

closed 15 July - 15 August, 24 December - 10 January, Saturday except dinner from October - February and Sunday **B3**

Rest – Menu 110 CHF – Carte 63/140 CHF

♦ French traditional ♦ Rustic ♦

This traditional restaurant is divided up into three visually separate dining areas. Remarkable choice of wines to go with a range of classic dishes.

XX **Il Gattopardo** VISA

Rotwandstr. 48 ✉ 8004 – ✆ 0434 434 848 – Fax 0432 438 5 51

closed 23 July - 13 August, Saturday lunch and Sunday except dinner from October - March **A3**

Rest – Menu 48 CHF (lunch)/100 CHF – Carte 68/126 CHF

♦ Italian ♦ Formal ♦

High quality classic Italian cuisine, served in an elegant atmosphere. Wine cellar open to diners (groups).

XX **Restaurant Greulich** – Hotel Greulich VISA

Herman Greulich-Str. 56 ✉ 8004 – ✆ 0432 434 243 – mail@greulich.ch – Fax 0432 434 2 00 – www.greulich.ch

closed Christmas, Saturday lunch and Sunday lunch **A3**

Rest – Menu 80 CHF – Carte 73/111 CHF

♦ Innovative ♦ Trendy ♦

Parquet floors, warm colours and clean lines define the ambiance of this restaurant, serving Spanish-inspired cuisine.

XX **Lake Side** < Lake Zurich, 600 VISA

Bellerivestr. 170 ✉ 8008 – ✆ 0443 858 600 – info@lake-side.ch – Fax 0443 858 6 01 – www.lake-side.ch **B3**

Rest – Carte 58/123 CHF

♦ Contemporary ♦ Trendy ♦

Choose from contemporary cooking or sushi at this modern restaurant in Seepark Zürichhorn. The large lakefront terrace is particularly appealing in summer.

X **Josef** VISA

Gasometerstr. 24 ✉ 8005 – ✆ 0442 716 595 – info@josef.ch – Fax 0444 405 5 64 – www.josef.ch

closed New Year, Saturday lunch and Sunday **A2**

Rest – Menu 59 CHF (dinner) – Carte 45/55 CHF

♦ Contemporary ♦ Friendly ♦

This contemporary place with a relaxed atmosphere offers a convincing blend of well-sourced modern cooking and helpful, personable service.

Caduff's Wine Loft

Kanzleistr. 126 ✉ 8004 – ✆ 0442 402 255 – caduff@wineloft.ch – Fax 0442 402 2 56 – www.wineloft.ch

closed 24 December-3 January, Saturday lunch and Sunday **A3**

Rest – *(booking essential)* Menu 52 CHF (lunch)/115 CHF – Carte 76/129 CHF

◆ Contemporary ◆ Trendy ◆

This former wholesale flower market now serves tasty morsels at the long bar and well-sourced dishes accompanied by a fine wine from the famous cellars.

Zentraleck

Zentralstr. 161 ✉ 8003 – ✆ 0444 610 800 – restaurant@zentraleck.ch – www.zentraleck.ch

closed 23 July - 5 August, 1 - 7 January, Saturday and Sunday **A3**

Rest – Menu 95 CHF – Carte 58/103 CHF

◆ Contemporary ◆ Bistro ◆

Pale walls and wood floors both add to the pleasantly smart, up-to-date feel of the Zentraleck, where little pots of kitchen herbs decorate the tables. Contemporary menus.

Ciro

Militärstr. 16 ✉ 8004 – ✆ 0442 417 841 – ciro@swissonline.ch – Fax 0442 911 4 24 **A3**

Rest – *(closed Sunday)* Carte 49/92 CHF

◆ Italian ◆ Friendly ◆

In the welcoming interiors of this restaurant close to the station guests are served with a variety of Italian dishes and the wines to accompany them.

Bistro Quadrino – Rigiblick

Germaniastr. 99 ✉ 8006 – ✆ 0432 551 570 – eppisser@restaurantrigiblick.ch – Fax 0432 551 5 80 – www.restaurantrigiblick.ch

closed Sunday and Monday **B2**

Rest – Carte 51/79 CHF

◆ Contemporary ◆ Trendy ◆

A bistro with a clean-lined design, successfully combining the Ess-Bar, lounge and the walk-in wine display and serving contemporary cuisine. Terrace with a view overlooking Zurich.

Blaue Ente

25

Seefeldstr. 223 (mill Tiefenbrunnen) ✉ 8008 – ✆ 0443 886 840 – info@blaue-ente.ch – Fax 0444 227 7 41 – www.blaue-ente.ch **B3**

Rest – *(booking essential)* Carte 64/107 CHF

◆ Contemporary ◆ Fashionable ◆

This trendy establishment with lots of glass, pipework, and gigantic gearwheels is housed in an old mill. Cheerful atmosphere and good, unfussy cooking in a modern style.

Giesserei

70

Birchstr. 108 ✉ 8050 Zürich-Oerlikon – ✆ 0432 051 010 – info@diegiesserei.ch – Fax 0432 051 0 11 – www.diegiesserei.ch

closed 24 December - 2 January, Sunday in summer and also Saturday in July - August **A2**

Rest – Carte 56/91 CHF

◆ Contemporary ◆ Trendy ◆

A restaurant with a simple setting in two former factories that feature old industrial architecture. Contemporary cuisine is served.

UNITED KINGDOM

UNITED KINGDOM

PROFILE

- **AREA:**
244 157 km²
(94 269 sq mi).
- **POPULATION:**
60 441 000 inhabitants (est. 2005), density = 248 per km².
- **CAPITAL:**
London (conurbation 9 332 000 inhabitants).
- **CURRENCY:**
Pound sterling (£); rate of exchange:
£ 1 = € 1.48 =
US$ 1.95
(Nov 2006).
- **GOVERNMENT:**
Constitutional parliamentary monarchy (since 1707). Member of European Union since 1973.

- **LANGUAGE:**
English.
- **SPECIFIC PUBLIC HOLIDAYS:**
Good Friday (Friday before Easter), first and last Monday in May, last Monday in August, Boxing Day (26 December).
- **LOCAL TIME:**
GMT in winter and GMT + 1 hour in summer.
- **CLIMATE:**
Temperate maritime with cool winters and mild summers (London: January: 3°C, July: 17°C), rainfall evenly distributed throughout the year.

- **INTERNATIONAL DIALLING CODE:**
00 44 followed by area or city code (London: **20**, Glasgow: **141**, etc.) and then the local number.
- **EMERGENCY:**
Police, Fire Brigade, Ambulance: ✆ **999**.
- **ELECTRICITY:**
240 volts AC, 50 Hz.
3 flat pin plugs.

FORMALITIES

Travellers from the European Union (EU), Switzerland, Iceland, the main countries of North and South America and some Commonwealth countries need a national identity card or passport (except for Irish nationals; America: passport required) to visit the United Kingdom for less than three months (tourism or business purpose). For visitors from other countries a visa may be required, in addition to a passport, especially for those wishing to stay for longer than three months. We advise you to check with your embassy before travelling.

Nationals of EU countries require a valid national driving licence. US citizens should hold a driving licence valid for 12 months. Insurance cover is compulsory and it is advisable to have an International Insurance Certificate (Green Card).

MAJOR NEWSPAPERS

The main national daily newspapers are *The Times*, *The Daily Telegraph*, *The Independent*, *The Guardian* and *The Financial Times*. *The Observer* is published on Sundays only and *The Evening Standard* is London's evening newspaper. In Scotland the major two newspapers are *The Herald* (Glasgow) and *The Scotsman* (Edinburgh).

HOTELS

→ CATEGORIES

Accommodation ranges from luxurious 5-star and boutique hotels with a wide choice of amenities to elegant country houses set in splendid grounds offering all kinds of sports and recreation. There are comfortable business hotels and moderately priced establishments as well as a great selection of bed and breakfasts and guesthouses. Some restaurants and pubs also have rooms.

→ PRICE RANGE

The price is per room. Special rates may be on offer at weekends or in quiet periods. There is very little difference between the cost of a single and a double room. A supplement is usually charged for single occupancy of a double room.

→ TAX

Tax (VAT) and service charges are included in the room price.

→ CHECK OUT TIME

Between 10.30am and noon. It is usually possible for luggage to be left with the concierge for collection later in the day.

→ RESERVATIONS

You can book your accommodation by phone or Internet. Ask for written confirmation by fax or email. Some hotels may require a deposit which may be forfeited in the event of a late cancellation. A credit card number is usually required as a guarantee.

→ TIPS FOR HANDLING LUGGAGE

It is usual to give a gratuity to luggage porters at the customer's discretion.

→ BREAKFAST

Breakfast is often not included in the price of the room. It is served between 6.30-7am and 10am. A full cooked English breakfast is generally on offer. Continental breakfast and a self-service buffet with hot dishes are also available.

RESTAURANTS

In addition to the conventional **restaurants** serving international cuisine, there is a multitude of brasseries, ethnic eating places, pizzerias and steak houses. **Gastropubs**, which offer food of an excellent quality at reasonable prices in simple surroundings, have become increasingly popular. In pubs and wine bars you will find less elaborate dishes: pies, steaks, jacket potatoes, pasta dishes, ploughman's lunch (cheese, pickle, bread), sausages and mashed potatoes, stews and curries. Fish and chips shops are an institution: fish in a crisp fried batter and served with golden chipped potatoes.

→ RESERVATIONS

Reservations can be made by phone or by Internet. For gourmet and smart restaurants, it is advisable to book well in advance. A telephone number is usually required and you may also be asked for a credit card number as a guarantee.

Some restaurants may impose a charge if you do not show up or if you do not give adequate notice in the event of a cancellation.

→ THE BILL

The bill (check) usually includes an optional service charge (10-15%) which you may choose not to pay if you are not satisfied with the service. Credit cards are widely accepted. Some restaurants leave the total open so make sure you check before signing the voucher. Occasionally a cover charge is levied for bread and canapés which are offered at the start of the meal.

Breakfast	7am – 10am
Lunch	12.30pm – 2-3pm
Dinner	6.30pm – 10-11pm sometimes later

LOCAL CUISINE

Although the United Kingdom is known for its cosmopolitan and fusion food, many British chefs have become very successful in recent years and modern British cuisine has become fashionable. However there are many regional dishes, all using fresh local products to best advantage, which reflect the nation's history.

The British are very fond of pies of all sorts. **Melton Mowbray pies** consist of succulent lean pork in jelly, with a little anchovy flavouring in a pastry case. Steak and kidney, steak and onion, chicken and mushroom or leek are some of the many varieties of pie baked in puff or shortcrust pastry. **Cornish pasty** is made with beef (skirt), turnip or swede, potatoes and onion baked in a pastry case, shaped like a half-moon, so that it could be carried down the mine to be eaten at midday; sometimes fruit was put at one end to provide a sweet. **Sherwood venison pie** is eaten hot or cold with redcurrant jelly. Game pies are very tasty. Cumberland sauce is not to be missed as an accompaniment to ham or game pies.

→ THE NATIONAL DISHES

Roasted joints of meat are great favourites. The national dish is undoubtedly **roast beef and Yorkshire pudding** – a succulent batter pudding on which the juices of the roasting beef have been allowed to drip – served with horseradish sauce. Lamb is usually eaten with mint sauce, mutton with redcurrant jelly and pork with golden crackling and apple sauce. Other meat dishes include **Dorset jugged steak**, cooked with sausage meat and port; **stuffed chine of pork**, a piece of back of fat pig, stuffed with green herbs; **Welsh honey lamb** cooked in cider with thyme and garlic and basted with honey. **Aylesbury duck** is prepared with green peas. Rabbit is served with forcemeat balls. **Veal collops with orange** are said to have been a favourite dish of Oliver Cromwell. Stews and casseroles are wholesome dishes often served with dumplings: steak and onion, lamb and carrots and in particular, the tasty **Lancashire hotpot. Pigeon casserole** is flavoured with cider and orange.

→ FISH AND SEAFOOD

Fish and seafood dishes include **Dover sole, 'Arnold Bennett omelette'** with haddock and cheese, **mussels in cider and mustard, samphire**, 'poor man's asparagus' eaten with melted butter, **spicy shrimp pie** cooked with wine, mace and cloves in a puff pastry case, **herrings** baked with mint, sage and pepper. **Baked crab and cockle pie** is a Welsh dish and the local sea trout – **sewin** – is stuffed with herbs before cooking. **Char**, a freshwater fish, is either cooked straight from the lakes or potted. Whitstable and Colchester oysters, Cromer crabs, Manx kippers, cockles, scallops, potted shrimps in butter, fresh and potted mackerel, potted salmon are some of the local delicacies. **Fish and chips** is a traditional dish which is popular all over the country.

→ SCOTTISH FLAVOURS

Scotland is renowned for its beef and lamb, for venison and grouse in season and wild and farmed salmon. **Partan Bree**, a tasty crab soup, **Arbroath smokies**, kippers, mutton pies are some of the specialities. **Haggis** served with swede and potatoes – 'haggis, neeps and tatties' – is a tasty dish often accompanied with a dram of whisky. **Kedgeree** is made with salmon, haddock or other fish, rice, hard-boiled eggs and butter and is usually served at breakfast.

→ CHEESE...

Cheese and biscuits are an essential part of a meal, which usually comes after the pudding or sweet course. There is an increasing variety of cheeses on offer as producers are encouraged to innovate. The traditional **Cheddar** is named after the caves in which it is ripened; the blue-veined **Stilton**, Red Leicester, sage Derby, Gloucester, Cheshire (white and blue vein), the delicate Wensleydale and Caerphilly are enjoyed nationwide.

→ ... AND DESSERTS

You should always leave space for a pudding at the end of a meal. **Fruit pies and crumbles** – apple, apple and blackcurrant, gooseberry, plum, cherry, rhubarb – creamy rice puddings, jam roly-poly, spotted dick, steamed jam puddings are delicious with custard. **Trifle** laced with sherry, **bread and butter pudding** and **lemon meringue pie** are scrumptious. **Bakewell tart** is made of shortcrust pastry with an almond and jam filling. **Black caps** are large baked apples filled with brown sugar, citrus peel and raisins. **Devon junket** is laced with rum and brandy. **Cranachan** made with soft fruit and cream and **Atholl Brose**, a mixture of honey, oatmeal, malt whisky and cream are Scottish desserts.

Rich fruit cakes and sponge cakes are teatime treats. Buttery **scones** are served with strawberry jam and clotted cream. Regional specialities include **parkin**, a dark oatmeal cake made with cinnamon, ginger, nutmeg and treacle from Yorkshire; **Bucks cherry bumpers**, cherries in shortcrust pastry; **Goosnargh cakes**, **gingerbread** from the Lake District; Welsh **crempog**, small soft pancakes, eaten hot with butter, and **Bara brith**, a rich moist cake bread, full of raisins, currants, sultanas and citrus peel. **Pikelets** are a cross between a crumpet and a pancake. **Taunton cider cake** includes raisins and a large apple, and the cider is reduced to concentrate the apple flavour.

DRINK

→ WINE

The British have a reputation as serious wine drinkers as is evident from the large quantities imported from all over the world. The local wine industry has improved by leaps and bounds and there are notable wine makers particularly in the south of the country. White wines are often blended from one or more varieties of grape to produce light, dry, fruity wines similar to German wines; red wines are fairly light. A range of fruit-flavoured liqueurs is also available: sloe gin, ginger whisky, whisky mead, raspberry brandy, etc.

→ BEER

However, the most popular alcoholic drink is **beer**, which can be divided into two principal types: **ales** and **lagers**. It can also be described as keg or cask; there are several different beer styles in Britain and Ireland. **Keg beer** is filtered, pasteurised and chilled and then packed into pressurised containers from which it gets its name. **Cask beer** or 'Real Ale' is not filtered, pasteurised or chilled and is served from casks using simple pumps. It is considered by some to be a more characterful, flavoursome and natural beer. **Bitter** is the most popular traditional beer in England and Wales. It is usually paler and drier than **Mild** with a high hop content and slightly bitter taste. **Mild**, which is largely found in Wales, the West Midlands and the North West of England, is a gentle, sweetish and full-flavoured beer. It is generally lower in alcohol and sometimes darker in colour, owing to the addition of caramel or the use of dark malt. **Stout** has a pronounced roast flavour with plenty of hop bitterness. The best dry stouts are brewed in Ireland and are instantly recognisable by their black colour and creamy head. Sweet stouts, including milk or cream stout are sweetened with sugar before being bottled. In addition there are Pale Ales, Brown Ales and Old Ales whilst the term Barley Wine is frequently used by English breweries to describe their strongest beer.

Although Ireland is most famous for its stouts, it also makes a range of beers which have been variously described as malty, buttery, rounded and fruity with a reddish tinge. In Scotland the beers produced are full bodied and malty.

→ WHISKY

The term **whisky** is derived from the Scottish Gaelic *uisage beatha* and the Irish Gaelic *uisce beathadh*, both meaning 'water of life'. When spelt without an *e* it usually refers to **Scotch Whisky** which can be produced only in Scotland by the distillation of malted and unmalted barley, maize, rye and mixtures of two or more of these. It can be divided into 2 basic types: malt whisky and grain whisky. **Malt whisky** is produced from malted barley, traditionally dried over peat fires. After fermentation and two distilling processes using a pot still, the whisky is matured in oak, ideally sherry casks, for at least three years which affects both its colour and flavour. A single malt is the product of an individual distillery. All malts have a distinctive smell and intense flavour. Malt whiskies can be divided into 4 classic regions: the Lowlands, the Highlands, Campbeltown and the Isle of Islay. There are approximately 100 malt whisky distilleries in Scotland. Each distillery produces a completely individual whisky of great complexity. **Grain whisky** is made from a mixture of any malted or unmalted cereal such as maize or wheat and is distilled by a continuous process. It matures more quickly than malt whisky. Very little grain whisky is ever drunk unblended. **De Luxe whiskies** are special because of the ages and qualities of the malts and grain whiskies used in them. They usually include a higher proportion of malts than in most blends. **Irish whiskey** is traditionally made from cereals, distilled three times and matured for at least seven years. The different brands are as individual as straight malt and considered by some to be smoother in character.

→ CIDER

Cider is said to have been brewed from apples since Celtic times. Only bitter apples are used for 'real' West Country cider which is dry in taste, flat and with an alcoholic content of 5.5-5.8%. Full-bodied draught cider is available in pubs. A sparkling cider is produced by fermenting the brew a second time in the bottle. There is also a small production of a strong cider brandy. Genuine perry is made from bitter perry pears.

LONDON

LONDON

Population: 2 914 000 (conurbation 9 332 000) – Altitude: sea level

P./Age Adams/HOA QUI

London is not only the capital of the United Kingdom, but also an international financial centre, a focus of fashion and entertainment, and an important centre for the arts. Before the Middle Ages, the City of London was already a busy commercial centre, while the royal palace and the abbey built by King Edward the Confessor marked the start of the City of Westminster. The differences between them are still evident: the City is the hub of trade and finance, while the West End is renowned for its elegant shops, theatres, clubs, parks, Buckingham Palace and the Houses of Parliament.

This great conurbation started as a Roman settlement on the north bank of the Thames, which evolved into the City of London, the famous square mile of banking houses and commerce. In the 12C London had replaced Winchester as the capital of England and by the 19C was the capital of a worldwide empire. It has grown, without much formal planning, by absorbing the surrounding villages but retained many green open spaces in its extensive royal parks, old commons, churchyards and municipal parks.

London is a great attraction for its tradition and its pageantry, its theatres and concerts, its great range of national and ethnic restaurants and its reputation for clubbing.

WHICH DISTRICT TO CHOOSE

For business visitors it may be best to choose a **hotel** near the City *Plan IX* **L2** or Canary Wharf, whereas for tourists there is a selection of expensive hotels in the West End and cheaper hotels in the neighbouring suburbs. There are also **B&Bs (bed-and-breakfast)** addresses.

The widest range of choice of **restaurants** is to be found in the West End (Soho *Plan II* **H3**, Covent Garden *Plan III* **J3**, South Kensington *Plan X* **DE6**) and Bloomsbury (Charlotte Street) but there are also good places on the South Bank *Plan III* **J4**. Smarter restaurants are in Mayfair *Plan II* **GH3** and St James's *Plan II* **HI4**.

If you are going out for a **drink** the West End, particularly Covent Garden, Soho and Shepherd Market, is well provided

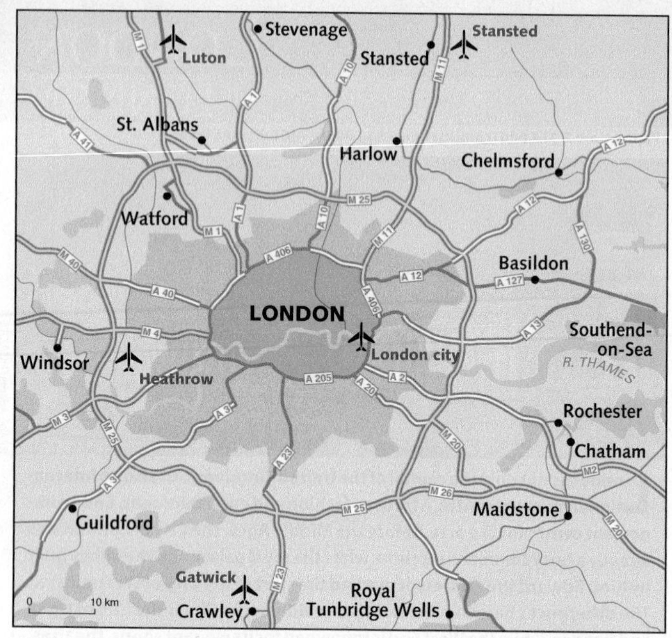

with traditional pubs, wine bars and clubs; the City and Canary Wharf have many pubs and wine bars, although some are closed in the evenings. In Central London or the suburbs, there is a local pub on almost every corner.

PRACTICAL INFORMATION

ARRIVAL – DEPARTURE

Heathrow Airport – About 32 km (20 mi) west of London. ✆ 08700 000 123 (flight information).

From the airport to Central London – By **rail**: **Heathrow Express** (15min) to Paddington Railway Station (5.10am-11.25pm); £14.50, return £27; ✆ 0845 600 1515; www.heathrowexpress.com. By **underground**: Piccadilly Line (50min) to Piccadilly Circus (Mon-Fri 5.15am-11.50am, Sun 7am-11.30pm); £3.80 (Zone 1-6 ticket); ✆ 020 7222 1234; www.tfl.gov.uk. By **bus**: at night N9 shuttles between Heathrow and Central London every 30min. By **taxi**: 40min to 1hr (depending on traffic conditions), £55 approx.

Gatwick Airport – 48 km (30 mi) south of London. ✆ 08700 002 468.

From the airport to Central London – By **rail**: Gatwick Express (30min) to Victoria Station (5am-11.45pm, every 15min); £14, return £25; ✆ 0845 600 1515; www.gatwickexpress.com By **rail**: Southern Trains (40min) to Victoria Station (every 15min); £9; ✆ 0870 830 6000; www.southernrailway.com. By **rail**: Thameslink Rail (30min) to London Bridge or (40min) to King's Cross (day time every 15min; at night every 1hr; £10; ✆ 0845 330 3660). By **coach**: National Express Speedlink (1hr 20min) to Victoria Coach

Station (7am-11.30pm); £6, return £11; ✆ 08705 757 747; www.nationalexpress.com/airport By **taxi**: 90min (subject to traffic conditions), £77 approx.

City Airport – About 13 km (6 mi) east of London. ✆ 020 7646 0000.

From the airport to Central London – By **bus**: Airport Shuttle (10min) to Canning Town and Canary Wharf and (25min) to Liverpool Street (6am-9pm); £3, £3.50, £6.50; ✆ 020 7222 1234; www.tfl.gov.uk; www.londoncityairport.com By **rail**: Docklands Light railway to Bank Station on the underground. By **taxi**: 30min (depending on traffic), £30 approx.

Luton Airport – About 56 km (35 mi) northwest of London. ✆ 01582 405 100.

From the airport to Central London – By **rail**: Thameslink (40min) to King's Cross Station (4.30am-1.30am, 1-3 times per hr); £10.40, return £10.60; ✆ 0845 330 6333; www.thameslink.co.uk By **coach**: Greenline (1hr) to Buckingham Palace Road (near Victoria Station) (4.30am-1.30am, 1-3 times per hr); £9, return £12; ✆ 0870 608 7261; www.greenline.co.uk

Stansted Airport – About 56 km (34 mi) northeast of London. ✆ 0870 000 0303, 01279 680 500.

From the airport to Central London – By **rail**: Stansted Express (45min) to Liverpool Street Station (5.30-0.30am, every 15min); £15; return £25; ✆ 0845 850 0150, www.stanstedexpress.com By **coach**: National Express (1hr 45min) to Victoria Coach Station (24hr service, every 15min); £10, return £15; ✆ 08705 757 747; www.nationalexpress.com By **coach**: Terravision (1hr 15min) to Victoria and (1hr) to Liverpool Street (7.30-1am); £8, return £14; ✆ 020 7630 7196; www.terravision.it

Railway Stations – There are 8 London termini: **Charing Cross** *Plan III* **IJ4** (via London Bridge) Southeast England. **Euston** *Plan VI* **I1** North West England; North Wales. **King's Cross** *Plan VI* **J1** Thameslink to St Albans, Hatfield, Brighton; Northeast England; East Scotland; **Liverpool Street** East Anglia. **Marylebone** *Plan V* **F1** Chiltern Lines to Warwick and Stratford. **Paddington** *Plan VIII* **DE2** Thames Valley; Cotswolds; West of England; South Wales. **St Pancras** *Plan VI* **IJ1** Nottingham; the Peak District. **Victoria** *Plan IV* **GH6** Gatwick Express: Southern England. **Waterloo** *Plan III* **JK45** Southwest England. National Rail Enquiry Line ✆ 08457 484 950; www.nationalrail.co.uk

TRANSPORT

→ UNDERGROUND, DLR, BUS AND TRAMLINK

The underground network is divided into 6 concentric charging zones. The Docklands Light Railway, 5 lines east of Central London, is linked to the underground network. Single tickets can be bought in underground stations at automatic ticket vending machines or the ticket office; at DLR ticket machines; at bus stops at automatic ticket vending machines or from the bus driver. Day Travelcard (off-peak Zones 1 & 2) £5 approx.; 3-day Travelcard (off-peak Zones 1-6) £20 approx. Bus Saver (6 tickets) £6. ✆ 020 7222 1234; www.tfl.gov.uk

→ TAXIS

Taxis are distinctive black cabs, with room for 4 passengers in the back and luggage beside the driver. They are numerous and can be hailed in the street, at a stand, at railway stations and at Heathrow Airport; they are occupied if the illuminated sign on the roof is not lit. Minimum charge £2; £4 for 1 mile, £6.40 for 2 miles, £11 for

4 miles, higher tariff 8pm-6am, at week ends and on public holidays. Tipping is not obligatory but 10% is usual. Tariff by negotiation for journeys outside Greater London. ✆ 020 7222 1234; www.tfl.gov.uk One Number Taxi bookings ✆ 0871 871 8710 (+ £2 if booked by phone).

USEFUL ADDRESSES

→ TOURIST INFORMATION

British Travel Centre, 1 Regent Street *Plan II* **H3**, SW1Y 4XT; Mon-Fri 9am (9.30 Tues)-6.30pm, Sat-Sun 10am-4pm (5pm Sat June-Sept); ✆ 020 8846 9000; Fax 020 7808 3801; www.visitbritain.com **City of London Information Centre** *Plan IX* **L3**, St Paul's Churchyard, EC4; May-Oct daily 9.30am-5pm; otherwise Mon-Sat 9.30am-5pm (12.30pm Sat). ✆ 020 7332 1456/7; www.visitlondon.com; www.london.gov.uk **Southwark Information Centre**, Vinopolis *Plan IX* **L4** 1 Bank End, SE1 9BU; all year, Tues-Sun, 10am-6pm; ✆ 020 7357 9168; www.visitsouthwark.com

→ POST OFFICES

Mon-Fri 9am-5.30pm. Main Post Office, William IV Street, Mon-Fri 8.30am-6.30pm, Sat 9am-5.30pm. Stamps can be bought at post offices, newsagents and supermarkets. Currency exchange without commission.

→ BANKS/CURRENCY EXCHANGE

Open generally Mon-Fri (except public holidays) 9.30am-5pm; some are also open on Saturday mornings. There are 24-hr cash machines (ATMs).

→ EMERGENCY

✆ **999** for Police, Fire Brigade, Ambulance.

EXPLORING LONDON

DIFFERENT FACETS OF THE CITY

It requires four to six days to visit the main sights and museums.

Museums and sights are usually open in summer from 10am to 5pm. Some places close on bank holidays.

London Pass – Free admission to museums, galleries, historic buildings and other attractions; discounts and enhancements; 1-day, 2-day, 3-day and 6-day passes (adult and child); www.leisurepassgroup.com

WESTMINSTER *Plan IV* **HI5** – **Westminster Abbey**: masterpiece of Gothic architecture, the burial place of kings and queens and the setting for state occasions as well as daily worship. **Houses of Parliament**: Royal palace, rebuilt after a fire in 1834 in Victorian Gothic style to contain the House of Commons and the House of Lords. **Whitehall** *Plan IV* **I4**: Broad street lined with government offices and the **Banqueting House** (1619).

MUSEUMS AND GALLERIES – **British Museum** *Plan VI* **I2**: Egyptian antiquities (Rosetta Stone), Oriental artefacts and Greek and Roman exhibits (Elgin marbles from the Parthenon, Roman Portland vase). **Victoria and Albert Museum** *Plan VII* **E5**: Treasures from the Middle Ages to the Renaissance: British works from 1500 to 20C, musical instruments; 18C French furniture. **Science Museum**: Scientific activity of all kinds with practical applications. **National Gallery** *Plan II* **I3**: Major British and European artists, one of the world's finest collections of works of art. **Tate Britain** *Plan IV* **I6**: British School – Gainsborough, Turner, William Blake, Constable, Stubbs, the Pre-Raphaelites and a major collection of 20C work. **Tate Modern** *Plan IX* **L4**: handsome power station converted to display modern art.

ROYAL RESIDENCES – **Buckingham Palace** *Plan II* **H5**: the London home of the monarch set in own garden and flanked by St James's Park and Green Park. **Tower of London** *Plan IX* **N4**: the Tower, where famous prisoners languished in fear of execution, now houses the Crown Jewels, guarded by Yeomen Wardens in Tudor costume. **Kensington Palace** *Plan VII* **D4**: a royal residence with State Apartments by Sir Christopher Wren, Colen Campbell and William Kent. **Clarence House** *Plan IV* **H4**: the residence of the Prince of Wales.

CITY OF LONDON – **St Paul's Cathedral** *Plan IX* **L3**: Baroque masterpiece (1675-1708) by Sir Christopher Wren, setting for the funerals of Nelson, Wellington and Churchill and also daily worship; acoustic effect in the **Whispering Gallery** in the dome; many neighbouring churches also designed by Wren.

THE THAMES – Magnificent view of the river and Central London from the **London Eye** *Plan III* **J4**. River boat cruises from one of the piers downstream past HMS Belfast to **Greenwich** (Cutty Sark, Observatory, Queen's House, National Maritime Museum) and on past the Dome to the **Thames Barrier** or upstream to **Kew** (Kew Gardens), **Richmond** (Marble Hill House, Ham House, Richmond Park) and **Hampton Court** (historic royal palace).

GOURMET TREATS

Afternoon tea, cucumber sandwiches, scones and clotted cream with jam, and cakes with Indian or China tea: *Fortnum & Mason*, 181 Piccadilly; *Richoux*, 172 Piccadilly or 86 Old Brompton Road; most large hotels: some small bakeries and patisseries. **Lunch** in the distinctive ambiance of some museums, galleries and department stores: *V&A Museum* courtyard in summer; the smart frescoed restaurant at *Tate Britain Plan IV* **I6**, *National Portrait Gallery Plan III* **I3**, *Harvey Nichols Plan VII* **F4**, *Fortnum & Mason Plan II* **H3**, *Selfridges Plan II* **G3**. **Brunch**, a halfway meal between breakfast and lunch, and **tea dances**, afternoon tea with live music: some of the larger hotels. **Lunch or dinner cruise** on the Thames. A drink in a pub is a traditional way of starting or rounding off an evening.

SHOPPING

Shops are usually open Mon-Sat 10am to 6/6.30pm; Sun 11am-4pm; late night shopping until 8pm in Knightsbridge (Wed) and in West End (Thurs). Food shops often close later.

The main shopping locations are **Oxford Street** *Plan II* **GH23**: department stores; **Regent Street** *Plan II* **H3**: smarter department stores; **Knightsbridge** *Plan VII* **FG45**: smarter department stores *(Harvey Nichols, Harrods)*; **Jermyn Street** *Plan II* **HI34** and **Savile Row** *Plan II* **H3** men's outfitters and tailors. For luxury goods: **Bond Street** *Plan II* **GH34**, **Jermyn Street**, **Burlington Arcade** *Plan II* **H3**, **Princes Arcade**, **Halkin Street** *Plan II* **G5**. Smaller specialist and trendy shops can be found in **Covent Garden, Neal's Yard** and **Seven Dials**. The main auction houses and art galleries are located in the **West End** (Bond Street, Cork Street and St James's).

MARKETS – Portobello Road *Plan XI* **BCI23** (Sat) may be the best known street market but **Petticoat Lane** *Plan IX* **N23** (Sun-Fri), **Brick Lane** *Plan I* **D2**, **Camden Passage** *Plan I* **C1** (Wed-Thu-Sat), **Charing Cross Collectors Market** *Plan III* **J4** (Sat) and **Greenwich Antiques Market** (Thu-Fri) provide a show and perhaps a bargain too.

WHAT TO BUY – Fashion: knitwear, tweeds, woollen garments; porcelain by Wedgwood, Royal Doulton, Minton, Royal Worcester, glassware by Dartington, marmalade, marmite, tea, whisky; books; art and antiques.

ENTERTAINMENT

Current events – plays, shows, films, concerts etc. – are listed in the following publications: *The London Planner* and *The London Guide* (www.visitlondon.com), both published monthly and available free of charge from Tourist Information Centres, *Welcome to London* (www.welcometolondon.com), *Time Out* (www.timeout.com) and *What's On?*, published weekly and on sale in street kiosks and newsagents. Theatre tickets can be obtained at the theatre, from agents (10% booking fee) or, for same day performances, from the Half-Price Ticket Booth in Leicester Square. Most of the numerous West End theatres are located in and around Shaftesbury Avenue.

Royal Opera House, Covent Garden *Plan III* **J3** – Opera and ballet

London Coliseum *Plan III* **I3** – Opera in English

Royal Albert Hall *Plan X* **E45** – Venue for many events including the Henry Wood Promenade Concerts (mid-July to mid-September)

Royal Festival Hall *Plan III* **J4** – Home to the **London Philharmonic Orchestra**: concerts of orchestral and chamber music and organ recitals; also Queen Elizabeth Hall and Purcell Room

Barbican *Plan IX* **L2** – Home to the **London Symphony Orchestra** and venue for visiting orchestras

Royal National Theatre *Plan III* **J4** – Three stages – **Olivier, Lyttleton** and **Cottesloe** – varied programme

Barbican Arts Centre *Plan IX* **L2** – Varied programme of plays

NIGHTLIFE

The list of venues is so eclectic and fluid, including river boat parties,that it is best to consult the listings publications or their websites *(see Entertainment above)*.

HOTELS – ALPHABETIC LIST

O - P

R

S

T - W

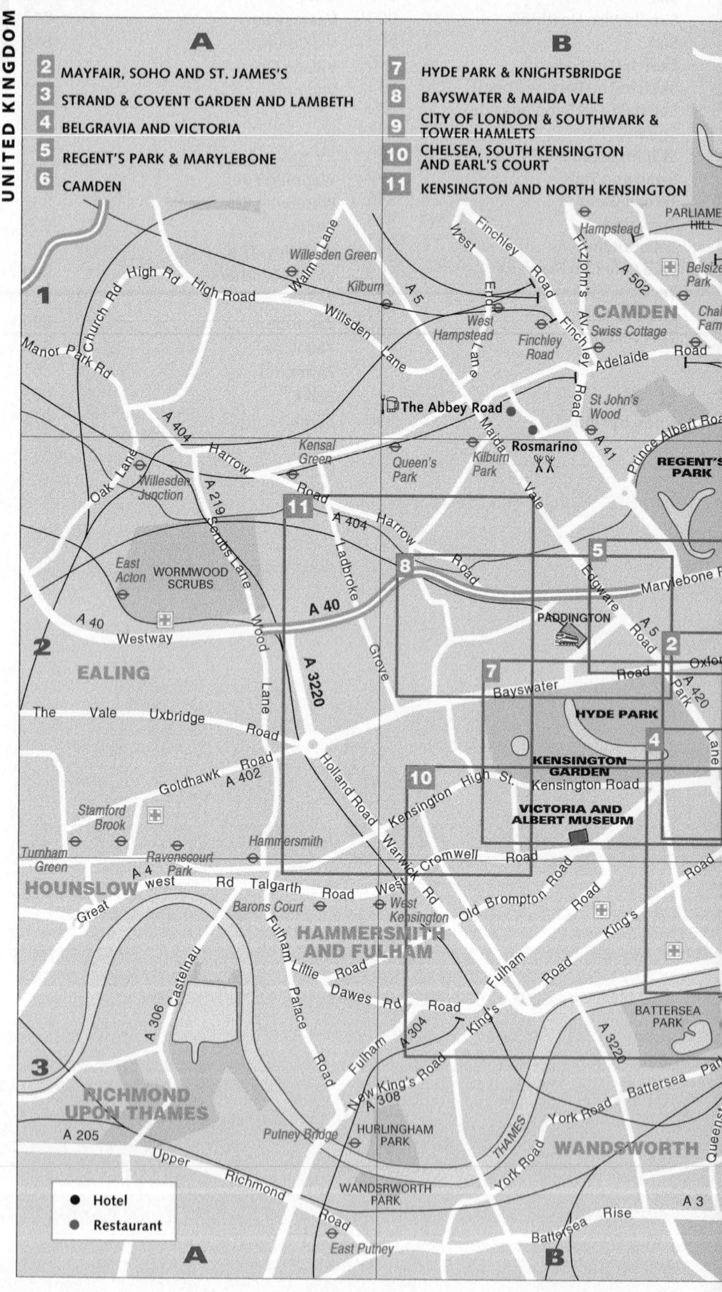
A
B
2 MAYFAIR, SOHO AND ST. JAMES'S
3 STRAND & COVENT GARDEN AND LAMBETH
4 BELGRAVIA AND VICTORIA
5 REGENT'S PARK & MARYLEBONE
6 CAMDEN
7 HYDE PARK & KNIGHTSBRIDGE
8 BAYSWATER & MAIDA VALE
9 CITY OF LONDON & SOUTHWARK & TOWER HAMLETS
10 CHELSEA, SOUTH KENSINGTON AND EARL'S COURT
11 KENSINGTON AND NORTH KENSINGTON
The Abbey Road
Rosmarino
CAMDEN
REGENT'S PARK
WORMWOOD SCRUBS
PADDINGTON
EALING
HYDE PARK
KENSINGTON GARDEN
VICTORIA AND ALBERT MUSEUM
HOUNSLOW
HAMMERSMITH AND FULHAM
BATTERSEA PARK
RICHMOND UPON THAMES
HURLINGHAM PARK
WANDSWORTH
WANDSRWORTH PARK
Hotel
Restaurant

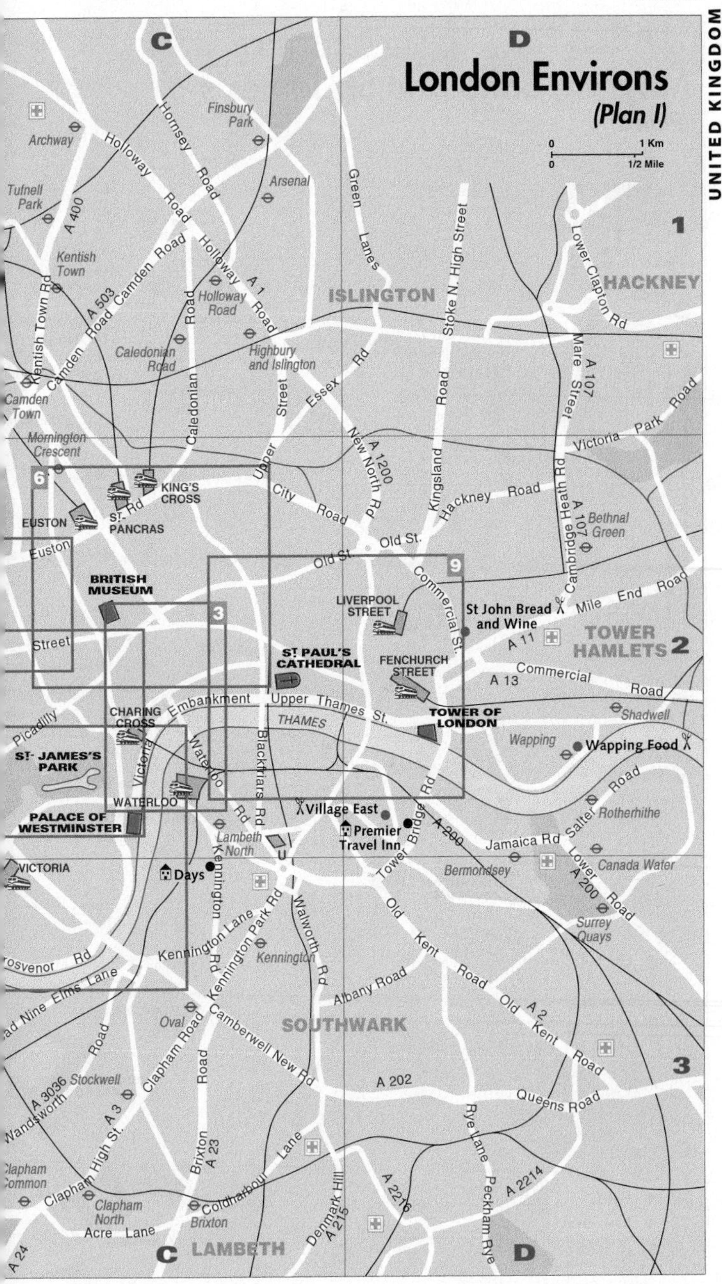
London Environs
(Plan I)
0 1 Km
0 1/2 Mile
C
D
1
2
3
ISLINGTON
HACKNEY
TOWER HAMLETS
SOUTHWARK
LAMBETH
Archway
Tufnell Park
Kentish Town
Camden Town
Mornington Crescent
Finsbury Park
Arsenal
Holloway Road
Caledonian Road
Highbury and Islington
Bethnal Green
Shadwell
Wapping
Rotherhithe
Canada Water
Surrey Quays
Bermondsey
Lambeth North
Kennington
Oval
Stockwell
Clapham Common
Clapham North
Brixton
KING'S CROSS
ST. PANCRAS
EUSTON
BRITISH MUSEUM
LIVERPOOL STREET
ST. PAUL'S CATHEDRAL
FENCHURCH STREET
TOWER OF LONDON
CHARING CROSS
ST. JAMES'S PARK
WATERLOO
PALACE OF WESTMINSTER
VICTORIA
THAMES
St John Bread and Wine
Wapping Food
Village East
Premier Travel Inn
Days
6
9
3

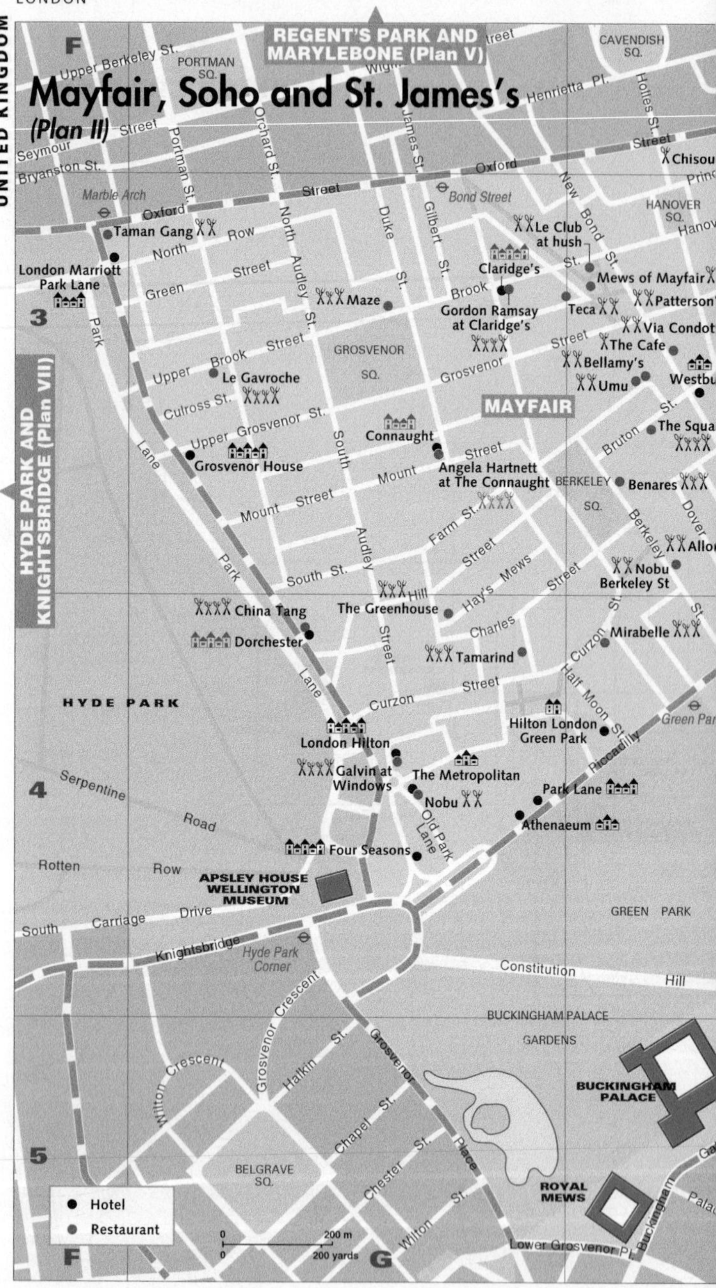
Mayfair, Soho and St. James's
(Plan II)
REGENT'S PARK AND MARYLEBONE (Plan V)
HYDE PARK AND KNIGHTSBRIDGE (Plan VIII)
Taman Gang
London Marriott Park Lane
Maze
Claridge's
Gordon Ramsay at Claridge's
Le Club at hush
Mews of Mayfair
Teca
Patterson
Via Condot
The Cafe
Bellamy's
Umu
Le Gavroche
Grosvenor House
Connaught
Angela Hartnett at The Connaught
The Squa
Benares
Allo
Nobu Berkeley St
Mirabelle
China Tang
Dorchester
The Greenhouse
Tamarind
London Hilton
Hilton London Green Park
Galvin at Windows
The Metropolitan
Nobu
Park Lane
Athenaeum
Four Seasons
APSLEY HOUSE WELLINGTON MUSEUM
MAYFAIR
HYDE PARK
GREEN PARK
BUCKINGHAM PALACE
BUCKINGHAM PALACE GARDENS
ROYAL MEWS
Hotel
Restaurant
200 m
200 yards

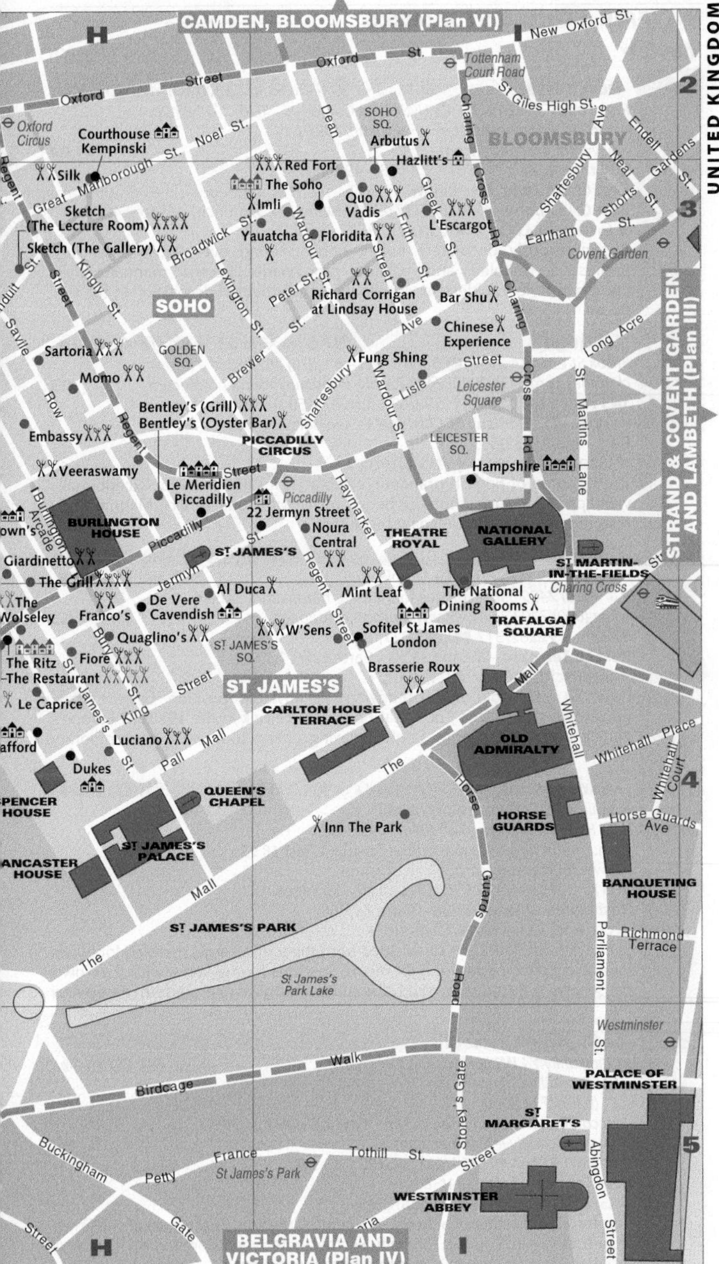
CAMDEN, BLOOMSBURY (Plan VI)
BELGRAVIA AND VICTORIA (Plan IV)
STRAND & COVENT GARDEN AND LAMBETH (Plan III)
SOHO
BLOOMSBURY
ST JAMES'S
PICCADILLY CIRCUS
LEICESTER SQ.
GOLDEN SQ.
SOHO SQ.
ST JAMES'S SQ.
Courthouse Kempinski
Silk
Sketch (The Lecture Room)
Sketch (The Gallery)
Red Fort
The Soho
Imli
Yauatcha
Floridita
Arbutus
Hazlitt's
Quo Vadis
L'Escargot
Richard Corrigan at Lindsay House
Bar Shu
Chinese Experience
Fung Shing
Sartoria
Momo
Bentley's (Grill)
Bentley's (Oyster Bar)
Embassy
Veeraswamy
Le Meridien Piccadilly
22 Jermyn Street
Noura Central
Hampshire
Giardinetto
The Grill
The Wolseley
Franco's
De Vere Cavendish
Al Duca
Mint Leaf
The National Dining Rooms
W'Sens
Sofitel St James London
Brasserie Roux
Quaglino's
The Ritz
The Restaurant
Fiore
Le Caprice
Luciano
Dukes
Inn The Park
BURLINGTON HOUSE
THEATRE ROYAL
NATIONAL GALLERY
ST MARTIN-IN-THE-FIELDS
TRAFALGAR SQUARE
CARLTON HOUSE TERRACE
OLD ADMIRALTY
QUEEN'S CHAPEL
HORSE GUARDS
BANQUETING HOUSE
ST JAMES'S PALACE
SPENCER HOUSE
LANCASTER HOUSE
ST JAMES'S PARK
St James's Park Lake
PALACE OF WESTMINSTER
ST MARGARET'S
WESTMINSTER ABBEY
Oxford Circus
Tottenham Court Road
Covent Garden
Leicester Square
Piccadilly
Charing Cross
Westminster
St James's Park
New Oxford St.
Oxford Street
St Giles High St.
Charing Cross Rd
Shaftesbury Ave
Long Acre
Earlham St.
Regent Street
Haymarket
Piccadilly
Jermyn St.
Pall Mall
The Mall
Whitehall
Horse Guards Road
Birdcage Walk
Tothill St.
Parliament St.
Abingdon Street
Storey's Gate
Buckingham Gate
Petty France
H
I
2
3
4
5

MAYFAIR, SOHO & ST JAMES'S

Mayfair

Plan II

Dorchester

Park Lane ✉ W1A 2HJ – Ⓜ Hyde Park Corner – ✆ (020) 7629 8888 – info@thedorchester.com – Fax (020) 7409 01 14 – www.thedorchester.com **G4**

200 rm – †£423 ††£617, ☕ £28 – 49 suites

Rest *China Tang* – see below

Rest *Grill Room* – *✆ (020) 7317 6336* – Menu £27.50 (lunch) – Carte £40/80

♦ Grand Luxury ♦ Classic ♦

A sumptuously decorated, luxury hotel offering every possible facility. Impressive marbled and pillared promenade. Rooms quintessentially English in style. Faultless service. Bold Scottish-themed decoration in the Grill Room.

Claridge's

Brook St ✉ W1A 2JQ – Ⓜ Bond Street – ✆ (020) 7629 8860 – info@claridges.com – Fax (020) 7499 22 10 – www.maybournehotels.com **G3**

143 rm – †£480/562 ††£598/621, ☕ £27 – 60 suites

Rest *Gordon Ramsay at Claridge's* – see below

Rest – Menu £32/35

♦ Grand Luxury ♦ Art Deco ♦

The epitome of English grandeur, celebrated for its Art Deco. Exceptionally well-appointed and sumptuous bedrooms, all with butler service. Magnificently restored foyer. Relaxed, elegant restaurant.

Grosvenor House

Park Lane ✉ W1K 7TN – Ⓜ Marble Arch – ✆ (020) 7499 6363 – grosvenor.house@marriotthotels.com – Fax (020) 7493 33 41 – www.marriott.com/longh **G3**

378 rm – †£282/317 ††£282/317, ☕ £22 – 74 suites

Rest *La Terrazza* – Menu £25.50 – Carte £27/44.50

♦ Grand Luxury ♦ Classic ♦

Over 70 years old and occupying an enviable position by the Park. Edwardian-style décor. The Great Room, an ice rink in the 1920s, is Europe's largest banqueting room. Bright, relaxing dining room with contemporary feel.

Four Seasons

Hamilton Pl, Park Lane ✉ W1A 1AZ – Ⓜ Hyde Park Corner – ✆ (020) 7499 0888 – fsh.london@fourseasons.com – Fax (020) 7493 18 95 – www.fourseasons.com **G4**

185 rm – †£394/429 ††£458, ☕ £25 – 35 suites

Rest *Lanes* – Menu £28/38 – Carte £47/68

♦ Grand Luxury ♦ Classic ♦

Set back from Park Lane so shielded from the traffic. Large, marbled lobby; its lounge a popular spot for light meals. Spacious rooms, some with their own conservatory. Restaurant's vivid blue and stained glass give modern yet relaxing feel.

Le Meridien Piccadilly

21 Piccadilly ✉ W1J 0BH – Ⓜ Piccadilly Circus – ✆ (020) 7734 8000 – piccadilly.sales@lemeridien.com – Fax (020) 7437 35 74 – www.piccadilly.lemeridien.com **H3**

248 rm – †£364 ††£364/411, ☕ £23 – 18 suites

Rest *Terrace* – Carte £34/38

♦ Grand Luxury ♦ Classic ♦

Comfortable international hotel, in a central location. Boasts one of the finest leisure clubs in London. Individually decorated bedrooms with first class facilities. Modern cuisine in comfortable surroundings.

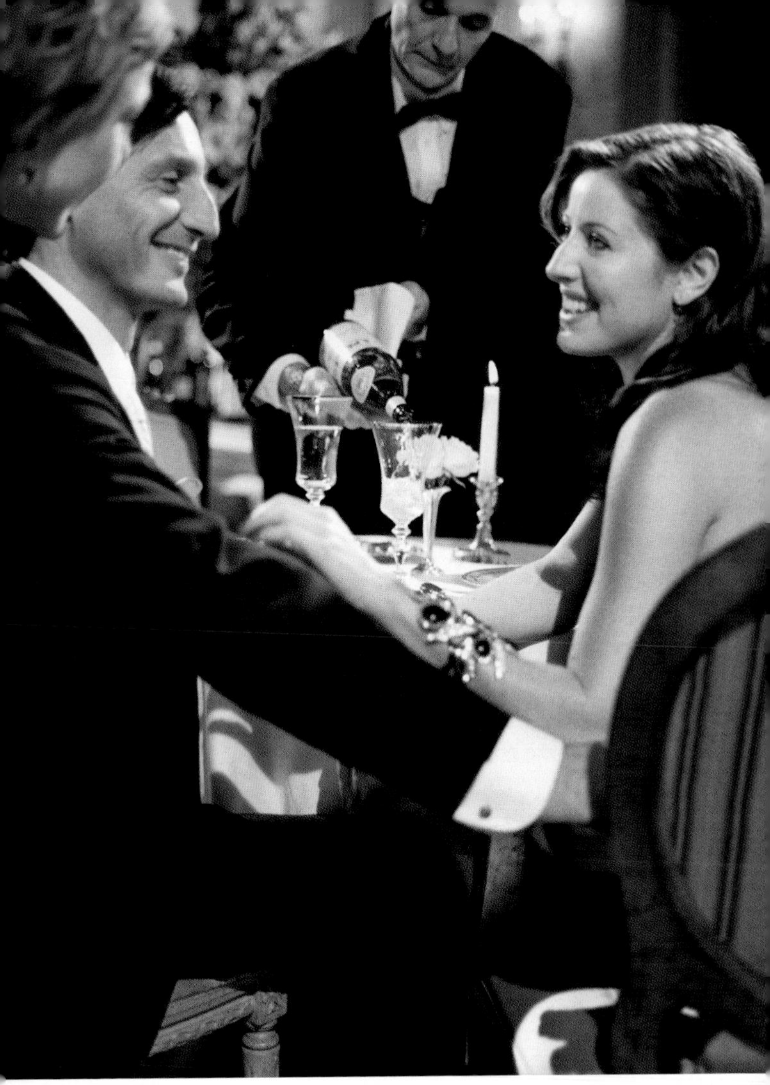

Live in Italian

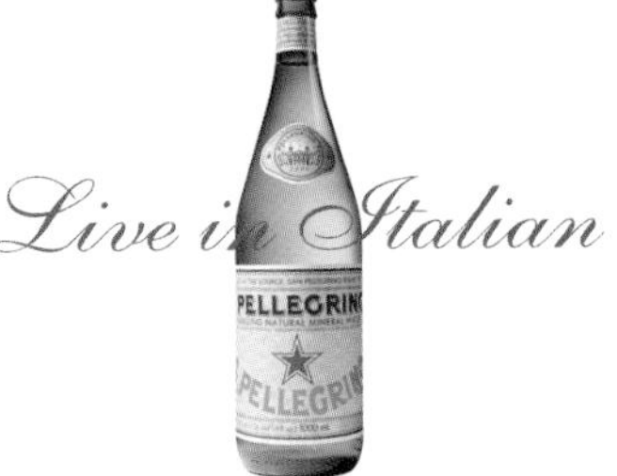

At finer restaurants in Paris, London, New York and of course, Milan.

London Hilton ≤ London, rm

22 Park Lane ✉ W1K 1BE – Ⓜ Hyde Park Corner 1000
– ✆ (020) 7493 8000 – reservations.parklane@hilton.com – Fax (020) 7208 41 42 – www.hilton.co.uk/londonparklane **G4**

395 rm – †£269/434 ††£269/434, ☕ £22 – 55 suites
Rest *Galvin at Windows* – see below – **Rest *Trader Vics*** – ✆ (020) 7208 4113 *(closed lunch Saturday and Sunday)* Carte £32/47
Rest *Park Brasserie* – Carte £29/40

♦ Business ♦ Classic ♦

This 28 storey tower is one of the city's tallest hotels, providing impressive views from the upper floors. Club floor bedrooms are particularly comfortable. Exotic Trader Vics with bamboo and plants. A harpist adds to the relaxed feel of Park Brasserie.

Connaught

16 Carlos Pl ✉ W1K 2AL – Ⓜ Bond Street – ✆ (020) 7499 7070 – info@the-connaught.co.uk – Fax (020) 7495 32 62 – www.maybournegroup.com
68 rm – †£363/480 ††£504, ☕ £29 – 24 suites **G3**
Rest *Angela Hartnett at The Connaught* – see below

♦ Luxury ♦ Classic ♦

19C quintessentially English hotel with country house feel. The grand mahogany staircase leads up to antique furnished rooms. One of the capital's most exclusive addresses. Planned closure March-September for renovation.

Brown's

Albemarle St ✉ W1S 4BP – Ⓜ Green Park – ✆ (020) 7493 6020 – reservations.browns@roccofortehotels.com – Fax (020) 7493 93 81 – www.roccofortehotels.com **H3**
105 rm – †£364 ††£723, ☕ £27 – 12 suites – **Rest *The Grill*** – see below

♦ Luxury♦ Stylish ♦

After a major refit, this urbane hotel offers a swish bar featuring Terence Donovan prints, up-to-the minute rooms and, of course, a quintessentially English lounge for tea.

Park Lane rm 500

Piccadilly ✉ W1J 7BX – Ⓜ Green Park – ✆ (020) 7499 6321 – reservations.theparklane@sheraton.com – Fax (020) 7499 19 65 – www.sheraton.com/theparklane **G4**
285 rm – †£222/341 ††£222/341, ☕ £21 – 20 suites
Rest *Citrus* – ✆ (020) 7290 7364 – Carte £28/35

♦ Luxury ♦ Art Deco ♦

The history of the hotel is reflected in the elegant 'Palm Court' lounge and ballroom, both restored to their Art Deco origins. Bedrooms vary in shape and size. Summer pavement tables in restaurant opposite Green Park.

London Marriott Park Lane

140 Park Lane ✉ W1K 7AA – Ⓜ Marble Arch 75
– ✆ (020) 7493 7000 – mhrs.parklane@marriotthotels.com – Fax (020) 7493 83 33 – www.marriotthotels.com/lonpl **F3**
148 rm – †£276/335 ††£276/335, ☕ £21 – 9 suites
Rest *140 Park Lane* – *(bar lunch Saturday)* Menu £18.50 (lunch) – Carte £30/47

♦ Luxury ♦ Design ♦

Superbly located 'boutique' style hotel at intersection of Park Lane and Oxford Street. Attractive basement health club. Spacious, well-equipped rooms with luxurious elements. Attractive restaurant overlooking Marble Arch.

Westbury rm 120

Bond St ✉ W1S 2YF – Ⓜ Bond Street – ✆ (020) 7629 7755 – sales@westburymayfair.com – Fax (020) 7495 11 63 – www.westburymayfair.com
233 rm – †£152/311 ††£152/311, ☕ £24 – 21 suites **H3**
Rest – *(closed Sunday and Saturday lunch)* Menu £24.50 – Carte £33/49

♦ Business ♦ Modern ♦

Surrounded by London's most fashionable shops; the renowned Polo bar and lounge provide soothing sanctuary. Some suites have their own terrace. Bright, fresh restaurant enhanced by modern art.

UNITED KINGDOM

The Metropolitan

Old Park Lane ✉ W1Y 1LB – Ⓜ Hyde Park Corner – ✆ (020) 7447 1000 – res.lon@metropolitan.como.bz – Fax (020) 7447 11 00 – www.metropolitan.como.bz **G4**

147 rm – £376/411 £411, ☕ £25 – 3 suites – **Rest *Nobu*** – see below

♦ Luxury ♦ Minimalist ♦

Minimalist interior and a voguish reputation make this the favoured hotel of pop stars and celebrities. Innovative design and fashionably attired staff set it apart.

Athenaeum

116 Piccadilly ✉ W1J 7BS – Ⓜ Hyde Park Corner – ✆ (020) 7499 3464 – info@athenaeumhotel.com – Fax (020) 7493 18 60 – www.athenaeumhotel.com

124 rm – £347 £452, ☕ £22 – 33 suites **G4**

Rest *Damask* – *(closed lunch Saturday and Sunday)* Menu £21 (lunch) – Carte £33/43

♦ Luxury ♦ Classic ♦

Built in 1925 as a luxury apartment block. Comfortable bedrooms with video and CD players. Individually designed suites are in an adjacent Edwardian townhouse. Conservatory roofed dining room renowned for its mosaics and malt whiskies.

Hilton London Green Park

Half Moon St ✉ W1J 7BN – Ⓜ Green Park – ✆ (020) 7629 7522 – reservations.greenpark@hilton.com – Fax (020) 7491 89 71 – www.hilton.co.uk **H4**

162 rm – £245/304 £304, ☕ £20 – **Rest** – *(bar lunch)* Carte £25/43

♦ Business ♦ Functional ♦

A row of sympathetically adjoined townhouses, dating from the 1730s. Discreet marble lobby. Bedrooms share the same décor but vary in size and shape. Monet prints decorate light, airy dining room.

Le Gavroche (Roux)

43 Upper Brook St ✉ W1K 7QR – Ⓜ Marble Arch – ✆ (020) 7408 0881 – bookings@le-gavroche.com – Fax (020) 7491 43 87 – www.le-gavroche.co.uk closed Christmas-New Year, Sunday, Saturday lunch and Bank Holidays

Rest – *(booking essential)* Menu £46 (lunch) – Carte £60/117 **G3**

Spec. Foie gras chaud et pastilla de canard à la cannelle. Râble de lapin et galette au parmesan. Le palet au chocolat amer et praline croustillant.

♦ French ♦ Formal ♦

Long-standing, renowned restaurant with a clubby, formal atmosphere. Accomplished classical French cuisine, served by smartly attired and well-drilled staff.

Angela Hartnett at The Connaught

16 Carlos Pl ✉ W1K 2AL – Ⓜ Bond Street – ✆ (020) 7592 1222 – reservations@angelahartnett.com – Fax (020) 7592 12 23 – www.angelahartnett.com

Rest – *(booking essential)* Menu £30/70 **G3**

Spec. Farfalle with roasted ceps and langoustine, truffle shavings. Veal fillet, Parmesan cream, new season peas and leeks. Coconut parfait, exotic fruit salsa and pineapple.

♦ Italian influences ♦ Formal ♦

Stylishly updated landmark, respectful of its history; mahogany panelling softened by enticing artwork. Accomplished modern European cooking with elegant Italian overlay.

Gordon Ramsay at Claridge's

Brook St ✉ W1A 2JQ – Ⓜ Bond Street – ✆ (020) 7499 0099 – reservations@gordonramsay.com – Fax (020) 7499 30 99 – www.gordonramsay.com

Rest – *(booking essential)* Menu £30/70 **G3**

Spec. Roast foie gras with cherries, pickled ginger, cauliflower and almond cream. Braised turbot with caviar, lettuce, root vegetables and coriander sauce. Assiette of pineapple.

♦ Modern ♦ Formal ♦

A thoroughly comfortable dining room with a charming and gracious atmosphere. Serves classically-inspired food executed with a high degree of finesse.

XXXX ✿✿ **The Square** (Howard) — AC 18 VISA MC AE D

6-10 Bruton St ✉ W1J 6PU – Ⓜ Green Park – ✆ (020) 7495 7100 – info@squarerestaurant.com – Fax (020) 7495 71 50 – www.squarerestaurant.com closed 24-26 December, 1 January and lunch Saturday, Sunday and Bank Holidays **H3**

Rest – Menu £30/60

Spec. Lasagne of crab with shellfish and basil cappuccino. Saddle of lamb with shallot purée and rosemary. Assiette of chocolate.

♦ Modern ♦ Formal ♦

Varnished wood and bold abstract canvasses add an air of modernity. Extensive menus offer French-influenced cooking of the highest order. Prompt and efficient service.

XXXX **The Grill** – (at Brown's H.) — AC VISA MC AE D

Albemarle St ✉ W1S 4BP – ✆ (020) 7518 4004 – reservations.browns@roccofortehotels.com – Fax (020) 7518 40 64 **H3-4**

Rest – Menu £25 (lunch) – Carte £38/50

♦ English ♦ Formal ♦

Cavernous room decorated by Olga Polizzi to reflect hotel's heritage: dark wood panelling, lime green banquettes. Well executed and unashamedly traditional English cooking.

XXXX ✿ **Sketch (The Lecture Room)** — AC VISA MC AE D

First Floor, 9 Conduit St ✉ W1S 2XG – Ⓜ Oxford Street – ✆ (0870) 777 4488 – Fax (0870) 777 44 00 – www.sketch.uk.com – closed 25 December, 1 January, Sunday, Monday, Saturday lunch and Bank Holidays **H3**

Rest – *(booking essential)* Menu £35 (lunch) – Carte £39/90

Spec. Custard of foie gras, crab and eel, broccoli and cauliflower. Grilled sea bass with dried fruit marmalade. Chocolate dessert

♦ French ♦ Design ♦

Stunning venue, combining art and food, creating an experience of true sensory stimulation. Vibrant dining options: Lecture Room or Library. Highly original, complex cooking.

XXXX **China Tang** – at Dorchester H. — AC 16 VISA MC AE D

Park Lane ✉ W1A 2HJ – Ⓜ Hyde Park Corner – ✆ (020) 7629 9988 – Fax (020) 7629 95 95 – closed 25 December **G4**

Rest – Carte £35/70

♦ Chinese ♦ Fashionable ♦

A striking mix of Art Deco, Oriental motifs, hand-painted fabrics, mirrors and marbled table tops. Carefully prepared, traditional Cantonese dishes using quality ingredients.

XXXX **Galvin at Windows** – at London Hilton H. — < London,

22 Park Lane ✉ W1Y 1BE – Ⓜ Hyde Park Corner — AC VISA MC AE D

– ✆ (020) 7208 4021 – windows.parklane@hilton.com – Fax (020) 7208 41 42 – www.hilton.co.uk/londonparklane – closed Saturday lunch and Sunday dinner

Rest – Menu £40/60 – Carte £37/65 **G4**

♦ Modern ♦ Formal ♦

On the 28th floor, so the views are spectacular. Contemporary makeover includes silk curtains and opulent gold leaf effect sculpture on ceiling. Upmarket brasserie dishes.

XXX ✿ **The Greenhouse** — AC 12 VISA MC AE D

27a Hay's Mews ✉ W1X 7RJ – Ⓜ Hyde Park Corner – ✆ (020) 7499 3331 – reservations@greenhouserestaurant.co.uk – Fax (020) 7499 53 68 – www.greenhouserestaurant.co.uk closed Christmas-New Year, Sunday, Saturday lunch and Bank Holidays

Rest – Menu £32/60 **G4**

Spec. Atlantic cod with hummus, chickpeas and chicken jus. Anjou pigeon, pomegranate and baby daikon. Poularde de Bresse with black truffle and chestnut.

♦ Innovative ♦ Fashionable ♦

A pleasant courtyard, off a quiet mews, leads to this stylish, discreet restaurant where an elaborate, innovative blend of flavours is much in evidence on inventive menus.

UNITED KINGDOM

XXX ✿

Mirabelle AC 48 VISA MC AE

56 Curzon St ✉ W1J 8PA – Ⓜ Green Park – ☎ (020) 7499 4636 – sales@whitestarline.org.uk – Fax (020) 7499 54 49 – www.whitestarline.org.uk

closed 26 December and 1 January **H4**

Rest – Menu £21 (lunch) – Carte £33/50

Spec. Tarte Tatin of endive with scallops, beurre à l'orange. Bresse pigeon with foie gras and Madeira sauce. Lemon tart

♦ Modern ♦ Design ♦

As celebrated now as it was in the 1950s. Stylish bar with screens and mirrors, leather banquettes and rows of windows. Modern interpretation of some classic dishes.

XXX ✿

Maze AC 10 VISA MC AE

10-13 Grosvenor Sq ✉ W1K 6JP – Ⓜ Bond Street – ☎ (020) 7107 0000 – maze@gordonramsay.com – Fax (020) 7107 00 01 – www.gordonramsay.com **G3**

Rest – Carte £24/35

Spec. Bacon and onion cream, lettuce velouté and tomato. Beef "tongue 'n cheek" with capers, raisins and ginger carrots. Peanut butter and cherry jam sandwich with salted nuts and cherry sorbet .

♦ Contemporary ♦ Fashionable ♦

Part of the Gordon Ramsay empire; a stylish, sleek restaurant. Kitchen eschews usual three-course menus by offering a number of small dishes of variety, precision and flair.

XXX ✿

Benares (Kochhar) AC 22 VISA MC AE

12 Berkeley House, Berkeley Sq ✉ W1J 6BS – Ⓜ Green Park – ☎ (020) 7629 8886 – enquiries@benaresrestaurant.com – Fax (020) 7491 88 83 – www.benaresrestaurant.com

closed 25-26 December, 1 January, lunch Saturday and Sunday **H3**

Rest – Carte £30/44

Spec. Crispy soft shell crab with spicy squid, passion fruit dressing. Ground lamb kebabs with mint and tamarind chutney and green mango salad. Sea bass in coconut milk with coconut kedgeree.

♦ Indian ♦ Formal ♦

Indian restaurant where pools of water scattered with petals and candles compensate for lack of natural light. Original Indian dishes; particularly good value at lunch.

XXX ✿

Embassy AC VISA MC AE

29 Old Burlington St ✉ W1S 3AN – Ⓜ Green Park – ☎ (020) 7851 0956 – embassy@embassylondon.com – Fax (020) 7734 32 24 – www.embassylondon.com

closed 25 December, 1 January, Sunday, Monday and Saturday lunch **H3**

Rest – Menu £23 (lunch) – Carte dinner £27/49

♦ Modern ♦ Trendy ♦

Marble floors, ornate cornicing and a long bar create a characterful, moody dining room. Tables are smartly laid and menus offer accomplished, classic dishes.

XXX ✿

Tamarind AC VISA MC AE

20 Queen St ✉ W1J 5PR – Ⓜ Green Park – ☎ (020) 7629 3561 – manager@tamarindrestaurant.com – Fax (020) 7499 50 34 – www.tamarindrestaurant.com

closed 25-26 December, 1 January and lunch Saturday and Bank Holidays **G4**

Rest – Menu £19 (lunch) – Carte £38/55

Spec. Fillet of John Dory with coconut and coriander, wrapped in banana leaf. Grilled scallops with green, pink and black peppercorns and fenugreek. Leg of lamb with cinnamon, bayleaf, rose petals and spices.

♦ Indian ♦ Fashionable ♦

Gold coloured pillars add to the opulence of this basement room. Windows allow diners the chance to watch the kitchen prepare original and accomplished Indian dishes.

XXX **Bentley's (Grill)** AC ⇸ ⌂6 VISA MC AE

11-15 Swallow St. ✉ W1B 4DG – Ⓜ Piccadilly Circus – ✆ (020) 7734 4756 – www.bentleysoysterbarandgrill.co.uk **H3**

Rest – Carte £34/49

♦ Traditional ♦ Elegant ♦

Entrance into striking bar; panelled staircase to richly decorated restaurant. Carefully sourced seafood or meat dishes enhanced by clean, crisp cooking. Unruffled service.

XXX **Sartoria** AC VISA MC AE

20 Savile Row ✉ W1X 1AE – Ⓜ Green Park – ✆ (020) 7534 7000 – sartoriareservations@conran-restaurants.co.uk – Fax (020) 7534 70 70 – www.conran.com

closed 25-27 December, Sunday, Saturday lunch and Bank Holidays **H3**

Rest – Menu £22 – Carte £30/43

♦ Italian ♦ Formal ♦

In the street renowned for English tailoring, a coolly sophisticated restaurant to suit those looking for classic Italian cooking with modern touches.

XX ✿ **Umu** AC ⇸ VISA MC AE ⓘ

14-16 Bruton Pl ✉ W1J 6LX – Ⓜ Bond Street – ✆ (020) 7499 8881 – enquiries@umurestaurant.com – www.umurestaurant.com

closed between Christmas and New Year, Sunday and Bank Holidays **H3**

Rest – Menu £22/60 – Carte £50/70 ✿

Spec. Sesame tofu with wasabi and sea urchin. Rice with marinated sea bream and pickled vegetables. Grilled toro teriyaki with radish and wasabi.

♦ Japanese ♦ Fashionable ♦

Exclusive neighbourhood location: stylish, discreet interior with central sushi bar. Japanese dishes, specialising in Kyoto cuisine, employing highest quality ingredients.

XX **Bellamy's** AC VISA MC AE

18 Bruton Pl. ✉ W1J 6LY – Ⓜ Bond Street – ✆ (020) 7491 2727 – Fax (020) 7491 99 90 – www.bellamysrestaurant.co.uk **H3**

Rest – Menu £28.50 – Carte £35/57

♦ French ♦ Brasserie ♦

French deli/brasserie tucked down a smart mews. Go past the caviar and cheeses into the restaurant proper for a very traditional, but well-executed, range of Gallic classics.

XX **Giardinetto** AC VISA MC AE ⓘ

39-40 Albermarle St ✉ W1S 4TE – Ⓜ Green Park – ✆ (020) 7493 7091 – info@giardinetto.co.uk – Fax (020) 7493 70 96 – closed Saturday lunch **H3**

Rest – Menu £22 (lunch) – Carte £33/46

♦ Italian ♦ Cosy ♦

Manages to mix a smart, stylish interior with a neighbourhood intimacy. Three dining areas, front being largest. Genoese chef/owner conjures up well-presented Ligurian dishes.

XX **Patterson's** AC ⌂30 VISA MC AE

4 Mill St ✉ W1S 2AX – Ⓜ Oxford Street – ✆ (020) 7499 1308 – pattersonmayfair@btconnect.com – Fax (020) 7491 21 22 – www.pattersonsrestaurant.com

closed Sunday and Saturday lunch **H3**

Rest – Menu £20/35

♦ Contemporary ♦ Intimate ♦

Stylish modern interior in black and white. Elegant tables and attentive service. Modern British cooking with concise wine list and sensible prices.

XX **Teca** AC VISA MC AE

54 Brooks Mews ✉ W1Y 2NY – Ⓜ Bond Street – ✆ (020) 7495 4774 – Fax (020) 7491 35 45 – closed 1 week January, Sunday and Saturday lunch

Rest – Menu £34 (dinner) – Carte lunch £30/49 **GH3**

♦ Italian ♦ Trendy ♦

A glass-enclosed cellar is one of the features of this modern, slick Italian restaurant. Set price menu with the emphasis on fresh, seasonal produce.

UNITED KINGDOM

XX **Alloro** AC 16 VISA MC AE

19-20 Dover St ✉ W1S 4LU – Ⓜ Green Park – ✆ (020) 7495 4768 – Fax (020) 7629 53 48 – closed 25 December-2 January, Saturday lunch, Sunday and Bank Holidays – **Rest** – Menu £26/36 **H3**

♦ Italian ♦ Fashionable ♦

One of the new breed of stylish Italian restaurants with contemporary art and leather seating. A separate, bustling bar. Smoothly run with modern cooking.

XX **Hush** AC VISA MC AE

8 Lancashire Court, Brook St ✉ W1S 1EY – Ⓜ Bond Street – ✆ (020) 7659 1500 – info@hush.co.uk – Fax (020) 7659 15 01 – www.hush.co.uk closed 24-26 December, 31 December-3 January, Sunday and Saturday lunch **Rest** – *(booking essential)* Menu £27 (lunch) – Carte £30/50 **H3**

♦ Modern ♦ Fashionable ♦

Tucked away down a delightful mews courtyard, this brasserie - with sunny courtyard terrace - is an informal and lively little place to eat rustic Mediterranean fare. Upstairs, Le Club serves slightly more refined dining menus.

XX **Nobu** – at The Metropolitan H. AC 40 VISA MC AE

19 Old Park Lane ✉ W1Y 4LB – Ⓜ Hyde Park Corner – ✆ (020) 7447 4747 – confirmations@noburestaurants.com. – Fax (020) 7447 47 49 – www.noburestaurants.com – closed 25 December **G4**

Rest – *(booking essential)* Menu £30/70 – Carte £34/40

Spec. Yellowtail with jalapeño. Black cod with miso. Sashimi salad.

♦ Japanese ♦ Fashionable ♦

Its celebrity clientele has made this one of the most glamorous spots. Staff are fully conversant in the unique menu that adds South American influences to Japanese cooking.

XX **Via Condotti** AC 18 VISA MC AE

23 Conduit St ✉ W1S 2XS – Ⓜ Oxford Circus – ✆ (020) 7493 7050 – info@viacondotti.co.uk – www.viacondotti.co.uk **H3**

Rest – Menu £25

♦ Italian ♦ Fashionable ♦

Chic bar-room leads to restaurant with Italian prints and leather banquettes. Full-flavoured rustic dishes with most ingredients from Italy; chef/owner makes his own breads.

XX **Taman Gang** AC VISA MC AE

141 Park Lane ✉ W1K 7AA – Ⓜ Marble Arch – ✆ (020) 7518 3160 – info@tamangang.com – Fax (020) 7518 31 61 – www.tamangang.com **F3**

Rest – *(dinner only and Sunday lunch)* Carte £26/87

♦ South-East Asian ♦ Exotic ♦

Basement restaurant with largish bar and lounge area. Stylish but intimate décor. Informal and intelligent service. Pan-Asian dishes presented in exciting modern manner.

XX **Mews of Mayfair** VISA MC AE

10-11 Lancashire Court, New Bond St. ✉ W1S 1EY – Ⓜ Bond Street – ✆ (020) 7518 9388 – Fax (020) 7518 93 89 – www.mewsofmayfair.com **H3**

Rest – Menu £19.50/40 – Carte £28/42

♦ Friendly ♦

Converted mews houses once used as storage rooms for Savile Row. Ground floor bar with French windows. Pretty first floor restaurant where eclectic modern menus are served.

XX **Sketch (The Gallery)** AC VISA MC AE

9 Conduit St ✉ W1S 2XG – Ⓜ Oxford Street – ✆ (0870) 777 4488 – info@sketch.uk.com – Fax (0870) 777 44 00 – www.sketch.uk.com closed 25 December, 1 January, Sunday and Bank Holidays **H3**

Rest – *(booking essential) (dinner only)* Carte £30/48

♦ Modern ♦ Trendy ♦

On the ground floor of the Sketch building: daytime video art gallery metamorphoses into evening brasserie with ambient wall projections and light menus with eclectic range.

Nobu Berkeley St

15 Berkeley St ✉ W1J 8DY – Ⓜ Green Park – ✆ (020) 7290 9222 – nobuberkeley@noburestaurants.com – Fax (020) 7290 92 23 – www.noburestaurants.com
closed Sunday and Bank Holidays **H3**
Rest – *(dinner only)* Carte £39/76
Spec. Wood roasted steak with truffles. Toro with miso and jalapeño salsa. Crispy pork belly with spicy miso.
♦ Japanese ♦ Fashionable ♦
In a prime position off Berkeley Square: downstairs 'destination' bar and above, a top quality, soft-hued restaurant. Innovative Japanese dishes with original combinations.

Momo

25 Heddon St ✉ W1B 4BH – Ⓜ Oxford Circus – ✆ (020) 7434 4040 – info@momoresto.com – Fax (020) 7287 04 04 – www.momoresto.com
closed 24-26 and 31 December, 1 January and Sunday lunch **H3**
Rest – Menu £14 (lunch) – Carte £27/40
♦ Moroccan ♦ Exotic ♦
Elaborate adornment of rugs, drapes and ornaments mixed with Arabic music lend an authentic feel to this busy Moroccan restaurant. Helpful service. Popular basement bar.

Veeraswamy

Victory House, 99 Regent St (entrance on Swallow St) ✉ W1B 4RS – Ⓜ Piccadilly Circus – ✆ (020) 7734 1401 – veeraswamy@realindianfood.com – Fax (020) 7439 84 34 – www.realindianfood.com **H3**
Rest – Menu £18 (lunch) – Carte £23/41
♦ Indian ♦ Design ♦
The country's oldest Indian restaurant enlivened by vivid coloured walls and glass screens. The menu also combines the familiar with some modern twists.

Bentley's (Oyster Bar)

11-15 Swallow St. ✉ W1B 4DG – Ⓜ Piccadilly Circus – ✆ (020) 7734 4756 – www.bentleysoysterbarandgrill.co.uk **H3**
Rest – Carte £27/39
♦ Seafood ♦ Bistro ♦
Ground floor location, behind the busy bar. White-jacketed staff open oysters by the bucket load. Interesting seafood menus feature tasty fish pies. Hearty Sunday roasts.

The Cafe – at Sotheby's

34-35 New Bond St ✉ W1A 2AA – Ⓜ Bond Street – ✆ (020) 7293 5077 – Fax (020) 7293 59 20 – www.sothebys.com
closed last 2 weeks August, 22 December-3 January, Saturday, Sunday and Bank Holidays **H3**
Rest – *(booking essential) (lunch only)* Carte £20/31
♦ Modern ♦ Friendly ♦
A velvet rope separates this simple room from the main lobby of this famous auction house. Pleasant service from staff in aprons. Menu is short but well-chosen and light.

Soho

Plan II

The Soho

100

4 Richmond Mews ✉ W1D 3DH – Ⓜ Tottenham Court Road – ✆ (020) 7559 3000 – soho@firmdale.com – Fax (020) 7559 30 03 – www.sohohotel.com **I3**
83 rm – †£282 ††£346, ☕ £19 – 2 suites
Rest *Refuel* – Menu £19.95 (lunch) – Carte £27/35
♦ Luxury ♦ Stylish ♦
Opened in autumn 2004: stylish hotel with two screening rooms, comfy drawing room and up-to-the-minute bedrooms, some vivid, others more muted, all boasting hi-tec extras. Contemporary bar and restaurant.

UNITED KINGDOM

Hampshire
100 VISA

Leicester Sq ✉ WC2H 7LH – Ⓜ Leicester Square – ☎ (020) 7839 9399 – reshamp@radisson.com – Fax (020) 7930 81 22 – www.radissonedwardian.com **I3**

119 rm – £208/282 £270/320, £19 – 5 suites

Rest *The Apex* – *(closed Sunday) (dinner only)* Menu £29.50 – Carte £25/34

◆ Luxury ◆ Classic ◆

The bright lights of the city are literally outside and many rooms overlook the bustling Square. Inside it is tranquil and comfortable with well-appointed bedrooms. Formal yet relaxing dining room with immaculately dressed tables.

Courthouse Kempinski
180 VISA

19-21 Great Marlborough St ✉ W1F 7HL – Ⓜ Oxford Circus – ☎ (020) 7297 5555 – info@courthouse-hotel.com – Fax (020) 7297 55 66 – www.courthouse-hotel.com **H3**

107 rm – £317 £317, £19 – 5 suites

Rest *Silk* – see below

Rest *The Carnaby* – Menu £15.95/18.95 – Carte £22/30

◆ Business ◆ Classic ◆

Striking Grade II listed ex magistrates' court: interior fused imaginatively with original features; for example, the bar incorporates three former cells. Ultra stylish rooms. Informal Carnaby offers extensive French, modern and British menu.

Hazlitt's without rest
VISA

6 Frith St ✉ W1D 3JA – Ⓜ Tottenham Court Road – ☎ (020) 7434 1771 – reservations@hazlitts.co.uk – Fax (020) 7439 15 24 – www.hazlittshotel.com **I3**

22 rm – £206/240 £240 – 1 suite

◆ Townhouse ◆ Historic ◆

A row of three adjoining early 18C town houses and former home of the eponymous essayist. Individual and charming bedrooms, many with antique furniture and Victorian baths.

L'Escargot
60 VISA

48 Greek St ✉ W1D 5EF – Ⓜ Tottenham Court Road – ☎ (020) 7437 2679 – sales@whitestarline.org.uk – Fax (020) 7437 07 90 – www.whitestarline.org.uk **I3**

Rest – *(closed 25-26 December, 1 January, Sunday and Saturday lunch)* Menu £18 (lunch) – Carte £27/29

Rest *Picasso Room* – *(closed August, Sunday, Monday and Saturday lunch)* Menu £26/42

Spec. Escargots en coquille Bordelaise. Smoked haddock with crushed Jersey potatoes, poached egg, mustard sauce. Chocolate fondant, milk ice cream.

◆ Modern ◆ Fashionable ◆

Soho institution. Ground Floor is chic, vibrant brasserie with early-evening buzz of theatre-goers. Finely judged modern dishes. Intimate and more formal upstairs Picasso Room famed for its limited edition art.

Quo Vadis
VISA

26-29 Dean St ✉ W1D 3LL – Ⓜ Tottenham Court Road – ☎ (020) 7437 9585 – whitestarline@org.uk – Fax (020) 7734 75 93 – www.whitestarline.org.uk closed 24-25 December, 1 January, Sunday and Saturday lunch **I3**

Rest – Menu £20 (lunch) – Carte £22/36

◆ Italian ◆ Formal ◆

Stained glass windows and a neon sign hint at the smooth modernity of the interior. Modern artwork abounds. Contemporary cooking and a serious wine list.

Red Fort
VISA

77 Dean St ✉ W1D 3SH – Ⓜ Tottenham Court Road – ☎ (020) 7437 2525 – info@redfort.co.uk – Fax (020) 7434 07 21 – www.redfort.co.uk closed lunch Saturday, Sunday and Bank Holidays **I3**

Rest – Carte £26/46

◆ Indian ◆ Formal ◆

Smart, stylish restaurant with modern water feature and glass ceiling to rear. Seasonally changing menus of authentic dishes handed down over generations.

XX ✿

Richard Corrigan at Lindsay House

AC VISA MC AE

21 Romilly St ✉ W1D 5AF – Ⓜ Leicester Square – ✆ (020) 7439 0450 – richardcorrigan@lindsayhouse.co.uk – Fax (020) 7437 73 49 – www.lindsayhouse.co.uk

closed Christmas, Sunday, Saturday lunch and Bank Holidays **I3**

Rest – Menu £27/52

Spec. Roast scallops with pea gnocchi and crispy bacon. Smoked eel and foie gras terrine with sour apple. Grouse en croute with wild mushroom duxelle.

♦ Contemporary ♦ Intimate ♦

One rings the doorbell before being welcomed into this handsome 18C town house, retaining many original features. Skilled and individual cooking with a subtle Irish hint.

XX

Floridita

AC ⌂8 VISA MC AE

100 Wardour St ✉ W1F 0TN – Ⓜ Tottenham Court Road – ✆ (020) 7314 4000 – Fax (020) 7314 40 40 – www.floriditalondon.com – closed Sunday **I3**

Rest – *(live music and dancing) (dinner only and lunch mid November-December)* Carte £33/39

♦ Latin American ♦ Musical ♦

Buzzy destination where the Latino cuisine is a fiery accompaniment to the vivacious Cuban dancing. Slightly less frenetic upstairs in the Spanish tapas and cocktail bar.

XX

Silk – at Courthouse Kempinski H.

AC VISA MC AE

19-21 Great Marlborough St ✉ W1F 7HL – Ⓜ Oxford Circus – ✆ (020) 7297 5555 – Fax (020) 7297 55 66 – www.courthouse-hotel.com – closed Sunday

Rest – *(dinner only)* Menu £45 – Carte £40/52 **H3**

♦ International ♦ Formal ♦

Stunningly unique former courtroom with original panelling, court benches and glass roof. Menu follows the journey of the Silk Route with Asian, Indian and Italian influences.

X ✿

Arbutus (Demetre)

AC ⁄ VISA MC AE

63-64 Frith St. ✉ W1D 3 JW – Ⓜ Tottenham Court Rd. – ✆ (020) 7734 4545 – info@arbutusrestaurant.co.uk – Fax (020) 7287 86 24 – www.arbutusrestaurant.co.uk **I3**

Rest – Menu £15.50 (lunch) – Carte £26/33

Spec. Chicken oysters with macaroni, lemon thyme and hazelnuts. Saddle of rabbit, cottage pie of shoulder and mustard sauce. Floating Island with pink pralines.

♦ Modern European ♦ Bistro ♦

Dining room and bar that's bright and stylish without trying too hard. Bistro classics turned on their head: poised, carefully crafted cooking - but dishes still pack a punch.

X ✿

Yauatcha

AC ⁄ VISA MC AE

15 Broadwick St ✉ W1F 0DL – Ⓜ Tottenham Court Road – ✆ (020) 7494 8888 – mail@yauatcha.com – Fax (020) 7494 88 89

closed 25-26 December **I3**

Rest – Carte £18/46

Spec. Scallop shumai. Chilean sea bass mooli roll. Stir fry of Mongolian rib-eye beef.

♦ Chinese (Dim Sum) ♦ Fashionable ♦

Converted 1960s post office in heart of Soho. Choose between darker, atmospheric basement or lighter, brighter ground floor. Refined Chinese dishes served on both levels.

X

Imli

AC ⁄ ⌂40 VISA MC AE

167-169 Wardour St ✉ W1F 8WR – Ⓜ Tottenham Court Road – ✆ (020) 7287 4243 – info@imli.co.uk – Fax (020) 7287 42 45 – www.imli.co.uk **I3**

Rest – Carte £14/18

♦ Indian ♦ Bistro ♦

Long, spacious interior is a busy, buzzy place to be: not the venue to while away an evening! Good value, fresh and tasty Indian tapas style dishes prove a popular currency.

UNITED KINGDOM

Bar Shu

28 Frith St ✉ W1D 5LF – Ⓜ Leicester Square – ✆ (020) 7287 8822 – Fax (020) 7287 88 58 – **Rest** – Menu £19.50/24.50 **I3**

◆ Chinese (Szechuan) ◆ Exotic ◆

Three floors decorated in carved wood and lanterns. Truly authentic Szechuan cooking typified by intense heat generated by peppers and chillies. Not for the faint hearted!

Chinese Experience

118 Shaftesbury Ave. ✉ W1D 5EP – Ⓜ Leicester Square – ✆ (020) 7437 0377 – www.chineseexperience.com **I3**

Rest – Menu £23 (dinner) – Carte approx. £17

◆ Chinese ◆ Fashionable ◆

Bright, airy restaurant: sit at long bench or chunky wood tables. Large, good value menus cover a wide range of Chinese dishes. Knowledgable service. A buzzy, informal place.

Fung Shing

15 Lisle St ✉ WC2H 7BE – Ⓜ Leicester Square – ✆ (020) 7437 1539 – Fax (020) 7734 02 84 – www.fung.shing.co.uk – closed 24-26 December and lunch Bank Holidays – **Rest** – Menu £17/35 – Carte £13/24 **I3**

◆ Chinese (Canton) ◆ Friendly ◆

A long-standing Chinese restaurant on the edge of Chinatown. Chatty and pleasant service. A mix of authentic, rustic dishes and the more adventurous chef's specials.

St James's *Plan II*

The Ritz

150 Piccadilly ✉ W1J 9BR – Ⓜ Green Park – ✆ (020) 7493 8181 – enquire@theritzlondon.com – Fax (020) 7493 26 87 – www.theritzlondon.com **H4**

116 rm – †£294/470 ††£352/470, ☕ £30 – 17 suites

Rest ***The Restaurant*** – see below

◆ Grand Luxury ◆ Classic ◆

Opened 1906, a fine example of Louis XVI architecture and decoration. Elegant Palm Court famed for afternoon tea. Many of the lavishly appointed rooms overlook the park.

Sofitel St James London

6 Waterloo Pl ✉ SW1Y 4AN – Ⓜ Piccadilly Circus – ✆ (020) 7747 2200 – h3144@accor-hotels.com – Fax (020) 7747 22 10 – www.sofitelstjames.com **I4**

179 rm – †£417/464 ††£493, ☕ £21 – 7 suites – **Rest** ***Brasserie Roux*** – see below

◆ Luxury ◆ Classic ◆

Grade II listed building in smart Pall Mall location. Classically English interiors include floral Rose Lounge and club-style St. James bar. Comfortable, well-fitted bedrooms.

Stafford

16-18 St James's Pl ✉ SW1A 1NJ – Ⓜ Green Park – ✆ (020) 7493 0111 – info@thestaffordhotel.co.uk – Fax (020) 7493 71 21 – www.thestaffordhotel.co.uk

75 rm – †£282/323 ††£376/393, ☕ £20 – 6 suites **H4**

Rest – *(closed Saturday lunch)* Menu £29.50 (lunch) – Carte £50/62

◆ Traditional ◆ Luxury ◆ Classic ◆

A genteel atmosphere prevails in this elegant and discreet country house in the city. Do not miss the famed American bar. Well-appointed rooms created from 18C stables. Refined, elegant, intimate dining room.

Dukes

35 St James's Pl ✉ SW1A 1NY – Ⓜ Green Park – ✆ (020) 7491 4840 – bookings@dukeshotel.com – Fax (020) 7493 12 64 – www.dukeshotel.com **H4**

82 rm – †£346/370 ††£493, ☕ £20 – 7 suites

Rest – Menu £20 (lunch) – Carte approx. £38

◆ Traditional ◆ Luxury ◆ Classic ◆

Privately owned, discreet and quiet hotel. Traditional bar, famous for its martinis and Cognac collection. Well-kept spacious rooms in a country house style. Refined dining.

De Vere Cavendish

81 Jermyn St ✉ SW1Y 6JF – Ⓜ Piccadilly Circus
– ✆ (020) 7930 2111 – cavendish.reservations@devere-hotels.com
– Fax (020) 7930 21 25 – www.cavendish-london.co.uk **H4**

227 rm – †£305 ††£305, ☐ £21 – 3 suites

Rest – *(closed lunch Saturday, Sunday and Bank Holidays)* Carte £26/38

♦ Business ♦ Design ♦

Modern hotel in heart of Piccadilly. Contemporary, minimalist style of rooms with moody prints of London; top five floors offer far-reaching views over and beyond the city. Classic-styled restaurant overlooks Jermyn Street.

22 Jermyn Street

22 Jermyn St ✉ SW1Y 6HL – Ⓜ Piccadilly Circus
– ✆ (020) 7734 2353 – office@22jermyn.com
– Fax (020) 7734 07 50 – www.22jermyn.com
closed 24-25 December **I3**

5 rm – †£258 ††£258 – 13 suites ††£364/411, ☐ £13

Rest – *(room service only)*

♦ Townhouse ♦ Classic ♦

Discreet entrance amid famous shirt-makers' shops leads to this exclusive boutique hotel. Stylishly decorated bedrooms more than compensate for the lack of lounge space.

The Restaurant – at The Ritz H.

150 Piccadilly ✉ W1V 9DG – Ⓜ Green Park – ✆ (020) 7493 8181
– Fax (020) 7493 26 87 – www.theritzlondon.com **H4**

Rest – *(dancing Friday and Saturday evenings)* Menu £45/65
– Carte £52/89

♦ Traditional ♦ Formal ♦

The height of opulence: magnificent Louis XVI décor with trompe l'œil and ornate gilding. Delightful terrace over Green Park. Refined service, classic and modern menu.

The Wolseley

160 Piccadilly ✉ W1J 9EB – Ⓜ Green Park – ✆ (020) 7499 6996
– Fax (020) 7499 68 88 – www.thewolseley.com
closed dinner 24-25 December, 1 January and August Bank Holiday **H4**

Rest – *(booking essential)* Carte £28/54

♦ Modern ♦ Fashionable ♦

Has the feel of a grand European coffee house: pillars, high vaulted ceiling, mezzanine tables. Menus range from caviar to a hot dog. Also open for breakfasts and tea.

W'Sens

12 Waterloo Pl ✉ SW1Y 4AU – Ⓜ Piccadilly Circus
– ✆ (020) 7484 1355 – info@wsens.co.uk
– Fax (020) 7484 13 66 – www.wsens.co.uk
closed Saturday lunch and Sunday **I4**

Rest – Menu £23/30 – Carte £27/50

♦ Inventive ♦ Trendy ♦

Impressive 19C façade; contrastingly cool interior: dive bar is a destination in its own right and the wildly eclectic restaurant is matched by three intriguing menu sections.

Fiore

33 St James's St ✉ SW1A 1HD – Ⓜ Green Park
– ✆ (020) 7930 7100 – info@fiore-restaurant.co.uk
– Fax (020) 7930 40 70
closed 25 December and 1 January **H4**

Rest – Menu £22/45 – Carte £26/37

♦ Italian ♦ Formal ♦

Formal restaurant with affluent feel appropriate to its setting: full linen cover and smart banquettes. Traditional Italian regional cooking with contemporary embellishments.

XXX **Luciano**

72-73 St. James's St. ✉ SW1A 1PH – Ⓜ Green Park – ☎ (020) 7408 1440 – www.lucianorestaurant.co.uk **H4**

Rest – Menu £22.50 (lunch) – Carte £34/46

♦ Italian ♦ Brasserie ♦

Art Deco, David Collins styled bar leads to restaurant sympathetic to its early 19C heritage. Mix of Italian and English dishes cooked in rustic, wholesome and earthy manner.

XX **Le Caprice**

Arlington House, Arlington St ✉ SW1A 1RT – Ⓜ Green Park – ☎ (020) 7629 2239 – Fax (020) 7493 90 40

closed 25-26 December, 1 January and August Bank Holiday **H4**

Rest – *(Sunday brunch)* Carte £22/54

♦ Modern ♦ Fashionable ♦

Still attracting a fashionable clientele and as busy as ever. Dine at the bar or in the smoothly run restaurant. Food combines timeless classics with modern dishes.

XX **Quaglino's**

16 Bury St ✉ SW1Y 6AL – Ⓜ Green Park – ☎ (020) 7930 6767 – Fax (020) 7839 28 66 – www.conran.com

closed 25 December and 1 January **H4**

Rest – *(booking essential)* Menu £19 (lunch) – Carte £22/38

♦ Modern ♦ Design ♦

Descend the sweeping staircase into the capacious room where a busy and buzzy atmosphere prevails. Watch the chefs prepare everything from osso bucco to fish and chips.

XX **Mint Leaf**

Suffolk Pl ✉ SW1Y 4HX – Ⓜ Piccadilly Circus – ☎ (020) 7930 9020 – reservations@mintleafrestaurant.com – Fax (020) 7930 62 05 – www.mintleafrestaurant.com

closed Bank Holidays and lunch Saturday and Sunday **I4**

Rest – Carte £25/45

♦ Indian ♦ Design ♦

Basement restaurant in theatreland. Cavernous dining room incorporating busy, trendy bar with unique cocktail list and loud music. Helpful service. Contemporary Indian dishes.

XX **Brasserie Roux**

8 Pall Mall ✉ SW1Y 5NG – Ⓜ Piccadilly Circus – ☎ (020) 7968 2900 – h3144-fb4@accor-hotels.com – Fax (020) 7747 22 42 **I4**

Rest – Menu £25 – Carte £23/32

♦ French ♦ Brasserie ♦

Informal, smart, classic brasserie style with large windows making the most of the location. Large menu of French classics with many daily specials; comprehensive wine list.

XX **Franco's**

61 Jermyn St ✉ SW1Y 6LX – Ⓜ Green Park – ☎ (020) 7499 2211 – Fax (020) 7495 13 75 – www.francoslondon.com **H4**

Rest – *(booking essential)* Carte £30/35

♦ Italian ♦ Brasserie ♦

Great all-day menu at 'the café'. Further in, regulars have taken to smart refurbishment. Classic/modern Italian cooking allows bold but refined flavours to shine through.

XX **Noura Central**

22 Lower Regent St ✉ SW1Y 4UJ – Ⓜ Piccadilly Circus – ☎ (020) 7839 2020 – Fax (020) 7839 77 00 – www.noura.co.uk **I3**

Rest – Menu £15/34 – Carte £15/35

♦ Lebanese ♦ Exotic ♦

Eye-catching Lebanese façade, matched by sleek interior design. Buzzy atmosphere enhanced by amplified background music. Large menus cover all aspects of Lebanese cuisine.

Al Duca

4-5 Duke of York St ✉ SW1Y 6LA – Ⓜ Piccadilly Circus – ☏ (020) 7839 3090 – info@alduca-restaurant.co.uk – Fax (020) 7839 40 50 – www.alduca-restaurant.co.uk

closed 23 December-4 January, Sunday and Bank Holidays **H4**

Rest – Menu £21/24

◆ Italian ◆ Friendly ◆

Relaxed, modern, stylish restaurant. Friendly and approachable service of robust and rustic Italian dishes. Set priced menu is good value.

Inn The Park

St James's Park ✉ SW1A 2BJ – Ⓜ Charing Cross – ☏ (020) 7451 9999 – info@innthepark.co.uk – Fax (020) 7451 99 98 – www.innthepark.co.uk

closed 25 December **I4**

Rest – Carte £23/40

◆ Modern ◆ Design ◆

Eco-friendly restaurant with grass covered roof; pleasant views across park and lakes. Super-heated dining terrace. Modern British menus of tasty, wholesome dishes.

Portrait

3rd Floor, National Portrait Gallery, St Martin's Pl ✉ WC2H 0HE – Ⓜ Charing Cross – ☏ (020) 7312 2490 – portrait.restaurant@searcys.co.uk – Fax (020) 7925 02 44 – www.searcys.co.uk *Plan III* **I3**

Rest – *(lunch only Monday-Friday and dinner Thursday-Friday)* Carte £25/39

◆ Modern European ◆ Brasserie ◆

On the top floor of National Portrait Gallery with rooftop local landmark views: a charming spot for lunch. Modern British/European dishes find favour with hungry tourists.

National Dining Rooms

Sainsbury Wing, The National Gallery, Trafalgar Sq ✉ WC2N 5DN – Ⓜ Charing Cross – ☏ (020) 7747 2525 – www.thenationaldiningrooms.co.uk **I34**

Rest – Menu £19.95 – Carte £23/38

◆ British ◆

Set on the East Wing's first floor, you can tuck into cakes in the bakery or grab a prime corner table in the restaurant for great views and proudly seasonal British menus.

STRAND, COVENT GARDEN & LAMBETH

Strand and Covent Garden *Plan III*

Savoy

Strand ✉ WC2R 0EU – Ⓜ Charing Cross – ☏ (020) 7836 4343 – info@the-savoy.co.uk – Fax (020) 7240 60 40 – www.savoy-group.co.uk **J3**

236 rm – †£246/457 ††£269/480, ☕ £25 – 27 suites

Rest *The Savoy Grill* – see below

Rest *Banquette* – Carte £19/40

◆ Grand Luxury ◆ Art Deco ◆

Famous the world over, since 1889, as the epitome of English elegance and style. Celebrated for its Art Deco features and luxurious bedrooms. Banquette is bright, airy, upmarket American diner.

Swissôtel The Howard

Temple Pl ✉ WC2R 2PR – Ⓜ Temple – ☏ (020) 7836 3555 – reservations.london@swissotel.com – Fax (020) 7379 45 47 – www.london.swissotel.com **J3**

177 rm – †£370/541 ††£370/541, ☕ £24 – 12 suites

Rest *Jaan* – see below

◆ Luxury ◆ Modern ◆

Cool elegance is the order of the day at this handsomely appointed hotel. Many of the comfortable rooms enjoy balcony views of the Thames. Attentive service.

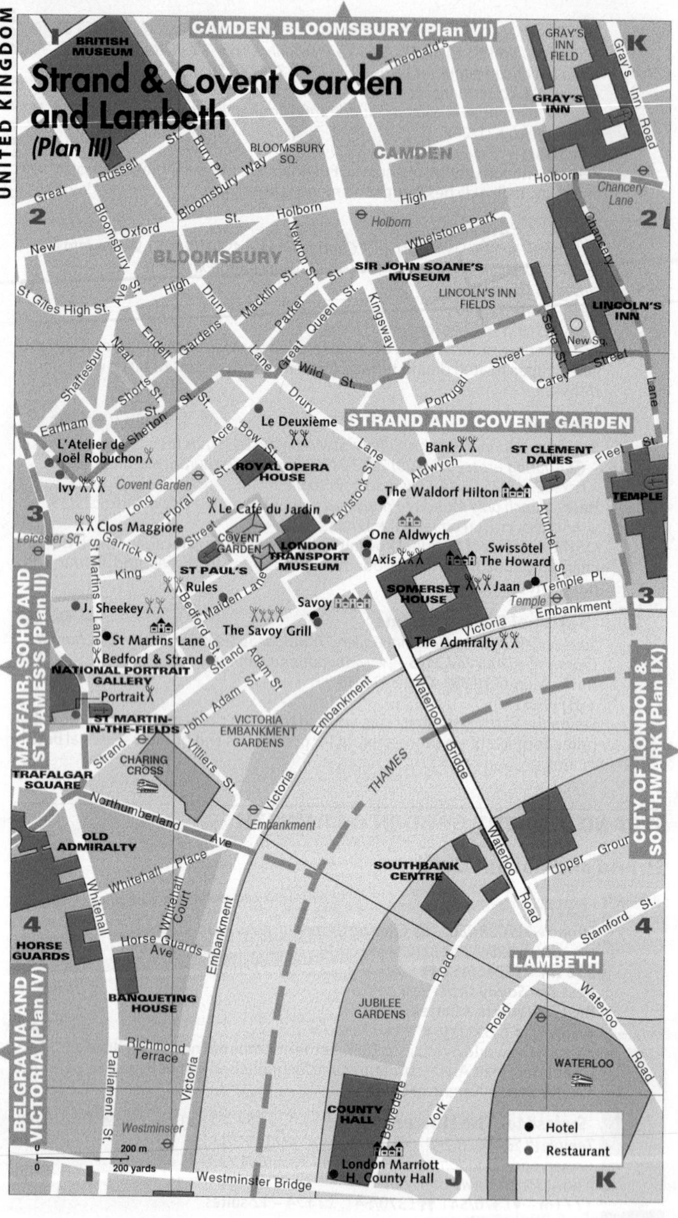
Strand & Covent Garden and Lambeth
(Plan III)
CAMDEN, BLOOMSBURY (Plan VI)
MAYFAIR, SOHO AND ST JAMES'S (Plan II)
CITY OF LONDON & SOUTHWARK (Plan IX)
BELGRAVIA AND VICTORIA (Plan IV)
BRITISH MUSEUM
BLOOMSBURY SQ.
CAMDEN
GRAY'S INN FIELD
GRAY'S INN
BLOOMSBURY
SIR JOHN SOANE'S MUSEUM
LINCOLN'S INN FIELDS
LINCOLN'S INN
STRAND AND COVENT GARDEN
Le Deuxième
L'Atelier de Joël Robuchon
Ivy
Bank
ST CLEMENT DANES
ROYAL OPERA HOUSE
The Waldorf Hilton
TEMPLE
Le Café du Jardin
Clos Maggiore
COVENT GARDEN
LONDON TRANSPORT MUSEUM
One Aldwych
Axis
Swissôtel The Howard
ST PAUL'S
Rules
SOMERSET HOUSE
Jaan
J. Sheekey
Savoy
The Savoy Grill
St Martins Lane
The Admiralty
Bedford & Strand
NATIONAL PORTRAIT GALLERY
Portrait
ST MARTIN-IN-THE-FIELDS
VICTORIA EMBANKMENT GARDENS
CHARING CROSS
TRAFALGAR SQUARE
THAMES
OLD ADMIRALTY
SOUTHBANK CENTRE
HORSE GUARDS
LAMBETH
BANQUETING HOUSE
JUBILEE GARDENS
WATERLOO
COUNTY HALL
London Marriott H. County Hall
Hotel
Restaurant
200 m
200 yards

The Waldorf Hilton

Aldwych ✉ WC2B 4DD – Ⓜ Covent Garden 400 VISA MC AE
– ✆ (020) 7836 2400 – waldorflondon@hilton.com – Fax (02) 7836 72 44
– www.hilton.co.uk/waldorf J3

290 rm – †£233/375 ††£233/375, ☕ £22 – 10 suites – **Rest *Homage*** – *(closed lunch Saturday and Sunday)* Menu £19.50 (lunch) – Carte £29/44

♦ Luxury ♦ Modern ♦

Impressive curved and columned façade: an Edwardian landmark. Basement leisure club. Ornate meeting rooms. Two bedroom styles: one contemporary, one more traditional. Large, modish brasserie with extensive range of modern menus.

One Aldwych

1 Aldwych ✉ WC2B 4RH – Ⓜ Covent Garden – ✆ (020) 7300 1000
– reservations@onealdwych.com – Fax (020) 7300 10 01
– www.onealdwych.com J3

96 rm – †£400 ††£423, ☕ £22 – 9 suites

Rest *Axis* – see below – **Rest *Indigo*** – Carte £30/39

♦ Luxury ♦ Stylish ♦

Decorative Edwardian building, former home to the Morning Post newspaper. Now a stylish and contemporary address with modern artwork, a screening room and hi-tech bedrooms. All-day restaurant looks down on fashionable bar.

St Martins Lane

45 St Martin's Lane ✉ WC2N 4HX – Ⓜ Charing Cross – ✆ (020) 7300 5500
– sml@morganshotelgroup.com – Fax (020) 7300 55 01
– www.morganshotelgroup.com I3

202 rm – †£235/370 ††£259/394, ☕ £19 – 2 suites

Rest *Asia de Cuba* – Carte £36/84

♦ Luxury ♦ Design ♦

The unmistakable hand of Philippe Starck evident at this most contemporary of hotels. Unique and stylish, from the starkly modern lobby to the state-of-the-art rooms. 350 varieties of rum at fashionable Asia de Cuba.

The Savoy Grill – at Savoy H.

Strand ✉ WC2R 0EU – Ⓜ Charing Cross – ✆ (020) 7592 1600 – savoygrill@marcuswareing.com – Fax (020) 7592 16 01 – www.marcuswareing.com J3

Rest – Menu £30/65

Spec. Omelette Arnold Bennett with Scottish lobster and hollandaise. Fillet of beef with potato galette and truffle sauce. Earl Grey tea cream and Garibaldi biscuits.

♦ Modern ♦ Formal ♦

Seamlessly conserving its best traditions, the Grill buzzes at midday and in the evening. Formal service; menu of modern European dishes and the Savoy classics.

Ivy

1 West St ✉ WC2H 9NQ – Ⓜ Leicester Square – ✆ (020) 7836 4751
– Fax (020) 7240 93 33
clodes 25-26 December, 1 January and August Bank Holiday I3

Rest – Carte £24/54

♦ Modern ♦ Fashionable ♦

Wood panelling and stained glass combine with an unpretentious menu to create a veritable institution. A favourite of 'celebrities', so securing a table can be challenging.

Axis – at One Aldwych H.

1 Aldwych ✉ WC2B 4RH – Ⓜ Covent Garden – ✆ (020) 7300 0300 – axis@onealdwych.com – Fax (020) 7300 03 01 – www.onealdwych.co.uk
closed 24 December-4 January, Easter, Sunday, Saturday lunch and Bank Holidays J3

Rest – *(live jazz at dinner Tuesday and Wednesday)* Menu £20 (lunch) – Carte £24/40

♦ Modern ♦ Design ♦

Lower-level room overlooked by gallery bar. Muted tones, black leather chairs and vast futuristic mural appeal to the fashion cognoscenti. Globally-influenced menu.

XXX **Jaan** – at Swissôtel The Howard

Temple Pl ✉ WC2R 2PR – Ⓜ Temple – ☎ (020) 7300 1700 – jaan.london@swissotel.com – Fax (020) 7240 78 16 – www.swissotel-london.com
closed lunch Saturday and Sunday – **Rest** – Menu £33 **J3**

♦ Innovative ♦ Design ♦

Bright room on the ground floor of the hotel with large windows overlooking an attractive terrace. Original cooking - modern French with Cambodian flavours and ingredients.

XX **J. Sheekey**

28-32 St Martin's Court ✉ WC2N 4AL – Ⓜ Leicester Square – ☎ (020) 7240 2565 – Fax (020) 7240 81 14 – closed 25-26 December, 1 January and August Bank Holiday – **Rest** – *(booking essential)* Carte £25/48 **I3**

♦ Seafood ♦ Fashionable ♦

Festooned with photographs of actors and linked to the theatrical world since opening in 1890. Wood panels and alcove tables add famed intimacy. Accomplished seafood cooking.

XX **Rules**

35 Maiden Lane ✉ WC2E 7LB – Ⓜ Leicester Square – ☎ (020) 7836 5314 – info@rules.co.uk – Fax (020) 7497 10 81 – www.rules.co.uk – closed 4 days
Rest – *(booking essential)* Carte £29/40 **J3**

♦ English ♦ Formal ♦

London's oldest restaurant boasts a fine collection of antique cartoons, drawings and paintings. Tradition continues in the menu, specialising in game from its own estate.

XX **Clos Maggiore**

33 King St ✉ WC2 8JD – Ⓜ Leicester Square – ☎ (020) 7379 9696 – enquiries@maggiores.uk.com – Fax (020) 7379 67 67 – www.maggiores.uk.com
closed 24-26 December and 1 January **IJ3**
Rest – Menu £18 (lunch) – Carte £32/43

♦ Innovative ♦ Formal ♦

Walls covered with flowering branches create delightful woodland feel to rear dining area with retractable glass roof. Seriously accomplished, original, rustic French cooking.

XX **The Admiralty**

Somerset House, The Strand ✉ WC2R 1LA – Ⓜ Temple – ☎ (020) 7845 4646 – Fax (020) 7845 46 58 – www.somerset-house.org.uk – closed 23-26 December and dinner Sunday and Bank Holidays – **Rest** – Carte £37/42 **J3**

♦ French ♦ Brasserie ♦

Interconnecting rooms with bold colours and informal service contrast with its setting within the restored Georgian splendour of Somerset House. 'Cuisine de terroir'.

XX **Bank**

1 Kingsway, Aldwych ✉ WC2B 6XF – Ⓜ Covent Garden – ☎ (020) 7379 9797 – aldres@bankrestaurants.com – Fax (020) 7379 50 70 – www.bankrestaurants.com
closed 25 December, 1-2 January and Sunday dinner **J3**
Rest – Menu £16 (lunch) – Carte £24/45

♦ Modern ♦ Brasserie ♦

Ceiling decoration of hanging glass shards creates a high level of interest in this bustling converted bank. Open-plan kitchen provides an extensive array of modern dishes.

XX **Le Deuxième**

65a Long Acre ✉ WC2E 9JH – Ⓜ Covent Garden – ☎ (020) 7379 0033 – Fax (020) 7379 00 66 – www.ledeuxieme.com – closed 25-26 December **J3**
Rest – Menu £15 (lunch) – Carte £24/30

♦ Modern ♦ Brasserie ♦

Caters well for theatregoers: opens early, closes late. Buzzy eatery, quietly decorated in white with subtle lighting. Varied international menu: Japanese to Mediterranean.

L'Atelier de Joël Robuchon

13-15 West St ✉ WC2H 9NE
– Ⓜ Leicester Square – ✆ (020) 7010 8600
– Fax (020) 7010 86 01 **I3**

Rest – Menu £30/60 – Carte £33/79

Rest *La Cuisine* – *(booking essential)* Menu £30/80 – Carte £36/82

Spec. Warm foie gras with roasted peaches. Lamb cutlets with fresh thyme. Crispy frog's legs with sweet garlic mash and parsley coulis.

♦ Innovative ♦ Fashionable ♦

Entrance into trendy atelier with counter seating; upstairs the more structured La Cuisine has wonderfully delicate, precise modern French cooking. Cool top floor lounge bar.

Le Café du Jardin

28 Wellington St ✉ WC2E 7BD – Ⓜ Covent Garden – ✆ (020) 7836 8769
– Fax (020) 7836 41 23 – www.lecafedujardin.com
closed 25-26 December **J3**

Rest – Menu £15 (lunch) – Carte £24/29

♦ Modern ♦ Bistro ♦

Divided into two floors with the downstairs slightly more comfortable. Light and contemporary interior with European-influenced cooking. Ideally placed for the Opera House.

Bedford & Strand

1a Bedford St ✉ WC2E 9HH – Ⓜ Charing Cross – ✆ (020) 7836 3033
– www.bedford-strand.com **J3**

Rest – *(booking essential)* Menu £15.50 – Carte £17/27

♦ Traditional ♦ Wine bar ♦

Basement bistro/wine bar with simple décor and easy-going (if somewhat smokey) atmosphere; kitchen sources well and has a light touch with Italian, French and British dishes.

Lambeth *Plan III*

London Marriott H. County Hall

Westminster Bridge Rd ✉ SE1 7PB – Ⓜ Westminster 70
– ✆ (020) 7928 5200 – mhrs.lonch.salesadmin@marriotthotels.com
– Fax (020) 7928 53 00 – www.marriott.com/lonch **J5**

195 rm – †£281/327 ††£281/327, ☐ £21 – 5 suites

Rest *County Hall* – Menu £23 – Carte £26/44

♦ Luxury ♦ Classic ♦

Occupying the historic County Hall building. Many of the spacious and comfortable bedrooms enjoy river and Parliament outlook. Impressive leisure facilities. World famous views from restaurant.

BELGRAVIA & VICTORIA

Belgravia *Plan IV*

The Berkeley

rm 250

Wilton Pl ✉ SW1X 7RL – Ⓜ Knightsbridge
– ✆ (020) 7235 6000 – info@the-berkeley.co.uk
– Fax (020) 7235 43 30 – www.the-berkeley.com **G4**

189 rm – †£539 ††£598, ☐ £29 – 25 suites

Rest *Pétrus* – see below

Rest *Boxwood Café* – *✆ (020) 7235 1010* – Carte £28/36

♦ Grand Luxury ♦ Stylish ♦

A gracious and discreet hotel. Relax in the gilded and panelled Lutyens lounge or enjoy a swim in the roof-top pool with its retracting roof. Opulent bedrooms. Split-level basement restaurant, divided by bar with modern stylish décor; New York-style dining.

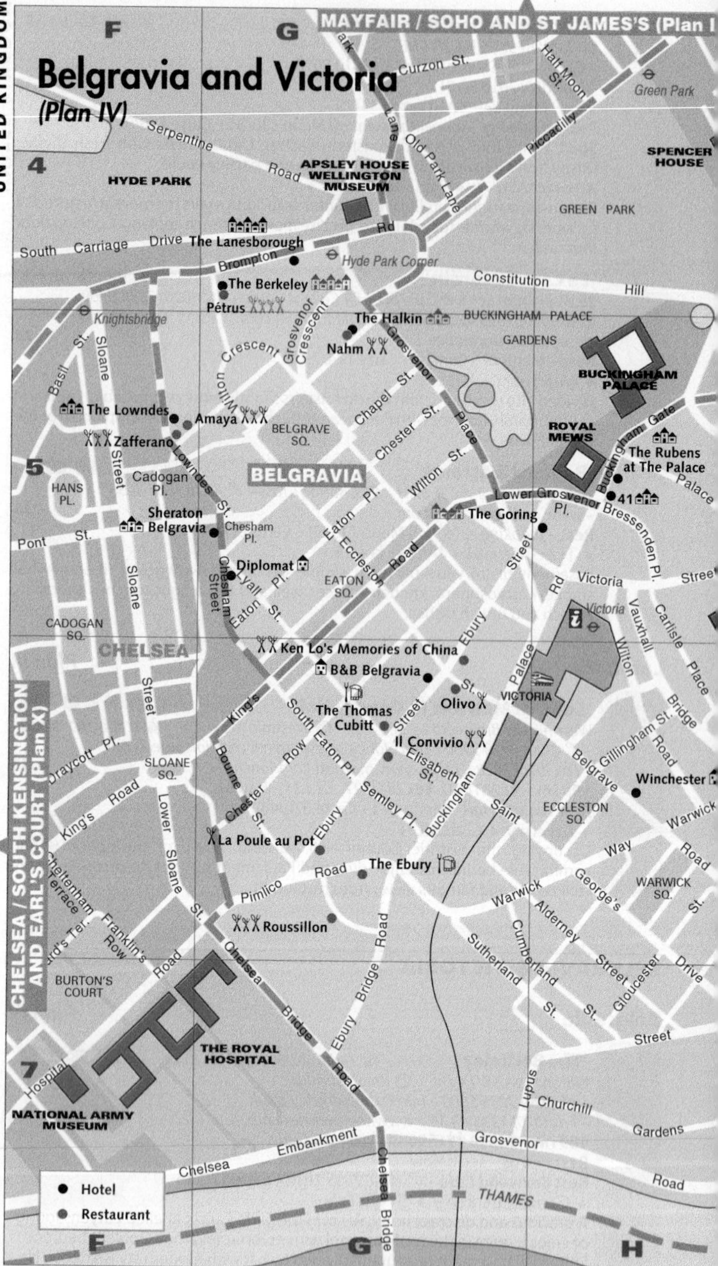
Belgravia and Victoria
(Plan IV)
MAYFAIR / SOHO AND ST JAMES'S (Plan I
CHELSEA / SOUTH KENSINGTON AND EARL'S COURT (Plan X)
HYDE PARK
APSLEY HOUSE WELLINGTON MUSEUM
GREEN PARK
SPENCER HOUSE
BUCKINGHAM PALACE GARDENS
BUCKINGHAM PALACE
ROYAL MEWS
BELGRAVE SQ.
BELGRAVIA
EATON SQ.
HANS PL.
CADOGAN SQ.
CHELSEA
SLOANE SQ.
ECCLESTON SQ.
WARWICK SQ.
BURTON'S COURT
THE ROYAL HOSPITAL
NATIONAL ARMY MUSEUM
VICTORIA
THAMES
The Lanesborough
The Berkeley
Pétrus
The Halkin
Nahm
The Lowndes
Amaya
Zafferano
Sheraton Belgravia
Diplomat
The Rubens at The Palace
41
The Goring
Ken Lo's Memories of China
B&B Belgravia
The Thomas Cubitt
Olivo
Il Convivio
Winchester
La Poule au Pot
The Ebury
Roussillon
Hotel
Restaurant

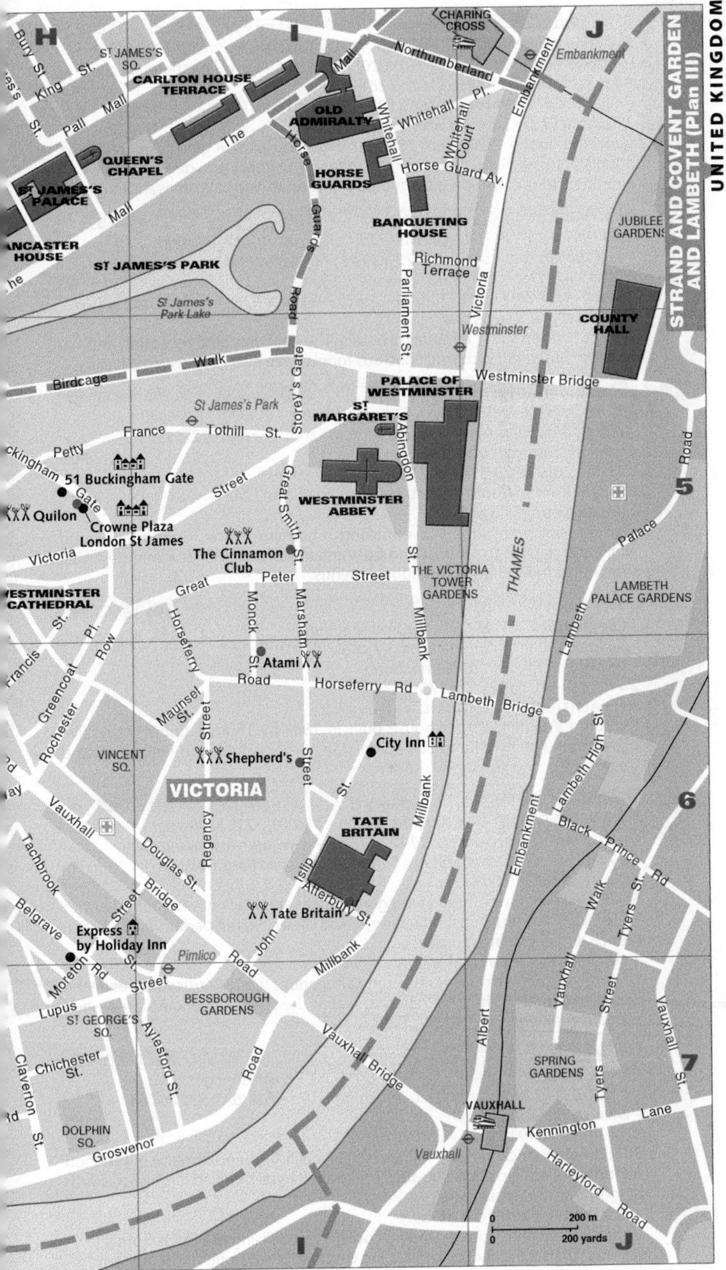

CHARING CROSS
Embankment
Northumberland
Whitehall Pl.
Whitehall Court
Whitehall
Horse Guard Av.
OLD ADMIRALTY
HORSE GUARDS
BANQUETING HOUSE
ST JAMES'S SQ.
CARLTON HOUSE TERRACE
King St.
Bury St.
Pall Mall
The Mall
QUEEN'S CHAPEL
ST JAMES'S PALACE
LANCASTER HOUSE
ST JAMES'S PARK
St James's Park Lake
Horse Guards Road
Storey's Gate
Birdcage Walk
St James's Park
Richmond Terrace
Parliament St.
Victoria Embankment
Westminster
Westminster Bridge
COUNTY HALL
JUBILEE GARDENS
STRAND AND COVENT GARDEN AND LAMBETH (Plan III)
UNITED KINGDOM
PALACE OF WESTMINSTER
ST MARGARET'S
Abingdon St.
WESTMINSTER ABBEY
Petty France
Tothill St.
Buckingham Gate
51 Buckingham Gate
Quilon
Crowne Plaza London St James
Victoria Street
The Cinnamon Club
Great Smith St.
Great Peter Street
THE VICTORIA TOWER GARDENS
THAMES
Lambeth Palace Road
LAMBETH PALACE GARDENS
WESTMINSTER CATHEDRAL
Francis St.
Greencoat Pl.
Rochester Row
Horseferry Road
Monck St.
Marsham St.
Atami
Millbank
Lambeth Bridge
Maunsel St.
Page Street
Shepherd's
City Inn
VINCENT SQ.
VICTORIA
John Islip St.
TATE BRITAIN
Lambeth High St.
Black Prince Rd
Vauxhall Bridge Road
Tachbrook Street
Douglas St.
Regency Street
Atterbury St.
Tate Britain
Belgrave Road
Express by Holiday Inn
Moreton St.
Pimlico
Lupus Street
St. George's Sq.
BESSBOROUGH GARDENS
Vauxhall Walk
Tyers St.
Tyers Street
Vauxhall St.
Albert Embankment
SPRING GARDENS
Chichester St.
Aylesford St.
Claverton St.
DOLPHIN SQ.
Grosvenor Road
VAUXHALL
Vauxhall
Kennington Lane
Harleyford Road
0 200 m
0 200 yards
H
I
J
5
6
7

UNITED KINGDOM

The Lanesborough

VISA AE 90 rm

Hyde Park Corner ✉ SW1X 7TA – Ⓜ Hyde Park Corner – ☎ (020) 7259 5599 – info@lanesborough.com – Fax (020) 7259 56 06 – www.lanesborough.com

86 rm – £370/511 £511, ☕ £28 – 9 suites **G4**

Rest *The Conservatory* – Menu £24/48 – Carte £46/79

◆ Grand Luxury ◆ Classic ◆

Converted in the 1990s from 18C St George's Hospital. A grand and traditional atmosphere prevails. Butler service offered. Regency-era decorated, lavishly appointed rooms. Ornate, glass-roofed dining room with palm trees and fountains.

The Halkin

VISA AE

5 Halkin St ✉ SW1X 7DJ – Ⓜ Hyde Park Corner – ☎ (020) 7333 1000 – res@halkin.como.bz – Fax (020) 7333 11 00 – www.halkin.como.bz

closed 25-26 December and 1 January **G5**

35 rm – £288/411 £370/500, ☕ £25 – 6 suites – **Rest *Nahm*** – see below

◆ Luxury ◆ Stylish ◆

One of London's first minimalist hotels. The cool, marbled reception and bar have an understated charm. Spacious rooms have every conceivable facility.

Sheraton Belgravia

rm 25 VISA AE

20 Chesham Pl ✉ SW1X 8HQ – Ⓜ Knightsbridge – ☎ (020) 7235 6040 – reservations.sheratonbelgravia@sheraton.com – Fax (020) 7259 62 43 – www.sheraton.com/belgravia **FG5**

82 rm – £199/329 £247/376, ☕ £20 – 7 suites

Rest *The Dining Room* – Menu £20 (lunch) – Carte £24/33

◆ Business ◆ Classic ◆

Modern corporate hotel overlooking Chesham Place. Comfortable and well-equipped for the tourist and business traveller alike. A few minutes' walk from Harrods. Modern, international menus.

Diplomat without rest

VISA AE

2 Chesham St ✉ SW1X 8DT – Ⓜ Sloane Square – ☎ (020) 7235 1544 – diplomat.hotel@btinternet.com – Fax (020) 7259 61 53 – www.btinternet.com/diplomat.hotel **G5**

26 rm ☕ – £95/115 £175

◆ Traditional ◆ Classic ◆

Imposing Victorian corner house built in 1882 by Thomas Cubitt. Attractive glass-domed stairwell and sweeping staircase. Spacious and well-appointed bedrooms.

Pétrus (Wareing) – at The Berkeley H.

14 VISA AE

Wilton Pl ✉ SW1X 7RL – Ⓜ Knightsbridge – ☎ (020) 7235 1200 – petrus@marcuswareing.com – Fax (020) 7235 12 66 – www.marcuswareing.com

closed 1 week Christmas, Sunday, Saturday lunch and Bank Holidays **G4**

Rest – Menu £30/80

Spec. Roast veal sweetbread with garden peas and black olives. Braised turbot with wild asparagus, poached quail egg and caviar. Peanut parfait with rice crisp crunch and chocolate mousse.

◆ Modern ◆ Formal ◆

Elegantly appointed restaurant named after one of the 40 Pétrus vintages on the wine list. One table in the kitchen to watch the chefs at work. Accomplished modern cooking.

Amaya

14 VISA AE

Halkin Arcade, 19 Motcomb St ✉ SW1X 8JT – Ⓜ Knightsbridge – ☎ (020) 7823 1166 – info@realindianfood.com – Fax (020) 7259 64 64 – www.realindianfood.com **F5**

Rest – Menu £19 (lunch) – Carte £25/50

Spec. Punjabi chicken wing "lollipops" with chilli, lime and cinnamon. Tandoori tiger prawn, scallops in herb sauce and grilled oyster. Grilled lamb chops with ginger, lime and coriander.

◆ Indian ◆ Fashionable ◆

Light, piquant and aromatic Indian cooking specialising in kebabs from a tawa skillet, sigri grill or tandoor oven. Chic comfortable surroundings, modern and subtly exotic.

XXX ✿

Zafferano AC ⅟ 18 VISA MC AE ①

15 Lowndes St ✉ SW1X 9EY – Ⓜ Knightsbridge – ✆ (020) 7235 5800
– Fax (020) 7235 19 71 – www.zafferanorestaurant.com
closed 1 week Christmas and Bank Holidays **F5**

Rest – Menu £30/40

Spec. Scallops in saffron vinaigrette. Veal shank ravioli in saffron. Chargrilled monkfish with courgettes and sweet chilli.

♦ Italian ♦ Fashionable ♦

Forever busy and relaxed. No frills, robust and gutsy Italian cooking, where the quality of the produce shines through. Wholly Italian wine list has some hidden treasures.

XX ✿

Nahm – at The Halkin H. AC 30 VISA MC AE ①

5 Halkin St ✉ SW1X 7DJ – Ⓜ Hyde Park Corner – ✆ (020) 7333 1234
– Fax (020) 7333 11 00 – www.halkin.co.uk
closed lunch Saturday and Sunday and Bank Holidays **G5**

Rest – *(booking essential)* Menu £26/50 – Carte £31/41

Spec. Red curry of minced quail with ginger and Thai basil. Crunchy prawn cake salad with green mango. Lychees, mangosteens and rambutans in perfumed syrup.

♦ Thai ♦ Design ♦

Teak furniture and honey-coloured walls add up to sleek, understated decor. Menu offers the best of Thai cooking with modern interpretations and original use of ingredients.

Victoria *Plan IV*

The Goring AC SAT 50 VISA MC AE ①

15 Beeston Pl, Grosvenor Gdns ✉ SW1W 0JW – Ⓜ Victoria – ✆ (020) 7396 9000
– reception@goringhotel.co.uk – Fax (020) 7834 43 93 – www.goringhotel.co.uk
– **65 rm** – †£347/405 ††£541, ☕ £24 – 6 suites **H5**

Rest – *(closed Saturday lunch)* Menu £31/46

♦ Traditional ♦ Luxury ♦ Classic ♦

Opened in 1910 as a quintessentially English hotel. The fourth generation of Goring is now at the helm. Many of the attractive rooms overlook a peaceful garden. Elegantly appointed restaurant provides memorable dining experience.

Crowne Plaza London St James AC ⅟rm SAT

45 Buckingham Gate ✉ SW1E 6AF – Ⓜ St James's Park 180 VISA MC AE ①
– ✆ (020) 7834 6655 – sales@cplonsj.co.uk – Fax (020) 7630 75 87
– www.london.crowneplaza.com **H5**

323 rm – †£323 ††£323, ☕ £16 – 19 suites

Rest *Quilon* – see below – **Rest *Bistro 51*** – Menu £15 (lunch) – Carte £21/46

♦ Luxury ♦ Classic ♦

Built in 1897 as serviced accommodation for visiting aristocrats. Behind the impressive Edwardian façade lies an equally elegant interior. Quietest rooms overlook courtyard. Bright and informal café-style restaurant.

51 Buckingham Gate without rest AC SAT VISA MC AE ①

51 Buckingham Gate ✉ SW1E 6AF – Ⓜ St James's Park – ✆ (020) 7769 7766
– info@51-buckinghamgate.co.uk – Fax (020) 7828 59 09
– www.51-buckinghamgate.com – **82 suites** – †£360 ††£975, ☕ £19 **H5**

♦ Luxury ♦ Classic ♦

Canopied entrance leads to luxurious suites: every detail considered, every mod con provided. Colour schemes echoed in plants and paintings. Butler and nanny service.

41 without rest AC SAT VISA MC AE ①

41 Buckingham Palace Rd ✉ SW1W 0PS – Ⓜ Victoria – ✆ (020) 7300 0041
– book41@rchmail.com – Fax (020) 7300 01 41 – www.41hotel.com **H5**

27 rm – †£264/347 ††£288/382, ☕ £18 – 1 suite

♦ Luxury ♦ Classic ♦

Discreet appearance; exudes exclusive air. Leather armchairs; bookcases line the walls. Intimate service. State-of-the-art rooms where hi-tec and fireplace merge appealingly.

UNITED KINGDOM

The Rubens at The Palace AC 90 VISA MC AE

39 Buckingham Palace Rd ✉ SW1W 0PS – Ⓜ Victoria – ✆ (020) 7834 6600 – bookrb@rchmail.com – Fax (020) 7828 54 01 – www.redcarnationhotels.com **H5**

170 rm – †£153/259 ††£188/317, ☕ £18 – 2 suites

Rest – *(closed lunch Saturday and Sunday) (carvery)* Menu £22.50/29 – Carte £34/40

♦ Traditional ♦ Classic ♦

Traditional hotel with an air of understated elegance. Tastefully furnished rooms: the Royal Wing, themed after Kings and Queens, features TVs in bathrooms. Smart carvery restaurant. Intimate, richly decorated Library restaurant has sumptuous armchairs.

City Inn AC 150 VISA MC AE

30 John Islip St ✉ SW1P 4DD – Ⓜ Pimlico – ✆ (020) 7630 1000 – westminster.res@cityinn.com – Fax (020) 7932 46 09 – www.cityinn.com **I6**

444 rm – †£311 ††£311, ☕ £19 – 16 suites

Rest *City Cafe* – Menu £17.50 – Carte £22/33

♦ Business ♦ Functional ♦

Modern hotel five minutes' walk from Westminster Abbey and Tate Britain. Well-appointed bedrooms with high-tech equipment and some with pleasant views of London. Brasserie serving modern-style food next to a glass-covered terrace with artwork feature.

B+B Belgravia without rest VISA MC

64-66 Ebury St ✉ SW1W 9QD – Ⓜ Victoria – ✆ (020) 7259 8570 – info@bb-belgravia.com – Fax (020) 7259 85 91 – www.bb-belgravia.com **G6**

17 rm ☕ – †£94 ††£99

♦ Townhouse ♦ Personalised ♦

Two houses, three floors, and, considering the location, some of the best value accommodation in town. Sleek, clean-lined rooms. Breakfast overlooking little garden terrace.

Winchester without rest

17 Belgrave Rd ✉ SW1V 1RB – Ⓜ Victoria – ✆ (020) 7828 2972 – winchesterhotel17@hotmail.com – Fax (020) 7828 51 91 – www.winchester-hotel.net **H6**

18 rm ☕ – †£75 ††£85

♦ Traditional ♦ Functional ♦

Behind the portico entrance one finds a friendly, well-kept private hotel. The generally spacious rooms are pleasantly appointed. Comprehensive English breakfast offered.

Express by Holiday Inn without rest VISA MC AE

106-110 Belgrave Rd ✉ SW1V 2BJ – Ⓜ Pimlico – ✆ (020) 7630 8888 – info@hiexpressvictoria.co.uk – Fax (020) 7828 04 41 – www.hiexpressvictoria.co.uk **H6**

52 rm – †£99/135 ††£99/135

♦ Chain hotel ♦ Functional ♦

Converted Georgian terraced houses a short walk from station. Despite property's age, all rooms are stylish and modern with good range of facilities including TV movies.

The Cinnamon Club AC 50 P VISA MC AE

Great Smith St ✉ SW1P 3BU – Ⓜ St James's Park – ✆ (020) 7222 2555 – info@cinnamonclub.com – Fax (020) 7222 13 33 – www.cinnamonclub.com
closed Saturday lunch, Sunday and Bank Holidays **I5**

Rest – Menu £22 (lunch) – Carte £26/49

♦ Indian ♦ Formal ♦

Housed in former Westminster Library: exterior has ornate detail, interior is stylish and modern. Walls are lined with books. New Wave Indian cooking with plenty of choice.

XXX **Quilon** – at Crowne Plaza London St James H.
45 Buckingham Gate ✉ SW1E 6AF – Ⓜ Victoria
– ✆ (020) 7821 1899 – Fax (020) 7828 58 02
– www.thequilonrestaurant.com
closed Sunday and Saturday lunch **H5**
Rest – Menu £16 (lunch) – Carte £18/36
◆ Indian ◆ Formal ◆
A selection of Eastern pictures adorn the walls in this smart, modern and busy restaurant. Specialising in progressive south coast Indian cooking.

XXX **Shepherd's**
Marsham Court, Marsham St ✉ SW1P 4LA – Ⓜ Pimlico – ✆ (020) 7834 9552
– www.langansrestaurants.co.uk – Fax (020) 7233 60 47
– www.langansrestaurants.co.uk
closed Saturday, Sunday and Bank Holidays **I6**
Rest – *(booking essential)* Menu £30
◆ English ◆ Formal ◆
A truly English restaurant where game and traditional puddings are a highlight. Popular with those from Westminster - the booths offer a degree of privacy.

XXX ✿ **Roussillon**
16 St Barnabas St ✉ SW1W 8PE – Ⓜ Sloane Square – ✆ (020) 7730 5550
– alexis@roussillon.co.uk – Fax (020) 7824 86 17 – www.roussillon.co.uk
closed 27 August-4 September, 25 December-3 January, Sunday and lunch Saturday-Tuesday **G6**
Rest – Menu £30/45
Spec. Wild asparagus with poached quail eggs and lemon zest. Venison with caramelised pumpkin and poached pear. Apricot soufflé with dark chocolate sauce.
◆ French ◆ Neighbourhood ◆
Tucked away in a smart residential area. Cooking clearly focuses on the quality of the ingredients. Seasonal menu with inventive elements and a French base.

XX **Atami**
37 Monck St ✉ SW1P 2BL – ✆ (020) 7222 2218 – mail@atami-restaurant.com
– Fax (020) 7222 27 88 – www.atami-restaurant.com **I6**
Rest – Carte £19/41
◆ Japanese ◆ Design ◆
Clean, modern lines illuminated by vast ceiling orbs induce a sense of calm. Menus true to Japanese roots feature sushi and sashimi turning down interesting modern highways.

XX **Il Convivio**
143 Ebury St ✉ SW1W 9QN – Ⓜ Sloane Square – ✆ (020) 7730 4099
– comments@etruscarestaurants.com – Fax (020) 7730 41 03
– www.etruscarestaurants.com
closed Sunday and Bank Holidays **G6**
Rest – Menu £20/33
◆ Italian ◆ Design ◆
A retractable roof provides alfresco dining to part of this comfortable and modern restaurant. Contemporary and traditional Italian menu with home-made pasta specialities.

XX **Tate Britain**
Tate Britain, Millbank ✉ SW1P 4RG – Ⓜ Pimlico – ✆ (020) 7887 8825
– tate.restaurant@tate.org.uk – Fax (020) 7887 89 02 – www.tate.org.uk
closed 24-26 December **I6**
Rest – *(booking essential) (lunch only)* Menu £27
◆ English ◆ Brasserie ◆
Continue your appreciation of art when lunching in this basement room decorated with original Rex Whistler murals. Forever busy, it offers modern British fare.

Ken Lo's Memories of China

65-69 Ebury St ✉ SW1W 0NZ – Ⓜ Victoria – ✆ (020) 7730 7734 – Fax (020) 7730 29 92 – closed Sunday lunch **G6**

Rest – Carte approx. £28

♦ Chinese ♦ Neighbourhood ♦

An air of tranquillity pervades this traditionally furnished room. Lattice screens add extra privacy. Extensive Chinese menu: bold flavours with a clean, fresh style.

Olivo

21 Eccleston St ✉ SW1W 9LX – Ⓜ Victoria – ✆ (020) 7730 2505 – maurosanna@oliveto.fsnet.co.uk – Fax (020) 7823 53 77 – closed lunch Saturday and Sunday and Bank Holidays – **Rest** – Menu £19 (lunch) – Carte £27/31 **G6**

♦ Italian ♦ Neighbourhood ♦

Rustic, informal Italian restaurant. Relaxed atmosphere provided by the friendly staff. Simple, non-fussy cuisine with emphasis on best available fresh produce.

La Poule au Pot

231 Ebury St ✉ SW1W 8UT – Ⓜ Sloane Square – ✆ (020) 7730 7763 – Fax (020) 7259 96 51 – closed 25 December **G6**

Rest – Menu £17 (lunch) – Carte £26/41

♦ French ♦ Bistro ♦

The subdued lighting and friendly informality make this one of London's more romantic restaurants. Classic French menu with extensive plats du jour.

The Ebury

Ground Floor, 11 Pimlico Rd, ✉ SW1W 8NA – Ⓜ Sloane Square – ✆ (020) 7730 6784 – info@theebury.co.uk – Fax (020) 7730 61 49 – www.theebury.co.uk – closed 24-26 December and 1 January **G6**

Rest – Menu £21/34

♦ Modern ♦ Pub ♦

Victorian corner pub restaurant with walnut bar, simple tables and large seafood bar. Friendly service. Wide-ranging menu from snacks to full meals.

The Thomas Cubitt

First Floor, 44 Elizabeth St. ✉ SW1W 9PA – Ⓜ Sloane Square – ✆ (020) 7730 6060 – Fax (020) 7730 60 55 – www.thethomascubitt.co.uk

Rest – *(booking essential)* Menu £21.50 (lunch) – Carte £27/47 **G6**

♦ Gastropub ♦

Georgian pub refurbished and renamed after master builder. He'd approve of elegant, formal dining room. Carefully supplied ingredients underpin tasty, seasonal English dishes.

REGENT'S PARK & MARYLEBONE *Plan V*

Landmark London

rm 350

222 Marylebone Rd ✉ NW1 6JQ – Ⓜ Baker Street – ✆ (020) 7631 8000 – reservations@thelandmark.co.uk – Fax (020) 7631 80 80 – www.landmarklondon.co.uk **F1**

290 rm – †£217/288 ††£247/305, ☕ £25 – 9 suites

Rest ***Winter Garden*** – Menu £25.75/33.45 – Carte £29/47

♦ Grand Luxury ♦ Classic ♦

Imposing Victorian Gothic building with a vast glass enclosed atrium, overlooked by many of the modern, well-equipped bedrooms. Winter Garden popular for afternoon tea.

Langham

rm 250

1c Portland Pl, Regent St ✉ W1B 1JA – Ⓜ Oxford Circus – ✆ (020) 7636 1000 – info@langhamhotels.com – Fax (020) 7323 23 40 – www.langhamlondon.com **H2**

409 rm – †£411 ††£411, ☕ £25 – 20 suites – **Rest** – Menu £37.50/45 – Carte £39/47

♦ Luxury ♦ Classic ♦

Opposite the BBC, with Colonial inspired décor. Polo themed bar and barrel vaulted Palm Court. Concierge Club rooms offer superior comfort and butler service. Memories is a bright, elegant dining room.

The Cumberland

300 VISA

Great Cumberland Pl ✉ *W1A 4RF* – Ⓜ *Marble Arch* – ✆ *(0870) 333 9280 – enquiries@thecumberland.co.uk – Fax (0870) 333 92 81 – www.guoman.com* **FG3**

1019 rm – †£370 ††£382, ☕ £17

Rest *Rhodes W1* – see below

♦ Business ♦ Design ♦

Fully refurbished, conference oriented hotel whose vast lobby boasts modern art, sculpture and running water panels. Distinctive bedrooms with a host of impressive extras.

Hyatt Regency London-The Churchill

rm 250 VISA

30 Portman Sq ✉ *W1A 4ZX* – Ⓜ *Marble Arch – ✆ (020) 7486 5800 – london.churchill@hyattintl.com – Fax (020) 7486 12 55 – www.london-churchill.hyatt.com* **G2**

397 rm – †£399 ††£423, ☕ £15 – 40 suites

Rest *The Montagu* – Menu £22.50 (lunch) – Carte £35/47

♦ Luxury ♦ Classic ♦

Modern property overlooking attractive square. Elegant marbled lobby .Cigar bar open until 2am for members. Well-appointed rooms have the international traveller in mind. Restaurant provides popular Sunday brunch entertainment.

Charlotte Street

65 VISA

15 Charlotte St ✉ *W1T 1RJ* – Ⓜ *Goodge Street* – ✆ *(020) 7806 2000 – charlotte@firmdale.com – Fax (020) 7806 20 02 – www.charlottestreethotel.co.uk* **I2**

44 rm – †£229/240 ††£335, ☕ £19 – 8 suites

Rest *Oscar* – see below

♦ Luxury ♦ Stylish ♦

Interior designed with a charming and understated English feel. Welcoming lobby laden with floral displays. Individually decorated rooms with CDs and mobile phones.

Sanderson

rm VISA

50 Berners St ✉ *W1T 3NG* – Ⓜ *Oxford Circus* – ✆ *(020) 7300 1400 – sanderson@morganshotelgroup.com – Fax (020) 7300 14 01 – www.morganshotelgroup.com* **H2**

150 rm – †£264/441 ††£294/499, ☕ £22

Rest *Spoon+* – Carte £36/84

♦ Luxury ♦ Minimalist ♦

Designed by Philippe Starck: the height of contemporary design. Bar is the place to see and be seen. Bedrooms with minimalistic white décor have DVDs and striking bathrooms. Stylish Spoon+ allows diners to construct own dishes.

The Leonard

VISA

15 Seymour St ✉ *W1H 7JW* – Ⓜ *Marble Arch* – ✆ *(020) 7935 2010 – reservations@theleonard.com – Fax (020) 7935 67 00 – www.theleonard.com* **G2**

25 rm – †£176 ††£276, ☕ £19.50 – 20 suites

Rest – *(room service only)*

♦ Townhouse ♦ Classic ♦

Around the corner from Selfridges, an attractive Georgian townhouse: antiques and oil paintings abound. Informal, stylish café bar offers light snacks. Well-appointed rooms.

Radisson SAS Portman

rm 650 VISA

22 Portman Sq ✉ *W1H 7BG* – Ⓜ *Marble Arch – ✆ (020) 7208 6000 – sales.london@radissonsas.com – Fax (020) 7208 60 01 – www.radisson.com* **G2**

265 rm – †£222 ††£234, ☕ £18 – 7 suites

Rest – *(buffet lunch)* Carte dinner £24/33

♦ Business ♦ Classic ♦

This modern, corporate hotel offers check-in for both British Midland and SAS airlines. Rooms in attached towers decorated in Scandinavian, Chinese and Italian styles. Restaurant renowned for its elaborate buffet lunch.

Montcalm
AC rm 80 VISA

Great Cumberland Pl ✉ *W1H 7TW* – Ⓜ *Marble Arch* – ✆ *(020) 7402 4288 – montcalm@montcalm.co.uk – Fax (020) 7724 91 80 – www.montcalm.co.uk*
110 rm – †£176/294 ††£200/294, ☕ £18 – 10 suites – **Rest *The Crescent*** – *(closed lunch, Saturday, Sunday and Bank Holidays)* Menu £26/29.50 **F2**

♦ Business ♦ Classic ♦

Named after the 18C French general, the Marquis de Montcalm. In a charming crescent a short walk from Hyde Park. Spacious bedrooms with a subtle oriental feel. Discreetly appointed room favoured by local residents. Best tables overlook a pretty square. Frequently changing fixed price modern menu includes half bottle of house wine.

Durrants
AC rest 55 VISA

26-32 St George St ✉ *W1H 5BJ* – Ⓜ *Bond Street* – ✆ *(020) 7935 8131 – enquiries@durrantshotel.co.uk – Fax (020) 7487 35 10 – www.durrantshotel.co.uk* – **88 rm** – †£105/155 ††£175, ☕ £15 – 4 suites
Rest – Menu £19.50/22 (lunch) – Carte £29/38 **G2**

♦ Traditional ♦ Classic ♦

First opened in 1790 and family owned since 1921. Traditionally English feel with the charm of a bygone era. Cosy wood panelled bar. Attractive rooms vary somewhat in size. Semi-private booths in quintessentially British dining room.

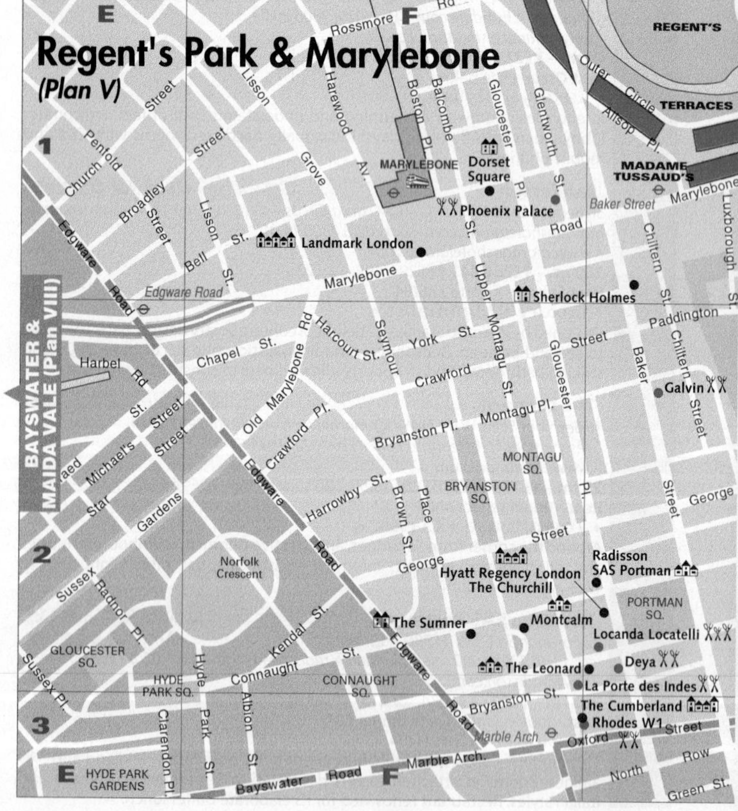

The Mandeville

40 VISA

Mandeville Pl ✉ W1V 2BE – Ⓜ Bond Street – ☎ (020) 79355599 – info@mandeville.co.uk – Fax (020) 79 35 95 88 **G2**

135 rm – †£250/275 ††£275/450, ☕ £20 – 7 suites

Rest *de Ville* – *(closed Sunday)* Menu £19/23 – Carte £30/39

♦ Chain hotel ♦ Design ♦

Fashionably located hotel, refurbished in 2005 with marbled reception and strikingly colourful bar. Stylish rooms have flatscreen TVs and make good use of the space available. Informal restaurant serving modern British cuisine.

Dorset Square

VISA

39-40 Dorset Sq ✉ NW1 6QN – Ⓜ Marylebone – ☎ (020) 7723 7874 – reservations@dorsetsquare.co.uk – Fax (020) 7724 33 28 – www.dorsetsquare.co.uk closed 25-26 December **F1**

37 rm – †£176/258 ††£306/411, ☕ £16 – **Rest *The Potting Shed*** – *(closed Saturday lunch and Sunday dinner) (booking essential)* Menu £21.95/24.85 – Carte £25/36

♦ Townhouse ♦ Classic ♦

Converted Regency townhouses in a charming square and the site of the original Lord's cricket ground. A relaxed country house in the city. Individually decorated rooms. The Potting Shed features modern cuisine and a set business menu.

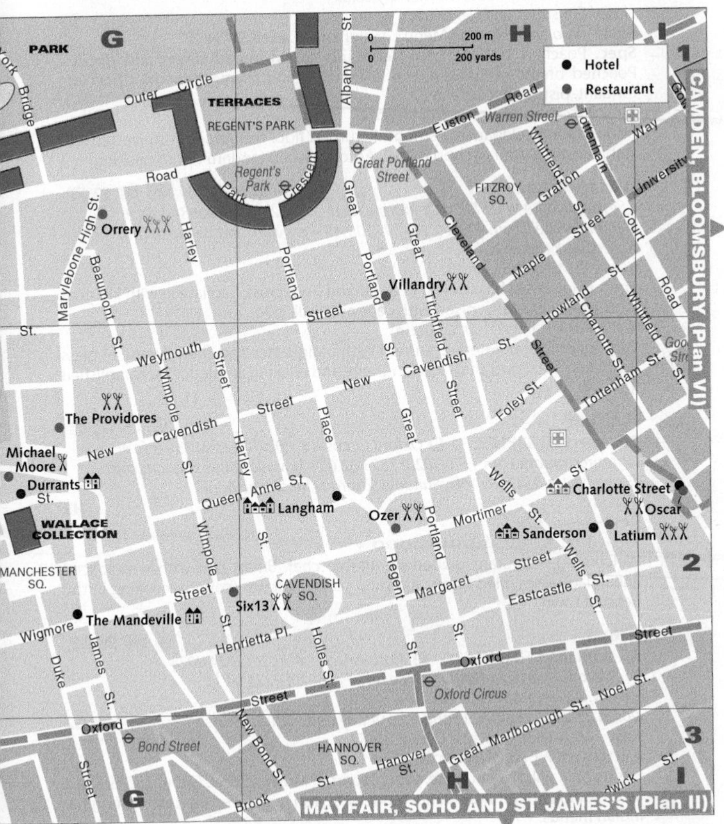

UNITED KINGDOM

The Sumner without rest

54 Upper Berkeley St ✉ W1H 7QR – Ⓜ Marble Arch – ✆ (020) 7723 2244 – enquiry@thesumner.com – Fax (020) 705 86 79 – www.thesumner.com

20 rm – ♦£116/152 ♦♦£116/152 **F2**

♦ Townhouse ♦ Personalised ♦

Two Georgian terrace houses in developing area of town. Comfy, stylish sitting room; basement breakfast room. Largest bedrooms, 101 and 201, have sunny, full-length windows.

Sherlock Holmes

108 Baker St ✉ W1U 6LJ – Ⓜ Baker Street – ✆ (020) 7486 6161 – info@sherlockholmeshotel.com – Fax (020) 7958 52 11 – www.sherlockholmeshotel.com **G1**

116 rm – ♦£176/294 ♦♦£176/294, £16.50 – 3 suites

Rest – Menu £14.50 (lunch) – Carte £25/44

♦ Business ♦ Modern ♦

A stylish building with a relaxed contemporary feel. Comfortable guests' lounge with Holmes pictures on the walls. Bedrooms welcoming and smart, some with wood floors. Brasserie style dining.

Orrery

55 Marylebone High St ✉ W1U 5RB – Ⓜ Regent's Park – ✆ (020) 7616 8000 – Fax (020) 7616 80 80 – www.orrery.co.uk

closed Christmas and New Year **G1**

Rest – *(booking essential)* Menu £25 (lunch) – Carte £37/54

Spec. Poached scallops with Vermouth cream, broad beans and girolles. Poached breast of chicken, truffle bouillon and thyme gnocchi. Chocolate fondant, pistachio ice cream.

♦ Contemporary ♦ Design ♦

Contemporary elegance: a smoothly run 1st floor restaurant in converted 19C stables, with a Conran shop below. Accomplished modern British cooking.

Locanda Locatelli

8 Seymour St ✉ W1H 7JZ – Ⓜ Marble Arch – ✆ (020) 7935 9088 – info@locandalocatelli.com – Fax (020) 7935 11 49 – www.locandalocatelli.com

closed Bank Holidays **G2**

Rest – Carte £33/52

Spec. Fillet of sea bass baked in a salt and herb crust. Tagliatelle with kid goat ragu. Medallions of venison with ceps and radicchio.

♦ Italian ♦ Fashionable ♦

Very stylishly appointed restaurant with banquettes and cherry wood or glass dividers which contribute to an intimate and relaxing ambience. Accomplished Italian cooking.

Latium

21 Berners St ✉ W1T 3LP – Ⓜ Oxford Circus – ✆ (020) 7323 9123 – info@latiumrestaurant.com – Fax (020) 7323 32 05 – www.latiumrestaurant.com

closed Easter, 25 December, Sunday, Saturday lunch and Bank Holidays **H2**

Rest – Menu £29

♦ Italian ♦ Neighbourhood ♦

Welcoming restaurant owned by affable chef. Smart feel with well-spaced linen-clad tables, tiled floors and rural pictures. Italian country cooking in the heart of town.

Deya

34 Portman Sq ✉ W1H 7BY – Ⓜ Marble Arch – ✆ (020) 7224 0028 – reservations@deya-restaurant.co.uk – Fax (020) 7224 04 11 – www.deya-restaurant.co.uk

closed 25-26 December, 1 January, Sunday and Saturday lunch **G2**

Rest – Menu £20 (lunch) – Carte £23/32

♦ Indian ♦ Fashionable ♦

Has its own pillared entrance, though part of Mostyn hotel. Grand 18C Grade II listed room with ornate ceiling. Modern, stylish makeover. Interesting, original Indian menus.

XX **Rhodes W1** – at The Cumberland H.

Great Cumberland Pl ✉ W1A 4RF
– Ⓜ Marble Arch – ✆ (020) 7479 3838
– rhodesw1@thecumberland.co.uk – Fax (020) 7479 38 88
– www.garyrhodes.com
Rest – Menu £22 (lunch) – Carte £20/42 **FG3**
♦ English ♦ Brasserie ♦

In the heart of the Cumberland Hotel, a very stylish dining experience with impressively high ceiling and classical Gary Rhodes dishes bringing out the best of the seasons.

XX **Galvin**

66 Baker St ✉ W14 7DH – Ⓜ Baker Street
– ✆ (020) 7935 4007 – info@galvinbistrotdeluxe.co.uk
– Fax (020) 7486 17 35 – www.galvinbistrotdeluxe.co.uk
closed 25-26 December and 1 January **G2**
Rest – Menu £16 (lunch) – Carte £20/32
♦ Modern ♦ Bistro ♦

A modern take on the classic Gallic bistro with ceiling fans, globe lights, rich wood panelled walls and French influenced dishes where precision and good value are paramount.

XX **Six13**

19 Wigmore St ✉ W1H 9UA – Ⓜ Bond Street – ✆ (020) 7629 6133
– jay@six13.com – Fax (020) 7629 61 35 – www.six13.com
closed Jewish Holidays, Friday dinner and Saturday **G2**
Rest – Menu £25 (lunch) – Carte £29/41
♦ Kosher ♦ Friendly ♦

Stylish and immaculate with banquette seating. Strictly kosher menu supervised by the Shama offering interesting cooking with a modern slant.

XX **Oscar** – at Charlotte Street H.

15 Charlotte St ✉ W1T 1RJ – Ⓜ Goodge Street
– ✆ (020) 7907 4005 – charlotte@firmdale.com
– Fax (020) 7806 20 02 – www.charlottestreethotel.co.uk
closed Sunday lunch **I2**
Rest – *(booking essential)* Carte £33/49
♦ Modern ♦ Trendy ♦

Adjacent to hotel lobby and dominated by a large, vivid mural of contemporary London life. Sophisticated dishes served by attentive staff: oysters, wasabi and soya dressing.

XX **The Providores**

109 Marylebone High St ✉ W1U 4RX – Ⓜ Bond Street – ✆ (020) 7935 6175
– anyone@theprovidores.co.uk – Fax (020) 7935 68 77
– www.theprovidores.co.uk
closed 25-26 and 31 December and 1 January **G2**
Rest – Carte £30/43
♦ Innovative ♦ Trendy ♦

Swish, stylish restaurant on first floor; unusual dishes with New World base and fusion of Asian, Mediterranean influences. Tapas and light meals in downstairs Tapa Room.

XX **La Porte des Indes**

32 Bryanston St ✉ W1H 7EG – Ⓜ Marble Arch
– ✆ (020) 7224 0055
– london.reservation@laportedesindes.com
– Fax (020) 7224 11 44
closed 25-27 December and Saturday lunch
Rest – Carte £22/45 **F2**
♦ Indian ♦ Exotic ♦

Don't be fooled by the discreet entrance: inside there is a spectacularly unrestrained display of palm trees, murals and waterfalls. French influenced Indian cuisine.

XX

Rosmarino

1 Blenheim Terrace ✉ NW8 0EH – Ⓜ St John's Wood – ✆ (020) 7328 5014 – Fax (020) 7625 26 39
closed Easter Monday, 25 December and 1 January — *Plan I* **B1-2**
Rest – Menu £25/30
♦ Italian ♦ Neighbourhood ♦
Modern, understated and relaxed. Friendly and approachable service of robust and rustic Italian dishes. Set priced menu is carefully balanced.

XX

Ozer

4-5 Langham Pl, Regent St ✉ W1B 3DG – Ⓜ Oxford Circus – ✆ (020) 7323 0505 – info@sofra.co.uk – Fax (020) 7323 01 11 – www.sofra.co.uk **H2**
Rest – Menu £17/22 – Carte £17/35
♦ Turkish ♦ Design ♦
Behind the busy and vibrantly decorated bar you'll find a smart modern restaurant. Lively atmosphere and efficient service of modern, light and aromatic Turkish cooking.

XX

Roka

37 Charlotte St ✉ W1T 1RR – Ⓜ Goodge Street – ✆ (020) 7580 6464 – info@rokarestaurant.com – Fax (020) 7580 02 20 – www.rokarestaurant.com
closed Sunday lunch — *Plan VI* **I2**
Rest – Carte £36/79
♦ Japanese ♦ Fashionable ♦
Striking glass and steel frontage. Airy, atmospheric interior of teak, oak and paper wall screens. Authentic, flavoursome Japanese cuisine with variety of grill dishes.

XX

Phoenix Palace

3-5 Glentworth St. ✉ NW1 5PG – Ⓜ Baker Street – ✆ (020) 7486 3515 – phoenixpalace@btconnect.com – Fax (020) 7486 34 01 **F1**
Rest – Menu £16/27 – Carte £20/55
♦ Chinese ♦ Friendly ♦
Tucked away near Baker Street; lots of photos of celebrities who've eaten here. Huge room for 200 diners where authentic, fresh, well prepared Chinese dishes are served.

X

Villandry

170 Great Portland St ✉ W1W 5QB – Ⓜ Regent's Park – ✆ (020) 7631 3131 – bookatable@villandry.com – Fax (020) 7631 30 30 – www.villandry.com
closed Sunday dinner and Bank Holidays **H1**
Rest – Carte £23/38
♦ Modern ♦ Rustic ♦
The senses are heightened by passing through the well-stocked deli to the dining room behind. Bare walls, wooden tables and a menu offering simple, tasty dishes.

The Abbey Road

63 Abbey Rd ✉ NW8 0AE – Ⓜ St John's Wood – ✆ (020) 7328 6626 – theabbeyroadpub@btconnect.com – Fax (020) 7625 91 68
closed 25 and 31 December — *Plan I* **B1**
Rest – *(closed Monday lunch)* Carte £20/25
♦ Modern ♦ Pub ♦
Grand Victorian pub appearance in bottle green. Busy bar at the front; main dining room, in calm duck egg blue, to the rear. Modern menus boast a distinct Mediterranean style.

CAMDEN

Bloomsbury

Plan VI

Covent Garden 50 VISA

10 Monmouth St ✉ WC2H 9HB
– Ⓜ Covent Garden
– ✆ (020) 7806 1000
– covent@firmdale.com
– Fax (020) 7806 11 00
– www.coventgardenhotel.co.uk

I3

56 rm – **†**£258/311 **††**£358/364, ☐ £20 – 2 suites

Rest *Brasserie Max* – *(booking essential)* Carte £29/50

◆ Luxury ◆ Stylish ◆

Individually designed and stylish bedrooms, with CDs and VCRs discreetly concealed. Boasts a very relaxing first floor oak-panelled drawing room with its own honesty bar. Informal restaurant.

Marlborough rest rm 250 VISA

9-14 Bloomsbury St ✉ WC1B 3QD
– Ⓜ Tottenham Court Road
– ✆ (020) 7636 5601 – resmarl@radisson.com
– Fax (020) 7636 05 32
– www.radissonedwardian.com

I2

171 rm – **†**£154/220 **††**£216/257, ☐ £17 – 2 suites

Rest *Glass* – *(closed lunch Saturday-Sunday)* Carte £25/34

◆ Business ◆ Classic ◆

A Victorian building around the corner from the British Museum. The lobby has been restored to its original marbled splendour and the bedrooms offer good comforts. Bright, breezy restaurant with suitably modish cooking.

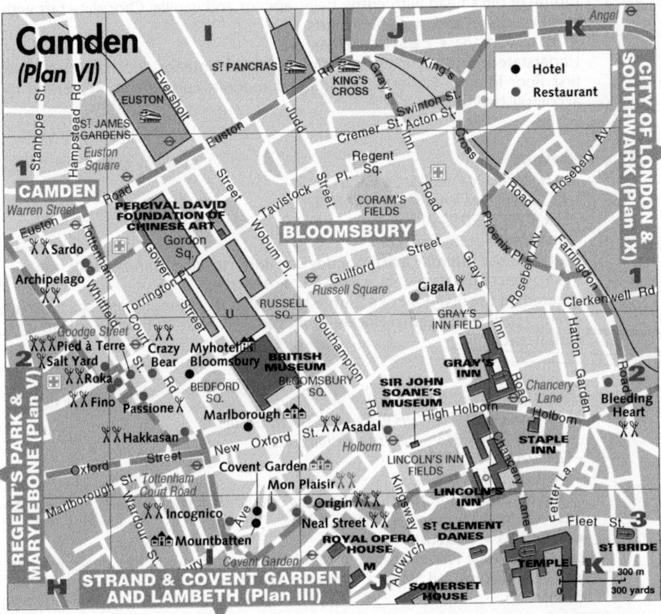

Mountbatten

20 Monmouth St ✉ WC2H 9HD – Ⓜ Covent Garden – ☎ (020) 7836 4300 – Fax (020) 7240 35 40 – www.radissonedwardian.com I3

149 rm – †£171/245 ††£220/282, ☕ £17 – 2 suites

Rest *Dial* – *(closed lunch Friday-Sunday)* Menu £25 (dinner) – Carte £25/34

◆ Business ◆ Classic ◆

Photographs and memorabilia of the eponymous Lord Louis adorn the walls and corridors. Ideally located in the heart of Covent Garden. Compact but comfortable bedrooms. Bright, stylish restaurant.

Myhotel Bloomsbury

11-13 Bayley St, Bedford Sq ✉ WC1B 3HD – Ⓜ Tottenham Court Road – ☎ (020) 7667 6000 – res@myhotels.co.uk – Fax (020) 7667 60 01 – www.myhotels.com I2

77 rm – †£147/266 ††£266/305, ☕ £18

Rest *Yo! Sushi* – Carte £15/22

◆ Business ◆ Minimalist ◆

The minimalist interior is designed on the principles of feng shui; even the smaller bedrooms are stylish and uncluttered. Mybar is a fashionable meeting point. Diners can enjoy Japanese food from conveyor belt.

Pied à Terre (Osborn)

34 Charlotte St ✉ W1T 2NH – Ⓜ Goodge Street – ☎ (020) 7636 1178 – p-a-t@dircon.co.uk – Fax (020) 7916 11 71 – www.pied.a.terre.co.uk

closed 10 days Christmas, Saturday lunch, Sunday and Bank Holidays I2

Rest – Menu £29/60

Spec. Ceviche of scallop, avocado and crème fraîche purée, sesame filo. Warm terrine of pig's head with crispy belly, apricot and vanilla. Chocolate tart with stout ice cream and macadamia nuts.

◆ Innovative ◆ Fashionable ◆

Understated, discreet exterior; intimate, stylish interior, incorporating sleek first floor lounge. Elaborate yet refined modern cuisine complemented by accomplished service.

Origin

The Hospital, 24 Endell St ✉ WC2H 9HQ – Ⓜ Covent Garden – ☎ (020) 7170 9200 – Fax (020) 71 70 92 21 – www.origin-restaurant.com J3

Rest – *(closed Saturday lunch, Sunday and Bank Holidays)* Carte £33/49

◆ Modern European ◆ Fashionable ◆

Located on the first floor of a former hospital. Buzzy lounge/bar leads to smart dining room with original Hockneys on the wall. Modern British cooking with global reach.

Mon Plaisir

21 Monmouth St ✉ WC2H 9DD – Ⓜ Covent Garden – ☎ (020) 7836 7243 – eatafrog@mail.com – Fax (020) 7240 47 74 – www.monplaisir.co.uk

closed Christmas, Saturday lunch, Sunday and Bank Holidays I3

Rest – Menu £16 (lunch) – Carte £26/38

◆ French ◆ Family ◆

London's oldest French restaurant and family-run for over fifty years. Divided into four rooms, all with a different feel but all proudly Gallic in their decoration.

XX

Incognico

117 Shaftesbury Ave ✉ WC2H 8AD – Ⓜ Tottenham Court Road
– ✆ (020) 7836 8866 – Fax (020) 7240 95 25
closed 1 week Christmas, Sunday and Bank Holidays I3
Rest – Carte £21/32
♦ Modern ♦ Brasserie ♦
Firmly established with robust décor of wood panelling and brown leather chairs. Downstairs bar has a window into the kitchen, from where French and English classics derive.

XX

Neal Street

26 Neal St ✉ WC2H 9QT – Ⓜ Covent Garden
– ✆ (020) 7836 8368
– Fax (020) 7240 39 64 – www.carluccios.co.uk
closed 24 December-2 January, Sunday and Bank Holidays I3
Rest – Menu £25 (lunch) – Carte £28/45
♦ Italian ♦ Brasserie ♦
Light, bright and airy; tiled flooring and colourful pictures. Dishes range from the simple to the more complex. Mushrooms a speciality. Has its own shop next door.

XX

Sardo

45 Grafton Way ✉ W1T 5DQ – Ⓜ Warren Street
– ✆ (020) 7387 2521 – info@sardo-restaurant.com
– Fax (020) 7387 25 59 – www.sardo-restaurant.com
closed Saturday lunch and Sunday H1
Rest – Carte £25/34
♦ Sardinian ♦ Family ♦
Simple, stylish interior run in a very warm and welcoming manner with very efficient service. Rustic Italian cooking with a Sardinian character and a modern tone.

XX

Hakkasan

8 Hanway Pl ✉ W1T 1HD – Ⓜ Tottenham Court Road – ✆ (020) 7927 7000
– mail@hakkasan.com – Fax (020) 7907 18 89
closed 24-25 December I2
Rest – Carte £29/78
Spec. Peking duck with Beluga caviar. Stir-fry black pepper rib-eye beef. Pan-fried silver cod in XO sauce.
♦ Chinese (Canton) ♦ Fashionable ♦
A distinctive, modern interpretation of Cantonese cooking in an appropriately contemporary and cavernous basement. The lively, bustling bar is an equally popular nightspot.

XX

Fino

33 Charlotte St (entrance on Rathbone St) ✉ W1T 1RR – Ⓜ Goodge Street
– ✆ (020) 7813 8010 – info@finorestaurant.com – Fax (020) 7813 80 11
– www.finorestaurant.com
closed 25 December, Sunday and Bank Holidays I2
Rest – Carte £17/50
♦ Spanish ♦ Fashionable ♦
Spanish-run basement bar with modern style décor and banquette seating. Wide-ranging menu of authentic dishes; 2 set-price selections offering an introduction to tapas.

XX

Crazy Bear

26-28 Whitfield St ✉ W1T 2RG – Ⓜ Goodge Street – ✆ (020) 7631 0088
– enquiries@crazybeargroup.co.uk – Fax (020) 7631 11 88
– www.crazybeargroup.co.uk
closed 1 week Christmas, Saturday lunch and Sunday I2
Rest – Carte £23/32
♦ South-East Asian ♦ Trendy ♦
Exotic destination: downstairs bar geared to fashionable set; ground floor dining room is art deco inspired. Asian flavoured menus, with predominance towards Thai dishes.

UNITED KINGDOM

Archipelago

110 Whitfield St ✉ W1T 5ED – Ⓜ Goodge Street – ✆ (020) 7383 3346 – archipelago@onetel.com – Fax (020) 7383 71 81
closed 25 December, Saturday lunch, Sunday and Bank Holiday Mondays
Rest – Carte £26/37 H1
◆ Innovative ◆ Exotic ◆
Eccentric in both menu and décor and not for the faint hearted. Crammed with knick-knacks from cages to Buddhas. Menu an eclectic mix of influences from around the world.

Passione

10 Charlotte St ✉ W1T 2LT – Ⓜ Goodge Street – ✆ (020) 7636 2833 – liz@passione.co.uk – Fax (020) 7636 28 89 – www.passione.co.uk
closed Saturday lunch and Sunday I2
Rest – *(booking essential)* Carte £41/46
◆ Italian ◆ Friendly ◆
Compact but light and airy. Modern Italian cooking served in informal surroundings, with friendly and affable service. Particularly busy at lunchtime.

Cigala

54 Lamb's Conduit St ✉ WC1N 3LW – Ⓜ Holborn – ✆ (020) 7405 1717 – tasty@cigala.co.uk – Fax (020) 7242 99 49 – www.cigala.co.uk
closed 25-26 December, 1 January and Easter Sunday J1
Rest – Menu £18 (lunch) – Carte £19/35
◆ Spanish ◆ Rustic ◆
Spanish restaurant on the corner of attractive street. Simply furnished with large windows and open-plan kitchen. Robust Iberian cooking. Informal tapas bar downstairs.

Salt Yard

54 Goodge St ✉ W1T 4NA – Ⓜ Goodge Street – ✆ (020) 7637 0657 – info@saltyard.co.uk – Fax (020) 7580 74 35 – www.saltyard.co.uk
closed 2 weeks Christmas-New Year, Sunday, Saturday lunch and Bank Holidays H2
Rest – Carte £15/30
◆ Mediterranean ◆ Tapas bar ◆
Vogue destination with buzzy downstairs restaurant specialising in inexpensive sharing plates of tasty Italian and Spanish dishes: try the freshly cut hams. Super wine list.

Hatton Garden — *Plan VI*

Bleeding Heart

Bleeding Heart Yard (off Greville St) ✉ EC1N 8SJ – Ⓜ Farringdon – ✆ (020) 7242 8238 – bookings@bleedingheart.co.uk – Fax (020) 7831 14 02 – www.bleedingheart.co.uk
closed 24 December-3 January, Saturday, Sunday and Bank Holidays K2
Rest – Carte £25/36
◆ French ◆ Romantic ◆
Wood panelling, candlelight and a heart motif; a popular romantic dinner spot. By contrast, a busy City restaurant at lunchtime. French influenced menu. Weighty wine list.

Holborn — *Plan VI*

Asadal

227 High Holborn ✉ WC1V 7DA – Ⓜ Holborn – ✆ (020) 7430 9006 – info@asadal.co.uk – www.asadal.co.uk J2
Rest – Menu £17.50 – Carte £9/25
◆ Korean ◆ Friendly ◆
A hectic, unprepossessing location, but delivers the authenticity of a modest Korean café with the comfort and service of a proper restaurant. Good quality Korean cooking.

HYDE PARK & KNIGHTSBRIDGE

Plan VII

Mandarin Oriental Hyde Park

66 Knightsbridge ✉ SW1X 7LA – Ⓜ Knightsbridge – ✆ (020) 7235 2000 – molon-reservations@mohg.com – Fax (020) 7235 20 01 – www.mandarinoriental.com

220 VISA MC AE

F4

177 rm – †£464/488 ††£587/617, ☕ £26 – 23 suites

Rest *Foliage* – see below

Rest *The Park* – Menu £33 (lunch) – Carte £20/47

◆ Grand Luxury ◆ Classic ◆

Built in 1889 this classic hotel, with striking façade, remains one of London's grandest. Many of the luxurious bedrooms enjoy Park views. Immaculate and detailed service. Smart ambience in The Park.

Knightsbridge Green without rest

A/C VISA MC AE

159 Knightsbridge ✉ SW1X 7PD – Ⓜ Knightsbridge – ✆ (020) 7584 6274 – reservations@thekghotel.co.uk – Fax (020) 7225 16 35 – www.thekghotel.com

F4

16 rm – †£105/160 ††£140/160, ☕ £12 – 12 suites

◆ Traditional ◆ Classic ◆

Privately owned hotel, boasting peaceful sitting room with writing desk. Breakfast - sausage and bacon from Harrods! - served in the generously proportioned bedrooms.

Foliage – at Mandarin Oriental Hyde Park H.

A/C VISA MC AE

66 Knightsbridge ✉ SW1X 7LA – Ⓜ Knightsbridge – ✆ (020) 7201 3723 – Fax (020) 7235 45 52

F4

Rest – Menu £25 (lunch) – Carte £48/50

Spec. Smoked belly of ham, date marmalade, black pudding and cauliflower cream. Roast loin of venison, wild mushrooms and smoked artichoke purée. Pumpkin treacle tart with pecans and orange marmalade mousse.

◆ Inventive ◆ Formal ◆

Reached via a glass-enclosed walkway that houses the cellar. Hyde Park outside the window reflected in the foliage-themed décor. Gracious service, skilled modern cooking.

Zuma

A/C VISA MC AE

5 Raphael St ✉ SW7 1DL – Ⓜ Knightsbridge – ✆ (020) 7584 1010 – info@zumarestaurant.com – Fax (020) 7584 50 05 – www.zumarestaurant.com

F5

Rest – Carte £27/46

◆ Japanese ◆ Fashionable ◆

Strong modern feel with exposed pipes, modern lighting and granite flooring. A theatrical atmosphere around the Sushi bar and a varied and interesting modern Japanese menu.

Mr Chow

A/C VISA MC AE

151 Knightsbridge ✉ SW1X 7PA – Ⓜ Knightsbridge – ✆ (020) 7589 7347 – mrchow@aol.com – Fax (020) 7584 57 80 – www.mrchow.com closed 24-26 December, 1 January and Easter Monday

F4

Rest – Menu £22 (lunch) – Carte £44/51

◆ Chinese ◆ Friendly ◆

Cosmopolitan Chinese restaurant with branches in New York and L.A. Well established ambience. Walls covered with mirrors and modern art. House specialities worth opting for.

Hyde Park & Knightsbridge
(Plan VII)

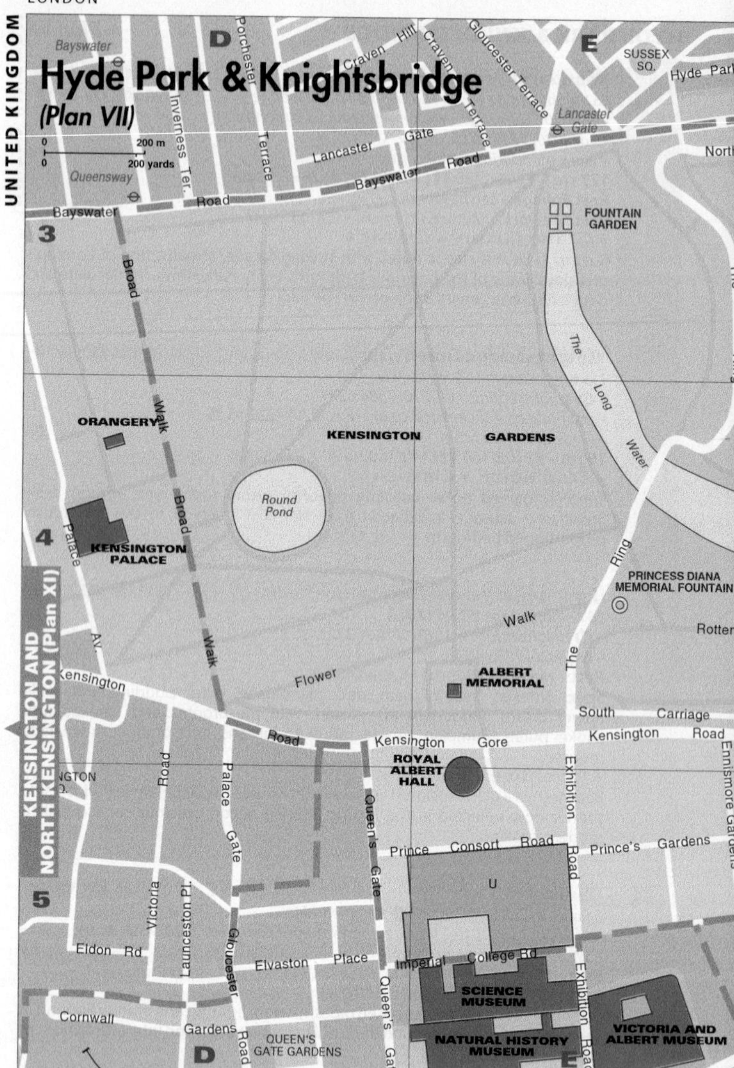

KENSINGTON AND NORTH KENSINGTON (Plan XI)

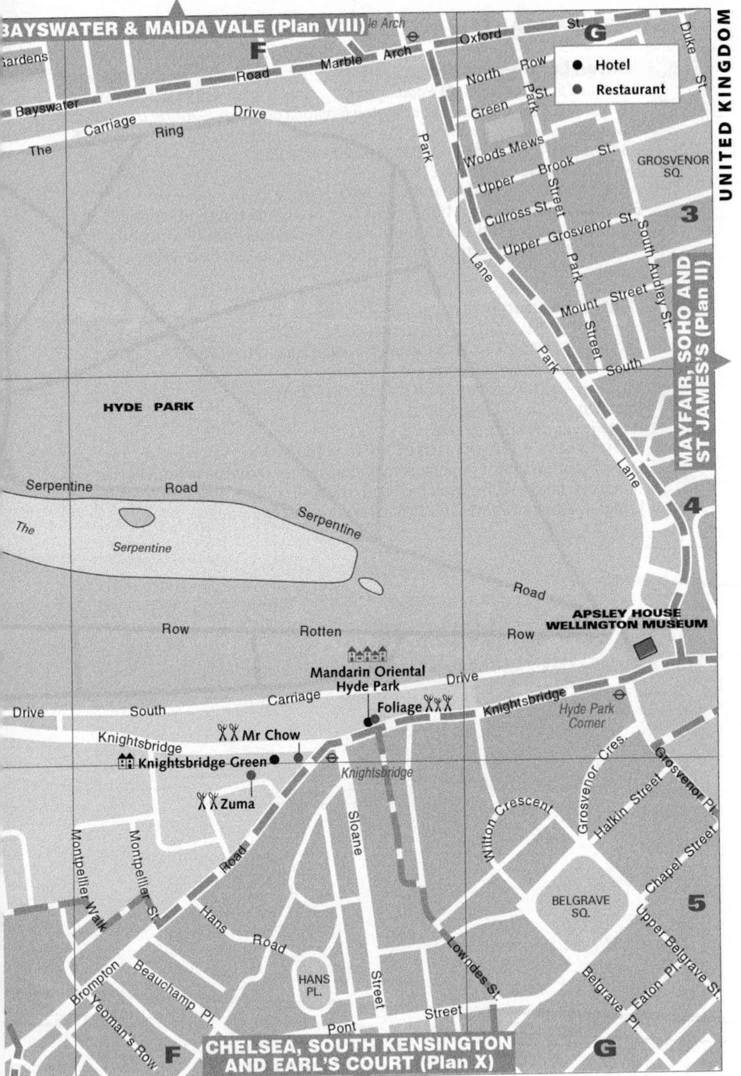

BAYSWATER & MAIDA VALE (Plan VIII)
F
G
Hotel
Restaurant
Oxford St.
Marble Arch
North Row
Green St.
Park St.
Duke St.
Bayswater Road
The Ring
Carriage Drive
Park Lane
Woods Mews
Upper Brook St.
Street
Culross St.
Upper Grosvenor St.
South Audley St.
GROSVENOR SQ.
3
Mount Street
Park Street
South
MAYFAIR, SOHO AND ST JAMES'S (Plan II)
HYDE PARK
Serpentine Road
The Serpentine
Serpentine Road
4
APSLEY HOUSE WELLINGTON MUSEUM
Rotten Row
Mandarin Oriental Hyde Park
Foliage
South Carriage Drive
Knightsbridge
Hyde Park Corner
Mr Chow
Knightsbridge Green
Zuma
Grosvenor Cres.
Grosvenor Pl.
Halkin Street
Wilton Crescent
Sloane Street
Brompton Road
Montpellier Walk
Montpellier St.
Chapel Street
BELGRAVE SQ.
5
Upper Belgrave St.
Hans Road
HANS PL.
Lowndes St.
Belgrave Pl.
Eaton Pl.
Beauchamp Pl.
Yeoman's Row
Pont Street
CHELSEA, SOUTH KENSINGTON AND EARL'S COURT (Plan X)

BAYSWATER & MAIDA VALE

Plan VIII

Hilton London Paddington

146 Praed St ✉ W2 1EE – Ⓜ Paddington
– ✆ (020) 7850 0500 – sales.paddington@hilton.com – Fax (020) 7850 06 00
– www.hilton.co.uk/paddington

350 VISA MC AE

E2

334 rm – †£140/311 ††£140/311, ☕ £20 – 20 suites
Rest *The Brasserie* – Carte £20/54

◆ Business ◆ Chain hotel ◆ Modern ◆

Early Victorian railway hotel, sympathetically restored in contemporary style with Art Deco details. Co-ordinated bedrooms with high tech facilities continue the modern style. Contemporarily styled brasserie offering a modern menu.

Hilton London Metropole

Edgware Rd ✉ W2 1JU – Ⓜ Edgware Road
– ✆ (020) 7402 4141 – cbs-londonmet@hilton.com – Fax (020) 7724 88 66
– www.hilton.co.uk/londonmet

1600 P VISA MC AE

E2

1033 rm – †£149/294 ††£149/294, ☕ £18 – 25 suites
Rest *Nippon Tuk* – Carte £22/41
Rest *Fiamma* – Carte £17/28

◆ Business ◆ Chain hotel ◆ Functional ◆

One of London's most popular convention venues by virtue of both its size and transport links. Well-appointed and modern rooms have state-of-the-art facilities. Vibrant Nippon Tuk. Italian favourites at Fiamma.

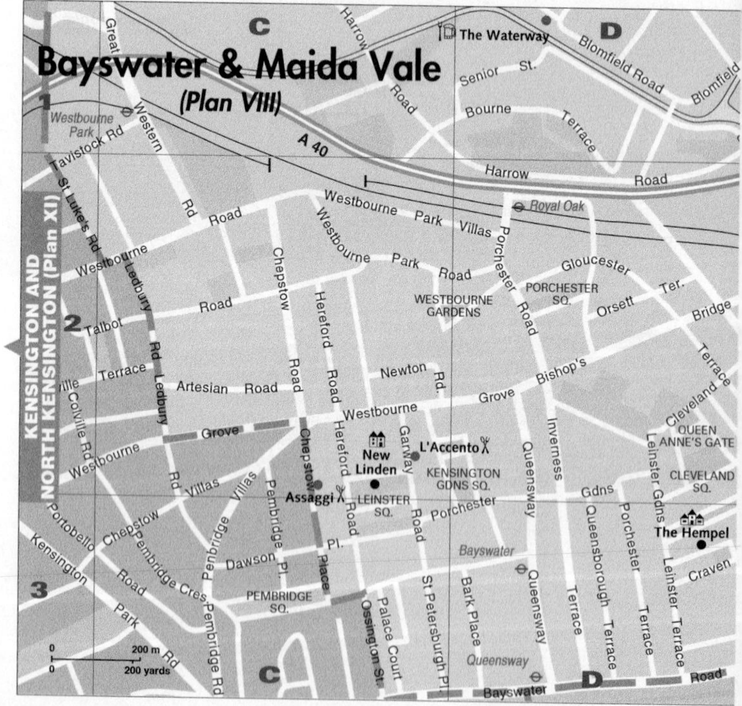

Royal Lancaster

1200 P VISA AE

Lancaster Terrace ✉ W2 2TY – Ⓜ Lancaster Gate – ✆ (020) 7262 6737 – sales@royallancaster.com – Fax (020) 7724 31 91 – www.royallancaster.com **E3**

394 rm – †£304 ††£304, ☕ £19 – 22 suites – **Rest *Island*** and ***Nipa*** – see below

♦ Business ♦ Classic ♦

Imposing 1960s purpose-built hotel overlooking Hyde Park. Some of London's most extensive conference facilities. Well-equipped bedrooms are decorated in traditional style.

The Hempel

VISA AE

31-35 Craven Hill Gdns ✉ W2 3EA – Ⓜ Queensway – ✆ (020) 7298 9000 – hotel@the-hempel.co.uk – Fax (020) 7402 46 66 – www.the-hempel.co.uk

closed Christmas – **37 rm** – †£194/335 ††£247/347, ☕ £15 – 4 suites **D3**

Rest *I-Thai* – *(closed Sunday)* Carte £35/56

♦ Luxury ♦ Minimalist ♦

A striking example of minimalist design. Individually appointed bedrooms are understated yet very comfortable. Relaxed ambience. Modern basement restaurant.

Colonnade Town House without rest

VISA AE

2 Warrington Crescent ✉ W9 1ER – Ⓜ Warwick Avenue – ✆ (020) 7286 1052 – rescolonnade@theetoncollection.com – Fax (020) 7286 10 57 – www.theetoncollection.com *Plan XI* **D1**

43 rm – †£164/211 ††£188/211, ☕ £15

♦ Townhouse ♦ Classic ♦

Two Victorian townhouses with comfortable well-furnished communal rooms decorated with fresh flowers. Stylish and comfortable bedrooms with many extra touches.

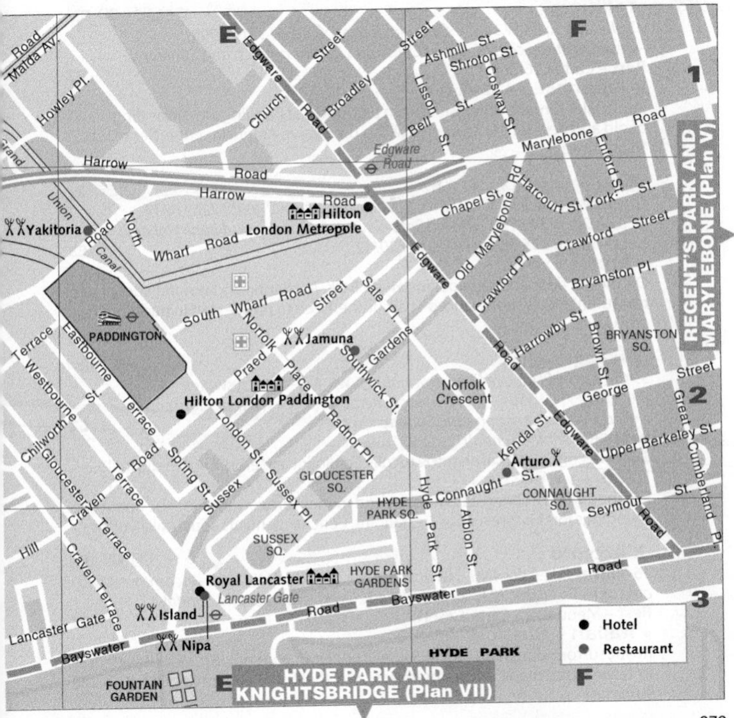

UNITED KINGDOM

New Linden without rest

58-60 Leinster Sq, ✉ W2 4PS – Ⓜ Bayswater – ✆ (020) 7221 4321 – newlindenhotel@mayflower-group.co.uk – Fax (020) 7727 31 56 – www.newlinden.co.uk

46 rm – †£69/85 ††£85/95, ☕ £7 C2

◆ Family ◆ Functional ◆

Smart four storey white stucco façade. Basement breakfast room with sunny aspect. Bedrooms are its strength: flat screen TVs and wooden floors; two split level family rooms.

Jamuna

38A Southwick St ✉ W2 1JQ – Ⓜ Edgware Road – ✆ (020) 7723 5056 – info@jamuna.co.uk – Fax (020) 7706 18 70 – www.jamuna.co.uk

closed 25-26 December, 1 January and Sunday E2

Rest – Carte £23/43

◆ Indian ◆ Neighbourhood ◆

Don't be put off by the unprepossessing nature of the area: this is a modern out of the ordinary Indian restaurant with cooking that's well presented, refined and flavoursome.

Island – at Royal Lancaster H.

Lancaster Terrace ✉ W2 2TY – Ⓜ Lancaster Gate – ✆ (020) 7551 6070 – eat@islandrestaurant.co.uk – Fax (020) 7551 60 71 – www.islandrestaurant.co.uk

Rest – Menu £15 (lunch) – Carte £25/35 E3

◆ Modern ◆ Brasserie ◆

Modern, stylish restaurant with buzzy open kitchen. Full length windows allow good views of adjacent Hyde Park. Seasonally based, modern menus with wide range of dishes.

Yakitoria

25 Sheldon Sq ✉ W2 6EY – Ⓜ Paddington – ✆ (020) 3214 3000 – www.yakitoria.co.uk – closed Christmas, Saturday lunch and Sunday

Rest – Carte £26/36 E2

◆ Japanese ◆ Design ◆

Funky, sleek interior accessible from platform 8 at Paddington. Appealing blend of old and new Japanese menus with a distinctive American edge. Bento boxes to take away.

Nipa – at Royal Lancaster H.

Lancaster Terrace ✉ W2 2TY – Ⓜ Lancaster Gate – ✆ (020) 7262 6737 – Fax (020) 7724 31 91 – closed Saturday lunch, Sunday and Bank Holidays

Rest – Menu £15 (lunch) – Carte £29/42 E3

◆ Thai ◆ Exotic ◆

On the 1st floor and overlooking Hyde Park. Authentic and ornately decorated restaurant offers subtly spiced Thai cuisine. Keen to please staff in traditional silk costumes.

Assaggi (Sassu)

39 Chepstow Pl (above Chepstow pub) ✉ W2 4TS – Ⓜ Bayswater – ✆ (020) 7792 5501 – nipi@assaggi.demon.co.uk – www.assaggi.com

closed 2 weeks Christmas and Sunday C2

Rest – *(booking essential)* Carte £37/39

Spec. Pecorino con carpegna & rucola. Tagliolini alle erbe. Fegato di vitello.

◆ Italian ◆ Rustic ◆

Polished wood flooring, tall windows and modern artwork provide the bright surroundings for this forever busy restaurant. Concise menu of robust Italian dishes.

L'Accento

16 Garway Rd ✉ W2 4NH – Ⓜ Bayswater – ✆ (020) 7243 2201 – laccentorest@aol.com – Fax (020) 7243 22 01 – closed 25-26 December and Sunday

Rest – Menu £19 – Carte £26/31 C2

◆ Italian ◆ Rustic ◆

Rustic surroundings and provincial, well priced, Italian cooking. Menu specialises in tasty pasta, made on the premises, and shellfish. Rear conservatory for the summer.

Arturo

23 Connaught St ✉ W2 2AY – Ⓜ Marble Arch – ☎ (020) 7706 3388
– Fax (020) 7402 91 95 – www.arturorestaurant.co.uk F2
Rest – Menu £16 (lunch) – Carte £16/27
♦ Italian ♦ Friendly ♦
On a smart street near Hyde Park: sleek, modish feel imbues interior with intimate, elegant informality. Tuscan and Sicilian dishes cooked with confidence and originality.

The Waterway

54 Formosa St ✉ W9 2JU – Ⓜ Warwick Avenue
– ☎ (020) 7266 3557 – info@thewaterway.co.uk – Fax (020) 7266 35 47
– www.thewaterway.co.uk D1
Rest – Carte £19/27
♦ Modern ♦ Pub ♦
Pub with a thoroughly modern, metropolitan ambience. Spacious bar and large decked terrace overlooking canal. Concise, well-balanced menu served in open plan dining room.

CITY OF LONDON, SOUTHWARK & TOWER HAMLETS

City of London

Plan IX

Great Eastern

rm 250

Liverpool St ✉ EC2M 7QN – Ⓜ Liverpool Street
– ☎ (020) 7618 5000 – info@great-eastern-hotel.co.uk
– Fax (020) 7618 50 01 – www.great-eastern-hotel.co.uk M2
264 rm – †£118/370 ††£118/370, ☕ £22 – 3 suites
Rest *Aurora* – see below
Rest *Fishmarket* – *(closed Saturday-Sunday)* Carte £25/48
Rest *Miyabi* – *(closed Christmas, Saturday lunch and Sunday) (booking essential)* Menu £18 (lunch) – Carte £24/44
♦ Luxury ♦ Modern ♦
A contemporary and stylish interior hides behind the classic Victorian façade of this railway hotel. Bright and spacious bedrooms with state-of-the-art facilities. Fishmarket based within original hotel lobby. Miyabi is compact Japanese restaurant.

Crowne Plaza London-The City

rm 180

19 New Bridge St ✉ EC4V 6DB – Ⓜ Blackfriars
– ☎ (0870) 400 9190 – loncy.info@ichotelsgroup.com – Fax (020) 7438 80 80
– www.crowneplaza.com K3
201 rm – †£358 ††£358, ☕ £17 – 2 suites
Rest *Refettorio* – *(closed Sunday, Saturday lunch and Bank Holidays)* Menu £20 (dinner) – Carte £33/37
Rest *Spicers* – Carte £22/28
♦ Business ♦ Chain hotel ♦ Modern ♦
Art deco façade by the river; interior enhanced by funky chocolate, cream and brown palette. Compact meeting room; well equipped fitness centre. Sizeable, stylish rooms. Modish Refettorio for Italian cuisine. British dishes with a modern twist at Spicers.

Threadneedles

35

5 Threadneedle St ✉ EC2R 8AY – Ⓜ Bank – ☎ (020) 7657 8080
– resthreadneedles@theetoncollection.com – Fax (020) 7657 81 00
– www.theetoncollection.com M3
68 rm – †£347 ††£347, ☕ £17 – 1 suite
Rest *Bonds* – see below
♦ Business ♦ Modern ♦
A converted bank, dating from 1856, with a stunning stained-glass cupola in the lounge. Rooms are very stylish and individual featuring CD players and Egyptian cotton sheets.

UNITED KINGDOM

City of London, Southwark & Tower Hamlets

(Plan IX)

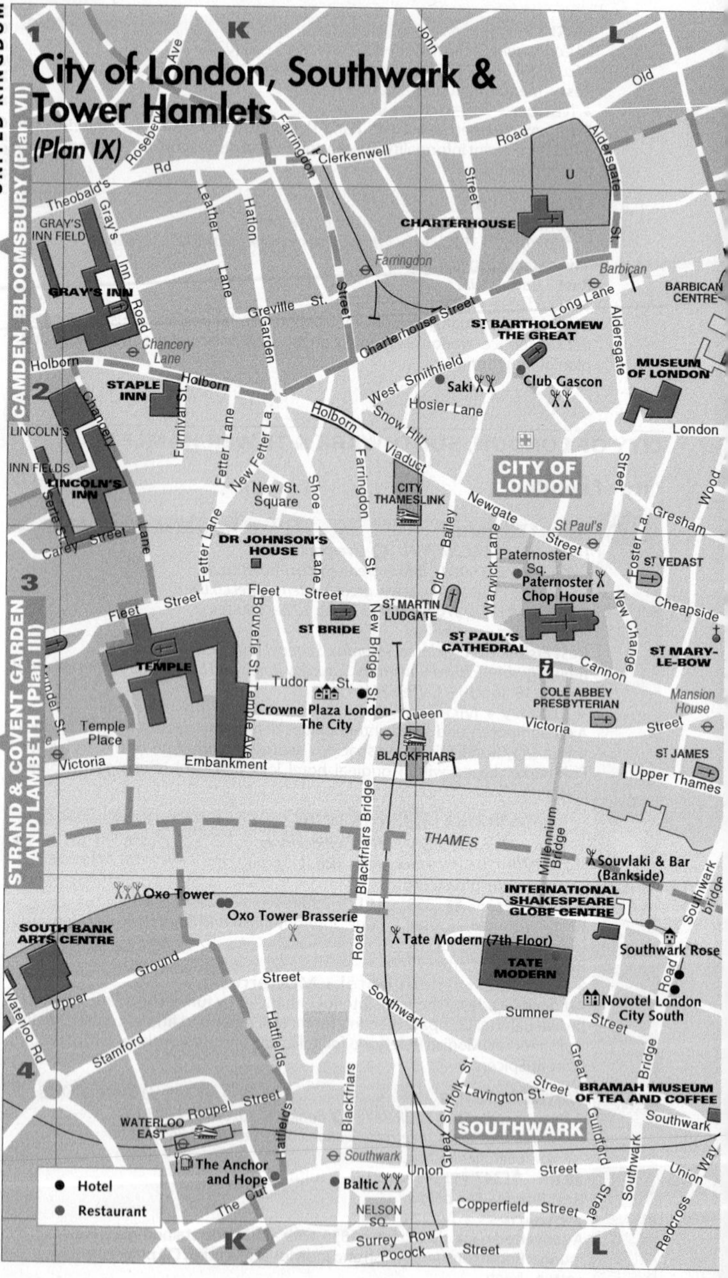

CAMDEN, BLOOMSBURY (Plan VII)

STRAND & COVENT GARDEN AND LAMBETH (Plan III)

K
L
1
2
3
4

GRAY'S INN FIELD
GRAY'S INN
STAPLE INN
LINCOLN'S INN FIELDS
LINCOLN'S INN
CHARTERHOUSE
ST BARTHOLOMEW THE GREAT
BARBICAN CENTRE
MUSEUM OF LONDON
Saki
Club Gascon
CITY THAMESLINK
CITY OF LONDON
DR JOHNSON'S HOUSE
ST BRIDE
ST MARTIN LUDGATE
ST PAUL'S CATHEDRAL
Paternoster Chop House
ST VEDAST
ST MARY-LE-BOW
COLE ABBEY PRESBYTERIAN
ST JAMES
TEMPLE
Crowne Plaza London-The City
BLACKFRIARS
THAMES
Souvlaki & Bar (Bankside)
INTERNATIONAL SHAKESPEARE GLOBE CENTRE
Oxo Tower
Oxo Tower Brasserie
SOUTH BANK ARTS CENTRE
Tate Modern (7th Floor)
TATE MODERN
Southwark Rose
Novotel London City South
BRAMAH MUSEUM OF TEA AND COFFEE
SOUTHWARK
WATERLOO EAST
The Anchor and Hope
Baltic
NELSON SQ.

Chancery Lane
Farringdon
Barbican
St Paul's
Mansion House
Southwark

- ● Hotel
- ● Restaurant

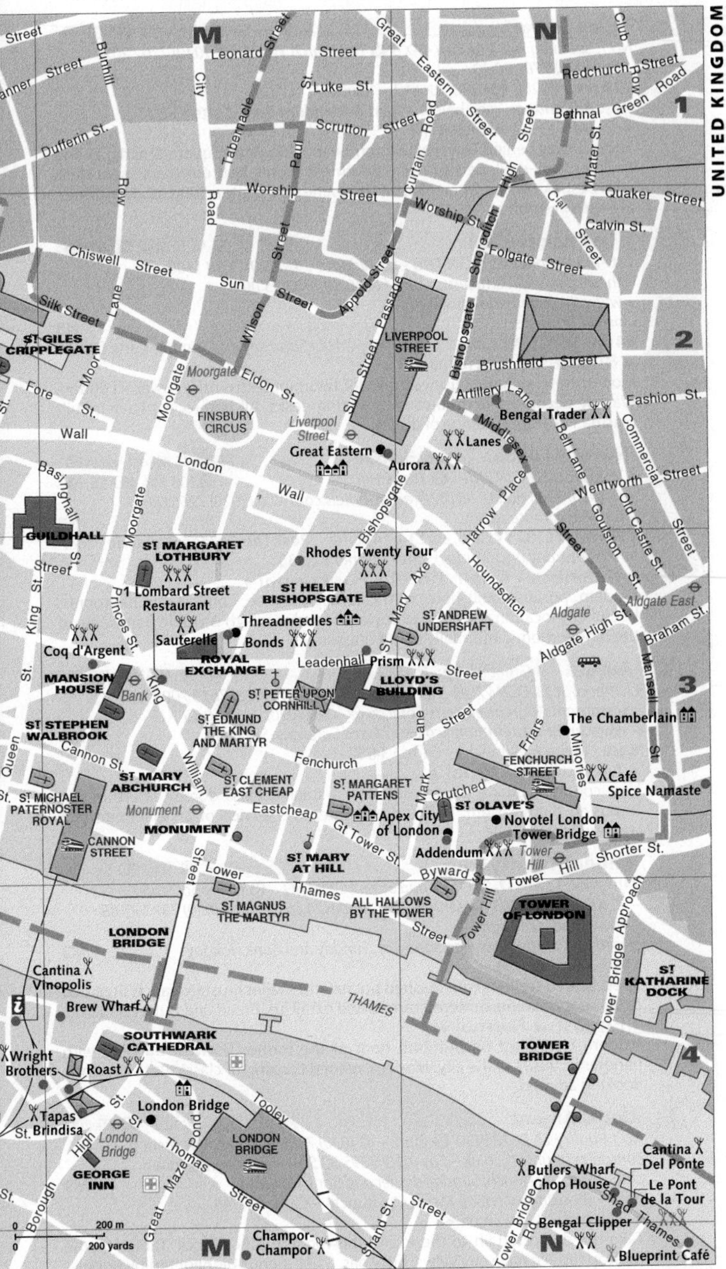
M
N
1
2
3
4
Street
Leonard Street
Street
Great Eastern Street
Club Row
Redchurch Street
Bunhill Row
City Road
Tabernacle Street
St. Luke St.
Bethnal Green Road
Dufferin St.
Scrutton Street
Curtain Road
Paul Street
High Street
Whater St.
Worship Street
Worship St.
Quaker Street
Calvin St.
Chiswell Street
Sun Street
Appold Street
Shoreditch
Folgate Street
Silk Street
Moor Lane
Wilson Street
Sun Street Passage
LIVERPOOL STREET
Bishopsgate
ST GILES CRIPPLEGATE
Brushfield Street
Moorgate
Eldon St.
Artillery Lane
Fashion St.
Fore St.
FINSBURY CIRCUS
Liverpool Street
Bengal Trader
Wall
Middlesex
Commercial Street
Great Eastern
Lanes
London Wall
Aurora
Bell Lane
Basinghall St.
Wentworth Street
Old Castle St.
Harrow Place
Goulston St.
GUILDHALL
Moorgate
ST MARGARET LOTHBURY
Rhodes Twenty Four
Houndsditch
Street
Aldgate East
King St.
1 Lombard Street Restaurant
ST HELEN BISHOPSGATE
St Mary Axe
ST ANDREW UNDERSHAFT
Aldgate
Braham St.
Princes St.
Threadneedles
Aldgate High St.
Coq d'Argent
Sauterelle
Bonds
Mansell St.
ROYAL EXCHANGE
Leadenhall
Prism
Street
MANSION HOUSE
Bank
King
ST PETER UPON CORNHILL
LLOYD'S BUILDING
ST STEPHEN WALBROOK
ST EDMUND THE KING AND MARTYR
Lime Street
The Chamberlain
Queen St.
Cannon St.
William
Fenchurch
Friars
Minories
ST MARY ABCHURCH
FENCHURCH STREET
Café Spice Namaste
ST MICHAEL PATERNOSTER ROYAL
ST CLEMENT EAST CHEAP
ST MARGARET PATTENS
Mark Lane
Crutched
ST OLAVE'S
Monument
Eastcheap
Apex City of London
Novotel London Tower Bridge
MONUMENT
Gt Tower St.
CANNON STREET
ST MARY AT HILL
Addendum
Tower Hill
Shorter St.
Street
Lower Thames Street
Byward St.
Tower Hill
ST MAGNUS THE MARTYR
ALL HALLOWS BY THE TOWER
TOWER OF LONDON
Tower Bridge Approach
LONDON BRIDGE
ST KATHARINE DOCK
Cantina Vinopolis
Brew Wharf
THAMES
SOUTHWARK CATHEDRAL
TOWER BRIDGE
Wright Brothers
Roast
Tooley
Tapas Brindisa
St.
London Bridge
St. Thomas Street
Pond
London Bridge
LONDON BRIDGE
High
Cantina Del Ponte
GEORGE INN
Maze
Butlers Wharf Chop House
Le Pont de la Tour
Borough
Shad Thames
0 200 m
0 200 yards
Great
Street
Shand St.
Tower Bridge Rd
Bengal Clipper
Champor-Champor
Blueprint Café

UNITED KINGDOM

Apex City of London 80 VISA

No 1, Seething Hill, ✉ EC3N 4AX – Ⓜ Fenchurch Street – ✆ (020) 7702 2020 – Fax (020) 7702 20 20

N3

129 rm – £288 £288, £17 – 1 suite

Rest *Addendum* – see below – **Rest *Addendum Bar*** – Carte £17/27

♦ Business ♦ Modern ♦

Tucked away behind Tower of London, overlooking leafy square. Smart meeting facilities, well-equipped gym and treatment rooms. Bedrooms are super sleek with bespoke extras. Open plan bar/brasserie serves interesting modern dishes; al fresco in summer.

The Chamberlain 50 VISA

130-135 Minories ✉ EC3N 1NU – Ⓜ Aldgate – ✆ (020) 7680 1500 – thechamberlain@fullers.co.uk – Fax (020) 7702 25 00 – www.thechamberlainhotel.com

closed Christmas

N3

64 rm – £225 £255, £15 – **Rest** – *(in bar Saturday and Sunday)* Carte £20/31

♦ Business ♦ Functional ♦

Modern hotel aimed at business traveller, two minutes from the Tower of London. Warmly decorated bedrooms with writing desks. All bathrooms have inbuilt plasma TVs. Popular range of dishes.

Novotel London Tower Bridge rest rm 100 VISA

10 Pepys St ✉ EC3N 2NR – Ⓜ Tower Hill – ✆ (020) 7265 6000 – h3107@accor-hotels.com – Fax (020) 7265 60 60 – www.accorhotels.com

N3

199 rm – £185 £205, £14 – 4 suites – **Rest *The Garden Brasserie*** – *(bar lunch Saturday and Sunday)* Carte /dinner £21/30

♦ Business ♦ Chain hotel ♦ Functional ♦

Modern, purpose-built hotel with carefully planned, comfortable bedrooms. Useful City location and close to Tower of London which is visible from some of the higher rooms. Informally styled brasserie.

XXX

Aurora – at Great Eastern H. VISA

Liverpool St ✉ EC2M 7QN – Ⓜ Liverpool Street – ✆ (020) 7618 7000 – restaurants@great-eastern-hotel.co.uk – Fax (020) 7618 50 35 – www.great-eastern-hotel.co.uk – closed Saturday-Sunday

M2

Rest – Menu £28 (lunch) – Carte £34/53

♦ Modern ♦ Formal ♦

Vast columns, ornate plasterwork and a striking glass dome feature in this imposing dining room. Polished and attentive service of an elaborate and modern menu.

XXX

Rhodes Twenty Four London, VISA

24th floor, Tower 42, 25 Old Broad St ✉ EC2N 1HQ – Ⓜ Liverpool Street – ✆ (020) 7877 7703 – reservations@rhodes24.co.uk – Fax (020) 7877 77 88 – www.rhodes24.co.uk

closed Christmas-New year, Saturday, Sunday and Bank Holidays

M3

Rest – Carte £27/33

Spec. Seared scallops with mashed potato and shallot mustard sauce. Steamed oxtail suet pudding, buttered carrots and oxtail jus. Bread and butter pudding.

♦ English ♦ Formal ♦

Modern restaurant on the 24th floor of the former Natwest building with panoramic views of the city. Modern, refined cooking of classic British recipes. Booking advised.

XXX

Coq d'Argent VISA

No 1 Poultry ✉ EC2R 8EJ – Ⓜ Bank – ✆ (020) 7395 5000 – coqdargent@conran-restaurants.co.uk – Fax (020) 7395 50 50 – www.conran.com

closed Saturday lunch, Sunday dinner and Bank Holidays

M3

Rest – *(booking essential)* Menu £27 (lunch) – Carte £37/44

♦ French ♦ Design ♦

Take the dedicated lift to the top of this modern office block. Tables on the rooftop terrace have city views; busy bar. Gallic menus highlighted by popular shellfish dishes.

XXX ✿ **1 Lombard Street Restaurant** AC ⁄ ⇔25 VISA MC AE ①

1 Lombard St ✉ EC3V 9AA – Ⓜ Bank – ✆ (020) 7929 6611 – hb@1lombardstreet.com – Fax (020) 7929 66 22 – www.1lombardstreet.com closed Saturday, Sunday and Bank Holidays **M3**

Rest – *(booking essential at lunch)* Menu £39/45 – Carte £53/62

Spec. Carpaccio of tuna with Oriental spices, ginger and lime vinaigrette. Beef tournedos with wild mushrooms, parsley purée and oxtail sauce. Feuillantine of apple, Guinness ice cream and glazed hazelnuts.

♦ Modern ♦ Formal ♦

A haven of tranquillity behind the forever busy brasserie. Former bank provides the modern and very comfortable surroundings in which to savour the accomplished cuisine.

XXX **Prism** AC VISA MC AE ①

147 Leadenhall ✉ EC3V 4QT – Ⓜ Aldgate – ✆ (020) 7256 3875 – Fax (020) 7256 38 76 – www.harveynichols.com closed 23 December-2 January, Saturday, Sunday and Bank Holidays **M3**

Rest – Carte £33/43

♦ Innovative ♦ Trendy ♦

Enormous Corinthian pillars and a busy bar feature in this capacious and modern restaurant. Efficient service of an eclectic menu. Quieter tables in covered courtyard.

XXX **Addendum** – at Apex City of London H AC ⁄ VISA MC AE ①

No. 1 Seething Lane ✉ EC3N 4AX – Ⓜ Fenchurch Street – ✆ (020) 7977 9500 – londonevents@apexhotels.co.uk – www.addendumrestaurant.co.uk closed 23 December-3 January, Saturday, Sunday and Bank Holidays **N3**

Rest – Carte £39/55

♦ Modern European ♦

Intimate and elegant with chocolate leather banquettes, fresh flowers and modern mirrors. Precise service of robust, earthy dishes which often rejoice in the use of offal.

XXX **Bonds** – at Threadneedles H. AC ⁄ VISA MC AE ①

5 Threadneedle St ✉ EC2R 8AY – Ⓜ Bank – ✆ (020) 7657 8088 – bonds@theetongroup.com – Fax (020) 7657 80 89 – www.theetoncollection.com closed 2 weeks Christmas-New Year, Sunday and Bank Holidays **M3**

Rest – Menu £20/25 – Carte £30/48

♦ Modern ♦ Retro ♦

Modern interior juxtaposed with the grandeur of a listed city building. Vast dining room with high ceiling and tall pillars. Attentive service of hearty, contemporary food.

XX ✿ **Club Gascon** (Aussignac) AC VISA MC AE

57 West Smithfield ✉ EC1A 9DS – Ⓜ Barbican – ✆ (020) 7796 0600 – Fax (020) 7796 06 01 closed 22-31 December, Sunday, Saturday lunch and Bank Holidays **L2**

Rest – *(booking essential)* Menu £38/60 – Carte £33/79

Spec. Saffron duck foie gras, crispy chicory. Grilled wild salmon, smoked violet tea and aubergine. Glazed veal sweetbread, Bergamot and artichoke barigoule.

♦ French ♦ Fashionable ♦

Intimate restaurant on the edge of Smithfield Market. Specialises in both the food and wines of Southwest France. Renowned for its tapas-sized dishes.

XX **Sauterelle** AC ⁄ ⇔24 VISA MC AE ①

The Royal Exchange ✉ EC3V 3LR – Ⓜ Bank – ✆ (020) 7618 2483 – www.conran-restaurants.co.uk closed Christmas and New Year, Saturday and Sunday **M3**

Rest – Carte £28/41

♦ French ♦ Design ♦

Located on mezzanine level of Royal Exchange, a stunning 16C property with ornate columns and pillars. Typically Conran rustic French menus attract smart lunchtime diners.

XX **Lanes** AC 28 VISA MC AE

109-117 Middlesex St. ✉ E1 7JF – Ⓜ Liverpool Street – ✆ (020) 7247 5050 – Fax (020) 7247 80 71 – www.lanesrestaurant.co.uk

closed 25 December, Saturday lunch, Sunday and Bank Holidays **N2**

Rest – Menu £22 (dinner) – Carte £28/44

♦ Modern European ♦

Busy lunchtimes and more sedate evenings at this bright destination with subterranean bar, where art displays are a regular backdrop. Modern British/European menus hold sway.

XX **Saki** AC 12 VISA MC

4 West Smithfield ✉ EC1A 9JX – Ⓜ Barbican – ✆ (020) 7489 7033 – info@saki-food.com – Fax (020) 7489 16 58 – www.saki-food.com **L2**

Rest – Menu £25/55 – Carte £22/60

♦ Japanese ♦ Fashionable ♦

Uber-stylish bar/restaurant below a Japanese deli. Incorporates a sushi bar, communal 'garden table' and impressive Japanese dishes based on seasonality and healthy eating.

X **Paternoster Chop House** AC VISA MC AE

Warwick Court, Paternoster Square ✉ EC4N 7DX – Ⓜ St Paul's – ✆ (020) 7029 9400 – Fax (020) 7029 94 09 – www.conran.com

closed 23 December-3 January, Saturday and Sunday **L3**

Rest – Carte £31/36

♦ English ♦ Brasserie ♦

A modern ambience holds sway, while there's a reassuringly resolute British classic style to the dishes. Back to basics menu relies on seasonality and sourcing of ingredients.

Southwark *Plan IX*

Bermondsey

London Bridge AC rm 100 VISA MC AE

8-18 London Bridge St ✉ SE1 9SG – Ⓜ London Bridge – ✆ (020) 7855 2200 – sales@london-bridge-hotel.co.uk – Fax (020) 7855 22 33 – www.londonbridgehotel.co.uk **N4**

135 rm – †£199 ††£199, ☐ £15 – 3 suites

Rest *Georgetown* – Menu £25 – Carte £20/29

♦ Business ♦ Classic ♦

In one of the oldest parts of London, independently owned with an ornate façade dating from 1915. Modern interior with classically decorated bedrooms and an impressive gym. Restaurant echoing the colonial style serving Malaysian dishes.

XXX **Le Pont de la Tour** 24 VISA MC AE

36d Shad Thames (Butlers Wharf) ✉ SE1 2YE – Ⓜ London Bridge – ✆ (020) 7403 8403 – Fax (020) 7403 02 67 – www.conran.com **N4**

Rest – Menu £30 (lunch) – Carte dinner £41/83

♦ Modern ♦ Formal ♦

Elegant and stylish room commanding spectacular views of the Thames and Tower Bridge. Formal and detailed service. Modern menu with an informal bar attached.

XX **Bengal Clipper** AC VISA MC AE

Cardamom Building, Shad Thames, Butlers Wharf ✉ SE1 2YR – Ⓜ London Bridge – ✆ (020) 7357 9001 – mail@bengalclipper.co.uk – Fax (020) 7357 90 02 – www.bengalclipper.co.uk **N4**

Rest – Carte £17/27

♦ Indian ♦ Friendly ♦

Housed in a Thames-side converted warehouse, a smart Indian restaurant with original brickwork and steel supports. Menu features Bengali and Goan dishes. Evening pianist.

Blueprint Café
Tower Bridge, VISA MC AE

Design Museum, Shad Thames, Butlers Wharf ✉ SE1 2YD – Ⓜ London Bridge – ✆ (020) 7378 7031 – Fax (020) 7357 88 10 – www.conran.com

closed 25-28 December, 1-2 January and Sunday dinner **N5**

Rest – Carte £24/38

◆ Modern ◆ Design ◆

Above the Design Museum, with impressive views of the river and bridge: handy binoculars on tables. Eager and energetic service, modern British menus: robust and rustic.

Village East
AC ⇸ ⇔18 VISA MC AE

171 Bermondsey St ✉ SE1 3UW – Ⓜ London Bridge – ✆ (020) 7357 6082 – info@villageeast.co.uk – Fax (020) 7403 33 60 – www.villageeast.co.uk *Plan I* **D2**

Rest – Carte £24/36

◆ Modern European ◆

In a glass fronted block sandwiched by Georgian townhouses, this trendy restaurant has two loud, buzzy bars and dining areas serving ample portions of modern British fare.

Cantina Del Ponte
VISA MC AE

36c Shad Thames, Butlers Wharf ✉ SE1 2YE – Ⓜ London Bridge – ✆ (020) 7403 5403 – Fax (020) 7403 44 32 – www.conran.com

closed 25-26 December **N4**

Rest – Carte £16/28

◆ Italian ◆ Bistro ◆

Quayside setting with a large canopied terrace. Terracotta flooring; modern rustic style décor, simple and unfussy. Tasty, refreshing Mediterranean-influenced cooking.

Butlers Wharf Chop House
Tower Bridge, VISA MC AE

36e Shad Thames, Butlers Wharf ✉ SE1 2YE – Ⓜ London Bridge – ✆ (020) 7403 3403 – Fax (020) 7403 34 14 – www.conran.com

closed 25-26 December, 1-3 January and Sunday dinner **N4**

Rest – Menu £26 (lunch) – Carte dinner £25/38

◆ English ◆ Rustic ◆

Book the terrace in summer and dine in the shadow of Tower Bridge. Rustic feel to the interior, with obliging service. Menu focuses on traditional English dishes.

Rotherhithe

Hilton London Docklands
AC ⇸rm 350 P VISA MC AE

265 Rotherhithe St, Nelson Dock ✉ SE16 5HW – ✆ (020) 7231 1001 – sales-docklands@hilton.com – Fax (020) 7231 05 99 – www.hilton.co.uk/docklands

closed 22-30 December

361 rm – †£112/194 ††£112/194, ☕ £15 – 4 suites

Rest *Traders Bistro* – *(dinner only)* Menu £24

◆ Business ◆ Chain hotel ◆ Functional ◆

Redbrick group hotel with glass façade. River-taxi from the hotel's own pier. Extensive leisure facilities. Standard size rooms with all mod cons. Eat on board Traders Bistro, a reconstructed galleon moored in dry dock.

Southwark

Novotel London City South
AC ⇸rm 100 VISA MC AE

53-61 Southwark Bridge Rd ✉ SE1 9HH – Ⓜ London Bridge – ✆ (020) 7089 0400 – h3269@accor.com – Fax (020) 7089 04 10 – www.novotel.com **L4**

178 rm – †£180/200 ††£200/220, ☕ £14 – 4 suites

Rest *The Garden Brasserie* – Carte £17/32

◆ Business ◆ Chain hotel ◆ Functional ◆

The new style of Novotel with good business facilities. Triple glazed bedrooms, furnished in the Scandinavian style with keyboard and high speed internet. Brasserie style dining room with windows all down one side.

UNITED KINGDOM

Southwark Rose

60 VISA AE

43-47 Southwark Bridge Rd ✉ SE1 9HH – Ⓜ London Bridge – ✆ (020) 7015 1480 – info@southwarkrosehotel.co.uk – Fax (020) 7015 14 81 – www.southwarkrosehotel.co.uk

L4

78 rm – †£170 ††£170, ☕ £13 – 6 suites – **Rest** – *(dinner only)* Carte £13/19

◆ Business ◆ Functional ◆

Purpose built budget hotel south of the City, near the Globe Theatre. Top floor dining room with bar. Uniform style, reasonably spacious bedrooms with writing desks.

XXX

Oxo Tower

< London Skyline and River Thames,

(8th Floor) Oxo Tower Wharf, Barge House St, ✉ SE1 9PH VISA AE *– Ⓜ Southwark – ✆ (020) 7803 3888 – oxo.reservations@harveynichols.co.uk – Fax (020) 7803 38 38 – www.harveynichols.com – closed 25-26 December*

Rest *Oxo Tower Brasserie* – see below

K4

Rest – Menu £30 (lunch) – Carte dinner £42/57

◆ Modern ◆ Formal ◆

Top of a converted factory, providing stunning views of the Thames and beyond. Stylish, minimalist interior with huge windows. Smooth service of modern cuisine.

XX

Roast

VISA AE

The Floral Hall, Borough Market ✉ SE1 1TL – Ⓜ London Bridge – ✆ (020) 7940 1300 – info@roast-restaurant.com – Fax (020) 7940 13 01 – www.roast-restaurant.com – closed Sunday dinner and Bank Holidays

Rest – Menu £21 (lunch) – Carte £32/47

M4

◆ British ◆

Set into the roof of Borough Market's Floral Hall. Extensive cocktail list in bar; split-level restaurant has views to St. Paul's. Robust English cooking using market produce.

XX

Baltic

VISA AE

74 Blackfriars Rd ✉ SE1 8HA – Ⓜ Southwark – ✆ (020) 7928 1111 – info@balticrestaurant.co.uk – Fax (020) 7928 84 87 – www.balticrestaurant.co.uk

Rest – Menu £14 (lunch) – Carte £23/28

K4

◆ Eastern European ◆ Brasserie ◆

Set in a Grade II listed 18C former coach house. Enjoy authentic and hearty east European and Baltic influenced food. Interesting vodka selection and live jazz on Sundays.

X

Oxo Tower Brasserie

< London Skyline and River Thames,

(8th Floor) Oxo Tower Wharf,Barge House St ✉ SE1 9PH VISA AE *– Ⓜ Southwark – ✆ (020) 7803 3888 – oxo.reservations@harveynichols.co.uk – Fax (020) 7803 38 38 – www.harveynichols.com – closed 25-26 December*

Rest – Menu £22 (lunch) – Carte £30/41

K4

◆ Modern ◆ Brasserie ◆

Same views but less formal than the restaurant. Open-plan kitchen, relaxed service, the modern menu is slightly lighter. In summer, try to secure a table on the terrace.

X

Cantina Vinopolis

VISA AE

No 1 Bank End ✉ SE1 9BU – Ⓜ London Bridge – ✆ (020) 7940 8333 – cantina@vinopolis.co.uk – Fax (020) 7940 83 34 – www.cantinavinopolis.com closed 24 December-2 January and Sunday dinner

L4

Rest – Menu £18 (lunch) – Carte £20/28

◆ Modern ◆ Bistro ◆

Large, solid brick vaulted room under Victorian railway arches, with an adjacent wine museum. Modern menu with a huge selection of wines by the glass.

X

Tate Cafe (7th Floor)

< London Skyline and River Thames,

Tate Modern, Bankside ✉ SE1 9TG – Ⓜ Southwark VISA AE *– ✆ (020) 7401 5020 – Fax (020) 7401 51 71 – www.tate.org.uk closed 24-26 December*

L4

Rest – *(lunch only and dinner Friday-Saturday)* Carte £20/32

◆ Innovative ◆ Design ◆

Modernity to match the museum, with vast murals and huge windows affording stunning views. Canteen-style menu at a sensible price with obliging service.

Souvlaki & Bar (Bankside)

Units 1-2, Riverside House, 2A Southwark Bridge Rd ✉ SE1 9HA – ✆ (020) 7620 0162 – Fax (020) 7620 02 62 – www.therealgreek.co.uk

Rest – Carte £14/25 L4

◆ Greek ◆ Bistro ◆

Overlooking the Thames, two minutes from Globe Theatre: a casual, modern restaurant with excellent value menus featuring totally authentic Greek dishes and beers.

Wright Brothers

11 Stoney St, Borough Market ✉ SE1 9AD – Ⓜ London Bridge – ✆ (020) 7403 9554 – Fax (020) 7403 95 58 – www.wrightbros.eu.com

Rest – Carte £23/43 L4

◆ Seafood ◆ Wine bar ◆

Classic style oyster and porter house - a large number of porter ales on offer. Simple settings afford a welcoming ambience to enjoy huge range of oysters and prime shellfish.

Anchor and Hope

36 The Cut ✉ SE1 8LP – Ⓜ Southwark – ✆ (020) 7928 9898 – Fax (020) 7928 45 95

closed Christmas-New Year, last 2 weeks August, Sunday, Monday lunch and Bank Holidays K4

Rest – *(bookings not accepted)* Carte £20/30

◆ Modern ◆ Pub ◆

Close to Waterloo, the distinctive dark green exterior lures visitors in droves. Bare floorboards, simple wooden furniture. Seriously original cooking with rustic French base.

Tower Hamlets

Canary Wharf

Four Seasons

Westferry Circus, ✉ E14 8RS – Ⓜ Canary Wharf – ✆ (020) 7510 1999 – sales.caw@fourseasons.com – Fax (020) 7510 19 98 – www.fourseasons.com/canarywharf

128 rm – †£388/447 ††£408/467, ☕ £22 – 14 suites

Rest Quadrato – see below

◆ Grand Luxury ◆ Classic ◆

Sleek and stylish with striking river and city views. Atrium lobby leading to modern bedrooms boasting every conceivable extra. Detailed service.

Circus Apartments without rest

39 Westferry Circus, ✉ E14 8RW – Ⓜ Canary Wharf – ✆ (020) 7719 7000 – res@circusapartments.co.uk – Fax (020) 7719 70 01 – www.circusapartments.co.uk

45 suites – †£229/276, ☕ £8

◆ Business ◆ Modern ◆

Smart, contemporary, fully serviced apartment block close to Canary Wharf: rooms, comfortable and spacious, can be taken from one day to one year.

Plateau (Restaurant)

Canada Place, Canada Square, ✉ E14 5ER – Ⓜ Canary Wharf (DLR) – ✆ (020) 7715 7100 – Fax (020) 7715 71 10 – www.conran.com

closed 25 December, 1 January, Saturday lunch and Sunday

Rest – Menu £25 (dinner) – Carte £40/51

◆ Modern ◆ Design ◆

Fourth floor restaurant overlooking Canada Square and The Big Blue art installation. Glass-sided kitchen; well-spaced, uncluttered tables. Modern menus with classical base.

XX **Ubon by Nobu** — River Thames and city skyline, AC

39 Westferry Circus, ✉ E14 8RR – Ⓜ Canary Wharf (DLR) P VISA MC AE
– ☎ (020) 7719 7800 – ubon@noburestaurants.com – Fax (020) 7719 78 01
– www.noburestaurants.com
closed Saturday lunch, Sunday and Bank Holidays
Rest – Menu £45/70
♦ Japanese ♦ Trendy ♦
Light, airy, open-plan restaurant, with floor to ceiling glass and great Thames views. Informal atmosphere. Large menu with wide selection of modern Japanese dishes.

XX **Quadrato** – at Four Seasons H. AC P VISA MC AE

Westferry Circus, ✉ E14 8RS – Ⓜ Canary Wharf (DLR)
– ☎ (020) 7510 1999 – Fax (020) 7510 19 98
– www.fourseasons.com/canarywharf
Rest – Menu £27/33 – Carte £27/41
♦ Italian ♦ Design ♦
Striking, modern restaurant with terrace overlooking river. Sleek, stylish dining room with glass-fronted open-plan kitchen. Menu of northern Italian dishes; swift service.

XX **Plateau (Grill)** AC VISA MC AE

Canada Place, Canada Square, ✉ E14 5ER – Ⓜ Canary Wharf (DLR)
– ☎ (020) 7715 7100 – Fax (020) 7715 71 10 – www.conran.com
closed 25 December, 1 January and Sunday dinner
Rest – Menu £20/35 – Carte £24/35
♦ Modern ♦ Design ♦
Situated on fourth floor of 21C building; adjacent to Plateau Restaurant, with simpler table settings. Classical dishes, with seasonal base, employing grill specialities.

The Gun VISA MC AE

27 Coldharbour ✉ E14 9NS – Ⓜ Blackwall (DLR)
– ☎ (020) 7515 5222 – info@thegundocklands.com
– www.thegundocklands.com
closed 25-26 December and 1 January
Rest – Carte £20/33
♦ Modern ♦ Pub ♦
Restored historic pub with a terrace facing the Dome: tasty dishes, including Billingsgate market fish, balance bold simplicity and a bit of French finesse. Efficient service.

Spitalfields

XX **Bengal Trader** AC VISA MC AE

44 Artillery Lane ✉ E1 7NA – Ⓜ Liverpool Street
– ☎ (020) 7375 0072 – mail@bengalclipper.co.uk – Fax (020) 7247 10 02
– www.bengalclipper.co.uk **N2**
Rest – Carte £13/25
♦ Indian ♦ Brasserie ♦
Contemporary Indian paintings feature in this stylish basement room beneath a ground floor bar. Menu provides ample choice of Indian dishes.

X **St John Bread and Wine** AC VISA MC AE

94-96 Commercial St ✉ E1 6LZ – Ⓜ Shoreditch
– ☎ (020) 7247 8724
– Fax (020) 7247 89 24
– www.stjohnbreadandwine.com
closed 24 December-2 January, Sunday dinner and Bank Holiday Mondays *Plan I* **D2**
Rest – Carte £25/29
♦ Innovative ♦ Bistro ♦
Very popular neighbourhood bakery providing wide variety of home-made breads. Appealing, intimate dining section: all day menus that offer continually changing dishes.

Wapping

Wapping Food

Wapping Wall ✉ E1W 3ST – Ⓜ Wapping – ✆ (020) 7680 2080 – info@wapping-wpt.com – www.thewappingproject.com – closed 24 December-2 January and Sunday dinner – **Rest** – Carte £26/42 *Plan I* **D2**

◆ Modern ◆ Design ◆

Something a little unusual; a combination of restaurant and gallery in a converted hydraulic power station. Enjoy the modern menu surrounded by turbines and TV screens.

Whitechapel

Cafe Spice Namaste

16 Prescot St, ✉ E1 8AZ – Ⓜ Tower Hill – ✆ (020) 7488 9242 – info@cafespice.co.uk – Fax (020) 7481 05 08 – www.cafespice.co.uk closed Christmas-New Year, Sunday and Bank Holidays **N3**

Rest – Menu £30 – Carte £17/29

◆ Indian ◆ Neighbourhood ◆

A riot of colour from the brightly painted walls to the flowing drapes. Sweet-natured service adds to the engaging feel. Fragrant and competitively priced Indian cooking.

CHELSEA, SOUTH KENSINGTON & EARL'S COURT

Chelsea

Plan X

Jumeirah Carlton Tower

Cadogan Pl ✉ SW1X 9PY – Ⓜ Knightsbridge – ✆ (020) 7235 1234 – jctinfo@jumeirah – Fax (020) 7235 91 29 – www.jumeirah.com **F5**

rm 400

190 rm – †£410/563 ††£563, ☕ £30 – 30 suites – **Rest *Rib Room*** – Carte £45/76

◆ Grand Luxury ◆ Classic ◆

Imposing international hotel overlooking a leafy square. Well-equipped roof-top health club has funky views. Generously proportioned rooms boast every conceivable facility. Rib Room restaurant has a clubby atmosphere.

Conrad London

Chelsea Harbour ✉ SW10 0XG – Ⓜ Fulham Broadway – ✆ (020) 7823 3000 – lonch-rs@hilton.com – Fax (020) 7352 81 74 – www.conradlondon.com **D8**

rm 250

160 suites – †£558, ☕ £23 – **Rest *Aquasia*** – Carte £25/45

◆ Luxury ◆ Modern ◆

Modern, all-suite hotel within an exclusive marina and retail development. Many of the spacious and well-appointed rooms have balconies and views across the Thames.

Sheraton Park Tower

101 Knightsbridge ✉ SW1X 7RN – Ⓜ Knightsbridge – ✆ (020) 7235 8050 – central.london.reservations@sheraton.com – Fax (020) 7235 82 31 – www.luxurycollection.com/parktowerlondon **F4**

100

275 rm – †£294/476 ††£294/476, ☕ £22 – 5 suites

Rest *One-O-One* – see below

◆ Luxury ◆ Business ◆

Built in the 1970s in a unique cylindrical shape. Well-equipped bedrooms are all identical in size. Top floor executive rooms have commanding views of Hyde Park and City.

Capital

22-24 Basil St ✉ SW3 1AT – Ⓜ Knightsbridge – ✆ (020) 7589 5171 – reservations@capitalhotel.co.uk – Fax (020) 7225 00 11 – www.capitalhotel.co.uk **F5**

25

49 rm – †£247/335 ††£385, ☕ £19 – **Rest *The Capital Restaurant*** – see below

◆ Luxury ◆ Traditional ◆ Classic ◆

Discreet and privately owned town house with distinct English charm. Individually decorated rooms with plenty of thoughtful touches.

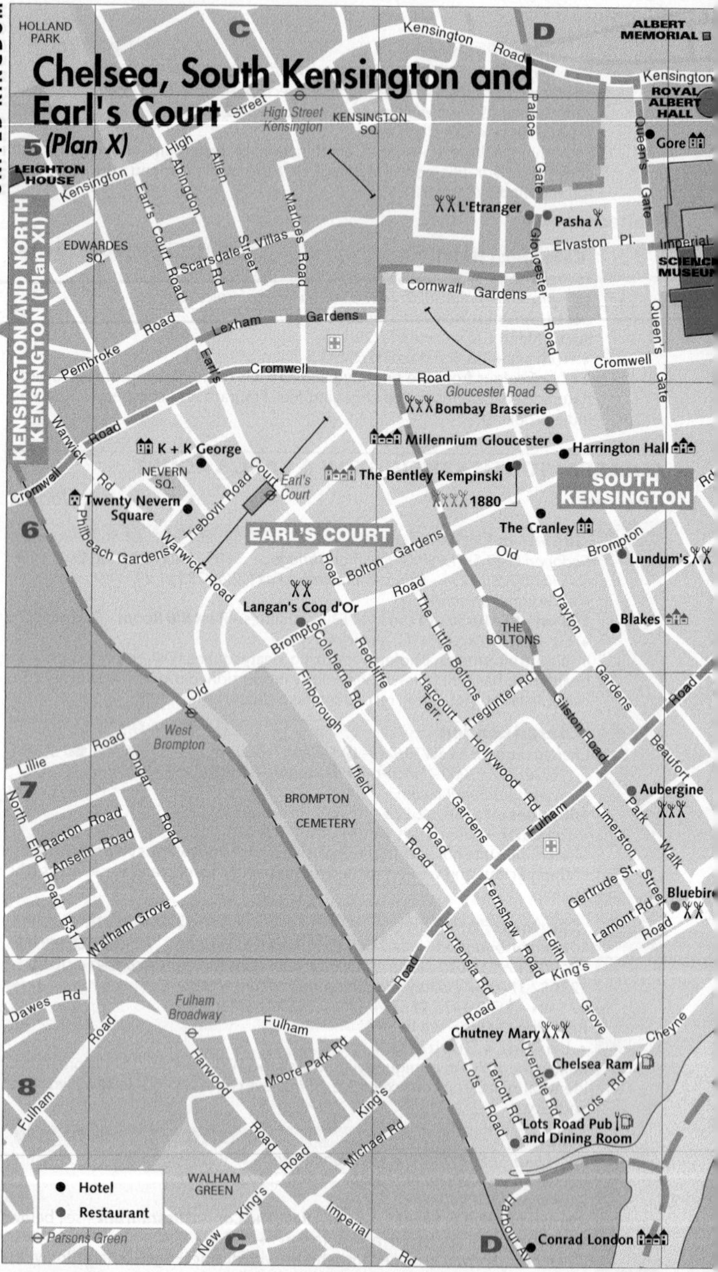
Chelsea, South Kensington and Earl's Court
(Plan X)
HOLLAND PARK
LEIGHTON HOUSE
KENSINGTON AND NORTH KENSINGTON (Plan XI)
EDWARDES SQ.
KENSINGTON SQ.
High Street Kensington
Kensington Road
ALBERT MEMORIAL
ROYAL ALBERT HALL
Gore
L'Etranger
Pasha
Elvaston Pl.
Imperial
SCIENCE MUSEUM
Cornwall Gardens
Lexham Gardens
Cromwell Road
Gloucester Road
Bombay Brasserie
Millennium Gloucester
Harrington Hall
K + K George
NEVERN SQ.
Twenty Nevern Square
The Bentley Kempinski
1880
SOUTH KENSINGTON
EARL'S COURT
Earl's Court
The Cranley
Lundum's
Langan's Coq d'Or
Blakes
THE BOLTONS
West Brompton
BROMPTON CEMETERY
Aubergine
Bluebird
Fulham Broadway
Chutney Mary
Chelsea Ram
Lots Road Pub and Dining Room
WALHAM GREEN
Conrad London
Parsons Green
Hotel
Restaurant

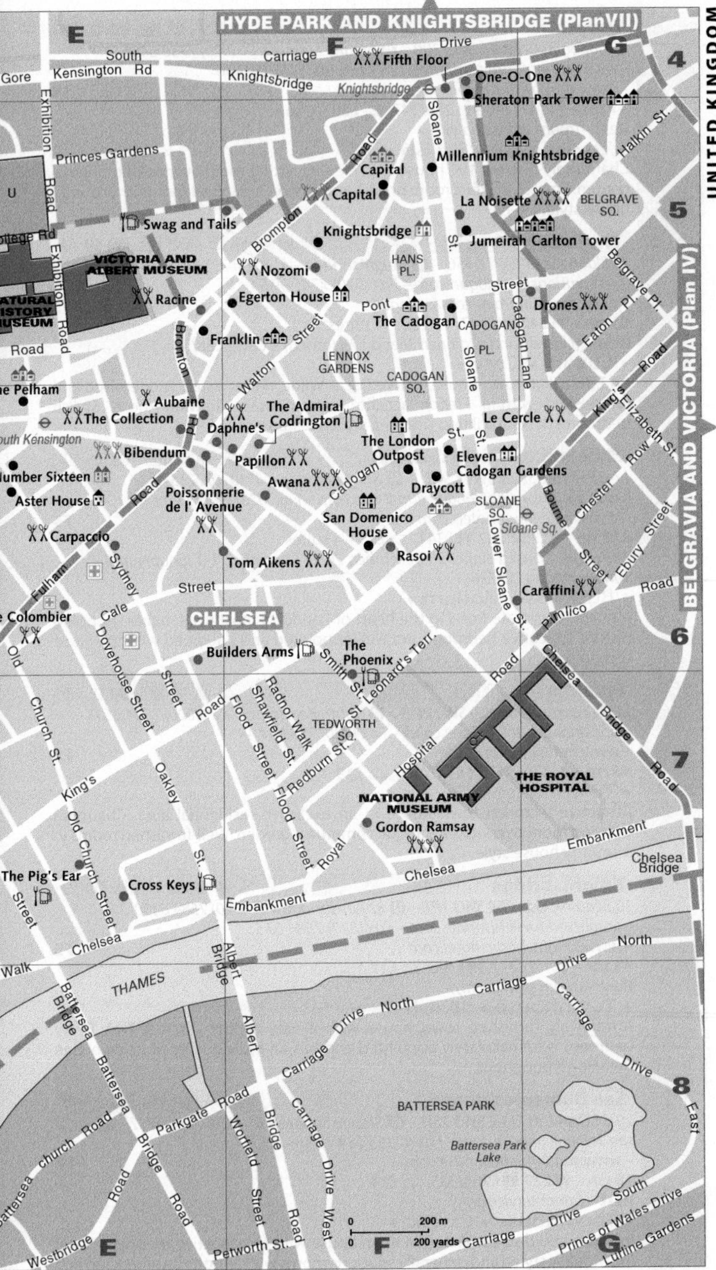
HYDE PARK AND KNIGHTSBRIDGE (Plan VII)
BELGRAVIA AND VICTORIA (Plan IV)
Fifth Floor
One-O-One
Sheraton Park Tower
Millennium Knightsbridge
Capital
La Noisette
Swag and Tails
Knightsbridge
Jumeirah Carlton Tower
VICTORIA AND ALBERT MUSEUM
Nozomi
Racine
Egerton House
The Cadogan
Drones
Franklin
The Pelham
Aubaine
The Collection
Daphne's
The Admiral Codrington
The London Outpost
Le Cercle
Eleven Cadogan Gardens
Bibendum
Papillon
Number Sixteen
Awana
Draycott
Aster House
Poissonnerie de l' Avenue
San Domenico House
Carpaccio
Tom Aikens
Rasoi
Caraffini
Le Colombier
CHELSEA
Builders Arms
The Phoenix
THE ROYAL HOSPITAL
NATIONAL ARMY MUSEUM
Gordon Ramsay
The Pig's Ear
Cross Keys
THAMES
BATTERSEA PARK
Battersea Park Lake
200 m
200 yards

Draycott AC rm VISA MC AE

26 Cadogan Gdns ✉ SW3 2RP – Ⓜ Sloane Square – ✆ (020) 7730 6466
– reservations@draycotthotel.com – Fax (020) 7730 02 36
– www.draycotthotel.com **F6**

31 rm – †£147/206 ††£288/347, ☕ £20 – 4 suites
Rest – *(room service only)*

♦ Townhouse ♦ Stylish ♦

Charmingly discreet 19C house with elegant sitting room overlooking tranquil garden. Smart breakfast room or 24-hour service. Individual rooms in a country house style.

The Cadogan AC 40 VISA MC AE

75 Sloane St ✉ SW1X 9SG – Ⓜ Knightsbridge – ✆ (020) 7235 7141
– reservations@cadogan.com – Fax (020) 7245 09 94
– www.thesteingroup.com/cadogan **F5**

61 rm – †£347 ††£347, ☕ £20 – 4 suites
Rest – *(closed Sunday dinner)* Menu £23 (lunch) – Carte £38/50

♦ Luxury ♦ Cosy ♦

An Edwardian town house, where Oscar Wilde was arrested; modernised and refurbished with a French accent. Contemporary drawing room. Stylish bedrooms; latest facilities. Discreet, stylish restaurant.

Millennium Knightsbridge AC 120 VISA MC AE

17-25 Sloane St ✉ SW1X 9NU – Ⓜ Knightsbridge – ✆ (020) 7235 4377
– reservations.knightsbridge@mill-cop.com – Fax (020) 7235 37 05
– www.millenniumhotels.com **F5**

218 rm – †£259/282 ††£341, ☕ £15 – 4 suites
Rest *Mju* – *(closed dinner 25 December, 26-27 December, 1-3 January and Sunday)* Menu £24/36

♦ Business ♦ Modern ♦

Modern, corporate hotel in the heart of London's most fashionable shopping district. Executive bedrooms are well-appointed and equipped with the latest technology.

Franklin without rest AC VISA MC AE

22-28 Egerton Gdns ✉ SW3 2DB – Ⓜ South Kensington – ✆ (020) 7584 5533
– bookings@franklinhotel.co.uk – Fax (020) 7584 54 49
– www.franklinhotel.co.uk **E5**

46 rm – †£176/347 ††£347/464, ☕ £19

♦ Townhouse ♦ Classic ♦

Attractive Victorian town house in an exclusive residential area. Charming drawing room overlooks a tranquil communal garden. Well-furnished rooms in a country house style.

Knightsbridge AC VISA MC AE

10 Beaufort Gdns ✉ SW3 1PT – Ⓜ Knightsbridge – ✆ (020) 7584 6300
– knightsbridge@firmdale.com – Fax (020) 7584 63 55
– www.knightsbridgehotel.com **F5**

44 rm – †£176/212 ††£306, ☕ £17
Rest – *(room service only)*

♦ Townhouse ♦ Stylish ♦

Attractively furnished town house with a very stylish, discreet feel. Every bedroom is immaculately appointed and has an individuality of its own; fine detailing throughout.

San Domenico House AC rm VISA MC AE

29-31 Draycott Pl ✉ SW3 2SH – Ⓜ Sloane Square – ✆ (020) 7581 5757 – info@sandomenicohouse.com – Fax (020) 7584 13 48
– www.sandomenicohouse.com **F6**

18 rm – †£229 ††£264/335, ☕ £14
Rest – *(room service only)*

♦ Townhouse ♦ Classic ♦

Intimate and discreet Victorian town house with an attractive rooftop terrace. Individually styled and generally spacious rooms with antique furniture and rich fabrics.

The London Outpost without rest

69 Cadogan Gdns ✉ SW3 2RB – Ⓜ Sloane Square
– ✆ (020) 7589 7333 – info@londonoutpost.co.uk – Fax (020) 7581 49 58
– www.londonoutpost.co.uk **F6**

11 rm – †£235 ††£273/387, ☕ £17

♦ Townhouse ♦ Cosy ♦

Classic town house in a most fashionable area. Relaxed and comfy lounges full of English charm. Bedrooms, named after local artists and writers, full of thoughtful touches.

Egerton House

17-19 Egerton Terrace ✉ SW3 2BX
– Ⓜ South Kensington – ✆ (020) 7589 2412
– bookings@egertonhousehotel.co.uk – Fax (020) 7584 65 40
– www.egertonhousehotel.co.uk **F5**

29 rm – †£276 ††£300/464, ☕ £17

Rest – *(room service only)*

♦ Townhouse ♦ Classic ♦

Stylish redbrick Victorian town house close to the exclusive shops. Relaxed drawing room. Antique furnished and individually decorated rooms.

Eleven Cadogan Gardens

11 Cadogan Gdns ✉ SW3 2RJ
– Ⓜ Sloane Square – ✆ (020) 7730 7000
– reservations@number-eleven.co.uk – Fax (020) 7730 52 17
– www.number-eleven.co.uk **F6**

55 rm – †£182/276 ††£381, ☕ £14 – 5 suites

Rest – *(residents only)* Carte £26/33

♦ Townhouse ♦ Classic ♦

Occupying four Victorian houses, one of London's first private town house hotels. Traditionally appointed bedrooms vary considerably in size. Genteel atmosphere. Light and airy basement dining room exclusively for residents.

Gordon Ramsay

68-69 Royal Hospital Rd ✉ SW3 4HP
– Ⓜ Sloane Square – ✆ (020) 7352 4441
– reservations@gordonramsay.com – Fax (020) 7352 33 34
– www.gordonramsay.com
closed 2 weeks Christmas-New Year, Saturday and Sunday **F7**

Rest – *(booking essential)* Menu £40/70

Spec. Ballotine and sautéed foie gras. Fillets of John Dory with crab, caviar and crushed new potatoes. Chocolate and amaretto biscuit soufflé with cinnamon ice cream.

♦ Modern ♦ Formal ♦

Elegant and sophisticated room. The eponymous chef creates some of Britain's finest, classically inspired cooking. Detailed and attentive service. Book two months in advance.

La Noisette

164 Sloane St ✉ SW1X 9QB – Ⓜ Knightsbridge – ✆ (020) 7750 5000
– lanoisette@gordonramsay.com – Fax (020) 7750 50 01
– www.gordonramsay.com **F5**

Rest – Menu £21/50

Spec. Seared foie gras with coffee and Amaretto. Slow cooked Atlantic cod with Jabugo ham and squid. Fromage blanc soufflé, apricots and toasted almond ice cream.

♦ Innovative ♦ Formal ♦

From the Ramsay portfolio, with Art Deco and hazelnut meeting at the top of the stairs. Confident service of highly accomplished original/classical dishes with bold flavours.

UNITED KINGDOM

XXX ꕥꕥ **The Capital Restaurant** - at Capital H.

22-24 Basil St ✉ SW3 1AT – Ⓜ Knightsbridge
– ✆ (020) 7589 5171 – caprest@capitalhotel.co.uk
– Fax (020) 7225 00 11 – www.capitalhotel.co.uk **F5**

Rest – *(booking essential)* Menu £30/55

Spec. Salmon with deep-fried soft shell crab. Honey roast pork belly with horseradish pommes mousseline. Iced coffee parfait with chocolate fondant.

♦ Modern ♦ Formal ♦

A hotel restaurant known for its understated elegance, discretion and graceful service. Cooking blends the innovative with the classic to create carefully crafted dishes.

XXX **Bibendum**

Michelin House, 81 Fulham Rd ✉ SW3 6RD
– Ⓜ South Kensington – ✆ (020) 7581 5817
– manager@bibendum.co.uk – Fax (020) 7823 79 25
– www.bibendum.co.uk
closed 25-26 December and 1 January **E6**

Rest – Menu £29 (lunch) – Carte dinner £32/60

♦ Modern ♦ Design ♦

A fine example of Art Nouveau architecture; a London landmark. 1st floor restaurant with striking stained glass 'Michelin Man'. Attentive service of modern British cooking.

XXX ꕥ **Tom Aikens**

43 Elystan St ✉ SW3 3NT – Ⓜ South Kensington
– ✆ (020) 7584 2003 – info@tomaikens.co.uk
– Fax (020) 7584 20 01 – www.tomaikens.co.uk
closed last two weeks August, 2 weeks Christmas-New Year, Saturday and Sunday **E6**

Rest – Menu £29/60

Spec. Frogs legs with chervil, white onion velouté and morels. Roast pork cutlet with pork lasagna and pearl barley. Passion fruit jelly and mousse with passion fruit syrup.

♦ Innovative ♦ Fashionable ♦

Smart restaurant; minimalist style decor with chic tableware. Highly original menu of individual and inventive dishes; smooth service. Book one month in advance.

XXX ꕥ **Aubergine**

11 Park Walk ✉ SW10 0AJ – Ⓜ South Kensington – ✆ (020) 7352 3449
– Fax (020) 7351 17 70
closed 23 December -3 January, Sunday, Saturday lunch and Bank Holidays **D7**

Rest – *(booking essential)* Menu £34/60

Spec. Mousse of salmon and langoustine, basil and tomato emulsion. Roast grouse with blackberries and thyme. Dark chocolate chiboust with poached cherries.

♦ Modern ♦ Formal ♦

Intimate, refined restaurant where the keen staff provide well drilled service. French influenced menu uses top quality ingredients with skill and flair. Extensive wine list.

XXX **One-O-One** - at Sheraton Park Tower H.

William St ✉ SW1X 7RN – Ⓜ Knightsbridge
– ✆ (020) 7290 7101
– Fax (020) 7235 61 96
– www.luxurycollection.com/parktowerlondon **F4**

Rest – Menu £25 (lunch) – Carte approx. £54

♦ Seafood ♦ Design ♦

Modern and very comfortable restaurant overlooking Knightsbridge decorated in cool blue tones. Predominantly seafood menu offers traditional and more adventurous dishes.

XXX **Drones** AC 40 VISA MO AE D

1 Pont St ✉ SW1X 9EJ – Ⓜ Knightsbridge – ✆ (020) 7235 9555
– sales@whitestarline.org.uk – Fax (020) 7235 95 66
– www.whitestarline.org.uk
closed 26 December, 1 January, Saturday lunch and Sunday dinner **G5**

Rest – Menu £18 (lunch) – Carte £28/44

◆ Modern ◆ Formal ◆

Smart exterior with etched plate-glass window. U-shaped interior with moody film star photos on walls. French and classically inspired tone to dishes.

XXX **Fifth Floor** – at Harvey Nichols AC VISA MO AE D

Knightsbridge ✉ SW1X 7RJ – Ⓜ Knightsbridge – ✆ (020) 7235 5250
– Fax (020) 7235 78 56 – www.harveynichols.com
closed Christmas, Sunday dinner and Monday **F4**

Rest – Menu £20/40 – Carte £30/48 ✿

◆ Modern ◆ Fashionable ◆

On Harvey Nichols' top floor; elevated style sporting a pink-hued oval shaped interior with green frosted glass. Chic surroundings with food to match and smooth service.

XXX **Awana** AC VISA MO AE D

85 Sloane Ave ✉ SW3 3DX – Ⓜ South Kensington
– ✆ (020) 7584 8880 – info@awana.co.uk
– Fax (020) 7584 61 88 – www.awana.co.uk **F6**

Rest – Menu £15 (lunch) – Carte £23/32

◆ Malaysian ◆ Exotic ◆

Enter into stylish cocktail bar. Traditional Malay elements adorn restaurant. Satay chef cooks to order. Malaysian dishes authentically prepared and smartly presented.

XXX **Chutney Mary** AC VISA MO AE D

535 King's Rd ✉ SW10 0SZ – Ⓜ Fulham Broadway – ✆ (020) 7351 3113
– chutneymary@realindianfood.com – Fax (020) 7351 76 94
– www.realindianfood **D8**

Rest – *(dinner only and lunch Saturday and Sunday)* Menu £17 (lunch)
– Carte dinner £25/47

◆ Indian ◆ Exotic ◆

Soft lighting and sepia etchings hold sway at this forever popular restaurant. Extensive menu of specialities from all corners of India. Complementary wine list.

XX **Daphne's** AC VISA MO AE D

112 Draycott Ave ✉ SW3 3AE – Ⓜ South Kensington – ✆ (020) 7589 4257
– office@daphnes-restaurant.co.uk – Fax (020) 7225 27 66
– www.daphnes.co.uk
closed 25-26 December, 1 January and August Bank Holiday **E6**

Rest – *(booking essential)* Carte £27/43

◆ Italian ◆ Fashionable ◆

Positively buzzes in the evening, the Chelsea set gelling smoothly and seamlessly with the welcoming Tuscan interior ambience. A modern twist updates classic Italian dishes.

XX ✿ **Rasoi** (Bhatia) AC VISA MO AE D

10 Lincoln St ✉ SW3 2TS – Ⓜ Sloane Square – ✆ (020) 7225 1881
– Fax (020) 7581 02 20 – www.vineetbhatia.com
closed Saturday lunch, Sunday and Bank Holidays **F6**

Rest – Menu £24 (lunch) – Carte £46/61

Spec. Chicken tikka flavoured with mustard seeds and curry leaves. Ginger and chilli lobster dusted with spiced cocoa powder. Chocolate and almond samosa, walnut and coffee mousse.

◆ Indian ◆ Neighbourhood ◆

Elegant mid-19C townhouse off King's Road with L-shaped dining room and attractive friezes. Seamlessly crafted mix of classic and contemporary Indian flavour combinations.

UNITED KINGDOM

XX

Racine

239 Brompton Rd ✉ SW3 2EP – Ⓜ South Kensington – ✆ (020) 7584 4477 – Fax (020) 7584 49 00 – closed 25 December **E5**

Rest – Menu £18 (lunch) – Carte £25/38

◆ French ◆ Brasserie ◆

Dark leather banquettes, large mirrors and wood floors create the atmosphere of a genuine Parisienne brasserie. Good value, well crafted, regional French fare.

XX

Papillon

96 Draycott Ave. ✉ SW3 3AD – Ⓜ South Kensington – ✆ (020) 7225 2555 – info@papillonchelsea.co.uk – Fax (020) 7225 25 54 – www.papillonchelsea.co.uk **F6**

Rest – Menu £16.50 (lunch) – Carte £27/36

◆ French ◆

Feels like a Parisian brasserie: large arched windows, brown décor, fleur-de-lys green banquettes and leather chairs. Classic French menus please the smart Chelsea set.

XX

Nozomi

15 Beauchamp Pl, ✉ SW3 1NQ – Ⓜ Knightsbridge – ✆ (020) 7838 1500 – Fax (020) 7838 10 01

closed 2 weeks January, 2 weeks August and Sunday **F5**

Rest – Carte £27/42

◆ Japanese ◆ Minimalist ◆

DJ mixes lounge music at the front bar; up the stairs in the restaurant the feeling is minimal with soft lighting. Innovative Japanese menus provide an interesting choice.

XX

Bluebird

350 King's Rd ✉ SW3 5UU – ✆ (020) 7559 1000 – Fax (020) 7559 11 11 – www.conran.com **E7**

Rest – Carte £22/37

◆ Modern ◆ Design ◆

A foodstore, café and homeware shop also feature at this impressive skylit restaurant. Much of the modern British food is cooked in wood-fired ovens. Lively atmosphere.

XX

Poissonnerie de l'Avenue

82 Sloane Ave ✉ SW3 3DZ – Ⓜ South Kensington – ✆ (020) 7589 2457 – info@poissonnerie.co.uk – Fax (020) 7581 33 60 – www.poissonneriedel'avenue.co.uk

closed dinner 24 December, 25 December, Sunday and Bank Holidays **E6**

Rest – Menu £22 (lunch) – Carte £25/36

◆ Seafood ◆ Formal ◆

Long-established and under the same ownership since 1965. Spacious and traditional French restaurant offering an extensive seafood menu. An institution favoured by locals.

XX

Le Cercle

1 Wilbraham Pl ✉ SW1X 9AE – Ⓜ Sloane Square – ✆ (020) 7901 9999 – info@lecercle.co.uk – Fax (020) 7901 91 11

closed Sunday-Monday **F6**

Rest – Menu £20 (lunch) – Carte £12/48

◆ French ◆ Fashionable ◆

Discreetly signed basement restaurant down residential side street. High, spacious room with chocolate banquettes. Tapas style French menus; accomplished cooking.

XX

Le Colombier

145 Dovehouse St ✉ SW3 6LB – Ⓜ South Kensington – ✆ (020) 7351 1155 – Fax (020) 7351 51 24 **E6**

Rest – Menu £15 (lunch) – Carte £27/34

◆ French ◆ Neighbourhood ◆

Proudly Gallic corner restaurant in an affluent residential area. Attractive enclosed terrace. Bright and cheerful surroundings and service of traditional French cooking.

Caraffini

61-63 Lower Sloane St ✉ SW1W 8DH – Ⓜ Sloane Square – ✆ (020) 7259 0235 – info@caraffini.co.uk – Fax (020) 7259 02 36 – www.caraffini.co.uk

closed 25 December, Easter, Sunday and Bank Holidays **F6**

Rest – Carte £24/32

♦ Italian ♦ Friendly ♦

The omnipresent and ebullient owner oversees the friendly service in this attractive neighbourhood restaurant. Authentic and robust Italian cooking; informal atmosphere.

The Collection

264 Brompton Rd ✉ SW3 2AS – Ⓜ South Kensington – ✆ (020) 7225 1212 – office@thecollection.co.uk – Fax (020) 7225 10 50 – www.the-collection.co.uk

closed 25-26 December, 1 January and Bank Holidays **E6**

Rest – *(dinner only)* Menu £40 – Carte £29/41

♦ Modern ♦ Trendy ♦

Beyond the impressive catwalk entrance one will find a chic bar and a vast split level, lively restaurant. The eclectic and global modern menu is enjoyed by the young crowd.

Carpaccio

4 Sydney St ✉ SW3 6PP – Ⓜ South Kensington – ✆ (020) 7352 3433 – eat@carpaccio.uk.com – Fax (020) 7352 34 35 – www.carpaccio.uk.com **E6**

Rest – Carte £32/40

♦ Italian ♦ Neighbourhood ♦

Fine Georgian exterior housing James Bond stills, 1920s silent Italian comedies, Ayrton Senna's Honda cockpit, witty waiters, and enjoyable, classical Trattoria style cooking.

Admiral Codrington

17 Mossop St ✉ SW3 2LY – Ⓜ South Kensington – ✆ (020) 7581 0005 – admiralcodrington@longshotplc.com – Fax (020) 7589 24 52 – www.theadmiralcodrington.co.uk **F6**

Rest – Carte £20/35

♦ Modern ♦ Pub ♦

Aproned staff offer attentive, relaxed service in this busy gastropub. A retractable roof provides alfresco dining in the modern back room. Cosmopolitan menu of modern dishes.

Chelsea Ram

32 Burnaby St ✉ SW10 0PL – Ⓜ Fulham Broadway – ✆ (020) 7351 4008 – pint@chelsearam.com – Fax (020) 7349 08 85 – www.chelsearam.com **D8**

Rest – Carte £18/21

♦ Modern ♦ Pub ♦

Wooden floors, modern artwork and books galore feature in this forever popular pub. Concise menu of modern British cooking with daily changing specials. Friendly atmosphere.

Swag and Tails

10-11 Fairholt St ✉ SW7 1EG – Ⓜ Knightsbridge – ✆ (020) 7584 6926 – theswag@swagandtails.com – Fax (020) 7581 99 35 – www.swagandtails.com

closed Saturday, Sunday and Bank Holidays **EF5**

Rest – Carte £24/32

♦ Modern ♦ Pub ♦

Attractive Victorian pub close to Harrods and the fashionable Knightsbridge shops. Polite and approachable service of a blackboard menu of light snacks and seasonal dishes.

Builders Arms

13 Britten St ✉ SW3 3TY – Ⓜ South Kensington – ✆ (020) 7349 9040
closed 25-26 December and 1 January **E6**
Rest – Carte £17/26
◆ Modern ◆ Pub ◆
Extremely busy modern 'gastropub' favoured by the locals. Eclectic menu of contemporary dishes with blackboard specials. Polite service from a young and eager team.

The Pig's Ear

35 Old Church St ✉ SW3 5BS – ✆ (020) 7352 2908
– hello@thepigsear.co.uk
– Fax (020) 7352 93 21 – www.thepigsear.co.uk **E7**
Rest – Carte £16/22
◆ Modern ◆ Pub ◆
Corner pub that gets very busy, particularly for downstairs bar dining. Upstairs, more sedate wood panelled dining room. Both menus are rustic, robust and seasonal in nature.

The Phoenix

23 Smith St ✉ SW3 4EE – Ⓜ Sloane Square
– ✆ (020) 7730 9182 – mail@geronimo-phoenix.fsnet.co.uk
– www.geronimo-inns.co.uk
closed 25-26 December **F67**
Rest – Carte £15/28
◆ Modern ◆ Pub ◆
Tile-fronted pub with al fresco seating area, very popular in summer. Shabby chic décor that's been modernised but feels retro. Modern British repertoire on extensive menus.

Cross Keys

1 Lawrence St ✉ SW3 5NB – Ⓜ South Kensington – ✆ (020) 7349 9111
– cross-keys@fsmail.net – Fax (020) 7349 93 33 – www.thexkeys.co.uk
closed 23-28 December, and Bank Holidays **E7**
Rest – Menu £25/28
◆ Modern ◆ Pub ◆
Hidden away near the Embankment, this 18C pub has period furniture and impressive carved stone fireplaces. Interesting, modern menus include blackboard of daily specials.

Lots Road Pub and Dining Room

114 Lots Rd ✉ SW10 0RJ – Ⓜ Gloucester Road
– ✆ (020) 7352 6645 – lotsroad@thespiritgroup.com
– Fax (020) 7376 49 75 – www.thespiritgroup.com **D8**
Rest – Carte £18/26
◆ Modern ◆ Pub ◆
Traditional corner pub with an open-plan kitchen, flowers at each table and large modern pictures on the walls. Contemporary menus change daily.

South Kensington *Plan X*

The Bentley Kempinski

80 VISA

27-33 Harrington Gdns ✉ SW7 4JX
– Ⓜ Gloucester Road – ✆ (020) 7244 5555
– info@thebentley-hotel.com – Fax (020) 7244 55 66
– www.thebentley-hotel.com **D6**
52 rm – †£340/458 ††£458, ☐ £20 – 12 suites
Rest ***1880*** – see below – **Rest** ***Peridot*** – *(lunch only and dinner Sunday-Monday)* Menu £27/52 – Carte £29/52
◆ Grand Luxury ◆ Classic ◆
A number of 19C houses have been joined to create this opulent, lavish, hidden gem, decorated with marble, mosaics and ornate gold leaf. Bedrooms with gorgeous silk fabrics. Airy, intimate Peridot offers brasserie menus.

Millennium Gloucester

4-18 Harrington Gdns ✉ SW7 4LH – Ⓜ Gloucester Road – ✆ (020) 7373 6030 – reservations.gloucester@mill-cop.com – Fax (020) 7373 04 09 – www.millenniumhotels.com D6

604 rm – †£223 ††£223, ☕ £16 – 6 suites

Rest *Bugis Street* – Menu £17

Rest *South West 7* – *(closed Sunday-Monday) (dinner only)*

♦ Luxury ♦ Classic ♦

A large international group hotel. Busy marbled lobby and vast conference facilities. Smart and well-equipped bedrooms are generously sized, especially the 'Club' rooms. Dinner or buffet at South West 7. Informal, compact Bugis Street.

The Pelham

15 Cromwell Pl ✉ SW7 2LA – Ⓜ South Kensington – ✆ (020) 7589 8288 – pelham@firmdale.com – Fax (020) 7584 84 44 – www.pelhamhotel.co.uk

50 rm – †£188/229 ††£294, ☕ £18 – 2 suites E6

Rest *Kemps* – Menu £18 – Carte £25/33

♦ Luxury ♦ Stylish ♦

Attractive Victorian town house with a discreet and comfortable feel. Wood panelled drawing room and individually decorated bedrooms with marble bathrooms. Detailed service. Warm basement dining room.

Blakes

33 Roland Gdns ✉ SW7 3PF – Ⓜ Gloucester Road – ✆ (020) 7370 6701 – blakes@blakeshotels.com – Fax (020) 7373 04 42 – www.blakeshotels.com

45 rm – †£206/323 ††£417, ☕ £25 – 3 suites D6

Rest – *(closed 25-26 December and 1 January)* Carte £63/80

♦ Luxury ♦ Design ♦

Behind the Victorian façade lies one of London's first 'boutique' hotels. Dramatic, bold and eclectic décor, with oriental influences and antiques from around the globe. Fashionable restaurant with bamboo and black walls.

Harrington Hall

5-25 Harrington Gdns ✉ SW7 4JB – Ⓜ Gloucester Road – ✆ (020) 7396 9696 – book.london@nh-hotels.com – Fax (020) 7396 17 19 – www.nh-hotels.com

closed 25 December D6

200 rm – †£215 ††£215, ☕ £17

Rest *Wetherby's* – Menu £20 (lunch) – Carte dinner £30/40

♦ Business ♦ Functional ♦

A series of adjoined terraced houses, with an attractive period façade that belies the size. Tastefully furnished bedrooms, with an extensive array of facilities. Classically decorated dining room.

Number Sixteen

16 Sumner Pl ✉ SW7 3EG – Ⓜ South Kensington – ✆ (020) 7589 5232 – sixteen@firmdale.com – Fax (020) 7584 86 15 – www.numbersixteenhotel.co.uk E6

42 rm – †£118/206 ††£300, ☕ £13 – **Rest** – *(room service only)*

♦ Townhouse ♦ Stylish ♦

Enticingly refurbished 19C town houses in smart area. Discreet entrance, comfy sitting room and charming breakfast terrace. Bedrooms in English country house style.

The Cranley

10 Bina Gdns ✉ SW5 0LA – Ⓜ Gloucester Road – ✆ (020) 7373 0123 – info@thecranley.com – Fax (020) 7373 94 97 – www.thecranley.com D6

38 rm – †£159/258 ††£241/276, ☕ £10 – 1 suite

Rest – *(room service only)*

♦ Townhouse ♦ Stylish ♦

Delightful Regency town house that artfully combines charm and period details with modern comforts and technology. Individually styled bedrooms; some with four-posters.

UNITED KINGDOM

The Gore rest rm 70

190 Queen's Gate SW7 5EX – Gloucester Road
– (020) 7584 6601 – reservations@gorehotel.co.uk
– Fax (020) 7589 81 27 – www.gorehotel.com **D5**
49 rm – £170/235 £211/235, £17
Rest *190 Queensgate* – *(booking essential)* Menu £16 (lunch) – Carte £31/51
◆ Townhouse ◆ Personalised ◆
Opened its doors in 1892; has retained its individual charm. Richly decorated with antiques, rugs and over 4,000 pictures that cover every inch of wall. 190 Queensgate boasts French-inspired décor.

Aster House without rest

3 Sumner Pl SW7 3EE – South Kensington – (020) 7581 5888
– asterhouse@btinternet.com – Fax (020) 7584 49 25
– www.asterhouse.com **E6**
13 rm – £93/159 £128/182
◆ Townhouse ◆ Cosy ◆
End of terrace Victorian house with a pretty little rear garden and first floor conservatory. Ground floor rooms available. A wholly non-smoking establishment.

1880 – at The Bentley Kempinski H.

27-33 Harrington Gdns SW7 4JX
– Gloucester Road – (020) 7244 5555
– info@thebentley-hotel.com – Fax (020) 7244 55 66
– www.thebentley-hotel.com
closed Sunday and Monday **D6**
Rest – *(dinner only)* Menu £45
◆ Innovative ◆ Formal ◆
Luxurious, opulently decorated room in Bentley basement: silk panels, gold leaf, Italian marble, chandeliers. Extensive "grazing" menu up to 10 courses.

Bombay Brasserie

Courtfield Rd SW7 4QH
– Gloucester Road – (020) 7370 4040
– bombay1brasserie@aol.com – Fax (020) 7835 16 69
– www.bombaybrasserielondon.com
closed 25-26 December **D6**
Rest – *(buffet lunch)* Menu £19 – Carte dinner £28/36
◆ Indian ◆ Exotic ◆
Something of a London institution: an ever busy Indian restaurant with Raj-style décor. Ask to sit in the brighter plant-filled conservatory. Popular lunchtime buffet.

Lundum's

119 Old Brompton Rd SW7 3RN – Gloucester Road – (020) 7373 7774
– Fax (020) 7373 44 72 – www.lundums.com
closed Sunday dinner **D6**
Rest – Menu £19/25 – Carte £27/49
◆ Modern Danish ◆ Family ◆
A family run Danish restaurant offering an authentic, traditional lunch with a more expansive dinner menu. Comfortable room, with large windows. Charming service.

L'Etranger 12

36 Gloucester Rd SW7 4QT – Gloucester Road
– (020) 7584 1118 – sasha@etranger.co.uk – Fax (020) 7584 88 86
– www.etranger.co.uk
closed lunch Saturday and Sunday **D5**
Rest – *(booking essential)* Menu £17 (lunch) – Carte £31/54
◆ French ◆ Neighbourhood ◆
Corner restaurant with mosaic entrance floor and bay window. Modern décor. Tables extend into adjoining wine shop. French based cooking with Asian influences.

XX **Pasha** AC 20 VISA MC AE

1 Gloucester Rd ✉ SW7 4PP South Kensington – Ⓜ Gloucester Road – ☎ (020) 7589 7969 – Fax (020) 7581 99 96 – www.pasha-restaurant.co.uk closed Sunday lunch **D5**

Rest – Carte £35/40

♦ Moroccan ♦ Exotic ♦

Relax over ground floor cocktails, then descend to mosaic floored restaurant where the rose-petal strewn tables are the ideal accompaniment to tasty Moroccan home cooking.

Earl's Court *Plan X*

K + K George AC SAT 30 P VISA MC AE

1-15 Templeton Pl ✉ SW5 9NB – Ⓜ Earl's Court – ☎ (020) 7598 8700 – hotelgeorge@kkhotels.co.uk – Fax (020) 7370 22 85 – www.kkhotels.com **C6**

154 rm – †£182 ††£217

Rest – *(in bar)* Carte £17/29

♦ Business ♦ Modern ♦

Five converted 19C houses overlooking large rear garden. Scandinavian style to rooms with low beds, white walls and light wood furniture. Breakfast room has the garden view. Informal dining in the bar.

Twenty Nevern Square without rest SAT P VISA MC AE

Nevern Sq ✉ SW5 9PD – Ⓜ Earl's Court – ☎ (020) 7565 9555 – hotel@twentynevernsquare.co.uk – Fax (020) 7565 94 44 – www.twentynevernsquare.co.uk **C6**

19 rm – †£79/99 ††£95/109, £9

♦ Townhouse ♦ Functional ♦

In an attractive Victorian garden square, an individually designed, privately owned town house. Original pieces of furniture and some rooms with their own terrace.

XX **Langan's Coq d'Or** AC VISA MC AE

254-260 Old Brompton Rd ✉ SW5 9HR – Ⓜ Earl's Court – ☎ (020) 7259 2599 – admin@langansrestaurant.co.uk – Fax (020) 7370 77 35 – www.langansrestaurants.co.uk closed 25-26 December and 1 January **C6**

Rest – Menu £21

♦ Traditional ♦ Brasserie ♦

Classic, buzzy brasserie and excellent-value menu to match. Walls adorned with pictures of celebrities: look out for more from the enclosed pavement terrace. Smooth service.

KENSINGTON, NORTH KENSINGTON & NOTTING HILL

Kensington *Plan XI*

Royal Garden AC rm SAT 550 P VISA MC AE

2-24 Kensington High St ✉ W8 4PT – Ⓜ High Street Kensington – ☎ (020) 7937 8000 – sales@royalgardenhotel.co.uk – Fax (020) 7361 19 91 – www.royalgardenhotel.co.uk **D4**

376 rm – †£317/388 ††£388/476, £18 – 20 suites

Rest *Park Terrace* – Carte £24/33

Rest *The Tenth* – *(closed Saturday lunch, Sunday and Bank Holidays)* Menu £23/65 – Carte £36/45

♦ Luxury ♦ Classic ♦

A tall, modern hotel with many of its rooms enjoying enviable views over the adjacent Kensington Gardens. All the modern amenities and services, with well-drilled staff. Bright, spacious, large-windowed Park Terrace. Modern menu and commanding views from the top floor Tenth restaurant.

UNITED KINGDOM

The Milestone

1-2 Kensington Court ✉ W8 5DL – Ⓜ High Street Kensington – ✆ (020) 7917 1000 – bookms@rchmail.com – Fax (020) 7917 10 10 – www.milestonehotel.com **D4**

52 rm – †£235/294 ††£235/294, ☕ £22 – 5 suites

Rest – *(booking essential for non-residents)* Menu £19/24 – Carte £46/58

◆ Luxury ◆ Stylish ◆

Elegant 'boutique' hotel with decorative Victorian façade and English feel. Charming oak panelled lounge and snug bar. Meticulously decorated bedrooms with period detail. Panelled dining room with charming little oratory for privacy seekers.

Baglioni

60 Hyde Park Gate ✉ SW7 5BB – Ⓜ High Street Kensington – ✆ (020) 7368 5700 – info@baglionihotellondon.com – Fax (020) 7368 57 01 – www.baglionihotellondon.com **D4**

53 rm – †£370 ††£529, ☕ £25 – 15 suites

Rest *Brunello* – Menu £24/48 – Carte £47/72

◆ Luxury ◆ Stylish ◆

Opposite Kensington Palace: ornate interior, trendy basement bar. Impressively high levels of service. Small gym/sauna. Superb rooms in cool shades boast striking facilities. Restaurant specialises in rustic Italian cooking.

Belvedere

Holland House, off Abbotsbury Rd ✉ W8 6LU – Ⓜ Holland Park – ✆ (020) 7602 1238 – sales@whitestarline.org.uk – Fax (020) 7610 43 82 – www.whitestarline.org.uk

closed 26 December, 1 January and Sunday dinner **B4**

Rest – Menu £18/23 (lunch) – Carte £26/36

◆ Modern ◆ Romantic ◆

Former 19C orangery in a delightful position in the middle of the Park. On two floors with a bar and balcony terrace. Huge vases of flowers. Modern take on classic dishes.

Babylon

(at the Roof Gardens) Kensington High St ✉ W8 5SA – Ⓜ High Street Kensington – ✆ (020) 7368 3993 – Fax (020) 7368 39 95 – www.roofgardens.com **C4**

Rest – Menu £21 (lunch) – Carte £30/59

◆ International ◆ Fashionable ◆

Situated on the roof of this pleasant London building affording attractive views of the London skyline. Stylish modern décor in keeping with the contemporary, British cooking.

Ribbands

147-149 Notting Hill Gate ✉ W11 3LF Kensington – Ⓜ Notting Hill Gate – ✆ (020) 7034 0301 – Fax (020) 7229 42 59 – www.ribbandsrestaurants.com

closed Sunday, Monday and Bank Holidays **C3**

Rest – Menu £25/48 – Carte £40/56

◆ French ◆ Neighbourhood ◆

Coffee shop/bar at the front; step down to the serious eating areas. Range of menus to wade through. Dishes are elaborately detailed, buttressed by first-rate ingredients.

Clarke's

124 Kensington Church St ✉ W8 4BH – Ⓜ Notting Hill Gate – ✆ (020) 7221 9225 – restaurant@sallyclarke.com – Fax (020) 7229 45 64 – www.sallyclarke.com

closed 10 days Christmas-New Year, Monday dinner, Sunday and Bank Holidays **C4**

Rest – *(set menu only at dinner)* Menu £44 (dinner) – Carte lunch £27/32

◆ Modern ◆ Neighbourhood ◆

Forever popular restaurant, now serving a choice of dishes boasting trademark fresh, seasonal ingredients and famed lightness of touch. Loyal following for over 20 years.

XX **Zaika**

A/C VISA MC AE D

1 Kensington High St ✉ W8 5NP
– Ⓜ High Street Kensington – ✆ (020) 7795 6533
– info@zaika-restaurant.co.uk – Fax (020) 7937 88 54
– www.zaika-restaurant.co.uk
closed 25-26 December and Saturday lunch **D4**
Rest – Menu £18 (lunch) – Carte £27/42
◆ Indian ◆ Exotic ◆

A converted bank, sympathetically restored, with original features and Indian artefacts. Well organised service of modern Indian dishes.

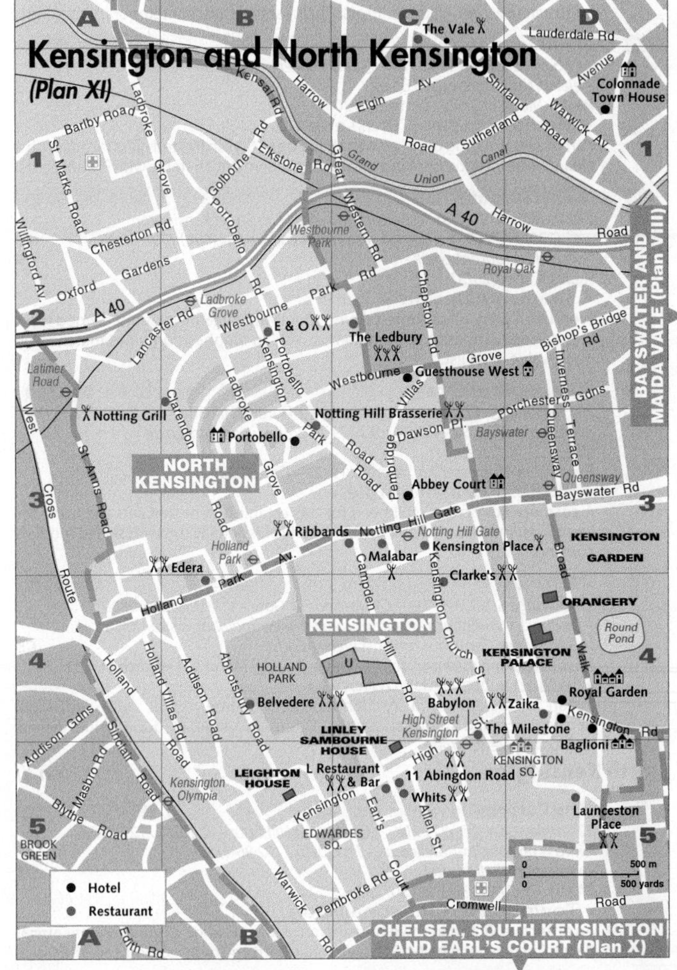

XX **Whits**

21 Abingdon Rd ✉ W8 6AH – Ⓜ High Street Kensington – ☎ (020) 7938 1122 – eva@whits.co.uk – Fax (020) 7937 61 21 – www.whits.co.uk **C5**

Rest – Menu £17.50/22.50 – Carte £26/36

♦ Modern European ♦ Neighbourhood ♦

Buzzy destination: bar runs length of lower level. Most diners migrate upstairs with its modish art work, intimate tables and modern dishes: do check out the souffles!

XX **Launceston Place**

1a Launceston Pl ✉ W8 5RL – Ⓜ Gloucester Road – ☎ (020) 7937 6912 – Fax (020) 7938 24 12

closed 24-28 December, 1 January, Saturday lunch and August Bank Holiday

Rest – Menu £19 (lunch) – Carte £31/38 **D5**

♦ English ♦ Neighbourhood ♦

Divided into a number of rooms, this corner restaurant is lent a bright feel by its large windows and gilded mirrors. Chatty service and contemporary cooking.

XX **11 Abingdon Road**

11 Abingdon Rd ✉ W8 6AH – Ⓜ High Street Kensington – ☎ (020) 7937 0120 – eleven@abingdonroad.co.uk **C5**

Rest – Menu £17.50 – Carte £21/30

♦ Mediterranean ♦ Brasserie ♦

Part of a little 'eating oasis' off Ken High Street. Stylish frosted glass façade with a clean, white interior. Cooking's from the modern British stable with Euro accents.

XX **L Restaurant & Bar**

2 Abingdon Rd ✉ W8 6AF Kensington – Ⓜ High Street Kensington – ☎ (020) 7795 6969 – info@l-restaurant.co.uk – Fax (020) 7795 66 99 – www.l-restaurant.co.uk **C5**

Rest – Carte £25/37

♦ Spanish ♦ Design ♦

Wonderfully airy glass-roofed dining room with tastefully designed wood work and mirrors. Authentic Iberian menus with an emphasis on tapas matched by good-value wine list.

X **Kensington Place**

201 Kensington Church St ✉ W8 7LX – Ⓜ Notting Hill Gate – ☎ (020) 7727 3184 – kpr@egami.co.uk – Fax (020) 7229 20 25 – www.egami.co.uk

closed 24-26 December **C3**

Rest – *(booking essential)* Menu £19/25 – Carte £29/46

♦ Modern ♦ Fashionable ♦

A cosmopolitan crowd still head for this establishment that sets the trend for large, bustling and informal restaurants. Professionally run with skilled modern cooking.

X **Malabar**

27 Uxbridge St ✉ W8 7TQ – Ⓜ Notting Hill Gate – ☎ (020) 7727 8800 – feedback@malabar-restaurant.co.uk – www.malabar-restaurant.co.uk

closed 1 week Christmas and last week August **C3**

Rest – *(booking essential) (buffet lunch Sunday)* Menu £21 – Carte £17/31

♦ Indian ♦ Neighbourhood ♦

Indian restaurant in a residential street. Three rooms with individual personalities and informal service. Extensive range of good value dishes, particularly vegetarian.

North Kensington *Plan XI*

The Portobello without rest

22 Stanley Gdns ✉ W11 2NG – Ⓜ Notting Hill Gate – ☎ (020) 7727 2777 – info@portobello-hotel.co.uk – Fax (020) 7792 96 41 – www.portobello-hotel.co.uk **B3**

24 rm – †£140/180 ††£180/290, ☐ £12

♦ Townhouse ♦ Personalised ♦

An attractive Victorian town house in an elegant terrace. Original and theatrical décor. Circular beds, half-testers, Victorian baths: no two bedrooms are the same.

Abbey Court without rest

20 Pembridge Gdns ✉ W2 4DU – Ⓜ Notting Hill Gate – ✆ (020) 7221 7518 – info@abbeycourthotel.co.uk – Fax (020) 7792 08 58 – www.abbeycourthotel.co.uk **C3**

22 rm – 🚹£75/125 🚹🚹£110/145, ☕ £8

◆ Townhouse ◆ Classic ◆

Five-storey Victorian town house with individually decorated bedrooms, with many thoughtful touches. Breakfast served in a pleasant conservatory. Friendly service.

Guesthouse West

163-165 Westbourne Grove ✉ W11 2RS – Ⓜ Notting Hill Gate – ✆ (020) 7792 9800 – reception@guesthousewest.com – Fax (020) 7792 97 97 – www.guesthousewest.com **C2**

20 rm – 🚹£147/170 🚹🚹£147/200, ☕ £8

Rest – *(closed lunch Monday-Wednesday)* Carte £18/22

◆ Townhouse ◆ Stylish ◆

Attractive Edwardian house in the heart of Notting Hill, close to its shops and restaurants. Contemporary bedrooms boast the latest in audio visual gadgetry. Chic Parlour Bar for all-day light dishes in a tapas style.

The Ledbury

127 Ledbury Rd ✉ W11 2AQ – Ⓜ Notting Hill Gate – ✆ (020) 7792 9090 – info@theledbury.com – Fax (020) 7792 91 91 – www.theledbury.com

closed 25-26 December, 1 January and August Bank Holiday **C2**

Rest – Menu £25/45

Spec. Scallops roasted in liquorice with fennel and white onion purée. Lamb baked in hay with creamed potato, truffle and celery. Chicory crème brûlée with coffee ice cream and chocolate Madeleine.

◆ Modern ◆ Neighbourhood ◆

Converted pub whose cool décor fits seamlessly into the neighbourhood it serves. Confident, highly accomplished cooking using first-rate ingredients; portions are generous.

XX **Notting Hill Brasserie**

92 Kensington Park Rd ✉ W11 2PN – Ⓜ Notting Hill Gate – ✆ (020) 7229 4481 – enquiries@nottinghillbrasserie.com – Fax (020) 7221 12 46

closed Sunday dinner **B3**

Rest – Menu £20 (lunch) – Carte dinner £30/40

◆ Modern ◆ Neighbourhood ◆

Modern, comfortable restaurant with quiet, formal atmosphere set over four small rooms. Authentic African artwork on walls. Contemporary dishes with European influence.

XX **Edera**

148 Holland Park Ave ✉ W11 4UE – Ⓜ Holland Park – ✆ (020) 7221 6090 – Fax (020) 7313 97 00 **B4**

Rest – Carte £23/35

◆ Italian ◆ Neighbourhood ◆

Split level restaurant with 4 outdoor tables. Attentive service by all staff. Interesting menus of modern Italian cooking with some unusual ingredients and combinations.

XX **E & O**

14 Blenheim Crescent ✉ W11 1NN – Ⓜ Ladbroke Grove – ✆ (020) 7229 5454 – Fax (020) 7229 55 22 – www.eando.nu **B2**

Rest – Carte £22/34

◆ South-East Asian ◆ Minimalist ◆

Mean, dark and moody: never mind the exterior, we're talking about the A-list diners. Minimalist chic meets high sound levels. Menus scour Far East: cutlery/chopstick choice.

UNITED KINGDOM

Notting Grill

123A Clarendon Rd ✉ W11 4JG – Ⓜ Holland Park – ✆ (020) 7229 1500 – nottinggrill@aol.com – Fax (020) 7229 88 89
closed 24 December-3 January, 27-28 August and Monday lunch **B2**
Rest – Carte £23/39
◆ Beef specialities ◆ Neighbourhood ◆
Converted pub that retains a rustic feel, with bare brick walls and wooden tables. Specialises in well sourced, quality meats.

LONDON AIRPORTS

Heathrow Airport West : 17 m. by A 4 and M 4

London Heathrow Marriott

Bath Rd, Hayes ✉ UB3 5AN – ✆ (020) 8990 1100 – salesadmin.heathrow@marriotthotels.com – Fax (020) 8990 11 10 – www.marriott.co.uk/lhrhr
391 rm – £145 £145 – 2 suites
Rest ***Tuscany*** – *(closed Sunday) (dinner only)* Carte £25/38
Rest ***Allie's Grille*** – Menu £22 – Carte £19/33
◆ Chain hotel ◆ Business ◆ Functional ◆
Built at the end of 20C, this modern, comfortable hotel is centred around a large atrium, with comprehensive business facilities: there is an exclusive Executive floor. Tuscany is bright and convivial. Grill favourites at Allie's.

Crowne Plaza London - Heathrow

Stockley Rd, West Drayton ✉ UB7 9NA – ✆ (0870) 400 9140 – reservations.cplhr@ichotelsgroup.com – Fax (01895) 44 51 22 – www.crowneplaza.com/lon-heathrow
457 rm – £210 £210, £16 – 1 suite
Rest ***Simply Nico Heathrow*** – see below
Rest ***Concha Grill*** – Menu £15/20
◆ Chain hotel ◆ Business ◆ Functional ◆
Extensive leisure, aromatherapy and beauty salons make this large hotel a popular stop-over for travellers. Club bedrooms are particularly well-equipped. Bright, breezy Concha Grill with juice bar.

Radisson Edwardian

140 Bath Rd, Hayes ✉ UB3 5AW – ✆ (020) 8759 6311 – resreh@radisson.com – Fax (020) 8759 45 59 – www.radissonedwardian.com
442 rm – £142/208 £178/246, £15 – 17 suites
Rest ***Henleys*** – *(dinner only Monday-Friday)* Menu £30
Rest ***Brasserie*** – Carte £19/28
◆ Chain hotel ◆ Business ◆ Functional ◆
Capacious group hotel with a huge atrium over the leisure facilities. Plenty of comfortable lounges, well-appointed bedrooms and attentive service. Henleys boasts oil paintings and cocktail bar.

Sheraton Skyline

Bath Rd, Hayes ✉ UB3 5BP – ✆ (020) 8759 2535 – res268-skyline@sheraton.com – Fax (020) 8750 91 50 – www.sheraton.com/skyline
348 rm – £257 £257, £17 – 2 suites
Rest ***Sage*** – Carte £15/32
◆ Chain hotel ◆ Business ◆ Functional ◆
Well known for its unique indoor swimming pool surrounded by a tropical garden which is overlooked by many of the bedrooms. Business centre available. Classically decorated dining room.

Hilton London Heathrow Airport

Terminal 4 ✉ *TW6 3AF* – ✆ *(020) 8759 7755 – sales.heathrow@hilton.com – Fax (020) 8759 75 79 – www.hilton.com*

Lб ☰ ⛆ ♿ AC ⁄rm SAT 250 P VISA MC AE D

390 rm – †£209 ††£209/256, ☕ £20 – 5 suites

Rest *Brasserie* – *(closed lunch Saturday and Sunday) (buffet lunch)* Menu £27/33 – Carte £30/52

Rest *Zen Oriental* – Menu £30 – Carte £23/52

♦ Chain hotel ♦ Business ♦ Functional ♦

Group hotel with a striking modern exterior and linked to Terminal 4 by a covered walkway. Good sized bedrooms, with contemporary styled suites. Spacious Brasserie in vast atrium. Zen Oriental offers formal Chinese experience.

Simply Nico Heathrow – at Crowne Plaza London - Heathrow

Stockley Rd, West Drayton ✉ *UB7 9NA – ✆ (01895) 437564 – heathrow.simplynico@corushotels.com – Fax (01895) 43 75 65 – www.simplyrestaurants.com*

AC P VISA MC AE D

closed Sunday

Rest – *(dinner only)* Carte £23/44

♦ French ♦ Brasserie ♦

Located within the hotel but with its own personality. Mixes modern with more classically French dishes. Professional service in comfortable surroundings.

Gatwick Airport South : 28 m. by A 23 and M 23

Hilton London Gatwick Airport

South Terminal ✉ *RH6 0LL* – ✆ *(01293) 518080 – londongatwick@hilton.com – Fax (01293) 52 89 80 – www.hiltongatwick.com*

Lб ♿ AC ⁄rm 500 P VISA MC AE D

791 rm – †£199/285 ††£285, ☕ £19

Rest – Menu £17 (dinner) – Carte £35/40

♦ Chain hotel ♦ Business ♦ Functional ♦

Large, well-established hotel, popular with business travellers. Two ground floor bars, lounge and leisure facilities. Older rooms co-ordinated, newer in minimalist style. Restaurant enlivened by floral profusions.

Renaissance London Gatwick

Povey Cross Rd ✉ *RH6 0BE* – ✆ *(01293) 820169 – reservations.gatwick@renaissancehotels.com – Fax (01293) 82 02 59 – www.renaissancelondongatwick.co.uk*

Lб ☰ ⛆ ♿ AC ⁄rm 220 P VISA MC AE D

253 rm – †£115/135 ††£115/165, ☕ £17 – 1 suite

Rest – *(bar lunch)* Menu £27 (dinner)

♦ Chain hotel ♦ Business ♦ Functional ♦

Large red-brick hotel. Good recreational facilities including indoor pool, solarium. Bedrooms are spacious and decorated in smart, chintzy style. Small brasserie area open all day serving popular meals.

Luton Airport North : 32 m. by M 1 and A 505

Express by Holiday Inn without rest

2 Percival Way (East : 2m by A505) ✉ *LU2 9GP – ✆ (0870) 4448920 – lutonairport@expressbyholidayinn.net – Fax (0870) 4 44 89 30 – www.hiexpressluton.co.uk*

♿ AC ⁄ 50 P VISA MC AE D

147 rm – †£95 ††£95

♦ Chain hotel ♦ Business ♦ Functional ♦

Purpose-built hotel handily placed beside the airport. Inclusive contenental breakfasts, plus 24 hour snack menus. Rooms are modern and well-equipped.

UNITED KINGDOM

Stansted Airport North : 37 m. by M 11 and A 120

Radisson SAS
400 VISA AE

Waltham Close ✉ *CM24 1PP* – ✆ *(01279) 661012 – info.stansted@radissonsas.com – Fax (01279) 66 10 13 – www.stansted.radissonsas.com*

484 rm – †£125 ††£125, ☕ £15 – 16 suites

Rest *New York Grill Bar* – Carte £23/31

Rest *Wine Tower* – Carte £11/13

Rest *Filini* – Carte £16/25

♦ Chain hotel ♦ Business ♦ Functional ♦

Impressive hotel just two minutes from main terminal; vast open atrium housing 40 foot wine cellar. Extensive meeting facilities. Very stylish bedrooms in three themes. Small, formal New York Grill Bar. Impressive Wine Tower. Filini for Italian dishes.

Hilton London Stansted Airport
rest rm 250 VISA AE

Round Coppice Rd ✉ *CM24 1SF – ✆ (01279) 680800 – reservations.stansted@hilton.com – Fax (01279) 68 08 90*

237 rm – †£94/146 ††£94/146, ☕ £18 – 2 suites

Rest – *(closed lunch Saturday, Sunday and Bank Holidays)* Menu £14/20 – Carte dinner £24/35

♦ Chain hotel ♦ Business ♦ Functional ♦

Bustling hotel whose facilities include leisure club, hairdressers and beauty salon. Modern rooms, with two of executive style. Transport can be arranged to and from terminal. Restaurant/bar has popular menu; sometimes carvery lunch as well.

Express by Holiday Inn without rest
60 VISA AE

Thremhall Ave. ✉ *CM24 1PY – ✆ (01279) 680015 – stansted@kewgreen.co.uk – Fax (01279) 68 08 38*

183 rm – †£80/96 ††£80/96

♦ Chain hotel ♦ Functional ♦

Adjacent to the airport and medium term parking facilities, so useful for leisure and business travellers. Functional rooms provide good value accommodation.

BIRMINGHAM

Population (est. 2005): 889 000 (conurbation 2 371 000) – Altitude: 98m

Duclerc/COLORISE

Birmingham, Britain's flourishing second city, is characterised by its cultural diversity and dynamic fusion of tradition and modernity. It takes pride in its manufacturing past while forging a new identity as a leader in leisure, entertainment, sport, commercial and industrial activities. The attractive squares adorned with modern sculpture and floral displays, the fine museums, theatres and art galleries, the profusion of shopping arcades and eating and drinking establishments as well as a thriving nightlife with one of the best club scenes, justify its designation as a World City.

The canals that weave their way through and beneath the city, played an essential role in the transport of products that made Birmingham a centre of trade and commerce. They are now the focal point for the cultural quarter and provide a pleasant waterfront setting for the many entertainment venues.

WHICH DISTRICT TO CHOOSE

Birmingham offers ample choice of **accommodation** in the city centre and surrounding area to suit every taste and budget. Luxury and boutique hotels are located around Broad Street *Plan II* **D2**, Wharfside Street *Plan II* **E2**, New Street and Church Street *Plan I* **A1**. For hotels with a country house ambience look on the outskirts. There are comfortable business hotels near the airport and the National Exhibition Centre (NEC).

The city's amazing diversity is reflected in the cosmopolitan array of places to eat (modern British, French, Italian, Irish, Japanese, Indian, Chinese, Thai, South American, Caribbean, Mediterranean). The Water's Edge *Plan II* **E1** and Brindley Place *Plan II* **D2** are the areas to explore for **cafés, gastro bars, brasseries** and **restaurants**. The city is famous for its Indian and Chinese restaurants. You may wish to visit Ladypool Road *Plan I* **B2** and Storey Lane at the heart of the Balti Triangle and the Arcadian Centre and the area around Hurst Street *Plan II* **F3** in the Chinese Quarter but there are some stylish ethnic establishments in the city centre.

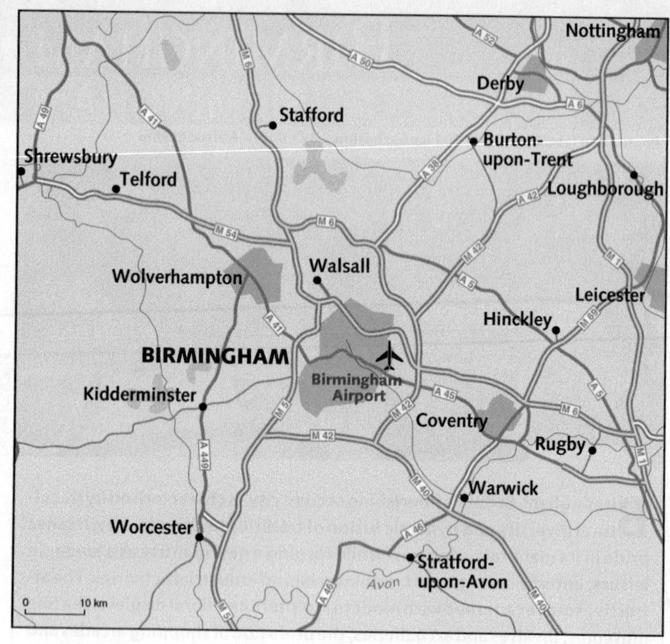

PRACTICAL INFORMATION

ARRIVAL – DEPARTURE

Birmingham International Airport – 13 km (8 mi) east of the city. ✆ 08707 335 511; www.bhx.co.uk

From the airport to the city centre – By **free Air-Rail** to Birmingham International Station: every 2min, time: 90sec; then frequent **trains** to New St Station, time: 20min. Fare: £2.80. ✆ 0845 748 4950. By **taxi**: Black cabs take up to 5 people with luggage. Credit cards are accepted. Fare: about £16. ✆ 0121 782 3744. **By bus**: local buses link the airport to the surrounding districts; all stop outside Terminal 2. Line 900 to Digbeth Coach Station (stop K), every 20-30min, time: 20min; fare: £1.20 single. ✆ 0870 608 2608; www.centro.org.uk; www.travelwm.co.uk

Railway Stations – Birmingham International Station (in the borough of Solihull, just east of the city) and New Street Station *Plan II* **E2** for main-line trains. www.nationalrail.co.uk

TRANSPORT

→ BUSES AND METRO

The integrated public transport system is a convenient way to get about. £2.70 single ticket. **Day Network** £5.60, off-peak weekly £8.10. Tickets can be purchased at rail stations, on buses, at the Centro Information Centre at New Street Station and at Travel WM Travelcard and Information Centres.

→ TAXIS

There is a good taxi service in the city. Allow £5-6 for a short journey. It is customary to add a tip (10%).

USEFUL ADDRESSES

→ TOURIST OFFICES

Tourism Centre & Ticket Shop, The Rotunda, 150 New Street, Birmingham B2 4TA *Plan II* **F2** (open Mon-Sat 9.30am-5.30pm, Sun and Bank hols 10.30am-4.30pm); **Welcome Centre**, Junction of New Street and Corporation Street *Plan II* **E2** (open Mon-Sat 9am-6pm, Sun and Bank hols 10am-4pm). ✆ 0121 202 5099; www.beinbirmingham.com

→ POST OFFICES

The main post offices are at 1 Pinfold St *Plan II* **E2** and 19 Union Passage *Plan II* **F2**. Open Mon-Fri 9.30am-5.30pm, Sat 9.30am-1.30pm.

→ BANKS/CURRENCY EXCHANGE

Banks open Mon-Fri, 9.30am-4.30pm. Some offer a limited service on Saturday mornings. There are cash dispensers (ATM) all over the city that accept international credit cards (PIN required).

→ EMERGENCY

Police, Fire Brigade and Ambulance Service ✆ **999**.

EXPLORING BIRMINGHAM

It is possible to visit the main sights and museums in two days.

Museums and other sights are usually open from 10am to 5pm. Some close on Mondays.

VISITING

Canal trips from Gas Street Basin *Plan II* **D3**, The International Convention Centre Quay *Plan II* **D2** and National Sea Life Centre.

The Wheel *Plan II* **D2** – Panoramic views of the city.

Birmingham Museum and Art Gallery *Plan II* **E2** – A fine building houses an outstanding collection of Pre-Raphaelite paintings as well as works of art by English and European masters.

Barber Institute of Fine Arts *Plan I* **A2** – An excellent collection of French, Italian, Flemish and English paintings as well as furniture and art objects.

St Philip's Cathedral *Plan II* **E2** – A Baroque cathedral (18C) adorned with splendid Pre-Raphaelite stained glass.

Thinktank *Plan I* **B2** – A museum devoted to scientific and technological invention.

Jewellery Quarter *Plan II* **D1** – A survival of early industrial Birmingham: visit the **Museum of the Jewellery Quarter** for the story of the area and for a demonstration of traditional skills and techniques as well as the Georgian **St Paul's Church**, the centrepiece St Paul's Square, the only remaining 18C square in the city.

Back-to-Backs *Plan II* **F3** – Discover the past way of life in an industrial town.

Soho House *Plan I* **A1** – The elegant Georgian home of the industrialist Matthew Boulton.

Aston Hall *Plan I* **B1** – A fine Jacobean house with original furnishings.

Bournville – *6km (4 mi) SW.* The planned estate was a progressive social achievement: workers' cottages, Rest House, school, Selly Manor. A visit to **Cadbury World** is a must for chocoholics.

SHOPPING

Birmingham is a shoppers' paradise. *The Pallasades*, New St, *Pavilion Central*, High St, *Arcadian Centre*, Pershore St, *Martineau Place*, near High St, and *The Mailbox*, Wharfside St are trendy shopping centres with designer shops, department stores, young fashions and accessories. The pedestrianised **Bullring** *Plan II* **F2** boasts the spectacular Selfridges store and other fashion shops. **The Burlington Arcade**, New Street *Plan II* **E2**, has a good selection of stylish shops. You will find that special gift or you may commission your own jewellery in silver, gold, platinum and diamonds in the numerous shops in the **'Golden Triangle'** bounded by Waterstone Lane and Vyse Street *Plan I* **A1**.

ANTIQUES – For arts and crafts visit **The Custard Gallery**, Gibb St (Urban Village, Fragile Design, Sarah Priesler), *Birmingham Antiques*, 68m Wyrley Road, *The Art Lounge*, 28-30 Wharfside Street, *Temple Gallery*, 5 Great Western Arcade and *Vesey Manor*, 62-64 Birmingham Road, Sutton Coldfield.

MARKETS – The Bullring area has a longstanding market tradition: **St Martin's Market** (Tue, Fri-Sat 9am-5pm), produce, clothing, antiques; **Indoor Market**, Edgbaston Street (Mon-Sat 9am-5.30pm); **Farmers' Market**, New St/Victoria Sq (first and third Wed of every month, 9am-5pm).

ENTERTAINMENT

Symphony Hall (ICC) *Plan II* **D2** – concerts of classical, folk, rock, pop, world music and stand-up comedy.

The Hippodrome *Plan II* **F3** – Ballet, opera, musicals and pantomimes.

Alexandra *Plan II* **E3** and **Repertory** *Plan II* **D3 Theatres** – Drama, musicals, comedies, dance.

NEC Arena – Pop and rock concerts, sporting events.

The Drum *Plan I* **A1** – African, Asian and Caribbean Arts and Culture: music, comedy, dance, drama.

Mac Midlands Arts Centre *Plan I* **B2** – Visual and performance arts.

NIGHTLIFE

Visit the Water's Edge and Brindley Place developments in the **Gas Street Basin** area *Plan II* **D2** and the **Jewellery Quarter** *Plan I* **A1** for trendy wine bars, café bars, restaurants and traditional English pubs. Some of the lively venues which attract a young crowd are: *The Jam House*, St Paul's Sq; *Dome II*, Horsefair, the largest discotheque in the city; *The Works* nightclub, Broad St; *The Canal Club*, Broad Street for dancing; *Mechu* and *Après*, 38-59 Summer Row for bars and clubs. **Starcity Entertainment Centre**, Watson Road, offers all kinds of entertainment: cinemas, restaurants, bowling, snow slope, casino.

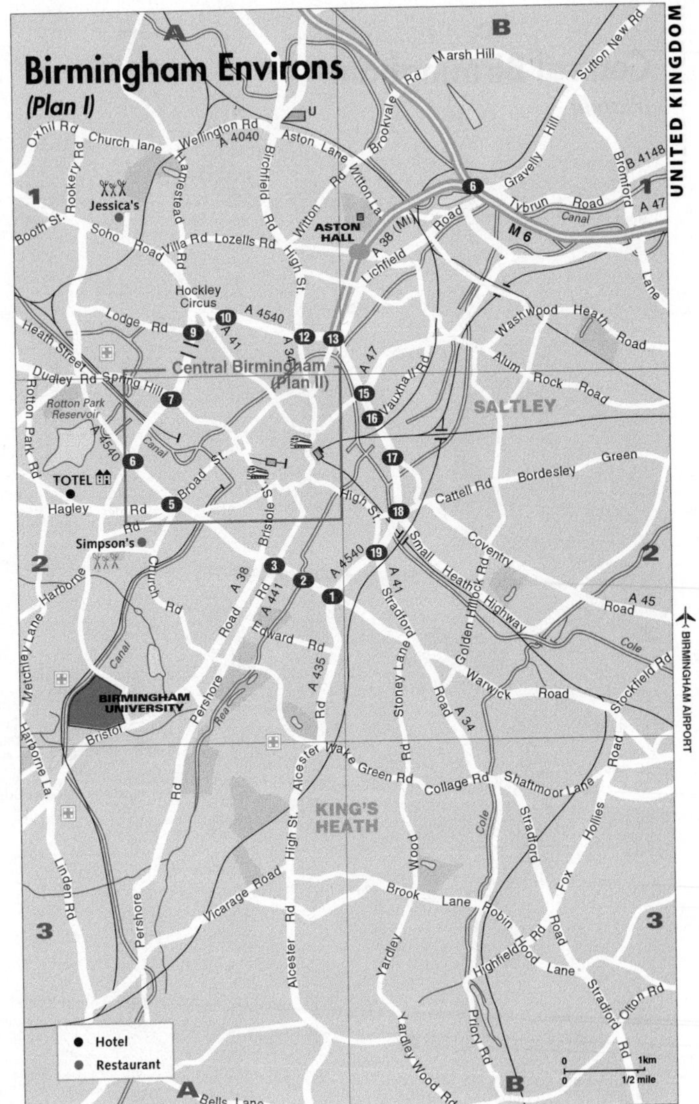
Birmingham Environs
(Plan I)
Central Birmingham
(Plan II)
Jessica's
TOTEL
Simpson's
ASTON HALL
BIRMINGHAM UNIVERSITY
SALTLEY
KING'S HEATH
BIRMINGHAM AIRPORT
Hotel
Restaurant
0 1km
0 1/2 mile

Central Birmingham
(Plan II)

C D

1 2 3

BROOKFIELDS

LADYWOOD

NATIONAL INDOOR ARENA

INTERNATIONAL CONVENTION CENTRE

CENTENARY SQUARE

SEA LIFE

Brindley Place

Spring Hill Circus

Ladywood Circus

Fiveways

Bank

Hyatt Regency

Zinc Bar and Grill

City Inn

Novotel

- Hotel
- Restaurant

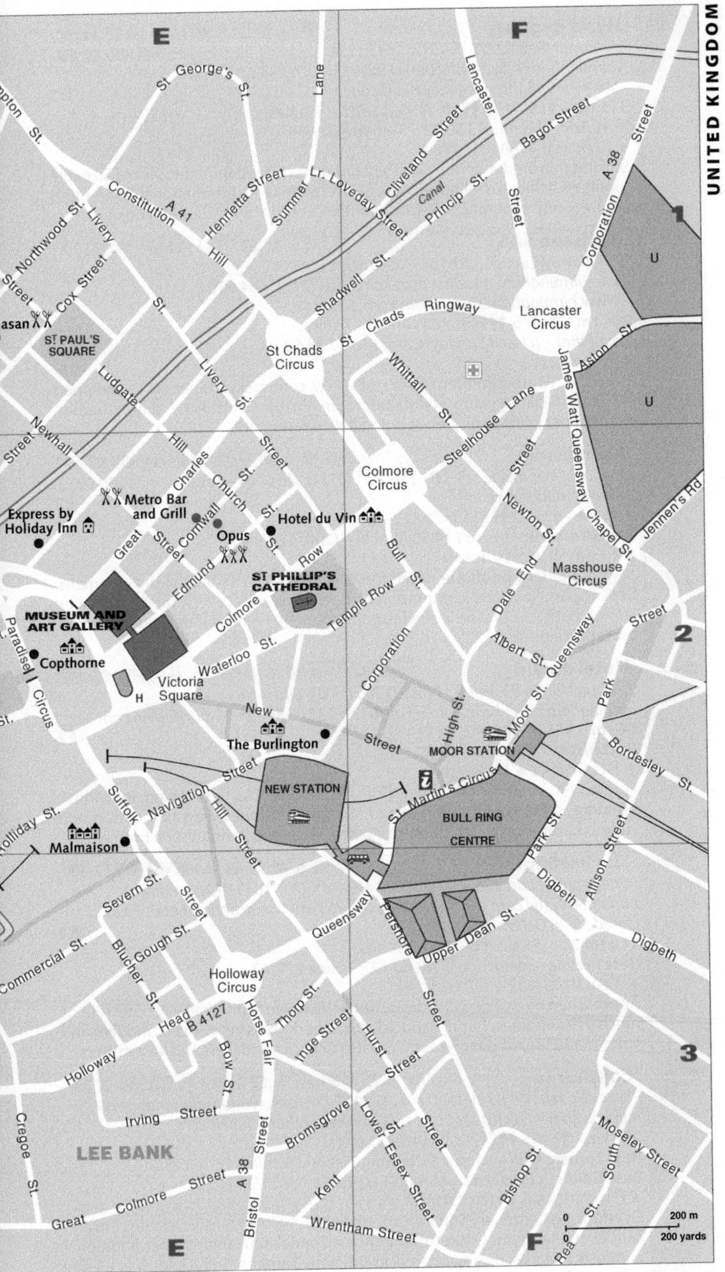
St Chads Circus
Lancaster Circus
Colmore Circus
Masshouse Circus
ST PAUL'S SQUARE
ST PHILLIP'S CATHEDRAL
MUSEUM AND ART GALLERY
Victoria Square
Metro Bar and Grill
Express by Holiday Inn
Hotel du Vin
Opus
Copthorne
The Burlington
Malmaison
NEW STATION
MOOR STATION
BULL RING CENTRE
Holloway Circus
LEE BANK
0 200 m
0 200 yards

UNITED KINGDOM

Hyatt Regency 200
2 Bridge St B1 2ZJ – (0121) 643 1234
– birmingham@hyattintl.com – Fax (0121) 616 23 23
– www.birmingham.regency.hyatt.com **D2**
315 rm – £99/199 £99/199, £15 – 4 suites
Rest *Aria* – Menu £13.50/16.75 – Carte £29/34
♦ Luxury ♦ Modern ♦
Striking mirrored exterior. Glass enclosed lifts offer panoramic views. Sizeable rooms with floor to ceiling windows. Covered link with International Convention Centre. Contemporary style restaurant in central atrium; modish cooking.

Radisson SAS 130 VISA
12 Holloway Circus B1 1BT – (0121) 654 6000
– info.birmingham@radissonsas.com – Fax (0161) 654 60 01
– www.birmingham.radissonsas.com
204 rm – £135 £135, £14.50 – 7 suites
Rest *Filini* – *(closed Sunday)* Carte £18.50/34.50
♦ Modern ♦
Occupies 18 uber-modern floors of a city centre skyscraper. Well-equipped business facilities; ultra stylish bedrooms in three distinctly slinky themes. Modern bar leads to airy, easy-going Italian restaurant.

Malmaison 45 VISA
Mailbox, 1 Wharfside St B1 1RD – (0121) 246 5000 – Fax (0121) 246 50 02
– www.malmaison.com **E2**
184 rm – £140 £140, £13 – 5 suites
Rest *Brasserie* – Menu £14.50 (lunch) – Carte £25/44
♦ Luxury ♦ Stylish ♦
Stylish, modern boutique hotel, forms centrepiece of Mailbox development. Stylish bar. Spacious contemporary bedrooms with every modern facility; superb petit spa. Brasserie serving contemporary French influenced cooking at reasonable prices.

Hotel du Vin rest 85 VISA
25 Church St B3 2NR – (0121) 200 0600 – info@
birmingham.hotelduvin.com – Fax (0121) 236 08 89 – www.hotelduvin.com **E2**
66 rm – £140 £140, £14
Rest *Bistro* – Carte £28/31
♦ Business ♦ Design ♦
Former 19C eye hospital in heart of shopping centre; has relaxed, individual, boutique style. Low lighting in rooms of muted tones: Egyptian cotton and superb bathrooms. Champagne in "bubble lounge"; Parisian style brasserie.

The Burlington 400 VISA
Burlington Arcade, 126 New St B2 4JQ – (0121) 643 9191 – mail@
burlingtonhotel.com – Fax (0121) 643 50 75 – www.macdonaldhotels.co.uk
closed 25-26 December **E2**
110 rm – £165 £175 – 2 suites
Rest *Berlioz* – *(dinner only)* Menu £27 – Carte £27/42
♦ Traditional ♦ Classic ♦
Approached by a period arcade. Restored Victorian former railway hotel retains much of its original charm. Period décor to bedrooms yet with fax, modem and voice mail. Elegant dining room: ornate ceiling, chandeliers and vast mirrors.

Copthorne rest 250 P VISA
Paradise Circus B3 3HJ – (0121) 200 2727 – reservations.birmingham@
mill-cop.com – Fax (0121) 200 11 97 – www.copthornehotels.com **E2**
209 rm – £155 £175, £16 – 3 suites
Rest *Turners Grill* – *(closed Saturday lunch and Sunday)* Carte £23/29
Rest *Goldie's Brasserie* – Menu £11/19 – Carte £21/34
♦ Business ♦ Functional ♦
Overlooking Centenary Square. Corporate hotel with extensive leisure club and cardiovascular gym. Cricket themed bar. Connoisseur rooms offer additional comforts. Flambé dishes offered in intimate Turner's Grill. Goldies is all-day relaxed brasserie.

City Inn rm 100 VISA
1 Brunswick Sq, Brindley Pl ✉ B1 2HW – ✆ (0121) 643 1003 – birmingham.reservations@cityinn.com – Fax (0121) 643 10 05 – www.cityinn.com
D2
238 rm – †£159 ††£159, ☕ £13
Rest *City Café* – Menu £13/17 – Carte £17/40
♦ Chain hotel ♦ Business ♦ Functional ♦
In heart of vibrant Brindley Place; the spacious atrium with bright rugs and blond wood sets the tone for equally stylish rooms. Corporate friendly with many meeting rooms. Eat in restaurant, terrace or bar.

TOTEL without rest VISA
19 Portland Rd, Edgbaston ✉ B16 9HN – ✆ (0121) 454 5282 – info@toteluk.com – Fax (0121) 456 46 68 – www.toteluk.com
Plan I **A2**
1 rm – 9 suites – †£75 ††£105
♦ Business ♦ Design ♦
19C house converted into comfortable, spacious fully-serviced apartments, individually styled with modern facilities. Friendly service. Continental breakfast served in room.

Novotel 300 VISA
70 Broad St ✉ B1 2HT – ✆ (0121) 643 2000 – hlo77@accor.com – Fax (0121) 643 97 86 – www.novotel.com
D3
148 rm ☕ – †£65/145 ††£95/155
Rest – Carte £20/32
♦ Chain hotel ♦ Business ♦ Functional ♦
Well located for the increasingly popular Brindleyplace development. Underground parking. Modern, well-kept, branded bedrooms suitable for families. Modern, open-plan restaurant.

Express by Holiday Inn without rest 30 VISA
65 Lionel St ✉ B11JE – ✆ (0121) 200 1900 – ebhi-bhamcity@btconnect.com – Fax (0121) 200 19 10 – www.hiexpress.co.uk
E2
120 rm – †£55/95 ††£55/95
♦ Chain hotel ♦ Functional ♦
Well-kept, well-managed hotel situated in a handy location for visitors to the city centre. Tidy, comfortable accommodation to suit tourists or business travellers alike.

Simpsons (Antona) with rm rest 18 VISA
20 Highfield Rd, Edgbaston ✉ B15 3DU – ✆ (0121) 454 3434 – info@simpsonsrestaurant.co.uk – Fax (0121) 454 33 99 – www.simpsonsrestaurant.co.uk
closed 24-27 December and 31 December-3 January
Plan I **A2**
4 rm – †£95/125 ††£160/225
Rest – *(closed Sunday dinner)* Menu £27.50/30 – Carte £41/47
Spec. Crab Cocktail, Granny Smith jelly, crab spring roll. Roast loin of venison, butternut squash, cabbage, truffle sauce. Chocolate délice, salted pine nuts.
♦ Innovative ♦ Fashionable ♦
Restored Georgian residence; its interior a careful blend of Victorian features and contemporary style. Refined, classically based cooking. Elegant bedrooms.

Jessica's (Purnell) VISA
1 Montague Rd ✉ B16 9HN – ✆ (0121) 455 0999 – www.jessicasrestaurant.co.uk
closed last 2 weeks July, 1 week Easter , 1 week Christmas, Saturday lunch, Sunday and Monday
Plan I **A2**
Rest – Menu £24.95/36.95
Spec. Ham hock with salad of cockles, gooseberries and pickle. Poached cod, vanilla and lettuce. Ravioli of lavender and strawberry.
♦ Innovative ♦ Formal ♦
Georgian 'outbuilding' and conservatory offering excellently presented, highly original French influenced modern British cooking sourced from quality Midland suppliers.

UNITED KINGDOM

XXX

Opus

A/C 64 VISA AE

54 Cornwall St ✉ B3 2DE – ✆ (0121) 200 2323 – restaurant@ opusrestaurant.co.uk – Fax (0121) 200 20 90 – www.opusrestaurant.co.uk closed 25 December-1 January, Saturday lunch, Sunday and Bank Holidays

E2

Rest – Menu £15/17.50 – Carte £25/35

♦ Modern ♦ Design ♦

Restaurant of floor-to-ceiling glass in evolving area of city. Seafood and shellfish bar for diners on the move. Assured cooking underpins modern menus with traditional base.

XX

Lasan

VISA AE

3-4 Dakota Buildings, James St ✉ B3 1SD – ✆ (0121) 212 3664 – info@ lasan.co.uk – Fax (0121) 212 36 65 – www.lasan.co.uk closed 25-27 December and Saturday lunch

E1

Rest – Carte £18/21

♦ Indian ♦ Design ♦

Jewellery quarter restaurant of sophistication and style; good quality ingredients allow the clarity of the spices to shine through in this well-run Indian establishment.

XX

Bank

A/C 100 VISA AE

4 Brindleyplace ✉ B1 2JB – ✆ (0121) 633 4466 – birmres@bankrestaurants.com – Fax (0121) 633 44 65 – www.bankrestaurants.com closed 26 December and 1 January

D2

Rest – Menu £15 (lunch) – Carte £24/36

♦ Modern ♦ Brasserie ♦

Capacious, modern and busy bar-restaurant where chefs can be watched through a glass wall preparing the tasty modern dishes. Pleasant terrace area.

XX

Metro Bar and Grill

A/C VISA AE

73 Cornwall St ✉ B3 2DF – ✆ (0121) 200 1911 – Fax (0121) 200 16 11 – www.metrobarandgrill.co.uk closed 25 December-1 January, Sunday and Bank Holidays

E2

Rest – *(booking essential)* Carte £22/30

♦ Modern ♦ Brasserie ♦

Gleaming chrome and mirrors in a bright, contemporary basement restaurant. Modern cooking with rotisserie specialities. Spacious, ever-lively bar serves lighter meals.

XX

Zinc Bar and Grill

A/C 40 VISA AE

Regency Wharf, Broad St, ✉ B1 2DS – ✆ (0121) 200 0620 – Fax (0121) 200 06 30 closed 25-26 December and Sunday

D2

Rest – Menu £14.50 – Carte £17/35

♦ Modern ♦ Brasserie ♦

Purpose-built restaurant in lively pub and club area of city. Spiral staircase leads to dining area, including terrace overlooking canal. Modern, classically toned, dishes.

at Birmingham Airport

Novotel Birmingham Airport

35 VISA AE

Passenger Terminal ✉ B26 3QL – ✆ (0121) 782 7000 – h1158@accor.com – Fax (0121) 782 04 45 – www.novotel.com

195 rm – †£129 ††£129, ☕ £13

Rest – *(bar lunch Saturday, Sunday and Bank Holidays)* Menu £17.95/24.95 – Carte £18/33

♦ Chain hotel ♦ Business ♦ Functional ♦

Opposite main terminal building: modern hotel benefits from sound proofed doors and double glazing. Mini bars and power showers provided in spacious rooms with sofa beds. Open-plan garden brasserie.

at National Exhibition Centre

Crowne Plaza 200 P VISA

Pendigo Way ✉ *B40 1PS* – ✆ *(0870) 400 9160 – necroomsales@ichotelsgroup.com – Fax (0121) 781 43 21 – www.birminghamnec.crowneplaza.com*

242 rm – £195/240 £195/240, ☕ £16

Rest – *(closed Saturday lunch)* Carte £29/32

◆ Business ◆ Modern ◆

Modern hotel adjacent to NEC. Small terrace area overlooks lake. Extensive conference facilities. State-of-the-art bedrooms with a host of extras. Basement dining room: food with a Yorkshire twist.

Express by Holiday Inn without rest 100 P

Bickenhill Parkway, Bickenhill, ✉ *B40 1QA Birmingham* – ✆ *(0870) 720 2297 – exhi-nec@foremosthotels.co.uk – Fax (0870) 7 20 22 98 – www.exhi-nec.co.uk*

179 rm – £115 £115

◆ Chain hotel ◆ Functional ◆

Handy for the NEC and airport. Modern budget hotel ideal for the corporate traveller. Extensive cold buffet breakfast included.

EDINBURGH

EDINBURGH

Population (2001): 430 082 (conurbation 452 194) – Altitude: 50m

J. Fuste Raga / HOA QUI

Set on a series of volcanic hills, Edinburgh, the capital of Scotland, is renowned for its cool elegance and sophistication. The Old Town, huddled on the ridge running down from Castle Rock contrasts with the New, with its elegant Georgian streets and squares. The numerous monuments, evidence of its rich historical past, the outstanding museum collections, its colourful traditions and its perennial zest for enjoyment are all reasons to visit this beautiful city. The Edinburgh Festival confirms its status as a cultural capital. The historic opening of the Scottish Parliament in 1999 has further enhanced the city's prestige.

The Castle Rock had been a secure refuge for generations and in the 11C it was chosen as the site for a residence by Malcolm Canmore and his Queen Margaret. Their son, David I, favoured the site by founding the Abbey of the Holy Rood. During the reign of the early Stuarts Edinburgh gradually assumed the roles of royal residence, seat of government and capital of Scotland. With the Union of the Crowns (1603) and subsequent departure of James VI of Scotland (James I of England) for London, Edinburgh lost most of its pageantry, cultural activity and in 1707, with the Union of the Parliaments, its parliament.

WHICH DISTRICT TO CHOOSE

There are several classic **hotels** with impressive amenities around Princes St *Plan II* **G2**, North Bridge and near Charlotte Square *Plan II* **F2**. Comfortable hotels and guest houses with good facilities are located in the New Town, Calton Hill *Plan II* **G2**, around Lauriston Place *Plan II* **G3**, Shandwick Place *Plan II* **F2** and near Ocean Drive *Plan I* **C1** in Leith.

Restaurants of some of the large hotels and museums in the city centre are famous for their imaginative cooking. There are pleasant eateries and pubs serving good food in Princes St, along the Royal Mile and in neighbouring streets, as well as around Rose St *Plan II* **F2**. Leith is a trendy area with many eating places.

ARRIVAL – DEPARTURE

Edinburgh International Airport – 12 km (8 mi) west of the city. ✆ 0870 040 0007; www.edinburghairport.com

From the airport to the city centre – By **bus**: Airlink services (line 100) every 10min to Waverley Bridge. Time: 35min. Fare: £3 one-way, £5 round trip. By **taxi**: time 25min. Fare: about £16.

Railway Stations – Waverley Station, Princes St *Plan II* **G2** and **Haymarket Station**, Haymarket Terrace *Plan II* **E2** for mainline trains. ✆ 08457 484 950; www.nationalrail.co.uk

TRANSPORT

→ BUSES

An efficient bus service operates in the city. A single ticket costs £1. Make sure you have the right money. **Daysaver** tickets £2.50 (£2 after 9.30am and all day Sat-Sun).

→ TAXIS

Metered taxis may be hailed from taxi ranks, outside rail and bus stations and at the airport. You can also order a taxi by phone: *Citycabs Edinburgh Ltd* ✆ 0131 228 1211; *Computer Cabs* ✆ 0131 228 2555.

USEFUL ADDRESSES

→ TOURIST OFFICES

Edinburgh & Scotland Information Centre, 3 Princes Street, Edinburgh EH2 2QP ✆ 0845 22 55 121; *Plan II* **G2**. **Edinburgh Airport**, Tourist Information Desk; www.edinburgh.org

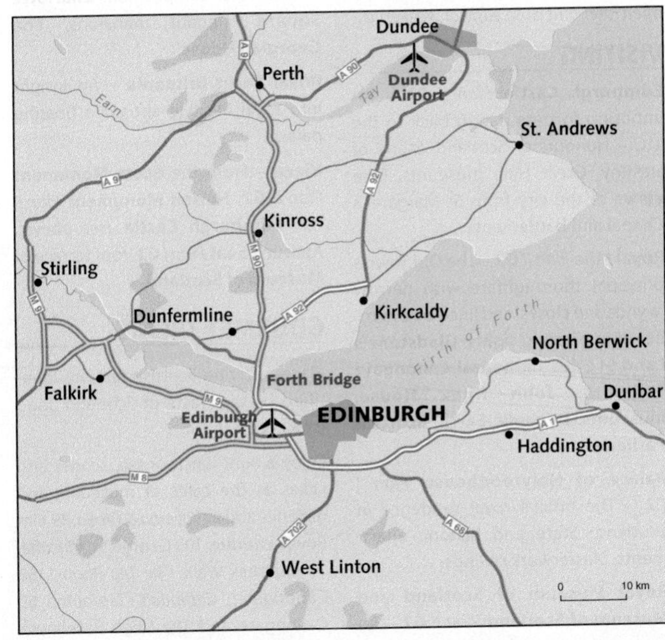

→ POST OFFICES

Opening times Mon-Fri 9am-5.30pm, Sat 9am-noon. Main post offices are at 8-10 St James' Centre *Plan II* **G1** and 40 Frederick St *Plan II* **F2**.

→ BANKS/CURRENCY EXCHANGE

Opening times, Mon-Fri 9.30am to 4-5.30pm; some banks open on Sat 9.30am to 12.30pm but offer a limited service. Cash machines (ATM) are available all over the city. There are foreign exchange offices in the city centre, at post offices, at the airport and train stations, in some stores and at the main tourist office.

→ PHARMACIES

Pharmacies open Mon-Fri, 9.30am-5.30pm, Sat, 9.30am-12.30pm. Boots, 48 Shandwick Place *Plan II* **F2** opens longer hours and on Sunday. There is also a list of pharmacies which open in rotation on Sundays displayed in the window of pharmacies.

BUSY PERIODS

It may be difficult to find a room when special events are held in the city:

Edinburgh International Festival: 3 weeks in August.

Royal Highland Show: late June.

Hogmanay: late December-1 January.

EXPLORING EDINBURGH

It is possible to visit the main sights and museums in Edinburgh in two days.

Museums and sights are usually open daily 9.30-10am to 5pm. Some may have longer opening hours and some may open later and close early at weekends.

VISITING

Edinburgh Castle *Plan II* **F2** – An imposing fortress dating back to the 11C – Honours of Scotland, Stone of Destiny, Great Hall, museums. Fine **views** of the city from St Margaret's Chapel and battlements.

Royal Mile *Plan II* **G2** – The Old Town's principal thoroughfare with narrow 'wynds and closes' and lined by a number of interesting sights: **Gladstone's Land, St Giles' Cathedral, Canongate Tolbooth, John Knox House, museums, Dynamic Earth, Scottish Parliament.**

Palace of Holyroodhouse *Plan I* **C2** – The official royal residence in Scotland: State and historic apartments, plasterwork ceilings.

Royal Museum of Scotland and **Museum of Scotland** *Plan II* **G2** – An enlightening presentation of the comprehensive art collections and of the history of Scotland.

New Town *Plan II* **F2** – An harmonious architectural composition: **Charlotte Square**, elegant mansions, **The Georgian House**.

Royal Yacht Britannia – An insight into royal lifestyle aboard a floating palace.

Views – From the **Scott Monument** *Plan II* **G2, Nelson Monument** *Plan II* **H2**, **Edinburgh Castle** *(see above)*, **Arthur's Seat** *Plan I* **C2**, roof terrace of **Museum of Scotland**.

GOURMET TREATS

Places offering Scottish fare are identified by the 'Taste of Scotland' logo (stockpot).

Enjoy a light lunch or tea, scones and cakes at the cafés of museums and galleries and at *Valvona & Crolla*, 19 Elm Row; *Centrotre*, 103 George St; *Vincaffe*, 11 Multrees Walk; *The Tea Room*, 158 Canongate; *Clarinda's Tearoom*, 69 Canongate and *The Laigh Bakehouse*,

17a Hanover St are all well worth a visit. *The Oyster Bar* at the Café Royal, Register Place is a stylish place. You can book whisky tastings at *The Scotch Malt Whisky Society Ltd*, 87 Giles St, Leith.

SHOPPING

Stores are usually open Mon-Sat, 9-10am to 5.30-6.30pm. Some shops open Sun, 11am to 4.30-5.30pm.

DESIGNER SHOPS, BOUTIQUES AND FASHION OUTLETS – For designer shops visit **The Walk**, off St Andrews Square *Plan II* **G1**, **William Street** *Plan II* **E2** and **Victoria St** *Plan II* **G2**. **Princes Street** is lined with quality stores such as *Jenners, House of Fraser* and trendy shops are located in **George Street** and **Rose St** *Plan II* **F2**.

SPECIALIST SHOPS – Tweed, tartan, cashmere, wool garments: *Romanes Paterson*, 62 Princes St; *Kinloch Anderson*, Commercial/Dock St, Leith; *The Cashmere Store*, 2 Saint Giles St, *Ragamuffin*, Canongate and *Troon*, 1 York Place. Crystal: *Edinburgh Crystal Visitor Centre*, Eastfield, Penicuik. Fossils and minerals: *Mr Wood's Fossils*, 5 Cowgatehead, Grassmarket. Jewellery: *Scottish Gems*, 24 High St; *The Tappit Hen*, 89 High St. Crafts: *The Ceramic Experience*, Hopetoun St. There are specialist food shops along the Royal Mile and *Baxters* is at Ocean Terminal in Leith. Malt whisky: *Royal Mile Whiskies*, 379 High St.

ANTIQUE SHOPS – Explore the area around the **Royal Mile, Victoria St** and **Grassmarket** in the Old Town and in **Dundas** *Plan II* **G1** and **Thistle Streets** *Plan II* **G2**. Also visit *Georgian Antiques*, 10 Pattison St, Leith Links.

MARKETS – **Leith Market**, Commercial Quay, Ocean Drive *Plan I* **C1**, Leith – food, art, fashion, flowers – open Sat 9am-5.30pm; Sun 10am-4pm. **Farmers' Market**, Castle Terrace: open Sat 9am-2pm.

WHAT TO BUY – Edinburgh crystal, ceramics, tartan, knitwear, malt whisky, smoked fish, shortbread, oatcakes, marmalade and jams, Dundee cake, crafts and jewellery.

ENTERTAINMENT

For listings consult the fortnightly magazine, The List. The Edinburgh pages of the weekly *Time Out* give useful information.

Usher Hall *Plan II* **F2** – Concerts.

Royal Lyceum Theatre *Plan II* **F2** – Scottish drama and dance.

Edinburgh Playhouse *Plan II* **H1** – Musicals.

King's Theatre *Plan II* **F3** and **Edinburgh Festival Theatre** *Plan II* **H3** – Plays, ballet, opera.

Traverse Theatre *Plan II* **F2** – Experimental theatre.

Corn Exchange, 11 Newmarket Rd – Live music.

Assembly Rooms *Plan II* **G2** – Ceilidhs.

NIGHTLIFE

Edinburgh **pubs** have a great atmosphere: *Abbotsford*, 3-5 Rose St *Plan II* **F2**; *Deacon Brodie* and *Ensign Ewart*, Lawnmarket; *Greyfriars Bobby*, 34 Candlemaker Row; *Bow Bar*, 80 West Row; *Oxford Bar*, 8 Young St; *Halfway House*, Fishmarket Close. Pubs in Grassmarket *Plan II* **G2** are popular with students and there are fashionable pubs and wine bars on the quayside at Leith. For live music, go to *Bannerman's*, 212 Cowgate; *Whistle Binkies*, 6 Niddry St; *Bongo Club*, 37 Holyrood Rd. A young and trendy crowd flocks to *Po Na Na*, 43b Frederick St;*The City Club*, 1a Market St; *The Subway*, 69 Cowgate; *The Vaults*, 15-17 Niddry St. Jazz fans will enjoy *Henry's Jazz Cellar*, 8 Morrison St. The *George Inter-Continental Hotel*, 19-21 George St and *Thistle Hotel*, 107 Leith St organise Scottish evenings.

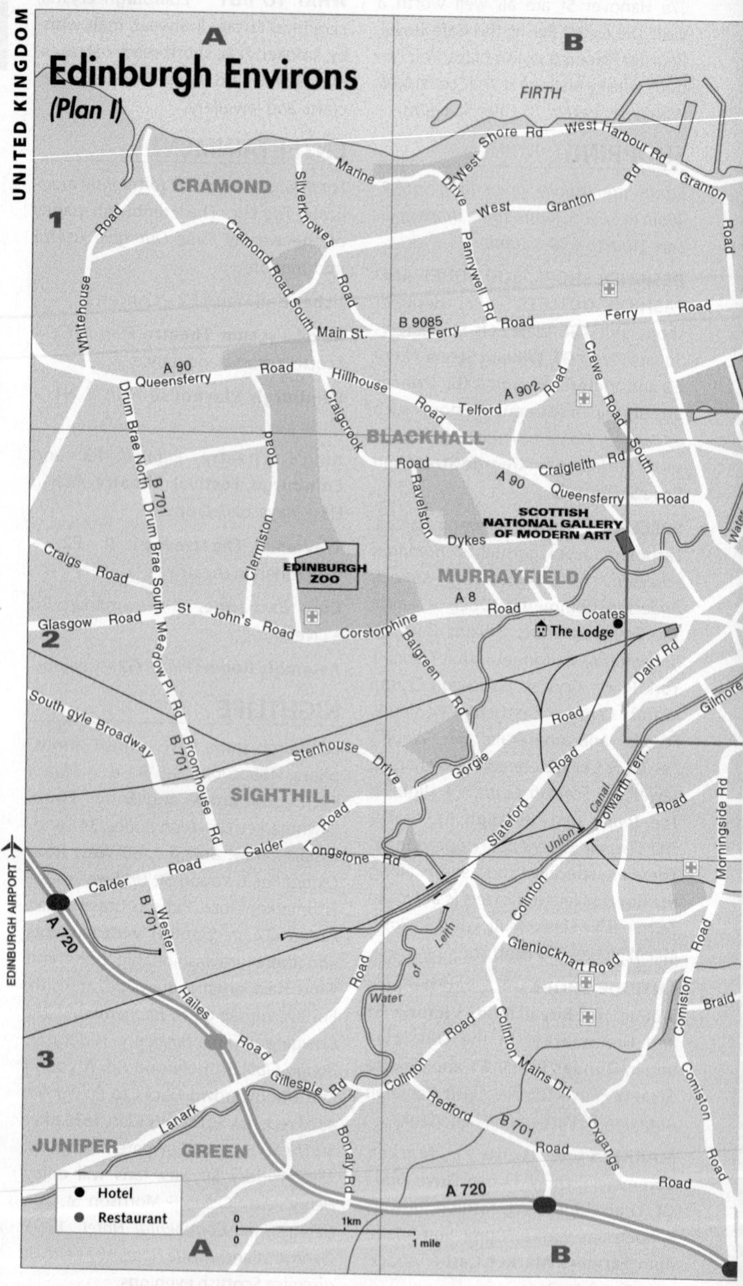
Edinburgh Environs
(Plan I)
A
B
1
2
3
FIRTH
CRAMOND
BLACKHALL
MURRAYFIELD
SIGHTHILL
JUNIPER
GREEN
EDINBURGH ZOO
SCOTTISH NATIONAL GALLERY OF MODERN ART
The Lodge
EDINBURGH AIRPORT
Hotel
Restaurant
1km
1 mile

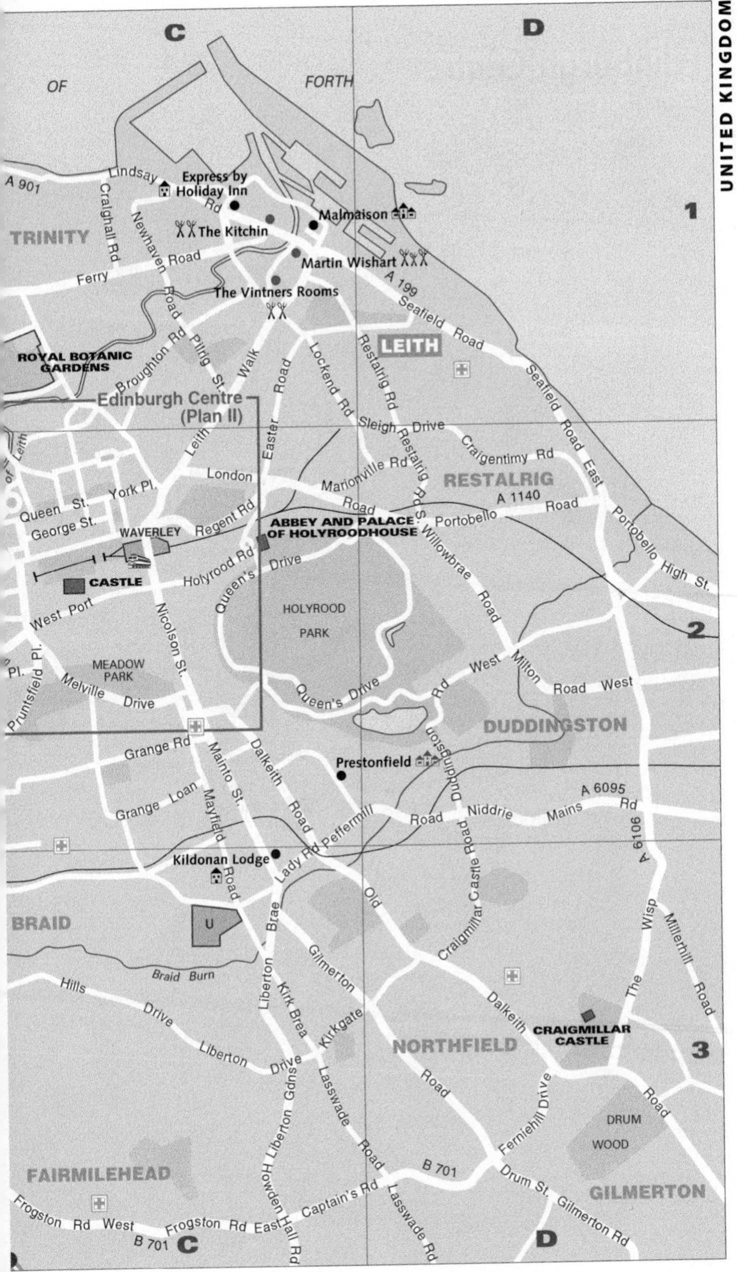
C
D
OF
FORTH
A 901
Lindsay Rd
Express by Holiday Inn
Malmaison
TRINITY
Craighall Rd
Newhaven Road
The Kitchin
Martin Wishart
Ferry Road
The Vintners Rooms
A 199
Seafield Road
LEITH
ROYAL BOTANIC GARDENS
Broughton Rd
Pilrig St.
Leith Walk
Easter Road
Lockend Rd
Restalrig Rd
Edinburgh Centre (Plan II)
Sleigh Drive
Restalrig Rd S.
Craigentimy Rd
Seafield Road East
Marionville Rd
RESTALRIG
London Road
York Pl.
Queen St.
George St.
Regent Rd
A 1140
Portobello Road
WAVERLEY
ABBEY AND PALACE OF HOLYROODHOUSE
Willowbrae Road
Portobello High St.
CASTLE
Holyrood Rd
Queen's Drive
West Port
HOLYROOD PARK
Nicolson St.
MEADOW PARK
Melville Drive
Pruntsfield Pl.
West Milton Road West
Queen's Drive
DUDDINGSTON
Duddingston Rd West
Grange Rd
Dalkeith Road
Mainto St.
Prestonfield
A 6095
Grange Loan
Mayfield Road
Peffermill Road
Niddrie Mains Rd
A 6106
Kildonan Lodge
Lady Rd
Old Dalkeith Road
Craigmillar Castle Road
BRAID
U
Braid Burn
Liberton Brae
Gilmerton
The Wisp
Millerhill Road
Hills Drive
Kirk Brea
Kirkgate
Liberton Drive
CRAIGMILLAR CASTLE
NORTHFIELD
Liberton Gdns
Lasswade Road
Ferniehill Drive
DRUM WOOD
FAIRMILEHEAD
B 701
Drum St.
Gilmerton Rd
GILMERTON
Frogston Rd West
Frogston Rd East
Howden Hall Rd
Captain's Rd
Lasswade Rd
1
2
3

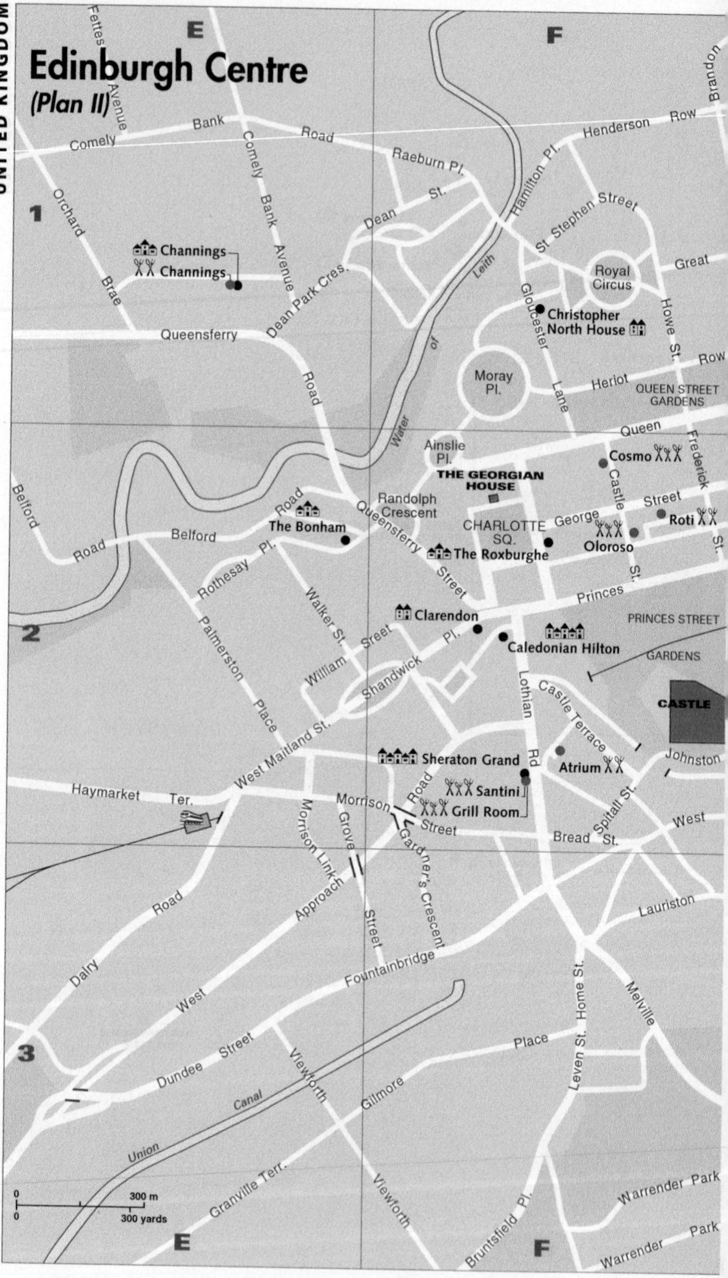

Edinburgh Centre
(Plan II)

E
F
1
2
3

Channings
Channings
Christopher North House
Cosmo
The Bonham
The Roxburghe
Oloroso
Roti
Clarendon
Caledonian Hilton
Sheraton Grand
Atrium
Santini
Grill Room
THE GEORGIAN HOUSE
CASTLE
Royal Circus
Moray Pl.
Ainslie Pl.
Randolph Crescent
CHARLOTTE SQ.
QUEEN STREET GARDENS
PRINCES STREET GARDENS

Fettes Avenue
Comely Bank Road
Comely Bank Avenue
Orchard Brae
Raeburn Pl.
Dean St.
Dean Park Cres.
Queensferry Road
Water of Leith
Hamilton Pl.
Henderson Row
Brandon
St. Stephen Street
Great
Gloucester Lane
Howe St.
Heriot Row
Queen
Frederick St.
Castle St.
George Street
Princes
Belford Road
Rothesay Pl.
Queensferry Street
Walker St.
William Sreet
Shandwick Pl.
Palmerston Place
West Maitland St.
Haymarket Ter.
Lothian Rd
Castle Terrace
Johnston
Spittall St.
West
Bread St.
Morrison Street
Morrison Link
Grove Street
Gardner's Crescent
Approach
Dalry Road
West
Fountainbridge
Lauriston
Home St.
Leven St.
Melville
Place
Dundee Street
Viewforth
Gilmore
Canal
Union
Granville Terr.
Bruntsfield Pl.
Warrender Park
Warrender Park

0 300 m
0 300 yards

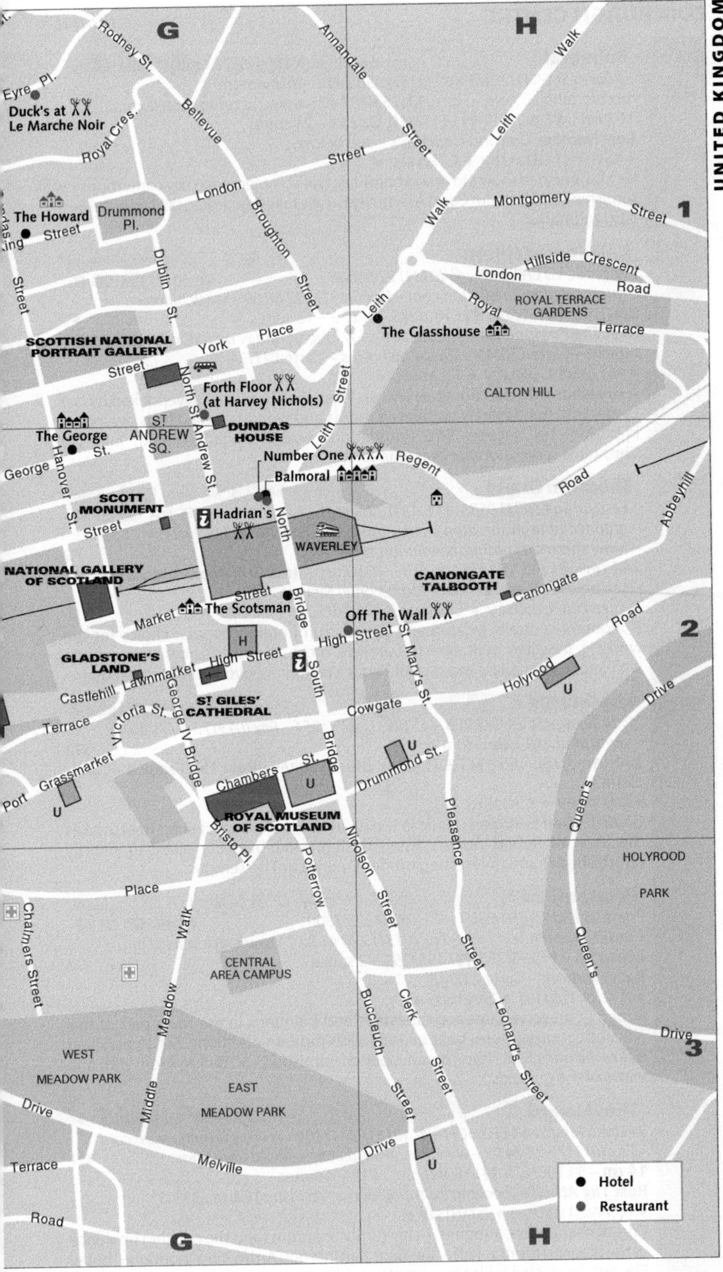
G
H
1
2
3
Duck's at Le Marche Noir
The Howard
Drummond Pl.
SCOTTISH NATIONAL PORTRAIT GALLERY
Forth Floor (at Harvey Nichols)
The Glasshouse
ROYAL TERRACE GARDENS
CALTON HILL
ST ANDREW SQ.
DUNDAS HOUSE
The George
Number One
Balmoral
SCOTT MONUMENT
Hadrian's
WAVERLEY
NATIONAL GALLERY OF SCOTLAND
CANONGATE TALBOOTH
The Scotsman
Off The Wall
GLADSTONE'S LAND
ST GILES' CATHEDRAL
ROYAL MUSEUM OF SCOTLAND
HOLYROOD PARK
CENTRAL AREA CAMPUS
WEST MEADOW PARK
EAST MEADOW PARK
Hotel
Restaurant

UNITED KINGDOM

EDINBURGH CENTRE

Plan II

Balmoral

1 Princes St ✉ EH2 2EQ – ✆ (0131) 556 2414 – thebalmoral@roccofortehotels.com – Fax (0131) 557 87 40 – www.roccofortehotels.com
350 VISA AE

167 rm – £290/450 £345/510, £19 – 21 suites **G2**

Rest *Number One* and ***Hadrian's*** – see below

♦ Grand Luxury ♦ Classic ♦

Richly furnished rooms in grand baronial style complemented by contemporary furnishings in the Palm Court exemplify this de luxe Edwardian railway hotel and city landmark.

Caledonian Hilton

Princes St, ✉ EH1 2AB – ✆ (0131) 222 8888 – guest.caledonian@hilton.com – Fax (0131) 222 88 89 – www.hilton.co.uk
rest rm 300 P VISA AE

238 rm – £150/245 £180/275, £20 – 13 suites **F2**

Rest *The Pompadour* – *(closed Saturday lunch, Sunday and Monday)* Menu £21 (lunch) – Carte £30/41 – **Rest *Chisholms*** – Carte £27/34

♦ Grand Luxury ♦ Classic ♦

A city landmark, affectionately known locally as "The Cally". Overlooked by the castle, with handsomely appointed rooms and wood-panelled halls behind an imposing 19C façade. The Pompadour boasts elegant dining. Informal Chisholms serves popular brasserie fare.

Sheraton Grand

1 Festival Sq ✉ EH3 9SR – ✆ (0131) 229 9131 – grandedinburgh.sheraton@sheraton.com – Fax (0131) 229 96 31 – www.sheraton.com/grandedinburgh
rm 500 P VISA AE

244 rm – £245 £275, £18 – 16 suites – **Rest *Grill Room*** and ***Santini*** – see below – **Rest *Terrace*** – *(buffet only)* Menu £21/22 **F2**

♦ Grand Luxury ♦ Business ♦ Modern ♦

A modern, centrally located and smartly run hotel. A popular choice for the working traveller, as it boasts Europe's most advanced urban spa. Comfy, well-kept rooms. Glass expanse of Terrace restaurant overlooks Festival Square.

The George

19-21 George St ✉ EH2 2PB – ✆ (0131) 225 1251 – Fax (0131) 2 40 71 19 – www.principal-hotels.com
rm 200 VISA AE

192 rm – £80/165 £100/175, £16 – 3 suites – **Rest *The Tempus*** – Carte £24/33 **G2**

♦ Luxury ♦ Classic ♦

Grade II listed Georgian classic in the heart of the city's most chic street; makes the most of Robert Adam's listed design. Modern decor allied to smartly refurbished rooms. Interesting modern menus at The Tempus.

Prestonfield

Priestfield Rd ✉ EH16 5UT – ✆ (0131) 225 7800 – mail@prestonfield.com – Fax (0131) 220 43 92 – www.prestonfield.com
rm 900 P VISA AE

20 rm – £195/255 £195/295 – 2 suites *Plan I* **C2**

Rest *Rhubarb* – Carte £32/45

♦ Traditional ♦ Stylish ♦

Superbly preserved interior, tapestries and paintings in the main part of this elegant country house, built in 1687 with modern additions. Set in parkland below Arthur's Seat. Two-roomed, period-furnished 18C dining room with fine views of the grounds.

The Howard

34 Great King St ✉ EH3 6QH – ✆ (0131) 2747402 – reserve@thehoward.com – Fax (0131) 2 74 74 05 – www.thehoward.com – closed Christmas
rest 30 P VISA AE

14 rm – £108/175 £180/265, £17 – 4 suites **G1**

Rest *The Atholl* – *(booking essential for non-residents)* Carte £33/43

♦ Townhouse ♦ Stylish ♦

Crystal chandeliers, antiques, richly furnished rooms and the relaxing opulence of the drawing room set off a fine Georgian interior. An inviting "boutique" hotel. Elegant, linen-clad tables for sumptuous dining.

The Scotsman — 80 P VISA

20 North Bridge ✉ EH1 1YT – ✆ (0131) 556 5565 – reservations@thescotsmanhotelgroup.co.uk – Fax (0131) 652 36 52 – www.thescotsmanhotel.co.uk **G2**

57 rm – †£270 ††£295, ☕ £18 – 12 suites

Rest *Vermilion* – *(closed Monday and Tuesday) (dinner only)* Carte £32/45

Rest *North Bridge Brasserie* – Carte £19/33

♦ Luxury ♦ Classic ♦

Imposing former offices of "The Scotsman" newspaper, with marble reception hall and historic prints. Notably impressive leisure facilities. Well-equipped modern bedrooms. Vibrant, richly red Vermilion. North Bridge Brasserie boasts original marble pillars.

Channings — 35 VISA

15 South Learmonth Gdns ✉ EH4 1EZ – ✆ (0131) 3152226 – reserve@channings.co.uk – Fax (0131) 3 32 96 31 – www.channings.co.uk **E1**

41 rm ☕ – †£125/195 ††£235/275 – 3 suites

Rest *Channings* – see below

♦ Townhouse ♦ Stylish ♦

Sensitively refurbished rooms and fire-lit lounges blend an easy country house elegance with original Edwardian character. Individually appointed bedrooms.

The Bonham — 50 P VISA

35 Drumsheugh Gdns ✉ EH3 7RN – ✆ (0131) 2747400 – reserve@thebonham.com – Fax (0131) 2 74 74 05 – www.thebonham.com **E2**

46 rm – †£145/165 ††£195, ☕ £12 – 2 suites

Rest – Menu £16 (lunch) – Carte dinner £26/37

♦ Townhouse ♦ Stylish ♦

A striking synthesis of Victorian architecture, eclectic fittings and bold, rich colours of a contemporary décor. Numerous pictures by "up-and-coming" local artists. Chic dining room with massive mirrors and "catwalk" in spotlights.

The Glasshouse without rest — 70 VISA

2 Greenside Pl ✉ EH1 3AA – ✆ (0131) 525 8200 – resglasshouse@theetongroup.com – Fax (0131) 525 82 05 – www.theetoncollection.com **H1**

65 rm – †£250 ††£270, ☕ £17

♦ Business ♦ Modern ♦

Glass themes dominate the discreet style. Modern bedrooms, with floor to ceiling windows, have views of spacious roof garden or the city below. Breakfast room to the rear.

The Roxburghe — rest 300 VISA

38 Charlotte Sq ✉ EH2 4HG – ✆ (0131) 240 5500 – roxburghe@macdonald-hotels.co.uk – Fax (0131) 240 55 55 – www.macdonaldhotels.co.uk/roxburghe **F2**

197 rm ☕ – †£90/200 ††£90/250 – 1 suite

Rest *The Melrose* – *(dinner only and Sunday lunch)* Menu £21.50/26.50 – Carte £25/32

♦ Business ♦ Classic ♦

Attentive service, understated period-inspired charm and individuality in the British style. Part modern, part Georgian but roomy throughout; welcoming bar. Restaurant reflects the grandeur of architect Robert Adam's exterior.

Christopher North House without rest — VISA

6 Gloucester Pl ✉ EH3 6EF – ✆ (0131) 225 2720 – reservations@christophernorth.co.uk – Fax (0131) 220 47 06 – www.christophernorth.co.uk **F1**

30 rm ☕ – †£88/110 ††£98/220

♦ Townhouse ♦ Classic ♦

Georgian house on cobbled street in quiet residential area; a chintzy feel overlays the contemporary interior. Eclectically styled bedrooms feature homely extra touches.

UNITED KINGDOM

Clarendon without rest

25 Shandwick Pl ✉ EH2 4RG – ☎ (0131) 229 1467 – res@clarendonhoteledi.com – Fax (0131) 229 75 49 – www.clarendonhoteledi.com **F2**

66 rm – ♦£40/130 ♦♦£60/160

♦ Business ♦ Modern ♦

Two minutes' walk from Princes Street, tastefully updated, this smart hotel boasts bright, vivid colours, a cosy, contemporary bar and well-presented rooms.

The Lodge without rest

6 Hampton Terrace, West Coates ✉ EH12 5JD – ☎ (0131) 337 3682 – info@thelodgehotel.co.uk – Fax (0131) 313 17 00 – www.thelodgehotel.co.uk *Plan I* **B2**

12 rm – ♦£60/80 ♦♦£80/135

♦ Family ♦ Classic ♦

A converted Georgian manse, family owned and immaculately kept. Individually designed bedrooms and lounge decorated with taste and care; close to Murrayfield rugby stadium.

Kildonan Lodge without rest

27 Craigmillar Park ✉ EH16 5PE – ☎ (0131) 667 2793 – info@kildonanlodgehotel.co.uk – Fax (0131) 667 97 77 – www.kildonanlodgehotel.co.uk

closed 25 December *Plan I* **C3**

15 rm – ♦£58/98 ♦♦£78/138

♦ Family ♦ Cosy ♦

Privately managed, with a cosy, firelit drawing room which feels true to the Lodge's origins as a 19C family house. One room has a four-poster bed and a fine bay window.

Number One – at Balmoral H.

1 Princes St ✉ EH2 2EQ – ☎ (0131) 622 8831 – numberone@roccofortehotels.com – Fax (0131) 557 87 40 – www.roccofortehotels.com **G2**

Rest – *(dinner only and lunch in December)* Menu £55/65

Spec. Seared scallops with chestnut purée, smoked bacon and shellfish velouté. Poached fillet of beef with horseradish glaze and mushroom emulsion. Caramelised hazelnut and chocolate frangipane with banana cream

♦ Modern ♦ Formal ♦

Edinburgh's nonpareil for polished fine dining and immaculate service; spacious basement setting. Original dishes with a well-balanced flair showcase Scottish produce.

Oloroso

14

33 Castle St ✉ EH2 3DN – ☎ (0131) 226 7614 – info@oloroso.co.uk – Fax (0131) 226 76 08 – www.oloroso.co.uk

closed first week January and 25-26 December **F2**

Rest – Carte £29/45

♦ Innovative ♦ Design ♦

Modish third floor restaurant in heart of city. Busy, atmospheric bar. Lovely terrace with good castle views to the west. Stylish, modern cooking with Asian influence.

Grill Room – at Sheraton Grand H.

1 Festival Sq ✉ EH3 9SR – ☎ (0131) 221 6422 – Fax (0131) 229 62 54 – www.sheraton.com/grandedinburgh

closed Saturday lunch, Sunday and Monday **F2**

Rest – Carte £29/50

♦ Modern ♦ Formal ♦

Ornate ceilings, wood panels and modern glass make an ideal setting for imaginative, well presented cooking. Local ingredients with a few European and Pacific Rim elements.

XXX **Santini** – at Sheraton Grand H. AC P VISA MC AE D

8 Conference Sq ✉ EH3 8AN – ✆ (0131) 221 7788 – Fax (0131) 221 77 89 – www.sheraton.com/grandedinburgh

closed Saturday lunch and Sunday F2

Rest – Menu £25 (lunch) – Carte £28/47

♦ Italian ♦ Formal ♦

The personal touch is predominant in this stylish restaurant appealingly situated under a superb spa. Charming service heightens the enjoyment of tasty, modern Italian food.

XXX **Cosmo** VISA MC AE D

58A North Castle St. ✉ EH2 3LU – ✆ (0131) 2266743 – info@cosmo-restaurant.co.uk

closed first 2 weeks January, Saturday lunch, Sunday dinner and Bank Holidays F2

Rest – Menu £21.50 (lunch) – Carte dinner £34/50

♦ Traditional ♦ Formal ♦

Off busy city centre street into a vividly red, leather furnished lounge and dining room in similar opulent style. Traditional menus served in pleasant, relaxing ambience.

XX **Off The Wall** VISA MC AE

105 High St ✉ EH1 1SG – ✆ (0131) 558 1497 – otwedinburgh@aol.com – www.off-the-wall.co.uk

closed 24-26 December, 1-3 January, Sunday and Monday G-H2

Rest – Menu £19.95 (lunch) – Carte dinner £35/42

♦ Scottish ♦ Formal ♦

Located on the Royal Mile, though hidden on first floor away from bustling crowds. Vividly coloured dining room. Modern menus underpinned by a seasonal Scottish base.

XX **Channings** – at Channings H. VISA MC AE D

12-16 South Learmonth Gdns ✉ EH4 1EZ – ✆ (0131) 623 9302 – Fax (0131) 623 93 06 – www.channings.co.uk E1

Rest – Menu £15 (lunch) – Carte dinner £21/33

♦ Mediterranean ♦ Fashionable ♦

A warm, contemporary design doesn't detract from the formal ambience pervading this basement restaurant in which classic Gallic flavours hold sway.

XX **Forth Floor (at Harvey Nichols)** < Castle and city skyline,

30-34 St Andrew Sq ✉ EH2 2AD – ✆ (0131) 524 8350 AC VISA MC AE D

– Fax (0131) 524 83 51 – www.harveynichols.com

closed 25 December, 1 January and dinner Sunday-Monday G1

Rest – Menu £17.50/31 – Carte £24/36

♦ Modern ♦ Brasserie ♦

Stylish restaurant with delightful outside terrace affording views over the city. Half the room in informal brasserie-style and the other more formal. Modern, Scottish menus.

XX **Atrium** AC VISA MC AE D

10 Cambridge St ✉ EH1 2ED – ✆ (0131) 228 8882 – eat@atriumrestaurant.co.uk – Fax (0131) 228 88 08 – www.atriumrestaurant.co.uk

closed 25-26 December, 1-2 January, Sunday and Saturday lunch except during Edinburgh Festival F2

Rest – Menu £17.50/27 – Carte £31/44

♦ Modern ♦ Design ♦

Located inside the Traverse Theatre, an adventurous repertoire enjoyed on tables made of wooden railway sleepers. Twisted copper lamps subtly light the ultra-modern interior.

UNITED KINGDOM

XX **Duck's at Le Marche Noir** 24 VISA MC AE

2-4 Eyre Pl ✉ EH3 5EP – ✆ (0131) 558 1608 – enquiries@ducks.co.uk – Fax (0131) 556 07 98 – www.ducks.co.uk
closed 25-26 December and lunch Saturday-Monday **G1**
Rest – Menu £15 (lunch) – Carte £22/38
♦ Innovative ♦ Bistro ♦
Confident, inventive cuisine with a modern, discreetly French character, served with friendly efficiency in bistro-style surroundings - intimate and very personally run.

XX **Hadrian's** – at Balmoral H. AC VISA MC AE

2 North Bridge ✉ EH1 1TR – ✆ (0131) 557 5000 – Fax (0131) 557 37 47 – www.roccofortehotels.com **G2**
Rest – Menu £16.95/20.95 – Carte £24/39
♦ Modern ♦ Brasserie ♦
Drawing on light, clean-lined styling, reminiscent of Art Deco, and a "British new wave" approach; an extensive range of contemporary brasserie classics and smart service.

XX **Roti** VISA MC AE

70 Rose St., North Lane ✉ EH2 3DX – ✆ (0131) 2251233 – info@roti.uk.com – Fax (0131) 2 25 53 74
closed Saturday lunch, Sunday and Monday **F2**
Rest – Carte £23/26
♦ Indian ♦ Friendly ♦
Though set in an unprepossessing backstreet, this is an out-of-the-ordinary Indian restaurant in two sparse rooms serving authentic dishes with satisfyingly original elements.

LEITH

Plan I

Malmaison rm 70 P VISA MC AE

1 Tower Pl ✉ EH6 7DB – ✆ (0131) 468 5000 – edinburgh@malmaison.com – Fax (0131) 468 50 02 – www.malmaison.com **C1**
95 rm – †£145 ††£145, ☐ £13 – 5 suites
Rest *Brasserie* – Menu £13.95/14.95 – Carte £26/41
♦ Business ♦ Stylish ♦
Imposing quayside sailors' mission converted in strikingly elegant style. Good-sized rooms, thoughtfully appointed, combine more traditional comfort with up-to-date overtones. Sophisticated brasserie with finely wrought iron.

Express by Holiday Inn without rest 25

Britannia Way, Ocean Drive ✉ EH6 6JJ P VISA MC AE
– ✆ (0131) 555 4422 – info@hiex-edinburgh.com – Fax (0131) 555 46 46 – www.hiex-edinburgh.com **C1**
145 rm – †£76 ††£89
♦ Business ♦ Chain hotel ♦ Functional ♦
Modern, purpose-built hotel offering trim, bright, reasonably-priced accommodation. Convenient for Leith centre restaurants and a short walk from the Ocean Terminal.

XXX **Martin Wishart** VISA MC AE

54 The Shore ✉ EH6 6RA – ✆ (0131) 553 3557 – info@martin-wishart.co.uk – Fax (0131) 467 70 91 – www.martin-wishart.co.uk
closed 1 week January, 1 week September, Christmas-New Year, Sunday and Monday **C1**
Rest – *(booking essential)* Menu £22.50/50
Spec. Lobster and smoked haddock soufflé, lobster cappuccino. John Dory with almonds and leeks, poached apricots and curry jus. Braised cheek and rib of beef, veal sweetbreads, wild mushroom ravioli.
♦ Innovative ♦ Formal ♦
Simply decorated dockside conversion with a fully formed reputation. Modern French-accented menus characterised by clear, intelligently combined flavours.

XX ✿

The Kitchin

78 Commercial Quay ✉ EH6 6LX – ✆ (0131) 5551755 – info@thekitchin.com – Fax (0131) 5 53 06 08 – www.thekitchin.com
closed 2-4 January, 1-15 July and Sunday-Monday **C1**
Rest – Menu £20 (lunch) – Carte £35/45
Spec. Langoustine with braised pork belly with Mesclun salad. Seared halibut with ginger tomato chutney and herb beurre blanc. Poached pear with mint and chocolate sorbet.
♦ Contemporary ♦ Design ♦
Former dockside warehouse, the industrial feel enhanced by original metal supports and battleship grey décor. Well-priced menus offering skilful, accomplished, modern cooking.

XX

The Vintners Rooms

The Vaults, 87 Giles St ✉ EH6 6BZ – ✆ (0131) 554 6767 – enquiries@thevintnersrooms.com – Fax (0131) 555 56 53 – www.thevintnersrooms.com
closed 25-26 December, Sunday and Monday **C1**
Rest – Menu £19 (lunch) – Carte £33/38
♦ Mediterranean ♦ Rustic ♦
Atmospheric 18C bonded spirits warehouse with high ceilings, stone floor, rug-covered walls and candlelit side-room with ornate plasterwork. French/Mediterranean cooking.

GLASGOW

GLASGOW

Population (est. 2005): 616 000 (conurbation 1 228 000) – Altitude: 8m

AGE Atlantide SNC/HOA QUI

The dynamic image which Glasgow has projected in recent years is in sharp contrast to its robust reputation as a populous, industrial city and major port. It is now enjoying a growing popularity as a cultural centre and evidence of a resolutely modern outlook is to be found in the eye-catching buildings on the banks of the Clyde which punctuate the Glasgow skyline. There is much animation in the city centre with the smart shopping centres and numerous places to eat and drink and have a good time.

St Mungo became its first bishop in the mid-6C and later its patron saint. In the 17C Glasgow – always a radical city – became the centre of the Protestant cause. By the 18C the city was rich from trade in textiles, sugar and tobacco, her wealth increasing in the 19C through banking, shipbuilding and heavy industry.

The arts prospered amid the wealth as the rich merchants proved to be enlightened patrons. In the late 19C a progressive outlook was fostered by the Glasgow Boys and a pioneer modern movement led by Charles Rennie Mackintosh, who was responsible for a renewal in fine and applied arts. Today the realism and radicalism of contemporary Glasgow artists are acclaimed. Glasgow is the home of Scottish Opera, Scottish ballet and several notable art collections.

WHICH DISTRICT TO CHOOSE

You will find luxury **accommodation** from 5-star hotels to stylish, boutique hotels around George Square *Plan II* **E2** and Argyle St *Plan II* **C2** in the city centre and around Great Western Road *Plan I* **A1** in the fashionable West End. For good accommodation at reasonable prices in a central location look around Sauchiehall St *Plan II* **C1**, Renfrew St *Plan II* **D1** and Hope St *Plan II* **D2**. There are comfortable business hotels near Central Station, near Finnieston Quay *Plan I* **A2** and along the riverside near the Scottish Exhibition and Conference Centre.

There is a fine selection of quality **restaurants** along Bath Street *Plan II* **D2** and in the parallel West Regent, West George and St Vincent streets as well as Albion St *Plan II* **E3** and Candleriggs. Tucked behind Byres Lane *Plan I* **A1** are cobblestone lanes with lively bistros and cafés. Some of the best restaurants and pubs are in charming Ashton Lane. For Glasgow's thriving pavement café culture, explore Merchant Square *Plan II* **E3**, Candleriggs, Royal Exchange Square *Plan II* **D2** in The Merchant City.

PRACTICAL INFORMATION

ARRIVAL – DEPARTURE

Glasgow International Airport – 13km (8mi) west of the city centre. ✆ 0870 040 0008; www.baa.co.uk/lasgow

Prestwick International Airport – 48km (30mi) southwest of the city. ✆ 01292 511 000 (outside the UK), 0871 223 0700 (inside the UK); www.gpia.co.uk

From Glasgow airport to the city centre – By **taxi**: about £18-20. By **bus**: No 905 and 950 from the front of the terminal building to stops close to Central Station, Queen Street Station and Buchanan Bus Station. City bus stops have an airport logo on them. Mon-Fri 6am-midnight, every 10min at peak times and 15-30min the rest of the day; Sat-Sun every 15-30min. Fare £3.50 single, £5.30 round trip. ✆ 0870 550 5050; www.travellinescotland.co.uk; www,citylink.co.uk

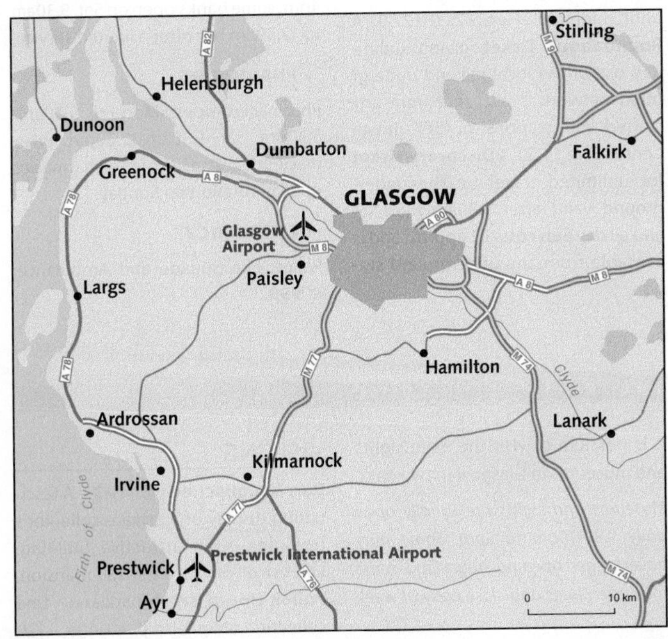

From Prestwick Airport to the city centre – By **rail** via Paisley Gilmour St Station: every 30 min (hourly on Sun). Time 45min. Fare: 50% reduction on standard rail fare for air passengers. By **bus** to Buchanan Bus Station via Kilmarnock: every 30min at peak times. Time 50min. £7, return £12. ✆ 0870 608 2608; www.travellinescotland.co.uk

Railway Stations – Central Station *Plan II* **D2** – Services from the south and England. **Queen Street Station** *Plan II* **E2** – Trains from Edinburgh and the north. ✆ 08457 484 950; www.nationalrail.co.uk

TRANSPORT

→ UNDERGROUND AND BUS

Glasgow and its environs have a very comprehensive public transport network. A **FirstDay** ticket for First Day services is available from bus drivers on the day of travel and is valid until midnight. Fare £2.20-£2.50. A **Roundabout Ticket** giving unlimited use of the local rail and undergr ound network is available from any staffed rail stations or SPT Travel Centre. Fare £4.50. A **Discovery Ticket** for unlimited travel on the underground valid after 9.30am Mon-Sat and all day Sun costs £2 approx. and is available from any underground station.

♦ TAXIS

Metered taxis can be picked up at taxi ranks in the town centre, outside the main rail and bus stations, at the airport or can be ordered by phone. Additional charges are levied for luggage, night travel and extra passengers. Many taxis accept credit cards.

USEFUL ADDRESSES

→ TOURIST OFFICES

Glasgow TIC, 11 George Square, Glasgow G2 1DY *Plan II* **E2**. ✆ 0141 204 4400. **Glasgow Airport TIC**, International Arrivals Hall, Glasgow. ✆ 0141 848 4400; www.seeglasgow.com

→ POST OFFICES

The main post office at 47 St Vincent St *Plan II* **D2** is open Mon-Fri, 8.30am-5.30pm and Sat, 9am-5.30pm.

→ BANKS/CURRENCY EXCHANGE

Opening times, Mon-Fri 9.30am to 4pm; some banks open on Sat, 9.30am to 12.30pm but offer a limited service.

→ PHARMACIES

Pharmacies open Mon-Fri, 9.30am-5.30pm, Sat, 9.30am-12.30pm. Pharmacies display a list of the pharmacies open in rotation on Sunday.

→ EMERGENCY

Police, Fire Brigade and Ambulance: ✆ **999**.

EXPLORING GLASGOW

It is possible to visit the main sights and museums in Glasgow in two days.

Museums and sights are usually open daily 9.30-10am to 5pm. Some may have longer opening hours and some may open later and close early at week ends.

VISITING

Burrell Collection *Plan I* **A3** – A fascinating display of a private collector's treasures in an attractive building. Later stroll down to the 18C mansion, **Pollok House**, set in parkland – fine collection of Spanish paintings.

Glasgow Cathedral *Plan II* **F2** – A magnificent medieval building marking the birthplace of the city. View from the Necropolis. Proceed to Cathedral Square with its original buildings and visit **Provand's Lordship.**

George Square *Plan II* **E2** – A splendid Victorian square lined with ornate buildings: **City Chambers, Merchants' House**, Post Office.

Glasgow University district *Plan I* **A1** – Grand university buildings. Do not miss the **Art Gallery and Museum Kelvingrove** (British and European paintings, arms and armour), the **Hunterian Museum and Art Gallery** (Whistler collection, Scottish paintings) and the **Mackintosh Wing** (interiors, furnishings, drawings, watercolours).

Museum of Transport *Plan I* **A1** – A comprehensive collection of trams and trolley buses, Scottish-built cars, fire vehicles and bicycles as well as model ships illustrating Scottish shipbuilding.

Gallery of Modern Art *Plan II* **E2** – A great 18C mansion houses a collection of contemporary art from around the world.

Glasgow Science Centre *Plan I* **A2** – Explore the wonders of science and technology in three sleek modern buildings on the river bank.

Tenement House *Plan II* **C1** – A piece of social history. Life in a tenement house in the early 20C.

Mackintosh Trail – *Ticket for bus travel and admission from SPT travel centres, tourist offices and participating sights.* A must for Mackintosh fans: **The Glasgow School of Art** *Plan II* **D1**, **The Lighthouse** *Plan II* **D2**, **Queen's Cross Church**, **Mackintosh Wing** *(see above)*, **Scotland Street School Museum** *Plan I* **A2**, **The Willow Tea Rooms** *(Sauchiehall Street) Plan II* **C1**, **House for an Art Lover** and **Hill House** in Helensburgh.

Boat trip along the Firth of Clyde starting from Waverley Terminal, Anderston Quay *Plan II* **C3** and from Broomielaw *Plan II* **D3** to Braehead with commentary on the history of the Clyde.

GOURMET TREATS

Establishments which offer the best Scottish fare are identified by a 'stockpot' sign. Take a break at the delightful *Willow Tea Rooms* at 217 Sauchiehall Street and 97 Buchanan Street which serve breakfast, light meals and afternoon tea.

SHOPPING

Stores are usually open Mon-Sat, 9-10am to 5.30-6.30pm. Some shops open Sun, 11am to 4.30-5.30pm.

LUXURY SHOPS, BOUTIQUES – **Sauchiehall** *Plan II* **D1** and **Argyle** *Plan II* **D2 Streets** are pedestrian shopping precincts. Exclusive shops and elegant malls line **Buchanan St** (*St Enoch Centre, Buchanan Galleries* and *Princes Square*) *Plan II* **D2**. Stylish shops are to be found in **John Street** *Plan II* **E2** and **Ingram Street** in the Merchant City. The **Braehead** shopping centre, Kings Inch Road, has a huge number of shops.

SCOTTISH CRAFTS AND GIFTS – *Mackintosh Shop* at Glasgow School of Art. *Hutchesons' Hall shop*, 158 Ingram St. *Form, The Lighthouse Shop*, 11 Mitchell Lane. For handcrafted jewellery, go to *Orro*, 12 Wilson St; *Nancy Smillie Shop & Gallery*, 53 Creswell St; *Starry, Starry Night*, 21 Dowanside Lane.

ANTIQUES – Take time to browse at *DeCourcy Arcade*, 5-12 Creswell St; *Victorian Village*, 93 West Regent St; *Tim Wright Antiques*, 147 Bath St.

MARKETS – **The Barras** *Plan II* **F3** is a lively flea market, full of local colour. Open Sat-Sun, 10am-5pm.

WHAT TO BUY – Tartans, knitwear, Scottish crafts, shortbread and cakes, marmalade and jams, whisky, Mackintosh-inspired jewellery and other gifts.

ENTERTAINMENT

For listings of what's on in Glasgow consult the daily papers, The Herald and The Evening Times or the fortnightly magazine The List. The Glasgow pages of the weekly Time Out also give useful information.

Glasgow Royal Concert Hall *Plan II* **D2** – Concerts.

Royal Scottish Academy of Music and Drama *Plan II* **D1** – National Conservatoire and performing arts centre.

Theatre Royal *Plan II* **D2** – Performances of Scottish Opera and Scottish Ballet.

Scottish Exhibition and Conference Centre *Plan I* **A2** – Live music, pop and rock concerts.

St Andrews in the Square *Plan II* **E3** – Folk and traditional Scottish music.

Centre for Contemporary Arts *Plan II* **C1** – Live music and cutting-edge theatre.

Mitchell Theatre *Plan II* **C2** – Drama and live music.

King's Theatre *Plan II* **D2** – Musicals, dance, drama.

Citizens' Theatre *Plan I* **B2**, **Tron Theatre** *Plan II* **E3**, **Tramway Theatre** *Plan I* **A2** – Experimental drama.

NIGHTLIFE

The lively atmosphere of **Glasgow pubs** is famous. Visit *Rab-Ha's*, 83 Hutchenson St;*Times Square*, St Enoch's Square, *Bonhams*, 194 Byres Rd and *Dows*, 9 Dundas St. Pubs with folk music include *Scotia Bar* and *Clutha Vaults*, both in Stockwell St (112 and 167); *Molly Malone's*, 224 Hope St.

For **live music and nightclubs**, a trendy crowd frequents *Archaos*, 25-37 Queen St; *Sub Club*, 22 Jamaica St; *The Tunnel*, 38 Mitchell St; while a young crowd dances the night away at *The Arches*, 253 Argyle St; *Barrowlands*, 244 Gallowgate; *The Garage*, 490 Sauchiehall St; and *The Carling Academy*, 121 Eglinton Rd. *The Riverside Club*, 33 Fox St and *Park Bar*, 1202 Argyle St have folk evenings at weekends.

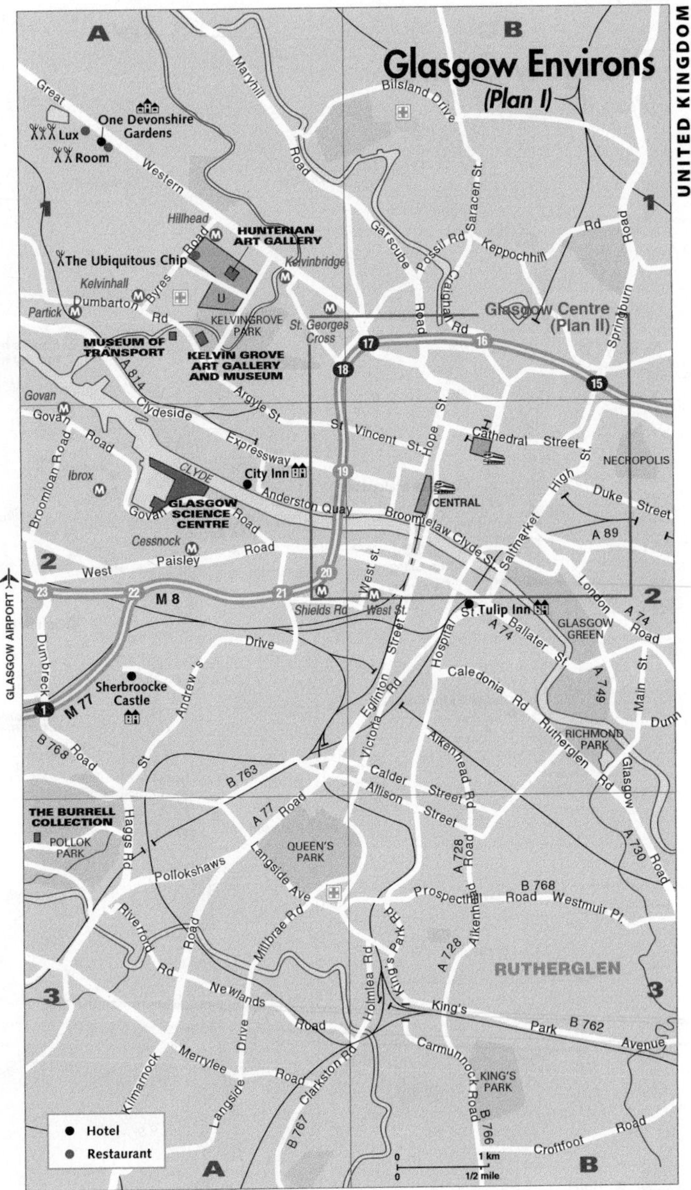
Glasgow Environs
(Plan I)
A
B
1
2
3
One Devonshire Gardens
Lux
Room
The Ubiquitous Chip
HUNTERIAN ART GALLERY
MUSEUM OF TRANSPORT
KELVIN GROVE ART GALLERY AND MUSEUM
KELVINGROVE PARK
City Inn
GLASGOW SCIENCE CENTRE
Glasgow Centre (Plan II)
CENTRAL
NECROPOLIS
Tulip Inn
GLASGOW GREEN
RICHMOND PARK
Sherbroocke Castle
THE BURRELL COLLECTION
POLLOK PARK
QUEEN'S PARK
KING'S PARK
RUTHERGLEN
GLASGOW AIRPORT
Great Western Road
Maryhill Road
Bilsland Drive
Garscube Road
Possil Rd
Saracen St.
Keppochhill Rd
Springburn Road
Craighall Rd
Hillhead
Kelvinbridge
Kelvinhall
Partick
Byres Road
Dumbarton Rd
St. Georges Cross
Argyle St.
Clydeside Expressway
Govan
Govan Road
Broomloan Road
Ibrox
CLYDE
Anderston Quay
Broomielaw
Clyde St.
St. Vincent St.
Hope St.
Cathedral Street
High St.
Duke Street
Saltmarket
A 89
A 814
Cessnock
Paisley Road West
M 8
M 77
Shields Rd
West St.
London Road
A 74
Ballater St.
Hospital St.
Caledonia Rd
Main St.
A 749
Rutherglen Rd
Glasgow Road
A 730
Dumbreck Road
B 768
St. Andrew's Drive
Eglinton Street
Victoria Rd
Aikenhead Rd
Calder Street
Allison Street
B 763
A 77 Road
Haggs Rd
Pollokshaws Road
Langside Ave
Millbrae Rd
A 728
Prospecthill Road
Westmuir Pl.
Riverford Rd
Newlands Road
Holmlea Rd
King's Park Rd
King's Park Avenue
B 762
Carmunnock Road
B 766
Croftfoot Road
Merrylee Road
Kilmarnock Road
Langside Drive
Clarkston Rd
B 767
Dunn
Hotel
Restaurant
1 km
1/2 mile

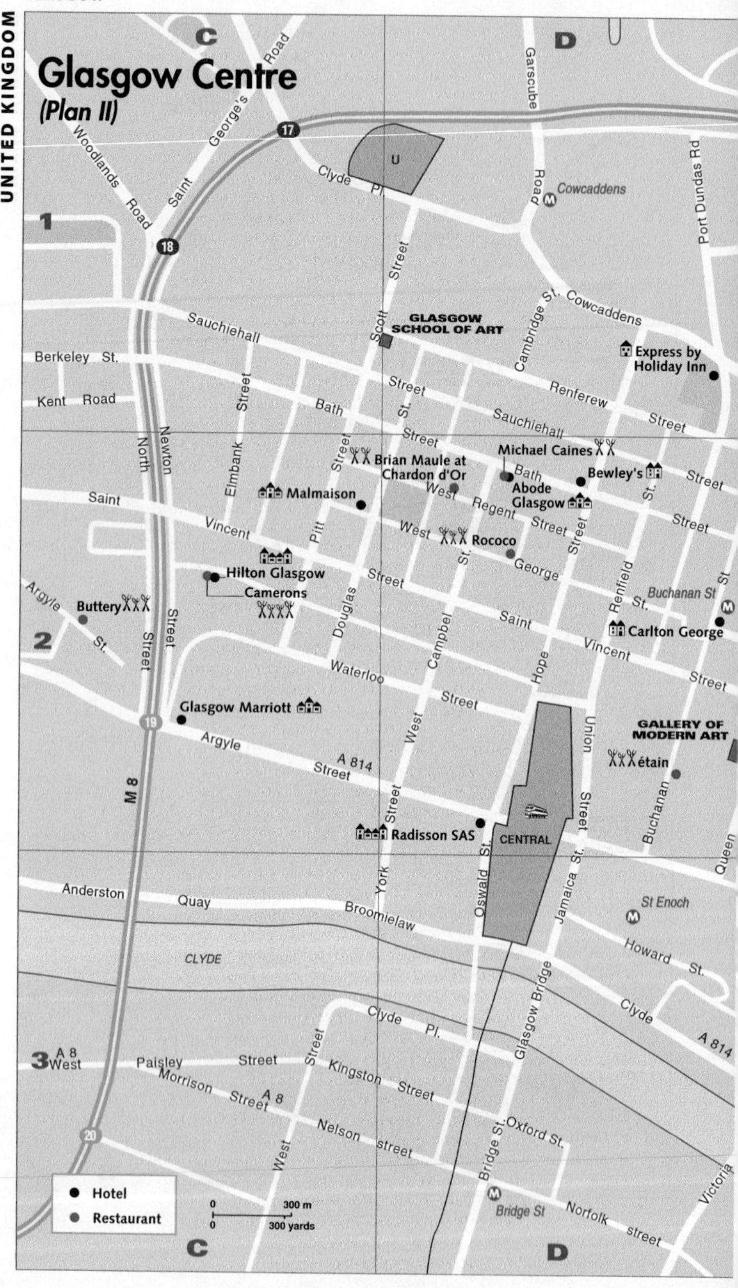
Glasgow Centre
(Plan II)
GLASGOW SCHOOL OF ART
Express by Holiday Inn
Michael Caines
Brian Maule at Chardon d'Or
Bewley's
Abode Glasgow
Malmaison
Rococo
Hilton Glasgow
Camerons
Buttery
Carlton George
Glasgow Marriott
GALLERY OF MODERN ART
étain
Radisson SAS
CENTRAL
Cowcaddens
Buchanan St
St Enoch
Bridge St
CLYDE
Sauchiehall Street
Bath Street
West Regent Street
West George Street
Saint Vincent Street
Waterloo Street
Argyle Street
A 814
Anderston Quay
Broomielaw
Clyde Pl.
Paisley Street
Kingston Street
Morrison Street
A 8
Nelson street
Norfolk street
Oxford St.
Howard St.
Renfrew Street
Cowcaddens
Berkeley St.
Kent Road
Woodlands Road
Saint George's Road
North Street
Newton Street
Elmbank Street
Pitt Street
Douglas
Scott Street
Cambridge St.
Garscube Road
Port Dundas Rd
Hope Street
Renfield St.
Union Street
Jamaica St.
Oswald St.
York Street
West Street
Campbel St.
Buchanan
Queen St
Glasgow Bridge
Bridge St.
Victoria
M 8
A 8 West
Hotel
Restaurant
300 m
300 yards

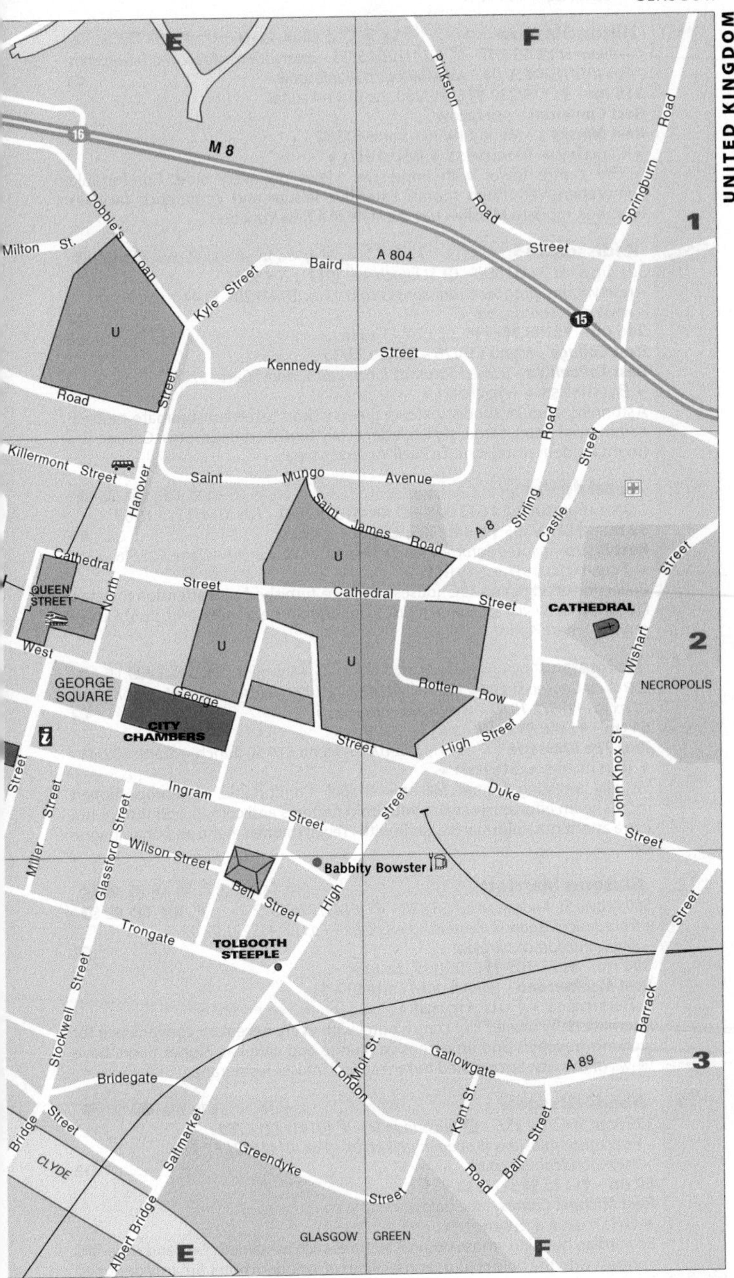
E
F
M 8
16
15
Pinkston Road
Springburn Road
Dobbie's Loan
Milton St.
Baird Street
A 804
Kyle Street
Kennedy Street
Road
Street
U
Killermont Street
Hanover Street
Saint Mungo Avenue
Saint James Road
A 8
Stirling Road
Castle Street
Cathedral Street
North
QUEEN STREET
West George Street
GEORGE SQUARE
CITY CHAMBERS
CATHEDRAL
NECROPOLIS
Wishart Street
Rotten Row
High Street
Duke Street
John Knox St.
Ingram Street
Miller Street
Glassford Street
Wilson Street
Bell Street
Babbity Bowster
Trongate
TOLBOOTH STEEPLE
Stockwell Street
Barrack Street
Gallowgate
A 89
Moir St.
London Road
Kent St.
Bain Street
Bridgegate
Bridge Street
CLYDE
Saltmarket
Greendyke Street
Albert Bridge
GLASGOW GREEN
1
2
3

UNITED KINGDOM

Hilton Glasgow

1000 P VISA AE

1 William St ✉ *G3 8HT – ✆ (0141) 204 5555 – reservations.glasgow@hilton.com – Fax (0141) 204 50 04 – www.hilton.co.uk/glasgow* **C2**

315 rm – †£179/230 ††£179/230, ☕ £18 – 4 suites

Rest *Camerons* – see below

Rest *Minsky's* – Menu £19/25 – Carte £27/37

♦ Luxury ♦ Business ♦ Modern ♦

A city centre tower with impressive views on every side. Comfortable, comprehensively fitted rooms. Extensive leisure and conference facilities. Spacious, modern Minsky's has the style of a New York deli.

Radisson SAS

rm 800 P VISA AE

301 Argyle St ✉ *G2 8DL* – Ⓜ *St Enoch – ✆ (0141) 204 3333 – reservations.glasgow@radissonsas.com – Fax (0141) 204 33 44 – www.radissonsas.com* **D2**

246 rm – †£198 ††£198, ☕ £14 – 1 suite

Rest *Collage* – Menu £19/26 – Carte £23/35

Rest *TaPaell'Ya* – *(closed Saturday lunch and Sunday)* Carte £20/31

♦ Business ♦ Modern ♦

A stunning, angular, modish exterior greets visitors to this consummate, modern commercial hotel. Large, stylish, eclectically furnished bedrooms. Collage is a bright modern restaurant. Ta Paell'Ya serves tapas.

Hotel du Vin

50 VISA AE

1 Devonshire Gdns ✉ *G12 0UX – ✆ (0141) 339 2001 – Fax (0141) 337 16 63*

32 rm – †£140/305 ††£140/305, ☕ £17 – 3 suites *Plan I* **A1**

Rest *Bistro* – *(closed Saturday lunch)* Menu £17.50 (lunch) – Carte £25/46

♦ Townhouse ♦ Stylish ♦

Collection of adjoining 19C houses in terrace, furnished with attention to detail. Elegantly convivial drawing room, comfortable bedrooms and unobtrusive service. Smart Bistro.

Malmaison

rm 25 VISA AE

278 West George St ✉ *G2 4LL – ✆ (0141) 572 1000 – glasgow@malmaison.com – Fax (0141) 572 10 02 – www.malmaison.com* **C2**

64 rm – †£140 ††£140, ☕ £13 – 8 suites

Rest *The Brasserie* – ✆ *(0141) 572 1001* – Menu £14.50 (lunch) – Carte £32/41

♦ Business ♦ Stylish ♦

Visually arresting former Masonic chapel. Comfortable, well-proportioned rooms seem effortlessly stylish with bold patterns and colours and thoughtful extra attentions. Informal Brasserie with French themed menu and Champagne bar.

Glasgow Marriott

600 P VISA AE

500 Argyle St, Anderston ✉ *G3 8RR – ✆ (0141) 226 5577 – frontdesk.glasgow@marriotthotels.co.uk – Fax (0141) 221 92 02 – www.marriott.co.uk/gladt* **C2**

300 rm – †£95/105 ††£105/115, ☕ £15

Rest *Mediterrano* – *(dinner only)* Carte £17/23

♦ Business ♦ Functional ♦

Internationally owned city centre hotel with every necessary convenience for working travellers and an extensive lounge and café-bar. Upper floors have views of the city. Strong Mediterranean feel infuses restaurant.

Abode Glasgow

70 VISA AE

129 Bath St ✉ *G2 2SZ* – Ⓜ *Buchanan St – ✆ (0141) 221 6789 – reservationsglasgow@abodehotels.co.uk – Fax (0141) 221 67 77 – www.abodehotels.co.uk* **D2**

60 rm – †£125 ††£125, ☕ £13

Rest *Michael Caines* – see below

♦ Business ♦ Stylish ♦

Edwardian building whose original features such as stained glass and cage-lifts contrast with the bold colours and facilities of a modern hotel. Smartly designed bedrooms.

Carlton George
44 West George St ✉ G2 1DH – Ⓜ Buchanan St – ✆ (0141) 353 6373 – resgeorge@carltonhotels.co.uk – Fax (0141) 353 62 63 – www.carltonhotels.co.uk
closed 23-27 December and 1-2 January **D2**
64 rm – †£185 ††£185, ☐ £14
Rest *Windows* – Menu £16.50/21.50 – Carte dinner £22/34
◆ Business ◆ Classic ◆
A quiet oasis away from the city bustle. Attractive tartan decorated bedrooms bestow warm tidings. Comfortable 7th floor business lounge. An overall traditional ambience. Ask for restaurant table with excellent view across city's rooftops.

Sherbrooke Castle rest 300
11 Sherbrooke Ave, Pollokshields ✉ G41 4PG – ✆ (0141) 427 4227 – mail@sherbrooke.co.uk – Fax (0141) 427 56 85 – www.sherbrooke.co.uk Plan I **A2**
22 rm ☐ – †£95/110 ††£160 – 2 suites
Rest *Morrisons* – Carte £16/34
◆ Castle ◆ Classic ◆
Late 19C baronial Romanticism given free rein inside and out. The hall is richly furnished and imposing; rooms in the old castle have a comfortable country house refinement. Panelled Victorian dining room with open fire.

City Inn 50
Finnieston Quay ✉ G3 8HN – ✆ (0141) 240 1002 – glasgow.reservations@cityinn.com – Fax (0141) 248 27 54 – www.cityinn.com Plan I **A2**
closed 26 December
164 rm – †£135 ††£135, ☐ £13
Rest *City Cafe* – Menu £15/16.50 – Carte £19/34
◆ Chain hotel ◆ Business ◆ Functional ◆
Quayside location and views of the Clyde. Well priced hotel with a "business-friendly" ethos; neatly maintained modern rooms with sofas and en suite power showers. Restaurant fronts waterside terrace.

Bewley's rest rm
110 Bath St ✉ G2 2EN – Ⓜ Buchanan St – ✆ (0141) 353 0800 – gla@bewleyshotels.com – Fax (0141) 353 09 00 – www.bewleyshotels.com
closed 24-29 December **D2**
103 rm – †£69 ††£69, ☐ £7
Rest *Loop* – Carte £18/22
◆ Business ◆ Functional ◆
A well-run group hotel, relaxed but professional in approach, in the middle of Glasgow's shopping streets. Upper rooms boast rooftop views and duplex apartments. People-watch from glass-walled eatery.

Tulip Inn rest 180
80 Ballater St ✉ G5 0TW – Ⓜ Bridge St – ✆ (0141) 429 4233 – info@tulipinnglasgow.co.uk – Fax (0141) 429 42 44 – www.tulipinnglasgow.co.uk Plan I **B2**
114 rm – †£59.50/85 ††£59.50/85, ☐ £8
Rest *Bibo Bar and Bistro* – *(dinner only)* Carte £16/26
◆ Chain hotel ◆ Business ◆ Functional ◆
Sensibly priced hotel appealing to cost-conscious business travellers. Good access to motorway and city centre. Bedrooms have working space and most modern conveniences. Informal, bright eatery serves a varied menu.

Express by Holiday Inn without rest
Theatreland, 165 West Nile St ✉ G1 2RL – Ⓜ Cowcaddens – ✆ (0141) 331 6800 – express@higlasgow.com – Fax (0141) 331 68 28 – www.hiexpressglasgow.co.uk
closed 25-26 December **D1**
118 rm ☐ – †£65 ††£77
◆ Chain hotel ◆ Functional ◆
Modern accommodation - simple and well arranged with adequate amenities. Equally suitable for business travel or leisure tourism.

XXXX **Camerons** – at Hilton Glasgow H. AC P VISA MO AE

1 William St ✉ G3 8HT – ✆ (0141) 204 5511 – Fax (0141) 204 50 04 – www.hilton.co.uk/glasgow

closed Saturday lunch, Sunday and Bank Holidays **C2**

Rest – Menu £19.50 (lunch) – Carte dinner £30/45

♦ Modern ♦ Formal ♦

Carefully prepared and full-flavoured modern cuisine with strong Scottish character. Very formal, neo-classical styling and smart staff have advanced its local reputation.

XXX **Buttery** P VISA MO AE

652 Argyle St ✉ G3 8UF – ✆ (0141) 221 8188 – the-buttery@hotmail.co.uk – Fax (0141) 204 46 39

closed Sunday, Monday and Saturday lunch **C2**

Rest – Menu £22/38

♦ Modern ♦ Formal ♦

Established, comfortable restaurant away from the bright lights; red velour and ageing bric-a-brac reveal its past as a pub. Ambitiously composed modern Scottish repertoire.

XXX **étain** AC VISA MO AE

The Glass House, Springfield Court ✉ G1 3JN – Ⓜ St Enoch – ✆ (0141) 225 5630 – etain@zincbar.com – Fax (0141) 225 56 40 – www.zincbar.com

closed 25 December, 1 January, Saturday lunch and Sunday dinner **D2**

Rest – Menu £29/32

♦ Modern ♦ Brasserie ♦

Comfortable, contemporary restaurant in unusual glass extension to Princes Square Centre. Well-sourced Scottish ingredients prepared in a modern, interesting way.

XXX **Rococo** AC VISA MO AE

202 West George St ✉ G2 2NR – Ⓜ Buchanan St – ✆ (0141) 221 5004 – info@rococoglasgow.co.uk – Fax (0141) 221 50 06 – www.rococoglasgow.co.uk

closed 26 December and 1 January **D2**

Rest – Menu £19/39.50 – Carte lunch £19/34 ❀

♦ Contemporary ♦ Design ♦

In style, more like studied avant-garde: stark, white-walled cellar with vibrant modern art and high-backed leather chairs. Accomplished, fully flavoured contemporary menu.

XXX **Lux** AC P VISA MO AE ①

1051 Great Western Rd ✉ G12 0XP – ✆ (0141) 576 7576 – enquiries@luxstazione.co.uk – Fax (0141) 576 01 62 – www.lux.5pm.co.uk

closed 25-26 December, 1-2 January and Sunday *Plan I* **A1**

Rest – *(dinner only)* Menu £30/34

♦ Modern ♦ Design ♦

19C railway station converted with clean-lined elegance: dark wood, subtle lighting and vivid blue banquettes. Fine service and flavourful, well-prepared modern menus.

XX **Michael Caines** – at Abode Glasgow H. AC VISA MO AE ①

129 Bath St ✉ G2 2SZ – Ⓜ Buchanan Street – ✆ 572 6011

Rest – *(closed Sunday)* Menu £12.50/17.50 – Carte £30/40 **D2**

♦ Modern ♦ Fashionable ♦

Smart, stylish restaurant in boutique hotel, a mirrored wall creating impression of size. Quality décor matched by clean, unfussy cooking with a degree of originality.

XX

Brian Maule at Chardon d'Or

VISA MC AE ①

176 West Regent St ✉ G2 4RL – Ⓜ Buchanan St – ✆ (0141) 248 3801 – info@brianmaule.com – Fax (0141) 248 39 01 – www.brianmaule.com

closed 2 weeks January, 25-26 December, 1 January, Saturday lunch, Sunday and Bank Holidays **D2**

Rest – Menu £18.50 (lunch) – Carte approx. £36

♦ Modern ♦ Brasserie ♦

Large pillared Georgian building. Airy interior with ornate carved ceiling and hung with modern art. Modern dishes with fine Scottish produce; substantial wine list.

X

The Ubiquitous Chip

AC VISA MC AE ①

12 Ashton Lane ✉ G12 8SJ, off Byres Rd – Ⓜ Kelvinhall – ✆ (0141) 334 5007 – mail@ubiquitouschip.co.uk – Fax (0141) 337 13 02 – www.ubiquitouschip.co.uk

closed 25 December and 1 January *Plan I* **A1**

Rest – Menu £28.65/39.85 – Carte £12/31

♦ Traditional ♦ Bistro ♦

A long-standing favourite, "The Chip" mixes Scottish and fusion styles. Well known for its glass-roofed courtyard, with a more formal but equally lively warehouse interior.

Babbity Bowster

VISA MC AE ①

16-18 Blackfriars St ✉ G1 1PE – ✆ (0141) 552 5055 – Fax (0141) 552 77 74 – www.babbity.com

closed 25 December **E3**

Rest – Carte £13/26

♦ Traditional ♦ Pub ♦

Well regarded pub of Georgian origins with columned façade. Paradoxically simple ambience: gingham-clothed tables, hearty Scottish dishes, slightly more formal in evenings.

at Glasgow Airport West : 8m by M8

Express by Holiday Inn

AC rest 75 P VISA MC AE ①

St Andrews Drive ✉ PA3 2TJ – ✆ (0141) 842 1100 – info@hiex-glasgow.com – Fax (0141) 842 11 22 – www.hiex-glasgow.com

143 rm – †£99/109 ††£99/109

Rest – *(dinner only)* Carte £16/22

♦ Chain hotel ♦ Functional ♦

Ideal for both business travellers and families. Spacious, carefully designed, bright and modern bedrooms with plenty of work space. Complimentary continental breakfast. Traditional and busy buffet-style restaurant.

Eurozone : €

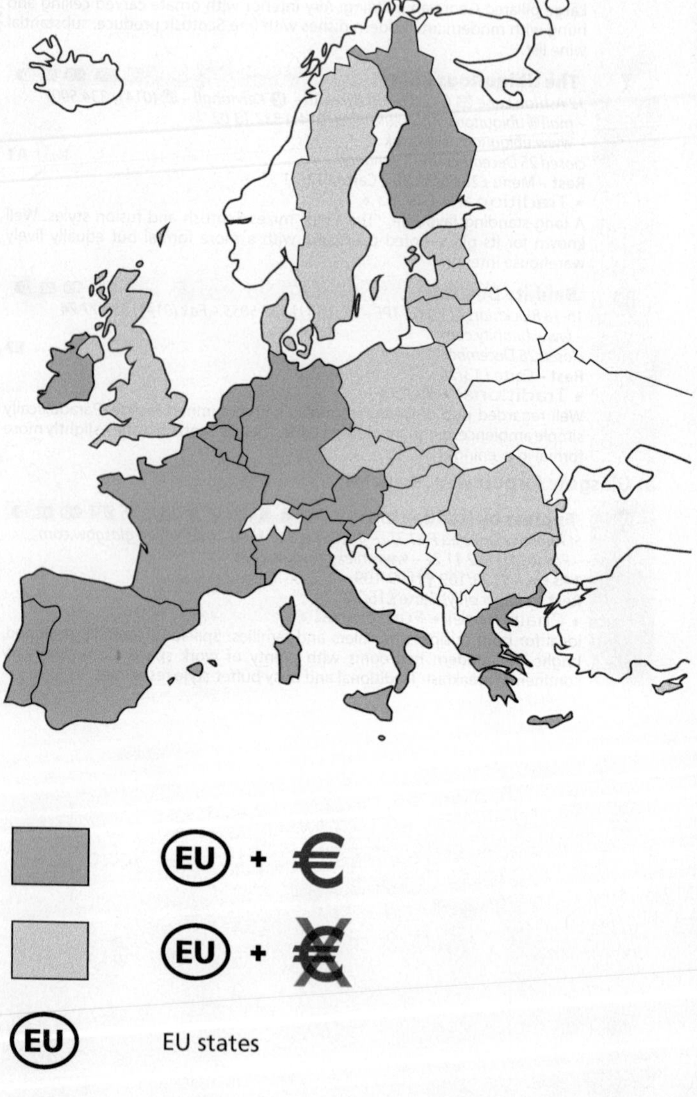

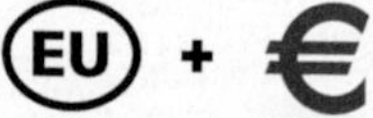

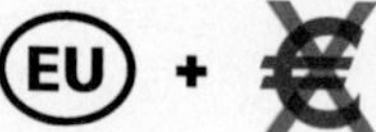

EU states

Schengen Countries

Area of free movement between member states

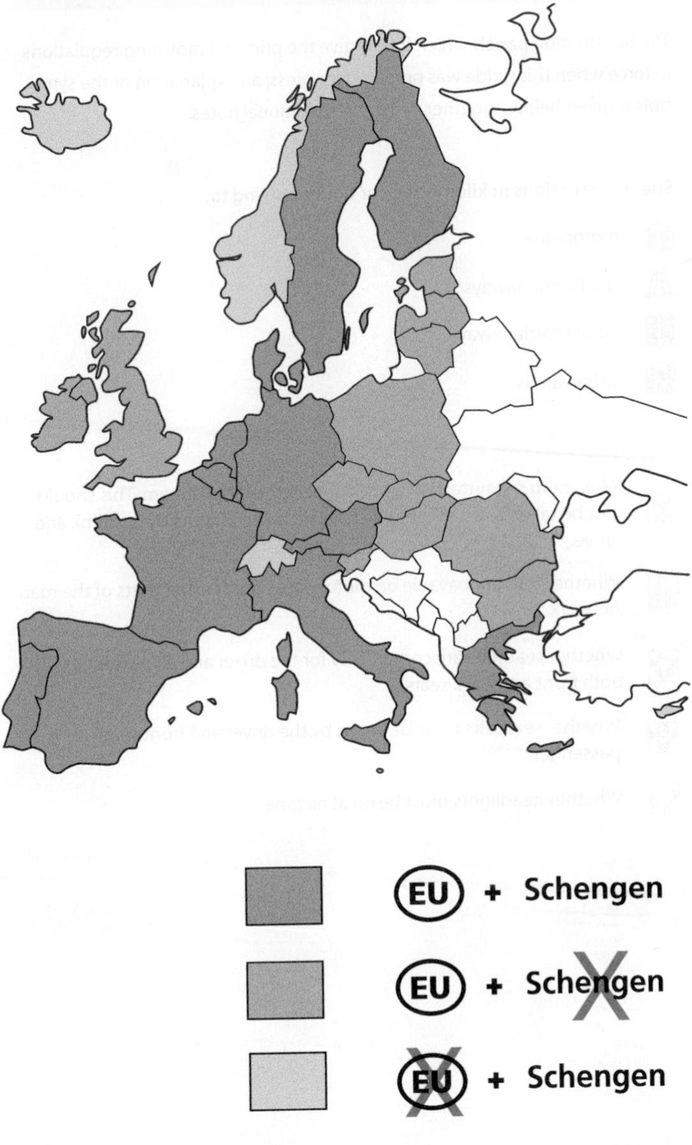

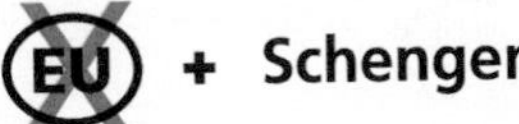

Driving in Europe

KEY

The information panels which follow give the principal motoring regulations in force when this guide was prepared for press; an explanation of the symbols is given below, together with some additional notes.

Speed restrictions in kilometres per hour applying to:

 motorways

 dual carriageways

 single carriageways

 urban areas

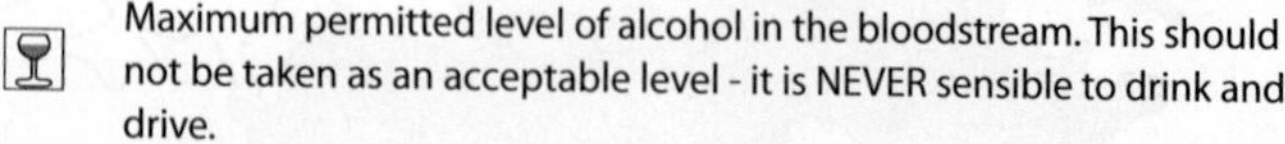 Maximum permitted level of alcohol in the bloodstream. This should not be taken as an acceptable level - it is NEVER sensible to drink and drive.

 Whether tolls are payable on motorways and/or other parts of the road network.

 Whether seatbelts are compulsory for the driver and all passengers in both front and back seats

 Whether seatbelts must be worm by the driver and front seat passenger

 Whether headlights must be on at all time

Driving in Europe

AUSTRIA	A	130		100	50	0,05	●	●	
BELGIUM	B	120	120	90	50	0,05		●	
CZECH REPUBLIC	CZ	130		90	50	0,00	●	●	31/10 -31/3
DENMARK	DK	130		80	50	0,05		●	●
FINLAND	FIN	120		80	50	0,05		●	●
FRANCE	F	130	110	90	50	0,05	●	●	
GERMANY	D			100	50	0,05		●	
GREECE	GR	120		90	50	0,05	●	●	
HUNGARY	H	130	110	90	50	0,00	●	●	●
IRELAND	IRL	120		80	50	0,08		●	
ITALY	I	130		90	50	0,05	●	●	●
LUXEMBOURG	L	130		90	50	0,08		●	
NETHERLANDS	NL	120	100	80	50	0,05		●	
NORWAY	N	90		80	50	0,02	●	●	●
POLAND	PL	130	120	90	50	0,02	●	●	1/10 -28/2
PORTUGAL	P	120	100	90	50	0,05	●	●	
SPAIN	E	120		90	50	0,05	●	●	
SWEDEN	S	110		70	50	0,02		●	●
SWITZERLAND	CH	120	100	80	50	0,05	●	●	
UNITED KINGDOM	GB	112		96	48	0,08		●	

● Compulsory

1/11-30/4 Period of regulation enforcement

Distances

123 : distances by road in kilometers

- (A) AUSTRIA
- (AL) ALBANIE
- (B) BELGIUM
- (BG) BULGARIA
- (BIH) BOSNIA-HERZEGOVINA
- (BY) BELORUSSIA
- (CZ) CZECH REPUBLIC
- (CH) SWITZERLAND
- (D) GERMANY
- (DK) DENMARK
- (E) SPAIN
- (EST) ESTONIA
- (F) FRANCE
- (FIN) FINLAND
- (GB) UNITED KINGDOM
- (GR) GREECE
- (H) HUNGARY
- (HR) CROATIA
- (I) ITALY
- (IRL) IRELAND
- (L) LUXEMBOURG
- (LT) LITHUANIA
- (LV) LATVIA
- (M) MALTA
- (MD) MOLDAVIA
- (MK) MACEDONIA (F.Y.R.O.M.)
- (N) NORWAY
- (NL) NETHERLANDS
- (P) PORTUGAL
- (PL) POLAND
- (S) SWEDEN
- (RO) ROMANIA
- (RUS) RUSSIA
- (SCG) SERBIA AND MONTENEGRO
- (SK) SLOVAK REPUBLIC
- (SLO) SLOVENIA
- (TR) TURKEY
- (UA) UKRAINE

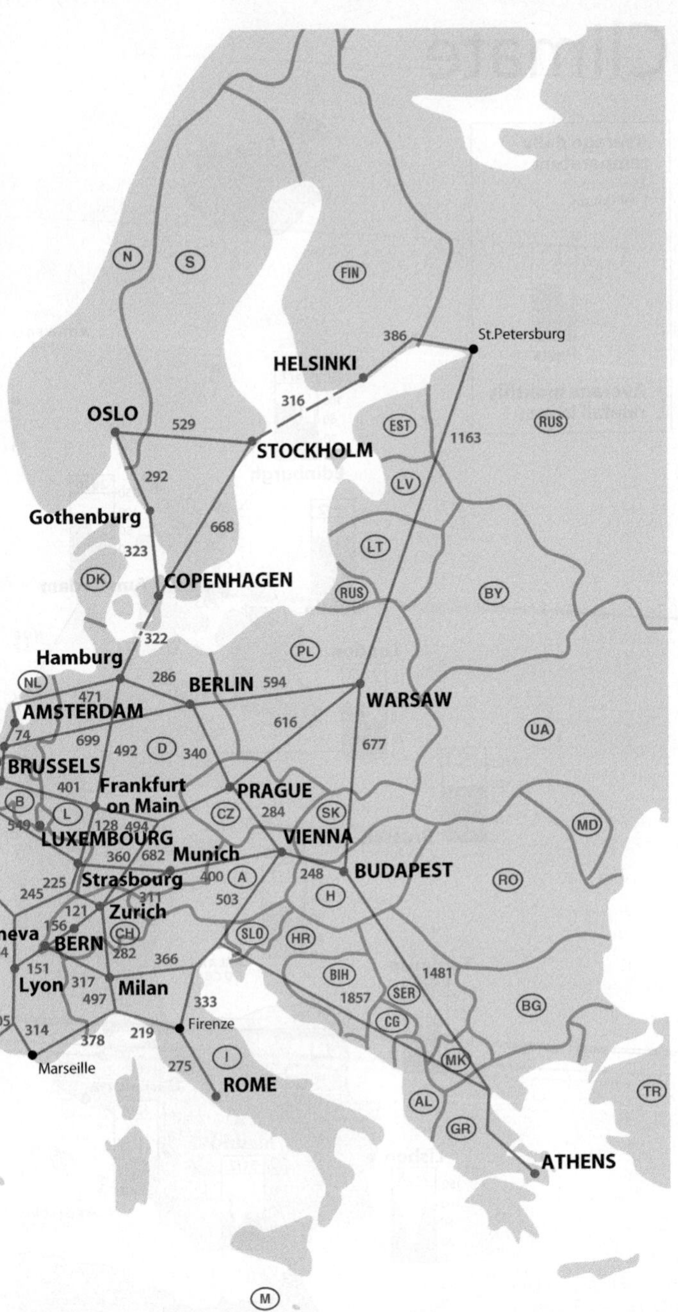
N
S
FIN
St.Petersburg
386
HELSINKI
316
OSLO
529
STOCKHOLM
EST
RUS
1163
292
LV
Gothenburg
668
LT
323
DK
COPENHAGEN
RUS
BY
322
PL
Hamburg
286
BERLIN
594
NL
471
WARSAW
AMSTERDAM
616
UA
74
699
492
D
340
677
BRUSSELS
401
Frankfurt on Main
PRAGUE
B
L
CZ
284
SK
MD
128
494
549
LUXEMBOURG
VIENNA
360
682
Munich
248
BUDAPEST
RO
225
Strasbourg
400
A
245
311
503
H
121
Zurich
156
CH
SLO
HR
BERN
282
366
151
BIH
1481
Lyon
317
Milan
497
1857
SER
333
BG
314
CG
219
Firenze
378
Marseille
I
MK
275
ROME
TR
AL
GR
ATHENS
M

Climate

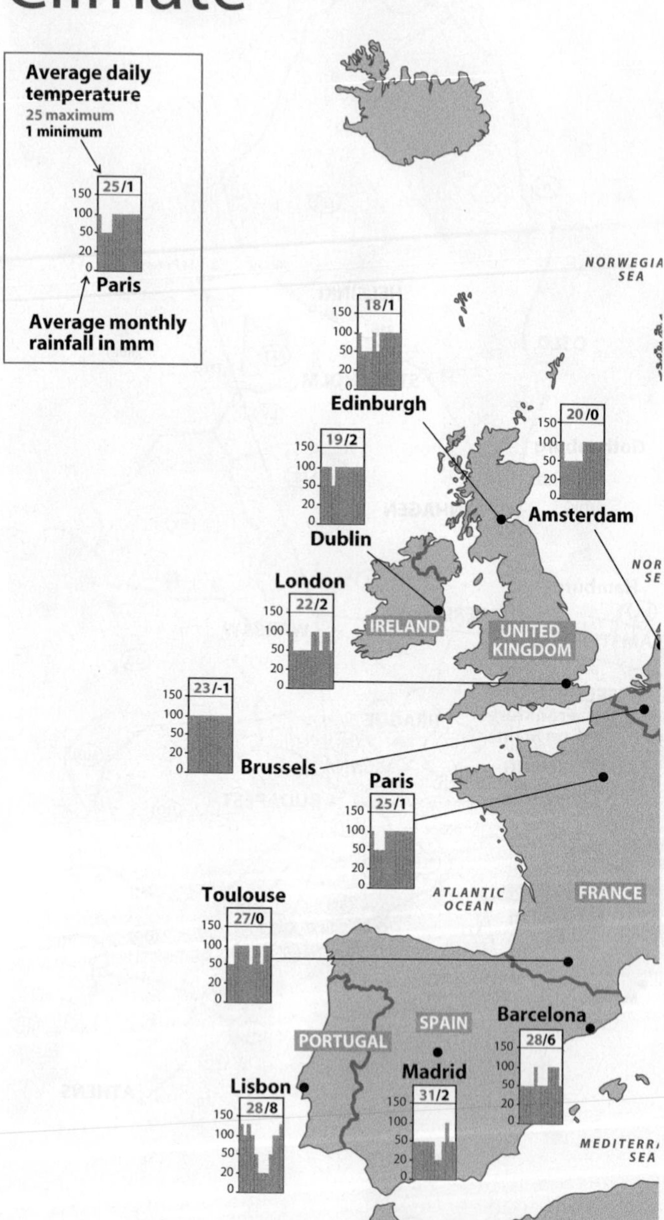

Average daily temperature
25 maximum
1 minimum
25/1
Paris
Average monthly rainfall in mm
NORWEGIA
SEA
18/1
Edinburgh
20/0
19/2
Amsterdam
Dublin
NOR
SE
London
22/2
IRELAND
UNITED
KINGDOM
23/-1
Brussels
Paris
25/1
ATLANTIC
OCEAN
FRANCE
Toulouse
27/0
SPAIN
Barcelona
PORTUGAL
28/6
Madrid
Lisbon
31/2
28/8
MEDITERR
SEA

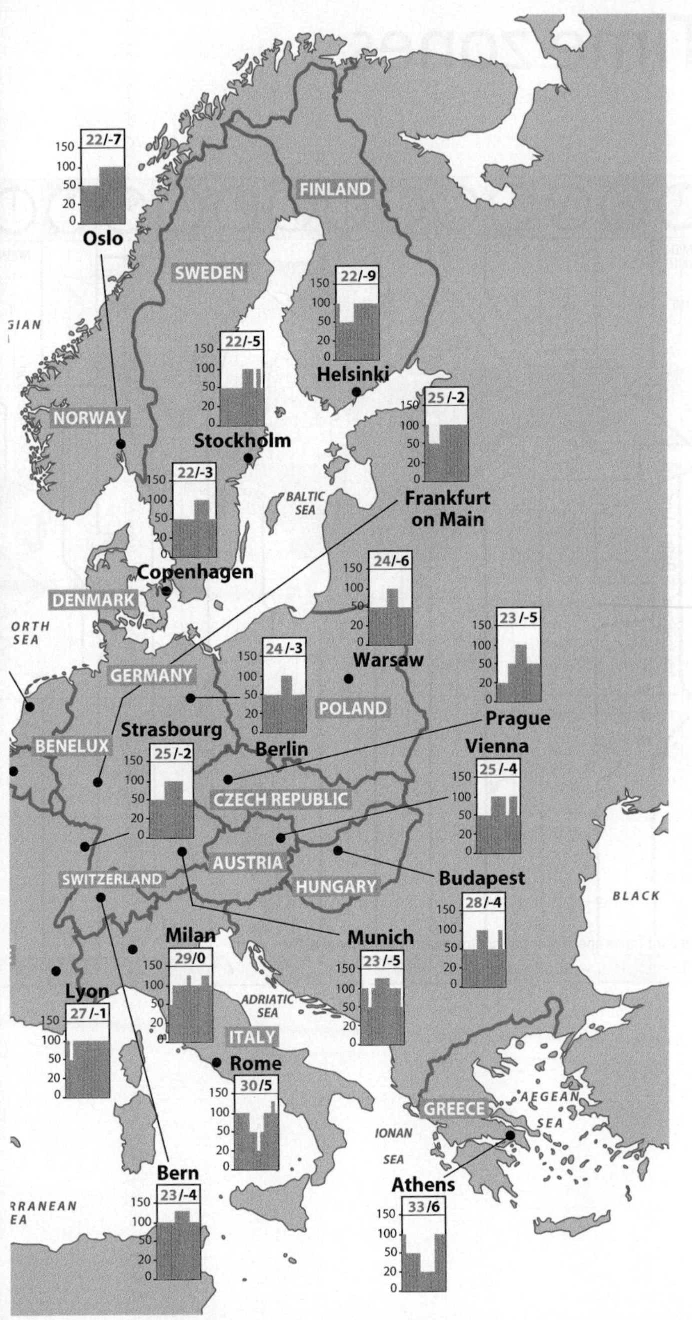
22/-7
Oslo
FINLAND
SWEDEN
22/-9
22/-5
Helsinki
25/-2
NORWAY
Stockholm
22/-3
BALTIC SEA
Frankfurt on Main
24/-6
Copenhagen
DENMARK
ORTH SEA
23/-5
24/-3
Warsaw
GERMANY
POLAND
Prague
Strasbourg
BENELUX
25/-2
Berlin
Vienna
25/-4
CZECH REPUBLIC
AUSTRIA
SWITZERLAND
HUNGARY
Budapest
28/-4
BLACK
Milan
Munich
29/0
23/-5
Lyon
ADRIATIC SEA
27/-1
ITALY
Rome
30/5
AEGEAN SEA
GREECE
IONAN SEA
Bern
Athens
23/-4
33/6
RRANEAN EA
GIAN

Time zones

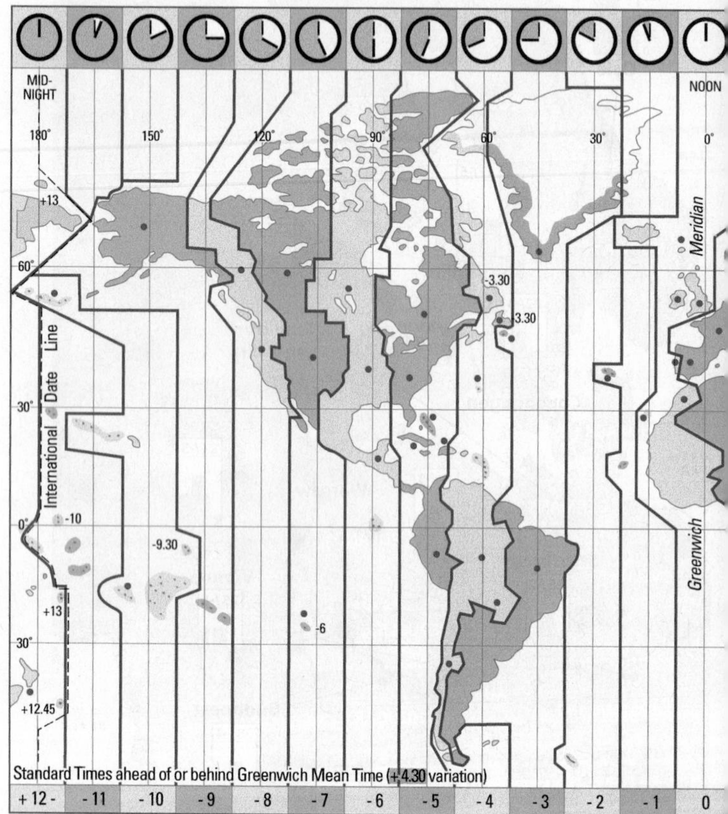

MID-NIGHT
NOON
180°
150°
120°
90°
60°
30°
0°
60°
30°
0°
30°
+13
-3.30
3.30
International Date Line
Meridian
Greenwich
-10
-9.30
+13
-6
+12.45
Standard Times ahead of or behind Greenwich Mean Time (+4.30 variation)
+ 12 -
- 11
- 10
- 9
- 8
- 7
- 6
- 5
- 4
- 3
- 2
- 1
0

Time zones

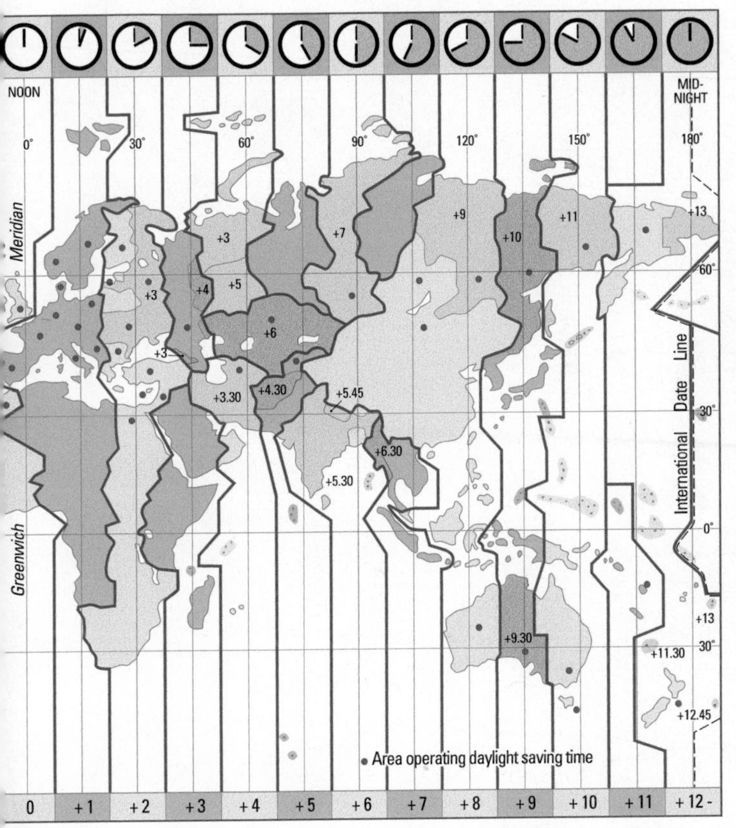
NOON
MID-NIGHT
0°
30°
60°
90°
120°
150°
180°
Meridian
Greenwich
International Date Line
+3
+7
+9
+10
+11
+13
+3
+4
+5
+6
+3
+3.30
+4.30
+5.45
+6.30
+5.30
+9.30
+11.30
+13
+12.45
60°
30°
0°
30°
Area operating daylight saving time
0
+ 1
+ 2
+ 3
+ 4
+ 5
+ 6
+ 7
+ 8
+ 9
+ 10
+ 11
+ 12 -

Town plans

MAIN CONVENTIONAL SIGNS

- Hotels
- Restaurants

Sights

- Place of interest
- Interesting place of worship

Roads

- Motorway
- Dual carriageway
- Pedestrian street
- 1 Junctions: complete
- 1 Junctions: limited
- Station and railway

Various Signs

- Tourist Information Centre
- Mosque
- Synagogue
- Ruins
- Garden, Park, Wood
- Coach station
- Airport
- Underground station
- Underground station (London)
- Hospital
- Covered market
- Public buildings:
- H Town Hall
- R Town Hall (Germany)
- M Museum
- U University

Manufacture française des pneumatiques Michelin
Société en commandite par actions au capital de 304 000 000 EUR
Place des Carmes-Déchaux – 63 Clermont-Ferrand (France)
R.C.S. Clermond-Fd B 855 200 507

Michelin et Cie, Propriétaires-éditeurs, 2007
Dépôt légal : mars 2007

"Based on Ordnance Survey Ireland by permission of the Government Permit No 8208 © Government of Ireland"

Town plans of Bern, Basle, Geneva and Zürich : with the permission of Federal directorate for cadastral surveys

"Based on Ordnance Survey of Great Britain with the permission of the Controller of Her Majest'ys Stationery Office, © Crown Copyright 60194"

Printed in Belgium : 02-2007/5-1

Compogravure : MAURY Imprimeur S.A., Malesherbes

Impression : CASTERMAN, Tournai (Belgium)

Reliure : CLÉMENT S.A. – Seichamps

Our editorial team has taken the greatest care in writing this and checking the information in it. However, pratical information (administrative formalities, prices, addresses, telephone numbers, Internet addresses, etc) is subject to frequent change and such information should therefore be used for guidance only.
it is possible that some of the information in this guide may not be a accurate or exhaustive as of the date of publication. Before taking action (in particular in regard to administrative and customs regulations and procedures), you should contact the appropriate official administration.
We hereby accept no liability in regard to such information